CONTENTS

INTRODUCTORY NOTE

he New Encyclopedia of the Occult is a reference work for practitioners of the many occult traditions of the Western world, as well as for people who are simply curious about magic, alchemy, astrology, Pagan spirituality, or any of the other fields of lore and practice that make up the complex, lively realm of modern Western occultism. Within the pages that follow, you'll find the essential knowledge you need to make sense of the occult, along with references to further reading that will show you where to look if you want to find out more.

This volume attempts to cover the whole range of occult tradition, lore, history, philosophy, and practice in the Western world. It includes magic in its various branches; alchemy; astrology; other methods of divination, including tarot cards, palmistry, geomancy, and many others; magical orders such as the Golden Dawn and the Rosicrucians; religions and spiritual traditions associated with occultism, such as Wicca, Thelema, Theosophy, and the modern Pagan movement; biographies of important occultists; and many other topics that relate to Western occultism in one way or another. In terms of geography, western Europe and North America are the core areas covered, as the heartlands of modern Western cultures and the areas in which most of their occult traditions have emerged and flourished. Perhaps the most noticeable exclusion is that, for a variety of reasons, I have not included biographies of anyone who is still living.

An encyclopedia of this kind could not have been written before the present time. Until recently, most occult traditions hoarded their teachings, restricting them to a handful of initiates sworn to secrecy. Until even more recently, professional historians looked down their noses at occultism; some actually tried to pretend that occult traditions didn't exist at all in the modern industrialized world. How times have changed! Nowadays, the secrets of the ages can be found lining the shelves at any well-stocked bookstore, and the history of occultism is a busy academic specialty with its own journals and conferences.

As a result, it's possible for the first time to collect a good deal of accurate information about occultism. It's also possible for the first time to compare occult traditions effectively with what's known about the history of ideas and of societies. The result has been unsettling; plenty of cherished illusions on all sides have had to be abandoned. Occultists have had to let go of the old claim that their teachings and organizations have endured unchanged since the dawn of history; historians have had to deal with the fact that much-praised historical figures such as Isaac Newton were deeply involved in occult practices.

This is all for the best. The occult traditions of the Western world have no need to be ashamed of their real history, which is far more interesting and dramatic than the fictional histories constructed by some occult groups in the past. A body of thought and practice that has evolved over more than twenty-five centuries in the Western world, changing and growing but still maintaining an impressive continuity, will stand comparison with the spiritual traditions of any culture on Earth. Nor do professional historians need to apologize for their interest in a set of living traditions that have played a vitally important part in shaping the cultures, the ideas, and the history of Western civilization and the world as a whole.

This encyclopedia differs significantly from other reference works on Western occult traditions. First, it is written by an occult practitioner, from a practitioner's point of view. While there can be some value in the "beginner's mind" of the writer who has no background in his or her subject, there is a great deal more to be said for writing about things one has actually done. We normally expect biology texts to be written by biologists, books on library science to be written by librarians, books on music to be written by people who have spent plenty of time listening to music (if not playing it themselves), and so forth. That most scholarly books on magic have been written by people who literally don't know which end of a wand to grab does not speak well of current academic attitudes to the occult —and it has produced a bumper crop of avoidable errors.

At the same time, unlike most books written by occult practitioners, this encyclopedia draws extensively from the scholarly literature on the history and development of occult traditions. If most scholars have no practical experience of magic, it's equally true that books on occultism written by occultists are routinely full of embarrassing historical errors that even the most basic research would catch at once.

You'll still find books on the stands, for example, claiming that the name of the tarot deck comes from the ancient Egyptian words *tar*, "road," and *rosh*, "royal." It takes five minutes with a dictionary of ancient Egyptian to find out that *tar* and *rosh* aren't ancient Egyptian words at all, and that the actual ancient Egyptian words for "road" and "royal" are *w3t* and *nsw* respectively. It may take a little longer, but not much, to find out that the etymology of tarot as *tar-rosh* was first proposed by an eighteenth-century French dilettante, Antoine Court de Gebelin (1728–1784), more than forty years before Champollion first deciphered Egyptian hieroglyphs ... at a time, in other

THE NEW
ENCYCLOPEDIA

Photograph by Robert Carroll

ABOUT THE AUTHOR

John Michael Greer is an occult scholar and the award-winning author of more than a dozen books on esoteric topics. A practitioner of magic and the Western mystery traditions for more than thirty years, his background combines academic study with training and initiation in several occult and Druid orders, including the Hermetic Order of the Golden Dawn and the Order of Bards, Ovates, and Druids. Greer currently serves as Grand Archdruid of the Ancient Order of Druids in America. He lives in Oregon.

THE NEW ENCYCLOPEDIA

of the Occult

JOHN MICHAEL GREER

Llewellyn Publications
Woodbury, Minnesota

FIRST EDITION
Sixth Printing, 2010

Book design and editing by Rebecca Zins
Cover design by Kevin R. Brown
Interior illustrations by Llewellyn Art Department
Universal Tarot by Roberto De Angelis used by permission of Lo Scarabeo ©2000

Llewellyn is a registered trademark of Llewellyn Worldwide Ltd.

Library of Congress Cataloging-in-Publication Data
   Greer, John Michael.
     The new encyclopedia of the occult / John Michael Greer.
       p. cm.
     Includes bibliographical references.
     ISBN 13: 978-1-56718-336-8
     ISBN 10: 1-56718-336-0
     1. Occultism—North America—Encyclopedias. 2. Occultism—Western Europe—Encyclopedias. 3. Occultism—History—North America—Encyclopedias. 4. Occultism—History—Western Europe—Encyclopedias.
I. Title.

   BF1407.G74 2003
   133'.03—dc21
                                2003054504

Llewellyn Publications
A Division of Llewellyn Worldwide Ltd.
2143 Wooddale Drive
Woodbury, MN 55125-2989
www.llewellyn.com

 Printed in the United States of America on recycled paper

OTHER BOOKS BY
JOHN MICHAEL GREER

Paths of Wisdom:
The Magical Cabala in the Western Tradition

Circles of Power:
Ritual Magic in the Western Tradition

Inside a Magical Lodge:
Group Ritual in the Western Tradition

Natural Magic:
Potions and Powers from the Magical Garden

Earth Divination, Earth Magic:
A Practical Guide to Geomancy

Sacred Geometry Oracle:
Become the Architect of Your Life

Monsters:
An Investigator's Guide to Magical Beings

Encyclopedia of Natural Magic

Atlantis:
Ancient Legacy, Hidden Prophecy

Secrets of the Lost Symbol
The Unauthorized Guide to Secret Societies, Hidden Symbols & Mysticism

The UFO Phenomenon
Fact, Fantasy and Disinformation

words, when neither Court de Gebelin nor anyone else knew a single word of the ancient Egyptian language.

Misinformation of this sort should have no place in serious occult study. To be honest, it's embarrassing that occultists who would never consecrate a talisman with misspelled words of power are perfectly comfortable repeating such things without making any effort to doublecheck their sources. This encyclopedia, among other things, will make it a good deal easier to do so, if the will is there.

By convention, the names of sacred texts such as the Corpus Hermeticum, the Zohar, and the Bible are capitalized but not put into italics, while the names of technical handbooks of magic and other inner practices, such as the *Lesser Key of Solomon* and the *Spiritual Exercises* of Ignatius Loyola are italicized.

As (among other things) a Druid, a Freemason, a geomancer, a Cabalistic ceremonial magician, and an ordained minister of a church with roots in traditional Louisiana hoodoo, my occult background is fairly broad, but the occult traditions of the West cover more ground than any one person can possibly master. In many fields, I have inevitably had to call on the expertise of people more knowledgeable than myself. Similarly, my personal background in historical research does not begin to cover the millennial sweep and global scale of Western occultism as a whole, and I have relied extensively on the work of competent scholars in areas of detail outside my own knowledge base.

In one way or another, I have thus had the help of well over a hundred people in this project. Rather than filling pages with a list of names (and finding some way to give equal thanks to those who would prefer that their names not be mentioned), I would like simply to offer all of you my thanks and gratitude here. You know who you are!

I would also like to encourage readers who disagree with points made in the following pages, or who have information on subjects I don't cover adequately, to contact me through the publisher of this volume and pass on the information you have. Circumstances permitting, I hope to bring out a revised edition of *The New Encyclopedia of the Occult* a few years down the line, with new material brought in and errors corrected. Any help that can be provided will be greatly appreciated. (On the other hand—and unfortunately, this does have to be said—if you claim to be a 2,318th-generation practitioner of an authentic Neanderthal family tradition of spirituality, handed down to you by your now-deceased third degree Neanderthal grandmother, and the only evidence you have is the oral tradition you claim to have received and a book written on mammoth hide that is too sacred to show to me or anyone else, I may not be in a hurry to get your alleged tradition's alleged history into the revised *Encyclopedia*.)

As this may suggest, the realm of the occult contains truth and nonsense, profound wisdom and prodigious folly. When human beings confront the realms of transformative power that lie just outside the ambit of ordinary consciousness, they reveal their humanity most completely—with all the strengths and weaknesses, brilliance and blundering that this implies. I have tried to present all sides of the picture as clearly as possible; the traditions themselves deserve no less. I hope you, the reader, find the result as entertaining and enlightening to read as it was for me to research and write.

A.˙. A.˙. *SEE* ARGENTEUM ASTRUM.

Aarab Tzereq. (Hebrew AaRB ZRQ, "ravens of dispersion") In Cabalistic teaching, the Qlippoth or demonic powers corresponding to Netzach, the seventh Sephirah of the Tree of Life. Their traditional form is that of demon-headed ravens emerging from an erupting volcano, the latter itself a demonic power named Getzphiel. Their cortex or realm in the Kingdom of Shells is Theumiel, and their archdemon is Baal Chanan. *SEE* QLIPPOTH.

Aatik Yomin. (Hebrew AaThIK IVMIN) "Ancient of Days," a title of Kether. *SEE* KETHER.

Ab. (Hebrew AaB, "darkness, obscurity") In the Cabala, the secret name of the world of Atziluth. The numerical values of its letters add up to seventy-two, which is also the sum of IVD HIH VIV HIH, the spelling of the Tetragrammaton in Atziluth. *SEE* ATZILUTH; TETRAGRAMMATON.

Abaris. According to legends recounted in ancient Greek sources, a Scythian magician who possessed a magical arrow that could ride through the air. He was said to have lived in the time of Pythagoras, the Greek mathematician and mystic, and visited the latter at his school in Crotona, Italy. Writers from the eighteenth century onward converted Abaris into a Druid, as part of a claim that Pythagoras had studied with the Druids (or vice versa). *SEE* DRUIDS; PYTHAGORAS.

Abba. (Hebrew, "father") In Cabalistic symbolism, a title of the Sephirah Chokmah, and also of the first letter of the Tetragrammaton. *SEE* CHOKMAH; TETRAGRAMMATON.

Abbadon. (Hebrew ABDVN, "destruction") The name of a demon, whose attributes have been variously described, or of a part or level of hell, defined with equal variability. In Cabalistic lore, Abbadon is the name of the sixth hell, which corresponds to the Sephirah Chesed. *SEE* HELLS, SEVEN.

Abel. The second son of Adam, according to the Book of Genesis, slain by his brother Cain. In Gnostic thought, Abel became the original of the "psychic" class of humanity, those who had the potential to achieve gnosis but did not have gnosis innately. *SEE* GNOSTICISM.

Abracadabra. A traditional word of power, used by Western magicians from classical times to the present. Written in the following way, it was used in talismans to cure fevers and asthma:

In recent times, Abracadabra has mostly been used by stage magicians. English mage Aleister Crowley (1875–1947) altered the spelling to make it fit his new magical religion of Thelema, and in this new form the word has been much used in the Thelemite community; SEE ABRAHADABRA. SEE ALSO BARBAROUS NAMES.

Abrahadabra. Aleister Crowley's reformulation of the older magical name Abracadabra, rewritten to place the name *Had*—the shorter form of *Hadith*, the second person of the Thelemite trinity—at its center. SEE CROWLEY, ALEISTER; THELEMA.

Abramelin the Mage, The Sacred Magic of. A grimoire preserved in a single eighteenth-century copy in the Bibliotheque de l'Arsenal in Paris. Written in French, it claims to be a translation of a Hebrew original dating from 1458, although scholars have cast doubt on this claim.

According to the long preface, it represents the teachings of a Jewish magician named Abramelin, passed on by him to his student Abraham, and by the latter to his son Lamech. These teachings, which Abraham describes as the only valid magical system in the world, require the student to devote six months of prayer, repentance, and ritual to obtain the "Knowledge and Conversation of the Holy Guardian Angel." After this accomplishment, the student gains the power to command evil spirits through talismans composed of letter combinations.

The Sacred Magic was rediscovered in the late 1890s by Golden Dawn founder Samuel Mathers (1854–1918), and Mathers' English translation was published in 1898. It has had a major impact on magical thinking ever since, especially through its influence on Aleister Crowley (1875–1947), who used it as the template for much of his own understanding of magic. To this day the idea that magic is or should be directed toward the knowledge and contemplation of one's Holy Guardian Angel—a concept not found outside this work in older sources—is commonplace in magical writings.

The book itself, however, developed a sinister reputation among occultists in the early part of this century. Dire accidents and mental imbalance were held to have befallen many of those who owned a copy of the original printing, or who tried to use the talismans contained in it. SEE ALSO HOLY GUARDIAN ANGEL. FURTHER READING: MATHERS 1974.

Abrasax. SEE ABRAXAS.

Abraxas. A popular magical deity in the ancient world, Abraxas (also called Abrasax) was depicted on classical amulet gems as a humanlike figure with a rooster's head and serpents for feet, wielding a charioteer's whip. The letters of his name in Greek add up to 365, the number of days in a year, which marked him as a solar deity and a lord of time. SEE GEMATRIA.

In modern times Abraxas has achieved a new popularity by way of the writings of the psychologist Carl Jung, who gave him a central place in his Gnostic work *The Seven Sermons to the Dead* and elsewhere in his writings. SEE JUNG, CARL GUSTAV.

Abred. In Druidry, one of the Three Worlds; the realm of plant and animal life through which souls journey in the course of their spiritual evolution. Each soul begins its incarnations in the simplest form of single-celled organism, and progress step by step, learning the lessons of every kind of plant and animal life, until they reach the human level, on the border between Abred and the higher life of Gwynfydd. SEE DRUIDRY; THREE WORLDS.

Abulafia, Abraham. Jewish Cabalist, 1240–after 1292. Born in Saragossa in Spain, he studied the Jewish scriptures and Talmud with his father until the latter's death in 1258. In 1260 he left Spain for the Holy Land, arriving in the city of Acre, but the outbreak of war between Christian Crusaders and Arabs forced him to leave. After a short stay in Greece, he went to Capua, Italy, where he encountered a distinguished rabbi, Hillel, who taught him philosophy, particularly the writings of Moses Maimonides.

His travels took him to Rome and then back to Spain, and it was in Barcelona, in 1271, that "God awakened me from my sleep, and I learned the Sepher Yetzirah and its commentaries," as he noted in his autobiography. This occurred under the guidance of Baruch Togarmi, a Cabalist about whom almost nothing is known. Abulafia's spiritual awakening ushered in a period of intense mystical experience, during which he wrote several books on the mysteries of the Cabala, teaching a highly idiosyncratic system of meditation on combinations of Hebrew letters. After this period he claimed prophetic powers, a claim that did not endear him to more orthodox Jews.

In 1279, convinced that God had commanded him to convert Pope Nicholas III to Judaism, he traveled to Rome, and then to Saronno, where the pope was staying at that time. Word of his mission preceded him, and the pope ordered that he should be seized and burned at the stake if he presented himself for an audience. Abulafia was informed of this, and showed up anyway—to find that the pope had died during the night. He was imprisoned by the Franciscans for a month and then released.

He returned to Barcelona, but in 1280 Rabbi Shlomo ben Adret (1235–1310), a distinguished legalist and scholar who was also a Cabalist, became chief rabbi of Barcelona's Jewish community. Rabbi Shlomo had no time whatsoever for Abulafia's prophetic claims and denounced him as a fraud and a lunatic. Abulafia moved to Sicily, living first in Palermo and then in Messina, and gained a number of followers, but here, too, opposition from more orthodox rabbis mounted, and he was forced to move to the little island of Comino, near Malta, where he spent the rest of his life. The date of his death is not known.

Abulafia's prophetic and messianic claims were too much for most Jews (and even most Cabalists) to swallow during his lifetime, but his writings on the *Derek ha-Shemoth* or "Way of the Names," his methods of contemplation using combinations of the Hebrew letters, were gradually adopted in Cabalistic circles in the century after his death. SEE ALSO CABALA; HEBREW ALPHABET. FURTHER READING: IDEL 1988, A. KAPLAN 1982, SCHOLEM 1974.

Ac. (Old English, "oak") The twenty-fifth rune of the Anglo-Saxon futhorc, described in the Old English rune-poem as "fodder for pigs and timber for ships on spear-sharp seas." It represents the sound *ai*. SEE ALSO ANGLO-SAXON FUTHORC.

Rune Ac

Achad, Frater. (Jones, Charles Stansfield) Canadian occultist, 1886–1950. Born in London, the son of an engineer, he ran a tobacco shop as a young man while study-

ing accounting. In 1906, he started investigating spiritualism with an eye to debunking it, but in the process developed an interest in the occult. This led him to Aleister Crowley's magical order, the Argenteum Astrum (A∴A∴), which he joined as a Probationer in 1909. Moving to Canada in 1910, he continued his studies with Crowley's associate J. F. C. Fuller. He was initiated into Crowley's other magical order, the Ordo Templi Orientis (OTO), in 1911, and proceeded to found the first OTO lodge in North America, Agape Lodge, in 1914. *SEE* ORDO TEMPLI ORIENTIS (OTO).

Their correspondence, and Crowley's visit to Vancouver in 1915, greatly impressed Crowley with Jones' mastery of Cabala. The younger man's interpretation of a cryptic passage in the *Book of the Law* led Crowley to acclaim the younger man as his "magical son."

Under Crowley's tutelage, Jones progressed to the grade of Magister Templi in the A∴A∴, and his work was serialized in Crowley's periodical *The Equinox* under the title "A Master of the Temple." In 1921, he became head of the Ordo Templi Orientis for North America, receiving a charter from OTO head Theodor Reuss, and for a time was involved in the Byzantine politics of that order. Like nearly all of Crowley's disciples, though, Jones found it impossible to put up with the Beast for long, and his approach to the Cabala also moved in directions incompatible with Crowley's own opinions.

As a result of his Cabalistic studies, Jones devised an entirely new set of attributions of the tarot trumps to the Tree of Life, and thus a distinctive Cabala, which is still used by some magicians today. His attributions are as follows:

> The Fool. *Path:* 11. *Letter:* Aleph.
>   *Connecting:* Malkuth-Yesod.
> The Magician. *Path:* 12. *Letter:* Beth.
>   *Connecting:* Malkuth-Hod.
> The High Priestess. *Path:* 13. *Letter:* Gimel.
>   *Connecting:* Yesod-Hod.
> The Empress. *Path:* 14. *Letter:* Daleth.
>   *Connecting:* Malkuth-Netzach.
> The Emperor. *Path:* 15. *Letter:* Heh.
>   *Connecting:* Tiphareth-Geburah.

The Hierophant. *Path:* 16. *Letter:* Vau.
Connecting: Hod-Netzach.

The Lovers. *Path:* 17. *Letter:* Zayin.
Connecting: Hod-Tiphareth.

The Chariot. *Path:* 18. *Letter:* Cheth.
Connecting: Yesod-Netzach.

Strength. *Path:* 19. *Letter:* Teth.
Connecting: Netzach-Tiphareth.

The Hermit. *Path:* 20. *Letter:* Yod.
Connecting: Hod-Geburah.

Wheel of Fortune. *Path:* 21. *Letter:* Kaph.
Connecting: Chokmah-Kether.

Justice. *Path:* 22. *Letter:* Lamed.
Connecting: Netzach-Chesed.

The Hanged Man. *Path:* 23. *Letter:* Mem.
Connecting: Yesod-Tiphareth.

Death. *Path:* 24. *Letter:* Nun.
Connecting: Geburah-Chesed.

Temperance. *Path:* 25. *Letter:* Samech.
Connecting: Chesed-Chokmah.

The Devil. *Path:* 26. *Letter:* Ayin.
Connecting: Tiphareth-Binah.

The Tower. *Path:* 27. *Letter:* Peh.
Connecting: Geburah-Binah.

The Star. *Path:* 28. *Letter:* Tzaddi.
Connecting: Binah-Chokmah.

The Moon. *Path:* 29. *Letter:* Qoph.
Connecting: Tiphareth-Chesed.

The Sun. *Path:* 30. *Letter:* Resh.
Connecting: Tiphareth-Chokmah.

Judgement. *Path:* 31. *Letter:* Shin.
Connecting: Tiphareth-Kether.

The Universe. *Path:* 32. *Letter:* Tau.
Connecting: Binah-Kether.

After his attainment of the Magister Templi grade, Jones returned briefly to England and joined the Roman Catholic Church in an attempt to convince Catholics to accept Crowley's Law of Thelema. This had predictably little effect, and he returned to Vancouver, where he wandered about the streets for a time dressed only in a raincoat, which he threw off in public, proclaiming that he had cast aside all the veils of illusion. This led to a brief stay in a mental institution.

In the 1920s Jones lived in Detroit and New York, and wrote several books expounding his system of Cabalistic mysticism, including *Q. B. L., or the Bride's Reception* (1923); *Chalice of Ecstasy* (1923), a study of the mystical dimensions of Wagner's opera *Parsifal*; and *The Anatomy of the Body of God* (1925), a study of the geometries of the Tree of Life. He was back in British Columbia by 1930, and gradually became convinced that Crowley had failed to proclaim the Word of the Aeon of Horus, and that he himself was destined to proclaim a different aeon, that of Maat or Ma-Ion. A series of mystical experiences in the 1930s and 1940s convinced him of this mission, and in April 1948, Jones formally announced that the New Aeon had arrived. He started a magical order called the Fellowship of Ma-Ion, devoted to the coming "Ma-Ion era of truth and justice," which survived his death and still has lodges in North America. SEE ALSO CROWLEY, ALEISTER.

Acquisitio. (Latin, "gain") A geomantic figure governed by Jupiter. Acquisitio signifies good fortune, especially in practical matters. SEE GEOMANCY.

Geomantic figure Acquisitio

Adam. (Hebrew ADM, "red") In the Book of Genesis and later Jewish and Christian tradition, the first human being, created by God on the sixth day of Creation. The orthodox account holds that he was created out of the dust of the earth. In the accounts of Gnosticism, the Cabala, and many other occult traditions, by contrast, Adam at his making was a luminous spiritual being possessed of nearly divine qualities.

A legend much repeated in the Middle Ages held that Seth, the third son of Adam and Eve, returned to the gate of the Garden of Eden and received from the angelic guardians three seeds from the Tree of Life. When Adam died, Seth placed these three seeds in the mouth of the corpse before its burial. From the seeds grew a tree which, after many other adventures, provided the wood for the cross on which Jesus of Nazareth was crucified.

In later Cabalistic writing, Adam is often interpreted as humanity as a whole, sometimes as a collection of souls, sometimes as a single entity—the so-called Adam Qadmon or "Primordial Adam"—of whom each human soul is a miniscule part. SEE ALSO EVE; FALL, THE.

Adamah. (Hebrew ADMH, "red clay") The second of the seven earths of Cabalistic lore, corresponding to Chesed. SEE EARTHS, SEVEN.

adept. (from Latin *adeptus*, "skillful") In most systems of Western occult thought, a title or grade used for (and by) advanced students of magic, alchemy, and other occult subjects. In alchemical tradition, only those capable of making the Philosopher's Stone were considered adepts. SEE PHILOSOPHER'S STONE. In modern ceremonial magic, similarly, the title is usually reserved for those who have penetrated the Veil of the Sanctuary and entered into contact with their Higher Genius or Holy Guardian Angel. SEE HOLY GUARDIAN ANGEL.

Some confusion has been caused over the years by the use of "adept" in occult lodges as a grade of initiation, since those who have passed through a given grade ritual may or may not have attained the spiritual experience that grade represents. As a result, the term has passed out of use in many parts of the magical community, except as a label for these grades. SEE ALSO MASTERS.

Adeptus Exemptus. The ninth grade in the Golden Dawn system of initiation, corresponding with the Sephirah Chesed. SEE CHESED; GOLDEN DAWN, HERMETIC ORDER OF THE.

Adeptus Major. The eighth grade in the Golden Dawn system of initiation, corresponding to the Sephirah Geburah. SEE GEBURAH; GOLDEN DAWN, HERMETIC ORDER OF THE.

Adeptus Minor. The seventh grade in the Golden Dawn system of initiation, corresponding to the Sephirah Tiphareth. This was the highest grade generally worked in Golden Dawn temples, and its initiation ritual—which takes place in a reconstruction of the Vault of Christian Rosencreutz—is considered by many to be the best of the Golden Dawn grade ceremonies. SEE GOLDEN DAWN, HERMETIC ORDER OF THE; TIPHARETH.

ADF. SEE AR NDRAIOCHT FEIN.

Adocentyn. In the *Picatrix*, an Arabic manual of Hermetic magic much used in medieval and Renaissance Europe, a walled city said to have been built by Hermes Trismegistus in the east of Egypt, its four gates guarded by talking magical statues, its citadel topped with a lighthouse tower that illuminated the city with one of the seven planetary colors, and its walls engraved with magical images that kept the inhabitants virtuous and safe from harm. The city of Adocentyn seems to have inspired many of the Hermetic Utopian schemes of the later Renaissance, such as Campanella's *City of the Sun* and J. V. Andreae's *Christianopolis*. SEE ALSO HERMETICISM; PICATRIX. FURTHER READING: YATES 1964.

Adonai. (Hebrew ADNI, "Lord") One of the traditional Hebrew names of God, usually assigned to the tenth Sephirah of the Tree of Life, Malkuth. In reading the Bible aloud in Jewish religious services, this name is used whenever the text gives YHVH, the Tetragrammaton, which is considered too sacred to vocalize. SEE TETRAGRAMMATON.

Adonai was among the first of the Jewish divine names to be taken up by non-Jewish magicians, and appears frequently in classical magical texts such as the Graeco-Egyptian magical papyri. SEE GRAECO-EGYPTIAN MAGICAL PAPYRI. The relation of this name to the God of the Old Testament was sometimes remembered and sometimes completely forgotten; in some sources, Adonai or Adonaios is an angel, in others an independent divine being, and in still others an archon—that is, a power of ignorance or evil. SEE ALSO CABALA.

Adonai ha-Aretz. (Hebrew, "Lord of Earth") In Cabala, one of two divine names attributed to the Sephirah Malkuth; the other is Adonai Malak. SEE MALKUTH.

Adonai Malak. (Hebrew, "Lord King") In Cabala, one of two divine names attributed to the Sephirah Malkuth; the other is Adonai ha-Aretz. SEE MALKUTH.

Adoptive Masonry. Any of several quasi-Masonic lodge systems for women, usually organized and run by male Freemasons. Many such systems came into existence in the eighteenth century, spurred by the success of the Mopses and other orders open to both genders. The Grand Orient of France in 1774 organized these into a rite of three degrees called the Rite of Adoption.

In the United States, the Order of the Eastern Star is the most popular adoptive rite, although there are several others. None of these rites seems to have included much in the way of occult content, but adoptive lodges once played an important role in training women in initiatory ritual and lodge management—skills that were sometimes put to use in more explicitly magical contexts. *SEE ALSO* EASTERN STAR, ORDER OF THE; FREEMASONRY; MOPSES, ORDER OF.

adytum. In ancient Greek and Roman religion, a shrine built into the basement level of a temple and used for ceremonies not open to the general public. The term has been used in several occult organizations, either as a synonym for "temple" or in a more metaphorical sense. *SEE* BUILDERS OF THE ADYTUM (BOTA).

aeon. (Greek *aion*, "age, world") A word with several different meanings in the occult traditions of the West. In Gnosticism and related traditions, the aeons were the powers of the transcendent spiritual realms of being, often equated with the stars or constellations of the zodiac. The aeons were distinct from and opposed to the archons, the diabolical and ignorant planetary powers of the corrupt created world in which human souls are now imprisoned. *SEE* GNOSTICISM.

In some sources, including the Graeco-Egyptian magical papyri, Aeon or Aion is a god, the ruler of eternity, and may be a Greek version of the Zoroastrian supreme god Zurvan Ahankara, lord of time.

In Thelema, the religious and magical system devised by Aleister Crowley, an aeon is a period of some two thousand years governed by a particular divine force. According to Crowley, the revelation of the *Book of the Law* in 1904 marked the end of the Aeon of Osiris and the coming of the Aeon of Horus, the Crowned and Conquering Child. *SEE* THELEMA.

On Crowley's death in 1947, Crowley's student and erstwhile "magical son" Charles Stansfield Jones announced that since Crowley had failed to properly proclaim the Word of the Aeon, the Aeon of Horus was cancelled; Jones then proclaimed a different new aeon, that of Maat, Goddess of Justice. *SEE* ACHAD, FRATER.

aerial niter. In alchemy, another term for niter. *SEE* NITER.

Aesc. (Old English, "ash tree") The twenty-sixth rune of the Anglo-Saxon futhorc, described in the Old English rune-poem as "a shield protecting man from all attacks." It represents the sound *ae*. *SEE* ANGLO-SAXON FUTHORC.

Rune Aesc

Aesh. (Hebrew ASh, "fire") The Hebrew word for the element of fire, often used in Cabalistic magic. *SEE* FIRE.

aethaevoyance. In the writings of American magician P. B. Randolph (1825–1875), the form of clairvoyance that allows access to the "ineffable Beyond"—in more standard magical terminology, the mental and spiritual planes. *SEE* CLAIRVOYANCE; MENTAL PLANE; RANDOLPH, PASCHAL BEVERLY; SPIRITUAL PLANE. *SEE ALSO* ZORVOYANCE.

aett. (Old Norse, "eight") In runelore, one of three divisions of the elder futhark; *SEE* ELDER FUTHARK. The same term is also used for the eight directions or airts; *SEE* AIRT.

African Architects, Order of. A semi-occult order founded in Germany in the late eighteenth century by C. F. Koffen, a government official. At its height it had lodges in Worms, Cologne, and Paris. Members were required to be Master Masons in good standing. It worked the following grades:

Lower

1. Apprentice of Egyptian Secrets
2. Initiate into Egyptian Secrets

3. Cosmopolitan
4. Christian Philosopher
5. Alethophilos ("Lover of Truth")

Higher

1. Esquire
2. Soldier
3. Knight

The order seems to have gone out of existence during the Napoleonic wars. *SEE ALSO* FREEMASONRY.

Agathodaemon. (Greek, "good spirit") Originally a spirit invoked at Greek banquets, Agathodaemon evolved into a guardian deity frequently invoked by late classical magicians. His name appears throughout the Graeco-Egyptian magical papyri; *SEE* GRAECO-EGYPTIAN MAGICAL PAPYRI.

Agharta. An underground city of Masters said to be located somewhere in central Asia, a fixture of late nineteenth- and twentieth-century occult mythology and New Age legend, also spelled Aghartta, Agharti, Agartha, and Arghati. Agharta is one of the most remarkable products of occult history—a rich fabric of legend woven out of a mixture of Victorian anthropology, occult politics, and thin air.

The origins of Agharta can be traced back to nineteenth-century attempts to interpret mythology in euhemerist terms as a record of the history of forgotten ages; *SEE* EUHEMERISM. For reasons having much to do with the racist ideologies popular at that time, ancient Germanic myth was a popular source for such projects, and Odin and the other gods and goddesses of Asgard were turned into pseudohistorical figures by a number of authors.

One of these was Louis Jacolliot (1837–1890), a French colonial official in Chandernagor, India, who wrote a great many popular books on myth, history, and religion. In his book *Le Fils de Dieu* (*The Son of God*, 1873), Jacolliot claimed to have been shown ancient manuscripts by friendly Brahmins revealing the 15,000-year history of India. Jacolliot's "ancient manuscripts" seem to have come out of his own head; the history he recounts has very little in common with the traditional history of India as recorded in Hindu scriptures and epic

literature, and a good deal more to do with Norse mythology and nineteenth-century speculations about prehistory.

According to Jacolliot, the capital of India in ancient times had been the city of Asgartha—which is simply Asgarth, an alternative spelling of Asgard, with a final *a* added to make it look like Sanskrit. His "Hindu sources" also provided a detailed history of Asgartha and the rise and fall of its great empire, most of which bears a suspiciously close resemblance to the attempts to historify Norse mythology mentioned above.

Jacolliot's book had a wide circulation in France, carrying his claims about "Asgartha" to a large audience. It's uncertain, however, just how those claims came into the hands of the next major figure in the genesis of Agharta, the French occultist J. A. Saint-Yves d'Alveydre. Saint-Yves, a dedicated if eccentric student of the occult and a proponent of exotic political schemes, claimed to have learned of Aghartta (his usual spelling) while learning Sanskrit from one Haji Sharif, whom he described as "a high official of the Hindu church" but who seems to have been a parrot-shop proprietor in Le Havre (and whose name is decidedly Muslim rather than Hindu). The balance of evidence suggests that it was Haji Sharif who introduced Agharta to Saint-Yves, but it was Saint-Yves himself who reshaped it into what would be its standard form.

In 1886 Saint-Yves had a book on Agharta, *Mission de l'Inde en Europe* (*The Mission of India in Europe*), printed at his own expense. Fearing that he had said too much about the hidden city, he then abruptly had all but two copies destroyed. In 1910, a year after Saint-Yves' death, the book was reissued. It described how Saint-Yves had mastered the art of astral travel as a result of his studies with Haji Sharif. This had allowed him to make his way to Aghartta and report back on what he had found: a vast underground city inhabited by millions of people, under the absolute rule of a Sovereign Pontiff wielding advanced technologies as well as mystical powers. The whole tale is marked by heavy borrowings from Jacolliot, Bulwer-Lytton's novel *The Coming Race*, and the Theosophical "Mahatma letters."

Saint-Yves' works were standard reading in Martinist circles in Paris and elsewhere, and information about Agharta and its marvels was in circulation there long before the republication of *Mission de l'Inde*. It was probably by way of Martinist channels that Saint-Yves' description of Agharta made its way into the hands of the hidden city's great publicist, the Polish Ferdinand Ossendowski. In 1922, after traveling in a central Asia wracked by the aftermath of the Russian Revolution, Ossendowski published the sensationally successful *Beasts, Men and Gods*, a book about his adventures. The first three chapters of this book are basically a summary of Saint-Yves' opus, although many of the terms are spelled differently; Saint-Yves' Aghartta, for example, has become Agharti. Though Ossendowski vigorously denied ever encountering Saint-Yves' book, the marks of plagiarism are fairly clear, and Ossendowski's honesty and accuracy have been sharply challenged on other counts; *SEE* PALLIS 1983.

Ossendowski's book gave the mythology of Agharta the form it has taken ever since. In the hands of Traditionalist philosopher René Guénon, who devoted his book *Le Roi du Monde* (*The King of the World*, 1927) to the subject, it became the basis for a subtle exploration of metaphysics and myth. Most of its later propagation, though, was filtered through channels such as the science-fiction magazine *Amazing Stories*, which made room for stories about Agharta in the 1940s along with accounts of sinister subterranean deros (dwarfs), fringe science, and technologies for which the world was not yet prepared; *SEE* DEROS; SHAVER MYSTERY.

Agharta soon became a fixture of New Age and alternative reality circles in America and elsewhere, a position it has held ever since. It has been frequently associated, and just as frequently confused, with that other mysterious city of central Asia, Shambhala; *SEE* SHAMBHALA. Among serious occult students, however, accounts of Agharta have found little support in recent decades. *SEE ALSO* MASTERS; OCCULT HISTORY; SAINT-YVES D'ALVEYDRE, JOSEPH-ALEXANDRE. FURTHER READING: J. GODWIN 1993, GUENON 1983, KAFTON-MINKEL 1989, OSSENDOWSKI 1922, PALLIS 1983.

Agiel. In ceremonial magic, the planetary intelligence of Saturn. Its subordinate spirit is Zazel. *SEE* INTELLIGENCE, PLANETARY.

AGLA. A Cabalistic divine Name formed by notariqon from the Hebrew sentence *Ateh Gibor Le-olam, Adonai* ("Mighty art Thou forever, Lord"). It was much used in medieval ceremonial magic as a word giving power over demons. In Golden Dawn magic, this name governs the passive aspect of the element of spirit, and is also used in the northern quarter in the Lesser Ritual of the Pentagram. *SEE* NOTARIQON.

Agrippa, Heinrich Cornelius. German occultist, 1486–1535. Born to a noble but relatively poor family, Agrippa showed promise as a scholar from childhood, and attended the University of Cologne, where he first encountered books on magic. After finishing his course of studies at Cologne, he spent some time as a soldier, and then began a series of journeys that took him over most of Europe. There were plenty of footloose scholars on the move during the Renaissance, but Agrippa was among the most constant travelers of the time, and he always seemed to have well-organized circles of friends and supporters wherever he went. The possibility that he was the emissary of a secret magical society has been considered even by entirely orthodox historians.

In 1509 and 1510 he visited the wizard-abbot Johannes Trithemius at Sponheim, and there wrote the first draft of his massive *De Occulta Philosophia Libri Tres* (*Three Books of Occult Philosophy*), which circulated in manuscript among a small circle of friends. *SEE* TRITHEMIUS, JOHANNES. Later in 1510 he was in England, where he met with important scholars, and then traveled to Italy in 1511, where he met with Francesco Giorgi, the Venetian Cabalist and author of *De Harmonia Mundi*, and other Cabalistic and Hermetic scholars and practitioners. *SEE* GIORGI, FRANCESCO.

After some years in Italy, Agrippa was back in Germany by 1520, where he stayed for a while in Metz, and then moved on to Geneva in Switzerland where he stayed with occultist friends. 1524 saw him in France, where he published a satirical book called *De Vanitate Scientiarum* (*On the Vanity of Knowledge*); this argued that all human knowledge is flawed and uncertain.

In 1528 Agrippa was in Antwerp, where he revised the *Three Books of Occult Philosophy* and prepared them for their long-delayed publication. Traveling to France thereafter, he made an incautious remark about the French Queen Mother, Louise of Savoy, and spent a short time in prison as a result. On his release, he continued his journeys until his death at Grenoble in 1535. *SEE ALSO* CEREMONIAL MAGIC; HERMETICISM. FURTHER READING: NAUERT 1965, YATES 1979.

Agshekelah. *SEE* GA'ASHEKLAH.

Ahephi. *SEE* HAPI.

Ahriman. The spirit of the lie in Zoroastrian theology, source of all evil and relentless foe of the one true god Ormuzd, Ahriman is the probable ancestor of the Christian devil. The original form of his name, in the archaic Avestan language of the oldest Zoroastrian scriptures, is Angra Mainyu. His servants include a vast array of fiends and archfiends, of whom Aeshma Daeva is the chief; this latter name, rounded off by time, became Asmodeus, one of the standard demons of later magical tradition. *SEE* ZOROASTER.

In the teachings of Anthroposophy, the system of spiritual theory and practice created by Rudolf Steiner, Ahriman is one of two powers of evil blocking the course of human evolution, and represents attachment to material desires and experiences. *SEE* ANTHROPOSOPHY; LUCIFER.

Aia Aziz. *SEE* THEON, MAX.

Ailm. (Old Irish, "fir tree") The sixteenth letter of the Ogham alphabet, with the sound-value *a*. It corresponds to the silver fir among trees, the lapwing among birds, the color piebald, and the number one. In Robert Graves' version of the Ogham tree-calendar, this letter is associated with the winter solstice. *SEE* OGHAM.

Ogham letter Ailm

Aima. (Hebrew AIMA, "mother") The maternal principle in Cabalistic thought, associated with Binah, the third Sephirah of the Tree of Life, and paired with Abba, "father," an aspect of the second Sephirah Chokmah. Some Cabalistic writings draw a distinction between Aima, the bright fertile mother, and Ama, the dark sterile mother; this is based on gematria, since the values of the letters in Aima add to fifty-two, the number of Ben, "son," while those of Ama add to forty-two, a number associated with severity. *SEE* CABALA; GEMATRIA.

Aima Elohim. (Hebrew AIMA ALHIM, "mother of the gods and goddesses") Another title of Aima, used in the Golden Dawn tradition and other branches of occult Cabala. *SEE* AIMA.

Ain. (Hebrew AIN, "not, nothing") The third and highest of the Three Veils of the Unmanifest, which are located above Kether on the Tree of Life and represent the inability of created beings to experience the divine as it actually is. The other two Veils are Ain Soph and Ain Soph Aur. *SEE* CABALA; TREE OF LIFE.

Ain Soph. (Hebrew AIN SVP, "no limit, infinity") The second of the Three Veils of the Unmanifest; the other two are Ain and Ain Soph Aur. *SEE* AIN.

Ain Soph Aur. (Hebrew AIN SVP AVR, "light without limit, infinite light") The first and lowest of the Three Veils of the Unmanifest; the other two are Ain and Ain Soph. *SEE* AIN.

Aiq beker. A method of Cabalistic number analysis, also known as the Cabala of Nine Chambers and theosophical reduction. It is based on the numerical values of the Hebrew letters. In Aiq beker, Aleph (which has a value of 1), Yod (with a value of 10), and Qoph (with a value of 100) all equal 1; Beth (2), Kaph (20), and Resh (200) all equal 2; Gimel (3), Lamed (30), and Shin (300) all equal 3, and so on up the alphabet to Teth (9), Tzaddi (90), and Tzaddi final (900), which all equal 9. Each of these groups of numbers is a "chamber," and the nonsense-words "Aiq beker" are simply what happens when a speaker of Hebrew pronounces the letters in the first two chambers, AIQ BKR. Aside from its use as a tool for gematria, Aiq beker has also been put to use as the basis for ciphers and other methods of secret communication. *SEE ALSO* CABALA; GEMATRIA.

air, element of. In magical symbolism, one of the four (or five) elements, corresponding to matter in the gaseous state, to the warm and moist qualities, and to the sanguine humor. As with all the elements, there are varying attributions to the element of air, but the following are standard in most current Western occult systems:

Symbol: △

Letter of Tetragrammaton: ו, Vau

Name of God: יהוה, YHVH, Tetragrammaton

Archangel: רפאל, RPAL, Raphael

Angel: חשן, ChShN, Chassan

Ruler: אריאל, ARIAL, Ariel

Elemental King: Paralda

Elementals: Sylphs

Hebrew Name of Element: רוח, RVCh, Ruach

Direction: מזרח, MZRCh, Mizrach, the East

Season: Spring

Time of Day: Dawn

Qualities: Hot and wet

Nature: Separation

SEE ALSO DIRECTIONS IN OCCULTISM; ELEMENTS, MAGICAL; HUMORS.

Aire. (also Aethyr) In the Enochian magical system of John Dee, one of thirty realms forming the subtle atmosphere of the Earth, and located between the Earth's surface and the orbit of the moon. A "call" or "key" in the Enochian language, the longest piece of connected Enochian prose, is used to command the spirits and angels of the various Aires. SEE ENOCHIAN LANGUAGE; ENOCHIAN MAGIC.

airt. In the folk traditions of northwestern Europe, one of the eight directions and eight corresponding times of the day. *Airt* is the Gaelic term; the corresponding Norse term is *aett*.

Direction	Time of Day
East	Morntide (4:30 AM–7:30 AM)
Southeast	Daytide (7:30 AM–10:30 AM)
South	Midday (10:30 AM–1:30 PM)
Southwest	Undorne (1:30 PM–4:30 PM)
West	Eventide (4:30 PM–7:30 PM)
Northwest	Nighttide (7:30 PM–10:30 PM)
North	Midnight (10:30 PM–1:30 AM)
Northeast	Uht (1:30 AM–4:30 AM)

SEE ALSO DIRECTIONS IN OCCULTISM. FURTHER READING: PENNICK 1989.

Aiwass. The entity who communicated the Book of the Law to Aleister Crowley. SEE BOOK OF THE LAW; CROWLEY, ALEISTER.

akasha. In Hindu philosophy, the element of spirit, one of five tattvas or elemental forces in the universe. Its symbol is a black or indigo oval. SEE TATTVAS.

Borrowed by Theosophists and then by the Golden Dawn, the term *akasha* entered into common use in Western occult and quasi-occult circles. It is commonly used as a synonym either for spirit in general, for the "astral light" or subtle substance of the astral plane, or for ether, the subtle substance/energy of the etheric plane. SEE ASTRAL LIGHT; ETHER; SPIRIT, ELEMENT OF.

akashic records. In occult lore of the Theosophical period and modern New Age teachings, the permanent trace of all past events, preserved in the *akasha* or astral light. Many occult teachers of the last hundred and fifty years have claimed to be able to view the akashic records, and most versions of occult history derive at least part of their backing from this unverifiable but appealing source. SEE ALSO ASTRAL PLANE; OCCULT HISTORY.

Akhenaten. Egyptian pharaoh, reigned c.1370–c.1353 B.C.E. The discovery of Akhenaten's existence was one of the major surprises of nineteenth-century Egyptology. Starting in the 1840s, surveys of the Amarna plateau—a desolate site across the Nile from the ancient city of Hermopolis—turned up carvings of figures worshipping a sun-disk. The archeologists noted with surprise that the style of these carvings violated many of the standard principles of ancient Egyptian art, and that the names and faces of the figures had been systematically erased some time after they were originally carved. Interest in these so-called "disk worshippers" led to a series of digs at

Amarna, to the discovery of a lost city and a forgotten pharaoh, and to controversies that have yet to be settled.

Much of the confusion around Akhenaten is a product of modern interpretations heavy with bias. Nineteenth-century Egyptologists such as William Flinders Petrie projected their own Christian beliefs onto Akhenaten, and presented a glorified and largely inaccurate picture of his reign and his ideas. In the twentieth century, people ranging from the neo-Nazi theorist Savitri Devi to certain modern Rosicrucian figures have co-opted Akhenaten for their own points of view; *SEE* DEVI, SAVITRI; ANCIENT MYSTICAL ORDER ROSAE CRUCIS (AMORC). Ideas such as these are still current in many circles, and have done much to obscure the life of one of ancient Egypt's most complex figures.

Akhenaten was the second son of Amenhotep III, among the greatest kings of Egypt's Eighteenth Dynasty, and was originally named Amenhotep after his father. There may have been ill feeling between father and son, as the young Amenhotep—unlike his siblings—is not named or portrayed on his father's surviving monuments. Some modern researchers, noting some of the odder details of portraits of Akhenaten made during his reign, have suggested that he may have suffered from a serious hormonal disorder called Fröhlich's syndrome. Still, he became crown prince upon the death of his elder brother Thutmose, and ascended to the throne a few years later as Amenhotep IV.

Shortly after his coronation, according to an inscription that survives in fragmentary form, he proclaimed that the traditional gods and goddesses of Egypt were lifeless and powerless; the only true god was Aten, the disk of the sun. Over the next few years, he pushed through a religious revolution, abolishing the temples and priesthoods of all gods but his own, erasing the names of the old gods from monuments throughout Egypt, and changing his own name from Amenhotep, "Amun is satisfied," to Akhenaten, "Spirit of Aten."

In the first years of his reign, he built four massive temples for Aten in the capitol city of Thebes, and in the fifth year abandoned Thebes altogether and moved to the Amarna plateau to build a new city called Akhetaten, "Horizon of Aten." There he oversaw the construction of an immense temple to Aten and a lavish palace for himself, built and decorated in a new style that owed nothing to the traditional sacred geometries of classic Egyptian art and architecture.

Akhenaten was apparently the closest thing to a complete materialist that ancient Egypt ever produced. Mythic and symbolic modes of human experience passed him by completely. To other ancient Egyptians, the sun could be seen as a hawk hovering in the air, a celestial boat, a lion-headed or cat-headed goddess, or the right eye of a god; on its way through the sky, it did battle against a celestial serpent, risked running aground in the shoals of heaven, and carried the spirits of the dead to paradise.

To Akhenaten, none of this was true. The sun was a shining disk in the sky and nothing else, and its actions were limited to those that could be seen and measured with ordinary vision: rising, shining, nourishing plants, and so on. The gods of the temples, in turn, were nothing but dead statues. In place of the rich mythic texture of Egyptian religion, Akhenaten proclaimed his own teaching of the supremacy of Aten, the solar disk, as the one living god and source of all life. He was apparently a poet of some talent—an impressive hymn to Aten found in Amarna-period tombs is believed to have been written by the pharaoh himself—but his view of the world stopped at the edge of the visible.

The last years of his reign were troubled. The soaring taxes and forced labor needed for the pharaoh's massive building projects left Egypt in a state of economic crisis, and large parts of the Egyptian empire fell under the control of the expanding Hittite kingdom in the north. To make matters worse, epidemic disease swept the country. Many Egyptians felt that just as Egypt had abandoned the gods, the gods had abandoned Egypt.

Akhenaten's death, in the seventeenth year of his reign, brought his religious revolution to a halt. Three short-lived successors—Smenkhare, the boy-king Tutankhamen, and Ay—tried to find middle ground, maintaining the cult of Aten while permitting the old temples to be reopened. None of the three left heirs, and on Ay's death the double crown of Egypt passed to Horemheb, the commander of the army.

Horemheb has been made into a villain in many modern accounts of Akhenaten's reign and its aftermath. In reality, he was a shrewd realist who saw that cooperation between the military and the temple priesthoods was essential to Egypt's survival. His reign of twenty-five years restored Egypt to stability and prosperity, and laid the foundations for the successes of the Nineteenth Dynasty, founded by his adopted son and heir Rameses I. He cut taxes and reformed the court system to win popular support, and ensured the backing of the temple priesthoods by restoring the old temples to their original splendor and position in society. The complete termination of Akhenaten's religious revolution was an essential part of Horemheb's work. By the new pharaoh's command, the temples of Aten were systematically destroyed, and the city of Akhetaten—which had already been abandoned in Tutankhamen's reign—was razed to the ground. In the same way that Akhenaten himself had attempted to erase the names of the Egyptian gods, Horemheb ordered every trace of Akhenaten's god, his religion, his reign, his image, and his name erased from records and monuments throughout Egypt. The work was done thoroughly enough that only scattered references to "the accursed one of Akhetaten" remained to puzzle historians until the excavations at Amarna began to reveal what had happened. *SEE ALSO* EGYPTIAN OC-CULTISM. FURTHER READING: ALDRED 1988, ASSMAN 1995, HORNUNG 1983, REDFORD 1984.

Alban Arthuan. In modern Druidry, one of the four Alban Gates, the festival of the winter solstice; the name is traditionally translated as "the Light of Arthur." *SEE* ALBAN GATES; DRUIDRY; SABBAT.

Alban Eiler. In modern Druidry, one of the four Alban Gates, the festival of the spring equinox; the name is traditionally translated as "the Light of the Earth." *SEE* ALBAN GATES; DRUIDRY; SABBAT.

Alban Elued. In modern Druidry, one of the four Alban Gates, the festival of the fall equinox; the name is traditionally translated as "the Light of the Water." *SEE* ALBAN GATES; DRUIDRY; SABBAT.

Alban Gates. In modern Druidry, the four solar festivals of Alban Eiler, Alban Heruin, Alban Elued, and Alban Arthuan, which are held on or around the solstices and equinoxes. Until the 1950s these were the annual celebrations held by most Druid groups in England, but the four fire festivals or cross-quarter days—Imbolc (Candlemas), Beltane, Lughnasadh (Lammas), and Samhain—have been added to the ritual calendars of many Druid orders, making the Druid calendar and the Wiccan year-wheel essentially identical. *SEE* DRUIDRY; FIRE FESTIVALS; SABBAT.

Alban Heruin. In modern Druidry, one of the four Alban Gates, the festival of the summer solstice; the name is traditionally translated as "the Light of the Shore." *SEE* ALBAN GATES; DRUIDRY; SABBAT.

Albertus, Frater. (Reidel, Albert Richard) German-American alchemist, 1911–1984. The most important figure in twentieth-century American alchemy, Albert Reidel was born in Dresden, Germany, in 1911, and grew up in the middle of the burgeoning German occult scene between the wars. As a young man, he made connections with French and German alchemical circles, and claimed in later years to have met the mysterious adept Fulcanelli in 1937. *SEE* FULCANELLI.

He immigrated to America just before the outbreak of the Second World War and settled in California, where he made contact with the Rosicrucian order AMORC; *SEE* ANCIENT MYSTICAL ORDER ROSAE CRUCIS (AMORC). During the war years, he attended classes in practical alchemy offered at the Rose-Croix University, a school based at AMORC's San Jose headquarters. Later, he moved to the Salt Lake City area, where in 1960 he organized the Paracelsus Research Society to teach alchemy, Cabala, and a science of "astro-cyclic pulsations." The Paracelsus Research Society, later renamed Paracelsus College, was the most important center for alchemical instruction in twentieth-century America, and most of the major figures in the current American alchemical scene got their start attending classes there. Frater Albertus, as he preferred to call himself, focused on the practice of spagyrics (herbal alchemy) as the foundation for the more advanced alchemy of metals, and his extremely influential *Alchemist's Handbook* (1960) gave the basic details of several simple spagyric operations.

By the early 1980s Paracelsus College was on the verge of establishing its own campus, with buildings in the Gothic style, supported by the sale of spagyric medicines. Albertus' sudden death in 1984 brought these plans to a halt, and despite efforts on the part of several students to keep the college going, it folded shortly thereafter. SEE ALSO ALCHEMY; SPAGYRICS. FURTHER READING: ALBERTUS 1960.

Albertus Magnus. German monk, scholar, alchemist, and natural magician, 1206–1280. Born to a noble family at Lauringen in the German province of Swabia, Albertus traveled to Padua in Italy to pursue an education, concentrating on the teachings of the Greek philosopher Aristotle. He entered the Dominican Order in 1223 and rose swiftly through the ranks of the Catholic Church, rising to the position of bishop of Ratisbon in 1260. In 1262 he resigned from this position in order to pursue his scholarly interests, and spent the rest of his life writing and teaching.

Like many devout Catholics in the Middle Ages, Albertus rejected ceremonial magic as a diabolical art, but saw nothing wrong with astrology, natural magic, or alchemy. He studied and practiced all three of these arts, and wrote detailed studies of natural magic that became a major source for later writers on the subject. SEE ALCHEMY; ASTROLOGY; NATURAL MAGIC.

His alchemical work earned him a place in histories of modern chemistry, where he is cited as the discoverer of metallic arsenic and caustic potash, as well as the first person to determine the chemical composition of cinnabar, minium, and white lead. His book *On Alchemy*, which advised would-be alchemists on lifestyle issues as well as alchemical processes, became a model for many later treatises.

These interests did not cause him any difficulty with his superiors in the church, and his posthumous career was just as successful as his earthly one. He was beatified in 1622 and canonized as a saint in 1932 by Pope Pius XI. Some modern esoteric Christians consider him to be the patron saint of occultism. SEE ALSO CHRISTIAN OCCULTISM.

His reputation as a magician, while it did not hinder his sainthood proceedings, did earn him immortality of another sort in the European and American magical communities. An important seventeenth-century French handbook of magic, *Les admirables secrets d'Albert le Grand* (*The admirable secrets of Albertus Magnus*), borrowed him as author in the traditional style, as did the nineteenth-century German-American magical text *Albertus Magnus: Being the Approved, Verified, Sympathetic and Natural Egyptian Secrets; Or White and Black Art for Man and Beast*, which went on to become a major influence in American folk magic circles. SEE GRIMOIRE.

Albigensians. SEE CATHARS.

Albus. (Latin, "white") A geomantic figure governed by Mercury. Albus is a favorable figure, especially for economic questions. SEE GEOMANCY.

Geomantic figure Albus

alchemy. One of the principal branches of Western occult theory and practice, alchemy is the occult science of matter and its transformations. Commonly misunderstood as a futile effort to turn lead into gold, as a precursor of modern chemistry, or as a primitive form of depth psychology, alchemy is actually a complex, wide-reaching, and subtle assemblage of disciplines, united by a common theoretical structure but extending into nearly every imaginable field of human experience.

The basic concept of alchemy is the idea of transmutation. In alchemical thought, every material thing comes into being out of a common substance or combination of substances. This common basis follows patterns laid down by nature, but cannot always complete its natural course. Thus, for example, all metals start out as a fusion of two principles, usually called "sulphur" and "mercury" (but not identical to the minerals now called by the same names). Given the right proportions of these principles, moderate heat beneath the earth, and enough time, the result of the combination is gold.

As the alchemical proverb has it, though, "Nature unaided fails." Most of the time, sulphur and mercury are not present in the right proportions or degree of purity, the subterranean heat is either inadequate or excessive, or the veins of the rock are broken open by human action before the substance has matured into gold. When this happens, the alchemist must complete Nature's work.

This is done by separating the substance into its components, purifying them, and recombining them under the right conditions to bring them to their perfection. The Latin words *solve*, "dissolve," and *coagula*, "coagulate," are standard alchemical terms for the first and last stage of the essential alchemical process. When this is done with metals, according to alchemical tradition, the result is the transmutation of base metals into gold or silver. When it is done with healing herbs, the result is a powerful medicine. When it is done with the human mind, the result is spiritual enlightenment.

These changes, important as they are, are the lesser work of alchemy. They require that each substance to be transmuted has to pass through the whole slow process of separation and recombination. The Great Work of alchemy is the production of a substance that brings perfection to matter quickly, by simple contact: the Philosopher's Stone.

The Philosopher's Stone, or Stone of the Wise, is the result of the Great Work of metals; heated together with lead, mercury, or some other base metal, it is held to transmute the entire mass of base metal to gold in a matter of minutes. *SEE* PHILOSOPHER'S STONE. While current scientific theories insist that this is impossible, the process of transmutation by means of the Stone was witnessed repeatedly by reputable observers in the Renaissance and early modern periods. It remains possible, despite modern scientific advances, that matter has possibilities that have not yet been discovered—although, of course, this by itself does not prove the reality of transmutation.

The word "alchemy" has complex origins. Its English form comes from the Latin *alchemia*, which is from the Arabic *al-kimiyya*, which in turn comes from a Greek word spelled two different ways—*chymia* or *chemeia*. Chymia means "smelting" or "casting," and is related to *chyma*, "fluid." Chemeia, on the other hand, probably descends from the ancient Egyptian word *Khem*, "the Black Land," which is what Egyptians in pharaonic times called their own country; chemeia thus means something close

to "the Egyptian art." While some scholars have insisted on one or the other of these origins as the "real" one, the traditional literature of alchemy is full of meaningful puns and wordplay of this sort, and it's quite possible that the creators of alchemy relished the idea of a term that implied both what they were doing and where they originally learned to do it.

The origins of alchemy, like those of the Western occult tradition as a whole, are to be found in the fusion of Greek philosophy with the ancient cultural legacies of Egypt and Mesopotamia. The two older cultures brought a wealth of practical experience and a strong connection with spirituality to this union. Throughout the ancient world, the craft of the metalworker had been deeply interwoven with magic and religion. In ancient Egypt, the god Ptah was the master goldsmith of Heaven, and the chief priests of his primary temple in Memphis had titles such as Great Wielder of the Hammer and He Who Knows the Secret of the Goldsmiths. In the equally ancient cultures of Mesopotamia, the secrets of metalworking were sacred mysteries guarded by elusive language; copper was called "the eagle," crude mineral sulphur was referred to as "bank of the river," and so on. To this fusion of sacred and practical concerns Greek philosophy brought an insistent search for fundamental unities. The Greek philosophers constantly searched for one substance or one process that could explain the world. By the time of alchemy's emergence, the most important school of philosophical thought in the Greek-speaking world was Stoicism, with its teaching of a semi-material *pneuma* or "breath" that shaped all things; *SEE* STOICISM. This concept of the "One Thing" that produced all things became deeply woven into alchemical thought.

The actual genesis of alchemy out of these disparate currents of thought and practice was apparently the work of one man, a Greek-speaking Egyptian named Bolos of Mendes. Essentially nothing is known for sure about Bolos' life. He probably lived in the second century B.C.E., and he wrote several books, which he published under the name of the fifth-century Greek philosopher Democritus of Abdera. He is said to have studied with the Persian magus Ostanes, about whom even less is known. After his time, perhaps in the first century, were two famous female alchemists, Maria and Cleopatra, who were respectively Jewish and Egyptian and were confused by later writers with Miriam, sister of Moses, and Cleopatra the Egyptian queen. Maria was particularly influential as a major theorist as well as the inventor of several important items of alchemical equipment; *SEE* MARIA.

Later, in the early third century C.E., Zosimos of Panopolis wrote a number of important alchemical texts and codified the work of many anonymous alchemists who had gone before him; *SEE* ZOSIMUS OF PANOPOLIS. Other later Greek alchemists include Olympiodorus of Thebes, who lived in the early fifth century C.E. and wrote an important commentary, and Stephanos of Alexandria, one of the first Christian alchemists, who lived in the early eighth century C.E.

By that time, on the verge of the great Arab conquests, alchemy was already making its transition out of Greek culture into the Middle East as a whole. An important alchemical school had been established at Harran, on the road east from the Mediterranean coast to India, sometime in late Roman times. The Harranian alchemists pioneered the use of copper as an ingredient in alchemical processes, and left some important books. *SEE* HARRAN.

By the middle of the fifth century, additionally, Pagans and Christian heretics had begun to flee the Roman Empire in large numbers to escape religious persecution; many of them ended up in the Persian Empire, where they taught Greek philosophy and alchemy, among other things, to their hosts. When the Arabs conquered the Persian Empire in the eighth century, the exiles and their descendants began passing on the same lore to their new Muslim overlords, and launched the long and highly creative tradition of Arabic alchemy. Arab alchemists such as Geber (Jabir ibn Hayyan, 720–800 C.E.) and Rhazes (Abu-Bakr Muhammad ibn-Zakariya al-Razi, 850–923 C.E.) made massive improvements in alchemical theory and practice alike. Geber, among the most influential of all alchemists, wrote a crucial work on furnaces, providing detailed information on most of the furnace types that would be used until the end of the Renaissance, and was the first writer to describe the preparation of nitric acid. His contributions to theory were equally substantial; he introduced the sulphur-mercury theory of metals,

holding that all metals were formed from the fusion of sulphur, the principle of dryness and flammability, and mercury, the principle of moisture and volatility. *SEE* GEBER; MERCURY; SULPHUR. Rhazes, for his part, was a physician with an international reputation, and the author of medical works that were prized from Spain to India; his alchemical contributions included important works on the interface between alchemy and medicine.

Western Europe had little contact with alchemy during the time of the Roman Empire, and Rome's fall cut off contact between the West and the areas where alchemical research and writing were still continuing. It was not until 1144, when Robert of Chester made the first translation of an Arabic alchemical text into Latin, that European scholars and occultists began to get access to alchemical lore. The work Robert translated was a dialogue between the alchemist Morienus and King Khalid of Egypt—both of them, in typical alchemical style, fictional characters—in which some of the basic alchemical terms and processes are outlined. Where many other branches of Arabic learning found an instant audience in the West, alchemy was slower to catch on, partly because of the obscurity of alchemical literature and partly because alchemical practice required a great deal of expensive, complicated equipment. Still, an alchemical subculture gradually emerged, and within a century or so of Robert of Chester's translation, the first European works on alchemy were in circulation.

The alchemy of Europe started out as a tradition closely derived from its Arabic sources, but by the fourteenth century original ideas were entering into it, and the great flowering of alchemical writing and research in the Renaissance and early modern periods saw the emergence of original alchemical theories and operations. The Arabic theory of the two principles, sulphur and mercury, was widely used, but later adapted by Paracelsus (1493–1541), who added salt as a third principle. *SEE* PARACELSUS; SALT. Another important approach was the Central Niter theory of Michael Sendivogius (1566–1636), which postulated a single substance linked with life energy that made all things by its transformations. *SEE* NITER; SENDIVOGIUS, MICHAEL.

In the last centuries of its prevalence in the West, alchemy expanded into many other fields of knowledge, and for a time seemed likely to become the foundation of a universal science embracing every possible field of knowledge. Approaches to economics based on alchemical ideas were current, and traced out paths that would be followed for centuries to come: in Germany, the alchemist Johann Joachim Becher (1632–1682) argued for an alchemical view of trade that prefigured mercantilist economic theory and modern "Free Trade" ideology, while in England, the radical theoretician Gerrard Winstanley (1609–c. 1676) proposed a form of alchemical communism, complete with a labor theory of value closely akin to that of Karl Marx.

Alchemical interpretations of agriculture and biology were common, and gave rise to alchemical fertilizers and a wide range of alchemical medicines. Even theology was not immune—there were entire Christian theologies based on alchemy, of which the writings of Jakob Böhme are the most important. SEE BÖHME, JAKOB; THEOSOPHY (CHRISTIAN MYSTICAL).

This final blossoming of alchemical thought was followed, throughout nearly all of the Western world, by a near-total eclipse. The rise of scientific ideologies to dominance in the late seventeenth and early eighteenth centuries forced alchemy underground. There it survived mostly in the German-speaking areas of central Europe.

German Romanticism, with its extensions into science and nature philosopy, drew to some extent on alchemical ideas, and figures of the stature of Johann Wolfgang von Goethe dabbled in the Great Art; SEE GOETHE, JOHANN WOLFGANG VON. Several German occult orders, most prominently the Orden des Gold- und Rosenkreuz of the late eighteenth century, also included alchemical lore in their secret teachings; SEE ORDEN DES GOLD- UND ROSENKREUZ. Homeopathy, a health-care system that emerged in nineteenth-century Germany, also drew substantially on older alchemical ideas, especially those of Paracelsus; SEE HOMEOPATHY.

Alchemy also survived for a time in the American colonies, with their close cultural ties to Germany and their openness to almost any form of radicalism. Alchemy reached America at a fairly early date—John Winthrop Jr. (1606–1676), governor of the Massachusetts Bay colony, was an ardent Hermeticist and a student of alchemy who amassed an impressive collection of al-

chemical writings—and by the eighteenth century had given rise to an alchemical underground that combined Hermetic and alchemical studies with mystical offshoots of Christianity and attempts to find buried treasures by magical means. This underground eventually gave rise to the Mormon Church, among other American spiritual movements; SEE SMITH, JOSEPH. By the nineteenth century, however, practical laboratory alchemy was rarely practiced even in America.

Renewed interest in alchemy in recent years has mostly come out of the work of the Swiss psychologist Carl Jung and his followers, who interpreted alchemy as an ancient art of psychological transformation wrapped up in the language of metalworking. This view has become extremely popular in the twentieth century, at least in part because it allows alchemy to be reinterpreted in a way that doesn't come into conflict with the concepts of modern materialist science. By way of Jung's theories, alchemical ideas and imagery have been borrowed wholesale for a variety of psychological and spiritual projects, many of which have nothing to do with alchemy in any sense that the old alchemists would have understood.

In the meantime, traditions of alchemical practice have been revived and are practiced today. The work of Frater Albertus (Albert Reidel, 1911–1984), whose Paracelsus Research Society offered one of the first public instructional programs in alchemy in the Western world, was crucial in bringing alchemy into a renewed popularity in the latter half of the twentieth century; SEE ALBERTUS, FRATER. Reidel's teachings, like those of most recent alchemists, take spagyrics as the starting point, and his *Alchemist's Handbook* (1960) is one of the few practical handbooks of spagyric alchemy available in English. FURTHER READING: ALBERTUS 1960, BROOKE 1994, T. HAYES 1979, KIECKHEFER 1989, LINDSAY 1970, PATAI 1994, SMITH 1994.

alectryomancy. Divination by chicken, a very common mode of divination in the ancient world. To perform it, the diviner marks out a circle, dividing it into segments corresponding to the letters of the alphabet. A grain of wheat is placed on each letter while an incantation is recited. A white chicken is then set in the middle of the circle, to the accompaniment of further incantations. The chicken proceeds to eat the grains of wheat, and the letters corresponding to the grains it chooses are noted down. An additional grain is placed on each letter when one has been eaten, to allow it to spell out words that contain the same letter more than once. The letters chosen spell out the answer to the divination.

A very famous example of this art was practiced by a group of Roman courtiers during the reign of the Emperor Valens (364–378 C.E.). The information wanted was the name of Valens' successor—a significant question at a time when the Roman Empire was in chaos. The chicken chose the wheat grains corresponding to the letters *T, H, E, O,* and *D.* The courtiers took this to refer to Theodotus, an important official who was widely expected to seek the imperial purple. Unfortunately Valens got wind of the divination, ordered all the courtiers present at the ceremony killed, and had Theodotus executed for good measure. A few years later, Valens and his army were slaughtered by the Visigoths, and after a brief period of chaos a new emperor took the imperial throne; his name was Theodosius. *SEE ALSO* DIVINATION.

Detail from an illustration depicting alectryomancy, circa 250–325 C.E.

alembic. (Arabic *al-anbiq,* "still") In traditional alchemy, a device for distillation, consisting of a cap-shaped or globe-shaped vessel, open at the bottom, with a channel around the inside, above the opening, and a spout leading off from the channel. In alchemical distillation, the alembic was sealed on top of the cucurbite, or vessel containing the substance to be distilled. When the cucurbite was heated, vapors rose into the alembic, condensed into liquid, flowed down into the channel, and were led off by the spout to a receiving vessel. *SEE* ALCHEMY; CUCURBITE.

Aleph. (Hebrew ALP, "ox") The first letter of the Hebrew alphabet, one of the three mother letters, Aleph represents a glottal stop in classical and modern Hebrew (not, as often claimed, the sound *a*). Its numerical value is one. Its most common correspondences are as follows:

> *Path of the Tree of Life:* Path 11, Kether to Chokmah.
>
> *Astrological Correspondence:* Air.
>
> *Tarot Correspondence:* Trump 0, the Fool.
>
> *Part of the Cube of Space:* Above-below axis.
>
> *Colors:* in Atziluth—bright pale yellow.
> in Briah—sky blue.
> in Yetzirah—bluish emerald green.
> in Assiah—emerald green, flecked with gold.

Its text from the *Thirty-Two Paths of Wisdom* runs: "The Eleventh Path is the Scintillating Intelligence, because it is the essence of that curtain which is placed close to the order of the disposition, and this has a special dignity given to it that it may be able to stand before the face of the Cause of Causes."

In Cabalistic lore, Aleph represents the hidden essence of the divine, as distinct from the creative power represented by the letter Beth. Renaissance Cabalists also drew a distinction between the bright Aleph, the aspect of the divine essence from which Creation proceeds, and the dark Aleph, the aspect of the divine essence from which chaos and destruction proceed. *SEE ALSO* CABALA; HEBREW ALPHABET.

Hebrew letter Aleph

Alexandria. City in Egypt, on the Nile Delta, founded in 323 B.C.E. by Alexander the Great after his conquest of Egypt. It soon became the most important trade center in the eastern Mediterranean, and the site of a major university and library. In the city, Greek philosophy and Egyptian religious magic combined freely, and many scholars suggest that much of Western magic and alchemy have their roots in this combination. SEE ALSO ALCHEMY; EGYPTIAN OCCULTISM.

Alexandrian Wicca. A branch of Wicca either founded or made public by Alec Sanders in the early 1960s. As with most of Wicca, its origins are a matter of dispute; Sanders claimed to have been initiated by his grandmother at the age of seven, while members of rival traditions have insisted that he was never initiated at all, but simply obtained a copy of the Gardnerian Book of Shadows and proclaimed himself a Third Degree initiate. Documentary evidence suggests that he was actually initiated by a Gardnerian coven in the early 1960s. SEE SANDERS, ALEC.

The Alexandrian tradition is close to standard Gardnerian Wicca, but its teachings include material on fluid condensers, Golden Dawn–derived ceremonial magic, and Enochian conjurations—subjects normally part of Hermetic magic rather than Wicca, at least in recent times. SEE ENOCHIAN MAGIC; FLUID CONDENSER; GOLDEN DAWN, HERMETIC ORDER OF THE. Alexandrian covens are autonomous, with some variation in ritual and practice from coven to coven; most covens meet at the new and full moons, as well as for the eight sabbats. The standard three-degree system is worked, although some covens have added an introductory degree of Dedicant.

Highly successful in the first decade or so of Wicca's modern expansion, Alexandrian Wicca seems to have lost some of its momentum with the rise of feminist Wicca in the 1980s, but remains a significant force in the Pagan community. Alexandrian covens remain active in Great Britain, the United States, Australasia, and several European countries, and there is a magazine, *The Guardian*, which circulates among Alexandrian initiates. SEE ALSO WICCA. FURTHER READING: DAVIES 2001, VALIENTE 1987.

Alfassa, Mira. French occultist and spiritual leader, 1878–1973. Born in Paris and raised in a rationalist milieu, Alfassa nonetheless began receiving occult instruction from guides in her dreams in childhood. In 1900 she encountered Max Theon, formerly the major force behind the Hermetic Brotherhood of Luxor and at that time head of a new organization, the Groupe Cosmique, headquartered in what was then the French colony of Algeria. Eager for occult knowledge, Alfassa devoted herself to the Groupe's work, and became an editor of its journal. SEE ALSO HERMETIC BROTHERHOOD OF LUXOR (H. B. OF L.); THEON, MAX.

In 1914, she and her second husband Paul Richard traveled to India, hoping to meet an authentic Hindu yogi. This ambition was more than satisfied when they encountered Aurobindo Ghose, who had just finished a year in prison for revolutionary activities against the British Raj and had decided to give up politics and concentrate on spiritual issues. Alfassa recognized in Aurobindo one of the guides from her childhood dreams. She was forced to leave India by the outbreak of the First World War, but was back in 1920 and worked with Aurobindo continuously until his death in 1950.

Known from the mid-1920s on as "the Mother," Alfassa made major contributions to the development of Aurobindo's system of Integral Yoga, which has substantial similarities to the *Philosophie Cosmique* she learned from Max Theon. She was also the moving force behind the growth of Auroville, a thriving international spiritual community in Pondicherry, India. In her later years, she concentrated much of her energies on intensive inner workings designed to speed up the evolutionary process and bring about the birth of a new, physically immortal human species. These workings were interrupted by her own death at the age of ninety-five. FURTHER READING: RHONE 2000.

Algard Wicca. Founded in 1972 by Mary Nesnick, an American initiate of both Alexandrian and Gardnerian Wicca, the Algard tradition was an important force in the American Wiccan community during the 1970s. Like most traditionalist Wiccan systems, it lost much of its popularity in the following decades, but there are still some covens in North America working in the Algard tradition as of this writing. Their rituals and teachings are based on a combination of Alexandrian and Gardnerian traditions. SEE ALEXANDRIAN WICCA; WICCA.

Algiz. (Old Germanic, "elk") The fifteenth rune of the elder futhark, also called Elhaz, corresponding to the elk and the concepts of protection and defense. It represents the sound *z*. Some modern Pagan runemasters have associated this rune with the god Heimdall. *SEE* ELDER FUTHARK.

The same rune, named Eolh (Old English, "elk"), is the fifteenth rune of the Anglo-Saxon futhorc. The Old English rune-poem relates it to the elk-sedge, a plant with leaf-edges sharp enough to draw blood. *SEE* ANGLO-SAXON FUTHORC.

Rune Algiz (Elhaz, Eolh)

alkahest. A term used in alchemy with various meanings. In some writings, it means the Universal Solvent, a substance that was believed to dissolve all metallic and semimetallic substances; in others, it is a specialized menstruum used to extract only one of the three principles of a substance. *SEE* ALCHEMY; MENSTRUUM; THREE PRINCIPLES.

Allan, William Frederick. *SEE* LEO, ALAN.

almadel. In the traditions of medieval goetic magic, a wax square inscribed with magical figures and names, supported by projections from the bases of four candles, and used in a specific set of evocations. The grimoire providing these instructions, the *Art Almadel*, was in circulation by the early thirteenth century, when William of Auvergne, Bishop of Paris, denounced it. The almadel is sometimes called "almandel" or "amandel." *SEE ALSO* GOETIA; GRIMOIRE; LEMEGETON.

Alpha et Omega. English occult order, founded after the breakup of the Hermetic Order of the Golden Dawn in 1900 by former GD head Samuel Liddell Mathers and his supporters. There were two temples in Great Britain, one in London and the other in Edinburgh. The former Golden Dawn temples in the United States—Thme No. 8 in Chicago and Thoth-Hermes No. 9 in New York City—sided with Mathers during the breakup and became part of the Alpha et Omega afterwards. Three other American temples were founded after the First World War: Ptah No. 10 in Philadelphia in 1919, Atoum No. 20 (sic) in Los Angeles in 1920, and Themis No. 30 (sic) in San Francisco in 1921.

The history of the Alpha et Omega is uncertain at best, as few documents survive. All of the temples of the order appear to have gone out of existence by the Second World War. *SEE ALSO* GOLDEN DAWN, HERMETIC ORDER OF THE.

Alpha Galates. French esoteric secret society active in the 1930s and 1940s. Alpha Galates was apparently founded by Georges Monti, former personal secretary to the Sâr Peladan and longtime minor player in French occult circles, sometime before 1934. Other members of the group included conservative political activist Louis Le Fur and Pierre Plantard, later the founder and head of the Prieure de Sion. During the Nazi occupation, Alpha Galates published a magazine, *Vaincre* (*Conquer*), which combined anti-Semitic diatribes with articles on Celtic lore and chivalry. The society apparently went out of existence after the end of the Second World War. *SEE ALSO* PRIORY OF SION; PELADAN, JOSÉPHIN.

alraun. In central European folk magic, a humanlike image made from the root of the rowan or mountain ash, and used as the dwelling of a spirit. They were said to answer questions by moving their heads. If neglected, they would cry out and bring ill luck to the household.

Primarily used in Germany, alrauns were all but forgotten by the end of the nineteenth century, but the practice has been included in some modern Pagan books and has experienced a modest revival.

The rituals and practices surrounding the alraun are closely related to those of the mandrake. *SEE* MANDRAKE.

altar. A flat-topped item of ritual furniture, used in many different occult traditions as a support for ritual tools and other symbolic objects. Altars have been a nearly universal feature in Western (and Eastern) religious practice for thousands of years. In ancient times, the altar was primarily used as a place where sacrifices were offered to the gods. *SEE* SACRIFICE.

Most modern Pagan and magical traditions place an altar at the center of the ritual circle. The altar in most ceremonial magic traditions is square-topped and twice as high as it is across the top; this duplicates the proportions of a double cube. The altar may be covered with a black cloth to symbolize the *prima materia* or unformed first matter of the alchemists; a white cloth to represent purity; or a cloth of elemental, planetary, or sephirothic color, depending on the force to be invoked in any given working. *SEE* COLOR SCALES.

In modern Pagan practice, round altars are common, but square, rectangular, and other shapes are also found. Typical Wiccan altar furnishings include an altar cloth; two candles, to represent the God and Goddess; the working tools of the four elements; a censer for incense; and a bell. Different traditions add additional items to this collection. The altar may be oriented to east or north, depending on the tradition.

Many modern Pagans also establish one or more household altars in their homes, decorated and equipped with statues, images, magical working tools, crystals, and the like. The diversity of the Neopagan movement is more than equalled by the diversity of design and arrangement in these altars.

In those traditions based on the work of Robert Cochrane (1931–1966), an influential British witch of the first decades of the Neopagan revival, many of the functions of the altar are carried out by the stang, a wooden staff with a forked top. The stang is placed in a direction corresponding to the season of the year—east in spring, south in summer, west in autumn, and north in winter—and decorated with symbolically appropriate items. *SEE* COCHRANE, ROBERT; STANG.

In traditional Satanism, a naked woman is typically used as the altar for a parody of the Catholic Mass. *SEE* BLACK MASS.

alu. (Old Germanic, meaning uncertain) A word of power found in runic inscriptions in the elder futhark, the oldest known system of runes, dating between the beginning of the Common Era and around 700 C.E. Its meaning has been hotly debated by scholars. The most common opinion is that it means "ale," and links with the use of ale and beer as sacred beverages among the ancient Germanic peoples. A subtler analysis suggests that both ale and alu may be derived from an ancient root meaning "ecstasy, magical power," which kept its old meaning in

alu and shifted to "drunkenness" and then to "alcoholic beverage" to give rise to the word "ale." Hittite parallels and connections from even further afield have also been proposed. *SEE* RUNES. FURTHER READING: FLOWERS 1986.

aludel. In alchemy, a pear-shaped vessel open at both ends, with a lid to cover the top opening. The aludel was placed atop a cucurbite for the process of sublimation, and used to condense the sublimed vapors back into solid form. *SEE* ALCHEMY; SUBLIMATION.

Alverda, Hugo. A Rosicrucian pseudonym of the period of the original manifestos, also used in certain symbolic contexts by later Rosicrucians. A pamphlet titled *Fortalitium scientiae* (*Fortress of the Sciences*), published in 1617, was allegedly by Alverda. Johannes Comenius, who discussed the Rosicrucian furor a few years later in his *Labyrinth of the World*, refers to a "Hugo Alvarda" as the *praepositus* of the order, and gives his age at that time as 562 years. *SEE* ROSICRUCIANS.

In the Golden Dawn Adeptus Minor ceremony, Hugo Alverda is named as one of the three "Highest Chiefs of the Order," along with Franciscus de Bry and Elman Zata. He is identified as a "Phrisian," and his age at the time of the sealing of the Vault of Christian Rosenkreutz is given as 576 years. *SEE* ADEPTUS MINOR.

Ama. In Cabalistic teaching, the dark, sterile aspect of the feminine principle. *SEE* AIMA.

amber. Fossilized resin from ancient pine trees, amber has been used for magical purposes for thousands of years. Large amounts of it were traded in prehistoric times from the deposits around the North Sea south into the Mediterranean world. In Roman times, a phallus carved from amber was a common amulet to counteract the evil eye; *SEE* EVIL EYE. In later traditions of natural magic, it was much used to bring good health and good fortune and to assist women in labor. *SEE ALSO* NATURAL MAGIC.

Amentet. (ancient Egyptian, "west") The realm of the honored dead in ancient Egyptian mythology and magic. Originally the place where the sun set, it later came to be associated with the great cemetery areas in the hills to the west of the Nile. *SEE* EGYPTIAN OCCULTISM.

Ameset. (ancient Egyptian *ameset* or *amesti*) One of the four sons of Horus, his name is often spelled Ameshet in older sources and sometimes appears as Imseti in recent ones. He had the head of a man and the body of a mummy, and was the lord of the southern quarter of the world. He had guardianship of the stomach and small intestine of the deceased, and was called "the Carpenter." He was associated with the goddess Isis. *SEE* CANOPIC GODS; ISIS.

In the Golden Dawn system of magic, Ameset was called Ameshet or Amesheth, and served as one of the invisible guardians of the temple. He was stationed in the northeast. *SEE* GOLDEN DAWN, HERMETIC ORDER OF THE; INVISIBLE STATIONS. FURTHER READING: BUDGE 1967, REGARDIE 1971.

Amesheth. *SEE* AMESET.

Amissio. (Latin, "loss") A geomantic figure governed by Venus. Amissio is an unfavorable figure for material pursuits, but fortunate in questions relating to love. *SEE* GEOMANCY.

Geomantic figure Amissio

AMORC. *SEE* ANCIENT MYSTICAL ORDER ROSAE CRUCIS (AMORC).

amulet. A magical device for general protection and good fortune. An amulet differs from a talisman in that talismans are made and ritually consecrated for specific, tightly focused purposes, while amulets are more general, and are often not formally consecrated at all. *SEE* TALISMAN.

The use of amulets goes back far into prehistoric times, and the oldest known civilizations are rich in amulet lore. The ancient Egyptians fashioned amulets of gold, precious and semiprecious stones, as well as less expensive materials. The ankh, the hieroglyph for "life," was among the most common Egyptian amulets, but there were many others, including the Udjat or Eye of Horus and the scarab beetle, a symbol of the sun. *SEE* ANKH; EGYPTIAN OCCULTISM. The ancient cultures of Mesopotamia had a rich amulet lore of their own, as did ancient Greece and Rome. In the Greek world, the *ephesia grammata* or "Ephesian letters" were among the most important ingredients in amulets; *SEE* EPHESIA GRAMMATA.

The great monotheistic faiths of the Piscean age—Judaism, Christianity, and Islam—brought their own traditions to bear on the lore and use of amulets. Texts from various sacred scriptures came to play a large part in amulets; in Christianity, which did not forbid the use of sacred images, pictures, or statues of the Trinity or the saints had a similar role. To this day many conservative Catholics keep a plastic statue of Jesus, the Virgin Mary, or a patron saint in their cars to ward off auto accidents. *SEE* CHRISTIAN OCCULTISM.

In modern ceremonial magic, amulets are somewhat neglected in favor of talismans and other, more focused magical devices. The modern Pagan scene, on the other hand, has made much more use of amulets, with the silver pentagram as the most common amulet. Amulets from other magical traditions, especially mojo bags from hoodoo, are also much used in the Pagan scene in North America. *SEE* HOODOO; MOJO.

analytic psychology. The formal name for the psychological theories of C. G. Jung. *SEE* JUNG, CARL GUSTAV; JUNGIAN PSYCHOLOGY.

Ancient Mystical Order Rosae Crucis (AMORC). An internationally active Rosicrucian order, as of this writing AMORC is among the largest occult organizations in the world. Founded in the United States but currently based in France, AMORC offers correspondence courses to a nearly worldwide audience, and has lodges in most American states and a number of foreign countries.

AMORC traces its own history, and that of Rosicrucianism, back to the "heretic pharaoh" Akhenaten, and claims a direct succession from the historical Rosicrucians. *SEE* AKHENATEN; ROSICRUCIANS. H. Spencer Lewis, AMORC's founder, is said to have received authority from a variety of European Rosicrucian bodies. Historians outside the order, however, date its origins to 1915, when H. Spencer Lewis received a charter from Theodor

Reuss, head of the Ordo Templi Orientis (OTO), and went to work trying to found a lodge. *SEE* ORDO TEMPLI ORIENTIS (OTO). After several false starts, the new organization was incorporated in Florida in 1925. Two years later Spencer and his family, who among themselves filled most of the offices of the fledgling order, moved operations to San Jose and acquired a printing plant and a radio transmitter.

Lewis and his order had a complicated relationship with its parent body, the Ordo Templi Orientis. The 1915 charter from Reuss was part of an intended collaboration between Lewis and the OTO, and was part of Reuss' efforts to regain control of the order from Aleister Crowley and his protegé Charles Stansfield Jones. *SEE* CROWLEY, ALEISTER; ACHAD, FRATER. Crowley, for his part, made overtures to Lewis in 1918 and offered him membership in the OTO or the A∴A∴, but Lewis turned him down. Reuss granted Lewis the honorary degrees of 33°, 90°, 95°, and VII° in 1921, the same year he formally expelled Crowley from the OTO, but his constant requests for money alienated Lewis and led to a parting of the ways between them.

To his occult background, Lewis added marketing and advertising talents of a high order, and once AMORC was on its feet it attracted a growing stream of students. This brought the new order the unwanted attention of R. Swinburne Clymer, head of the Pennsylvania-based Fraternitas Rosae Crucis (FRC), who claimed exclusive rights to the term "Rosicrucian." For much of the 1930s the two orders fought a furious but inconclusive pamphlet war over their respective pedigrees, which ended up in the courts. *SEE* FRATERNITAS ROSAE CRUCIS (FRC). During the midst of this, Aleister Crowley offered Lewis his support against Clymer. Lewis, sensibly, did not take the Beast up on his offer.

On Lewis' death in 1939, the position of Imperator passed to his son, Ralph Maxwell Lewis. Most of the original AMORC monographs and rituals were withdrawn from circulation shortly afterwards and have not been used since. Working with a new set of rituals and teachings, AMORC went on to become perhaps the most successful of all of the twentieth-century occult orders, with local chapters in most American cities and a substantial overseas presence as well.

On Ralph Maxwell Lewis' death in 1987, the position of Imperator passed to Gary L. Stewart. Three years later, in 1990, Stewart was removed by the AMORC board of directors on charges of embezzlement, amid a flurry of accusations, countercharges, and legal maneuvering. Stewart was replaced by Christian Bernard, the present Imperator. Despite these upheavals, AMORC remains an active presence today, and is probably the largest American occult order in existence as of this writing. *SEE ALSO* LEWIS, HARVEY SPENCER. FURTHER READING: AMORC 1948, MCINTOSH 1987.

Andreae, Johann Valentin. German scholar and theologian (1586–1654), a central figure in the genesis of the original Rosicrucian manifestos. His grandfather Jakob Andreae (1529–1590) was a close friend of Martin Luther and an important early Lutheran theologian, who adopted as his family coat of arms a red St. Andrew's Cross and four red roses. His father Johann Andreae (1554–1601), a clergyman as well, was also a practicing alchemist who received patronage from Friedrich, Duke of Württemberg, a prominent supporter of alchemical studies. Johann Valentin thus grew up in an environment saturated with Lutheran theology and Hermetic alchemy.

He entered Tübingen University in 1602, receiving his baccalaureate there in 1603 and his master of arts in 1605, and was on his way to a doctorate in theology when he was caught up in a scandal over a student prank in 1607 and expelled. He returned to the university in 1611, failed his ordination exams the next year, and finally passed them and entered the Lutheran ministry in 1614. Thereafter he settled down to a life of sober scholarship and religious orthodoxy, serving in a succession of church offices until his death.

His involvement in the occult was limited to his college days, when he belonged to a circle of Christian Hermeticists that formed around the Paracelsian physician Tobias Hess (1568–1614). This circle produced two Rosicrucian manifestos, the *Fama Fraternitatis* and the *Confessio Fraternitatis*, while the *Chymische Hochzeit* (*Chemical Wedding*)—the "third manifesto," an elaborate alchemical fable—was written by Andreae himself around 1605, although it was published without his permission (and to his extreme embarrassment) in 1616, at the height of the Rosicrucian furor.

Andreae's later attitude toward the manifestos is telling. He referred to them consistently as a "joke" or "comedy"—the Latin word he used, *ludibrium*, has both meanings—and, from the standpoint of the Lutheran orthodoxy of his mature years, sharply criticized those who "preferred some artificial and unusual way to the simple way of Christ" (Dickson 1998, p. 82). At the same time, he was at the center of several later projects to establish secret or semisecret societies of Lutheran scholars, dedicated to much the same principles as the mysterious fraternity of the manifestos. SEE ALSO ROSENCREUTZ, CHRISTIAN; ROSICRUCIANS. FURTHER READING: DICKSON 1998, MONTGOMERY 1973, YATES 1972.

angel. (Greek *angelos*, "messenger") In most Western occult teachings, as well as in the orthodox theologies of Judaism, Christianity, and Islam, a spiritual being in the service of God. Detailed discussions of the nature and powers of angels fill many pages of theological textbooks. The lore of angels is one of the places where Western occult tradition comes closest to the religious mainstream—although, as with all things occult, there are important exceptions.

Angels are divided into various classes or orders. Most Christian analyses, occult or otherwise, follow the nine orders of angels first outlined by Dionysius the pseudo-Areopagite in the fifth century:

Seraphim, the highest class, who are angels of radiant love, and contemplate the divine order and providence;

Cherubim, angels of absolute wisdom, who contemplate the divine essence and form;

Thrones, who also contemplate, though some proceed from contemplation to action;

Dominations, who are like architects, and plan what the lower orders carry out;

Virtues, who move the stars and planets, and serve as instruments of the divine in the working of miracles;

Powers, who maintain the universe in harmony with the divine will, and some of whom descend to interact with human beings;

Principalities, who have nations and their rulers in their keeping;

Archangels, who have responsibility for religion and look after holy things;

Angels, the lowest class, who take care of minor affairs and serve as guardian angels to individual human beings.

The Jewish tradition, followed by most Cabalistic magical systems, divides angels into ten orders corresponding to the ten Sephirah of the Tree of Life:

Chaioth ha-Qodesh, "Holy Living Creatures," the highest of the angels, who bear the throne of the Divine;

Auphanim, "Wheels" or "Whirling Forces," angels of wisdom, described as "wheels within wheels" covered everywhere with eyes;

Aralim, "Mighty Ones," angels of understanding;

Chashmalim, "Shining Ones," angels of mercy and magnificence;

Seraphim, "Burning Ones," angels of severity and justice;

Malekim, "Kings," angels of beauty and harmony;

Tarshishim, "Sparkling Ones," angels of victory;

Beni Elohim, "Children of the Divine," angels of glory;

Kerubim, "Strong Ones," angels of the foundation of the universe;

Ishim, "Human Beings," angels of the material world.

It is worth noting that in the Cabalistic system, archangels are a separate and higher class of being, dwelling in the world of Briah, while angels of the ten orders dwell in Yetzirah. Depending on your choice of system, then, archangels are either the second lowest class of angels or the highest of all. This sort of uncertainty is common in angel lore.

While most occult writings accept the standard religious view of the nature of angels, there are alternative views. In some occult traditions, particularly those derived from Theosophy, angels are held to be part of the Devic kingdom—an alternate track of spiritual evolution that starts with elementals, rises through faeries and devas, and culminates with angels and archangels. This parallels the human kingdom, which starts with one-celled organisms, rises through animals and ordinary human beings, and culminates in adepts and Masters. SEE ADEPT; DEVA; MASTERS; THEOSOPHY.

Angels play an important role in the Cabala and related magical systems; SEE CABALA. They are also central to most Christian magical systems as the only spiritual entities other than God whom Christian magicians are supposed to consort with; *SEE* CHRISTIAN OCCULTISM. In the New Age movement, finally, angels have become popular in recent years, and a flood of recent angel books from a New Age perspective can be found on bookstore shelves; *SEE* NEW AGE MOVEMENT. FURTHER READING: G. DAVIDSON 1967, GREER 2001, HODSON 1976B.

angles, astrological. *SEE* CARDINES.

Anglo-Saxon futhorc. The runic alphabet of the Anglo-Saxon tribes, a coalition of Germanic peoples who invaded Britain in the fifth and sixth centuries of the Common Era and became the ancestors of the modern English. The Anglo-Saxon futhorc evolved out of the elder futhark by the addition of several new runes needed to express sounds not shared by other Germanic languages. Related changes shifted the sound value of the fourth rune to *o* and the sixth to *c*; thus the term "futhorc" is commonly used for this runic system, while "futhark" is used for those that retained the Old Germanic sound values. *SEE* FUTHARK.

Different versions of the Anglo-Saxon futhorc give different numbers of runes. The Old English rune-poem, the most detailed surviving source on the Anglo-Saxon futhorc's symbolism, includes twenty-nine runes, while other sources from the north of England give up to thirty-three.

Rune	Sound Value	Name	Meaning
ᚠ	F	Feoh	Wealth
ᚢ	U	Ur	Wild Ox
ᚦ	Th	Thorn	Thorn
ᚩ	O	Os	Mouth
ᚱ	R	Rad	Journey
ᚳ	C	Cen	Torch
ᚷ	G	Gyfu	Gift
ᚹ	W	Wynn	Joy
ᚻ	H	Haegl	Hail
ᚾ	N	Nyd	Trouble
ᛁ	I	Is	Ice
ᛄ	J	Ger	Harvest
ᛇ	E	Eoh	Yew Tree
ᛈ	P	Peorth	(unknown)
ᛉ	Z	Eolh	Elk-sedge
ᛋ	S	Sigil	Sun
ᛏ	T	Tir	Planet Mars
ᛒ	B	Beorc	Birch Tree
ᛖ	E	Eh	Horse
ᛗ	M	Mann	Man
ᛚ	L	Lagu	Ocean
ᛜ	Ng	Ing	The Hero Ing
ᛟ	Oe	Ethel	Home
ᛞ	D	Daeg	Day
ᚪ	Ai	Ac	Oak Tree
ᚫ	Ae	Aesc	Ash Tree
ᛠ	Ye	Yr	Axe
ᛡ	Io	Ior	Beaver
ᛠ	Ea	Ear	Grave
ᛢ	Q	Cweorp	Fire-stick
ᛣ	C	Calc	Cup
ᛥ	St	Stan	Stone
ᚸ	G	Gar	Spear

Like the other runic alphabets, the Anglo-Saxon futhorc went out of use with the coming of Christianity and the introduction of the Latin alphabet. It has been brought back into use in recent years by people in the modern Pagan revival, but so far has received much less attention than the elder futhark. *SEE ALSO* ELDER FUTHARK; RUNES. FURTHER READING: PENNICK 1989.

anima mundi. (Latin, "soul of the world") In ancient, medieval, and Renaissance philosophy, the indwelling consciousness of the world, which acts through the *spiritus mundi* or vital force of the world on the *corpus mundi* or physical body of the world. The concept is an ancient one, dating back at least to Plato and probably much earlier. It played a very large role in both the Platonic and the Stoic schools of philosophy. *SEE* PLATONISM; STOICISM.

In late alchemical writings such as the *Aurea Catena Homeri,* the anima mundi was identified with the central niter, the essential principle of fire and transformation in the universe. *SEE* NITER.

animal body of transformation. *SEE* LYCANTHROPY.

animal magnetism. In the writings of Franz Anton Mesmer and his followers, a subtle energy closely related to biological life, which behaves in ways similar to magnetism. Mesmer held that animal magnetism was an omnipresent force supporting life, and that it could be concentrated, dispersed, stored, and transmitted by a variety of methods. He used it for healing purposes, and apparently accomplished some impressive cures, although scientific critics of the time (including Benjamin Franklin) dismissed his work as nonsense.

Most modern occult writers who deal with the subject suggest that animal magnetism—like od, orgone, vril, and many other terms proposed down through the years—is simply another term for etheric energy. *SEE* ETHER. *SEE ALSO* MESMER, FRANZ ANTON; MESMERISM.

ankh. The ancient Egyptian symbol and hieroglyph for "life," a Tau cross with a loop above, it can be found in Egyptian texts and religious art from the Old Kingdom onwards, and was much used as an amulet throughout Egyptian history; *SEE* AMULET. In modern use, it has come to be associated with the beliefs of Akhenaten, the "heretic pharaoh" of the New Kingdom, who attempted to proscribe traditional Egyptian religion and replace it with the monotheistic cult of Aten, the deified sun and source of life. *SEE* AKHENATEN.

Various magical traditions have adopted the ankh as a symbol in modern times, including the Golden Dawn (which uses it in its Adeptus Minor ritual) and the Ancient Mystical Order Rosae Crucis (AMORC). *SEE* ANCIENT MYSTICAL ORDER ROSAE CRUCIS (AMORC); GOLDEN DAWN, HERMETIC ORDER OF THE. It was also a common ornament in the American Pagan community in the last few decades of the twentieth century.

Ankh symbol

anointing. The application of oil to a person or object. The act of anointing has been a part of magical practice for thousands of years. In ancient Greece, magicians who wished to consecrate a stone as a dwelling for a spirit or god would anoint it with olive oil and drape it with a garland of flowers while reciting an appropriate spell. Similar rites were used in many ancient cultures to consecrate statues of the gods and goddesses; *SEE* STATUES, MAGICAL.

The Catholic Church uses consecrated oil in three of the seven sacraments—baptism, confirmation, and ordination of priests—and many other Christian churches have retained some aspects of this tradition. Medieval and Renaissance forms of magic often use anointment with oils as a way of consecrating working tools for magical use. In modern magical practice, anointing is used in initiation rituals, blessings, and Wiccaning ceremonies, as well as for a range of practical magical workings. Candle magic, in particular, generally involves anointing one or more candles with scented oil; *SEE* CANDLE MAGIC.

Ansuz. (Old Germanic, "god") The fourth rune of the elder futhark, associated with the god Odin, the element of air, and the ideas of consciousness and communication. It represents the sound *a*. *SEE* ELDER FUTHARK.

Rune Ansuz

Anthroposophical Society. The organization created by Austrian occultist Rudolf Steiner (1861–1925) as a vehicle for his "spiritual science" of Anthroposophy. Well before Steiner's 1913 break with the Theosophical Society, he had become a noted figure in European Theosophical circles, lecturing to large audiences in Berlin and elsewhere on topics that would later become central to Anthroposophy.

In 1906 he was invited to give a series of lectures at a major Theosophical conference in Paris that attracted more attention than the conference itself, and he began to win a sizeable personal following. By 1912, his supporters made up a majority of German Theosophists. In that year, Annie Besant's claims concerning the Order of the Star in the East and the messiahship of Jiddu Krishnamurti became too much for Steiner (among many others) to stomach, and a massive schism split the Theosophical Society in Germany and elsewhere. SEE STAR IN THE EAST, ORDER OF THE; THEOSOPHICAL SOCIETY.

Steiner's Anthroposophical Society was founded early the next year, and attracted a substantial membership in Germany and elsewhere. It also attracted a great deal of hostility from the remaining old-line Theosophists, from Christian groups, and from Ariosophist occultists such as Gregor Schwartz-Bostunich. SEE ARIOSOPHY.

After being refused government permission to establish a headquarters near Munich, Steiner settled in Dornach, Switzerland. A massive wooden building, the Goetheanum, was designed by Steiner and built by his followers, but one or more arsonists burned it to the ground just before its completion on New Year's Eve of 1922. A second Goetheanum of less flammable materials was built thereafter. There Steiner established a School for Spiritual Science, which continues to operate today.

The Anthroposophical Society was never much more than a mouthpiece for Steiner's teachings and ideas, and after his death in 1925 it continued along much the same course. Currently there are branches of the Society throughout Europe, the Americas, and Australasia. Local groups operate study circles that read and discuss Steiner's major books, and there are also programs for those interested in pursuing anthroposophical medicine, biodynamic agriculture, eurhythmy, Waldorf education, and other Steinerian teachings. SEE ALSO ANTHROPOSOPHY; STEINER, RUDOLF. FURTHER READING: WEBB 1976, STEINER 1933.

Anthroposophy. The system of "spiritual science" created by German occultist Rudolf Steiner (1861–1925) and discussed at length in his voluminous books. In the early phases of his career, Steiner had passed through a varied series of involvements with occult and quasi-occult teachings, from boyhood encounters with a local herbalist and folk healer through a stint editing the scientific writings of Johann Wolfgang von Goethe (1749–1832) to a position as General Secretary of the German section of the Theosophical Society. SEE GOETHE, JOHANN WOLFGANG VON; THEOSOPHICAL SOCIETY. All these contributed to Steiner's system, as did Steiner's contact

with the Ordo Templi Orientis, which he joined in 1906, despite a history of denials by Anthroposophists. SEE ORDO TEMPLI ORIENTIS (OTO).

The basic framework of Anthroposophy can be traced back directly to Theosophical sources. Like the Theo-sophists, Steiner was a believer in karma and reincarnation, Atlantis and Lemuria, the akashic records, and the process of spiritual evolution by which human beings ascend to higher and higher levels of consciousness; SEE ROOT RACE; LOST CIVILIZATIONS. Unlike orthodox Theosophy, though, Steiner combined this with a devout if rather unorthodox Christianity in which the incarnation of Christ was the equivalent, for the entire world, of the mystery initiations of ancient Greece. Steiner connected the Christian dimension of his teaching with the Rosicrucian movement. His first public discussions of Rosicrucian ideas, interestingly, date from 1907, the year after he was initiated into the OTO. SEE CHRISTIAN OCCULTISM; ROSICRUCIANS.

Unlike many currents in Theosophy, which treated speculations about root races and lost continents as ends in themselves, Anthroposophy also includes a distinct set of practical methods of spiritual training. These are meditative exercises designed to open up hidden faculties of spiritual perception in the human soul, making it possible for the individual to perceive spiritual realities directly. Several of Steiner's most popular books include detailed directions for these practices; SEE STEINER 1994; STEINER 1999.

Steiner's work, unlike most other occult systems of his time, also spilled over the borders of occultism into a range of other subjects. His work with agriculture set in motion the biodynamic agriculture movement and played a central part in launching modern organic agriculture. His educational theories were responsible for starting the Waldorf schools, the world's largest alternative education system. Other Steiner creations such as eurhythmy, a performance art coordinating physical gestures with the sounds of words, and anthroposophical medicine have also remained popular. Ironically, these offshoots of his teachings have been far more influential in the modern world than the occult philosophy at their foundation. SEE ALSO ANTHROPOSOPHICAL SOCIETY; STEINER, RUDOLF. FURTHER READING: STEINER 1994, STEINER 1999.

Anubis. (ancient Egyptian *Anup*) The messenger of Osiris and protector of the dead, Anubis was among the more important deities of the ancient Egyptian funerary rituals, and plays a major role in the myths of Osiris; *SEE* OSIRIS. In the Golden Dawn, two officers in the Outer Order made use of the visualized godform of Anubis during ritual workings. The Kerux, who guards the inner side of the portal in the Neophyte Grade, is "Anubis of the East" (in Coptic, *Ano-oobist em-Pe-eeb-tte*). The Sentinel, who guards the outer side of the portal and prepares the candidate, is "Anubis of the West" (in Coptic, *Ano-oobi em-Pementte*). *SEE* GOLDEN DAWN, HERMETIC ORDER OF THE.

aor. *SEE* AUR.

apas. (Sanskrit, "water") The tattva of water, represented by a silver crescent with its points upward. *SEE* TATTVAS.

Apep. *SEE* APOPHIS.

apocatastasis. The theory that all things at the end of time will return to their original perfection. The doctrine of apocatastasis was held by a variety of different groups at various times, and has been interpreted in at least as many different ways.

Among the Stoics, a belief in the absolute power of fate led some theorists to suggest that at the end of vast cycles of time, the planets would return to some original configuration. Since in Stoic theory all earthly things were completely controlled by astrological factors, this would cause everything on earth to return to its state at the beginning of time. Thereafter, history would repeat itself exactly, in every detail, until the planets again returned to their primal positions and the cycle began yet again. *SEE* STOICISM. This doctrine of the Eternal Return was resurrected by Nietzsche in the late nineteenth century, as part of his revolt against Christian attitudes, but found few takers.

In heretical Christian circles from ancient times to the present, the doctrine of apocatastasis took on a different form. The early theologians Clement of Alexandria and Origen had speculated that at the end of time, even Satan and his fallen angels would be redeemed in a return to the primal perfection of Creation. This view was de-clared heretical by church councils and repeatedly denounced, but has continued to find adherents ever since, especially in Gnostic and quasi-Gnostic traditions. *SEE* GNOSTICISM. *SEE ALSO* CYCLES, COSMIC.

Apollonius of Tyana. Greek magician, first century C.E. A major figure in the lore of ancient and modern magical traditions, Apollonius was almost certainly a historical figure, but little is actually known about his life and activities. Most of what passes for biographical information about him is thickly encrusted with myth, folklore, and outright fiction. The same, of course, is true of other figures of the same period with connections to the occult; *SEE* JESUS OF NAZARETH.

Most of what is known about Apollonius comes to us by way of a biography written by Philostratus more than a century after his death, packed with mythic details but somewhat short on historical ones. He was born in the city of Tyana, near the southern coast of what is now Turkey, and received the standard Hellenistic education. Deeply impressed by what he could learn of the teachings of Pythagoras, he devoted himself to the Pythagorean tradition while still in his teens, vowing himself to silence for five years while practicing austerities. Later, he traveled through much of the Roman Empire and, if Philostratus is to be believed, east as far as India, seeking wisdom.

He apparently found it, to judge not only by Philostratus' account but by his broader reputation throughout the Roman world. He was credited with healings, exorcisms, and a variety of other miracles, including raising a girl from the dead. When a jealous rival had him charged with treason and necromancy, he is said to have gone to the imperial court in Rome, won acquittal by means of cogent arguments, and then vanished suddenly from the middle of the court and appeared the same day in Dicaearchia, many miles away. A list of the evil spirits he was said to have banished would fill several pages. For several centuries after his time, talismans made according to his designs were still being used to ward off shipwreck, vermin, and attacks by wild beasts.

In the late nineteenth century, the magician Eliphas Lévi attempted to summon the spirit of Apollonius. According to his account, he succeeded in evoking a spirit, but refused to say whether or not he believed it to be Apollonius or not. *SEE* LÉVI, ELIPHAS. FURTHER READING: E. BUTLER 1948, DZIELSKA 1986, MEAD 1966.

Apophis. (ancient Egyptian *'Apef* or *'Apep*) In Egyptian mythology, the great enemy of the solar god Re, a monstrous serpent who attempted to swallow the sun at various points along its daily and nightly journey. The efforts of several warrior gods were needed to keep Apophis at bay. In the Litany of Re, performed every day in temples of the sun god throughout Egypt, the priests helped out by fashioning a wax "voodoo doll" of Apophis, stabbing it with knives, and burning it over a fire of bryony roots. *SEE* EGYPTIAN OCCULTISM.

In the Golden Dawn system of magic, Apophis was used as a symbol of the powers of unbalanced force, and formed part of the Evil Triad evoked and overcome in the Neophyte Grade ritual. *SEE* GODFORMS; INVISIBLE STATIONS.

apple. (*Pyrus malus*) An important fruit in magical traditions, apples were associated with the faery folk in old folklore, and also had an important role in many European Pagan traditions. Its use in love spells dates back hundreds of years at least. It is also one of the trees associated with the Irish Ogham alphabet; *SEE* OGHAM, QUERT.

In modern Paganism, the apple is sacred, since the five seeds of an apple form a pentagram when the apple is cut crosswise. *SEE* PENTAGRAM.

Apuleius, Lucius. North African author and philosopher, second century C.E. Born in the town of Madauros in what is now Algeria, Apuleius studied at Carthage and the Academy in Athens, where he became an adherent of Platonic philosophy; *SEE* PLATONISM. After finishing his studies, he returned to Africa, and then set out for Alexandria, but fell ill on the road and stayed with Socinius Pontianus, a fellow student from the Academy.

Pontianus' mother, Aemilia Pudentilla, was still young, well educated, recently widowed, and very rich. She and Apuleius fell in love and were married. Her relatives accused Apuleius of using love magic to bring about the marriage, and he was brought to trial before the Roman proconsul, who acquitted him. Apuleius' oration at the

trial has survived, and is an important source for scholars of classical magic.

After his acquittal, he and Pudentilla moved to Carthage, where he became an important teacher, orator, and author. His most important work, *The Golden Ass*, is the only surviving Roman novel; it tells the story of a young man named Lucius who falls in love with the servant of a Thessalian witch, ends up being turned into a donkey, and undergoes a series of adventures before finally being restored to human form by the goddess Isis. It has been suggested by a number of magical authors that Apuleius was himself an initiate of the mysteries of Isis, and included elements of their sacred lore in his novel. FURTHER READING: GRAF 1997, KNIGHT 1985.

aqua fortis. (Latin, "strong water") The alchemical name for nitric acid, an important menstruum in the alchemy of metals. *SEE* ALCHEMY; MENSTRUUM.

aqua regia. (Latin, "royal water") In alchemy, a mixture of nitric and hydrochloric acids, made by distilling nitric acid together with salt. It was called "royal" because of its power to dissolve gold. *SEE* ALCHEMY.

Aquarius. (Latin, "water carrier") The eleventh sign of the zodiac, symbolized by a person carrying a jug of water. Aquarius is a fixed air sign of masculine polarity. In Aquarius, Saturn (or, in modern writings, Uranus) is the ruler and the sun is in its detriment. It rules the shins, ankles, and circulatory system. *SEE ALSO* ZODIAC.

The sun is in this sign approximately from January 21 to February 18. People born with this sun placement are traditionally outgoing, creative, highly intellectual, and have strong humanitarian tendencies; they can also be unstable and emotionally distant.

In the Golden Dawn tarot system, Aquarius corresponds with Trump XVII, the Star. *SEE* STAR, THE; TAROT.

Astrological symbol of Aquarius

Aquarius, Age of. In astrology as well as popular culture, the approaching age of the world, which will supplant the present Piscean Age. The astrological ages are marked out by precession, a slow wobble in the Earth's axis that moves the position of the sun at solstices and equinoxes slowly backwards through the zodiac; SEE PRECESSION OF THE EQUINOXES.

The Piscean Age, in occult philosophy, is seen as the age of Christianity, dominated by Pisces at the spring equinox and Virgo at the autumn; it is no accident, according to this way of thinking, that the Fish and the Virgin are among the most ancient Christian symbols, or that Piscean self-sacrifice and Virgoan purity have been the core spiritual themes of the last two thousand years. With the coming of Aquarius, the Water-carrier and the Lion move into the equinoctial stations, and Aquarian benevolence and Leonine self-assertion are expected to come to the fore in the spiritual traditions of the next 2,150 years. The exact date of the arrival of the Age of Aquarius has been subject to a great deal of speculation, however. Much depends on whether Aquarius is seen as the actual constellation of stars, on the one hand, or as a thirty-degree section of the heavens more or less overlapping the position of the constellation, on the other; SEE ZODIAC.

Some accounts would place the beginning of the Aquarian Age some years in the past; Swiss psychologist and astrologer Carl Jung, for example, saw 1940 as the beginning of the New Age. The movement of major stars across the cusps of the existing signs has been used as a predictive measure, and the crossing of Regulus, the great star at the heart of Leo, into the sign of Cancer in 2012 has been cited by numerous astrologers as the beginning of the Aquarian Age.

On the other hand, those writers who rely on the actual constellations have noted that the sun's position at the spring equinox will not leave the sprawling constellation of Pisces for well over a century, with estimates ranging from 2157 to 2374 C.E. for the starting date. SEE ALSO CYCLES, COSMIC.

aqua toffana. In nineteenth-century occult tradition, a lethal and undetectable poison, the recipe for which was believed to be the property of certain secret magical orders. Aqua toffana had its start as one of the stage props of the political conspiracy theories of the time; a recipe for a poison of that name had allegedly been found by Bavarian police among papers seized at the home of Xavier Zwack, a member of the Bavarian Illuminati, in 1786. The deaths of several heads of state, including the Austrian emperors Joseph II and Leopold II, were credited to Illuminati agents dealing out aqua toffana. Later on, as writers in the occult revival of the late nineteenth century borrowed these conspiracy theories for their own purposes, aqua toffana put in an appearance in a number of books on occultism, notably those of Eliphas Lévi. SEE ALSO BAVARIAN ILLUMINATI; LÉVI, ELIPHAS. FURTHER READING: LÉVI 1972, J. ROBERTS 1972.

aqua vitae. (Latin, "waters of life") The alchemical term for distilled alcohol, an important menstruum in spagyric (herbal) alchemy. SEE ALCHEMY; MENSTRUUM; SPAGYRICS.

Ar. Ar is the tenth rune of the younger futhark, standing for harvest and plenty, the cycles of nature and reward for the actions of the past. It represents the sound *a*. SEE YOUNGER FUTHARK.

Ar is also the tenth rune of the Armanen runic alphabet, corresponding to the solar light. Its power, according to the rune-charm from the Old Norse *Havamal*, is to banish spirits from the house. It corresponds to the god Forseti, to the child, and to the zodiacal sign Capricorn, and represents the sound *a*. SEE ARMANEN RUNES.

Rune Ar

Arabian Parts. In astrology, a set of points calculated by measuring the distance between two planets and measuring the same distance from the ascendant; SEE ASCENDANT. For example, the Part of Fortune is calculated by measuring the distance around the curve of the zodiac from the sun to the moon, and going the same distance from the ascendant. Other combinations of planets produce other parts, each of which governs a different aspect of human life. In Arabic and medieval astrology, the parts were much used and played an important role in astrological prediction. Most modern astrologers ignore them completely. SEE ALSO ASTROLOGY; PART OF FORTUNE. FURTHER READING: ZOLLER 1988.

Araboth. (Hebrew AaRBVTh, "plains") In Cabalistic lore, the seventh and highest Heaven, corresponding to the three Supernals. *SEE* HEAVENS, SEVEN.

Arachne. A proposed thirteenth sign of the zodiac, located between Taurus and Gemini. The sign Arachne was originally proposed by science-fiction writer John Sladek, using the pseudonym James Vogh, in his 1977 book *Arachne Rising: The Search for the Thirteenth Sign of the Zodiac.* Sladek, who has also written a book attacking astrology and the paranormal, has since claimed in published interviews that he made the whole thing up as a prank. This has not kept the book from being cited as a serious source, especially by the creators of the modern system of Celtic astrology. *SEE* CELTIC ASTROLOGY. FURTHER READING: VOGH 1977.

Aradia. According to Charles Godfrey Leland's *Aradia, The Gospel of the Witches* (1899), a goddess worshipped by witches in Italy in the late nineteenth century. Leland, a folklorist with an interest in the occult, claimed that he received from Maddalena, a Tuscan witch whom he had befriended, a handwritten text containing the mythology of the witches' cult. According to this document, Aradia was the daughter of Diana, goddess of the Moon, and her brother and son Lucifer. Because Diana pitied the poor and oppressed on earth, she sent her daughter to become the first witch, and to teach witchcraft to those who were willing to learn it. The text presents witchcraft as a deeply political, peasant-oriented alternative to Christianity, and includes many details that have since been adopted into modern Wicca and Neopaganism generally, such as meetings on the night of the full moon and ritual nudity.

The authenticity of Leland's lore is open to question, and there is some evidence that he made up some of the material he passed on as relics of the witches' cult. There is also no way of knowing just how old Maddalena's lore actually was, even if it was authentic, since oral traditions are notoriously hard to date. The possibility that the witch cult might have been an offshoot of the Carbonari, an early nineteenth-century radical Italian secret society, deserves particular investigation. Still, the name Aradia is at least plausible as an Italian slurring of Herodias, the

goddess worshipped by some medieval Pagan sects. *SEE* HERODIAS.

English scholar T. C. Lethbridge, and a number of modern Pagan writers following his lead, have suggested that Aradia may have been a historical person, an Italian peasant prophet of the late Middle Ages who founded the folk religious movement later chronicled by Leland. While there is essentially no documentary evidence to support this claim, such a figure would not have been out of place in the complex cultural scene of medieval Italy, where several goddess-worshipping sects are known to have existed. *SEE* BENSOZIA; MADONA HORIENTE. *SEE ALSO* PAGANISM. FURTHER READING: LELAND 1974, LETHBRIDGE 1962.

Aral. In Cabalistic magic, ruler of the element of air. His name derives from that of the Aralim, the angelic host attributed to the Sephirah Binah. In a number of sources, including the Golden Dawn knowledge lectures, this name has been exchanged with that of Ariel, who is properly the angel of the element of fire. *SEE ALSO* ARALIM; ARIEL; RULER, ELEMENTAL.

Aralim. (Hebrew ARALIM, "Mighty Ones") In Cabalistic lore, the third order of angels, corresponding to the Sephirah Binah. They are said to be composed of white fire, dwell in the third heaven, and have special charge over grass, trees, fruit, and grain. *SEE* ANGEL.

ARARITA. A Cabalistic Name of God, created from the initials of the Hebrew sentence *achad resh achdotho resh yechodo temurahzo achad,* "One is His beginning, one is His individuality, His permutation is One." In medieval traditions of magic, this name is to be written on a golden plate and worn on the body to prevent sudden death. *SEE* GRIMOIRE.

In the Golden Dawn tradition, this name is used in the Rituals of the Hexagram, and each of its seven letters is assigned to one of the seven planets. *SEE* HEXAGRAM, RITUALS OF THE; NOTARIQON.

Aratron. One of the seven Olympian spirits, Aratron is associated with the planet Saturn. He rules over 49 of the 196 provinces of Heaven, and was ruler of the universe from 550 B.C.E. to 60 B.C.E. *SEE* OLYMPIAN SPIRITS.

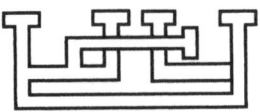

Olympian spirit Aratron

Arbatel of Magic, the. Grimoire first published at Basle, Switzerland, in 1575, and reprinted numerous times since then. Written in Latin, it consists of an introduction to magic, followed by information on the seven Olympian Spirits who govern the world. *SEE* OLYMPIAN SPIRITS. Popular as a guide to magical practice, the *Arbatel* has had a good deal of influence over Western magical practice, and many more recent texts draw on ideas from it. *SEE ALSO* GRIMOIRE.

Arcane School, the. Occult teaching organization founded by Alice Bailey and her husband, Foster Bailey, in 1923. Based on the teachings received by Alice Bailey via telepathic communication from her inner plane teacher, "the Tibetan," it seeks to develop a New Group of World Servers to accomplish the work of the Hierarchy of Masters under the guidance of its head, the Christ. According to its literature, it presents the principles of the Ageless Wisdom through esoteric meditation, study, and service as a way of life.

The Arcane School seems to have avoided many of the organizational extravagances of other occult teaching bodies in the last century or so, and consists of small groups and individual students studying by correspondence. The writings of Alice Bailey, as dictated by the Tibetan, form the curriculum. Details of the size and activities of the Arcane School are hard to come by and harder to verify, but the complexity of Bailey's teachings and the dryness of the prose in which they are expressed make it unlikely that the school is very large at present. *SEE ALSO* BAILEY, ALICE. FURTHER READING: BAILEY 1950.

archangel. A member of a class of angels variously placed in the celestial hierarchies, according to different systems of angelology. In the angel lore of the Cabala, which is standard in modern magical circles, archangels are the ruling powers of the angelic world, with a place in the scheme of things midway between God and the angels. There are ten of them, according to the usual scheme, corresponding to the ten Sephiroth of the Tree of Life in the world of Briah. *SEE* BRIAH.

In Christian angelology, by contrast, archangels are the eighth of nine choirs of angels, outranked not only by cherubim and seraphim but by thrones, dominations, virtues, powers, and principalities. Their special duty is to attend to the spiritual needs of religious rituals and the church.

Three archangels—Michael, Gabriel, and Raphael—are named in the Old Testament. The number named in less official religious sources, not to mention magical texts, is probably beyond calculation. *SEE ALSO* ANGEL. FURTHER READING: G. DAVIDSON 1967.

Archdruid. In many traditions of Druidry, the chief Druid of a grove or an order of Druids. The term seems to be a seventeenth-century invention, but has been widely adopted even among those modern Druid groups most insistent on their rejection of the Druid Revival. *SEE* DRUIDS.

archetype. In Jungian psychology, a "psychic dominant," a center of psychological energy that tends to surface in human consciousness through similar forms and images around the world and throughout time. According to Jung and his followers, the archetypes are inner, psychological expressions of the fundamental human instincts. They correspond precisely to the gods, goddesses, and other mythic figures of the world's religions. *SEE* JUNGIAN PSYCHOLOGY.

arch-fay. In Golden Dawn terminology, one of a class of nature spirits corresponding to the High Elves, trooping faeries, or Tuatha de Danaan of folklore. In the original Golden Dawn tarot deck, the chariot of the Prince of Swords is drawn by "Arch Fays, Archons or Arch Faeries" (Regardie 1971, p. 548). *SEE* FAERY.

archon. (Greek, "ruler") In Gnostic thought, one of the evil (or at least ignorant) ruling powers of the fallen material world. The archons were either opposed or oblivious to the aeons, the ruling powers of the higher, spiritual world. Many versions of Gnostic theology identified the archons with the gods or intelligences of the seven planets, just as the aeons were often identified with the stars.

The chief of the archons was Ialdabaoth, also called Saklas and Samael.

In certain other traditions, the same word is used as a synonym for "archangel," or as a term for angels having rulership over human nations. One Golden Dawn instructional paper seems to equate archons with fays—a suggestion which puts an entirely different light on much of traditional faery lore. *SEE* ARCH-FAY. *SEE ALSO* GNOSTICISM; IALDABAOTH. FURTHER READING: LAYTON 1987, ROBINSON 1988.

Aretz. (Hebrew ARTz, "dry earth, soil") The Hebrew term for the element of earth; also the first of the seven earths of Cabalistic theory, corresponding to the three supernal Sephiroth. *SEE* EARTH, ELEMENT OF; EARTHS, SEVEN.

Argenteum Astrum (A∴A∴) (Latin, "silver star") Magical order founded by English occultist Aleister Crowley (1875–1947) to promote his religion of Thelema. Based in some ways on the Hermetic Order of the Golden Dawn, the A∴A∴ was (and is) far less structured, and its work consisted of individual magical study and practice according to Crowley's curriculum in place of the formal lodge work beloved by the Golden Dawn. *SEE* GOLDEN DAWN, HERMETIC ORDER OF THE.

Despite Crowley's often sweeping claims for its size and influence, the A∴A∴ during his lifetime never amounted to more than Crowley himself and a small circle of students, few of whom were able to put up with the Beast's behavior for more than a short time. After Crowley's death, several of his disciples found students of their own, and there are several different lineages of the A∴A∴ presently in existence, mostly in North America and continental Europe. *SEE ALSO* CROWLEY, ALEISTER.

Argyraigis. (Greek, "silver shield") In the Aurum Solis system of magic, a term used for the aura when charged with energy and used as a protective barrier. *SEE* AURA; AURUM SOLIS.

Ariel. (Hebrew, "Lion of God") In Cabalistic magic, angel of the element of fire. In a number of sources, including the Golden Dawn knowledge lectures, this name has been exchanged with that of Aral, who is properly the ruler of the element of air. *SEE ALSO* ANGEL; ARAL.

Aries. (Latin, "ram") The first sign of the zodiac, symbolized by the energetic ram. Aries is a cardinal fire sign of masculine polarity. In Aries, Mars rules, the sun is exalted, Venus is in its detriment, and Saturn in its fall. It rules the head. *SEE* ZODIAC.

The sun is in this sign approximately from March 21 to April 20. People born with this sun placement are traditionally lively, enthusiastic, assertive, and brave; they can also be selfish and impatient.

In the Golden Dawn tarot system, Aries corresponds to the Emperor, Trump IV. *SEE* EMPEROR, THE; TAROT.

Astrological symbol of Aries

Arikh Anpin. (Hebrew, "great face") In Cabalistic teaching, the Macroprosopus or Greater Countenance, one of five *Partzufim* or aspects of the divine, identified with Kether. Arikh Anpin represents the highest, most transcendent aspect of God, that which cannot be grasped by human consciousness in any way. It is also associated with divine mercy. *SEE* PARTZUFIM.

Ariosophy. A tradition of racist occultism that arose in central Europe at the beginning of the twentieth century, Ariosophy was in many ways an offshoot of the Theosophical movement, but rejected Theosophy's commitment to human brotherhood in favor of a belief system claiming that only people of northern Indo-European ("Aryan") descent were actually human and capable of spiritual development. Ariosophy was rooted in racist ideologies common to most Western countries in the nineteenth century, but took shape around the writings of Guido von List (1848–1919) and Jörg Lanz von Liebenfels (1874–1954), two Austrian occultists who published their most important works in the first decade of the twentieth century. *SEE* LANZ VON LIEBENFELS, JÖRG; LIST, GUIDO VON.

Like most occult movements, Ariosophy was never a single coherent system, and there were many different versions of the basic set of beliefs. In most of its forms, though, it held that modern humanity was descended from two different species—Aryans, who were the true human beings, and non-Aryans, who were soulless animals who happened to look human. Modern Europeans were the descendants of interbreeding between these two species, while peoples of other races were simply animals with no human (i.e., Aryan) blood at all. Interbreeding with non-Aryans had caused the original Aryans to lose supernatural powers that were once their birthright, and occult training was directed toward restoring these lost powers.

Ariosophy played a large part in popularizing the sort of mystical racism later identified with Nazism, and in fact much of the Nazi program of the 1920s and 1930s was simply a restatement of Ariosophical ideas. Hitler himself is known to have subscribed to an Ariosophical magazine while living in Vienna, and many other figures in the upper levels of the Third Reich had their own connections to the movement. *SEE* HITLER, ADOLF; NATIONAL SOCIALISM.

Similar ideas, although derived from different historical roots, underlie the Christian Identity movement, an occult-influenced religious and political movement that emerged in North America in the middle of the twentieth century. *SEE* CHRISTIAN IDENTITY. FURTHER READING: GOODRICK-CLARKE 1992.

arithmancy. Divination by means of numbers. This is the proper term for what is now usually called "numerology," that is, divination using the numerical value of a person's name, but it was once given much broader applications in occult theory and practice.

In Greek, Hebrew, and several other ancient languages, every letter has a numerical value. (Fans of jargon will be delighted to learn that languages with this peculiarity are called *isopsephic languages*.) The habit of adding up the values of the letters of a word, and drawing conclusions about the word based on numerical connections with other words, was an obvious development in these languages, and it was heavily used by Jewish Cabalists, Greek and Hellenistic mystics, and early Christians; the famous enigma from the Book of Revelation, the "number of a man" 666, derives from this practice. The Cabala still uses arithmantic methods heavily; *SEE* GEMATRIA.

The oldest known reference to arithmancy is found in an inscription of Sargon II, king of Assyria from 727 to 707 B.C.E. According to the inscription, the city wall of the new Assyrian capitol, Dur Sharrukin, was made to measure 16,283 cubits long, since this number was the value of Sargon's name. The origins of the system are thus probably to be found in Mesopotamian occult tradition; *SEE* MESOPOTAMIAN OCCULTISM.

Attempts have been made since ancient times to work out methods of arithmancy for languages that are not isopsephic. In Latin, where only certain letters (*I, V, X, L, C,* and so on) have numerical values, medieval and Renaissance writers took up the habit of counting up the number values of these particular letters when they occurred in a word or phrase. For example, IVDICIVM, "judgment" in Latin, can be added up to 1613—a detail that gave a certain amount of impetus to sixteenth-century speculations about the approaching Last Judgment, and may have played a role in setting off the Rosicrucian furor. *SEE* ROSICRUCIANS.

In modern languages such as English, many different systems of arithmancy have been produced, none of them entirely satisfactory. The most basic, which is much used in popular numerology but can also be found in Renaissance occult writings, simply gives each letter the number of its place in the alphabet; thus *A*, the first letter, is 1, and *Z*, the twenty-sixth, is 26. A variation on this adds together the digits of any two-digit number; thus *Z* in this system would equal 8 (26 becomes 2 + 6 = 8). Other systems, based on analogies between English sounds and those of Hebrew, Greek, and other languages, are also in circulation. FURTHER READING: HULSE 1994.

arithmology. The esoteric science of number, sometimes confused with arithmancy or "numerology." Arithmology is the application of occult principles to number (or vice versa), so that numerical relationships become symbols of magical and spiritual forces. Arithmology is to number what sacred geometry is to geometrical form, and both are part of the quadrivium, the four sciences of occult mathematics. *SEE* QUADRIVIUM; SACRED GEOMETRY.

The differences between arithmology and arithmancy are easy to trace out in the abstract, but often become complicated in practice. In arithmancy, numbers are used to translate letters—for example, a Hebrew or Greek word may be converted to its numerical equivalent, and then compared to other words with the same numerical value. In arithmology, on the other hand, the numerical properties of the number itself are the key to its meaning; thus two, for example, is associated with ideas of division and polarity, while three represents the resolution of polarity by a third conecting factor. While these differences are fairly straightforward, it has been common since ancient times to use arithmological ideas to decipher arithmantic relationships, to construct arithmantic word-conundrums to conceal arithmological secrets, and to mix the two together in any number of other ingenious ways.

The origins of the Western tradition of arithmology are not known for certain, although both Egypt and Mesopotamia had advanced mathematical knowledge closely interwoven with spiritual teachings early enough to be responsible. The Greek philosopher and mystic Pythagoras of Samos (c. 570–c. 495 B.C.E.), who traveled and studied in both these countries, is the first clearly known figure in the tradition. His students, who scattered across the Mediterranean world after the anti-Pythagorean riots of the early fifth century B.C.E., passed on elements of his teachings to others. SEE PYTHAGORAS.

The Neoplatonists of the early centuries of the Common Era played a major role in reviving arithmological studies; from them, the tradition passed down to the Middle Ages, which included arithmology in ordinary arithmetic in the same way that it fused astrology and astronomy. The Renaissance occult revival drew heavily on ancient arithmological works and on medieval developments of the tradition, and Renaissance texts of arithmology—most of which have never been translated or even reprinted since the Scientific Revolution—represent in many ways the high-water mark of the tradition. The Scientific Revolution, here as elsewhere in the occult tradition, brought an end to this flourishing of arithmological studies. Still, a slow but steady trickle of books on the subject has continued to appear up to the present time.

By way of Freemasonry, which absorbed certain elements of traditional arithmology at an early date, arithmological symbolism still plays an important role in many fraternal and magical lodge systems. The number of officers in a lodge, degrees or grades in a system,

knocks upon a door, rungs on a symbolic ladder, or stripes upon a robe in a traditional lodge generally has a specific arithmological meaning. SEE BATTERY; LODGE, FRATERNAL; LODGE, MAGICAL. SEE ALSO QUADRIVIUM; SACRED GEOMETRY. FURTHER READING: MICHELL 1972, TAYLOR 1972, THEON 1979, WATERFIELD 1988.

Arktogäa. (from Greek *arktos*, "bear, Big Dipper" and *gaia*, "earth, land") In Ariosophical writings, the supposed homeland of the Aryans, a vanished continent now covered by the Arctic Ocean. SEE ARIOSOPHY.

Armanen. According to the Ariosophical doctrines of Guido von List, an order of ancient Germanic Pagan priest-kings who ruled the Teutonic tribes in the era before the coming of Christianity. List derived the concept from a passage by the Roman historian Tacitus, who described the ancient Germans as composed of three tribes: the Ingaevones on the North Sea coast, the Istaevones in the south, and the Hermiones in between. List's reconstruction equated these three tribes with the three *arya* castes of Vedic Hindu society—respectively, the farmers, the warriors, and the priest-intellectuals—and derived the term "Hermiones" from an invented proto-German word *Armanen*.

According to List and his followers, the ancient Armanen were divided into three degrees of initiation, each with the full nineteenth-century lodge equipage of signs, grips, and passwords. Candidates of sufficient racial purity spent seven years in each of the lower grades of Novice and Brother before finally advancing to the status of Master. In the Armanist high places or *Halgadome*, masters dispensed justice, enforced laws against racial mixing, and studied the secrets of the universe, which List described along essentially Theosophical lines.

The coming of Christianity, according to List's theory, forced the Armanen into concealment but did not eliminate them. The Knights Templar, the operative Freemasons, the Rosicrucians, and the Holy Vehm were all instanced by List as Armanen organizations operating under concealment, and Renaissance humanists such as Johann Reuchlin and Cornelius Agrippa also found a place in the ranks of secret Armanist initiates. List also claimed that the Armanist teachings had been passed on to Jewish rabbis in the Rhineland during the ninth century, in an effort to preserve them against Christian persecution; this claim allowed List and other Ariosophists to claim that the Cabala was not really Jewish in origin, and enabled them to identify nearly the entire body of Western ceremonial magic as Armanist wisdom.

There seems to be no evidence whatsoever that the Armanen had any historical existence outside the imaginations of List and his followers, and it's not hard to trace the genesis of these ideas in a free mix of Theosophy, nineteenth-century occultism, early twentieth-century central European racist ideology, and borrowings from the Druid revival. The Armanist ideology was nonetheless highly influential in central Europe between the two world wars, and groups drawing on List's ideas are still active today. List's theories may also have played a part in the development of the historical mythology of modern Wicca, which includes similar (and similarly unverified) claims about the continuity of Pagan religious traditions from prehistoric times to the present. SEE ALSO ARIOSOPHY; DRUIDS; LIST, GUIDO VON; THEOSOPHY. FURTHER READING: GOODRICK-CLARKE 1992.

Armanen runes. Runic alphabet devised by Guido von List, who believed it to be part of the ancient wisdom of the Armanen priesthood; SEE ARMANEN. In 1902, while recovering from an eye operation, List had a mystical experience in which he saw connections between eighteen of the runes of the elder futhark and the eighteen verses of the rune charm of the *Havamal*, a section of the Elder Edda. Upon his recovery, he published the correspondences, and expanded them substantially in his 1908 book *The Secret of the Runes*. While there is no historical evidence that the Armanen futhark existed at all before List, it is a well-developed magical alphabet and remains in use among rune practitioners in the German-speaking countries.

Rune	Sound Value	Name	Meaning
ᚠ	F	Fa	Transitory
ᚢ	U	Ur	Primordial
ᚦ	Th	Thorn	Thunderbolt
ᚨ	O	Os	Mouth
ᚱ	R	Rit	Wheel
ᚲ	K	Ka	Maiden
ᚻ	H	Hagal	Introspection
ᚾ	N	Not	Need
ᛁ	I	Is	Will
ᛅ	A	Ar	Solar Light
ᛋ	S	Sig	Victory
ᛏ	T	Tyr	Sword
ᛒ	B	Bar	Song
ᛚ	L	Laf	Law
ᛘ	M	Man	Mothering
ᛦ	Y	Yr	Rainbow
ᛂ	E	Eh	Marriage
ᚷ	G	Gibor	Gift

SEE ALSO RUNES. FURTHER READING: LIST 1988, THORSSON 1989B.

Ar nDraiocht Fein (ADF). (Irish, "Our Own Druidism") American Neopagan organization founded in 1983 by Pagan writer and practitioner P. E. I. Bonewits, formerly an Archdruid of the Reformed Druids of North America. ADF's founding was inspired by a widespread interest in Druidism among American Pagans, combined with the frustration Bonewits and others felt about the misinformation and inaccurate scholarship relied on by many Neopagan systems. ADF thus draws heavily on orthodox historical scholarship about the Druids and other ancient Indo-European religious traditions.

ADF is organized in self-governing Groves, which observe the eight High Days (identical to the Wiccan sabbats) and also hold regular meetings, at least twice a month. ADF as a whole is incorporated as a religious nonprofit organization, headed by an Archdruid; Bonewits was the first Archdruid, but stepped aside in 1993. A succession of elected Archdruids have held the post since that time.

The practices, liturgy, and training curriculum of the ADF is largely based on scholarly research into Indo-European traditions, and is heavily influenced in particular by the work of French mythologist Georges Dumezil. The three worlds of Earth, Sea, and Sky are central to ADF ritual, and the three kindreds—the gods, the ancestors, and the nature spirits—are invoked. ADF writings make something of a point of rejecting the four elements and four quarters used by most other Neopagan groups; some claim (inaccurately) that these are Judeo-Christian and thus unacceptable in a Pagan setting, while others simply point out (accurately) that there is no evidence for their use among prehistoric Indo-European peoples. *SEE* ELEMENTS, MAGICAL.

Dumezil's division of ancient Indo-European social structures into three functions—priest-king, warrior, and peasant—is echoed in the ADF training program. There are a series of guilds, or special interest groups within ADF, which are assigned to the various functions, and each has an extensive training program.

The Earth Mother is invoked at every ritual, and the God of the Sea is called on to open the gates between the worlds. The specific names used for these deities, and for other gods and goddesses who may be invoked in ADF ritual, vary from Grove to Grove and often from ceremony to ceremony; any Indo-European pantheon can be used in an ADF setting, and in fact rituals are performed in languages ranging from Irish through Old Common Slavic to Proto-Indo-European.

As of this writing, the ADF is among the largest Neopagan groups in North America, with Groves, Proto-Groves, and individual practitioners in most U.S. states and Canadian provinces as well as several other countries. *SEE ALSO* DRUIDS; REFORMED DRUIDS OF NORTH AMERICA (RDNA).

Aroueris. (ancient Egyptian *Heru-ur*, "Horus the Great") Horus the Elder, an ancient and complex Egyptian god partly conflated with his nephew Horus the Younger, the son of Isis and Osiris. Aroueris is a warrior god whose two eyes are the sun and the moon; according to the theology of Heliopolis, he is one of the five children of Nut and Geb. *SEE* OSIRIS.

In the Golden Dawn system of magic, the godform of Aroueris was used by the Hierophant when that officer moved off the dais in the east. *SEE* GODFORMS. *SEE ALSO* HORUS.

Arqa. (Hebrew ARQA, "earth") One of the seven earths of Cabalistic lore, corresponding to Hod. *SEE* EARTHS, SEVEN.

Ars Notoria. *SEE* NOTORY ART.

Art of Memory. Originally developed in ancient Greece, the Art of Memory is a system for expanding the capacity and accuracy of human memory by the use of visualization. Its connections to the occult traditions of the West were somewhat limited until the Renaissance, and in classical and medieval times it was an ordinary part of most educated people's knowledge set, with no connection at all to occultism. During the Renaissance, however, a number of major occult figures practiced it extensively, and Giordano Bruno and Robert Fludd both contributed important works on the subject. *SEE* BRUNO, GIORDANO; FLUDD, ROBERT.

A practitioner of the Art of Memory in its classical form starts by memorizing the inside of a building, walking through it physically and then, repeatedly, in imagination until he or she can recall it in detail. A set of *loci* ("places") within the building are chosen so that when the practitioner walks through the building in imagination, he or she will pass by each *locus*. Each "place" is then stocked with a visualized image representing something the practitioner wants to remember. The image should be striking and memorable, and it should suggest the thing to be memorized in some unmistakable way; visual puns and the use of "alphabets" of images were a standard way of doing this. Once the images are in place, the practitioner simply has to walk through the building once again in imagination and take note of the images to remember what they are intended to convey.

All this seems extremely complicated and roundabout to modern minds, but it works extremely well in practice. Modern practitioners have found that with practice, an enormous amount of information can be quickly and accurately stored and recalled by these methods. During its Renaissance interaction with the Western occult traditions, the Art of Memory left several important traces behind. Mnemonic habits of constructing striking visual images had a major impact on occult symbolism, and the tarot cards themselves may have started out life as images in someone's private memory system; *SEE* TAROT. By way of Giordano Bruno's student Alexander Dicson, the Art of Memory also came into use in stonemasons' craft lodges in Scotland, and thus may have had an important role in shaping the symbolism and ritual of Freemasonry; *SEE* FREEMASONRY. FURTHER READING: YATES 1966.

Arthur, King. Roman-British war leader, fl. fifth–sixth centuries C.E. Next to nothing is actually known about this most famous of legendary kings. His name was probably Artorius, a Roman name attested in Roman-British sources, and he is mentioned in a handful of early chronicles as "leader in the battles" (*dux bellorum*), a Roman military rank more or less equivalent to "general." He may have been the nephew of Ambrosius Aurelianus, a slightly less shadowy historical figure in post-Roman Britain.

According to the chronicles, he fought a series of battles against Saxon invaders of Britain on behalf of the Romanized Celtic inhabitants of the island, the ancestors of the later Welsh and Cornish peoples. The final decisive battle was at a place called Mount Badon, which has not been identified with any degree of certainty. Evidence suggests that the Saxons made no headway for a period of some fifty years in the early sixth century, and many historians give Arthur credit for this.

Despite efforts to connect him with southern Scotland, Brittany, and places even further afield, most historians agree that his activities and battles were centered on the region traditionally associated with him—the land of Logres, now southwestern England. Cadbury Castle, a prehistoric hill-fort in that area that was massively refortified in post-Roman times, has been proposed as a plausible site for his home base. Glastonbury, where his body was allegedly excavated in medieval times, is also in Logres. *SEE* GLASTONBURY.

In the difficult years after the mid-sixth century, when most of Britain fell under Saxon control and many refugees fled to Brittany in northwestern France, stories of the glorious years when Celtic forces had held the invaders at bay were told and retold, and combined with older, mythological material from pre-Christian Celtic religion. It was these materials, reworked in the twelfth century and later by medieval minstrels and poets, that gave rise to the Arthurian legends that have come down to us; *SEE* ARTHURIAN LEGENDS. FURTHER READING: DARRAH 1994.

Arthurian legends. The most famous of all medieval stories, the tales that comprise the Arthurian legends center on King Arthur of Britain, his queen Guinevere, his court wizard Merlin, and the knights of his Round Table. Few tales in all of history have had so wide a distribution or so impressive a continuity through time.

The Arthurian legends crystallized in the early Middle Ages around the shadowy figure of a Roman-British general, probably named Artorius, who defended Britain's Celtic inhabitants against Saxon invaders in the late fifth and early sixth centuries. *SEE* ARTHUR, KING. Tales of his exploits and the deeds of his warriors circulated in oral tradition in Wales and Cornwall, and in Brittany in northwestern France, where many British refugees fled during the Saxon invasions. In the process, these tales picked up elements from older, pre-Christian Celtic mythology.

During the early twelfth century, some of this material came to the attention of Geoffrey of Monmouth, a Welsh scholar in the service of the Norman overlords of England, who set out to write a definitive history of Britain. His *Historia Regum Britanniae* (*History of the Kings of Britain*) was based, according to his own account, on "a certain very ancient book written in the British (i.e., Welsh) language." Modern scholars have argued endlessly over whether he was telling the truth or not, for the *Historia* is a wild mix of fantasy, fact, fiction, myth, and prophecy. (In this it has much in common with most medieval histories.) Whether or not the "ancient book" existed, though, it's clear that Geoffrey drew extensively on sources outside his own imagination, and many odd details of his book have been verified by later archeological research.

Geoffrey's book vaulted Arthur at once to the center stage of medieval literature, and with him a handful of other characters: Guinevere, Merlin, Gawain, Kay, Bedivere, and Mordred. By twelfth-century standards, the *Historia* was a runaway bestseller, and it inspired several generations of poets and prose writers to seek out more details about Arthur and his warriors. The result, after several centuries of effort, was the full-blown Arthurian legend as it exists in its massive late medieval versions—Thomas Malory's *Le Morte D'Arthur* in English, the *Prose*

Lancelot in French, and equivalents in many other European languages. Later versions, such as Tennyson's and T. H. White's English reworkings and the flurry of modern historical fiction on Arthurian themes, are almost entirely derivative from these earlier sources.

The occult dimensions of Arthurian legend are many-sided. First of all, the long process of oral transmission that shaped the earliest Arthurian tales mixed them thoroughly with elements of Pagan Celtic myth that did not survive in any other form. The landscape of Arthur's kingdom is thickly populated with Celtic gods. Kings such as Brandegore, Brandiles, and the Fisher King Bron are the Welsh god Bran the Blessed in various forms (the first two, for example, are simply "Bran of Gower" and "Bran of the Isles" filtered through medieval French). Similarly, the god Beli became Sir Balin, and the Irish goddess Morrigan took a new shape as Morgan le Fay. The adventures of Arthur and his knights also echo older mythologies in many places.

The legends of the Holy Grail, which may not originally have been connected with Arthur but were caught up in the construction of the legend at an early point, provide another major magical dimension to the Arthurian tales. The origins, history, and meaning of the Grail are complex enough to require separate examination; SEE GRAIL, HOLY.

Another magically significant aspect of the legends deals with the knights Sir Pellinore and Sir Palomides and their never-ending pursuit of Glatisant, the mysterious Questing Beast; SEE QUESTING BEAST.

The magical revival of the nineteenth and early twentieth centuries, with its strong tinge of Romanticism, found new occult dimensions in Arthurian legend. The imagery of the Grail Quest was particularly attractive to occult writers, especially after its reformulation by Richard Wagner in his final opera, *Parsifal*. An entire literature of occult Arthurianism emerged out of this movement, extensive and diverse enough that it is impossible to summarize here. British occult groups in particular were especially active in this field, and Dion Fortune's Society of the Inner Light produced an extensive body of magical work on the subject, which was later written up and published by Gareth Knight as *The Secret Tradition in Arthurian Legend* (1983). British Druid orders

such as the Order of Bards Ovates and Druids (OBOD) have also devoted much time and effort to expounding the occult dimensions of Arthurian legend. In addition, there have been a number of orders—in Britain and elsewhere—specifically built up around the Arthurian legend. SEE ORDER OF BARDS OVATES AND DRUIDS (OBOD); INNER LIGHT, SOCIETY OF THE.

The Neopagan revival has also adopted the Arthurian legend in various forms and guises, especially as filtered through the lens of modern fantasy fiction; Marion Zimmer Bradley's *The Mists of Avalon*, a feminist revision of the legend, has been particularly influential here. At least one offshoot of Wicca based on Bradley's version of the classic Arthurian themes has emerged in the American Pagan scene, and there will no doubt be others. FURTHER READING: DARRAH 1994, GEOFFREY 1966, KNIGHT 1983, NICHOLS 1990.

As. (Old Norse, "god") The fourth rune of the younger futhark, the special rune of the god Odin. It stands for inspiration, wisdom, and knowledge, and represents the sound *a*. SEE YOUNGER FUTHARK.

Rune As

asana. In yoga, a body posture used for meditation or psychophysical exercise. The term has been borrowed by some Western occult systems for meditation postures or static exercise positions. SEE MEDITATION; YOGA.

Asatru. (Old Norse, "faith of the Aesir") The most common modern term for Norse and Germanic Pagan religion, primarily used for its modern revivals but also applied, mostly by Asatruar (followers of Asatru), to the ancient worship of the Germanic deities. In its original form, Asatru was the tribal religion of the Germanic peoples, a branch of the Indo-European family of nations, who came spilling westward out of Asia sometime around 1000 B.C.E. and established themselves in what is now central and northern Europe. Like nearly all Pagan traditions in the ancient Western world, Germanic religion was a loose polytheism that revered a wide array of gods, spirits, and other supernatural entities. Its primary rites included sacrificial offerings of livestock, beer, and valuables; divination by a variety of means, including the use of the runic alphabet; and a variety of quasi-shamanic trance practices. *SEE* RUNES; SACRIFICE.

Few Germanic peoples were ever conquered by the Romans, even in the days of the empire's greatest power, and so Christianity was slow to make inroads in the German lands. By the fall of Rome in 476 C.E., however, a number of the more Romanized Germanic tribes had already converted to Christianity, and the church spread steadily northwards, finally converting the last entirely Pagan countries in Scandinavia in the eleventh century. *SEE* PAGANISM. Pagan minorities continued in existence until much later, and it has been claimed that a continuous tradition of Norse Paganism survived in Iceland up to the present day.

Be this as it may, the revival of Asatru in the twentieth century had essentially nothing to do with these survivals. Rather, it arose from the rediscovery of Old Norse myth and literature in the nineteenth century. Romantic writers and poets in Germany, England, and several other countries drew heavily on these sources, and produced a flood of major works of literature and art, among them German composer Richard Wagner's phenomenally popular four-opera series *Der Ring des Nibelungen* (*The Ring of the Nibelung*) and English author J. R. R. Tolkien's equally successful trilogy *The Lord of the Rings*.

The revival of Pagan ideas in the twentieth century made it inevitable that the ancient Germanic traditions would sooner or later be taken up by modern worshippers. Unfortunately, this first happened in Germany and Austria among right-wing racist occult circles that were directly ancestral to the National Socialist (Nazi) movement in Germany. *SEE* ARIOSOPHY; NATIONAL SOCIALISM. While the Nazi movement was hardly an accurate reflection of the older tradition, it played a large role in discouraging an Asatru revival until several decades after other Pagan revivals had gotten off the ground. *SEE* DRUIDRY; WICCA.

The first significant Asatru movement outside of the Ariosophical fold got underway in the 1970s, when several small groups in Europe and America began exploring a new Germanic Paganism. A major boost was given to the fledgling movement by the publication of Ralph Blum's *The Book of Runes* in 1978; Blum's work has been sharply criticized by Asatruar as shallow and inaccurate, but it brought Germanic spiritual traditions into a sudden glare of mostly positive publicity. *SEE* RUNES.

The 1980s and 1990s were the great seedtime of Asatru in the Western world, and saw the founding of a series of organizations that have played a major role in developing a coherent body of practice and theory for modern Asatru. The first of these, the Rune-Gild, was launched in America by Edred Thorsson (Stephen Flowers) in 1980. The sort of organizational upsets universal in modern Pagan circles have enlivened the history of the Rune-Gild and its successors, but do not seem to have greatly hindered the spread of Asatru.

At the present time Asatru is still in the midst of major developments. The eight sabbats of Wiccan practice have been taken over by a number of Asatru groups, although there is some debate over this and alternative ritual calendars have been proposed. Runic lore, the original focus of most Asatru activity in the Western world, remains a strong theme, but rituals of worship for the gods and goddesses have become increasingly prominent, and galdor—traditional Norse magical practice, heavily supplemented by borrowings from other magical systems—also has a growing place. Most recent has been the spread of *seidhr* or *seith*, a system of trance work based largely on current ideas about shamanism, which was introduced in the 1990s by American writer and priestess Diana Paxson; *SEE* SEIDHR. Further developments can probably be expected in the near future. *SEE ALSO* NEOPAGANISM. FURTHER READING: ASWYNN 1998, THORSSON 1989A, THORSSON 1998.

ascendant. In astrology, the point on the ecliptic on the eastern horizon at any specific point in time. In natal astrology, the ascendant plays a crucial role, as it marks the orientation of the subject to the entire pattern of fixed stars and zodiacal constellations. In ancient and early medieval astrology, the ascendant was termed the horoscope; the importance of this point may be judged by the fact that, by the late Middle Ages, it had given its name to the entire chart. *SEE* ASTROLOGY; HOROSCOPE.

In the Golden Dawn system, the Sphere of Sensation or aura mirrors the sphere of the heavens as it was at the time of birth, with the point of the ascendant in front of the physical body's midline throughout life. *SEE* SPHERE OF SENSATION.

Ascended Masters. *SEE* MASTERS.

Ascended Masters' teachings. In popular occultism from the middle of the twentieth century onward, a system of esoteric theory and practice based on the writings of Guy Ballard and several other occult authors; *SEE* BALLARD, GUY. The Ascended Masters are believed to be an association of advanced spiritual beings dedicated to uplifting the human race, who communicate their teachings via mediumship and other means. Jesus of Nazareth is generally considered to be the highest of the Masters, with the Comte de Saint-Germain a close second. *SEE* MASTERS.

The teachings, like so much of popular American occultism in the last century, are largely a mix of Theosophy with Christian elements; *SEE* THEOSOPHY. The supreme being, I AM, is present in the higher self of each individual as the I AM presence. Human souls pass through many incarnations, burdened with the karma of their actions, until they realize the I AM presence and undergo ascension, leaving behind their material bodies. The Ascended Masters are simply those souls who have already accomplished this and now form the Great White Brotherhood, the secret spiritual government of the universe.

Practical methods of the Ascended Master teachings center on decreeing and the use of the Violet Flame. Decrees are prayers to the I AM presence and to one or more of the Ascended Masters; spoken in a meditative state along with visualizations, they are often repeated many times over like mantras. The Violet Flame is an expression of the Violet Ray, one of the Seven Rays; *SEE* RAYS, SEVEN. It represents the power of freedom, transmutation, and healing. Visualized along with the repetition of appropriate decrees, the Violet Flame is held to cleanse away the karma of past errors, bring healing, and foster spiritual development. Daily practice of decrees and the Violet Flame is considered by most followers of the Ascended Masters' teachings to be the most effective route to ascension.

The Ascended Masters' teachings are at the center of a diffuse but lively movement, and several dozen organizations exist to promote them. There have been some well-publicized problems with authoritarian behavior and financial exploitation in some groups associated with the teachings, but it's hard to find a spiritual tradition of which this is not true nowadays. On the whole, the teachings and the movement that has grown up around them represent an original and largely positive addition to the Western magical traditions. *SEE ALSO* THEOSOPHICAL SOCIETY.

ash. The ash tree (*Fraxinus* spp.) is among the more important trees in Western myth and folk magic. Preeminently a wizard's tree, it was associated with the Norse god Odin and his Welsh semi-equivalent, the enchanter Gwydion son of Don; the world-tree of ancient Norse mythology, Yggdrasil, was an ash. The ash is also an Ogham tree, associated with Nion, the fifth letter of the Ogham alphabet. *SEE* NION.

In folk magic the ash has countless uses. Burning an ash log at Yuletide is held to bring prosperity for the coming year, and eating the red buds of ash on St. John's Eve (June 24) is a sure preventive against hostile magic. Axles and tool handles of ash make a vehicle go faster or a tool accomplish more than those made of any other wood. *SEE ALSO* NATURAL MAGIC.

Ashim. (Hebrew AShIM, "flames") According to some accounts, the order of angels attributed to Malkuth, the tenth sphere of the Tree of Life; other accounts assign Malkuth to the Ishim. *SEE* ANGEL; ISHIM; MALKUTH.

Ashmole, Elias. English scholar and occultist, 1617–1692. The most important occult scholar of his generation, Ashmole was born in the country town of Lichfield, Staffordshire, and attended the famous Lichfield Grammar School. He worked as an attorney until his marriage, when his wife's fortune made it possible for him to devote his time entirely to scholarly and occult pursuits.

Ashmole's interests included alchemy, ritual magic, and astrology. He was responsible for collecting most of what survives of the magical manuscripts of the great Elizabethan magus John Dee; *SEE* DEE, JOHN. His collection of English alchemical poems, *Theatrum Chemicum Britannicum* (1652), preserves several important medieval texts of alchemy, including Norton's *Ordinall of Alchemy*; *SEE* NORTON, THOMAS. He also wrote what is still the single best work on the origins and early history of the Order of the Garter.

Although a committed Royalist, Ashmole managed to survive the troubled years of the English Civil War and the Interregnum without serious trouble. One of his close friends was the Parliamentary astrologer William Lilly, with whom he cooperated on a variety of astrological research projects; Lilly's friendship may have helped keep him safe during the war years, and he returned the favor at the Restoration, when his influence kept Lilly out of legal jeopardy. *SEE* LILLY, WILLIAM.

After the Restoration Ashmole received numerous favors from King Charles II and several lucrative government offices. He was also a founding member of the Royal Society. In 1677 he donated a large collection of antiquities, partly inherited from his friend John Tradescant, to the University of Oxford, where it became the nucleus of the Ashmolean Museum. He died in 1692. *SEE ALSO* ALCHEMY. FURTHER READING: ASHMOLE 1652.

Ashurbanipal. Assyrian king, reigned 668–627 B.C.E.. Much of his reign was spent in wars at the frontiers of the Assyrian empire, which included all of Mesopotamia and Palestine, and had expanded to northern Egypt in the reign of his father Esarhaddon. He finished the conquest of Egypt, put down a widespread rebellion led by his brother Shamashumukin, conquered Elam, and brought Arabia and Armenia under Assyrian control. Unlike most Assyrian kings, though, he was a scholar as well as a warrior, and in the peaceful years toward the end of his reign he devoted much of his time to literary and historical pursuits.

His importance for the history of magic lies in his systematic efforts to collect ancient clay-tablet records from the old Babylonian and Sumerian towns in his empire. Tablets copied by his scribes, and found in the ruins of his palace in the Assyrian capital of Nineveh, include a large part of the surviving literature of Mesopotamian magic.

Whether Ashurbanipal himself practiced any of the material he preserved is not recorded, but certainly the rituals were not simply there for antiquarian purposes. A set of five terra-cotta statues of dogs was found buried in the entrance to the west wing of Ashurbanipal's palace in Nineveh; their colors, and the inscriptions on their shoulder blades, match exactly the instructions for manufacturing magical guardian statues from a clay-tablet ritual text in his library. *SEE* STATUES, MAGICAL. *SEE ALSO* MESOPOTAMIAN OCCULTISM.

Asmodeus. (from Persian *Aeshma Daeva*) One of the important figures of Jewish and Christian demonology, Asmodeus has various jobs and attributes in different authors. In most sources, he is listed as the archdemon of Geburah, the seventh sphere of the Cabalistic Tree of Life; *SEE* CABALA; GEBURAH. According to the *Lemegeton*, he appears as a man with three heads—those of a bull, a ram, and a man—with a serpent's tail and feet like a goose, mounted on a dragon and breathing fire. He is said to be an excellent teacher of arithmetic, astronomy, geometry, and handicrafts.

Cabalistic lore claims that the name Asmodeus, or Ashmedai, is actually a title rather than a name, and is held in turn by each king of the demons. This claim is related to the Cabalistic art of gematria, because Ashmedai and the word "pharoah," the title of the king of Egypt, add up to the same number in gematria.

An odd Jewish legend claims that Asmodeus is or was the leader of a class of demons that converted to Judaism and accepted the Torah. These "Jewish demons" were thought to be descendants of matings between demons and human beings, and were long-lived but not immortal. Asmodeus himself was thought to be the son of King David and Agrath, queen of the demons, or the son of Naamah, the sister of Tubalcain, by an unnamed demonic father. According to one account, he was caught in the Jewish community of Mainz, Germany, in the terrible pogrom of 1096 and killed.

His name is sometimes given as Asmodai or Asmoday. *SEE ALSO* DEMON. FURTHER READING: SCHOLEM 1974.

aspect, astrological. One of a number of angular relationships between planets and/or other astrologically important points, measured from the standpoint of the

Earth, which are considered meaningful in astrology. The aspects of traditional astrology are conjunction, in which two bodies are in the same degree of the zodiac at the same time; opposition, in which they are 180 degrees apart; trine, 120 degrees apart; square, 90 degrees apart; and sextile, 60 degrees apart.

Each aspect has an *orb*, a certain number of degrees before and after the exact aspect in which it has effect. The size of the orb differs from aspect to aspect, with conjunction and opposition having a relatively large orb and the others progressively less. The exact size of the orb for a given aspect is a subject of much dispute among astrologers, but one common scheme gives an orb of 7 degrees for conjunction and opposition, 5 degrees for trine and square, and 3 degrees for sextile.

Beginning in the seventeenth century, astrologers have proposed a number of additional aspects. The first major effort in this direction was the work of the German astronomer and astrologer Johannes Kepler (1571–1630), who introduced the biquintile (144 degrees), sesquisquare (135 degrees), sesquiquintile (108 degrees), quintile (72 degrees), semisquare (45 degrees), and semiquintile (36 degrees). Kepler's contemporary, the French astrologer Jean-Baptiste Morin (1583–1656), provided the semisextile (30 degrees) and quincunx (150 degrees). All of these are considered relatively weak aspects, and most modern astrologers treat them as background factors at most.
SEE ENTRIES UNDER THE NAME OF EACH ASPECT; SEE ALSO ASTROLOGY.

Assessors, Forty-two. In ancient Egyptian mythology, divine beings who assisted Osiris in judging the souls of the dead. To each Assessor corresponded a sin, and the deceased had to be able to deny that he had committed each of these sins to avoid being condemned by the Assessors and devoured by the monstrous Eater of Souls. The entire process is detailed in the Egyptian Book of the Dead. *SEE* EGYPTIAN BOOK OF THE DEAD; OSIRIS.

In the Neophyte Grade ceremony of the Golden Dawn, the Forty-two Assessors form part of the structure of invisible stations built up by the Hierophant and other officers before the rite, used to channel energies during it. *SEE* INVISIBLE STATIONS.

Assiah. The world of action, the fourth of the four worlds in Cabalistic theory, corresponding to the material level of being. It is represented on the Tree of Life as a whole by the ten celestial spheres, and corresponds most closely with Malkuth, the tenth and last Sephirah. In Assiah, the Tetragrammaton is spelled YVD HH VV HH, and the secret name of Assiah is BN, Ben. *SEE* BEN; CABALA; TETRAGRAMMATON.

Astarte. An ancient Canaanite goddess of love and war, Astarte appears in records dating back to the middle of the second millennium B.C.E., and is mentioned in the Jewish scriptures. She was apparently the most popular goddess among the various Semitic peoples of the ancient Near East. As such, she has been borrowed by a number of modern Pagan traditions as a name for the Goddess of current Neopagan theology. *SEE* GODDESS, THE.

Astaroth. An important demon in Jewish and Christian demonology, Astaroth is probably based on the Canaanite goddess Astarte, but seems to have suffered a sex change somewhere along the line; *SEE* ASTARTE. According to Cabalistic lore, he is the archdemon of Chesed, the fourth Sephirah of the Cabalistic Tree of Life; the *Lemegeton* describes him as a duke of Hell, appearing as an angel riding a dragon and carrying a viper in his right hand. He has the power to tell fortunes and teach the liberal arts. *SEE ALSO* DEMON; LEMEGETON.

asteroids. An assortment of small planetoids orbiting the Sun, ranging from grains of dust up to rocky masses several hundred miles across. There are at least 40,000 of them large enough to be seen from Earth by telescope; most, but not all, circle between the orbits of Mars and Jupiter, and it has been suggested that they may be the remains of a destroyed planet that once filled this orbit.

Astrologers ignored the asteroids almost completely until 1973, when American astrologer Eleanor Bach arranged to have an astronomer prepare an accurate ephemeris of the four most prominent—Ceres, Vesta, Pallas, and Juno. All four were considered by Bach to correspond to the zodiacal sign Virgo, although some later astrologers have assigned the last two to Libra.

The giant comet Chiron, which follows an unstable orbit between Saturn and Uranus, was originally thought to be an asteroid, and is sometimes classed with the asteroids for astrological purposes. *SEE* CHIRON.

A certain number of modern astrologers have come to include the asteriods in their work. Even the proponents of asteriod astrology admit that they are relatively minor factors in the chart, however, and most astrologers ignore them completely. *SEE ALSO* ASTROLOGY.

astral body. In magical philosophy, the aspect of the human individual on the astral plane or level of concrete consciousness. It is the vehicle of emotions and desires, and of all the activities of the mind that deal with sensory perceptions. The five aspects of the lower self—memory, will, imagination, emotion, and thinking—operate entirely on an astral level until access to the mental level is achieved by meditation and inner development.

The most widely known feature of the astral body is its ability to separate from the physical and etheric bodies and travel through the astral plane. This ability, the power of astral projection, is a conscious and developed version of something every human being does during sleep. *SEE* ASTRAL PROJECTION.

In the process of entering into incarnation before birth, according to occult teachings, the astral body is built up from the energies of the seven planets of traditional astrological theory as the soul descends toward incarnation. After death, these same energies are returned to their sources in the period after the Second Death, when the etheric body has been discarded and no longer binds the astral energies in place. *SEE* ETHERIC BODY; SECOND DEATH. *SEE ALSO* ASTRAL PLANE.

astral light. In the writings of Eliphas Lévi and other nineteenth- and twentieth-century occultists, the Great Magical Agent, the substance of stellar influence through which every magical operation has its effect. Lévi and his followers identified the astral light with od, animal magnetism, and other Western terms for etheric energy, a usage that has helped add to the already confused terminology of the planes of being. *SEE* ETHER; LÉVI, ELIPHAS. FURTHER READING: LÉVI 1972.

astral plane. In occult philosophy, the realm of concrete consciousness, the level of reality that corresponds to the human experiences of dream, vision, out-of-body experience, and ordinary consciousness. The astral plane is located between the etheric plane, the level of subtle life-energy, and the mental plane, the level of abstract consciousness and meaning. As with all the planes of occult theory, the astral is "above" or "below" other planes only in a metaphorical sense; in reality, all the planes interpenetrate the realm of physical matter experienced by the senses.

The astral plane is the most important of the planes from the point of view of the practicing magician, since it is on the astral level that most magical energies come into manifestation. It stands on the border between the timeless and spaceless mental and spiritual planes, on the one hand, and the etheric and physical planes within space and time, on the other. It is on the astral level, therefore, that patterns from the higher planes take shape before descending fully into space and time, and the magician who can access this plane freely and effectively can influence the way these patterns work out in the world of ordinary experience. *SEE ALSO* ASTRAL BODY.

astral projection. The process of separating the astral body from the physical and etheric bodies, producing what is often referred to as an out-of-body experience, or OBE. *SEE* ASTRAL BODY. Methods of astral projection have been taught in magical traditions for many centuries, at least, and most of the magical systems active at present include effective techniques for this operation.

According to magical theory, astral projection happens naturally every night during sleep, and is responsible for the experience of dreaming. Controlled (so-called "lucid") dreaming is thus one common way to develop the knack of astral projection. Other methods range from the induction of trance states to the construction of a Body of Light by visualization and controlled breathing, followed by the transfer of consciousness to the secondary body by an act of will.

Different magical traditions place widely different levels of importance on the art of astral projection. In some systems it is considered to be little more than a stunt, useful primarily as a way to develop will and imagination. In others, the capacity to leave one's physical body at will is seen as a central goal of magical practice, or even as the essential requirement of magical initiation.

In the alchemical writing of Mary Ann Atwood, the entire body of alchemical teaching and symbolism is reinterpreted as a cryptic way of talking about astral projection. SEE ATWOOD, MARY ANNE. SEE ALSO ETHERIC PROJECTION. FURTHER READING: BARDON 1962, W. BUTLER 1962, CROWLEY 1976.

Astrampsychus, Lots of. A divination system invented in the second or third centuries of the Common Era, attributed to a (probably fictional) Astrampsychus the Magician, and much used in late Roman and early medieval times. The Lots start with ninety-two questions; the querent chooses one, and then randomly picks a number between one and ten. The chosen number is added to the number of the question, and the sum is looked up in a table of oracular gods (in the Pagan version of the Lots) or Christian saints (in the Christian version). Each god or saint has a table of ten answers, and the randomly chosen number is used to pick the correct answer.

The basic structure of the Lots is similar to that of Napoleon's *Book of Fate*, although the latter also draws on the divinatory art of geomancy. SEE GEOMANCY; NAPOLEON'S BOOK OF FATE. SEE ALSO DIVINATION; ORACLES. FURTHER READING: R. STEWART 2001, VAN DER HORST 1998.

astrology. The art and science of divination by the position of sun, moon, planets, and stars relative to a position on the surface of the Earth, astrology is among the most ancient branches of occultism still being practiced today. Its essential concept is that the position of stars and planets at any given moment can be interpreted as a map of the subtle forces and factors in play at that moment. When a person is born, an event takes place, or a question is asked, the characteristics of the exact moment in time when these things happen are mirrored in the heavens, and can be read by those who know how.

Central to traditional Western astrology is a vision of the universe as a matrix of forces in which everything affects everything else. The same energies that flow through stars and planets also pulse through the minds and bodies of individual human beings, and the movements of the heavens are thus mirrored in subtle ways by events on Earth. Many older accounts of astrology approach this awareness by way of the Neoplatonist philosophy that underlies most Western occultism, while many modern astrologers prefer to speak in terms of psychologist Carl Jung's concept of "synchronicity"; either way, the basic concept is the same.

The origins of astrology can be found in the ancient city-states of Mesopotamia, where Pagan religious beliefs held that the planets were gods and goddesses, and where priests began tracking the movements of the deities in heaven at a very early date. The oldest surviving record of planetary movements, the Venus tablet of Ammishaduqa, dates from approximately 1650 B.C.E., but there is every reason to think such records once reached many centuries further back. The recorded movements of the planets, along with many other omens and signs, were compared with earthly events and the results recorded. By the seventh century B.C.E., when the 7,000-omen collection *Enuma Anu Enlil* was compiled, this huge project had reached the stage where systematic conclusions could be drawn, and it was in the centuries immediately following that astrology as we know it first took shape. SEE MESOPOTAMIAN OCCULTISM.

The oldest known horoscopes, as suggested above, are Babylonian, and date from the end of the fifth century B.C.E. Shortly thereafter, the art was transmitted to the rising new power of Greece, and when Alexander the Great conquered Mesopotamia in 331 B.C.E. the resulting political and cultural shifts spread astrology throughout the Mediterranean world.

It was one among many systems of divination until the reign of Augustus, the first emperor of Rome (63 B.C.E.–19 C.E.). Augustus found astrology useful as a propaganda tool in his quest to legitimatize his rule over the former republic, and published his horoscope to back up his claim that the stars destined him to rule Rome. His patronage and that of his successor Tiberius made astrology the most prestigious of divination systems, and sparked a golden age of astrological practice and study.

Many important textbooks of astrology were written in the following two centuries, including the books of Manilius, Dorotheus of Sidon, Vettius Valens, and above all Claudius Ptolemy, whose *Tetrabiblos* (*Four Books*) was the most important manual of astrology for more than a thousand years thereafter. Passed on to the Arabs during the declining years of Rome, astrology underwent further refinements as generations of Arab astronomers and mathematicians worked out new tools for calculating the exact positions of planets and signs and for extracting meaning from the chart.

Astrology underwent a partial eclipse in Europe during the early Middle Ages, largely as a result of Christian prejudices against divination. The basic elements of the art were preserved, however, and contemporary records indicate that most of the French nobility as early as the ninth century C.E. sought advice from private astrologers. Most of early medieval astrology had to depend on night-by-night observations of the stars and planets, since much of the mathematical knowledge needed to erect a horoscope accurately was lost with the fall of Rome, and had to be reimported from the Arabic world. Early medieval astrologers paid a great deal of attention to the phases and positions of the moon, which could be easily tracked by eye, and an entire literature of lunar astrological almanacs came into being; *SEE* BOOK OF MOONS.

By the end of the eleventh century C.E., however, Arabic astrological and mathematical books were being translated into Latin, and soon became available to scholars throughout Europe. While many church officials were suspicious of the astrological revival, many others were enthusiastic supporters of the new art, and astrology became extremely popular.

By the early part of the twelfth century, detailed astrological tables became available in Western Europe and removed the last serious barrier in the way of astrological practice. With the new Alphonsine Tables—so called because they were compiled under the direction of King Alfonso I of Aragon—anyone with a basic knowledge of Latin and mathematics could erect a horoscope accurate to within a degree or so.

From this point on, astrology was, for all practical purposes, an everyday part of life until the coming of the Scientific Revolution. A small number of scholars denounced it or challenged its assumptions, but most people treated it as part of the basic nature of reality. It's typical of the age that during the middle of the sixteenth century, when the Reformation was heating up, Protestant and Catholic astrologers worked up and circulated sharply different horoscopes of Martin Luther, respectively praising or damning him by means of the stars.

The sixteenth century also saw the beginning of a movement to put astrological knowledge into the hands of the public. Jerome Cardan (1501–1576), an Italian astrologer and scholar, was instrumental in starting this process with his book *Libelli Duos* (*Two Booklets*, 1538), which contained the first widely circulated collection of horoscopes and their interpretations in print. The greatly expanded 1547 edition of the *Libelli* also included a set of aphorisms meant to serve as a detailed guide to chart interpretation. *SEE* CARDAN, JEROME.

Later figures expanded this project by translating astrological texts out of Latin into the languages of the common people. William Lilly (1602–1681) was the most important of these in the English-speaking world, publishing the first English textbook of astrology, *Christian Astrology* (1647; the title was an attempt to counter claims that astrology was a Satanic art). *SEE* LILLY, WILLIAM. At the same time, however, the first stirrings of the Scientific Revolution were underway, and with it a complete rejection of astrology and the rest of the Western occult tradition.

The scientific rejection of astrology primarily affected the educated upper classes, however, and astrologers continued their practice lower down the social ladder. All through the so-called Age of Reason, a succession of popular almanacs in most Western countries carried on the traditions of astrology, and works such as Lilly's were much in demand in the underworld of cunning folk, occult secret societies, and magical lodges. *SEE* CUNNING MAN/WOMAN; LODGE, MAGICAL.

With the beginning of the occult revival of the late nineteenth century, astrology was among the first occult sciences to begin the climb back into wider publicity. The work of English astrologer Alan Leo was central in launching this astrological renaissance; *SEE* LEO, ALAN. That climb accelerated in the twentieth century, which saw the emergence of professional organizations such as the American Federation of Astrologers, the development of a sizeable industry in astrological books and magazines, and—especially in the wake of the Sixties—the return of astrology to social acceptability in many circles. The revelation that American president Ronald Reagan planned many of the events of his presidency according to the advice of a California astrologer made headlines, but significantly it seems to have had little impact on his popularity—even with conservative Christian supporters who might have been expected to protest. The place of astrology in the Western world thus seems secure for the time being.

The essential medium of the astrologer's art is the astrological chart, which provides an abstract map of the heavens for a given moment from the standpoint of a particular place on the Earth's surface. The chart includes the following features:

a) twelve houses, which are abstract divisions of the sky as seen from Earth, each representing some aspect of human life. The modern system of twelve houses is partly descended from an older system of eight houses, the octatopos, used in Greek and Roman times; *SEE* OCTATOPOS. There are various ways of dividing the heavens mathematically into twelve sections, but in all but a few exotic systems the first house begins at the ascendant—the point rising above the eastern horizon at the moment for which the horoscope is drawn up—and the houses proceed counterclockwise around the chart. *SEE* HOUSE, ASTROLOGICAL; HOROSCOPE.

b) four cardines or cardinal points—the ascendant, zenith or midheaven, descendent, and nadir—which represent the eastern horizon, the middle of the sky overhead, the western horizon, and the point in the sky directly beneath the Earth. *SEE* CARDINES.

c) twelve signs of the zodiac, which are divisions of the heavens marked out by twelve constellations close to the ecliptic, the track of the sun among the stars. Due to the rotation of the Earth, the entire zodiac passes over each spot on the Earth's surface in a little less than twenty-four hours. The relation between the signs and the houses provide the basic framework of the horoscope. *SEE* ZODIAC.

d) seven or more planets, which move against the background of the zodiac in patterns determined by their orbits and the orbit and rotation of the Earth. In astrological terms, the sun and the moon are planets, and at least five others—Mercury, Venus, Mars, Jupiter, and Saturn, the five planets visible from Earth without a telescope—also play an important role in all forms of Western astrology. Many astrologers include the more recently discovered planets Uranus, Neptune, and Pluto in the astrological chart, some include the larger asteroids, and a few keep track of other, hypothetical bodies such as Lilith, an invisible moon said to be orbiting the Earth, and Transpluto, a planet out beyond the orbit of Pluto. *SEE* ASTEROIDS; PLANETS.

e) an assortment of other points, including the north and south nodes of the moon, which represent the points where the moon's and sun's tracks through the zodiac intersect; the Arabian parts, mathematically calculated points that are of high importance in Arabic astrology; and others. *SEE* NODES, LUNAR; ARABIAN PARTS.

f) aspects—geometrical angles—between any two planets, parts, lunar nodes, or cardines, which determine the relationship between the different energies active in the chart. *SEE* ASPECT, ASTROLOGICAL.

While most people think of astrology primarily as a way of determining character and destiny by reading a person's birth chart, there are many different applications of the art. The most important branches of astrological practice are as follows:

Electional astrology is astrology in reverse; instead of erecting a chart for a particular time and interpreting its meaning, the electional astrologer tries to find a particular time when the astrological influences will most strongly favor some particular action. This system is among the most important in occult practice, as many systems of magic require the time of ritual workings to be selected astrologically. *SEE* ELECTIONAL ASTROLOGY.

Genethliac astrology is an older term for natal astrology (see below).

Horary astrology is a strictly divinatory use of the art. A chart is erected for the moment when a particular question is asked, and various rules are used to work out a favorable or unfavorable answer to the question. *SEE* HORARY ASTROLOGY.

Mundane astrology is the astrology of nations and the world as a whole, and uses special tools such as eclipses and conjunctions of Jupiter and Saturn to trace out grand cycles of time. *SEE* MUNDANE ASTROLOGY.

Natal astrology is the most famous form of the art, where an astrological chart is drawn up for the moment and place of a person's birth to divine details of their character and destiny in life. The oldest surviving horoscopes are natal horoscopes, a fact which testifies to the enduring interest of this branch of astrology. SEE NATAL ASTROLOGY. FURTHER READING: BARTON 1994A, BARTON 1994B, GENEVA 1995, KIECKHEFER 1998, LINDSAY 1972, TESTER 1987, THORNDYKE 1923.

astrosome. (Greek, *astron* "star" + *soma* "body") An alternative term for the astral body used in certain occult traditions, including Martinism and the Aurum Solis. SEE ASTRAL BODY; AURUM SOLIS; MARTINISM.

athame. The knife, usually black-hilted, that serves as the primary magical working tool in Wicca. In Wiccan ritual and magical practice, the athame is used to channel and direct magical energies. Many modern Wiccans and Pagans also use their athames for more prosaic tasks such as cutting herbs, although traditionally other tools—a white-handled knife and the bolline or curved knife—were used for such purposes. SEE BOLLINE.

The word "athame" seems to have been introduced to Western magical practice by Gerald Gardner, the founder of modern Wicca. The origins of the word are French: *arthame* is an old word for a dagger in that language. The use of a black-hilted knife for ritual can be found in the *Key of Solomon*, and in the *Bok of the Art Magical*—Gardner's first draft of the Wiccan Book of Shadows—the instructions for making and consecrating the black-hilted knife are largely copied from S. L. Mathers' English translation of the *Key*. Some elements from this source remain in use in many traditional Wiccan lineages. SEE KEY OF SOLOMON.

While the dagger or knife was a relatively minor tool in most earlier traditions of magic, the popularity of Wicca and its offshoots in twentieth-century occult circles has made the athame among the most common magical working tools as of this writing, and versions of it are used in most modern Pagan traditions. SEE ALSO WICCA.

athanor. (Arabic *al-tannur*, from Babylonian *utunu*, "furnace") The standard furnace of classical alchemy, the athanor appeared in several different forms, and much research in the early days of alchemy went into its proper design; a work by Geber, *On Furnaces*, has survived. An athanor usually consisted of a brick or earthenware body with a firebox in the middle, several receptacles for alchemical glassware on the top, and various arrangements for piping away the smoke.

In modern practical alchemy, laboratory hot plates and Bunsen burners are generally used in place of the old athanor, as they provide steadier heat with much less effort. SEE ALSO ALCHEMY.

Atkinson, William Walker. (Yogi Ramacharaka) American businessman, author, and occultist, 1862–1932. Born in middle-class circumstances in Baltimore, Maryland, Atkinson started a business career and studied law, but suffered a breakdown due to stress in the late 1890s. Self-help ideas learned from the New Thought movement helped him recover, and in 1900 he decided to put his talents to work in this field. He moved to Chicago and became an editor at *New Thought* magazine. A few years later, he founded the Atkinson School of Mental Sciences, and began publishing two series of books, one on New Thought under his own name, and one on yoga under the pen name of Yogi Ramacharaka.

Both he and his books soon became fixtures in the occult community of the time. In 1907 he was contacted by the young Paul Foster Case and the two entered into a long correspondence, eventually cowriting, along with Michael Whitty, *The Kybalion*, one of the classic works of American occultism. SEE KYBALION, THE. Whitty was American head of the Alpha et Omega, one of the successor orders of the Hermetic Order of the Golden Dawn, and Atkinson seems to have been a member of Thme Temple No. 8 in Chicago, but the details of his involvement have not surfaced.

His series on yoga played an important part in introducing Americans to Hindu spiritual traditions. This is ironic, as Atkinson's earlier books on the subject show no sign of any actual knowledge of yoga; instead, they are capable textbooks of the physical culture exercises then being practiced over much of the English-speaking world; SEE PHYSICAL CULTURE. His later books on yoga are much closer to actual yoga, suggesting that by this time he had been able to locate teachers or published works on the subject.

Atkinson retired to California in the 1920s and died there in 1932. While his occult and New Thought books have been almost entirely forgotten, the Yogi Ramacharaka books are still in print as of this writing. *SEE ALSO* NEW THOUGHT; YOGA. FURTHER READING: RAMACHARAKA 1905, "THREE INITIATES" 1912.

Atlantis. A hypothetical lost continent said to have existed in the middle of the Atlantic Ocean, Atlantis had little if any place in Western occult traditions before the Theosophical movement of the late nineteenth century. Since that time, however, it has been the subject of an enormous amount of occult theory, speculation, visionary narrative, outright forgery, and complete hokum. While its popularity has faded in recent years in the occult community, it has been adopted with enthusiasm by the New Age movement and remains one of the most potent of all modern mythologies.

The first references to Atlantis are found in two of Plato's dialogues, the *Timaeus* and the *Critias*. In these, one of the characters—a philosopher named Critias—recounts a story which he claims was passed down in his family from the time of Solon, the famous Athenian lawgiver. According to Critias, Solon learned from an Egyptian priest of the city of Sais that in the distant past, the people of a prehistoric Athens had fought against an empire based on an island "beyond the pillars of Hercules" (that is, the Straits of Gibraltar). This island, Atlantis, had afterwards been overwhelmed by violent earthquakes and floods in a single day, and vanished beneath the sea about 9,000 years before Solon's time. In the *Timaeus*, Critias simply outlined the story; the dialogue named after him—in which the story of Atlantis was to have been central—was never finished, and ends just after Critias completes his description of Atlantean geography and politics.

These two passages, a few pages in length, are the sum total of ancient writings concerning the lost continent. Very little further discussion of Atlantis appears until the Renaissance, when a handful of writers borrowed the concept from Plato. The one figure of major importance in Western occult circles to make use of it before the nineteenth century was John Dee, the court astrologer and magus of Queen Elizabeth I, who suggested that the newly discovered American continents were actually the fabled Atlantis. *SEE* DEE, JOHN.

Several seventeenth-, eighteenth-, and nineteenth-century historical theorists, however, borrowed Atlantis for various purposes, and their work ended up being incorporated into the occult traditions at several points. The *Oera Linda Book*, a nineteenth-century forgery, relocated Atlantis (or "Atland") to the middle of the North Sea; *SEE* OERA LINDA BOOK. Popular among Ariosophical occultists in Germany in the early twentieth century, it has been adopted by at least one modern Neopagan organization in more recent times. *SEE* ARIOSOPHY. The *Oera Linda Book* drew on a series of earlier attempts to move Atlantis north, starting with the Swedish scholar Olaus Rudbeck, who in 1675 had identified Atlantis with Sweden.

The great revival of Atlantean speculation began with the American lawyer and politician Ignatius Donnelly (1831–1901), whose best-selling *Atlantis, or the Antediluvian World* (1882) argued for the lost continent's reality by way of Victorian scientific speculation. He also launched another major element of alternative history by arguing, in his book *Ragnarok: The Age of Fire and Gravel*, that the Earth had been struck by a comet in prehistoric times. Donnelly's theories were eagerly adopted by H. P. Blavatsky, the founder of Theosophy, who included both Atlantis and Lemuria, as well as two additional lost continents called Hyperborea and the Imperishable Sacred Land, in her massive synthesis of occultism. *SEE* BLAVATSKY, HELENA PETROVNA; THEOSOPHY.

During what might be called the "Theosophical Century"—the period from 1875 to 1975, when the ideas of Blavatsky and her successors dominated most of Western occultism—it was a rare system of occult theory that did not make room for Atlantis. The trickle of Atlantean books became a flood tide, as occult writers and teachers vied with one another to bring out ever more elaborate accounts of the history of the lost continent.

Rudolf Steiner, whose system of Anthroposophy started as a schism from Theosophy and developed into a complex spiritual method all its own, had much to say on Atlantis, most of it along Theosophical lines. *SEE* ANTHROPOSOPHY; STEINER, RUDOLF. His student Max

Heindel (Carl Louis Grashof) expanded on the same theories in his massive *The Rosicrucian Cosmo-Conception* (1909); *SEE* ROSICRUCIAN FELLOWSHIP. Both of these accounts of Atlantis, like Blavatsky's, are closely tied into the Theosophical concept of root races; *SEE* ROOT RACES.

Another important Atlantis theorist was Edgar Cayce, whose comments in trance states played a major role in shaping the underpinnings of modern New Age beliefs. His version of the Atlantean legend included three separate destructions, caused by the struggle between the Children of the Law of One and the evil Sons of Belial. Cayce also predicted that Atlantis would resurface in 1968 or 1969—a prophecy that, like most of his predictions, stubbornly failed to come to pass. *SEE* CAYCE, EDGAR.

English magician and self-proclaimed Antichrist Aleister Crowley wrote what was perhaps the strangest occult version of the Atlantis legend. His *Liber LI, The Lost Continent* described the Atlanteans as sex magicians busily creating the mysterious substance Zro, in order to escape from the Earth and migrate en masse to the planet Venus. *SEE* CROWLEY, ALEISTER.

Dion Fortune, founder of the Society of the Inner Light, was another active theorist on Atlantean themes. Her books presented a historical lineage for all the world's religious and magical traditions that traced them to one of three groups of survivors who left the lost continent before its demise. Her extremely influential occult novels also had much to say about Atlantis. *SEE* FORTUNE, DION; INNER LIGHT, SOCIETY OF THE.

The last decades of the twentieth century saw a reappraisal of Atlantis and its importance, as part of a general movement away from grand schemes of occult history and toward a greater focus on practical applications of occultism. Most of the occult traditions founded or reformulated during this period paid little attention to Atlantis, and the rise of the Neopagan revival turned the attention of the more imaginative away from lost continents and toward a very different scheme of alternative history, one in which ancient matriarchies and Pagan survivals played the central roles. *SEE* MATRIARCHIES, ANCIENT; PAGANISM.

Ironically, this shift in the occult community simply passed on the topic of Atlantis to new hands. In the New Age movement, which developed from older currents in the 1970s and surged into the public eye in the 1980s, Atlantis found a new source of support, and a flurry of new books on the lost continent emerged. Many of these headed in novel directions; claims were circulated that placed Atlantis in Antarctica, for example, or the Andes mountains of South America—two locations impossible to justify from Plato's original statements, since (among other things) neither of these locations is under water at present. *SEE* NEW AGE MOVEMENT.

As a quiet counterpoint to all this fanfare, scientists for the last hundred and fifty years have been exploring the possibility that there might have been an advanced culture of some sort in areas now covered by the Atlantic Ocean. Plato's date for the lost continent's submergence is strongly suggestive, since the same date—around 9600 B.C.E.—is considered by current geologists to be right about the time when the last Ice Age ended, global temperatures soared dramatically upward, and sea levels rose some 300 feet over the space of a few centuries. Recent shifts in geological science, away from models of slow change and toward a recognition of the roles of sudden catastrophes in shaping the Earth, have also given the idea of Atlantis a degree of intellectual respectability it did not have before. Still, none of this justifies the extraordinary marketing of Atlantean nonsense that has occurred over the last century and a quarter. *SEE ALSO* LOST CIVILIZATIONS; MU; OCCULT HISTORY. FURTHER READING: BLAVATSKY 1888, CROWLEY 1970, DE CAMP 1970, DONNELLY 1973, FORTUNE 1987B, FREJER 1995, HAPGOOD 1979, HEINDEL 1909, SCHOCH 1999, SCOTT-ELLIOTT 1925, SPENCE 1921, STEINER 1972.

atmic plane. In Theosophical cosmology, the highest plane of existence, corresponding with the upper levels of the spiritual plane; also called the nirvanic plane. *SEE* SPIRITUAL PLANE; THEOSOPHY.

atout. A traditional term for the trumps or Major Arcana of the tarot. A number of authors trace this back to a (nonexistent) ancient Egyptian word *Atu*, supposedly meaning "key." It is actually French, and comes from the cards' use in the game of Tarocchi, where they are good "for all" (*à tout*) suits. *SEE* TAROT.

atrilism. In the writings of American occultist P. B. Randolph (1825–1875), a state of possession in which a spiritual entity or the consciousness of a living magical adept takes control of another person's mind and body. In atrilism, the ordinary personality and consciousness are completely absent, and the possessing entity has full control; this distinguishes it from blending, in which the ordinary self and the outside entity are both present. *SEE* BLENDING. *SEE ALSO* POSSESSION, DEMONIC; RANDOLPH, PASCHAL BEVERLY.

Atwood, Mary Ann. English author and occultist, 1817–1910. The only child of Thomas South, a reclusive and eccentric country squire who devoted his life to the study of alchemy and metaphysics, she grew up in an environment full of Mesmerism and occult philosophy. Fluent in Latin and Greek, she took an active part in her father's researches from an early age. In 1846, under the pseudonym θΥΟΣ ΜΑθΟΣ, she published her first book on the subject, *Early Magnetism, In Its Higher Relations to Humanity As Veiled in the Poets and the Prophets.* Three years later, she and her father set out to write definitive works on their discoveries, he in verse, she in prose. Her work, a dense volume entitled *A Suggestive Inquiry Into the Hermetic Mystery*, was finished first, and was published at her father's expense in 1850.

Within a few weeks of the book's release, both father and daughter became convinced that they had revealed too much. The entire edition was recalled by Mr. South at substantial expense. Except for a few copies that had already been sold and a few others kept by the author, every copy was burnt, along with the manuscript of Mr. South's uncompleted poem.

Mr. South died a few years later, leaving his library to his daughter. In 1859, Mary Ann married the Rev. Thomas Atwood, an Anglican clergyman who lived in Thirsk, Yorkshire, where she spent the rest of her life. She continued to read occult and alchemical writings, and corresponded with several important early Theosophists until her death. Several of her friends received copies of her second book, which had been preserved from the fire, and it was from one of these that a new edition was printed in 1918.

The secret she had revealed was simply that alchemy was a process of transforming the human soul through trance, in which the soul separated from the body, ascended into the spiritual realm, and then returned to the body. Her book argued that every detail of alchemical symbolism and practice should be interpreted in this way, and that references to metals, chemical processes, and the like were simply code words for the real materials and processes of a spiritual alchemy. *SEE ALSO* ALCHEMY; ASTRAL PROJECTION; MESMERISM. FURTHER READING: ATWOOD 1918.

Atziluth. (Hebrew ATzILVTh, "nearness") The first and highest of the four worlds of Cabalistic theory, corresponding to the divine level of being. It is represented on the Tree of Life as a whole by ten Names of God, and corresponds most closely with Kether, the first Sephirah. In Atziluth, the Tetragrammaton is spelled IVD HIH VIV HIH, and the secret name of the world of Atziluth is Ab. *SEE* AB; CABALA; TETRAGRAMMATON.

aub. *SEE* OB.

aud. *SEE* OD.

Augiel. (Hebrew AaVGIAL, "hinderers") In Cabalistic demonology, the Qlippoth or demonic powers associated with Chokmah, the second Sephirah of the Tree of Life. They have the appearance of giants twined about with serpents. Their name is variously spelled Ghagiel, Chaigiel, Ghogiel, and Chaigidiel. *SEE* CHOKMAH; QLIPPOTH.

augoeides. (Greek, "shining image") A term that has had various meanings in Western occult tradition over the last two thousand years. In the Greek Neoplatonist writers of the late Roman period, who first used it, it refers to the Body of Light or transformed spiritual body worn by the initiate who has overcome the material world. *SEE* BODY OF LIGHT; PLATONISM.

In recent occult writings, the augoeides is used as a synonym for the Holy Guardian Angel, and shares in all the ambiguities of that term. *SEE* HOLY GUARDIAN ANGEL.

aum. The principal mantra in Hindu and Tantric Buddhist practice, also transliterated as *om* in some sources. It has been adopted by a large number of Western occult systems since the rise of Theosophy in the late nineteenth century. In Hindu writings, it is considered to be the origin of the alphabet and of speech. *SEE ALSO* BARBAROUS NAMES.

Auphanim. (Hebrew AVPNIM, "wheels") In Cabalistic lore, the order of angels assigned to the second Sephirah, Chokmah. Their traditional form is that of many-eyed wheels. *SEE* ANGEL; CHOKMAH.

aur. (Hebrew AVR, "light") One of the three forms of fire in magical philosophy, identified with sunlight and the sun on the physical plane, and with the light of spirit and illumination on the higher planes. Aur is generally understood as a higher form of light bringing balance to the other two forms of light, ob and od, which are respectively negative and positive, death and life, white and black magic. Aur is occasionally spelled *or* or *aor*. *SEE* ETHER; OB; OD.

aura. The outermost layer of the human subtle body, an egg-shaped zone extending two or three feet out from the physical body in all directions. Occult theorists disagree about whether the aura is part of the etheric body, the astral body, or both.

In clairvoyant vision, the aura is a many-colored zone of light; its hues and shades reflect the physical, mental, and emotional tone of the person. Reading the aura— viewing the auric colors and interpreting them as a guide to medical and psychological diagnosis—has been a specialty of psychics for more than a century.

In Theosophy, the aura is divided into several different aspects, which include every plane from the dense etheric well up into the spiritual levels of being. The health aura, the densest aspect, is a nearly transparent layer close to the physical body, and corresponds closely to the etheric double of other systems; *SEE* ETHERIC BODY. The vital aura, which comes next, is the usual egg-shaped zone of energies, described as pink or reddish toward the physical body and bluish toward its outer edges. Next is the karmic aura, which manifests every thought and feeling by means of constantly changing colors. Then comes the aura of character, which shows the basic emotional and intellectual patterns of the personality by its colors. Finally is the aura of the spiritual nature, which can only be seen clearly in those who have accomplished a great deal of spiritual development, and in such cases shines with intense brilliance.

In the Golden Dawn tradition, the aura is known as the Sphere of Sensation, and is described as an etheric structure filled with astral energies; it serves as the "magical mirror of the universe," in which all objects of perception and all inner activities of thought and feeling are reflected. In terms of the Theosophical analysis just given, the Sphere of Sensation is equivalent to the vital aura, and the perceptions and thoughts reflected there correspond to the karmic aura. *SEE ALSO* SUBTLE BODIES.

Auriel. (Hebrew AVRIAL, "light of God") In ceremonial magic, archangel of the element of earth, invoked in the northern quarter in the Lesser Ritual of the Pentagram. *SEE* ARCHANGEL.

Aurum Solis. (Latin, "gold of the sun") A Hermetic magical order whose teachings and practices were first made public in a series of books by Melita Denning and Osborne Phillips (Vivian and Leon Barcynski) beginning in the mid-1970s. According to its own published history, the Aurum Solis was originally founded in 1897 by English occultists Charles Kingold and George Stanton, and remained in existence through the twentieth century, with brief periods of inactivity during the two world wars. A schism in 1957 over issues of initiatory ritual led to the rise of a separate group, the Ordo Sacri Verbi (Order of the Sacred Word), which rejoined the main body of the Aurum Solis in 1971.

The Aurum Solis claims to draw on a magical and philosophical current—the Ogdoadic Tradition—which can be traced back through the centuries to classical times, and descended to Kingold and Stanton by way of a lineage of previous orders whose membership includes such luminaries as Marsilio Ficino; *SEE* FICINO, MARSILIO. Such older esoteric bodies as the Knights Templar, the Fideli d'Amore, and the Elizabethan-era Order of the Helmet are considered to have been in the Ogdoadic Tradition.

In actuality, no trace of a self-identified Ogdoadic Tradition can be found anywhere in the history of Western occultism and philosophy before the publication of the first Aurum Solis book, nor does Aurum Solis material appear in those earlier organizations named in its pedigree whose existence can be traced at all. Like many other "traditions" described in occult writings, it is almost certainly the product of the sort of retrospective recruitment common in occult history; *SEE* OCCULT HISTORY.

The Aurum Solis system is very closely modeled on that of the Hermetic Order of the Golden Dawn. In terms of theory and symbolism, it shares many distinctive features—the same unusual blend of Cabalistic and Enochian magic, the same distinctive attribution of planets and tarot trumps to the Hebrew letters, the same use of Tantric tattwas to track elemental cycles of time, and others—while in terms of magical practice, it has a precise equivalent of every significant Golden Dawn ritual practice, including the Pentagram and Hexagram rituals, the Middle Pillar exercise, the Vibratory Formula, and others. This sort of point-for-point equivalence is not found in any magical system that can be reliably dated to the nineteenth century. It has thus been suggested by occult scholars that the entire system was created about the time of the order's reconstitution in 1971, based on published accounts of Golden Dawn lore.

Whatever its origins, however, the Aurum Solis is a fully detailed and effective system of Hermetic magic, and the books describing the system are far more coherent than the somewhat disorganized papers that make up published versions of the original Golden Dawn system. It has its own distinctive symbolism and practice, which a significant number of modern Hermetic magicians have found preferable to the Golden Dawn's version. The system has also been broadened intellectually with the addition of Greek and Latin materials, and aesthetically with the use of Hermetically inspired art, especially from the Renaissance.

The initiatory structure of the Aurum Solis is distinctly different from the Golden Dawn. There are three levels or, in Aurum Solis terminology, Halls: the First Hall or Neophytus Grade, the Second Hall or Servitor Grade, and the Third Hall or Adeptus Grade, each with its own initiation ritual.

The Aurum Solis currently has five Commanderies (local lodges) in England and the United States. It accepts members by invitation only. The Aurum Solis books, however, have been influential across the modern magical scene, and a noticeable number of modern Hermetic magicians with no connection to the order use its methods and rituals as the basis for their own practice. *SEE ALSO* GOLDEN DAWN, HERMETIC ORDER OF THE; ROUSING OF THE CITADELS; VELOCIA; WARDS, SETTING. FURTHER READING: DENNING AND PHILLIPS 1974, DENNING AND PHILLIPS 1975A, DENNING AND PHILLIPS 1975B, DENNING AND PHILLIPS 1978, DENNING AND PHILLIPS 1981, PHILLIPS 2001.

automatic writing. Writing which is not directed by the conscious will of the writer, but by some other entity, internal or external to the writer. Like most practices that involve the surrender of the will to another consciousness, automatic writing is strongly discouraged by many Western magical teachings, but practiced by a large minority as a convenient way to contact spirits and receive large amounts of information in a short time.

In alternative religious movements in the Western world, as elsewhere, automatic writing has played a large role in providing scriptures in volume for nearly two hundred years. Andrew Jackson Davis, whose automatic writings played an important part in creating the philosophy of the Spiritualist movement, was among the major early practitioners. *SEE* DAVIS, ANDREW JACKSON.

Avalon. *SEE* GLASTONBURY.

Ave. In the Enochian system of magic, an important angel who had a large role in revealing the system to John Dee and Edward Kelly, its original discoverers. *SEE* ENOCHIAN MAGIC.

Awen. (Welsh, "spirit, inspiration") In medieval Welsh sources and in modern Druidry, a term for spiritual energy. The word itself, pronounced "ah-oh-en," is also commonly used as a chant in many modern Druidic traditions. *SEE* AWENYDDION; DRUIDRY.

Awenyddion. (Welsh, "those with Awen") In medieval sources, a class of mediumistic diviners in Wales in the

Middle Ages, apparently tolerated by the church. According to Giraldus Cambrensis, who provides the most detailed description, the *awenyddion* repeated a prayer to the Holy Trinity and then entered into a trance, in which they spoke incoherent and seemingly meaningless words. Careful attention to the words, however, revealed the answer to whatever question had been asked by the querent. The diviner had to be thoroughly shaken in order to return to ordinary consciousness, and had no memory of what had occurred during the trance.

It seems likely that this practice can be traced back to Pagan Celtic traditions, but as usual with such matters, no solid evidence for such a connection seems to be available. *SEE ALSO* AWEN. FURTHER READING: GERALD OF WALES 1978.

Ayin. (Hebrew AaIN, "eye") The sixteenth letter of the Hebrew alphabet, a single letter representing a silent "back stop," with the numerical value of seventy. Its standard magical symbolism is as follows:

> *Path of the Tree of Life:* Path 26, Tiphareth to Hod.
>
> *Astrological Correspondence:* Capricorn.
>
> *Tarot Correspondence:* Trump XV, the Devil.
>
> *Part of the Cube of Space:* Upper north edge.
>
> *Colors:* in Atziluth—indigo.
>> in Briah—black.
>> in Yetzirah—blue-black.
>> in Assiah—cold dark gray.

The corresponding text in the *Thirty-two Paths of Wisdom* runs: "The Twenty-sixth Path is called the Renovating Intelligence, because the Holy God renews by it all the changing things which are renewed by the creation of the world." *SEE ALSO* HEBREW ALPHABET.

Hebrew letter Ayin

azoth. Composed from the first and last letters of the Latin, Greek, and Hebrew alphabets (*A* and *Z*, alpha and omega, aleph and tau), this word has many different meanings in alchemical and occult writings. In the Golden Dawn and related traditions, it was taken to mean "essence."

B

Ba'al Shem Tov. (Rabbi Israel ben Eliezer) Jewish Cabalist, 1698–1760. Born in a small village on what is now the Polish-Russian border, he was orphaned at an early age, and spent his teen years working as a synagogue caretaker while studying the scriptures. Later, after his marriage to Hannah, daughter of the influential Rabbi Ephraem of Brody, he spent seven years in intensive meditation and study, and then took a position as teacher and kosher butcher in the Polish town of Koslowitz. In 1734 he moved to Talust, and a short time later to Medzyboz, in the Ukraine, where he began to teach Cabala publicly. He died peacefully in Medzyboz in 1760.

His qualities as a teacher, a scholar, and a person attracted a remarkable number of students, including some of the most highly regarded rabbinical minds of the period. Unlike the previous Cabalistic movements within Judaism, however, the Hasidic movement launched by Rabbi Israel spread outside scholarly and rabbinic circles to include much of the Jewish population of Eastern Europe.

By all accounts, Rabbi Israel was accomplished in the practical Cabala—that is, Cabalistic magic—as well as the Cabala's more philosophical and mystical sides. The title by which he is nearly always known, Ba'al Shem Tov or "Master of the Good Name," refers to his mastery of the secret powers of the Name of God, by which he is said to have performed many miracles. *SEE ALSO* CABALA. FURTHER READING: BUBER 1955, A. KAPLAN 1982.

Babalon. In the Enochian language, the word for "harlot." This is probably connected with Christian symbolism in which the city of Babylon is pictured as a harlot. *SEE* ENOCHIAN LANGUAGE.

In Aleister Crowley's religion of Thelema, the Enochian term was reconnected with its probable origins and used as a title for the Scarlet Woman, an important figure in Thelemite theology. *SEE* THELEMA.

Bacon, Francis. English statesman and philosopher, 1561–1626. The youngest child of Sir Nicholas Bacon, Lord Keeper of the Privy Seal under Queen Elizabeth I, Bacon grew up in the highest levels of Elizabethan society. He received his education at Trinity College, Cambridge, studied law at Gray's Inn, and was admitted to the bar in 1582. In 1584 he was elected to Parliament and began a long and checkered political career.

Despite a series of setbacks, mostly occasioned by backing the wrong figure in the complicated court politics of the time, he made his way up the social ladder step by step; he was knighted in 1603 by King James I, and worked his way up through a variety of posts in the royal government, finishing with a stint as Lord Chancellor in 1618–1621. In this latter year, however, he was charged and convicted of taking bribes, spent a short time in the Tower of London, and was released with his career in ruins. He retired to his country estate and spent his time in scholarly and scientific pursuits until his death.

Along with his political activities, Bacon devoted much time to philosophical writings, and his treatise *Of the Advancement of Learning* (1605) was an important early manifesto of the philosophy of modern science. His *Novum Organum* was among the most important treatises on inductive logic—the key element of scientific method—and his one work of fiction, the incomplete *New Atlantis*, was a utopian romance centered around the "House of Salomon," an Elizabethan vision of what we would now call a scientific think tank.

Bacon's involvement with occult traditions was minimal at best, and in his writings he dismisses the entire Renaissance occult tradition as superstitious nonsense, at most suggesting that alchemy ought to be rationally studied in order to uncover any useful chemical processes the old alchemists may have found. This attitude has not kept him from from being turned into a Rosicrucian adept by nineteenth- and twentieth-century practitioners of occult history. In Theosophical circles, he is identified with the Comte de Saint-Germain; *SEE* SAINT-GERMAIN, COMTE DE.

The bizarre history of the Bacon-Shakespeare controversy—the insistence by a long line of fringe scholars, on miminal evidence, that Francis Bacon actually wrote the plays attributed to William Shakespeare—has also added to Bacon's stature in some occult circles. The tendency to confuse him with his partial namesake, the Franciscan friar Roger Bacon, has also played a role. *SEE* BACON, ROGER.

Bacon, Roger. English philosopher, 1214–1294. Born at Ilchester, he studied mathematics and medicine at Oxford and Paris. Returning to England, he entered the Franciscan Order and taught at Oxford. At this time the European intellectual scene was full of controversy over the works of Aristotle, which were eagerly accepted by some scholars and rejected by others as incompatible with Christianity. Bacon was an ardent proponent of the Aristotelian view, and his scientific experiments (which included some of the first European experiments with gunpowder) brought him under the suspicion of practicing magic. In 1257 he was sent to Paris by the Franciscan Order, where he spent many years in penance, forbidden to write.

This prohibition was lifted in 1266 by Pope Clement IV, and Bacon thereafter wrote his most important works,

Opus Majus, *Opus Minus*, and *Opus Tertius*, a discussion of the relation between philosophy and theology, and of the importance of scientific studies. The pope's approval allowed him to return to Oxford and his studies, but after Clement's death in 1268 Bacon once again found himself in difficulties with the church. In 1278 he was again imprisoned, and did not win release again until 1292, two years before his death.

Bacon's interest in occult traditions was minimal; like nearly all intellectuals of his time, he accepted alchemy and astrology as valid, but he seems to have been innocent of the charges of magic leveled against him, and readers of his works will search in vain for esoteric teachings. None of this prevented him from gaining, especially after his death, a wide reputation as a sorcerer. In the reign of Queen Elizabeth I, he became the hero of a popular novel and play. More recently, he was adopted as a predecessor by a number of Rosicrucian orders, and has been constantly confused with his partial namesake Francis Bacon by occultists with a limited grasp of history. *SEE* BACON, FRANCIS.

Bahir. (Hebrew BHIR, "brilliance") The first important treatise of Cabalistic philosophy, assembled in southern France between 1150 and 1200 out of older, fragmentary material. It is the oldest surviving source for many of the basic ideas of the Cabala, including the names and basic structure of the ten Sephiroth. Although relatively short for a Cabalistic treatise, the book is difficult, highly symbolic, full of parables and allusions. It includes references to the much older Sepher Yetzirah, which dates from pre-Cabalistic systems of Jewish mysticism; *SEE* SEPHER YETZIRAH. *SEE ALSO* CABALA. FURTHER READING: A. KAPLAN 1979, SCHOLEM 1974.

Bailey, Alice. American occultist, 1880–1949. Born in Manchester, England, the daughter of an engineer, Bailey became involved in Christian evangelism as a young woman, and traveled to India on missionary work. In 1907 she married Walter Evans, whom she had met in India, and they emigrated to America, where he found a position as an Episcopalian minister. The marriage resulted in three daughters but little happiness, and she separated from her husband and later obtained a divorce.

Shortly after her arrival in America, Bailey encountered the works of H. P. Blavatsky and threw herself into Theosophy with the same energy she had previously applied to Protestantism. She soon discovered that she had been guided by the Master Koot Hoomi since the age of fifteen, and in 1919 was contacted by another inner plane entity, called simply "the Tibetan," who wished her to write and publish his teachings. *SEE* DJWAL KUL, MASTER.

In 1920 she married another Theosophist, Foster Bailey, and in 1923 they founded the Arcane School to promote the Tibetan's teachings and instruct disciples in spiritual discipline and service. She pursued an active career of occult writing and teaching for nearly twenty years thereafter until her death in 1949. The Arcane School survived her death and remains active today. *SEE ALSO* ARCANE SCHOOL, THE. FURTHER READING: BAILEY 1951.

Ballard, Guy. American occultist, 1878–1939. Born in Kansas, Ballard worked as a mining engineer until the Great Depression, then turned his longtime interest in occultism into a new profession. In 1934, under the pen name Godfré Ray King, he published his first book, *Unveiled Mysteries*, recounting his meeting with the Ascended Master Saint Germain on the slopes of Mount Shasta and his subsequent education by the Masters in the secrets of the supreme power of the universe, the I AM presence.

With the assistance of his wife Edna and son Donald, who took active roles in promoting his teachings, Ballard soon gathered a substantial following, establishing a widespread organization under the name of the I AM Activity. He proclaimed himself to be the reincarnation of George Washington, while Edna was the reincarnation of Joan of Arc.

Ballard's teachings had much to do with the occult influences of color and light; he wore pastel suits while working as the one and only "Accredited Representative of the Masters," and multimedia presentations including colored lights and banners played an important role at public meetings.

By the time of his death in 1939, the Activity could count some 400,000 members worldwide. It shrank substantially after Ballard's death and a series of scandals that followed shortly thereafter, but remains active on a smaller scale today. Ballard's writings and ideas have also been a central inspiration to numerous other groups and individuals since his time, and have given rise to one of the most lively branches of contemporary popular occultism; *SEE* ASCENDED MASTERS' TEACHINGS. *SEE ALSO* SAINT-GERMAIN, COMTE DE; SHASTA, MOUNT. FURTHER READING: KAFTON-MINKEL 1989, G. KING 1934.

balneum arenae. (Latin, "bath of sand") In alchemy, a container filled with sand and placed on top of a heat source, with one or more alchemical vessels partly or wholly buried in the sand. This arrangement provided the even, steady heat needed for alchemical processes, and could be raised to higher temperatures than the more common balneum Mariae. *SEE ALSO* BALNEUM MARIAE.

balneum Mariae. (Latin, "bath of Mary") In alchemy, a vessel of water placed on top of a heat source, with one or more alchemical vessels either immersed in the water or suspended above in the steam. This provided the even, steady heat needed for alchemical processes.

The balneum Mariae derives its name from the early Jewish-Egyptian alchemist Maria, who is traditionally credited with its invention. *SEE* MARIA.

The balneum Mariae is the ancestor of the modern double boiler, which is still called *bain-Marie* in French. *SEE ALSO* ALCHEMY; BALNEUM ARENAE.

banishing. The process of causing a spirit or nonphysical force to depart or withdraw from manifestation. Effective methods of banishing are essential in magical practice. As the story of the sorcerer's apprentice points out, being able to stop a magical process is just as important as being able to start it in the first place! There are at least two effective ways to banish an entity or energy, one using ceremonial magic, the other relying on natural magic.

The ceremonial method relies on specific banishing rituals such as the Banishing Ritual of the Pentagram, which uses geometrical symbols and divine names to persuade reluctant or intrusive spirits to depart. The method of natural magic, by contrast, relies on the use of physical substances that are held to be inimical to the entities to be banished. Thus iron or steel is traditionally used to banish nature-spirits of the faery type, and noxious herbs such as asafoetida are burned to drive away spirits of all kinds. In ancient times, this latter approach was taken to much further extremes, as in this recipe from Egyptian sources for an incense to exorcise evil spirits:

> Pound together honey, fresh olives, northern salt, piss of a menstruating woman, ass-shit, tomcat-shit, pig-shit, the plant ewnek . . . so as to make a compact mass and use for fumigation around the man [who is possessed by spirits] (quoted in Lindsay 1970, p. 234).

As the above suggests, banishing is closely related to exorcism; *SEE* EXORCISM. *SEE ALSO* CEREMONIAL MAGIC; NATURAL MAGIC; PENTAGRAM, RITUALS OF THE.

Baphomet. The idol supposedly worshipped by the Knights Templars, according to confessions extracted by torture during the trials of members of the order after its condemnation in 1307. The name "Baphomet" is simply the medieval French misspelling of Muhammad (cf. the medieval English misspelling "Mahound"), and its place in the Templar Order is likely an invention of the French government as part of its publicity campaign to justify the Templars' suppression. As with most of the claims made for Templar heresy or magical practices, there is no evidence that anything of the sort ever actually existed.

Once the Templars had been adopted as forebears by nineteenth-century occultists, the same process of redefinition that converted the Templars of history into grail-worshipping Gnostic magicians also drove attempts to make sense of Baphomet in overtly occult terms. Friedrich Nicolai, a German Masonic bookseller and theorist, proposed that the name was a fusion of Greek words for "color" (or, by an unlikely extension, "baptism") and "spirit." Eliphas Lévi's suggestion was that it should be read backwards as a Latin abbreviation, TEM. O.H.P.AB., *Templi omnium hominum pacis abbas* ("abbot of the temple of peace of all men")—which is at least creative. Another explication suggests that the name comes from an old phrase meaning "Father Mithras." *SEE* MITHRAIC MYSTERIES.

As history or etymology, these suggestions have little value, but they gave the image and concept of Baphomet entry into the world of magical theory, where it quickly took on a range of important meanings. In the writings of Eliphas Lévi, Baphomet represents the pantomorphous Astral Light—the central concept in Lévi's magical synthesis. Later theorists, building on Lévi's work, have used Baphomet as a symbol of the astral level as a whole, of Earth's astral atmosphere, or of the planetary spirit of the Earth. *SEE* ASTRAL LIGHT.

Most recently, writers involved in the current wave of Templar speculations have suggested that Baphomet may have been identical to the Shroud of Turin, a piece of cloth supposedly imprinted with the image of the face of Jesus. There is, as usual with occult history of this sort, no real evidence for the claim. *SEE ALSO* KNIGHTS TEMPLAR; LÉVI, ELIPHAS; OCCULT HISTORY. FURTHER READING: LÉVI 1972, PARTNER 1982, SADHU 1962.

baptism. The first of the seven Christian sacraments, baptism in water was developed by John the Baptist (fl. first century C.E.) from the older Jewish tradition of purification through bathing, and then adopted by early Christianity. The full ritual of baptism includes a formal renunciation of the Devil and all his works. According to a variety of occult writings, not all of them by Christian occultists, the rite of baptism has significant magical effects, and those who have received it are both protected from and shut out from participation in certain magical energies connected with earth magic and the like. *SEE* CHRISTIAN OCCULTISM.

Bar. *SEE* BERKANA.

barbarous names. A standard term for the words of power used in many traditional magical rituals. The term originated with the ancient Greeks, for whom *barbaroi* (the source of our word "barbarian") simply meant anyone who didn't speak Greek, and the phrase "barbarous name" was used by them for any word of power in magical ritual that didn't make sense in their language.

The barbarous names used in magic derive from many different sources, including religious and magical terminology in ancient Egyptian, Hebrew, and Old Persian. Some cannot be traced to any known source at all. Most have been reshaped and distorted over the centuries, to the point that attempts to decipher them rarely produce useful results. Interestingly, this was as true in ancient times as it is in more recent sources; many of the spells in the Graeco-Egyptian magical papyri contain barbarous names that baffle any attempt at interpretation. *SEE* GRAECO-EGYPTIAN MAGICAL PAPYRI.

Examples of barbarous names from the ancient world are *ablanathanalba, sesengenbarpharanges,* and *akrammacha-marei.* By the Middle Ages, somewhat shorter names with a Greek or Hebrew flavor were more common, such as *anexhexeton, baldachia,* and *anabona.*

In the modern magical renaissance, barbarous names have been somewhat neglected. A few traditional rituals and systems, such as the ritual of the Bornless One or the Goetia, retain ancient or medieval barbarous names; *SEE* BORNLESS ONE RITUAL; GOETIA. The Enochian language, which derives from a series of magical rituals performed by the Elizabethan occultists John Dee and Edward Kelly, serves as a major source of barbarous names in modern magical practice; *SEE* ENOCHIAN MAGIC.

According to ancient as well as modern magical theory, the effect of barbarous names is a function of their sound rather than of their meaning. Thus classical theorists of magic such as Iamblichus of Chalcis instruct the student not to translate them into a more familiar language, even when their meaning can be deciphered. In practice, certainly, the sonorous thunder of the barbarous names adds much to the psychological and magical effect of ritual. *SEE ALSO* PALINDROMES. FURTHER READING: BETZ 1986, E. BUTLER 1949.

bard. (Welsh *bardd*, "poet, musician") Title of the traditional poets and musicians of Wales and, by extension, other Celtic areas. Bards were required to memorize a great deal of poetic and mythological lore in order to complete their training, and such fragments of bardic lore as have survived have been an important resource in attempts to reconstruct Pagan Celtic religion since the seventeenth century.

In the Druid revival of the eighteenth century, Welsh bardic lore (real and forged) played a central part. Iolo Morganwg, who produced several large volumes of bardic lore and may or may not have invented most of it, provided a great deal of the material that was taught by later Druid orders. His works made the bardic tradition important to nearly all Druidry after his time. Later, in the nineteenth and twentieth centuries, Druid groups

and Celtophiles generally began drawing on the very substantial corpus of surviving Irish bardic lore for similar purposes.

In many modern Druid orders and traditions, the grade of Bard is one of three levels of initiation, either first or second in a sequence that culminates in the rank of Druid. The grade of Ovate fills out the sequence. *SEE* OVATE. *SEE ALSO* DRUIDRY. FURTHER READING: MATTHEWS 1998.

Bardon, Franz. (Frantisek Bardon) Czech occultist and healer, 1909–1958. One of the major influences on twentieth-century occultism, Franz Bardon was one of thirteen children, the only son of Viktor Bardon, a devout Christian mystic. He was born in what is now the town of Opava, in the Czech Republic just south of the Polish border, and spent much of his life there.

At the time of his birth, Opava was called Troppau and was a provincial capital in the Austro-Hungarian Empire. Little is known about his childhood and education, but he probably served in the Austrian army during the First World War. After the war, he had a career as a stage magician in Germany under the stage name Frabato.

His background in the occult is almost completely unclear. Some sources have claimed that he belonged to the Fraternitas Saturni, an important German occult lodge of the period between the wars, but Bardon himself claimed that he did not belong to any magical order. Certainly, however, the books he published later in life show a very detailed knowledge of the occult literature of the time and a mastery of a wide range of magical practices. *SEE* FRATERNITAS SATURNI.

In 1938, as a result of the Munich peace accords, German troops seized control of Czechoslovakia. Like many other occultists caught up in the maelstrom of the Third Reich, Bardon was arrested and imprisoned by the Gestapo, and spent the time from late 1941 or early 1942 until the end of the war in a concentration camp. After the war, he returned to Opava and worked for a time as a hospital administrator, then settled into a career as a natural healer using herbal medicines.

It was in the postwar years that he published the books that would be his legacy. His first book, *Der Weg zum wahren Adepten* (*Initiation into Hermetics*) was published in

Germany in 1954; *Die Praxis der magischen Evokation* (*The Practice of Magical Evocation*) followed in 1956, and *Der Schlüssel zur wahren Quabbalah* (*The Key to the True Quabbalah*) in 1957. In the depths of the Cold War, this was a risky act, both because of the topic—occultism was officially frowned upon by the Communist government of Czechoslovakia—and because it involved dealings with one of the Western nations. Bardon's activities as an herbal healer may also have brought him to the attention of the official medical service. In 1958, he was arrested by the Czechoslovakian secret police and died while in custody.

Beginning in the 1960s, his books were translated into English and sold in America and elsewhere. Although the translations were in a garbled English that was barely readable, the amount of detailed practical information on occult meditation, training, and ritual made them widely popular. Large portions of his teachings, especially from *Initiation into Hermetics*, were borrowed without acknowledgement by many American Wiccan groups, and remain in many covens' Books of Shadows and training programs to this day. FURTHER READING: BARDON 1962, BARDON 1967, BARDON 1971.

Barrett, Francis. English scholar and occultist, active 1801–1802. Little biographical information is known about this important English magician, whose 1801 manual of magic *The Magus, or Celestial Intelligencer* played a crucial role in jumpstarting the nineteenth-century revival of magic. He is known to have lived in Marylebone in London, and had a reputation as an eccentric.

In his book, which consists almost entirely of passages borrowed from Cornelius Agrippa's *Three Books of Occult Philosophy*, he invited up to twelve students to contact him and begin training in occult theory and practice. At least one person did so, a Dr. John Parkins of Grantham, Lincolnshire. A surviving letter from Barrett to Parkins gives detailed instructions for scrying with a crystal, and offers Parkins the opportunity to be initiated "into the highest Mysteries of the Rosycrucian Discipline" (quoted in J. Godwin 1994, p. 116). FURTHER READING: BARRETT 1968, J. GODWIN 1994.

Bar Shachath. (Hebrew BAR ShChTh, "pit of ruin") One of the seven hells of Cabalistic lore, corresponding to Geburah. *SEE* HELLS, SEVEN.

Bartzabel. In ceremonial magic, the planetary spirit of Mars. Its governing intelligence is Graphiel. *SEE* PLANETARY SPIRIT.

battery. In magical ritual, a sequence of knocks used for symbolic purposes. Different numbers of knocks, patterned in different ways, are common in lodge workings—fraternal as well as magical. In the latter, they may be used to symbolize the grade or degree being worked, or (via some system of arithmology) the forces being invoked in a particular ritual. *SEE* ARITHMOLOGY; LODGE, MAGICAL.

Bavarian Illuminati. A short-lived political secret society founded in 1776 by Adam Weishaupt (1748–1830), then a college professor at the University of Ingolstadt in the kingdom of Bavaria (now part of Germany). Weishaupt was an advocate of the sceptical, secular Enlightenment thought of French writers such as Voltaire and Diderot, but both Bavaria and the university where he taught were strongholds of Catholic orthodoxy and conservatism. Inspired by Freemasonry, by the various quasi-Masonic orders then flourishing in central Europe, and by the Jesuits, he set out to create a secret society to advance a progressive political and social agenda in Bavaria and elsewhere.

From an original membership of five, it grew rapidly and by 1784 had more than six hundred members spread through Bavaria, the other German states, Austria, Hungary, Poland, and northern Italy. A policy of recruiting Freemasons and taking control of existing Masonic lodges assisted the order's spread, and a habit of disguising lodges under a variety of names was put in place in the hope of avoiding detection.

The grading system is as follows:

Nursery:	1. Preparation
	2. Novice
	3. Minerval

Masonry:	(Symbolic)	1. Apprentice
		2. Fellow Craft
		3. Master Mason
	(Scottish)	4. Illuminatus Minor or Scottish Novice
		5. Illuminatus Dirigens or Scottish Knight
Mysteries:	(Lesser)	1. Presbyter or Priest
		2. Prince or Regent
	(Greater)	3. Magus
		4. Rex

By 1782, rumors about the Illuminati were already in circulation through much of Europe, and the important Mason and Martinist J.-B. Willermoz included a denunciation of the Illuminati in his publications after the great Masonic conference at Wilhelmsbad in that year, at which Illuminati members made strenuous efforts to recruit Masonic members and lodges. In 1794 rumors and accusations had reached a high pitch in Bavaria itself. The Bavarian government responded with edicts prohibiting the order, and arrests and searches by the Bavarian police turned up hundreds of pages of Illuminati documents, including rituals, letters to and from Weishaupt, and recipes for secret inks and poisons.

Despite the organizational success of the Illuminati, its political activities never seem to have gotten past the amateur stage, and it collapsed quickly once the machinery of official repression went to work on it. Weishaupt and a few other senior members managed to get out of Bavaria in advance of the police raids, but many other Bavarian members ended up in prison, and Illuminati-run Masonic lodges in other areas were closed by the authorities. There is no evidence that the order itself survived, although many former Illuminati went on to become significant figures in the upheavals of the next thirty years.

The transformation of the Illuminati from a footnote in European political history to the centerpiece of two centuries of paranoid speculation was the work of Augustin de Barruel (1741–1821), a Catholic priest and conservative journalist who fled France in 1791 during the Revolution. In 1797, he published the first two volumes (of five) of his major work, *Mémoires pour servir à l'histoire du jacobinisme* (*Memoirs Serving as a History of Jacobinism*). This work claims that the French Revolution was the result of a deliberate conspiracy against Catholicism, the French monarchy, and Western civilization as a whole, carried out by Freemasons and liberal intellectuals but conceived and orchestrated by the Bavarian Illuminati, who had simply gone underground. Despite severe evidential and logical weaknesses, Barruel's case was accepted almost at once by many European conservatives, and continues to play a significant role in ideologies on the fringes of modern political opinion. *SEE ALSO* FREEMASONRY; OCCULT HISTORY. FURTHER READING: J. ROBERTS 1972.

Beans. (*Vicia* spp.) An important source of food and livestock fodder since ancient times, beans have long been at the center of an equally important complex of myth, folklore, and magic. Traditions in many Indo-European cultures, including ancient Greece, ancient Rome, and much of modern India associate beans with the souls of the dead, who are held to hover around the flowers or dwell within the beans themselves.

Folklore of this sort seems to have played a significant role in the Pythagorean tradition, a central current of Western occultism in classical times. According to surviving records, Pythagoras himself and a number of later Pythagorean teachers, including Empedocles, specifically forbade their students to eat beans. The reason for this ban has been much disputed, in ancient times and in the present, but the ancient connection between beans and the souls of the dead is probably at the root of the matter. The modern claim that beans were banned by Pythagoras in an attempt to avoid favism, a disease that affects some people who eat fava beans, has been effectively disproven by Simoons (1998). *SEE* PYTHAGORAS. FURTHER READING: SIMOONS 1998.

Beith. (Old Irish, "being") The first letter of the Ogham alphabet, also spelled Beth and Beithe, with the sound-value *b*. It corresponds to the birch among trees, the pheasant among birds, the color white, and the number five. According to Robert Graves' version of the Ogham calendar, its month runs from December 24 to January 20. *SEE* OGHAM.

Ogham letter Beith

Belial. (Hebrew BLIAL, "without God") A major demon in Jewish and Christian demonology, assigned in Cabalistic demonology to Ain Soph, the second of the Three Veils of the Unmanifest; *SEE* AIN SOPH. According to the *Lemegeton*, he is a king among demons, commands fifty legions, and appears as two angels with beautiful voices, sitting in a chariot of fire. He has the power to give excellent familiars. *SEE ALSO* DEMON.

Belial, Sons of. In the recorded trance records of Edgar Cayce, whose revelations had a significant impact on later occult and New Age movements, the Sons of Belial were the villains of the Atlantis legend, whose activities led to the sinking of the lost continent. *SEE* ATLANTIS; CAYCE, EDGAR.

bell, book, and candle. Originally a phrase from the Catholic ritual of excommunication, a ceremony used to expel a baptized person from the community of Christians and condemn him or her to eternal damnation. Like the phrase "hocus pocus," which was originally a phrase from the Latin Mass, the phrase "bell, book, and candle" became associated with magic after the Scientific Revolution made all supernatural concepts suspect, and some recent Pagan and magical traditions have come up with ceremonies incorporating a bell, a book, and a candle in response. *SEE ALSO* HOCUS POCUS.

Beltane. (Gaelic *bealteinne*, "fire of Bel") One of the eight great festivals of the modern Pagan calendar, celebrated on or around May 1. In many Pagan traditions this festival represents the marriage or mating of the God and Goddess. As with all things Pagan, details of the celebrations vary widely, but dancing around a maypole is a common practice. Those traditions that practice a real, rather then symbolic, Great Rite often class Beltane as the most sacred time for it; *SEE* GREAT RITE. *SEE ALSO* SABBAT.

ben. In English folk magic, an effigy of the grain spirit, placed in the wagon in front of the last load of the harvest. Similar customs are found all over Europe, and probably can be traced back to Pagan ritual practices. *SEE* PAGANISM. FURTHER READING: PENNICK 1989.

Ben. (Hebrew BN, "son") A name of Tiphareth, the sixth Sephirah of the Tree of Life; also the secret name of the world of Assiah. The numerical values of its letters add up to fifty-two, which is also the sum of YVD HH VV HH, the spelling of the Tetragrammaton in Assiah. *SEE* ASSIAH; TETRAGRAMMATON; TIPHARETH.

benandanti. (Italian, "good walkers") Members of a Pagan magical cult in northeastern Italy, discovered by the Inquisition in 1575. The benandanti were active in Friulia, a region in the far northeast of the country where Italian, German, and Slavic traditions had mingled since the early Middle Ages. It was only open to those "born with a caul"—that is, born with a piece of amniotic membrane over their heads—and included both men and women.

According to the Inquisition records, the benandanti believed that they left their bodies on the ember days and traveled in animal form through the air to the Valley of Josaphat at the center of the world; *SEE* EMBER DAYS. There, armed with fennel stalks, they did battle with the *malandanti* or "evil walkers," destructive sorcerers who carried sorghum stalks; *SEE* FENNEL. The two armies would battle for an hour or more in the night. If the benandanti won, there would be a good harvest, while if the malandanti won, bad weather would ruin the crops and famine would follow. Benandanti also had powers of magical healing, and could cure bewitched persons.

The Inquisition found these stories completely baffling, since they did not correspond to the patterns of witchcraft or non-Christian religion covered in Inquisitorial manuals. More than a hundred benandanti were brought before the Inquisition in Friuli and Venice between 1575 and 1644, and confessions of more conventional witchcraft were extracted from a handful of prisoners. As with most Italian Inquisitorial activities, though, torture was not used and those found guilty were punished with penance, prison sentences, or banishment, rather than execution. The entire affair petered out in the late 1600s as the Inquisition found more pressing challenges to confront.

The benandanti are of high importance in the history of European Paganism, as they demonstrate the survival of complex Pagan traditions up to the beginning of the modern period. The activities of the benandanti have much in common with the traditions mentioned in the Canon *Episcopi*, which dates from the ninth century C.E., and with other Pagan survivals recorded in medieval sources. SEE CANON EPISCOPI; MADONA HORIENTE; STOECKHLIN, CHONRAD. At the same time, the sharp differences between these traditions and those of modern Pagan groups cast strong doubt on the claims of ancient roots made by the latter. SEE NEOPAGANISM; PAGANISM. FURTHER READING: GINZBURG 1985.

benefic. (Latin *beneficus*, "doing good") In older traditions of astrology, a term for those planets and aspects that have a generally positive influence on the chart. Jupiter and Venus are the primary benefic planets, and trine and sextile are the main benefic aspects. The opposite of benefic is malefic; SEE MALEFIC. SEE ALSO ASPECT, ASTROLOGICAL; ASTROLOGY; JUPITER; VENUS.

Beni Elohim. (Hebrew BNI ALHIM, "sons of the gods/goddesses") In some versions of Cabalistic angel lore, the order of angels corresponding to Netzach, the seventh Sephirah of the Tree of Life. SEE ANGEL; NETZACH.

Benjamine, Elbert. SEE C. C. ZAIN.

Bennett, Allan. English occultist and Buddhist monk, 1872–1923. His life is poorly documented, and little seems to be known about his childhood, education, and early career. He joined the Hermetic Order of the Golden Dawn in 1894 as Frater Voco, and reached the grade of Adeptus Minor the next year, taking the new motto *Iehi Aour* (Hebrew, "let there be light"). While in the Golden Dawn he met Aleister Crowley and roomed with the younger man for a time, teaching him magic in exchange for free rent.

In 1900, during the political crisis that led to the order's dissolution, Bennett left for Ceylon, where he took the Three Refuges and became a Theravada Buddhist, receiving the religious name Ananda Metteya. He was the first Englishman to become an accredited Buddhist teacher, and on his return to England he founded a Buddhist study circle and taught meditation. His lifelong poor health, worsened by poverty, brought about his death in 1923. SEE ALSO CROWLEY, ALEISTER; GOLDEN DAWN, HERMETIC ORDER OF THE.

Bensozia. A goddess worshipped in southern France in the twelfth and thirteenth century, according to Inquisition records. Her worship appears to have been much the same as that chronicled several centuries earlier by the author of the Canon *Episcopi*. SEE CANON EPISCOPI.

Beorc. SEE BERKANA.

Berkana. (Old Germanic, "birch tree") The eighteenth rune of the elder futhark, associated with the birth goddess Berchta, with nurturing and women's mysteries, and with shamanism. SEE ELDER FUTHARK. This rune, under the name Beorc ("Birch"), is the eighteenth rune in the Anglo-Saxon futhorc, with similar meanings. Under the name Bjarkan (again, "birch") it is the thirteenth rune of the younger futhark. SEE ANGLO-SAXON FUTHORC; YOUNGER FUTHARK.

In the Armanen rune system devised by Guido von List, this rune is called Bar, and means "song"; its correspondences include the god Skirnir, the father, and the power to protect a warrior in battle by casting water, as described in the *Havamal* rune-poem. SEE ARMANEN RUNES.

Rune Berkana (Beorc, Bjarkan, Bar)

berserker. (Old Icelandic *berserkr*, "bear shirt") According to Icelandic sagas dating from the end of the Viking Age, berserkers were warriors who had mastered a form of shamanistic trance in which they took on the character, and sometimes the quasi-physical form, of a bear. They were held to be all but invulnerable, and in their trance states became filled with murderous rage. The sagas and other sources have little to say about how berserkers were trained or how they went into their battle-rages, which may be just as well.

Closely associated with berserkers were the *Ulfhednarr* or "wolf-coats," who practiced a similar trance discipline but had the wolf rather than the bear as a totem animal. *SEE ALSO* LYCANTHROPY.

Besant, Annie. English social reformer and Theosophist, 1847–1933. One of the most astonishing figures in an astonishing movement, Annie Besant was born in London to a middle class family and married an Anglican minister in 1867. The marriage soon failed, and Besant migrated out of the Church of England toward atheism, becoming a leading figure in the National Secular Society and publishing *The Gospel of Atheism* in 1877. That same year, her efforts to promote birth control—another liberal cause she espoused—made her the target of an unsuccessful prosecution for selling "obscene literature."

The 1880s saw her active in Socialist, feminist, and labor circles, and she led the famous London match girl's strike of 1888. In the following year, however, she announced that she had abandoned atheism and joined the Theosophical Society. Her personality and organizational skills took her swiftly to the top of the society, and on H. P. Blavatsky's death in 1891 Besant and C. W. Leadbeater took control of most of the society.

With Leadbeater, Besant played a central role in proclaiming Jiddu Krishnamurti, the son of one of the servants at the Theosophical headquarters in Adyar, India, the World Teacher of the coming age. In 1911, the Order of the Star in the East was founded by Besant and Leadbeater, and once Leadbeater had bowed out—a series of scandals caused by his taste for young boys had made him a major liability—the order remained under Besant's control until Krishnamurti dissolved it in 1929. *SEE* THEOSOPHY.

Besant also played an important role in bringing Co-Masonry, into which she was initiated in 1906, into the Theosophical fold, and encouraged Leadbeater's efforts to spread the Liberal Catholic church through Theosophical channels as well. *SEE* FREEMASONRY; LIBERAL CATHOLIC CHURCH (LCC).

In her last years Besant was active in Indian nationalist politics, helping to build opposition to the British Raj. She died in 1933, convinced that she would be reincarnated soon. FURTHER READING: NETHERCOT 1961, NETHERCOT 1963.

besom. A broom, particularly the old-fashioned type with a round rather than a flattened head, used in many modern Pagan traditions as a magical working tool. A circle may be purified by sweeping outwards around its edge in a deosil (clockwise) circle. The besom is also used in ritual dances, and in many rituals for handfasting; "jumping over the broom" is an old Celtic custom still practiced among Appalachian people of Scotch-Irish descent, and has been borrowed into many Pagan traditions. *SEE* HANDFASTING.

The besom or broom is a major element in traditional folklore about witchcraft, and images of witches flying on broomsticks have survived even into present-day media culture. Medieval and Renaissance sources, however, picture witches flying on any number of objects, including pitchforks, shovels, staffs, and animal-shaped demons. Many old depictions also show witches riding brooms brush-side forward, often with a candle perched on the bristles to light the way.

Lore current in several modern Pagan systems states that a magical besom should be made of birch twigs, an ash stave (handle), and willow bindings. FURTHER READING: VALIENTE 1987.

Beth. (Hebrew BTh, "house") The second letter of the Hebrew alphabet, a double letter with the sounds *b* and *v*. Its numerical value is two. Its standard correspondences are as follows:

Path of the Tree of Life: Path 12, from Kether to Binah.

Astrological Correspondence: Mercury.

Tarot Correspondence: Trump I, the Magician.

Part of the Cube of Space: The upper face of the cube.

Colors: in Atziluth—yellow.

in Briah—purple.

in Yetzirah—gray.

in Assiah—indigo, flecked with violet.

Its text from the *Thirty-two Paths of Wisdom* reads: "The Twelfth Path is the Intelligence of Transparency, because it is that species of Greatness called 'visionary' (*chazchazit*), which is named the place whence issues the vision of those seeing in apparitions."

Beth is the first letter of the Torah, starting off the word *berashith* ("in the beginning"). In traditional Cabalistic lore it represents the creative activity of the divine, as distinct from the hidden divine essence represented by the letter Aleph. *SEE ALSO* CABALA; HEBREW ALPHABET.

Hebrew letter Beth

Beth. (Ogham letter) *SEE* BEITH.

Beth-Luis-Nion. One of the two systems of Ogham. *SEE* OGHAM.

Bethor. One of the seven Olympian spirits, Bethor is associated with the planet Jupiter, and rules over 32 of the 196 provinces of Heaven. The period of history ruled by Bethor extends from 60 B.C.E. to 430 C.E. *SEE* OLYMPIAN SPIRITS.

Olympian spirit Bethor

bibliomancy. (Greek, "book divination") A system of divination in which a book is opened and a passage pointed out at random; the words thus pointed out are read as an answer to the querent's question. The Bible was much used as a resource for bibliomancy, on the grounds that divination using it could not possibly be considered diabolic magic. Among the educated classes, classical works such as Vergil's *Aeneid* were used in the same way.

Bibliomancy with the Bible often carried the Latin name of *sortes apostolorum* ("Apostle's lots"); bibliomancy with Vergil's *Aeneid* was called *sortes Vergilianae*. *SEE ALSO* DIVINATION.

Binah. (Hebrew BINH, "understanding") The third Sephirah of the Cabalistic Tree of Life and the highest Sephirah of the Pillar of Severity. Binah is the primary feminine power on the tree, associated with Aima Elohim the Divine Mother, and its symbols include the sea and the womb. Its standard correspondences are as follows:

Name of God: YHVH ALHIM, Tetragrammaton Elohim.

Archangel: TzPQIAL, Tzaphqiel (Contemplation of God).

Angelic Host: ARALIM, Aralim (Valiant Ones).

Astrological Correspondence: ShBThAI, Shabathai (Saturn).

Tarot Correspondence: The four Threes and four Queens of the pack.

Elemental Correspondence: Water.

Magical Image: An old woman with long white hair.

Additional Symbols: All cteic (vaginal) symbols.

Additional Titles: AMA, Ama, the dark sterile mother; AIMA, Aima, the bright fertile mother; MRH, Marah, the Great Sea.

Colors: in Atziluth—crimson.

in Briah—black.

in Yetzirah—dark brown.

in Assiah—gray flecked with pink.

Correspondence in the Microcosm: Neshamah, the spiritual understanding.

Correspondence in the Body: The right side of the head.

Grade of Initiation: 8=3, Magister Templi.

Qlippoth: SAThARIAL, Satariel, the Concealers.

The text of the *Thirty-two Paths of Wisdom* associated with Binah runs, "The Third Path is the Sanctifying Intelligence, and it is the foundation of Primordial Wisdom; it is called the creator of faith, and its roots are in Amen. It is the parent of faith, and from its virtues faith emanates." *SEE ALSO* CABALA; TREE OF LIFE.

binding tablet. (Greek *katadesmos*, "binding"; Latin *defixio*, "fixation") In Greek and Roman times, a common means of hostile magic for cursing, seducing, or controlling other people. Normally a binding tablet was text written on a piece of lead, which was ritually consecrated and then dropped into a well, a spring, a tomb, the opening of a cave, or some other point of access to the underworld. In many cases, the text called upon deities of the underworld, especially Persephone, to grant the magician power over someone, or bound the intended victim to the powers of the realm of the dead. A wide range of symbols and words of power, including the famous Ephesia grammata, often appear on binding tablets. SEE EPHESIA GRAMMATA.

The chemical stability of lead, especially when safely preserved underwater or underground, has made binding tablets among the most durable artifacts of classical culture, and more than fifteen hundred of them have been excavated and catalogued by scholars over the last century and a half. The oldest known examples occur in Sicily and Attica (the area of Greece near Athens) and date from the fifth century B.C.E.

By Roman times (first century C.E. and after) they had become very widespread. Instructions for their manufacture and consecration appear in the Graeco-Egyptian magical papyri; SEE GRAECO-EGYPTIAN MAGICAL PAPYRI. They were made in a dizzying array of languages; two lead binding tablets from Roman Gaul, for example, provide the longest surviving prose texts of the ancient Gaulish language.

The purposes for which they were made and used cover a range familiar to any student of practical magic: love, revenge, justice, success in business or legal matters, luck in gambling and sports, and so on. Chariot racing, the most popular sport of Roman times, was particularly common as a focus of binding tablets, and in at least one case a binding tablet was smuggled into the race course and buried under the starting gate before an important race.

Binding tablets remained a common feature of life in the Mediterranean world until Christian and Islamic religious prohibitions finally forced them out of common use sometime around the eighth century C.E. A puzzling collection of late examples dates from seventeenth-century England, probably as part of the major magical revival of the period; it seems possible that documents relating to this very old magical method might have surfaced at that time, but no evidence beyond the tablets themselves has surfaced. FURTHER READING: GAGE 1992, MERRIFIELD 1987.

biquintile. In astrology, a minor aspect, formed by two planets at an angle of 144 degrees. It was introduced by the German astrologer Johannes Kepler (1571–1630) in the seventeenth century. It is held to indicate talent. SEE ASPECT, ASTROLOGICAL.

Bjarkan. SEE BERKANA.

Black Lodges. In the folklore of nineteenth- and early twentieth-century occultism, organized magical lodges serving the powers of evil. Also known as the Brothers of the Shadow, the Black Lodges were said to be in opposition to the forces of spiritual evolution, and thus to the Masters and the Great White Lodge. In the Hermetic Brotherhood of Luxor and traditions descending from it, the Black Lodges were associated with the mysterious Dark Satellite and its sinister hierarch, Ob. SEE DARK SATELLITE; HERMETIC BROTHERHOOD OF LUXOR (H. B. OF L.); OB.

Theosophical writings of the time claim that the ideology of the Black Lodges glorified the infinite assertion of separate individuality, as opposed to the teachings of the Great White Lodge, which sought to lead all souls into the Divine Unity.

Evidence for the actual existence of Black Lodges along these lines during the late nineteenth and early twentieth centuries seems to be entirely absent—although, of course, there were a certain number of Satanist organizations during that time, and many more occult lodges of dubious character. Ironically, though, some of the magical orders that emerged from Satanist circles in America in the late twentieth century have teachings identical to those Theosophists once attributed to the Black Lodges. Whether this is a case of life imitating art, whether Satanist organizations such as the Temple of Set were influenced by Theosophical literature, or whether some other factor was at work is hard to say. SEE ALSO SATANISM; TEMPLE OF SET; THEOSOPHY. FURTHER READING: FORTUNE 1930, GODWIN ET AL. 1995, LEADBEATER 1925.

Black Man. SEE SUMMONER.

Black Mass. The central rite of some traditional forms of Satanism, the Black Mass is a parody of the Catholic Mass in which a nude woman is used as the altar and the symbols and actions of the mass are inverted or desecrated; for example, urine is often used in place of holy water, and the consecrated Host (the wafer of unleavened bread which represents the body of Christ) is defiled in various ways. The proceedings usually end with an orgy.

One specialized form of the Black Mass is the Mass of St. Secaire, which dates from the High Middle Ages and originated in the French province of Gascony. This rite is used to curse an enemy to a fatal wasting illness. It makes use of black, triangular communion wafers, and water drawn from a well in which the corpse of an unbaptised infant has been tossed.

While much of the lore surrounding the Black Mass seems to be the product of the overheated imaginations of Catholic Inquisitors, those who rejected the Catholic Church at various periods have borrowed these ideas and acted them out. In the sixteenth and seventeenth centuries, many French priests were convicted of performing Black Masses and executed by the church, and evidence suggests that some of these prosecutions may actually have been based on real activities.

More certain was the role of Black Masses in the "Affair of the Poisons" during the reign of Louis XIV of France. An active circle of Parisian Satanists, headed by a fortuneteller and abortionist who went by the nickname La Voisin, existed in Paris and was patronized by the nobility. Louis' mistress, Mme. de Montespan, sought out their help when she suspected that the king was becoming interested in another woman, and served as the altar in three Black Masses, in which communion wafers allegedly made with infants' blood were consecrated over her genitals and inserted into her vagina.

Whatever the titillation value of these ceremonies, they were magically ineffective. The entire proceeding came to light shortly afterwards, La Voisin and thirty-five other people were burned alive, and Mme. de Montespan lost her place in the king's affections and left the court.

The Black Mass was also much practiced by the Hell Fire Club in late eighteenth-century England, although here it was mostly an excuse for heavy drinking and sex; *SEE* HELL FIRE CLUB. During the heyday of *fin de siecle*

decadence in France before the First World War, there was a substantial Satanist scene that enacted various forms of the Black Mass, and these spilled over into the realm of literature by way of novelist J.-K. Huysmans, whose novel *La-Bàs* remains the best literary expression of the Decadent esthetic.

For obvious reasons, the Black Mass was rarely popular outside of Catholic countries, and lost most of its popularity once its shock value slipped away. It seems to have been largely abandoned by Satanists in recent years. *SEE ALSO* SATANISM.

Black Pillar. *SEE* BOAZ.

Black Staff. *SEE* SUMMONER.

Blavatsky, Helena Petrovna. Russian occultist, 1831– 1891. Born to a German family that had lived in Russia for several generations, the daughter of a provincial official, she was married at age seventeen to a very much older man, General Nikefor Blavatsky, but ran away after a few months and left Russia.

Her whereabouts for the next ten years are a matter of some dispute, Theosophists claiming that she was in Tibet studying with Mahatmas, while researchers from outside the Theosophic fold have come up with uncomfortable scraps of evidence about a career as a circus performer, fraudulent medium, and adventuress. While she always denied having any children, circumstantial evidence points to the existence of an illegitimate son who died in childhood. In later years, she herself refused to discuss this period of her life.

Certainly she was in Cairo in 1871, where she founded a Spiritualist organization, the Societé Spirite, aided by a M. and Mme. Coulomb. This blew up after a short time amid charges of fraud and embezzlement, and Blavatsky left Egypt shortly thereafter. She arrived in New York in 1873 and spent a while supporting herself as a dressmaker before venturing into journalism.

It was at this point, while investigating a pair of mediums in Vermont, that she met Col. Henry Steel Olcott, whose talents as an organizer and publicist filled the gaps in Blavatsky's own abilities. The two were soon living together, and drew up plans for a new organization, to be called the Theosophical Society. The society was duly founded in 1875, and while Olcott arranged meetings and publications, Blavatsky devoted her time to a massive work of occult philosophy, *Isis Unveiled*, which was published in 1877 and brought the new society a great deal of favorable publicity.

In 1878 the footloose Blavatsky, accompanied by Olcott and a few other Theosophists, traveled to India by way of England and set up a headquarters for the society at Adyar, near Bombay. Here Blavatsky, joined again by her old confederates the Coulombs, impressed the local English upper class with a display of miracles. This attracted the attention of the Society for Psychical Research, however, and in 1884, when Blavatsky and Olcott were away from Adyar on a fundraising trip, the society sent an investigator who turned up conclusive evidence of fraud. In this he was assisted by the Coulombs, who passed on details of their own involvement in manufacturing Blavatsky's "miracles."

The publication of the SPR report caused a widespread scandal and marked a parting of the ways between Blavatsky and Olcott, who banished her from Adyar. She went to London, where she lectured, taught, and wrote voluminously, producing another massive book, *The Secret Doctrine* (1877), and several smaller works. By the time of her death the Theosophical Society had close to 100,000 members and was again the dominant presence in the occult scene throughout Europe and North America. *SEE ALSO* THEOSOPHICAL SOCIETY; THEOSOPHY.

blending. In the writings of American occultist P. B. Randolph (1825–1875), a state of quasi-possession in which another entity—a spiritual being, the soul of a dead human, or the consciousness of a living adept—enters into another person's body and mind without interrupting the host's awareness or mental activities. In blending, two souls share one body and mind, and both are active.

Randolph held that the state of blending was the key to communicating with higher spiritual intelligences. He drew a sharp distinction between this state and ordinary spiritualistic trance, on the one hand, and the state of full possession or atrilism on the other. *SEE* ATRILISM; RANDOLPH, PASCHAL BEVERLY.

Blood of the Lion. In alchemical symbolism, a symbol of sulphur, one of the two (or three) essential constituents of metals. *SEE* SULPHUR.

Blue Ray. In occult philosophy, the second of the Seven Rays, the primary creative energies of the cosmos. The Blue Ray is the ray of wisdom. In Theosophical lore, the Blue Ray is under the direction of the Master Kuthumi, a Chohan of the Great White Lodge. Its symbolic gem is the sapphire. *SEE* KUTHUMI, MASTER. *SEE ALSO* RAYS, SEVEN.

Boaz. (Hebrew, "in it is strength") One of the two pillars at the door of the Temple of Solomon, an important element of Cabalistic, magical, and Masonic symbolism. The pillar Boaz stood at the left of the entrance of the temple. In symbolism, it is often shown as black, and corresponds to the receptive or passive, the material, and the feminine, as the pillar Jachin corresponds to the active, the spiritual, and the masculine.

Cabalists associate Boaz with the left-hand pillar of the Tree of Life, the Pillar of Severity. *SEE* TREE OF LIFE.

In many Masonic lodges, the pillar Boaz is topped with a globe of the earth, representing its association with the material world. *SEE* FREEMASONRY. *SEE ALSO* JACHIN; TEMPLE OF SOLOMON.

Body of Light. In occult writings, a common term for one or more of the subtle bodies of the individual human being, especially the astral body. *SEE* ASTRAL BODY.

Böhme, Jakob. (also Boehme) German shoemaker and mystic, 1575–1624. Born to a peasant family in the eastern German province of Upper Lusatia, Böhme spent most of his childhood herding livestock, with a brief period spent at the village school. At the age of thirteen, he left home to seek his fortune in the nearby city of Görlitz, where he became an apprentice cobbler, rising to the status of master cobbler in 1599. Shortly thereafter he married the daughter of a Görlitz butcher.

As he approached middle age, however, Böhme's mental horizons widened in a direction far from the ordinary middle-class life he was leading. Evidence from his later writings suggests that he read extensively in alchemical literature, including the writings of Paracelsus. *SEE*

ALCHEMY; PARACELSUS. Around 1610, he underwent a mystical experience in which he became aware of the hidden "signatures" of all things, and this gave rise to his first book *Aurora, oder die Morgenröte und Aufgang* (*Aurora, or the Dawn and Beginning*). Copies of it were circulated in manuscript, and Böhme found himself at the center of a circle of local scholars and philosophers who were fascinated by his work. The local Lutheran Church was less impressed, denounced his work as heretical, and forbade him from writing.

Böhme obeyed this injunction for a short time, and then returned to writing in secret, turning out a flood of treatises on mystical Christian spirituality that were secretly circulated among his friends. Towards the end of his life, his supporters had become sufficiently strong that he was able to publish several essays expounding his own unusual take on Christian theology. Invited to the Prussian capital at Dresden in 1624, he found himself surrounded by admirers, but contracted a fever and died of it a short time after his return to Görlitz.

His writings played a primary role in initiating the tradition of Christian theosophy, and essentially all the later figures in this movement drew on his work to one degree or another; SEE THEOSOPHY. His works are also sometimes thought to have influenced the Rosicrucian movement; SEE ROSICRUCIANS. FURTHER READING: BENZ 1983, BÖHME 1978, BÖHME 1989.

bolline. A knife with a curved blade, used in some modern Pagan traditions to harvest herbs for magical use. SEE NATURAL MAGIC.

Book of Moons. In the Middle Ages, an almanac-style book of divination based on the phases of the moon; also known as a lunary. There were many different versions. According to the standard system, each day of the thirty-day lunar cycle was held to be fortunate for some purposes and unfortunate for others, and the *Book of Moons* gave detailed charts of favorable and unfavorable days for different activities. The day of the moon on which a person was born was also used as a basis for a rough and ready birth horoscope by many lunaries.

Alternative systems of lunar interpretation, which were also popular, paid attention to the movement of the moon through the twelve signs of the zodiac or the twenty-eight lunar mansions. Some *Books of Moons* were organized on this basis, or combined zodiacal signs or lunar mansions with the days of the moon. SEE MANSIONS OF THE MOON; ZODIAC.

The lunary tradition dates back well into the early Middle Ages; in England, examples survive from Anglo-Saxon times. Despite the importation of more exact astrology from the Arabic world, starting in the twelfth century, the *Book of Moons* remained popular because of its simplicity. Where an astrological chart could only be cast by someone with access to planetary tables and a grasp of mathematics, a lunary could be read and used by any literate person, and many of them were in local languages rather than in Latin—another feature that made them more accessible.

Nearly the only trace of the *Book of Moons* to survive into modern times is a line from an Elizabethan song, "Tom O' Bedlam's Song":

> *From the hag and the hungry goblin*
> *That into rags would rend ye,*
> *The spirit that stands by the naked man*
> *In the Book of Moons defend ye.*

The Cabalistic symbolism of this image—the spirit is presumably the archangel Gabriel, ruler of Yesod and protector against insanity, next to the Beautiful Naked Man who is the magical image of the moon-sphere Yesod—suggests that by Elizabethan times, at least, the *Book of Moons* had absorbed significant elements of astrological and Cabalistic magic. SEE CABALA; YESOD. SEE ALSO MOON. FURTHER READING: KIECKHEFER 1989, MEANS 1993, TAAVITSAINEN 1988.

Book of Secrets. In the Middle Ages and Renaissance, one of a class of popular books that purported to teach the occult mysteries of the cosmos to one and all. The most famous of these books, the *Book of Secrets* falsely attributed to Albertus Magnus, was compiled late in the thirteenth century and was translated into all major (and most minor) European languages in the three centuries that followed. Readers of this *Book of Secrets* learned, among other wonders, that daffodils banish devils, that a lapwing's head in the purse keeps the bearer from being tricked by merchants, and that if marigolds be brought into a church during the service, no adulterous woman will be able to leave until it is removed—"and this last point has been proved, and is very true," the book insists.

With the coming of the Renaissance, books of secrets gradually turned into collections of household hints, early scientific treatises, or manuals for the practical joker—or sometimes all three at once. The greatest example of the last type is Giambattista Della Porta's *Natural Magic*, a bestseller of the sixteenth century, which delighted readers with an assortment of scientific marvels and oddball pranks. One recipe gives a fair taste of the whole; it suggests that violin strings be cut up into short pieces and sprinkled on roast meat hot out of the oven; the bits of string, twisting and stretching in the heat and moisture, would look like live maggots infesting the meat. FURTHER READING: BEST AND BRIGHTMAN 1973, DELLA PORTA 1954.

Book of Shadows. In modern Wicca, the standard title for a book of Wiccan rituals and teachings. Traditionally each witch was required to copy out his or her own Book of Shadows by hand from the copy owned by his or her initiator. This is still commonly done in the more traditional covens, although many modern Wiccans and other Pagans use published books for the bulk of their ritual and instructional work.

The first known Book of Shadows under that name was compiled by Gerald Gardner, and consists of lengthy excerpts from the writings of Aleister Crowley, Charles Godfrey Leland's *Aradia, or the Gospel of the Witches*, and the *Key of Solomon*, along with borrowings from other sources and a few pieces of original material. Later, in the 1950s, Gardner's high priestess Doreen Valiente insisted on removing most of Crowley's contribution in order to shield the Craft from too close a connection with the Beast's very dubious reputation. These two versions of Gardner's are the basis for many Books of Shadows now in circulation, while a large number of others are collections of material plagiarized or adapted from current published sources.

The term "Book of Shadows" does not occur in Western occult lore or the literature of witchcraft before Gardner introduced it sometime around 1950. The title may have been borrowed from a 1949 article in the *Occult Observer*, "The Book of Shadows" by Mir Bashir, about a supposed system of Hindu divination by the measurement of the querent's shadow. *SEE ALSO* WICCA. FURTHER READING: LADY SHEBA 2000.

Book of the Dead, Egyptian. *SEE* EGYPTIAN BOOK OF THE DEAD.

Book of the Law. The channeled volume received by Aleister Crowley in 1904, proclaiming the arrival of the New Aeon of Horus. According to Crowley, it was dictated to him over a three-day period by a disembodied voice that identified itself as Aiwass, minister of Ra-Hoor-Khuit, the lord of the New Aeon. The relatively short text contains prose, poetry, and several cryptograms; it denounces Christianity and conventional morality, praises passion and violence, and includes what would later be Crowley's most famous phrase, "Do what thou wilt shall be the whole of the law."

The *Book of the Law* is treated as revealed scripture by many current followers of Thelema, the religion Crowley founded, although Crowley himself prohibited discussion of it, apparently feeling that each person should figure out what it means by himself or herself.

Sizeable portions of the *Book of the Law* were borrowed by Gerald Gardner for the first version of the *Gardnerian Book of Shadows*, but these were excised in the 1950s by Doreen Valiente, one of Gardner's High Priestesses, who felt that the plagiarism would be recognized and bring discredit on the Craft. *SEE* BOOK OF SHADOWS; GARDNER, GERALD BROUSSEAU; VALIENTE, DOREEN.

The original manuscript of the *Book of the Law* was sent on Crowley's death to Karl Germer, the executor of his will and head of the A∴A∴. On Germer's death no trace of it could be found in his papers. There matters rested until 1984, when Tom Whitmore, the new owner of a house in Berkeley, California, began searching through the junk left in the basement by the previous owner. Among the used mattresses, lumber, and outdated high school textbooks were two boxes of assorted papers and newspaper clippings dealing with Germer's affairs, the original charter of the OTO, and an envelope containing the manuscript of the Book of the Law. Whitmore donated the papers to the OTO. How they found their way to a Berkeley basement remains a complete mystery. *SEE ALSO* CROWLEY, ALEISTER; ORDO TEMPLI ORIENTIS (OTO); THELEMA. FURTHER READING: CROWLEY 1991.

Bornless One ritual. A magical ceremony from the Graeco-Egyptian magical papyri which entered into nineteenth-century English occultism and has become one of the standard rituals in current Golden Dawn and Thelemic magical practice. The ritual is found in a papyrus now in the British Museum in London, known to scholars as PGM V. Its original title is "the Stele of Jeu the Hieroglyphist."

In its original form it was a ritual of exorcism, calling on a mysterious god, the Headless or Beginningless One, to drive a demon out of a possessed person. Like many of the Graeco-Egyptian workings, it includes a section in which the magician takes on the identity and powers of the god.

This ritual was first published and translated by the British antiquarian Charles Wycliffe Goodman (1817–1878) in 1853, and borrowed by the English magical community in the latter years of the nineteenth century. By 1890 at the latest, it had been thoroughly reworked and expanded, and had entered into use among a small circle of Golden Dawn members. *SEE* GOLDEN DAWN, HERMETIC ORDER OF THE.

This expanded version first saw print in 1903, when Aleister Crowley used it as the "Preliminary Invocation" in his pilfered edition of Samuel Mather's translation of the *Goetia*. Later, Crowley revised it further to suit his own magical and sexual interests, and published this as *Liber Samekh*; this last form is popular mostly among Thelemites. *SEE* CROWLEY, ALEISTER; THELEMA. *SEE ALSO* GRAECO-EGYPTIAN MAGICAL PAPYRI. FURTHER READING: BETZ 1986, REGARDIE 1980.

BOTA. *SEE* BUILDERS OF THE ADYTUM (BOTA).

Boullan, Joseph-Antoine. French priest and occultist, 1824–1893. Pious as a boy, he entered the seminary in his teens and was ordained to the priesthood at the age of twenty-five. Around 1854, he became the father confessor of a nun named Adéle Chevalier, but his relation with her did not stay fatherly for long; she became his mistress and bore him two children. The two of them founded an organization called the Society for the Reparation of Souls, which specialized in exorcising possessed nuns; reports claim that these ceremonies involved feeding the victim consecrated Communion wafers mixed with human feces.

By the 1860s, rumors about Boullan's activities came to the attention of church authorities, and a local investigation found evidence that he and Chevalier had murdered one of their children in a satanic Black Mass. *SEE* BLACK MASS. His case was referred to Rome, where Boullan was cleared of the charges. Information continued to surface, however, and in 1875 he was defrocked.

In the wake of the church's action, Boullan announced that he was a reincarnation of John the Baptist sent to proclaim a new way of salvation for human beings. He took over the Work of Mercy, a schismatic sect founded by an eccentric Norman miracle-worker named Pierre Vintras, who had died that same year. In Boullan's hands, the Work became even odder than it had been under Vintras' leadership. Boullan held that the way to salvation consisted of lovemaking sessions with archangels and other spiritual entities. There is some reason to think that the "spiritual entities" may have consisted of Boullan and Chevalier themselves.

In 1886 Boullan fell afoul of the Rose+Croix Kabbalistique, France's major occult order at that time. Two of its members, Stanislaus de Guaita and Oswald Wirth, had contacted Boullan and obtained details of his practices, which they brought before their order's Council of Twelve. The council condemned him to "death by the [magical] fluids." There followed a magical battle royale in which J.-K. Huysmans, a friend of Boullan's, was also involved. When Boullan died suddenly in 1893, Huysmans accused Guaita of causing his death by magic. *SEE ALSO* GUAITA, STANISLAUS DE.

bow. *SEE* QESHETH.

brass. An alloy of copper and zinc or other metals, known since ancient times and much used in statuary and metalwork. In natural magic, brass is used as the metal of Mercury (the actual metal of Mercury, mercury or quicksilver, is a liquid at room temperature and thus impossible to make into solid objects). *SEE* MERCURY; NATURAL MAGIC.

breast divination. Among the more unlikely systems of divination invented over the years, breast divination claims to be able to read a woman's personality by the shape of her breasts. The inventor (and apparently sole practitioner) of the system was one Timothy Burr, whose detailed book on the subject can occasionally be met with in the used book trade. FURTHER READING: BURR 1965.

breastplate of the High Priest. In the Old Testament (Exodus 28:17–20), the High Priest of the Israelites was instructed to wear a breastplate or lamen (Hebrew ChShN, *choshen*) with twelve jewels on it. Like all the priestly furnishings of the Israelites, the breastplate has been studied at great length by Cabalists down through the years, but there is a good deal of uncertainty about its symbolism and use.

The twelve jewels themselves are not certain, as some of the Hebrew words have multiple or uncertain meanings. The most common interpretations are sard, topaz, carbuncle, emerald, sapphire, jasper, jacynth, agate, amethyst, chrysolite, onyx, and beryl.

Exodus 28:21 indicates that the twelve stones represent the twelve tribes of Israel, but fails to mention which stone goes with each tribe. As usual with such symbolism, there have been several different attributions proposed. SEE ALSO TRIBES OF ISRAEL. FURTHER READING: D. GODWIN 1992, HALEVI 1980.

breath. In occult theory, the breath is the main channel for the movement of etheric energy into and out of the human body. Many of the ancient words for "breath" are also words for "spirit": Hebrew *ruach*, Greek *pneuma*, and Latin *spiritus* are all examples. A wide range of breathing exercises, some independently developed and others imported from Asian spiritual systems, have been used in Western occult practice for several centuries as a way to direct, balance, and make use of the etheric effects of breath. SEE ETHER. SEE ALSO EXSUFFLATION; INSUFFLATION.

breath, alternate nostril. SEE PRANAYAMA.

breath, fourfold. SEE PRANAYAMA.

Briah. (Hebrew BRIAH, "creation") The second of the four worlds of Cabalistic theory, corresponding to the archangelic level of being and the first Heh of Tetragrammaton. It is represented on the Tree of Life as a whole by ten archangels, and corresponds most closely with Chokmah and Binah, the second and third Sephiroth of the tree. In Briah, the Tetragrammaton is spelled YVD HI VAV HI, and the secret name of the world of Briah is Seg. SEE CABALA; SEG; TETRAGRAMMATON.

Bride, the. In Cabalistic symbolism, a title of Malkuth, the tenth Sephirah. SEE MALKUTH.

Britten, Emma Hardinge. English occultist and spiritualist, 1823–1899. The daughter of a ship's captain, she showed musical abilities at an early age and by the age of eleven, after her father's death, was helping to earn a respectable living for her family as a music teacher. She also came to the attention of a circle of English occultists, who used her as a clairvoyant. After a few years in Paris, where she continued her musical studies, she returned to England, where she pursued a career as an opera singer and actress.

In 1856, she obtained a lucrative contract with a theatrical company and traveled to the United States, where she became a convert to Spiritualism. She soon became one of the most celebrated mediums in the English-speaking world, as well as a fervent propagandist and public speaker in the Spiritualist cause. By 1860 she was publishing essays rejecting orthodox religion in favor of an version of Spiritualism heavily flavored with the occult philosophy of the time.

In 1872 she married Dr. William Britten, a Mesmerist physician, and settled down with him in New York City, becoming active in occult circles there. In 1875 she became one of the founding members of the Theosophical Society, but soon found H. P. Blavatsky's activities too much to tolerate and left the organization. SEE THEOSOPHICAL SOCIETY. She continued her work on behalf of Spiritualism until her death in 1899. FURTHER READING: BRITTEN 1900, J. GODWIN 1994.

Brodie-Innes, John Williams. Scottish lawyer and occultist, 1848–1923. Born in rural Morayshire, he studied law at Cambridge and moved to Edinburgh after graduating. He was active in Scottish occult and Masonic circles, and helped found the Scottish Lodge of the Theosophical Society in 1884 and later became its president, contributing many essays to its transactions. *SEE* THEOSOPHY.

In 1890 he joined the Hermetic Order of the Golden Dawn, taking the motto *Sub Spe* ("With hope"). He rose quickly through the grades of the order, and became an Adeptus Minor in 1893. That same year he helped found Amen-Ra Temple in Edinburgh, becoming its Imperator, a position he held for the rest of his life. As such, he was deeply involved in the crises that shook the order in 1900–1903, navigating the Edinburgh temple through a series of complex political shifts that took it into and then out of the Stella Matutina, one of the GD successor orders, before finally bringing it into the rival Alpha et Omega. *SEE* GOLDEN DAWN, HERMETIC ORDER OF THE.

Brodie-Innes was also an active writer on occult subjects, producing a book on mystical Christianity, *The True Church of Christ* (1893), and numerous articles for the occult press of the time. He was interested in Celtic and Gypsy lore, the traditions of medieval witchcraft, and many other occult topics, and his essays (most of them long out of print and difficult to find) are full of unusual information on occultism of various kinds. FURTHER READING: GILBERT 1983.

broom. *SEE* BESOM.

Bruno, Giordano. Italian magician and mnemonist, 1548–1600. Born in Nola, a little town on the foothills of the volcano Vesuvius, Bruno entered the Dominican Order as a novice in 1563 and resided at the Dominican monastery in Naples. He made a special study of the Art of Memory, a specialty of the Dominican Order at that time, and achieved so high a level of skill that he was one of a small group of young friars taken to Rome to display their talents to the pope. In 1576, however, charged with heresy, he abandoned the Dominican Order and fled from Italy. He spent a short time in Geneva, then under the control of radical Protestants led by Jean Calvin, and spent two years lecturing on astronomy at the University of Toulouse, then moved on to Paris.

There, in 1582, he published *De Umbris Idearum* (*On the Shadows of Ideas*), his first work on the Art of Memory. This book made it clear that the heresy that sent Bruno fleeing from the convent had a great deal to do with magic, and with the Hermetic tradition of magical philosophy. In it, Bruno fused the traditional Art of Memory with the Renaissance Hermetic magic pioneered by Marsilio Ficino, using magical images out of Cornelius Agrippa's *Three Books of Occult Philosophy*. This same fusion dominates his later books on the Art of Memory, published during his travels through England, France, and Germany, along with other books teaching a more straightforward Hermetic philosophy.

Arrogant, demanding, and convinced of his own brilliance, Bruno was a difficult man who kept few friends for long. He had at least one known follower, the Scotsman Alexander Dicson, who taught the Art of Memory to some of the first known Freemasons' lodges; *SEE* FREEMASONRY. Rumors recorded by the Inquisition at the time of his trial suggest that he may have founded secret circles of "Giordanists" in Germany, and it has been suggested—though without any supporting evidence—that these may have played a role in the genesis of the Rosicrucian movement a few decades later.

Like many Renaissance magicians, Bruno spent much of his time searching for an aristocratic patron who would support him in the grand style to which he aspired. In 1591, after receiving an invitation from the Venetian nobleman Zuan Mocenigo, he returned to Italy with high hopes of finding such a position. This proved to be a fatal mistake. Mocenigo betrayed him to the Inquisition, and he spent eight years in ecclesiastical dungeons in Venice and Rome before being burnt as a heretic at the Campo de' Fiori in Rome in 1600.

Bruno's impact on the magical tradition of his time was minor, and the propagandists of the Scientific Revolution turned him into a martyr to rationalism, burying his occult involvements as thoroughly as possible. It was only with the beginning of serious scholarly study of Western magical traditions in the middle of the twentieth century that the dimensions of Bruno's occult activities became visible. Since that time, his work has become far better known than it was during his lifetime, and at least one important modern occultist—the scholar and magician Ioan Culianu—was heavily influenced by Bruno's work. *SEE* CULIANU, IOAN PETRU. *SEE ALSO* ART OF MEMORY; HERMETICISM. FURTHER READING: YATES 1964.

Bry, Franciscus de. According to Golden Dawn tradition, one of the three highest chiefs of the order, who was a Frisian and lived to the age of 495 years. The name "de Bry," interestingly, was that of a famous firm of German printers who were important publishers of Rosicrucian literature in the seventeenth century. Like the other two highest chiefs, Hugo Alverda and Elman Zata, Franciscus de Bry appears to be entirely mythical. *SEE* ALVERDA, HUGO; GOLDEN DAWN, HERMETIC ORDER OF THE; ZATA, ELMAN.

Bryony. (*Bryonia alba, B. dioica*) One of the most important plants in Western magical tradition, with a history going back to ancient Egypt, bryony is a relative of the cucumber; it is a vine found in woods and hedges, with small yellow or green flowers in the summer months. The root is the part used in magical practice.

In ancient Egyptian magic, a fire of bryony was used to burn wax figures of the enemies of the gods as a way to banish evil influences, and was also used in the same way to curse human targets. *SEE* EGYPTIAN OCCULTISM.

Later magical traditions in the West treated bryony as a close equivalent of mandrake; *SEE* MANDRAKE. Typically a fresh root was carved into the shape of a human being and then buried in wet sand until the cut surfaces grew over with bark, and the resulting poppet was treated as a familiar spirit and given daily offerings of wine; in return, it would carry out its master's wishes. A wreath of the leaves was also used as far back as Roman times to protect against lightning.

Bryony is attributed to Mars in Gemini, and is of fiery temperature, warm and dry in the third degree. *SEE* HUMORS. FURTHER READING: GREER 2000, GRIEVE 1931.

Builders of the Adytum (BOTA). American esoteric order founded by Paul Foster Case (1884–1956). It originated in 1921 as the Hermetic Order of Atlantis, a working group within the Thoth-Hermes Temple of the Alpha et Omega, one of the successor orders of the Hermetic Order of the Golden Dawn. *SEE* ALPHA ET OMEGA;

GOLDEN DAWN, HERMETIC ORDER OF THE. After Case resigned from the Thoth-Hermes Temple in 1922, he began work on what later became the BOTA correspondence course, and founded the School of Ageless Wisdom in 1923, later changing the name to Builders of the Adytum; *SEE* ADYTUM.

In its early days, BOTA was simply a correspondence school, but in 1926, after becoming a Freemason, Case created a set of rituals for BOTA chapters, basing them on the Alpha et Omega rituals but making substantial changes in keeping with his own approach to Hermetic philosophy. In 1927, the correspondence course was thoroughly rewritten, and in 1928, the first chapter was founded in Boston, with others appearing the same year in Washington, D.C., New York City, Buffalo, and Rochester, N.Y.

In 1932, Case moved to Los Angeles and established the new headquarters of BOTA there, where it still remains. In the years that followed, BOTA established chapters in most American cities and became a major presence in the American occult scene. As in most of the successful orders of the time, members started work with the correspondence course, and could begin attending chapter meetings and receiving initiations after reaching a certain point in their studies.

After Case's death in 1954, his student Ann Davies became the head of BOTA, and added several sections to the correspondence course. The order remains active today, with students across North America and chapters active in most large American cities. *SEE ALSO* CASE, PAUL FOSTER.

Bureus, Johannes. Swedish scholar and occultist, 1568–1652. Born into a middle class family, Bureus learned Hebrew from a local minister in his teens, and on reaching adulthood went to the Swedish royal court at Stockholm, hoping for a career as a scribe and artist. His interest was caught by the runic inscriptions that still could be found throughout Sweden at that time, and by 1600 he had learned to translate them. The Swedish government sent him around the country to inventory and translate runestones, and this work—the first significant study of the runes in modern times—earned him the post of royal antiquarian in 1602. *SEE* RUNES.

These runic activities did not exhaust his range of interests. His background in Hebrew led him to the Cabala and ceremonial magic, and during the Rosicrucian furore of 1616–1618, he published three pamphlets supporting and defending the mysterious order; SEE ROSICRUCIANS. Earlier, by 1610, he had obtained a copy of John Dee's enigmatic book *Monas Hieroglyphica* and used its complex geometries as a key to unlock mysteries he was convinced were hidden within the runic script. After a series of intense visionary experiences, he became convinced that he had discovered the secret template for the runic alphabet, the Adulruna, a fusion of symbolism and sacred geometry that also provided a key to the prophetic interpretation of Scripture.

These ideas were taken up with enthusiasm by mystics and occultists across northern Europe. Bureus attempted to interest the Swedish government in them, with limited success. A first draft of his magnum opus, *Adulruna Rediviva*, was presented by him to Gustavus Adolphus, king of Sweden, when he took the throne in 1611, and the final version went to Queen Christina, Gustavus Adolphus' daughter, in 1643. Neither monarch seems to have done much with the material covered in the book.

Bureus' work with the runes was taken up after his death by early students of Scandinavian folklore and history, but the magical dimension of his work was all but forgotten. Like many occultists of his generation, he had the misfortune to live just before the beginning of the Scientific Revolution, which forced the entire Western occult tradition underground and made the complex occult philosophies of the late Renaissance incomprehensible to most of those who came after. SEE ALSO ASATRU; SACRED GEOMETRY. FURTHER READING: ÅKERMAN 1998.

Burgoyne, Thomas Henry. (Thomas Dalton) English occultist, 1855–1895. Of working-class origins, Burgoyne worked as a grocer in the city of Leeds before taking up the study of occultism. Little is known about his early life. In 1882 he first surfaced in English occult circles, contacting William Ayton and other well-known students of the occult. In this same year he served as a scryer for Max Theon, and made contact with Peter Davidson; these three later went on to found the Hermetic Brotherhood of Luxor (H. B. of L.).

In 1883 his occult studies were interrrupted when he was convicted of petty fraud and served seven months in jail. After his release, taking the alias "Thomas Burgoyne," he became the secretary of the H. B. of L. and helped produce its monthly journal, *The Occult Magazine*. In 1886, however, Burgoyne's identity as the convicted con man Dalton became public, and the resulting scandal all but swamped the H. B. of L. Both Davidson and Burgoyne left England for America, where, after several false starts, Burgoyne found a home in Carmel, California.

There he met Norman Astley, a retired British Army officer who had studied occultism in India. (Astley later married Genevieve Stebbins, a famous teacher of physical culture and elocution and a member of the H. B. of L.; SEE STEBBINS, GENEVIEVE.) At the behest of Astley and a circle of his friends, all students of occultism, Burgoyne wrote his one book, *The Light of Egypt*, which was published in 1889. His health failed him a few years thereafter and he died in Carmel. SEE ALSO HERMETIC BROTHERHOOD OF LUXOR (H. B. OF L.); THEON, MAX.

Burning Times. In current Pagan and magical use, the period of European history in which large numbers of people were arrested, tortured, and executed as witches. The collective memory of the Burning Times plays a large role in the group identity of many modern Pagan traditions, especially in Wicca and other systems claiming descent from medieval witches. References to "nine million dead" (an early and inaccurate estimate) and similar Burning Times themes are common throughout modern Pagan literature.

Although many of these are exaggerated, the reality of the Burning Times was horrific enough. For a period of nearly four hundred years, starting in the early 1400s and ending in the late 1700s, people in most of the European countries lived under the threat of being accused of witchcraft, tortured until they confessed, and burned at the stake. While the intensity of witch hunting varied drastically over time and also from place to place, few parts of Europe were spared. The exact toll in lives cannot be known for certain, but most scholars nowadays agree on a figure around 50,000 deaths.

The witch hunts began in what is now western Switzerland and the nearby areas of France in the early

1400s. Church and local government officials reported that a frightening new heresy had appeared in the area around 1375. In this heresy, according to the claims, people made pacts with the Devil in exchange for worldly wealth and the power to do harm by magic. As the hunts spread, further details took their place in an expanding mythology; it was held the Devil's servants met at regular intervals in isolated places to feast, fornicate, and worship their master. SEE WITCHES' SABBATH.

From the first areas affected, the hunts spread up the Rhine, expanding through much of what is now western Germany, and outwards from the Rhine to east and west. Around 1500, for reasons that are not clear, the hunt slackened; writing in 1516, Martin Luther commented that witches had been common in his youth but were rarely heard of in more recent times.

This decline in witch hunting reversed around 1550, and the next several decades saw steady increases in witch trials. The 1580s marked the beginning of the worst part of the Burning Times, with mass trials and executions in Switzerland and Belgium. By the 1590s France and Scotland were in the grip of witch panics, and in the early 1600s Germany was the scene of massive witch hunts, with victims being burnt by the hundreds in some areas. During the seventeenth century, few countries in Europe escaped the witch-hunting hysteria, and hunts continued into the eighteenth century. England saw its last legal witchcraft execution in 1682, Scotland in 1722, France in 1745, Germany in 1775, and Switzerland in 1782.

While witch hunting went on through most of Europe over a span of more than three centuries, individual hunts were a far more sporadic affair. Some areas suffered only a single outbreak of witch-killing during the entire period, while others underwent hunts three or four times in as many decades. Some hunts involved one or two trials, while others spun out of control into massive panics in which hundreds of people were arrested, tortured, and burned. The age and sex of victims also varied wildly; while the majority of victims across Europe were women, and elderly unmarried women were especially at risk, some countries executed more men than women, and in the most extreme panics, men, women, and children from every level of society might be put to death.

Two major factors made the witch hunts possible. First, legal codes in much of Europe had changed in important ways during the late Middle Ages. Up to that point, prosecutions for crimes followed what was called "accusatorial procedure," which meant that charges had to be brought by a private citizen, who risked the same punishment as the accused if the accusation was judged to be false. In most of Europe, torture was actually illegal in judicial proceedings, and either a confession or the testimony of two witnesses was required for a conviction—all of which made prosecutions for witchcraft a difficult operation. With the rediscovery of Roman law toward the end of the Middle Ages, though, the accusatorial procedure was replaced in most areas with "inquisitorial procedure," in which charges were brought by a public official who was shielded from legal consequences if the charges turned out to be false; torture was also reintroduced, and the requirements for conviction became much looser. This made witchcraft prosecutions much easier and safer to carry out.

The second major factor was a reinterpretation of magic that made it, in the eyes of educated people, a sign of heresy. Magical practices had a complex status in Christian Europe until the fourteenth century; those that strayed too close to old Pagan traditions were outlawed, but the penalties were generally light, and magical practice of this sort was seen as a mark of ignorance and superstition. There was also a flourishing realm of Christian magic that was either tacitly permitted or openly approved. SEE CHRISTIAN OCCULTISM; MAGIC, PERSECUTION OF.

Religious heresy, on the other hand, had been treated with the utmost savagery ever since the Roman Empire became Christian and the church first gained the power to back up its edicts with the legal machinery of the state. SEE CATHARS; PAGANISM. When church officials came to believe that witchcraft was a heresy—an organized system of religious belief opposed to Christian orthodoxy—this made any evidence of magical practice look like a sign of heretical beliefs, and brought the full power of church and state to bear on the supposed heretics. In the process, theologians and intellectuals throughout Europe transformed the image of the witch from a superstitious and deluded old peasant to a secret participant in a diabolic conspiracy against the entire world.

These two factors worked together to create witch hunts. In many cases, the spark that lit a witch panic was an accusation by one peasant that another peasant had cast a harmful spell. Once such an accusation came to the ears of a local court, judges and officials who were used to thinking of magic as a sign of heresy rushed in, seized the accused person, and tortured him or her until he or she confessed to participating in witchcraft as they understood it. Given the degree of pain that could be inflicted by the very effective torture methods of the time, it's not surprising that many people ended up confessing to whatever the torturers wanted to hear.

A whole literature of witch-hunters' handbooks provided lists of detailed questions to be asked during torture—when had the accused made a pact with the Devil, when had she or he attended the sabbath, who else had she or he seen there, what were the names of other witches in the area, and so on. Once other people had been named, they might be arrested and tortured as well. In this way a single accusation of magic could be transformed into a massive panic in which hundreds of people were rounded up and burnt.

It is possible that an additional factor was at work. Many fourteenth- and fifteenth-century writers on the subject of witchcraft insisted that it was relatively new. Johannes Nider, a German Dominican monk writing in the 1430s, quoted experienced inquisitors of his time who held that witchcraft had been in existence for only about sixty years. The inquisitor Ponce Fougeyron, writing in the early fifteenth century, commented on "new sects and prohibited rites" flourishing in his time, and the inquisitor Bernardo de Rategno, at the start of the sixteenth century, dated the great expansion of witchcraft to around 150 years before his time. To these writers, in other words, witchcraft was a recently founded religious sect, not an ancient tradition that had never quite been rooted out.

The Inquisition was bigoted but not stupid, and it's possible that it was on to something. The late fourteenth century, in the aftermath of the great bubonic plague epidemic of 1347–1351, was a turbulent time in which many different political, intellectual, and religious currents clashed. Many heretical offshoots of Christianity emerged around this time, and peasant revolts against the feudal nobility were common. A new religious movement among the peasantry, overtly opposed to the religion of the ruling classes and drawn in part from folk customs and beliefs with a Pagan or quasi-Pagan cast, would not have been out of place in a fourteenth-century setting. At least one nineteenth-century claim concerning Pagan survivals may relate to this; *SEE* ARADIA.

The hunt for witches now and then clearly did turn up rituals and traditions that had survived from Pagan times. In northeastern Italy, officials of the Inquisition stumbled across a group called the benandanti or "good walkers," who went into trance four times a year and journeyed astrally to do battle with evil witches to preserve the crops; *SEE* BENANDANTI. The baffled inquisitors ended up labeling the whole matter as superstition, and none of the benandanti were burnt. People in other European countries who held similar shamanistic beliefs were not always so lucky; Chonrad Stoeckhlin, a Bavarian peasant who held beliefs related to those of the benandanti, was burnt at the stake in 1587 along with sixteen other people; *SEE* STOECKHLIN, CHONRAD. Witch trial records from all over Europe provide intriguing glimpses of folk magic and belief from the early modern period, although these elements vanish quickly once the torture equipment and the lists of standard questions appear. *SEE ALSO* CANON EPISCOPI.

Despite this, the evidence doesn't support the often-made claims that the witch hunts were an organized attempt to wipe out surviving organized Pagan groups, or that many or most of the people burned as witches were actually followers of a Pagan religion. The obliteration of the Knights Templar in 1307–1314 shows that European governments on the eve of the first witch hunts were perfectly capable of the sort of police-state tactics necessary to uncover and wipe out actual organizations; *SEE* KNIGHTS TEMPLAR. Wherever claims of witchcraft were subject to judicial oversight, wherever actual evidence was required or torture was barred, witch hunts tended to fizzle out quickly. This strongly suggests that the evidence for witchcraft as an organized religious movement simply didn't exist.

The case of the one major Spanish witchcraft panic, which spilled across the French border in 1610–1614, is relevant. The Spanish Inquisition by that time had spent centuries hunting out underground religious groups that actually existed—Jews and Muslims who had feigned conversion to Christianity but kept up their own religious practices in secret—and also had a long history of prosecuting people who practiced magic. On being informed of a flurry of witchcraft accusations in the Basque country, the Inquisition's supreme tribunal in Madrid sent out Fray Alonso Salazar, an experienced inquisitor, to look into the matter.

After an exhaustive investigation, Salazar reported back that the whole thing was nonsense, that he could find no evidence whatsoever that any heretical or non-Christian movement was afoot, and that the Inquisition had better ways to spend its time and resources. The supreme tribunal reviewed his findings, agreed with them, and imposed stringent new procedural requirements on future witchcraft trials that effectively brought Spanish witch hunting to a permanent halt. Given the Spanish Inquisition's ferocity toward real heretics and Jews, it's hard to imagine that an actual Pagan religious movement would come in for gentle treatment at its hands—but easy to see how competent investigators could recognize the difference between heresy and fantasy. *SEE ALSO* CECCO D'ASCOLI; WICCA; WITCHCRAFT. FURTHER READING: GINZBURG 1991, KIECKHEFER 1989, LEVACK 1995.

Butler, W. E. (Walter Ernest) English occultist, 1898–1978. Born and raised in rural Yorkshire, he made contact with a Spiritualist circle in 1914 and the next year joined the Theosophical Society, becoming a pupil of Robert King, a bishop of the Liberal Catholic Church. He remained a student of King until the latter died, and spent the rest of his life as a member of the LCC, receiving ordination as a priest.

After serving in the First World War, he went to India with the British Army. He continued his Theosophical studies, and applied for membership in the Theosophical Society's Esoteric Section, but was turned away. *SEE* LIBERAL CATHOLIC CHURCH (LCC); THEOSOPHICAL SOCIETY.

He returned to England in 1924 and made contact with Dion Fortune the next year. In 1930, he was initiated into the Fraternity of the Inner Light, and became a regular lecturer on its behalf. In 1938, he founded a subsidiary FIL lodge at Guildford, which remained active until the war forced its closure in 1941. He gradually moved out of Fortune's ambit during the war years, although he rejoined the FIL in 1965 and remained a member until his death; *SEE* INNER LIGHT, SOCIETY OF THE.

In 1962 he met Gareth Knight and other disaffected members of the FIL, who had formed the Helios Book Service to publish occult works. The two of them created a correspondence course, the Helios Course on the Practical Qabalah, and published a journal for its students, *Round Merlin's Table*. Over the course of the decade the course and its students evolved into a contacted magical order, the Servants of the Light, with Butler as its head. He held this position until 1977, when he turned over the order to Dolores Ashcroft-Nowicki. *SEE* SERVANTS OF THE LIGHT (SOL).

Butler was afflicted with difficult health for much of his life; in his later years heart disease and diabetes took a severe toll on him, and he had one leg amputated. During the last year of his life, he nonetheless founded another magical order, the Ibis Fraternity. He died of complications of diabetes in 1978. FURTHER READING: W. BUTLER 1990, CHAPMAN 1993, KNIGHT 2000.

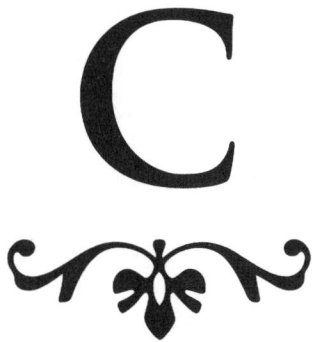

C

Cabala. (Hebrew, "oral tradition") One of the core elements of Western occultism, the Cabala began as a mystical movement in Jewish communities in Spain and southern France. Adopted first by Christian mystics, then by Hermetic magicians, and finally by almost every branch of Western occultism, it became the dominant occult philosophy in the West for several centuries, while remaining a central part of Jewish mystical belief and practice. Jewish, Christian, Hermetic, and Pagan versions of Cabala are still very much in use today.

The word *Cabala* is a Latin transliteration of the Hebrew word QBLH, "tradition," in the sense of unwritten tradition. Other transliterations include Kabbalah, Qabalah, and Kabala. In recent years, some writers have attempted to draw distinctions among these terms, using Kabbalah for the original Jewish version of the tradition, Cabala for the Christian version, and Qabalah for the Hermetic version. Others have ignored these attempts at classification, and the boundaries between the different aspects of Cabala have rarely been firm enough to justify hard and fast divisions. Cabala, the oldest and most common spelling of the word, will be used here for all branches of the tradition.

The origins of the Cabala are variously given in the old sources. Some texts claim that the original Cabala was transmitted to Adam, either by God or by the angel Raziel, at the beginning of time. Adam's son Seth is another candidate for the founder of the Cabalistic tradition. Nearly all sources record the claim that Moses, while on Mount Sinai, received from God two different sets of teachings—the written law, enshrined in the first five books of the Old Testament, and a secret oral law, passed on by word of mouth, which included the hidden meanings and interpretations of the written law. From that time, the legends claim, the Cabala was passed down continuously from master to pupil until the present.

Turning from these mythic perspectives to those of history, the first versions of Cabala actually emerged in Jewish mystical groups in Provence, in the south of France, during the eleventh century C.E. These groups drew heavily on older Jewish mystical traditions such as the Ma'aseh Merkabah and the Ma'aseh Berashith, and were also deeply familiar with the Neoplatonist tradition. *SEE* MA'ASEH BERASHITH; MA'ASEH MERKABAH; PLATONISM. At some point around 1150, they also obtained a fragmentary book or collection of books which, via a process of editing, became the first major text of Cabalistic theory, the Bahir; *SEE* BAHIR.

Isaac the Blind, a rabbi of Narbonne who died around 1235, was the crucial figure in the formulation of this early Cabala. He had disciples throughout Spain and southern France, who passed on his teachings. Centers of Cabalistic study founded by his pupils sprang up in Gerona, Burgos, and Toledo in Spain.

What set these teachings apart from other, earlier versions of Jewish mysticism was a new set of doctrines about the nature of God and the world, and a new approach to religious practice. To the Cabalist, God in himself is utterly hidden behind the three veils of Ain (Nothing), Ain Soph (Infinity), and Ain Soph Aur (Limitless Light); *SEE* AIN; AIN SOPH; AIN SOPH AUR. In manifestation, God expresses himself through the Sephiroth, ten creative powers that came forth from the divine unity and formed the Tree of Life. *SEE* SEPHIROTH; TREE OF LIFE. The Sephiroth are connected by twenty-two Paths, which correspond to the twenty-two letters of the Hebrew alphabet; *SEE* HEBREW ALPHABET. The Tree of Life also maps out the stages of ascent in the spiritual path, which can unfold over many lives; unlike other Jews, Cabalists accept reincarnation, although there have been far-reaching disputes about how reincarnation works and how it relates to more orthodox ideas of heaven and hell.

Cabalists do not differ from other Jews in their religious practices or their daily life—in fact, from the beginning, the Cabala tended to be a conservative force within Judaism, favoring strict obedience to tradition and custom. The difference in practice lies in the way that Cabalists use traditional religious duties as a vehicle for meditative practice and mystical experience. In Cabalistic practice, every one of the rituals and customs surrounding Jewish life has a mystical meaning, and should be done with that meaning in mind. In reciting prayers or reading from the scriptures, each word of the Hebrew text is used as a focus for concentrated attention and devotional meditation.

The Cabalistic tradition went through an important series of developments in Spain, where it became popular in large parts of the Jewish community and won the support of many of the best rabbinic scholars and legalists of the thirteenth and fourteenth centuries. During this time, many of the details of later Cabalistic teachings were worked out, and in particular the order and relationships of the Sephiroth took on a standard form, the Cabalistic Tree of Life; *SEE* TREE OF LIFE. The eccentric but brilliant mystic Abraham Abulafia was initiated into this Spanish tradition of Cabala, and many of his handbooks of meditation became standard after his death in Spanish Cabalistic circles and elsewhere. *SEE* ABULAFIA, ABRAHAM. Two main currents emerged; the school of Gerona, which focused on a more philosophical approach, and the school of Burgos, which had a more ecstatic and magical bent.

These currents were fused in the greatest text of Spanish Cabala, the Zohar. Attributed to the third-century mystic Simeon bar Yochai, it was actually the creation of Moses de Leon, a Spanish Cabalist who spent most of his life in the small town of Guadalajara, north of Madrid. A huge, complex, many-layered book written over a period of some thirty years, the Zohar presents the Cabala in a deeply mythic vein. It quickly became the standard text of Cabalistic study, and brought Cabalistic ideas to Jewish communities all over the Mediterranean basin and beyond. *SEE* ZOHAR.

Spain continued to be the center of Cabalistic study and development until 1492, when the Spanish government ordered all Jews expelled from the country. It was also in Spain, in the years before the expulsion, that the first stirrings of Christian Cabala emerged. The earliest movements in this direction were on the part of Christian missionaries, who sought to learn enough about Judaism to make efforts to convert Jews to Christianity more successful. In the Cabala, they found not only a potential tool for proselytizing, but a new way to look at their own religious tradition. The "combinatorial art" of Ramon Lull (1235–1315), which later played a significant role in Renaissance occult philosophies, was inspired at least partly by Cabalistic teachings about the Hebrew alphabet and its combinations; *SEE* LULL, RAMON.

The expulsion was a tremendous shock to the Jewish community throughout Europe, and it turned Cabalistic thought into more prophetic and messianic directions. Cabalistic works predicting the coming of the Messiah and the redemption of Israel began to circulate in the decades after 1492. By scattering Spanish Cabalists across much of Europe, the expulsion also gave a major boost to the Christian Cabala.

Before the expulsion, in 1486, the Italian philosopher Giovanni Pico della Mirandola (1463–1494) had begun studying Cabalistic texts with the Jewish Christian convert Samuel ben Nissim Abulfaraj (also known as Flavius Mithridates), and launched a furor that echoed across Europe by proclaiming that "no science can better convince us of the divinity of Jesus Christ than magic and the Cabala." *SEE* PICO DELLA MIRANDOLA, GIOVANNI. In the year of Pico's death, the German scholar Johannes Reuchlin (1455–1522) published his *De Verbo Mirifico* (*On the Wonder-Working Word*), an introduction to Christian Cabala, which focused on the Cabalistic interpretation of the name of Jesus. *SEE* PENTAGRAMMATON; REUCHLIN, JO-HANNES. Reuchlin followed this up in 1517 with the far more comprehensive *De Arte Cabalistica* (*On the Art of the Cabala*), which has been called the first serious Cabalistic treatise in any Western language.

After Reuchlin, the Christian Cabala was the subject of a flood of publications, and the first traces of a purely Hermetic, magical Cabala appeared in 1533 with the publication of Cornelius Agrippa's *Three Books of Occult Philosophy*; *SEE* AGRIPPA, HEINRICH CORNELIUS. For several centuries thereafter, this magical Cabala remained at least nominally Christian, just as most versions of Hermeticism from the Renaissance until the beginning of the twentieth century had some degree of Christian gloss; *SEE* HERMETICISM.

After the expulsion of the Jews from Spain, the center of Jewish Cabalistic studies shifted eastward, and the town of Safed in Israel became the site of the most important Cabalistic schools from 1530 onward. Other centers came into existence in Italy, North Africa, and Turkey, where large numbers of exiled Spanish Jews settled.

The most important Cabalist of the Safed school was Rabbi Isaac Luria (1534–1572), a brilliant and charismatic mystic who radically reshaped the Cabala. Many of the basic concepts of later Cabalistic thought were first introduced by Luria: *tzimtzum*, the "contraction" of the divine at the very beginning of the process of Creation; the primal worlds of unbalanced force, which were destroyed, giving rise to the Qlippoth, the "husks" or "shells" that are the demons of Lurianic Cabala; the five *partzufim* or personifications in the Tree of Life; and the process of *tikkun* or redemption, in which all the sparks of light lost amid the world of the Qlippoth are to be restored to the world of light. *SEE* LURIA, ISAAC. Luria also introduced new meditative techniques to Cabala, foremost among them the practice of *Yichud* or Unification, a system of meditation on divine names.

The teachings of Isaac Luria became widespread throughout the Jewish world within a generation of his early death. They combined with the intense messianic expectations of the time in the career of Shabbatai Zevi (1626–1676). Zevi was proclaimed as the Messiah in 1665 by the noted Cabalist Nathan of Gaza, and hun-dreds of thousands of Jews throughout Europe and the Middle East accepted the claim and prepared for the messianic kingdom. The sordid end of the whole affair—seized by the Turkish government in 1666, Zevi was offered a choice between execution and conversion and renounced Judaism on the spot—did much to diminish the messianic expectations of the time, but little to weaken the place of Cabala in Jewish thought and religious practice. A hard core of Zevi's followers continued to believe in their Messiah, arguing that his apostasy was somehow part of his messianic mission, and many of these converted to Islam or Christianity over the next century or so, bringing with them a set of radical Cabalistic teachings associated with the Shabbatean movement.

For some three hundred years, from the middle of the sixteenth to the middle of the nineteenth century, Cabalistic approaches were at the core of Judaism as it was practiced throughout Europe and the Middle East. During this period, a more popular version of Cabala became common in eastern European Judaism, fostered by the Hasidic movement founded by Rabbi Israel Ba'al Shem Tov (1698–1760). *SEE* BA'AL SHEM TOV. Only with the eighteenth century and the rise of the *Haskalah* ("Enlightenment") movement among Jews in western Europe did the Cabala begin to lose its importance in Jewish circles. To this day there are still many Hasidic and Cabalistic schools in Jewish communities throughout the world, preserving the traditions of Jewish Cabala and communicating them to new generations of students.

The history of Christian and Hermetic Cabala in recent centuries has been more complex. While orthodox Christian denominations rid themselves of Cabalistic elements by 1650, the Cabala kept the dominant role it held in the Renaissance all through the later development of Western occultism, and both Christian mysticism and Hermetic magic remained closely linked with Cabala. The writings of Jakob Böhme (1575–1624), the mystical shoemaker of Görlitz, do not seem to have been directly influenced by Cabalistic writings, but the alchemical Christian theosophy Böhme taught could easily be combined with Cabalistic ideas. *SEE* BÖHME, JAKOB; THEOSO-PHY (CHRISTIAN MYSTICAL). Alchemy, astrology, magic and many other branches of the occult traditions of the

West flowed into the Cabalistic tradition toward the end of the Renaissance, and inspired the great Hermetic encyclopedias of Robert Fludd; SEE FLUDD, ROBERT. This same fusion of traditions continued at the core of the Western occult movement thereafter.

The Hermetic tradition of the Cabala was recognized by Eliphas Lévi (1810–1875), the founder of the modern occult renaissance, as the core of the tradition he hoped to revive. It was Lévi who first connected the letters of the Hebrew alphabet with the twenty-two Major Arcana of the tarot, setting in motion a major new direction in Cabalistic symbolism. SEE HEBREW ALPHABET; LÉVI, ELIPHAS; TAROT.

After Lévi, a series of occultists in France and England, most of them associated with the major occult orders of the late nineteenth and early twentieth century, developed new variations on the old Cabalistic themes, or veered off in new directions entirely. Very few traditional Cabalistic sources were known to these Hermetic Cabalists, few of whom were literate in Hebrew. On the other hand, Latin translations made during the Renaissance and early modern periods were much used, and the ancient Sepher Yetzirah was also closely studied; SEE SEPHER YETZIRAH. A good deal of the material in the new Hermetic Cabala, however, came from Renaissance magical writings with little relationship to the Cabala, and another major source was the field of comparative religion and mythology, which led Hermetic Cabalists to propose directions—such as the attribution of Pagan gods and goddesses to the Tree of Life—that were unthinkable in classic Jewish Cabala.

The work of the Hermetic Order of the Golden Dawn, the most significant of these orders, was largely based on this new Hermetic Cabala, and the publication of most of the Golden Dawn legacy over the course of the twentieth century led its particular take on Cabalistic matters to become all but universal in the magical community throughout the English-speaking world. SEE GOLDEN DAWN, HERMETIC ORDER OF THE. The French magical tradition of Lévi and Papus (Gerard Encausse, 1868–1916) also became popular in many parts of the Western world; SEE PAPUS.

These developments led, for the first time, to versions of the Cabala that had no connection whatsoever to ei-

ther Judaism or Christianity—first in the Hermetic tradition, with the works of such figures as Aleister Crowley (1875–1947) and Manly Palmer Hall (1901–1990), and then in the last decades of the twentieth century with the first Neopagan versions of the Cabala; SEE CROWLEY, ALEISTER; HALL, MANLY PALMER. Many of these were based on the work of the Hermetic Order of the Golden Dawn and its offshoots, and adapted this material to a dizzying assortment of new spiritual and symbolic approaches. FURTHER READING: BLAU 1944, DENNING AND PHILLIPS 1988, J. GODWIN 1994, GREER 1996, A. KAPLAN 1982, PAPUS 1977, REGARDIE 1974, SCHAYA 1958, SCHOLEM 1941, SCHOLEM 1974, D. WALKER 1958.

Cabalistic Cross. In the Golden Dawn magical tradition, a fundamental ritual practice used to open and close ceremonies. It is performed by making the sign of the cross over the body while vibrating the Hebrew words *Ateh* ("Unto thee"), *Malkuth* ("kingdom"), *ve-Geburah* ("and power"), *ve-Gedulah* ("and glory"), *le-Olahm, amen* ("forever, amen"). Specific visualizations accompany each word and gesture.

The Cabalistic Cross first appears in print in the Golden Dawn papers published by Aleister Crowley, but references to a special mode of making the Christian sign of the cross in the writings of Eliphas Lévi may well refer to it, or an earlier form of it. SEE ALSO GOLDEN DAWN, HERMETIC ORDER OF THE; PENTAGRAM, RITUALS OF THE. FURTHER READING: REGARDIE 1970.

Cabeiri. A group of minor Greek gods, worshipped in Boeotia, Lemnos, Thessaly, and Samothrace. According to ancient sources there were four of them: Axieros, Axiokersos, Axiokersa, and Kasmillos. They were powerful in magical rites, and initiates of their mysteries were held to be safe against all forms of misfortune. Their mythology and most of their symbolism have been forgotten for centuries, although eighteenth- and nineteenth-century speculations abound.

Allusions and comments in classical sources reveal a few details about the Samothracian Mysteries, in which the Cabeiri played a central role. The initiate was crowned with an olive wreath, dressed in a purple garment, and seated on a throne at one point in the ceremony; sacred dance also had a role.

The Hermetic Order of the Golden Dawn did not leave the Cabeiri out of its synthesis, and three of the officers in the Order's Practicus grade impersonated Axieros, Axiokersa, and Axiokersos, while the candidate represented Kasmillos. SEE GOLDEN DAWN, HERMETIC ORDER OF THE.

caduceus. The traditional emblem and tool of the Greek god Hermes, a winged staff with two snakes twined about it. The caduceus has been used in a variety of ways in Hermetic magical symbolism. In the Hermetic Order of the Golden Dawn, it was mapped onto the Cabalistic Tree of Life, and its top, middle, and bottom were also related to the Hebrew mother letters Shin, Aleph, and Mem, respectively. SEE GOLDEN DAWN, HERMETIC ORDER OF THE.

Two interpretations of the caduceus

Cagliostro, Count Alessandro. (Balsamo, Giuseppe) Sicilian adventurer, 1743–1795. Born in Palermo, he spent a brief period in his youth as a novice of the Brothers of Mercy, a Catholic order of monks, where he studied medicine. A succession of scandals forced him out of the cloister, and he took up a new career as a forger and con artist. Magic played some role in these enterprises; he claimed vast occult powers, particularly the ability to find buried treasure. Whether or not he had any actual magical training or knowledge is anyone's guess.

He fled Palermo after being implicated in forging the title deed to an estate, and went to Rome, where he met and married a beltmaker's daughter named Lorenza Feliciani, a beautiful girl in her teens whose moral standards matched his own. He and Lorenza were soon traveling from city to city throughout Europe. He played the part of a man of rank, first calling himself Marquis Pellegrini, then Count Alessandro Cagliostro; Lorenza took the name Serafina. He specialized in selling bogus medicines and elixirs of life, while she made herself available as a mistress to a succession of rich noblemen—a line of work that also provided lucrative opportunities for blackmail.

In 1777, while in London, he joined a Masonic lodge belonging to the Strict Observance, receiving the four degrees then being worked. SEE FREEMASONRY. Shortly thereafter he claimed to have found an old manuscript at a London bookstall, and proceeded to launch a system of occult Egyptian Freemasonry, allegedly as old as the Pyramids, with himself at its head as Grand Copht.

This new scheme proved far more profitable than his previous trade in elixirs, and for the following decade Cagliostro was a spectacular success, fabulously wealthy and surrounded with a reputation as a man of miracles. He spent money lavishly, and to his credit gave just as lavishly to charitable causes. He also apparently worked with Rabbi Falk of London, whose Cabalistic and Masonic connections covered much of Europe; SEE FALK, SAMUEL JACOB HAYIM.

His arrival in Paris in 1785 marked the zenith of his career. He dazzled the French royal court and Parisian society, and became a close associate of the powerful Cardinal de Rohan. In August of that year, however, he became entangled in the "affair of the diamond necklace," a disastrous scandal involving Rohan and the French royal house, and was arrested and imprisoned in the Bastille. Though he was freed in June of the next year, his reputation suffered sharply; he was banished from France, and shortly thereafter the hack journalist Théveneau de Morande published an exposé that identified "the divine Caglistro" as Giuseppe Balsamo, the small-time crook from Palermo.

This revelation was a disaster for the Grand Copht. He fled from London to Switzerland and then to Italy, and Lorenza—who wished to see her family again—talked him into going to Rome. This proved to be a fatal mistake. In 1789 he was arrested by the Inquisition and condemned to death as a heretic and a Freemason. The pope commuted the sentence to life imprisonment, and Balsamo lingered in the dungeons of the papal fortress of San Leo until 1795, when he died of a stroke. Both his Egyptian Freemasonry and his reputation survived his death in a small way, and a certain number of European occult writers have continued to insist that Cagliostro the Masonic adept and Balsamo the petty con artist were two different people. FURTHER READING: E. BUTLER 1948, SCHUCHARD 1995, TROWBRIDGE 1910.

Calc. (Old English, "cup") The thirty-first rune of the Anglo-Saxon futhorc. Its meaning is not included in surviving texts of the Old English rune-poem; it represents the sound *c*. *SEE* ANGLO-SAXON FUTHORC.

Rune Calc

calcination. In alchemy, the process of heating something to a high temperature in order to convert it to a calx, or powder. Calcination is an important process in metallic alchemy and spagyrics, where it is used to prepare materials for the extraction of soluble salts.

In some accounts of the alchemical process, calcination is the first stage, and corresponds to the zodiacal sign Aries. *SEE* ALCHEMY; SALT; SPAGYRICS.

Campanella, Tommaso. Italian writer, revolutionary, and magician, 1568–1639. Born in the small town of Stilo in southern Italy, Campanella showed intellectual promise as a boy and entered the Dominican Order at the age of fourteen, studying philosophy and theology. In 1589, he left his convent and came to Naples, where he was arrested on charges of heresy. Released after a short time, he traveled to Padua in 1592 and was again arrested, but freed in 1595.

The year 1597 saw him traveling south, first to Naples and then further south into Calabria, where he set to work organizing a revolt against the Spanish, who controlled all of southern Italy at that time. Campanella proclaimed that the sun was coming closer to the Earth, that this portended the coming of a new Golden Age, and that he himself was the magician-prophet destined to lead Calabria to freedom. Backed by a group of heretical Dominicans and supported by the local peasantry, the uprising began in 1599 but was easily crushed by Spanish forces. Campanella and his surviving followers were rounded up, tortured, and jailed, with Campanella being condemned to life in prison.

During his imprisonment, Campanella wrote an enormous number of philosophical, theological, magical, and poetic works, most of them heavily influenced by the Hermetic tradition. The most important of these was his *Civitas Solis* (*City of the Sun*), a utopian work describing a splendid city governed by astrological magic, divided into seven planetary circles and ruled by a Sun-Priest.

In 1626, after publishing a book calling upon the Spanish monarchy to establish a universal theocratic state along the lines of his *City of the Sun*, Campanella was released from prison and traveled to Rome. There, in 1628, he was contacted by Pope Urban VIII, who was a student of astrology and feared that an approaching eclipse might mean his death. Together, the magician and the pope worked a ritual of planetary magic to ward off the baleful effects of the eclipse—a scene that points out the complexities of attitudes to magic in the Renaissance.

For several years after this, Campanella remained in Rome and had high hopes of influencing the church to reform itself along Hermetic lines. In 1634, however, he moved to Paris and became associated with King Louis XIII and his powerful minister, Cardinal Richelieu, in their drive to centralize France's government. In 1639, noting the approach of another dangerous eclipse, he performed a ritual of the sort he had worked for the pope eleven years before. This was apparently less successful, for Campanella died shortly thereafter. *SEE ALSO* HERMETICISM. FURTHER READING: CAMPANELLA 1981, D. WALKER 1958, YATES 1964.

Cancer. (Latin, "crab") The fourth sign of the zodiac, a cardinal water sign of feminine polarity. In Cancer the moon has rulership, Jupiter is exalted, Saturn is in his detriment, and Mars is in his fall. Cancer rules the breasts, esophagus, and stomach. *SEE ALSO* ZODIAC.

The sun is in this sign approximately from June 22 to July 22. People born with this sun placement are traditionally sensitive and protective, with a strong emotional nature and a tendency to act in unexpected ways. Thay can also be moody, easily offended, and clingy.

In the Golden Dawn tarot system, Cancer corresponds to Trump VII, the Chariot. SEE CHARIOT, THE; TAROT.

Astrological symbol of Cancer

candle magic. The use of candles in magic dates back many centuries, but the specific system of magic in which colored, anointed candles are the primary tools is a relatively recent innovation, developed in the nineteenth century out of Catholic devotional practices using candles of various kinds. The southern United States, with its rich heritage of hoodoo magic and African tradition, seems to be the homeland of candle magic, with New Orleans probably the original place of invention.

The basic practices of candle magic involve a detailed color symbolism in which red candles represent sexual desire, green stand for money, white for spirituality and healing, black for cursing and banishing, and so forth. Candles used in magic are "dressed" or anointed with specific oils, which are typically rubbed onto the candle from the middle out to both ends. A candle magic working may simply involve lighting one or more candles and reciting a charm while it burns; it may also involve rearranging candles on an altar to represent the rearrangement in the world that the working is intended to bring about.

Originally, candle magic was mostly practiced among Southern folk magicians of various kinds, but in recent decades it has spread far more widely. Many witches and Pagans in the current Pagan revival movements make use of it, as do a great many occultists who simply picked up a book on the subject and found it to their liking. *SEE ALSO* HOODOO. FURTHER READING: BUCKLAND 1970, MALBROUGH 1998, MALBROUGH 1999.

Canon Episcopi. The most important text in Catholic canon law concerning witchcraft before the age of the great persecutions, the Canon *Episcopi* (its title comes from its first word, "bishops") was written in what is now France sometime in the ninth century. Under the mistaken belief that it came from the fourth-century Council of Ancyra, it found its way into several of the most important medieval collections of canon law and was accepted as an authoritative text.

While it covers a wide range of folk beliefs condemned by the church, its most famous passage runs as follows:

> Some wicked women . . . believe and profess that in the hours of the night they ride out on certain animals with Diana, the goddess of the pagans, and an innumerable multitude of other women, and in the silence of the dead of night they journey over vast distances of the earth, and to obey her commands as of their mistress, and to be summoned to her service on certain nights.

The canon condemns this belief as superstitious and impossible, suggesting that at most, the Devil might delude sleeping people with false visions of traveling in the night. It urges priests to teach their congregations that such nocturnal journeys cannot happen, and imposes a relatively mild penance on those who hold the belief in question.

With its ninth-century date, the Canon *Episcopi* is among the oldest surviving records of a set of beliefs widespread in Europe in the Middle Ages—beliefs which held that certain people were summoned by supernatural beings to travel great distances at night, usually leaving their physical bodies in a trance state. The purpose and nature of these nocturnal journeys varied somewhat in different accounts, as did the name of the entity—usually, but not always, female—who led the journeyers. The traditions involved played a complex but significant role in the development of European witchcraft folklore, and some scholars have argued that they formed the core around which Christian ideas of the Witches' Sabbath originally coalesced. SEE SABBATH, WITCHES'. The radical differences between these traditions and the modern Pagan revival, on the other hand, cast doubt on the claims of ancient ancestry made by Wicca and other Neopagan movements; *SEE* NEOPAGANISM; WICCA.

The Canon *Episcopi* shaped official Catholic policy toward many surviving Pagan or quasi-Pagan traditions through the high Middle Ages, and encouraged an attitude that saw Pagan survivals as a matter for the ignorant and the deluded. In the early stages of the great persecutions, as a result, many theologians found it necessary to argue against the canon, or insist that it didn't apply to the case under discussion, in order to justify witch hunting. *SEE ALSO* BURNING TIMES; MAGIC, PERSECUTION OF. FURTHER READING: BEHRINGER 1998, GINZBURG 1991.

Canopic gods. In ancient Egyptian mythology, the four sons of Horus: Hapi, Ameset, Duamutef, and Qebehsenuf. Originally the four pillars of the sky and the four *khu* or luminous spiritual forms of Horus, they came to play an important role in the funeral cult, guarding the internal organs of the deceased, serving as guides and bodyguards on the difficult journey through the underworld, and taking away hunger and thirst from the virtuous soul. They were under the protection of four powerful goddesses. See the entry for each god for their specific functions and symbolism.

In the Golden Dawn system of magic, the four Canopic gods were among the invisible stations of the temple, placed in the four corners as guardians. *SEE* INVISIBLE STATIONS. FURTHER READING: BUDGE 1967, REGARDIE 1971.

Canopic jars. In ancient Egyptian mummification procedure, jars used to contain the internal organs of the deceased, which were removed from the body and stored separately. There were four jars, each under the guardianship of one of the four Canopic gods. *SEE* CANOPIC GODS.

Capricorn. (Latin, "goat horn") The tenth sign of the zodiac, a cardinal earth sign of masculine polarity. In Capricorn, Saturn has the rulership and Mars is exalted; the moon is in her detriment and Jupiter in his fall. Capricorn rules the knees, skin, bones, and teeth. *SEE ALSO* ZODIAC.

The sun is in Capricorn approximately from December 22 to January 20. People born under this sun placement are traditionally practical, patient, and organized, with a strong sense of discipline and an unexpectedly keen sense of humor. They can also be pessimistic, rigid, and prone to grumble.

In the Golden Dawn tarot system, Capricorn corresponds to Trump XV, the Devil. *SEE* DEVIL, THE; TAROT.

Astrological symbol of Capricorn

Caput Draconis. (Latin, "head of the dragon") A geomantic figure governed by the North Node of the Moon, and harmonious with Jupiter and Venus. In divination, Caput Draconis is a favorable figure, especially for beginnings. *SEE* GEOMANCY.

Geomantic figure Caput Draconis

caput mortuum. (Latin, "dead head") In alchemy, the mass of waste material left behind after maceration, distillation, or any other process of separation. The caput mortuum is usually symbolized in alchemical art by a skull, bones, or a dead body.

In spagyrics, the most common form of alchemical practice nowadays, the vegetable matter that remains after herbs are macerated is sometimes called the caput mortuum. Properly, though, this term should be used only for what is left over when the vegetable matter has been burned to ashes, calcined, and macerated again to extract the salt. *SEE* SPAGYRICS. *SEE ALSO* ALCHEMY.

Carcer. (Latin, "prison") A geomantic figure governed by Saturn. In divination, Carcer is usually an unfavorable figure, symbolizing restriction and hindrance. *SEE* GEOMANCY.

Geomantic figure Carcer

Cardan, Jerome. (Girolamo Cardano) Italian astrologer, physician, and scholar, 1501–1576. Born in Pavia and raised in Milan, Cardan was the son of Milanese scholar and occultist Fazio Cardano, who was an expert in goetic magic and carried on conversations with spirits over a period of thirty years. Cardan himself studied medicine at the Universities of Pavia and Padua, graduating in 1524, and began a career as a physician. In the difficult times afflicting northern Italy in the early sixteenth century, he had difficulty establishing a practice, and launched a second career as a writer on astrology.

His first significant publication was *Libelli Duo* (*Two Booklets*, 1538), a pair of essays on astrological practice, which included one of the first collections of horoscopes and their interpretations ever to be put in print. A bestseller by the standards of the time, *Libelli Duo* won Cardan a large readership. The original edition had only ten horoscopes, but later editions expanded the collection substantially—67 in the 1543 edition, 100 in the 1547 edition—including major political and cultural figures from all over Europe.

In 1552 Cardan traveled north to Scotland on the invitation of John Hamilton, the last Catholic archbishop of Edinburgh, who sought his advice on health problems. On the way, he traveled through France and England, and met the great English occultist John Dee, then in the early years of his career; *SEE* DEE, JOHN.

In his later years Cardan was accused of heresy, in part because he had tried to calculate the horoscope of Jesus, and was barred from teaching and placed under house arrest in Rome, where he occupied himself studying the Stoic writings of Marcus Aurelius; *SEE* STOICISM. He was finally pardoned by Pope Gregory XIII, who ordered him admitted to the College of Physicians in Rome. He remained a member until his death. FURTHER READING: CARDAN 1931, GRAFTON 1999.

cardinal points. *SEE* CARDINES; DIRECTIONS IN OCCULTISM.

cardines. The four principal points in an astrological chart. They are the ascendant, the point of the zodiac rising above the eastern horizon at the time and place for which the chart is erected; the zenith or midheaven, the point of the zodiac highest in the sky; the descendant, the point of the zodiac setting beneath the western horizon; and the nadir, the point furthest below the Earth.

These points are also known as the angles or cardinal points of a chart.

In modern astrology, the ascendant and midheaven are considered most important, and many astrologers nowadays attribute little influence to the descendant and nadir. *SEE* ASCENDANT; DESCENDANT; MIDHEAVEN; NADIR.

Carey, George Washington. American physician and occultist, 1845–1924. Born in Dixon, Illinois, to a farming family, he traveled west to Oregon in a covered wagon with his parents before his second birthday, and spent most of his youth farming in what was then the wildest of frontier country. In the 1880s he became the first postmaster of Yakima, Washington, but he later became interested in the biochemic system of medicine, which had been introduced by the German physician Wilhelm Schüssler in 1873, and which used twelve homeopathically prepared mineral salts to treat diseases. *SEE* CELL SALTS.

He resigned his position in order to devote himself to the study and practice of biochemic medicine and, along with several other Yakima physicians, founded the College of Biochemistry. The sleepy farm town of Yakima proved too small and remote to attract many students, though, and the venture went under after a few years. Carey also wrote a book on the subject, *The Biochemic System of Medicine*, which became one of the most popular textbooks of biochemic medicine and went through dozens of editions in the early twentieth century.

Carey's interests also extended to occultism, and he combined this with his medical work in a short book, *The Relation of the Mineral Salts of the Body to the Signs of the Zodiac*. He became convinced that biochemic medicine was the key not only to health but to spiritual regeneration, and reinterpreted the Bible, Pagan mythologies, and many other forms of traditional lore in the light of the twelve cell salts. His works are eccentric and difficult, but most have been kept in print by small publishing houses ever since their publication.

Carey lived in Los Angeles for the last few decades of his life. He lectured frequently on biochemic medicine, and wrote and published several books exploring the cell salts as tools of physical and spiritual transformation. His disciple Inez Perry cowrote several of these books with him, and took over his medical practice after his death. FURTHER READING: CAREY 1996, CAREY AND PERRY 1932.

Carpocratians. A quasi-Gnostic Christian sect discussed in the writings of St. Irenaeus that was active in the second century of the Common Era. Founded by Carpocrates of Alexandria, it taught that Jesus of Nazareth was an initiate of Isis who had studied for six years at a temple in Egypt, and had derived his inner teachings from that source; these had been passed on to the apostles, and from them to Carpocrates. These claims are surprisingly close to those made by modern scholars who have explored the possibility that Jesus of Nazareth was a magician rather than a messiah; *SEE* JESUS OF NAZARETH.

The Carpocratians also believed in reincarnation and practiced theurgic rituals. They appear, like most of the Gnostic sects, to have been driven out of existence by orthodox Christian persecution in the fourth and fifth centuries. *SEE ALSO* GNOSTICISM.

Case, Paul Foster. American musician and occultist, 1884–1956. Born in Fairport, N.Y., the son of the town librarian and his half-Gypsy wife, Case was something of a child prodigy, learning to read by the age of two and starting piano and organ lessons at three. By his teens he was a professional musician. While performing at a charity concert in 1900, he met the occultist Claude Bragdon, and their conversation launched Case on a study of the tarot and occultism in general.

By 1905, Case was studying yoga intensively, and made contact in 1907 with William W. Atkinson (Yogi Ramacharaka), an influential figure in the occult community at the time. With Atkinson and Michael Whitty, the American head of the Alpha et Omega—one of the successor orders of the Hermetic Order of the Golden Dawn—Case wrote *The Kybalion*, which was published pseudonymously in 1912 and became one of the most influential works in the American occult scene. *SEE* ATKINSON, WILLIAM WALKER; KYBALION, THE. It was around this time, according to his later statements, that Case first came into contact with the Master Rakoczy, who would later become the source of Case's teachings. *SEE* MASTERS; SAINT-GERMAIN, COMTE DE.

This was not his only source of occult training, however. During the First World War, while living in New York City, he met Aleister Crowley and was initiated into the Ordo Templi Orientis by the Beast himself, rising to the Third Degree. Case found little of interest in the OTO, however, and left it after a few years. More important was his contact with Michael Whitty, then Praemonstrator of the Thoth-Hermes Temple No. 9 of the Alpha et Omega, one of the successor orders of the Hermetic Order of the Golden Dawn. Case was initiated into the Alpha et Omega in 1918, taking the motto *Perseverantia* ("Perseverance"), and received the Adeptus Minor degree in 1920. *SEE* ALPHA ET OMEGA; GOLDEN DAWN, HERMETIC ORDER OF THE.

Later that same year, Whitty died, and Case was advanced to the office of Praemonstrator. Disagreements with Moina Mathers, the Imperator of the Order, led him to resign in 1922, and in 1923 Case launched an occult school of his own, the School of Ageless Wisdom, later renamed Builders of the Adytum (BOTA). At first largely a correspondence school, BOTA established its first local chapter in 1928, and has since become one of the leading American occult orders; *SEE* BUILDERS OF THE ADYTUM (BOTA).

Case moved to Los Angeles in 1932, and spent the rest of his life there, teaching and writing on occult subjects. He died on a train vacation in Mexico in 1954. FURTHER READING: CASE 1947, CASE 1985.

Cassiel. In Cabalistic magic, the angel of the planet Saturn. *SEE* ANGEL.

Castle of Heroes. Irish magical order designed by poet and Golden Dawn member W. B. Yeats, with the help of a number of fellow GD members and other students of Celtic tradition. Yeats' longtime interest in the Celtic mysticism of his homeland had led him to consider the possibility of an Irish magical order even before he was initiated into the Hermetic Order of the Golden Dawn in 1890, but the decision to actually do so took shape in 1895, when he discovered a small, abandoned castle on an island in Lough Key, Co. Roscommon, and decided it would be perfect for the project.

To help create the Castle of Heroes, he enlisted the help of Samuel Liddell Mathers, then acting head of the Golden Dawn; Mathers' wife Moina, a skilled clairvoyant; Maud Gonne, an Irish political activist whom Yeats loved hopelessly for decades; George Pollexfen, Yeats' uncle and a fellow Golden Dawn member; George Russell, an Irish mystic and activist who wrote Theosophical prose under the pen name "AE"; and several others. With their aid, and in some cases in their company, Yeats carried out a series of clairvoyant workings and magical rituals that brought through the raw material for a set of initiation rituals paralleling those of the Golden Dawn.

The following degree rituals were drafted for the Castle of Heroes:

Outer Order

1. The Cauldron (Grade of Water)
2. The Stone (Grade of Earth)
3. The Sword (Grade of Air)
4. The Spear (Grade of Fire)

Inner Order

5. The Spirit (Grade of Spirit)

Along with each of these went a curriculum of magical, philosophical, and Celtic studies.

The Castle of Heroes might well have become an actual magical order if not for the great schism in the Golden Dawn in 1900, which put Yeats and the Matherses on opposite sides of a bitter political struggle, and Maud Gonne's marriage to John MacBride in 1903. Yeats continued working on drafts of the rituals, but seems to have made no further attempt to put the plan into operation. Still, at the last meeting between Yeats and Gonne before his death in 1939, he is reported to have said, "Maud, we should have gone on with our Castle of Heroes, we might still do it." *SEE ALSO* GOLDEN DAWN, HERMETIC ORDER OF THE; NEOPAGANISM; YEATS, WILLIAM BUTLER. FURTHER READING: KALOGERA 1977.

Cathars. (Greek *catharoi*, "pure") A Gnostic sect, the Cathars or Albigensians were the largest and most important Christian heretic group in the Western world between the fall of Rome and the dawn of the Reformation. Their origins go back to Gnostic movements of the late Roman period such as the Paulicians and the Messalians, which insisted that the visible world was the creation of the Devil and that humans were spiritual beings trapped in the prison of matter. There is some evidence that the Cathar teachings may have been at least partly based on those of Manichaeism, the most successful of all the Gnostic sects, but this is hotly disputed by scholars. *SEE* GNOSTICISM; MANICHAEISM.

Around 950 C.E., these teachings were circulated in what is now Bulgaria by a priest named Bogomil. Despite persecution, the Bogomil sect (as it came to be called) spread widely in what is now Greece and the Balkans, and established a sizeable presence in Constantinople itself. The Bogomils believed in reincarnation, rejected the sacraments of the mainstream Christian churches as valueless, and particularly condemned marriage, since to them sexuality was the way that souls were kept trapped in a succession of physical bodies.

According to the *Discourse Against the Bogomils* of Cosmas the Priest, written between 969 and 972, the Bogomils believed that Satan and Jesus were the two sons of God; that Satan had fallen from grace, created the material world, ensnared the angels who fell with him in material bodies, and became the God of the Old Testament; and that Jesus had come to enable the trapped angelic spirits to free themselves and return to heaven. Later, after Cosmas' time, a split opened up in the Bogomil community between those who believed in the moderate dualism that saw Jesus and Satan as brothers, the sons of a good God, and a more radical sect, which held that the powers of good and evil had existed at war since the beginning. It was this radical approach that became central to Catharism in the West.

The first reports of dualist heretics in western Europe date from a little after 1000 C.E. Northern Italy, with its close trade contacts with the Byzantine Empire, was the first area reached by dualist missionaries, and southern France was next. By the early twelfth century there were underground communities of Cathars, "pure ones," over much of Catholic Europe, and the south of France was particularly active. The Catholic Church there was weak and notoriously corrupt. The town of Albi became a center for Cathar activities, and Albigenses, "those born in Albi," became a common term for the heretics.

By 1176 there were two Cathar bishops in France and one in northern Italy, all connected to the moderate dualist tradition. In that year, however, the Bogomil missionary Nicetas came through Italy to southern France.

An adherent of the radical dualist position, Nicetas was an effective speaker and converted most of the French Cathars to his view. He also consecrated new bishops for Toulouse, Carcassone, and Agen, doubling the number of Western bishoprics. The aftermath of Nicetas' visit was a surge in Cathar proselytising and conversions, and the explosive spread of the Cathar faith in southern France.

The teachings and rituals of the Cathars have survived in a fair amount of detail. Three full texts of the central Cathar rite, the *Consolamentum*, and two complete books of Cathar theology, the *Questions of John* and the *Book of the Two Principles*, escaped the flames of the Inquisition; see Wakefield and Evans 1969 for translations. Cathar beliefs were identical in essence with those of the more radical Bogomils; they believed in the "two principles"— that is, in eternally separate powers of good and evil at war in the universe—and held that human souls were entities from the side of good who had been imprisoned in the evil world of matter.

The *Consolamentum*, the main Cathar sacrament, was a spiritual baptism by laying-on of hands, which, according to Cathar teaching, conferred the Holy Spirit and made it possible to escape from the material world at death. Those who had received the *Consolamentum* were called *perfecti*, "perfect ones," vowed to celibacy and a mostly vegetarian diet. Those who were not ready for this were called *credentes*, "believers," and generally received the *Consolamentum* on their deathbeds. The supreme sacrament, undertaken by the most zealous *perfecti*, was the *endura*, a process of suicide by starvation that guaranteed an instant trip to Heaven.

The Cathar Church posed a massive and spreading threat to the Catholic Church, but it took some time for the latter to notice. Missionaries were sent, public debates were held, and in 1179, the Third Lateran Council condemned Catharism in harsh terms. None of this slowed the spread of Catharism noticeably. In 1198, however, a new pope—Innocent III—took the papal throne. A strong-minded and intolerant man, he became convinced that force would have to be used to restore the Catholic Church's position. The murder of a papal legate in 1208 provided a pretext, and that year Innocent declared a crusade against the heretics.

The war that followed lasted some thirty-five years, from the siege of Beziers in 1209 to the fall of the last Cathar fortress, Montségur in the Pyrenees, in 1244. The south of France was devastated by the fighting and the calculated brutality of the Crusaders. In the wake of the Crusade came a new organization, the Holy Office of the Inquisition, which evolved out of older and less efficient structures in the 1230s and was formally established by Innocent's successor, Gregory IX, in 1239. Under constant pressure from the Inquisition, the last known Cathar *perfecti* in France were hunted down by 1330, although a few small groups of Cathars may have survived in hiding in the Piedmont region, on what is now the border with Switzerland.

Like the Knights Templar, who were destroyed by charges of heresy during the same period, the Cathars ended up experiencing an afterlife that is in many ways more interesting, and far more closely linked to the occult. They received little attention during the later Middle Ages and the Renaissance, and their place in Reformation and early modern scholarship was mostly limited to attempts by Catholics and Protestants alike to use the history of the Cathars as ammunition in theological warfare. The Romantic movement of the late eighteenth and nineteenth centuries, however, brought on a fascination with the outcast, the heretical, and the medieval, and the Cathars benefited posthumously from all these. Political currents supporting regional independence in the south of France also fed into a revival of interest in the Cathars and, in time, a revival of Catharism itself.

Unfortunately much of this was shaped by the same sort of carelessness with facts that has bedeviled the occult field for centuries; SEE OCCULT HISTORY. The Cathars have been presented as anything and everything from Theosophist mystics to extraterrestrial contactees, and the actual nature of their teachings and rites—which are recorded in great detail in surviving Cathar documents—have usually been ignored by writers more interested in importing their pet concerns into Catharism or simply telling a romantic story.

The Cathars came to play a particularly important role in the British occult scene during the early and middle twentieth century. Numerous members of the Society of the Inner Light, the magical order founded by Dion Fortune, claimed Cathar past lives and communicated supposedly Cathar material to the Society; *SEE* INNER LIGHT, SOCIETY OF THE. Another important source was London psychiatrist Arthur Guirdham, who encountered a patient with mediumistic abilities, engaged in dialogues with the spirits of dead Cathars by this means, and eventually became an important influence on the English esoteric scene by way of numerous books discussing his experiences and the Cathar teachings he received. *SEE ALSO* KNIGHTS TEMPLAR. FURTHER READING: BARBER 2000, GUIRDHAM 1977, VAN DEN BROECK 1998, WAKEFIELD AND EVANS 1969.

catoptromancy. The art of divination by use of a magical mirror. *SEE* MIRROR, MAGICAL.

Cauda Draconis. (Latin, "tail of the dragon") A geomantic figure governed by the South Node of the moon, and harmonious with Saturn and Mars. In divination, Cauda Draconis is an unfavorable figure in most contexts, good only for endings and departures. *SEE* GEOMANCY; NODES, LUNAR.

Geomantic figure Cauda Draconis

cauldron. One of the tools of the stereotypical Halloween witch, and made famous by the witches' chant in Shakespeare's *Macbeth*, the cauldron has an important place in myth and magical practice alike. In earlier times, the cauldron was an essential part of household equipment, in constant use for cooking, washing, bathing, and other chores, and it also made a convenient and symbolically rich tool for magical workings.

The Celts were particularly fond of cauldron lore in their mythologies and legends, and a good half-dozen magical cauldrons appear in the old sources. The cauldron of the Dagda, the Irish father-god, would provide food for any number of people. The same power was also possessed by the cauldron of Tyrnog, listed in Welsh bardic lore as one of the thirteen treasures of Britain. Other Welsh cauldrons include the cauldron of Cerid-

wen, in which she used to brew a potion of wisdom; the cauldron of the Underworld in the second branch of the *Mabinogion*, which returns the dead to a half-life in which they move but cannot speak; and the mysterious pearl-rimmed cauldron, warmed by the breath of nine maidens, for which Arthur and his men quested in the ancient Welsh poem *Preiddeu Annwn*. The sacrificed hero Llew Llaw Gyffes, who features in the fourth branch of the *Mabinogion*, met his ritual death standing on the edge of a stream with one foot on the rim of a cauldron and the other on the back of a goat; this is astrological symbolism, and locates Llew's death at the cusp of the zodiacal signs Capricorn the goat and Aquarius the water bearer. *SEE* ASTROLOGY; MABINOGION.

In modern Pagan practice, the cauldron is often used as an emblem of the Goddess in ritual. *SEE* NEOPAGANISM.

Cayce, Edgar. American healer and psychic, 1877–1945. The son of a Kentucky farmer, he had little formal education. His childhood was marked by visions and other psychic experiences, and by the age of sixteen he had begun to diagnose diseases and prescribe treatments by psychic means. With the help of a local hypnotist, he learned to put himself into a light trance to assist this process, and within a few years his successes brought him thousands of patients a year.

Cayce sought to work with orthodox medical practitioners but was repeatedly rebuffed; a small number of alternative practitioners worked with him, however, and one—Dr. Wesley Ketchum, a homeopath—investigated his record of cures and reported favorably on them to the American Society of Clinical Research. The financial support provided by his steady stream of patients allowed Cayce to set up his own hospital in Virginia Beach, Virginia, and an organization—the Association for Research and Enlightenment (ARE)—to record and study his work.

In addition to diagnosis and treatment of diseases, Cayce used his trance states to bring through information about the past lives of some of his patients, as well as prophecies of the near and far future. Atlantis, ancient Egypt, and the Yucatan played a significant role in his account of human history, which has many similarities to

the Theosophical version of the world's history. *SEE* AT-
LANTIS; THEOSOPHY.

While his medical powers seem to have helped a great
many people, his prophecies have not stood the test of
time well. For example, he predicted that Atlantis would
begin to surface in 1968 or 1969, in the context of Earth
changes that would begin in 1958 and end in 1998. FUR-
THER READING: FREJER 1995, SUGRUE 1973.

Cecco d'Ascoli. Italian astrologer and magician, 1257–
1327. Little in the way of detailed information has survived about Cecco, who was apparently the first victim
of the great campaign against magic that modern Pagans
call the Burning Times. He was born in the town of Ascoli, and in 1322 was appointed to a position as professor
of astrology at the University of Bologna.

Not long thereafter he published a commentary on the
De Sphaera of John of Sacrobosco, the standard text of astronomy used at the time. His commentary was full of references to occult practices and quotations from magical
books, and included among other things detailed instructions on how to create a magical statue in order to call
down the spirit Floron for divinatory purposes; *SEE* STAT-
UES, MAGICAL. Although it also contained the usual condemnations of magic on religious grounds, the Inquisition
was not fooled; the Inquisitor of Bologna condemned
him as a heretic, expelled him from his university position, and forbade him from teaching astrology again.

After this Cecco moved to Florence, and apparently
took up a position as court astrologer to Charles of Calabria, Duke of Florence. He also wrote a long and bitter
poem titled *l'Acerba*, "The Acerbic One," which was at
least in part a parody of Dante's *Divine Comedy*. Whether
this or his continued astrological activities brought him
to the attention of the Inquisition again is uncertain, but
in 1327 the Florentine Inquisition arrested him, tried and
convicted him as a relapsed heretic, and had him burned
at the stake. All available copies of his works were destroyed, and a sentence of excommunication was imposed
on anyone who kept a copy of any of them. *SEE ALSO*
BURNING TIMES; MAGIC, PERSECUTION OF. FURTHER
READING: THORNDYKE 1923.

cell salts. Twelve minerals that are used in biochemic
medicine, a system of alternative health care related to

homeopathy and also influential in some alchemical and
occult systems. If all the organic substances and water
were to be removed from the human body, twelve mineral compounds make up the vast majority of the remainder. The German homeopathic physician Wilhelm
Schüssler proposed in 1873 that these minerals prepared
in a homeopathic manner could be used as the basis of a
system of healing, arguing that deficiencies in these minerals were at the root of most human illnesses.

Schüssler's system readily won adherents in the days
before current legal restrictions on health care, and in the
decades around 1900 it was popular in most of the Western world, as well as in India. Like most traditions of alternative medicine, it was forced underground in the
middle of the twentieth century by pressure from conventional physicians, but has remained popular in Britain
and India. Some naturopathic physicians in America also
use the cell salts.

The connection between cell salts and Western occult
traditions was the creation of Dr. George W. Carey
(1845–1924), a biochemic physician and occultist who
assigned the twelve cell salts to the signs of the zodiac as
part of a complex system of mystical healing that reinterpreted the Bible as a manual for the transformation of the
human body. *SEE* CAREY, GEORGE WASHINGTON. Carey's
approach to the cell salts was taken up by many astrologers and students of the occult, and discussions of
the cell salts in relation to astronomy, alchemy, and personal transformation can still be found in some occult
traditions today. *SEE ALSO* HOMEOPATHY. FURTHER READ-
ING: BOERICKE AND DEWEY 1925, CAREY AND PERRY
1932.

Celtic astrology. A recently devised system of astrology
using a thirteen-sign zodiac based on the Ogham tree-
calendar of Robert Graves. It was invented by British astrologer Helena Patterson in the 1980s, and has been
used by a growing number of astrologers in the last
decade or so. *SEE* OGHAM TREE-CALENDAR.

Birch. *Dates:* Dec. 24–Jan. 20. *Degrees:* 2°00'
  Capricorn–29°59' Capricorn.
Rowan. Dates: Jan. 21–Feb. 17. *Degrees:* 0°00'
  Aquarius–27°59' Aquarius.

Ash. *Dates:* Feb. 18–March 17. *Degrees:* 28°00' Aquarius–25°59' Pisces.

Alder. *Dates:* March 18–April 14. *Degrees:* 26°00' Pisces–23°59 Aries.

Willow. *Dates:* April 15–May 12. *Degrees:* 24°00' Aries–20°59 Taurus.

Hawthorn. *Dates:* May 13–June 9. *Degrees:* 21°00' Taurus–17°59' Gemini.

Oak. *Dates:* June 10–July 7. *Degrees:* 18°00' Gemini–14°59' Cancer.

Holly. *Dates:* July 8–Aug. 4. *Degrees:* 15°00' Cancer–11°59' Leo.

Hazel. *Dates:* Aug. 5–Sept. 1. *Degrees:* 12°00 Leo–8°59 Virgo.

Vine. *Dates:* Sept. 2–Sept. 29. *Degrees:* 9°00' Virgo–6°59' Libra.

Ivy. *Dates:* Sept. 30–Oct. 27. *Degrees:* 7°00 Libra–4°59 Scorpio.

Reed. *Dates:* Oct. 28–Nov. 24. *Degrees:* 5°00 Scorpio–2°59' Sagittarius.

Elder. *Dates:* Nov. 25–Dec. 23. *Degrees:* 3°00 Sagittarius–1°59 Capricorn.

This system of astrology has been harshly criticized by some historians, who point out that Graves' tree-calendar was a product of his own imagination fired by incomplete descriptions of traditional Irish Ogham, and that the historical pre-Christian Celts used a very different astrological system, of which traces appear in old Irish texts. Less often pointed out is the fact that Patterson credits her initial inspiration to the book *Arachne Rising*, which was an extended practical joke on astrologers, written under a pseudonym by debunker and science-fiction writer John Sladek. *SEE* ARACHNE.

The irony of all this, though, is that the thirteen-sign zodiac works as well as the older twelve-sign version, producing clear and accurate meanings when applied to natal charts. *SEE ALSO* ASTROLOGY; ZODIAC. FURTHER READING: PATTERSON 1997, PATTERSON 1998.

Celtic reconstructionism. Modern Neopagan movement dedicated to the reconstruction of ancient, pre-Christian Celtic spirituality. A product of the 1980s and 1990s, the Celtic reconstructionist movement is among the smaller branches of Neopaganism, but has had a significant impact on the broader tradition by way of several influential groups and teachers.

The basic thrust of the Celtic reconstructionist movement is an attempt to work out, largely from scholarly sources, what exactly the religion of the ancient Celts was, and to try to reformulate that for modern times. This has involved the rejection of much of the "Celtic" lore of the Druid Revival, and thus of most of British traditional Druidry, until recently the major claimant to Celtic connections in the occult community; *SEE* DRUIDRY. Another source that has been largely rejected is Wicca, which has claimed Celtic roots but seems to have little connection to actual Celtic traditions; *SEE* WICCA.

As of this writing the Celtic reconstructionist movement appears to consist mostly of scattered groups and individuals with widely varying ideas and agendas. Communication, and what organization exists, is largely by way of the Internet. The movement is in a relatively early stage, though. *SEE ALSO* NEOPAGANISM.

Cen. (Old English, "torch") The sixth rune of the Anglo-Saxon futhorc, associated in the Old English rune-poem with the flame of a torch illuminating the hall of a king. Its sound-value is hard *c*. *SEE* ANGLO-SAXON FUTHORC.

Rune Cen

central gaze. In European magical traditions of the nineteenth and twentieth centuries, a method of using the eyes to prevent another magician from gaining control of one's mind and will. To use the central gaze, the magician focuses his or her eyes intently on a point between the attacker's eyebrows, at the location of the "third eye" center. The crucial point lies in not allowing oneself to meet the attacker's gaze directly, even for a moment; concentration must be maintained on the chosen point. FURTHER READING: LOMER 1997; SADHU 1962.

ceremonial magic. One of the major divisions of Western magic, also known as ritual magic. As the name implies, ceremonial magic uses ritual or ceremonial means as its primary approach to working with magical energies and entities. The main traditions of ceremonial magic in the Western world have long been deeply intertwined with the Hermetic tradition on the one hand, and the Cabala on the other, and the term "ceremonial magic" is often used as a label for these traditions in modern occult parlance. *SEE* CABALA; HERMETICISM.

The concept of ceremonial magic, as distinct from other kinds of magical practice, emerged in the Middle Ages and was heavily influenced by the legal strictures on magical practice imposed by the Catholic Church. The church's main concern was to prohibit the worship of Pagan deities, and any form of magic that could be construed as a mode of worship was strictly prohibited unless it dealt strictly with the Christian Trinity or the saints. Thus all magic that dealt with spirits of any kind was forbidden, while approaches such as natural magic and religious magic were generally permitted. *SEE* CHRISTIAN OCCULTISM; NATURAL MAGIC.

The prohibited forms of magic formed the first nucleus of what developed into the ceremonial magic of the later Middle Ages and Renaissance. Heavily supplemented by material from Arabic magical manuals such as the *Picatrix*, ceremonial magic developed a literature of its own, consisting of the famous *grimoires* or "grammars" of magical practice. *SEE* GRIMOIRE; PICATRIX. Some of these were openly demonological works of goetic magic that aimed at summoning the powers of evil and exploiting them for the magician's benefit; *SEE* GOETIA. Others dealt with planetary spirits and other ethically neutral powers, and still others were works of angel magic of a more or less austere character. The church predictably classified them all as demonic, and until the Renaissance the whole tradition was relatively secret.

During the Renaissance occult revival, attitudes toward the old ceremonial magic of the grimoires varied widely. Some of the important Renaissance magi rejected the medieval tradition completely, turning instead to Hermetic and Cabalistic sources in an attempt to produce a new, theologically untainted magic. Others borrowed freely from the grimoires. In this latter camp was Cornelius Agrippa, whose *De Occulta Philosophia Libri Tres* (*Three Books of Occult Philosophy*, 1533) was among the central texts of magicians for several centuries thereafter. *SEE* AGRIPPA, HEINRICH CORNELIUS.

The ceremonial magic of the modern occult revival drew heavily on these medieval and Renaissance sources, but was profoundly reshaped by the writings of Eliphas Lévi (1810–1875). Lévi's works argued for a higher, spiritual dimension to magical practice, seeing the goal of magic as the spiritual transformation of the magus, rather than simply as the accomplishment of practical goals. *SEE* LÉVI, ELIPHAS. This approach became extremely common after his death, partly through the influence of the Hermetic Order of the Golden Dawn and its many offshoots, and partly as the increasing Western knowledge of Eastern traditions such as yoga influenced the way Western occultists thought about their own traditions. *SEE* GOLDEN DAWN, HERMETIC ORDER OF THE; YOGA.

The rise of the Neopagan movement in the second half of the twentieth century brought about another change, one that is still reshaping the ceremonial magic tradition. The efforts of Pagans to define their religions as something different from other occult traditions led, particularly in the English-speaking countries, to a division of the magical community into Pagan and "ceremonialist" wings, with this latter term meaning "practitioner of ceremonial magic." From the Renaissance to the 1950s, Pagan religious practice of one form or another was a common element of many currents of ceremonial magic, but this has become increasingly uncommon in recent years as Neopagan writers and practitioners have staked out their own claims to the territory. *SEE* NEOPAGANISM.

At present, in the English-speaking world, the system of ceremonial magic created by the Hermetic Order of the Golden Dawn is the most popular, although several others are widely practiced. *SEE* AURUM SOLIS; BARDON, FRANZ; CHAOS MAGIC; THELEMA. Recent decades have seen a great deal of research and exploration by ceremonial magicians, especially into the older byways of ritual magic and similar traditions from other cultures, and new developments in the field seem likely. *SEE ALSO* MAGIC; NATURAL MAGIC. FURTHER READING: BUTLER 1949, GREER 1997, LÉVI 1972.

Ceres. An asteroid sometimes used in astrology, assigned to the zodiacal sign Virgo. *SEE* ASTEROIDS.

Ceridwen. *SEE* GODDESS, THE.

Cernunnos. *SEE* GOD, THE.

ceration. In alchemy, the process of softening a hard substance by heat and other processes. *SEE* ALCHEMY.

ceromancy. Divination by melted wax, also known as ceroscopy. The diviner melted wax in a brass container until it was entirely liquid, then poured the wax into another container of cold water. The wax congealed into shapes floating on the surface of the water, which were then interpreted by the diviner. Ceromany was relatively common in ancient and medieval times and has survived in some folk cultures until modern times, but has received essentially no attention by the modern occult revival. *SEE* DIVINATION.

ceroscopy. *SEE* CEROMANCY.

Ceugant. In Druidry, one of the three circles of existence, the transcendant realm which can be traversed only by the divine. Some traditions of Druidry influenced by Judeo-Christian theories of the Fall hold that the journey of souls through Abred was caused by an attempt by those souls to traverse Ceugant. *SEE* CIRCLES OF EXISTENCE; DRUIDRY.

Chaeremon. Egyptian priest and philosopher, fl. first century C.E. Little is known about his life. Head of the Alexandrian School of Grammarians, and possibly keeper of the Museum of Alexandria, he was also an important member of the native priesthood. He was part of an embassy of Alexandrian notables to the court of the Roman emperor Claudius in 40 C.E., and at some point before 49 C.E. served for a time as a teacher to the future emperor Nero. He is known to have written a history of Egypt, a book about comets, and a treatise on hieroglyphics; this last was influential all through the late classical period and was still being read and cited in the twelfth century C.E. Unfortunately only scattered quotations from his books have survived.

His career is important in the history of magic, even given the little that is known about it, because it demonstrates the complete interpenetration of Greek and Egyptian thought that had occurred in Egypt by Roman times. The fact that a fully consecrated Egyptian temple priest could also be a notable Stoic philosopher says much about the cultural politics of Alexandria during the period that saw the birth of the Western occult traditions. *SEE ALSO* ALEXANDRIA; EGYPTIAN OCCULTISM; STOICISM. FURTHER READING: VAN DER HORST 1984.

Chaioth ha-Qodesh. (Hebrew ChIVTh HQDSh, "Holy Living Creatures") In Cabalistic lore, the order of angels associated with Kether, the first Sephirah of the Tree of Life. Their traditional form, as described in the first chapter of the Book of Ezekiel, is humanoid, with four wings, four faces—of a man, a lion, an eagle, and an ox—and hooves like a calf's, but of glowing brass. *SEE* ANGEL; KETHER.

chakra. (Sanskrit, "wheel") One of a set of energy centers or vortices located in the human body, according to Hindu philosophy and a variety of Western systems influenced by it. In Hindu writings, the number and position of the chakras varies widely. The version of the chakra system popular in the Western world is considerably more uniform, with seven chakras located at various points along the length of the central nervous system, as follows:

> *Number:* 1. *Name:* Muladhara. *Translation:* Root. *Location:* Base of Spine. *Color:* Red.★
>
> *Number:* 2. *Name:* Svadhisthana. *Translation:* Sweetness. *Location:* Genitals. *Color:* Orange.
>
> *Number:* 3. *Name:* Manipura. *Translation:* Jewel. *Location:* Solar Plexus★★. *Color:* Yellow.
>
> *Number:* 4. *Name:* Anahata. *Translation:* Unstruck. *Location:* Heart. *Color:* Green.
>
> *Number:* 5. *Name:* Vishuddha. *Translation:* Purification. *Location:* Throat. *Color:* Blue.
>
> *Number:* 6. *Name:* Ajna. *Translation:* Perception. *Location:* Brow. *Color:* Indigo.
>
> *Number:* 7. *Name:* Sahasrara. *Translation:* Thousandfold. *Location:* Top of Head. *Color:* Violet.

★ The colors given here are standard in most Western versions of the chakra system, but differ sharply from those given in traditional Hindu writings. Different chakra color systems also exist in Western sources.

★★ The location of the third chakra varies in different sources. The navel, the *hara* or *tan t'ien* (an important point in Japanese and Chinese martial arts, just below the navel), and the spleen are also common locations given for this center.

The chakras were introduced to Western audiences by a variety of nineteenth- and early twentieth-century European writers, of whom Arthur Avalon (Sir John Woodroffe) and the Theosophist C. W. Leadbeater were the most influential. The popularity of Asian spiritual teachings at that time, fostered by the influential Theosophical Society, encouraged many Western occultists to borrow the chakra system in one form or another, with the somewhat odd result that it's not hard to find Wiccans, Druids, Hermetic alchemists, and other practitioners of Western occult traditions using what was originally a Hindu system of subtle-body work.

A wide range of different correspondences have been worked out to fit the chakras into Western occult philosophy. Connections between the seven chakras and the seven planets have played an important role in most of these, but attributions differ widely. The following table gives the versions developed by Paul Foster Case, Jean Dubuis, Dion Fortune, Jon Mumford, and Ross Nichols, all twentieth-century Western occultists:

Chakra: 1. *Case:* Saturn. *Dubuis:* Sun. *Fortune:* Sun. *Mumford:* Saturn. *Nichols:* Moon.

Chakra: 2. *Case:* Sun. *Dubuis:* Moon. *Fortune:* Jupiter. *Mumford:* Jupiter. *Nichols:* Mercury.

Chakra: 3. *Case:* Mars. *Dubuis:* Mercury. *Fortune:* Mercury. *Mumford:* Mars. *Nichols:* Venus.

Chakra: 4. *Case:* Jupiter. *Dubuis:* Venus. *Fortune:* Saturn. *Mumford:* Venus. *Nichols:* Sun.

Chakra: 5. *Case:* Venus. *Dubuis:* Mars. *Fortune:* Venus. *Mumford:* Mercury. *Nichols:* Mars.

Chakra: 6. *Case:* Moon. *Dubuis:* Jupiter. *Fortune:* Mars. *Mumford:* (none). *Nichols:* Jupiter.

Chakra: 7. *Case:* Mercury. *Dubuis:* Saturn. *Fortune:* Moon. *Mumford:* (none). *Nichols:* Saturn.

There have also been a variety of proposed correlations between the seven chakras and the Sephiroth of the Tree of Life. One approach, pioneered by English magician Dion Fortune, aligns the midline of the body with the central pillar of the Tree of Life, and uses the intersection of the three horizontal paths with the Middle Pillar as locations for centers; this system correlates closely with the set of energy centers used in the Middle Pillar exercise, and Fortune assigns Malkuth to an extra center below the feet to complete the correspondence. *SEE* MIDDLE PILLAR EXERCISE; TREE OF LIFE. Another system, more popular in European magical circles, assigns the seven Sephiroth below the Veil to the seven chakras; the version presented by Rafal Prinke is given here:

Chakra: 1. *Fortune:* Yesod. *Prinke:* Malkuth.

Chakra: 2. *Fortune:* Hod and Netzach. *Prinke:* Yesod.

Chakra: 3. *Fortune:* Tiphareth. *Prinke:* Hod.

Chakra: 4. *Fortune:* Geburah and Chesed. *Prinke:* Netzach.

Chakra: 5. *Fortune:* Daath. *Prinke:* Tiphareth.

Chakra: 6. *Fortune:* Binah and Chokmah. *Prinke:* Geburah.

Chakra: 7. *Fortune:* Kether. *Prinke:* Chesed.

In its original Hindu context, the chakras play a role in the exercises used to awaken the *kundalini* or "serpent fire" at the base of the spine. This connection has also found its way into some Western occult traditions. *SEE ALSO* SUBTLE BODIES; THEOSOPHY. FURTHER READING: AVALON 1974, CASE 1985, JUDITH 1987, JUDITH AND VEGA 1993, LEADBEATER 1971, LEADBEATER 1974.

Chakshusha Manu. According to Theosophical lore, the manu or ruler of the fourth root race. *SEE* MANU; ROOT RACE.

Chaldean Oracles. A collection of revelations from the gods, written down in Greek verse by Julianus the Theurgist (fl. second century C.E.). The *Oracles* survive only in fragmentary form, preserved in quotations in a variety of ancient Platonist authors. Little is known about the circumstances of their writing. Murky and difficult to interpret, they appear to teach a magical vision of the universe based on Platonism; *SEE* PLATONISM.

The *Oracles* were the subject of much interest among the Pagan Platonists of the last century or so of Pagan classical civilization. Porphyry, Iamblichus, and Proclus all wrote extensively on them, and Julian, the last Pagan emperor, refers to concepts from the *Oracles* in his surviving writings. They were nearly lost in the Middle Ages but came to light again in the Renaissance, and have been used extensively since that time in magical systems, including that of the Golden Dawn; SEE GOLDEN DAWN, HERMETIC ORDER OF THE.

The *Oracles* were at times considered to have been written by Zoroaster, the prophet of the Zoroastrian religion, and references to the "Chaldean Oracles of Zoroaster" are still not hard to find in occult literature. SEE ZOROASTER. SEE ALSO JULIANUS THE CHALDEAN; JULIANUS THE THEURGIST. FURTHER READING: LEWY 1978.

chalybs. (Greek, "steel") In alchemy, another term for niter. SEE NITER.

Chaos magic. A diverse occult movement born in the last quarter of the twentieth century, sometimes spelled "Xaos magic"—apparently on the principle that rejection of authority should be carried into the realm of spelling as well as that of spells. Chaos magic owes its origins largely to a work of science fiction, the Illuminatus! trilogy by Robert Shea and Robert Anton Wilson. The trilogy, a dizzying mixture of satire, put-on, pop culture, and occultism, attacked all conceivable belief systems, presented a theory of magic that centered on sex, and drew heavily on the writings of the previously obscure Discordian movement, which worships the goddess of chaos; SEE DISCORDIANISM. All three of these features went on to become essential to Chaos magic.

The first significant publication in the Chaos magic field seems to have been Peter Carroll's *Liber Null*, originally published in 1978, which combined the above ideas with Thelemic magic, tantra, Taoism, and the masturbation mysticism of British artist-occultist Austin Osman Spare; SEE SPARE, AUSTIN OSMAN. The same year also saw the first public announcement of Carroll's magical organization for Chaos magicians, the Illuminates of Thanateros (IOT); SEE ILLUMINATES OF THANATEROS (IOT). A second major Chaos magic organization, Thee Temple ov Psychick Youth (TOPY), was founded in 1980 by British performance artist Genesis P-Orridge; SEE TEMPLE OV PSYCHICK YOUTH, THEE (TOPY). Other groups and approaches followed, especially by way of computer bulletin boards and the Internet, which became the preferred habitat of many Chaos magicians years before the rest of the world found out about them.

Chaos magic differs from other occult traditions in its exclusive focus on magical technique and its rejection of theory and philosophy. Beliefs, according to Chaos magic proponents, are tools used to attain specific mental effects and nothing more; they have no validity or truth in themselves, merely usefulness for particular tasks. "Nothing is true; everything is permitted"—a saying attributed to Hassan-i-Sabbah, the founder of the Order of Assassins, and repeated often in Discordian writings and the novels of American writer William S. Burroughs—is often cited as a summary of the Chaos magic viewpoint.

In keeping with their rejection of the validity of belief systems, Chaos magicians have made much use of symbolism drawn from fantasy fiction. Many Chaos magicians use, as a symbol of their approach, some variant of the "Banner of Chaos" from the fantasy novels of British author Michael Moorcock, which consists of eight arrows radiating from a common center. The works of Peter Carroll also include such fantasy-fiction elements as references to "octarine," the eighth color of the spectrum in Terry Pratchett's Discworld fantasy-satires, and an invocation of Azathoth, the idiot-god of primal chaos in the horror fiction of H. P. Lovecraft. SEE FANTASY OCCULTISM. FURTHER READING: CARROLL 1980, SHEA AND WILSON 1975A, SHEA AND WILSON 1975B, SHEA AND WILSON 1975C.

Chapter of Perfection. Rosicrucian order, founded in Germany in the late seventeenth century by the Pietist theologian and alchemist Johann Jakob Zimmerman. Little is known for certain about the chapter's teachings, but they are believed to include Christian Cabalistic mysticism, alchemy, and astrology, along with a lively conviction that the end of the world was at hand. The membership was exclusively male, and celibate.

Upon hearing that the English Quaker nobleman William Penn had invited religious minorities of all kinds to his new American colony of Pennsylvania, Zimmerman and his group decided to emigrate, but Zimmerman died shortly before the group embarked in 1694. Under the leadership of Johannes Kelpius (1673–1708), the chapter sailed for the New World and settled in what is now Germantown Creek, Pennsylvania.

The chapter established what would now be called a commune in the Pennsylvania wilderness, with all property shared in common and all members living together in a communal house. An observatory on the top floor of the house allowed members to keep track of the heavens for astrological purposes, as they believed that the heavens would soon announce the Second Coming of Christ. Kelpius died as a result of extreme austerities in 1708, and Conrad Matthai became the head of the community. Under his management, the communal structure was dissolved and the group's members became hermits, pursuing their salvation individually. Some of the members took up careers as folk healers and magicians in the German emigrant communities nearby, and contributed much to the later Pennsylvania Dutch magical traditions. *SEE ALSO* ROSICRUCIANS.

Charge of the Goddess. A ritual text much used in modern Wiccan practice, the Charge of the Goddess was originally written in the late 1940s by Gerald Gardner, based on the writings of Charles Godfrey Leland and Aleister Crowley. *SEE* CROWLEY, ALEISTER; LELAND, CHARLES GODFREY. In the 1950s, Gardner's High Priestess, Doreen Valiente, convinced him that recognizeable quotes from Crowley would bring bad publicity to the Craft, and rewrote the Charge to exclude most of Crowley's contribution. This later version of the Charge has become standard in most modern Wiccan traditions, where it is often presented as an ancient Wiccan text passed down for generations. *SEE* GARDNER, GERALD BROUSSEAU; VALIENTE, DOREEN; WICCA.

Chariot, the. The seventh Major Arcanum of the tarot, usually showing the image of a man on a chariot. In the Golden Dawn system, this Arcanum is assigned to the Hebrew letter Cheth, while the French system assigns it to Zayin. In divination, it means victory and success, though potentially not stable or lasting.

Its magical title is "Child of the Power of the Waters, Lord of the Triumph of Light." *SEE ALSO* CHETH; TAROT.

Tarot trump the Chariot (Universal Tarot)

Charnock, Thomas. English alchemist, 1524–1581. Very little is known about the biography of this important figure in the evolution of the English alchemical tradition. He was born on the Isle of Thanet in Kent, and after a range of travels settled in Oxford, where he became the friend and assistant of an older alchemist whose name has not survived. In 1557 he was pressed into the English army and served in France for several years. By 1562 he was back in England, for in that year parish records report that he married one Agnes Norton, and settled in Stockland in Somerset, where he spent the rest of his life in alchemical research and writing. His books *Aenigma ad Alchimiam* (*Enigma of Alchemy*, 1572) and *The Breviary of Naturall Philosophy* (1577) were important influences on later alchemical writers in England and throughout Europe. *SEE ALSO* ALCHEMY.

charter. The formal document that authorizes a lodge to meet and initiate members. In fraternal lodges such as Freemasonry, charters are issued by a Grand Lodge or other supervising body, and confer various rights and duties on the lodge members. During the eighteenth and nineteenth centuries, when many occult organizations based their structure on the fraternal lodge model, forged charters supposedly issued by "secret chiefs" were a common feature of many magical lodges. *SEE* LODGE, FRATERNAL; LODGE, MAGICAL.

Chartres Cathedral. Built in the twelfth and thirteenth century in the French city of Chartres, on a site that was considered the spiritual center of France in Druidic times, Chartres Cathedral is one of the masterpieces of early Gothic church architecture. A number of modern occultists have argued that important esoteric teachings are concealed within its design and decoration. *SEE* SACRED GEOMETRY. FURTHER READING: CHARPENTIER 1972.

Chashmalim. (Hebrew, "shining ones") The order of angels assigned to Chesed, the fourth Sephirah of the Cabalistic Tree of Life. They are equated with the order of Dominations in Christian angelology. *SEE* CHESED; CABALA.

Chashmodai. In ceremonial magic, the planetary spirit of the moon. It is governed by the Spirit of Spirits of the moon, Shad Barshemoth ha-Shartathan, and the Intelligence of Intelligences of the moon, Malkah be-Tarshishim ve-ad Ruachoth Shechalim. *SEE* SPIRIT, PLANETARY.

Chassan. In Cabalistic magic, the angel of the element of air. *SEE* ANGEL; AIR, ELEMENT OF.

Cheiro. (William John Warner) Irish adventurer and diviner, 1866–1936. Very little is known for sure about this major figure in the history of modern palmistry, although a wide range of romantic stories are in circulation—many of them started by Cheiro himself. According to his birth certificate, he was born in 1866 in Bray, Ireland, just south of Dublin; his mother was allegedly an Irishwoman of French ancestry, and had an informal relationship with one Count Louis Hamon. Warner himself first seems to have surfaced in England in the 1880s as a stagehand in London theaters, using the name Louis Warner. Later, he worked as a chemical manufacturer, a spy, and the head of the postal service in Tsarist Russia, before settling down to a career as a palmist.

As Count Louis Hamon, a name he took in England shortly before the First World War, he traveled to America in 1930, where he made his reputation reading the palms of Hollywood film stars. He wrote several books on palmistry that are still much studied today. Rumors in the palmistry community have long claimed that he died in abject poverty, but the evidence suggests that he was still relatively well off when he died of lung disease in his own home in Los Angeles in 1936. *SEE ALSO* PALMISTRY. FURTHER READING: CAMPBELL 1996, CHEIRO 1987.

Cheled. (Hebrew ChLD, "world") One of the seven earths of Cabalistic lore, corresponding to the Sephirah Malkuth; our own Earth. *SEE* EARTHS, SEVEN.

cherubim. *SEE* KERUBIM.

Chesed. (Hebrew ChSD, "mercy, love") The fourth Sephirah of the Tree of Life, at the center of the Pillar of Mercy, Chesed is the great center of expansive and creative forces on the tree. Its alternate name is Gedulah, GDVLH, which means "greatness, magnificence." Its standard symbolism is as follows:

> *Name of God:* AL, El (God).
> *Archangel:* TzDQIAL, Tzadkiel (Justice of God).
> *Angelic Host:* ChShMLIM, Chashmalim (Shining Ones).
> *Astrological Correspondence:* TzDQ, Tzedek (Jupiter).
> *Tarot Correspondence:* The four Fours of the pack.
> *Elemental Correspondence:* Water.
> *Magical Image:* An old but mighty king sitting on a throne.
> *Colors:* in Atziluth—deep violet.
> in Briah—blue.
> in Yetzirah—deep purple.
> in Assiah—deep azure, flecked with yellow.
> *Correspondence in the Microcosm:* The memory in Ruach.
> *Correspondence in the Body:* The left shoulder.
> *Grade of Initiation:* 7=4, Adeptus Exemptus.
> *Qlippoth:* GAaShKLH, Ga'ashekelah, the Breakers in Pieces.

Its text from the *Thirty-two Paths of Wisdom* runs, "The Fourth Path is called the Cohesive or Receptacular Intelligence, and is so called because it contains all the Holy Powers, and from it emanate all the spiritual virtues with the most exalted essences. These emanate, one from another, by the power of the Primordial Emanation, the Highest Crown." *SEE ALSO* CABALA; TREE OF LIFE.

chess, Enochian. A variant of chess practiced in the Hermetic Order of the Golden Dawn, and devised by the order's cofounder William Wynn Westcott. Based on *chaturanga*, the ancient Hindu version of chess, it is a game for four players in which the pieces are Egyptian gods and the board is derived from one of the four Enochian elemental tablets. A detailed description of the game can be found in published collections of Golden Dawn papers. *SEE ALSO* ENOCHIAN MAGIC. FURTHER READING: REGARDIE 1974, WESTCOTT 1983.

Cheth. (Hebrew ChITh, "fence, enclosure") The eighth letter of the Hebrew alphabet, a single letter with the sound-value of *ch* (as in "Bach" or the Scottish word "loch") and the number-value of eight. Its standard correspondences are as follows:

> *Path of the Tree of Life:* Path 18, Binah to Geburah.
> *Astrological Correspondence:* Cancer, the Crab.
> *Tarot Correspondence:* Trump VII, the Chariot.
> *Part of the Cube of Space:* Lower east edge.
> *Colors:* in Atziluth—amber.
>> in Briah—maroon.
>> in Yetzirah—rich bright russet.
>> in Assiah—dark greenish brown.

The text from the *Thirty-two Paths of Wisdom* corresponding to this Path runs: "The Eighteenth Path is called the Intelligence of the House of Influence, by the greatness of whose abundance the influx of good things on created beings is increased, and from its midst by investigation are drawn forth the arcana and hidden senses, which dwell in its shadow and which cling to it, from the cause of all causes." *SEE ALSO* CHARIOT, THE; HEBREW ALPHABET.

Hebrew letter Cheth

chiah. (Hebrew ChIH, "life") In Cabalistic lore, the second highest element of the human soul, the essential energy or dynamism of the eternal aspect of the self, the neshamah. The chiah corresponds to Chokmah, and in many current magical traditions, it is identified with the true will. *SEE* CABALA; NESHAMAH; WILL.

chiromancy. *SEE* PALMISTRY.

Chiron. Quasi-planetary body located in an orbit between Saturn and Uranus, which plays a role in some modern versions of astrology. Chiron was discovered in 1977 by Charles Kowal. It is around 150–200 kilometers in diameter, and has a "coma" or tail like a comet. Current research suggests that it is, in fact, a giant comet rather than an asteroid. Its orbit is unstable and may eventually send it into the inner solar system; at the moment, it takes some fifty years to complete an orbit around the sun.

The existence of a planetary or quasi-planetary body had been predicted well in advance of Kowal's discovery by two astrologers—Dane Rudhyar in 1936 (see Rudhyar 1970) and Charles Jayne in 1961—and the latter also accurately predicted its orbital period. *SEE* RUDHYAR, DANE.

Its symbolism in modern astrology is largely based on the myth of Chiron the centaur, legendary for his healing powers. On this mythic basis, the planetoid has been assigned rulership over healing, shamanic transformation, psychic experiences, and transitions between various states of being. It has been proposed as the ruling planet of the sign Virgo, although this is far from being generally accepted. *SEE ALSO* ASTEROIDS; ASTROLOGY. FURTHER READING: CLOW 1988.

Chnoubis. Also known as Chnouph, a lion-headed serpent who appears on many ancient magical amulets. He seems to have been a combination of the Egyptian creator god Khnum, the divine serpent Kneph, and a star god named Kenem. Most of the traditions that once surrounded him were forgotten centuries ago.

The "lion-serpent" occurs with some frequency in the writings of Aleister Crowley, who, predictably enough, used it as a symbol of his penis. *SEE* CROWLEY, ALEISTER.

Chokmah. (Hebrew ChKMH, "wisdom") The second Sephirah of the Tree of Life, the primary masculine power of the tree, and the head of the Pillar of Mercy. Its usual symbolism is as follows:

Name of God: YH, Yah (God).

Archangel: RZIAL, Raziel (Secret of God).

Angelic Host: AVPNIM, Auphanim (Wheels).

Astrological Correspondence: MZLVTh, Mazloth (the zodiac).

Tarot Correspondence: The four Twos and four Kings of the pack.

Elemental Correspondence: Fire.

Magical Image: An old man.

Additional Symbols: All phallic symbols.

Additional Title: Abba, the Supernal Father.

Colors: in Atziluth—pure soft blue.

in Briah—gray.

in Yetzirah—iridescent pearl gray.

in Assiah—white, flecked with red, blue, and yellow.

Correspondence in the Microcosm: Chiah, the Spiritual Will.

Correspondence in the Body: The left side of the head.

Grade of Initiation: 9=2, Magus.

Qlippoth: Augiel, the Hinderers.

The text of the *Thirty-two Paths of Wisdom* corresponding to this Sephirah is: "The Second Path is called the Illuminating Inteligence; it is the Crown of Creation, the Splendor of the Unity, equalling it. It is exalted above every head, and named by Cabalists the Second Glory." *SEE ALSO* CABALA; TREE OF LIFE.

Cholem Yesodoth. A common misprint for Olam Yesodoth, "World of the Elements," the correspondence in the World of Assiah for the Sephirah Malkuth. *SEE* CABALA; MALKUTH; OLAM YESODOTH.

Christian Identity. A modern religious movement, strongly influenced by traditions of Gnostic thought and racist occultism, which was responsible for a good deal of right-wing political violence in the United States in the 1980s and 1990s. It is closely akin to Ariosophy, the occult philosophy underlying German National Socialism, although it has different historical roots; *SEE* ARIOSOPHY.

Christian Identity has an unusually complex pedigree even by the standards of modern quasi-occult movements. It emerged in the middle decades of the twentieth century from an unlikely mixture of sources. One of these was a movement in Protestant Christian theology that borrowed the ancient Gnostic idea of two bloodlines descended from Eve: an evil one via Cain, who was supposedly fathered by the Serpent, and a good one via Seth, who was fathered by Adam. *SEE* GNOSTICISM. The Baptist theologian Daniel Parker (1781–1844) was a major American proponent of this belief. Predictably, this "two seeds" doctrine was put to work in the service of Southern racism, and by 1900 racist ideologue Charles Campbell was claiming that the children of Cain were black, those of Seth white.

Another source of Christian Identity was to be found in a series of occult ideologies with ties to American fascism. The most important figure in this context was William Dudley Pelley (1890–1965), whose Silver Legion was the most successful of the fascist groups in America between the two world wars. *SEE* PELLEY, WILLIAM DUDLEY. Pelley's teachings, which were inspired by a mystical experience he underwent in 1925, also borrowed from many different occult sources but blended these with intense anti-Semitism and attitudes that would now be called "survivalist." Pelley's role as a forerunner of Christian Identity was direct; many of the leading figures in Christian Identity at the end of the twentieth century, including Aryan Nations founder Richard Girnt Butler, started out as Silver Legion members.

The final element in the creation of Christian Identity was the British Israelite movement—a small but vocal fringe group claiming that the British people are descended from one or more of the ten lost tribes of Israel. By a complicated series of doctrinal shifts, British Israelite groups in Canada and the United States managed to convince themselves by the late 1930s that they were descended from the ancient Israelites—but modern Jews were not.

During the 1950s and 1960s, mostly on the West Coast, British Israelite ideas of this sort blended with Pelley's mystical survivalism and racist versions of the "two seeds" theory to give rise to the Christian Identity movement. Wesley Swift (1913–1970), the most important Identity leader in the 1950s and 1960s, taught what has since become standard Identity theology: white "Aryans" are the true Israelites, the children of God, while other races are subhuman animals, and Jews are literally the biological offspring of Satan. All this has been combined, by Swift and his successors, with a radical right-wing political stance, a conviction that an apocalyptic war of the races is close at hand, and a obsession with guns and violence.

The results have been predictably bloody. Most notable among violent Identity groups has been the Bruders Schweigen or Silent Brotherhood, better known in the media as the Order. Founded in Metaline Falls, Idaho, in 1983, the Order carried out an armored-car robbery, counterfeited money, and assassinated Alan Berg, a Jewish radio talk-show host in Denver, in an effort to launch a guerrila war against the U.S. government. The leader of the Order, Robert Mathews, was killed in a shootout with federal agents in 1984, while other members were arrested in 1985 and 1986 and are serving long prison terms. Other Identity groups have proclaimed a policy of peaceful territorial separation in place of a more violent approach. FURTHER READING: AHO 1990, BARKUN 1994.

Christian occultism. Despite two thousand years worth of stereotypes, Christianity and the occult are far from strangers to each other, and there have been many different traditions of magic, divination, and occult practice founded on Christian principles. The existence of Christian occultism is one of the major blind spots in both contemporary Christian thinking and that of the occult community.

The occult dimensions of Christianity, in all probability, go all the way back to its founder. Rumors that Jesus of Nazareth was a magical practitioner, rather than a prophet, religious reformer, or deity, were apparently in circulation within a short time of his crucifixion, and several modern studies have shown that there is good reason to think that these rumors had a basis in fact. *SEE* JESUS OF NAZARETH.

Certainly practices that would normally be called magic and divination were in use in the earliest years of the Christian Church, among people who had known

Jesus or his personal followers. Acts 1:23–26 documents the use of divination by lots to select a new apostle to replace Judas Iscariot, while Paul of Tarsus in 1 Corinthians 12:8–10 enumerates a set of gifts of the Holy Spirit that includes healing powers, the ability to prophesy, and the power to work miracles. While modern Christian theology draws a sharp distinction between these activities and occult practices, there is no real basis for that distinction; *SEE* MAGIC. There is also some evidence that geometrical and numerical symbolism can be found in numerous passages of the New Testament, suggesting that Pythagorean and Platonic mysticism was present in Christian circles from a very early period. *SEE* QUADRIVIUM; PLATONISM.

During the first few centuries of its existence, the Christian Church held attitudes toward magic that were fairly close to those of Roman society as a whole. The Roman state viewed all magical practices with suspicion, and prosecutions of people who practiced magic, divination, or related arts were a relatively common event in Roman times. *SEE* MAGIC, PERSECUTION OF. At the same time, certain kinds of magical practice were considered acceptable: medical magic, weather magic, and most kinds of natural magic were exempt from Roman prohibitions, and most of the other types of magic were permitted unofficially so long as the magicians did not stray too close to the realm of politics. These same divisions, reshaped into church policy, became standard through most of the early Middle Ages.

With the collapse of Roman power in the West, the Christian Church found itself practically the sole custodian of classical learning in most of Europe. During the difficult years from the Visigothic sacking of Rome in 410 C.E. to the Carolingian revival of learning in the early ninth century, Christian monks, nuns, and church officials carried out what amounted to a vast salvage operation on what remained of Greek and Roman culture, and among the things that were preserved were magical documents and traditions.

A simple but straightforward rule seems to have governed the incorporation of magic into the new culture of Christian Europe: any magical working that avoided references to non-Christian spirits or deities was acceptable; any working that invoked a non-Christian spirit or deity was either eliminated or reformulated in a Christian mode. This was made much easier by the large-scale transformation of Pagan gods into Christian saints, which allowed prayers to Apollo and Woden to be turned without much difficulty to St. Apollinaris and St. Swithold. Many magical and divinatory practices were Christianized in this way but otherwise left entirely intact. For example, the Lots of Astrampsychus, a popular divination system in late Roman times, was lightly revised by replacing its lists of oracular gods with equivalent lists of Christian saints, and remained equally popular in the early Middle Ages. SEE ASTRAMPSYCHUS, LOTS OF.

The result was the emergence of an extensive tradition of Christian magic in medieval Western cultures, entirely acceptable to the church and practiced by all levels of society throughout the medieval world. That tradition included astrology and other forms of divination, weather magic, agricultural magic, healing magic, and a wide range of assorted charms for luck, protection, and success. Even goetic magic, which involved summoning spirits and thus fell under the prohibition of the Christian church, took on a strong Christian coloration during the Middle Ages; many surviving goetic rituals include Christian holy names and symbols, and operate entirely within the mental universe of medieval Christianity.

This Christian magical tradition remained an important and largely public current in Western cultures until the fourteenth century. Thereafter, attitudes against magic hardened. The first signs of what was to come were a series of heresy trials in which the main evidence for heresy was the practice of magic. The prosecution of Dame Alice Kyteler in 1324-5 and the burning of the Italian astrologer Cecco d'Ascoli in 1327 marked the opening of a large-scale assault on magic. During the four centuries that followed, the assault grew in scope and severity until some fifty thousand people had been killed. SEE BURNING TIMES; MAGIC, PERSECUTION OF.

Under these conditions Christian occultism faced a brutal struggle for survival. In the handbooks produced and used by inquisitors and witch-hunters, any ritual activity outside of those specifically sanctioned by the church was demon worship; the fact that many accused sorcerers and witches worked magic in the name of Christ and the saints was irrelevant. Still, nearly all oc-cultists of the time continued to claim that they and their art were entirely Christian.

Some occult writers during the Burning Times included harsh condemnations of witchcraft in their works, as a way of drawing distinctions between what they were teaching and the ideas of magic in general circulation at the time. Others criticized the witch-hunting mania, and Cornelius Agrippa—author of the most important Renaissance handbook of ceremonial magic—is known to have successfully defended an accused witch in court.

The impact of the Burning Times on Christian occult traditions was profound. Of the rich traditions of Christian magic and divination before the fourteenth century, very little survived. The exceptions were at opposite ends of the social scale. On the one hand, the vast majority of ceremonial magicians—who came from the educated upper classes—continued to think of themselves as Christian magicians, and to use Christian holy names and symbols in their workings. Ceremonial occult traditions such as Martinism and the Rosicrucian movement, in particular, drew heavily on Christian theology and practice. SEE MARTINISM; ROSICRUCIANS. Among the poor, especially in isolated areas, folk magic with Christian elements continued to be practiced quietly.

Both of these currents faded out to a large extent with the coming of industrialization in the nineteenth century, and the rise of alternatives to Christianity in the late nineteenth and twentieth centuries took care of much of what remained. While the Hermetic Order of the Golden Dawn, founded in 1888, originally required its members either to be Christian or to "be prepared to take an interest in Christian symbolism," many of its twentieth-century successor orders have been non-Christian or even anti-Christian.

Similarly, the penetration of Theosophy, Asian religions, and Neopaganism into popular culture throughout the Western world in the twentieth century has had a strong impact on folk traditions of magic. It's not hard to find people in America who come from families with more or less Christian traditions of folk magic but who encountered the Neopagan movement, decided that this was what their family traditions were actually about, and systematically replaced references to God and the saints with the Goddess and an assortment of Pagan divinities.

There are still, as of this writing, a number of occult orders that continue to work within the Christian magical tradition. Notable are occult Christian bodies drawing on the lineages of independent bishops, a number of English magical orders with a comfortable relationship with the Anglican Church, and the system of focused contemplative prayer, using the ancient name of theurgy, which evolved in nineteenth-century French occult circles and is still practiced in a variety of countries. SEE THEURGY. Churches and other religious bodies with a Gnostic focus have moved in this direction as well, buoyed by the soaring interest in Gnosticism set off by the translation of the Nag Hammadi scriptures; SEE GNOSTICISM. The last decade of the twentieth century also saw the emergence of a new current of Christian occultism, in the form of the Christian Wicca movement; SEE CHRISTIAN WICCA. Whether any of this will survive the rising popularity of Neopaganism remains to be seen. SEE ALSO CROMLECH TEMPLE. FURTHER READING: COHN 1975, FIDELER 1993, ROSSNER 1989, SADHU 1965, WHITEHEAD 1995.

Christian, Paul. (Jean-Baptiste Pitois) French occultist, 1811–1877. He was born in the rural Vosges district of France; very little seems to be known about his parents, other than the fact that they were not married. He attended Catholic schools in Harcourt and Paris, and entered the Trappist Order in 1828, but decided that he was unsuited to the monastic life and left a year later. Thereafter he traveled to Strasbourg, Martinique, and Spain before settling in Paris, where he spent the rest of his life.

A capable and prolific writer, he edited several magazines and published translations of English, German, and Italian literature, while publishing his first occult writings under a pseudonym. In the early 1850s he met and studied with Eliphas Lévi, and thereafter became more deeply involved in occultism. SEE LÉVI, ELIPHAS. Thereafter he developed a highly idiosyncratic version of astrology based on the thirty-six Egyptian decans; SEE DECANS.

Much of his fame rests on his massive *History of Magic*, originally published in 1870. Rambling, uneven, and historically inaccurate, it includes a detailed account of an "Egyptian initiation" based on the tarot, which is credited to Iamblichus of Chalcis but was made up out of whole cloth by Christian. SEE IAMBLICHUS OF CHALCIS. It also includes a long account of Cagliostro's prediction of the French Revolution; again, the entire scene is an invention of Christian's. SEE CAGLIOSTRO, COUNT ALESSANDRO. FURTHER READING: CHRISTIAN 1952, DECKER ET AL. 1996.

Christian Science. Founded by Mary Baker Eddy (1821–1910), the Church of Christ Scientist teaches that all disease and death are the product of human ignorance and sin. The essential theme of Christian Science teaching is that humanity, being made in the image of God, is spiritual rather than material, and so is not actually subject to material conditions and illnesses.

According to the church's official accounts, the key tenets of Christian Science were discovered by Eddy in 1866, when she was instantly healed of an injury after turning to the Bible. Her most important book, *Science and Health with Key to the Scriptures*, was published in 1875, and the first Christian Science church was founded in Boston in 1879. The organization grew rapidly in the late nineteenth and early twentieth centuries, but lost membership just as rapidly in the latter part of the twentieth century.

Eddy claimed that the entire body of Christian Science teaching was her own original discovery, but much of the material in *Science and Health* is closely parallel to the work of P. P. Quimby, a Mesmerist who treated Eddy in the 1860s. SEE QUIMBY, PHINEAS PARKHURST.

The ideas and teachings of Christian Science have played a noticeable part in the twentieth-century occult renaissance, and several major occultists—including Dion Fortune, arguably the most important magical theorist of the century—came out of a Christian Science background. SEE FORTUNE, DION. Eddy's ideas, by way of the New Thought movement, have had an even more pronounced influence on the modern New Age movement, and much of Christian Science teaching is also common parlance in New Age circles. SEE NEW AGE MOVEMENT. SEE ALSO CHRISTIAN OCCULTISM.

Christian Wicca. One of the most original offshoots of the current Neopagan ferment, Christian Wicca emerged in the 1990s in America, as people interested in Neopagan ways of practice but strongly attracted to traditional

Christian images of the divine sought to create a bridge between the two. As of this writing, the Christian Wicca (or Christo-Wiccan) movement is relatively small even by Neopagan standards and very diffuse, with few public spokespeople and fewer significant publications to its credit.

While generalizations are risky—no two Christian Wiccans seem to approach it in the same way—the movement centers on the use of Wiccan patterns of ritual and practice to worship the Trinity, the Virgin Mary, and the saints. The Virgin Mary and Mary Magdalene commonly fill the same role as the Goddess in other forms of Wicca, and God the Father seems to be less emphasized than in most other Christian denominations. The Christian ritual year and the eight Wiccan sabbats are typically combined, often by moving Christian feasts to coincide with the closest sabbat.

Christian Wicca has not been well received by the wider Pagan community, with responses ranging from reasoned criticisms to hysterical (and sometimes hysterically funny) denunciations. Many modern Pagans have incorporated a highly dualistic attitude toward religions, and react to the idea of worshipping Christ in a Wiccan circle the way fundamentalist Christians would react to worshipping the Horned God in church. Still, given that modern Paganism champions absolute religious freedom (and makes room for such dubious creations as Klingon Wicca; *SEE* FANTASY OCCULTISM), it's hard to come up with a meaningful reason why Christian Wicca should be excluded. *SEE ALSO* CHRISTIAN OCCULTISM; NEOPAGANISM; WICCA.

Church of Illumination. Religious body connected to the Fraternitas Rosae Crucis (FRC), an American Rosicrucian order. The Church of Illumination serves as an outer court to the FRC and presents an exoteric version—the "Divine Law"—of the FRC's esoteric teachings. *SEE* FRATERNITAS ROSAE CRUCIS (FRC).

Church of Light. American esoteric order, founded in 1932 by Elbert Benjamine (C. C. Zain) in Los Angeles. According to its traditions, the Church of Light descends from the Brotherhood of Light, a secret order that separated from the ancient Egyptian priesthood in 2440 B.C.E. and has remained active ever since, counting Akhenaten, Thales, Pythagoras, Plato, Eudoxus, and Hypatia among its initiates. In 1900, it contacted Benjamine, a young student of the occult; in 1909, after the death of one of the three heads who governed the brotherhood on the material plane, Benjamine was elected to the vacant spot and charged with the task of communicating the brotherhood's teachings to the world. This took the form of a correspondence course and school, which remains active today.

On the plane of ordinary history, the Church of Light can trace its antecedents to the Hermetic Brotherhood of Luxor (H. B. of L.), one of the major occult orders of the late nineteenth century, which claimed ancient Egyptian roots. *SEE* HERMETIC BROTHERHOOD OF LUXOR (H. B. OF L.). After the breakup of the H. B. of L., one of its members—Thomas Burgoyne—went to America, where he attempted to restart the order under the name of the Brotherhood of Light. This was the organization that Benjamine came into contact with; it seems certain that Benjamine was acting in good faith in repeating the traditional history of the brotherhood, and simply gave the account of its origins as he received it.

The Church of Light, according to its official publications, is dedicated to teaching the "Religion of the Stars," a spiritual approach to life based on astrology and occult philosophy. Members of the church who practice the Religion of the Stars are called "Stellarians."

The teachings of the Church of Light are still based on Benjamine's 21-volume, 210-lesson correspondence course, which covers astrology, alchemy, and magic in a great deal of detail. The entire correspondence course, or individual volumes of it, can be purchased by nonmembers, but there are special papers for members only. Those who complete the relevant lessons and pass an examination can work their way through the first twenty-one degrees of initiation; the second twenty-one require evidence of certain types of psychic experience, while the remaining eight depend on the attainment of advanced spiritual states. Members of the church who have completed the course can join a higher organization, the Order of the Sphinx.

The church maintained its headquarters in Los Angeles until 1998, when the head office moved to a new location in the Los Angeles suburbs. It remains active in a quiet way as of this writing. *SEE ALSO* ZAIN, C. C. FURTHER READING: GIBSON 1996, ZAIN 1914–1934.

Church of Satan. Satanist religious organization founded by Anton Szandor LaVey in 1966, based in San Francisco. Easily the most colorful and public of the modern Satanist organizations, the Church of Satan teaches a philosophy of "rational selfishness" based largely on the writings of Aleister Crowley, Friedrich Wilhelm Nietzche, and Ayn Rand. The existence of Satan as an actual being is not an article of belief. The traditional imagery and trappings of Satanism, by contrast, are very much a part of the church's ambience; inverted pentagrams, black robes, nude women on the altar, and the like are much in evidence in church publicity.

At one point, the church had a network of grottoes located in various American cities, but these were dissolved by LaVey, who felt that they had become social clubs rather than hotbeds of Satanism. For the last quarter century, as at present, the church consists primarily of a small group of active members in the San Francisco area, and a looser network of supporters spread more widely around the country and the world. *SEE ALSO* LAVEY, ANTON SZANDOR; SATANISM.

cibation. (Latin *cibatio*, "feeding") In alchemy, adding additional material to an alchemical vessel while it is partway through an alchemical process such as distillation. *SEE* ALCHEMY.

Cipher manuscript. A collection of loose papers, which are the original source of the Golden Dawn ritual and magical system, and which played a complex and still uncertain role in the founding of the Hermetic Order of the Golden Dawn. The manuscript is written on paper with a watermark of 1809, in a cipher borrowed from the cryptographic writings of Johannes Trithemius, and gives outlines of the rituals for what became the Outer Order of the Golden Dawn. *SEE* TRITHEMIUS, JOHANNES.

Several different stories were circulated in the Golden Dawn at different times to explain the origins of the manuscript. It was claimed, among other things, that it had been found in a used book shop, or that it had been given to Golden Dawn founder William Wynn Westcott by the Rev. A. F. A. Woodford, an elderly Freemason of magical and Rosicrucian interests. More recently, several writers have suggested on plausible grounds that it was

originally written by Kenneth Mackenzie, and reached Westcott along with papers relating to the Swedenborgian Rite of Masonry, which Westcott headed after Mackenzie's death. *SEE* FREEMASONRY; MACKENZIE, KENNETH ROBERT HENDERSON; WESTCOTT, WILLIAM WYNN.

Along with the manuscript, according to the accounts circulated in the Golden Dawn, was the name and address of an adept in Germany named Anna Sprengel. Westcott supposedly contacted her, and received from her the right to found the Hermetic Order of the Golden Dawn. The letters from "Anna Sprengel" have been shown conclusively to be forgeries, written in poor German by a native speaker of English. *SEE* SPRENGEL, ANNA. *SEE ALSO* GOLDEN DAWN, HERMETIC ORDER OF THE; PICKINGILL, GEORGE. FURTHER READING: KÜNTZ 1996.

circle, magical. An essential element in medieval and Renaissance ceremonial magic, the magical circle is still used by more traditional magicians today. It consists of a barrier of magically effective words and symbols that is laid out on the floor and surrounds the magician during his or her ritual work, providing protection against hostile spirits and forces. The magical circle may be drawn on the floor with chalk, painted or embroidered on a cloth background that can be put away between rituals, or permanently painted in place.

The magical circle seems to have entered use in Western occultism with some of the early grimoires; its roots are probably in Arabic magic. Many different designs can be found in medieval grimoires and books of goetic magic. *SEE* GOETIA; GRIMOIRE.

A circle for evocation; center square is the altar, top of circle is in the east

A somewhat different form of magical circle is used nowadays by modern Pagan and Wiccan practitioners. Traced out by a variety of means, it functions as a container for energy; thus its purpose is to keep things in, rather than to keep them out. As with all things relating to modern Pagan practice, there are a dizzying variety of ways to cast a circle of this kind; sprinkling ashes, sweeping with a broom, and tracing the circle in the air with an athame are all common methods.

In modern Pagan practice, the magical circle is often used in ritual as the basis for a cone of power. *SEE* CONE OF POWER.

Circles of Existence. In many traditions of modern Druidry, especially those influenced by Welsh Druid writer Iolo Morganwg (Edward Williams, 1747–1826), a system of reincarnation involving three states of being. The first, the Circle of Abred, consists of animal and plant incarnations, up to the human level, and is characterized by suffering, ignorance, and compulsion. The second, the Circle of Gwynfydd, consists of spiritual states of being from the human level on up, and is characterized by joy, knowledge, and freedom. The third, the Circle of Ceugant, is infinite, and may only be traversed by the divine.

Some accounts of the Three Circles hold that souls come into existence at the lowest level of Abred out of the cauldron of Annwn, which represents inanimate matter, and work their way up from there. Other accounts, influenced by Judeo-Christian beliefs in the Fall, claim that souls started out higher up but fell into Abred through attempting to traverse the unattainable realm of Ceugant. *SEE* ABRED; CEUGANT; DRUIDRY; GWYNFYDD. FURTHER READING: WILLIAMS AB ITHEL 2004.

circulation. In alchemy, a method by which the transformative powers of a substance can be steadily increased. Circulation is a form of distillation in which the distilled substance is either poured back onto the leftover, undistilled substance and distilled again, or piped back into the original distilling vessel while the distillation is still going on. In either case the same substances are distilled over and over again. The process is also known as cohobation.

Circulation is much used in the more advanced levels of spagyrics, the alchemical art of making medicines from herbs. It is also used in some approaches to making the Philosopher's Stone. *SEE* ALCHEMY; SPAGYRICS. *SEE ALSO* OUROBOROS.

circumambulation. The act of moving in a circle, an important element of some magical rituals. The direction and number of circumambulations is important in many systems of magic. In many modern occult systems, clockwise movement (referred to as "deosil" in Pagan parlance) is used to generate power and counterclockwise motion ("widdershins") is used to disperse it. *SEE* DEOSIL; WIDDERSHINS.

clairvoyance. (French, "clear seeing") The psychic ability to see events occurring at a distance in space or time, or on other planes of reality besides the physical. The term was invented in the late eighteenth century by the followers of Franz Anton Mesmer, who found that persons placed into trance by means of Mesmeric methods sometimes reported seeing things that were not present to the ordinary sense of vision, some of which proved to be accurate reflections of events going on elsewhere or at other times.

Methods for developing clairvoyant powers have been part of the stock in trade of occult traditions for many centuries, and a wide range of these methods have been published in the last century or so. Many of these relate to scrying—the traditional occult art of attaining visions in a crystal or other reflecting surface—or the related art of "scrying in the spirit vision," which uses the imagination as a vehicle for visionary experience. *SEE* SCRYING.

In the work of American occultist P. B. Randolph (1825–1875), two different forms of clairvoyance were distinguished: zorvoyance, the power to perceive the "middle Spaces" or astral plane, and aethaevoyance, the power to perceive the "ineffable Beyond" or mental and spiritual planes. This distinction is recognized in many occult writings, although Randolph's colorful terminology has not caught on. *SEE* RANDOLPH, PASCHAL BEVERLY.

Related to clairvoyance, and usually occurring together with it, are clairaudience, the power of psychic hearing, and clairsentience, which includes all other ways of sensing what is not apparent to the physical senses. FURTHER READING: BARDON 1962, W. BUTLER 1987, DEVENEY 1997.

Clan of Tubal-Cain. English witchcraft tradition founded by Robert Cochrane in the late 1950s and early 1960s, and reorganized by several of his students after Cochrane's death in 1966. The term "clan" was used by Cochrane in preference to "coven"; Cochrane felt the latter was too closely associated with Gerald Gardner's version of witchcraft, which Cochrane claimed to despise. The tradition is still practiced in England, and is the basis for the Plant Bran, a tradition mostly active in Britain, and the 1734 Tradition, practiced by many North American covens at present; SEE PLANT BRAN; 1734 TRADITION (UNDER S).

The Clan of Tubal-Cain claims roots in the family tradition inherited by Robert Cochrane, as well as in Cochrane's contacts with the folk magic of English blacksmiths and canal boatmen. It differs from Gardnerian Wicca in a number of ways. The most obvious difference is that nude ritual is not a part of the Tubal-Cain system; all workings are done in hooded black robes. The same calendar of sabbats and esbats is celebrated, but the rituals differ significantly, being simpler and more shamanistic. There is only one degree of initiation. The assignment of elements to the quarters is also different, with fire assigned to the east, air to the south, water to the west, and earth to the north. SEE DIRECTIONS IN OCCULTISM.

The working tools used in the Tubal-Cain tradition are the knife, the stang (a staff with a forked top, used as a symbol of the Horned God), the cord, the cup (usually made of horn), and the whetstone. The cauldron is also used in ritual as a symbol of the Goddess. SEE ALSO COCHRANE, ROBERT. FURTHER READING: JONES AND VALIENTE 1990, VALIENTE 1989.

cledonomancy. The art of divination by overhearing words by chance. A branch of omen divination, cledonomancy was much used by the ancient Greeks and Romans, and references to it can be found all through classical literature.

In his treatise *De Divinatione* (*On Divination*), the Roman writer Marcus Tullius Cicero cites the example of the consul Lucius Paulus, who was preparing to lead the Roman armies against Perseus, king of Macedonia, in 168 B.C.E. As he said his farewells to his family, he noted that his young daughter Tertia looked very sad, and asked her the reason. Her reply was "*Mi pater, Persa periit*" ("My father, Persa has died"). Persa was the name of her pet puppy, but Paulus took it as an omen that he would defeat Perseus—as in fact he did.

The practice of cledonomancy was common enough in classical times that some oracles were designed around it. The oracle of Hermes at Pharai in Greece, for example, required seekers to burn incense and light lamps to the god, place an offering of money, and then whisper their question into the ear of the god's statue. They would then cover their own ears, leave the oracle, and walk some distance away. When they uncovered their ears, the first words they heard were to be interpreted as the answer to their question.

Cledonomancy fell out of widespread use with the coming of Christianity, although it has been practiced now and again by people with a background in classical learning. It remains among the least widely known forms of divination at present. SEE ALSO DIVINATION; OMENS. FURTHER READING: FLACELIERE 1965.

Clutterbuck, Dorothy. English witch?, 1880–1951. Very little is known about her early life, beyond the fact that she was born in India to English parents. She returned to England with her parents when her father retired from the army, and settled in the New Forest region near Christchurch. She had a long-term relationship with a local landowner, Rupert Fordham, but had no children. Both she and Fordham were important figures in the Conservative Party and attended the local Anglican church regularly. Their joint gravestone is a large memorial cross with an inscription of perfect Christian orthodoxy.

According to Gardner, on the other hand, Clutterbuck was a member of the Rosicrucian Order of the Crotona Fellowship, an occult lodge that operated a "Rosicrucian Theatre"; SEE ROSICRUCIAN ORDER OF THE CROTONA FELLOWSHIP (ROCF). She was also, he claimed, the High Priestess of a coven of witches that had been active in the New Forest for many years. She and several other members of the coven, who were also active in the ROCF, approached Gardner and initiated him into Wicca in 1939, shortly after the beginning of the Second World War. She is also said to have played a central role in the famous working at Lammas of 1940, carried out by several covens in southern England, that sought to prevent a Nazi invasion of England.

It must be said that the evidence for Clutterbuck's activities as an occultist and a witch consists entirely of Gardner's unsupported word. Despite decades of searching, no other evidence for her involvement in Wicca or occultism has yet surfaced. Her private diaries from 1942 and 1943, when she was allegedly an active participant in Wiccan activities, make no references whatsoever to occultism, Pagan deities, the sabbats, or anything else relevant to Wicca. Gardner's own honesty and accuracy are highly suspect—he claimed doctorates he didn't have, and apparently forged his famous "OTO Charter"—and it is possible that his claims of Clutterbuck's involvement in Wicca were sheer inventions. *SEE ALSO* GARDNER, GERALD BROUSSEAU; WICCA. FURTHER READING: FARRAR 1984, HUTTON 1999.

clyssus. In spagyrics, an alchemical medicine made from a single plant. Traditionally all parts of a plant—root, stem, leaf, flower, and seed—were included in a clyssus.

An alchemical medicine made from several different plants is called an elixir. *SEE* SPAGYRICS.

Cochrane, Robert. English witch, 1933–1966. Of working-class background, Cochrane had a varied career, working as a blacksmith, a canal boatman, and a graphic designer at different times in his life. He claimed to have been initiated into a family tradition of witchcraft by a great-uncle, and also claimed to have learned magical traditions associated with the canal-boat and smithying subcultures.

A significant player in the witchcraft revival of the early 1960s, he organized a coven, the Clan of Tubal-Cain, around a system of witchcraft sharply different from the Gardnerian and Alexandrian approaches popular at that time. He insisted that witchcraft was not a Pagan religion, although it retained memories of ancient Pagan faiths. Rather, it was a mystery cult and a tradition of magic. *SEE* CLAN OF TUBAL-CAIN.

By all accounts, Cochrane was a brilliant magician and witch. Unfortunately he also had a strong authoritarian streak, and he became increasingly embroiled in disputes with those who disagreed with his version of witchcraft.

He was particularly virulent in his denunciation of Gardnerian Wicca. Several of the members of his coven left over these issues. He also began an affair with another member of the coven, and his wife, the coven's High Priestess, left him.

Cochrane was fascinated with the ritual use of traditional European psychedelic drugs, most of which are extremely poisonous. On midsummer of 1966, he ingested a lethal dose of deadly nightshade. He was found outside his house by a neighbor at 4 A.M., and taken to the hospital, but died three days later without regaining consciousness. The official verdict was suicide, although some have speculated that he may have died from an accidental overdose.

Despite his short and troubled career within the witchcraft movement, Cochrane left behind a substantial legacy. The Clan of Tubal-Cain was reorganized after his death and remains active as of this writing. Two other traditions—the Plant Bran, active mostly in Britain, and the 1734 Tradition, active mostly in America—also trace their roots to students of Cochrane. *SEE* PLANT BRAN; 1734 TRADITION (UNDER S). FURTHER READING: JONES AND VALIENTE 1990, VALIENTE 1989.

cohobation. *SEE* CIRCULATION.

Coligny calendar. The only legible example of a Celtic calendar from pre-Christian times, the Coligny calendar is a broken bronze plaque measuring 148 cm by 90 cm (about 4½ by 3 feet). The style of writing and the objects buried with the calendar date it to around the second century of the Common Era, but it is believed to be a late copy of a long-established calendar system almost certainly dating to Druidic times. Fragments of a similar calendar have been found at Lac d'Antre in the Jura Mountains.

The calendar follows a combined lunar-solar pattern, and is based on a repeating five-year cycle. Each year has twelve months of twenty-eight, twenty-nine, or thirty days each, arranged to track the lunar cycle of approximately 29.5 days. Twice in each five-year cycle—at the beginning of the first year and in the middle of the third—an additional, unnamed month is added to bring the cycles of moon and sun back into synchronization.

The twelve regular months are as follows:

1. Samonios (fortunate; 30 days)
2. Dumannos (unfortunate; 29 days)
3. Riuros (fortunate; 30 days)
4. Anaganios (unfortunate; 29 days)
5. Ogronnios (fortunate; 30 days)
6. Cutios (fortunate; 30 days)
7. Giamonios (unfortunate; 29 days)
8. Simivisonna (fortunate; 30 days)
9. Equos (unfortunate; variable)
10. Elembiu (unfortunate; 29 days)
11. Aedrini (fortunate; 30 days)
12. Cantlos (fortunate; 29 days)

According to the calendar, the thirty-day months of Samonios, Riuros, Ogronnios, Cutios, Simivisonna, and Aedrini are *mat* or fortunate, while the others are *anmat* or unlucky. The month of Equos, which has thirty days in the first, third, and fifth years of the cycle, and twenty-eight in the second and fourth, is anmat. The additional months have thirty days each, and are thus mat. The individual days in each month also have various characteristics, not all of which can be translated.

The Coligny calendar is unrelated to the Ogham tree-calendar, which is thought to be an ancient Druidic calendar by modern Pagans but was actually invented by English poet Robert Graves in the 1940s. *SEE* OGHAM; OGHAM TREE-CALENDAR.

The Coligny calendar does, however, have connections to authentic Celtic folklore and tradition. The month of Samonios is evidently related to the Irish Samhain; the seventeenth day of Samonios in the Coligny calendar is marked *trinox. samon. sindiu*—"the three nights of Samonios begin today"—and it's known that in Ireland the feast of Samhain traditionally lasted for three nights. The Celts' use of a lunar calendar is known from Greek and Roman sources, and each month in the Coligny calendar is divided into two fortnights, another detail attested in the classical sources. *SEE ALSO* DRUIDS.

Coll. (Old Irish, "hazel") The ninth letter in the Ogham alphabet, with the sound-value *k*. It corresponds to the hazel among trees, the crane among birds, the color

brown, and the number nine. In Robert Graves' version of the Ogham tree-calendar, its month runs from August 6 to September 2. *SEE* OGHAM.

Ogham letter Coll

collective unconscious. In the writings of psychologist Carl Jung and his followers, the deepest stratum of the unconscious that contains material relating not to the individual but to humanity as a whole. The most important presences in the collective unconscious are the archetypes. According to Jungian theory, these are reflections of primal instincts, and also the patterns on which gods and other mythic entities are based. Contacting the archetypal patterns of the collective unconscious in a conscious and balanced way is an important part of the process of individuation, the goal of Jungian psychological work. *SEE* INDIVIDUATION.

The concept of the collective unconscious, like that of the archetype, is in many ways a rephrasing in psychological language of the older Platonic concept of the world of forms or ideas, the realm of primal patterns that are reflected in ordinary life. *SEE* PLATONISM. *SEE ALSO* ARCHETYPE; JUNG, CARL GUSTAV; JUNGIAN PSYCHOLOGY.

color scales. In the lore of Cabalistic magic, tables of colors that are related to the different Sephiroth and Paths of the Tree of Life in each of the Four Worlds. The Golden Dawn magical tradition includes the most commonly used set of color scales, which are also used by followers of Aleister Crowley's religion of Thelema. The Ogdoadic tradition of the Aurum Solis has a somewhat different set of color scales. *SEE* AURUM SOLIS; CABALA; GOLDEN DAWN, HERMETIC ORDER OF THE. FURTHER READING: CROWLEY 1973, DENNING AND PHILLIPS 1988, REGARDIE 1974.

Co-Masonry. *SEE* FREEMASONRY.

Companions of the Coinherence. (Order of the Coinherence) Esoteric Christian order founded by English poet and occultist Charles Williams in 1939. Williams spent ten years (1917–1927) as a member of A. E. Waite's Fellowship of the Rosy Cross, an offshoot of the Hermetic Order of the Golden Dawn; *SEE* GOLDEN DAWN, HERMETIC ORDER OF THE; WAITE, ARTHUR EDWARD. Later he developed a more mystical approach to Christian theology based on the doctrines of coinherence—the idea that all beings share a common life and attain salvation through one another—and substitution—the idea that Christians are called to take on each other's psychological and spiritual burdens, in the same way that Christian theology holds Christ took on the sins of the world. These became the central principles of the Companions of the Coinherence.

The structure of the order is very simple, especially when compared to the elaborate Masonic structures of the Golden Dawn and its successor orders. There are no officers or formal rituals, and no laws or rules other than a set of seven guiding principles. Williams proclaimed that "the order has no constitution except in its members," and membership is conferred by each individual's decision to belong to it. The Companions meet four times a year, at the church feasts of the Annunciation, the Trinity, the Transfiguration, and All Souls. It remains quietly active at present, although by the nature of the order details are not easy to come by. *SEE ALSO* CHRISTIAN OCCULTISM; WILLIAMS, CHARLES.

Comte de Gabalis, Le. Occult novel by the Abbé N. de Montfaucon de Villars (1635–1673), a French ecclesiastic of markedly sceptical beliefs. His novel was originally published in 1670. It recounts the conversations of a nameless narrator, who pretends a knowledge of occultism, with a German adept of noble birth—the Comte of the title—about elemental spirits. The Comte's teachings have to do with the value, and indeed the necessity, of frequent sexual relations between human beings and elementals. The entire book is written in a tone of high hilarity and mockery—a detail which has not prevented some occultists from claiming it as a deep magical allegory. *SEE ALSO* ELEMENTAL; SEX AND OCCULTISM. FURTHER READING: DE MONTFAUCON DE VILLARS 1963.

condenser. *SEE* FLUID CONDENSER.

cone of power. In modern Wiccan and Pagan practice, a pattern of energy formulated in and above a magical circle. The cone uses the outer edge of the circle as its base, and a point high above the circle's center as its apex. Building a cone of power is done in different ways by different traditions; dancing, chanting, visualization, drumming, and other methods of altering consciousness are used for this purpose. Once built, the cone of power is released so that its energies can accomplish the purpose of the ritual.

According to Gerald Gardner, the founder of modern Wicca, the cone of power is one of the "old ways" inherited from witches of the Middle Ages and before. As with so many of the claims of ancient roots for modern Pagan practices, the evidence to support this claim is conspicuously absent; no reference to cones of power in older sources on witchcraft or Paganism has come to light, despite many years of searching on the part of modern Pagans. It is thus probable that the cone of power is one of Gardner's major contributions to modern magical practice. *SEE* GARDNER, GERALD BROUSSEAU. *SEE ALSO* CIRCLE, MAGICAL; NEOPAGANISM; WICCA.

congelation. In alchemy, the process of allowing a liquid or molten substance to cool gradually and solidify. Alchemical symbolism relates this process to the zodiacal sign Taurus. *SEE* ALCHEMY.

Conjunctio. (Latin, "conjunction") A geomantic figure governed by Mercury. In divination, it represents meetings and combinations of forces, either for good or ill. *SEE* GEOMANCY.

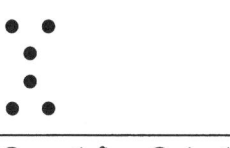

Geomantic figure Conjunctio

conjunction. In astrology, the aspect between two planets or other important points that occupies the same degree of the zodiac. Two or more factors that are in conjunction are allied and aligned, working in such close harmony that they cannot usually be untangled from one another. Like most astrological aspects, a conjunction has an "orb" or area around the exact point of conjunction in which the energies of the aspect are still felt; most atrologers give a conjunction an orb of eight degrees. *SEE* ASTROLOGY.

conjure magic. *SEE* HOODOO.

consecration. The process of charging an object with magical or spiritual energies, either to transform it into a working tool or to empower it to perform some specific work of magic. The art of consecration is central to many modes of magical practice.

The methods of consecration used in most current systems of ceremonial magic are relatively complex, and call on the full armamentarium of ritual magic methods. In a standard consecration ritual, the magician begins by preparing the space and banishing unwanted influences, then invokes the energies that will charge the object, tracing geometrical figures in the air, pronouncing divine names and words of power, burning appropriate incenses, and so forth. Once the desired energy has reached a high enough level of intensity, it is then projected into the object. The consecrated object is then wrapped in silk or some other insulating material to keep its energies from being discharged by the closing phases of the ceremony, excess energies are banished, and the ritual is brought to an end.

In modern Pagan practice, a simpler approach is generally used to consecrate working tools, altar furnishings, and the like. The object to be consecrated is sprinkled with salt or salted water, blessed with smoke from incense, and anointed with a specially prepared oil. The words used to consecrate range from a simple statement that negative energies are being expelled and replaced by positive ones on up to extensive invocations of one or more deities. *SEE ALSO* CEREMONIAL MAGIC; TALISMAN.

Constant, Alphonse Louis. *SEE* LÉVI, ELIPHAS.

Coptic. A medieval and modern language descended from ancient Egyptian, and still spoken by the Coptic minority in Egypt. The Coptic language is written with an alphabet derived from Greek. In the Hermetic Order of the Golden Dawn, Coptic spellings of the names of Egyptian gods were taught and used, and some efforts were made to develop the Coptic alphabet as a symbolic system parallel to the Hebrew alphabet; very little work

seems to have been done in this direction since the order's collapse in 1900. *SEE* GOLDEN DAWN, HERMETIC ORDER OF THE; HEBREW ALPHABET.

cord. A working tool and item of regalia in modern occult systems. In many current Pagan traditions, a variety of colored cords are used as regalia for the three degrees of initiation. In many Wiccan traditions, for example, first degree initiates wear a white cord, second degree initiates a red cord, and third degree initiates a blue or black cord. Given the diversity of modern Paganism, varying explanations for these colors have been circulated, and many other color sequences also exist. Some magical lodge organizations have also taken to using colored cords as regalia for the degrees of initiation. *SEE* DEGREE(S).

In modern Pagan practice, the ritual cord (or other cords) are often used for various sorts of spellwork. Knots may be tied into a cord to hold magical energies in place, or a cord may be wrapped around a magically consecrated object as a binding.

Cornua Lunae. (Latin, "horns of the moon") In the Aurum Solis system of magic, the second lowest of the six energy centers of the human body, related to the Sephirah Yesod and located at the genitals. In the Rousing of the Citadels, an Aurum Solis exercise equivalent to the Middle Pillar exercise, it is visualized as a radiant lavender sphere, half of which projects from the front of the body. Its Name of Power is ShDI AL Chi, Shaddai El Chai.

It corresponds to the second chakra and to the Yesod center of the Middle Pillar exercise. *SEE* AURUM SOLIS; MIDDLE PILLAR EXERCISE; ROUSING OF THE CITADELS.

Corona Flammae. (Latin, "crown of flames") In the Aurum Solis system of magic, the highest of the six energy centers of the human body, related to the Sephirah Kether and located above the crown of the head. In the Rousing of the Citadels, an Aurum Solis exercise equivalent to the Middle Pillar exercise, it is visualized as a brilliant white sphere above the head. Its Name of Power is AHIH, Eheieh.

It corresponds to the crown chakra and to the Kether center of the Middle Pillar exercise. *SEE* AURUM SOLIS; MIDDLE PILLAR EXERCISE; ROUSING OF THE CITADELS.

Corpus Christi. In the Catholic Church, a festival held on the first Thursday after Trinity Sunday, celebrating the mystery of the Eucharist. Originally proposed by Saint Juliana (1193–1258) and first celebrated in Belgium in 1247, it was added to the liturgical calendar in 1264. It seems to have had no connection whatsoever with the Western occult traditions until the emergence of the Hermetic Order of the Golden Dawn.

In Golden Dawn rituals and knowledge lectures, the mysterious "Day C" of the Rosicrucian manifestoes is identified as the festival of Corpus Christi, and most currently active Golden Dawn temples follow this tradition. *SEE* GOLDEN DAWN, HERMETIC ORDER OF THE; ROSICRUCIANS.

Corpus Hermeticum. A collection of fifteen treatises attributed to Hermes Trismegistus, originally written in Egypt at some point between the first and third centuries of the Common Era. The surviving set of treatises are only a small part of what was once a very large literature produced by Egyptian Hermeticists. *SEE* HERMETICISM.

After the triumph of Christianity in the Mediterranean world and the suppression of Pagan religious traditions, the *Corpus Hermeticum* survived in a few collections in the Byzantine Empire, which retained enough interest in Neoplatonist philosophy to value it. A copy is known to have been in the possession of the Greek Neoplatonist Michael Psellus.

Around 1460, a copy of the *Corpus Hermeticum* was obtained by one of the agents of Cosimo de Medici, ruler of Florence, who was amassing western Europe's largest library of Greek works. When this copy came to Cosimo's attention in 1463, he asked Marsilio Ficino—the young head of Florence's Platonic Academy, then about to start work on the first Latin translation of the complete works of Plato—to put Plato aside and translate Hermes first. *SEE* FICINO, MARSILIO. The translation was finished in 1464, and became an immediate bestseller by the standards of the time, going through sixteen editions before the end of the sixteenth century.

This popularity was in part the result of a mistake in dating. Until 1614, when Isaac Casaubon demonstrated the real date of the treatises on linguistic grounds, scholars across Europe believed that the Hermetic writings dated from far more ancient times. Hermes Trismegistus himself was usually thought to be a contemporary of Moses, and thus the first philosopher and theologian in human history. Hermetic writings were cited by a number of early Christian writers, including Lactantius and Augustine, who accepted the same early date. During the century and a half after Ficino's translation was published, therefore, educated Europeans saw the *Corpus Hermeticum* as nothing less than the oldest wisdom in the world. The magical doctrines included in the treatises thus played a major role in laying the foundation for the Renaissance magical synthesis.

The great popularity of the *Corpus Hermeticum* came to an end in 1614 with the publication of a detailed study of its origins by Isaac Casaubon (1559–1614), a Swiss Protestant scholar living in England. (It is an interesting detail that his son, Meric Casaubon, carried on the family tradition of hostility to occultism and was responsible for publishing the diaries of John Dee's angelic workings in an attempt to discredit the great Elizabethan magus; *SEE* DEE, JOHN.) Casaubon pointed out that the treatises mention the Greek sculptor Phidias and the Pythian games, quote from many Greek authors dating from long after Hermes' supposed lifetime, and are written in a late style of Greek using words that do not appear until Christian times.

Casaubon's conclusions were almost universally accepted at the time and, with some modifications, are still accepted by scholars today. A few stalwart Hermeticists such as Robert Fludd dismissed or denied Casaubon's arguments, but with very little effect. The Hermetic treatises received very little attention until recent times, when the writings of historians such as Frances Yates pointed out their importance to the history of magic, and a small but significant number of modern magicians began to include Hermetic materials in their work. *SEE ALSO* HERMES TRISMEGISTUS. FURTHER READING: YATES 1964.

corpus mundi. (Latin, "body of the world") In Renaissance magical philosophy, the physical universe, which relates to the spiritus mundi and anima mundi in exactly the same way that the human body relates to its vital energy and soul. *SEE* ANIMA MUNDI; SPIRITUS MUNDI.

coscinomancy. (Greek, "sieve divination") Divination with sieve and shears, an extremely ancient form of divination still practiced by folk diviners in several European countries, and used principally to detect the guilty party in criminal cases. A pair of shears are opened to form an X shape, and balanced on the thumbnails of two persons; a winnowing sieve is placed on top of the shears, balanced on the center. The two people supporting the shears look into each others' eyes. After a prayer or incantation is recited, the names of all those suspected of the crime are read aloud. When the guilty party's name is read, the sieve will turn or shift.

Coscinomancy was much used by the ancient Greeks, and is referred to by the Greek poet Theocritus in his *Third Idyll*. SEE ALSO DIVINATION.

cosmic cycles. SEE CYCLES, COSMIC.

coven. In Scottish folklore and modern Pagan practice, a group of witches. The traditional number of members in a coven is thirteen, and Margaret Murray, whose writings on medieval witchcraft were a major source for modern Wicca, insisted that this was an absolute rule. The medieval evidence does not support her claim, however, as groups of thirteen are hard to find in pre-Murray discussions of witchcraft lore or the witch trials.

The word *coven* is a Scots English version of *convent* or *conventicle*, and simply means "gathering." It appears in the records of a few Scottish witchcraft trials, and was taken from these sources by Murray.

In modern Wicca and many other Pagan traditions, the coven is the basic unit of organization, and consists of three or more people who meet at least often enough to celebrate the eight sabbats. While thirteen is considered the optimum number of members, this requirement is usually honored in the breach, and covens range in size from three members to twenty or more. In most Wiccan traditions, the leadership of a coven is centered in the High Priestess, who may or may not share her authority with a High Priest. Other officers include a Maiden, who is female and assists the High Priestess, and a Summoner or Guardian, who is male and assists the High Priest; these positions are often held by members in training to become High Priestesses or High Priests themselves. SEE ALSO WICCA.

covendom. In Wicca, the geographical area over which a coven has authority and from which it draws its members, supposedly one league (three miles) in all directions from the covenstead, which is the place where a coven meets. Covendoms have little relevance to the present-day realities of Wicca and the rules governing them are rarely observed. SEE COVEN.

covener. In Wicca, a member of a coven. SEE COVEN.

covenstead. In Wicca, the meeting place of a coven. SEE COVEN.

cowan. A Scots dialect term meaning a person who builds drystone walls (that is, stone walls without mortar). In the days when Freemasons actually made things out of stone, it came to be used as a label for those who worked as stonemasons but were not members of the mason's guild. Inherited by later Freemasons as a label for those outside their order, it was borrowed by Wicca in the mid-twentieth century and now appears in most Neopagan traditions as a general label for "outsider." There are few better examples of the way that the meanings of a word in occult circles can mutate over time. SEE FREEMASONRY; WICCA.

Craft, the. A term used by modern Wiccans to refer to their religious and magical traditions; also a term used by Freemasons to refer to Freemasonry. The Wiccan usage is a shortened form of "the Craft of the Wise," Gerald Gardner's (inaccurate) translation of the Anglo-Saxon original of the word *witchcraft*. SEE FREEMASONRY; WICCA; WITCH.

craft name. In most modern Pagan traditions, a name taken by an initiate for Pagan use. In the early days of the Pagan revival, craft names were generally kept secret from everyone except members of one's own coven, but this tradition has largely gone by the boards in recent years, and many modern Pagans seem to treat their craft names as something like fashion accessories.

Craft names are often assembled from a variety of words that are meaningful to the bearer, with animal names especially common; Starhawk and Silver Ravenwolf (the craft names of two famous contemporary Wiccans) are good examples of the type.

The term "craft name" may have been borrowed by the Pagan revival of the late twentieth century from the Woodcraft movement, which used the phrase "woodcraft name" for essentially the same concept. The magical mottoes used in many Hermetic and Rosicrucian magical orders may also have had an influence. *SEE* MOTTO, MAGICAL; WOODCRAFT. *SEE ALSO* NEOPAGANISM; WICCA.

Cremer, John. English alchemist, fl. fourteenth century C.E. Nothing at all is known about his life. According to references in his brief alchemical work, *The Testament of Cremer*, he was a Benedictine monk and the abbot of Westminster Abbey, although no John Cremer appears on the records of Westminster's abbots. The same document claims that Cremer studied with Ramon Lull (1232–1315), the brilliant Spanish mystic, who was reputed to be an alchemist; it has been suggested by Raphael Patai, in a recent book on the history of alchemy, that Cremer may actually have studied with Ramon de Tarrega, an alchemist whose works were later attributed to Lull. *SEE* TARREGA, RAMON DE. *SEE ALSO* ALCHEMY.

Cromlech Temple. British occult group founded about 1900, with a membership largely drawn from Golden Dawn circles and a semi-official connection to the Alpha et Omega—the section of the Golden Dawn that remained loyal to Samuel Mathers after the revolt of 1900.

Despite its Celtic-sounding name, the Cromlech Temple was devoted to Christian occultism and mysticism, and its initiatory rituals drew on Zoroastrian elements—not an unusual mix for a British occult group at the time. Members practiced a variety of rituals, including a thoroughly Christianized ceremony based on the Lesser Ritual of the Pentagram. Much of this material was received from an inner plane source calling itself Ara ben Shemesh, a Sun Master.

The Cromlech Temple appears to have died out around World War II in England, although a group in New Zealand connected to the Smaragdum Thalasses branch of the Golden Dawn kept working the rituals until the 1960s. It has recently been revived in England. *SEE ALSO* CHRISTIAN OCCULTISM; GOLDEN DAWN, HERMETIC ORDER OF THE. FURTHER READING: KING 1971A.

croomstick. In English folk magic, a staff with a curved upper end, like a conventional cane or shepherd's crook, but longer. It is used for a wide range of magical and practical purposes. The upper end should be sized so that when the user holds it at arm's length, one-sixteenth of the circle of the horizon is visible within the curve. *SEE ALSO* STAFF. FURTHER READING: PENNICK 1989.

cross. A geometrical figure much used in some branches of magic, the cross is by no means entirely a Christian symbol, although for the last two thousand years in the Western world it has often been associated with the cross on which Jesus of Nazareth was executed. A cross with four equal arms is often used as an emblem of the four elements; *SEE* ELEMENTS, MAGICAL. *SEE ALSO* CHRISTIAN OCCULTISM.

crossing. In hoodoo, a curse, or the process of putting a curse on somebody; the removal of a curse is called "uncrossing." Both these terms have been adopted into several other magical traditions in North America. *SEE* CURSE; HOODOO; UNCROSSING.

crossroads. The place where two or more roads cross has been a place of magic since ancient times. The Greek goddess of magic, Hekate, ruled over crossroads where three roads met, and sacrifices were offered to her at such places. Later, in the Middle Ages, folklore claimed that sorcerers went to crossroads to conjure the Devil. Suicides and suspected vampires were buried there, and to this day practitioners of hoodoo and other forms of folk magic make use of crossroads as a place for various types of magical workings. *SEE ALSO* CROSS; HOODOO.

crow. In alchemy, a symbol of the nigredo or black phase of the work, the dissolution and putrefaction of the First Matter. *SEE* ALCHEMY.

Crowley, Aleister. (Edward Alexander Crowley) English writer, occultist, Antichrist, and self-proclaimed messiah of the New Aeon, 1875–1947. Easily the most controversial figure in the recent history of Western occultism, Crowley was born into the Plymouth Brethren, a small and deeply puritanical Protestant sect that originated most of modern Fundamentalist Christian theology. His father, a wealthy brewer, died when Crowley was five years old, leaving him to be raised by his mother and uncle. He had an excellent (and expensive) public school education and went to Trinity College, Cambridge, where he dabbled in chemistry but left without taking a degree.

While at college, he wrote and self-published his first books, a collection of philosophical poetry entitled *Aceldama* and a volume of pornographic verse entitled *White Stains*. Upon encountering a copy of A. E. Waite's *Book of Black Magic and of Pacts*, however, his interests turned to the occult, and in 1898 he was initiated into the Hermetic Order of the Golden Dawn. *SEE* GOLDEN DAWN, HERMETIC ORDER OF THE.

As a member of the order, he studied with the occultist and Buddhist Allan Bennett (1872–1923), but was denied advancement to the Adeptus Minor grade and the order's inner magical teachings because the senior adepts of the order in London disapproved of his behavior. *SEE* BENNETT, ALLAN. The order's chief, Samuel Liddell Mathers (1854–1918), proceeded to initiate him into the Adeptus Minor grade in Paris, an act that helped bring about the schism in the order in 1900. During the schism Crowley remained loyal to Mathers and acted as the chief's emissary, although his inept handling of his mission and his insistence on parading about in full Highland dress through the whole affair did not help Mathers' cause. *SEE* MATHERS, SAMUEL LIDDELL.

Crowley's lifestyle at this time was still fueled by his inherited money, and he traveled widely, went on mountain climbing expeditions, and devoted much of his time to chess, poetry, and a variety of sexual liaisons. It is entirely in character that he paid the chef of a London hotel to name a dish after him, *sole à lá Crowley*, and commissioned Augustus John—the most prestigious portraitist of the time—to paint his portrait.

In 1903 he married Rose Kelly, the daughter of a portrait painter, and took her on a world tour by way of honeymoon. The next year, while in Cairo, he received—according to his account, via a disembodied but clearly audible voice—a communication from a spirit named Aiwass, who claimed to be the representative of the spiritual powers governing the next age of world his-

tory, the Aeon of Horus. Over a three-day period, Aiwass dictated to Crowley the text of *Liber AL vel Legis*, the Book of the Law, and proclaimed Crowley the Beast 666 from the Book of Revelation. *SEE* BOOK OF THE LAW.

Thereafter, as his marriage disintegrated and his literary career ground to a halt, Crowley's involvement in magic became steadily more intense, and he gradually became convinced of the accuracy of Aiwass' message and his own messianic role. With the last of his inherited money, he founded and ran a lavish magazine—*The Equinox*—devoted to the occult. In its pages, he published many of the Golden Dawn papers and brought them for the first time to the attention of the broader occult community. A variety of intensive magical workings, alone or with others, convinced him that he was working his way up the grades of magical attainment. He also accepted initiation into the Ordo Templi Orientis, a small quasi-Masonic organization run by a dubious character named Theodor Reuss, and went on to take over large parts of the order and reshape it to fit his philosophy. *SEE* ORDO TEMPLI ORIENTIS (OTO).

At the outbreak of World War I he moved to the United States, where he supported himself by journalism, pursued his magical training, and involved himself in the politics of the American occult scene. In 1920 he and a small group of followers moved to Cefalu, in Sicily, where they established what would now be called a commune and devoted their time to sex, magic, and drugs. There Crowley went through an experience that, in his opinion, marked his ascent to the grade of Ipsissimus, the highest level of magical attainment. Shortly thereafter Raoul Loveday, one of the community's members, died of food poisoning. The result was a public scandal in Great Britain and Italy, and the Italian dictator Mussolini ordered Crowley expelled from the country.

After the collapse of the Cefalu community, Crowley spent a while in Tunisia and France, becoming a heroin addict in the process, and finally returned to England. Not long after his return, he happened to read a passage in the autobiography of British sculptor Nina Hammett that referred to him as a "black magician." Crowley reacted by suing her for libel. Unfortunately for him, British libel law required her to prove the accuracy of her statement in order to defend herself. This she did, in the eyes of the jury, the press, and the public, in a sensational trial that left Crowley's reputation and finances in shreds.

Crowley spent the remainder of his life in cheap lodgings, first in London and later in Hastings, on the Sussex coast, corresponding with a small circle of students and scrambling to support his drug habit. While rumors in the occult community have claimed for decades that he was hired to write the original Wiccan Book of Shadows by Gerald Gardner, there is no evidence that this is true, and a good deal of evidence that Gardner wrote it himself after Crowley's demise. SEE BOOK OF SHADOWS; GARDNER, GERALD BROUSSEAU. On Crowley's death, his estate was valued at fourteen shillings. SEE ALSO THELEMA. FURTHER READING: CAMMELL 1951, CROWLEY 1989, FULLER 1990, KING 1977, KING 1991.

crucible. In alchemy, a small container of heat-proof ceramic used to melt metals. Most modern crucibles are made of porcelain. SEE ALCHEMY.

crucifixion. The act of fastening a person to a cross, usually as a means of execution. While Jesus of Nazareth is the most famous victim of this procedure, he was far from the first or the only one. Like hanging, it may derive from old traditions of human sacrifice in which the person being killed had to be kept from touching the ground.

In the hands of the Romans, who perfected it as a means of capital punishment, it became an exercise in slow and painful death. The crucified person was tied or nailed to the cross, raised up in the air, and left to die from a combination of thirst, exposure, and suffocation (since the weight of the body pulling down on the arms makes expanding the chest steadily more difficult as exhaustion sets in).

In some initiation rituals drawing on Christian symbolism, such as the Adeptus Minor grade of the Hermetic Order of the Golden Dawn, the candidate is briefly crucified, using ropes rather than nails. SEE ADEPTUS MINOR; GOLDEN DAWN, HERMETIC ORDER OF THE.

crystallomancy. The art of divination by scrying in a crystal. SEE DIVINATION; SCRYING.

Cthulhu. In the supernatural horror fiction of H. P. Lovecraft and a variety of magical and pseudo-magical systems derived from this source, Cthulhu is a vast, bat-winged, tentacled horror, the most widely known of the nightmarish Elder Gods described in the *Necronomicon*. SEE NECRONOMICON.

Cube of Space. In the Cabala, a symbolic structure for the Hebrew alphabet that functions, in some ways, as an alternative to the Cabalistic Tree of Life. The Cube of Space is based on the Sepher Yetzirah, the oldest surviving proto-Cabalistic document; SEE SEPHER YETZIRAH.

In the Sepher Yetzirah, nineteen of the twenty-two Hebrew letters are assigned to directions in space. The seven double letters go with the six primary directions (up, down, east, west, north and south) and the center; the twelve single letters go with the "angles" between these (northeast, north above, and so on). Thus the single and double letters trace out the boundaries of a cube: the double letters are the six faces and the center, and the single letters are the twelve edges. This cube was visualized in Jewish methods of meditation based on the Sepher Yetzirah.

The American Cabalist and magician Paul Foster Case (1884–1956) was responsible for reshaping the cube of letters from the Sepher Yetzirah into the Cube of Space as currently used among Western ceremonial magicians. He made two major additions to the system, adding the three mother letters as the three dimensions (up-down, east-west, and north-south), and applying the Major Arcana of the Tarot to the Cube. With these additions, the Cube has gone on to become a significant part of modern Cabalistic studies within the occult community.

Aleph	Up/down axis
Beth	Upper face
Gimel	Lower face
Daleth	Eastern face
Heh	Northeast edge
Vau	Southeast edge
Zayin	Upper east edge
Cheth	Lower east edge
Teth	Upper north edge

Yod	Lower north edge
Kaph	Western face
Lamed	Northwest edge
Mem	East/west axis
Nun	Southwest edge
Samech	Upper west edge
Ayin	Lower west edge
Peh	Northern face
Tzaddi	Upper south edge
Qoph	Lower south edge
Resh	Southern face
Shin	North/south axis
Tau	Center

SEE ALSO CABALA; HEBREW ALPHABET. FURTHER READING: HULSE 2000, KAPLAN 1990, TOWNLEY 1993.

cucurbite. (Latin *cucurbitus*, "cucumber") In alchemical parlance, a vessel of glass or fireproof pottery shaped roughly like a cucumber and used for holding substances to be heated on the athanor, or alchemical furnace. The cucurbite is the lower half of the traditional alchemical distillation equipment; when used for this purpose, it was topped with an alembic. In modern sexual theories of alchemy, it is sometimes used as a symbol of the vagina. *SEE* ALCHEMY; ALEMBIC.

Culianu, Ioan Petru. Romanian scholar and occultist, 1950–1991. Born into a former aristocratic family in Iasi, in eastern Romania, he entered the University of Bucharest in 1967. There he encountered the writings of Romanian expatriate Mircea Eliade on yoga and religion, and became an avid student of yoga and Hindu philosophy, practicing yogic postures for hours each day. His academic studies in Renaissance literature and philosophy brought him into contact with the writings of major magical theorists such as Marsilio Ficino and Giordano Bruno, and this sparked a lifelong interest—both academic and practical—in Renaissance magic. *SEE* BRUNO, GIORDANO; FICINO, MARSILIO. From Bruno's work, he derived a particular interest in the Art of Memory, which he practiced systematically; *SEE* ART OF MEMORY.

In 1972, after graduating, he won a scholarship to Italy for a summer program, and while there defected. After eight months in a refugee camp, he found a position as a teaching assistant in Milan and began a meteoric scholarly career. Living in Italy gave him access to the entire range of Renaissance magical writings, and he honed his mastery of the Art of Memory. A friend during this period later recalled Culianu routinely studying for fifteen or sixteen hours at a stretch without taking notes, using the Art of Memory to store what he learned (Anton 1996, p. 83).

He received a doctorate in 1975, became a professor at Groningen University in Holland in 1976, received two additional doctorates from the Sorbonne, and published his magnum opus, *Eros and Magic in the Renaissance*, in 1984. In 1988, after several stints as a guest lecturer there, he was hired as a professor of history of religions at the University of Chicago. At Chicago, he became well-known among students for giving highly accurate tarot and geomancy divinations at parties, and taught classes in which Western occult traditions and practices were a major feature.

The late 1980s were a period of increasing repression in Romania as the communist government of Nicolae Ceausescu lurched from crisis to crisis, and as a prominent Romanian exile, Culianu was drawn into the political fray. The exact details of his involvement are unclear, but he was active in circulating petitions against the Ceausescu regime, and his family in Romania played a significant role in the revolution when it broke out in 1989. After the revolution, he played a prominent role in denouncing the new government's attempts to maintain its power and preserve elements of the communist system. He published numerous articles in the Romanian emigré press attacking the new regime, and become one of its foremost critics.

On May 21, 1991, Culianu was murdered in a restroom on the University of Chicago campus. The killing was execution-style, a single bullet to the back of the head. No suspects were ever apprehended. The theory that the murder was done by Romanian security forces remains unproved, but no other motive has surfaced. FURTHER READING: ANTON 1996, CULIANU 1987.

culmination. The position of a star or planet when it reaches the midheaven or zenith; SEE MIDHEAVEN. A star or planet that is culminating is considered to be at the summit of its power and effect. Some magical operations are timed to take place when a particular star or planet is culminating; SEE ELECTIONAL ASTROLOGY.

cunning man/woman. English term for a practitioner of folk magic, commonly used during the period when "witch" was equated with "worshipper of Satan." During the Burning Times, in fact, cunning men and women were often hired by peasants or local governments to locate the evil witches in whose existence most people devoutly believed. They also practiced healing, using herbs as well as magical charms, and carried out divination to find lost objects, identify suitable marriage partners, predict the success of the year's crops, and the like. Some practiced astrology, crystal scrying, or card divination for clients.

There is no evidence that cunning men and women were practitioners of a non-Christian religion. On the contrary, many were devout Christians who attended the same churches as their neighbors. Detailed information on the magical techniques used by cunning folk has been gathered by British folklorists in the last century or so, and again, no trace of Paganism appears; in fact, prayers to the Trinity and the saints, quotations from the Bible, and other details of Christian folk magic are a frequent feature.

A number of the standard handbooks of Renaissance high magic, such as Cornelius Agrippa's *Three Books of Occult Philosophy*, and astrological textbooks and almanacs, were popular resources among cunning folk. Some apparently had access to ancient magical traditions that have since been lost; it is hard to find any other explanation of the seventeenth-century lead binding tablets, made according to ancient Greek specifications, found in several places in England. SEE BINDING TABLET. On the other hand, standard folk magic such as witch bottles and herbalism also entered into the repertoire of the cunning folk. SEE NATURAL MAGIC; WITCH BOTTLE.

Cunning men and women were also called conjurers, white witches, wizards, and similar titles. They remained active in rural England up until the first decades of the twentieth century, and can still be found in some rural districts today. SEE ALSO WITCH. FURTHER READING: HUTTON 1999, MACFARLANE 1991, MAPLE 1970, MERRIFIELD 1987.

Cunningham, Scott. American writer and occultist, 1956–1993. Born in a middle-class California family, Cunningham became interested in witchcraft in his teen years and was initiated into the Standing Stone tradition of Wicca in 1973. He later took initiation into three other Wiccan traditions, but shifted to a solitary approach to magic beginning in 1982. He was among the first public Pagan figures in America to espouse solitary practice as an option for Pagans; this stance brought him into conflict with many defenders of the older, coven-based approach to Pagan training and worship, but proved enormously popular in the American Pagan community as a whole.

After a brief period in the navy, he embarked on a writing career, publishing in a range of popular genres. His first book on occult topics, *Magical Herbalism*, was published in 1982, and became a major success. This and several of his later books, including *Cunningham's Encyclopedia of Magical Herbs* (1985) and the controversial *Wicca: A Guide for the Solitary Practitioner* (1989), made him a household name in the American Pagan scene.

Even as Cunningham's career was expanding, however, his health was beginning to fail due to HIV infection. He survived a bout with cancer in 1983, but came down with meningitis in 1990 and nearly died. After a brief recovery, the meningitis returned, along with other opportunistic infections, and he died of AIDS complications in 1993. SEE ALSO NEOPAGANISM; SOLITARY PRACTITIONER; WICCA. FURTHER READING: CUNNINGHAM 1982, CUNNINGHAM 1988, HARRINGTON AND REGULA 1996.

cup. In ceremonial magic, the elemental weapon or working tool of water. The use of the cup as a ritual tool was introduced by Eliphas Lévi (1810–1875), who was inspired by the four suits of the tarot deck. By way of the Hermetic Order of the Golden Dawn, which adopted and expanded on Lévi's invention, the use of the cup as a magical implement has become all but universal in modern magical circles. *SEE* LÉVI, ELIPHAS; WATER, ELEMENT OF.

In Wicca, the cup or chalice is used as a symbol of the feminine powers and the Goddess. In some Wiccan traditions, the Great Rite (ritual sexual intercourse) is performed symbolically by dipping the athame, the witch's dagger, into the chalice. *SEE* GREAT RITE; WICCA.

The cup as a symbol of elemental water

curse. A magical working intended to bring misfortune, sickness, injury, or death to its target. Among the most common kinds of magic in folklore and magical tradition alike, curses can be found in every tradition of magic, from around the world and throughout time.

Methods of cursing vary as widely as magical traditions, but there are common threads. Figures of wax, clay, or cloth—called voodoo dolls in popular culture, and poppets in magical jargon—are one common medium for a curse. Objects associated with the victim, such as hair, nail clippings, or clothing, are also commonly used. Magically charged objects can be placed in the victim's house, or simply in a place where he or she will step over them; alternatively, if one can find the victim's footprint, a nail or a knife can be driven into it, accompanied by the proper incantation. In ancient Greece and Rome, the standard approach to cursing was to write a letter to the powers of the underworld on a sheet of lead; the lead sheet was folded and dropped into a well, a cave, a tomb, or some other entrance to the underworld; *SEE* BINDING TABLET.

The methods used to break curses are as varied as those used to inflict them. If a magically charged object has been hidden in or around the victim's house, it may be located by divination or clairvoyance and ceremonially destroyed. Otherwise, banishing rituals or other pro-

tective workings can be used to overpower the curse, protective talismans or amulets can be worn, magical oils or washes can be used to lift the curse's effects, and so on. One side effect of such operations can make cursing a dangerous occupation: when a curse is broken, its energies generally recoil on the person who cast it, and if that person fails to take adequate precautions, he or she can end up receiving the full effect intended for the curse's victim.

In many traditional societies, witches and magicians offer cursing and curse removal as a professional service, available to anyone for a price. This was (and may still be) the case among British cunning men and women, and folklorists over the last century have collected detailed price lists; see Hutton 1999, p. 105, for examples.

In the modern world, such services are still offered by hoodoo doctors, practitioners of Pennsylvania Dutch magic, and many other ethnic magical traditions. Few ceremonial magicians and even fewer modern Pagans will engage in such practices, though, and most Pagan traditions consider casting curses to be a violation of the ethical principles of their religion. *SEE* NEOPAGANISM.

Cweorp. (Old English, "fire-stick") The thirtieth rune of the Anglo-Saxon futhorc. Its meaning is not given in surviving texts of the Old English rune-poem; it represents the sound *q. SEE* ANGLO-SAXON FUTHORC.

Rune Cweorp

cycles, cosmic. Among the common features of occult philosophy since ancient times are systems of cosmology in which the universe moves through vast cycles of time in which worlds are created and destroyed. It would be impossible to review more than a few of the most popular systems of cyclical history used in Western occult traditions; a large book could be filled to bursting on the subject. A general outline and a few examples will be presented here.

The oldest and, until recent times, most popular teaching of cosmic cycles in the Western world dates from ancient Greece, where it first appears in the works of the poet Hesiod (c. eighth century B.C.E.). This divides history into five ages: the golden age of happiness, the silver age of folly, the bronze age of violence, the heroic age of great quests and adventures, and the present age of iron, an age of suffering, toil, and decay. This system was part of the mental furniture of most ancient, medieval, and Renaissance occultists.

Similar to this, and probably linked to it via a common Indo-European ancestor, is the Hindu tradition of the four *yugas* or ages of the world: the Satyayuga or golden age of truth, lasting 1,728,000 years; the Tretayuga or silver age, lasting 1,296,000 years; the Dvaparayuga, lasting 864,000 years; and the bitter Kaliyuga, the age of decay and darkness, lasting a mere 432,000 years.

The four yugas are fairly widely known in the Western world these days, having been popularized by Theosophy, borrowed by hippie culture in the Sixties, and circulated through New Age channels in recent years. *SEE* NEW AGE MOVEMENT; THEOSOPHY. Less widely known, although they were also taken up by Theosophy from Hindu sources, are the Mahayuga of 4,320,000 years; the Manvantara or Day of Brahma, which runs 4,320,000,000 years; and the Kalpa or Age of Brahma, which comes out to a dizzying 311,040,000,000,000 years. All of these are part of a cyclic vision of the cosmos in which worlds, suns, and universes come into being out of the primal unity of Brahman and return to unity again after vast periods of time.

Astrological thinking also made a substantial contribution to early Western occult theories of cosmic cycles. A theory dating back to Roman times, if not before, suggested that after a certain vast period of time all the planets would return to their original positions in the zodiac. Once this happened, it was suggested, time would start over and exactly the same events would be played out all over again, driven by the merciless determinism of the stars. This idea was popular among the Stoics, and mathematically inclined Stoic philosophers devoted a good deal of effort to calculating out the length of time after which the entire cosmos would start over again. *SEE* APOCATASTASIS; STOICISM.

Another astrological factor that became important in theories of cosmic cycles was the precession of the equinoxes, a slow wobble in the tilt of the Earth's axis that causes the sun's apparent movement against the zodiac to shift backwards one degree or so every seventy-two years. References to the Age of Aquarius, popular in the Sixties and at other recent times of social change, actually refer to this process—at present, the sun's position at the spring equinox is moving out of Pisces and into Aquarius. Such a shift happens every 2,160 years, and ancient and modern astrologers alike agree that it portends vast changes; the rise of Christianity, for example, corresponds to the last such shift. On a larger scale is the Great Year of 25,920 years, the time needed for the equinoctial point to shift all the way around the zodiac, and another popular focus for cosmic cycle theorists. *SEE* ASTROLOGY; PRECESSION OF THE EQUINOXES.

The Cabala has its own speculations about cosmic cycles, drawn largely from scriptural passages. Rabbinic lore from long before the origins of the Cabala mentioned worlds that had been created and destroyed before our present world came into being. This gave rise to the idea of the Primal Worlds of unbalanced force, the source of the Qlippoth or demons, but it also spurred thought about shemittoth or cycles of time. Some Jewish Cabalists suggested that the world would exist for a total of 49,000 years—7,000 years for each of the days of Creation—and then be destroyed in the fiftieth millennium. By the thirteenth century, these calculations gave rise to even vaster ones, in which 18,000 periods of 50,000 years each measured the total time span of the cosmos. Much speculation was also directed toward figuring out where contemporary history fit into these vast cycles; the standard Cabalistic assessment was that the present world was in the period of Geburah, or strict judgment, and would eventually pass into that of Tiphareth or beauty. *SEE* CABALA; GEBURAH; QLIPPOTH; TIPHARETH.

Still other systems of cosmic cycles entered the occult tradition from scientific speculations of the eighteenth, nineteenth, and twentieth centuries. The polar-tilt theories of Sampson Mackey (1765–1843), a self-taught cosmologist from Norwich, England, were borrowed by the Hermetic Brotherhood of Luxor and included in its teachings. Mackey believed that the poles gradually turned over, so that at some points in Earth's history the poles were at right angles to the Earth's orbit around the sun, and the Earth basked in a perpetual springtime; at other times—the "Age of Horror"—the poles were parallel to the plane of orbit, resulting in six-month summers of perpetual sunlight and six-month winters of endless darkness. The wide membership and influence of the H. B. of L. allowed this idea to spread widely through the occult scene of the late nineteenth century. *SEE* HERMETIC BROTHERHOOD OF LUXOR (H. B. OF L.).

More recent contenders in the cosmic-cycle sweepstakes include the Mayan calendar, current scientific theories about the cycles that drive Ice Ages, speculations about the frequency of meteor impacts on the Earth, and a variety of purely visionary accounts. It seems likely that the fascination with vast cycles of time will continue to be a part of occult theory into the foreseeable future. *SEE ALSO* OCCULT HISTORY. FURTHER READING: BARBORKA 1964, CAMPION 1994, GODWIN 1993, HESIOD 1973, SCHOLEM 1974.

Cyprian of Antioch, Saint. The legendary Christian patron saint of sorcerers and a character in a central Christian legend about magic, Cyprian supposedly lived in the third century C.E. There is no reason to believe that he actually existed, and no Bishop Cyprian occurs in the records of the Church of Antioch. Stories about him appear to have gone into circulation in the fourth century, and the legend was put in its final form by Simon Metaphrastes, the great Byzantine compiler of saints' lives, in the latter part of the tenth century.

According to the story, a Christian virgin named Justina refused the marriage proposal of Acladius, a Pagan. Acladius went to Cyprian, a magician, and offered him two talents (sixty pounds) of gold if he could change the lady's mind. Cyprian proceeded to summon a variety of devils to afflict Justina. The virgin, however, banished all of them with the Sign of the Cross. Cyprian, convinced that he obviously needed to learn this more powerful magic, went at once to the bishop of Antioch and was baptized. His intellectual and spiritual talents were such that he was ordained a priest within a year, and became bishop of Antioch on the retirement of the incumbent sixteen years later. He and Justina were beheaded together during the persecution of Diocletian in 280 C.E.

In Christian occult circles during the Middle Ages and thereafter, it was alleged that Cyprian had continued to practice magic after his conversion, but had given up his Pagan magic in favor of proper Christian magic. *SEE* CHRISTIAN OCCULTISM. *SEE ALSO* THEOPHILUS OF ADANA. FURTHER READING: P. PALMER 1936.

Daath. (Hebrew, "knowledge") In the Cabala, the non-Sephirah in the midst of the Abyss, situated on the Middle Pillar of the Tree of Life between Kether and Tiphareth. In many ways Daath is the most complex and obscure element of the Cabalistic tree, and it has provoked a great deal of confusion and argument over the years. In one sense, it is a downward reflection of Kether, the first Sephiroth, and represents the closest thing to knowledge of Kether that can be attained below the Abyss. In another, it is the knowledge, in the biblical sense, of Chokmah and Binah, the primal male and female centers of the tree. Its symbolism is much debated, but a common version runs as follows:

> *Astrological Correspondence:* Sirius, the Dog Star.
>
> *Tarot Correspondence:* The trumps as a whole.
>
> *Elemental Correspondence:* Air.
>
> *Magical Image:* A head with two faces.
>
> *Additional Symbols:* The empty room; the pyramid; the absence of all symbolism.
>
> *Colors:* in Atziluth—lavender.
>
> in Briah—pale silver-gray.
>
> in Yetzirah—pure violet.
>
> in Assiah—gray flecked with gold.
>
> *Correspondence in the Microcosm:* The conjunction of ruach (the conscious self) and neshamah (the higher spiritual self).
>
> *Correspondence in the Body:* The neck.

The mysteries of Daath are a central topic of discussion in the traditional Jewish Cabala, but have received little attention in the modern magical Cabala. *SEE ALSO* CABALA; TREE OF LIFE.

Dadouchos. (Greek, "torchbearer") The title of an officer in the Eleusinian Mysteries of ancient Greece. As with so much relating to the Eleusinian Mysteries, little is known for sure about the duties and symbolism of this officer, other than the fact that he probably carried a torch. *SEE* ELEUSINIAN MYSTERIES.

In the Hermetic Order of the Golden Dawn, the Dadouchos is a minor officer with a role in the Neophyte and Zelator grade rituals. She stands in the south, and wears a lamen bearing a swastika made of seventeen squares corresponding to the sun, the elements, and the signs of the zodiac. The duties of the Dadouchos are to purify the hall and the candidate with fire, and to have charge of all lights, fires, and incense in the temple. Titles of the Dadouchos are "Goddess of the Scale of the Balance of the White Pillar" and "Perfection through Fire manifesting on Earth." She corresponds to the Egyptian goddess-form Thaum-Aesch-Niaeth. *SEE* GOLDEN DAWN, HERMETIC ORDER OF THE.

Daeg. *SEE* DAGAZ.

Dagaz. (Old Germanic, "day") The twenty-third (or twenty-fourth) rune of the elder futhark, corresponding to the ideas of day, light, change, and the beginnings and endings of cycles. It represents the sound *d*. *SEE* ELDER

FUTHARK. In the Anglo-Saxon futhorc, this rune is called Daeg (also "day"); it is the twenty-fourth rune and has the same symbolism and sound. *SEE* ANGLO-SAXON FUTHORC.

Rune Dagaz (Daeg)

dagger. In ceremonial magic, and in many other branches of the Western occult traditions, one of the principal working tools of the magician. In the Golden Dawn and related traditions, it is the elemental weapon of air, and is used to invoke and command the powers of that element. *SEE* AIR, ELEMENT OF. Some other magical traditions reject this attribution and assign the dagger to the element of fire.

The athame, the primary working tool in Wicca and most other Neopagan traditions, is usually a double-edged dagger; *SEE* ATHAME.

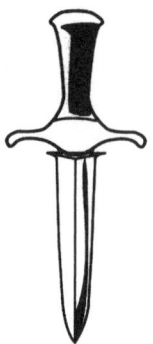

The dagger as a symbol of elemental air

Daleth. (Hebrew DLTh, "door") The fourth letter of the Hebrew alphabet, a double letter with the sounds *d* and *dh.* Its numerical value is four. Its standard correspondences are as follows:

> *Path of the Tree of Life:* Path 14, Chokmah to Binah.
>
> *Astrological Correspondence:* Venus.
>
> *Tarot Correspondence:* Trump III, the Empress.
>
> *Part of the Cube of Space:* The eastern face.

Colors: in Atziluth—emerald green.

> in Briah—sky blue.
>
> in Yetzirah—pale spring green.
>
> in Assiah—bright rose or cerise, rayed with pale green.

The text of the *Thirty-two Paths of Wisdom* assigned to Daleth runs: "The Fourteenth Path is the Illuminating Intelligence, and is so called because it is that Brilliance which is the founder of the concealed and fundamental ideas of holiness and of their stages of preparation." *SEE ALSO* CABALA; HEBREW ALPHABET.

Hebrew letter Daleth

Dalton, Thomas. *SEE* BURGOYNE, THOMAS HENRY.

Damcar. *SEE* DAMEAR.

Damear. In the *Fama Fraternitatis* and *Confessio Fraternitatis,* the original Rosicrucian manifestoes, and in later Rosicrucian literature, a city in Arabia governed by the wise, where Christian Rosenkreutz studied Cabala, magic, and alchemy. The name of this city has generally been misspelled "Damcar." This error appears in the second printed version of the *Fama Fraternitatis* and has been consistently repeated since that time, at least in part because "Damcar" is said to derive from the Hebrew words for "blood of the lamb."

Damear itself is an old spelling of the name of Dhamar, a city in Yemen, on the southwestern corner of the Arabian peninsula. Dhamar, located in Yemen's central plateau region, is an important local center of horse breeding and rug weaving, and an Islamic theological school has been located there for some centuries. The entire area has a complex cultural and religious history, involving Pagan, Jewish, Christian, and Islamic traditions; the Queen of Sheba (ancient Saba) came to Solomon's court from this region. *SEE* ROSENKREUTZ, CHRISTIAN; ROSICRUCIANS.

Dark Night of the Soul. In the writings of the Christian contemplative mystic Saint John of the Cross (1542–1591), a period of spiritual "dryness" and depression that occurs in the course of mystical development. It is marked by a loss of the sense of the presence of God, and the absence of mystical experiences, and must be undergone in order to attain the higher levels of attainment. *SEE* MEDITATION.

In occult writings of the nineteenth and twentieth centuries, the Dark Night of the Soul is identified with the journey across the Abyss—the gap on the Tree of Life between the seven lower and three higher Sephirah. Aleister Crowley seems to have been the first to suggest this equation. *SEE* CROWLEY, ALEISTER; TREE OF LIFE.

Dark Satellite. In the teachings of the Hermetic Brotherhood of Luxor and occult groups derived from it, an invisible, "semi-spiritual" planet. The Dark Satellite is the place where souls that have failed to make contact with their higher selves, and so gain immortality, sink gradually into oblivion. Its exact location varies in different presentations, but it is sometimes associated with the shadow cast by the Earth in space.

The Dark Satellite's "ruling spiritual hierophant" is named Ob, and its influence is said to be the source of power for the sinister Black Lodges. *SEE* BLACK LODGES; OB. *SEE ALSO* HERMETIC BROTHERHOOD OF LUXOR (H.B. OF L.).

Davis, Andrew Jackson. American mesmerist, socialist, and occult philosopher, 1826–1910. Born into a poor and mostly illiterate family in New York State, he displayed clairvoyant gifts and received guidance from disembodied voices from childhood on. He became a shoemaker's apprentice, and worked at that trade for two years. In 1843, however, a traveling Mesmerist came to Poughkeepsie, where Davis was then living, and Davis was among the subjects who volunteered at public lectures. He did not go into trance on this occasion, but a short time later, a local tailor made another attempt and was able to put Davis into trance. In this state Davis was able to diagnose diseases, and soon developed a reputation as a seer.

In 1844 Davis underwent an experience in which he claimed to have met and spoken with the spirits of Galen and Swedenborg, and to have entered into an illuminated state. *SEE* SWEDENBORG, EMMANUEL. Thereafter he began teaching and lecturing, and in 1845 began work on his most important book, *The Principles of Nature, Her Divine Revelations, and a Voice to Mankind*, which was published in 1847. This book was written entirely in trance, and includes a complex mystical philosophy, arguments against the infallibility of the Old Testament and the divinity of Jesus, and a system of socialist economic theory partly drawn from the work of Charles Fourier; *SEE* FOURIER, CHARLES. It went through more than thirty editions in the next three decades, and established Davis as one of the most important figures in the American occult scene.

Davis continued to write, lecture, and diagnose diseases by means of his clairvoyant abilities for many years. His writings were enthusiastically taken up by the Spiritualist movement, although he remained skeptical of some aspects of Spiritualism and wrote a book, *The Diakka and their Earthly Victims* (1873), arguing that many Spiritualist manifestations were the result of evil spirits called Diakka, whose lies and distortions had to be guarded against in trance work. Late in life he obtained a medical degree, and in his last years ran a bookstore in Boston, where he sold occult literature and prescribed herbal remedies to patients. *SEE ALSO* MESMERISM; SPIRITUALISM. FURTHER READING: KERR AND CROW 1983, MOORE 1977.

Death. The thirteenth Major Arcanum of the tarot, usually showing a conventional figure of death as a skeleton. In the Golden Dawn system, this Arcanum is assigned to the Hebrew letter Nun, while the French system assigns it to Mem. In divination, it generally means change or transformation—not death as such.

Its magical title is "Child of the Great Transformers, Lord of the Gates of Death." *SEE ALSO* TAROT.

Tarot trump Death (Universal Tarot)

Death of the Soul, Book of the. A mysterious text of evil magic referred to by Roger Bacon and some other medieval Christian writers. Nothing seems to be known for sure about it, including whether or not it ever existed, and it may simply have been a figment of the imaginations of clerics hostile to magic. *SEE* GRIMOIRE; BACON, ROGER.

de Bry, Franciscus. According to the Golden Dawn Adeptus Minor ritual, one of the three Highest Chiefs of the order, along with Hugo Alverda and Elman Zata. He is identified as a Gaul, and his age at the time of the sealing of the Vault of Christian Rosenkreutz is given as 495 years. *SEE* ROSICRUCIANS; VAULT OF CHRISTIAN ROSEN-KREUTZ.

decans. Divisions of the zodiac of ten degrees each; there are three decans in each zodiacal sign, thirty-six in all. The decans are one of the few contributions of Egyptian starlore to make an impact on later astrology and magic. Originally they formed the basic framework of ancient Egyptian star symbolism and teaching, and are pictured on the inside lids of Egyptian mummy cases to assist the dead in journeying through the heavens. In ancient Greek and Roman astrology, the decans were used as an additional way of measuring planetary influences on the chart, along with terms and dodecatemories. *SEE* DO-DECATEMORY; TERMS, ASTROLOGICAL.

Adopted by Arabic magicians and astrologers after the Muslim comquest of Egypt, they were transmitted to medieval Europe in the pages of the *Picatrix*, the most famous of the Middle Ages' books of magic. *SEE* PICATRIX. Each decan has a figure or magical image associated with it, and these were much used in magical practice during the Renaissance.

Later, in the nineteenth-century occult revival, the decans were associated with the Minor Arcana of the tarot. Two different attributions are still in use—that of Papus (Gerard Encausse, 1865–1916), the French occultist, included in his book *Le Tarot du Bohemiens*, and that of the Golden Dawn, which is standard in the English-speaking world and can be found in works on the Golden Dawn tarot tradition. *SEE* TAROT.

In astrology, two different systems of assigning the planets to the decans are in use. One, the so-called Western system, assigns the planets in descending order, beginning with the first decan of Aries, which is assigned to Mars; the second decan of Aries thus goes to the sun, the third to Venus, the first decan of Taurus to Mercury, the second to the moon, the third to Saturn, and so on around the circle of decans. The last decan of Pisces, like the first of Aries, is assigned to Mars. This Western system is the most common among magicians working with the decans, and is standard in Golden Dawn magic.

More common among astrologers is the Eastern system, which assigns the first decan of each sign to the planet ruling that sign, and the other two decans to the planets ruling the other two signs that share the same element. Thus in Aries, Mars again rules the first decan and the Sun (the ruler of Leo) the second, but Jupiter (the ruler of Sagittarius) rules the third; in Taurus, Venus rules the first decan, Mercury (ruler of Virgo) the second, and Saturn (ruler of Capricorn) the third, and so on. FURTHER READING: PAPUS N.D., REGARDIE 1971, YATES 1964.

decile. *SEE* SEMIQUINTILE.

decree. In the Ascended Masters teachings, a system of twentieth-century American popular occultism, a prayer combined with meditation and visualization. Decrees invoke the I AM presence, the divine presence in the higher self, as well as Ascended Masters and other spiritual beings. Students of the teachings use a variety of decrees for different purposes, such as protection, purification, physical and mental healing, and spiritual development. SEE ASCENDED MASTERS' TEACHINGS; VIOLET FLAME.

Decretism. In the teachings of American occultist P. B. Randolph (1825–1875), the second stage in the process of magic, the act of active concentration on an act of will. It is preceded by Volantia and followed by Posism. SEE POSISM; RANDOLPH, PASCHAL BEVERLY; VOLANTIA.

In the teachings of the Hermetic Brotherhood of Luxor, which drew heavily on Randolph's work, Decretism was renamed Execution. The other phases were named Formation and Reception. SEE HERMETIC BROTHERHOOD OF LUXOR (H. B. OF L.).

Dee, Arthur. English physician and alchemist, 1579–1651. The son of John Dee, the great Elizabethan astrologer and occultist, Dee was born into a milieu saturated with magic. When he was four years old, he accompanied his parents, his father's scryer Edward Kelly, and their households to Europe. The next six years of his life were spent in Poland, Hungary, Germany, and Bohemia, where his father visited many of the most important alchemists and magicians of the time. While staying in Prague, according to his later recollections, he and the other children in the Dee household played with toys of alchemical gold. His father also attempted to train him as a scryer, but without success.

In 1589 the Dee household returned to England, and Arthur attended Westminster School and Oxford University. In 1600, he became chapter clerk of the Collegiate Church in Manchester, where his father was Warden of Christ's College, and married Isabella Prestwich in 1602. He fathered four children, and began a career in medicine, moving to London in 1605 and establishing a successful practice. This was despite the opposition of the Royal College of Physicians, which summoned him for practicing illegally on several occasions. His avowal of Paracelsian medicine, which was anathema to the orthodox physicians of the time, had much to do with these difficulties.

In 1621, Dee accepted a position as royal physician to Mikhail Romanov, tsar of Russia. This appointment was part of a broad recruitment program that brought dozens of English scholars and technicians to Russia in the six-teenth and seventeenth centuries. During the fourteen years he spent in Russia, Dee practiced alchemy as well as medicine, and edited a collection of alchemical texts, *Fasciculus Chemicus*, which was published in Paris in 1631.

He returned to England in 1635 to take up a position as royal physician-in-ordinary to King Charles I. He renewed his contacts in English medical circles; when he himself came down with a liver complaint, he was cured by the famous Nicholas Culpeper, and gave the latter one of John Dee's shewstones out of gratitude for the cure.

The execution of the king in 1649, in the aftermath of the English Civil War, deprived Dee of his position, and he moved to Norwich, where he continued to practice medicine until his death in 1651. While at Norwich, he became a close friend of writer and physician Thomas Browne, who inherited many of his alchemical books after Dee's death. SEE ALSO DEE, JOHN. FURTHER READING: ABRAHAM 1994.

Dee, John. English astrologer, magician, and polymath, 1527–1608. The son of a minor official in the court of Henry VIII, he entered Cambridge in 1542, receiving his B.A. in 1546 and his M.A. in 1548. In the latter year he traveled to Louvain in Belgium, then a center for mathematical and scientific research, where he continued his studies until 1551. Returning to England that year, he became a consultant to the English merchant fleet, providing geographical and navigational information and introducing new navigational instruments.

These practical interests went hand in hand with a lifelong interest in occult subjects, dating back to his first days at college. Two of his teachers, John Cheke and Thomas Smith, had their own connections to the occult; Cheke was more than casually interested in astrology, and Smith was not only an active astrologer but a practicing alchemist as well. Dee's first book, *Propaedumata Aphoristica* (*Aphoristic Introductions*, 1558), presented a theoretical basis for astrology based on optics, Arabic astrological writings, and the quasi-alchemical *Voarchadumia* of Johannes Pantheus. SEE ASTROLOGY; VOARCHADUMIA. His second book, the enigmatic *Monas Hieroglyphica* (*Hieroglyphic Monad*, 1564), united astrology, alchemy, sacred geometry, symbolism, and Cabala in an arcane synthesis that has resisted more than four centuries of attempted explanations. SEE MONAS HIEROGLYPHICA.

His involvement in astrological studies led to his arrest in 1555, on the charge of casting spells against the Catholic Queen Mary in favor of her Protestant half-sister, Elizabeth. While the charges were ultimately dismissed, he spent several months in prison. Elizabeth's accession in 1559 made Dee's position more secure, and sometime in the late 1560s, after another trip to Europe, he settled at Mortlake.

There his library soon became Elizabethan England's largest, and court officials, merchant adventurers, and ordinary tradesmen came for information and instruction. His "Mathematicall Praeface" to the first English translation of Euclid's *Elements of Geometry* (1570) helped introduce practical mathematics for the first time to an audience outside the universities. During the Mortlake years, he also wrote several important works on navigation and drew maps for English explorers.

This same period saw his occult studies in full flower. The house at Mortlake allowed Dee the space to set up a complete alchemical laboratory, and records from the 1570s and early 1580s show him busily pursuing various alchemical processes. Sometime in the 1560s, Dee also began experimenting with theurgy, using prayer and devotional techniques to call angels to visible appearance in crystal shewstones, and from 1581 on this became an increasingly central part of his life. Since Dee himself lacked the ability to scry effectively, he hired a succession of scryers, of whom Edward Kelly was the most effective. With Kelly's sometimes unwilling help, Dee conversed with a variety of angelic entities, who revealed to him the complex system now known as Enochian magic. *SEE* ENOCHIAN MAGIC; KELLY, EDWARD.

When Dee returned to Europe in 1583, accompanied by Kelly and their families, his magical and alchemical work continued in full spate. Strains between Dee and the often unstable Kelly, though, made the working relationship between the men a difficult one, and when Dee returned to England in 1589, Kelly remained behind.

Dee's homecoming was an unhappy one. His house at Mortlake had been looted during his absence, and Queen Elizabeth's government offered him little support or encouragement. He continued to petition the court for financial help, and was finally made warden of a college in Manchester. He retired from this position in 1605, and in the same year his wife Jane died of the plague. He continued practicing magic and alchemy until his own death three years later. FURTHER READING: CLULEE **1988**, DEE **1986**, JOSTEN **1964**, MEBANE **1989**, TURNER **1989**, YATES **1969**, YATES **1979**.

defixio. *SEE* BINDING TABLET.

degree(s). In fraternal and magical lodge systems, levels of initiation, each of which has its own ceremony, symbolism, and traditional lore. The term "grades" is also used with the same meaning.

The system of degrees was originally inspired by the three-level structure of the medieval guild system, in which a member could expect to pass through the stages of apprentice, journeyman, and master in the course of his career. Apprentices were taught the basics of a craft in exchange for room and board, and were bound to work for a master for a fixed period of years. Journeymen, companions, or fellows—the terms for this stage varied—had completed an apprenticeship and worked for masters for wages, developing their skills in the guild's trade. Upon completion of a "master piece"—an item of work that showed complete mastery of the craft—journeymen advanced to the rank of master, gained voting rights in the guild, and took on apprentices and journeymen of their own.

This same three-level structure was used by the operative stonemasons' guilds that turned into Freemasonry, and gave rise to the Masonic degree structure of Entered Apprentice, Fellow Craft, and Master Mason. Many other groups that borrowed Masonic methods took on versions of the same system, and a three-degree structure of initiations is still the most common both in fraternal lodges and in magical ones. It has also been adopted into Wicca and Druidry, along with a surprising amount of Masonic symbolism and terminology. *SEE* DRUIDRY; WICCA.

Later, with the development of additional Masonic degrees, more elaborate degree structures made their appearance. The most extravagant example is the ninety-nine degrees of the Masonic Rite of Memphis and Mizraim, although very few of these degrees were ever developed beyond a very basic framework. In the Masonic Scottish Rite of thirty-three degrees, on the other hand, every degree has its own fully developed ritual, symbolism, and teachings.

Other systems, some modeled on Masonry and others deriving from different sources, have different degree structures, although none seem to have attempted the complexity of these latter Masonic systems. One worth mentioning is the Golden Dawn system of twelve grades, based on the Cabalistic Tree of Life, which is itself derived from an older Rosicrucian scheme of nine grades used by the German Order of the Gold and Rosy Cross. SEE GOLDEN DAWN, HERMETIC ORDER OF THE; ORDEN DES GOLD- UND ROSENKREUTZ. Another is that of the Independent Order of Odd Fellows (IOOF), the largest non-Masonic fraternal order, which has a total of ten degrees of initiation divided into three levels, and has influenced a number of American occult orders. SEE ODD FELLOWSHIP. The nine-degree structure of the Ordo Templi Orientis (OTO) has also been much copied over the last century; SEE ORDO TEMPLI ORIENTIS (OTO). SEE ALSO LODGE, FRATERNAL; LODGE, MAGICAL.

demon. (Greek *daimon*, "spirit") In most current magical traditions, a nonphysical creature of (usually) malign nature. Demons have been conceptualized in a dizzying diversity of ways over the centuries, but nearly all magical traditions include lore about their nature and actions. The demon-lore of ancient Egypt and Mesopotamia is extremely complex and detailed, and includes quite a range of blood-curdling entities. Much of this lore has its echoes in Greek and Latin sources as well.

There is an equally huge demonological literature dating from the Middle Ages, the Renaissance, and the early modern period, packed with details about demons, their activities, their hierarchies, and their interactions with human beings. This literature is a very mixed bag; some of it is based purely on Scripture and scholastic philosophy, with little connection to the realities of human contact with hostile spirits. Other sources are more useful to the modern student of the subject. Two of the latter that are heavily used in current magical practice are the demonology of the Cabala and that of medieval goetia.

Cabalistic demonology dates back to the earliest phase of the tradition, and plays a very large role in the litera-ture of the Jewish Cabala. The early Spanish Cabalists of the School of Burgos devoted many pages to lengthy expositions of the *sitra achra* or "Other Side"—the usual Cabalistic term for the powers of evil in the cosmos.

Demons, according to this lore, are to be found in ruins, deserts, and especially in the northern countries. Their bodies are composed of fire and air. Like humans, they are born, reproduce, and die, and some Cabalistic sources give detailed family trees of the various demonic royal houses. They are surrounded by an intense coldness that is among their most terrifying features.

According to some Cabalistic writings, many so-called demons are actually half-breeds, the offspring of matings between human beings and demons. Most, but not all, are malevolent; there is an entire class of demons who have converted to Judaism and accept the Torah, and are prepared to do favors for devout Jews. Their leader is (or was) Ashmedai or Asmodeus; SEE ASMODEUS. Other demons have crooked feet and no thumbs, and delight in playing pranks on human beings. It seems likely that these "demons" should actually be identified with the faery folk, and are not demons at all; SEE FAERY.

On the other hand, the demon-lore of the Cabala also contains far less amusing entities such as the Tzephariron, who look like half-decayed corpses, and the Behemiron, who resemble elephants or hippopotami squashed flat, but crawl over the ground with immense strength. These demons belong to the Qlippoth, the Lords of Unbalanced Force who play a central role in Cabalistic analyses of evil; SEE QLIPPOTH.

The demonological lore of the goetic underground mostly takes the form of grimoires, or handbooks of magical practice. The goetic tradition's interest in demons was practical, not academic; goetic magicians wanted to know about demons in order to summon them and make use of them. Here the names, ranks, powers, appearance, rulerships, and former position among the angels of several hundred demons are given in great detail. One example from the *Lemegeton* will suffice:

Caim is a great President taking the form of a thrush, but when he putteth on a man's shape he answereth in a voice of burning ashes, carrying in his hands a sharp sword, and giving the understanding of all birds, the lowing of bullocks and the barking of dogs. He was of the Order of Angels and ruleth thirty legions of devils.

All the various classes of demonology—classical, Pagan, Gnostic, Cabalistic, goetic, and Christian—interpenetrate to a very great degree. Later demonologies tended to borrow heavily from earlier ones, completely ignoring boundaries of faith and culture. Jewish and Christian demon lore also tended to pick up the folk demonology of local cultures, so that evil spirits rooted in Pagan folk traditions found themselves pitchforked into the Christian hell or the Cabalistic Kingdom of Shells.

Current magical traditions differ sharply on the nature of demons, to say nothing of the advisability of magical practices that call on them. Even those traditions that make use of goetic rituals for summoning demons, however, stress that this is not work for magical beginners, and carries very substantial risks. SEE ALSO CABALA; GOETIA; GRIMOIRE. FURTHER READING: E. BUTLER 1949, GREER 2001, MCLEAN 1990, SCHOLEM 1974.

deosil. This Irish Gaelic word for clockwise circular motion has been borrowed by most traditions in the modern Pagan revival. In the American Pagan community, it is usually mispronounced "dee-o-sill" or "day-o-sill"; the correct Gaelic pronunciation is "jeshel." The opposite of deosil is *tuathil*, although the Lowland Scots term *widdershins* is much more common in current Pagan circles. SEE CIRCUMAMBULATION; WIDDERSHINS.

deros. In the writings of Richard Shaver and other contributors to the "Shaver mystery," psychotic subterranean dwarfs who dwell in the abandoned caverns of the ancient Lemurian civilization, far beneath the surface of the Earth, and torment surface-dwellers with the help of castoff Lemurian technology. Their name supposedly comes from the Lemurian language, Mantong, and means "*de*trimental *ro*bots." SEE MANTONG; SHAVER MYSTERY.

descendant. In an astrological chart, the point of the zodiac on the Western horizon at the moment for which the chart is cast. The descendant is little used in modern astrological analysis, but received more attention in earlier times. SEE ASCENDANT; ASTROLOGY.

deva. (Sanskrit, "god") In Theosophy and occult traditions influenced by it, a class of spiritual beings midway between angels and elemental spirits, having special authority over the world of nature. As with all things Theosophical, the lore of devas has been worked out in elaborate detail by means of the akashic vision of early Theosophical writers, although this information has all the usual drawbacks of clairvoyant material. SEE CLAIRVOYANCE.

At Findhorn, a spiritual community on the Scottish coast, much of the community's work has been devoted to the interface between deva lore and organic agriculture. The results have been impressive enough to spark a wide range of occult approaches to gardening. SEE ALSO ANGEL; SPIRIT; THEOSOPHY. FURTHER READING: FINDHORN COMMUNITY 1975, HODSON 1976A, PETTIS 1999, WRIGHT 1987.

Devachan. In Theosophical terminology, the realm of the devas. SEE DEVA; THEOSOPHY.

Devi, Savitri. (Savitri Devi Mukherji) French author, 1905–1982. Born Maximiani Portas to a family of mixed English, Italian, and Greek origin in the French city of Lyons, she spent several long stays in Greece after leaving secondary school, returning at intervals to attend the University of Lyons. After finishing two doctoral dissertations in 1931, she traveled to India, where she settled, marrying Asit Krishna Mukherji, a publisher and political activist in the movement for Indian independence, and taking the Sanskrit name under which her later books were published. While she traveled extensively, she made her home in India until shortly before her death.

Like many European intellectuals of the early twentieth century, Devi held strong racist and anti-Semitic views, along with a contempt for democracy and the mass cultures of the West. These views combined readily with the caste-bound, elitist traditions of the conservative Hindu circles she frequented in India. She was also a lifelong vegetarian and a proponent of animal rights.

All these ideological positions were shared by Adolf Hitler and other important figures in the Nazi movement in Germany. The connection was not lost on Devi, who became a vocal supporter of Hitler in the 1930s, distributed pro-German propaganda before the war, and spied on British activities in India for the Axis powers once war broke out. In the meantime she wrote three books and a play about Akhenaten, the heretic pharaoh of Egypt's eighteenth dynasty, whose solar religion appealed strongly to her. *SEE* AKHENATEN.

In the aftermath of the German surrender, Devi wrote a book on animal rights, *The Impeachment of Man*, which was published a decade later in 1959. She then returned to Europe, where she made three visits to occupied Germany, talking to former Nazis and handing out pro-Nazi leaflets; arrested by the British occupation government, she spent six months in prison before being expelled. She was back again in 1952, having obtained a Greek passport under her birth name, and from that time until her death in 1982 she traveled, lectured, and wrote in support of neo-Nazi movements in Europe and North America.

Her beliefs developed into a full-blown mystical theology of Nazism, which can be found in her major work *The Lightning and the Sun* (1958). Combining Hindu myth and Nazi ideology, she identified Hitler as an avatar of the divine collective of Aryan humanity, come into the world to vanquish the powers of evil (which she identified, predictably, as the Jews) in the Kali Yuga, the last degenerate age of the Hindu world-cycle. Hitler's defeat and suicide became, in her eyes, a sacrificial death that would lead ultimately to the end of the Kali Yuga and the renewal of Aryan humanity.

These ideas have been taken up by other Nazi and neo-Nazi thinkers, including the Chilean diplomat and author Miguel Serrano. Her less controversial writings have had an even wider influence; *The Impeachment of Man* was reprinted as recently as 1991 and has had a significant impact on the animal rights movement in North America and Europe, and her most important work on Akhenaten is kept in print by the American Rosicrucian order AMORC. *SEE* ANCIENT MYSTICAL ORDER ROSAE CRUCIS (AMORC). *SEE ALSO* NATIONAL SOCIALISM. FURTHER READING: DEVI 1958; GOODRICK-CLARKE 1998.

Devil, the. The fifteenth Major Arcanum of the tarot, usually showing the image of a conventional devil, with horns and hooves. The Golden Dawn system assigns this Arcanum to the Hebrew letter Ayin, while the French system assigns it to Samekh. In divination, it has a wide range of meanings, ranging from fate through the power of the unconscious mind to supernatural evil.

Its magical title is "Lord of the Gates of Matter, Child of the Forces of Time." *SEE ALSO* AYIN; TAROT.

Tarot trump the Devil (Universal Tarot)

Devil's shoestring. (*Viburnum* spp.) Much used in traditional Americal hoodoo, Devil's shoestring is the root of any of several closely related *Viburnum* species. The roots are long, thin, and flexible. In hoodoo lore, they are used for protection against crossing (magical attack) and malicious gossip, for gambling luck, and for success in finding a job. *SEE* HOODOO.

devil trap. The usual term for a class of amulets found in Babylonia and other parts of the Middle East, and used between the third century B.C.E. and the sixth century C.E. Despite the location of most finds, they were principally a Jewish custom, and most surviving examples are written in Hebrew. They consist of terra-cotta bowls inscribed with magical incantations, which were buried upside down at the four corners of a house or other buildings. Many quote passages of the Hebrew scriptures and include holy names of various kinds. They were held to drive away demons, counteract curses, and protect the inhabitants of the house from the evil eye. *SEE* AMULET; EVIL EYE.

dew. As water vapor that condenses out of the night air onto cold surfaces at or near ground level, dew has been an important element in occult practices for many centuries. In alchemy, dew is considered to be one of the chief sources of the mysterious central niter, the subtle form of the primal fire of nature. During the two months that the sun is in the astrological signs Aries and Taurus (roughly March 21–May 21), alchemists gather dew by dragging sheets across clean grass, placing metal bowls out overnight to serve as condensation surfaces, or shaking dewdrops off the leaves of the herb lady's mantle. Once collected, the dew is used as a solvent for many alchemical processes. *SEE* ALCHEMY; NITER.

In traditional folk magic from several parts of the world, dew was held to have important fertilizing powers. In Italy, a woman who wished to become pregnant would lay naked on her back on the night of the full moon, remaining there until the sun rose, so that her body was covered with dew. *SEE ALSO* WATER, ELEMENT OF.

Dhyan Chohans. In Theosophy, a general term for all those entities who have transcended the human level and serve as divine intelligences charged with supervising different aspects of the universe. There are three classes of Dhyan Chohans, although within this general division there are countless subdivisions and categories. The Masters of the Great White Lodge, who are still incarnate in human form, are apparently the lowest rung on the ladder of Dhyan Chohans. Others are discarnate but can still be contacted by human beings, while still others are completely imperceptible and incomprehensible to human beings. *SEE ALSO* GREAT WHITE LODGE; MASTERS; THEOSOPHY.

diakka. In the writings of "the Poughkeepsie Seer," Andrew Jackson Davis, a class of ignorant and evil spirits who are responsible for much of the fraud and trickery that surrounds many Spiritualist séances. According to Davis' theory, unprincipled and selfish human beings become unprincipled and selfish spirits upon their deaths, and these—the diakka—remain close to earth until they give up their bad habits and progress to higher levels of being. Davis recommended a pure, refined, and religious life as a way to avoid diakka activities, since they are drawn to those whose minds are most in harmony with their own. *SEE* DAVIS, ANDREW JACKSON. *SEE ALSO* DEMON.

Diana. A Roman goddess closely linked with the traditions of ancient and medieval witchcraft, Diana seems originally to have been a native Italian goddess paired with Dianus or Janus, the god of doors and beginnings. Her name is derived from the very oldest Indo-European name for divinity, and in all probability she and her male equivalent were worshipped in Italy centuries or millennia before the first written records of her presence.

Later, with the expansion of Roman Paganism, she absorbed many of the legends and traditions associated with the Greek goddess Artemis, and in this form she was worshipped over much of the ancient world before the emergence of Christianity; *SEE* PAGANISM. The worship of Diana seems to have endured longer than that of most other Pagan divinities. Churchmen in parts of rural Italy in the fifth and sixth centuries of the Common Era—long after the official Christianization of the area—were still expostulating against the worship of Diana by local peasants.

In what is now France, during the ninth century, the famous Canon *Episcopi* was written, denouncing "wicked women" who believe that they travel through the air at night "with Diana, goddess of the pagans, and an innumerable multitude of other women"; *SEE* CANON EPISCOPI. This tradition of nocturnal, spectral journeys in the company of a goddess does not seem to have existed in Roman times, but it spread over much of Europe in the early Middle Ages; sometimes associated with Diana and sometimes not, it survived in some parts of Europe through the Middle Ages and Renaissance, and may not have been stamped out until the worst part of the Burning Times; *SEE* BURNING TIMES.

According to the writings of Charles Godfrey Leland, whose *Aradia, or the Gospel of the Witches* (1899) played a central role in launching the modern Pagan revival, Diana was the goddess worshipped by the Italian witches whom he researched. Currently a number of modern Pagan traditions worship Diana as their primary form of the Goddess; *SEE* GODDESS, THE. FURTHER READING: FRAZER 1922, LELAND 1974.

Dianic Wicca. A movement within modern Wicca dedicated to a purely feminine and politically feminist vision of Pagan spirituality. Originally set in motion by

Zsuzsanna Budapest (1940–), who founded Susan B. Anthony Coven No. 1 in California in the early 1970s, it has remained mostly an American movement, though there are Dianic covens in a few other countries.

Diverse even by Neopagan standards, Dianic Wicca includes a wide range of different rituals, traditions, and approaches, united mostly by a commitment to a woman-centered spiritual vision, a feminist political stance, and the exclusion of men and of masculine images of the divine from Dianic rituals and teachings.

Despite the implications of the movement's name, the goddess Diana is far from the only deity worshiped by Dianic witches. Attitudes toward divinity vary widely; some Dianic witches see the Goddess as a real entity, others relate to her as a metaphor for the power of woman. Similarly, magic is practiced as an occult discipline with real powers by some Dianic witches, while others approach ritual purely as a tool for psychological self-empowerment or a mode of propaganda. Many of the standard elements of other Wiccan traditions—for example, the calendar of eight sabbats and the assignment of directions to the elements—are common in Dianic circles as well. *SEE ALSO* NEOPAGANISM; WICCA. FURTHER READING: BUDAPEST 1989, WALKER 1990.

diaphane. In the writings of Eliphas Lévi and other Hermetic occultists, the human aura as the interface between the imagination and the astral world. *SEE* AURA.

dibbuk. *SEE* DYBBUK.

digestion. In alchemy, the process of exposing a substance to gentle, steady heat for an extended period. Many substances treated in this way will go through a complex series of chemical and energetic changes, which are of the highest importance in some alchemical methods. Alchemical symbolism assigns this process to the zodiacal sign Leo. *SEE* ALCHEMY.

Din. (Hebrew DIN, "justice") An alternative name for Geburah, the fifth Sephirah of the Cabalistic Tree of Life. *SEE* GEBURAH.

direction. In astrology, a mode of predicting future events in a person's life from the birth chart. There are various ways of handling directions, some of which involve extremely complicated mathematics. In all forms of direction, the planets are moved a fixed amount along one of the coordinates of the heavens for each year in the life of the person whose chart is being directed.

The relationship between the new, directed positions of the planets and their original positions is crucial. In a primary direction, for example, if one planet has to cover a distance of thirty degrees before it comes into aspect with the second planet, the relationship between the two will have most of its influence in the thirtieth year of the person's life.

Directions are closely related to progressions, another form of prediction using the birth chart. *SEE* PROGRESSIONS. *SEE ALSO* ASTROLOGY.

directions in occultism. The assignment of meanings to the four directions is an important part of occult symbolism, but one subject to many variations. The idea that there were four and only four directions is a recent one in the Western world; as recent as the early Middle Ages, many peoples divided the horizon into eight rather than four divisions. Medieval Christian culture recognized four directions (along with four Gospels, evangelists, elements, humors, etc.), but combined these in ways that do not always correspond with modern assumptions; see the table below.

Source:	East	South	West	North
Renaissance:	Fire	Air	Water	Earth
Golden Dawn Elemental:	Air	Fire	Water	Earth
Golden Dawn Zodiacal:	Fire	Earth	Air	Water
Wiccan:	Air	Fire	Water	Earth
Cochrane (1):	Fire	Air	Water	Earth
Cochrane (2):	Fire	Earth	Water	Air

In modern magical practice, the standard version of directional symbolism is that devised by Eliphas Lévi and popularized by the Hermetic Order of the Golden Dawn. Nearly all modern ceremonial magic systems use this. Most traditions of modern Wicca and witchcraft follow the lead of Gerald Gardner, who used the standard

Golden Dawn correspondences in his creation (or reformulation) of Wicca. SEE WICCA. The major exceptions are the traditions rooted in the work of Robert Cochrane (1931–1966), which include the Clan of Tubal-Cain and the 1734 Tradition; some of these place fire in the east and air in the south, as in the standard Renaissance model, leaving water and earth in their standard positions, while others move air to north and earth to south. SEE CLAN OF TUBAL-CAIN.

Discordianism. Somewhere in the space between a religious movement and a practical joke, Discordianism had its origins in the late 1950s, when its founders Greg Hill and Kerry Thornley developed the concept of a religion worshipping Eris, the Greek goddess of chaos, discord, and confusion. According to published accounts, the theology of Discordianism was originally either created by Hill and Thornley, or revealed to them by a spectral chimpanzee, late one night in a Los Angeles–area bowling alley. It caught on among the founders' friends, but remained the private joke of a small circle until 1970, when Rip Off Press in San Francisco issued the first widely available edition of the *Principia Discordia*, the scriptures of the movement. In 1975, Robert Shea and Robert Anton Wilson published the Illuminatus! trilogy, a science-fiction spoof of conspiracy theories that drew heavily on Discordian material. The trilogy became a cult classic and thrust Discordianism into the spotlight throughout the alternative scene.

As befits a religion worshipping chaos, the theology, teachings, rituals and practices of Discordianism range from the weird through the impossible to the downright silly. Discordians are forbidden from eating hot dog buns; accordingly, every Discordian is required to go off and eat a hot dog, bun and all, during his or her self-initiation. The pages of the *Principia* include such oddities as the Book of Uterus, the Epistle to the Paranoids, and the dread Discordian Turkey Curse. Would-be Chaplins (as in Charlie) of the Paratheoana-metomystik-hood of Eris Esoteric, one of a flurry of Discordian orders, are instructed to copy out the Erisian Affirmation five times, signing and noseprinting each copy; the copies are respectively mailed to the president of the United States, sent to a minor California state government office, nailed to a telephone pole, hidden, and burned.

While Discordianism is on the periphery of Western occultism, and of much else as well, it has been a major source of inspiration to the Chaos magic movement; SEE CHAOS MAGIC. FURTHER READING: MALACLYPSE 1970, SHEA AND WILSON 1975.

dissolution. In alchemy, the process of dissolving a substance in a suitable fluid; the fluid used is referred to as a menstruum. Alchemical symbolism assigns this process to the zodiacal sign Cancer; in some accounts, it is listed as the second operation of the Great Work, the preparation of the Philosopher's Stone. SEE ALCHEMY; MENSTRUUM.

distillation. In alchemy, the process of extracting the volatile parts of a solution by heating it and condensing the steam into liquid in another container. Distillation is among the most used of alchemical processes, and is particularly useful in spagyrics—the medicinal alchemy of herbs—which is the most commonly practiced form of alchemy at present. Alchemical symbolism assigns it to the zodiacal sign Virgo; in some accounts, it is listed as the sixth operation of the Great Work. SEE ALCHEMY; SPAGYRICS.

dittany of Crete. A perennial herb (*Origanum dictamnus*) native to the Mediterranean area, closely related to oregano and marjoram. It has a strong materializing quality, and is therefore common as an incense in the evocation of spirits to visible appearance. SEE EVOCATION.

divination. The art and science of obtaining information by occult means, divination has been practiced in every culture in the world throughout history. The receptive side of occult practice, as magic is the active side, divination is a basic skill used by most magicians, witches, and other occult practitioners in one form or another.

There are four basic types of divination. *Omen divination* consists of ways of reading signs that are naturally present in the world of human experience—for example, a Roman augur observing the flight of birds, or an astrologer using a computer to calculate the positions of the stars and planets. *Pattern divination* consists of articifial methods of producing a pattern or image that can be read according to fixed rules—for example, a modern fortuneteller reading the patterns of tea leaves, or a medieval wizard pouring hot wax into cold water and interpreting the blobby shape that results. *Symbol divination* consists of methods to select one or more of a fixed set of divinatory symbols, each with its own interpretation—for example, a Chinese sage consulting the I Ching or a tarot reader shuffling and dealing the cards. *Trance divination*, finally, consists of methods that put a human being into an altered state of consciousness—for example, a shaman using hallucinogenic mushrooms to induce visionary trance, or anyone who has every awakened suddenly from an intense dream and tried to figure out what it meant.

Within these four classes of divination, techniques have multiplied almost to infinity. Different methods have played widely different roles in the occult traditions as well as the popular imagination. Astrology, geomancy, and the tarot have been important influences on Western occultism, to the extent that it is difficult or impossible to work with many occult systems without some background in one or more of these. Others have been almost completely ignored by the occult community.

There are also systems that have become closely associated with one particular branch of modern occultism or magical spirituality. For example, the Ogham—an archaic Celtic alphabet used in modern times as a set of divinatory symbols—is mostly used by practitioners of Druidry and other Celtic and quasi-Celtic paths, and seidhr—a system of trance work partly based on Old Norse materials—is almost entirely practiced within the Asatru community. *SEE* OGHAM; SEIDHR.

A surprising number of divination systems are closely associated with games of chance or strategy. Tarot, with its close connection to playing cards, and dice, which have been used for divination at least as long as for gambling, are two widely known examples. Attempts have also been made to work the process in reverse; the most widely known example is the "Enochian chess" devised in the Hermetic Order of the Golden Dawn, which was used for divinatory purposes. *SEE* AUGURY; CHESS, ENOCHIAN. *SEE ALSO* ALECTRYOMANCY; ASTROLOGY; BREAST DIVINATION; CEROMANCY; CLEDONOMANCY; COSCINOMANCY; CRYSTALLOMANCY; DOWSING; DREAMS AND DREAMING; GEOMANCY; INTELLIGENCE; OMENS; ORACLES; PALMISTRY; PHYSIOGNOMY; RUNES; SACRIFICE; SCRYING; TAROT; TASSOMANCY. FURTHER READING: FLACELIERE 1965, LOEWE AND BLACKER 1981, PENNICK 1989.

Djin. In ceremonial magic, the king of the salamanders or elementals of fire. His name may derive from the Arabic word *jinn*, "demon." *SEE* ELEMENTAL.

Djwal Kul, Master. In the lore of Theosophy and related systems of occult philosophy, a Master of the Great White Lodge, the secret brotherhood that superintends the spiritual evolution of the Earth. The Master Djwal Kul (also spelled Djwal Kuhl) was a Tibetan mystic who was the chief pupil of the Master Kuthumi, and advanced to the position of Master in the early twentieth century. He has been identified as "the Tibetan" who dictated to Alice Bailey her voluminous works on occult philosophy and practice. *SEE* BAILEY, ALICE; KUTHUMI, MASTER; MASTERS; THEOSOPHY.

dobbie stone. In English folk magic, a stone with a natural or artificial hollow on its upper surface, into which liquid offerings can be poured. In a traditional spell for raising a wind, milk is poured into a dobbie stone from the direction out of which the desired wind is to come, and then left for cats to drink; in gratitude, the cats will raise the desired wind. It has been suggested that this spell was originally an invocation of the Nordic goddess Freya, whose sacred animal was the cat; however, no reference to this or any other Pagan deity is included with the spell. *SEE ALSO* CUNNING MAN/WOMAN. FURTHER READING: PENNICK 1989.

Doctor John. (Jean Montancé) African-American hoodoo doctor, ?–1885. Born in Senegal, he was enslaved in his youth but either escaped or purchased his freedom. He arrived in New Orleans from Cuba as a ship's cook, worked on the docks for some years, and owned a coffeehouse at the time of the 1850 census. By the 1860 census he gave his profession as "physician" and owned real estate worth $12,000, a very substantial sum at that time. According to an 1885 magazine article, he gambled away his wealth in his last years and was living in the home of his daughter Alicia when he died.

Doctor John was a powerfully built man with parallel scars on his cheeks, which he claimed were marks of royal birth. Along with Marie Laveau, he was the most famous of New Orleans hoodoo practitioners in the nineteenth century. In the late twentieth century his name was borrowed by New Orleans musician Mac

Rebennack. *SEE ALSO* HOODOO. FURTHER READING: LONG 2001.

dodecatemory. (ancient Greek, "twelfth part") In ancient astrology, a fraction of an astrological sign, usually one-twelfth of a sign or 2.5 degrees. The dodecatemories were assigned to the signs of the zodiac in sequence, from Aries to Pisces, and tracked subtle variations in the sign's energies—thus the Aries dodecatemory of each sign was its first forceful onset, the Taurus dodecatemory was the solid establishment of its energies, and so on. Dodecatemories have been largely forgotten in modern astrology and it is rare to come across a present-day astrologer who uses them. *SEE ALSO* ASTROLOGY; ZODIAC.

Doreal, Maurice. American occultist, 1898–1963. Born Claude Doggins in Oklahoma, Doreal took his new name and established his order, the Brotherhood of the White Temple, in 1929 in Denver, Colorado. He claimed to have spent eight years studying with the Dalai Lama in Tibet, but much of his order's teachings seem to have come from his substantial library (some 30,000 volumes) of occult and science-fiction books. He attracted around a thousand followers, who went with him in the late 1940s to a small town southwest of Denver to build a city that would survive a predicted atomic holocaust. He lived there, writing and teaching, until his death in 1963. FURTHER READING: KAFTON-MINKEL 1989.

dowsing. Also known as radiesthesia and "water witching," dowsing is a traditional art of divination originally used to find underground water sources, but more recently used for a wide range of other divinatory purposes. In its classic form, dowsing is done with a Y-shaped hazel branch. The dowser holds two ends in his or her hands with the third pointing more or less straight out in front. The hands are pulled slightly apart so that there is some tension on the dowsing rod. The dowser then walks over the land to be dowsed. When he or she crosses an underground water course, the free end of the dowsing rod will typically jerk downwards, sometimes with great force.

Many modern dowsers use pendulums or L-shaped wire rods in place of the traditional dowsing stick. The pendulum gives answers by moving in various directions; the wire rods, which are used in pairs and held by the short end of the L with the long end level, pivot toward each other and cross to indicate that something has been found. Dowsing over a map, rather than over the territory itself, has become popular in recent years.

Dowsing has a complicated relation to the broader Western occult traditions. Up until modern times it was usually carried on by folk practitioners who had little contact with other occult practices. Occasionally, however, dowsing entered the magical mainstream. For example, the occult treasure-hunting circles in which Joseph Smith, later the founder of the Mormon Church, learned magic were also active dowsers using dowsing sticks for general divination. *SEE* SMITH, JOSEPH.

One significant interface between dowsing and occultism has been in the field of leys and other Earth mysteries. A variety of English dowsers in the twentieth century have explored the network of leys (prehistoric alignments), which, according to Alfred Watkins and other researchers, crisscross the British countryside, and found that they correspond to networks of subtle energy detectable by dowsing. The adoption of Earth-mysteries research and its conclusions by many modern Pagan and occult traditions has brought dowsing into the toolkit of a number of modern Druid and other Pagan traditions, in Britain and elsewhere. *SEE* DRUIDRY; LEYS.

To many dowsers, on the other hand, their art is unconnected to occultism, and many dowsers with Christian or scientific belief systems are horrified by what they see as the intrusion of occultism into their art. *SEE ALSO* DIVINATION. FURTHER READING: BARRETT AND BESTERMAN 1968, FIDLER 1983, UNDERWOOD 1973.

drawing down the moon. In modern Wiccan and Pagan practice, the invocation of the Goddess into a member of a coven, usually the coven's High Priestess. In most cases, the High Priestess takes up a posture traditionally associated with the Goddess, while the High Priest invokes the Goddess into her by ritual means. Drawing down the moon plays an important part in many rituals, particularly those involving the Great Rite. *SEE* GREAT RITE.

In ancient times, the sorceresses of Thessaly were reputed to be able to call the moon down out of the sky. It has been suggested that this refers to rituals, known from surviving texts, in which the full moon's light was reflected by a mirror into water or oil as a way of consecration. *SEE ALSO* INVOCATION.

dreams and dreaming. Most versions of magical theory consider dreaming to be a form of awareness of the astral realm, and deliberate control of dreams has been practiced by a variety of different magical traditions as a way of astral travel. *SEE* ASTRAL PLANE.

The study and interpretation of dreams is also a very old and widely practiced form of divination. Handbooks of dream interpretation have been available since ancient Greek times, if not before; most of them, like their modern equivalents, give long lists of objects or persons, along with the meaning of each if it appears in a dream. The focus on dreams in modern psychology is thus only a recent form of a very old (and generally occult) tradition. *SEE ALSO* DIVINATION.

Drebbel, Cornelis. Dutch alchemist and inventor, 1572–1633. Born in Alkmaar in northern Holland and educated in the Netherlands, Drebbel left his homeland at the conclusion of the wars with Spain, settling first in Prague and then in England. During his Prague stay, he became principal alchemist to the Holy Roman Emperor Rudolf II, who was devoted to alchemy and the occult. Thereafter he moved to England, where he served as court alchemist to the Stuart kings James I and Charles I; *SEE* STUART, HOUSE OF.

His most famous feat took place in 1621, when he and twelve oarsmen climbed into a wooden submarine and rowed their way underwater on a three-hour voyage down the Thames from Westminster to Greenwich under the astonished gaze of King James I, the nobles of his court, and several thousand Londoners. The small vessel had no snorkel or outside air supply, but all aboard emerged alive and healthy at the end of the voyage. According to contemporary accounts, Drebbel had bottles of an unknown "quintessence of air" aboard the submarine, which he opened at intervals to keep the atmosphere breathable during the voyage. Several historians have argued that Drebbel's "quintessence" was oxygen, which was not officially discovered for another 150 years.

Drebbel also devised an effective mordant for cochineal dye, created a number of meteorological devices, and produced fireworks. He wrote two small books, one of them a treatise on meteorology that makes reference to Michael Sendivogius' influential aerial niter theory; *SEE* SENDIVOGIUS, MICHAEL. Since the aerial niter theory was based on experiments with saltpeter, which gives off large quantities of oxygen when heated, the claim that Drebbel knew how to make oxygen alchemically may not be unfounded. *SEE ALSO* ALCHEMY. FURTHER READING: HARRIS 1961, SZYDLO 1994.

Druidic witchcraft. A movement within modern Neopaganism that combines elements of Wicca with various Celtic material, mostly from Ireland and Wales. While some traditions within Druidic witchcraft claim to have survived since Pagan times, this is at least open to question. In practice, Druidic witchcraft is a highly eclectic mix of contemporary Wicca and Celtic lore drawn from published sources, with little in common either with what is known about the ancient Druids, or with older traditions of modern Druidry. *SEE* DRUIDS; WICCA.

Druidry. A modern religious, spiritual, philosophical, and magical movement that has attempted, with varying degrees of success, to revive the teachings and practices of the ancient Celtic Druids. For information on the ancient Druids, *SEE* DRUIDS.

Many modern Druid organizations, though not all, claim one form or another of direct descent from the ancient Celtic Druids, and it's just barely possible that one or another of these claims might have something behind it. Still, the rise of Druidry had much more to do with cultural and religious trends in the early modern and modern worlds than with whatever fragments of ancient tradition may have survived fifteen hundred years of Roman and Christian persecution.

The arrival of Renaissance culture in England and France forced educated people in those countries to confront the awkward reality of ancient Greek and Roman cultures artistically and intellectually far in advance of anything the early modern world had managed. A revived interest in the past led early scholars to rediscover surviving references to the ancient Druids, as well as sprawling megalithic ruins such as Stonehenge and Carnac. In England, sixteenth- and seventeenth-century occult traditions were already drawing on Celtic faery lore; *SEE* FAERY. The result was a climate ripe for a Druid revival.

That revival began sometime in the early eighteenth century. A traditional account current in modern Druid orders claims that John Toland (1670–1722), an Irish author and philosopher, organized a Druid grove at a meeting in London in the autumn of 1717, though no contemporary record of this meeting or the resulting grove survives. By the middle of the same century, William Stukeley (1687–1765) and his friends in the Society of Antiquaries were carrying out detailed studies of Stonehenge, Avebury, and other megalithic ruins. Stukeley himself was convinced that the ancient Druids were not merely the builders of these sites, but also the inheritors of an proto-Christian religious revelation handed down from the family of Noah. He and a number of other writers of the same sort made the ancient Druids respectable and encouraged others to explore, or invent, Druid traditions.

One such creation was the Ancient Order of Druids, founded in 1781 in London by English carpenter Henry Hurle. Modeled on Freemasonry, the AOD used elements of Druid tradition to fill out the standard fraternal-lodge system. A schismatic movement, the United Ancient Order of Druids (UAOD), was founded in 1833 and went on to become an organization of respectable size, especially in America. *SEE* LODGE, FRATERNAL.

Another nineteenth-century Druidry was produced by the brilliant if eccentric Welsh polymath Edward Williams (1747–1826), who under his pen name Iolo Morganwg turned out poetry, essays, and rituals he claimed to have inherited from the bardic traditions of his native Glamorganshire. Most of this material is now generally held to have originated in Williams' own fertile imagination, but his substantial grasp of Welsh tradition and literature enabled him to graft his creations effectively onto the Welsh *eisteddfodau* (bardic assemblies), where his rituals and symbolism are used to this day. His posthumous book *Barddas* (1862), a collection of manuscripts on bardic and Druidic traditions, had a massive impact on Druidry for a century thereafter.

Williams' example and writings launched a successful Druid organization based at Pontyprydd in Wales under successive Archdruids Myfyr Morganwg (Edward Davies) and Morien (Owen Morgan). The Druids of Pontyprydd were strongly influenced by current theories of phallic religion, which held that all religion was actually the worship of the life force in sexual form. Though their worship of sex never seems to have gone past the limits of Victorian propriety, the Druids of Pontyprydd were the subject of scandalized gossip, but they had a membership that extended to America, and a significant influence on many later Druid groups.

Other influences on the British Druid movement came from elsewhere in the occult scene. In the early twentieth century, the collapse of the Hermetic Order of the Golden Dawn sent many English occultists looking for other organizations in which to work. A surprising number of them seem to have ended up in one or another Druid order—a shift that was made easier by the strong interest in Celtic tradition among a number of major Golden Dawn figures. *SEE* CASTLE OF HEROES; GOLDEN DAWN, HERMETIC ORDER OF THE. This influx of trained ceremonial magicians led to the birth of new, syncretic Druid orders during the twentieth century; the Cabbalistic Order of Druids and the Ancient Order of Druid Hermetists, both of which flourished in London between the two world wars, are examples of the type.

The second major influence on twentieth-century British Druidry came from the broader Pagan revival that swung into motion throughout the Western world after the First World War. Woodcraft, a quasi-Pagan back-to-nature program for youth launched by Canadian nature writer Ernest Thompson Seton, had a particularly large impact from the 1920s on, and later Druid orders such as the Order of Bards Ovates and Druids (OBOD) drew members directly from the Woodcraft movement. *SEE* KIBBO KIFT, KINDRED OF THE; ORDER OF BARDS OVATES AND DRUIDS (OBOD); WOODCRAFT. Later on, the rise of Wicca brought a different mode of Pagan spirituality into contact with Druidry, and in particular brought the image of the Goddess into new prominence in Druid circles. *SEE* DRUIDIC WITCHCRAFT; GODDESS, THE; WICCA.

Outside of Britain, the Druid tradition put down roots in France early on. Brittany, a Celtic nation now part of the French Republic, had Druid orders as early as 1855, when a branch of the Welsh Eisteddfod was organized there. The UAOD reached France in 1869, and the first mystically oriented Druid organization, the Eglise Drudique et Nationale (Druidic and National Church), was founded in Paris in 1885. Since the Second World War, the French Druid scene has been busy, with dozens of active groups of various kinds, some related to British Druid traditions and others entirely home-grown.

America had Druid organizations as early as the 1780s, and both the UAOD and the Druids of Pontyprydd had a substantial presence in North America. Still, one of the most influential twentieth-century Druid organizations in America started as a joke. Students at Carleton College in Northfield, Minnesota, required to attend religious services, organized the Reformed Druids of North America (RDNA) as a mocking protest in 1963. The requirement was dropped, but a number of the members decided to take the joke seriously; the RDNA still exists. SEE REFORMED DRUIDS OF NORTH AMERICA (RDNA). An offshoot of the RDNA, the New Reformed Druids of North America, shifted the RDNA's eccentric approach in a more Neopagan direction, but attracted few members. In 1983 a former NRDA Archdruid, P. E. I. (Isaac) Bonewits (1949–), founded a more successful effort along the same lines, Ar nDraiocht Fein (ADF), which has become one of the more influential Druid groups in North America. SEE AR NDRAIOCHT FEIN (ADF).

The 1980s and 1990s, which saw an explosion of new groups in every branch of the modern Pagan revival, produced the same effect in the realm of Druidry, and a great many new Druid organizations and traditions emerged during this time. As with other modern Pagan movements, many of these fell apart almost as soon as they were started, but some have remained in existence to the present time and have produced some impressive work.

The sheer diversity of Druid organizations and traditions makes it impossible to describe "typical" Druid ritual, teaching, or practice; no such animal exists. Druid organizations disagree, sometimes violently, about whether Druidry is a religion, a spiritual path, a philosophy, or a magical tradition. Some modern Druid organizations

worship one or another set of ancient Celtic deities, while others do not; many, but not all, are deeply involved in the ecological movement; some have an interest in megaliths, ley lines, and other earth mysteries, while others consider these totally unrelated to Druidry. Druid rituals range from primeval sacrificial rites in which offerings of ale and silver are made to the gods, through vaguely Unitarian religious services in which passages from assorted mystical literature are read and a chalice of whiskey is passed around as a communion, to formal Hermetic rituals in which the guardian powers of the elements are invoked and figures in flowing white robes intone words of power.

Many students of traditional Celtic lore, especially those involved in the Celtic Reconstructionist movement, tend to dismiss modern Druid organizations as "modern fakery," and there is some basis for this charge, especially among those groups that make unverified claims of direct descent from the original Druids. On its own terms as a modern spiritual movement, however, Druidry has no reason for shame. As one of the first modern Pagan revival movements, with close to three hundred years of its own history and a rich legacy of philosophy, theory, and practice to its credit, it can stand comparison with most other spiritual traditions in the Western world. SEE ALSO CELTIC RECONSTRUCTIONISM; NEOPAGANISM. FURTHER READING: CARR-GOMM 2002, HANSEN 1995, JENKINS 1997, MILES 1992, MORGAN N.D., NICHOLS 1990, OWEN 1962, RAOULT 1996, REFORMED DRUIDS OF NORTH AMERICA 2003.

Druids. Members of a religious caste of at least some Celtic peoples of western Europe. Very little is known about them, since they had a taboo against keeping written records. The sum total of surviving information on the subject comes from ancient Greek and Roman writers, and later Christian missionaries and chroniclers, and fills a few dozen pages at most. Archeology provides a little more information, but the only accurate answer to most questions about them is "we don't know."

The Druids were probably the priests of the Pagan Celts, although even this is disputed, since none of the ancient writers who refer to them actually call them "priests." Their origins and history are anyone's guess;

Julius Caesar, the one ancient writer who discusses the issue, claimed that the Druidic system originated in Britain and spread from there to Gaul (present-day France). Druids also existed in Ireland and Scotland, but there are no ancient references to them in Central Europe or Asia Minor, where other Celtic peoples lived in ancient times.

According to Greek and Roman authors, the Druids were a privileged caste, exempt from taxation and military service. Their teachings were contained in verses, which had to be memorized by their students; some took as much as twenty years to finish this task. Those teachings apparently included a belief in reincarnation; *SEE* REINCARNATION.

Greek and Roman writers divide the Druids into three classes—Ovates, who practiced divination and studied nature; Bards, whose poetry and music formed the living memory of Pagan Celtic culture; and Druids proper, who taught students and superintended at sacrifices to the gods. Whether these were different levels of initiation, as most modern Druid traditions have supposed, or simply occupational specializations, is unknown. *SEE* BARD; OVATE.

Early Christian writers who mention Druids portray them as sorcerers who call on demons in a vain attempt to hinder the spread of Christianity. This parallels Christian rhetoric about other Pagan priesthoods, but there may well be a core of truth to the image of Druids as magicians; certainly folklore in Ireland and Wales for centuries thereafter saw Druidry as primarily a matter of magical power, and the Irish word *draiocht* means both "druidry" and "magic."

The Druids of Gaul and Britain suffered persecution in Roman times, since the Druids were identified as potential leaders of rebellion against Rome. In Ireland and Scotland, which never fell under Roman control, Druid traditions flourished until the coming of Christianity. The fragmentary historical records from the early Middle Ages, when Christianity finally penetrated the Celtic lands of northwestern Europe, provide only rough dates, but by 800 or so it seems clear that Druidry in its original form had died out. Some amount of Druid lore may have survived in the native poetic and scholarly traditions of Wales, Ireland, and the Scottish Highlands, though this is a subject of bitter argument by contemporary scholars.

Like most ancient people with a reputation for wisdom, the Druids were caught up early and often in the speculations of occult historians, and have played any number of roles in this context. Suggestions in one ancient source that Pythagoras may have studied with the Druids of Marseilles, or perhaps vice versa, have been enthusiastically repeated by occult authors from the Renaissance onwards; *SEE* PYTHAGORAS. Druids have also been associated with the lost continent of Atlantis, with ancient Egypt, and with a variety of more exotic origin theories as well; the one thing that seems to be missing is a claim that the ancient Druids came from outer space—though this will no doubt be forthcoming.

The ancient Druids have also served as primary inspiration to the modern tradition of Druidry; *SEE* DRUIDRY. *SEE ALSO* CELTIC RECONSTRUCTIONISM. FURTHER READING: BERESFORD ELLIS 1994, PIGGOTT 1968.

Dryhten. (Old English, "lord") In some modern Wiccan traditions, the primal divine unity which divides into the God and the Goddess. Dryhten is more a philosophical concept than a deity who is actually worshipped, and plays little part in Wiccan ritual and practice even in those traditions that include it. *SEE* GOD, THE; GODDESS, THE; WICCA.

Duamutef. (ancient Egyptian *dwamtf*) One of the four sons of Horus, Duamutef had the head of a jackal, ruled over the eastern quarter of the world, and had guardianship of the heart and lungs of the deceased. His name is spelled Tuamautef, Ttoumathph, and Tmooumathv in various older sources. He was associated with the goddess Neith, and was also called "the Cutter." *SEE* CANOPIC GODS.

In the Golden Dawn magical system, under the name Ttoumathph, he is one of the invisible guardians of the temple, stationed in the southeast. *SEE* GOLDEN DAWN, HERMETIC ORDER OF THE; INVISIBLE STATIONS.

Duir. (Old Irish, "oak") The seventh letter of the Ogham alphabet, with the sound-value *d*. It corresponds to the oak among trees, the wren among birds, the color black, and the number twelve. In Robert Graves' version of the Ogham tree-calendar, its month runs from June 11 to July 8. *SEE* OGHAM.

Ogham letter Duir

Dweller on the Threshold. *SEE* WATCHER ON THE THRESHOLD.

dybbuk. In Jewish folklore and magic, a demon or ghost that possesses a living person. Dybbuks became a common feature in Jewish lore before the start of the Common Era. In earlier writings they were held to be demons, but by the Middle Ages they were understood to be the souls of those too evil to be allowed to reincarnate. These "naked spirits" sought shelter inside the bodies of living persons, but could only enter if the person had committed a secret sin. They could be exorcized by Cabalistic magical methods, and detailed manuals for banishing dybbuks were in circulation from the fifteenth century on. *SEE ALSO* DEMON; POSSESSION, DEMONIC. FURTHER READING: SCHOLEM 1974.

Eadha. (Old Irish, meaning uncertain) The nineteenth letter of the Ogham alphabet, with the sound-value *e*. It corresponds to the aspen among trees, the swan among birds, the color red, and the number two. In Robert Graves' version of the Ogham tree-calendar, it is associated with the autumn equinox. *SEE* OGHAM.

Ogham letter Eadha

eagle. In magical symbolism, the Kerubic emblem of the element of water (not air, as one might suspect); it derives from the complex magical symbolism of the zodiacal sign Scorpio. *SEE* SCORPIO; WATER, ELEMENT OF.

In alchemy, the eagle is a common symbol, and usually represents mercury. Paired with the lion, it represents mercury and sulphur, the basic principles of all metallic substances. *SEE* ALCHEMY; MERCURY.

Ear. (Old English, "grave") The twenty-ninth rune of the Anglo-Saxon futhorc. The Old English rune-poem relates this rune to the idea of death as the common fate of all. *SEE* ANGLO-SAXON FUTHORC.

Rune Ear

earth, element of. In magical symbolism, one of the four (or five) elements, corresponding to matter in the solid state, to the cold and dry qualities, and to the melancholic humor. As with all the elements, there are varying attributions to the element of earth, but the following are standard in most current Western occult systems:

> *Symbol:* ∀
> *Letter of Tetragrammaton:* ה, final Heh
> *Name of God:* אדני, ADNI, Adonai (Lord)
> *Archangel:* אוריאל, AVRIAL, Auriel (Light of God)
> *Angel:* פורלאכ, PVRLAK, Phorlakh
> *Ruler:* כרוב, KRVB, Kerub
> *Elemental King:* Ghob
> *Elementals:* Gnomes
> *Hebrew Name of Element:* ארץ, ARTz, Aretz
> *Direction:* צפון, TzPVN, Tzaphon, the North
> *Season:* Winter
> *Time of Day:* Midnight
> *Qualities:* Cold and dry
> *Nature:* Stability

SEE ALSO DIRECTIONS IN OCCULTISM; ELEMENTS, MAGICAL; HUMORS.

earths, seven. According to Cabalistic lore, there are seven earths, seven heavens, and seven hells. The seven earths are worlds inhabited either by human beings or by other intelligent creatures not descended from Adam. According to Golden Dawn sources, which derive from the Zohar, the seven earths and their correspondences are as follows:

Name	Translation	Sephirah
1. Aretz	dry earth	the Supernals
2. Adamah	red clay	Chesed
3. Gia	valley	Geburah
4. Neshiah	pasture or meadow	Tiphareth
5. Tziah	desert	Netzach
6. Arqa	earth	Hod
7. Thebel	world	Yesod and Malkuth or Cheled

Our own Earth is Cheled, and is described as mixed earth and water—which seems fairly accurate. The seven hells are located in Arqa, the world corresponding to Hod. SEE ALSO HEAVENS, SEVEN; HELLS, SEVEN.

Eastern Star, Order of the. An auxiliary of American Freemasonry, the Order of the Eastern Star admits Master Masons and women connected to them by birth or marriage. Christian, charitable, and utterly proper, it has nothing at all to do with the occult, but its emblem—an inverted pentagram bearing an assortment of symbols, and letters spelling the word FATAL—has caused a good deal of confusion and suspicion. FATAL stands for the sentence "Fairest Among Ten thousand, Altogether Lovely," which may give some sense of the order's general flavor. SEE FREEMASONRY; PENTAGRAM.

Ebad. SEE KOAD.

Ebhadh. SEE KOAD.

ecliptic. The apparent path of the sun against the background of stars as seen from Earth, the ecliptic is a great circle passing through the twelve constellations of the zodiac. The term "ecliptic" comes from the fact that eclipses occur when the moon is also on this line. Because of the tilt of Earth's axis, the ecliptic appears to be tilted a little over twenty-three degrees from the celestial equator (the projection of the Earth's equator in space). The ecliptic plays a significant role in many ancient mythologies, which encode astronomical and astrological information in narrative form. SEE ALSO PRECESSION OF THE EQUINOXES; ZODIAC. FURTHER READING: DE SANTILLANA AND VON DECHEND 1977.

ectoplasm. In Spiritualism and many other modern occult traditions, a subtle substance that is extruded from certain mediums during their séances, and provides the semimaterial basis for certain mediumistic phenomena. Invisible and intangible in its ordinary form, it can become a mistlike vapor, a fluid, or a gelatinous semisolid. During a séance, it oozes from all the orifices of the medium's body, including the pores of the skin. It smells of ozone, and breaks up readily when exposed to light. Exactly what it is, if it actually exists, is a riddle, though concentrated and condensed etheric substance might be a good working hypothesis.

According to several exposés of fraudulent mediums, the standard way to fake ectoplasm is to wad up fine cotton chiffon and hide it in a body orifice, then extract it as needed. SEE ALSO SPIRITUALISM.

Eden. According to biblical mythology, the garden in which the first man and woman lived after they were created, and from which they were expelled after tasting the fruit of the Tree of the Knowledge of Good and Evil. Eden has played varying roles in occult symbolism and teaching since that time. As the primary origin myth of the Western world, it remains a living presence, and it continues to crop up in many different forms all through modern folk spirituality and popular culture.

In the Western occult traditions themselves, Gnostic lore includes many alternative versions of the Eden story, which relate to the biblical version roughly the way conspiracy theories about the Kennedy assassination relate to the official Warren Commission report. SEE GNOSTICISM. In the Cabala, by contrast, the story is used as the basis for complex cosmological speculations, Eve is turned into the goddess of nature, and Adam becomes the collective soul of humanity as a whole; SEE CABALA. In Christian occultism, finally, the story is taken more or less as given; SEE CHRISTIAN OCCULTISM. SEE ALSO ADAM; EVE; FALL, THE.

Edom. (Hebrew ADVM, "red") An ancient kingdom located in the desert country east of Israel, in what is now Jordan. Edom had a succession of kings before the time of Saul, the first King of Israel. In Cabalistic symbolism, these kings were equated with the Lords of Unbalanced Force, the ruling powers of the Primal Worlds which passed away before the birth of the present universe.

There were eight kings and eleven dukes of Edom, and they were assigned to the Tree of Life as follows:

1. Bela, son of Beor. *City:* Dinhabah. *Duke:* Timnah, Alvah, Jetheth. *Sephirah:* Daath.

2. Jobab, son of Zerah. *City:* Bozrah. *Duke:* Aholibamah. *Sephirah:* Chesed.

3. Husham. *City:* Temani. *Duke:* Elah. *Sephirah:* Geburah.

4. Hadad son of Bedad. *City:* Avith. *Duke:* Pinon. *Sephirah:* Tiphareth.

5. Samlah. *City:* Masrekah. *Duke:* Kenaz. *Sephirah:* Netzach.

6. Saul. *City:* Rehoboth. *Duke:* Teman. *Sephirah:* Hod.

7. Baal-Hanan son of Achbor. *City:* {none}. *Duke:* Mibzar and Magdiel. *Sephirah:* Yesod.

8. Hadar. *City:* Pau. *Duke:* Eram. *Sephirah:* Malkuth.

Note: The wife of Hadar, the last of the kings, was Mehitabel, daughter of Matred, daughter of Mezahab.

The connection between the kings of Edom and the powers of the primal worlds plays a role in several Golden Dawn rituals, which quote passages about the Edomite kings drawn from the Bible and various Cabalistic texts. SEE GOLDEN DAWN, HERMETIC ORDER OF THE. SEE ALSO QLIPPOTH.

egregor. Also spelled "egregore," this is a common term in modern magical practice for the artificial group soul brought into being by any working magical or spiritual group—or, for that matter, any group of people united by emotional ties of any sort. The word originally meant "watcher," and referred to an artificial elemental built up by a magical group to keep watch over its workings and ward off physical and nonphysical intruders. Over time, the meaning of the term shifted to its present use.

In some modern Pagan writings, the gods and goddesses of traditional Paganism are identified as egregors constructed jointly by divine beings and their human worshippers. This corresponds closely to older Hermetic discussions of the same subject. SEE ALSO GROUP SOUL.

Egyptian Book of the Dead. Known to the ancient Egyptians as *Pert em Hru,* "coming forth by day," the Book of the Dead was the most important of a whole family of texts designed to help the dead navigate their way through the underworld to the paradise of Amentet. Substantial parts of it date from the very beginnings of Egyptian civilization. It consists of a series of prayers, hymns, spells, and invocations to be used by a dead person on the underworld journey.

There are four known versions of the text. The oldest version is found in the Pyramid Texts, which were carved on the walls of the tombs of pharaohs of the fifth and sixth dynasties from around 2300 B.C.E. Starting in the time of the eighteenth dynasty, around 1500 B.C.E., the Theban version came into circulation, along with another closely related to it. The fourth version was a product of the Saite period, the last period of Egyptian independence, which began in 550 B.C.E.; this Saite version was carefully revised and expanded by the scholar-priests of the period, and it remained in use until the last traces of ancient Egyptian culture went under in the first centuries of the Common Era.

The Book of the Dead was completely forgotten until Champollion's decipherment of Egyptian hieroglyphics in 1822 opened the door to the rediscovery of ancient Egyptian culture. Lepsius' German translation of the Turin papyrus in 1842 was followed by numerous translations of other texts into German and French. The classic English version is E. A. Wallis Budge's translation of the Papyrus of Ani, the longest known copy of the Theban version, which had a powerful influence on magical circles throughout the English-speaking world. SEE ALSO EGYPTIAN OCCULTISM. FURTHER READING: BUDGE 1967.

Egyptian calendar. The ancient Egyptians seem to have been the first culture in history to establish a solar calendar with twelve months. Each Egyptian month has thirty days, with an additional five days—the so-called epagomenal days—at the end of the year to fill out the total of 365. The names of the Egyptian months are as follows:

1. Thoth
2. Phaophi
3. Athyr
4. Choiak
5. Tybi
6. Mecheir
7. Phamenoth
8. Pharmuthi
9. Pachon
10. Payni
11. Epiphi
12. Mesore

The five epagomenal days were the birthdays of the deities Osiris, Aroueris, Set, Isis, and Nephthys, respectively. According to Egyptian myth, the sky-goddess Nut was the wife of Ra, but loved the earth-god Geb and became pregnant by him. When Ra learned of the pregnancy, he cursed Nut and ordained that she would not give birth in any day of any month of the year. Thoth, the god of wisdom, who was also a lover of Nut, gambled with the goddess of the moon and won from her one-seventieth of each day. Together, these made up five full days, which Thoth then added on to the year; since they did not belong to any month, Nut gave birth to her children by Geb on those days. *SEE ALSO* OSIRIS.

Because the Egyptian calendar lacks a leap year system, or any other way to make up for the fraction of a day left over at the end of each 365-day year, dates in the Egyptian calendar move backwards through the seasons over time. In the year 2000 of the modern (Gregorian) calendar, for example, the first day of Thoth fell on April 8. To determine the Gregorian date of Thoth 1 for any year thereafter, subtract one day for each leap year between 2000 and the year for which you're trying to calculate. For dates before 2000, add one day for each leap year (including one for 2000 itself). FURTHER READING: BUDGE 1967, EVANS 1998.

Egyptian days. In medieval folklore, thirty-two days in each year that are full of misfortune. To do nearly anything on these days was to risk disaster. According to one fifteenth-century manuscript, "whoso weddeth a wife on any of those days, he shall not long have joy of her; and who that taketh any journey, shall never come (back) again, or some misfortune shall befall him; and he that beginneth any great work shall never make end thereof; and he that letteth him blood shall soon die, or never be whole" (Dawson 1934, pp. 328–329).

The particular days thus marked vary from source to source. The manuscript mentioned above lists the Egyptian days as follows:

January 1, 2, 4, 5, 10, 11, 15
February 1, 7, 10
March 2, 11
April 16, 21
May 6, 15, 20
June 4, 7
July 15, 20
August 19, 20
September 6, 7
October 6
November 15, 19
December 6, 7, 9

In the later Middle Ages and the Renaissance, the Egyptian days were one target of the church's crackdown on popular magic and divination. Those who openly kept track of the Egyptian days risked falling afoul of the Inquisition; inquisitors' handbooks from the thirteenth century and after include the Egyptian days in lists of prohibited "superstitious" practices. FURTHER READING: DAWSON 1934, KIECKHEFER 1989.

Egyptian occultism. From the time of the pharaohs to the present, ancient Egypt has had a reputation as the homeland of magic par excellence. A proverb from the Talmud claims that all the magic in the world is divided into ten parts; Egypt got nine, and the rest of the world split up the one remaining part. Similar comments can be found throughout ancient, medieval, and early modern literature.

Many Western occult systems, including some with roots very far from the banks of the Nile, trace themselves back to alleged Egyptian origins. While most of these accounts are mythic rather than historical, and some are fairly straightforward examples of fakery, there is a core of truth behind them: to a very large degree, the Western occult tradition itself began in the country its ancient inhabitants called Khem, "the Black Land."

The origins of ancient Egyptian civilization are traced by modern archeologists to 4000 B.C.E., rooted in tribal cultures that were established along the banks of the Nile for many centuries before that time. By 3200 B.C.E., a plethora of small kingdoms had given way to two—Lower Egypt, comprising the Nile Delta, and Upper Egypt, extending south from the beginning of the delta to the First Cataract near Aswan. The two kingdoms were united by Narmer, the founder of the First Dynasty. By the Third Dynasty, the first pyramids were being built, and much of ancient Egyptian civilization was already solidly in place. That civilization persisted through some thirty dynasties reaching from 3200 B.C.E. to the first centuries of the Common Era, when the impact of Roman rule, the coming of Christianity, and finally the arrival of Islam brought it to an end.

Magic was pervasive throughout Egyptian religion, philosophy, and daily life. For example, part of the daily temple liturgy to the sun god Re—performed in temples throughout Egypt from Middle Kingdom times onward—used a wax "voodoo doll" of Re's great enemy, the underworld serpent Apophis. The Apophis figure was impaled with copper knives and then burned, to vanquish the serpent and assist Re in his voyage through the heavens. At the same time, the priests performing this rite also sacrificed other wax figures, who stood for the political and military enemies of the reigning pharaoh; they also offered still more figures, representing the personal enemies of the donors who paid for the ritual's daily performance. Separating out "religion" from "magic" in a ceremony of this sort is a futile process, as the ancient Egyptians themselves drew no such distinction. Although there is an Egyptian word for magic—heka—there is no ancient Egyptian term that can be translated as "religion."

The primary practitioners of magic in ancient Egypt, in fact, were the temple priests themselves. Surviving records from pharaonic through Ptolemaic times show no sign of a separate class of magicians, of the sort found in most other ancient and modern societies. Instead, the priesthoods themselves worked magic. Magical practices were an important part of the seshtau, "that which is hidden"—the inner rituals of the temple cult, which were enacted in the inner sanctuaries of Egyptian temples.

Except for those at the very top of the hierarchy, Egyptian priests served at the temples in rotation, and performed ritual workings for private clients in the intervals between periods of temple duty. It's indicative that the standard late Egyptian word for "magician," hariteb, is descended from the older phrase hari-heb hari-tep, "chief lector priest," an important Egyptian priestly rank. (The same Egyptian word gave rise to the biblical Hebrew word hartum, a common Old Testament term for "magician.")

The Egyptian word for magic, heka, was also the name of a god—Heka, "Magic" or "the Magician," who had shrines in the Egyptian cities of Heliopolis and Memphis, and a festival on the twenty-second day of the month of Athyr; SEE EGYPTIAN CALENDAR. Coffin texts from the Old Kingdom describe Heka as the first creation of the primordial god Atum. Later texts describe him as the ka or vital spirit of the solar god Re, traveling in Re's sunboat and helping him vanquish the evil serpent Apophis. Other gods and goddesses also claimed the title werethekau, "great of magic," and the Tenth Dynasty text "Instructions for King Merikare" includes magic as one of the great gifts—together with Heaven, Earth, air, food, and good government—that the gods had given to human beings.

As the place of pharaoh's enemies in the ritual against Apep shows, magical practices were an important part of the political structure. Magical operations against Egypt's military and political opponents were a common event. Ritual "execration figures"—that is, small statues of domestic and foreign enemies of the state—were used in a variety of magical practices, and the pharaohs even had such figures painted on their sandals, so they could symbolically trample their enemies with each step. (A pair of such sandals were found in the tomb of Tutankhamun.)

Cursing ceremonies were also much used against opponents of the Egyptian state; these included the *Sed deseru* or "Breaking of the Red Vases," in which pottery vessels were inscribed with the names of intended targets and then shattered, and the custom of writing letters to the dead, who were asked either to carry out various activities themselves or to appeal to the gods on the magician's behalf. This latter method seems to have been ancestral to the later Greek and Roman use of *defixiones* or binding tablets; *SEE* BINDING TABLET.

The same practices were also turned against the regime on occasion. When Queen Tiye, one of the wives of Rameses III, set out to murder her husband by magic and put her son on the throne, the ritual scrolls used in the plot were stolen from the pharaoh's own library.

Not all Egyptian magic had such hostile intentions behind it. Healing magic was much practiced, especially for victims of scorpion stings and snakebite, and overlapped considerably with the abundant lore of ancient Egyptian medicine and surgery. A great deal of magic also found a place in the elaborate rituals for the dead, and texts such as the *Pert em Hru* or "Book of Coming Forth by Day", the so-called Egyptian Book of the Dead, are important repositories of magical ritual. *SEE* EGYPTIAN BOOK OF THE DEAD.

The impact of Egyptian magical traditions on the other peoples of the ancient world was considerable. During the last period of Egyptian independence, the Saite period (663–525 B.C.E.), the political and military alliance between Egypt and the city-states of Greece made it possible for a number of Greek intellectuals, Pythagoras foremost among them, to study Egyptian temple lore; *SEE* PYTHAGORAS. The Persian invasion of 525 B.C.E. closed off this option, but Alexander the Great's conquest of Egypt in 332 B.C.E. opened the door wide again and ushered in the Ptolemaic period, a span of three centuries in which a Greek-Egyptian hybrid culture came into being on the banks of the Nile. During this period, the Egyptian city of Alexandria became a center of Greek culture and philosophy, and several important currents of Greek thought absorbed a significant amount from Egyptian sources. *SEE* ALEXANDRIA. In particular, the Pythagorean tradition—itself rooted in Egypt-

ian soil—flourished under the Ptolemies, and the foundations of Neoplatonism were also laid in Alexandrian philosophical circles. The fusion between Greek and Egyptian culture extended far enough that Egyptian priests could and did become Greek philosophers as well; *SEE* CHAEREMON. It was also in Alexandria during the same period that alchemy first appeared in the Western world; *SEE* ALCHEMY.

The Roman conquest in 30 B.C.E. marked the beginning of the end for ancient Egyptian culture. While the Roman government was willing to permit many Egyptian religious practices to continue, anything that strayed too close to what Romans understood as magic ran into increasing legal difficulties; *SEE* MAGIC, PERSECUTION OF. Edicts of 199 and 359 C.E. prohibited the traditional *peheneter* oracles, and all magical practices were forbidden by imperial legislation starting in the time of Augustus and frequently renewed by his successors. In response, Egyptian priests carried on their more obviously magical practices in secret, and a class of full-time magicians operating on the far side of the law began to emerge.

It was in this context that ritual texts from the ancient temple lore made their way into the assortment of spellbooks from Roman Egypt now known as the Graeco-Egyptian magical papyri; *SEE* GRAECO-EGYPTIAN MAGICAL PAPYRI. The same forces shaped the Hermetic and Gnostic movements, which fused Egyptian ritual, Greek philosophy, and Hebrew theology into a religious approach that replaced much of what remained of the moribund temple traditions. On a more intellectual level, the diffusion of Egyptian temple lore into late classical magic had a potent influence on Neoplatonist philosophy, and became a central factor in the theurgic Neoplatonism of Iamblichus and Proclus. *SEE* HERMETICISM; PLATONISM; THEURGY.

The new, secretive magical spirituality proved both more durable and easier to export beyond Egypt's borders. When the last Egyptian temples went out of existence in the fifth century, it remained for these later systems to carry on what remained of Egypt's magical legacy. FURTHER READING: ASSMANN 1995, BUDGE 1967, HARRIS 1998, RITNER 1993.

Eh. (Anglo-Saxon rune) *SEE* EHWAZ.

Eh. (Armanen rune) The seventeenth rune of the Armanen rune system, Eh corresponds to the concept of marriage, the god Loki, and the magical power, from the *Havamal* rune-verses, to make girls not hate the runemaster. *SEE* ARMANEN RUNES.

Rune Eh

Ehwaz. (Old Germanic, "horse") The nineteenth rune of the elder futhark, corresponding to the horse, and particularly to the god Odin's magical eight-legged horse Sleipnir; other ideas connected with this rune include marriage, partnerships of all kinds, and transformations. It represents the sound *e*. *SEE* ELDER FUTHARK.

The same rune, named Eh (Old English, "horse") is the nineteenth rune of the Anglo-Saxon futhorc. The Old English rune-poem relates this rune to the warrior's horse, "whose pride is in its hoofs, a joy to man." *SEE* ANGLO-SAXON FUTHORC.

Rune Ehwaz (Eh)

eight. In Pythagorean number symbolism, eight—the octad—is the first cube and the number of harmony. It is called "mother," "safety," and "foundation," and is associated with the Muse Euterpe. *SEE* PYTHAGORAS.

In the Cabala, eight is Hod, the eighth Sephirah, and also the number of the letter Cheth. Names of God with eight letters include ALVH VDAaTh, Eloah Va-Daath, and YHVH VDAaTh, Tetragrammaton Va-Daath. *SEE* CABALA.

In Renaissance magical symbolism, eight is the number of health and preservation, and represents eternity. *SEE ALSO* ARITHMOLOGY. FURTHER READING: MCLEAN 1994, WATERFIELD 1988, WESTCOTT 1984.

Eihwaz. (Old Germanic, "yew tree") The thirteenth rune of the elder futhark, corresponding to the yew tree,

the god Ullr, the craft of hunting, and also to rune staves and calendars. It represents the sound *ei*. In some modern Pagan accounts, this rune is identified with the world-tree Yggdrasil of Norse myth, but as Yggdrasil was traditionally an ash tree rather than a yew this seems somewhat far-fetched. *SEE* ELDER FUTHARK.

The same rune, with the name Eoh (Old English, "yew"), is the thirteenth rune of the Anglo-Saxon futhorc. The Anglo-Saxon rune-poem gives it a special role as guardian of fire. *SEE* ANGLO-SAXON FUTHORC.

Rune Eihwaz (Eoh)

elder futhark. The oldest known runic alphabet, the elder futhark entered into use among most of the ancient Germanic tribes sometime between 200 B.C.E. and 50 C.E. Its historical origins are still a matter of dispute; one hypothesis traces it to an alphabet used in northern Italy around 500 B.C.E., close to German territory and well within reach of Germanic traders and adventurers, while the Greek and Latin alphabets have also been proposed as sources.

The elder futhark consists of twenty-four runes, divided into three groups or *aettir* of eight runes each:

First Aett

Rune	Sound Value	Name	Meaning
ᚠ	F	Fehu	Cattle
ᚢ	U	Uruz	Wild Ox
ᚦ	Th	Thurisaz	Giant
ᚨ	A	Ansuz	God Odin
ᚱ	R	Raido	Journey
ᚲ	K	Kaunaz	Torch
ᚷ	G	Gebo	Gift
ᚹ	W	Wunjo	Joy

Second Aett

Rune	Sound Value	Name	Meaning
ᚺ	H	Hagalaz	Hail
ᚾ	N	Nauthiz	Need
ᛁ	I	Isa	Ice

ᛃ	J	Jera	Year
ᛇ	Ei	Eiwaz	Yew Tree
ᛈ	P	Perth	(unknown)
ᛉ	Z	Algiz	Elk
ᛋ	S	Sowelu	Sun

Third Aett

ᛏ	T	Teiwaz	God Tyr
ᛒ	B	Berkana	Birch Tree
ᛖ	E	Ehwaz	Horse
ᛗ	M	Mannaz	Man
ᛚ	L	Laguz	Lake
◊	Ng	Inguz	God Ing (Frey)
ᛟ	O	Othila	Home
ᛞ	D	Dagaz	Day

There is some question about the proper order of the last two runes in the sequence. Most accounts, ancient and modern, give the order shown here, but the oldest complete futhark—carved on the Gotland stone in Sweden around 425 C.E.—places Dagaz before Othila. *SEE ALSO* ANGLO-SAXON FUTHORC; RUNES; YOUNGER FUTHARK.

elder tree. (*Sambucus* sp.) The elder tree is important in folk magic over much of Europe. It was planted at the corners of gardens as a protection against evil. To burn an elder log, however, was to invite the Devil into the house, and cradles were never made of elder wood because any child put in one would be pinched black and blue by the faery folk. *SEE* FAERY. *SEE ALSO* NATURAL MAGIC. Under the name Ruis, the elder is also an Ogham tree. *SEE* OGHAM; RUIS.

electional astrology. The art of choosing the most favorable time for events using astrological cycles. Electional astrology is essentially ordinary astrology turned upside down. Instead of starting with a given time and place, and working out the astrological factors in play then and there, the electional astrologer starts out with a set of desired astrological factors and sets out to find a time and place when those factors are present. For exam-

ple, a marriage might be scheduled for a time when Venus is strong and in positive aspects.

Electional astrology can range from relatively simple approaches up to exhaustive calculations involving many factors. Many of the complexities involve using the birth chart of the person seeking to plan the event, and working out a time when the planets and signs are in placements that not only favor the event in question, but also harmonize with the person's birth chart. In the case of a wedding, in turn, both spouses' charts need to be taken into account.

Electional astrology has been in common use since ancient times. It played an important role in society in the Middle Ages and Renaissance, when few significant events would be planned without the advice of an astrologer. While the decline of astrology at the time of the Scientific Revolution affected electional astrology at least as much as any other branch of the art, it has staged an impressive comeback in the last century and is actively studied and pursued by many astrologers today.

Electional astrology also has a direct application to magical practice. Traditional textbooks of magic such as the *Key of Solomon* and H. Cornelius Agrippa's *Three Books of Occult Philosophy* routinely instruct the magician to do certain rituals at times chosen for astrological reasons. For example, Agrippa instructs the magician to make a magical ring to bring prophetic dreams when either the sun or Saturn is in the ninth house, favorably aspected, and in the sign that was in the ascendant in the birth chart of the person for whom the ring is made (Agrippa 1993, p. 404). In medieval and Renaissance magic, this sort of electional astrology was the most common way to calculate the proper time of a magical ritual, and some magicians still use this method at present. *SEE* CEREMONIAL MAGIC. *SEE ALSO* ASTROLOGY. FURTHER READING: AGRIPPA 1993.

electric fluid. In nineteenth- and early twentieth-century magical writings, a term for the positive mode or aspect of etheric energy. The corresponding negative mode or aspect was called the "magnetic fluid." *SEE* ETHER.

elemental. A spirit inhabiting one of the four magical elements. Elementals play a very important part in modern magical theory and practice, but are actually quite a recent addition to the traditional lore. Some material on elemental spirits can be found in medieval sources, but it was Paracelsus (1493–1541) who defined the elementals in the terms used ever since: gnomes, the elementals of earth; undines, elementals of water; sylphs, elementals of air; and salamanders, elementals of fire. SEE PARACELSUS. The vast influence of Paracelsus' works on early modern occult traditions ensured that his account of the elementals would become standard throughout the Western world, and most magical traditions from the sixteenth century onward repeat his material with additions.

A surprisingly influential source of these additions was a satirical story entitled *Le Comte de Gabalis* by the Abbé Montfaucon de Villars. In this tale, the Comte of the title propounds to the main character the theory that the point of all occult practice was sexual relations with the spirits of the elements. Though the entire tale is written in tones of broad farce, and in fact the Western occult traditions have few funnier satires, the story has been treated by many occultists with deadpan seriousness, and there is good reason to think that all through the eighteenth and nineteenth century, there were plenty of magicians who devoted all their time and efforts to achieving such a "counterpartal marriage." SEE COMTE DE GABALIS, LE.

In modern magical philosophy, elementals are seen as conscious entities inhabiting the four elements of the physical world. They have limited intelligence but extensive powers over the element they indwell, and their powers are at the disposal of a magician who has mastered the corresponding elemental force in himself or herself. According to some sources, elementals are dependent on human beings for some aspects of their spiritual evolution, and respond willingly to human attempts at contact. As creatures of a single element, though, they have an unbalancing effect on the human psyche, and too much contact with elementals of a particular type can lead to a range of problems. SEE ALSO ELEMENTS, MAGICAL. FURTHER READING: FORTUNE 1930, GREER 2001.

elemental king. In the lore of ceremonial magic, one of four beings who are held to govern the elemental spirits; SEE ELEMENTAL. Their nature and place in the hierarchies of spiritual beings is uncertain, though many authorities suggest that an elemental king is essentially the collective mind of an entire class of elemental spirits. The elemental king of air is Paralda, that of fire is Djin, that of water is Nichsa, and that of earth is Ghob. SEE ALSO ELEMENTS, MAGICAL.

elementary spirit. In most versions of occult philosophy, another term for elementals; SEE ELEMENTAL. In some sources, the term "elementary" is used for those spirits who have bodies formed from two or three elements, while the term "elemental" is reserved for those with bodies of a single element. Just to add to the confusion, still other sources use the term to refer to the souls of deceased human beings.

Elementaries and fays are often confused with one another, and may actually be the same. SEE FAERY.

elements, magical. Central elements of magical philosophy since ancient times, the four elements—earth, water, fire, air—and the "fifth element" of spirit were introduced into the Western occult tradition in ancient Greek times. The four elements were apparently first devised by Empedocles of Acragas (fifth century B.C.E.), a follower of Pythagoras, and popularized by Plato and Aristotle in the fourth century. SEE EMPEDOCLES OF ACRAGAS. Aristotle defined earth as the union of cold and dry qualities, water as cold and moist, air as warm and moist, and fire as warm and dry; this set the stage for humoral medicine, the traditional healing system of the West, and also had a powerful influence on alchemy. SEE ALCHEMY; HUMORS.

Another important transformation of elemental theory that can be credited to Aristotle is the doctrine of the "fifth element," variously called the quintessence, spirit, ether, and akasha. Not actually an element at all, spirit is the background unity out of which the four elements come into manifestation and into which they return. In Aristotle's cosmology, the planets and stars were thought to be made of the quintessence. This notion was discarded by magical theorists at the end of the Renaissance in favor of an approach that sees spirit or ether as the subtle patterning energy underlying all physical matter, here on Earth as well as out among the stars. SEE ETHER.

It is important to understand that the elements are not simply the physical substances of the same names. Each element is a basic category of existence, which can be traced in any realm of experience. Earth represents the solid, stable, and enduring; water, the receptive, responsive, and fluid; air, the mediating, pervading, and embracing; fire, the active, energizing, and transforming; and spirit as the transcendent, the factor that influences the system of elements from another level. In the human psyche, for example, earth appears as sensory perception, water as feeling (which includes both emotion and intuition), air as intellect, fire as will, and spirit as awareness itself. In society, similarly, earth is expressed by the producers of useful goods and services; water by the artists, poets, and performers; air by the scientists, scholars, and teachers; fire by the politicians and soldiers; and spirit as the priests, priestesses, mystics, and occultists. In modern physics, finally, earth appears as the solid state of matter, water as the liquid state, air as the gaseous state, fire as energy, and spirit as the underlying fabric of space-time.

The applicability of the elements to nearly every field of human experience has given rise to a vast array of symbolism and correspondences, shot through (like many elements of occult symbolism) with contradictions and perplexities. *SEE* AIR, ELEMENT OF; EARTH, ELEMENT OF; FIRE, ELEMENT OF; SPIRIT, ELEMENT OF; *AND* WATER, ELEMENT OF for the common elemental correspondences of each element in modern occult theory. *SEE ALSO* ELEMENTAL.

Eleusinian Mysteries. The most important of the ancient Mysteries, celebrated for nearly two thousand years in the village of Eleusis, not far from Athens. Archeological evidence suggests that it was originally founded sometime before 1500 B.C.E. An open space for ritual dancing seems to have existed in Eleusis at that time; in the following century, the first small temple was built there, surrounded by a rough stone wall. This temple, the Telesterion, was gradually expanded over the years until, by Roman times, a huge roofed space half the size of a modern football field awaited the initiates. At its center was a small, rectangular building, the Anaktoron.

For close to two millennia, candidates for initiation into the Eleusinian Mysteries went through essentially the same process. First came the Lesser Mysteries, the *Myesis*. This was originally enacted at Eleusis but later moved to the banks of the river Ilissos, closer to the city of Athens. There, on a day in the Athenian month of An-

thesterion (our February), the candidates each sacrificed a pig, bathed in the icy waters of the Ilissos, and listened to instruction. No record has survived of what exactly was taught there, but it seems to have involved myths concerning the earth goddess Demeter and her daughter Persephone. Those who had passed through the Lesser Mysteries were forbidden to attend the Greater in the same year; they had to wait at least a full year before going to Eleusis to complete the process.

The Greater Mysteries, or *Teletai*, were held in the Telesterion at Eleusis, but the process began in Athens. On the fourteenth of the Athenian month Boedromion—approximately our September—priestesses left Eleusis carrying sacred objects whose nature remains unknown to this day; these were stored in a temple, the Eleusinion, in Athens. The candidates for initiation had already begun fasting on the tenth; on the sixteenth, they bathed in the sea to purify themselves further, and then remained indoors in seclusion for the next two days.

In the early morning of the nineteenth, they formed a procession at the *Stoa Poikile* or Painted Portico in Athens along with the priestesses and the sacred objects, left Athens by the Sacred Gate, and marched along the Sacred Road to Eleusis. The candidates wore myrtle wreaths on their heads and carried boughs of the same tree in their hands. At the first bridge on the road, over the river Kephisos, they were given the *kykeon* ("mixture") to drink—a special beverage that is known to have contained roasted barley, pennyroyal, and water. Each candidate received a carefully measured dose, which suggests that some psychoactive compound might also have been part of the drink.

At a second bridge, over the river Rheitoi, each candidate had a thread tied to his or her right hand and left foot. Then came Eleusis itself. By the time the candidates reached the sacred site, evening had arrived, and torches lit the way to the great outer gate of the temple complex. The Dadouchos, one of the priestly officials in charge of the Mystery, led the way in, carrying a torch in each hand. The crowd of candidates passed through an inner gate and moved forward, following the Dadouchos, to the huge Telesterion. Inside waited the Hierophant, the highest priest of the Mysteries, seated on a throne just outside the entrance to the Anaktoron.

What followed remains, in every sense of the word, a mystery. We know that a brilliant light shone out of the Telesterion; many ancient authors mention it, and comment that it could be seen for miles. By that light, the Anaktoron was opened, and the candidates saw—something. We simply don't know what. One late and questionable source suggests that it might have been a single ear of grain, held up in silence.

A few people in ancient times were known to have broken the oath of secrecy demanded of initiates. One, Diagoras of Melos, called "the godless," even wrote a book about what went on at Eleusis, though every copy of it was hunted down and destroyed. No trace of what the oathbreakers said or Diagoras wrote has survived. A great deal of speculation by non-initiates was current even in the ancient world, and practitioners of occult history in more recent times have filled books with their guesses; *SEE* OCCULT HISTORY. Eleusis still keeps its secrets.

The initiates were taught a test of recognition, the *synthema*: "I have fasted, drunk the kykeon, taken things out of the large basket, performed a rite, put them into the small basket, and then back into the large basket."

The Mysteries continued to be celebrated at Eleusis well into the Christian period. In the year 364 C.E. the Roman Emperor Valentinian, a Christian, sent out an edict prohibiting all nocturnal Pagan ceremonies. The proconsul of Greece, Vettius Agorius Praetextatus, refused at the risk of his life and position to enforce the order at Eleusis, and the Mysteries were still celebrated for a time. Internal rivalries and pressure from the growing power of the Christians made the last years of the Mysteries difficult ones. Finally, in 396, the Visigoths invaded Greece. Converted to Christianity earlier in the century, they looted and devastated Pagan sanctuaries throughout Greece. The entire temple complex at Eleusis was destroyed, and the Mysteries lost.

A number of attempts have been made to reconstruct the Eleusinian Mysteries over the years. The Patrons of Husbandry, an American fraternal order founded in 1867 and still active, includes a Victorian-era reenactment of the Eleusinian Mysteries as its seventh and highest degree of initiation. *SEE* PATRONS OF HUSBANDRY (GRANGE). *SEE ALSO* MYSTERIES, THE. FURTHER READING: KERENYI 1967, MYLONAS 1961.

eleven. In the Cabala, eleven is the number of the Qlipphoth, and of the eleven curses of Mount Ebal. *SEE* CABALA.

In Renaissance magical symbolism, eleven is the number of sin and penitence, and was held to have no virtue or connection with the Higher. *SEE ALSO* ARITHMOLOGY. FURTHER READING: MCLEAN 1994, WATERFIELD 1988, WESTCOTT 1984.

elixir. In spagyrics, an alchemical medicine made from several different herbs. A product made from a single herb is called a clyssus. *SEE* SPAGYRICS.

elixir of life. In the lore of alchemy, a special preparation of the Philosopher's Stone that would grant eternal (or very long) life, and cure all diseases. *SEE* ALCHEMY; PHILOSOPHER'S STONE.

El Morya, Master. In Theosophy and related systems of occult teaching, one of the Masters of the Great White Lodge, the secret brotherhood that oversees the spiritual evolution of the Earth. El Morya is the Chohan or chief Adept of the First or Red Ray, the ray of power, and is thus the immediate subordinate of the Lord Vaisvavata, the manu of the current root race. In the approaching period of the sixth root race, which is expected to begin sometime in the twenty-sixth century, El Morya will become the manu. *SEE* MANU; RED RAY; ROOT RACE.

According to modern historian K. Paul Johnson, "El Morya" was an alias used by Blavatsky for Ranbir Singh, maharaja of Kashmir, an Indian aristocrat who supported her when she was in India. Ranbir Singh was apparently part of a network of Indian leaders who worked with Blavatsky in opposition to the British raj and the attempted Christianization of India. This identification has been strongly opposed by Theosophists. *SEE ALSO* GREAT WHITE LODGE; MASTERS; THEOSOPHY. FURTHER READING: JOHNSON 1994, LEADBEATER 1925.

Elohim. (Hebrew ALHIM, "deities") One of the most important of the Names of God in Cabala and ceremonial magic, the word *Elohim* is a grammatical oddity in Hebrew, made from the feminine noun *Elohe*, "goddess," and the masculine plural ending -*im*. As the third word in the Book of Genesis, it is the first divine name that occurs in the Bible.

On the Tree of Life, the name Elohim occurs in combination with other words and names in all of the Sephiroth of the Pillar of Severity: as YHVH ALHIM, Tetragrammaton Elohim, the divine name in Binah; as ALHIM GBVR, Elohim Gibor, the divine name in Geburah; and as ALHIM TzBAVTh, Elohim Tzabaoth, the divine name in Hod. It is also sometimes used as the name of an order of angels assigned to Netzach. SEE BINAH; GEBURAH; HOD; NETZACH. SEE ALSO CABALA.

Élus Coens. (French and Hebrew, "chosen priests") A quasi-Masonic magical order founded by Martines de Pasqually in 1767, and active in various forms since that time; its full name was *La Franc-Maçonnerie des Chevaliers Maçons Élus Coens de l'Univers* ("Freemasonry of the Knight Masons, Chosen Priests of the Universe"). The founding of the order dates to 1754, when Pasqually began establishing a series of lodges in France; the first, in Montpellier, went under the name of *Juges Ecossais* ("Scottish Judges") and claimed a connection with the Scottish Rite of Masonry, the branch of the Craft most closely associated with the torrent of higher degrees then in production in France and elsewhere. The first lodge founded by Pasqually with a name referring to the *Élus Coens* came into being in Toulouse in 1760. In 1766, Pasqually went to Paris in an effort to interest the Grand Lodge of France in his system; the venture failed, largely due to discords within the Grand Lodge itself, but in the process Pasqually met Jean-Baptiste Willermoz, an influential Mason from Lyon, who embraced Pasqually's system enthusiastically and assisted him in setting up the order on a national basis.

As practiced, the Élus Coens system had four grades, of which the first three—*Apprenti* (Apprentice), *Compagnon* (Fellow Craft), and *Maitre* (Master)—were identical to the three grades of standard Freemasonry, but initiates at each of these levels were provided with instructional materials and taught various preparatory disciplines. The fourth grade, that of *Élu Coen* or *Grand Profès*, brought with it access to the secret magical rituals of the order, referred to as *La Chose* ("The Thing"). This, the core of Pasqually's system, was a ritual of invocation performed within a consecrated circle on the day of the equinox, conjuring spirits and intelligences into visual and audible presence. The "passes" of these entities—mysterious lights and sounds experienced by the Élu Coen during the ritual—were seen not only as a demonstration of the reality of spiritual beings, but also as proof that the initiate had transcended matter and accomplished the reintegration of his being.

Pasqually's one writing, the *Traité de la Réintégration des etres* (*Treatise of the Reintegration of Beings*, 1769) presents a remarkable Gnostic cosmology as the basis for this system. According to the *Treatise*, the material world was originally created by God as a prison for evil spirits who had rebelled against the divine will. Adam Cadmon, the Primordial Man, was placed in the material world as its guardian and master, but desired to create beings in his own image, and so fell in turn. He and his first creation, Eve, mated without divine blessing and produced the evil Cain. Their second child, Abel, was conceived with the help of God but was killed by Cain. The third child, Seth, was again conceived with God's help and received all the divine knowledge once possessed by Adam. In later generations, the descendants of Cain, who were materialistic and evil, mated with the descendants of Seth, who were spiritual and good, and produced the present human race. Among the latter, a handful remembered fragments of the divine knowledge and sought reintegration with the divine will and purpose; these were the *Amis de la Sagesse*, the "Friends of Wisdom," and Pasqually himself claimed to be the latest of these.

The order itself barely survived its founder's death in 1774 due to inadequate organization and no arrangements for a successor. In the hands of Willermoz and other members, however, large elements of Pasqually's system were absorbed into high-grade Masonry across Europe, while Louis-Claude de Saint-Martin used many of the same concepts as a foundation for Martinism, a system of Christian esotericism that remains an active force in the occult scene in France and elsewhere. Texts of the Élus Coens rituals and *La Chose* have also survived, and practitioners of Pasqually's rites in their original form have been a presence in French and German occult circles since the middle of the nineteenth century, if not before. SEE ALSO MARTINISM; PASQUALLY, MARTINES DE. FURTHER READING: BENZ 1983, HUBBS 1971.

ember days. (Old English *ymbrene daeg*, "circuit day") The Wednesday, Friday, and Saturday of the first week in Lent, the week after Pentecost, the third week in September, and the third week of Advent in the Catholic religious calendar. The ember days were days of fasting, and folk traditions in much of Europe claimed that spirits appeared on these days. Their closeness to the solstices and equinoxes suggests a possible connection with surviving Pagan beliefs. At an earlier time, before the church calendar achieved its modern form, the ember days were the three days before an equinox or solstice, and this usage has been revived in some modern Pagan traditions.

The ember days were also important in a number of medieval European Pagan traditions. In particular, groups such as the benandanti and the Pagan cult described in the Canon *Episcopi* commonly went on their visionary journeys at or near the ember days each year. *SEE* BENANDANTI; CANON EPISCOPI; STOECKHLIN, CHONRAD.

emblem books. In the Renaissance, a literary genre in which visual emblems were paired with titles and brief verses. The genre came into existence in response to the discovery of an ancient text, the *Hieroglyphica* of Horapollo, which was found on the Greek island of Andros in 1419 and sold to the Medici, the ruling family of Florence. Its arrival in Florence in 1422 caused a major stir in scholarly circles throughout Europe, since it appeared to offer the key to Egyptian hieroglyphics.

The *Hieroglyphica* was actually a product of the fifth century of the Common Era, when the actual meaning of the hieroglyphics had been lost. Instead, Horapollo interpreted the hieroglyphic letters as allegorical images—thus a circle meant eternity, a dog watchfulness, and so on. While it had nothing to do with the actual meanings of Egyptian hieroglyphics, this way of looking at visual imagery became extremely popular in Renaissance Europe following the rediscovery of Horapollo's work. It is possible that the popularity of Horapollo helped inspire the invention of the tarot, which emerged in Italy in the middle decades of the fifteenth century; *SEE* TAROT.

The first actual emblem book was the *Emblemata Liber* of Italian lawyer Andrea Alciati (1492–1550), which was published in 1531 and became an international bestseller.

Many other emblem books were published over the century and a half between Alciati and the fading out of the tradition in the early eighteenth century.

The emblem book tradition had a powerful influence on alchemical writings. Before Alciati's time, alchemical books contained few illustrations, only those most practical. The visual punning of the emblem books, however, was quickly adopted by alchemical writers, who came to use a wide range of emblems and visual symbols in their difficult art of writing about alchemy without revealing any of its secrets. The alchemical emblem books of Michael Maier (1568–1622) are considered to be among the supreme examples of the art. *SEE* ALCHEMY; MAIER, MICHAEL. FURTHER READING: ADAMS AND LINDEN 1998, ALCIATUS 1985, BATH 1994.

Emerald Tablet. The most famous of all alchemical texts, supposedly written on a slab of emerald by Hermes Trismegistus and discovered by one of several legendary figures in Hermes' tomb. In its standard English translation, it runs as follows:

> True, without error, certain and most true: that which is above is as that which is below, and that which is below is as that which is above, to perform the miracles of the One Thing. And as all things were from One, by the mediation of One, so from this One Thing come all things by adaptation. Its father is the Sun; its mother is the Moon; the wind carried it in his belly; the nurse thereof is the Earth. It is the father of all perfection and the consummation of the whole world. Its power is integral if it be turned to earth. Thou shalt separate the earth from the fire, the subtle from the gross, gently and with much ingenuity. It ascends from Earth to Heaven and descends again to Earth, and receives the power of the superiors and the inferiors. Thus thou hast the glory of the whole world; therefore let all obscurity flee before thee. This is the strong fortitude of all fortitude, overcoming every subtle and penetrating every solid thing. Hence are all wonderful adaptations, of which this is the manner. Therefore am I called Hermes Trismegistus, having the three parts of the philosophy of the whole world. That is finished which I have to say concerning the operation of the Sun.

The origins of the Emerald Tablet are unknown. It first surfaced in Europe in the thirteenth century, when it is cited in a book by Albertus Magnus, and a garbled version in Arabic dates from around 900 C.E. Joseph Needham, the distinguished scholar of Chinese science, has pointed out that its basic concepts can be found in Chinese alchemical writings from a much older period, and suggests that there may have been a Chinese original, but this remains pure speculation.

Whatever its source and early history, it became a central text to medieval, Renaissance, and modern European alchemists, and remains much in use in Hermetic circles today. *SEE ALSO* ALCHEMY; HERMES TRISMEGISTUS; HERMETICISM. FURTHER READING: ANONYMOUS 1988, LINDSAY 1970, READ 1937, SMOLEY 1996.

Emeth-Achavah, Ancient Order of. (Hebrew, "truth love") An occult society founded in 1898 in Denver, Colorado, by Franklin P. White, the Ancient Order published a magazine titled *The Light of Kosmon*. The order was apparently devoted to the study of *Oahspe, the Kosmon Bible*, a work of automatic writing produced by John Ballou Newbrough (1828–1891) in 1881. It went out of existence sometime in the 1920s. *SEE ALSO* LODGE, MAGICAL.

Empedocles of Acragas. Greek philosopher and magician, fifth century B.C.E. Very little is known for certain about his biography, but it is recorded that he was born into a wealthy family in the Greek colonial city of Acragas in Sicily around the beginning of the fifth century, and died around the age of sixty. Traditions known to later Greek authors claim that he took an active role in Acragan politics, supporting the democratic side in the political convulsions of the period, and also worked as a physician.

He wrote two long philosophical poems, *On Nature* and *The Purifications*, which survive only in fragments quoted by other authors. *On Nature* presents a detailed theory of the origin and nature of the universe, based on a theory of four elements—the first appearance of this concept in the historical record—which are united and separated in complicated cyclic patterns by the powers of love and strife. Knowledge of the elements and their cycles, according to the opening section of the poem, opens the door to magical abilities over weather and grants the power to defeat old age, sickness, and death.

The Purifications, of which much less survives, describes the descent of souls from an original state of unity and blessedness into the cycle of reincarnation, and the long process of purification by which they rise back up to dwell among the gods. Passages from *The Purifications* condemn animal sacrifice and the eating of beans, and insist on the value of a vegetarian diet. Ancient and modern scholars alike have recognized substantial links between these ideas and those of Pythagoras, the Orphics, and other mystical and occult traditions in the ancient Greek world; a number of ancient writers simply refer to Empedocles as a Pythagorean. *SEE ALSO* BEANS; PYTHAGORAS; VEGETARIANISM.

Empedocles' role in the Western occult tradition is a significant one, not only as the apparent originator of the doctrine of the four elements—a central factor in later magic, alchemy, astrology, and occult philosophy—but as a major figure in the chain of philosopher-mystics that established the core ideas and approaches from which essentially all Western occult systems have unfolded. His poems were still in use in a religious context in the late first or early second century C.E. in Panopolis in southern Egypt, a major center of alchemical studies then and later, and it has been argued that otherwise lost details of his teaching can be found in a variety of Greek and Arabic alchemical sources. *SEE* ALCHEMY. FURTHER READING: BARNES 1987, KINGSLEY 1995.

Emperor, the. The fourth Major Arcanum of the tarot, generally showing the image of a crowned and enthroned man. In the Golden Dawn system, this Arcanum is assigned to the Hebrew letter Heh, while the French system assigns it to Daleth. In divination, its common meaning is power, authority, and fatherhood.

Its magical title is "Son of the Morning, Chief among the Mighty." *SEE ALSO* TAROT.

Tarot trump the Emperor (Universal Tarot)

Empress, the. The third Major Arcanum of the tarot, generally showing the image of a crowned and enthroned woman. In the Golden Dawn system, this Arcanum is assigned to the Hebrew letter Daleth, while the French system assigns it to Gimel. In divination, its usual meanings include fertility, productiveness, happiness, and motherhood.

Its magical title is "Daughter of the Mighty Ones." *SEE ALSO* TAROT.

Tarot trump the Empress (Universal Tarot)

enneagram. According to the writings of Caucasian mystic G. I. Gurdjieff and his followers, the emblem of the Sarmoun Brotherhood, an ancient occult order active in the Middle East. Used by Gurdjieff as a symbolic structure of existence in his teaching, it remained little known until Claudio Naranjo, a student of the Chilean esotericist Oscar Ichazo, began giving seminars on the subject in Berkeley, California, in 1970.

The particular interpretation of the enneagram taught by Naranjo focused on the symbol as a map of personality, with different character types assigned to the points of the symbol. This approach caught on with American students, many of whom were interested in psychology, and with liberal Catholics who noted the similarity between enneagram character types and the seven deadly sins of traditional Christian moral thought. The first popular book on the subject was published in 1984, and was followed by a torrent of others. The popularization of the enneagram also saw, predictably, quite a bit of squabbling among various people involved in the development of the system over who did or did not have the right to teach (and profit from) the enneagram.

Various attempts, some more successful than others, have been made to connect the enneagram to the various symbolic systems of traditional Western occultism, or simply to import it directly into a Western occult context. It has also become very popular in certain aspects of the New Age community; *SEE* NEW AGE. As of this writing, though, it remains on the fringes of the occult tradition—belonging to the distinctive Gurdjieff system of mysticism, on the one hand, and to the realm of pop psychology on the other. FURTHER READING: BENNETT **1983**, PALMER **1988**.

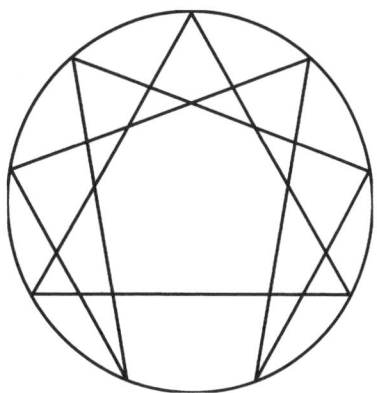

Enneagram

Enoch. According to the Book of Genesis, the great-great-great-great-grandson of Adam. He was the son of Jared and the father of Methuselah, and lived for 365 years. An enigmatic comment in the Bible suggests something unusual around his death: "He walked with God, and was not, for God took him" (Genesis 5:24).

Later Jewish commentaries and apocryphal writings expanded this brief mention into an entire mythology, according to which Enoch had not died, but was carried off bodily by God to Heaven, where he became the mighty archangel Metatron. *SEE* METATRON. His reputation for wisdom led Jewish writers to identify him with Hermes Trismegistus, and this led him to be incorporated into Western occult traditions in the Renaissance. *SEE* CABALA; HERMES TRISMEGISTUS.

Enochian language. The language of the Enochian calls and other related material, received by John Dee in a series of occult workings extending over more than thirty years. *SEE* DEE, JOHN; ENOCHIAN MAGIC. It has its own script, the appearance (at least) of grammar and syntax, and its own system of numerology and Cabalistic symbolism, similar to that of Hebrew but by no means identical with it.

Enochian	Title	English
Ⅴ	Pe	B
₿	Veh	C or K
↳	Ged	G
Ↄ	Gal	D
⅄	Orth	F
⅂	Un	A
⅂	Graph	E
Ɛ	Tal	M
Ⅼ	Gon	I, Y, or J
⋔	Na-hath	H
⊂	Ur	L
∩	Mals	P
Ⅱ	Ger	Q
Ⱬ	Drun	N
Γ	Pal	X
Ⅼ	Med	O
Ɛ	Don	R
Ρ	Ceph	Z
∂	Vau	U, V, W
⅂	Fam	S
⅃	Gisa	T

The Enochian language does not seem to be closely related to any human language, although a few of its words are similar to roots derived from a scattering of other languages. Scholars have quarreled over whether it has the grammatical structure and syntax of a true language or not. In magical circles, however, its reputation as an effective tool for summoning spirits is extremely high.

The following passage from the *Second Key* will give some sense of the language's flavor. The first version is as spelled in Dee's writings, transcribed directly from the Enochian script; the second is the Golden Dawn pronunciation, while the third is Dee's English translation.

In Enochian spelling: *torzu gohe L zacar eca c noqod zamran micalzo od ozazm vrelp lap zir Io-Iad.*

As pronounced: *Torzodu gohe El; zodacare, eca, ca noqoda. Zodameranu micaelzodo oda ozodazodme vurelpe lape zodire Io-Iada.*

Translated: "Arise, saith the First; move, therefore, unto my servants. Show yourselves in power and make me a strong seer of things, for I am of Him that liveth forever."

A few words that sound very like Enochian can also be found in the *Voarchadumia* of Johannes Pantheus, a handbook of mystical alchemy published in 1530 and closely studied by Dee. *SEE* VOARCHADUMIA. FURTHER READING: HARKNESS 1999.

Enochian magic. A system of magical working developed out of the writings of John Dee (1527–1608), the most important English occultist of the Elizabethan period. With the help of a series of scryers, of whom Edward Kelly was the most famous, Dee carried out a massive series of theurgic workings in search of hidden wisdom about the nature of God, the universe, and humanity. According to his detailed journals, angels who appeared to his scryers communicated hundreds of pages of complex material, which formed the raw material for Enochian magic.

The first version of the Enochian system, the one used by Dee himself under the angels' guidance, was theurgic rather than magical; *SEE* THEURGY. Dee used prayers and Christian devotional exercises to attune himself and his scryers to the angelic presences with whom he communicated, and the commands and technical methods of Renaissance magic were notable by their absence. Following the angels' instructions, he constructed a special table with complicated signs and symbols painted on it, its four legs resting on wax pentacles, and another wax disk inscribed with the complex Sigillum Dei Aemeth (Sigil of the God of Truth) set on the table as the base for his scrying crystal. Long passages in a previously unknown language, called Enochian, a series of complex tables of letters and numbers, a ring, and a golden lamen were also part of this first version of Enochian working.

From the material he received, Dee assembled several manuscript books—*Heptarchia Mystica* (*Mystic Sevenfold Rulership*), *Liber Scientiae Auxilii et Victoriae Terrestris* (*Book of Earthly Knowledge, Help and Victory*), *48 Claves Angelicae* (*48 Angelic Keys*), and others. These formed the basis of a complex system of mystical philosophy and theurgic practice.

After Dee's death, portions of his journals surfaced and were published by Meric Casaubon in 1659. Casaubon hoped to use this publication to discredit Dee and, more importantly, magic as a whole. Unwittingly, he succeeded in ensuring that Dee's workings would be preserved and revived. At least two groups of English occultists in the late seventeenth century are known to have carried out further work with the Enochian system, using Casaubon's book as a guide.

There may well have been other groups over the next century and a half, but no trace of them seems to have survived. The Enochian system did not surface again until the time of the Hermetic Order of the Golden Dawn, founded in 1887. The Enochian elemental tablets are mentioned in the original Cipher Manuscript that provided the basis for the order's workings, and appear in Outer Order rituals. It was not until sometime after the Inner Order was founded in 1892, however, that the Golden Dawn's chiefs presented their students with detailed information on the Enochian system.

The Golden Dawn Enochian papers marked a complete reshaping of Dee's original system. The theurgic dimension had been almost completely removed, replaced by full-blown ritual magic using the Enochian language

and symbols together with other Golden Dawn techniques. The angelic keys or calls, the five tablets assigned to the elements, and the angels and spirits derived from these latter made up the first level of Golden Dawn Enochian magic; the *Heptarchia Mystica*, which describes forty-nine spirits assigned to the seven planets, was taught to more advanced students. A system of Enochian chess, played with pieces representing Egyptian gods and used as a system of divination, was also developed and put to use. *SEE* CHESS, ENOCHIAN.

Much of the basic Golden Dawn Enochian material was published by Aleister Crowley, the first Golden Dawn member to go public with his knowledge, in the early years of the twentieth century. The entire body of calls, tables, spirits, and related material, along with the instructions for Enochian chess, was included in volume IV of Israel Regardie's landmark *The Golden Dawn*, published in 1940. In the last decades of the twentieth century, finally, a handful of magical scholars returned to the original source—Dee's own writings—and these, along with several books of previously unpublished Golden Dawn Enochian material, have sparked a modest renaissance in Enochian magic. *SEE ALSO* DEE, JOHN; SMITH, HARRY. FURTHER READING: HARKNESS 1999, REGARDIE 1971.

Eoh. *SEE* EIHWAZ.

Eolh. *SEE* ALGIZ.

Ephesia grammata. (Greek, "Ephesian letters") The most celebrated words of power in the classical world, the Ephesia grammata were used in a wide range of magical applications and even gave rise to a slang term for magic itself. Two different versions of the Ephesia grammata survive from ancient times, differing only in the ending of the last word; one version gives the words as *askion, kataskion, lix, tetrax, damnameneus, aision*, while the other ends the sequence *aisia*. Greek boxers, in particular, were said to carry rolls of parchment wearing the Ephesia grammata to give them magically heightened strength in combat.

The use of the Ephesia grammata was so widespread that *aski kataski*, a shortened version of the first two words, was used as a slang term for magic in the Greek-speaking world, with much the same connotations that "hocus pocus" has in modern English. No convincing interpretation of the words has yet been proposed.

In modern scholarly works on magic, the term *ephesia grammata* is sometimes used to refer to any incomprehensible magical word or words. SEE BARBAROUS NAMES. SEE ALSO AMULET; BINDING TABLET. FURTHER READING: GAGER 1992.

equinox. (Latin, "equal night") The two days each year, one in spring and one in fall, in which day and night are exactly the same length. At the moment of equinox, the sun crosses the celestial equator (the projection of Earth's equator into space).

In tropical astrology—the most common modern form of astrology—the spring equinox is considered to mark the entry of the sun into the first degree of Aries, and the fall equinox the sun's entry into the first degree of Libra, even though the precession of the equinoxes has moved the two constellations of the same name nearly thirty degrees away from the equinoctial points as of the present writing. SEE PRECESSION OF THE EQUINOXES.

In the system of magic taught by Martines de Pasqually (1727–1774) to the members of the Élus Coens, his magical order, the equinox was the proper time for attempts to perform ritual invocation of spiritual beings. SEE ÉLUS COENS; PASQUALLY, MARTINES DE.

In the Golden Dawn system of magic, the equinoxes are two of the three most important holy days of the year. The spiritual energies of the sun are held to descend to Earth directly at these times, and rituals are held to draw on these energies. The installation of temple officers is a part of the ritual work done at the equinox. SEE GOLDEN DAWN, HERMETIC ORDER OF THE.

In traditional Druidry, the equinoxes are two of the four Alban Gate festivals; the spring equinox is called Alban Eiler, the Light of the Earth, and the autumn Alban Elued, the Light of the Water. SEE ALBAN GATES; DRUIDRY.

In most modern Pagan traditions, the equinoxes are among the eight celebrations of the year. Their names vary widely, reflecting the fact that very few traditional cultures in Europe celebrated the equinoxes in any form. SEE SABBAT; WICCA. FURTHER READING: FARRAR AND FARRAR 1981, REGARDIE 1971.

esbat. In the writings of Margaret Murray, the routine meeting of a coven of witches. Borrowed by some modern Wiccan groups, it now commonly means the monthly coven meeting on the night of the full moon, as distinct from the sabbats, the eight major festivals of the Wiccan year. The term appears to be of Murray's invention and does not appear in older sources. Murray derived it from the medieval French word *s'esbattre*, "to frolic."

In current practice, an esbat is part business meeting, part social evening, and part religious event, and most of the activities of a coven are coordinated by way of these monthly meetings. It has substantial similarities to the regular meetings of fraternal lodges; SEE LODGE, FRATERNAL. SEE ALSO SABBAT; WICCA.

Esoteric Fraternity. American occult organization founded in 1887 by Hiram E. Butler, a sawmill worker turned mystic who studied the teachings of the Hermetic Brotherhood of Luxor (H. B. of L.) but radically reformulated its sexual occultism, becoming convinced that complete celibacy was the only path to spiritual awareness. Butler spent fourteen years living in semi-isolation in the New England forests, studying astrology and publishing works on "solar biology," and gradually attracted a following.

His first attempt at a group to carry on his teachings was the oddly named group "Genii of Nations, Knowledge and Religions" or G. N. K. R., which he headed under the mystic name of "Adhy-apaka, the Hellenic Ethnomedon." This organization had the distinction of being personally attacked by H. P. Blavatsky, who identified it with the H. B. of L. and insisted that the initials actually stood for "Gulls Nabbed by Knaves and Rascals." SEE BLAVATSKY, HELENA PETROVNA. In 1887, the G. N. K. R. was reorganized as the Esoteric Fraternity, and issued a magazine, *The Esoteric*, for a short time.

Near the end of the nineteenth century, the fraternity moved to Applegate, California, where a handful of members still live. Celibacy, reincarnation, New Thought, and esoteric Christianity make up the framework of their creed. SEE ALSO CHRISTIAN OCCULTISM; HERMETIC BROTHERHOOD OF LUXOR (H. B. OF L.); NEW THOUGHT.

Ethel. *SEE* OTHILA.

ether. The substance/energy of the etheric level of existence in magical theory, also known by dozens of other names, such as akasha, od, orgone, vital life force, and vril. According to recent writers, it is identical with the prana of Hindu philosophy and the ch'i of Chinese medicine and martial arts. It is the basis of life and physical form, can be concentrated and directed by breath and intention, and can be felt directly by the human skin through the use of certain exercises. Magical lore relates it to the moon, which generates tides in the etheric atmosphere of the Earth; *SEE* MOON.

The word "ether" was borrowed by nineteenth-century occultists from contemporary science, which postulated a "luminiferous ether" to explain the wavelike qualities of light and other electromagnetic radiation. This concept was discarded by scientists after the emergence of relativity theory at the beginning of the twentieth century, but the term was useful enough that it has been kept by many occultists. *SEE ALSO* ETHERIC BODY; ETHERIC PLANE.

etheric body. In modern magical lore, the densest level of the human subtle body, closely connected to the physical body. As with all modern subtle-body lore, accounts differ, but most distinguish two layers or aspects of the etheric body. The first of these, the etheric double, occupies the same space as the physical body, extending no more than an inch or two beyond the skin. It is a lattice of forces shaping and sustaining the physical body, and has its own complicated structure of channels and centers; many magical scholars identify these with the nadis and chakras of Hindu theory, and with the meridians of Chinese medicine.

The second aspect of the etheric body is the aura or Sphere of Sensation, a roughly egg-shaped zone of energies surrounding the physical body, extending out to a distance of several feet in all directions. The aura serves as the interface between the individual etheric body and the universe of etheric forces surrounding the self. It also serves as a vessel for the forces of the individual's astral body, and the patterns of astral force in the aura can be perceived and read by clairvoyants. *SEE* AURA.

While the presence and proper functioning of the etheric body is essential for physical life, it is possible under some conditions to project a portion of etheric substance as a vehicle for out-of-body experience. *SEE* ETHERIC PROJECTION.

In the dying process, the separation of the higher bodies from the etheric body is the point of no return. This separation is traditionally called the Second Death. *SEE* SECOND DEATH. Prior to this stage, individuals who have shed their physical bodies may appear to the living as ghosts; afterwards, the cast-off etheric body may remain in the vicinity of the corpse for a time, giving rise to other forms of ghostly phenomena. *SEE* GRAVEYARD SPECTER. FURTHER READING: BENDIT 1977, LEADBEATER 1971.

etheric double. *SEE* ETHERIC BODY.

etheric plane. In occult theory, the level of reality consisting of etheric forces and entities midway between the astral plane (the level of concrete consciousness) and the physical plane (the level of substances that can be perceived by the senses). As with all the planes of the occult universe, the etheric plane is "above" the physical and "below" the astral only in metaphorical terms; in reality, the etheric (and all other planes) interpenetrate the world of ordinary experience.

As described by visionaries and discussed in occult textbooks, the etheric plane is a realm of currents and tides, powerfully influenced by the moon—the great ruler of the etheric world—and by the other astrological planets as well. Patterns of elemental, planetary, and zodiacal energies sweep through the etheric realm in cycles that are tracked by various systems of calculation. *SEE* ASTROLOGY; TATTVAS.

The etheric plane in the macrocosm—that is, the universe as a whole—has its equivalent in the etheric body of each living being. *SEE* ETHERIC BODY. FURTHER READING: BENDIT 1977.

etheric projection. The type of out-of-body experience in which the practitioner forms a secondary body out of etheric energy as a vehicle; it thus differs from astral projection, in which the vehicle is made purely out of astral patterns. *SEE* ASTRAL PROJECTION. The etheric material used for the projection is typically taken from the practitioner's etheric body, but can also come from other sources.

In etheric projection, the projected body has a much higher degree of solidity than in astral projection; the practitioner can affect physical objects to some degree, and can also be affected by them. It is therefore more dangerous, due to the potential for repercussion if the projected body is damaged in any way by conductive materials such as metals. *SEE* REPERCUSSION.

The practice of etheric projection has had a large role to play in traditions of shapeshifting and lycanthropy. *SEE* LYCANTHROPY. *SEE ALSO* ASTRAL PROJECTION.

etheric revenant. In occult lore, a dead person who has prevented himself or herself from passing through the Second Death, the separation of the soul from the etheric body. A variety of magical means were once taught to allow individuals to achieve this state as a way of prolonging existence after death and avoiding the potential difficulties of the afterlife. In one interpretation, much of the magical lore of ancient Egypt had the goal of allowing the dead to linger on as etheric revenants.

The existence of a revenant depends on three factors. First, the former physical body must be preserved. Second, the revenant must avoid direct sunlight and other factors that tend to disperse etheric structures. Third, the revenant must have a regular source of etheric energy. In many cultures, these needs were met by methods of embalming, burial practices involving earth mounds or stone structures surrounded by taboos, and regular offerings of food and drink.

In historical times, the collapse of these customs forced would-be revenants into progressively more dangerous practices, of which vampirism is perhaps the most common; *SEE* VAMPIRE. *SEE ALSO* ETHERIC BODY. FURTHER READING: GREER 2001.

Etteila. (Jean-Baptiste Aliette) French diviner and occultist, 1738–1791. The first person known to history who made his living by card divination, Etteila was born to working-class parents in Paris, and worked as a seed merchant. He married sometime before 1763 and had a son, but the marriage was not a success and the couple separated in 1767.

How and where he learned to divine using cards is unknown, although a comment in one of his books suggests that he was introduced to the art by an old man from the Piedmont region of Italy sometime in the 1750s.

In 1770 he published his first book on the subject, *Etteila, ou maniere de se récréer avec un jeu de cartes par M ✱✱✱* (*Etteila, or A Way of Entertaining Oneself with a Pack of Cards, by Mr.* ✱✱✱). The method in this book used the standard playing card deck of the time. A book of astrological predictions followed in 1772, and an expanded version of *Etteila* in 1773. Thereafter he worked as a print seller in Paris and Strasbourg for some years.

He returned to the world of publishing in 1783 with two pamphlets on cartomancy, and in the same year published the first of four volumes of his masterwork, *Manière de se récréer avec le jeu de cartes nomées Tarots* (*A Way of Entertaining Oneself with the Pack of Cards called Tarot*). In this work, Etteila argued for the Egyptian origin of the tarot deck, and presented a new version of the deck with the cards renumbered and the symbolism changed to reflect the "Egyptian" philosophy he saw in the tarot. By this time he had become a student of the entire occult tradition, and later years saw him publish books on astrology, alchemy, physiognomy, and chiromancy.

In 1788 he founded an organization, *Société des Interprètes du Livre de Thot* ("Society of the Interpreters of the Book of Thoth"), to promote his deck and his system of interpretation. 1790 saw the creation of a more ambitious project, the *Nouvelle Ecole de Magie* ("New School of Magic"). He died the next year, although details such as cause of death remain unknown. A student of his, a Lyonnais bookseller named Hugand, continued his school for a short time, but it vanished in the confusions of the French Revolution around 1794. *SEE ALSO* TAROT. FURTHER READING: DECKER ET AL. 1996.

Eucharist. A ceremony in which one or more items of food or drink are consecrated with the energies of a divinity or spiritual power, and then ingested by the participants. The most famous version of the Eucharist, and the one most often copied by occultists over the last few centuries, is the Christian Mass, in which bread and wine are transformed into the body and blood of Jesus and consumed by the faithful.

Some versions of the Wiccan feast of cakes and wine, a common element of Wiccan ceremony, function as a form of Eucharist, although most simply treat it as a symbolic sharing of food and drink; *SEE* WICCA.

In the Golden Dawn tradition, every Neophyte Grade initiation and Equinox ceremony ends with a Eucharistic rite in which a rose, a flame, wine, and bread and salt are consecrated as the elements of the body of Osiris, and then partaken by those present. *SEE* EQUINOX; GOLDEN DAWN, HERMETIC ORDER OF THE.

euhemerism. The theory that the gods and events of mythology are simply dim memories of people and events of the distant past, magnified through much retelling. The theory takes its name from the Greek writer Euhemerus, who proposed it in the fourth century B.C.E. It was an extremely popular viewpoint in the late classical period, among cultured Pagans who sought an intellectualized version of their traditional faith, as well as among Christians who used it to dismiss Pagan gods as lifeless figures who did not deserve worship. Ironically, this strategy backfired by allowing myths and legends of the Pagan gods to survive intact through the Middle Ages into the Renaissance, when they stimulated the first attempts at reviving Pagan religion. *SEE* NEOPAGANISM; PAGANISM.

Euhemerist approaches to mythology have played a central part in occult history, particularly in the nineteenth century, and can still be found in various corners of occult lore. *SEE* AGHARTA; OCCULT HISTORY. It has also been enthusiastically adopted by the modern New Age movement, which has reinterpreted ancient myths as surviving memories of extraterrestrial visits to the Earth, among other things; *SEE* NEW AGE MOVEMENT. Most current scholars of mythology, however, tend to reject euhemerism as a misinterpretation of myth. FURTHER READING: SEZNEC 1953.

Eulis, Brotherhood of. Magical order founded by the American occultist Paschal Beverly Randolph (1825–1875). The Provisional Grand Lodge of Eulis was founded by Randolph in March of 1874 in Tennessee, and dissolved by him in June of the same year due to personality conflicts with its other members. That same year he traveled to England, where he probably initiated

Peter Davidson, later a founder of the Hermetic Brotherhood of Luxor. September of 1874 saw him in California, where he stayed until May of the next year, setting up lodges of the brotherhood and initiating new members. His further activities on behalf of the brotherhood were cut short by his suicide on July 29, 1875.

The brotherhood taught Randolph's system of sexual occultism, and for this reason remained largely out of the public eye. It appears to have survived Randolph's death, however, and lodges claiming to belong to the original brotherhood were active in upstate New York as late as the 1950s. At least two other occult orders—the Hermetic Brotherhood of Luxor and the Fraternitas Rosae Crucis—developed out of the brotherhood and continued to teach some elements of its system. *SEE* FRATERNITAS ROSAE CRUCIS (FRC); HERMETIC BROTHERHOOD OF LUXOR (H. B. OF L.). *SEE ALSO* RANDOLPH, PASCHAL BEVERLY. FURTHER READING: J. GODWIN 1994, RANDOLPH 1978.

Eve. According to the Book of Genesis, the second human being created by God in the Garden of Eden. In occult symbolism and teaching, Eve fills a variety of roles. Gnostic rewrites of Genesis give her roles ranging from world-redeeming goddess to willing minion of evil; *SEE* GNOSTICISM. More recent occult traditions have tended to follow the first of these options, and the "Great Goddess Eve" is a presence in many different systems of occult lore, including that of the Hermetic Order of the Golden Dawn. More recently, the rejection of Christian symbolism by most aspects of the occult community has turned Eve into little more than a pale reflection of the Goddess of modern Paganism; *SEE* GODDESS, THE. *SEE ALSO* ADAM; FALL, THE.

evil eye. In folk magic around the world, a cursing power that operates through the glance. Belief in the evil eye is extremely ancient and widespread. Some folk traditions believe that it is a magical power deliberately used, while others hold that it is inborn, automatic, and nearly unconscious. It brings bad luck, impotence, sterility, miscarriage, sickness, and death in various combinations. A wide range of amulets and protective spells are used to ward off the evil eye's insidious effects. *SEE* AMULET. *SEE ALSO* CURSE. FURTHER READING: ELWORTHY 1971, MALBROUGH 1986.

Evil Persona. In Golden Dawn magical theory, the negative or destructive aspect of the individual human being, which fills the same role in the microcosm as the Qlippoth or demonic powers in the microcosm. Golden Dawn instructional papers teach that the Evil Persona is to be disciplined and enlightened rather than destroyed: "The evil persona can be rendered as a great and strong, yet trained, animal whereupon the man rideth, and it then becometh a strength unto his physical base of action" (Regardie 1971, I:215–218). Once this is accomplished by the adept, his or her nephesh (subtle body) takes on the role of the genius or guardian spirit of the Evil Persona, and the Evil Persona itself becomes a servant and manifestation of the divine in the realm of the Qlippoth. SEE GOLDEN DAWN, HERMETIC ORDER OF THE; NEPHESH; QLIPPOTH. FURTHER READING: REGARDIE 1971.

evocation. (Latin *evocatio*, "calling forth") In ritual magic, the process of summoning a spirit into a manifestation external to the magician. It is distinguished from invocation, which is the process of summoning a spirit (usually a god or divine aspect) into the magician. SEE INVOCATION.

Evola, Julius. (Baron Julius–Césare Andrea Evola) Italian philosopher and occultist, 1898–1974. The eldest son of an aristocratic Sicilian family, Evola was born in Rome. He became fluent in French and German as well as his native Italian at an early age, and read widely in philosophy and literature. At the outbreak of the First World War he enlisted in the Italian Army and served with distinction in a battalion of mountain artillery in the Alpine front.

After the war, he met Arturo Reghini (1878–1946), an important figure in the occult wing of Italian Freemasonry at the time, and was introduced by Reghini to the ideas of René Guénon, the Traditionalist philosoper. SEE REGHINI, ARTURO. His practical studies in occultism were carried out at first with the UR Group, a loose association of students of magic in which Reghini was involved, but he found it impossible to run in harness with anyone else for long. On his own, Evola studied oriental mystical teachings as well as alchemy and other branches of Western occultism, and synthesized an occult philosophy based on radical individualism and the rejection of Christian thought in favor of a warrior paganism with Aryan racial roots.

Starting in the late 1920s, Evola became increasingly interested in Fascist politics. At the time, Mussolini's "corporative state" seemed to offer a welcome alternative to capitalist and communist ideologies, and Evola hoped to see it evolve into a spiritual movement along the lines of his own ideas. The rising power of Nazi Germany to the north, with its warrior ethos and its uncompromising rejection of Christianity, caught his attention in the 1930s. His interest was shared; several of his books were translated into German under Nazi auspices, and he contributed to several important Nazi journals, including *Deutsches Volkstum* (*German Folkdom*) and the widely respected *Europaeische Revue* (*European Review*).

During the war years he was recruited by the Ahnenerbe, the research branch of Heinrich Himmler's SS, and spent most of the war working at an Ahnenerbe research post in Vienna, collecting information on Masonic lodges and secret societies. SEE SS.

During the closing months of the war, his apartment took a direct hit from an Allied bomb, and he was crippled from the waist downwards. After the war, he made his way back to Rome, where his lodgings in the Corso Vittorio Emmanuele became a meeting place for many of the founders of the European neofascist movement. He continued to write and speak on esoteric topics until shortly before his death in 1974. FURTHER READING: DRAKE 1986, EVOLA 1992, EVOLA 1995, WATERFIELD 1990.

evolution. The theory of evolution, as introduced to Western scientific thought by Charles Darwin, has few equivalents in earlier occult thought. Most Western occult traditions before the middle of the nineteenth century either accepted the concept of fall and redemption common to more orthodox faiths, or affirmed the essential goodness of humanity as it is and saw no need for progress.

There were a few eighteenth- and early nineteenth-century exceptions, however. One of these was the work of Emmanuel Swedenborg (1688–1772), whose complex theology includes the idea that human beings are capable of progressing after death into angelic states of being; *SEE* SWEDENBORG, EMMANUEL. Another was the system of transmigration found in the writings of the Welsh Druid revivalist Iolo Morganwg (1747–1826), who postulated a system of spiritual evolution in which every soul starts out at the simplest, single-celled form of life and works its way upwards through every living creature to the human level and beyond. *SEE* DRUIDRY.

Almost immediately after the publication of Darwin's *Origin of Species* in 1859, however, people began to redefine a wide range of spiritual traditions in evolutionary terms. Spiritualists and occult theorists of various kinds began fitting their beliefs into various schemes of evolution in which disembodied intelligences were the next stage above the human. This involved significant reshapings of older traditions; for example, believers in reincarnation redefined that process in terms of spiritual evolution, and discarded the essentially negative view of the subject held in traditional Hindu and Buddhist writings. *SEE* REINCARNATION.

The most spectacular example of this trend was the dizzying evolutionary system of H. P. Blavatsky, expounded in her massive work *The Secret Doctrine* (1888). *SEE* BLAVATSKY, HELENA PETROVNA. Blavatsky's system stands most of Victorian science on its head, postulating a series of root races, from the barely physical Polarians to the Aryans of the present epoch, whose physical and spiritual evolution stretches across billions of years and an assortment of lost continents. One curious feature of her system is that instead of humanity evolving out of animals, animals devolved out of humanity; every species of mammal, in this scheme, represents an offshoot of one of the previous root races which had degenerated to its present status.

The popularity of Theosophy helped put similar schemes of evolution into most occult writings of the late nineteenth and twentieth centuries. Many branches of the magical and Pagan communities, though, have abandoned these themes as part of the widespread rejection of the Theosophical legacy, and evolutionary schemes are becoming hard to find in modern occult writings as a result. They remain extremely popular in the modern New Age movement, however, which in this as so many other ways has borrowed heavily from the Theosophy-influenced occultism of the early twentieth century; *SEE* NEW AGE MOVEMENT. *SEE ALSO* LOST CIVILIZATIONS; ROOT RACE; THEOSOPHY.

execution. *SEE* DECRETISM.

exorcism. The process by which a possessing or obsessing spirit is driven out of a person, object, or place. Rituals of exorcism have played an important part in magical practices around the world since very ancient times, and most of the world's magical systems include rituals for driving away spirits. The Graeco-Egyptian magical papyri, the best surviving source for ancient Western magical practices, contain a selection of exorcism rituals; one of these, "the Stele of Jeu the Hieroglyphist," is the raw material from which the modern Bornless One ritual was created. *SEE* BORNLESS ONE RITUAL; GRAECO-EGYPTIAN MAGICAL PAPYRI.

After the coming of Christianity, exorcism became primarily a specialty of Christian priests, although rural folk magicians also practiced it. In the Christian church the power to exorcise evil spirits was given to a specific class of clergy by the end of the third century, and for many centuries the office of exorcist was one of the minor orders of the church, conferred in a ceremony in which the new exorcist was given a book of exorcistic rituals by his local bishop. It was largely among exorcists, or priests and monks who also practiced exorcism, that the more Christian branches of medieval ceremonial magic flourished; *SEE* GOETIA.

During the Reformation, most of the churches that retained the traditional priesthood and sacraments turned exorcism into a specialty practiced by a small number of ordained priests alone. Some recent systems of Christian magic, especially those connected to the world of independent bishops, have gone back to the older tradition. *SEE* CHRISTIAN OCCULTISM; HOLY ORDERS.

The rites of exorcism have close parallels to methods of banishing; *SEE* BANISHING. FURTHER READING: GOODMAN 1988.

exsufflation. (Latin *exsufflatio*, "blowing out") A form of magical breathwork in which subtle energy in another body or object is drawn into the magician's mouth or lungs by drawing in the breath; it may then either be absorbed, or expelled by a sudden sharp outbreath combined with focused intent and visualization. *SEE* BREATH; INSUFFLATION.

eye-biter. In Irish magical lore, a person with the power to curse cattle so that they go blind. There was a major eye-biter panic in Ireland in the late sixteenth century, in which more than a dozen people were accused of being eye-biters, and executed. *SEE ALSO* BURNING TIMES; EVIL EYE.

Fa. *SEE* FEHU.

face reading. *SEE* PHYSIOGNOMY.

Faery. A realm of nonhuman entities associated with the natural world; also, the entities themselves. Technically speaking, an inhabitant of Faery is a fay, not a faery or fairy, but the terms have become totally confused over the last half-dozen centuries or so. The exact nature of Faery and its inhabitants has been a subject of quite a bit of debate down through the years, in and out of the Western occult traditions.

Entities of the sort later known as fays, elves, and the like can be found in ancient Greek and Roman sources, where they blend in seamlessly with the realm of nature spirits and minor gods—the background fabric of classical religion. This same attitude can be found in Germanic and Celtic traditions, where the boundaries between gods and elves are impossible to draw.

The coming of Christianity, here as in so much else, forced a division down the middle of this easy unity. Christian dualism demanded that all entities be either good or evil, servants of God or of the Devil, and most orthodox accounts of Faery assigned it firmly to the Devil's camp. The idea of morally neutral spirits persisted, however, and both these attitudes can be found in medieval and Renaissance writings on the subject.

In England, which evolved and passed on magical traditions not found elsewhere, rites for summoning fays were in circulation by the sixteenth century, if not before. Rituals published in skeptic Reginald Scot's *Discov-erie of Witchcraft* (1584) include a ceremony for calling on three faery sisters, Milia, Achilia, and Sybilia, to provide a magical ring of invisibility. The 1665 edition of the same book, which was expanded by the addition of a huge collection of magical rites, includes another rite for the summoning of Luridan, a helpful spirit who is associated with Welsh bards, and announced by a group of gnome-like entities who speak ancient Irish! Contemporary records show that rites of this sort were being practiced in England through the end of the seventeenth century, and ceremonies for summoning the local faery folk were in use in Germany by the beginning of the sixteenth, when one was published in *The Threefold Harrowing of Hell*, the most famous of the grimoires attributed to Faust. *SEE* FAUST LEGEND.

These sources classified fays as simply one more type of spirit. The rise of a different approach, one that saw fays as a distinct class of entity, had to wait for the end of the Renaissance. The writings of Jerome Cardan (1501–1576), which included references to his father's magical work with a variety of spirits, helped introduce these ideas, which were relatively common by the time Robert Kirk (1644–1697) wrote his influential book *The Secret Commonwealth* in 1690. In this view, fays were not spirits as such, but intelligent living beings with bodies that happened to be subtler than ours.

This was the majority opinion among educated magicians at the time of the Scientific Revolution, when the entire subject dropped out of general awareness even in the occult community. Faery became a subject of interest again in the late nineteenth and early twentieth centuries, as Spiritualist and Theosophical writers broadened the range of spiritual beings under discussion. Thomas Lake Harris, an American Unitarian minister turned occult philosopher, included fays in his eccentric but influential theories, claiming that celibacy and "demagnetizing" practices allowed the human body to become home to swarms of health-giving faeries. *SEE* HARRIS, THOMAS LAKE. Similarly, the Golden Dawn papers include brief comments on "Fays and Arch-Fays," and examples of the species appear on the Prince of Swords card in the original Golden Dawn tarot deck.

W. Y. Evans-Wentz, a Theosophist who later became famous for his translations of Tibetan Buddhist scriptures, published a large and still valuable study—*The Fairy-Faith in Celtic Countries*—in 1912, including over one hundred eyewitness accounts of fays and detailed arguments supporting their reality. In 1920, a set of alleged photographs of fays taken by two small children were made public; although they have since been proven to be clever fakes, the Cottingsley fairy photographs stirred up further interest in fays and ensured them a place in modern New Age thought.

Current ideas about faery in the occult community range across the spectrum from Jungian analyses that conceptualize them as psychological realities through Theosophically derived teachings that see them as participants in another current of evolution (one that starts with elementals and proceeds through faeries, devas, and angels to archangels and beyond), to Pagan conceptions that interpret them as simply one part of the conplex fabric of spiritual reality, bringing the wheel around full circle. Which of these is closest to the truth, only the fays know—and they're not saying. *SEE ALSO* DEVA; ELEMENTARY SPIRIT. FURTHER READING: EVANS-WENTZ 1912, GREER 2001, MCLEAN 1990, STEWART 1990, TOLKIEN 1966.

Fairy. *SEE* FAERY.

Falk, Samuel Jacob Hayim. Jewish rabbi and Cabalist, c. 1710–1782. He was born in Podolia, Poland, in an area where the Jewish communities had been powerfully influenced by the teachings of the Cabalist messiah Sabbatai Zevi, and devoted himself to scriptural studies from an early age. *SEE* CABALA. He developed a reputation as a

Baal Shem or "Master of the Name," an expert in the practical Cabala, and was sought out by Christians as well as Jews for his occult help. He is recorded as having performed marvels in the presence of a variety of German noblemen. In 1740, while he was traveling in Germany, the archbishop of Cologne condemned him to death as a sorcerer. He was able to escape to safety in the more tolerant setting of Amsterdam, where he was welcomed by the local Jewish community.

Shortly thereafter, he moved to London, where he settled at Wellclose Square in the East End. There he became the center of a Cabalistic circle that included both Jews and Christians, and also established an alchemical laboratory. He was also heavily involved in Masonic circles in London; the details of his initiation have not survived, but he was sought out by Masons from England and overseas as an expert in Cabala and occult studies, and seems to have been tangled up in the murky Masonic and magical intrigues that surrounded the Jacobite risings of 1715 and 1745. *SEE* FREEMASONRY; STUART, HOUSE OF.

He was widely rumored to be one of the "Unknown Superiors" who were believed to govern high-grade Masonry in the 1770s, and was associated with both Cagliostro and Swedenborg, both of whom were also on the short list of suspected Secret Chiefs. *SEE* CAGLIOSTRO, COUNT ALESSANDRO; SWEDENBORG, EMMANUEL. He died in London in 1782, just before the great Masonic conventicle of Wilhelmsbad in that year.

According to later accounts in the English magical community, Falk's circle of Cabalistic students was the original version of the Hermetic Order of the Golden Dawn. Whether this has any truth to it, or whether it is another example of the occult history surrounding the Golden Dawn, is anybody's guess. *SEE* GOLDEN DAWN, HERMETIC ORDER OF THE; OCCULT HISTORY. FURTHER READING: PATAI 1994, SCHUCHARD 1995.

Fall, the. In Christian mythology, the process by which human beings became subject to death, suffering, and eternal damnation, and snakes lost their feet. The original story appears in the Old Testament (Genesis 3:1–19). Adam and Eve, the first two humans, were forbidden to eat the fruit of the Tree of Knowledge of Good and Evil.

A serpent convinced Eve to eat, and then she convinced Adam to do so; afterwards, they both realized that they were naked, and hid themselves in the undergrowth. God then cursed the serpent to travel on his belly from then on, Eve to have labor pains in childbirth and to be subject to Adam, and Adam to have to work for a living and to die. God then made Adam and Eve leather clothing to wear, and threw them out of the Garden of Eden.

The myth in its Old Testament form is a straightforward origin story, clearly meant to explain the origin of death, labor pains, work, clothing, and other unpleasant facts of life, as well as why snakes have no feet. Early Christian theologians, however, claimed that the side effects of eating the fruit also included damnation to everlasting torture in Hell for all Adam and Eve's descendants, except for believers in the right version of Christianity. This new interpretation was written into the New Testament and has been a central claim of Christianity ever since.

Both versions of the Fall have played a dizzying array of roles in occult teachings. The ancient Gnostics exercised an extraordinary amount of ingenuity on the story of the Fall, creating versions of "what really happened" that often read like the religious equivalent of conspiracy theories. *SEE* GNOSTICISM. Many other occult traditions have interpreted and reinterpreted the brief account of Genesis in different ways.

One common interpretation places Eden on the astral plane, rather than the physical world. The leather garments or "coats of skins" given by God to Adam and Eve after the Fall are interpreted as physical bodies, and the expulsion from Eden as the descent of humanity to the physical plane. *SEE* ASTRAL PLANE.

Most recently, theories in the New Age community have tended to interpret the entire story of Eden and the Fall in terms borrowed from science fiction, with extraterrestrials filling in for God. While this sort of approach is hard to justify on the basis of evidence or tradition, it has been understandably popular in a culture obsessed with its own technological toys. *SEE ALSO* ADAM; EDEN; EVE.

Fama Fraternitatis. (Latin, "report of the brotherhood") The commonly used short form of the title of the first Rosicrucian manifesto. *SEE* ROSICRUCIANS.

familiar. Also "familiar spirit," a spiritual being who associates itself with certain kinds of magical practitioners. The Old Testament refers to people who have familiar spirits; from context, and from other sources dating from the ancient Middle East, these people seem to have been something not unlike Spiritualist mediums, and their spirits were usually the ghosts of dead human beings, often those who had died violently. *SEE* SPIRITUALISM.

In Europe during the Middle Ages, these scriptural passages were reinterpreted in the light of ancient European folklore about magical animal guides who accompanied folk magicians and shamans. The result was the concept of the "witch's familiar," a demon in the form of an animal who assisted and protected the witch. While most familiars were believed to take relatively conventional animal forms—cats, toads, mice, rats, flies, and the like—witch trial reports include some exotic forms as well.

Familiars were believed to live by sucking blood from their master or mistress by way of a "witch's teat," a spot on the body that was discolored, icy cold, and insensitive to pain. Testing for the "witch's teat" or "witch mark" played an important part in many witchcraft trials during the Burning Times, with suspected witches being jabbed many times with sharp instruments. Some witch hunters made use of trick bodkins with retractable points to produce the illusion of a pain-free spot.

Some modern Wiccans and witches consider their pets to be familiars, and make use of their sensitivity to subtle energies in magical work. *SEE ALSO* WITCHCRAFT.

family tradition. In Wicca and other modern Pagan movements, a family tradition (often shortened to "famtrad") is a system of teaching and practice said to have been handed down from one generation to the next in a particular family since ancient times. Authentic traditions of this sort certainly exist, in branches of the occult traditions ranging from hoodoo to Rosicrucian mysticism. However, "fam-trad" claims have been so frequently used to provide a fictitious history for newly minted systems, especially among Wiccan and Neopagan groups in America, that the concept has fallen into disrepute in large parts of the occult community. *SEE ALSO* GRANDMOTHER STORY; OCCULT HISTORY; WICCA.

fantasy occultism. The interface between the worlds of literature and magic has been relatively complex all through history. One of the best sources in existence for the traditions of magic current in the Roman Empire, for example, is Lucius Apuleis' novel *The Golden Ass*; SEE APULEIUS, LUCIUS. Similarly, the historical Johann Georg Faustus and the legendary and literary figure of Faust are very difficult to tease apart.

The Faust legends gave rise to an entire literature of demon-summoning handbooks, based on older grimoires but attributed to Faust. These "Faustbooks" were popular for several centuries all through central Europe among would-be magicians who hoped to win Faust's supposedly limitless wealth while avoiding the inconvenience of eternal damnation. SEE FAUST LEGEND; FAUSTUS, JOHANN GEORG.

In the same way, the great magical revival of the nineteenth century was heavily influenced by writers of occult fiction such as Edward Bulwer-Lytton and Joséphin Peladan. The American occult community of the late twentieth century thus had quite a few precedents behind it when it began to come up with systems of magic and magical religion based on the imaginary worlds of fantasy and science fiction.

Several factors played a part in the emergence of this sort of fantasy magic. One is the massive popularity of science fiction and fantasy among people in the American Neopagan scene. Another is the Society for Creative Anachronism, also hugely popular in the Neopagan subculture, which provided a venue for medieval make-believe on a grand scale. Still another is the profusion of roleplaying games such as Dungeons & Dragons, nearly all of which contained detailed systems of "magic" that have little or nothing to do with actual occult tradition, and also vary widely among themselves. All these factors made it increasingly easy to lose track of the difference between authentic magic and the various simulations of the occult in literature, gaming, and medieval reenactments.

The most widely known of the resulting fantasy-magic systems is probably Klingon Wicca, which was created around 1995 by Pagan fans of the *Star Trek* TV and movie series. The rituals of this system were translated into the language invented for the warlike Klingon aliens of the *Star Trek* universe; participants brandish Klingon weapons, and wear armor and clothing copied from movies and TV episodes, while performing what are more or less standard Wiccan rituals. SEE WICCA.

Other forms of fantasy occultism have grown up around Wiccan reworkings of several very popular series of fantasy-fiction novels—the Darkover novels of Marion Zimmer Bradley, the Deryni Chronicles of Katherine Kurtz, and the Valdemar novels of Mercedes Lackey. All three of these series include detailed systems of magic as a central plot element, and one author (Kurtz) has actually published a "grimoire" of her characters' magical methods. Attempts to put these fictional magical systems into practice have been fairly common in recent decades.

Still another form of fantasy occultism has emerged around the Cthulhu mythos, a literary mythology created by American pulp writer H. P. Lovecraft and his colleagues in the 1930s. The mythos is based on the idea that a collection of evil entities from outer space, the Old Ones, once ruled the Earth, and now wait for the chance to wrap their slimy tentacles around the planet once again. The Cthulhu mythos presents magic as the debased remnants of Old One science, used by sinister cultists who seek to call the Old Ones back.

While Lovecraft's relentlessly negative attitude toward magic may seem to provide little incentive to the fantasy occultist, materials from the Cthulhu mythos have been in use in the occult community since the 1960s. As of this writing, no fewer than three purported versions of Lovecraft's imaginary magical tome, the *Necronomicon*, have been concocted and marketed in the occult book trade. SEE NECRONOMICON.

As a form of recreation, these various styles of fantasy occultism are relatively harmless. As forms of magical practice, on the other hand, they are almost entirely useless. Methods of magic created purely for fictional effect have, as one might expect, purely fictional effects when put into practice. The extent to which this was lost sight of does not speak well for the seriousness or the sophistication of some elements of the American occult scene.

A slightly more serious use of fantasy and science fiction in current occult circles is the work of adherents of Chaos magic. A central idea of Chaos magic is that belief systems are simply tools for attaining certain mental states, and have no truth or validity in themselves; a fictional god or symbol is thus just as good as one with a long historical pedigree. On this principle, Chaos magicians have borrowed extensively from fantasy and science fiction. The "Banner of Chaos" from English writer Michael Moorcock's Eternal Champion novels, the magical color "octarine" from Terry Pratchett's Discworld fantasy-satires, and the eldritch deities of H. P. Lovecraft's horror fiction have made an appearance in Chaos magic writings.

There is a certain irony in this, since the entire Chaos magic movement was arguably launched by another work of science fiction—the Illuminatus! trilogy by Robert Shea and Robert Anton Wilson. Still, whatever their choice of symbolism, most Chaos magicians make use of tested and effective magical methods. SEE ALSO CHAOS MAGIC; DISCORDIANISM.

Farrar, Stewart. English writer and witch, 1916–2000. Born in London, Farrar grew up in a family involved in Christian Science, and served as an antiaircraft gun instructor in the Second World War. He joined the Communist Party in the early 1950s, but became disillusioned and quit at the time of the Hungarian revolt in 1956. He went on to become a journalist and writer, publishing several popular novels.

In 1970, he contacted Alec Sanders, the self-proclaimed "King of the Witches," as a reporter for the British magazine *Reveille*. This contact led to Farrar's own involvement in witchcraft, as well as his first book on the subject, *What Witches Do* (1971). He was initiated into Sanders' coven in 1970. He and another coven member, Janet Owen (later Farrar), left the coven to found their own after receiving their third degree initiations; they were married in 1972.

In 1976 the Farrars moved to Ireland, where they organized a coven and wrote numerous books on witchcraft and related subjects. Their publications and lectures were among the major influences on the development of Wicca during the last quarter of the twentieth century, and they also played a central role in starting the Neopagan movement in Ireland where, according to some accounts, three-quarters of all Wiccans can trace their initiation lineage back to the Farrars. When Stewart Farrar died in Ireland in 2000, the news saddened Wiccans and Pagans around the globe. SEE ALSO SANDERS, ALEC; WICCA. FURTHER READING: FARRAR AND FARRAR 1984.

fascination. (Latin *fascinatio*, "binding") Originally a term of magic before it gained its more recent (and more watered-down) meaning, fascination referred to the power of enchanting or controlling another person through the glance. SEE EVIL EYE.

Faust legend. The most famous of all stories about a man who sold his soul to the Devil in exchange for wealth and power, the Faust legend had its origins in the career of Johann Faustus (c. 1480–c. 1540), a German who may have been an actual occultist, a charlatan, or both at once. SEE FAUSTUS, JOHANN GEORG. Stories about him, heavily influenced by earlier legends about pacts with the Devil, were in circulation during his lifetime, and seem to have spread widely throughout Germany in the years after his death. SEE PACT; THEOPHILUS OF ADANA.

In 1587, Faust's posthumous career was launched by a German hack writer named Johann Spiess, whose *Geschichte der Doktor Johannes Fausten* (*History of Doctor Johannes Fausten*) was an international bestseller, translated into every major European language. Spiess' account included most of the elements of the later legend, presenting Faust as a sorcerer who sold his soul to the Devil in exchange for magical powers, wallowed in sensual delights for twenty-four years with the aid of the familiar spirit Mephistopheles, and was then dragged off to Hell.

Two years after the publication of Spiess' book, the Elizabethan dramatist Christopher Marlowe used it as the basis for one of the great plays of his career, *The Tragicall History of Doctor Faustus* (1589). Marlowe's Faust was lured by a desire for forbidden knowledge into a pact with the demon Mephistopheles, enjoys seven years of power and luxury, and then is carried away to Hell. Marlowe was associated with the so-called School of Night, a circle of noblemen and scholars interested in occultism and religious heresy, and it has been suggested that Marlowe's play was influenced by this connection. SEE SCHOOL OF NIGHT.

Marlowe's play was only the first, though arguably the best, of a torrent of dramatic productions based on the

Faust legend, including everything from a grand opera (Charles Gounoud's *Faust*, first performed in 1859) to early modern German puppet plays. In the field of literature, Goethe's massive poetic rendition of the Faust legend, published in two parts (the first in 1808, the second in 1833) is the high point of the tradition, and one of the greatest works of German literature as well. *SEE* GOETHE, JOHANN WOLFGANG VON.

One of the minor comedies of magical history is the extent to which fictions about magic, even those circulated by people violently opposed to every kind of occultism, tend to inspire attempts at magical practice; *SEE* FANTASY OCCULTISM. In the late sixteenth and seventeenth centuries, a variety of magical textbooks allegedly by Faust made their appearance in Germany and were widely circulated among would-be sorcerers. The most famous of these "Faustbooks" is the *Magia Naturalis et Innaturalis* (*Natural and Unnatural Magic*), subtitled *The Threefold Harrowing of Hell*, but there were many others—including, predictably, a *Fourfold Harrowing of Hell*.

These Faustian grimoires all draw heavily on older magical handbooks, and are very much within the tradition of Christian ceremonial magic, with substantial elements of Catholic legend and devotional practice put to work for the purpose of summoning and commanding demons. The goal of the conjurations is almost always cold, hard cash in sizeable amounts. The famous pact with the Devil that plays a central role in the Faust legend rarely appears in the Faustbooks, which seem much more interested in getting something for nothing by browbeating the hosts of Hell. *SEE ALSO* DEMON; GOETIA. FURTHER READING: BARON 1978, BUTLER 1949, BUTLER 1952, PALMER 1936.

Faustus, Johann Georg. German magician, c. 1480–c. 1540. Little is known about the life and times of this person, who set in motion the most famous of all magical legends. He was apparently born in the German town of Knittlingen, and probably died in Staufen. The years between these two somewhat vague markers are even less well documented, but a variety of letters and local chronicles testify to his activities.

Faustus advertised himself as a physician, alchemist, soothsayer, astrologer, and magician, and claimed, among other things, to be able to perform all the miracles of

Jesus of Nazareth. He is said to have referred to the Devil as his brother-in-law. What actual degree of magical knowledge and ability he may have had is anybody's guess, but it may not have been much.

Certain scholars have argued that there may have been two Fausts, Johann and Georg, the first an actual occultist of the classic Renaissance type and the other a charlatan, but the evidence is far from conclusive. *SEE ALSO* FAUST LEGEND. FURTHER READING: BARON 1978, PALMER 1936.

fay. *SEE* FAERY.

Fe. *SEE* FEHU.

Fearn. (Old Irish, "alder") The third (in Boibeloth) or fourth (in Beth-Luis-Nion) letter of the Ogham alphabet, with the sound-value *v*. It corresponds to the alder among trees, the gull among birds, the color red, and the number eight. In Robert Graves' version of the Ogham tree-calendar, its month runs from March 18 to April 14. *SEE* OGHAM.

Ogham letter Fearn

Fehu. (Old Germanic, "cattle") The first rune of the elder futhark, associated with cattle and other forms of wealth, with the god Njord, and with creativity and prosperity. Its sound-value is *f*. *SEE* ELDER FUTHARK.

The same rune, under the name Feoh (Old English, "cattle, wealth"), is the first rune of the Anglo-Saxon futhorc, and has the same sound-value. The Old English rune-poem relates it to wealth, which must be freely given for the sake of honor. *SEE* ANGLO-SAXON FUTHORC.

Under the name Fe (Old Norse, "cattle, wealth"), with the same implications and sound-value, this rune also begins the younger futhark. As befits the character of the Viking age, the Danish and Norwegian rune-poems relate the concept of wealth to strife between kinfolk. *SEE* YOUNGER FUTHARK.

The same rune, finally, also begins the Armanen runic alphabet, but here it has the name Fa and stands for the concept of transitoriness. It is associated with Alfheim (the realm of the *ljos-alfar* or Light-Elves), with the father in the family, and the sign Aries in the zodiac, and the power, derived from Odin's rune-charm in the *Havamal*, to bring help in time of anguish and trial. *SEE* ARMANEN RUNES.

Rune Fehu (Feoh, Fe, Fa)

fennel. (*Foeniculum vulgare*) A magical herb important in Mediterranean lore, fennel is a tall plant—reaching six to eight feet high—with blue stripes on its stems, large umbels of yellow flowers, and a strong licorice scent. It was used in spells for fertility and virility, and was hung above the door on midsummer's eve to banish hostile entities and bad luck from the house.

A related plant, the giant fennel, was famous in ancient times but is now extinct. It had important medicinal uses as an effective contraceptive, and played an important role in symbolism.

The benandanti, a northern Italian Pagan movement of the sixteenth and seventeenth centuries C.E., used fennel stalks as weapons in their spectral forays against the powers of evil. *SEE* BENANDANTI. *SEE ALSO* NATURAL MAGIC. FURTHER READING: GREER 2000.

Feoh. *SEE* FEHU.

fermentation. In alchemy, a process in which a small portion of an active substance is added to a larger amount of inert substance in order to transform the latter. The fermentation of beer and wine is considered, by alchemists, to be a simple form of alchemical transformation.

In alchemical symbolism, this process is associated with the zodiacal sign Capricorn; in some accounts, it is listed as the fifth operation of the Great Work. *SEE* ALCHEMY.

fetch. In English and American occult folklore, the image of a person about to die, seen by the person's friends and family. In some modern Pagan traditions the term is also used for the projected astral body of a magical practitioner; *SEE* ASTRAL PROJECTION.

Fez. City in Morocco, an important center of trade and scholarship since the early Middle Ages. According to the *Fama Fraternitatis*, Christian Rosenkreutz studied magic and Cabala in Fez after his departure from Damcar in Arabia. *SEE* ROSENKREUTZ, CHRISTIAN.

According to a much-circulated story, the tarot was originally devised by a convention of sages and adepts who met in Fez in the year 1300 C.E. As with most accounts of the tarot's origin circulated in the occult community, there is no evidence whatsoever for this claim. *SEE* TAROT.

Ficino, Marsilio. Italian scholar, physician, and magician, 1433–1499. His father was the personal physician to Cosimo de Medici, the ruler of the city-state of Florence, and he was raised in the midst of the most vigorous cultural, artistic, and literary scene of Renaissance Europe. A child prodigy, he had a fluent command of Latin and classical Greek by his teen years, and became one of Europe's most distinguished classical scholars while still in his twenties.

While he was still in his teens he was selected by Cosimo de Medici as the head of a new Florentine Academy, and given access to the Medici collection of Greek manuscripts salvaged from the crumbling Byzantine Empire to the east. The jewel among these was a complete collection of the works of Plato, which included books few European scholars had ever seen. For his first major project, Ficino was set to work on making the first translation of these precious works into Latin.

But in 1453, as Ficino was about to begin work on Plato, word came from Cosimo de Medici that something more important had been found and needed to be done first. This was the Corpus Hermeticum, a collection of writings attributed to Hermes Trismegistus. *SEE* CORPUS HERMETICUM. Ficino translated it in a few months, and his translation was widely distributed, both in manuscript and in printed form—the first printed edition came out in 1471, and it went through sixteen editions before the end of the sixteenth century. More than any other factor, this translation jumpstarted the Renaissance revival of Hermetic magic.

It also led Ficino himself straight into magical practices. His major original work, *Libri de Vita* (*Books on Life*, 1489), is a handbook of medicine and health care for scholars. According to Renaissance medical thought, intensive intellectual work made scholars vulnerable to melancholy and several other "occupational diseases," which Ficino's handbook sought to prevent or cure. The methods he proposes, however, are full to the brim with astrological magic and planetary talismans, which are used to draw down the beneficent energies of the Sun, Venus, and Jupiter and overcome the influence of Saturn.

The publication of the overtly magical *Libri de Vita* brought Ficino a certain amount of criticism, although the protection of the House of Medici kept him safe from any real danger. He had entered holy orders in the Catholic Church in 1473, becoming a canon in the Cathedral of Florence, but the relaxed attitude of the church toward Hermeticism in the fifteenth century helped to blunt the attacks aimed at him. He remained an active figure in scholarly circles until his death in Florence in 1499. *SEE ALSO* HERMETICISM; PLATONISM. FURTHER READING: M. ALLEN 1984, MEBANE 1989, D. WALKER 1958, WALKER 1972, YATES 1964.

Fionn's window. Mandala-like diagram found in the *Book of Ballymote*, a fourteenth-century Irish manuscript of bardic lore. The "window" is made up of the letters of the Ogham alphabet, arranged on a set of five concentric circles. Its connection to the legendary Irish hero Fionn mac Cumhaill, who is also credited with many other elements of bardic lore, is almost certainly apocryphal. Fionn's window has been brought back into use in a few modern Druid and Celtic groups. *SEE ALSO* OGHAM. FURTHER READING: CALDER 1917.

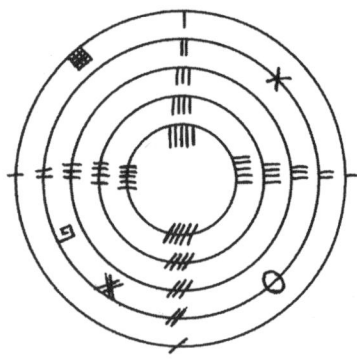

Fionn's window

fire, element of. In magical symbolism, one of the four (or five) elements, corresponding to energy, to the warm and dry qualities, and to the choleric humor. As with all the elements, there are varying attributions, but the following are standard in most current Western occult systems:

Symbol: △

Letter of Tetragrammaton: י, Yod.

Name of God: אלהים, ALHIM, Elohim (gods and goddesses).

Archangel: מיכאל, MIKAL, Michael (He Who Is As God).

Angel: אראל, ARAL, Aral.

Ruler: שרף, ShRP, Seraph.

Elemental King: Djin.

Elementals: Salamanders.

Hebrew Name of Element: אש, ASh, Aesh.

Direction: דרום, DRVM, Darom, the south.

Season: Summer.

Time of Day: Noon.

Qualities: Hot and dry.

Nature: Energy.

SEE ALSO DIRECTIONS IN OCCULTISM; ELEMENTS, MAGICAL; HUMORS.

fire festivals. The four cross-quarter sabbats of Samhain, Imbolc (Candlemas), Beltane, and Lammas (Lughnassadh). *SEE* SABBAT.

First Matter. In alchemy, the substance from which the Philosopher's Stone is made. Its identity is perhaps the central secret of the alchemist's art. Alchemical texts suggest that the First Matter is everywhere, in plain sight, and considered worthless by all but alchemists. *SEE* ALCHEMY.

Firth, Violet. *SEE* FORTUNE, DION.

fith-fath. In traditional Irish magic, the practice of shapeshifting into an animal form. *SEE* LYCANTHROPY.

In some traditions of modern Wicca and Paganism, the term is used for a wax or clay poppet into which pins, needles, or thorns are stuck. The flamboyant but not always accurate Alec Sanders seems to have been originally responsible for this use of the term. *SEE* POPPET; SANDERS, ALEC.

five. In the Cabala, five is Geburah, Severity, the fifth Sephirah, and also the number of the letter Heh. Names of God with five letters include ALHIM, Elohim, and ALIVN, Elyon. The Christian and Hermetic versions of the Cabala add the two forms of the Pentagrammaton—YHShVH, Yeheshuah, and YHVShH, Yehowashah. *SEE* CABALA.

In Christian symbolism, five is the number of the wounds of Christ.

In Renaissance magical symbolism, five is sacred to Mercury, and is the number of woman and of the sea. FURTHER READING: MCLEAN 1994, WATERFIELD 1988, WESTCOTT 1984.

Fivefold Kiss. In Wiccan initiation rituals and other magical practices, a pattern of kisses applied to an initiate or witch. There are several different versions in common use at present. One involves kisses on both feet, both knees, and the genitals, forming a pentagram. Another expands the pentagram, and places the kisses on head, hands, and feet. *SEE* PENTAGRAM. Still another places the kisses on feet, knees, genitals, breasts, and lips. In many traditions, the Fivefold Kiss is given by a woman to a man or by a man to a woman, but not by people of the same gender to one another. *SEE ALSO* WICCA.

fixation. In alchemy, the process of transforming a volatile substance into a form that does not change or dissipate when exposed to heat. This was considered to be an important stage in the alchemical process, which some texts describe as "fixing the volatile and volatilizing the fixed." Alchemical symbolism assigns this process to the zodiacal sign Gemini. *SEE* ALCHEMY.

Flamel, Nicholas. French scrivener and alchemist, c. 1330–1418. Born in Pontoise to poor but educated parents, he came to Paris as a young man and took up a position as a scrivener or public scribe, eventually winning the post of official scrivener to the University of Paris. In the course of his work he dealt with a variety of old

books, and one day—according to his own account, which is the only source of information about his alchemical work—came across an unusual book of twenty-one pages, bound in brass and written on the inner bark of some sort of tree.

Its first page had large gold letters reading *Abraham the Jew Prince, Priest, Levite, Astrologer, and Philosopher, to the nation of the Jews, by the wrath of God dispersed among the Gauls, sendeth health*, followed by formal curses against anyone but a priest or scribe who cast eyes on it. The remaining pages contained a set of emblems with no explanations, which seemed to have to do with alchemy. He bought the book for two florins and began what would be a long quest for the secrets of alchemy.

His wife Perenelle, whom he had recently married, took an interest in the subject as well, and soon became his coworker in the full range of alchemical experiments. For many years, though, they were unable to decipher the meanings hidden in the mysterious book. The best scholars in Paris were unable to help them. Finally, with Perenelle's agreement, he set out as a pilgrim to the great shrine of Saint James at Compostela, in the hope of finding an adept of alchemy in Spain, where Arabs and Jews shared knowledge with Christian scholars from across Europe.

In the city of Leon, after a long search, he finally encountered a Jewish alchemist named Master Canches, who recognized the emblems with great excitement, began to decipher them, and agreed to accompany Flamel back to Paris. They set off at once, and Canches worked on the decipherment as they traveled. Unfortunately he took sick on the way and died at Orleans, having explained only the first principles of the art to Flamel.

Flamel returned home, and he and Perenelle went to work at once trying to build on the knowledge Canches had revealed. After three years of hard work, they succeeded in discovering the right way of preparing the First Matter. Within a short time thereafter they had mastered the rest of the art. Their first projection was around noon on Monday, January 17, 1382, when they used the White Stone—which transmutes base metal into silver—to turn half a pound of mercury into pure silver. On April 25 of the same year, around five o'clock in the evening, they projected the Red Stone—which transmutes base metal into gold—onto half a pound of mercury, transmuting it into pure gold. According to Flamel's account, they carried out two other transmutations later on.

Much of the income resulting from these successful transmutations went to charitable works, and Flamel mentions in his account that he and Perenelle founded and endowed no fewer than fourteen hospitals. Orthodox historians have noted that Flamel certainly did exist, and seems to have become very wealthy during his life; the sources of his wealth, of course, have been the subject of much speculation. *SEE ALSO* ALCHEMY; PHILOSOPHER'S STONE. FURTHER READING: FLAMEL 1994, PATAI 1994, READ 1937.

Flamel, Perenelle. The wife and alchemical partner of Nicholas Flamel, she became a capable alchemist in her own right and by Flamel's account played an important role in discovering the Philosopher's Stone. *SEE* FLAMEL, NICHOLAS; PHILOSOPHER'S STONE.

flamen. A priest in ancient Rome who was consecrated to the service of a specific divinity. There were originally three flamines: the Flamen Dialis who served Jupiter, the Flamen Martialis who served Mars, and the Flamen Quirinalis who served the deified Romulus, founder of Rome. Over the history of Pagan Rome additional flamines were added; by the time the empire was converted to Christianity, there were several dozen flamines in Rome. The wife of a flamen held the title of flaminica, and served as a priestess in her own right. When either a flamen or a flaminica died, the surviving spouse had to resign the office and was not permitted to remarry.

In some modern Pagan traditions, the title of flamen has been adopted as an equivalent of High Priest; *SEE* HIGH PRIEST. *SEE ALSO* PAGANISM.

Flaming Sword. In Cabala, the pattern formed by the sequence of Sephiroth on the Tree of Life, equated with the flaming sword that guarded the gate of Eden in Genesis 3:24. It is also called the Lightning Flash. *SEE* LIGHTNING FLASH; TREE OF LIFE.

flaminica. In ancient Rome, a priestess, the wife of a flamen; *SEE* FLAMEN. Some modern Pagan traditions have adopted this title (or the alternate spelling "flamenca") as an equivalent of High Priestess; *SEE* HIGH PRIESTESS.

flashing colors. In the Golden Dawn system of magic, colors that produce a flashing or "strobe" effect in the eyes of a viewer. If one stares fixedly at a color for a time and then looks at a white wall, an afterimage of the opposite color will appear before the eyes. If two colors are chosen so that each is the other's exact opposite, and the two are placed side by side, each will appear to pulse with the other after a short period of concentrated gaze. The Golden Dawn knowledge lectures stated that this effect was associated with a stirring up of etheric energy, and flashing colors were therefore used in consecrated working tools and talismans as a source of additional energy.

A somewhat more complex way of using flashing colors involved three colors rather than two; a principal color was chosen, and then two other colors—both of them nearly but not quite opposite to the principal color—were used with it. *SEE ALSO* COLOR SCALES. FURTHER READING: GREER 1997, REGARDIE 1971.

flashing tablet. In the Golden Dawn tradition of magic, a magical device used for practical magical workings. A flashing tablet is a square or rectangular piece of heavy paper, card, or wood, painted with the symbols of an element, planet, Sephirah, or other magical energy in flashing colors, and then consecrated like a talisman to accomplish some particular purpose. It is then wrapped in silk or linen.

Each day thereafter, the magician unwraps it and sets it upright on the altar, sits facing it, and passes through it in imagination, using it as a portal into the realm of the energy previously bound into it by the consecration. Once in that realm, the magician performs an invoking ritual of the same energy, calling in additional power for the fulfillment of the flashing tablet's purpose. This process charges the flashing tablet from within, giving it far more power than an ordinary talisman. *SEE ALSO* FLASHING COLORS; TALISMAN. FURTHER READING: GREER 1997, REGARDIE 1971.

Flos Abysmi. (Latin, "flower of the abyss") In the Aurum Solis system of magic, the third highest of the six energy centers of the human body, related to the quasi-

Sephiroth Daath and located at the throat. In the Rousing of the Citadels, an Aurum Solis exercise equivalent to the Middle Pillar exercise, it is visualized as a purple sphere located entirely in front of the middle of the throat; no part of it is inside the physical body. Its Name of Power is AaLIVN, Elyon.

It corresponds to the throat chakra and to the Daath center of the Middle Pillar exercise. *SEE* AURUM SOLIS; MIDDLE PILLAR EXERCISE; ROUSING OF THE CITADELS.

Fludd, Robert. English physician and occultist, 1574–1637. The son of a government official turned country squire, Fludd was born and grew up in rural Kent, and entered Oxford University in 1592, receiving his bachelor's degree in 1596 and his master's in 1598. After the latter, he traveled in Europe for six years, working as a tutor for aristocratic families in France and Italy. During these travels, he became interested in medicine, and when he returned to Oxford in 1604 he began formal medical studies, graduating with a doctorate in 1605. After some initial troubles with the College of Physicians, the medical trade organization in Britain at the time, he was admitted to practice in 1609 and began a successful medical career.

In addition to medicine, though, Fludd had a lifelong interest in astrology, occult philosophy, and Cabala, and also made important contributions to the Art of Memory; *SEE* ART OF MEMORY. In his undergraduate days he was already good enough at astrology to identify a thief by means of a horary chart; *SEE* HORARY ASTROLOGY. Later he mastered geomancy as well, and nearly got into serious trouble during his European travels when a group of Jesuits found out about his divinations and went to the papal vice-legate, a high church official, in an attempt to get Fludd arrested. The vice-legate, however, turned out to be just as interested in geomancy as Fludd, and invited the Englishman to dinner, where they spent a pleasant evening discussing the art. *SEE* GEOMANCY.

After his return to England and the beginning of his medical career, Fludd launched what would be his great contribution to Western occultism, a massive encyclopedia of all human knowledge from the perspective of Renaissance occult philosophy. The first volume of *Utriusque Cosmi Maioris scilicet et Minoris Metaphysica, Physica et Technica Historia* (*Metaphysical, Physical and Technical History of Both Universes, that is, the Greater and the Lesser*) was pub-

lished by Johann Theodor de Bry in 1617, and further volumes followed over the next few years.

A prolific writer and vigorous debater, Fludd was active in pamphlet debates (the Renaissance equivalent of modern Internet flamewars) with proponents of materialist science, such as the French priest Marin Mersenne and the English physician William Foster. He never quite finished the great encyclopedia, publishing several important books of Hermetic medicine and spagyric alchemy in the later part of his life. He died peacefully at his home in 1637 and was buried at the Fludd family parish church in Bearstead, Kent. *SEE ALSO* HERMETICISM. FURTHER READING: FLUDD 1992, J. GODWIN 1979.

fluid condenser. In European traditions of magic, a substance used to store etheric energy. The most common fluid condensers are liquid, and made by dissolving small amounts of gold in water, then combining this with herbal infusions of various kinds; there are also solid fluid condensers, which are less often used. The term *fluid condenser* derives from the concept of etheric energy as a subtle fluid. *SEE ALSO* ETHER. FURTHER READING: BARDON 1962.

flying roll. In the Hermetic Order of the Golden Dawn, various incidental papers and lectures were termed "flying rolls" and circulated among the adepti of the order. Most of these have been reprinted in King 1987. *SEE* GOLDEN DAWN, HERMETIC ORDER OF THE. FURTHER READING: KING 1987.

Fohat. In Theosophy, the primary cosmic energy that brings the manifested universe into being. It is closely related to the life-force or One Life. *SEE* THEOSOPHY.

Fool, the. Numbered zero, twenty-one, or twenty-two among the Major Arcana of the tarot, this trump shows the image of a court jester in the earlier tarot decks, while later decks give it a variety of images ranging from an old man in ragged clothing to a naked child holding a wolf by a leash. In the Golden Dawn system, it is assigned to the Hebrew letter Aleph, while the French system assigns it to Shin. In divination, its common meanings range from folly and madness to the highest levels of spiritual influence.

Its magical title is "The Spirit of Aether." *SEE* TAROT.

Tarot trump the Fool (Universal Tarot)

footprints. In many traditions of folk magic, a footprint can be used as a means of enchanting the person who made it. Thrusting a sharp object into someone's footprint can be used as part of a magical curse to bring lameness, while dirt from within someone's footprint can be used to establish a magical link with that person, for good or ill. *SEE* CURSE; NATURAL MAGIC.

Forman, Simon. English occultist and physician, 1552–1611. The fifth son of a peasant family in the little village of Quidhampton, near Salisbury, Forman spent his childhood pursuing the few educational opportunities open to him, and by the age of eighteen was employed as a schoolmaster. Around 1574 he met Francis Cox, a local physician who dabbled in astrology and magic, and became interested in medicine as well as occultism. In 1579 he was arrested—the charge is uncertain—and imprisoned for more than a year.

The next fifteen years saw Forman struggling to establish himself as a physician and an astrologer, living in Salisbury and London at varying times before finally settling for good in the London suburb of Lambeth. As an unlicensed physician, he faced constant legal trouble with the official College of Physicians, while a Salisbury official named Giles Estcourt tried numerous times to get him imprisoned for magical practices.

Forman's astrological business was already attracting clients in high places, however, and this helped him escape his legal difficulties. During this same time, he steadily expanded his magical knowledge and practices. His diary records for the year 1588: "This year I began to practice necromancy, and to call angels and spirits" (quoted in Rowse 1974, p. 38).

In 1592, bubonic plague struck London. Forman caught the disease but was able to cure himself and many other people with a distilled herb tincture of his own invention. This made his reputation as a physician, and his talents as an astrologer were also becoming widely known in the metropolis. Thereafter, prosperous and respected, he pursued his studies and catered to a growing clientele that included many aristocrats. His diary and case notes provide an astonishingly detailed look at the underside of the Elizabethan age—as well as plenty of information on his very active sex life.

Forman appears to have studied and practiced every branch of occultism known at his time. Besides astrology and geomancy, both of which he did professionally, he engaged in necromancy, evoked spirits and angels of various kinds, prepared talismans and charms, studied the Cabala, worked with natural magic, and was familiar with the Art of Memory. *SEE* ART OF MEMORY; ASTROLOGY; CABALA; EVOCATION; GEOMANCY; NECROMANCY; TALISMAN. His alchemical work included attempts to create the Philosopher's Stone, on the one hand, and the production of spagyric medicines on the other. *SEE* ALCHEMY; SPAGYRICS. After his death, his papers passed to his student Richard Napier, and from him to William Lilly, the most famous English astrologer of the next century; *SEE* LILLY, WILLIAM. FURTHER READING: ROWSE 1974, TURNER 1989.

Formation. *SEE* VOLANTIA.

Formation, Book of. *SEE* SEPHER YETZIRAH.

Fortuna Major. (Latin, "greater fortune") A geomantic figure governed by the sun. In divination, a favorable omen in nearly all matters. *SEE* GEOMANCY.

```
  •  •
  •  •
   •
   •
```

Geomantic figure Fortuna Major

Fortuna Minor. (Latin, "lesser fortune") A geomantic figure governed by the sun. In divination, a favorable omen, but unstable. *SEE* GEOMANCY.

Geomantic figure Fortuna Minor

fortune. *SEE* BENEFIC.

Fortune, Dion. (Firth-Evans, Violet Mary) English occultist, 1890–1946. Born to a middle-class family involved in Christian Science, she was something of a child prodgy, publishing two small books of poetry and prose in her teens. In 1911 she began studies at Studley Agricultural College for Women; graduating in 1913, she took a position on the college staff, but left a few months later after a confrontation with the warden of the college that, according to her account, escalated into a psychic attack.

The attack and the nervous breakdown that followed it sparked an interest in psychology, and in 1914 she enrolled as a student at the Medico-Psychological Clinic in London. Contacts with the Theosophical Society and with Dr. Theodore Moriarty, an occultist and Co-Mason, led her away from orthodox psychology and toward the occult dimensions of the mind. She became a Co-Mason in 1919 in a lodge run by Moriarty, and studied with him until his death in 1923.

In 1919 she also joined the Alpha et Omega, one of the orders descended from the Hermetic Order of the Golden Dawn. Her magical motto as an Alpha et Omega member was *Deo non Fortuna* ("by God, not by chance"); this was the source of her pseudonym "Dion Fortune." She remained a member of the Alpha et Omega until 1927, when she was expelled after a quarrel with Moina Mathers. *SEE* FREEMASONRY; GOLDEN DAWN, HERMETIC ORDER OF THE.

In 1921 she began work as a trance medium, and participated in trance work with Frederick Bligh Bond, whose excavations at Glastonbury had been largely guided by spirit communications. Her frequent visits to Glastonbury brought her into contact with Charles T.

Loveday (1874–1946), a Christian occultist who became one of her primary coworkers. Beginning in 1922, she and Loveday carried out a series of intensive inner plane workings that brought through the core teachings of a new magical order, the Fraternity of the Inner Light. The fraternity itself came into being in 1924 with six members, and became the primary focus of her work for the rest of her life.

In 1925, she and Loveday joined the Christian Mystical Lodge of the Theosophical Society, and took part in the controversies over Jiddu Krishnamurti and the Order of the Star in the East. *SEE* STAR IN THE EAST, ORDER OF THE. She resigned in 1927, taking many of the lodge's members with her into the Fraternity of the Inner Light. The year 1927 was also the year of her marriage to Dr. Thomas Penry Evans, and the publication of the first of her occult novels, *The Demon Lover*.

The years from 1928 to the beginning of World War II saw a steady stream of books, articles, and public lectures by Dion Fortune, the name she used consistently by this time. Her marriage ended with a separation in 1938, and this was also the publication date of *The Sea Priestess*, the last of her finished books; an unfinished novel, *Moon Magic*, was released posthumously in 1957.

The beginning of war in 1939 caused major disruptions to the fraternity's work, and paper rationing made further publication all but impossible. Still, she and the fraternity both remained active throughout the war years. Her health began to fail in 1945, although the leukemia that killed her was not diagnosed until a few weeks before her death in January of 1946. *SEE ALSO* INNER LIGHT, SOCIETY OF THE. FURTHER READING: CHAPMAN 1993, FIELDING AND COLLINS 1983, KNIGHT 2000, RICHARDSON 1987.

four. Four in the Cabala is Chesed, Mercy, the fourth Sephirah, and is also the number of the letter Daleth. Four angels support the Throne of God. The most powerful of the Names of God, the Tetragrammaton YHVH, has four letters; other names of four letters include AHIH, Eheieh, and AGLA, Agla. *SEE* CABALA.

In Christian symbolism, four is the number of the Evangelists.

Four in Renaissance magical symbolism is called the fount of nature and the root and foundation of numbers. It is the number of the elements, the seasons, the directions, and countless other correspondences. FURTHER READING: MCLEAN 1994, WATERFIELD 1988, WESTCOTT 1984.

Four Worlds. In Cabala, four fundamental levels of being. The first world is Atziluth (Hebrew, "nearness"), the archetypal or divine world; the second is Briah ("creation"), the archangelic world of eternal patterns, equivalent to Plato's world of Ideas; the third is Yetzirah ("formation"), the angelic world of interwoven force and form; and the fourth is Assiah ("action"), the material world of physical matter and energy.

The worlds relate to the Cabalistic Tree of Life in two different, although not mutually exclusive, ways. In one system, there is a different Tree of Life for each world. In the other, different levels of the Tree relate to different worlds. There are several different systems of correlation, but in the most common, the first Sephirah, Kether, corresponds to Atziluth; the second and third, Chokmah and Binah, correspond to Briah; the fourth through ninth, Chesed to Yesod, correspond to Yetzirah; and the last, Malkuth, corresponds to Assiah. *SEE* TREE OF LIFE.

These worlds have a special relationship to the Tetragrammaton, the four-lettered Name of God that plays a central role in Cabala. The worlds correspond to the four letters of the Tetragrammaton, and the Tetragrammaton itself has a different pronunciation in each of the worlds. *SEE* TETRAGRAMMATON. *SEE ALSO* CABALA. FURTHER READING: FORTUNE 1984, GREER 1996.

Fourier, Charles. French philosopher, 1772–1837. Fourier was born and grew up in the city of Lyons, a hotbed of occultism, and absorbed a good deal of esoteric philosophy and Mesmerist ideology in his youth, although there is no evidence he took an active part in the busy Lyonnais occult and Masonic scene. Employed as a traveling salesman for most of his life, he never married. In 1799, he began formulating the complex structure of his "Harmonial Philosophy," which first appeared in print in *Théorie des quatre mouvements* (*Theory of the Four Movements*) in 1809. Thereafter, he spent the rest of his life elaborating his theories in ever more detailed forms and passing on his teachings to his disciples.

Fourier's theories are almost unbelievably complicated, and cover every imaginable area of human thought. His cosmology traces the vast ages of evolution by which worlds coalesce out of the "interstellar aroma" as comets, becoming moons, worlds, and suns in turn. Interwoven with this process is the evolution of humanity, which passes from Savagery through Barbarism to Civilization, and then finally to Harmony—that is, to Fourierism.

Like so many eighteenth- and nineteenth-century visionaries, Fourier saw his own discoveries as the essential turning point in human evolution. Once even a small community committed itself to the Harmonial way of life, he insisted, Earth would become green and fruitful from pole to pole, the oceans would turn to lemonade through the descent of vast amounts of "cosmic citric acid" from space, and four stray moons that had graced the skies during Earth's infancy would return to their former orbits. All social problems would be solved by "passional attraction," and human life would focus on dining ("gastrosophy") and orgiastic sex, interspersed with modest periods of labor at frequently changing tasks.

These somewhat exotic notions had a surprisingly large impact on nineteenth-century thought. His writings and those of his followers are generally considered to be the first statements of what would later be called socialism. His cosmology, with its stress on evolution and cosmic cycles, had an influence on the development of similar ideas in Theosophy. *SEE* CYCLES, COSMIC. Several nineteenth-century occultists such as Andrew Jackson Davis made use of the less giddy parts of Fourier's thought. By the end of the nineteenth century, however, his ideas had been essentially forgotten, and despite an attempted revival in the 1960s they remain the province of historical specialists today. *SEE* DAVIS, ANDREW JACKSON; THEOSOPHY. FURTHER READING: J. GODWIN 1995.

frankincense. (*Boswellia thurifera*) The most important traditional incense for Western religious and magical uses, frankincense is the resin of a small tree native to the Arabian peninsula and northeastern Africa. Prized since ancient Egyptian times, it is considered to have strong spiritual energies and may be used for practically any form of magical working. Intensely solar, it is also associated with the Pleiades. *SEE ALSO* NATURAL MAGIC.

Fraternitas Rosae Crucis (FRC). An American Rosicrucian order, the FRC claims to have been founded by the African-American occultist Paschal Beverly Randolph (1825–1875) in 1858, based on a series of initiations into Rosicrucian orders and an Arabic secret society, the Ansairis, which Randolph allegedly received in Europe and Syria. *SEE* RANDOLPH, PASCHAL BEVERLY. On Randolph's death in 1875, the rank of Grand Master devolved on Freeman B. Dowd (1825–1910), who resigned in 1907 in favor of Edward H. Brown (1868–1922). Brown's death left the Grand Mastership in the hands of Reuben Swinburne Clymer.

In terms of historical fact, the connections between the FRC and Randolph are a good deal less structured. Randolph, who admitted having made up his "Rosicrucian" teachings on the basis of his own researches, did initiate Dowd into his system at some point in the 1860s. Like nearly all of Randolph's students, however, Dowd was soon driven away by Randolph's erratic moods and egotistical behavior, and went on to found several Rosicrucian lodges of his own. Neither these nor any of the several occult groups descended directly from Randolph appear to have survived into the twentieth century. It was from a handful of personal contacts and the papers of several defunct orders that Clymer succeeded in organizing the FRC and giving it an assumed history.

Under Clymer, an alternative physician and occultist with a flair for publicity, the FRC established its headquarters at Beverly Hall, Quakertown, Pennsylvania, and launched a successful correspondence school of occult studies. Clymer's claim to be the one and only Supreme Grand Master of the Rosicrucians in the New World brought him into conflict with the other major contender for that title, H. Spencer Lewis, whose Ancient Mystical Order Rosae Crucis (AMORC) was operating an equally successful correspondence school from the other end of the continent. *SEE* ANCIENT MYSTICAL ORDER ROSAE CRUCIS (AMORC). The rival Grand Masters engaged in a series of lawsuits and pamphlet wars in the

1920s and 1930s, in which neither one showed any great amount of dignity or restraint.

Clymer remained head of the FRC until his death in 1966. His son, Emerson Clymer, is currently the Grand Master of the order, which retains its Quakertown headquarters and is quietly active at present. Membership is by invitation only, and the nature of the FRC's current teachings is difficult to guess from its public presentations. *SEE ALSO* ROSICRUCIANS. FURTHER READING: DEVENEY 1997, MCINTOSH 1987.

Fraternitas Saturni. (Latin, "Brotherhood of Saturn") German occult order founded in 1925 by a collection of occultists interested in the work of Aleister Crowley. The Fraternitas had its roots in an earlier organization, the Collegium Pansophicum, founded in the early 1920s by the antiquarian bookseller Heinrich Tränker, who at that time was also the head of the Ordo Templi Orientis (OTO) in Germany. The Collegium claimed to be the last inheritor of the original Rosicrucian teachings, but seems to have been a fairly typical occult lodge of the time.

In 1925, Aleister Crowley came to Germany and stayed for a time with Tränker at the latter's country house in Thuringia. Many of the more important Collegium members came to visit, and went away impressed by Crowley's occult knowledge but irritated by his demands that they submit to his authority. Quarrels between Crowley and Tränker escalated, until the latter applied to the German government to have Crowley expelled from the country. In response, the Berlin lodge of the Collegium dissolved and reformulated itself as a new order, the Fraternitas Saturni, with Eugen Grosche as Grand Master. *SEE* CROWLEY, ALEISTER.

The new order drew heavily on Crowley's sexual magic, and expanded it in some new directions; for example, positions for ritual lovemaking were chosen based on the relative position of the planets at the time of the working. It soon became the most prominent of German magical lodges, and retained that status until 1933, when the Nazi government took power and forced the closure of all magical organizations but its own. In 1945, after the Nazi defeat, Grosche revived the Fraternitas and remained its Grand Master until his death in 1964. It remains active at present. *SEE ALSO* ORDO TEMPLI ORIENTIS (OTO). FURTHER READING: THORSSON 1990.

Fraternity of the Inner Light. *SEE* INNER LIGHT, SOCIETY OF THE.

Fratres Lucis. English esoteric order, founded by English Mason and occultist F. G. Irwin in 1874. The Fratres Lucis came into being as a result of a series of magical workings carried out by Irwin in 1872 and 1873, in which he communicated with a spirit who identified itself as Cagliostro. This entity passed on the traditional history and structure of the order, which was also called the Brethren of the Cross of Light.

The order, at least on paper, had four grades, of which the first three were derived from Mesmer's lodge system, the Swedenborgian Rite, and Cagliostro's Egyptian Rite respectively. It claimed to foster study in natural magic, Mesmerism, the nature of life after death, Cabala, alchemy, necromancy, astrology, and all branches of magic. There were four annual meetings, and a banquet of bread, butter, cheese, pastry, fruit, and wine was to be held each year.

How much of this structure actually existed outside of Irwin's imagination is anyone's guess, although the Fratres Lucis had at least four members. It apparently passed into abeyance with the death of Irwin in 1893. In 1970, however, an organization with the same name and repeating the same traditional history was active in London; whether this was a revival or a continuation of Irwin's brainchild is impossible to tell. *SEE ALSO* LODGE, MAGICAL. FURTHER READING: HOWE 1997.

Freemasonry. The Order of Free and Accepted Masons is an international fraternal order with massive historical connections to occultism. While not actually an occult organization, Freemasonry is the most important of the fraternal orders in the Western world, and the source of a very large percentage of occult ideas about lodges, degrees, initiations, symbolism, and the like. In its basic and essential form, Freemasonry consists of three degrees of initiation that draw their symbolism and teachings from the stonemason's trade, and from the biblical account of the building of King Solomon's Temple. On this rela-

tively simple foundation has been raised an immense structure of ritual, symbolism, philosophy, magic, philanthropy, spirituality, speculation, and sheer hogwash.

The origins of Freemasonry are wrapped in a thick fog of guesswork and wishful thinking. Masonic historians, at various points over the last three hundred years, have traced the origins of Freemasonry to ancient Egyptian priests, Roman colleges of architecture, and the medieval Knights Templar, as well as to King Solomon's Temple itself. *SEE* KNIGHTS TEMPLAR; TEMPLE OF SOLOMON. Many of these claims can still be found in popular literature today. There is, however, no actual evidence that any of these groups had anything to do with the historical origins of Freemasonry. Rather, the evidence of current research suggests that its roots can be found in the much more prosaic realm of late medieval stonemasons' guilds in Scotland and England.

Scottish records of working stonemasons' lodges provide the oldest known references to the Mason Word (the secret method of identifying oneself as a Mason to other Masons), permanent masons' lodges, multiple degrees of initiation, and the initiation of people who were not working stonemasons into lodges. As late as 1691, the Rev. Robert Kirk referred to the Mason Word as one of five "curiosities" common in Scotland but rare or nonexistent elsewhere. There is also documentary evidence that Scottish stonemasons were expected to study the Art of Memory as of 1599, the date of statutes issued by William Schaw, Master of Works to the King of Scotland. This points to a familiarity with traditions of Hermetic imagery that later played a central role in Masonic ritual and practice. *SEE* ART OF MEMORY.

These traditions, and the symbolic and ceremonial dimensions that ultimately became the core of the Masonic movement, took their place gradually over at least a century. In the early seventeenth century, most members of Mason's lodges were *operative* masons—that is, working men who made their living in the building trades. Starting around 1640, men who had no business connection to building, but were interested in the masons' rituals and symbols, began to join lodges; they were called *accepted* masons. By 1700, accepted masons were in the majority in most lodges, and there were many lodges without a single member who had ever spread mortar with a trowel.

In 1717, four London lodges came together to form the Grand Lodge of England (now the United Grand Lodge of England), the oldest Grand Lodge in Freemasonry. The next hundred years were a period of explosive growth, as lodges were founded throughout Britain, Europe, and the American colonies as well.

During this time Masonry became entangled in the complex net of political and magical intrigues surrounding the House of Stuart, which was driven off the British throne in 1688 and tried for most of a century to regain its former place. The Jacobites, as the pro-Stuart party was called, used the secrecy of Masonic lodges as a shield for their conspiracies against the House of Hanover, the new British royal house. The Hanoverian side responded in kind. The Grand Lodge of England, which was a stronghold of Hanoverian Masons, and the Scottish Rite, which developed out of Jacobite lodges in France, both took shape in the midst of these controversies. SEE STUART, HOUSE OF.

Central to these intrigues was Scottish Freemason Andrew Michael Ramsay (1686–1743), a Jacobite and Catholic convert who spent most of his life in exile in France. In the 1730s, as part of the preparations for the Stuart rising of 1745, Ramsay played a central role in creating a new, more complex system of "Scottish" Freemasonry closely allied to the Jacobite cause, and heavily loaded with Hermetic and occult material, in keeping with Ramsay's own interests. After Ramsay's death and the failure of the 1745 rising, Scottish Freemasonry regrouped into a Rite of Perfection of twenty-five degrees, which later evolved into the Scottish Rite of thirty-three degrees.

Another set of complexities emerged out of the relations between Freemasonry and the Catholic Church. These started off poorly and rapidly worsened. Anything associated with Protestant England was looked at suspiciously in Rome, and as Masonry spread in France and Italy, it drew most of its members from liberal circles who supported political reform and religious toleration—two things the church was not prepared to accept. The first Catholic condemnation of Masonry, the papal bull *In Eminente*, was promulgated in 1732, and followed by others. To this day a Catholic who becomes a Mason risks

excommunication. The Catholic condemnation of Freemasonry has at times risen to the level of claiming that Masonry is actually a front for the deliberate worship of Satan, a charge that has involved the church in extreme embarrassment at least once already in its history; SEE PALLADIAN ORDER.

Despite the tide of Catholic rhetoric, and more recent flurries of criticism from fundamentalist Protestants who have become convinced that Masonry is somehow connected to secular humanism and the Antichrist, the reality of the Masonic lodge is prosaic enough. Lodges hold business meetings for third-degree members at intervals ranging from once each week to once each month, usually with a dinner either before or after the meeting; perform traditional and rather verbose initiation rituals for new members; raise money to donate to a wide range of worthy causes; and behave like most other clubs. On initiation, members promise to keep the rituals, identification signals, and private business of the lodge secret from non-members, to follow the various rules and bylaws of the lodge and the order, and to maintain standards of good behavior with other Masons. The tone of the whole system can be measured adequately by the fact that an open Bible is part of the lodge furnishings, and the Pledge of Allegiance is recited by American Freemasons at the beginning of each meeting.

The degrees of initiation conferred in Freemasonry fall into two broad classes. The first, the Symbolic or "Blue Lodge" degrees, are the foundation of the entire system, and any person who has received them is considered to be fully initiated as a Freemason. They are:

1°: Entered Apprentice

2°: Fellow Craft

3°: Master Mason

Beyond this, matters get confusing very quickly. There are higher Masonic grades, assembled in a variety of rites, and there are also concordant bodies with their own degrees, which are not considered Masonic but which recruit members only among Master Masons. In the United States, two main rites—the York Rite and the Scottish Rite—attract most Masons interested in higher degrees, but other rites exist, and concordant bodies number in the dozens. None of these additional rites or bodies have any authority over the Blue Lodges that work the three degrees already mentioned.

The York Rite in North America offers the following degrees, divided up into three sets:

Chapter degrees

Mark Master

Past Master

Most Excellent Master

Royal Arch

Cryptic degrees

Royal Master

Select Master

Super Excellent Master

Knights Templar degrees

Order of the Red Cross

Order of the Knights of Malta

Order of Knights Templar

For its part, the Scottish Rite provides its initiates with a much more extensive set of degrees. The following degrees are offered in the Southern Jurisdiction of the Ancient and Accepted Scottish Rite, which includes most of the United States:

Lodge of Perfection degrees

4°: Secret Master

5°: Perfect Master

6°: Intimate Secretary

7°: Provost and Judge

8°: Intendant of the Building

9°: Elu of the Nine

10°: Elu of the Fifteen

11°: Elu of the Twelve

12°: Master Architect

13°: Royal Arch of Solomon

14°: Perfect Elu

Chapter of Rose Croix degrees

15°: Knight of the East, of the Sword, or of the Eagle

16°: Prince of Jerusalem

17°: Knight of the East and West

18°: Knight of the Rose Croix

Council of Kadosh degrees

19°: Pontiff

20°: Master of the Symbolic Lodge

21°: Noachite or Prussian Knight

22°: Knight Royal Axe, Prince of Libanus

23°: Chief of the Tabernacle

24°: Prince of the Tabernacle

25°: Knight of the Brazen Serpent

26°: Prince of Mercy or Scottish Trinitarian

27°: Knight Commander of the Temple

28°: Knight of the Sun or Prince Adept

29°: Scottish Knight of Saint Andrew

30°: Knight Kadosh or Knight of the White and Black Eagle

Consistory degrees

31°: Inspector Inquisitor

32°: Master of the Royal Secret

Supreme Council degree

33°: Sovereign Grand Inspector General

Many of these Scottish Rite degrees have fairly explicit occult content, and Albert Pike, who was reponsible for creating much of the present Scottish Rite system, expounded that system in occult terms in his massive *Morals and Dogma of the Ancient and Accepted Scottish Rite* (1871); SEE PIKE, ALBERT. Nonetheless, very few Scottish Rite Masons pay much attention to this aspect of the system, and there seems to be no reason to think that the present leaders of the Scottish Rite are occult adepts—or, for that matter, occultists at all.

The internal politics among the various Masonic bodies are extremely complex, involving overlapping jurisdictions, disputes as to who is or is not a valid Mason, and the like. There are also bodies such as Co-Masonry, a Masonic order open to women as well as men, which nearly all other Masonic bodies refuse to recognize, and Adoptive Masonry, open only to women, which has a complex relationship to the male-only Masonic Lodges.

SEE ALSO LODGE, FRATERNAL; LODGE, MAGICAL. FURTHER READING: CURL 1993, HALL 1937, MACNULTY 1991, PIKE 1871, SCHUCHARD 1975, SCHUCHARD 1995, STEVENSON 1988, WILMSHURST 1980.

Fulcanelli. French? alchemist, dates unknown. One of the great enigmas of modern alchemy, Fulcanelli is the apparent author of two books on alchemy, *Demeures Philosophales* (*Philosophical Dwellings*, 1921) and *Le Mystère des Cathédrales* (*The Mystery of the Cathedrals*, 1925), which are highly valued by many modern students of the art. He is also said to have actually accomplished the alchemical Great Work, producing the powder of transmutation and turning base metal into gold.

Precisely nothing is known for sure about Fulcanelli, including his actual name. According to his pupil Eugene Canseliet, who studied with him in the 1920s, Fulcanelli was then in his eighties, but French esotericist R. A. Schwaller de Lubicz, who was also in contact with him during that period, claimed that Fulcanelli was only in his fifties at that time. According to Canseliet and several other writers, Fulcanelli disappeared in the late 1920s, only to reappear decades later in an alchemically renewed body, but Schwaller de Lubicz claimed to witness Fulcanelli's death about the time of his "disappearance." SEE ALSO ALCHEMY. FURTHER READING: FULCANELLI 1986, VANDENBROEK 1987.

Furlac. SEE PHORLAKH.

futhark. The traditional term for a runic alphabet, derived from the sound-values of the first six runes in both elder and younger futharks: Fehu *(f)*, Uruz *(u)*, Thurisaz *(th)*, Ansuz *(a)*, Raido *(r)*, and Kenaz *(k)* in the elder futhark, and Fe *(f)*, Ur *(u)*, Thurs *(th)*, As *(a)*, Reidh *(r)*, and Kaun *(k)* in the younger.

In the Anglo-Saxon version of the runes, the fourth rune shifted to a sound value of *o* and the sixth to *c*; the spelling "futhorc" is thus commonly used for these runes, and some writers use it for all runic alphabets. SEE ALSO ANGLO-SAXON FUTHORC; ELDER FUTHARK; RUNES; YOUNGER FUTHARK.

futhorc. SEE FUTHARK.

Ga'ashekelah. (Hebrew GAaShKLH, "breakers") In Cabalistic lore, the Qlippoth or demonic power associated with the fourth Sephirah of the Tree of Life, Chesed. They are called the "Disturbers" or "Breakers in Pieces," and are pictured in the traditional lore as giants with the heads of cats. Their name is spelled Agshekeloh or Gog Sheklah in some sources, and they are also called Gamchicoth. The cortex or realm of the Ga'ashekelah is Azariel, and their archdemon is Astaroth. *SEE* QLIPPOTH.

Gabriel. (Hebrew GBRIAL, "strength of God") One of the principal archangels of Jewish, Christian, Islamic, Cabalistic, and magical lore, Gabriel is remembered by Christians as the heavenly herald who informed the Virgin Mary of her miraculous pregnancy, while Muslims revere him principally as the archangel who dictated the Quran to Muhammad. Rabbinic lore credits him with an enormous array of scriptural miracles, and places him at the left hand of God in Heaven.

In the Cabala, Gabriel is the archangel governing Yesod, the ninth Sephirah of the Tree of Life, in the world of Briah. *SEE* ARCHANGEL; BRIAH; YESOD.

Gaia hypothesis. A theory advanced by climatologist James Lovelock in the mid-1970s, proposing that the biosphere of the Earth can be understood as a single entity that preserves the chemical composition of the oceans and atmosphere by complex ecological feedback loops like those that balance blood chemistry in a living body. In his 1979 book *Gaia: A New Look at Life on Earth*, Lovelock proposed that human beings could be understood as the nervous system of Gaia.

This theory has been eagerly adopted by many Pagans, who have identified Gaia with the Goddess of modern Pagan theology; *SEE* GODDESS, THE. In 1970, well before Lovelock's first publications on the subject, American Pagan leader Tim Zell had already proposed a theory of "theagenesis," in which the collective life of the Earth would awaken as a conscious goddess as human beings achieved telepathic union with all other life forms. Zell's original name for this goddess was Terrebia (from Latin *terra*, "earth," and Greek *bios*, "life"); Lovelock's term (Gaia) was adopted shortly after his first publication and has been standard ever since. Zell's and Lovelock's ideas have been combined in various proportions, and with varying degrees of sophistication, to produce a range of Gaian attitudes and approaches that are highly influential in the modern Pagan community. *SEE ALSO* NEOPAGANISM. FURTHER READING: LOVELOCK 1979.

galdor. In ancient and modern Norse tradition, the art of ritual magic. Little is known about ancient galdor, and those sources that have survived (such as the *Galdrabók*, an Icelandic magical text) are heavily mixed with conventional European magical traditions.

In modern Asatru, galdor is nearly always related to the runes, and includes various forms of runic magic. A wide range of different methods and approaches have been invented or borrowed from other magical systems, and the field is still very much in the early stages of development. One common method is to "rist" (carve) one or more runes on a piece of wood or other material while concentrating intensely on the goal of the magical working. *SEE* RUNES. *SEE ALSO* ASATRU; SEIDHR. FURTHER READING: ASWYNN 1998, THORSSON 1998.

Gamaliel. (Hebrew GMLIAL, "Recompense of God") A name with decidedly mixed meanings in Cabalistic lore. On the one hand, it is the name of the "Obscene Ones," the Qlippoth or demonic power associated with Yesod, the ninth Sephirah of the Tree of Life. They are pictured in the traditional lore as "corrupting, loathsome bull-men, linked together." The cortex or realm of the Gamaliel is Ogiel, and their archdemon is Lilith. *SEE* QLIPPOTH.

On the other hand, some Cabalistic and Gnostic angelologies define Gamaliel as one of the great aeons or angelic powers of light. According to the Coptic *Revelation of Adam to His Son Seth*, Gamaliel is the angel who brings the souls of the elect to Heaven. *SEE* AEON; ANGEL.

Gar. *SEE* ANGLO-SAXON FUTHORC.

Gardner, Gerald Brousseau. English civil servant, author, occultist, and witch, 1884–1964. Easily the most important figure in the creation of modern Wicca, Gerald Gardner spent most of his life as an English colonial bureaucrat. Born to a wealthy family in England, near Liverpool, he suffered from severe asthma as a child and spent winters in southern Europe. Later, when his nurse married an English colonist from Ceylon and moved there, Gardner accompanied her and worked on a tea plantation, then took up positions with the British colonial administration in Borneo and Malaysia. Successful investments in the rubber industry made him a wealthy man, and enabled him to dabble in archeology and pursue his interest in native weapons. His first book, *The Kris and Other Malay Weapons*, was published in Singapore in 1939.

In 1936 he retired from government service and with his wife Donna, whom he married in 1927, he returned to England and settled in the New Forest area. He soon made contact with a group called the Rosicrucian Order of the Crotona Fellowship, a quasi-Theosophical organization based in the town of Christchurch. A branch of the ROCF called the Theatricum produced plays on occult themes, and has been discussed in Wiccan historical

works under the name of "The First Rosicrucian Theiatre in England." *SEE* ROSICRUCIAN ORDER OF THE CROTONA FELLOWSHIP (ROCF).

Gardner also joined the Folklore Society and became a close friend with one of its most controversial members, the former Egyptologist Margaret Murray, who had proposed in her 1921 book *The Witch-Cult in Western Europe* that medieval witchcraft was the survival of an ancient Pagan religious tradition. *SEE* MURRAY HYPOTHESIS.

According to Gardner, and to Gardnerian witches since his time, the Crotona Fellowship had an inner circle consisting of people who claimed to practice this same original witch-cult, a Pagan religion passed down in secret through the centuries. Dorothy Clutterbuck, the High Priestess of the coven, is said to have initiated Gardner in 1939. *SEE* CLUTTERBUCK, DOROTHY.

Despite half a century of effort, it has so far been impossible to determine whether this account is accurate or an invention of Gardner's. If it is accurate, the question still remains whether Clutterbuck and her associates were telling the truth about the origins of their rituals and traditions, or whether they passed on to Gardner a system they themselves had invented earlier—possibly in reponse to Murray's theories. The actual origins of Gardnerian Wicca thus remain shrouded in a fog of uncertainty.

In 1946, Gardner was introduced to Aleister Crowley, and apparently joined one of Crowley's magical orders, the Ordo Templi Orientis (OTO). Gardner's involvement was somewhat limited by the fact that, by the 1940s, the OTO itself was completely inactive in England, and the only initiation Crowley offered at the time consisted of being given copies of the rituals and other papers to read. Shortly after Crowley's death, Gardner tried to revive the OTO with himself as head, but Crowley's reputation was bad enough that Gardner was unable to attract any interest.

While Gardner claimed to have a valid charter for an OTO camp, the charter (now in a private collection) was apparently written and signed by Gardner himself; it is entirely in Gardner's distinctive handwriting, and starts off "Do what thou wilt shall be the Law" instead of Crowley's invariable "Do what thou wilt shall be the whole of the Law"—a mistake the Beast himself would never have made. *SEE* CROWLEY, ALEISTER; THELEMA.

There is thus some doubt that Gardner had much connection with the OTO at all—and good evidence that he was not above stooping to forgery.

Interestingly, 1946 also saw Gardner receive a very different form of initiation. This was the year in which he was ordained as a Christian priest in the Ancient British Church, an esoteric Christian church with loose connections to the Liberal Catholic Church. The bishop who ordained him was Dorian Herbert, titular bishop of Caerleon and head of the Ancient British Church. SEE INDEPENDENT BISHOPS; LIBERAL CATHOLIC CHURCH (LCC). Gardner was reordained *sub conditione* in 1949 by Bishop Colin Mackenzie Chamberlain of the Confraternity of the Kingdom of Christ, another esoteric Christian church, and in 1954 was consecrated as a Christian bishop.

These same years saw Gardner active in a range of other activities that may have some bearing on the origins of Wicca. He became a nudist (or Naturist, to use the euphemism of the time), and also came into contact with Woodcraft, a back-to-nature movement active in the New Forest area at the time. SEE WOODCRAFT. He also joined the Ancient Druid Order and became a close friend of another occultist and Naturist, Ross Nichols, who went on to found the Order of Bards Ovates and Druids after Gardner's death. SEE DRUIDRY; NICHOLS, PHILIP PETER ROSS; ORDER OF BARDS OVATES AND DRUIDS (OBOD).

In 1949, Gardner published his first work on occult subjects, a novel entitled *High Magic's Aid*, which was issued under the pseudonym Scire (Gardner's magical motto). He gave his rank as "4°=7□ OTO" on the title page; 4°=7□ is not an OTO degree, but a rank in Crowley's other magical order, the A∴A∴, which adds to the confusion. The novel includes detailed descriptions of initiation rituals into a medieval witch-cult; according to Doreen Valiente, these were nearly identical to the ones used when she was initiated into Gardner's coven in 1953.

In 1951, as a result of pressure brought by Spiritualist churches, England's laws against witchcraft were finally repealed. That same year, Gardner formed his own coven and moved to Castletown, on the Isle of Man, where he took up a position as resident witch at the Museum of

Magic and Witchcraft. A few years later Gardner bought the museum from its original owner, Cecil Williamson.

The year 1954 saw the publication of Gardner's first nonfiction work on witchcraft, *Witchcraft Today*. It presented Wicca (or, as Gardner spelled it at that time, Wica) as a healthy, life-affirming Pagan religious tradition, and attracted widespread attention from the media and the public. He followed it with his last book, *The Meaning of Witchcraft*, in 1959. All through the last decade of his life, he made frequent media appearances to promote witchcraft, initiated dozens of people into the Craft, and presided over the first Wiccan coven whose existence can definitely be proved. After a few years of failing health, he died in 1963 while returning by ship from a vacation in Lebanon. SEE ALSO WICCA. FURTHER READING: BRACELIN 1960, GARDNER 1954, GARDNER 1959, HESELTON 2000, HUTTON 1999, VALIENTE 1987.

garter. In Wicca and some other modern Pagan traditions, the "witch's garter" is one of the standard working tools, and often takes the form of a cord that is worn tied just above the left knee. A blue or green garter is the emblem of a High Priestess in some traditions, and may be ornamented with silver buckles, one for each coven over which the High Priestess has authority. SEE HIGH PRIESTESS; WICCA.

Geber. (Abu Musa Jabir ibn Hayyan) Arab alchemist, c. 720–c. 810 C.E. The details of his life are very poorly known, and different sources give a variety of dates for his birth and death. He was a native of the town of Kufa, in what is now Iraq, and became a widely respected physician there. He wrote more than a hundred books, twenty-two of them on alchemy; the remainder covered every branch of knowledge from philosophy and grammar to medicine and agriculture.

Geber spent some years in Baghdad, then the political capitol of the Muslim world, at the invitation of the Caliph Harun al-Rashid. There he established the most complete alchemical laboratory of the time and carried out extensive experimentation. He was the first person to describe the preparation of nitric acid, and marked several other firsts in alchemical (and chemical) history. One of his major interests was the proper design of furnaces, and his book on the subject was required reading for practicing alchemists until the time of the Scientific Revolution.

Geber's most influential contribution, though, was his sulphur-mercury theory of the formation of metals. According to this theory, every metal came into being out of the fusion and maturation of two factors, sulphur and mercury. Sulphur was the fiery, "male" principle, and mercury the watery, "female" one. When sulphur and mercury of a high enough degree of purity combined and matured properly, the result was gold. If the mercury was pure but the sulphur was slightly impure, the result was silver. All other metals represented different degrees of impurity of the original sulphur and mercury, combined in some cases (such as iron) with incomplete maturation. *SEE* MERCURY; SULPHUR.

In the early fourteenth century, a Spanish alchemist whose name remains totally unknown wrote several additional works under Geber's name. The most famous of them, the *Summa Perfectionis* (*Sum of Perfection*) and the *Liber Fornacum* (*Book of Furnaces*), were widely used by alchemists throughout the late Middle Ages, Renaissance, and early modern period. *SEE ALSO* ALCHEMY. FURTHER READING: HAQ 1994, HOLMYARD 1957.

Gebo. (Old Germanic, "gift") The seventh rune of the elder futhark, associated with the giving and receiving of gifts, with partnership and contracts, and with the reconciliation of opposites. Its sound-value is *g*. *SEE* ELDER FUTHARK.

The same rune, under the name Gyfu (Old English, "gift") is the seventh rune of the Anglo-Saxon futhorc, and has the same sound-value. The Old English rune-poem relates it to gifts charitably bestowed on the needy, which win honor for the giver. *SEE* ANGLO-SAXON FUTHORC.

Rune Gebo (Gyfu)

Geburah. (Hebrew GBVRH, "severity, harsh judgment") The fifth Sephirah of the Cabalistic Tree of Life, the center of the Pillar of Severity or Form. It is also called Pachad, "fear." In Cabalistic theory this Sephirah is ambivalent, "open to good and evil," and some sources suggest that it was by means of Geburah that the Qlippoth, the powers of evil, originally entered the universe. *SEE* QLIPPOTH. Its standard symbolism is as follows:

> *Name of God:* ALHIM GBVR, Elohim Gibor (Gods of Power).
>
> *Archangel:* KMAL, Kamael (He Who Sees God).
>
> *Angelic Host:* ShRPIM, Seraphim (Fiery Serpents).
>
> *Astrological Correspondence:* MDIM, Madim (Mars).
>
> *Tarot Correspondence:* The four Fives of the pack.
>
> *Elemental Correspondence:* Fire.
>
> *Magical Image:* A warrior king (in some versions, queen) in full armor, standing in a chariot.
>
> *Additional Symbol:* The pentagram.
>
> *Additional Title:* PChD, Pachad (Fear).
>
> *Colors:* in Atziluth—orange.
>
> in Briah—red.
>
> in Yetzirah—bright scarlet.
>
> in Assiah—red flecked with black.
>
> *Correspondence in the Microcosm:* The will in Ruach.
>
> *Correspondence in the Body:* The left shoulder.
>
> *Grade of Initiation:* 6=5, Adeptus Major.
>
> *Qlippoth:* GVLHB, Golohab (the Burners).

The corresponding text from the *Thirty-two Paths of Wisdom* runs as follows: "The Fifth Path is called the Radical Intelligence because it is itself the essence of Unity, uniting itself to Understanding, which emanates from the primordial depths of Wisdom." *SEE ALSO* CABALA; TREE OF LIFE.

Gedulah. *SEE* CHESED.

Gehenna. (Hebrew GIHNVM, "valley of Hinnom") Once the municipal garbage dump in ancient Jerusalem, a nearby valley where refuse was taken to be burned, Gehenna had already become a term for Hell in biblical times. In Cabalistic lore it is the first and shallowest of the seven hells, and corresponds to Malkuth and Yesod. *SEE* HELLS, SEVEN.

gematria. The art of Cabalistic numerology, a system for analysing Hebrew (and other) words by way of the numerical value of the letters of the Hebrew alphabet. Hebrew (like Greek and many other ancient languages) uses what is called an isopsephic alphabet—that is, an alphabet in which letters also stand for numbers. Where modern people write down numbers or do arithmetic using Arabic numerals (1, 2, 3, and so on), ancient and medieval Jews used letters of the Hebrew alphabet—א (Aleph) for 1, ב (Beth) for 2, and so on.

In the hands of Cabalists, this habit became a tool for subtle analyses of the scriptures. For instance, there is a scene in the story of the patriarch Abraham, in Genesis 18:2, in which three "men" come to visit him. They are representatives of God, and bring tidings that he and his wife Sarah will have a son. The passage starts off in Hebrew, *Ve-hineh shelshah* . . . ("And behold, three . . ."). The letters of this phrase, added up, equal 701. The sentence *Elu Michael Raphael ve-Raphael* ("These are Michael, Raphael, and Gabriel") also adds up to 701, and this has been used for centuries as a way of showing who the three "men" were.

This tool predictably led in some strange directions. For example, NChSh, *nachash*, "serpent," is equal to 358; so is MShICh, "messiah." On this basis some Cabalists argued that the serpent of the Garden of Eden was in some sense the Messiah—a suggestion that the Gnostics made a long time earlier. Equally odd is the equation that links *Qadosh ha-Qadoshim*, "Holy of Holies," the name of the inner chamber in the Temple of Jerusalem, and *Eisheth Zenunim*, "Woman of Whoredom," the archdemon of prostitution in Hebrew demonology; both phrases add up to 1424. Equations like these have led more cautious Cabalists to point out that while gematria can reveal truths, it can also lead to remarkable nonsense, and should be used with care and common sense. SEE ALSO ARITHMANCY; CABALA; HEBREW ALPHABET.

Gemini. (Latin, "twins") The third sign of the zodiac, a mutable air sign of masculine polarity. In Gemini, Mercury has rulership and Jupiter is in his detriment. Gemini rules the lungs, arms, and nervous system.

The sun is in Gemini approximately from May 22 to June 21. People with this sun placement are traditionally talkative, clever, versatile, and intellectual; they can also be superficial, tense, and deceptive.

In the Golden Dawn tarot system, Gemini corresponds to Trump VI, the Lovers. SEE LOVERS, THE; TAROT.

Astrological symbol of Gemini

geomancy. (Greek *ge*, "earth," + *manteia*, "divination") A system of divination using the sixteen geomantic figures—patterns of four lines of dots, with either one or two dots in each line. These are essentially four-digit binary numbers; in divination, four such patterns are produced by a random process, and then combined with others according to traditional methods to produce a geomantic chart.

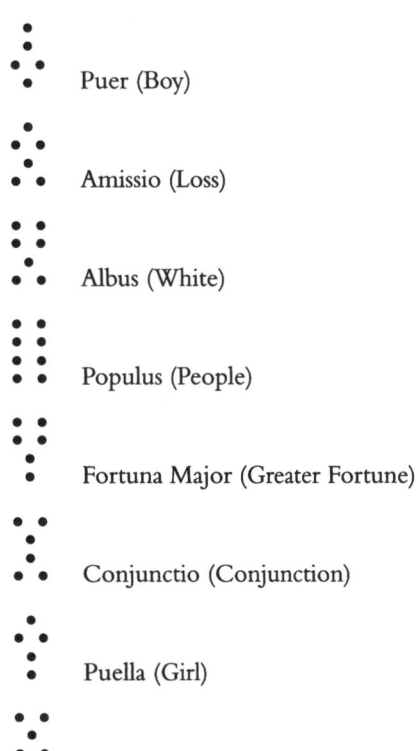

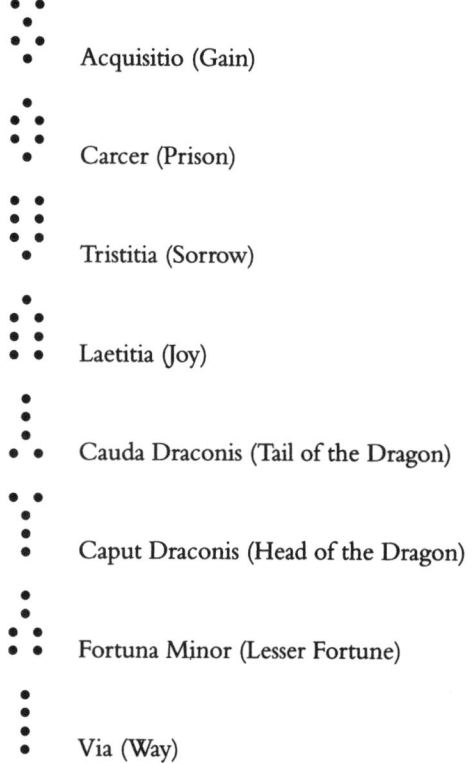

According to the oldest accounts of the art, the geomancer would take a wand or stick, smooth a patch of sand or earth, and poke the stick into the ground repeatedly, making a random number of marks in a line. The total number of dots was then counted; an odd number equalled one dot in the final figure, an even number two dots. A total of four lines were made for each figure, and four figures—or sixteen lines—were used for a single reading.

Later geomancers made marks with a pen on parchment or paper, but followed the same process. More recently, geomantic card decks have also been designed, and in the Renaissance it was possible to buy geomantic dice in sets of four, with a single or double point on each face.

The four figures produced randomly are called the Mothers. The Daughters are produced from them by taking the top row of dots from each of the four Mothers, in order, to form the First Daughter. The second row forms the Second Daughter, the third the Third Daughter, and the bottom row the Fourth Daughter.

The First and Second Mothers, Third and Fourth Mothers, First and Second Daughters, and Third and Fourth Daughters are then added together line by line. If there are two or four dots in the lines being added, the result is two dots; if three, one dot. The resulting four figures were called the Nieces in medieval sources, but are usually called the Nephews in modern books. The Nieces are then added together to produce two Witnesses, and the Witnesses to produce the Judge, the final figure. All these are written on the geomantic chart, and interpreted according to traditional rules.

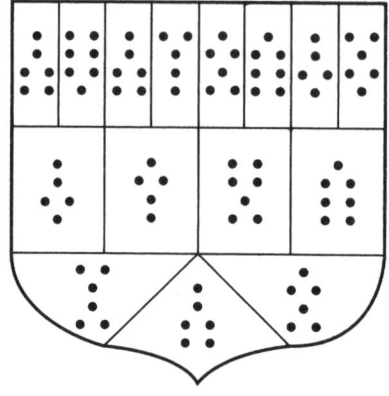

Example of a finished geomantic chart

The origins of geomancy are not known for certain, but one likely source is sub-Saharan Africa, where a wide range of binary divination systems using from one to eight digits have been in use for many centuries. Geomancy itself first appeared in written sources in Arabic North Africa around the ninth century C.E., and passed from there to medieval Europe with the first Latin translations from Arabic in the twelfth century. It went on to become one of the most popular divination systems in the late Middle Ages and Renaissance, and remained in frequent use until the Scientific Revolution. Thereafter, despite attempts to revive it in the nineteenth and twentieth centuries, it has remained nearly forgotten, and the term "geomancy" has come to be used for such unrelated topics as ley lines and other Earth mysteries, on the one hand, and methods of landscape design such as the Chinese art of feng shui, on the other. *SEE* LEYS. *SEE ALSO* DIVINATION, *AND ENTRIES UNDER THE NAMES OF*

EACH OF THE GEOMANTIC FIGURES. FURTHER READING: CHARMASSON 1980, GREER 1999, SKINNER 1980.

Georgian tradition. American Wiccan tradition founded in 1970 in Bakersfield, California, by George "Pat" Patterson. In 1971 it became one of the first American Wiccan groups to obtain legal status as a church by being chartered by the Universal Life Church as the Church of Wicca Bakersfield. Highly eclectic, it draws from Gardnerian, Alexandrian, and other English and American Wiccan traditions.

There are Georgian covens active in most parts of North America, as well as England and Australasia. The Georgian tradition has had particular success in the US armed forces; unlike many of the traditionalist Wiccan groups, it has seen a significant upsurge in activity and numbers in recent years. *SEE ALSO* WICCA.

Ger. *SEE* ANGLO-SAXON FUTHORC.

Germanenorden. (Order of Germans) The central link in the chain of secret societies and magical orders that led to the birth of the Nazi Party, the Germanenorden was founded in 1912 as the inner, initiatory circle of the *Reichshammerbund* ("Reich Hammer Society"), an important anti-Semitic and nationalist organization.

The idea of such a group had been in circulation for some years before its founding; many of those who believed in the existence of a vast, secret Jewish conspiracy against Aryans in general and Germany in particular—and there were plenty of people in early twentieth-century Germany who held this as an article of faith—seem to have decided that the same methods used by the alleged conspiracy could just as well be used against it.

The moving spirit in this project was Hermann Pohl, who devised a lodge ritual around 1910 and introduced it to a group of fellow anti-Semites in his home town of Madgeburg. In 1911 the group constituted itself as the Wotan Lodge, and later the same year Pohl contacted potential recruits around Germany to invite them to join the new organization. The idea proved popular, and the Germanenorden was formally founded in May of 1912; by the end of that year there were six lodges with a total membership of more than 300.

Much of Germanenorden ritual and practice was adapted from contemporary fraternal lodge sources, particularly the United Ancient Order of Druids, an English lodge organization that had established a substantial German presence in the late nineteenth century; *SEE* DRUIDS. An equally substantial amount was taken from the Ariosophical teachings of Guido von List, whose speculative reconstructions of ancient Germanic spirituality were extremely popular in the radical right all through central Europe. *SEE* ARIOSOPHY; LIST, GUIDO VON.

A surviving initiation ritual from the early years of the order describes a typical lodge setting, with the Master at one end of the room flanked by two Knights with horned helmets and swords, the Bard at the other end in the symbolic Grove of the Grail, and other officers in the usual stations. Candidates for initiation were blindfolded and dressed in pilgrims' cloaks for the ceremony, which was accompanied by music from Wagner's operas, sung by a chorus of "forest elves" accompanied by harmonium and piano.

The ritual side of the order was central to Pohl's conception of its work; he hoped, according to his 1912 manifesto, to foster an "Aryan-Germanic religious revival" through the order, and stressed that a fervent membership was more important than a numerous one. Many other members, however, saw less value in the ceremonial work, and tried to reposition the order along the more familiar lines of political conspiracy. These differences reached a breaking point in 1916, and Pohl left the order and founded a new group, the Germanenorden Walvater of the Holy Grail. A substantial minority of Germanenorden lodges joined the new organization, and new Walvater lodges came into existence in several cities—notably in Munich, where Rudolf von Sebottendorf played an important part in reviving the dormant lodge and making it into a significant force in Bavarian politics and culture. It was from this branch of the order that the *Thule-Gesellschaft* or Thule Society, and ultimately the Nazi Party, came into being; *SEE* THULE SOCIETY.

The original Germanenorden continued to operate throughout the period between the wars as well, and took an active part in the chaotic politics of the early

Weimar Republic. Both branches appear to have survived until the early years of the Third Reich, when they (like all other lodge organizations) were outlawed. *SEE ALSO* LODGE, MAGICAL; NATIONAL SOCIALISM. FURTHER READING: GOODRICK-CLARKE 1992.

Ghob. In ceremonial magic, the king of the earth elementals, or gnomes. *SEE* ELEMENTAL.

Gia. (Hebrew GIA, "valley") In Cabalistic lore, the third of the seven earths, corresponding to Geburah. *SEE* EARTHS, SEVEN.

Gibor. The eighteenth and last rune of the Armanen runic alphabet, meaning "gift." Its power, according to the rune-charm from the Old Norse *Havamal*, is to bind the runemaster's lover in his or her arms. It corresponds to Ginnungagap. *SEE* ARMANEN RUNES.

Rune Gibor

Gihon. (Hebrew GIHVN) According to Genesis 2:13, the second of the four rivers that flow out of Paradise. In the Golden Dawn tradition, Gihon is associated with the element of water, and with the Pillar of Mercy on the Tree of Life. *SEE* CABALA.

Gimel. (Hebrew GML, "camel") The third letter of the Hebrew alphabet, Gimel is one of the double letters; it represents the sounds *g* and *gh*, and has the numerical value of three. Its standard symbolism is as follows:

> *Path of the Tree of Life:* Path 13, Kether to Tiphareth.
> *Astrological Correspondence:* The Moon.
> *Tarot Correspondence:* Trump II, the High Priestess.
> *Part of the Cube of Space:* The lower face.
> *Colors:* in Atziluth—blue.
> in Briah—silver.
> in Yetzirah—cold pale blue.
> in Assiah—silver rayed with sky blue.

The corresponding text from the *Thirty-two Paths of Wisdom* runs as follows: "The Thirteenth Path is named the Uniting Intelligence, and is so called because it is itself the essence of glory; it is the consummation of truth of individual spiritual things." *SEE ALSO* CABALA; HEBREW ALPHABET.

Hebrew letter Gimel

Giorgi, Francesco. Italian friar and occultist, 1466–1540. Born in Venice to an aristocratic family, he entered the Franciscan Order at an early age. He spent most of his life at the Franciscan convent of San Francesco della Vigna in Venice. During his time, Venice was a major cultural center, enriched by trade links with the Muslim East and one of Europe's largest and least persecuted Jewish communities. He made the most of these opportunities and became one of the most famous scholars of his age.

Giorgi was fluent in many languages, and was especially noted for his mastery of Hebrew studies at a time when few Gentiles knew more than the rudiments of that language. During the dispute over the English King Henry VIII's divorce from Catherine of Aragon, he was consulted by the English government about details of Jewish divorce law. Giorgi was also a deep student of numerology and sacred geometry, and was famous enough in this latter capacity that when a dispute arose in 1534 about the proportions of a new church in Venice, the doge of Venice ordered the matter submitted to Giorgi for resolution.

Giorgi's most important contribution to the Renaissance occult movement was a massive book, *De Harmonia Mundi* (*On the Harmony of the World*), published in 1525. The most comprehensive manual of Renaissance occult philosophy ever written, it combined Hermetic and Neoplatonic philosophy with Pythagorean numerology, sacred geometry, and Christian Cabala, and became one of the standard texts for aspiring magicians for more than a century thereafter; it has, unfortunately, never been translated into any modern language. A later and shorter book, *In Scripturam Sacram Problemata* (*Problems in the Sacred Scriptures*, published in 1536), explored similar themes in less overwhelming detail. *SEE ALSO* CABALA; SACRED GEOMETRY. FURTHER READING: YATES 1979.

Glatisant. *SEE* QUESTING BEAST.

glamour. In folk traditions connected with faery, the power of illusion possessed by faery creatures, which is capable of confusing and deluding human beings to an almost unlimited extent. Glamour can be dispelled by cold iron, by magical amulets, and by certain odd actions such as taking off one's coat and putting it back on inside out. *SEE* FAERY.

In the writings of Alice Bailey, and in some other systems of occult philosophy influenced by her work, the word is used for the morass of illusion and delusion in which nearly all human beings spend their lives. It can be divided into four aspects: illusion, or fixation on false ideas; glamour proper, or fixation on distorted desires; maya, or fixation on inappropriate actions; and the Watcher on the Threshold, which is the sum total of illusion, glamour, and maya affecting a given person, and which must be overcome by that person in the process of initiation. *SEE* BAILEY, ALICE; WATCHER ON THE THRESHOLD. FURTHER READING: BAILEY 1950, GREER 2001, STEWART 1990.

Glastonbury. Located in the West Country of England, Glastonbury has long had a reputation as the major spiritual center of England. According to medieval legend, Joseph of Arimathea came to Glastonbury not long after the crucifixion of Jesus and there established Britain's first Christian church. Joseph's staff was said to have taken root on Wearyall Hill near the abbey, and gave rise to the Glastonbury Thorn, a hawthorn tree that blooms on Christmas Day. It was cut down by Puritans in the sixteenth century, but cuttings were replanted, and there is still a Glastonbury Thorn in the abbey ruins.

A monastery was founded by King Ine of Wessex around 705 C.E., and became an important English monastic center by the eleventh century. It remained among the most hallowed abbeys in England until the sixteenth century, when King Henry VIII abolished all Catholic religious orders in the country and seized their

property. After many years of neglect, Glastonbury received renewed interest in the early twentieth century, when English Theosophists and occultists were drawn by its connections to Arthurian legend. It is now the site of a thriving complex of occult and New Age organizations and businesses.

The old name for the Glastonbury area is the Isle of Avalon. This comes from the Welsh *ynys Avallach*, "isle of Avallach." Avallach is a medieval Welsh word for apple orchard, but it is also the name of an ancient Celtic god; Welsh bardic lore makes Avallach the son of Beli and Anna, who are the Celtic high god Belenos and the mother of the gods Ana or Danu respectively, and also names him as the father of Modron, who is Matrona, "the Mother," an important goddess in northeastern Gaul and the mother of the god Mabon or Maponos. *SEE* MABON AP MODRON. This sort of connection to ancient myth is typical for Glastonbury.

The great majority of Glastonbury's magical connections, though, have to do with Arthurian legend. The isle of Avalon is believed by some to be the burial place of King Arthur, a claim backed up by local monks in 1190, who found a hollow log coffin with two skeletons—a man nearly seven feet in height with a damaged skull, and a woman whose skull still bore a few wisps of blonde hair—with a leaden cross inscribed, "Here lies buried the renowned King Arthur in the Isle of Avalon." Most modern scholars, although not all, reject this claim as the sort of monastic fakery common across medieval Europe. *SEE ALSO* ARTHUR, KING. FURTHER READING: BROMWICH 1961, FORTUNE 1989.

gluten. In alchemical writings, any thick, viscous matter. *SEE* ALCHEMY.

Gluten of the Eagle. In alchemical jargon, an alternative name for mercury. Some modern writers who interpret alchemical writings in sexual terms have identified the Gluten of the Eagle as semen. *SEE* ALCHEMY; SEX AND OCCULTISM.

gnomes. In ceremonial magic, the elementals of earth. Their king is Ghob. The word "gnome" seems to have been invented by Paracelsus, and (like many of his technical terms) has no known etymology. *SEE* ELEMENTAL.

Gnosticism. (from Greek *gnosis*, "knowledge") Any of a set of wildly diverse spiritual traditions that emerged in the ancient world around the beginning of the Common Era. Their exact origins are the subject of violent disputes among modern scholars, but Greek mystical traditions, Zoroastrian dualism from Persia, Jewish teachings, and early Christian ideas may all have played some part in generating the Gnostic movement.

Their history is difficult to trace, since Gnosticism was violently opposed by the Christian church. Except for a collection of Gnostic scriptures recovered from Nag Hammadi in Egypt, nearly all the information we now have about Gnosticism thus comes from its bitter enemies. It is clear, though, that Gnostic sects were in existence in much of the Roman world by the second century of the Common Era, flourished in the third and early fourth centuries, and were eliminated or driven underground in the late fourth and fifth centuries.

The core theme uniting all Gnostic teachings is that of *gnosis*, "knowledge," which is not a matter of ordinary learning but a personal experience of spiritual truth. The Gnostic is not interested in belief; he or she wants to know, directly and personally, the spiritual realities of the cosmos.

Most Gnostic systems combine this stress on personal experience with a harshly dualistic and at least slightly paranoid vision of the universe. In this view, the entire material world is a prison created by evil powers, the archons, to entrap souls from a higher world of light. To be living in a material body in the world is to be trapped in an alien realm, at the mercy of the archons and their terrifying leader—the "blind god" Ialdabaoth, also known as Saklas and Samael, who is also the God of the Old Testament. *SEE* IALDABAOTH; ARCHON.

Beyond the false world of matter lies the true world, the world of light, ruled by the aeons, who are both beings and realms. The creation of the material world and the archons was considered by many Gnostics to be the result of a mistake by one of the aeons, Sophia ("Wisdom"), who desired to create something on her own, and managed only to give birth to a maimed, blind entity, shaped like a serpent with a lion's head: Ialdabaoth. Hoping to hide her deed from the other aeons, Sophia cast her creation out of the world of light into the void.

In the process, though, sparks of light from the true world entered the void, and when Ialdabaoth fashioned a world out of the substance of the void, the sparks were trapped in it. Ialdabaoth created the other archons; together they made physical bodies as prisons for the sparks of light, and created stars and planets to enmesh the sparks in a merciless net of astrological destiny. In this way the world we know came into being.

The goal of most versions of Gnosticism is to break free of Ialdabaoth's world and return to the world of light. This escape hatch is not open to all, however. Many Gnostic sources divide human beings into three classes: hylics (from *hyle*, "matter") who are robotic creations of the archons, and cannot escape the material world; psychics (from *psyche*, "mind") who have the potential to break free from matter and rise to the realm of light, but have to work at it; and pneumatics (from *pneuma*, "spirit") who have gnosis as an innate birthright and can count on returning to the world of light.

These basic principles seem to have been accepted by most (although not all) Gnostic systems as a common foundation. The structures built on that foundation, however, were fantastically diverse. Some Gnostic traditions were explicitly Christian, and taught that Jesus of Nazareth was an aeon of the world of light who descended into the false world of matter to liberate souls from the clutches of the Archons. Others pointed to Seth, the third son of Adam, as the one who opened the way of escape. Other Gnostics turned the villains of the Bible—Cain, Esau, the inhabitants of Sodom, and so forth—into heroes rebelling against the power of the evil creator.

There were a few Gnostic teachers and traditions that ignored the Bible and the imagery of standard Judeo-Christian thought altogether. Most Gnostic writings, however, kept a focus on these sources, reinterpreting them in various ways. To some extent, Gnosticism functioned as a sort of conspiracy theory of the spiritual realm, treating orthodox ideas as a theological "official account" that had to be seen through in order to get at the truth. Gnostic writers combed through the events of the Book of Genesis, in particular, in much the same way that modern conspiracy buffs pore over details of the Kennedy assassination—and their proposed interpretations varied just as widely.

Gnostic practice was as diverse as Gnostic theory. Magical rites were apparently much practiced; Plotinus, the great Platonist philosopher, criticizes their reliance on charms in his essay *Against the Gnostics*. A number of the surviving Gnostic scriptures include magical invocations and words of power closely related to those found in the Graeco-Egyptian magical papyri. *SEE* BARBAROUS NAMES; GRAECO-EGYPTIAN MAGICAL PAPYRI.

There were some Gnostics who argued in favor of a life of asceticism and spiritual discipline, and sex in particular was often roundly condemned, since it created new human bodies in which souls were imprisoned. Others argued that if the god of conventional religion was evil, what he prohibited must be good, and on this basis insisted that every kind of sexual activity was permitted. One middle ground between these positions was to prohibit forms of lovemaking that could lead to pregnancy but to consider anything else fair game.

After its suppression in the Roman world, Gnosticism continued to be taught and practiced in small underground sects in various parts of the Middle East. At least one of these sects, the Mandeans, has survived in southern Iraq to this day. Another, the Bogomils, flourished in the early Middle Ages in what is now Bulgaria, and missionaries from this sect traveled west to Italy and southern France in the twelfth and thirteenth centuries, launching the most widely known Gnostic movement in the West, the Cathar heresy; *SEE* CATHARS.

The Inquisition, formally established in 1239 as a weapon against Catharism, gradually eliminated what was left of the Cathars after the church-sponsored crusade that began in 1208. Gnosticism in the Western world thereafter existed primarily as a footnote in history books until the nineteenth century, when several small Gnostic sects were established in France as part of the early phases of the occult renaissance of that period.

Attitudes toward the Gnostics underwent a major change around that time, as part of the Romantic revaluation of outcast traditions and rejected knowledge. Many opponents of established versions of Christianity turned to Gnosticism, either as a polemic weapon or as a framework for new quasi-Christian approaches to spirituality. The Theosophical Society, which spearheaded the alternative spirituality movement in the late nineteenth and early twentieth centuries, portrayed the Gnostics as enlightened mystics slaughtered by bigoted orthodox fanatics; this portrayal became widespread throughout occult circles during the "Theosophical century" from 1875 to 1975. *SEE* THEOSOPHICAL SOCIETY. Swiss psychologist Carl Jung (1875–1961) also drew substantially on what was known of Gnosticism in his creation of analytic psychology; *SEE* JUNG, CARL GUSTAV.

It is worth noting, however, that all speculation and discussion of Gnosticism from the fall of Rome until the early 1970s was based on a handful of sources, nearly all of them written by early Christian clergymen who were far more interested in denouncing the Gnostics than understanding them. In 1945, however, farmers near the village of Nag Hammadi in Egypt came across a buried pottery jar in which were concealed twelve leather-bound volumes of ancient Gnostic scriptures. Scholarly turf wars delayed their publication and translation for more than two decades, but a complete facsimile edition was published in stages between 1972 and 1977, and a one-volume English translation was issued in 1977.

The result has been a great upsurge in interest in Gnosticism, and the rise and spread of a number of Gnostic religious and spiritual organizations. Several alternative branches of Christianity connected with the independent bishops movement have redefined themselves as Gnostic; *SEE* INDEPENDENT BISHOPS. Few of these recent Gnostics, though, have ventured into the profound dualism of ancient Gnostic thought—which may be just as well. *SEE ALSO* CHRISTIAN OCCULTISM; JESUS OF NAZARETH; HERMETICISM; PLATONISM. FURTHER READING: LAYTON 1987, PAGELS 1979, PLOTINUS 1992, ROBINSON 1988.

God, the. One of the two primary deities of modern Wicca, the male counterpart of the Goddess. Usually portrayed as an antlered man, the God is the lord of the forest and the animals, and is often seen as the spirit of vegetation and growth. His exact relationship to the Goddess varies somewhat from tradition to tradition, but he is always seen as her lover and usually as her child as well.

Wiccan tradition holds that the God is the oldest male deity worshipped by human beings. Since we know exactly nothing about the religious traditions of prehistory, it's anyone's guess whether or not this is true. In historical times, however, horned gods of fertility are few and far between. The most widely known examples are Pan, a minor Greek god from the region of Arcadia, and Cernunnos, a Celtic deity from Gaul.

The emergence of the God in his modern form seems to have started in England in the middle of the nineteenth century, when Pan became a favorite image among Romantic poets. The remarkable craze for Pan, fauns, and satyrs that swept English literary circles in the late nineteenth and early twentieth centuries has been the subject of more than one critical study; *SEE* MERIVALE 1969. The god of fertility worshipped by Margaret Murray's hypothetical medieval witch-cult was Pan's first cousin, although the Christian Devil (another close relative) also played a role in Murray's creation. *SEE* MURRAY HYPOTHESIS.

The transition between Pan and the Wiccan God was partly the work of Robert Graves (1895–1985), whose *The White Goddess* also played a central role in the creation of the Wiccan Goddess, and partly a result of the popularity of Celtic culture in the middle and late twentieth century, which made stag-antlered Cernunnos a more appealing image than goat-horned Pan. Further reworking and development of the God's image has gone on throughout the evolution of modern Paganism, in tune with (and quite probably caused by) the equally far-reaching redefinitions of male identity in many Western cultures during that same time.

In some traditions there are two Gods, or two forms of the God. These are the Oak King and the Holly King, who are respectively the powers of the waxing and waning year, and who fight and replace each other in turn for the favors of the Goddess.

Other Wiccan writers distinguish three aspects of the God, paralleling the three forms of the Goddess. The Hooded One is the Green Man of folklore, and also the source of the Robin Hood legend, a god of the forests. The Horned One is the god of the hunt and ruler over the animal kingdom; despite the name, he is usually portrayed with antlers rather than horns. The Old One, finally, is the god of death. *SEE ALSO* GODDESS, THE;

WICCA. FURTHER READING: FARRAR 1989, HUTTON 1999, MERIVALE 1969.

God posture. In Wiccan practice, a position taken when invoking the God. It is essentially identical with the Golden Dawn Sign of Osiris Slain—legs and ankles together, body erect, and arms folded across the chest. The head may be bowed to represent the God as dying Harvest God, or raised to represent the God reborn. *SEE ALSO* GOD, THE; GODDESS POSTURE; WICCA.

Goddess, the. The principal divinity of the modern Neopagan movement, associated with nature, fertility, the moon, the cycles of biological life, and the planetary ecosystem of Earth conceived as a single vast entity. In many Neopagan traditions, the Goddess has three forms—Maiden, Mother, and Crone—corresponding to the waxing, full, and waning phases of the moon.

Many of her modern votaries hold that the worship of the Goddess has been handed down continuously in its present form since prehistoric times. The actual history of the Goddess, however, is a good deal more complex. Goddesses of various kinds date back to before the beginning of recorded history, and some of these older goddesses played a role in the emergence of the Goddess of modern Neopaganism. The Goddess herself, though, is essentially a modern figure, and her emergence is the most recent and best documented example of the birth of a new divinity.

It is frequently claimed that Goddess worship is the world's oldest religion, dating to the Paleolithic hunter-gatherers whose "Venus figurines" carved of stone and bone are common modern icons in the Goddess spirituality movement. Still, despite an immense amount of speculation, we know precisely nothing about the religious traditions of prehistory. The fact that people in the Stone Age carved female figures tells nothing about what those figures meant. Were they goddesses, magical talismans, works of art, Stone Age erotica, or something else? We simply don't know, and attempts to cover that ignorance with sweeping statements about what "must have been" have much more to do with modern cultural politics than with honest scholarship.

What we do know is that at the time of the first historical records in the Middle East and elsewhere, a single universal lunar goddess of fertility is noticeably absent. Instead of the Goddess—or, for that matter, the God—the Pagan religions of the ancient world worshipped dozens or hundreds of gods, goddesses, spirits, and less easily defined supernatural entities. These beings ranged from minor local divinities up to the great creative and destructive powers of the cosmos, and they all had their own personalities, powers, and roles in the universe. It's worth noting that the ancient pantheons routinely violated modern assumptions about divine gender: in Egypt, for example, the earth was a god, the sky was a goddess, and the fiercest of the deities of war was the lion goddess Sekhmet, while the moon was male in the religions of Mesopotamia. This same sort of diversity was the rule, not the exception, all through the ancient world; *SEE* PAGANISM.

The first ancestral formulations of what became the Goddess of modern Neopaganism emerged among Platonist mystics around the beginning of the common era. During the period of Middle Platonism (roughly 300 B.C.E.–200 C.E.), philosophers of this tradition developed a theory of nature as a living, quasi-divine being, mediating between the transcendent world of Ideas and the realm of matter; *SEE* PLATONISM. Among students of theurgy—the magical wing of Platonism—nature came to be seen as a goddess, and gradually absorbed the characters and names of a variety of classical goddesses. The Chaldean Oracles of Julianus the Theurgist, a major source for later theurgic practice, linked nature with the shadowy figure of Hekate, an archaic Greek goddess mentioned in the writings of Hesiod; *SEE* CHALDEAN ORACLES.

More important for later developments was the Platonist writer Lucius Apuleius, who drew on Platonic ideas of nature in his portrayal of the Egyptian goddess Isis in his novel *The Golden Ass*. In a scene near the end of the novel, the goddess Isis appears to the main character and gives a long list of the names by which different peoples knew her, finishing up with her true name of Isis. This scene drew heavily on the teachings of the Isaic mysteries of the first few centuries of the Common Era,

in which Apuleius is thought to have been an initiate. *SEE* APULEIUS, LUCIUS; ISIS.

The adoption of Platonist philosophy by the early Christian church saw to it that a good deal of this material survived the fall of Rome. The idea of nature as a feminine creative power acting in the world can be found all through the Middle Ages in Christian writings of unquestioned orthodoxy. For complicated cultural reasons, Pagan gods and goddesses continued to be acceptable as poetic and philosophical symbols all through the Middle Ages. There was also a bevy of allegorical goddesses—Wisdom, Philosophy, Truth, Nature, and many others—were not confined to literature but routinely appeared in visionary experiences and received the prayers of many devout medieval Christians.

Goddess imagery also played a large role in Renaissance magic, which drew heavily on Platonist sources and resurrected the Platonist goddess of nature. It suffered some degree of eclipse, however, in the Reformation and Counter-Reformation movements that reshaped Western thought in the sixteenth and seventeenth centuries, discarding ideas of a living earth and a complex spiritual world in favor of more politically expedient images of God's autocracy over a universe of dead matter.

The revival of the Platonist and magical image of nature, and its transformation into the modern Goddess, was the work of the Romantic movement. Romanticism rebelled passionately against the entire structure of post-Reformation thought, valuing emotion above reason, nature above culture, woman over man, and very often magic over science. The old Platonist imagery of Nature as goddess was an obvious inspiration, especially since many of the Romantics drew heavily from Renaissance magical sources, and it led many Romantic writers straight back to classical Pagan traditions or to the few surviving scraps of Celtic or Germanic Pagan lore.

By the early 1800s, the Romantic movement was evolving a powerful goddess-image, effectively identical with the Goddess of modern Neopaganism: a lunar deity of nature and fertility, the great mother of the universe. This is the image that dominates the intensely Pagan poetry of figures such as Swinburne—who was the favorite poet, it may be worth adding, of Aleister Crowley, Dion

Fortune, and Gerald Gardner, among other magical luminaries of a later generation.

The Romantic goddess did not stay safely put in the realms of poetry for long. In 1849, the German scholar Eduard Gerhard proposed that the goddesses of the ancient Greeks were all descended from a single prehistoric goddess. Speculations about ancient matriarchies, an idea introduced by the Romantic historian J. J. Bachofen in the 1860s, were soon added to this concept; *SEE* MATRIARCHIES, ANCIENT. In 1903, the English classicist Jane Harrison drew all these threads together to produce a set of ideas very familiar to watchers of the Pagan scene today, arguing that prehistoric southeast Europe had been the site of an idyllic, peaceful, woman-centered civilization worshipping a threefold goddess of nature. This civilization, she claimed, had been destroyed by patriarchal invaders before the dawn of history.

These ideas were based on very little concrete evidence, and were fiercely contested by other scholars. Despite this, they had an enormous impact on the popular imagination. This was especially true in England, where Harrison's books were standard reading in Woodcraft and other quasi-Pagan movements in the early twentieth century, and where popular novels such as H. Rider Haggard's *She* brought the Romantic goddess-image into wide circulation. *SEE* WOODCRAFT.

The poetic and historical aspects of the Goddess were brought together in their definitive form by English poet Robert Graves, whose *The White Goddess* (1948) was the most influential source of Goddess imagery and ideology for the modern Pagan revival. Subtitled *An Historical Grammar of Poetic Myth*, Graves' work used the Goddess-worshipping matriarchies of old Europe and their suppression by patriarchal invaders as elements in an intensely personal and poetic vision of reality. This was missed by many of the book's readers, who took these and other elements of the book—such as the Ogham tree-calendar, which Graves invented from scratch—as simple matters of historical fact. *SEE* OGHAM TREE-CALENDAR. Within a few years of its publication, *The White Goddess* was joined by the first of Gerald Gardner's books on Wicca, and the modern revival of Paganism was born.

While a great deal has been written on the Goddess since Graves' time, very little of it has departed significantly from the themes and imagery he received from previous poets and scholars and passed on to the current Pagan movement. It thus seems probable that the basic images and attributes of the Goddess have crystallized for the foreseeable future. The fact that many people in today's Neopagan movement can testify to personal experiences of the Goddess argues forcefully for the idea that, whatever her historical origins, she is unquestionably a living presence in the inner realms of experience. *SEE ALSO* GAIA; GOD, THE; WICCA. FURTHER READING: ELLER 1993, FARRAR AND FARRAR 1986, GOODISON AND MORRIS 1998, GRAVES 1966, HARRISON 1903, HUTTON 1998, HUTTON 1999, NEWMAN 2001.

Goddess posture. In Wiccan practice, a position taken when invoking the Goddess, especially when drawing down the moon. It consists of standing with legs spread wide apart, body straight, and arms raised up at an angle so that the limbs form an X. *SEE ALSO* GOD POSTURE; GODDESS, THE; WICCA.

godforms. In Golden Dawn magic, the images of selected Egyptian deities that are built up in the imagination and used in ritual. Some godforms are inhabited by temple officers during initiation rituals—for example, the Hierophant in a Golden Dawn temple "wears" the godform of Osiris when in his or her station in the east of the temple—while others are part of the astral furniture of the temple, and are used as vessels for magical energies during the ceremony. *SEE* GOLDEN DAWN, HERMETIC ORDER OF THE.

Since the first publication of the Golden Dawn rituals by Aleister Crowley at the beginning of the twentieth century, the technique of using godforms in ritual has become relatively widespread, and deities from many different pantheons have been used for this purpose. *SEE ALSO* MEDIATION. FURTHER READING: CROWLEY 1976, REGARDIE 1971.

Goethe, Johann Wolfgang von. German poet, scholar, scientist, and occultist, 1749–1832. The son of a lawyer, Goethe was tutored at home and then sent to law school at the University of Leipzig, but after three years of study suffered severe health problems and had to return home to Frankfurt. While recovering, he was introduced to

Christian theosophy by a Fräulein von Klettenburg, a family friend. *SEE* THEOSOPHY (CHRISTIAN MYSTICAL). Recognizing the occult dimension behind the writings of Jakob Böhme and other theosophical writers, he went on to study Paracelsus, Van Helmont, and other alchemical writers, and established an alchemical laboratory in his parent's house, where he carried out experiments in search of the Philosopher's Stone. *SEE* ALCHEMY.

In 1770, having recovered his health, he moved to Strasbourg to resume his studies, and finally graduated in 1771 with a degree in law. While in Strasbourg he met Johann Gottfried von Herder, one of the first significant Romantic poets. Herder's ideas had a powerful effect on the young Goethe, who spent the next few years writing some of his best lyric poetry, a play, and the appallingly sentimental (but hugely successful) novel *The Sorrows of Young Werther*. He also began work on his version of the Faust legend.

In 1775 he was invited by the duke of Weimar, a seventeen-year-old boy, to visit the ducal court. He had planned to spend a few weeks there but, except for brief travels and one two-year visit to Italy, he remained there the rest of his life. As a member of the governing council of the duchy, director of the Weimar Theater, and the most famous author and poet in Germany, he had plenty to keep him occupied.

During his first decade at Weimar, however, he also found time to carry out scientific researches into geology, botany, and zoology, and in the process created an approach to science that had clear roots in his earlier occult and alchemical studies. His *naturphilosophie* or "natural philosophy" played an important part in launching modern ecological studies, and also served as a major inspiration to Rudolf Steiner (1861–1925), the creator of Anthroposophy. *SEE* ANTHROPOSOPHY; STEINER, RUDOLF.

The work of his later years included researches into light and color, which convinced him that Isaac Newton's theories of optics were fundamentally inaccurate, and the completion of his vast two-part play *Faust*. He died in 1832 in Weimar. FURTHER READING: MATTHAEI 1971, STEINER 1950.

goetia. From the Middle Ages to the present, a standard term for the branch of magic that deals with summoning demons. In classical Greek, *goeteia* was the art of the *goes*, originally a ritual mourner at funerals—*gôos* is an archaic Greek term for a lament for the dead—and later, according to literary sources, a *goes* was a necromancer who could call the spirits of the dead back from Hades. Later still, *goes* came to mean simply "sorcerer," and magic of all kinds was labeled *goeteia* as often as *mageia*. The word had strong negative connotations, and classical magicians usually insisted that they were not *goetes*.

Rituals for summoning spirits of various kinds, on the other hand, were very much a part of classical magic, as the Graeco-Egyptian magical papyri as well as other sources make clear; *SEE* GRAECO-EGYPTIAN MAGICAL PAPYRI. As the classical world disintegrated and the Middle Ages dawned, such rituals and their practitioners formed a secretive subculture, first in the Muslim cultures that took shape after the great Arab conquests of the eighth and ninth centuries, and then a little later in the Christian world of medieval Europe.

The spread of goetic magic in the Middle Ages actually took place within the Christian church itself, in a secret and loosely knit underworld of magical practitioners among priests, monks, and clerics in minor orders. Knowledge of Latin and familiarity with the Christian rituals of exorcism gave clerics the necessary background, and the shadowy literature of grimoires provided the rituals and technical information. To judge from contemporary writings, the goetic underground was probably in existence in the eleventh century, and by 1200 it was an active presence throughout western Europe. Despite constant pressure from the church, the goetic underground was able to survive the Middle Ages intact and contributed much to the magical synthesis of the Renaissance.

The details of medieval goetia can be studied in surviving grimoires such as the *Sworn Book of Honorius* and the *De Nigromancia* attributed to Roger Bacon. These are handbooks for the evocation of spirits; they include drawings of circles traced on the ground to protect the magician, conjurations and sacrifices to induce the spirit's presence, and instructions for the necessary tools and equipment of the goetic art.

Goetic magic remained an active presence in the occult field throughout the Renaissance and early modern periods, but lost popularity along with nearly all other branches of magic with the coming of the Scientific Revolution in the late 1600s. Because many goetic writings promised material wealth, goetic methods remained in use in some parts of the eighteenth- and early nineteenth-century magical underground, and folk traditions borrowed goetic methods among others; SEE CUNNING MAN/WOMAN.

The magical revival of the nineteenth century borrowed from goetic sources, but many nineteenth- and early twentieth-century magicians strove to distance themselves as far as possible from the goetic approach. The acceptance of some form of Christianity by many influential figures in the magical scene during this time played an important role in keeping goetia out of widespread open use. The rise of non-Christian and anti-Christian magical religion in the twentieth century, though, brought goetia into more widespread practice.

English mage and self-proclaimed Antichrist Aleister Crowley (1875–1947), among his other activities, plagiarized and published a major text of goetic magic and engaged in a fair amount of magical work with demons. His example has been followed by many modern magicians. By the last decades of the twentieth century, goetic magic had become a fairly common magical specialty in America and elsewhere, and a substantial number of books on the subject have been published in recent decades. SEE ALSO DEMON; EXORCISM; FAUST LEGEND; GRIMOIRE; MAGIC. FURTHER READING: GRAF 1997, KIECKHEFER 1990, KIECKHEFER 1998, KONSTANTINOS 1997, MACDONALD 1988.

Goetia, The. The first and largest portion of *The Lesser Key of Solomon*, one of the major medieval grimoires; SEE GRIMOIRE. *The Goetia* discusses seventy-two demons, giving their ranks in the infernal hierarchy and their powers when summoned and bound, and includes rituals for evoking and controlling them.

The Goetia was first translated out of Latin by Samuel Mathers in the last years of the nineteenth century, and first saw print in 1903, when Aleister Crowley published it as his own work, with the unrelated Bornless One ritual as a "Preliminary Invocation." SEE BORNLESS ONE RITUAL. Numerous editions have seen the light of day

since that time. SEE ALSO GOETIA; LEMEGETON. FURTHER READING: BUTLER 1949, DUQUETTE 1992.

gold. The most valuable of the metals known to the ancients, gold is usually assigned to the sun and put to use in solar talismans and other magical devices. Cabalists generally assign it to Tiphareth, the sixth Sephirah of the Tree of Life, although a minority assign it to the fifth Sephirah, Geburah. SEE CABALA.

The creation of gold from mercury or some other less valuable metal is one of the central goals of alchemy. Some alchemical texts, however, warn that "our gold is not the common gold," and references to gold in alchemical sources and other occult writings may not necessarily be about the metal in question. SEE ALCHEMY.

Golden Dawn, Hermetic Order of the. The most famous and influential occult order of modern times, the Hermetic Order of the Golden Dawn emerged from a complex underworld of quasi-Masonic magical lodges in Victorian England. The two main founders of the order, William Wynn Westcott (1848–1925) and Samuel Liddell Mathers (1854–1918), were Freemasons deeply involved in a variety of occult lodges in England; Westcott in particular had connections all over the English occult scene. SEE FREEMASONRY; MATHERS, SAMUEL LIDDELL; SOCIETAS ROSICRUCIANA IN ANGLIA (SRIA); WESTCOTT, WILLIAM WYNN.

Sometime in 1886, Westcott came into possession of a set of documents in cipher. When decoded, they turned out to be outlines for the rituals and teachings of a magical order called the Hermetic Order of the Golden Dawn, with a grade structure partly borrowed from an eighteenth-century German magical order, the Orden des Gold- und Rosenkreuz. SEE CIPHER MANUSCRIPT; ORDEN DES GOLD- UND ROSENKREUZ.

How exactly the documents came into Westcott's hands is anybody's guess at this point. He himself claimed that they had been found in a bookseller's stall by yet another magically inclined Mason, the Rev. A. F. A. Woodford (1821–1887), and there is nothing particularly improbable in this. Modern researchers have proposed a number of other possible origins, however.

Along with the papers, according to Westcott, was the name and address of one Fräulein Sprengel, a Rosicrucian adept in Germany. His account goes on to claim that he wrote to Sprengel and received permission from her to turn the rituals into a fully functioning magical order; Sprengel then died. This account will not hold water, for the letters from Sprengel to Westcott have survived, and were clearly written by someone whose first language was English and whose knowledge of German was limited. It has been suggested that Westcott himself wrote the letters, and this seems plausible although it has not been proved.

Westcott recruited Mathers and another Mason, Robert Woodman, and the Hermetic Order of the Golden Dawn was formally founded in March of 1888. Its initial membership came from the friends and associates of the founders, and gradually spread outwards to embrace, at its height, more than a hundred members.

The first public announcement of the Golden Dawn came in the form of a letter from one Gustav Mommsen, published in *Notes and Queries* on December 8, 1888, asking about a "society of Kabbalists" in which the famous Cabalist Rabbi Falk and the magician Eliphas Lévi had been involved; *SEE* FALK, SAMUEL JACOB HAYIM; LÉVI, ELIPHAS. Westcott wrote a reply, published two months later, stating that the society—"the Hermetic Students of the G. D."—still existed, and dropping some none too subtle hints about the order's activities. The result, predictably, was a flood of further inquiries and a sharp increase in membership.

In its early days the order offered the five grades of Neophyte, Zelator, Theoricus, Practicus, and Philosophus, and taught occult theory, astrology, geomancy, and tarot divination. Practical magic was not taught, and the level of instruction was fairly simple in the lower grades; initiates of the Neophyte grade, for example, were given a set of "knowledge lectures" for study containing nothing more earth-shaking than the Hebrew alphabet, the symbols and names of the planets, the names of the ten Sephiroth of the Tree of Life, and a few other scraps of occult lore. In the higher grades, initiates studied Cabala, astrology, alchemical symbolism, geomantic divination, and general occult philosophy; those who completed all the required studies, and passed an examination, were given the title of "Adept." *SEE* ADEPT; ALCHEMY; ASTROLOGY; CABALA; GEOMANCY.

Within a few years, however, a number of the order's members wanted to go beyond this level, and the order's chiefs—and in particular Mathers—were more than willing to oblige. Mathers created two additional grade rituals, the Portal grade and the Adeptus Minor grade, for the new second order, the Ordo Roseae Rubeae et Aureae Crucis ("Order of the Ruby Rose and Golden Cross") or RR+AC. Together, Mathers and Westcott compiled a massive curriculum of practical occultism for initiates to study. The new grades were first conferred in 1891, and by 1895 there were forty-five active members of the second order.

Other grades were planned, although the next—that of Adeptus Major—was apparently still in draft form at the time of the order's breakup. The full system of grades in the Golden Dawn system was as follows:

Outer Order: The Golden Dawn

Neophyte $0°=0^\square$

Zelator $1°=10^\square$

Theoricus $2°=9^\square$

Practicus $3°=8^\square$

Philosophus $4°=7^\square$

Inner Order: RR+AC

Portal

Adeptus Minor $5°=6^\square$

Adeptus Major $6°=5^\square$

Adeptus Exemptus $7°=4^\square$

Etheric Link

Third Order

Magister Templi $8°=2^\square$

Magus $9°=1^\square$

Ipsissimus $10°=1^\square$

Temples of the Golden Dawn included Isis-Urania No. 3 in London, which was the first founded (temples No. 1 and No. 2 seem to have been fictions invented by Westcott); Osiris No. 4 in Weston-super-Mare; Horus No. 5 in Bradford, Yorkshire; Amen-Ra No. 6 in Edinburgh; and Ahathoor No. 7 in Paris, which did at least some of its rituals in French. There were also two temples founded in the United States—Thme No. 8 in

Chicago and Thoth-Hermes No. 9 in New York, both chartered in 1897, shortly before the breakup of the order.

The second order and the studies connected with it were the true foundation of the order's later reputation and influence. The first order, the Golden Dawn proper, covered much the same ground as other occult lodge organizations of the same period. In the second order, by contrast, initiates were expected to master a curriculum that went far beyond anything else available at the time in its comprehensiveness and its practical focus. Members of this level were expected to make and consecrate seven different magical working tools, evoke spirits, consecrate talismans, practice alchemy, and carry out a wide range of similar occult practices. They were also expected to be ready to take a role in the order's grade rituals, in which second order members took on godforms and directed currents of magical energy to enhance the effect of the ceremonies. SEE EVOCATION; GODFORMS; TALISMAN.

Much of the material taught in the second order was derived from the large collection of magical manuscripts in the British Library, where Mathers in particular spent many hours. Other elements of the system, however, were the creation of Mathers and Westcott, or came by way of connections that have not yet been traced. Faced with the huge and diverse body of magical lore that had been inherited by the occult movement of their time, the senior members of the order attempted to draw all of it together into a unified system and succeeded to a remarkable degree.

Unfortunately these efforts could not guarantee the survival of the order itself. One of the three chiefs, Woodman, died in 1891, and was not replaced. Westcott, who was employed by the British government as a coroner, was forced to resign from the order in 1896 when his superiors got wind of his involvement in an occult order. That left Mathers, who was a brilliant magician but an unstable and domineering personality with few leadership skills. A succession of mismanaged crises led to a full-blown revolt in the order in 1900.

Mathers was effectively deposed in that year, although he and a few loyalists established a new order called the Alpha et Omega. The Adepti who had led the revolt were unable to agree on a leadership structure to replace him, and before long the order had broken apart into several quarreling factions. The largest, renaming itself the Stella Matutina, eventually came under the leadership of Robert W. Felkin and survived for most of the twentieth century; the last two of its temples went out of existence in the 1970s. By that date, the other fragments were long dead. SEE ALPHA ET OMEGA; STELLA MATUTINA, ORDER OF THE; WAITE, ARTHUR EDWARD.

The survival of the Golden Dawn tradition in the twentieth century was largely the result of three magicians who chose, for a variety of reasons, to break the vows of secrecy they took on initiation. The first of these was Aleister Crowley, who joined the order in 1898 and remained loyal to Mathers during the revolt of 1900. Shortly thereafter, though, he broke with Mathers and published substantial parts of the order's rituals and knowledge lectures in his magazine, *The Equinox.* SEE CROWLEY, ALEISTER.

The second was Dion Fortune, who joined the Alpha et Omega in 1919 and remained an active member until 1927. In 1935 she published her masterwork, *The Mystical Qabalah,* which included most of the Golden Dawn Cabalistic teaching and became the standard text on the subject for decades thereafter. SEE FORTUNE, DION.

The most important source for the later Golden Dawn revival, though, was Israel Regardie, an American student of magic who became Aleister Crowley's secretary for a time, then broke with the Beast and joined the Stella Matutina. He later fell out with the Stella Matutina's leadership and, convinced that the Golden Dawn system would perish unless it was made public, he gathered all the material he could find together and published it in four large volumes between 1937 and 1940. SEE REGARDIE, ISRAEL.

The Golden Dawn, Regardie's opus, went on to become the most influential work on occultism in the twentieth century. Most of the magical lodges in the English-speaking world borrowed heavily from it, but the mantle of the Golden Dawn itself was not picked up to any significant extent until the 1980s, when several different orders were founded to carry on its work. Most of these use the same name—the Hermetic Order of the Golden Dawn—which has made it difficult to keep track of them adequately.

Several of these new Golden Dawn orders were created by friends and students of Regardie in the United States. Among these were Chic Cicero and Sandra Tabatha Cicero, who founded an order in Florida, while another emerged in Arizona under the leadership of Christopher Hyatt. Another new Golden Dawn organization arose in New Zealand, where Pat and Chris Zalewski studied with surviving members of a defunct Stella Matutina temple. Still others were created by people who simply took the published material and went to work with it.

The results of the recent Golden Dawn revival have been mixed, as many of the new Golden Dawn temples have had the same troubles with internal politics as their ancestors, and this has not been helped by occasional squabbles among groups as to the validity of one another's lineage and teachings. Nonetheless, there are more people in the world actually practicing the Golden Dawn system of magic today than ever before in the past, and the quantity and quality of published material on the system has improved markedly in the last few decades. SEE ALSO ROSICRUCIANS. FURTHER READING: FORTUNE 1984, GILBERT 1983A, GILBERT 1986, GREER 1998, HOWE 1972, KING 1971A, KÜNTZ 1996A, KÜNTZ 1996B, REGARDIE 1971, TORRENS 1973.

Golden Dawn, New Reformed Orthodox Order of the (NROOGD). An American Neopagan tradition founded in 1968 in the San Francisco area, NROOGD began as a group of friends, one of whom was attending a class on ritual as art at San Francisco State College. As part of the classwork, the group concocted a Pagan ritual based on Robert Graves' *The White Goddess*. The first performance had no apparent effect on the participants, but the group found itself drawn more and more toward the study of the occult. A second performance was more effective, and at the third, on Lammas 1968, those present experienced what one participant described as a silence that "swelled into waves of unseen lightness, flooding our circle, washing about our shoulders, breaking over our heads" (Adler 1986, p. 164).

Over the next few years, the group took on most of the structure of a coven, initiated its members, and began regular meetings. Its name, according to a 1972 article in the NROOGD journal, was given to it by the Goddess. Whatever its source, it has caused a good deal of confusion, as NROOGD's workings, traditions, and symbolism are essentially unrelated to those of the Hermetic Order of the Golden Dawn; SEE GOLDEN DAWN, HERMETIC ORDER OF THE.

NROOGD seems to have invented the double spiral dance now common to many American Pagan traditions, and has given a larger role to poetry and performance art than many other branches of the Pagan movement. Their ritual began with a pastiche of the writings of Graves, Gerald Gardner, Margaret Murray, and T. C. Lethbridge, but a good deal of further material has been developed by NROOGD covens over the years since the tradition's founding.

From 1969 to 1976, it operated as a semiformal organization, with a Red Cord Council (composed of second degree members) as its governing body. In 1976, though, the Red Cord Council was dissolved and NROOGD transformed itself from an order into a tradition. As of this writing, NROOGD covens are active in half a dozen American states, although the bulk of the membership is still in the San Francisco Bay area. SEE ALSO NEOPAGANISM. FURTHER READING: ADLER 1986.

Golden Proportion. The most important of the proportions used in traditional sacred geometry, also known as φ (phi). The Golden Proportion is a ratio between two measurements, such that the smaller relates to the larger in the same ratio as the larger to the sum of both—in mathematical terms, A:B::B:A+B, "A is to B as B is to A+B." The only ratio that meets these criteria, worked out numerically, is 1 to 1.6180339 . . . and so on for an infinite number of digits that follow no repeating pattern. In geometrical terms, the Golden Proportion is the ratio between the side of a pentagon and the side of a pentagram drawn inside the pentagon; it can also be produced geometrically in several other ways.

Laboratory studies have shown that rectangles and other shapes based on the Golden Proportion are judged more balanced and attractive by most people than those based on any other proportion. In the natural world, the Golden Proportion appears in a profusion of different ways, from the arrangement of seeds in a sunflower head to the structure of nautilus shells. *SEE ALSO* PENTAGRAM; SACRED GEOMETRY. FURTHER READING: GHYKA 1977, LAWLOR 1982.

golem. In Jewish magical lore, an artificial person manufactured from clay and brought to life by magic. According to the traditional accounts, the body of a golem is formed from clay or earth, and complex ritual and contemplative processes are used to awaken the golem to life. The culmination of these workings involves writing the word *Ameth*, "truth," on the golem's forehead, and when this is done the golem awakes. If it is ever necessary to return the golem to dust, the first letter of the word is erased, leaving *meth*, "dead."

The first references to a golem in Jewish tradition are found in the Talmud, which dates from the first few centuries of the Common Era. The word itself, which literally means "unformed" or "incomplete," was first applied to the artificial human by Jewish mystics in Germany during the twelfth and thirteenth centuries. References to the golem in these earlier sources suggest that it was something much more like the ensouled magical statues of the ancient world than the clay robot of later legend. *SEE* STATUES, MAGICAL. The processes of creation are generally held to have involved the complex letter symbolism of the Sepher Yetzirah, the oldest of the Cabalistic texts; *SEE* SEPHER YETZIRAH.

By the fifteenth century the golem was at the center of a complex of legend and folklore, which had less and less to do with the original magical process as the years went on. These legends describe the golem as a creature like Frankenstein's monster, able to understand and obey orders but unable to speak, and usually getting out of control after a short time and having to be returned to earth. In the last few centuries, this process has completed itself with the transformation of the golem into a literary phenomenon. *SEE ALSO* CABALA; HEBREW ALPHABET. FURTHER READING: IDEL 1990, SCHOLEM 1974.

Golohab. (Hebrew GVLHB, "arsonists") In Cabalistic tradition, "the Burners," the Qlippoth or demonic powers associated with Geburah, the fifth Sephirah of the Tree of Life. They are also called Zaphiel. Their traditional image is that of enormous hideous heads with open mouths, like volcanoes belching smoke and flame. Their cortex or realm is Usiel, and their archdemon is Asmodeus. *SEE* QLIPPOTH.

goofer dust. In traditional hoodoo, a powder used for cursing and other forms of destructive magic. The word "goofer" is an Americanized version of the Kongo word *kufwa*, "to kill." According to tradition, people who have been "goofered" waste away slowly, acting increasingly erratic or "goofy," until they finally die. This sounds like the work of a slow poison; modern recipes for goofer dust, however, rarely contain any pharmacologically active ingredient, and graveyard dust is usually the chief component. *SEE* GRAVEYARD DUST. *SEE ALSO* HOODOO.

Gort. (Old Irish, "field") The twelfth letter of the Ogham alphabet, with the sound-value *g*. It corresponds to ivy among trees, the swan among birds, the color blue, and the number ten. In Robert Graves' version of the Ogham tree-calendar, its month runs from October 1 to October 28. *SEE* OGHAM.

Ogham letter Gort

grades. *SEE* DEGREE(S).

Graeco-Egyptian magical papyri. The single largest collection of sources for ancient magic, these are documents written on papyrus scrolls in Egypt during the first few centuries of the Common Era. Some are written entirely in Greek, while others are in ancient Egyptian or a mixture of the two. They were apparently the working handbooks of professional magicians.

The most important of the papyri came from a single source, probably in the Egyptian city of Thebes; scholars have speculated that they may have come from the library of an ancient magician-priest. They were obtained by an adventurer at the court of the pasha of Egypt, one Jean d'Anastasi (1780?–1857), who sold them to major European libraries. Most of the papyri were first published in collected form in 1928–1931 by Karl Priesendanz (1883–1968). References to his edition are still the standard way to refer to the papyri and their component spells.

The magic of the papyri is a free mix of ancient Egyptian, Greek, and Jewish lore, blended together into a working synthesis of theurgic and thaumaturgic magic. Rituals for spiritual development and the attainment of a guardian spirit sit cheek by jowl with recipes for love potions and spells for invisibility. Many of the rituals, however, are used to bring about a systasis or direct encounter between the magician and a deity or spirit, either for purposes of practical magic or to assist the magician's spiritual development; in this latter are the historical roots of the Holy Guardian Angel concept so popular in modern magical circles. *SEE* HOLY GUARDIAN ANGEL.

Most of the material from the papyri has been neglected by the current magical revival. One ceremony from the papyri, known to scholars as PGM V 96–172, and to its original users as "the Stele of Jeu the Hieroglyphist," was published by the British scholar Charles Wycliffe Goodwin (1817–1878) in 1853, and entered into the modern magical tradition shortly thereafter as the Bornless One ritual; *SEE* BORNLESS ONE RITUAL. FURTHER READING: BETZ 1986.

Grail, Holy. In the Arthurian legends, a mysterious object for which the Knights of the Round Table searched in the latter part of Arthur's reign. Usually described as a goblet or cup, it had the power to feed an unlimited number of people with the food and drink they most desired, and was capable of miraculous healing. It was carried by a woman, the grail bearer, in a procession in the hidden castle of Carbonek. In order to awaken its power and break an evil enchantment that was on the land, it was necessary for a wandering knight to ask the right question at the right time in this ceremony; the question varies from source to source, but the most common was "Whom does the grail serve?"

The roots of the grail legend reach back far into Celtic prehistory. Cauldrons of plenty that magically provide food for an army of warriors are a common feature of Celtic myth. Also related to the grail is a ritual attested in a handful of Celtic and Germanic sources, in which a woman bore a cup of mead to the king and proclaimed his kingship. This is allied to the Celtic idea of Sovereignty as a goddess of the land, an idea that can also be traced in old Germanic epics. The procession of the grail, with a woman bearing the sacred cup that brings healing to the wounded king and the land, may well be a dim memory of a once-potent magical ceremony of this kind.

The first known version of the grail legend, *Perceval*, was begun by Chrétien de Troyes around 1180 but was left incomplete at his death. In the forty years between 1180 and 1220, nearly the entire body of grail stories that still survive were produced. They range from Chrétien's relatively plain version, through the complex symbolism of Wolfram von Eschenbach's *Parzival* (1207), to a massive effort to reformulate the grail as an orthodox Christian allegory, which reached its full flower in the *Queste del Sant Graal* (1207) attributed to Walter Map.

The grail has been an important symbol in many branches of modern occult thought and practice, especially those which draw on some degree of Celtic or Arthurian lore. In occult lodges derived from or influenced by the work of British mage Dion Fortune (1890–1946), the grail is the symbol of spirit, and represents the Greater Mysteries of spiritual transformation. *SEE* FORTUNE, DION. In some modern Wiccan traditions, in much of Druidry, in many branches of esoteric Christianity, and in Christian Wicca, the grail is used as a symbol of the feminine aspect of the divine. *SEE* CHRISTIAN OCCULTISM; CHRISTIAN WICCA; DRUIDRY; WICCA. *SEE ALSO* ARTHURIAN LEGENDS; CUP. FURTHER READING: ENRIGHT 1996, KNIGHT 1983, MATTHEWS AND GREEN 1986.

gramarye. An old spelling of the word "grammar," used as a term for magic in medieval and Renaissance English and (as a deliberate archaism) in some more recent works. *SEE* GRIMOIRE.

Grand Grimoire. One of the more popular grimoires or "grammars" of magical practice in the early modern period, probably written in France sometime in the seventeenth century but attributed, like most grimoires, to King Solomon; *SEE* SOLOMON.

The *Grand Grimoire*, like most grimoires, includes a detailed description of the hosts of Hell, with instructions for preparing the necessary equipment and performing the rituals for summoning and commanding them. It differs in advising the magician, or Karcist (a term only used in this source), to make a pact with the demons—an idea that has no place in earlier grimoires, which teach the magician to master and command demons rather than to barter with them. *SEE* PACT. *SEE ALSO* GRIMOIRE. FURTHER READING: BUTLER 1949.

grandmother story. In modern Pagan parlance, a dubious claim to a hereditary Pagan lineage. A number of important figures in the early history of modern Wicca claimed to have been initiated into the Craft by third-degree grandmothers who had since died, thus putting their claims out of reach of cross-examination. While there may have been some truth to a handful of these claims, the practice of claiming a family tradition via a dead grandmother became a common strategy for poseurs and status seekers in the magical community all through the last quarter of the twentieth century. *SEE ALSO* FAMILY TRADITION.

Grange, the (Patrons of Husbandry). American fraternal order, founded in 1867 by a group of seven Masons and Odd Fellows. The Grange is unusual among fraternal lodge organizations in that it has admitted women as well as men to equal membership from the beginning. Its major focus, symbolic as well as practical, is agriculture, and to this day most Grange members are farmers or come from a farm background.

Although Granges, like nearly all American fraternal lodges, have an open Bible present in meetings and open and close with conventional prayers, Grange symbolism is decidedly Pagan. Three female officers, representing the three Graces Flora, Pomona, and Ceres, sit in the place usually reserved in lodge design for the presiding officer. The first four degrees, which are conferred in a subordinate (local) Grange, correspond to the four seasons of the year. The fifth degree, conferred in a Pomona (county) Grange, is that of Pomona; the sixth, conferred in a state Grange, is that of Flora.

The seventh and highest Grange degree, conferred only at meetings of the national Grange, is the degree of Ceres—a full-blown nineteenth-century reconstruction of the Eleusinian Mysteries. The ritual used in this last degree is not a Grange invention; it was apparently obtained by Grange founder Oliver Hudson Kelley from an Italian nobleman, and thus probably has its roots in European irregular Masonry. It is sufficiently Pagan that many Christian Grange members refuse to take it.

The Grange seems to have little contact with Western occult traditions since its founding, and appears here mostly as a demonstration of the impressive penetration of occult and Pagan ideas in nineteenth-century American culture. Surprisingly, despite its presiding Triple Goddess and its use of the symbolism of seasons and agricultural fertility, the Grange seems to have gone unnoticed by modern Pagans. *SEE ALSO* ELEUSINIAN MYSTERIES; FREEMASONRY; ODD FELLOWSHIP.

Graphiel. In ceremonial magic, the intelligence of Mars. Its subordinate planetary spirit is Bartzabel. *SEE* INTELLIGENCES, PLANETARY.

graveyard dust. Dirt from a graveyard, used as an ingredient in traditional hoodoo magical workings. When collected for magical purposes, hoodoo workers always leave a payment in exchange, usually a silver dime or some whiskey. *SEE* HOODOO.

graveyard specter. In magical theory, a dead person's cast-off etheric body, which sometimes can be seen hovering over cemeteries by the psychically sensitive. Graveyard specters are essentially harmless, although they can attract larvae and other less innocuous beings. *SEE* ETHERIC BODY.

Gray, William G. English magician, 1913–1992. Gray was born in Middlesex, England, to a family that combined Christian and occult connections; his father was descended from a long line of Anglican clergymen, while his mother was a professional astrologer with friends throughout the British occult scene of the time. He joined the British Army and served in Egypt as a communications technician in the late 1930s, then was sent to France in the opening phases of the Second World War and was among the soldiers evacuated from Dunkirk after the French collapse in 1940.

After the war, he took up occult studies and enrolled in Dion Fortune's Fraternity of the Inner Light, but left it not long after completing the initial correspondence course. SEE INNER LIGHT, SOCIETY OF THE. He also studied at length with a Martinist who had been previously associated with the French occultist Papus (Gérard Encausse). SEE MARTINISM; PAPUS.

In the late 1960s, encouraged by his friend and fellow occultist Gareth Knight, he began writing books on his personal system of occultism, which used a radically different attribution of the Tarot to the Cabalistic Tree of Life, and assigned the Paths to English rather than Hebrew letters. His first book, *The Ladder of Lights* (1968), became a widely used source for students of the Hermetic Cabala, while later books such as *The Talking Tree* and *Concepts of Qabalah* attracted students from Britain, the United States, and South Africa. His four-part *Sangreal Sodality* series provided the complete rituals and practices for a magical order of his own design, which promptly took shape and remains active today; SEE SANGREAL SODALITY.

Gray supported himself by working as a chiropodist, and his wife of many years, Bobbie, was a professional astrologer. Irascible and eccentric, he nonetheless was a major presence in the British occult scene during the last decades of the twentieth century, and some of his students have become important teachers and writers in their own right in recent years. He died in 1992. FURTHER READING: DECKER AND DUMMETT 2002, GRAY 1982, GRAY 1984.

Great Mother. SEE GODDESS, THE.

Great Rite. In Wicca and other modern Pagan traditions, ritual lovemaking, seen as the mating of the Goddess and the God. Either symbolically or in actual practice, it plays a central role in the third degree initiation in most Wiccan traditions, and also plays a role in sabbats and handfasting ceremonies in some traditions. SEE HANDFASTING; SABBAT.

When physically performed in a coven, it is often done in private, with the coveners who are not actively involved leaving the room during the performance of the rite, or simply going to the edge of the circle and turning their backs.

When symbolically acted out, the Great Rite is performed by lowering an athame into a chalice of wine, accompanied by words equating the athame with the penis or the God and the chalice with the vagina or the Goddess. SEE ATHAME; CUP. SEE ALSO SEX AND OCCULTISM; WICCA.

Great White Lodge. In Theosophy and many other occult traditions of the nineteenth and twentieth centuries, the body of benevolent Masters who are responsible for preserving the wisdom of the ages and superintending the evolution of humanity and the Earth. The Masters of the Great White Lodge, according to these traditions, are the real government of the world, guiding all of humanity along the paths of spiritual development. The terms "Great White Lodge" and "Great White Brotherhood" are used interchangeably.

Theosophical writings discuss the internal organization of the Great White Lodge in much detail. At its head is the Lord of the World, Sanat Kumara. Below him are Gautama, who is the buddha of the current root race, and three pratyeka buddhas, who assist the Lord of the World. Below these are the manu of the current root race, Vaivasvata; the bodhisattva, Maitreya; and the mahachohan, whose name does not seem to appear in published sources. Below these on the pyramid are the seven chohans or Lords of the Rays, and below these the ordinary Masters. All of this material was obtained by clairvoyance, and is subject to all the usual liabilities of clairvoyant information. SEE ALSO MASTERS; ROOT RACE; SANAT KUMARA; THEOSOPHY. FURTHER READING: LEADBEATER 1925.

green lion. In alchemy, a symbol which—like most alchemical symbols—has multiple meanings. In *The Dialogue of Morienus and King Khalid*, the first Arabic work of alchemy translated into Latin, Morienus defines the green lion as glass. Later alchemical writings use it to represent a solvent or menstruum, which is used to dissolve the basic materials of the art. Images of a green lion are common in alchemical emblems. SEE ALSO ALCHEMY.

Green Man. Woodland figure found in the folklore, art, and rituals of many European cultures from the Middle Ages to the present, usually pictured as a man wearing a mask and garments of leaves. Many modern Pagan writers have interpreted the Green Man as a deity of the forest, although there is very little evidence for such a god in surviving sources on European Pagan religion. He may well have been a spirit or a ritual personification.

In many English springtime dances and mummers' plays, the Green Man is represented by a man dressed in greenery, or covered by a frame to which branches in full leaf are fastened. The greenery, with or without its bearer, is often pushed into the water or treated to other forms of rough treatment. Some writers have suggested that this may be a survival of ancient traditions of human sacrifice. *SEE ALSO* PAGANISM. FURTHER READING: ANDERSON 1990.

Green Ray. In occult philosophy, the fourth of the Seven Rays, the primary creative energies of the universe. The Green Ray is the ray of beauty and the arts, and it also has a very strong link to the natural world. In Theosophical lore, the Green Ray is under the direction of the Master Serapis, a chohan of the Great White Lodge. Its symbolic gem is jasper. *SEE* SERAPIS, MASTER. *SEE ALSO* RAYS, SEVEN.

green witchcraft. A term used by and for a variety of modern Wiccan and quasi-Wiccan traditions that share a common focus on nature and the natural world, earth-oriented deities such as Gaia, and in many cases an involvement in ecological activism. Some green witches claim descent through family traditions from ancient or medieval Pagan herbalists, wise women, and midwives, while others treat these figures as their foremothers and role models but make no claim to an inherited lineage from such sources.

Diverse even by modern Pagan standards, green witchcraft is more a general category, or even a mood, than a specific tradition or set of traditions. It nonetheless forms one of the largest categories of Paganism at present. *SEE ALSO* GAIA HYPOTHESIS; NEOPAGANISM; WICCA. FURTHER READING: MOURA 1996, MOURA 2000.

Greenstein, Joseph L. Polish-American Cabalist and professional strongman, 1893–1977. A sickly child, Greenstein took up wrestling in his teen years. Later, after emigrating to America, he entered the vaudeville circuit

as a strongman under the stage name "The Mighty Atom." His signature feats included tying iron horseshoes into knots, biting through chains, pounding spikes through metal-covered boards with his bare hands, and towing trucks with his hair.

These and other accomplishments were based not only on physical training but also on Greenstein's lifelong study of Cabala, on which he based a unique system of subtle energy work. As a boy, he studied the Jewish scriptures in a Polish yeshiva, and continued his studies in America, branching out into natural medicine, hypnosis, and a variety of occult topics.

After the collapse of the vaudeville industry in the Great Depression, Greenstein entered the health products field, making and selling natural soap, liniment, laxative compound, and other products, and using his feats of strength as a sales tool at public markets up and down the East Coast. At the age of eighty-two, two years before his death, he was still able to perform his classic feats flawlessly before a Madison Square Garden audience. *SEE ALSO* PHYSICAL CULTURE. FURTHER READING: SPIELMAN 1998.

Grigori. *SEE* WATCHERS, THE.

grimoire. (Medieval French, "grammar") A handbook or "grammar" of magic from the Middle Ages or Renaissance periods. Grimoires make up the most significant body of medieval magical literature. Their focus is almost entirely on goetic magic—that is, the art of summoning spirits and demons to do the bidding of the magician—although a certain amount of natural magic appears in some examples as well. The most famous of the grimoires include the *Picatrix*, the *Key of Solomon*, the *Lemegeton*, the *Sworn Book of Honorius*, the *Grand Grimoire*, and the *Dragon Rouge* ("Red Dragon"); there were many others.

The magic of the grimoires is a free mix of methods from many different sources, of which Jewish, Arabic, Greek, and medieval Christian elements are the most visible. The magician was instructed to make and consecrate a variety of working tools, lay out a magical circle for protection against the spirits, and then repeat a series of prayers, conjurations, and commands to induce the desired spirit to appear. Once the spirit arrived, it could be commanded to consecrate talismans, prophesy the future, reveal the location of hidden treasure, and so on.

The popularity of the grimoires was at its height in the late Middle Ages, and began to wane with the spread of Renaissance high magic in the later sixteenth century. They have nonetheless remained in use up to the present time, and a number of more recent magical traditions have drawn heavily from one or another grimoire. Some of the magical handbooks presently used in American folk magic, such as the *Sixth and Seventh Books of Moses*, draw on the older grimoire lore. SEE SIXTH AND SEVENTH BOOKS OF MOSES. SEE ALSO FAUST LEGEND; GOETIA; KEY OF SOLOMON; LEMEGETON. FURTHER READING: E. BUTLER 1949, FANGER 1998, KIECKHEFER 1998, MATHERS 1888.

grip. In lodge terminology, a special mode of handshake used as a method of identification among lodge members. Like many other elements of the lodge system, grips were used as a form of symbolism from an early date in both fraternal and magical lodges. SEE LODGE, FRATERNAL; LODGE, MAGICAL.

group mind. In magical parlance, the collective consciousness of a group of people whose emotions and thoughts are focused in the same direction. Mob behavior and many other quirks of social psychology, according to occult teachings, are generated by group minds that are formed at random, generally by people who have no notion of what is going on. The deliberate construction of a group mind, on the other hand, is an important part in the construction of a working magical lodge. SEE LODGE, MAGICAL.

Group minds should not be confused with group souls, which are the overshadowing spiritual essence of a community, nation, or ethnic group. SEE GROUP SOUL. FURTHER READING: FORTUNE 1987B, GREER 1998.

group soul. In occult parlance, the collective spiritual essence of a community, nation, or ethnic group. (The term "race soul" was once used for ethnic group souls, but was dropped in the second half of the twentieth century for obvious reasons.) The group soul is a source of guidance for the group it overshadows, but it also has its own karma and may fall into imbalanced and destructive

states. The group overshadowed by a group soul is its body; the group soul "incarnates" when the group comes into being, gains and loses strength as the group does, and "dies" when the group becomes extinct or is absorbed by another.

Group souls should not be confused with group minds, which are a form of collective consciousness shared by individuals whose thoughts and emotions are focused in the same direction. SEE GROUP MIND. FURTHER READING: FORTUNE 1987B.

grove. In most modern Druid organizations, the word used for a local group of Druids; the term is equivalent to "coven" in Wicca or "lodge" in many magical orders. It appears to have entered common use by way of the fraternal Druid orders of the late eighteenth century. SEE DRUIDS.

Guaita, Stanislaus de. French poet and magician, 1860–1898. Descended from Alsatian nobility, de Guaita came to Paris in 1880 and set out to make a name for himself as a poet. In 1884 he read Joséphin Peladan's novel *Le Vice Suprême* and was captivated by its magical and Cabalistic symbolism. SEE PELADAN, JOSÉPHIN. He quickly became active in the Parisian occult scene, and first befriended and then broke with the scandalous Abbé Boullan, whom he visited in Lyon. SEE BOULLAN, JOSEPH-ANTOINE.

In 1888 he, along with Peladan, Papus, and several other notables of the Paris occult scene, founded the Ordre de la Rose+Croix Kabbalistique ("Order of the Cabalistic Rose+Cross"), taking a seat on its governing Council of Twelve. In the "War of the Two Roses" that followed Peladan's departure in 1890, he took an active role in defending the order in print.

In 1893, after Boullan's sudden death, de Guaita was accused by Jules Bois and J.-K. Huysmans of having caused the Abbé's death by magic. The ensuing quarrel led to a duel with pistols between de Guaita and Bois, in which neither party was hurt.

Like many of his contemporaries in the Decadent scene, de Guaita reveled in a sinister reputation that his publications on magic, including such titles as *Le Temple de Satan* (*The Temple of Satan*) and *La Clef de la Magie Noire* (*The Key to Black Magic*), did nothing to dispell. He lived in a ground-floor apartment draped entirely in red, sleeping by day and working by night. His addiction to morphine and cocaine—another common habit of the fin-de-siècle Decadents—wrecked his health, and he died at the age of thirty-eight. FURTHER READING: WEBB 1974.

Guardian. *SEE* SUMMONER.

Guardians. In some modern Pagan traditions, entities corresponding to the four elements, who are held to dwell in four elemental watchtowers at the four quarters of the world. The Guardians are called upon in the process of casting a circle and in a few other magical operations. *SEE ALSO* WATCHTOWERS.

guph. (Hebrew GVPh, "corpse") In Cabalistic theory, the physical body of a human being, understood as a structure of inert matter infused and animated by the higher-level bodies of the self. *SEE* SUBTLE BODIES.

gur. In alchemical theory, a soft buttery substance formed underground from the fusion of alchemical sulphur and alchemical mercury; the "first matter" of metals, which evolves through a variety of stages into metallic ores. *SEE* ALCHEMY.

Gwynfydd. In Druidry, one of the Three Circles of Existence, the realm of liberated spirits who have completed the journey through Abred, the realm of plant and animal life. Souls in Gwynfydd are held to possess complete memory of their previous incarnations—plant, animal, and human—and can enter into any form of incarnate life at will. Only Ceugant, the highest Circle traversed only by the divine, is closed to them, as to all created beings. *SEE* CIRCLES OF EXISTENCE; DRUIDRY.

Gyfu. *SEE* GEBO.

H

Haegl. (Old English, "hail") The ninth rune of the Anglo-Saxon futhorc. The Old English rune-poem relates it to hail as "the whitest of grain." *SEE* ANGLO-SAXON FUTHORC.

Rune Haegl

Hagalaz. (Old Germanic, "hail") The ninth rune of the elder futhark, corresponding to hail and the concepts of danger and disruption. It represents the sound *h*. *SEE* ELDER FUTHARK.

Rune Hagalaz

Hagall. (Old Norse, "hail") The seventh rune of the younger futhark, representing hail, "the coldest of grain," and the concepts of danger and crisis. Its sound-value is *h*. *SEE* YOUNGER FUTHARK.

The same rune, named Hagal, is the seventh rune of the Armanen rune system. Its meaning is introspection, and it corresponds to the god Balder, the father in the family, the zodiacal sign Libra, and the power, according to the rune-charm in the Old Norse *Havamal*, to stop hot flames. *SEE* ARMANEN RUNES.

Rune Hagall (Hagal)

Hagiel. In ceremonial magic, the planetary intelligence of Venus. Its subordinate spirit is Kedemel. *SEE* INTELLIGENCE, PLANETARY.

Hagith. One of the seven Olympian spirits, Hagith is associated with the planet Venus and rules over 21 of the 196 provinces of Heaven. The period of history governed by Hagith extended from 1410 to 1900 c.e. *SEE* OLYMPIAN SPIRITS.

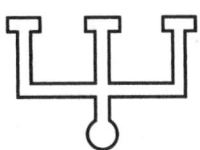

Olympic spirit Hagith

Hall, Manly Palmer. Canadian-American occultist, 1901–1990. Born in Peterborough, Ontario, Hall was raised by his maternal grandmother, who brought him to the United States in 1904. He grew up in Sioux Falls, South Dakota. Hall was interested in the occult from an early age and joined the Theosophical Society while still in his teens. In 1919 he came to Oceanside, California, where he studied with the Rosicrucian Fellowship of Max Heindel; *SEE* ROSICRUCIAN FELLOWSHIP. After a short time he moved to Los Angeles, where he spent the rest of his life.

He supported himself at first working as a screenwriter in the early days of the movie industry in Hollywood. In the fall of 1920, he was invited to give a lecture on reincarnation to a small audience in Santa Monica. His talk was well recieved, and led to a lecture series in Los Angeles the next year. In 1923 he was ordained as a minister in the Church of the People, a metaphysical church in Los Angeles.

In 1922, he began working on what would become his magnum opus, *An Encyclopedic Outline of Masonic, Hermetic, Qabbalistic, and Rosicrucian Symbolical Philosophy* (also published under the title *The Secret Teachings of All Ages*). Lavishly illustrated by Augustus Knapp and funded by a variety of wealthy subscribers, it was published in 1928 and gave Hall an international reputation. In 1934, hoping to create a modern equivalent to the ancient mystery school of Pythagoras, Hall launched the Philosophical Research Society (PRS). Construction began on its headquarters in Los Angeles the next year, and continued over the following decades. Hall traveled widely, visiting Europe and the Far East, but between trips could be found in Los Angeles, where he gave weekly lectures at the PRS and wrote more than 200 books on occult topics. He remained active at the PRS until a short time before his death. FURTHER READING: HALL 1988, HOELLER 1991.

hammer. The traditional weapon of the Norse god Thor, the hammer is used by Asatru priests as a working tool for tracing circles and signs, and for other religious and magical purposes. It serves essentially the same purposes in Asatru as the athame in Wicca and the wand in many ceremonial magic traditions. *SEE* ASATRU; ATHAME; WAND.

hand. *SEE* MOJO.

handfasting. The Wiccan form of wedding ceremony in which the hands of the couple being married are tied together with a cord. The old Celtic and Appalachian custom of jumping over a broom is also a common element of handfasting rituals. Wiccan handfasting ceremonies have been copied by many groups in the modern Pagan revival. *SEE* NEOPAGANISM; WICCA.

Hanged Man, the. The twelfth Major Arcanum of the tarot, bearing the image of a man hanged by one foot. This has been given a dizzying array of modern interpretations, but in Renaissance times, when the image was created, it was a well-known habit of the justice system, used for traitors and political criminals; as late as 1944, the corpse of Italian dictator Benito Mussolini was treated in exactly this way. In the Golden Dawn system, this Arcanum is assigned to the Hebrew letter Mem, while the French system assigns it to Lamed. Its common meanings in divination include sacrifice, initiation, a period of delay or suspension, reversal, and renunciation.

Aleister Crowley, in his book on the tarot (Crowley 1969, p. 98), refers the posture of the Hanged Man to the "Sleep of Shiloam," which is probably the same as the "Sleep of Sialam" much discussed by late nineteenth- and early twentieth-century occultists. *SEE* SIALAM, SLEEP OF.

Its magical title is "Spirit of the Mighty Waters." *SEE ALSO* TAROT.

Tarot trump the Hanged Man (Universal Tarot)

Haniel. (Hebrew HANIAL, "grace of God") The archangel of Netzach, the seventh Sephirah of the Tree of Life, and Netzach's manifestation in the world of Briah. *SEE* BRIAH; NETZACH. In some sources, Haniel is given as the angel who transported Enoch to Heaven; *SEE* ENOCH. *SEE ALSO* ARCHANGEL.

Hapi. (ancient Egyptian *hpy*) One of the four sons of Horus, also spelled Ahepi, Ahephi, or Ahaphix in some older sources. Hapi was the god of the Nile in flood; he had the head of an ape, ruled the northern quarter of the world, and had guardianship over the large intestine of the deceased. He was associated with the goddess Nephthys, and was also known as "the Digger." SEE CANOPIC GODS.

In the Golden Dawn magical tradition, Hapi (here spelled Ahephi) was one of the invisible guardians of the temple, and was stationed in the northwest. SEE GOLDEN DAWN, HERMETIC ORDER OF THE; INVISIBLE STATIONS. FURTHER READING: BUDGE 1967, REGARDIE 1971.

harmonic chart. In astrology, a chart created by taking the position of each planet and multiplying its celestial longitude by a given number, which is the "harmonic" being studied. Originally developed in Hindu astrology, where it has been used for centuries, the use of harmonics was introduced to Western astrology in the twentieth century and has had a strong influence, especially in English astrological circles. Each harmonic is held to have a particular influence. SEE ASTROLOGY.

Harpocrates. (ancient Egyptian *Heru-pe-khradj*, "Horus the Child") A form of the complex Egyptian god Horus, Harpocrates is Horus as a child in the marshes of the Nile delta, hiding from the forces of his uncle Set. In Egyptian art, he is sometimes shown seated or standing on a lotus blossom, sometimes standing on a pair of crocodiles.

In Golden Dawn magic, the godform of Harpocrates fills one of the invisible stations of a temple in the Neophyte grade, and is also important in individual ritual practice. One of the two signs of the Neophyte grade, the Sign of Silence, corresponds to Harpocrates, and a formula of invisibility is derived from this sign and its associated godform. SEE INVISIBILITY; INVISIBLE STATIONS.

In the magical religion of Thelema, as founded by Aleister Crowley, Harpocrates (under the old form Hoor-par-kraat) is one of the forms of Horus as Lord of the Aeon. SEE THELEMA. SEE ALSO HORUS.

Harran. In ancient and early medieval times, an important city in northern Mesopotamia, located on the main trade routes connecting the eastern Mediterranean with the valleys of the Tigris and Euphrates Rivers, and with Persia and India beyond; its site is presently in southeastern Turkey. The city of Harran was originally founded as

a trading post by Sumerian merchants sometime before 2000 B.C.E., and grew to become a metropolis of 20,000 people, centered on the great temple Ehulhul (Sumerian for "House of Rejoicing"), dedicated to the Sumerian moon god Sin.

Like the rest of the Middle East, Harran passed through a range of religious and cultural changes as Sumerian, Babylonian, Assyrian, Persian, Greek, and Roman empires rose and fell, bringing with them traditions from distant lands. The coming of Christianity, however, made little impact on Harran. Why this was so is unclear. The nearby city of Edessa (modern Urfa) became a center of Christian influence in the region, and the rest of the Roman province of Syria became a center of Christian monastic and theological activity.

Only Harran remained resolutely Pagan. Its location on the unsettled Roman-Persian border, in an area that changed hands from one empire to the other several times, made it impossible for the Roman government to enforce religious legislation banning Paganism there. Around the same time, or possibly earlier, it became an important center of alchemical studies; a good deal of original work in alchemy was done there, including some of the first experiments on the alchemical properties of copper. SEE ALCHEMY.

The arrival of Islam in 639 C.E., when the whole of northern Mesopotamia was conquered by Muslim armies under ʿIyadh ibn Ghanam, might have been expected to change this. The teachings of Islam require some degree of tolerance for Jews and Christians but do not extend the same privilege to Pagans, and surviving Pagan temples and communities throughout the area of the Muslim conquests faced a hard choice between conversion and death.

The passages of the Quran that require toleration of Christians and Jews also speak of another group, the *Sabiʿah* or Sabians, who are also considered "People of the Book" and protected by Islamic law. For reasons that are still unclear, the Harranians came to be identified with the Sabians of the Quran, and so were able to continue the practice of their Pagan religious traditions for centuries longer.

According to a Muslim source from around 1300 C.E., Harran under Muslim rule contained temples to each of the planetary gods. The temple of Saturn was black and hexagonal, with a statue of lead on a dais with nine steps; that of Jupiter was green and triangular, the statue was of tin and the number of steps eight; that of Mars, red and oblong, with an iron statue and seven steps; that of the Sun, square and golden, with a golden statue set with pearls and six steps; that of Venus, blue and triangular (with one side longer than the others), with a copper statue and five steps; that of Mercury, brown and hexagonal (with a square interior), with a statue of alloy filled with mercury set atop four circular steps; and that of the Moon, white and pentagonal, with a silver statue atop three steps.

Whether or not this account is correct, the inhabitants of Harran were famous as scholars and philosophers, and a number of them—including the famous philosopher and mathematician Thabit ibn Qurra (died 901 C.E.)—rose to important positions in the Islamic world. The historian Bar Hebraeus records a speech Thabit made defending Harran's religious traditions, which Thabit called *hanputho*; the meaning of this Syriac word is unclear, but like its Arabic cognate *hanif*, it is commonly used as a term for Pagan spiritual traditions.

The sources on what *hanputho* actually was are fragmentary and contradictory, but the picture that has been pieced together by scholars is a complicated mix of ancient Mesopotamian star religion with Greek Neoplatonic philosophy and Hermetic magical practice. Harranian scholars demonstrated a broad knowledge of Greek philosophy, as well as astrology and alchemy, and it has been suggested by more than one modern scholar that the Harranian religion was actually the last survival of the Neoplatonic Pagan spirituality followed by many people in the last centuries of the Roman Empire. *SEE* PLATONISM; THEURGY.

Harran remained an important city for several centuries after the Muslim conquest, but war between the Caliphate of Baghdad and the Byzantine Empire devastated the entire region, and internal warfare among different Muslim rulers increased the destruction. The last temple of the moon god in Harran, according to one chronicler, was destroyed in 1032 during one of these wars; another gives the date as 1081. The Mongol invasions of the thirteenth century completed the devastation

and disrupted the trade routes on which Harran's survival depended. In 1271, the city was finally abandoned and its unique religious traditions were lost.

Attempts have been made by several recent writers to connect Harran with various later Western esoteric traditions, including Wicca, arguing essentially that Pagan Platonism in the Western world had to come from somewhere. No evidence of a direct Harranian link has yet been brought forward, and the presence of intensely Pagan symbolism and philosophy within the Platonic traditions preserved in the Christian West makes it unnecessary to posit some additional source. It seems likely nonetheless that Harran may take an honored place in future versions of occult history; *SEE* OCCULT HISTORY. *SEE ALSO* MESOPOTAMIAN OCCULTISM; PAGANISM. FURTHER READING: FREW 1999, GREEN 1992, LINDSAY 1970.

Harris, Thomas Lake. American writer and occultist, 1823–1906. After a conventional upbringing and an early career as a Swedenborgian minister, Harris began to experiment with trance states around 1850, after meeting the Spiritualist philosopher Andrew Jackson Davis. *SEE* DAVIS, ANDREW JACKSON; SPIRITUALISM; SWEDENBORG, EMMANUEL. His visions led him to a series of intense inner experiences in which he cohabited with a spiritual lover, one "Queen Lily of the Conjugial [sic] Angels," and fathered three spirit-children.

On the basis of these visions, Harris founded an organization called the Brotherhood of the New Life, with headquarters at what would now be called a commune in upstate New York. Techniques of "open breathing" and "demagnetizing," borrowed from mesmerist circles, were taught to bring the Holy Spirit directly into the body and free it from harmful animal magnetism; according to Harris, this would allow the body to become home to thousands of happy, health-giving faeries. Physical celibacy allowed members of the brotherhood to form "counterpartal unions" with their angelic soul mates.

The brotherhood lasted until 1875, when a split among its members led Harris to move to California and set up a new community in Santa Rosa. There, despite a series of scandals sparked by claims that his "counterpartal marriages" were considerably less ethereal than they looked, he continued to teach and gather followers. In

1894 he announced that he had attained immortality through spiritual union with his angelic counterpart, and proclaimed the imminent end of the world. This failed to happen, and he spent the last years of his life in retirement in New York City.

Despite the oddity of his beliefs and a severe case of sugary Victorian sentimentality, Harris' ideas and voluminous writings had a surprisingly large influence in the late nineteenth and early twentieth centuries. Several important Golden Dawn members, including Percy Bullock, considered his teachings to be of central importance, and Bullock published a series of pamphlets on Harris' teachings and circulated them in Golden Dawn circles. *SEE* GOLDEN DAWN, HERMETIC ORDER OF THE. *SEE ALSO* FAERY; SEX AND OCCULTISM. FURTHER READING: SCHNEIDER AND LAWSON 1942.

hawthorn. (*Crataegus* spp.) An important tree in Western natural magic and in the Irish Ogham alphabet, the hawthorn is a small, shrubby tree with large, sharp thorns. Most varieties flower in May, giving the tree one of its other names, the may tree.

Hawthorns are traditionally linked with the faery folk and are hedged about with the usual range of taboos related to faery. *SEE* FAERY.

In the Ogham alphabet, the hawthorn corresponds to the letter Huath. *SEE* HUATH; OGHAM.

head, severed. An important element of ancient Celtic magic revolved around the cult of the severed head. The Pagan Celts were headhunters who, according to classical sources, preserved the severed heads of enemies and made use of them in magic. An echo of this appears in the Welsh Triads, in which the head of Bran the Blessed is said to have been buried beneath Tower Hill in London to keep away foreign invaders; *SEE* BRAN THE BLESSED. FURTHER READING: BROMWICH 1961.

heavens, seven. According to Cabalistic lore, there are seven earths, seven heavens, and seven hells. The seven heavens correspond to the Sephiroth of the Tree of Life as follows:

Name	Translation	Sephirah
7. Araboth	Plains	the Supernals
6. Makhon	Place	Chesed
5. Maon	Residence	Geburah
4. Zebul	Dwelling	Tiphareth
3. Shechaqim	Clouds	Netzach
2. Raqia	Firmament	Hod
1. Tebel Vilon Shamayim	Veil of Heaven	Malkuth

SEE ALSO EARTHS, SEVEN; HELLS, SEVEN.

Hebrew alphabet. The most important symbolic alphabet in Western magical tradition, the Hebrew alphabet entered occultism by way of the Cabala, a system of Jewish mystical thought and practice adopted by many non-Jewish magicians during and after the Renaissance. The Hebrew letters have a more extensive set of symbolic correspondences than any other alphabet used in Western magic.

Much of the basic symbolism of the Hebrew alphabet can be found in the Sepher Yetzirah, a pre-Cabalistic book of Jewish mysticism which was taken up by Cabalists; *SEE* SEPHER YETZIRAH. From this source comes the relationship between the letters and the Cube of Space, a basic diagram of Cabalistic theory; *SEE* CUBE OF SPACE. The link between the Hebrew letters and the Tree of Life, the other (and more widely known) Cabalistic diagram, emerged in the early stages of the development of the Cabala, and can be found in the Bahir—the oldest major text of the Cabala—and the Zohar, Moses de Leon's massive Cabalistic sourcebook. *SEE* BAHIR; ZOHAR.

Aleph, Ox

Letter: א, A

Path: 11

Number: 1

Astrological Correspondence: Air

Type: Mother

Beth, House

Letter: ב, B

Path: 12

Number: 2

Astrological Correspondence: Mercury

Type: Double

Gimel, Camel

Letter: ג, G

Path: 13

Number: 3

Astrological Correspondence: Moon

Type: Double

Daleth, Door

Letter: ד, D

Path: 14

Number: 4

Astrological Correspondence: Venus

Type: Double

Heh, Window

Letter: ה, H

Path: 15

Number: 5

Astrological Correspondence: Aries

Type: Single

Vau, Nail

Letter: ו, U, V

Path: 16

Number: 6

Astrological Correspondence: Taurus

Type: Single

Zayin, Sword

Letter: ז, Z

Path: 17

Number: 7

Astrological Correspondence: Gemini

Type: Single

Cheth, Fence

Letter: ח, Ch

Path: 18

Number: 8

Astrological Correspondence: Cancer

Type: Single

Teth, Serpent

Letter: ט, T

Path: 19

Number: 9

Astrological Correspondence: Leo

Type: Single

Yod, Fist

Letter: י, I, Y

Path: 20

Number: 10

Astrological Correspondence: Virgo

Type: Single

Kaph, Hand

Letter: כ, K

Path: 21

Number: 20

Astrological Correspondence: Jupiter

Type: Double

Lamed, Goad

Letter: ל, L

Path: 22

Number: 30

Astrological Correspondence: Libra

Type: Single

Mem, Water

Letter: מ, M

Path: 23

Number: 40

Astrological Correspondence: Water

Type: Mother

Nun, Fish

Letter: נ, N

Path: 24

Number: 50

Astrological Correspondence: Scorpio

Type: Single

Samech, Prop

Letter: ס, S

Path: 25

Number: 60

Astrological Correspondence: Sagittarius

Type: Single

Ayin, Eye

Letter: ע, Aa

Path: 26

Number: 70

Astrological Correspondence: Capricorn

Type: Single

Peh, Mouth

Letter: פ, P

Path: 27

Number: 80

Astrological Correspondence: Mars

Type: Double

Tzaddi, Hook

Letter: צ, Tz

Path: 28

Number: 90

Astrological Correspondence: Aquarius

Type: Single

Qoph, Back of the Head

Letter: ק, Q

Path: 29

Number: 100

Astrological Correspondence: Pisces

Type: Single

Resh, Head

Letter: ר, R

Path: 30

Number: 200

Astrological Correspondence: Sun

Type: Double

Shin, Tooth

Letter: ש, Sh

Path: 31

Number: 300

Astrological Correspondence: Fire

Type: Mother

Tau, Cross

Letter: ת, Th

Path: 32

Number: 400

Astrological Correspondence: Saturn

Type: Double

The following letters have different shapes and number values when written at the end of a word:

Letter	Final Form	Number
Kaph	ך	500
Mem	ם	600
Nun	ן	700
Peh	ף	800
Tzaddi	ץ	900

★ Note that Hebrew is written right to left, not left to right as English.

The twenty-two letters are divided into three mother letters, seven double letters, and twelve single letters; these groupings, as the table shows, signify the elements of fire, water, and air; the seven planets; and the twelve signs of the zodiac. Other correspondences include tarot trumps, colors, scents, musical notes, angels, divine names, Paths on the Tree of Life, and parts of the Cube of Space. These correspondences have developed over more than two thousand years of mystical speculation and occult practice in Jewish and non-Jewish communities alike, and they contain a good deal of internal confusion and contradiction.

According to Cabalistic thought, the Hebrew letters form the basic patterns and tools with which God created the universe. Specific combinations of letters form the Names of God, which have power over the universe when spoken correctly. Most important of the Names is the Tetragrammaton or four-lettered Name, יהוה or YHVH; *SEE* TETRAGRAMMATON. In orthodox Judaism this name is so sacred that it may not be spoken aloud. Cabalistic practitioners in and out of Judaism have recorded a wide range of pronunciations, which are used in magical practice, particularly to command spirits.

Another important Hebrew divine Name is the Shem ha Mephoresh or Shemhamphorash, the "Divided Name." According to legend, this Name is so powerful that to pronounce it correctly would destroy the universe. *SEE* SHEMHAMPHORASH.

According to some Cabalistic sources, one of the letters of the alphabet is missing in the current *shemittah* or cosmic cycle, and will be restored in the next. *SEE* CYCLES, COSMIC. *SEE ALSO* CABALA *AND THE NAMES OF INDIVIDUAL LETTERS.* FURTHER READING: D. GODWIN 1989, GREER 1996, SCHOLEM 1974.

hedge witch. In modern Paganism, a term used by and for solitary witches whose practices incorporate large amounts of natural magic, herb lore, and similar subjects, and who generally do not claim a connection with any particular tradition. *SEE ALSO* CUNNING MAN/WOMAN; WITCH.

Heh. (Hebrew HH, "window") Heh is the fifth letter of the Hebrew alphabet and the first of the twelve single letters. It represents the sound *h*, and its numerical value is five. Its standard correspondences are as follows:

> *Path of the Tree of Life:* Path 15, Chokmah to Tiphareth.
>
> *Astrological Correspondence:* Aries, the Ram.
>
> *Tarot Correspondence:* Trump IV, the Emperor.
>
> *Part of the Cube of Space:* The northeast edge.
>
> *Colors:* in Atziluth—scarlet.
>
> in Briah—red.
>
> in Yetzirah—brilliant flame red.
>
> in Assiah—glowing red.

Its text from the *Thirty-two Paths of Wisdom* runs: "The Fifteenth Path is the Constituting Inteligence, so called because it constitutes the substance of Creation in pure darkness, and it is said of these contemplations: it is that darkness spoken of in Scripture (Job 38:9), 'and thick darkness a swaddling band for it.'"

In the Cabalistic system of Aleister Crowley, the letter Heh is associated with tarot trump XVII, the Star. *SEE* CROWLEY, ALEISTER. *SEE ALSO* CABALA; HEBREW ALPHABET.

Hebrew letter Heh

Heka. The ancient Egyptian term for magic, and also the name of a god, one of three abstract powers who traveled with the solar god Re in the boat named "Millions of Years," giving Re the power to rule the universe. The other two were Hu, the primordial word, and Sia, the power of omniscience. *SEE* EGYPTIAN OCCULTISM.

Hell Fire Club. The Friars of Saint Francis of Wycombe, as the club was formally known, has developed a largely undeserved reputation in histories of Satanism. It was founded by Sir Francis Dashwood and a group of his friends in 1746, at the peak of the Gothic craze in English popular culture. Early meetings were held at the George and Vulture, a London tavern, but in 1752 the club moved operations to Medmenham Abbey and met there for the rest of its existence.

The Hell Fire Club was essentially a group of bored, wealthy Englishmen with a taste for orgies and a fondness for Gothic kitsch. Members attended meetings in black monastic robes and were accompanied by "nuns" who were either professional prostitutes or enthusiastic amateurs. Burlesque ceremonies, plenty of alcohol, and indiscriminate lovemaking were the chief orders of business at meetings.

The club's membership included some of the leading political and cultural figures of the time, including the Earl of Bute and George Wilkes. Benjamin Franklin, whose web of connections involved secret societies on two continents, was a member during his stay in England.

The club faded out of existence sometime around 1780. *SEE ALSO* SATANISM. FURTHER READING: MEDWAY 2001, TOWERS 1987.

hells, seven. According to Cabalistic lore, there are seven earths, seven heavens, and seven hells. The seven hells are located in Arqa, the sixth of the seven earths. They correspond to the Sephirah of the Tree of Life as follows:

Name	Translation	Sephirah
7. Sheol	abyss	the Supernals
6. Abbadon	destruction	Chesed
5. Bar Shachath	pit of ruin	Geburah
4. Tit ha-Yon	mire of mud	Tiphareth
3. Shaare Moth	gates of death	Netzach
2. Tzelmoth	shadow of death	Hod
1. Gehenna	valley of Hinnom	Yesod and Malkuth

The seventh hell is the deepest of these, and the first the closest to the surface. *SEE ALSO* EARTHS, SEVEN; HEAVENS, SEVEN.

hepatoscopy. *SEE* SACRIFICE.

herbalism, magical. *SEE* NATURAL MAGIC.

Hermes Trismegistus. (Greek, "Hermes Thrice Great") The mythical founder of Hermeticism, Hermes Trismegistus began his career as the ancient Egyptian god Djehuti or Thoth, among whose titles was "three times great." After the Greek conquest of Egypt under Alexander the Great, Thoth became identified with Hermes, the closest equivalent among the Greek gods, and his title was translated as well. Over time, with the emergence of a hybrid Greek-Egyptian culture in the Nile valley, the ancient Egyptian habit of crediting Thoth with the authorship of all books on magic carried over to Hermes, and a genre of Greek books on magic and mysticism took shape in what came to be called the Hermetic tradition. *SEE* HERMETICISM.

Few people in ancient times, and even fewer in the Middle Ages, doubted that Hermes Trismegistus had been a flesh-and-blood person who had lived at a distant time in the past and written important books of magic, astrology, alchemy, and theology. Efforts were made starting in Roman times to provide him with a biography,

and these accelerated as Pagan gods became less acceptable and human sages more so.

Even in the Hermetic writings themselves, the Hermes who appears is sometimes described as the grandson of an older Hermes, who is clearly enough the god Thoth; later on, efforts to reinterpret Hermes as a historical figure became all but universal. Thus, for example, Jewish writers commonly identified Hermes with Enoch, while Muslim scholars considered him to be the same person as the mysterious Idris who initiated Moses. Since Enoch was held to have become the mighty angel Metatron after his assumption into heaven, while Idris has nearly as exalted a status in Islamic legend and lore, both these identifications give the Thrice Great One as close to his former divine status as a monotheistic religion can provide. *SEE* ENOCH; METATRON.

By the early Middle Ages, the figure of Hermes had changed shape once again, and an entire literature of magical, astrological, and alchemical books was attached to his still-famous name. To the medieval mind, Hermes was a contemporary of Moses, an Egyptian priest, prophet, and king who had single-handedly invented alchemy, astrology, magic, and a variety of other arts.

Attempts to redefine Hermes Trismegistus in historical terms have continued up to the present. In the teachings of the American Rosicrucian order AMORC, for instance, the heretic pharaoh Akhenaten is defined as the "second Hermes," despite the fact that the teachings of Akhenaten, which are well attested historically, are about as far from Hermeticism as can be imagined; *SEE* AKHENATEN. FURTHER READING: FAIVRE 1995, FOWDEN 1986.

Hermetic Brotherhood of Luxor (H. B. of L.). Occult order founded in England sometime before 1884, when it first publicized its existence in an advertisement in an English translation of the *Corpus Hermeticum*. The H. B. of L. was the brainchild of the elusive adept Max Theon (1848?–1927), but was largely operated by his student Peter Davidson (1837–1915) and Davidson's associate Thomas H. Burgoyne (1855?–1895?).

The H. B. of L. was among the first examples of the occult correspondence school. Candidates for membership, who responded to its advertising or were recommended by a member, would be requested to send a photograph and an astrological birth chart; upon acceptance, the new member would be placed in contact with a mentor, who would send out a series of manuscripts covering the teachings and practical work of the brotherhood. A modest membership fee and annual dues were charged—in 1885, for American members, these were respectively $5.00 and $1.25.

In exchange for these and a pledge of secrecy, the member received the details of a system of occultism, which, while admittedly cobbled together out of materials in circulation at the time, was original compared to most occultism in the late nineteenth century. Members were taught how to make and use a magic mirror in order to develop clairvoyance and clairaudience, and instructed in a method of sexual magic derived from the writings of American occultist P. B. Randolph (1825–1875). *SEE* MIRROR, MAGIC; RANDOLPH, PASCHAL BEVERLY; SEX AND OCCULTISM. They also received documents outlining a somewhat idiosyncratic system of historical and cosmic cycles based largely on the theory of polar shifts propounded by the British shoemaker-scholar Samson Mackey (1765–1843).

The H. B. of L. engaged in a running feud with the Theosophical Society, the major player in contemporary occult circles. Unfortunately for the brotherhood, it had a skeleton in its closet: Thomas Burgoyne, the Private Secretary to the Council of the H. B. of L. and one of its two most prominent members, had been imprisoned briefly in 1883 for mail fraud. When this fact surfaced in 1886, the resulting scandal effectively sank the H. B. of L. in Britain. Activities in France continued for some time longer, and attracted occultists of the caliber of Papus, but by the first decade of the twentieth century the H. B. of L. current was all but extinct there as well. *SEE* PAPUS.

Only in Germany and the United States did the H. B. of L. attain a certain degree of longevity, and that was under new names and in different forms. In Germany, the Ordo Templi Orientis (OTO) was founded by ex-H. B. of L. members Theodor Reuss and Carl Kellner, and incorporated the H. B. of L.'s sexual magic as the secret teachings of its highest degrees. *SEE* ORDO TEMPLI ORIENTIS (OTO).

In America, where both Burgoyne and Davidson moved in the aftermath of the 1886 scandal, the H. B. of

L. set down deeper roots. Both men were able to recruit new students and continue teaching the brotherhood's lore, and Burgoyne wrote and published a book, *The Light of Egypt*, which became a popular work in American occult circles. Genevieve Stebbins, a successful teacher of physical culture and elocution, was also closely involved in H. B. of L. activities, in America; *SEE* STEBBINS, GENEVIEVE.

Burgoyne ended up at the center of a new organization, called the Brotherhood of Light, which was based in Denver, Colorado, and had its own publishing arm. In 1909, Elbert Benjamine (better known under his pen name, C. C. Zain) became head of the Brotherhood of Light and started a process of transformation that led to the birth of the Church of Light. *SEE* CHURCH OF LIGHT; ZAIN, C.C. *SEE ALSO* BURGOYNE, THOMAS HENRY; THEON, MAX. FURTHER READING: GODWIN ET AL. 1995.

Hermetic Order of the Golden Dawn. *SEE* GOLDEN DAWN, HERMETIC ORDER OF THE.

Hermeticism. One of the core elements in the Western occult tradition, Hermeticism had its roots in the fusion of Greek philosophy and Egyptian magic that took place in Egypt after its conquest by Alexander the Great in 332 B.C.E. While Egyptians were slow to accept the ways of their Greek conquerors, the Greeks themselves readily took up the worship of Egyptian gods, and the political advantages of fluency and literacy in Greek were not lost on the Egyptian priesthood.

Thus, over time, a bilingual and bicultural society emerged along the banks of the Nile in which millennia-old Egyptian magic and spirituality could be reformulated in the terms of Greek thought. The career of Chaeremon, an Egyptian priest of the first century C.E. who was also a Stoic philosopher of international fame, shows how far this process extended; *SEE* CHAEREMON.

At some point within a century or so of the beginning of the Common Era, this context began to respond to the same spiritual impulse that drove the rise of Neoplatonism, Gnosticism, Manichaeism, and Christianity—a sense of entrapment in the world of ordinary experience, and a longing for a way of escape. The causes of this trend are complex and still much debated. The results were equally complex and varied widely, depending on the resources available to philosophers and mystics in different parts of the ancient world. In the Nile valley, the central resources were those of ancient Egyptian spirituality, and the result was Hermeticism.

Very little trace has survived of the original Hermetic schools and teachings. From clues in the remaining writings, scholars have guessed that the Hermetic tradition was developed and transmitted in small, informal circles of students gathered around charismatic teachers. Mystical philosophy, ceremonial magic, astrology, and alchemy were all part of the course of study, and all these were intended to lead to an experience of rebirth in which the individual soul realized its connection with the supreme, nameless divine power of the universe. Just as ancient Egyptian books of magic were all credited to Thoth, rather than to their human authors, the books produced by these circles were attributed to Hermes Trismegistus, the Greek equivalent of Thoth. SEE HERMES TRISMEGISTUS.

The massive cultural charisma of Egypt in the ancient world gave these books, and the Hermetic tradition itself, a reputation for deep wisdom that made them attractive to students of many other spiritual traditions. Among Platonists and Neoplatonists, though there were always those who rejected overtly magical traditions such as Hermeticism, there were equally those who embraced them as a useful resource. This latter approach became increasingly common with the rise of Christianity, as Pagan traditions that had formerly spent much time quarreling with one another sought common ground in the face of a common threat. At the hands of Iamblichus of Chalcis, who sought to create a unified Pagan spirituality as a bulwark against the Christian tide, Hermetic magic became a key element in this system. SEE IAMBLICHUS OF CHALCIS.

The Christians themselves were not immune to the aura of wisdom that surrounded "Egyptian Mysteries," and a number of church fathers did their best to co-opt Hermetic writings in support of Christianity, going to the extent of forging "oracles of Hermes" that predicted the coming of Jesus. This had an unexpected effect; because Hermes Trismegistus ended up wearing the ill-fitting label of a prophet of Christ, Hermetic documents that might otherwise have been consigned to the flames

were preserved and copied through the Middle Ages. A good deal of Hermeticism thus survived in Christian garb, giving rise to Christian occult traditions; SEE CHRISTIAN OCCULTISM.

The Arab invasions of the eighth century replaced one dogmatic religion with another in Egypt and through much of the Mediterranean world. The Muslim conquerors absorbed many of the cultural traditions of the peoples they overran, however, and a large body of Hermetic practice was taken over both by mystically minded Muslims and by Arab magicians. The Quran, the holy book of Islam, also provided a loophole for Hermeticists by including "Sabians" among the Peoples of the Book, who were to be permitted to follow their own religions unmolested by good Muslims; exactly what the term "Sabians" meant has been a subject of centuries of argument, but in the centuries after the Muslim conquests it was widely interpreted to mean Hermeticists. The Pagan town of Harran took advantage of this to preserve their own religious traditions, which were heavily mixed with Hermeticism and Neoplatonism; SEE HARRAN.

Hermetic traditions of spiritual and practical magic thus became part of the broad current of Arabic magic that flowed into Europe beginning in the twelfth century C.E. The more theoretical side of Hermeticism was also preserved in a handful of books. During the Middle Ages, the most important of these was the *Asclepius*, which survived in a Latin translation in the West. Further east, in the Byzantine Empire, a collection of Hermetic texts later known as the *Corpus Hermeticum* was preserved, although it seems to have had little circulation; SEE CORPUS HERMETICUM.

Several astrological books under Hermes' name were also available early on, and Arabic magical handbooks such as the *Picatrix* also contained a certain amount of Hermetic philosophy; SEE PICATRIX. There were also purely magical texts to be had with Hermes' name on them, such as *Liber Hermetis de quindecim stellis* (*Book of Hermes on the fifteen stars*), a handbook of talismanic magic that was widely copied throughout the Middle Ages and Renaissance. Despite the occasional suspicions of the church, a steady undercurrent of interest in Hermes and his teachings continued in educated circles throughout the medieval period. Important Platonists such as Bernardus Sylvestris (fl. twelfth century) used it as a resource, though they rarely cited it by name. *SEE* PLATONISM.

The recovery of the *Corpus Hermeticum* by the West, by way of a single Greek manuscript obtained by Cosimo de Medici of Florence around 1460 and translated into Latin by Marsilio Ficino in 1463, transformed this undercurrent into a flood. Ficino himself, his pupil Giovanni Pico della Mirandola, and a constellation of later scholars and magicians used the Hermetic writings as the foundation for an ambitious attempt to create a new Christian occultism, drawing on magical techniques and directed toward spiritual and practical ends alike. *SEE* FICINO, MARSILIO; PICO DELLA MIRANDOLA, GIOVANNI. This program probably reached its zenith in 1591, when the Croatian Hermeticist Francesco Patrizi (1529–1597) formally proposed that the philosophy of Aristotle and Thomas Aquinas should be replaced by that of Hermes as the intellectual foundation of Catholic theology. The proposal was rejected, but only after serious consideration, and the fact that it was made at all shows the degree to which Hermetic thought had permeated the intellectual life of the Renaissance. *SEE* PATRIZI, FRANCESCO.

Not long after Patrizi's proposal, however, Hermeticism suffered a major blow when Isaac Casaubon demonstrated on linguistic grounds that the treatises of the *Corpus Hermeticum* dated not from the time of Moses, but from the early centuries of the Common Era. Casaubon's work, published in 1614, marks the effective end of Renaissance Hermeticism. Afterwards, though committed Hermeticists and occultists continued to study the Hermetic writings, European culture in general threw them aside as discredited forgeries.

Until very recently, although the label "Hermetic" was much used by a variety of magical societies, the actual teachings of classical Hermeticism received little attention. The nineteenth-century occult revival saw the reprinting of the *Corpus Hermeticum* and other ancient Hermetic documents, but for the most part the Hermetic teachings were reinterpreted through the filters of Theosophy and similar occult philosophies.

That began to change in the 1960s, as a new generation of occultists encountered the scholarly writings of Dame Frances Yates, who almost singlehandedly reintroduced the Hermetic tradition into the world of modern scholarship. Yates' writings argued that Hermeticism had a massive influence on all levels of Renaissance culture, and sparked a great deal of debate and further research in academic circles. At the same time, and without those circles' knowledge, these same books became required reading for educated magicians all over the Western world, and catalyzed a variety of efforts to explore older levels of magical tradition and reclaim Western occultism's own historical roots. FURTHER READING: FOWDEN 1986, MEAD 1992, YATES 1964.

Hermit, the. The ninth Major Arcanum of the tarot, usually showing the image of an old man in a hooded robe, bearing a staff and a lantern. The Hermit corresponds to the Hebrew letter Yod in the Golden Dawn system, and to the letter Teth in the French system. In divination, its common meanings include wisdom, prudence, secret knowledge, loneliness, and initiation.

Its magical title is "Magus of the Voice of Light, the Prophet of the Gods." *SEE* TAROT; YOD.

Tarot trump the Hermit (Universal Tarot)

Herne the Hunter. In English folklore, one version of the Wild Huntsman, sometimes portrayed with horns or antlers, and accompanied by a pack of spectral hounds. He is mentioned in Shakespeare's *Merry Wives of Windsor* and a range of other literary and folklore sources. Many modern Pagan writers have equated Herne with the Horned God of the hypothetical "Old Religion" that is believed to lie behind Wicca. *SEE* GOD, THE.

Herodias. Jewish queen, c. 14 B.C.E.–after 40 C.E. Herodias was a granddaughter of Herod the Great, king of Judea, and married two of her uncles in succession. She and her second husband, Herod Antipas, tetrarch of Galilee from 4 C.E. to 40 C.E., were denounced by John the Baptist on account of their marriage, which violated traditional Jewish law. According to the account in the Christian scriptures (Matthew 14:3–12), she was instrumental in having John put to death.

Her standing as the archvillainess of Christian legend may have led to her bizarre afterlife as a Pagan goddess in medieval France and Italy. According to a number of medieval sources, Pagan or quasi-Pagan cults in these countries worshipped a goddess named Herodias. It is quite possible that Aradia, the goddess allegedly worshipped by the witches documented by Charles Godfrey Leland, is derived from the same name. *SEE* ARADIA; CANON EPIS-COPI; LELAND, CHARLES GODFREY.

hexagram. One of the major symbols in Western magical practice, the hexagram is commonly used as a symbol of the sun, or of the seven traditional planets. Like the pentagram, with which it is often paired, it has a long and complex history; under the label of "Star of David" it has become the most widely recognized symbol of Judaism and appears on the flag of Israel.

In the Golden Dawn tradition and related magical systems, the points of the hexagram are assigned to the seven planets as follows:

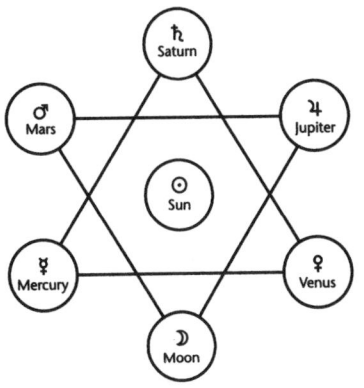

The assignment of planets to the points of the hexagram

This attribution is used when invoking and banishing planetary forces; a hexagram traced clockwise, beginning from any one point, invokes the planet assigned to that point, while one traced counterclockwise banishes the same planet. *SEE ALSO* HEXAGRAM, RITUALS OF THE; PENTAGRAM.

Hexagram, Rituals of the. A set of basic Golden Dawn magical rituals using hexagrams to invoke and banish planetary energies, similar to and probably modeled on the more commonly used Rituals of the Pentagram. In the standard Golden Dawn form, the magician begins by performing a complicated little rite called the Analysis of INRI, which combines words, gestures, and visualizations to invoke a pattern of forces associated with the Egyptian deities Isis, Apophis, and Osiris.

When this is completed, the magician goes to the eastern quarter of the working space and traces a hexagram in the air, visualizing it as it is traced. He or she then draws a line around the working space, about shoulder height, a quarter circle to the south. Another hexagram goes in the south, and then the next quarter circle is drawn to the west. The process is repeated twice more, until the magician is standing in the midst of a visualized circle with hexagrams at the four quarters. The magician then returns to the center of the circle and repeats the Analysis of INRI a second time, completing the ritual.

As with pentagrams in the pentagram rituals, the hexagrams used in the hexagram rituals can be drawn in a wide variety of ways, and each of these invokes or banishes a given planetary force. There are also four variations on the basic form of the hexagram, which are used in some forms of the hexagram ritual; these are assigned to the four elements, and allow the elemental and planetary forces to be brought into play together.

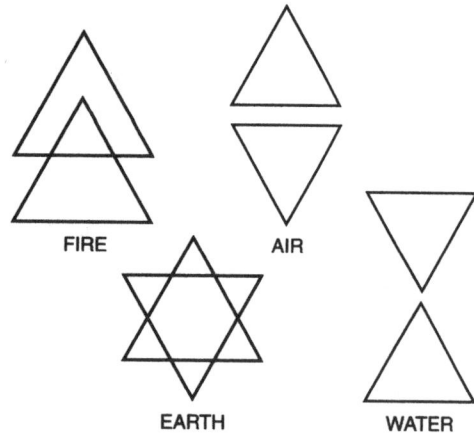

The four forms of the hexagram

As with the pentagram rituals, finally, there are a wide range of variations in the basic hexagram ritual, and new variants have been proposed by a number of recent writers. *SEE ALSO* PENTAGRAM, RITUALS OF THE. FURTHER READING: GREER 1997, REGARDIE 1971.

Hiddekel. (Hebrew HDQL) According to Genesis 2:14, the third of the four rivers that flow out of Paradise, identified with the actual river Tigris. In the Golden Dawn tradition, the river Hiddekel is associated with the element of air and the section of the Middle Pillar from Daath to Yesod. In earlier Rosicrucian tradition, the word *Hiddekel* was the symbol of the Adeptus Exemptus grade. *SEE* CABALA.

hieroglyphic monad. *SEE* MONAS HIEROGLYPHICA.

hieromancy. *SEE* SACRIFICE.

Hierophant, the. The fifth Major Arcanum of the tarot, appearing in some tarot decks as the Pope or Jupiter. The image on this card varies based on the title and the preferences of the designer, but a pope in his official garments, with the triple cross of the papacy in one hand and two kneeling monks at his feet, is the oldest and among the most common images. In the Golden Dawn tradition, this Arcanum corresponds to the Hebrew letter Vau, while in the French system it corresponds to Heh. Its common meanings include wisdom, spirituality, and authority.

Its magical title is "Magus of the Eternal Gods." *SEE ALSO* TAROT.

Tarot trump the Hierophant (Universal Tarot)

High John the Conqueror root. An important ingredient in traditional hoodoo, High John the Conqueror (the last word is always pronounced "conker") is also something of a historical mystery, as old accounts identify many different species of plants as High John. Cranesbill (*Geranium maculatum*), American ginseng (*Panax quinquefolium*), Jack-in-the-pulpit (*Arisaema triphyllum*), St. John's wort (*Hypericum perfoliatum*), Solomon's seal (*Polygonatum odoratum*), and wild morning glory (*Ipomoea macrorrhiza* or *I. violaceae*) are among the plants that have been identified as the elusive High John.

High John himself is at least as much of a mystery as the root bearing his name. Some accounts claim that he was an African king captured by slave traders, who used his strength, cunning, and mastery of hoodoo to outwit his white owner. Anthropologists suggest that he may be an African god or spirit under a new name.

There are also other roots associated with John, High or otherwise. "Chewing John" or "Little John to Chew" is usually galangal root (*Alpinia galanga*), and Southern John is usually beth root (*Trillium* sp.). One source from the 1940s refers to "Johnson's Conqueror Root"; what this might have been is unknown.

Present day High John roots are nearly always jalap (*Ipomoea jalapa*), a member of the bindweed family, closely related to the sweet potato. A vine native to Mexico and South America, jalap has heart-shaped leaves and red or purple cone-shaped flowers. Its root, a brown, wrinkled tuber ranging from the size of a walnut to that of an orange, is the part generally used in magic. Attributed to the sun, like most solar herbs it has protective powers against hostile magic, and can also be used in workings for love, for luck, and for all forms of success. *SEE ALSO* HOODOO. FURTHER READING: GREER 2000, HASKINS 1990, LONG 2001, MALBROUGH 1986.

High Priest. In Wicca, the title of a male initiate of the third degree; also the title of the male partner of the High Priestess of a coven. *SEE* HIGH PRIESTESS; WICCA.

High Priestess. In Wicca, and many other modern Pagan systems, the title of a female initiate of the third degree. This status brings with it the right to start and run a coven. Some Pagan traditions that lack a defined degree structure have borrowed this term as a simple title for the leader of a coven. *SEE* NEOPAGANISM; WICCA.

High Priestess, the. The second Major Arcanum of the tarot, called the Popess or Juno in many decks. The illustration on the card generally follows the title, showing either a seated High Priestess in front of a veil, a woman in pope's garments, or the goddess Juno on a throne. In the Golden Dawn tradition, it corresponds to the Hebrew letter Gimel, while the French system assigns it to Beth. Its common meanings include wisdom, revelation, intuition, and the ebb and flow of cyclical phenomena.

The magical title of this Arcanum is "Priestess of the Silver Star." *SEE ALSO* TAROT.

Tarot trump the High Priestess (Universal Tarot)

Hilarion, Master. In Theosophy and related systems of occult teaching, one of the Masters of the Great White Lodge, the secret brotherhood that oversees the spiritual evolution of the Earth. The Master Hilarion is the chohan or chief adept of the Fifth or Orange Ray, the ray of science and practical intellect. He is said to have been the great Greek Platonist Iamblichus of Chalcis in a former incarnation; *SEE* IAMBLICHUS OF CHALCIS; GREAT WHITE LODGE; MASTERS; THEOSOPHY. FURTHER READING: LEADBEATER 1925.

Hismael. In ceremonial magic, the planetary spirit of Jupiter. Its governing intelligence is Yophiel.

Hitler, Adolf. Austrian politician and occultist, 1889–1945. The occult involvements of the twentieth century's most destructive figure are still a matter of debate, and a good deal of misinformation, distortion, and sheer fantasy have been heaped over his biography during the half-century or so since his suicide. Documentary evidence is hard to come by, for the simple reason that Hitler was of no interest to anybody until he began his meteoric rise to power in 1920; after that time, his public appearance was carefully groomed to match the image that he and his associates wished to project. Nonetheless, some details are clear.

Hitler was born to a middle-class family in the Austrian town of Branau am Inn, and moved with his family to Linz during early childhood. A moody and difficult child, he showed impressive intellectual and artistic gifts but was uninterested in schoolwork, preferring to read voraciously on his own. According to his boyhood friend August Kubizek, Hitler as a teen was deeply influenced by the philosophy of Arthur Schopenhauer (1778–1856), the one significant nineteenth-century philosopher who accepted the effectiveness of magic. He left secondary school in 1905, and in 1907 left Linz for Vienna, where he hoped to enroll in the Vienna Academy of Art.

Hitler failed the entrance exams for the Academy, however, and spent the next six years in Vienna, eking out a living by painting postcards and doing odd jobs, and living in a series of cheap rented rooms. It was during these years, by his own account, that he became an anti-Semite. According to a friend of his Vienna days, books on occultism, astrology, hypnotism, and oriental religions made up a large part of Hitler's reading during that time. His reading also included *Ostara*, the racist magazine edited by the Ariosophical mystic Jörg Lanz von Liebenfels, and he once paid a visit to Lanz's offices in order to complete his collection of *Ostara* back issues. SEE ARIOSOPHY; LANZ VON LIEBENFELS, JÖRG.

He also began to develop his own approach to politics, one that combined anti-Semitism, nationalism, Schopenhauer's philosophy, and Aryan racism with ideas drawn from Ariosophical occult literature. In 1913 he emigrated to Germany, which he had come to see as the hope of the Aryan peoples. On the outbreak of the First World War in 1914, he enlisted in the German army and served with distinction on the Western Front, earning an Iron Cross for bravery under fire.

After Germany's defeat, while working for German Army intelligence in Munich, he visited a meeting of the newly founded Deutsche Arbeiterspartei or DAP (German Workers Party) and was invited to join. The party was an offshoot of the Thule-Gesellschaft, a partly political, partly occult organization linked with an Ariosophical magical order, the Germanenorden. SEE GERMA-NENORDEN (ORDER OF GERMANS); THULE-GESELLSCHAFT (THULE SOCIETY). While Hitler was not impressed with the party or its program, he saw its potential as a vehicle for his political and racial ideas. As a member of the DAP, he displayed an astonishing gift for oratory, and soon attracted large crowds to DAP rallies. His speaking style has been described as hypnotic and overwhelming by those whom it impressed, and as "verbal diarrhea" by those whom it did not.

As a result of his involvement in the DAP—later renamed the Nationalsozialistische Deutsche Arbeiterpartei (National Socialist German Workers Party) or NSDAP—Hitler also came to the attention of influential people in the Thule-Gesellschaft and the wider realm of Bavarian right-wing politics. Chief among these was Dietrich Eckart, whom Hitler later described as "the spiritual founder of the Nazi party" (Hitler 1974, p. 633). While Eckart was not a member of the Thule-Gesellschaft, he was deeply involved in Ariosophical and occult circles and knew most of the leading Thule members. Eckart

lent Hitler books, helped him polish his speaking style, and introduced him to the wealthy and powerful. It has been alleged that he also instructed Hitler in occultism, and while there is no conclusive evidence one way or another, Eckart was certainly qualified to do so.

The remainder of Hitler's career offers few clues to the occult researcher, if only because very little unedited material about his activities and ideas leaked out through the cracks of the Nazi propaganda machine, and even less survived the collapse of the Thousand-Year Reich. The reports of several people who knew Hitler in the early 1930s make it clear, though, that his occult interests were not simply a feature of his early years. The memoirs of Otto Wagener, chief of staff of the SA (Storm Troopers) in the early 1930s, include several conversations with Hitler about occult topics such as Odic force (H. Turner 1985, pp. 35–38, 103–104, 241–242). Hermann Rauschning, a former Nazi who broke with the Third Reich before the war and published several books denouncing Hitler, described similar conversations, and some disquieting stories. He reports:

> My informant described to me in full details a remarkable scene—I should not credit the story if it had not come from such a source [a friend of Rauschning's in Hitler's household]. Hitler stood swaying in his room looking wildly about him. "He! He! He's been here!" he gasped. His lips were blue. Sweat streamed down his face. Suddenly he began to reel off figures, and odd words and broken phrases, entirley devoid of sense. It sounded horrible. He used strangely composed and entirely un-German word-formations . . . then he gradually grew calm. After that he lay asleep for many hours. (Rauschning 1939, pp. 250–251.)

Rauschning's source reported that Hitler had such attacks frequently. From an occult standpoint, it sounds a good deal like demonic possession or obsession. This same conclusion was reached as early as 1939, when the French Martinist René Kopp wrote in an occult magazine that "[Hitler's] solitary nature and a special mysticism, together with other indicators, suggest the possibility of possession by a spirit of unknown origin" (quoted in Hakl 2000, p. 23).

Hitler remained at the peak of his considerable powers—intellectual, oratorical, and quite possibly occult as well—through the early part of the Second World War. After 1940, however, his formerly keen sense of timing and judgment failed him more and more often, and he committed Germany to a war on two fronts it could not possibly win. An assassination attempt by his own generals in 1944 left him permanently disabled, although he saw to the execution of hundreds of people involved in the plot. He committed suicide in his bunker in Berlin in 1945, a few days before the Russian army took control of the city.

Since the beginning of Hitler's rise to power, there has been quite a substantial industry of books devoted to his occult connections. Unfortunately most of these are examples of the worst sort of occult history, full of the usual collection of untraceable sources, allegations repeated by book after book with no effort to check their validity, and the like. Claims that Hitler's career was shaped by the quest for the spear that pierced the side of Jesus of Nazareth, that he was a puppet in the hands of mysterious and evil Tibetan adepts, or that he was an emissary of secret powers from within the Hollow Earth fall into this category and should be discarded unless actual evidence supporting these claims should surface. *SEE* OCCULT HISTORY.

The same sort of thinking applied in a different direction has given rise to books in which Hitler is presented as a holy avatar of Aryan humanity whose sacrificial death was necessary to bring on the end of the Kali Yuga. The writings of Savitri Devi and Miguel Serrano are among the most widely known example of this repellent literature. *SEE* DEVI, SAVITRI. In all of this farrago, whether pro–Hitler or anti-Hitler, the actual career of an extraordinary if corrupt and destructive man and magus has been effectively obscured. *SEE ALSO* NATIONAL SOCIALISM. FURTHER READING: GOODRICK-CLARKE 1992, HAKL 2000, HITLER 1974, RAUSCHNING 1939, TURNER 1985.

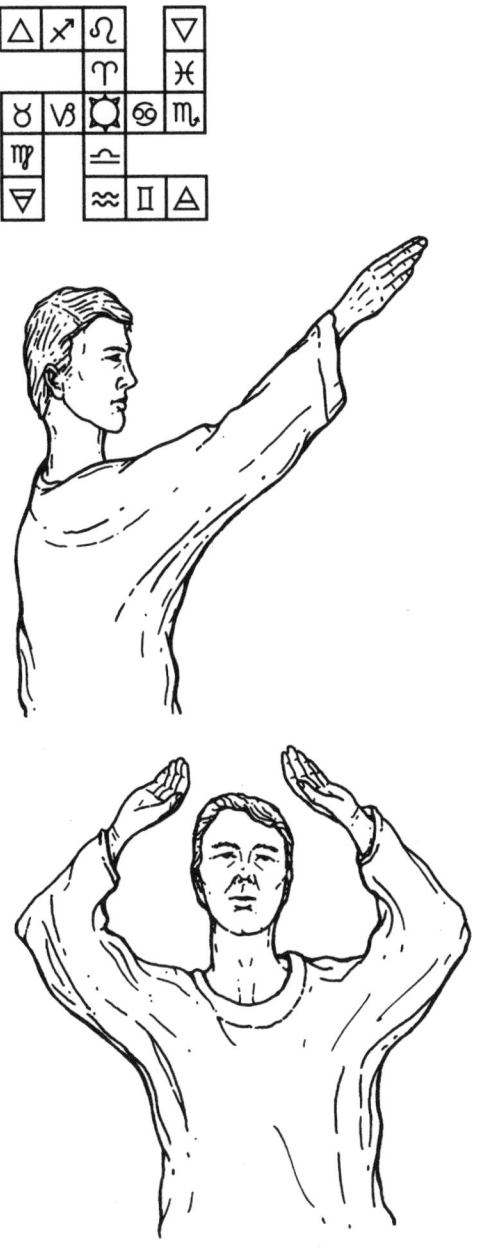

These symbols of the Golden Dawn tradition—the swastika/Fylfot cross, top, the Sign of Zelator, middle, and the Sign of Theoricus, below—may have been stolen and exploited by Hitler for magical reasons

Hockley, Frederick. English accountant and occultist, 1808–1885. Nothing is known about Hockley's origins or family, but he seems to have had the ordinary education of a middle-class Englishman of his time. In the early days of his business career, he apparently worked for a time for John Denley, the famous Covent Garden occult bookseller. His interest in the occult went back further, however; according to his own account, he began experimenting with scrying in crystals and magic mirrors at the age of sixteen.

In the 1840s he first began to publish accounts of his crystal visions in the occult press of the time. He became a noted figure in Spiritualist circles in the 1850s, famous for his immense library and his very wide knowledge of occult traditions. Most of his own work, however, remained (and remains) unpublished. His records of conversations with spirits in the crystal eventually filled some thirty manuscript volumes, but these were only shown to close friends.

Like most magicians working with crystal scrying, Hockley generally used a scryer, who entered into trance and saw visions in the crystal, while he conjured spirits and wrote down the results. His most successful scryer was Emma Louisa Leigh, the daughter of a friend, whose talents brought him into contact with an entity calling itself the Crowned Angel of the Seventh Sphere. By way of Ms. Leigh, the Crowned Angel dictated an extensive book on occultism, *Metaphysical and Spiritual Philosophy: Or the Connection with and Influence Over Material Bodies by Spirits*, which was received in the mid-1850s.

Though Hockley was in contact with many of the important occultists of his time, he seems to have had little interest in the host of occult orders and magical lodges active in England and elsewhere during his time. He was an active Freemason, and for a while belonged to the Societas Rosicruciana in Anglia (SRIA), a Masonic body with some occult involvements, but took little part in the latter's activities. He was allegedly a member of the Fratres Lucis, an order founded by Hockley's friend Francis Irwin, but (like almost everything else about the Fratres Lucis) it has been impossible to determine this for certain. *SEE* FRATRES LUCIS.

He died peacefully after a few years of ill health in 1885, and his library (of over 1,000 occult books) and his manuscripts were sold off. Most of the latter have never been traced. *SEE ALSO* SCRYING. FURTHER READING: J. GODWIN 1994, HAMILL 1986.

hocus pocus. This apparent nonsense word was originally the Latin phrase *hoc est corpus meus*, "this is my body"; it is part of the most solemn portion of the Catholic Mass, in which the officiating priest repeats the words of Jesus at the Last Supper to consecrate the communion bread, transforming it (according to Catholic belief) into the flesh of God. In the aftermath of the Reformation, Protestant writers attacked many Catholic beliefs as magical, and the words of consecration were garbled and converted into a term for "magical mumbo-jumbo." *SEE ALSO* BELL, BOOK, AND CANDLE.

Hod. (Hebrew HVD, "splendor") The eighth Sephirah of the Cabalistic Tree of Life, located at the base of the Pillar of Form or Severity. Its standard magical symbolism is as follows:

Name of God: ALHIM TzBAVTh, Elohim Tzabaoth (Gods of Armies).

Archangel: RPhAL, Raphael (Healing of God).

Angelic Host: BNI ALHIM, Beni Elohim (Sons of Elohim).

Astrological Correspondence: KVKB, Kokab (Mercury).

Tarot Correspondence: The four Eights of the pack.

Elemental Correspondence: Water.

Magical Image: A hermaphrodite.

Additional Symbol: The caduceus.

Colors: in Atziluth—violet purple.
> in Briah—orange.
> in Yetzirah—reddish russet.
> in Assiah—yellowish brown flecked with white.

Correspondence in the Microcosm: The intellect in Ruach.

Correspondence in the Body: The left hip.

Grade of Initiation: 3=8, Practicus.

Negative Power: SMAL, Samael (the Liars).

The corresponding text from the *Thirty-two Paths of Wisdom* reads as follows: "The Eighth Path is called the Absolute or Perfect Intelligence, because it is the mean of the Primordial; it has no root by which it can cleave or rest except the hidden places of Gedulah, which emanate from its own proper essence." *SEE ALSO* CABALA; TREE OF LIFE.

Hodos Chamelionis. (mixed Greek and Latin, "path of the chameleon") In Golden Dawn writings, the many-colored realms of the astral plane, associated with the bow or rainbow Qesheth, as well as with the color scales of Golden Dawn magical theory. *SEE* COLOR SCALES; QESHETH.

hof. (Old Norse, "hall") In modern Nordic Neopaganism, a common term for a temple or sacred space in which the ancient Germanic gods and goddesses are invoked. *SEE* ASATRU.

Holly King. In some modern Wiccan and Pagan traditions, the god of the dark half of the year, who fights the Oak King (the lord of the bright half of the year) in an eternal struggle for the favor of the Goddess. The concept of the Oak and Holly Kings is derived from the writings of English poet Robert Graves, whose *The White Goddess* (1948) is the source of much of modern Pagan imagery and tradition. *SEE ALSO* GOD, THE; OAK KING.

Holy Guardian Angel. In modern magical parlance, either a synonym for the higher self or a separate, angelic entity assigned to the self as a guardian and guide. The term entered common usage by way of *The Sacred Magic of Abramelin the Mage*, a grimoire which instructs the student to spend six months invoking his Holy Guardian Angel before attempting to summon and command demons; *SEE* ABRAMELIN THE MAGE, THE SACRED MAGIC OF. This text was discovered, translated, and published in 1898 by Samuel "MacGregor" Mathers (1854–1918) of Golden Dawn fame, and has been a popular sourcebook for ceremonial magicians ever since. It does not, however, define the nature of the entity the magician is told to invoke.

Some students of the text, borrowing the common Christian and Jewish notion of the guardian angel, have assumed that the Holy Guardian Angel is an angel in the precise sense of the word—that is, a conscious spiritual being, separate from the person who invokes it, and possessed of superior power, wisdom, and other angelic characteristics. *SEE* ANGEL. Others, borrowing the Golden Dawn concept of the Higher and Divine Genius, have assumed that the Holy Guardian Angel is another term for this entity—that is, a level of the self that is in complete contact with the divine, and can be contacted by the lower self through spiritual and magical practice.

The resulting confusion has led to a good deal of scrambled communication in magical circles. It may be worth noting that the Abramelin operation seems to work equally well when approached with either of these two concepts of the entity one is attempting to contact. *SEE ALSO* INVOCATION. FURTHER READING: MATHERS 1974.

holy orders. In Christian tradition, the ceremonies by which the spiritual power of the apostles of Christ is conferred on a Christian who is called to the clerical life; also the various stations or positions attained through these ceremonies. There are traditionally seven holy orders, four minor and three major. The minor orders are doorkeeper, lector, exorcist, and acolyte; the major orders are deacon, priest, and bishop. All were reserved for men until recent years, but a number of churches—some mainstream bodies, and others the creation of independent bishops—now confer some or all of the holy orders on women as well. *SEE* INDEPENDENT BISHOPS.

The seven holy orders parallel the grades of initiation in magical lodges, and a case could be made for holy orders transmitted by a bishop with valid apostolic succession as the logical framework for initiation in Christian occultism. Certainly they have been used in much this way among certain lines of independent bishops. *SEE* CHRISTIAN OCCULTISM.

homeopathy. One of the major systems of alternative medicine in the modern world, homeopathy has been heavily influenced by occult traditions at several points in its history. It was originally founded by Samuel Hahnemann (1755–1843), a German physician who discovered that substances which caused disease symptoms in large doses would cure diseases with similar symptoms when given in minute doses. From this experience, many times repeated, he formed the basic principle of homeopathy, *simila similibus curantur* ("like is cured by like").

Hahnemann claimed to have discovered homeopathy entirely out of his own researches, but footnotes in his major work, *Organon of the Rational System of Medicine*, show that he was deeply familiar with the writings of Paracelsian alchemists and healers, and the basic principles of homeopathy appear in these sources, as well as in the writings of Paracelsus himself. *SEE* PARACELSUS.

Homeopathic medicines are made by mixing one part of the basic substance with either nine or ninety-nine parts of an inert material (usually lactose), shaking or grinding these together for a period, and repeating the entire process several times—each time mixing one part of the mixture with nine or ninety-nine more parts of lactose. The different dilutions are referred to as "potencies," because the more dilute the original substance becomes, the stronger and longer-lasting its effects on the body become. This happens even though potencies above 12C (that is, the result of twelve successive 99-to-1 dilutions with lactose) literally may not contain a single molecule of the original substance. This effect has been repeatedly verified by controlled, double-blinded experiments, even though it violates some of the most basic scientific theories about the nature of matter.

After Hahnemann's time, homeopathy became one of several competing systems of medicine in the Western world, and succeeded in establishing a strong following in Europe and America before political pressure from orthodox medicine drove it underground in the early twentieth century. During its American heyday, which spanned the period from 1870 to 1910, homeopathy became closely associated with the Swedenborgian Church, and for some years most of the principal homeopathic physicians and teachers in the United States were Swedenborgians. This had a significant influence on homeopathic theory, especially in the hands of James Tyler Kent, whose deeply occult version of homeopathy became the most common approach by the beginning of the twentieth century and retains that status today. *SEE* KENT, JAMES TYLER; SWEDENBORG, EMMANUEL.

During the mid-twentieth century, when all alternative forms of health care were suppressed in most Western countries by political pressure from mainstream physicians and heavy legal penalties, homeopaths carried on a half-underground existence. Some amount of interaction with other underground traditions seems to have taken place during this time; the British magus W. E. Butler mentioned that some magical groups in his knowledge gave homeopathic doses of hallucinogenic drugs to initiates, as a way of developing inner powers. Some French alchemical schools also make use of the biochemic cell salts, which are related to homeopathy; *SEE* CELL SALTS.

With the weakening of orthodox dominance over medicine and the rise of alternative health care in recent years, homeopathy has again become common through much of the Western world, but its occult connections seem to be largely unrecognized in the magical community. FURTHER READING: BOYD 1981, W. BUTLER 1990, WOOD 2000.

homunculus. (Latin, "little human") In alchemy, a miniature but living human being created artificially by alchemical means. Recipes for creating a homunculus usually involved placing semen, alone or with other substances, in an alchemical vessel which was kept at very mild heat for forty days. At the end of this time a small, half-transparent human shape could be observed. The alchemist was then instructed to feed it each day with the Arcanum (an alchemical preparation) of human blood, keeping it at the same low heat, for forty weeks. At the end of this time it would have matured into a miniature human child, which could then be taken out of the vessel and raised like any other child.

The traditions concerning the homunculus are probably related to those of the golem, the artificial human whose construction is discussed in Jewish folklore and Cabalistic magical texts. *SEE* GOLEM. *SEE ALSO* ALCHEMY. FURTHER READING: EBERLY 1997.

Honorius of Thebes. The supposed author of the *Sworn Book of Honorius*, one of the most important medieval grimoires. *SEE* GRIMOIRE; SWORN BOOK OF HONORIUS.

hoodoo. The traditional folk magic of African-American culture, also known as conjure magic and rootwork. (The origin of the word "hoodoo" itself is uncertain, although it may derive from a West African source.) Hoodoo is to occultism what the blues are to music: rooted in African culture, transformed and reshaped through the long ordeal of slavery and segregation, drawing freely on a wide range of cultural influences but with a distinctive flavor of its own.

Hoodoo practices can be traced nearly as far back as the African presence in North America itself. Court records and other sources from the American colonies show that many of the basic practices of nineteenth- and twentieth-century hoodoo were already in existence well before the American Revolution. By around 1760, despite the brutal realities of slavery, Africans and African-Americans in the colonies had begun to adapt the magical heritage of their homeland to the New World, borrowing elements of folk Christianity, European magic, and Native American tradition in the process. The result was hoodoo.

Like most traditions of folk magic, hoodoo directs its workings primarily toward success in everyday life. Spells for drawing money, winning at gambling, attracting a mate or keeping one from straying, avoiding legal trouble, or winning court cases play a substantial role in the hoodoo repertoire. Methods for cursing or "crossing" another person are also an important part of the tradition, and there is a correspondingly rich lore of spells for "uncrossing" or countering curses, either by preventing hostile magic from being used in the first place by nullifying spells that have already been set in motion, or by "turning the trick" (that is, sending the spell back on its originator).

Much of hoodoo technique belongs to the broad realm of natural magic, relying on the magical powers of natural substances to accomplish the purposes of the magician. *SEE* NATURAL MAGIC. Powders, incenses, oils, floor washes, and many other preparations are used in hoodoo; among the most typical forms of hoodoo magic are "hands," also called "tobies" and "mojos," which are bags of flannel containing magically effective substances. Goofer dust, graveyard dust, High John the Conqueror (*Ipomoea jalapa*) root, Van Van oil, and lodestones are among the most typical ingredients in hoodoo preparations, but many other substances have a role as well. *SEE* GOOFER DUST; GRAVEYARD DUST; HIGH JOHN THE CONQUEROR ROOT; MAGNETITE; VAN VAN OIL.

During the late nineteenth and early twentieth centuries, hoodoo was a constant presence in most American communities with a sizeable African-American population. Practitioners—hoodoo doctors, as they were often called—carried on their trade in much the same way as magicians, witches, and shamans of other cultures, working out of their homes, consulting with clients and preparing charms as needed. The commercializing thrust of American culture, though, brought hoodoo into its orbit, and by the first decades of the twentieth century hoodoo preparations could be bought over the counter in ready-to-use form. The Cracker Jack Drugstore on Rampart Street in New Orleans was perhaps the most famous of America's hoodoo stores, but there were such stores in nearly every American city with a large African-American population by 1920, and many of them were still operating in the 1970s; some are still in existence today.

Despite legal troubles due to laws that classed magic as fraud by definition, the commercial hoodoo industry grew to respectable size, with dozens of manufacturers and several hundred stores selling "spiritual products" during the industry's heyday in the mid-twentieth century. The products offered in the hoodoo trade went considerably beyond the traditional repertoire, with High John the Conqueror air freshener among the new offerings, but the magical quality of these products often left much to be desired. Traditional ingredients have routinely been replaced by others; chicken bones are sold as black cat bones, for example, and herbs are quite commonly replaced on a "green for green and brown for brown" basis—that is, any herb may be replaced by another of the same approximate color. Very often, currently available commercial hoodoo products contain no trace of the magically effective ingredients so colorfully portrayed on their labels.

While hoodoo has always been rooted in the African-American community, there's also a long history of white participation, as clients and practitioners alike. During the twentieth century, increased urbanization and literacy among African-Americans have brought hoodoo practitioners into contact with other American occult traditions, and standard elements of Western high magic such as planetary days and hours have become widespread in hoodoo. Hoodoo stores in the mid-twentieth century routinely carried works on Cabalistic magic, yoga, and

Christian mysticism along with standard hoodoo texts. At the same time, access to religious traditions from West Africa, and from Carribean and Latin American cultures with African roots, has drawn hoodoo back toward its origins and enriched it substantially. It remains one of the most vital currents of American magic at present. FURTHER READING: J. BUTLER 1983, HASKINS 1978, LONG 2001, MALBROUGH 1986, PIERSEN 1995, YRONWODE 2002.

horary astrology. The art of astrological divination in which a chart is cast for the moment at which a specific question is asked, and interpreted as an answer to the question. Horary astrology was once among the most popular branches of astrology, and formed the bread and butter of astrological practice before the Scientific Revolution. It fell out of popularity with the rise of psychological approaches to astrology in the nineteenth century, but has experienced a modest revival in the latter part of the twentieth century.

Horary astrology starts with a specific question and a specific moment in time. The question must be one that can be assigned to one of the twelve astrological houses; SEE HOUSE, ASTROLOGICAL. The chart is erected just like a birth chart, using the place and time in which the question was asked. The person asking the question, who is called the querent, is symbolized by the first house of the chart; the subject of the question is called the quesited, and is represented by whatever astrological house the question relates to. For example, a question about a marriage relates to the seventh house, and this would be the house of the quesited in a horary chart drawn up to answer the question.

In astrology, the cusp of each house falls in one of the signs of the zodiac, and each zodiacal sign is ruled by a planet. This is the key to horary interpretation. The astrologer, having identified the houses of the querent and quesited, identifies the planets whose signs are on the cusps of the two houses in question, and looks for an astrological relationship between the planets in the chart. There are various possible relationships, each with its traditional interpretation. Reading off the meanings of the

relationships, or noting that there are none—traditionally a negative sign—the horary astrologer can provide the answer to the question.

There are strong similarities between horary astrology and geomancy. SEE GEOMANCY. SEE ALSO ASTROLOGY. FURTHER READING: APPLEBY 1985, DELUCE 1932.

horn crown. In modern Wiccan practice, a headdress bearing stag's antlers, worn by the High Priest of a coven, who represents the God in ritual. The equivalent headdress for the High Priestess is the moon crown. SEE HIGH PRIEST; MOON CROWN; WICCA.

Horned God. SEE GOD, THE.

horoscope. In modern astrological terminology, a chart of the heavens at a particular moment as they relate to a specific point on the surface of the Earth. The word *horoscope* originally meant what is now called the ascendant— that is, the degree of the zodiac at the eastern horizon at the moment for which the chart is cast—and took on its present meaning in the late Middle Ages.

Until recent times, the standard format for a horoscope was square, divided into twelve triangular areas and a central square by straight lines. In the days before preprinted blanks, this form of chart was much easier to draw. Over the last two centuries, a circle divided into twelve wedges has become more common.

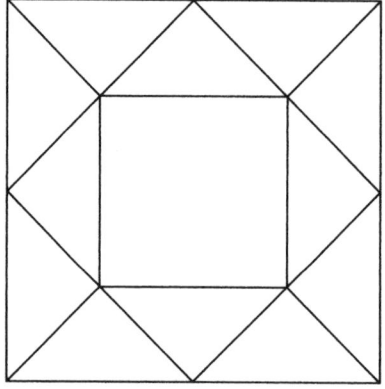

A medieval horoscope

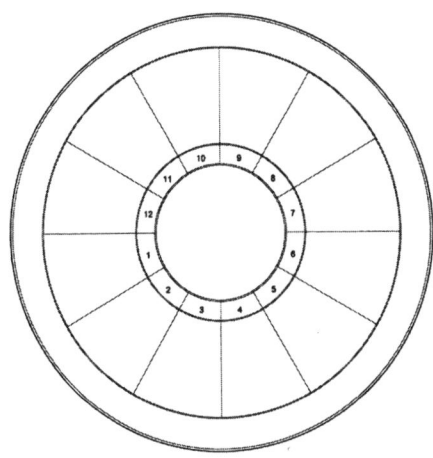

A modern horoscope

SEE ALSO ASTROLOGY. FURTHER READING: BARTON 1994A, KIECKHEFER 1989, TESTER 1987.

Horus. An ancient Egyptian solar god, usually portrayed as a hawk or a man with a hawk's head. Horus was among the most complex of the Egyptian gods, with many different aspects and forms. As Horus the Elder, he was the brother of Osiris and Set; as Horus the Younger, he was the child of Osiris and Isis, and the enemy and slayer of Set; as Horus of the Two Horizons, he was the supreme sky god, identified with Re the Sun. He played a significant role in some ancient Egyptian magical workings; SEE EGYPTIAN OCCULTISM.

In the Hermetic Order of the Golden Dawn, the visualized godform of Horus the Elder was used by the Past Hierophant in ritual, while that of Horus the Avenger was used by the Hiereus. The form of Horus the Child also appears in the Outer Order temple as one of the invisible stations. SEE AROUERIS; GOLDEN DAWN, HERMETIC ORDER OF THE; HARPOCRATES.

In Thelema, the magical-religious system devised by Aleister Crowley, Horus is held to be the divinity ruling over the current age of the world, the Aeon of Horus, which began with the revelation of the *Book of the Law* in 1904. Three different aspects of Horus are mentioned in the *Book of the Law* and Crowley's writings: Ra Hoor Khuit, who is the active aspect of the Lord of the Aeon; Hoor-par-kraat, who is the withdrawn aspect; and their unity, which is Heru-ra-ha. SEE THELEMA.

Hotfoot powder. In traditional American hoodoo, a powder used to make enemies and unwanted neighbors leave the area. Recipes vary widely, but cayenne pepper is a common ingredient. The powder may be sprinkled in the yard of the person to be affected, or mixed with dirt from one of his or her footprints. SEE HOODOO.

house, astrological. One of twelve sections of the heavens as seen from a particular place and time on Earth. The astrological houses were among the last ingredients to be added to classical astrology, and in Roman times they were still in competition with alternative divisions of the sky into four or eight sections.

There are a number of different systems of house division, based on different mathematical ways of dividing up the sky. Among the most common nowadays are the Placidus system, the Koch system, and the Equal House system. Different astrologers favor different systems, and there seems to be no basis for defining one or another as "right."

In medieval, Renaissance, and modern astrology, the twelve houses refer to twelve basic categories of things in human life, and a planet or sign in one of the houses will have its strongest influence on that part of the horoscope. There is some variation in the aspects of life that are assigned to different houses; the list given here is from medieval sources.

First House: the querent, or the person for whom the divination is performed.

Second House: goods, material wealth, gain, business transactions, material things the querent desires, and stolen property.

Third House: brothers and sisters, the querent's neighbors and environment, short journeys, letters, advice, news and rumors.

Fourth House: father and mother, inheritances from parents, land, agriculture, buildings, construction, treasures, anything underground, ancient places and things, old age, hidden things, and the end of any matter.

Fifth House: pregnancy, children, entertainments and feasts, bodies of water, and rain.

Sixth House: servants, employees, small animals, illness, and injuries.

Seventh House: the querent's spouse or lover, love relationships, marriage, partnerships, quarrels, any unidentified person.

Eighth House: suffering, death, dangers, inheritances (other than from parents).

Ninth House: religion, philosophy, learning and education, the arts, wisdom, long journeys, divination.

Tenth House: employment, position in society, people in positions of authority, courts and judges, and the weather.

Eleventh House: friends, sources of help, good fortune, the querent's hopes and wishes.

Twelfth House: enemies, suffering, difficulties, any secret matter, imprisonment, large animals, the querent's fears.

In the case of zodiacal signs, the cusp or beginning of the sign is the important point for determining its house placement; if a sign has its cusp in one house, that sign rules that house, even if most of the sign overlaps into another house. *SEE ALSO* ASTROLOGY.

Hru. In Golden Dawn ritual, a "Great Angel" set over the operations of the order's secret wisdom. Hru was invoked in the ceremony used to consecrate the Vault of the Adepti, and is also mentioned in the Golden Dawn tarot papers; as a result of this latter point, he is called upon by many tarot practitioners, in and out of the Golden Dawn tradition, for guidance in divination.

While nothing significant is said about Hru in the published Golden Dawn literature, his name is identical to that of the Egyptian deity Horus (ancient Egyptian *hru*); *SEE* HORUS. It has been suggested that he is the angelic guardian of the Golden Dawn tradition as a whole. *SEE ALSO* GOLDEN DAWN, HERMETIC ORDER OF THE; VAULT OF CHRISTIAN ROSENKREUTZ. FURTHER READING: REGARDIE 1971.

Hu Gadarn. In Welsh legend and bardic lore, the mythic chieftain who led the ancestors of the Welsh from the land of Hâv, which is called Defrobani (Taprobane, mod-

ern Sri Lanka), to the island of Britain. His appearances in medieval Welsh poetry are sometimes those of a hero, sometimes those of a god; thus wrote the fifteenth-century bard Rhys Brydydd:

> The smallest, if compared with small,
> Is the Mighty Hu, in the world's judgment
> And he is the greatest, and Lord over us,
> And our God of mystery.

Other poetry, written from a more orthodox Christian perspective, decries "the men of Hu, the usurping bards of Wales" and describes Hu as a source "of falsehood, and base omens." All this may represent the echoes of an attempt by medieval Welsh bards to preserve or revive pre-Christian religious traditions. *SEE* AWENYDDION; BARD. *SEE ALSO* PAGANISM.

Hua. (Hebrew HVA, "He") In the Cabala, a name for Kether, the first Sephirah of the Tree of Life. *SEE* KETHER.

In the Golden Dawn tradition, the name of a "Great Avenging Angel" who is invoked in the ritual for consecrating the Vault of the Adepti. *SEE* VAULT OF CHRISTIAN ROSENKREUTZ.

Huath. (Old Irish, "terror") The sixth letter of the Ogham alphabet, also spelled Uath and Huathe, with the sound-value *h*. It corresponds to the hawthorn among trees, the night-crow among birds, the color "terrible" (Gaelic *huath*), and no number. In Robert Graves' version of the Ogham tree-calendar, its month runs from May 14 to June 10. *SEE* OGHAM.

Ogham letter Huath

humors. (Latin *humor*, "moisture") In ancient, medieval, and Renaissance medical thought, four fluids present in the human body that brought physical and mental health when in balance and sickness when out of balance. They were closely associated with the four elements; *SEE* ELEMENTS, MAGICAL. The system of humors evolved in ancient Greek times, along with the theory of the elements themselves, and remained the foundation of Western medical thought until the eighteenth century.

Humor	Element	Qualities
Sanguine	Air	Hot and moist
Choleric	Fire	Hot and dry
Phlegmatic	Water	Cold and moist
Melancholic	Earth	Cold and dry

Nearly all herbals from before the Scientific Revolution refer to the humoral balance, or "temperature," of herbs and other natural medicines. Any given substance could be hot, cold, or temperate (neutral); it could also be moist, dry, or temperate. The balance of hot versus cold and moist versus dry determined whether the herb would stimulate the body in a sanguine, choleric, phlegmatic, or melancholic direction. Each quality could also be present in the first, second, third, or fourth degree, which determined the intensity of the herb's effect on the human body. This allowed a fine degree of definition and control of herbal effect.

Humoral medicine also paid close attention to diet, exercise, and other factors. It was a holistic medical system along the same lines as traditional Chinese medicine and Indian ayurveda. Like these two systems, it was very efficient at dealing with chronic illnesses and lifestyle problems but had few resources to deal with epidemic diseases, and this had much to do with its abandonment in the West during the eighteenth and nineteenth centuries.

A good deal of humoral medicine remains in half-remembered form in folklore in the United States. For example, the old adage "feed a cold and starve a fever" is classic humoral advice; digesting food heats the body, and so food is good for a cold illness but counterproductive in the heat of a fever. Despite the very large role of the four traditional elements in modern magical practice, however, the old system of humoral medicine remains essentially forgotten at present. FURTHER READING: FOSTER 1994, GREER 2000, GULLAN-WHUR 1987.

hunting lodges. According to Dion Fortune and several writers associated with her, hunting lodges were secretive magical lodges devoted to policing the occult community and combating corrupt magicians and magical organizations. They were said to use a combination of magical remedies and media campaigns to accomplish their work. The statements of Fortune and a few others are the only evidence for their reality, but the existence of one or even several such bodies in the very active English magical lodge scene of the late nineteenth and early twentieth centuries is well within the bounds of possibility. FURTHER READING: FORTUNE 1930.

hytersprite. In English folk belief, a beneficial earth spirit that can be summoned by magical rites. *SEE* GNOME; YARTHKIN.

Ialdabaoth. In Gnostic theology, the leader of the archons and creator of the fallen material world, also called Saklas and Samael. Ialdabaoth was the child or creation of Sophia, the lowest of the aeons of the spiritual realm, whose fall from primal perfection began the process of material creation. Hidden away by Sophia in the darkness of matter, Ialdabaoth could not perceive the spiritual realm; he became convinced that he was the supreme being in the universe, and shaped the substance of his hiding place into the world of matter we know. The remaining history of the cosmos, in Gnostic terms, is largely an account of the struggle of the emissaries of the spiritual realm, and those human beings who listen to them, against Ialdabaoth and his minions.

The origin and meaning of the name Ialdabaoth are unclear; suggestions include Aramaic *yaled aba'ot,* "begetter of Sabaoth," a name of the Jewish god. *SEE ALSO* ARCHON; GNOSTICISM.

Iamblichus of Chalcis. Greek philosopher, ?–c. 330. Little is known about the life of this great Neoplatonist theoretician. He was born to aristocratic parents in the town of Chalcis in Syria, and studied philosophy under Anatolius and Porphyry. He wrote many books on philosophical themes, most of which are now lost.

By Iamblichus' time, Christianity was a rising power throughout the Mediterranean world, and the whole range of Pagan religious traditions were coming under increasing pressure. Iamblichus made it his life's work to bring the wild diversity of classical Paganism together into a coherent intellectual unity, as a basis for coopera-tion and mutual defense against a common opponent. He sought to define a Pagan way of thought and life, broad enough to include every element of Pagan tradition within its scope, tolerant enough to prevent theological quarrels within the Pagan community, but also strong enough to counter the assaults of Christian propagandists and to bring the strengths of the Greek philosophical tradition to bear on the religious struggle. In the process, he systematized the emerging tradition of Platonist theurgy, which went on to become the last effective intellectual force to oppose Christianity in the ancient world.

The essence of his approach was the search for common ground between traditional Pagan practice and Platonist philosophy. Where some earlier Platonists had criticized elements of popular religion—for example, animal sacrifices—Iamblichus set out to embrace every detail of Pagan tradition. His philosophy showed how each element of Pagan ritual and custom could be explained and justified as a reflection, in the world of matter, of some important spiritual reality.

His writings and ideas had a major impact on their time. Throughout the fourth and fifth centuries of the Common Era, Pagan thinkers throughout the Mediterranean world turned to his works as a central resource in the struggle to define themselves and preserve their traditions against Christian attacks. His efforts were central to the great fourth-century revival of Paganism, and his writings were the chief inspiration of the Emperor Julian (331–363), who attempted to restore Pagan worship throughout the empire, and whose death marked the end of the last real hope of classical Paganism. Later Neoplatonists such as Proclus also drew heavily on his ideas; *SEE* PROCLUS.

Most of his writings were suppressed after the new religion triumphed, but several important books—*On The Mysteries, An Exhortation to Philosophy*, and his biography of Pythagoras—were preserved in Byzantium, and went on to play an important part in the revival of Neoplatonic theurgy in the Renaissance.

Like many important figures in the Western occult tradition, Iamblichus was recruited by the Theosophical Society as one of the Masters; he is considered to have been an incarnation of the Master Hilarion. *SEE* MASTERS. *SEE ALSO* HILARION, MASTER; PAGANISM; PLATONISM; PORPHYRY; THEURGY. FURTHER READING: GEFFCKEN 1978, IAMBLICHUS 1984, SHAW 1995.

IAO. One of the most important Gnostic words of power, IAO is probably derived from the Tetragrammaton, the most important of the Jewish names of God; *SEE* TETRAGRAMMATON. It first appears in magical writings from around the beginning of the Common Era, and can be found all through the Graeco-Egyptian magical papyri. It apparently fell from use with the demise of Gnosticism and the rise of a more orthodox Christian magic after the fall of the Roman Empire. *SEE* CHRISTIAN OCCULTISM; GNOSTICISM; GRAECO-EGYPTIAN MAGICAL PAPYRI.

It was rediscovered by early researchers into Gnosticism in the eighteenth and nineteenth centuries, however, and incorporated by the founders of the Hermetic Order of the Golden Dawn into their magical synthesis. In Golden Dawn usage, the three letters were assigned to the deities Isis, Apophis, and Osiris, and the name thus expanded plays an important part in Golden Dawn ritual. *SEE* GOLDEN DAWN, HERMETIC ORDER OF THE. *SEE ALSO* BARBAROUS NAMES; VOWELS.

iatrochemistry. An old term for spagyrics, or alchemical medicine. *SEE* SPAGYRICS.

iatromathematics. An old term for medical astrology. *SEE* ASTROLOGY.

Idad. *SEE* IDHO.

Idho. (Old Irish, "yew tree") The twentieth letter of the Ogham alphabet, also called Ioho, with the sound-value *i*. It corresponds to the yew among trees, the eaglet among birds, the color brilliant white, and the number three. In Robert Graves' version of the Ogham tree-calendar, it is associated (along with Ailm) with the winter solstice. *SEE* OGHAM.

Ogham letter Idho

Illuminates of Thanateros (IOT). International magical order, founded in Germany in 1976 by two Chaos magicians, one English and one German. Its formal name is "The Magical Pact of the Illuminates of Thanateros"; the word *Thanateros* is a fusion of Greek *thanatos* (death) and *eros* (sexual love). The IOT's central focus is Chaos magic; its teaching methods and practical work emphasize the use of altered states of consciousness, on the one hand, and the rejection of fixed patterns of belief, on the other.

The emblem of the pact is a black circle from which eight black arrows radiate. This is based on the "Banner of Chaos" from the fantasy novels of English author Michael Moorcock, and is one of several common Chaos magic borrowings from fiction; *SEE* FANTASY OCCULTISM. The pact offers four grades of initiation—Neophyte 4°, Initiate 3°, Adept 2°, and Magus 1°. The honorary grade of Supreme Magus 0° is held by the head of the pact as a whole. Ordination as a Priest or Priestess of Chaos is available to members at the 3° or 2° levels.

IOT's most important spokesman is Peter Carroll, one of the two founders and the author of several influential books on Chaos magic. According to Carroll, the IOT came into being out of a fusion of Thelemic magic, tantra, Taoism, and the work of English occultist Austin Osman Spare (1886–1956), whose Zos Kia Cultus was ancestral to most current Chaos magic systems. *SEE* SPARE, AUSTIN OSMAN.

According to a website updated shortly before this writing, the IOT currently has sixteen temples around the world. *SEE ALSO* CHAOS MAGIC. FURTHER READING: CARROLL 1978.

Illuminati, Bavarian. *SEE* BAVARIAN ILLUMINATI.

Imbolc. (Gaelic, "ewe's milk") In modern Pagan practice, one of the eight festivals of the year, celebrated on or about February 2. It is also called Oimelc, Brigid, and Candlemas. Many current Pagan traditions devote it to worship of the Goddess, or more specifically to the Irish goddess/saint Brigid or Bride. *SEE* SABBAT.

Imseti. *SEE* AMESET.

inceptional astrology. Another term for electional astrology. *SEE* ELECTIONAL ASTROLOGY.

incineration. In alchemy, the process of burning a substance until it is reduced to ashes, which are then used as raw material for other processes. Alchemical symbolism assigns this process to the zodiacal sign Sagittarius. *SEE* ALCHEMY.

incubation. In Greek Pagan tradition and some later systems, a process of divination and spiritual healing typically used by people suffering from chronic illness. The patient would go to the temple of a god or goddess with healing powers and, after appropriate sacrifices and ceremonies, would sleep through the night in the temple in the hope of receiving a dream from the deity. To judge from the surviving records, miraculous healings happened at incubation shrines at least as often as they do at Christian shrines such as Lourdes.

In modern times, the practice of incubation has been revived by some occult and Pagan groups. This has been at least in part inspired by the importance of dreamwork in Jungian and other modern psychological theories. *SEE* JUNGIAN PSYCHOLOGY. *SEE ALSO* PAGANISM.

incubus. (Latin, "one who lies upon") In Western demonology, a male spirit who seeks to have sexual relations with human women. Incubi were believed to put particular efforts into seducing nuns and other women committed to a celibate life. The counterpart on the other side of the gender line is a succubus; *SEE* SUCCUBUS.

independent bishops. Bishops who do not belong to any of the established Christian churches but who have been consecrated by a bishop possessing a valid line of apostolic succession—that is, a lineage that (at least in theory) can be traced back all the way to one of the original apostles of Jesus of Nazareth. Although most lines of apostolic succession are kept tightly within a small number of established Christian churches, several have slipped out over the centuries. At present there are more than twenty lines outside the established churches that are generally accepted to be valid.

The origins of the independent bishops go far back into church history. According to Christian theology, consecration as a bishop is permanent: once a bishop, always a bishop. From the Middle Ages onward, bishops who were expelled from their sees for misconduct of one sort or another were compelled to wander from place to place until they could find another setting to carry out their episcopal duties; this gave rise to the older term for independent bishops, *episcopi vagantes*, "wandering bishops." During the seventeenth and eighteenth centuries, a large number of Irish bishops left home and wandered through America and the Continent. Starting in the eighteenth century, too, lines of apostolic succession with their roots in the ancient churches of the Middle East and India came into play. The Old Catholic Church of Holland, a body that split from the Roman Catholic Church when the latter proclaimed the infallibility of the pope in 1870, has also contributed to the supply of independent bishops.

Adding to the complexity of the scene is the habit, common among independent bishops, of receiving consecrations in lineages other than their own. In Christian tradition, a second baptism, ordination, or consecration can be given *sub conditione*, "on condition"—that is, in case the first one was invalid for some reason. This has been taken to extremes, and nowadays independent bishops may have been consecrated *sub conditione* in as many as twenty-three lines of apostolic succession.

Many independent bishops are more or less orthodox in their theology, but a significant number have embraced some form of esoteric or Gnostic Christianity, and some have been deeply involved in Christian occultism. Many of the major figures in present-day Christian occult circles have some form of ordination from an independent bishop. *SEE ALSO* CHRISTIAN OCCULTISM; GNOSTICISM; LIBERAL CATHOLIC CHURCH (LCC). FURTHER READING: ANSON 1964, KEIZER 1976.

Indigo Ray. In occult philosophy, the seventh of the Seven Rays, the primary creative energies of the cosmos. The Indigo Ray is the most subtle and mysterious of the rays and is strongly associated with magic. In Theosophical lore, the Indigo Ray is directed by the Master Rakoczy, better known as the Comte de Saint-Germain, a chohan of the Great White Lodge. Its symbolic gem is amethyst. *SEE* SAINT-GERMAIN, COMTE DE. *SEE ALSO* RAYS, SEVEN.

individuation. In the psychological thought of Carl Jung, the process of personal development by which the ego comes into relationship with the Self, the essential core of the human psyche. The concept of individuation was largely borrowed from earlier occult models of spiritual development by way of Jung's substantial contacts with the European occult scene. *SEE* JUNG, CARL GUSTAV; JUNGIAN PSYCHOLOGY.

Infernal Palaces. *SEE* HELLS, SEVEN.

infortune. *SEE* MALEFIC.

Ing. (Old English, "the hero Ing") The twenty-second rune of the Anglo-Saxon futhorc, linked in the Old English rune-poem with the hero Ing the Dane, "who ever moved eastward." Its sound-value is *ng*. This rune is a close variant of the rune Inguz, which has the same position in the elder futhark. *SEE* ANGLO-SAXON FUTHORC; INGUZ.

Rune Ing

Inguz. (Old Germanic, "son, the god Frey") The twenty-second rune of the elder futhark, also called Ingwaz. It is associated with the fertility god Frey, traditionally portrayed with a large erect penis, and with ideas of fertility and growth. It represents the sound *ng*. *SEE* ELDER FUTHARK.

Rune Ingwuz (Ingwaz)

Ingwaz. *SEE* INGUZ.

initiation. (Latin *initiatio*, "beginning") One of the most confused and complex terms in modern occult parlance, the word "initiation" was originally borrowed from fraternal lodge organizations such as Freemasonry, where it was used to refer to the ceremony by which a member was advanced to a particular grade or degree, receiving the teachings, rights, and formal title of that level of membership. In the eighteenth and nineteenth centuries, the concept of lodge degrees became fused with ideas of the process of spiritual development, and this caused the concept of initiation to take on a great deal of additional baggage. As a result, nineteenth- and early twentieth-century writings often treat initiation as something vastly mysterious, involving Hidden Masters and out-of-body experience.

All this has very little to do with the reality of initiation as actually practiced by magical lodge organizations, Wiccan covens, and other occult groups. The ceremonies of initiation worked by such groups can have powerful psychological and spiritual effects on those who pass through them, especially when amplified by the technical methods of ritual magic. Still, they are not particularly complex in terms of their basic structure and operation.

Details vary widely, but in outline, most initiations start by secluding the candidate—the person to be initiated—while a space is prepared, physically and magically, for the ceremony. The candidate is commonly blindfolded before being brought into the space, and may be walked around in circles, startled by sudden noises or physical contact, or left in silence and darkness for a period. All this serves to create a state of heightened receptivity in the candidate.

While in this state, the candidate is taken through a set of symbolic experiences that encode the teachings of the degree through sounds, words, physical contact and movement, and other stimuli. The blindfold will usually be raised at one point or another to reveal important images. At some point during this process, the candidate takes an oath or obligation, binding himself or herself to abide by the rules of the order, coven, lodge, or other group.

At some point after the oath or obligation, the candidate receives the secrets of the degree—typically a set of grips, passwords, symbolic gestures, and other identifying signs. These ground the experience of initiation in the candidate's body; when the same signs are repeated by the candidate, as they will be at every subsequent working of that degree, they function as somatic triggers that reawaken the emotional states the candidate experienced during the initiation. The ritual typically closes with one or more lectures on the teachings of the degree, which serve to "talk the candidate down" from his or her altered state, and also to communicate useful information.

This pattern of initiation is all but universal in those Western occult traditions that practice ceremonial workings, although alternative methods based on the very different Hindu or Buddhist initiation patterns have been introduced by a few groups, especially in central Europe. Many initiation rituals have been published, including those of such influential groups as Gardnerian Wicca and the Hermetic Order of the Golden Dawn. SEE ALSO DEGREE(S); LODGE, FRATERNAL; LODGE, MAGICAL. FURTHER READING: GREER 1998.

Inner Light, Society of the. English magical order, founded in 1924 by Dion Fortune as the Fraternity of the Inner Light; the change from "Fraternity" to "Society" was carried out after Fortune's death in 1946. According to its current publications, it is "a Society for the study of Occultism, Mysticism, and Esoteric Psychology and the development of their practice. Its aims are Christian and its methods are Western."

The society's teachings derive from material brought through in trance by Dion Fortune, beginning in 1922, from a variety of inner plane contacts. Fortune's books *The Cosmic Doctrine* and *The Mystical Qabalah* are central texts. The society's grade structure includes three degrees of the Lesser Mysteries, which were originally derived from the degree rituals of Co-Masonry, and two degrees of Greater Mysteries.

The society has passed through a series of transformations over the years. During Dion Fortune's lifetime it

seems to have been primarily a vehicle for her own work and teaching, and changed in tune with her own changes in focus. After her death and a brief transitional period, Arthur Chichester became effective head of the society, with Margaret Lumley Brown serving as principal trance medium; during this period the society worked the full system of degrees and expanded considerably on Fortune's work.

In 1961, however, the society stopped working all but the First Degree of the Lesser Mysteries, and reformulated itself in a more Christian mystical direction. Many members left at this time, and a flurry of new magical lodges more or less based on the older system sprang up in England and America. More recently, beginning in 1990, the society has resumed work on something closer to its original lines, reestablishing the full degree structure and bringing out many of Dion Fortune's previously unpublished essays in book form. SEE ALSO FORTUNE, DION. FURTHER READING: FORTUNE 2000, KNIGHT 2000.

inner plane adepti. SEE MASTERS.

Instita Splendens. (Latin, "splendid border") In the Aurum Solis system of magic, the lowest of the six energy centers of the human body, related to the Sephirah Malkuth and located at the feet. In the Rousing of the Citadels, an Aurum Solis exercise roughly equivalent to the Middle Pillar exercise, it is visualized as a sphere of the seven colors of the rainbow, centered at a point between the feet. Its name of power is ADNI, Adonai.

It corresponds (roughly) to the root chakra and (more exactly) to the Malkuth center of the Middle Pillar exercise. SEE AURUM SOLIS; MIDDLE PILLAR EXERCISE; ROUSING OF THE CITADELS.

insufflation. (Latin *insufflatio*, "blowing in") A form of magical breathwork in which subtle energy from the magician's body is directed into another person or object by breathing upon it with focused intent and visualization. SEE BREATH; EXSUFFLATION.

intelligence. In magical lore, a spiritual entity of a high level, which appears to human beings as a pattern of ideas or states of consciousness. Intelligences have been described as "thoughts which think themselves"; they are assigned to the upper astral or mental levels of being, and they play an important part in the traditions of Platonic mysticism. *SEE* PLATONISM.

According to some magical writers, including Aleister Crowley, the information received in divination comes from intelligences, and each system of divination has a particular group of intelligences assigned to it. *SEE* DIVINATION. *SEE ALSO* SPIRIT. FURTHER READING: GREER 2001.

intelligence, planetary. In the lore of ceremonial magic, one of seven spiritual beings associated with the seven planets of ancient astrology, and ruling over the seven planetary spirits. In some traditional sources, the intelligence of each planet is described as good, while the spirit is considered evil; in others, the spirit is simply a blind force, which requires the guidance of the intelligence if it is to accomplish good. *SEE ALSO* INTELLIGENCE; SPIRIT, PLANETARY.

Planet	Intelligence
Saturn	Agiel
Jupiter	Iophiel
Mars	Graphiel
Sun	Nakhiel
Venus	Hagiel
Mercury	Tiriel
Moon	Malkah be-Tarshishim ve-ad Ruachoth Shechalim

(Note: The moon is governed by multiple intelligences. Malkah be-Tarshishim ve-ad Ruachoth Shechalim is the Intelligence of Intelligences, or collective consciousness of the intelligences of the moon.)

invisible stations. In Golden Dawn ritual, a series of images built up by the temple officers but not used directly as magical vehicles by any officer. Each initiation ritual has its own set of invisible stations. In the Neophyte grade, for example, there are a total of fourteen invisible stations: the four Kerubim, which are outside the hall in each of the four directions; the four children of Horus or Canopic gods, which are in the four corners of the hall; the Evil One, located at the base of the altar; Harpocrates, east of the altar; Hathor, in the east of the hall; Isis and Nephthys, at the two pillars; and the Forty-two Assessors, whose location is not specified but who salute the candidate as he or she passes them. All these are in addition to the eleven godforms formulated and used by the officers in the grade ceremony.

Many other magical lodge systems, some inspired by the Golden Dawn and others independently originated, also use invisible stations of one form or another in their initiation rituals and elsewhere. *SEE* INITIATION; LODGE, MAGICAL. *SEE ALSO* CANOPIC GODS; GODFORMS; GOLDEN DAWN, HERMETIC ORDER OF THE. FURTHER READING: REGARDIE 1971.

invisibility. One of the standard attainments of the magical adept in legend, a state of invisibility is actually a fairly common goal of working magical practice as well. Methods of ritual and natural magic aimed at invisibility are common in medieval sources and can also be found in detail in more recent works.

According to the teachings of the Hermetic Order of the Golden Dawn, which provided its members with full instructions on the process, invisibility is attained by establishing an astral and etheric shell—the so-called "Shroud of Concealment"—around the body of the magician. The shroud works by distorting the consciousness of those within sight of the magician; while their eyes receive the image of his or her presence, their minds do not process it, and the magician passes unnoticed.

A number of modern magicians have experimented with the technique and found it at least partly effective. The fact that the ninja assassin-mystics of feudal Japan used very similar methods to evade detection suggests that the method may have a good deal of potential. FURTHER READING: J. GREER 1997, REGARDIE 1971.

invocation. (Latin *invocatio*, "calling in") In ritual magic, the act of bringing a deity or other spiritual power into the magician. It is distinguished from evocation, which is the process of summoning a spirit into some form of manifestation external to the magician. *SEE* EVOCATION.

Ioho. *SEE* IDHO.

Iophiel. In ceremonial magic, the planetary intelligence of Jupiter. Its subordinate spirit is Hismael. *SEE* INTELLIGENCE, PLANETARY.

Iphin. The fourth of five additional Ogham letters, used to represent the vowel combination *io* or the consonant *ph*. It corresponds to the gooseberry among trees but lacks the extended symbolism of the twenty regular Ogham letters. It is also known in some versions of the Ogham as Phagos, and as such is assigned to the beech. *SEE* OGHAM.

Ogham letter Iphin

Is. *SEE* ISA.

Isa. (Old Germanic, "ice") The eleventh rune of the elder futhark, associated with ice, stasis, and cold. It represents the sound *i*. *SEE* ELDER FUTHARK.

The same rune, called Is (Old English, "ice"), is the eleventh rune of the Anglo-Saxon futhorc. The Old English rune-poem associates it with cold, slippery, glittering ice. *SEE* ANGLO-SAXON FUTHORC.

In the younger futhark, this rune has the name Iss (Old Norse, "ice") and is the ninth in the sequence. Its symbolism and sound-value are the same as above. *SEE* YOUNGER FUTHARK.

The Armanen rune system, finally, names this rune Is, and identifies it with the concept of will. Its correspondences include the goddess Freyja, the process of engendering, the zodiacal sign Sagittarius, and the power from the *Havamal* rune-charm of calming the winds and seas. *SEE* ARMANEN RUNES.

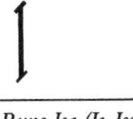

Rune Isa (Is, Iss)

Ishim. (Hebrew, "people") In Cabalistic theory, the tenth host of angels, consisting of the souls of righteous human beings. The Ishim correspond to the Sephirah Malkuth in the world of Yetzirah. The Ashim or Flames are sometimes assigned to this Sephirah in place of the Ishim. *SEE ALSO* MALKUTH, TREE OF LIFE.

Isis. (ancient Egyptian *Aset*) The most important of the goddesses of ancient Egyptian myth, Isis went on to become an even more significant figure in late classical Pagan religion. The wife of Osiris and mother of Horus the Younger, she was also one of the handful of Egyptian deities who had the title *weret-hekau*, "great of magic," and played a significant role in the priestly magic of ancient Egypt. *SEE* EGYPTIAN OCCULTISM.

In the last centuries of classical Paganism, priests and priestesses of Isis proselytized throughout the Roman world, and temples of Isis were built in Rome and other cities of the empire. Her legends and reputation were central to *The Golden Ass*, the famous occult novel by Roman writer (and Isiac initiate) Lucius Apuleius. Through this and other channels, Isis became an important source for the nineteenth- and twentieth-century creation of the Goddess of modern Paganism. *SEE* APULEIUS, LUCIUS; GODDESS, THE.

Isis played a relatively minor role among the godforms of the Hermetic Order of the Golden Dawn, being assigned to the Praemonstrator, one of the three Chiefs of a Golden Dawn temple, who has no active part in the initiation rituals. *SEE* GODFORMS; GOLDEN DAWN, HERMETIC ORDER OF THE. In more recent magical and Pagan practice, however, she has taken on steadily more importance, and several significant books have been written in recent years as guides to modern worshippers of Isis. *SEE ALSO* NEOPAGANISM; PAGANISM. FURTHER READING: FORREST 2000, GEFFCKEN 1978, MEEKS AND FAVARD-MEEKS 1996, REGULA 1994.

isopsephic alphabets. *SEE* ARITHMANCY.

Iss. (Younger futhark rune) *SEE* ISA.

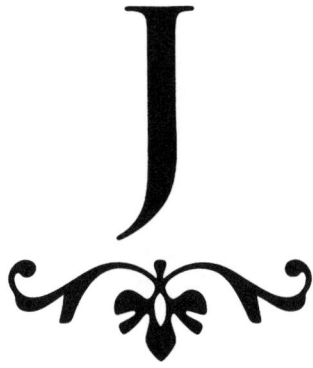

Jabir ibn Hayyan. *SEE* GEBER.

Jachin. (Hebrew, "he has established") One of the two pillars at the door of the Temple of Solomon, an important element of Cabalistic, magical, and Masonic symbolism. The pillar Jachin stood at the right of the entrance of the temple. In symbolism, it is often shown as white, and corresponds to the active, the spiritual, and the masculine, as the pillar Boaz corresponds to the receptive or passive, the material, and the feminine.

Cabalists associate Jachin with the right-hand pillar of the Tree of Life, the Pillar of Mercy. *SEE* TREE OF LIFE.

In many Masonic lodges, the pillar Jachin is topped with a globe of the heavens, representing its association with the celestial world. *SEE* FREEMASONRY. *SEE ALSO* BOAZ; TEMPLE OF SOLOMON.

jack ball. In traditional hoodoo, a charm made by taking magically powerful materials and wrapping them with a long piece of thread or string, usually cut to a particular measure (such as the height of the person for whom it is made). *SEE ALSO* HOODOO.

Jack-in-the-Green. In British folklore and folk custom, a figure representing springtime and new growth. Many British mummers' plays, spring parades, and dances include a Jack-in-the-Green, who is often a dancer concealed under a framework covered with fresh green boughs. In many such plays and dances, the Jack-in-the-Green is symbolically sacrificed, a custom that led many folklorists of the nineteenth and early twentieth cen-turies to suspect that an ancient custom of human sacrifice may be at the origin of the tradition.

In modern Pagan thought, Jack-in-the-Green is considered to be a manifestation of the God in his aspect of Green Man or Hooded One. *SEE* GOD, THE. FURTHER READING: ANDERSON 1990.

Jera. (Old Germanic, "year") The twelfth rune of the elder futhark, corresponding to the cycle of the year, to harvest, to fertility, and to time. Its element is earth, and some modern rune masters link it to the deities Frey and Freyja. Its sound-values are *j* and *y*. *SEE* ELDER FUTHARK.

Rune Jera

Jesus of Nazareth. (Yeshua bin Maryam) Jewish religious reformer and magician(?), c. 4 B.C.E.–c. 30 C.E. The life and activities of Jesus have been subject to ceaseless controversy since the beginning of his public career around 27 C.E. According to the version of his life accepted by most Christian churches, which may be found in the first four books of the New Testament, he was the son of God, born to a Jewish virgin, who performed miracles during his lifetime by divine power, founded the Christian religion, and suffered a sacrificial death by crucifixion at the age of thirty-three. Accounts found in Pagan, Jewish, Muslim, and heretical Christian sources take issue with every one of these details in one way or another, and a sizeable literature has grown up over the centuries arguing the matter. The role of occultism in these disputes is central, for many of the sources that reject the Christian theological doctrine of Jesus' divinity suggest that he was, instead, a magician.

Certainly rumors linking Jesus to magic were in circulation early on. Jewish literature from the first centuries of the Common Era refers to him as "Jesus son of Pantera" and knows him as a magician and religious heretic, the illegitimate son of a hairdresser and a Roman soldier, who learned magic in Egypt while working there as a migrant laborer. Passages in the Talmud refer, often evasively, to Jesus as a magician; the evasions are not difficult to understand when one recalls the brutal persecutions inflicted on anyone who questioned the doctrines of Christianity during the centuries when the church had effective political power.

Similar charges, a good deal less obscurely phrased, can be found in Greek and Roman sources from the same period. The Roman writers Suetonius, Tacitus, and Pliny the Younger, writing near the beginning of the second century, all refer to the early Christians in terms commonly used for practitioners of magic. Lucian the satirist, in the middle of the same century, discusses Jesus as the founder of a "new initiation." The Platonist Celsus, whose second-century treatise attacking Christianity survives only in quotations included in a Christian counterattack by Origen, knew of Jesus in terms identical to the Jewish account—the illegitimate child of a Jewish woman and a soldier named Panthera, who learned magic in Egypt, returned to Israel, collected a following from the dregs of society, was put to death by the Romans, and had his resurrection faked by his disciples.

These same beliefs are referred to in many early Christian writings, especially those of apologists and propagandists who were forced to argue against them. Quadratus, the first important Christian apologist, argued at length in a passage written around 125 C.E. against the idea that Jesus' miracles were performed by magic. Around 160 C.E., Justin Martyr's *Dialogue with Trypho* denounced Jewish leaders of his time for describing Jesus as a "Galilean magician." The Christian apologist Tertullian, around 200, referred to elements of the Jewish account.

Writing around 300, the Christian writer Arnobius records a belief that "he [Jesus] was a magus who performed all these [miracles] by means of secret arts," having learned hidden doctrines and the names of angelic powers in the underground temples of Egypt.

Another source of evidence can be found in classical occult writings and amulets, where the name of Jesus appears early and often as a word of power. Lead binding tablets and passages from the Graeco-Egyptian magical papyri refer to Jesus among the beings who can be invoked for magical power, and two of the three oldest images of Jesus' crucifixion are on magical amulets, surrounded with incantations. Oddly, a number of early images show Jesus with a donkey's head; whether this was a reference to the donkey-headed god Set, with whom Jesus was sometimes associated in Gnostic magical writings, or simply a visual insult, is uncertain at present. SEE BINDING TABLET; GNOSTICISM; GRAECO-EGYPTIAN MAGICAL PAPYRI.

The concept of Jesus the magician disappeared or went underground during the centuries of Christian domination of the Western world, although ironically Christianity soon developed its own rich traditions of magic; SEE CHRISTIAN OCCULTISM. The Renaissance revival of magic saw some further awareness of the possibility that Jesus' career might be understood as that of a magician, although most of the references are to attempts by Renaissance magi to back away from this suggestion as fast as possible; thus, for example, Giovanni Pico della Mirandola's nine hundred theses, unorthodox as many of them were, included a specific denial that Jesus' miracles were the product of magic; SEE PICO DELLA MIRANDOLA, GIOVANNI. Only after the political power of Christianity was finally broken in the nineteenth century did the image of Jesus as magical adept enter again into open discussion.

Much of this was the work of Theosophy. In this and related systems of occult teaching, Jesus of Nazareth has been enthusiastically adopted as one of the Masters of the Great White Lodge, the secret brotherhood that oversees the spiritual evolution of the Earth. In these teachings the Master Jesus is the chohan or chief adept of the Sixth or Violet Ray, the ray of devotion and spiritual love. In Theosophical thought, Jesus lived a century and a half earlier than the official version of history suggests. His role was primarily that of providing a body for the temporary incarnation of the Lord Maitreya, the bodhisattva of the current root race. He attained adeptship in a later incarnation as Apollonius of Tyana. *SEE* APOLLONIUS OF TYANA; MASTERS; ROOT RACE; THEOSOPHY.

This approach to a magical interpretation of Jesus was strongly contested by Christian occultists of a somewhat more orthodox stripe, such as Dion Fortune. There is still some dispute along these lines in certain conservative branches of the occult scene, but the wholesale rejection of Christianity by large parts of the occult community during the twentieth century has rendered the whole question of little interest to many modern students of the occult. At the same time, however, several scholars of early Christian history began to discuss Jesus as a magician in the last few decades of the twentieth century, launching a dispute in academic circles that has remarkable parallels to those set off by Theosophy in the occult world a hundred years earlier. *SEE ALSO* MAGIC. FURTHER READING: GALLAGHER 1982, GRAF 1997, HULL 1974, LEADBEATER 1925, M. SMITH 1978.

John Barleycorn. The hero of a Scottish song immortalized by Robert Burns, John Barleycorn is the barley grain that is planted, harvested, and turned into beer and whiskey; the verses of the song chronicle each stage of the process that turns a barley seed into an alcoholic drink. Many modern Pagan writers have identified John Barleycorn with the God, the male deity of Wicca and many other Neopagan religions. Close parallels between the events of the song and the myths of several ancient agricultural gods, including the Egyptian barley-god Osiris, suggest that this may not be entirely fanciful. *SEE* GOD, THE; OSIRIS. FURTHER READING: GREER 1998.

Jones, Charles Stansfield. *SEE* ACHAD, FRATER.

journal, magical. An important tool in modern magical practice, also known as a magical diary, the magical journal is simply a detailed record of practices and studies, kept daily in diary form. It allows the student to review his or her progress regularly, preserves important insights from study, meditation, and experience, and assists in the achievement of self-knowledge.

The magical journal appears to have become a standard part of the tradition during the great magical revival of the nineteenth century. There are, however, examples from before that time, of which the detailed magical diaries kept by the Elizabethan wizard John Dee (1527–1608) are the most famous. *SEE* DEE, JOHN.

Judgement. The twentieth Major Arcanum of the tarot, usually bearing the conventional Christian image of the resurrection of the dead, with an angel blowing a trumpet while the dead climb out of their graves. In the Golden Dawn system, this Arcanum is assigned to the Hebrew letter Shin, while the French system assigns it to Resh. In divination, it commonly means the final settlement or outcome of an affair, renewal, and rebirth.

Its magical title is "Spirit of the Primal Fire." *SEE ALSO* TAROT.

Tarot trump Judgement (Universal Tarot)

Julianus the Chaldean. Chaldean magician, fl. early second century C.E. Almost nothing is known for certain about this important figure, the coauthor of the *Chaldean Oracles,* beyond the facts that he lived in Rome for much of his adult life and was the father of Julianus the Theurgist. There are several stories about his magical powers. According to one, he was famous for being able to kill vermin in fields without the use of the sort of charms and incantations used by other mages of the time. Another—which combines figures who lived at different times—claims that he defeated Apuleius and Apollonius of Tyana in a struggle to see which one could magically halt a plague raging in Rome. Apuleius offered to stop it in fifteen days, Apollonius in ten, but Julianus stopped it instantly with a single word.

He and his son together wrote the *Chaldean Oracles*, a collection of mystical texts that became extremely popular to later Platonists and magicians. SEE CHALDEAN ORACLES. SEE ALSO JULIANUS THE THEURGIST. FURTHER READING: LEWY 1978.

Julianus the Theurgist. Chaldean magician, fl. second century C.E. Like his father, Julianus the Chaldean, Julianus the Theurgist left little trace in the historical record. SEE JULIANUS THE CHALDEAN. In 174, he accompanied the Emperor Marcus Aurelius on a campaign against the Marcomanni and, according to several ancient historians, successfully conjured up a thunderstorm that frightened away the Marcomanni army. He wrote several books on occult philosophy, of which the *Chaldean Oracles*, which he and his father wrote jointly, survives in fragmentary form. SEE CHALDEAN ORACLES. SEE ALSO PLATONISM; THEURGY. FURTHER READING: LEWY 1978.

Jung, Carl Gustav. Swiss psychologist and occultist, 1875–1961. Among the most influential figures in modern psychology, Carl Jung was born into a family whose backgrounds defined much of his future life. His father was a Protestant minister from a line of eminent scholars and theologians, while his mother came from a family deeply involved in occult and spiritualistic practices. He enrolled in the medical school of Basel University in 1895, and finished his studies there at the end of 1900. His dissertation, "On the Psychology and Pathology of So-Called Occult Phenomena," was based on séances he himself had conducted with members of his family, using his cousin Hélène Preiswerk as the medium.

Fresh out of medical school, he went to work at the Burghölzli Mental Hospital in Zurich, where he carried out widely acclaimed studies in word association as a diagnostic tool. He and the head of the hospital, Eugen Bleuler (1857–1939), were among the first physicians outside Vienna to take up psychoanalysis, the new and extremely controversial system of therapy then being developed by Sigmund Freud (1856–1939) in Vienna. From 1905 to 1912, Jung was among the most influential figures in the Freudian community, rising to the position of president of the International Psychoanalytic Association.

In 1912, however, Jung broke publicly with Freud, rejecting much of the older man's theories in favor of a more radical and in many ways more spiritual approach to psychotherapy. Jung argued that along with the personal unconscious, which consists of things forgotten or repressed during the individual's life, there is also a collective unconscious, which consists of archaic patterns—archetypes—that correspond to primitive human instincts, on the one hand, and the gods of Pagan religion, on the other. SEE ARCHETYPE; COLLECTIVE UNCONSCIOUS.

Lying behind Jung's theories was a long association with the occult. His library contained many books by Theosophical mystic and scholar G. R. S. Mead (1863–1933), and after his break with Freud he became a frequent visitor and speaker at the School of Wisdom in Darmstadt, a center for occult studies founded by Baltic occultist Count Hermann Keyserling (1880–1947). Like many German occultists, Jung was particularly interested in the ancient Persian traditions of Zoroastrianism and Mithraism, and also in Gnosticism. Jung himself recorded dreams and visionary experiences in which he encountered Gnostic deities and was transformed into Aion, the lion-headed Mithraic deity. SEE GNOSTICISM.

In his later career, Jung became deeply interested in the traditions of alchemy, and came to believe that the alchemists had been practicing psychotherapy, using chemical reactions as a blank slate on which to project psychological transformations. He was also a practicing astrologer, having learned to erect horoscopes from his colleague and lover Antonia Wolff (1888–1953) in 1911, and played a central role in introducing the Western world to the I Ching by writing an influential foreword to Richard Wilhelm's famous 1950 translation.

Jung left the Burghölzli in 1909 to go into private practice, and moved to Küsnacht, near Zurich, where he built a stone tower and led a busy career as therapist, teacher, and author. He became an increasingly famous public figure, not only in Europe but in North America as well, where Jungian ideas took hold in the 1920s and became extremely popular by the time of Jung's death. SEE ALSO JUNGIAN PSYCHOLOGY. FURTHER READING:

HOELLER 1982, JUNG 1962, NOLL 1994, NOLL 1997, WEHR 1989.

Jungian psychology. Officially known as "analytic psychology," the system of psychology developed by Swiss psychologist Carl Jung (1875–1961) became one of the most common interpretations of occult phenomena in the Western world during the second half of the twentieth century. The central concept of Jungian psychology is that the whole range of occult and religious phenomena are psychological in nature, and have to do with the relationship between the individual and the realm of the collective unconscious.

The concept of the collective unconscious marks the principal line of division between Jungian psychology and most other schools of psychotherapeutic thought. Freudian psychology, for example, treats the unconscious as little more than a dumping ground for repressed memories and desires. In Jungian thought, by contrast, the unconscious has a personal layer (corresponding to Freud's concept) and a deeper, collective side that is inborn and contains archaic forces as old as the human species. *SEE* COLLECTIVE UNCONSCIOUS.

The most important inhabitants of the collective unconscious are the archetypes, fundamental categories of human awareness that are closely linked to basic human instincts. Examples of commonly encountered archetypes are the Shadow, which represents all the aspects of the individual that the personality is not willing to face; the Anima (in men) and the Animus (in women), which represents the other gender; the Mother; the Father; and most important of all, the Self, the archetype of psychological wholeness. *SEE* ARCHETYPE.

According to Jungian theory, the archetypes are the deep structuring principles of human consciousness, and must be encountered in order for psychological growth and healing to take place. The goal of Jungian psychotherapy is individuation, a process of increasing self-knowledge and empowerment leading to inner wholeness. *SEE* INDIVIDUATION.

The traditions of alchemy and Gnosticism were important elements in Jung's development of his psychological system. In the process, Jung came to argue that these, and all other occult, mythic, and religious phenomena, were actually garbled attempts to deal with the same psychological factors he was exploring. In particular, he claimed that alchemy was only accidentally concerned with furnaces, chemicals, and reactions; the outer work of alchemy, he proposed, simply served as a convenient inkblot on which the alchemists projected archetypal symbols from within themselves. This view has been sharply challenged by modern practitioners of alchemy, who argue that such an interpretation misses the point of alchemical practice entirely. *SEE* ALCHEMY. *SEE ALSO* JUNG, CARL GUSTAV. FURTHER READING: HOELLER 1982, SINGER 1987, YOUNG-EISENDRATH AND DAWSON 1997.

Juno. An asteriod sometimes used in astrology. It is assigned to Virgo by some astrologers and to Libra by others. *SEE* ASTEROIDS.

Jupiter. One of the seven traditional planets of astrology, Jupiter in the birth chart represents expansion, good fortune, and happiness, and also has to do with learning. In astrological symbolism, Jupiter rules the signs Sagittarius and Pisces, although modern astrologers generally assign Pisces to the new planet Neptune. He is exalted in Cancer, in his detriment in Gemini and Virgo, and in his fall in Capricorn. *SEE* ASTROLOGY.

In alchemy, Jupiter is often used as a symbol for tin. *SEE* ALCHEMY.

♃

Astrological symbol of Jupiter

Justice. The eighth Major Arcanum of the traditional tarot, this card was moved to the eleventh place in the deck of the Hermetic Order of the Golden Dawn for reasons of Cabalistic symbolism, and this move has been copied by many other decks since that time. Its usual image is a woman seated on a throne, with a sword in one hand and a pair of scales in the other. In the Golden Dawn system, this Arcanum is assigned to the Hebrew letter Lamed, while the French system assigns it to Cheth. In divination, its common meanings are balance, equilibrium, and legal matters.

Its magical title is "Daughter of the Lords of Truth, the Holder of the Balances." *SEE ALSO* TAROT.

Tarot trump Justice (Universal Tarot)

K

Ka. (Armanen rune) The sixth rune of the Armanen runic system devised by Guido von List, it means "maiden," and corresponds to the goddess Skadi, the zodiacal sign Virgo, and the power to reverse a spell and turn it back on its sender, as described in the rune-poem in the Old Norse *Havamal*. It represents the sound *k*. *SEE* ARMANEN RUNES.

Rune Ka

Ka. (Egyptian spirit) One of the several subtle aspects of the human individual in ancient Egyptian theory, the Ka corresponds closely to the modern concept of the etheric body. It served as the vehicle of the *Ba*, or conscious self, and linked the Ba to the material body. After death, it had to be fed regularly with sacrificial meals. *SEE ALSO* EGYPTIAN OCCULTISM; ETHERIC BODY.

Kabala. *SEE* CABALA.

Kabbalah. *SEE* CABALA.

Kabexnut. *SEE* QEBEHSENUF.

Kabiri. *SEE* CABEIRI.

Kamael. (Hebrew KMAL, "He Who Sees God") In Cabalistic angel lore, the archangel of Geburah, fifth Sephirah of the Tree of Life. His name is also sometimes spelled Camael or Khamael. *SEE* ARCHANGEL; GEBURAH.

kamea. *SEE* MAGIC SQUARE.

Kaph. (Hebrew KP, "hand") The eleventh letter of the Hebrew alphabet, a double letter with the sounds *k* and *kh*. Its numerical value is 20 in its ordinary form, and 500 in its final form. Its standard magical symbolism is as follows:

> *Path of the Tree of Life:* Path 21, Chesed to Netzach.
> *Astrological Correspondence:* Jupiter.
> *Tarot Correspondence:* The Wheel of Fortune.
> *Part of the Cube of Space:* The western side.
> *Colors:* Atziluth—violet.
> > Briah—blue.
> > Yetzirah—rich purple.
> > Assiah—bright blue rayed with yellow.

The corresponding text of the *Thirty-two Paths of Wisdom* runs: "The Twenty-first Path is the Intelligence of Conciliation, and is so called because it receives the divine influence which flows into it from its benediction upon all and each existence." *SEE ALSO* HEBREW ALPHABET.

Hebrew letter Kaph, left, and its final form, right

Karcist. In the *Grand Grimoire*, a relatively late grimoire probably produced in France in the seventeenth century, the word used for the magician who summons spirits. The meaning and origin of the word are unknown. *SEE* GRAND GRIMOIRE.

Kardec, Allan. (Hippolyte Léon Denizard Rivail) French educator and Spiritist, 1804–1869. Born in Lyon, the perennial hotbed of French occultism, he was an unusually gifted child, and was sent at age ten to study with J. H. Pestalozzi, a major educational reformer of the time, in Yverdon, Switzerland. He returned to France at the age of eighteen and settled in Paris the next year, becoming an important writer and speaker on educational issues. Fluent in half a dozen languages, he taught mathematics, astronomy, physics, chemistry, anatomy, physiology, and French, and published successful textbooks of arithmetic and French grammar. In 1832 he married Amelie Boudet, an artist and writer nine years his senior.

In 1854 he first encountered Spiritualism, which was then nearing the crest of its first great wave of European popularity; *SEE* SPIRITUALISM. At first he dismissed it as nonsense, but in 1855 he attended a séance at which tables bounced across the room in apparent defiance of the laws of physics. This convinced him that the subject deserved research, and he began studying it intensively. With the aid of friends and associates who were also researching the subject, he amassed a collection of more than fifty notebooks full of questions and answers from séances. In these, he found a coherent philosophy and theology, which he compiled into his first Spiritist book, *Le Livre des Esprits* (*The Spirits' Book*, 1857).

The main difference between the material he received and what was developing into Spiritualist thought elsewhere was the issue of reincarnation. Most Spiritualists rejected the concept; by contrast, the revelations given to him strongly supported it, and he was told by the spirits that in a past life he had been a Breton Druid named Allan Kardec. On their advice, he adopted this as a nom de plume.

The question of reincarnation was a very heated one at the time; *SEE* REINCARNATION. The disputes over it forced Kardec to come up with a new label—Spiritism—for the teachings he had received. He went on to found

an association of Spiritists, and to publish a series of books on the subject, including *Le Livre des Mediums* (*The Medium's Book*, 1864), which was for many years the standard textbook for developing mediumship in much of the world, and is still popular in Latin America. He continued speaking and writing on Spiritism until his death in 1869.

Kardec's teachings dominated the French spiritualist scene in the late nineteenth and early twentieth centuries, but lost ground later on. It was in Latin America, and especially in Brazil, that his approach found its permanent home. To this day Kardec's books are among the most popular occult works in Brazil, and have inspired a substantial network of Spiritist churches. Spiritism also found a welcoming home in the Philippines. In both these areas, Kardec's teachings have fused with indigenous beliefs in spirits and spirit possession to create a variety of new religious and occult movements. *SEE* SPIRITISM. FURTHER READING: KARDEC **1989.**

Kaun. (Old Norse, "sore") The sixth rune of the younger futhark, associated with sickness, death, and decay; both the Norwegian and the Icelandic rune-poems relate it to fatal diseases of children. Modern runic magicians relate it to the destructive and purifying power of fire. Its sound-value is *k*. *SEE* YOUNGER FUTHARK.

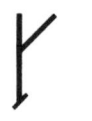

Rune Kaun

Kaunaz. *SEE* KENAZ.

Kedemel. In the lore of ceremonial magic, the planetary spirit of Venus, under the governance of the intelligence Hagiel. *SEE* SPIRIT.

Kelippoth. *SEE* QLIPPOTH.

Kelly, Edward. English magician and alchemist (1555–c. 1597). Kelly was born at Worcester, one of three children. His education was substantial enough to give him a fluent command of Latin, and it has been reported that he attended Oxford briefly, but left before matriculating.

At some point he had one of his ears cropped, a common legal punishment in England at that time; it has been claimed that he made his living for a time as a forger of title deeds, and lost his ear as a result, but no documentary evidence for this has surfaced. He is also believed to have practiced magic and necromancy. This may simply be a rumor, but it closely parallels the career of another working-class occultist of the same period, Simon Forman, and cannot therefore be dismissed out of hand. *SEE* FORMAN, SIMON; NECROMANCY.

Kelly also went by the name Edward Talbot, and it is under this name that he first appears in the diaries of Dr. John Dee, astrologer to Queen Elizabeth. In 1582, after a series of disappointing experiences, Dee was seeking a scryer and assistant for the practice of angel magic. The two were introduced by a mutual friend. Dee was suspicious of "Talbot," and the two of them quarreled frequently. Still, Kelly proved to be a highly capable scryer, and their magical work together continued for seven years.

At some point before 1583 Kelly married Jane Cooper. The marriage was a stormy one, and Jane Kelly spent much of the time living with her mother at Chipping Norton. In the fall of 1583, when Dee and Kelly left England in the company of the Polish nobleman Olbracht Laski, Kelly's marital relations were good enough that Jane accompanied the party. The next few years of Kelly's life are a chronicle of travels around Europe, promises of support from noblemen that rarely panned out, and an almost unbroken succession of magical workings in which the Enochian system of magic was communicated by a succession of spirits.

In the spring of 1583, while still in England, Kelly—according to his own account, under the direction of spirits—found a collection of alchemical manuscripts and a small quantity of powder buried at Northwick Hill near Blockley. Dee by that time was already deeply involved in the study of alchemy, but Kelly's own alchemical studies seem to have taken place later. It is not until 1586, when Dee and Kelly were living in Trebon, that the diaries record Kelly practicing alchemy. On December 19 of that year, he is recorded to have transmuted 1.25 ounces of mercury into fine gold. *SEE* ALCHEMY.

In 1587 Kelly and Dee performed their final magical working together, although they continued to practice alchemy. In the summer of 1588, Jane Kelly left her husband again, this time permanently, and in March of the next year Dee and his family left Trebona, also bound for England. Kelly stayed in Trebona. The two men would not see each other again.

Kelly, now making a living as an alchemist, became a favorite of the Holy Roman Emperor Rudolf II and a celebrity all over central Europe. He was reported to have transmuted mercury into gold in substantial amounts, and carried out transmutations in the presence of scholars and noblemen. Officials in the English government attempted to lure him back to England, without success. At some point between 1589 and 1591, he married Lady Joanna Weston, a widow with two children; two imperial ministers served as witnesses for the ceremony.

Kelly's period of prosperity was brief. In 1591 the emperor ordered his arrest. He fled, but was captured after a few days and was imprisoned in the castle of Pürglitz. It turned out that Kelly's vast "alchemical" wealth was the product of reckless borrowing, assisted by petty fraud. After two years, he was released by the emperor, but was back in prison again by 1595. In 1597, according to contemporary accounts, he tried to escape from prison, but fell from a wall during the attempt and died of his injuries. *SEE ALSO* DEE, JOHN; ENOCHIAN MAGIC. FURTHER READING: WILDING 1999.

Kenaz. (Old Germanic, "torch") The sixth rune of the elder futhark, associated with knowledge and illumination, with the element of fire, and with the god Heimdall; also known as Kaunaz. Its sound-value is *k*. As a verb, *kenaz* means "to know," and some modern runemasters have related this plausibly to "knowledge" in the sexual sense as well as the intellectual one. *SEE* ELDER FUTHARK.

Rune Kenaz (Kaunaz)

Kent, James Tyler. American homeopathic physician and occultist, 1849–1916. Born in Woodhull, N.Y., Kent attended college at what is now Colgate University and went on to study medicine at the Eclectic Medical Institute in Cincinnati, graduating in 1871. He married shortly after graduating, lost his wife after a few years, moved to St. Louis and married again.

At that time the medical profession in America was divided into many different schools and approaches. Kent began as a practitioner of the Eclectic school, which relied on traditional herbal medicines, but switched to homeopathy after homeopathic treatment cured his wife of a severe illness. He took a second medical degree at a homeopathic college in Missouri, became active as a teacher and propagandist for the homeopathic system, and in 1887 became president of the International Hahnemannian Association, a major homeopathic organization.

In 1888, after the death of his second wife, he married Clara Tobey, a fellow homeopath who also introduced him to the teachings of Emmanuel Swedenborg. Important elements of Swedenborgian teaching entered into his approach to homeopathic medicine thereafter. *SEE* SWEDENBORG, EMMANUEL.

Kent came to believe that homeopathic medicines work by way of an immaterial factor, "simple substance," which made up the inner spiritual essence of everything. In his view, simple substance possesses three qualities—existence, power, and intelligence or pattern—and serves as the "limbus" or vital body of every entity, mediating between spirit and matter. Disease consists of an imbalance in the spirit—a separation between the two spiritual faculties of will and understanding—that allows a foreign simple substance to enter the vital body. This interrupts the normal flow of simple substance from the center to the periphery of the body, and allows disease to manifest in the physical body. All these ideas are to be found in Swedenborgian as well as in many other occult traditions.

Teachings such as these were central to Kent's approach, and he presented them from a series of increasingly prestigious positions in homeopathic medical schools. He also wrote and published three books—*Lectures on Homeopathic Philosophy* (1900), *Repertory of Homeopathic Materia Medica* (1903), and *Lectures on Homeopathic*

Materia Medica (1905)—which became the most influential homeopathic textbooks of the twentieth century. He died in 1916.

Kent's ideas developed into the dominant force in twentieth-century homeopathy, and constitute much of what is now called "classical homeopathy." His essentially magical understanding of healing remains the standard approach to homeopathic medicine today. *SEE ALSO* HOMEOPATHY. FURTHER READING: KENT 1900, WOOD 2000.

Kepler, Johannes. German astrologer and astronomer, 1571–1630. Born in a peasant family, he showed a talent for mathematics in childhood that won him a series of scholarships, culminating in his admission to the University of Tübingen, where he graduated in 1593. The same year saw him appointed to a position as teacher of mathematics in Graz, Austria, where he devoted much time to astronomy and entered into correspondence with the great Danish astronomer Tycho Brahe, court astrologer to Emperor Rudolf II.

The outbreak of religious warfare near Graz in 1599 caused Kepler, a Protestant, to flee to the imperial court at Prague. Kepler became Brahe's assistant and then, on Brahe's death in 1601, court astrologer in his place. Working with Brahe's massive collection of planetary observations, Kepler was able to create his three famous laws of planetary motion, the foundation of modern astronomy. He also developed a general theory of astrological aspects, and introduced several new aspects into astrological practice. *SEE* ASPECT, ASTROLOGICAL.

After Rudolf II was deposed in 1611, Kepler found a new home in Linz, Austria, where he became a professor of mathematics and astronomy at Linz University. He died in Germany in 1630. *SEE ALSO* ASTROLOGY.

Kerub. In Cabalistic magic, ruler of the element of earth. Her name derives from that of the Kerubim, the angels attributed to the Sephirah Yesod. *SEE ALSO* KERUBIM; RULER, ELEMENTAL.

Kerubim. (Hebrew, from Akkadian *karibu*, "intercessor") In Judeo-Christian lore, one of the traditional hosts of angels, assigned in the Cabala to the ninth Sephirah, Yesod. Originally the Kerubim were winged, human-headed bulls, and in this form can be found throughout

Mesopotamian art and legend. Later, after their adoption into Jewish angel lore, they were reshaped into four-winged, four-faced angels and given their now-standard place on the Tree of Life. SEE YESOD.

Later still, after their absorption into Christian angelology, the word (usually spelled "Cherubim" in this context) became used for the highest class of angels, beings of pure love who were believed to contemplate the divine order and providence. SEE ANGEL.

Kether. (Hebrew KThR, "crown") The first and highest Sephirah of the Cabalistic Tree of Life and the highest Sephirah of the Middle Pillar. Kether is the first manifestation, the original unity from which all else unfolds, and the goal of the spiritual quest as understood by the Cabala. Its standard correspondences are as follows:

Name of God: AHIH, Eheieh (I Am).

Archangel: MITTRVN, Metatron, the Prince of Countenances.

Angelic Host: ChIVTh HQDSh, Chaioth ha-Qodesh (Holy Living Creatures).

Astrological Correspondence: RAShITh HGLGLIM, Rashith ha-Gilgalim (Beginnings of Turnings or Primum Mobile).

Tarot Correspondence: The four Aces of the pack.

Elemental Correspondence: Air.

Magical Image: A human face looking toward the viewer's right, seen through brilliant light. Some versions make this a bearded male face, others present it as androgynous.

Additional Symbols: The point, the crown.

Additional Titles: Macroprosopus, the Greater Countenance; Amen; the Primordial Point; the Head Which Is Not; Ancient of Days.

Colors: in Atziluth—pure brilliance.

in Briah—brilliant white.

in Yetzirah—brilliant white.

in Assiah—white, flecked with gold.

Correspondence in the Microcosm: Yechidah, the spiritual essence of the self.

Correspondence in the Body: Above the crown of the head.

Grade of Initiation: 10=1, Ipsissimus.

Qlippoth: ThAVMIAL, Thaumiel, the Divided Ones.

The text of the *Thirty-two Paths of Wisdom* associated with Kether runs, "The First Path is called the Admirable or Hidden Intelligence, for it is the Light giving the power of comprehension of that First Principle which has no beginning; and it is the Primal Glory, for no created being can attain to its essence." SEE ALSO CABALA; TREE OF LIFE.

Key of Solomon. The most famous of the medieval grimoires, the *Key of Solomon* (in Latin, *Clavicula Salomonis*) emerged sometime in the early Middle Ages; its author and early history are completely unknown, and attempts to trace it are confused by the fact that a number of different magical handbooks under Solomon's name were in circulation during medieval times. SEE SOLOMON.

The earliest surviving copies date from the twelfth or thirteenth century, and medieval manuscript versions can be found in Latin, Greek, Hebrew, Italian, French, English, and German. Despite the strenuous efforts of inquisitors, scores of manuscript copies have survived. The most readily available version is an English translation made by Golden Dawn founder Samuel Liddell Mathers (1854–1918) in 1888, with the garbled Hebrew words of power of the original manuscripts corrected; SEE MATHERS, SAMUEL LIDDELL.

The *Key*, like most grimoires, is a set of instructions for summoning and commanding a variety of spirits, in this case spirits associated with the seven astrological planets. Since the spirits in question are described as "evil and fallen spirits" and "animals of darkness" in the text of the ritual, there seems to be no doubt that the entities summoned are demonic in nature, and they may be related to the Maskim, the planetary archdemons who play a role in Mesopotamian occultism. SEE MASKIM.

In order to summon these entities, the user of the *Key* must fashion and consecrate an extensive toolkit of magical gear, including a robe, shoes, crown, white-handled knife, black-handled knife, four swords, sickle, poniard, dagger, scimitar, lance, wand, staff, burin, three pens, ink, censer, incense, holy water sprinkler, candles, virgin parchment, wrapping cloth, white book, black book, and several dozen pentacles.

An ornate magical circle full of Cabalistic Names of God must be traced, the correct planetary hours calculated, and a series of extensive invocations, prayers, and conjurations learned. Three, five, or seven companions accompany the magician in his work, and all must go through a rigorous process of fasting, bathing, confession of sins, and purification before the night of the ceremony.

Despite its demanding nature, the *Key* was extremely popular for several centuries, and had pride of place among the sizeable literature of medieval grimoires. At present there are still a few intrepid souls who work the rituals of the *Key*. SEE ALSO GRIMOIRE. FURTHER READING: E. BUTLER 1949, MATHERS 1888.

kia. In the Zos Kia Cultus magical system of British occultist Austin Osman Spare, the soul or "atmospheric self" of the individual, symbolized by the eye or penis. SEE SPARE, AUSTIN OSMAN; ZOS KIA CULTUS.

Kibbo Kift, Kindred of the. English quasi-Pagan organization, founded in 1920 by English occultist and Woodcraft leader John Hargrave (1894–1978). The Kibbo Kift (the name is from an English country dialect phrase meaning "proof of strength") was an offshoot of the Woodcraft movement, which may have been ancestral to several branches of modern Neopaganism; SEE WOODCRAFT. Like other Woodcraft organizations, it was a back-to-nature movement focusing on physical, mental, and spiritual regeneration. The Kibbo Kift also had substantial connections to the English occult scene of the time, mostly through Hargrave, who was deeply versed in occult lore and in later life wrote a book on Paracelsus.

Members of the Kibbo Kift wore an outfit somewhat reminiscent of Robin Hood's Merry Men, and gathered for hikes and camping weekends, archery competitions, and handcraft activities. There was also a great deal of ritual, much of it of an occult nature. Kindred member Vera Chapman, who later went on to join the Order of Bards

Ovates and Druids (OBOD), commented that there was "quite a little bit of mysticism, ritualism, what John Hargrave particularly called 'magik,' spelt with a k. He knew quite a lot, and still does, about occultism and had met a great many of the people who were moving in occultist circles at the time" (Drakeford 1997, p. 62).

In the 1930s Hargrave became convinced that the Kibbo Kift's approach was too slow and too limited to deal effectively with the degenerative forces of modern "civilized" life. He turned to political organizing, transforming the Kibbo Kift into the Green Shirt movement and then into the Social Credit Party of Britain and Northern Ireland. These failed to make a significant impact on the British political scene, and Hargrave dissolved the organization in 1951. Significant elements of Kibbo Kift ritual seem to have been taken up by the Druid movement, especially in the Order of Bards Ovates and Druids; SEE ORDER OF BARDS OVATES AND DRUIDS (OBOD). FURTHER READING: HARGRAVE 1927, DRAKEFORD 1997, WEBB 1976, WITEMEYER 1994.

Kingsford, Anna Bonus. English physician and occultist, 1846–1888. Born into a stifling middle-class family, she married an Anglican clergyman but found domestic life and motherhood intolerable, and took up vegetarianism and the campaign against vivisection as a way out. In 1870, she became a Roman Catholic and the editor of a women's rights magazine. Deciding on a medical career—nearly an impossible option for a woman in England at that time—she went to Paris in the company of Edward Maitland (1824–1897), a lawyer whom she met through her writing, and graduated with a medical degree in 1880.

By this time Kingsford was receiving visions and spiritual messages proclaiming a new version of Christianity, which reinterpreted the Bible in allegorical terms, denied the divinity of Jesus of Nazareth, and included reincarnation and vegetarianism as essential doctrines. Her revelations were largely a product of her use of nitrous oxide, the most popular "consciousness-raising" drug of the time. The visions were first made public in a course of lectures in London in 1881, and published as *The Perfect Way* the next year.

In 1883, in the midst of a furore over doctrinal issues, Kingsford became president of the British Theosophical Society. Her tenure there was brief and stormy, dogged by accusations that she was simply trying to take over Theosophy for the benefit of her own revelations. *SEE* THEOSOPHICAL SOCIETY. In 1884, she stepped down and became the head of her own organization, the Hermetic Society. There she tirelessly promoted her gospel until her death from tuberculosis four years later.

The Hermetic Society sank into unimportance shortly after her death. During its four years of operation, however, it featured lectures on Hermeticism and the Cabala by William Wynn Westcott and Samuel Mathers, the two chief moving spirits behind the Hermetic Order of the Golden Dawn, and played an important role in bringing together the group of occultists who made the GD a possibility. *SEE ALSO* CHRISTIAN OCCULTISM; GOLDEN DAWN, HERMETIC ORDER OF THE. FURTHER READING: GODWIN 1994, KINGSFORD AND MAITLAND 1882.

Knights Templar. The Order of Poor Knights of the Temple of Solomon was founded in 1118 in Jerusalem by a small group of knights under the leadership of Hugues de Payens, a minor nobleman of French birth. Their original purpose was the protection of Christian pilgrims on the road from the port of Jaffa to the holy city of Jerusalem. Few in number at first, the order grew spectacularly after 1128, when it was endorsed by St. Bernard of Clairvaux and received the formal approval of the Catholic Church.

By the end of the twelfth century it was able to field upwards of two thousand horsemen in the Holy Land, funded and supplied by a network of estates and chapter houses all over western Europe. A succession of popes granted the Templars a wide range of privileges, matched by royal grants in most European countries, exempting them and their lands not only from taxes but from nearly all civil laws and authority.

The Templars remained a major part of the military power of the Crusader Kingdom of Jerusalem as long as it lasted, but their efforts and those of the other great military order—the Knights Hospitaller—were able to do little more than slow the Arab reconquest. The fall of the last Crusader holdings in Palestine to the Mamluk Turks in 1291 relieved the Templars of their reason for existence. While the Hospitallers established new bases in Rhodes and Malta to carry on the war against the Muslim world, the Templars contented themselves with lobbying the royal courts of Europe for a new crusade. Their wealth and their political independence made them both envied and isolated, and this proved to be a fatal combination.

At dawn on Friday, October 13, 1307, servants of the French King Philip IV carried out coordinated raids on Templar establishments throughout France, and arrested every known member of the Templar Order they could find—about two thousand in all, of whom perhaps a hundred were full knights of the order. The official charge was heresy. Just under a year later, on August 12, 1308, Pope Clement V authorized similar arrests in all the other countries of the Catholic world.

Following the usual methods of the time, the suspects were tortured to produce confessions, which duly followed. According to the confessions, the Templar initiation ceremony required the novice to renounce Jesus, trample on the cross, and kiss the initiator on the anus, and Templar chapter meetings involved the worship of an idol known as Baphomet (a word which has seen many strange interpretations over the years, but which is simply the standard medieval French misspelling of the name "Muhammad"). *SEE* BAPHOMET. Various other forms of sexual, religious, and magical misconduct were also alleged.

The confessions in the trial records are stereotyped in a way that shows the presence of a standard list of leading questions—another common practice of the time, and one that would be used during the following century in the witch hunts. Similar accusations of blasphemy and magic had been brought against Jews and a variety of political enemies by the French government in the years leading up to the Templar purge, and would be brought against supposed witches in the first of the great witchcraft panics about a hundred years afterwards. *SEE* BURNING TIMES.

Outside of France and areas largely controlled by the French king, few of these charges were upheld. The attempt to organize prosecutions in Germany fizzled out—several German archbishops found the Templars in their jurisdictions innocent—and trials in England, Aragon, and Cyprus, among other places, produced no proof of wrongdoing. Even in France, no evidence besides confessions extracted through torture was ever produced, and the supposed "Baphomet" idols were conspicuous by their absence. Nonetheless, Pope Clement dissolved the order on March 20, 1312. The great majority of Templars were released after the trials. Some joined other military orders, while others returned to civilian life. Fifty-four Templars who had recanted their confessions were burned as relapsed heretics in 1310; two more, including the last Grand Master of the order, Jacques de Molay, met a similar fate on March 18, 1314. These and an uncertain number who died during torture were the only direct casualties of the purge—although legend lists two other deaths that resulted from it. The story has it that de Molay pronounced a curse on King Philip and Pope Clement as he was burnt. If so, it was an effective one, for both king and pope were dead before the year was out.

The question of the guilt or innocence of the Templars was much debated at the time. Outside France, most contemporary observers who commented on the trials suggested that the real motive behind the prosecution was King Philip's greed for Templar wealth. (Dante Alighieri, whose *Divine Comedy* commented on most of the political and social phenomena of his time, put a passage to this effect in Canto XX of the *Purgatorio*.) The same view persisted throughout the rest of the Middle Ages and into the Renaissance, although it was aggressively disputed by propagandists for a number of French kings and by the official historians of the Catholic Church.

It was not until the eighteenth century that a new interpretation of the Knights Templar came into play: the claim that the Templars were initiates of a secret wisdom tradition brought from the East, exterminated because of the threat they posed to the power of the Catholic Church. The seed of this concept was sown by Andrew Michael Ramsay (1686–1743), a Jacobite Freemason living in exile in France, in a famous oration to a group of French Masons in 1736. Ramsay traced the origins of Masonry back to the Crusades, where it had supposedly

been instituted by men who were both stoneworkers and knights. (That this was a social impossibility during the Middle Ages did not seem to occur to Ramsay's listeners.) Ramsay's oration did not mention the Templars at all; rather, he linked his supposed knightly stonemasons to the Knights Hospitaller. Still, the connection he drew between Masonry and knighthood, which inspired a host of new "chivalric" Masonic degrees, also made the invention of Masonic-Templar connections all but inevitable.

These possibilities were first pursued in Germany, where imagery of warfare and knightly rank had a strong appeal, and three different German Templar rituals had come into existence by 1760. Traditional connections between high-grade Masonry and Scotland, born of the Masonic conspiracies surrounding the exiled Stuart kings and also central in the founding and naming of the Scottish Rite of Masonry, were drawn upon to create a pedigree for these new degrees. *SEE* STUART, HOUSE OF. Claims were circulated that a handful of Templars in Scotland had survived the (imaginary) wholesale slaughter of the order's members, and preserved Templar wisdom and treasure in hiding. No evidence was ever forthcoming to support these ideas, a point which did little to slow their diffusion.

These Masonic Templar rites quickly spread outside Germany. There were Templar lodges in the American colonies by 1769, and in England by 1778. In the Anglo-Saxon world, however, the Templars quickly became another aspect of the burgeoning fraternal lodge scene, with little linkage to the occult. In Germany and France, by contrast, Templar lodges were as often as not centers of occult studies. This was especially true of the most important of the German Templar orders, the Strict Observance of Karl Gotthelf von Hund, which engaged in systematic alchemical experimentation.

By the early nineteenth century, Templar organizations had begun to surface outside the ambit of Masonry. The first of these appeared in France in 1804, when Bernard Fabré-Palaprat established a Templar order on the basis of a set of forged charters supposedly dating from 1324. By the 1820s Fabré-Palaprat's order had become deeply involved in a heterodox Gnostic version of Christianity, and for a few years in the early 1830s it ran a

"French Catholic Church" that attracted a handful of followers.

The connection between the Templars and the occult was also central to the flood of conspiracy literature that followed the French Revolution. Right-wing authors such as Louis Cadet de Gassicourt and the Abbé de Barruel claimed the Templars as an important link in the vast conspiracy against Christianity and monarchy they claimed to have uncovered. *SEE* BAVARIAN ILLUMINATI. The crucial figure in this redefinition of the Templars, though, was the Austrian scholar Joseph von Hammer-Purgstall, whose major article "The Mystery of Baphomet Revealed" was published in 1818. Hammer argued, using evidence that most later scholars have dismissed as blatant forgery, that the Templars had been secret Gnostics worshipping an androgynous idol by way of ritual orgies. He also seems to have been the first to suggest a connection between the Templars and the Holy Grail—a suggestion that was soon taken up by neo-Templar occultists, and has become a staple of later speculations.

By the late nineteenth century, the idea of the Templars as guardians of the Holy Grail and students of secret wisdom was securely in place in the occult community. To this day, many occult orders in France, Germany, Switzerland, and the Low Countries either claim Templar lineage or borrow Templar imagery and terminology for their own purposes. Organizations as different as the Ordo Templi Orientis and the ill-fated Temple Solaire have continued to draw on this common source.

More recently, the Templars have been adopted wholesale by the proponents of various schemes of alternative history, and the manufactured legends of eighteenth-century Masonic Templarism have been reissued alone or in combination with other standard motifs of occult history. To this genre belong books such as Baigent, Leigh, and Lincoln's best-selling *Holy Blood, Holy Grail*, Robinson's *Born In Blood*, and many others. Their popularity makes it likely that the Templars will remain a significant source of new legendry in the occult scene for some time to come. *SEE ALSO* FREEMASONRY; OCCULT HISTORY; ORDO TEMPLI ORIENTIS (OTO); PRIEURE DE SION; TEMPLE SOLAIRE. FURTHER READING: BAIGENT ET AL. 1982, PARTNER 1982, SEWARD 1995.

Koad. (Old Irish *choad*, "grove") The first of the five additional letters or *forfedha* of the Ogham alphabet, used for the vowel combination *ea* or the consonant *ch*; also called Ebad or Ebhadh, "aspen." It corresponds to all the trees, but lacks the more detailed symbolism of the twenty "regular" letters. *SEE* OGHAM.

Ogham letter Koad

Kokab. (Hebrew, "star") The eighth celestial sphere in Cabalistic cosmology, assigned to the Sephirah Hod in the world of Assiah. Its astrological equivalent is Mercury. *SEE* HOD; TREE OF LIFE.

Koot Hoomi, Master. *SEE* KUTHUMI, MASTER.

Krumm-Heller, Arnoldo. German-Mexican occultist, 1876–1949. Born in Salchendorf, Germany, in 1876, Krumm-Heller left home at age sixteen to make his fortune and traveled widely in Latin America and Europe. His interest in occultism developed fairly early, and by 1900 he was in Paris studying Martinism with the great French occultist Papus (1865–1916). *SEE* PAPUS.

In 1908, at a major Martinist conclave, Krumm-Heller was made the Martinist Order's representative to Chile, Bolivia, and Peru. Within a short time he was back in Latin America, teaching occultism and engaging in a range of business enterprises. Sometime around 1910, while in Mexico, he began to organize a magical order, the Fraternitas Rosicruciana Antiqua (FRA) or Ancient Rosicrucian Fraternity, and a few years later founded a Gnostic religous body, the Iglesia Gnostica. Both of these organizations found a ready audience throughout the Latin American countries.

In 1920 Krumm-Heller returned to Germany, where he bought a printing business and settled in the town of Marburg. He remained active in occult circles, making contact with Rudolf Steiner and Aleister Crowley, and remaining in touch with his pupils in Latin America. *SEE* CROWLEY, ALEISTER; STEINER, RUDOLF. During the years of Nazi rule, he kept a low profile and managed to survive. After the Second World War, he resumed contact with his overseas students and was active in the Red Cross. He died at home in Marburg in 1949. *SEE ALSO* MARTINISM; ROSICRUCIANS.

kundalini. (Sanskrit, "coiled one") In yogic theory, a primal energy in the lowest chakra at the base of the spine, symbolized by a coiled snake. Several different branches of yoga teach methods for awakening the kundalini and directing it up through the chakras or spinal centers to the crown of the head, bringing enlightenment and a range of supernormal powers.

While kundalini seems to be entirely a Hindu concept, and is not clearly traceable in other mystical traditions, the popularity of Hindu spiritual teachings in the wake of Theosophy caused many writers in the Western occult tradition to suggest that all spiritual exercises are aimed at awakening kundalini, and there are a bewildering variety of systems in the current occult scene that reinterpret and apply kundalini in Western occult terms. *SEE ALSO* CHAKRA.

Kuthumi, Master. In Theosophy and related systems of occult teaching, one of the Masters of the Great White Lodge, the secret brotherhood that oversees the spiritual evolution of the Earth; his name was spelled Koot Hoomi in Theosophical Society founder H. P. Blavatsky's own writings, but was later changed to Kuthumi for esthetic reasons.

Kuthumi is the chohan or chief adept of the Second or Blue Ray, the ray of wisdom, and is thus the immediate subordinate of the Lord Maitreya, the bodhisattva of the current root race. In the time of the sixth root race, which is scheduled to begin sometime in the twenty-sixth century, Kuthumi will advance to the position of bodhisattva of that race. *SEE* BLUE RAY; ROOT RACE.

According to Theosophical texts, Kuthumi was Pythagoras in a previous incarnation. *SEE* PYTHAGORAS.

According to the research of modern historian K. Paul Johnson, "Kuthumi" (or, rather, "Koot Hoomi") was Blavatsky's alias for Thakar Singh Sandhanwalia, an important Sikh leader of the time who cooperated with Blavatsky during her years in India. This identification has been strongly criticized by Theosophists. *SEE ALSO* GREAT WHITE LODGE; MASTERS; THEOSOPHY. FURTHER READING: BARBORKA 1964, JOHNSON 1994, LEADBEATER 1925.

Kybalion, The. Perhaps the most influential work to come out of the American occult scene in the twentieth century, *The Kybalion* was written by American occultists William Walker Atkinson (also known by his pen name Yogi Ramacharaka), Paul Foster Case, and Michael Whitty, then head of the Alpha et Omega magical lodges in North America. *SEE* ATKINSON, WILLIAM WALKER; CASE, PAUL FOSTER. Published anonymously in 1912 as the work of "Three Initiates," it quickly became standard reading in most American occult circles and remains popular in the more traditionally oriented magical groups to this day.

The Kybalion is organized as a commentary on a supposedly ancient collection of Hermetic axioms handed down from master to pupil for centuries; this collection is also (and confusingly) called *The Kybalion.* As usual in matters of this sort, no trace of a collection of this name appears in the very well-documented history of Hermeticism before 1912; *SEE* HERMETICISM. The commentary focuses on a set of seven "Hermetic Principles," as follows:

The Principle of Mentalism, which holds that all phenomena are ultimately mental, and that physical matter is a product of the universal Mind;

the Principle of Correspondence, which holds that the same principles and patterns hold true on every level of existence;

the Principle of Vibration, which holds that all the different levels of existence are simply different rates of vibration of one primary, mental substance;

the Principle of Polarity, which holds that all things contain two opposing aspects, and all opposites are aspects of some unity;

the Principle of Rhythm, which holds that all things have a rhythm between their two opposing aspects, which gives rise to an infinite number of rhythmic cycles of action and reaction;

the Principle of Cause and Effect, which holds that all things are the effect of some cause and the cause of some effect, and that nothing happens by chance; and the Principle of Gender, which holds that there are masculine and feminine principles in everything and on all planes, and that all creation takes place through contact between these two.

While *The Kybalion* almost certainly does not have the ancient origins claimed for it, these seven principles very adequately sum up the basic concepts of modern Hermetic philosophy, and the book has certainly earned its reputation among occultists as one of the fundamental texts of a modern magical education. FURTHER READING: "THREE INITIATES" 1912.

L

Lady's mantle. (*Alchemilla vulgaris*) An important herb in alchemical lore, as the first element of its scientific name ("little alchemist") suggests. Lady's mantle has deeply fringed leaves that collect water in beads along their edges. Alchemists reputedly used lady's mantle to gather dew for their work. Lady's mantle is also an important herb in medicinal herbalism, with particular value in healing the female reproductive system; its astrological correspondence is Venus in Scorpio. *SEE ALSO* ALCHEMY; DEW.

Laetitia. (Latin, "happiness") A geomantic figure governed by Jupiter, fortunate in all divinatory contexts. *SEE* GEOMANCY.

Geomantic figure Laetitia

Laf. *SEE* LAGUZ.

Lagu. *SEE* LAGUZ.

Laguz. (Old Germanic, "water") The twenty-first rune of the elder futhark. It is associated with the deity Nerthus or Njord, with water, with the tides, and with sorcery. It represents the sound *l*. *SEE* ELDER FUTHARK.

In the Anglo-Saxon futhorc, the same rune is called Lagu (Old English, "water, lake") and also occupies the twenty-first position. The Old English rune-poem associates this rune with the deep ocean and its terrifying waves. *SEE* ANGLO-SAXON FUTHORC.

In the younger futhark, the same rune comes fifteenth and is called Lögr (Old Norse, "water, sea, waterfall"). It represents water, vital strength, and intuition. *SEE* YOUNGER FUTHARK.

In the Armanen runic system, finally, this rune is fourteenth, and has the name Laf, meaning "Law"; its correspondences include the god Lodhurr, the mother, and the power to name all the gods and elves, as described in the *Havamal* rune-charm. *SEE* ARMANEN RUNES.

Rune Laguz (Lagu, Lögr, Laf)

Lamed. (Hebrew LMD, "Ox-goad") The twelfth letter of the Hebrew alphabet. One of the twelve single letters, Lamed represents the sound *l* and has the numerical value of thirty. Its most common correspondences are as follows:

Path of the Tree of Life: Path 22, Geburah to Tiphareth.

Astrological Correspondence: Libra, the Scales.

Tarot Correspondence: Trump XI, Justice.

Part of the Cube of Space: The northwestern edge.

Colors: in Atziluth—emerald green.

in Briah—blue.

in Yetzirah—deep blue-green.

in Assiah—pale green.

The associated text of the *Thirty-two Paths of Wisdom* is, "The Twenty-second Path is the Faithful Intelligence, and is so called because by it spiritual virtues are increased, and all dwellers on Earth are nearly under its shadow." *SEE* HEBREW ALPHABET.

Hebrew letter Lamed

lamen. (Latin, "plate") In ceremonial magic, a symbolic breastplate worn on the chest, supported by a ribbon, collar, or cord around the neck. In Cabalistic traditions of magic, the lamen is generally used to represent the forces of Tiphareth, the central unifying Sephirah of the Tree of Life, and carries the corresponding symbolism in one form or another; *SEE* TIPHARETH. In the practice of magical evocation, the sigil of the spirit to be evoked is sometimes worn as a lamen, to represent the power of the magician over the spirit; *SEE* EVOCATION.

The Abramelin system uses the term *lamen* in a different sense; here it is a silver plate on which the Holy Guardian Angel writes in letters formed of dew. *SEE* ABRAMELIN THE MAGE, THE SACRED MAGIC OF.

The Rose Cross Lamen used in the Hermetic Order of the Golden Dawn

Lammas. (Old English *hlaefmass*, "loaf mass") In modern Paganism, one of two common names for the celebration of the beginning of harvest on or around August 1; the other name is Lughnassadh. *SEE* SABBAT.

lamp. In several traditions of ceremonial magic, a working tool representing the presence of spirit or the divine in the temple. The magical lamp is similar to, and probably inspired by, the Presence lamp kept burning in some Christian denominations as a symbol of the presence of God. FURTHER READING: CROWLEY 1980.

Lanz von Liebenfels, Jörg. Austrian occultist, 1874–1954. Born to a middle-class Viennese family, Lanz (the "von Liebenfels" was a later affectation) was fascinated from childhood with the Middle Ages and the legends of knighthood. In 1893, despite the opposition of his family, he entered the Cistercian order as a novice at Heiligenkreuz Abbey near Vienna. He took final vows in 1897 and held a teaching position in the abbey seminary starting in 1898. His own religious beliefs, however, were already straying in directions far from Catholic orthodoxy, and in 1899 he renounced his vows and left the monastery.

He went public with his beliefs in a long 1903 article, "Anthropozoon Biblicum" ("Human Animals of the Bible"), and followed this up in 1905 with a book-length study under the remarkable title *Theozoologie oder die Kunde von den Sodoms-Äfflingen und dem Götter-Elektron* (*Theozoology, or the Lore of the Sodom-Apelings and the Electron of the Gods*). In these works, Lanz argued that the mystery cults of the ancient world were devoted to deviant intercourse with semi-human dwarfs (the "Sodom-Apelings" of the title); that interbreeding between these inferior beings and true Aryan humanity had caused the loss of mysterious electrical-psychic powers once possessed by the latter; and that Jesus, who had been an Aryan rather than a Jew, had come into the world to restore the sexual and racial gnosis to the Aryan chosen people.

Such opinions won Lanz a ready hearing in German nationalist circles, and from 1905 on he produced a magazine, *Ostara*, in which discussions of Lanz's "theozoology" blended with racist diatribes and conservative political and economic essays. Lanz became an early supporter of the Ariosophical ideas of Guido von List, which were popular in the same circles, and was a founding member of the Guido von List Society. *SEE* LIST, GUIDO VON.

In 1907, Lanz founded an organization of his own, the Ordo Novi Templi (Order of New Templars), or ONT. Headquartered at Burg Werfenstein, a medieval castle on the Danube donated by a wealthy follower, the ONT developed a complex ritual system partly modeled on the Cistercian liturgy of Lanz's monastic period, but devoted to the new racial gnosis of "the Electron and the Holy Grail." Full membership was limited to those who passed Lanz's tests of racial purity. The banner of the ONT, first unfurled over Werfenstein in 1907, bore a red swastika and four blue fleurs-de-lys on a golden field. *SEE* ORDO NOVI TEMPLI (ONT).

From the founding of *Ostara* until the end of World War I, Lanz was one of the major figures in Viennese far-right circles, and *Ostara* itself was required reading among German nationalists, anti-Semites, and racists in central Europe. During his Vienna years, according to several testimonies, Adolf Hitler read *Ostara* constantly and once visited Lanz at his office to fill out his collection of back issues. *SEE* HITLER, ADOLF.

At the end of World War I, Lanz moved to Hungary, where he took an active role in politics in the chaos that followed the collapse of the Austro-Hungarian Empire, and was twice nearly executed by Communist firing squads. After the victory of conservative forces in 1920, he settled down to a career in journalism, continued expanding and developing the ONT liturgy, and wrote several books on occult topics. In 1933 he left Hungary for Switzerland, where he stayed through the Second World War. A final move after the war brought him back to Vienna, where he died in obscurity in 1954. *SEE ALSO* ARIOSOPHY. FURTHER READING: GOODRICK-CLARKE 1992.

laukar. (Old Norse, "leek") A word of power found in runic inscriptions in both the elder and younger futharks. The leek was a symbol of male virility and fertility in Germanic and Norse cultures, at least in part due to its phallic shape. It was sometimes paired with *lina*, "flax, linen," which served a similar role as an emblem of female fertility. *SEE* LINA; RUNES.

Laveau, Marie. African-American priestess and hoodoo practitioner, 1801?–1881. Born in New Orleans, she was the daughter of Charles Laveau, a free African-American who owned considerable property, and one of his mistresses. She married Jacques Paris, an immigrant from Haiti, in 1819, but was widowed a few years later, and established a less formal relationship with Christophe Glapion, a white Louisianan, which lasted until Glapion's death in 1855.

The beginnings of her involvement in New Orleans' Voodoo community has not been traced. A number of sources claim that she originally worked as a hairdresser, and used information she received from her clients as a basis for blackmail and divination. By 1850, however, she was considered to be New Orleans' reigning Voodoo queen, a position she held until her retirement in 1869. During these years, in her cottage on St. Ann Street, she carried out magical workings and conducted Voodoo services for an extensive clientele.

After her retirement, she moved in with her daughter, Marie Philomene Glapion, and died in 1881 after a long illness. There is some reason to think that her daughter took over her practice and name after her death, since a number of people interviewed by the Works Project Administration writer's project during the Depression described a middle-aged and very active Marie Laveau as a hoodoo worker in the 1880s, well after the original had died. *SEE ALSO* HOODOO; VOODOO. FURTHER READING: FANDRICH 1994, LONG 2001.

LaVey, Anton Szandor. (Howard Stanton Levey) American Satanist, 1930–1997. Easily one of the most entertaining figures in the twentieth-century American occult scene, LaVey was born in Chicago to working-class parents who moved to the San Francisco Bay area during his childhood. He later claimed to have been a child prodigy who played the oboe with the San Francisco Ballet Symphony, a psychic investigator, a police photographer, an organist for a burlesque theater, and a circus lion tamer. Some of these claims appear to be complete inventions by LaVey, who was never averse to pulling a journalist's leg.

Documentation on LaVey's life is hard to come by, but some aspects of his occult career are tolerably clear. In the 1950s and 1960s, LaVey gave weekly lectures at his parents' house on California Street in San Francisco's Richmond neighborhood. (Later on, when it was the headquarters of the Church of Satan, LaVey claimed that the sprawling black house had once been a brothel operated by the legendary San Francisco madam Mammy Pleasant.) There, on Walpurgisnacht, April 30, 1966, LaVey formally founded the Church of Satan. Satanic weddings, funerals, and baptisms, conducted with an eye toward maximum publicity, attracted a swelling crowd of recruits, including such celebrities as Sammy Davis Jr. and Jayne Mansfield.

The late 1960s and early 1970s were LaVey's glory days. 1969 saw the publication of his million-copy bestseller *The Satanic Bible*, which presented a philosophy of radical self-interest and sensual gratification largely cribbed from Aleister Crowley and the Objectivist philosopher Ayn Rand; *SEE* CROWLEY, ALEISTER. The same year saw him appear on the *Tonight Show* with Johnny Carson, where he performed a Satanic ritual to summon success for the next year. By the early 1970s he had also established a network of "grottoes" (Satanic churches) across the United States, although he later closed these down, as they had become social clubs rather than centers of Satanic activity.

Starting in 1975, when Satanic priest Michael Aquino broke away from LaVey's church to found the rival Temple of Set, LaVey and his organization were bedeviled by schisms and disputes, and LaVey himself withdrew from the limelight. He surfaced again in the early 1990s, publishing a new book, *The Devil's Notebook* (1992), and hosting late-night discussions of Satanic subjects with a growing circle of younger aficionados, largely drawn from the alternative music scene. He died of heart disease in 1997. *SEE ALSO* CHURCH OF SATAN; SATANISM; TEMPLE OF SET.

Leek, Sybil. English witch and astrologer, 1923–1983. According to her autobiography, *Diary of a Witch* (1968), Sybil Leek was born to a family of hereditary witches of Irish and Russian origins, grew up in the New Forest, met Aleister Crowley at the age of nine, and spent a year living with the New Forest Gypsies in early adulthood. None of these claims can be documented. She first surfaced in occult circles in the early 1950s, when she oper-

ated an antique shop in the New Forest. After a mystical experience convinced her that she was meant to be an evangelist for witchcraft, she went public as a witch, attracting a great deal of media attention. Her landlord refused to renew her shop's lease unless she renounced witchcraft. She refused, closed up her shop, and embarked on a new career as a professional witch.

In the early 1960s she moved to the United States, living first in New York and then in Los Angeles. She established herself as an astrologer, publishing a successful astrological journal, and published her first book on witchcraft in 1968. Thereafter she was again much in the media spotlight, and published some sixty books on a variety of occult subjects.

Among the most colorful figures in the American occult scene, she kept a tame jackdaw and a pet boa constrictor. She divided her time in her later years between Texas and Florida, and died in the latter state in 1983 after several years of failing health. *SEE ALSO* ASTROLOGY; WITCHCRAFT. FURTHER READING: LEEK **1968**.

Leland, Charles Godfrey. American scholar and occultist, 1824–1903. Born into a wealthy Pennsylvania family, Leland displayed an interest in the occult from an early age, and absorbed Irish, African-American, and Pennsylvania Dutch magical ideas from the servants in his childhood home. At the age of eighteen, he made his own translation of the *Poimandres*—the first and most important tractate of the *Corpus Hermeticum*—from the original Greek. *SEE* CORPUS HERMETICUM.

In his early twenties he went to Paris to further his education at the Sorbonne. He was there in 1848 when revolution broke out across much of Europe, and he fought alongside the revolutionaries in Paris. Later, returning to the United States, he served on the Union side in the Civil War, traveled and prospected for oil in the West, and then took up a career as a writer and journalist.

In 1870 he moved to England and began researching Gypsy folklore and traditions, a study which led to his first publication on occult subjects, *Gypsy Sorcery and Fortune-Telling* (1891). He was widely reputed to practice the subjects he studied, and developed a reputation in scholarly circles as well as in his extended family as a sorcerer. Later he moved to Florence, Italy, where he lived for the rest of his life, carrying out researches into local folklore, with an emphasis on surviving Roman and Etruscan traditions.

In 1886, according to his later account, he first heard rumors of the existence of a book, preserved in manuscript copies, which set out the doctrines of Italian witchcraft. He made contact with a local *stregha*, a woman to whom he gave the pseudonym Maddalena, and finally managed to obtain from her a copy of the book, which he published in translation as *Aradia, or the Gospel of the Witches* (1899). SEE ARADIA.

Despite failing health, he remained active as a scholar of folklore until his death in 1903. FURTHER READING: LELAND 1974, LELAND 2002, PENNELL 1906.

Lemegeton, the. Among the most famous of the medieval grimoires, the *Lemegeton* consists of five books— the *Goetia*, the *Theurgia Goetia*, the *Art Pauline*, the *Art Almadel*, and the *Artem Novem*—each dedicated to a different branch of the art of evoking spirits. The meaning of the word "Lemegeton" remains unknown, and the collection is also known as the *Lesser Key of Solomon; SEE* SOLOMON.

The first book, the *Goetia*, is by far the most famous, and has been reprinted numerous times on its own. It consists of a list of seventy-two demons, along with their seals, their special powers, and full ritual instructions for summoning and commanding them.

The *Goetia* has retained its popularity as a source for evocations into modern times, and is still commonly used by a range of magical practitioners. Its list of spirits and their seals are included in the *Bok of the Art Magical*, the first version of Gerald Gardner's Book of Shadows. SEE BOOK OF SHADOWS; GARDNER, GERALD BROUSSEAU. The same collection of spirits and seals has also been made the basis for a divination system and a fantasy wargame.

The remaining portions offer additional rituals and smaller collections of spirits who can be summoned and commanded for a variety of special purposes. The *Theurgia Goetia* deals with aerial spirits, some good and some evil; the *Art Pauline* discusses the spirits governing the planetary hours, degrees of the zodiac, and planets; the *Art Almadel* concerns a set of twenty spirits associated

with the seasons, who can be summoned for certain specified purposes; and the *Artem Novem* or "New Art" consists of instructions for summoning good spirits through theurgic means. Much less attention has been paid to these latter sections in recent times. SEE ALSO GOETIA, THE; GRIMOIRE. FURTHER READING: E. BUTLER 1949, DUQUETTE 1992.

Lemuria. According to some versions of occult history, a lost continent—variously located in the Indian Ocean, the eastern Pacific, or portions of both—which sank before the heyday of Atlantis. The concept of a Lemurian continent was the creation of geologists in the 1860s and 70s, who noticed striking similarities in rocks and fossils from southern Africa and central India. As the modern theory of continental drift had not yet been proposed, much less accepted, the geologists suggested that the similarities showed the existence of a land bridge crossing the Indian Ocean. Biologists of the same period noted that such a bridge would explain the distribution of lemurs—primitive primates now found mostly on the island of Madagascar—and the British zoologist Philip Sclater gave the concept its permanent name by suggesting that the land bridge be called "Lemuria" after them.

Discoveries since Sclater's time—continental drift on the one hand, and lemur fossils over a much wider range on the other—made the theory of Lemuria unnecessary to scientists. In the meantime, though, it had been picked up by H. P. Blavatsky, the founder of Theosophy, who wove Lemuria into the Theosophical vision of cosmic history in her last book, *The Secret Doctrine*.

According to the Theosophical account, Lemuria in its prime reached from the Indian to the Pacific Oceans, including parts of what are now southern and eastern Africa, southeast Asia, Australia, and New Zealand. Its inhabitants were members of the third root race, hermaphrodite egg-laying apemen, some with four arms and others with an eye in the back of their heads.

By way of Blavatsky's opus, Lemuria found its way into most post-Theosophical versions of occult history. It can still be met with all through the New Age movement, in variously updated forms, and Lemurian adepts have played a significant role in the legendry of many occult groups over the last century or so.

It may be worth noting, in the light of all this, that there is no concrete evidence whatsoever that Lemuria or anything remotely like it actually existed, and occult traditions from before Blavatsky's time are as innocent of Lemuria as they are of root races, Cosmic Rounds, or any of the other colorful furniture of the Theosophical worldview. *SEE ALSO* ATLANTIS; LOST CIVILIZATIONS; SHASTA, MOUNT; OCCULT HISTORY; THEOSOPHY. FURTHER READING: DE CAMP 1970.

Lenormand, Marie-Anne. French diviner, 1772–1843. Born in Alençon, Normandy, the daughter of a draper, she lost both her parents by the age of five and was raised by her mother's second husband. She attended convent schools, and moved to Paris in 1786, where she may have worked in a dressmaker's shop. In 1797 she attempted to launch a daily newspaper for ladies, but it went under after eight issues.

At some point before 1800, she had begun working as a diviner, practicing palmistry and reading cards using what was then the standard thirty-two-card picquet deck. In France at the time, fortunetelling was officially against the law, but fines were low and the business was a very profitable one. Her talent soon brought her to the attention of high society, and by 1802 she was wealthy enough to buy a country house. A police note from 1809 comments that most of the figures of Napoleon's court consulted her on current affairs.

Her first book, a tell-all memoir titled *Les Souvenirs Prophétiques d'une Sibylle* (*The Prophetic Memoirs of a Sibyl*), was published in 1814, and was followed by a series of similar books combining court gossip, prophecies of the future, and stories detailing the brilliance of her own predictions and the stupidity of the police who harassed her. By the time of her 1817 *Les Oracles Sibyllins* (*The Sibylline Oracles*), she had added tarot cards to her repertoire.

She remained far and away the most famous of French diviners until her death in June of 1843, and over a hundred mourners attended her lavish funeral. For more than a generation thereafter, diviners in Paris were quarreling over the right to call themselves her successor. A fifty-two-card divination deck, the Lenormand deck, appeared two years after her death and is still in print as of this writing. There is no evidence that Lenormand herself

ever used this deck, and it seems to have been given its name as a simple sales gimmick. FURTHER READING: DECKER ET AL. 1996.

Leo. (Latin, "lion") The fifth sign of the zodiac, a fixed fire sign of masculine polarity. In Leo, the sun has rulership and Saturn is in his detriment. Leo rules the heart, spine, and back. *SEE* ZODIAC.

The sun is in Leo approximately from July 23 to August 23. People with this sun placement are traditionally creative, vital, generous, and enthusiastic; they can also be pompous, arrogant, overly dramatic, and as self-centered as a gyroscope.

In the Golden Dawn tarot system, Leo corresponds to Trump VIII, Strength. *SEE* STRENGTH; TAROT.

Astrological symbol of Leo

Leo, Alan. (William Frederick Allan) English astrologer, 1860–1917. Born in London to Scottish parents, Leo spent most of his adult life working as a traveling salesman. His interest in occultism led him to astrology early on, and in 1890 he and fellow astrologer F. W. Lacey launched the *Astrologer's Magazine*, a monthly later renamed *Modern Astrology*. The same year saw him join the Theosophical Society, in which he remained active for the rest of his life. *SEE* THEOSOPHICAL SOCIETY.

His wife Elizabeth, whom he married in 1895, was also an astrologer and soon took on a significant role in his work. In the twenty years after they married, he wrote some thirty books, some of which remain classics to this day. These books played a central role in launching the modern renaissance of astrology.

Leo had a passion for astrology, and was convinced that it could be brought back into general use in the modern world. His books presented astrology for the first time as a method of psychological analysis rather than a way of predicting the future. He also devoted much of his time to organizing astrologers throughout Britain, a task that finally bore fruit in the foundation of the Astrological Lodge of the Theosophical Society in 1915.

In 1914 he won an important legal victory for astrology when he won acquittal on a charge of fortune-telling. His last years were spent in retirement in Cornwall, where he continued to write and carry on an active correspondence with other astrologers until his death in 1917. SEE ALSO ASTROLOGY. FURTHER READING: LEO 1989A, LEO 1989B.

Lesser Key of Solomon. SEE LEMEGETON; SOLOMON.

Levanah. (Hebrew LBNH, "moon") The ninth celestial sphere in Cabalistic cosmology, corresponding to the Sephirah Yesod in the world of Assiah. Its astrological equivalent is the moon. SEE TREE OF LIFE, YESOD.

Lévi, Eliphas. (Alphonse Louis Constant) French magician and author, 1810–1875. The single most important figure in the modern revival of ceremonial magic, Constant was the son of a Paris shoemaker. A fragile and studious child, he was deeply moved by his early experiences with Catholicism and studied for the priesthood, but a platonic relationship with a member of a girls' catechism class convinced him that he was not suited for a celibate life and he left the seminary before receiving ordination. Afterwards, he supported himself by a succession of odd jobs while beginning a career as a writer. His first major work, *La Bible de la Liberté* (*The Bible of Liberty*), was a manifesto of Christian socialism; it was confiscated by the Paris police an hour after it went on sale, and Constant's trial and eleven-month imprisonment for advocating insurrection catapulted him into the public limelight.

While in prison, he encountered the works of Emmanuel Swedenborg, and after his release—while he continued to write and publish works on politics and his own somewhat quirky variety of Catholic mysticism—he went on to study Ramon Lull, Cornelius Agrippa, and other important Renaissance esotericists, as well as the writings of German philosopher Arthur Schopenhauer (1788–1860), whose doctrine of the will influenced him profoundly. SEE AGRIPPA, HEINRICH CORNELIUS; LULL, RAMON; WILL. He served two more terms in prison for advocating radical political doctrines. In 1848, in the midst of revolution, he ran for the new republican assembly but failed to win a seat. His personal life proved

equally frustrating; in 1846, he married a seventeen-year-old, Noémi Cadiot, but the marriage proved unsuccessful and they separated in 1853.

After the failure of Constant's marriage and political ambitions, he devoted himself fully to esoteric studies. He became a friend of Hoené Wronski, who instructed him in the Cabala; SEE WRONSKI, JOSEPH-MARIE-HOENÉ. His first and most important book on magical topics, *Dogme et Rituel de la Haute Magie* (*Dogma and Ritual of High Magic*, published in English as *Transcendental Magic*), appeared in installments from 1854–6 and was published in complete form in 1856. His magical pseudonym Eliphas Lévi Zahed—which was simply his legal name translated into Hebrew—appeared on this and all of his later works.

Dogme et Rituel includes nearly all the elements that have formed the core of ceremonial magic ever since. Lévi fused Cabala, the tarot, and magical ceremony to a degree no previous writer had done. He invented a substantial number of the basic concepts and approaches of modern magic—the use of the four suit markings of the tarot as the elemental weapons of the magician, for example, and the definition of the magical virtues as "to know, to will, to dare, and to be silent"—while presenting these as the elements of ancient Egyptian wisdom.

His later works, which included *Histoire de la Magie* (*The History of Magic*, 1860) and *La Clef des Grandes Mystères* (*The Key of the Great Mysteries*, 1861) were largely restatements of the material in *Dogme et Rituel*. The last two decades of his life were as calm and orderly as the rest had been turbulent; he lived quietly in apartments in Paris, writing and corresponding with students across Europe. He died quietly at home in 1875. SEE ALSO CEREMONIAL MAGIC; TAROT. FURTHER READING: LÉVI 1972, T. WILLIAMS 1975.

Lewis, Harvey Spencer. American occultist, 1883–1939. Born in Frenchtown, New Jersey, in comfortably middle-class surroundings, Lewis went into business in the advertising field. His interest in occultism blossomed in the heady climate of the early 1900s, when Theosophy was on the rise and America in particular was the scene of a wide range of occult movements. In 1904, Lewis founded the New York Institute for Psychical Research, which was essentially an occult research group with a particular focus on Rosicrucian traditions. Official AMORC histories recount a series of high-ranking initiations from European sources supposedly received by Lewis in these early years, but researchers outside the order have found no evidence for such connections from before 1915. In that year, Lewis contacted Theodor Reuss, head of the Ordo Templi Orientis, and received a charter for an OTO lodge. This put Lewis in the middle of the burgeoning quarrel between Reuss and the flamboyant Aleister Crowley, who had been made head of the order in Great Britain and was attempting to remake it along the lines of his new religion of Thelema. *SEE* CROWLEY, ALEISTER; ORDO TEMPLI ORIENTIS (OTO). In 1918, Lewis rebuffed an effort by Crowley to recruit him, and in 1921 Reuss made Lewis an honorary VII° in the OTO, as well as a 33°, 90°, and 95° in the Scottish Rite, Rite of Memphis, and Rite of Misraim respectively.

After several unsuccessful attempts to found a magical order of his own, Lewis incorporated the Ancient and Mystic Order Rosae Crucis (AMORC) in Florida in 1925. Two years later he and his family moved to San Jose, California, and laid the foundations for what would become one of the most successful of twentieth-century occult orders. Lewis' advertising background became a major asset for AMORC, which carried out a highly effective publicity campaign; for many years AMORC advertisements could be found in scores of American magazines, and attracted thousands of students to the organization.

During the 1920s and 1930s, Lewis was embroiled in a series of quarrels with R. Swinburne Clymer, the head of the rival Rosicrucian Brotherhood. Clymer claimed exclusive rights to the name "Rosicrucian" in the United States, and the dispute led to lawsuits and a vitriolic pamphlet war. None of this hindered the growth of Lewis' order, and the squabble may actually have helped him in his efforts to publicize AMORC.

The 1930s also saw Lewis make connections with a range of overseas occult bodies. In 1934, Lewis and the heads of several French and Belgian esoteric orders organized FUDOSI, the Fédération Universelle d'Ordres et Sociétés Initiatiques, in the hope of establishing a general umbrella organization for like-minded esoteric orders worldwide. FUDOSI never really developed much independent life, however, and went under at the beginning of the Second World War.

Lewis spent his last years promoting and running AMORC. On his death in 1939, his position as Imperator of the order passed to his son, Ralph Maxwell Lewis. *SEE ALSO* ANCIENT MYSTICAL ORDER ROSAE CRUCIS (AMORC).

leys. Prehistoric alignments, of much-disputed nature and purpose, said by proponents to determine the placement of ancient structures throughout England and elsewhere. The concept was the creation of Alfred Watkins (1855–1935), a commercial traveler and amateur archeologist, who discovered in the early 1920s that a very large number of prehstoric sites in the Hertfordshire countryside seemed to lie along a small number of straight lines. Tracing these lines on standard British Ordnance Survey maps, he came to believe that much if not all of England had once been covered with a network of alignments, marked by mounds, standing stones, ancient trackways, holy wells and pools, beacon hills, and old churches raised on pre-Christian sacred sites. Noting that many placenames with the element "ley" appeared on these alignment, Watkins began referring to them as "leys."

Watkins' original guess was that these alignments might once have served as a method of cross-country navigation in times when Britain had few if any roads. This idea was central to his book on the subject, *The Old Straight Track*, which appeared in 1925. Others who studied the phenomenon were less sure, as leys rountinely crossed bogs, lakes, mountain peaks, and the like. Members of the Straight Track Postal Club, which was founded by readers of *The Old Straight Track* shortly after its publication, discussed various odd phenomena related to the leys. Even Watkins, who had a lifelong distrust of the occult, commented: "I feel that ley-man, astronomer-priest, druid, bard, wizard, witch, palmer, and hermit, were all more or less linked by one thread of ancient knowledge and power, however degenerate it became in the end" (quoted in Michell 1969, p. 14).

Watkins died in 1935, and the Straight Track Postal Club ceased activities with the coming of war in 1939. Although some further research was done thereafter, especially on the connections between leys and astronomical alignments, it was not until 1969 that the ley hypothesis gained a wider public. This was largely the work of the fiery English visionary John Michell, whose *The View Over Atlantis* argued that the leys, along with the Great Pyramid and other ancient monuments, were part of a vast and ancient system based on sacred geometry that once channeled a subtle "dragon current" derived from polar magnetism over the entire world.

Despite strenuous opposition from more conservative ley researchers, Michell's approach to the leys became the dominant view by the early 1970s, and was adopted by many Druid traditions of that time; *SEE* DRUIDRY. It focused much research thereafter on the more occult dimensions of the lines, as well as on methods of research (such as dowsing) rejected by establishment science. Many New Age systems of the last thirty years have thus made use of leys, incorporating them into speculations about Lemuria, Atlantis, ancient astronauts, and so forth. Predictably, too, the great "crop circle" frenzy of the late 1980s and early 1990s drew on the more occult ley theories nearly as much as on UFO folklore. *SEE* DOWSING; NEW AGE MOVEMENT.

In reaction to the florid atmosphere of New Age claims that had come to surround the entire subject by the early 1990s, a new approach became popular among serious students of the ley phenomenon. This approach rejected the idea of leys as an energy grid, and proposed the *Doodwegen* or "dead roads" of Holland—traditional straight pathways along which corpses were brought to cemeteries—as a new model. The more hardline proponents of this view did their best to chase off the whole range of paranormal and magical ideas that had gathered around the "Old Straight Paths" first glimpsed by Watkins. This approach, though, fell foul of many of the same objections as Watkin's own thesis. Another side of the more serious attention to leys was an attempt to trace equivalents in other cultures, with some success. Complex mathematical and statistical methods have also been used to demonstrate that ley alignments occur in ways that cannot be ascribed to chance alone.

Despite all the attention that has been given to leys and related topics over the last three quarters of a century, then, very little can be said to be known for certain about them. Proponents have amassed impressive anecdotal and statistical evidence for the existence of some alignments, but the nature and original purpose of the leys remain mysteries. Meanwhile, leys remain an important element of modern occult folklore. The resolution of all this confusion awaits further research, archeological as well as occult. FURTHER READING: MICHELL 1969, PENNICK AND DEVEREAUX 1989, WATKINS 1925.

Liberal Catholic Church (LCC). A Christian church closely allied with Theosophy, the Liberal Catholic Church emerged out of the clerical underworld of independent bishops in the early twentieth century. Like many independent Catholic churches, it drew its apostolic succession from the Old Catholic Church of Holland, which had split off from Vatican control in 1739. *SEE* INDEPENDENT BISHOPS.

Arnold Harris Mathew (1852–1919), a clergyman of notably flexible beliefs—he had been a Catholic priest, a Unitarian minister, and an Anglican curate before finally becoming an Old Catholic bishop—was consecrated in 1908, and set out to create a new English Catholic Church by recruiting priests and bishops. Many of these came from the Theosophical Society, and in 1915 the Theosophical contingent took over Mathew's church. In 1918 the church took its present name.

Charles Leadbeater (1847–1934), one of the leaders of the Theosophical Society, became a bishop of the LCC in 1916 and wrote *The Science of the Sacraments*, a handbook of LCC ritual interpreted by way of Theosophical teachings. Under Leadbeater, the LCC became closely involved with the Order of the Star in the East and the attempt to promote Jiddu Krishnamurti as the new messiah; *SEE* STAR IN THE EAST, ORDER OF THE.

Like Theosophy itself, the Liberal Catholic Church has undergone several schisms, and remains active in a quiet way over much of the English-speaking world. Its rituals are closely akin to those of other traditional Christian churches, but its theology is drawn from Theosophy, with the Master Jesus as Lord of the Seventh Ray rather than the second person of the orthodox Christian trinity. *SEE ALSO* THEOSOPHY. FURTHER READING: KEIZER 1976, LEADBEATER 1920.

Libra. (Latin, "scales") The seventh sign of the zodiac, a cardinal air sign of masculine polarity. In this sign, Venus has rulership and Saturn is exalted; Mars is in his detriment and the sun in his fall. Libra rules the kidneys. *SEE* ZODIAC.

The sun is in Libra approximately from September 23 to October 23. People with this sun placement are traditionally gregarious, friendly, diplomatic and idealistic; they may also be indecisive, gullible, and self-indulgent.

In the Golden Dawn tarot system, Libra corresponds to Trump XI, Justice. *SEE* JUSTICE; TAROT.

Astrological symbol of Libra

license to depart. In ritual magic, an essential element of the closing phase of any ceremony in which spirits have been summoned. In this step, the magician formally permits the spirits to depart, and may command them to do so. The form of the license to depart is largely standardized; a good example is that from the *Key of Solomon*, which runs: "In the name of Adonai, the Eternal and Everlasting One, let each of you return unto his place; be there peace between us and you, and be ye ready to come when ye are called."

The Golden Dawn tradition's license to depart runs similarly: "Depart ye in peace unto your habitations. May the blessing of (insert the appropriate divine name) be upon you. Be there peace between us and you, and be ye ready to come when ye are called."

In modern magical practice, the license to depart is usually followed by a banishing ritual. *SEE ALSO* EVOCATION.

ligature. A magical working performed by tying a string, thread, or cord in one or more knots. Ligatures have traditionally been most often used for binding spells, for obvious symbolic reasons. In ancient Greek times, sorcerers used knotted cords to bind the winds to provide fair weather for sailors.

In many Wiccan traditions, each candidate for initiation is measured from head to toe with a cord, which is then used as a ritual belt. One, two or three knots are tied in the cord to mark the first, second, and third degrees of initiation; the knots serve to magically bind the initia-

tions in place and prevent their energies from being dispersed. *SEE* INITIATION; WICCA.

Lightning Flash. In Cabala, a diagram made by connecting the ten Sephiroth of the Tree of Life in their numerical order; also known as the Flaming Sword. Cabalistic theory envisions the Lightning Flash as a representation of the descent of creative power down the Planes of Being at the beginning of the universe. *SEE ALSO* CABALA; FLAMING SWORD; TREE OF LIFE.

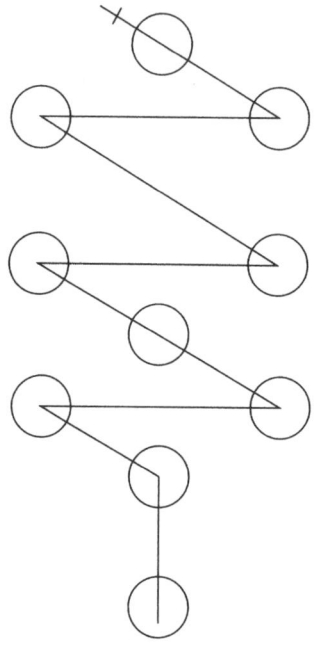

Lightning Flash

Lilith. (planet) In astrology, a hypothetical dark second moon of Earth, about one-fourth the size of the moon. The existence of Lilith was first proposed by eighteenth-century astronomers, on the basis of a few sightings (probably of an asteroid). Charts of Lilith's estimated positions have been drawn up, and a few modern astrologers make use of Lilith in chart interpretations. *SEE ALSO* ASTROLOGY; VULCAN.

Lilith. (spirit) In medieval Jewish legend, the first wife of Adam, who insisted on being treated as an equal and was therefore put aside and replaced by Eve. Her origins are uncertain: some sources claim that she was created by

God along with Adam, while others identify her as a demon from the beginning. After her separation from Adam, however, she became the mate of Samael and a demon who delighted in killing newborn infants and pregnant women.

The first reference to Lilith is in the *Alphabet of Ben Sira*, a Hebrew folktale dating from the tenth century. She may, however, descend from the Lilitu, who were female demons in Babylonian mythology. The angels Senoi, Sensenoi, and Semangelaph were invoked to drive her away from women in childbirth and from newborn infants. *SEE ALSO* DEMON.

Lilith later played a role in Cabalistic symbolism as the Qlippoth of Malkuth, the tenth sphere of the Tree of Life. *SEE* CABALA; MALKUTH; QLIPPOTH.

Lilly, William. English astrologer, 1602–1681. Far and away the most important figure in the British astrological revival of the seventeenth century, Lilly was born to a poor rural family in Diseworth, a small village near Derby. He learned Latin in the grammar school at Ashby de la Zouch, and hoped to attend Cambridge, but his family's poverty prevented this. Instead, Lilly went to London and became a servant to a wealthy businessman. When the latter died a few years later, Lilly married his widow and inherited the estate.

His wife's death in 1633 left him free to pursue his own interests, of which astrology soon became the most important. He bought a sizeable library of astrological books and devoted himself to study. He proved to have a genius for the art, and within a few years was much in demand as an astrologer, erecting and interpreting natal and horary charts for clients from all over Great Britain. He also benefited from access to the papers and case books of the successful Elizabethan astrologer and occultist Simon Forman (1552–1611); *SEE* FORMAN, SIMON.

In the political troubles that finally exploded into the English Civil War of 1640–1645, Lilly was a firm supporter of the Parliamentary side, and his astrological almanacs and pamphlets (which began appearing in print in 1644) predicted Parliamentary victory on the basis of the stars. His greatest success in this field was his prediction of the battle of Naseby (1645), in which Parliamentary forces crushed the Royalist army and ensured the defeat of King Charles I. Lilly also predicted Charles' violent death in a variety of publications beginning in 1639; this prediction, unlikely seeming at the time, was borne out with the king's execution in 1649. *SEE* STUART, HOUSE OF.

Lilly's radicalism extended to the practice of astrology in another way. In 1647 he published his masterpiece, the 841-page *Christian Astrology*, the first textbook of astrology ever published in the English language. (The title was intended to reassure readers who doubted astrology's religious bona fides.) This work became the standard introduction to astrological practice in the English-speaking world, and remained unrivaled until the beginning of the modern astrological revival in the late nineteenth century.

Lilly managed to escape the Royalist backlash at the restoration of Charles II to the English throne in 1660, largely through the efforts of his Royalist friend and fellow astrologer Elias Ashmole. *SEE* ASHMOLE, ELIAS. He remained the doyen of English astrologers, publishing regularly and earning the then-astonishing sum of £500 a year from horary consulations alone, until his death in 1681. *SEE ALSO* ASTROLOGY; HORARY ASTROLOGY. FURTHER READING: GENEVA 1995, PARKER 1975.

lily. An important symbolic flower in the Western tradition, the lily typically represents purity and virginity, and contrasts with the rose, the symbol of love. *SEE* ROSE.

lina. (Old Norse, "flax, linen") A word of power found in runic inscriptions in both the elder and younger futharks, usually paired with the word *laukar*, "leek." *Lina* was apparently a symbol of female fertility. *SEE* LAUKAR; RUNES.

List, Guido von. Austrian writer and occultist, 1848–1919. Born in Vienna to a prosperous merchant family, List was devoted to outdoor pursuits from an early age and hoped for a career as a writer and scholar. After an unsuccessful stint in the family leather-goods business, he earned a sparse living by writing articles on the Austrian countryside for popular magazines. In 1888, his novel *Carnutum*—a historical romance pitting heroic Germanic tribesmen against villainous Romans—won him widespread acclaim. It was followed by two other successful novels and a series of plays on similar themes. All these brought him a good deal of popularity, especially among German nationalist circles then struggling to define and defend a German identity within the polyglot Austro-Hungarian empire.

In 1902, after an eye operation left him blind for most of a year and sparked a mystical experience linked with the ancient Nordic runes, List's interests turned increasingly toward occultism. His studies of the fragmentary surviving materials on ancient Germanic paganism convinced him that a caste of priest-kings, the Armanen, had governed all the Germanic tribes in ancient times, and had preserved their secrets after the coming of Christianity by way of a series of secret societies, including the Knights Templar, the Masons, and the Rosicrucians. According to List, the Armanen had been forced to entrust their secrets to Jewish rabbis in the Rhineland in the eighth century, to preserve them from Christian persecution; this, he believed, was the origin of the Cabala. Nearly the entire Western magical tradition, in this way, was brought within the ambit of List's Armanist gnosis. *SEE* CABALA; FREEMASONRY; KNIGHTS TEMPLAR; ROSICRUCIANS.

List's research topics included the runic alphabet, on which he wrote the first significant modern occult work, *Das Geheimnis der Runen* (*The Secret of the Runes*, 1908), and the pagan roots of fairy tales and folklore. Out of his 1902 revelation, he devised a somewhat idiosyncratic approach to the runes, and made it one of the central elements of his magical system; *SEE* ARMANEN RUNES. He also dabbled in prophecy, predicting that a "Strong One from Above" would arise in the near future to reestablish the ancient Armanist state and lead the German people to the mastery of the world. This prophecy was arguably fulfilled by Hitler's rise a short time after List's own death.

List's influence on occultism throughout central Europe was profound, and was fostered by the Guido von List Society, founded in 1908 to promote his ideas. Large and well financed, with members drawn from German conservative and nationalist circles as well as the occult community, the society evolved an inner circle, the Höhere Armanen-Orden ("High Armanen Order") or HAO, which conducted pilgrimages to pagan religious sites. For decades after List's death, his ideas remained standard elements of occult theory and practice throughout the German-speaking countries. Most of the ideas that later became part of the magical dimension of the Nazi movement can be traced back to List, as can a good deal of modern Norse and Germanic neopaganism. *SEE ALSO* ARIOSOPHY; NATIONAL SOCIALISM; RUNES. FURTHER READING: GOODRICK-CLARKE 1992.

Litha. A name for the summer solstice used in many modern Pagan traditions. It has been claimed as the original Pagan name for this festival, but no evidence has been presented to back this up. The actual origin of the term appears to be J. R. R. Tolkien's fantasy trilogy *The Lord of the Rings*; in the calendar Tolkien devised for the fictional race of Hobbits, midsummer's day is named Lithe (Tolkien 1966 pp. 478 and 481–483).

This is not the only element of fantasy fiction to have found its way into current Pagan practice; *SEE* FANTASY OCCULTISM. *SEE ALSO* SABBAT.

lodestone. *SEE* MAGNETITE.

lodge, fraternal. The fraternal lodge is a form of social and community organization once all but universal in the English-speaking world, but almost forgotten today. The first fraternal lodges came into being in Britain sometime around 1600, when remnants of the medieval guild system were taken over and reshaped to meet the needs of a new mercantile society. Freemasonry, which evolved out of Scottish stonemasons' craft guilds, and Odd Fellowship, which has its roots in English journeymen's organizations of the late Middle Ages, are two of the very few orders to have survived from this earliest period. Later, especially between 1800 and 1920, they were joined by a vast number of other fraternal orders, ranging from sizeable orders such as the Knights of Pythias and the Grange to little-known oddities such as the Bagmen of Bagdad and the Concatenated Order of Hoo-Hoo.

The basic elements of lodge structure and process are common to all these organizations. A lodge is made up of a number of initiated members of a given fraternal order, who receive a charter from the order's Grand Lodge (or some similar supervisory body). The charter allows the lodge to meet, carry on business, elect representatives to the Grand Lodge, and—most importantly—to initiate new members into the order. The lodge elects its own officers and, for the most part, manages its own affairs, subject to rules and regulations enacted by the Grand Lodge, and to the supervision of Grand Lodge officers.

There are standard patterns for the ceremonies that open and close all lodge meetings, and the layout of the lodge room tends to be much the same from one order to another, with the members seated around the sides of a rectangular room, and the area in the middle left mostly clear for ritual work. Even small details are shared among different lodge organizations: three raps with a gavel, for instance, will call the members to their feet in most surviving lodges in North America.

The similarity in basic structure and process is balanced by a wide range of variation in symbolism and language. For instance, although "lodge" is the most common term for a local unit of a fraternal order, there are also orders whose local units are camps, commanderies, temples, cantons, bethels, granges, workshops, fortresses, encampments, circles, and groves, among other things. Titles for officers are even more diverse; an Oracle, a Noble Grand, a Worthy Master, and a Sachem, for example, are the presiding officers of a Camp of Royal Neighbors of America, a Lodge of the Independent Order of Odd Fellows, a Grange of the Patrons of Husbandry, and a Tribe of the Improved Order of Red Men respectively.

Initiation rituals, which form the core of the entire fraternal lodge system, reveal exactly the same combination of similar structure with wildly diverse symbolism and terminology; *SEE* INITIATION. In a fraternal initiation ritual, the candidates may find themselves reenacting a passage from the Bible, passing through the cycle of the agricultural year, venturing into a Native American camp or a Druid temple, or simply passing through a set of apparently unrelated incidents and events. In nearly all cases, though, they will be blindfolded on entrance, and will be guided on one or more circuits around the hall; they will be made to promise to keep secret the rituals and private business of the order; they will have the blindfold taken off at a visually and dramatically impres-

sive moment; and shortly thereafter, they will be taught the password, grip, sign, and other secrets of the degree of initiation they are receiving. These latter are repeated by all members present whenever the lodge is opened in that degree, and they form a set of somatic triggers which help the members to re-enter the state of consciousness induced by the initiation ceremony at will.

Most fraternal lodge organizations were open only to men, and many still are. Exceptions include the Patrons of Husbandry, which has admitted men and women on equal terms since its founding in 1867, and the Independent Order of Odd Fellows, which began admitting women to membership in 2001. One branch of Freemasonry, Co-Masonry, also admits women as well as men to membership, but nearly all other Masonic organizations refuse to accept the validity of Co-Masonic initiation. Most of the orders that admit only men to membership also have women's auxiliaries with their own rituals and traditions, although in many cases these have been heavily watered down compared to the men's rituals.

During the Golden Age of the fraternal lodge movement—roughly between 1750 and 1950—a very large percentage of male occultists belonged to one or more fraternal lodges, and a good deal of occult material found its way into even the most respectable lodge systems; thus, for example, the Patrons of Husbandry adopted a version of the Eleusinian Mysteries as its Seventh Degree, and large amounts of Hermetic tradition found their way into various Masonic degrees. Magical lodge organizations such as the Hermetic Order of the Golden Dawn and the Ordo Templi Orientis drew heavily on fraternal lodge practice, borrowing fraternal (especially Masonic) methods as a basic vocabulary of ceremonial working. More recently, however, with the drastic decline in fraternal lodge membership since 1950, the number of occultists who make use of this resource has also declined sharply. *SEE ALSO* FREEMASONRY; LODGE, MAGICAL; ODD FELLOWSHIP; GRANGE, THE (PATRONS OF HUSBANDRY). FURTHER READING: GREER 1998.

lodge, magical. The standard social form for Western occultism during most of the modern period, the magical lodge is an odd hybrid derived mostly from contemporary fraternal lodge systems. Occult writers during the Golden Age of magical lodges (roughly 1780–1950) claimed that their lodges, and the lodge system as a whole, dated to ancient times and had been preserved intact for thousands of years. This is inaccurate. The magical lodge system was borrowed almost entirely from fraternal lodge traditions such as Freemasonry, taking not only its basic structure but most of its details from this source. *SEE* FREEMASONRY; LODGE, FRATERNAL.

The earliest magical lodges took shape on the fringes of French and German Freemasonry around the middle of the eighteenth century. While there had been occult secret societies of various kinds before that time, of course, the standard toolkit of the magical lodge—ritual initiations, an ascending ladder of degrees, passwords, secret handshakes, and the like—were an eighteenth-century addition. This set of fraternal lodge methods was combined with older occult traditions by figures such as Martinez de Pasqually and Karl Gotthelf von Hund, founders respectively of the Élus Coens and the Strict Observance, two important early magical lodge organizations. *SEE* PASQUALLY, MARTINEZ DE.

Pasqually and von Hund, like many later magical lodge designers, also drew heavily on legends about various older secret societies such as the Rosicrucians and the Knights Templar. Early magical lodges also drew a surprising amount of their imagery and internal mythology from a far less reputable source—the vast structure of conspiracy theories that arose in Europe in the aftermath of the French Revolution, and blossomed into hysteria in the wake of the popular insurrections across Europe in the 1820s and 1840s; *SEE* ILLUMINATI, BAVARIAN. Whatever the political risks of borrowing such imagery, it was colorful, and it promoted the idea that magical orders were vast, powerful, and well organized—a claim that was useful for recruitment purposes. Thus staples of conspiracy literature such as *aqua toffana* entered into many of the texts of the nineteenth-century magical revival. *SEE* AQUA TOFFANA.

The result was the rise of a mythology of magical lodges, which can be seen in its full flower in fictional works such as Dion Fortune's "Doctor Taverner" short stories. According to the mythology, magical lodges had been in continuous existence since ancient Egyptian times, if not since Atlantis itself; they had worldwide connections, and exercised subtle but powerful influence over everything that happened in the world; they were led by mysterious, secluded adepts with superhuman abilities; and they guarded vast quantities of secret teachings which had never been revealed to outsiders, and which conferred miraculous powers over the physical world.

In point of actual fact, none of this was true. The magical lodges of the eighteenth, nineteenth, and early twentieth centuries were recent creations cobbled together from scraps of older lore, and few of them lasted beyond the lifespans of their original founders. Few had more than a dozen individual lodges, and fewer still had more than a hundred members. With a very small handful of exceptions—cases in which a member of one or another order happened to rise to an important political office—they had no noticeable political influence. Their leaders, like the rank-and-file members, were ordinary human beings whose interest in occultism did not keep them from having to earn a living or deal with the ordinary issues of everyday life. The teachings of the magical lodges, finally, were derived either from publicly available sources or from the personal research of the orders' founders and leading members, and constantly trickled out into print.

There have been three main waves of magical lodges over the years, each with its own characteristics. The first, which dates from the late eighteenth century, was essentially an offshoot of Freemasonry and drew nearly all its rituals and methods from that source. The lodges of this first wave tended to restrict membership to Master Masons, and were thus open to men only. Their occult teachings were generally very specialized—particular methods of alchemy, ritual magic, or other branches of occult practice were taught, but no attempt was made to present a complete study course in occultism. The initiations were the central feature of these lodges; the teachings were simply one of the benefits to be gained by being initiated. The Orden des Gold- und Rosenkreuz (Order of the Golden and Rosy Cross), a German order of the late eighteenth century, is a typical and well-documented example of this type; *SEE* ORDEN DES GOLD- UND ROSENKREUZ.

The second wave took shape in the second half of the nineteenth century, and was influenced both by the first wave and by the great European occult revival of the time. Lodges of the second wave varied widely in how much material they drew from Masonry; many did not require Masonic affiliation, and several opened their doors to women. Orders of this second wave put approximately equal stress on their initiations and their teachings. In many cases, the teachings themselves were expanded into full-scale study courses in occult theory and practice. The Hermetic Order of the Golden Dawn is far and away the best known of this type; SEE GOLDEN DAWN, HERMETIC ORDER OF THE.

The third wave began in the last years of the nineteenth century and reached full flood between the two world wars. Magical lodges of this third type generally had little if anything to do with Freemasonry or other fraternal orders, and their teachings were increasingly central to their work. Most of them functioned mainly as correspondence schools, and offered initiation and lodge activity as one of the benefits to be gained by advancing through the different lessons of the course. Examples of the type include such well-known modern orders as AMORC and BOTA; SEE ANCIENT MYSTICAL ORDER ROSAE CRUCIS (AMORC); BUILDERS OF THE ADYTUM (BOTA).

Like the fraternal lodges from which they borrowed so much, most magical lodges went into a steep decline in the second half of the twentieth century. The reasons for this are complex and still not well understood, but the somewhat stuffy ritual and hierarchical structures of many magical lodge organizations did not appeal to the young, counterculture-influenced people who flocked into occultism in the wake of the Sixties. Some magical lodges still remain active at the present time, and others have been revived on the basis of written materials. While they are unlikely to dominate the magical field they way they once did, magical lodges will probably be a noticeable element in the occult scene for some time to come. FURTHER READING: GREER 1998.

Logr. SEE LAGUZ.

Lomer, Georg. German occultist, 1877–1957. Born at Loosten near Wismar, Germany, Lomer studied medicine and worked as a physician in the years before and during World War I. After the war, he came into contact with Theosophical circles in Germany and began publishing books on a wide range of occult topics, including critiques of Christianity, dream interpretation, alternative medicine, astrology, and Germanic paganism. He also became a professional graphologist and astrologer in the 1930s.

Like many German occultists between the wars, he was influenced by the Ariosophical movement, which combined Germanic paganism and Theosophy with racism and anti-Semitism. A number of his books, including *Hakenkreuz und Sowjetstern* (*Swastika and Soviet Star*, 1925) and *Die Götter der Heimat* (*The Gods of the Homeland*, 1927), are heavily Ariosophical. From 1929 on he was the editor of *Asgard*, subtitled "A fighting sheet for the gods of the homeland," which published articles by Ariosophical authors such as F. B. Marby and Gregor Schwarz-Bostunitsch. Like nearly all occultists outside the Nazi party's inner circles, he and his periodical were silenced after Hitler's seizure of power in 1933, but he managed to survive the war years and was active in the postwar occult scene in Germany. He died in 1958.

At some point during the 1920s or 1930s, Lomer wrote a set of instructions for Hermetic students, *Lehrbriefe zur Geistigen Selbstschulung* (*Instructional Letters on Spiritual Self-training*), parts of which were first published anonymously as an appendix to Franz Bardon's book *Frabato the Magician*. The whole text has recently been issued in English translation. SEE ALSO ARIOSOPHY; BARDON, FRANZ. FURTHER READING: LOMER 1997.

Long Lost Friend, The. A magical handbook written by Pennsylvania Dutch magician Johann Georg Hohman and first published in 1820. Wildly popular in the American folk magic community, *The Long Lost Friend* gives magical cures for illnesses of people and livestock. It has been published under several titles, including *The Long Hidden Friend* and *Pow-Wows*. SEE ALSO SIXTH AND SEVENTH BOOKS OF MOSES. FURTHER READING: HOHMAN 1992.

lost civilizations. Occult theories since the late eighteenth century have included a range of claims about lost civilizations, some known to orthodox scholars (for example, the Maya) and others rejected by officially accepted versions of history (for example, the inhabitants of Atlantis). These claims have played an important role in various systems of occult history, and quite a number of occult systems have traced their roots back to one lost civilization or another; SEE OCCULT HISTORY.

The fascination with lost civilizations is a relatively new ingredient in the occult traditions of the West. Versions of Western occultism dating from before 1750 or so show few signs of it. It sprang out of the achievements of nineteenth-century archeology, and above all the rediscovery of ancient Egypt. In many ways, Egypt was the archetypal "lost civilization"—ancient, legendary, and (at least before the decipherment of hieroglyphics in 1822) sufficiently unknown to serve as a Rohrshach inkblot on which fantasies could be projected at will. It's typical that Antoine Court de Gébelin, a French savant of the late eighteenth century, could write an immense nine-volume work about ancient Egyptian culture at a time when hieroglyphics could not yet be read and nearly nothing was actually known about Egyptian culture. Most of Court de Gébelin's data came out of his own head—a point which has not stopped occultists from citing several of his most inaccurate claims as historical fact ever since. (It was Court de Gébelin, for instance, who was responsible for the wildly inaccurate claim that the word "tarot" is ancient Egyptian for "royal road"; SEE TAROT.)

Egypt has remained a happy hunting ground for occult history ever since, but other lost civilizations soon entered the fray. Nineteenth-century occult writings, in particular, were full of them; nearly every imaginable corner of the globe was assigned to some lost civilization or other. Large and detailed occult histories of the world were drawn up and published, tracking the rise and fall of forgotten empires and the emergence and sinking of lost continents. The sweeping planetary history traced out by H. P. Blavatsky in her immense tome *The Secret Doctrine* was the most famous of these, but it drew on many previous examples of the genre and inspired countless imitators.

Another lost-civilization theme of great current importance entered the picture in the middle of the nineteenth century, when J. J. Bachofen's book *Mutter-recht* introduced the idea that the first form of human culture had been matriarchal. In 1903, English classicist Jane Harrison proclaimed that Europe itself had been the location of an idyllic, goddess-worshipping, matriarchal civilization just before the beginning of recorded history, and spoke bitterly of the disastrous consequences of the Indo-European invasion that destroyed it. In the hands of later writers such as Robert Graves, Jacquetta Hawkes, and Marija Gimbutas, this lost "civilization of the Goddess" came to play the same sort of role in many modern Pagan communities that Atlantis and Lemuria played in Theosophy. For a time in the middle and late twentieth century, the idea of neolithic matriarchies was accepted by many conventional archeologists and prehistorians, although this support has faded in recent decades, and forceful challenges have been mounted by scholars claiming that the evidence for ancient matriarchies simply isn't there. SEE MATRIARCHIES, ANCIENT.

In defense of all these enterprises, it must be said that not all the evidence about the past fits gracefully into the accepted vision of the human past promulgated by orthodox scholars. In particular, there are a variety of facts which suggest, though they do not prove, the existence of cultures in prehistoric times a good deal more advanced than current archeological theory would admit. On the other hand, it has to be admitted that most accounts of lost civilizations are packed full of wishful thinking, circular argument, sheer fantasy, and complete ignorance of known historical facts. SEE ALSO AGHARTA; ATLANTIS; LEMURIA; MU. FURTHER READING: DE CAMP 1970, DONNELLY 1973.

lotus wand. In Golden Dawn magical practice, one of three primary magical working tools used by an adept, along with the magic sword and the lamen. The lotus wand has a top shaped like a lotus blossom, and a shaft divided into fourteen bands—the uppermost white, representing spirit; the lowest black, representing material force; and the twelve in between colored to represent the forces of the zodiac. In use, the magician holds the wand by the band corresponding to the force he or she wishes to invoke. SEE ALSO WAND. FURTHER READING: REGARDIE 1971.

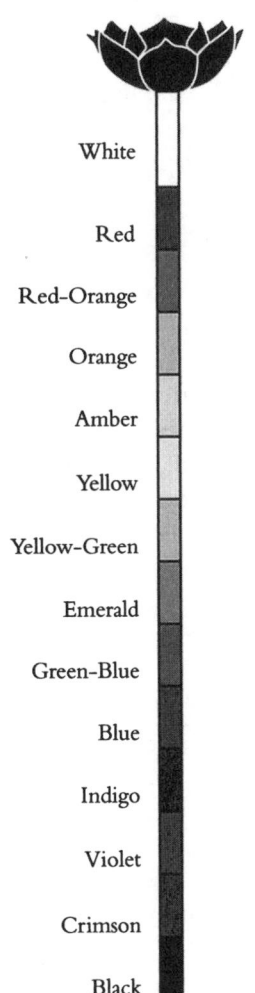

Lotus wand

Tarot trump the Lovers (Universal Tarot)

Lovers, the. The sixth Major Arcanum of the tarot, this card has among the more diverse collections of images associated with it. Many decks, including the oldest, show simply a young couple together; the Rider-Waite deck, and many decks based on it, show Adam and Eve in the Garden of Eden, while the Golden Dawn deck shows the scene of Andromeda's rescue from a sea monster by Perseus.

In the Golden Dawn system, this Arcanum corresponds to the Hebrew letter Zayin, while the Franch system assigns it to Vau. Its magical title is "Children of the Voice Divine, the Oracles of the Mighty Gods." *SEE* TAROT.

Lucifer. (Latin, "bearer of light") Originally a Latin name for the morning star, this word was mistakenly applied to the Christian Devil as a result of a misunderstood biblical verse (Isaiah 14:12) that referred to a king of Babylon. It is one of many names assigned to the Prince of Darkness. *SEE ALSO* SATAN.

In *Aradia, or the Gospel of the Witches* (1899), American folklorist Charles Godfrey Leland claimed to have discovered a manuscript containing myths and teachings of an ancient Italian witch-cult. In the central myth he presented, Lucifer was the son and mate of Diana, the goddess of the night. Aradia, the witch-messiah whose career is central to the myth, is the daughter of these two. *SEE* ARADIA; LELAND, CHARLES GODFREY.

In Anthroposophy, the occult philosophy created by Austrian occultist Rudolf Steiner (1861–1925), Lucifer is one of two powers of evil in the universe. He represents the temptation of intellectual arrogance, with its tendency to retreat from material existence into a purely mental life. *SEE* AHRIMAN; ANTHROPOSOPHY.

Lughnasadh. In modern Pagan practice, one of the festivals of the eightfold year-wheel, usually celebrated on or about August 1. The day is also known by the English name of Lammas. Lughnasadh is derived from an old Irish festival of the same name, celebrated in late summer with horse races and temporary "Teltown marriages" that lasted for one year.

In modern Irish Gaelic, Lughnasadh is the name for the month of August. *SEE ALSO* SABBAT.

Luis. The second letter of the Ogham alphabet, with the sound-value *l*. Luis' correspondences include the rowan among trees, the duck among birds, the color gray, and the number fourteen. In Robert Graves' version of the Ogham tree-calendar, its month runs from January 21 to February 17. *SEE* OGHAM.

Ogham letter Luis

Lull, Ramon. Spanish mystic, 1232–1315. Born to a noble family in the island of Majorca, off the Mediterranean coast of Spain, Lull pursued the ordinary lifestyle of his class at the court of King James I of Aragon, but the first of a series of intense religious experiences led him to withdraw to a hermit's cell on his estate, where he practiced ascetic disciplines. In 1272 he joined the tertiary order of St. Francis, and in 1274 he experienced a vision on Mount Randa, in which nine attributes or "dignities" of God were revealed. From this vision developed the Lullian Art, a system of contemplative philosophy with strong similarities to Cabala; *SEE* LULLIAN ART.

Further visionary experiences led Lull to believe that he had been divinely commissioned to convert the Muslim world to Christianity, and he studied Latin, Arabic, and logic in preparation for this mission. He went to Tunis three times to preach the Christian gospel, was imprisoned and banished twice, and the third time was stoned by a mob at Bugia, in what is now Tunisia, dying a short time later of his injuries.

During his lifetime Lull had a Europe-wide reputation as a scholar and a holy man, and the Lullian Art was taken up enthusiastically by students throughout the Western world. His books included several detailed studies of the art, of which the *Ars Magna* was perhaps the most important, and a very popular treatise on chivalry based on the art, *The Book of the Order of Chivalry*, which was translated into many languages.

After his death, Lull was also acclaimed as the author of more than ninety important works on alchemy. Many of these were actually written by a younger contemporary, Ramon de Tarrega (c. 1295–1371), who was condemned for heresy in 1371 and whose books were thus

potentially dangerous to own. They seem to have been assigned to the pen of Ramon Lull in the hope that his reputation as a martyr for the Christian faith would stave off difficulties with the Inquisition—as it indeed seems to have done. *SEE* ALCHEMY; TARREGA, RAMON DE. FURTHER READING: BONNER 1985, HILLGARTH 1971, PATAI 1994, PERIERA 1989, YATES 1979.

Lullian Art. A system of contemplative philosophy devised by the Spanish mystic Ramon Lull (1235–1315), as a result of a vision on Mount Randa in which nine attributes or "dignities" of God were revealed to him. These dignities were Goodness, Greatness, Eternity, Power, Wisdom, Will, Strength, Truth, and Glory (in Lull's Latin, *Bonitas, Magnitudo, Eternitas, Potestas, Sapeintia, Voluntas, Virtus, Veritas,* and *Gloria*).

Each of these were assigned to one of nine letters—B, C, D, E, F, G, H, I, and K respectively—and formed a set of fundamental ideas, which were reflected in each of the levels of being. For example, the nine dignities of God took shape on the angelic level as the nine orders of angels; on the celestial level they became the seven planetary spheres plus the sphere of stars and the *primum mobile*, the outermost sphere which moved the whole cosmos; and so on down the planes. The dignities (and their equivalents on each level) could also be combined, generating further concepts and correspondences.

All these processes were mapped out into geometrical patterns, concentric circles, and "trees" that mapped the relationships between different manifestations of the dignities. The result was a complicated algebra of ideas that could be used to analyze existing concepts and create new ones. The art also had its practical aspects. Lull's *Treatise on Astronomy* gave a system of astrological medicine in which the interplay of the elements, planets, and zodiacal signs was used to track cycles of human health. Lull also wrote a *Book of the Order of Chivalry*, a guide to the ethics of knighthood based on the art; this latter was wildly popular across Europe and was translated into most European languages.

The similarity of all this to the Cabala is probably not accidental. Lull's vision on Mount Randa was in 1274, one year before the publication of the Zohar, and the first versions of Christian Cabala were coming into being in Spain at this same time. The dignities correspond closely to the Sephiroth of the Cabalistic Tree of Life, and the method of using letter combinations to generate concepts was much used in early Cabala as well, having been developed by the Spanish Jewish Cabalist Abraham Abulafia less than a hundred years previously.

The Lullian Art became extremely popular in Spain, France, and Italy during Lull's lifetime, boosted by his reputation as a philosopher and holy man, and remained a significant intellectual force throughout Europe until the end of the Renaissance. Renaissance magi such as John Dee and Giordano Bruno studied the art closely. After the rise of scientific rationalism, however, the art was effectively forgotten. Some few references have been made to it in occult literature, but as yet no significant attempt to revive it seems to have occurred. SEE ALSO CA-BALA; LULL, RAMON. FURTHER READING: BONNER 1985, HILLGARTH 1971, YATES 1979.

Lunar Pitris. In Theosophy, a class of Dhyan Chohans who transcended the human level of being during the time of the Moon Chain, the planetary chain which was reincarnated as our present Earth (and its six invisible companions). The Lunar Pitris are responsible for forming the bodies of the different root races of humanity. SEE ROOT RACE; THEOSOPHY.

lunar return. SEE SOLAR RETURN.

lunary. SEE BOOK OF MOONS.

Luria, Isaac. Jewish Cabalist, 1534–1572. The most influential figure in the development of the modern Jewish Cabala, Luria was born in Jerusalem to a Jewish family of German origins. A child prodigy, he was already respected as a scholar of the Talmud by the age of eight. On his father's death, he went with the rest of his family to live with a wealthy uncle in Egypt. There Luria studied under Rabbi Betzalel Ashkenazi, one of the foremost Talmudic scholars of the period, and Rabbi David abu Zimra, the chief rabbi of Cairo.

At the age of seventeen, Luria discovered the Zohar and plunged into the study and practice of Cabalism, devoting fifteen years to Cabalistic meditation. His work culminated in two years of intensive meditation in soli-tude in a small hut by the edge of the Nile. At the end of this period, in 1570, he received a vision instructing him to return to the Holy Land.

He traveled at once to Safed, then an internationally famous center of Cabalistic study. There, Luria soon became the center of a small circle of disciples, to whom he passed on the details of a complex new approach to the Cabala. The most important of these disciples was Rabbi Chaim Vital, who was already an important Cabalistic scholar and teacher but who devoted much of the rest of his life to expounding Luria's teachings. Two years after his arrival in Safed, Luria died suddenly after a short illness.

Luria's Cabalistic teachings are all but impossible to summarize adequately in a brief space. He introduced a complex new understanding of the processes of fall and redemption in the universe, centered on the "Breaking of the Vessels," the primal catastrophe that overwhelmed the Primal Worlds of unbalanced force. The fragments of these worlds, in Luria's scheme, became the Qlippoth, the powers of evil in the cosmos. Since they were originally vessels of light in the world of Atziluth, however, the powers of evil can be redeemed. By special Cabalistic meditations, on the one hand, and obedience to traditional Jewish laws and religious customs, on the other, the Cabalist can help redeem the powers of evil and the universe as a whole.

Within a few generations of his death, Luria's approach to the Cabala was standard throughout the Jewish world, and it has remained the core of Jewish Cabalistic theory and practice ever since. The Christian and Hermetic currents of the Cabala were less strongly influenced by Luria's work, since both these currents began separating from the Jewish current before Luria's time, and few of the major writings of Lurianic Cabala have ever been translated out of Hebrew. Still, significant elements of Luria's approach have found their way into some traditions of magical Cabala, and the teachings of the Hermetic Order of the Golden Dawn in particular were significantly shaped by some of Luria's ideas. SEE GOLDEN DAWN, HERMETIC ORDER OF THE. SEE ALSO CABALA; QLIPPOTH.

lycanthropy. (from Greek *lykos*, "wolf," and *anthropos*, "man") The tradition of shapeshifting into a wolf's form, famous in European folklore and in modern horror-movie imagery. The oldest known records of lycanthropy date from classical times, when people (or whole tribes) that occasionally turned into wolves appeared in various works. Nearly all cultures around the world have legends of shapeshifting, and the wolf is a preferred form in most of the areas where wolves are found at all.

The lore of lycanthropy is deeply intertwined with that of magic, and a variety of magical methods for taking on a wolf-form have survived, especially in Norse and Slavic sources. Several old Russian *zagovori* (spells) for managing the transformation exist in folklore collections.

One feature of lycanthropy that was heavily discussed in medieval and Renaissance literature on the subject, and is also covered in some later magical literature, has to do with the nature of the wolf-body taken on by the lycanthrope. In contrast to modern horror-movie imagery, werewolves in traditional folklore and magical teachings alike do not physically transform into wolves; the wolf-form is constructed of a subtle substance, most often identified by occultists as ether. *SEE* ETHER. The human body of the lycanthrope is typically left behind in a trance state, and lycanthropy thus represents a somewhat specialized form of etheric projection; *SEE* ETHERIC PROJECTION. FURTHER READING: GREER 2001, LÉVI 1972.

Ma'aseh Berashith. (Hebrew, "Work of Creation") One of the two oldest known branches of Jewish mysticism, a system of theory and practice based on the account of the Creation of the world in the Book of Genesis. Little is known about the Ma'aseh Berashith nowadays, although many scholars believe that the Sepher Yetzirah was a text of this school. Much of the lore of the Ma'aseh Berashith was later absorbed into the Cabala. *SEE* CABALA; SEPHER YETZIRAH. *SEE ALSO* MA'ASEH MERKABAH.

Ma'aseh Merkabah. (Hebrew, "Work of the Chariot") One of the two oldest branches of Jewish mysticism, a system of theory and practice based on the description of the chariot of God in the first chapter of the Book of Ezekiel. In the Ma'aseh Merkabah, this chariot was interpreted as nothing less than the structure of the spiritual world itself, divided into seven heavens and staffed by a dizzying assortment of angelic powers. Detailed handbooks of the structure of the chariot were written and circulated during the heyday of the Ma'aseh Merkabah, which extended from perhaps 300 B.C.E. until the early Middle Ages.

Several of these handbooks survive in fairly complete form, but were clearly meant to be supplemented with oral instruction, and many of the details of theory and practice remain obscure. What is clear is that Merkabah mystics were not content to study or meditate about the structure of Heaven; they were interested in going there, in visionary journeys that are described in detail in several accounts.

The practice of the Merkabah was considered to be very holy and very dangerous. It is related in the Talmud that a child, studying the scriptures in his teacher's house, understood the secret meaning of the word *chashmal* ("radiance")—whereupon a fire came forth from the chashmal and burnt him to death.

The Ma'aseh Merkabah was still being practiced in some circles during the development of the Cabala, and substantial elements of the older system seem to have been brought into Cabalistic teaching. Unlike the Ma'aseh Merkabah, though, the Cabala mostly relies on meditation as a vehicle for spiritual development, rather than the ecstatic visionary experiences of the Merkabah mystics of old. *SEE ALSO* MA'ASEH BERASHITH.

Mabinogion. The chief surviving collection of Welsh legends, and one of the few significant sources of information on the religious traditions of pre-Christian Wales, the *Mabinogion* has been a principal source for many modern Pagan traditions. The earliest complete version is in the *Red Book of Hergest*, written around 1400, although manuscripts dating back to 1225 or so contain fragments. Scholars are agreed that the tales were in circulation for centuries before they were first written down, but the final form seems to have been thoroughly worked over by the unknown figure who committed the tales to writing.

The name "Mabinogion" is actually a misnomer, and does not occur in Welsh. There are eleven surviving tales in the complete collection, of which four—the tales of Pwyll Lord of Dyved, Branwen daughter of Llyr,

Manawyddan son of Llyr, and Math son of Mathonwy—are described in the text as "the four branches of the Mabinogi." The meaning of the word *mabinogi* is uncertain; it may mean "stories of childhood," or it may be related to the name of the ancient Celtic deity Maponos, who appears in one of the tales in the later Welsh form of Mabon ap Modron.

Several of the characters of the Four Branches are lightly disguised gods. Rhiannon, whose adventures are important in the First and Third Branches, is descended from the Gaulish horse-goddess Epona, whose cult title Rigantona ("great queen") is the source of her name. Manawyddan son of Llyr, who plays a role in the Second and Third Branches, is borrowed from the Irish god Manannan, while the wizard Gwydion son of Don is actually a close cognate of the Germanic deity Woden or Odin. Trying to tease out details of pre-Christian Celtic religion from the dizzying confusion of the Four Branches, however, is difficult at best and has tended to produce wildly variable results, depending mostly on the presuppositions of those who have attempted it.

The other tales are unrelated to the Four Branches and include two pieces of legendary history, four legends of King Arthur's court, and a strange visionary tale, the *Dream of Rhonabwy*. One of the Arthurian legends, the raucous and confused *Tale of Culhwch and Olwen*, also contains a vast array of ancient mythic and legendary lore, jumbled together in a degree of disarray that has confounded attempts at analysis. SEE ALSO CELTIC RECONSTRUCTIONISM; DRUIDS; PAGANISM; TRIADS. FURTHER READING: GANTZ 1976, GRUFFYDD 1953.

Mabon. In modern Paganism, a name for the autumn equinox, one of the eight festivals of the year-wheel that occurs on September 23 each year. The name is derived from the Welsh mythic figure Mabon ap Modron, who was stolen away from his mother at the age of three days, and imprisoned in a magical castle. This is sometimes used to represent the hiding away of the earth's power of growth during the dark half of the year.

The use of Mabon as a name for this festival is entirely modern, and seems to have originated in the United States sometime in the 1970s. SEE ALSO SABBAT.

maceration. In alchemy, the process of soaking a substance in a suitable fluid in order to extract substances from it. The process of maceration is much used in spagyrics, where alcohol is often used to dissolve the vegetable sulphur and mercury from herbs. SEE ALCHEMY; SPAGYRICS.

Mackenzie, Kenneth Robert Henderson. English writer, scholar, and occultist, 1833–1886. Born in London, Mackenzie spent his early childhood in Vienna, where his father worked as a physician, and was educated in Germany. Fluent in English, German, Latin, Greek, and Hebrew, Mackenzie was a child prodigy who was publishing in scholarly journals by the age of seventeen and was elected to the Society of Antiquaries before his twenty-first birthday. His interests included occultism, which he studied under the guidance of Frederick Hockley, and in 1861 Mackenzie traveled to Paris to meet Eliphas Lévi. SEE HOCKLEY, FREDERICK; LÉVI, ELIPHAS.

Mackenzie's gifts as a scholar were substantial, but he became an alcoholic in his twenties and produced only one significant work thereafter. While later writers have claimed that he helped found the Societas Rosicruciana in Anglia, he showed no interest in joining it until 1872, when he received the Zelator degree, and he resigned in 1875. SEE SOCIETAS ROSICRUCIANA IN ANGLIA (SRIA).

By that time he had already begun work on his most important contribution, the *Royal Masonic Cyclopaedia*. Large parts of this were plagiarized from Albert Mackey's recently published *Encyclopedia of Freemasonry*, but he enriched these borrowings with a great deal of occult tradition, and with details of various quasi-Masonic orders operating in the English occult community at the time. He himself was involved in several of these, including the Royal Oriental Order of the Sat B'hai; SEE SAT B'HAI, ROYAL ORIENTAL ORDER OF THE. The *Cyclopaedia* was published in installments from 1875 to 1877. By the time it was finished, Mackenzie's health had begun to fail, and he died in poverty in 1886.

macrocosm and microcosm. A fundamental doctrine of occult philosophy, the concept of macrocosm and microcosm proposes that the universe as a whole (the macrocosm—Greek *makrokosmos*, "great cosmos") and the individual human being (the microcosm—Greek *mikrokosmos*, "little cosmos") reflect one another in their essential nature.

The roots of the doctrine of macrocosm and microcosm go back into prehistoric times. Ancient mythologies found in many different cultures suggest that the universe was created from the body of a primal human being or giant—Prajapati in Hindu myth, Ymir in the Norse *Eddas*, and so on. By the time of the Greek alchemists, these mythic images had been formalized into a theory that every aspect of the universe had a reflection in the human body, soul, and spirit. This has been a central concept in Western occultism ever since, and serves as the core explanation for astrology and other occult sciences; since the individual mirrors every aspect of the cosmos, changes in the cosmos will be mirrored in the individual—and vice versa.

In the Golden Dawn tradition of magic, the process of reflection between macrocosm and microcosm is held to be mediated by the aura or Sphere of Sensation, the egg-shaped region of energies surrounding the human body. *SEE* SPHERE OF SENSATION. *SEE ALSO* ASTROLOGY; AURA.

Madhr. (Old Norse, "man") The fourteenth rune of the younger futhark, Madhr stands for humanity in all its forms and manifestations. The Old Norwegian rune-poem also compares it, because of its shape, to the claw of a great hawk. Its sound-value is *m*. *SEE* YOUNGER FUTHARK.

The same rune, under the name Man, is also the fifteenth rune of the Armanen runic alphabet. It represents the concept of mothering, and its divine equivalent is the Midgard Serpent. Its magical power, from the rune-charm of the Old Norse *Havamal*, is Odin's gift and power of foresight. Its sound-value is *m*. *SEE* ARMANEN RUNES.

Rune Madhr (Man)

Madim. (Hebrew MDIM) The Hebrew name of the planet Mars, used to represent the Sphere of Mars in magical workings. It is considered to be the manifestation of Geburah, the fifth Sephirah of the Tree of Life, in Cabalistic theory. *SEE* CABALA; GEBURAH.

Madimi. The principal spirit involved in the Enochian workings of John Dee and Edward Kelly. *SEE* ENOCHIAN MAGIC.

Madona Horiente. (Italian dialect, "Lady East") According to the records of the Milanese inquisition, a goddess worshipped by a group in Milan in the late fourteenth century. The followers of Madona Horiente called themselves the *bona gens* ("Good People") and engaged in visionary travels at night, in animal form, in the company of the dead. To her followers, Madona Horiente gave knowledge of herbs, powers of divination, and the ability to detect and counter sicknesses, thefts, and bewitchments. These practices were condemned by the Catholic Church in 1380 and 1390.

The Good People were one of many medieval groups with similar beliefs, and their practices compare closely with those described in the ninth-century Canon *Episcopi*. *SEE* CANON EPISCOPI; HERODIAS. FURTHER READING: BEHRINGER 1998.

magic. Perhaps the most complex concept in Western occultism, magic has been defined and understood in a dizzying variety of ways over the centuries. At present, there is no single meaning generally accepted, even within the occult community, and the definitions used by occultists differ immensely from those proposed by academics and those held by the man or woman in the street. A history of these different definitions is, to a large extent, a history of magic itself.

Originally, the word—in Greek, *mageia*; in Latin, *magia*—meant the knowledge or art of the *magoi* or *magi*, a hereditary caste of Persian holy men. The Greek historian Herodotus ascribes to the magoi the responsibility for sacrifices, funeral ceremonies, and divination at the Persian royal court, and Xenophon describes them as experts in all things concerning the gods. As a borrowed term in Greek and Roman society, it had something of the same cachet that the word "swami" had in twentieth-century America—suggesting something strange, mystical, possibly impressive, possibly suspect.

The word "magus" had several competitors in ancient times, each of which came to refer to a particular class of what we would now label "magicians." The Greek word *goes* originally referred to a type of professional mourner in archaic funeral rites, and gradually shifted meanings over time to refer to the lowest class of magical practitioner, a mediumistic communicator with the dead; it could also mean "charlatan." *SEE* GOETIA. On a much higher level was the *theios aner* or "divine man," a person who had gained magical powers by asceticism and devotion to the gods. Apollonius of Tyana is among the most widely known examples of the type, and Jesus of Nazareth may have been another. *SEE* APOLLONIUS OF TYANA; JESUS OF NAZARETH. The polemics over magic in ancient times made for a situation in which any or all of these labels might be applied to the same person; a given magician might well be called a *theios aner* by his clients and supporters, a *goes* by his enemies, and a *magos* by the population at large.

By the beginning of the Common Era, the words "magus" and "magic" had lost most of their Persian connotations, and were used for most of the same practices that are still called "magical" today—that is, ritual workings and special preparations of substances meant to affect the universe by methods that don't make sense in the framework of modern scientific thought. This widening of the concept of magic caused a certain degree of difficulty, because prohibitions of magic were on the lawbooks of Rome long before Christianity rose to dominance. The Roman state had a long-term paranoia about private spiritual activities, which burst out in such atrocities as the execution of thousands of Dionysian initiates in 186 B.C.E. and the persecution of Christians at various times in the first, second, and third centuries of the Common Era; all forms of magic potentially fell under the same draconian laws. Traditional practices in agriculture, medicine, and many crafts found themselves reclassified as magic, and hasty exemptions had to be granted in some cases to keep these from falling under the severe legal penalties for magical practice. *SEE* MAGIC, PERSECUTION OF.

This widened definition of magic went through several shifts as Christianity rose to dominance in the Roman world, the Roman state itself collapsed, and the new societies of medieval Europe took shape. Paradoxically, the rise of Christianity actually decreased the persecution of magic for some centuries, as the early church defined "magic" as any form of occult practice that called upon non-Christian deities or powers. Identical rituals invoking the Trinity or the saints were explicitly exempted, and so a huge body of Christian magical practice grew up, tacitly permitted (and on occasion, actively supported) by church officials and theologians. *SEE* CHRISTIAN OCCULTISM.

The later Middle Ages, however, saw a sharp upswing in the persecution of magic. Partly this was a function of the severe stress undergone by the medieval world in the fourteenth century, the age of the Black Death of 1347–1352 and the social convulsions that followed it. Much of the renewed assault on magic, though, was actually due to the revival of studies of ancient Roman law in the universities. The old Roman classification of magic was widely discussed, and the idea that magic was magic no matter what entities were invoked became common among European intellectuals and lawyers. This shift played a significant part in launching the age of witch hunting that modern Pagans call the Burning Times. *SEE* BURNING TIMES.

The same revival of classical learning that helped start the Burning Times also, paradoxically enough, set in motion a very different redefinition of magic. The recovery of ancient mystical and magical texts from Greece and Rome led to the burgeoning of Renaissance Hermeticism, which saw magical practice as a religious act, a way of participation in the divine. *SEE* HERMETICISM. In the hands of Christian Hermeticists such as Marsilio Ficino (1433–1499) and Giovanni Pico della Mirandola (1463–1494), Renaissance Hermeticism became a more literate and philosophically sophisticated version of the magical Christianity of the early Middle Ages. *SEE* FICINO, MARSILIO; PICO DELLA MIRANDOLA, GIOVANNI. In the hands of more radical figures such as Giordano Bruno (1548–1600), it became an independent religion in its own right, one that claimed to be older and wiser than Christianity. It was for making such claims that Bruno was burned at the stake; *SEE* BRUNO, GIORDANO. Both the

Christian and the non-Christian view of magic as a religious rite remained common in the occult community itself until the rise of new definitions of magic in the nineteenth and twentieth centuries.

The next great shift in opinions about magic started out with the Protestant Reformation of the sixteenth century, and was the product of a radical redefinition of religion that took root in the arguments between Protestant and Catholic factions in the years that followed. Protestant polemicists in England, seeking a way to denounce Catholic ritualism, argued that religion consists entirely of turning toward the divine in hope and trust, and waiting passively for a response. Any action that seeks to influence, direct, or command spiritual powers, they argued, was magic, not religion.

This line of argument was moderately effective as a way of attacking Catholicism, but its greatest impact was in another field. During the eighteenth and nineteenth century, a series of Protestant theologians and philosophers built an entire theory of religion on this basis, which went on to become standard throughout the English-speaking and German-speaking countries of the world. From there it passed into comparative religion and anthropology, not least because it allowed the religions of non-European peoples to be dismissed as magic, not religion. To this day, a noticeable percentage of books written about magic by academics quote this same distinction between magic and religion as though it were a universal truth. In fact, with the exception of a few forms of Protestant Christianity, every religion in the world deals with spiritual powers by a combination of approaches, some more passive, some less so.

The multiple impacts of the Reformation and the Scientific Revolution thus brought about vast shifts in the definitions of magic used in the Western world. While clergymen denounced magic as an affront to the omnipotence of the Christian god, and scientists scratched their heads wondering why people could believe something that so obviously couldn't be true, magical practitioners themselves gradually evolved definitions of their own. This project was launched primarily by the work of French magus Eliphas Lévi (1810–1875), whose synthesis and redefinition of traditional occultism kick-started the modern magical revival. Lévi defined magic as the art of manipulating the Astral Light, the mysterious substance-energy that in his view lay behind all magical activities. SEE ASTRAL LIGHT; LÉVI, ELIPHAS.

Later writers, drawing on Lévi's theory of the magical will, expanded the definition considerably. The English magus and self-proclaimed Antichrist Aleister Crowley (1875–1947) proclaimed that magic—or as he spelled it, "magick"—is "the science and art of causing change in conformity with will" (Crowley 1976, p. xii). This definition, of course, would include anything from evoking the fiends of Hell to buttering a slice of bread—a point that Crowley intended as part of an effort to break down the conceptual barriers between occultism and other forms of human action. SEE CROWLEY, ALEISTER; THELEMA. Crowley was also among the first major figures in the occult world to conceptualize magic as a discipline of spiritual transformation, along the lines of yoga or other Asian traditions of practice. English occultist Dion Fortune (1890–1946) provided a common phrasing for this concept by describing magic as "the yoga of the West"; SEE FORTUNE, DION. Both Fortune and Crowley were strongly influenced by the new psychology being developed in their time by Sigmund Freud (1856–1939) and Carl Jung (1875–1961), and this gave a strong impetus to their redefinition of magic as an essentially internal practice of self-development. The same was true of another highly influential figure of the same period, Israel Regardie (1907–1985), who studied the work of Freud and Jung and combined these with the concepts of Freud's oddest disciple, Wilhelm Reich (1897–1957). SEE REGARDIE, ISRAEL; REICH, WILHELM.

In the last half of the twentieth century, a number of magical theorists came to define magic in purely psychological terms, as a method of ritual psychodrama with no effects outside the psyches of the participants. This definition found few takers in the occult community as a whole. More popular was the proposal of American mage and Druid P. E. I. Bonewits (1949–), who borrowed concepts from parapsychology to propose that magic was a set of psychological tools for making use of psychic powers such as telepathy and telekinesis.

In the light of all these competing definitions of magic, it may be foolhardy to risk another. Still, the one thing that can be said for certain about magic is that it is what magicians do. Magic, in other words, is a social category, defined by the fact that it is practiced by a particular set of subcultures—many of which have existed, in one form or another, for at least two and a half millennia in the Western world. The Pythagoreans and Orphics of classical Greece, the Gnostic and Hermetic movements of the Roman world, the occult circles of the Arab Near East, the shadowy magical and alchemical underworld of medieval Europe, the esoteric schools of Renaissance Hermeticism, the secret societies of the early modern period, the occult lodges of the eighteenth and nineteenth centuries, and the magical societies and Pagan covens of the present day all represent a single broad social phenomenon—the magical underground—distinct and coherent enough to be discussed and explored in its own terms.

As the above suggests, magic is also a historical category. Modern Western magic consists of coherent bodies of theory and practice that can be traced back some two and a half millennia through history to the occult traditions of the ancient Greek world. The term *magic* itself, as shown above, originally evolved in that ancient setting, and has remained attached to the traditions in question ever since. It thus makes sense to use the term for the traditions as such, rather than for some proposed universal category that happens to include them.

Magic, in this view, is not an abstract category of human activity, to be found in all places and times. It is a specific set of traditions found in Western cultures, and recently exported elsewhere in the world. It is directed toward shaping the world of human experience through contact with nonphysical powers, but it does so in its own distinctive and historically conditioned ways. Ways of doing the same thing that evolved in other cultural and historical settings, from this viewpoint, should not be called "magic"—any more than it would make sense for Chinese or Haitian scholars to refer to Western magical traditions as "European Taoism" or "European Voodoo." FURTHER READING: CROWLEY 1976, M. SMITH 1978.

magic, persecution of. One of the continuing themes in the history of occultism in the West, the persecution of magic and magicians has ranged in intensity from mild social ostracism to the horrors of the Burning Times. Rarely in the last twenty-five centuries, however, have magicians been able to work without some degree of hostility from their neighbors.

The idea that magical practices as such should be outlawed was a relatively late growth, since it required (among other things) a concept of magic as something separate from religion, medicine, and ordinary skilled craftsmanship. This concept was completely foreign to most ancient cultures, and evolved only gradually in the classical world. Plato played a significant part in the development both of a concept of magic and of a hostile approach to it, arguing in *The Laws* that those who claimed to be able to influence gods and spirits for the private benefit of their clients should be imprisoned for life and left unburied at death; *SEE* PLATO.

More important than the diatribes of philosophers, though, was the paranoia of the Roman state, which gradually expanded its reach to include nearly all of the ancient Western world. The Roman attitude toward magic was complex, and certain types (for example, medical magic and agricultural magic) were considered harmless. The political implications of personal, secret access to nonphysical powers, however, were not lost on Roman legalists, and by the Imperial period laws were on the books forbidding not only the practice of magic but even the possession of knowledge about it.

Roman attitudes toward occult practices hardened sharply in 186 B.C.E., when practitioners of the Bacchic mysteries were accused of plotting to overthrow the Roman state. *SEE* MYSTERIES, THE. Exactly what, if anything, was behind it all is impossible to say, but some 6,000 people were put to death as a result. Later, the slave rebellion in Sicily from 136 to 132 B.C.E. was largely fostered by Eunous, a prophet of Dea Syria, the Syrian Goddess. These experiences made the Roman ruling classes deeply suspicious of any unauthorized dealings with the supernatural, and did much to lay the groundwork for the persecution of Christianity under the empire.

These attitudes were adopted by Christianity from an early date, at least in part because Christians themselves were believed to be magicians by many Pagans, and faced prosecution under Roman laws against magic. Accusations of magic also provided an effective way to counter claims that Pagan, Gnostic, and heretical figures had performed miracles equal to those of Jesus or the saints. By the time of Augustine of Hippo (354–430 C.E.), who wrote at length about the demonic nature of magic in his major work *The City of God*, it was accepted throughout the church that magic and Christianity were incompatible, and that magic and Paganism were synonymous.

Ironically, this led in the centuries that followed to a widespread accommodation between the church and many magical practices. Since the name of Jesus and the intercession of the saints were held to be omnipotent against magic, magical practices that replaced Pagan gods with Jesus or the saints rarely came in for theological criticism in the thousand years or so after Augustine. The same habit of accommodation that built Christian churches on the sites of Pagan temples, and moved Christmas to the date that Pagan Romans had used to celebrate the birth of the Unconquerable Sun, allowed impressive amounts of Pagan magical lore to put on Christian dress and pass unhindered into the Middle Ages. *SEE* CHRISTIAN OCCULTISM.

Nonetheless, the old Roman laws against magic made an effective tool that could be used against Christian heretics or political opponents as well as Pagans. Priscillian of Avila, a fourth-century Spanish bishop who fell afoul of church politics, found himself caught in this particular trap; he was accused of heresy and magical practices, tortured by the imperial government until he confessed, and executed around 385. Such prosecutions were rare at that time, and for centuries thereafter, but a dangerous precedent was set.

On the whole, however, the Middle Ages marked a period of truce between the Christian church and the magical traditions of the Western world. Attitudes toward Christian magic ranged from tacit approval to open support, and even less thoroughly baptized systems such as astrology suffered no more than the occasional clerical denunciation. In many contexts, old quasi-Pagan traditions blended seamlessly with Christian ritual and practice; in Anglo-Saxon England, for example, good Christians used lightly Christianized spells to protect themselves from elves, and saw nothing wrong with the practice.

Open Paganism was opposed, but church officials ridiculed it as ineffective, rather than denouncing it as diabolic; penalties for making Pagan offerings were relatively light. *SEE* CANON EPISCOPI; PAGANISM. The one form of magic that did fall under heavy penalties was *maleficium*, magic intended to harm or kill another person, which was punished like any other form of violence or murder; *SEE* MALEFICIUM.

But the magical Christianity of the Middle Ages came under increasing pressure in the thirteenth and fourteenth century. One major factor was the revival of ancient Roman legal doctrines, first by church scholars and then by civil governments over much of Europe. Roman law included severe penalties for magic, and it allowed the use of torture, which was forbidden in criminal cases in most of Europe before the thirteenth century. The prestige of ancient Rome gave these ideas widespread credibility at a time when the medieval world was under increasing strain.

Roman law also brought a major change in the way criminal charges were handled. Most of Europe before the revival of Roman law followed a traditional "accusatorial" process—that is, charges had to be brought by a person who had been harmed by the alleged crime, and if the charges proved false the person bringing them faced severe penalties. Roman law, by contrast, made use of an "inquisitorial" process—that is, charges were brought by a public official, who was exempt from penalties in the case of false accusations. The study of Roman law in the universities led to the adoption of inquisitorial procedure over much of Europe.

All these changes made heretics and magicians much easier to charge and convict. The rise and destruction of the Cathar heresy in southern France drove these trends; *SEE* CATHARS. As the most powerful challenge the Catholic Church faced between the fall of Rome and the beginning of the Protestant Reformation, the Cathar crisis called forth an extreme response and led to the formal founding of the Holy Office of the Inquisition in 1239. In a time of crisis, it was easy for many people to believe that Christendom was threatened by unseen conspiracies with mysterious powers.

Among the first victims of these new trends was the Italian astrologer and magician Cecco d'Ascoli (1257–1327), who was burned at the stake as a heretic for his occult activities. *SEE* CECCO D'ASCOLI. He was the first of a number of intellectuals who suffered a similar fate or, like Ramon de Tarrega (c. 1295–1371), died in the Inquisition's dungeons; *SEE* TARREGA, RAMON DE. The same charges were also used to target political figures, especially by King Philip IV of France; the dismemberment of the Templars in 1307–1314 on charges of sorcery and heresy was only one of several similar campaigns launched by this cynical monarch. *SEE* KNIGHTS TEMPLAR.

In 1320 the Inquisition was made responsible for prosecuting cases of magical practice, an expansion of its authority that was confirmed by a papal bull in 1327. The trial of Lady Alice Kyteler in Ireland in 1326–7 contained most of the accusations heard later on in the witchcraft trials of the Burning Times: evil magic, lovemaking with demons, worship of Satan, and the existence of an organized sect dedicated to these practices.

All that was needed was a period of social strain intense enough to bring these occasional accusations into the forefront of collective consciousness. This was provided by the Black Death of 1347–1352, a massive epidemic of bubonic plague that killed approximately one-third of the population of Europe. In the aftermath of this apocalyptic event, conspiracy theories and mass panics swept through the disorganized and terrified survivors. The idea of a horrific conspiracy eating away at the foundations of Christian Europe became widespread. Over the half century following the Black Death, these beliefs came more and more to focus on the idea that a secret society of witches existed throughout Europe, worshipping the Devil, sacrificing and eating infants, practicing magic, and violating every social and sexual taboo. As a result, the next three hundred years—the Burning Times—saw some 50,000 people executed for witchcraft in Europe and North America. *SEE* BURNING TIMES.

Ironically, the witch-hunting frenzy caught few actual magicians, and some of the major figures in the occult scene of the time actually supported the witch hunts. The Burning Times were also the period when Renaissance Hermeticism was at its height, and occult traditions made enormous inroads into Western culture at all levels. Still, accusations of witchcraft were sometimes directed against even the most scholarly and devoutly Christian of Hermetic magicians. Giordano Bruno (1548–1600), burned at the stake in Rome in 1600 for heresy, was only the most prominent of Renaissance magicians to be caught up in the Inquisition's net. *SEE* BRUNO, GIORDANO.

The coming of the Scientific Revolution brought massive changes in attitudes. By the eighteenth century, with the Scientific Revolution in full swing, witchcraft prosecutions stopped in nation after nation. In England, which saw its last execution for witchcraft in 1682, the change was marked by the passage of the Witchcraft Act of 1736. This law repealed all previous statutes on the subject, overturned the legal basis for witchcraft prosecutions, and made it an offense to accuse someone of being a witch.

At the same time, however, it established legal penalties for people who claimed to be able to work magic, defining such claims as a type of fraud. Similar legislation went into effect over the next century in many other countries. Prosecutions for magic thus continued, although the penalties were far less extreme than before; under the Witchcraft Act, for example, a magician faced a maximum of one year in jail.

These last legal prosecutions ground to a halt in most of the Western world in the twentieth century. In Britain, the repeal of the Witchcraft Act in 1951 made possible the public emergence of modern Wicca. Elsewhere, laws of the same sort were repealed or simply not enforced, although prosecution for fortunetelling still occasionally takes place in a few United States jurisdictions.

Astrology, which had been subject to the same penalties as other forms of divination, won a pair of victories in 1914, when the British astrologer Alan Leo and the American astrologer Evangeline Adams were both tried on charges of fortunetelling and won acquittals. Leo himself was tried again in 1917 and fined £30, but prosecutions dropped steeply in the years that followed. *SEE*

LEO, ALAN. In Communist societies, which condemned occultism of all kinds as relics of a feudal past, and in Nazi Germany, which sought to eliminate all occult activities outside of Nazi Party control, persecution of occultists continued, but the collapse of these regimes brought an end to this wave of persecutions.

The fading out of legal penalties, however, did not bring an end to all forms of opposition to occultism. Where the legal system bowed out, the media was all too eager to step in. Media campaigns against occultism have been a frequent event in the Western world since the nineteenth century. The emergence of Wicca in Britain in the 1950s sparked off a frenzy of lurid denunciations in the media, and the same thing was repeated in the late 1960s and 1970s in the United States. The widespread panic over so-called "Satanic ritual abuse" in the United States and elsewhere, which began in 1980, brought out another flurry of similar media campaigns, and managed a brief but dismaying resurgence of legally supported witch hunting; SEE SATANIC RITUAL ABUSE. While this latest wave of persecution appears to have lost its momentum as of this writing, the possibility that occult traditions may face further waves of persecution in the future cannot be ruled out. FURTHER READING: CHADWICK 1976, COHN 1975, GINZBURG 1991, HUTTON 1999, JOLLY 1996, PETERS 1978.

magic square. A set of whole numbers, starting with one, arranged so that when vertical, horizontal, or diagonal lines of numbers are added together, the total is always the same. A set of seven magic squares has been traditionally assigned to the seven planets since ancient times, and are much used in talismanic magic.

By the process of gematria, the letters of a word in Hebrew or other ancient alphabets can be converted into numbers. The name of any spirit connected to a planet, turned into a sequence of numbers, can be traced out on the magic square of that planet by a connect-the-dots process, resulting in a linear design called a sigil. In ceremonial magic, the sigil of a spirit is used to summon, command, or banish the spirit. SEE GEMATRIA.

Magic squares made of letters rather than numbers are also found in occult tradition—though this concept only makes sense in cultures that distinguish between the two; SEE ARITHMANCY. The so-called "Sator-Rotas" square, formed of the Latin sentence *sator arepo tenet opera rotas*, is perhaps the most famous of these; SEE SATOR AREPO TENET OPERA ROTAS. SEE ALSO ARITHMOLOGY; CABALA.

magical personality. In modern Hermetic traditions, an artificial personality created by the magician for use in magical practice. The magician's ordinary personality is seen as a haphazard structure cobbled together out of the assorted experiences of this and previous lives, insufficiently stable to handle the stresses of sustained magical training. The apprentice magician therefore creates an alternate personality, based on a balanced set of concepts such as Love, Wisdom, and Power, and practices moving into and out of this alternate personality at will, using as a cue some action such as putting on and taking off a ring.

The magical personality can be treated simply as a means of preventing the overinflation of the ego that can occur in magical training. In another sense, however, it is understood as "borrowing" from the Higher Genius those qualities of balanced power which, according to magical theory, the adept will have constantly at his or her disposal. SEE ADEPT. FURTHER READING: W. BUTLER 1959.

Magician, the. The first Major Arcanum of the tarot, this card is called the Mountebank or the Juggler in old decks; the present title is a product of the occult reinterpretation of the tarot and does not seem to be traceable before the middle of the nineteenth century. Older decks, and some recent ones, show a huckster in a broad-brimmed hat, standing behind a table covered with an assortment of items for sale; many modern decks turn the table into an altar, the objects on it into magical working tools, and the huckster into a mage clad in the robes of an adept.

In the Golden Dawn system, the Magician corresponds to the Hebrew letter Beth, while the French system assigns it to Aleph. In divination, common meanings of this card are the human will, intelligence, communication, skill, trickery, and deception.

Its magical title is "The Magus of Power." SEE BETH; TAROT.

Tarot trump the Magician (Universal Tarot)

magick. Obsolete spelling of the word "magic" adopted by Aleister Crowley "to distinguish the Science of the Magi from its counterfeits" (Crowley 1980, p. 53). Since Crowley's time it has been used by numerous magicians, writers, and groups, some with connections to Crowley's magical and religious system of Thelema, some without. The adjective "magickal" and the noun "magickian" have also seen use in recent years, although neither term has an actual pedigree as an English word. ("Magick" was used as adjective as well as noun in earlier times, and the spelling of "magician" contemporary with "magick" was actually "magitian").

Similar motives to Crowley's have generated several other attempted respellings of the word "magic," including "magik," "majick," and "majik." Fortunately for the language, none of these have caught on. *SEE ALSO* CROW-LEY, ALEISTER; MAGIC.

magister. (Latin, "master, teacher") In classical times, the Middle Ages, and the Renaissance, a title of respect given to any educated man; the equivalent term for a woman was *magistra*. Several different occult traditions have used it as a title. In some Pagan traditions, it serves as an alternative to High Priest; *SEE* HIGH PRIEST.

magistery. In alchemical parlance, a product of alchemy requiring a solid degree of competence in the art. Modern spagyric texts most often use the term for plant magisteries, which are concentrated alchemical extracts prepared from plants by a process of repeated maceration (steeping of the plant matter in fluid) and distillation. *SEE ALSO* ALCHEMY; SPAGYRICS. FURTHER READING: JUNIUS 1985.

magistra. (Latin, feminine of *magister*, "master") A term used by and for High Priestesses in some modern traditions of Wicca. *SEE* HIGH PRIESTESS; MAGISTER.

magnetic fluid. In some occult writings, a term for etheric energy, or for the negative polarity of etheric energy. *SEE* ETHER.

magnetism. In some occult writings, a term for etheric energy. *SEE* ANIMAL MAGNETISM; ETHER.

magnetite. This naturally magnetic form of iron ore, also known as lodestone, has an important role in several different traditions of folk magic. In hoodoo, pieces of magnetite are kept as amulets and "fed" iron filings in order to draw good luck, money, or love to their owner. *SEE ALSO* HOODOO.

Mah. (Hebrew MH, "what?") In the Cabala, the secret name of the world of Yetzirah. The numerical values of its letters add up to forty-five, which is also the sum of YVD HA VAV HA, the spelling of the Tetragrammaton in Yetzirah. *SEE* TETRAGRAMMATON; YETZIRAH.

Maiden. In many Wiccan traditions, a female member of a coven who assists the High Priestess, and who is usually at least a second degree initiate. She often runs the training circle of prospective initiates. *SEE* COVEN; WICCA.

Maier, Michael. German writer, physician, and alchemist, 1568–1622. Maier was born in Rendsburg in northern Germany. He attended the university at Rostock, where he graduated with a doctorate in medicine in 1597, and became a successful physician, serving for a time as personal physician and secretary to Emperor Rudolf II.

In 1614, two years after the emperor's death, he visited England, where he met the great English occultist Robert Fludd, and learned the English language in order to translate Thomas Norton's *Ordinall of Alchemy* into Latin. *SEE* FLUDD, ROBERT; NORTON, THOMAS. He returned to Germany in 1616, settling in Madgeburg, where he died in 1622.

Maier's books were the product of his last years; his first book was not published until 1614, and all his substantial output appeared over the seven years following. His most important writings include *Symbola Aurea Mensae Duodecim Nationum* (*Twelve Nations' Symbols of the Golden Table*, 1617), which presents the arguments in favor of alchemy in dialogue form, and *Atalanta Fugiens* (*Atalanta Fleeing*, 1618), a multimedia tour de force in which Maier presented fifty alchemical concepts, each with a lavishly engraved image, an epigram, a commentary, and a three-part musical fugue. Maier also edited and presented the works of other alchemists; his Latin translation of Norton's *Ordinall* was responsible for that work's European popularity, and he also played a central role in introducing the alchemical writings of Basilius Valentinus into circulation. *SEE* VALENTINUS, BASILIUS.

Maier's writings also included several major works dealing with the Rosicrucian furor, including his *Silentium Post Clamores* (*Silence After Noise*, 1617) and *Themis Aurea* (*Golden Themis*, 1618). The first of these was a defense of the Rosicrucian order, the second a detailed commentary on the six laws of the order as given in the *Fama Fraternitatis*, the first of the Rosicrucian manifestos. Like almost everyone who published on the Rosicrucian side of the debate, Maier denied that he himself was a Rosicrucian; he has nonetheless been included in most lists of probable Rosicrucians by those, in and out of the occult traditions, who hold that the mysterious fraternity had a real existence. *SEE* ROSICRUCIANS. *SEE ALSO* ALCHEMY. FURTHER READING: MAIER 1989, READ 1937.

Makon. (Hebrew MKVN, "place") In Cabalistic lore, the sixth of the seven heavens, corresponding to the Sephirah Chesed. *SEE* HEAVENS, SEVEN.

Malakim. (Hebrew MLKIM, "kings") The order of angels corresponding to Tiphareth, the sixth Sephirah of the Tree of Life, and forming Tiphareth's correspondence in the world of Yetzirah. The Malakim are sometimes considered to be the same as, or associated with, the elemental kings of the four races of elementals. *SEE* CABALA; ELEMENTAL; YETZIRAH.

malefic. (Latin *maleficus*, "doing evil") In older traditions of astrology, a planet or aspect that has a generally negative effect. Mars and Saturn were considered the two malefic planets, and opposition and square the malefic aspects. *SEE* ASPECT, ASTROLOGICAL; ASTROLOGY; MARS; SATURN.

maleficium. (Latin, "evil work"; plural *maleficia*) In the legal codes of the Middle Ages, the standard term for magic intended to harm or kill another person, directly or indirectly. During most of the Middle Ages, maleficium was the only form of magic as such that was punishable by law, and had the same penalties as non-magical forms of violence. Thus, for example, the sixth-century laws of the Salic Franks prescribe a fine to be paid by the offender to the victim's family in cases of murder by magic, just as in cases of murder with a sword or poison. In the same way, King Aethelstan of England (reigned 925–940 C.E.) decreed that someone who killed by means of maleficia was to be put to death if he or she pled guilty, while a suspected *maleficus* who pled innocent was to be freed after payment of wergild and a pledge by members of his or her family to guarantee the future good behavior of the accused.

To the church, on the other hand, maleficia were problematic because—at least according to church theorists—they required the cooperation of demons. Since many Christian scholars insisted that all Pagan gods were actually demons, the survival of Pagan magical practices lent some support to this view. By the beginning of the fourteenth century, the viewpoint of the church had hardened to the extent of considering all magic, without exception, to be maleficia, demon-worship, and thus also heresy. This led, in 1320, to a ruling by Pope John XXII turning over prosecutions for magic to the Inquisition, and played an important role in setting the stage for the Burning Times. *SEE ALSO* BURNING TIMES; MAGIC, PERSECUTION OF.

Malkah be-Tarshishim ve-ad Ruachoth Schechalim. (Hebrew MLKA BThRShYSYM VAaD RVChVTh ShChLIM, "Queen of Chrysolites and Spirits of Lions") In ceremonial magic, the Intelligence of Intelligences of the moon; her subordinate Spirit of Spirits is Shad Barshemoth ha-Shartathan, and both these govern the planetary spirit of the moon, Chashmodai. There are several different spellings of her name in circulation. *SEE* INTELLIGENCE, PLANETARY.

Malkuth. (Hebrew MLKVTh, "kingdom") The tenth and lowest Sephirah of the Cabalistic Tree of Life, representing the world of ordinary life. Its standard magical symbolism is as follows:

Name of God: ADNI, Adonai (Lord).

Archangels: MThThRVN, Metatron, Prince of Countenances; SNDLPVN, Sandalphon (Twin Brother).

Angelic Host: AIShIM, Ishim (Humanity).

Astrological Correspondence: AaVLM YSWDWTh, Olam Yesodoth (Sphere of the Elements).

Tarot Correspondence: The four Tens and four Pages or Princesses of the pack.

Elemental Correspondence: Earth.

Magical Image: A young woman sitting on a throne.

Additional Symbols: The altar, the equal-armed cross, the temple, the Tree of Knowledge of Good and Evil.

Colors: in Atziluth—clear yellow.

in Briah—citrine, olive, russet, and black.

in Yetzirah—as Briah, but flecked with gold.

in Assiah—black rayed with yellow.

Correspondence in the Microcosm: GVP, Guph, the physical body.

Correspondence in the Body: The feet.

Grade of Initiation: 1=10, Zelator.

Qlippoth: LILITh, Lilith, the Woman of Night.

The corresponding text from the *Thirty-two Paths of Wisdom* runs as follows: "The Tenth Path is the Resplendent Intelligence, because it is exalted above every head, and sits on the throne of Binah. It illuminates the splendor of all the Lights, and causes an influence to descend from the Prince of Countenances." *SEE ALSO* BRIDE, THE; CABALA; TREE OF LIFE.

Malleus Maleficarum. (Latin, "Hammer of Witches") Witch-hunting manual written by the German friars Heinrich Kramer and Jakob Sprenger, first published in 1486. The most popular of all the witch-hunting manuals of early modern Europe, the *Malleus* provided a de-tailed account of official Catholic beliefs about witches, their actions and motives, and the proper methods for identifying them and obtaining confessions through torture. *SEE ALSO* BURNING TIMES. FURTHER READING: KRAMER AND SPRENGER 1971.

Man. *SEE* MADHR.

Man in Black. *SEE* SUMMONER.

mandrake. (*Mandragora officinarum*). An important herb in Western magical tradition, mandrake is a member of the nightshade family, with leaves that lay flat on the ground, purple flowers, round yellow fruit, and a fleshy root that is commonly forked. The root often has at least a slight similarity to a human form, and like other human-shaped roots—ginseng is a good example—it has been held to contain a wide array of magical powers.

According to traditional plant lore, mandrakes grow beneath gallows and scream when they are uprooted. They must be harvested by means of a complex ceremony in which a dog is tied to the plant and lured with meat to pull it from the ground. Once harvested, they should be kept wrapped up and washed with wine every day; if this is done, the spirit of the mandrake will carry out magical tasks for its owner. Bryony is the center of a similar set of practices; *SEE* BRYONY. *SEE ALSO* NATURAL MAGIC. FURTHER READING: BRZUSTOWICZ 1974.

Manichaeism. Although it is almost forgotten today, Manichaeism was once a world religion with organized churches scattered across Eurasia from Spain to southern China. Its founder, Mani (216–276 C.E.), was born near the city of Ctesiphon, in what is now Iraq. He was brought up among the Elchasaites, a sect of Jewish-Christian Gnostics, but at the age of twelve received a revelation from the Tawm, his angelic companion. At the age of twenty-four, on the prompting of the Tawm, he left the Elchasaites and began the first of many journeys.

Like other prophets and messiahs of the same period, Mani attracted a circle of apostles, and a collection of accounts of his life—the so-called *Cologne Mani Codex*—was rediscovered in Egypt in 1970. He formally proclaimed his new religion in 240, and during the reign of Shapur I, emperor of Persia (reigned 242–272), preached freely throughout the sprawling Persian Empire, as well as in central Asia and northern India. After Shapur's death in 272, Mani and his followers came under increasing persecution at the hands of the Zoroastrian priesthood, and in 276 Mani was tortured to death and his skin, stuffed with straw, displayed in public.

The religion Mani founded was essentially Gnostic in outline; *SEE* GNOSTICISM. He taught that there were two worlds, a world of light and spirit opposed by a world of darkness and matter. The Father of Greatness, ruler of the world of light, sent forth the Primal Man to vanquish the world of darkness, but the Primal Man became entangled in matter and his soul remains there in fragments, each of which is a human soul. The Father of Greatness then called into being a series of spiritual beings—the Living Spirit, the Third Messenger, the Jesus of Light, and finally the Apostle of Light—to call the fragments of the soul of Primal Man back to the World of Light. Mani himself was the last incarnation of the Apostle of Light, who had earlier appeared in the world as the Buddha, Zoroaster, and Jesus of Nazareth.

The Manichaean Church was persecuted not only in the Persian Empire, but also in the Roman and Chinese empires as well. Despite this, it managed to establish itself across most of the Eurasian continent, and established a strong presence in central Asia, where the nomadic Uighur tribespeople converted en masse to the new faith. The Bogomils and Cathars, heretical Gnostic sects in medieval Europe, may have been Manichaean off-shoots, but this is hotly debated by modern scholars; *SEE* CATHARS. Manichaeism seems to have gradually gone out of existence by the fifteenth century, although attempts have been made to revive it in recent years. FURTHER READING: KLIMKEIT 1993, VAN OORT 1998.

Mann. *SEE* MANNAZ.

Mannaz. (Old Germanic, "man") The twentieth rune of the elder futhark, corresponding to humanity, companionship, social relations, and the community. Some modern runemasters relate it to the deity Heimdall. Its sound-value is *m*. *SEE* ELDER FUTHARK.

The same rune appears in the Anglo-Saxon futhorc under the name Mann, with the same meanings and sound-value.

Rune Mannaz (Mann)

mansions of the moon. In astrology and stellar magic, a set of twenty-eight constellations which track the moon's passage through the heavens. The mansions of the moon once served approximately the same purpose in lunar astrology that the signs of the zodiac served in solar astrology. In the days before written calendars, a person who had learned the mansions could compare the phase of the moon to the mansion it was in, and track the course of the seasons with a good deal of precision. Different versions of the mansions are found in Arabic, Hindu, and Chinese astrology, although the system as a whole seems to have been of Hindu origin.

In Arabic magic, the mansions of the moon play an important role, and each was assigned a name, a spirit, a magical image, a metal and incense, and a particular power or influence. Talismans of the metal, bearing the image, are consecrated by being censed with the incense when the mansion was rising above the eastern horizon. The *Picatrix*, an important Arabic magical text also much studied in medieval Europe, contains a good deal of lore on the mansions of the moon. *SEE* PICATRIX.

In medieval astrological tradition, the twenty-eight mansions of the moon were sometimes used to organize *Books of Moons*. *SEE* BOOK OF MOONS. *SEE ALSO* MOON.

Mantong. According to the writings of Richard Shaver and others involved in the "Shaver mystery" of the 1940s, the original language of mankind, dating to Lemurian times. The word itself literally means "man tongue," "human language." *SEE* SHAVER MYSTERY. The following definitions are Shaver's own:

A: Animal (used AN for short)

B: Be (to exist: often command)

C: See

D: (also used DE) Disintegrant energy; Detrimental (most important symbol in language)

E: Energy (an all concept, including motion)

F: Fecund (use FE as in female: fecund man)

G: Generate (used GEN)

H: Human (some doubt on this one)

I: Self; Ego (same as our I)

J: (see G) (same as generate)

K: Kinetic (force of motion)

L: Life

M: Man

N: Child; Spore; Seed (as ninny)

O: Orifice (a source concept)

P: Power

Q: Quest

R: (used as AR) Horror (symbol of dangerous quantity of dis force in the object)

S: (SIS) (an important symbol of the sun)

T: (used as TE) (the most important symbol; origin of the cross symbol) Integration; Force of growth (the intake of T is the cause of gravity; the force is T; tic meant science of growth; remains as credit word)

U: You

V: Vital (used as VI) (the stuff Mesmer calls animal magnetism; sex appeal)

W: will

X: conflict (crossed force lines)

Y: Why

Z: Zero (a quantity of energy of T neutralized by an equal quantity of D)

manu. In Theosophical lore, the ruler and ancestor of a root race. A manu is "the Representative Man of [his] Race, its prototype, and every member of that race is directly descended from him" (Leadbeater 1925, p. 28).

The manu of the fifth root race, the Aryan race, is Vaivasvata Manu, who is a mahachohan of the Great White Lodge. The manu of the fourth root race, which includes most of non-Aryan humanity, is Chakshusha Manu. Sometime in the twenty-sixth century, when the sixth root race appears in California, the Master El Morya will become its manu. *SEE* EL MORYA, MASTER. *SEE ALSO* MASTERS; ROOT RACE; THEOSOPHY.

manvantara. In Theosophy, a period of manifestation. Each manvantara alternates with pralaya, a period of dissolution and latency. Manvantaras and pralayas make up the building blocks of the Theosophical doctrine of cosmic cycles. *SEE* CYCLES, COSMIC; PRALAYA; THEOSOPHY.

Maon. (Hebrew MAaVN, "residence") In Cabalistic lore, the fifth of the seven heavens, corresponding to the Sephirah Geburah. *SEE* HEAVENS, SEVEN.

Maqlû rituals. (Akkadian, "burning") A type of magical ceremony practiced in Babylonia, Assyria, and several other Mesopotamian cultures, in which figurines of demons, ghosts, or human enemies were made, consecrated, and destroyed by fire. Detailed texts of a variety of Maqlû rituals were recovered from the royal library of the Assyrian king Ashurbanipal at Nineveh. *SEE ALSO* ASHURBANIPAL; MESOPOTAMIAN OCCULTISM.

Marby, Friedrich Bernhard. Danish occultist, 1882–1966. Born in Friesland, Marby encountered the writings of Guido von List while working as a printer's apprentice in Germany, and became an avid student of Ariosophy and runic lore. *SEE* ARIOSOPHY; LIST, GUIDO VON. In 1917 he moved to Stuttgart, pursued a career in the newspaper industry, and studied astrology. His researches and experiments led him to see the runes as basic patterns of cosmic energy that could be tapped by way of meditation and rune yoga exercises, in which the practitioner stands in rune-derived postures while intoning the corresponding sounds.

In 1936, as part of the Nazi regime's campaign against unauthorized occultists, he was arrested and interned at Welzheim concentration camp. He was transferred to Flossenbürg and then to Dachau, where he was among the survivors liberated by Allied troops in 1945. After the war he resumed his occult work, publishing a magazine and two new books before his death in 1966. FURTHER READING: GOODRICK-CLARKE 1992.

Maria. Jewish-Egyptian alchemist, first century B.C.E. One of the most important figures in the early history of alchemy, Maria is often called Maria Prophetissa or Maria the Jewess in older sources. Details of her life are entirely lacking, in large part because later writers confused her with Miriam, the sister of the Jewish prophet Moses. She wrote several books, portions of which survive as quotations in later alchemical works.

Maria was a brilliant inventor, and created many of the items of equipment that would be standard alchemical gear for the next two thousand years. Her creations include the *balneum Mariae* or water-bath, an early form of double boiler; the *balneum arenae* or sand-bath, another method of ensuring moderate heat; and the *kerotakis*, a device for treating metals with corrosive vapors. She also devised important new equipment for distillation, including a three-beaked still that is used for fractional distillation. *SEE ALSO* ALCHEMY; BALNEUM ARENAE; BALNEUM MARIAE. FURTHER READING: LINDSAY 1970.

Mars. One of the seven traditional planets of astrology, Mars in the birth chart represents sexuality, aggression, and will, as well as the masculine side of the personality. In astrological symbolism, Mars rules the signs Aries and Scorpio, although many modern astrologers assign Scorpio to the new planet Pluto. He is exalted in Capricorn, in his detriment in Libra and Taurus, and in his fall in Cancer. *SEE* ASTROLOGY.

In alchemy, Mars is commonly used as a symbol of iron. *SEE* ALCHEMY.

Astrological symbol of Mars

Martinism. A major Western magical and mystical tradition, rooted in the teachings of the great eighteenth-century French occultist and mystic Louis-Claude de Saint-Martin (1743–1803); *SEE* SAINT-MARTIN, LOUIS-CLAUDE DE. Saint-Martin began his esoteric career as a student of Martines de Pasqually (1727–1774), whose Ordre des Élus Coens (Order of Chosen Priests) taught a system of ceremonial magic rooted in an esoteric interpretation of Freemasonry. *SEE* FREEMASONRY; PASQUALLY, MARTINES DE. Later in his life, Saint-Martin turned away from this magical approach and became a student of the Christian mystical theosophy of Jakob Böhme; *SEE* BÖHME, JAKOB; THEOSOPHY (CHRISTIAN MYSTICAL). These two very different approaches, and the often difficult relation between them, have been important themes in the history of Martinism.

Saint-Martin himself, after his departure from the Elus Coens, opposed formal organizations and encouraged individuals to pursue their spiritual development in solitude. Still, his writings were extremely popular in occult Masonic circles, especially in Germany and Russia. The Strict Observance, a branch of Masonry based in Germany with strong occult connections, played an important part in spreading Saint-Martin's ideas throughout central and eastern Europe.

In Russia, where the Strict Observance had a significant presence, Saint-Martin's ideas were extremely influential throughout the Masonic scene, and moved from there into intellectual circles throughout Russian society. Martinism throughout that period was relatively unorganized, though, and existed in the form of individuals and small circles of students, some of whom used ritual forms while others did not.

In the late nineteenth-century revival of occultism, Martinism did not escape attention. Papus (Gérard Encausse, 1865–1916), a major figure in French occult circles at the turn of the century, was largely responsible for organizing the largest and most successful of these, the Martinist Order, which combined the ritual and contemplative aspects of the tradition. *SEE* PAPUS. Founded in 1884 by Papus and fellow Martinist Pierre Augustin Chaboseau, the Martinist Order worked four degrees:

Associate

Initiate

S.I. (*Superieur Inconnu*—Secret Chief)

S.I.I. (*Superieur Inconnu Initiateur*—Initiator Secret Chief)

According to some accounts, the ceremony of the Associate degree was borrowed from the "Egyptian" Masonry of Cagliostro, while that of the Initiate degree came from the Benevolent Knights of the Holy City, a quasi-Masonic order founded by Jean-Baptiste Willermoz, another student of Martinez de Pasqually.

In 1891 Papus and Chaboseau established a Supreme Council and set out to unite as many Martinists as possible under its umbrella. After Papus' death in 1916, however, the Martinist Order broke into several competing factions, and several attempts to bring about a renewed unity since then have had little effect. Most Martinist orders, although not all, accept the initiations of other orders as valid, but there has been a great deal of debate over which orders can and cannot trace a valid lineage back to Louis-Claude de Saint-Martin.

Martinism has undergone a modest renaissance in the 1980s and 1990s, with several new orders founded during that period and a noticeable spread in lodges and individuals working with Martinist teachings. Little has been published in English on the Martinist tradition, although Polish Martinist Dymitr Sudowski wrote two important books on the subject in the middle of the twentieth century under his pseudonym Mouni Sadhu. *SEE ALSO* LODGE, MAGICAL; SADHU, MOUNI. FURTHER READING: HUBBS 1971, SADHU 1962, SADHU 1965.

Maskim. In the occult traditions of Babylonia, seven evil spirits associated with the seven planets. They were said to rise in the west and set in the east, and brought every kind of sickness, calamity, and destruction. Impressive rituals to ward off the influence of the Maskim survive in Mesopotamian clay tablet records. *SEE* MESOPOTAMIAN OCCULTISM. FURTHER READING: E. BUTLER 1949.

Masters. In some branches of occult lore, especially those connected with Theosophy, highly evolved human (or quasi-human) beings who have attained enlightenment and supernormal powers over countless incarnations of spiritual striving. Much of the material circulated in occult circles over the last century and a quarter was said to derive from one or another Master, communicated by means of telepathy or mediumistic trance.

The list of known or suspected Masters in occult publications is a fairly extensive one. Among the most famous are Jesus of Nazareth, who is sometimes described as the Master of Masters; the Comte de Saint-Germain, often called the Master R. (that is, Rakoczy); and the Masters El Morya and Kuthumi (sometimes spelled Koot Hoomi), who were the principal Masters said to be behind the Theosophical movement.

A modern historian of Theosophy, K. Paul Johnson, has argued that Blavatsky's Masters were living individuals, whose real names and backgrounds can be teased out from contemporary sources. "El Morya," he suggests, was Blavatsky's alias for Ranbir Singh, maharajah of Kashmir, while "Kuthumi" was the Sikh leader Thakar Singh Sandhanwalia. Both of these men were supporters of Blavatsky during her years in India, when she was a vocal supporter of Indian autonomy and an opponent of Christian missionaries. Whatever the truth of their involvement, however, the concept soon spun out of Blavatsky's hands and took on its later, more mystical form—a process that annoyed Blavatsky endlessly. *SEE* BLAVATSKY, HELENA PETROVNA.

The concept of the Masters derives in part from the older idea, current in eighteenth-century occult lodges, of Secret Chiefs. It can also trace some of its roots back to the Buddhist conception of the bodhisattva, the enlightened being who returns from the edge of Nirvana in order to lead others to enlightenment. At the same time, contact with apparently real entities who have teachings to impart is a fairly common experience for students of many spiritual paths, and this experience is probably the core of the entire complex. That these teachings cover the spectrum from brilliant insights to gibberish is part of the mystery. *SEE ALSO* THEOSOPHY. FURTHER READING: J. GODWIN 1994, K. JOHNSON 1994, LEADBEATER 1925.

Mathers, Samuel Liddell. English occultist, 1854– 1918. Born in London and educated at Bedford Grammar School, he came from a background of poverty and never attended university. He spent his early adult years living with his mother in Bournemouth, working as a clerk and beginning his lodge involvements with his initiation into Freemasonry in 1877. *SEE* FREEMASONRY. In 1882 he became a member of the Societas Rosicruciana in Anglia, a Masonic Rosicrucian group whose leading light at that time was William Wynn Westcott, a rising star in English occult circles. *SEE* SOCIETAS ROSICRUCIANA IN ANGLIA (SRIA); WESTCOTT, WILLIAM WYNN.

In 1885 he moved to London and became a member of the Hermetic Society founded by Anna Kingsford; *SEE* KINGSFORD, ANNA BONUS. The same year saw the publication of his most significant book, *The Kabbalah Unveiled*, a translation of parts of the Zohar with accompanying commentary. *SEE* CABALA; ZOHAR. By this time he was working closely with Westcott on the development of the Hermetic Order of the Golden Dawn, which would go on to become the most influential occult order of its time. *SEE* GOLDEN DAWN, HERMETIC ORDER OF THE.

Well before the time the Golden Dawn was formally founded in 1888, Mathers had begun to insist that he was descended from the MacGregors, the outlaw "nameless clan" of Scottish Highlands legend, and adopted the title Comte de Glenstrae, which he claimed was conferred on an ancestor by Louis XV of France. His claims to Scottish ancestry have found little support from actual research: the list of known aliases of MacGregors does not include the name Mathers, and no trace of his title has surfaced in French records.

In 1890 he married Mina Bergson, the sister of French philosopher Henri Bergson, and was made curator of the Horniman Museum—which was, not coincidentally, owned by the father of fellow Golden Dawn initiate Anne Horniman. Mathers' unstable behavior lost him that position by 1892, however, and he and Mina (who changed her name to the more Celtic-sounding Moina) moved to Paris. Once there, Mathers became increasingly dictatorial and erratic, and Westcott's resignation from the order in 1897 left Mathers free of any outside control.

The result was a series of spiralling crises that ended in the open revolt of most of the order in 1900. Caught off guard, Mathers was able to preserve a fraction of the original order under the name Alpha et Omega; *SEE* ALPHA ET OMEGA. The defection of Aleister Crowley, an initiate of the order who had backed Mathers during the revolt and then turned on him in 1904, came as another blow.

In his last years Mathers continued to run the Alpha et Omega, and also wrote and performed a series of public rituals, the Rites of Isis, which attracted favorable attention from the Paris occult scene as well as the cultural avant-garde. He died in the great influenza epidemic of 1918. *SEE ALSO* ZANONI. FURTHER READING: COLQUHON 1975, GILBERT 1983A.

matriarchies, ancient. According to some writers and scholars of the nineteenth, twentieth, and twenty-first centuries, the original form of human society was politically dominated by women. This was first proposed by

the Swiss Romantic historian Johann Jakob Bachofen (1815–1887), who proposed in his 1861 book *Mutterrecht* (*Mother Right*) that human social evolution had passed through three stages, defined by the relation between the sexes. The first stage of "hetairism" was one of universal promiscuity and equality; it was followed by the stage of matriarchy, in which women dominated society, and finally by the stage of patriarchy, in which men dominated. Bachofen's work was extremely popular in the late nineteenth- and early twentieth-century counterculture, and played an important role in inspiring revivals of Pagan goddess worship during this time. *SEE* GODDESS, THE; NEOPAGANISM.

Other writers built on Bachofen's theory, and in 1903 the English classicist Jane Harrison presented the theory of ancient matriarchies in what is essentially its modern form. According to Harrison, southeastern Europe in the late Stone Age had been the site of a peaceful, harmonious, artistic culture centered on the worship of a universal mother goddess. In this utopian society, crime and warfare were unknown, and disputes were settled by female elders in accordance with traditional custom. This society was destroyed at the beginning of the Bronze Age by invading Indo-European tribesmen on horseback, who introduced warfare, social hierarchy, and the subjugation of women.

During her lifetime, Harrison's views were associated with conservative and even reactionary political movements; her interpretation of matriarchy was based on giving a privileged status to traditionally female roles of nurturing and childbearing, rather than on overturning Victorian ideas of gender identity. Harrison herself became a public figure of some importance on the British right wing, and took an active role in the struggle to deny women the vote in Britain.

Her historical theories were supported by later British academics of similarly conservative political stances, of whom the archeologist Jacquetta Hawkes is the best known. Despite claims that an "archeological establishment" has steadfastly refused to accept the matriarchal hypothesis, the idea that Neolithic Europe was a peaceful, goddess-worshipping society was actually the conventional wisdom in British archeology for most of the twentieth century. The hold of this theory was so strong that archeological evidence was sometimes bent to fit it; for example, sites showing evidence of warfare were assigned to the Bronze Age even when stone weapons were found and radiocarbon dates pointed to a Neolithic date; *SEE* KEELEY 1996.

Given the conservative role of the matriarchal theory in Britain, it is ironic that the same ideas in America came to be associated with the other end of the political spectrum. This transformation was largely the work of the Lithuanian archaeologist Marija Gimbutas (1921–1994). In a series of best-selling books, Gimbutas took over Harrison's matriarchal "Old Europe" and transformed it into a feminist utopia that appealed intensely to late twentieth-century liberal audiences.

Gimbutas' theory—that Neolithic Europe was a woman-centered but egalitarian society without crime or warfare—was backed up by a new methodology she called "archeomythology," which was largely borrowed from Jungian psychological theory. Gimbutas and her followers claimed that archeomythology allowed them to successfully recapture the intellectual world of Neolithic prehistory. Her many critics have suggested that it is nothing more than a method for projecting modern assumptions back onto a Rohrshach blot of prehistoric artifacts.

During the 1990s, when the popularity of Gimbutas' work reached its peak, few groups within the Pagan community or the broader cultural left wing in the United States failed to look back to ancient matriarchies for inspiration. By contrast, the same period saw the collapse of the last organized support for the theory of ancient, utopian matriarchies in the academic community. Archeological studies have shown in detail that, far from being a collection of peaceful and egalitarian societies, Neolithic Europe shows all the signs of having been as hierarchical and violent as the periods following it. Critiques of the matriarchal theory have also pointed out serious misstatements of evidence in the writings of Gimbutas and other proponents of the theory.

Believers in ancient matriarchies, for their part, have claimed that these critiques are simply products of patriarchal bias. The entire topic remains the subject of fierce debate within the Pagan community. *SEE ALSO* OCCULT HISTORY. FURTHER READING: EISLER 1987, ELLER 1993, ELLER 2000, GIMBUTAS 1989, GIMBUTAS 1991, KEELEY 1996.

Matronit. *SEE* SHEKINAH.

maypole. In English folk custom, a tall pole garlanded with flowers and greenery, and hung with ribbons that are plaited into patterns by dancers in traditional May Day dances. Many modern Pagan traditions have adopted the maypole as an element of Beltane celebrations, and linked it with Pagan traditions supposedly deriving from many different countries. However, the maypole dance seems to be a purely English creation and is not documented in authentic folklore from anywhere else. *SEE* BELTANE.

Mazloth. (Hebrew MZLVTh, "constellations") In Cabalistic lore, the sphere of fixed stars or sphere of the zodiac; the correspondence of the Sephirah Chesed in the world of Assiah. *SEE* ASSIAH; CHESED.

mediation. In modern magical theory, a process in which a magician represents a god or goddess, or some other spiritual power, in a ritual working. In mediation, the magician attunes to the being he or she intends to mediate, and then uses the framework of the ritual to express the energies of the being. The mediating magician remains fully conscious during this process; this marks the central difference between mediation and the forms of trance used in Spiritualism. *SEE* SPIRITUALISM; TRANCE.

The practice of mediation, at least in the particular form used in modern magical traditions, seems to have evolved largely from the use of godforms in the Golden Dawn and other magical lodge organizations; *SEE* GODFORMS. In all probability, however, one form of mediation or another has been part of most types of ritual working since ancient times. *SEE ALSO* THEURGY. FURTHER READING: R. STEWART 1987, R. STEWART 1988.

medicine of metals. In alchemy, another term for the Philosopher's Stone. *SEE* PHILOSOPHER'S STONE.

meditation. Despite the stereotype that claims meditation as a purely Eastern spiritual practice, the Western occult traditions have a long and complex history of meditative practices. Even the orthodox religions of the West have their own extensive meditative traditions. In Catholicism, for example, the spiritual exercises of Ignatius Loyola are still practiced by Jesuits and some other Catholics, and form only one small part of a much larger heritage of meditative disciplines.

One factor that tends to cause confusion in understanding Western systems of meditation is a core difference between these disciplines and those Asian methods of meditation that have become most popular in the modern world. In the latter, the goal of practice is the silencing of the thinking mind. In *shikan-taza* (the most common form of Zen meditation), for example, the meditator seeks to empty the mind of all thoughts; in mantrayana, a Hindu method of meditation marketed all over the Western world under the name "transcendental meditation," the meditator repeats a sacred word in Sanskrit over and over again as a way to stop the flow of thoughts.

In most Western meditative practices, by contrast, the goal is not to silence the thinking mind but to take control of the thinking process and use it as a vehicle for higher states of awareness. The meditator concentrates on a particular topic, following out all its implications and shades of meaning in his or her mind, while excluding all thoughts that do not relate to the topic. Using this method, the meditator gains the same powers of concentration and self-mastery as the practitioner of Eastern meditative arts, and also learns to use the thinking mind with far more efficiency and clarity.

Traditions of Western occult meditation date back to the beginnings of occultism in the West. In ancient times, both Platonism and Hermeticism—two of the fundamental traditions of Western occult philosophy—include references to meditation in their core writings: Plotinus, the great third-century Platonist, describes some of his own meditative experiences in his *Enneads*, while the *Corpus Hermeticum*, the basic collection of ancient Hermetic writings, has numerous passages discussing meditation and its results. *SEE* CORPUS HERMETICUM; HERMETICISM; PLATONISM; PLOTINUS.

In the traditional Jewish Cabala, meditation is one of the primary methods of practice, along with prayer and observance of scriptural and Talmudic commandments. Cabalists meditate on the Names of God, the structure of the Tree of Life, and the hidden meanings of scripture revealed through gematria and other methods of Cabalistic analysis. Meditative awareness is also focused on prayers and the details of Jewish religious ritual, so that every word and action is performed with full consciousness of its meaning and importance.

Meditative practices in the Cabala reach up to a high pitch of complexity and power, with the letter-combinations meditation of Abraham Abulafia and the unification meditations of Isaac Luria counting among the tradition's high points. *SEE* ABULAFIA, ABRAHAM; LURIA, ISAAC. Much of Cabalistic meditation tends to focus on abstract concepts, but visualized colors and Hebrew letters, breathing exercises, and similar details also play their part. *SEE* CABALA.

Meditation also plays a central part in theosophy, the tradition of Christian occultism that arose in the sixteenth century (and which should not be confused with the teachings of the Theosophical Society in the nineteenth and twentieth centuries), and in most other systems of Christian esoteric practice. *SEE* CHRISTIAN OCCULTISM; THEOSOPHY (CHRISTIAN MYSTICAL). In more recent occult systems, meditation has tended to take a back seat to the more colorful arts of ritual magic and clairvoyance, but even so such influential magical orders as the Hermetic Order of the Golden Dawn and the Society of the Inner Light included Western modes of meditation in their curriculum of occult training. *SEE* GOLDEN DAWN, HERMETIC ORDER OF THE; INNER LIGHT, SOCIETY OF THE.

Since the founding of the Theosophical Society in 1875, finally, material from Eastern systems of meditation has also been incorporated in the Western occult tradition. Besides Theosophy itself, which has included meditation among the few methods of occult practice it recommends to students, particular mention should be made here of the work of Aleister Crowley, whose work on yoga and Hindu methods of meditation has been widely copied in the occult community. *SEE* CROWLEY, ALEISTER; THEOSOPHY; YOGA. FURTHER READING: CROWLEY 1980, FORTUNE 1987A, FORTUNE 1987B, GARDNER 1968, GREER 1996, A. KAPLAN 1982, REGARDIE 1971, SCHOLEM 1974.

Melchizedek. (Hebrew, "king of righteousness" or "Tzedek is king") In the Book of Genesis, the priest-king of Salem, to whom the patriarch Abraham offered one tenth of the spoils won in the battle with the Kings of the Valley. Later Jewish and Christian speculation transformed Melchizedek into a strange entity outside of time; the Psalms refer to the priesthood of the order of Melchizedek as greater than the priesthood of Aaron (brother of Moses and founder of the Jewish priesthood), while the apostle Paul of Tarsus refers to him in the Epistle to the Hebrews as "Without father, without mother, without descent, having neither beginning of days, nor end of life; but made like unto the Son of God" (Hebrews 7:3). References to Melchizedek in one form or another can be found all through Gnostic and esoteric Christian writings, usually accompanied by some claim to the priesthood of Melchizedek. *SEE ALSO* CHRISTIAN OCCULTISM; GNOSTICISM.

Mem. (Hebrew MM, "sea") The thirteenth letter of the Hebrew alphabet, one of the three mother letters, Mem has the sound-value of *m*, and the numerical values of 40 and, in final form, 600. Its standard correspondences are as follows:

> *Path of the Tree of Life:* Path 23, Geburah to Hod.
>
> *Astrological Correspondence:* Water.
>
> *Tarot Correspondence:* Trump XII, the Hanged Man.
>
> *Part of the Cube of Space:* The east-west axis.
>
> *Colors:* in Atziluth—deep blue.
>
> > in Briah—sea green.
> >
> > in Yetzirah—deep olive green.
> >
> > in Assiah—white flecked with purple.

The text from the *Thirty-two Paths of Wisdom* corresponding to the letter runs as follows: "The Twenty-third Path is the Stable Intelligence, and it is so called because it has the virtue of consistency among all numerations." *SEE ALSO* CABALA; HEBREW ALPHABET.

Hebrew letter Mem, left, and its final form, right

menstruum. In alchemy, a fluid in which another substance is dissolved or macerated; *SEE* MACERATION. In modern spagyrics, alcohol is the most commonly used menstruum for work with herbs, although water and other fluids are also used. In the alchemy of metals, the proper menstruum is one of the most important secrets of the Great Work. *SEE* ALCHEMY; SPAGYRICS.

mental body. In occult philosophy, the aspect of the human individual on the mental plane or level of abstract consciousness. The mental body is the part of the self that allows awareness of meaning. It exists outside of space and time, and thus is the lowest part of the self that survives physical death. *SEE ALSO* MENTAL PLANE.

mental plane. In occult philosophy, the plane or level of existence above the astral level, a realm of abstract consciousness located between the astral plane, the level of concrete consciousness, and the spiritual plane, the level of primary creative being. As with all the planes of occult theory, the mental is "above" or "below" other planes only in a metaphorical sense; in reality, all the planes interpenetrate the realm of physical matter experienced by the senses.

The mental plane is the plane of meaning, pattern, and the laws of nature and mathematics; number, geometrical form, and music best communicate its nature. It is outside of space and time. Most methods of occult meditation are intended to raise the mind up from the concrete, quasi-sensory experiences of the astral level to the pure meanings and relationships of the mental level. *SEE ALSO* MENTAL BODY.

mercury. In alchemy, the principle of fluidity, one of the two principles of metals in traditional alchemy and one of the three principles in the Paracelsian system of alchemical philosophy. While the term "mercury" in alchemical writings sometimes refers to common mercury—the liquid metal quicksilver, Hg—more often it refers to something else. References to Our Mercury or the Mercury of the Philosophers sometimes help distinguish the two, but in most alchemical traditions operating with ordinary mercury was considered to be one of the most common blind alleys on the way to the Great Work.

In spagyrics, which follows the Paracelsian theory of the Three Principles closely, every substance is held to have its own mercury (along with its own sulphur and salt), but the mercuries of all plants are closely related, and alcohol—the product of the fermentation of plant juices—can be substituted for any plant mercury. *SEE* SPAGYRICS. *SEE ALSO* ALCHEMY.

Mercury. One of the seven traditional planets of astrology, Mercury in a birth chart represents the mind and intellectual side of the person. He rules the signs Gemini and Virgo, although some modern writers assign Virgo to the quasi-planet Chiron; he is exalted in Virgo, in his detriment in Sagittarius and Pisces, and in his fall in Pisces. *SEE* ASTROLOGY; CHIRON.

In alchemy, the planet Mercury is often used as a symbol for the liquid metal mercury or quicksilver. *SEE* MERCURY.

Astrological symbol of Mercury

Merkabah. *SEE* MA'ASEH MERKABAH.

Merlin. The supreme magician of the Arthurian legends, Merlin has been a major influence on the idea of the magician throughout the Western world since the Middle Ages. In the early Welsh sources, his name is given as *Myrddin* (pronounced *Mur-thin*, with the *th* voiced as in "these clothes").

According to the *Historia Regum Britanniae* (*History of the Kings of Britain*, 1136) of Geoffrey of Monmouth, the original Arthurian bestseller and the source of most later legends, Merlin was the child of a princess of southern Wales by an incubus; *SEE* INCUBUS. Gifted with visionary powers from childhood, he prophesied to three successive kings of Britain—Vortigern, Ambrosius, and Uther—and arranged for the conception of Uther's son Arthur. Later versions of the legend went on to make Merlin responsible for Arthur's upbringing and coronation, and for his victories in the wars that established him firmly on the British throne. At some point thereafter, he vanished from the scene into a hidden place—a cave or a tower of glass—either by his own will, or by the wiles of a young woman who used his own magic to imprison him.

Geoffrey of Monmouth himself, though, wrote a different account of Merlin's life, the *Vita Merlini* (*Life of Merlin*). In this version the mage outlived Arthur, went on to become a king, and went mad after seeing his nephews killed in battle. As a madman, he dwelt in the forests for many years before finally recovering his sanity and spending the remainder of his life in retirement and spiritual contemplation. This version of Merlin's life is given unexpected support by a collection of ancient Welsh poems attributed to Myrddin, and it has been argued that Geoffrey's biography and the Welsh poems both refer to an actual person, a poet and Druid who lived in what is now southern Scotland about a century after the time of Arthur.

The differences between the two sets of legends have suggested to many readers that there was more than one person involved, and as early as the Middle Ages there were writers who distinguished Merlin Ambrosius or Myrddin Emrys, the wizard and councillor of Arthur, from Merlin Sylvester or Myrddin Wyllt, the madman and poet. *The White Book of Rhydderch*, a collection of ancient Welsh lore, adds the curious detail that the oldest name given to the island of Britain, before it was settled by human beings, was *Clas Myrddin*—the Enclosure of Merlin.

It is hardly surprising that the name of Merlin has appeared a great deal in occult tradition over the centuries since his time. William Lilly (1602–1681), the great English astrologer, published an astrological almanac under the title *The English Merlin*; *SEE* LILLY, WILLIAM. The Druid revival, which has drawn heavily on Arthurian themes throughout its history, has made much use of Merlin as symbol and example, and the surge of interest in Celtic traditions and occultism in the twentieth century made his name indeed one to conjure with. At least one modern magical theorist, R. J. Stewart, has devised a complete system of magical and spiritual development based on the traditional accounts of Merlin in Welsh poetry and Geoffrey of Monmouth's writings. *SEE ALSO* ARTHUR, KING; ARTHURIAN LEGENDS. FURTHER READING: KNIGHT 1983, STEWART 1986A, STEWART 1986B, STEWART 1991, TOLSTOY 1985.

Mesmer, Franz Anton. Swiss physician and occultist, 1734–1815. Usually (and incorrectly) remembered in mainstream histories as the discoverer of hypnosis, Mesmer was a complex figure whose life and work are thoroughly interwoven with the occult scene of the late eighteenth century, and whose discoveries played a central role in launching the occult revival of the nineteenth century.

He was born in the small village of Iznang in southern Germany in 1734, and attended medical school in Vienna, receiving his doctorate in 1766 with a thesis on the influence of the planets on human illness. After receiving his doctorate, he established a medical practice in Vienna and began experimenting with the health effects of magnetism—a hot topic in medical research at the time.

Mesmer also established himself in the Viennese Masonic scene, where his friends included the composer Mozart, and in the occult scene as well. He is known to have joined the Order of the Gold and Rosy Cross (Orden des Gold- und Rosenkreuz), one of the most important esoteric orders in eighteenth-century Europe; SEE ORDEN DES GOLD- UND ROSENKREUZ. While Mesmer always claimed that his discoveries were entirely original, it seems likely that his ideas were shaped by the occult and alchemical lore passed on by the order.

In the mid–1770s, Mesmer came to the conclusion that the healing effects of magnets were not due to conventional magnetism but to another force, similar to magnetism but more closely connected to animal life. He named this force "animal magnetism" and began working on ways by which it could be directed, concentrated, and stored for healing purposes. SEE ANIMAL MAGNETISM. Never a modest man, Mesmer managed to alienate most of the Viennese physicians by his insistence that his was the only valid method of healing, and he decided to move on to greener pastures.

In 1778 he arrived in Paris, set up his equipment, and began treating patients and advertising his methods. The French Academy of Sciences and the Royal Society of Medicine both expressed cautious interest at first, then decided that Mesmer was a quack and refused to have anything further to do with him. As Mesmer's clientele and reputation both grew, this escalated into open attacks in magazine articles and the pamphlet press. Mesmer, his followers, and people whom he had cured responded by publishing pamphlets and articles of their own, denouncing the medical establishment of the time as a collection of venal incompetents fighting to maintain their monopoly at the expense of public health. The resulting frenzy kept the media busy and the Parisian public entertained until the beginning of the French Revolution nine years later brought other matters to the forefront of public attention.

In the midst of the controversy, Mesmer's close allies Nicolas Bergasse and Guillaume Kornmann founded an organization, the Société de l'Harmonie Universelle (Society of Universal Harmony), to pass on Mesmer's teachings. Mesmer agreed to turn over all his secrets to the Société for the sum of 2400 louis—quite a substantial sum in those days. In 1785, after the release of a government commission condemning his teachings, Mesmer left Paris for London, and proceeded from there to Austria, Italy, Switzerland, and Germany, continually trying to win the universal acclaim he believed he deserved. He died in 1815 in Meersburg, Germany, not far from his birthplace. SEE ALSO ANIMAL MAGNETISM; MESMERISM. FURTHER READING: BURANELLI 1975, DARNTON 1968.

mesmerism. The system of healing with subtle energies devised by Franz Anton Mesmer and his followers in the late eighteenth and early nineteenth centuries, mesmerism was strongly rooted in occult traditions. It is often confused with hypnotism, which was a later and very different development. Unlike hypnotism, mesmerism was never understood as a mental process; instead, it was a method of energy work, operating by means of the subtle forces of life, which Mesmer called "animal magnetism." SEE ANIMAL MAGNETISM.

According to Mesmer's book on the subject, *Mémoire sur la Découverte du Magnétisme Animal* (*Memoir on the Discovery of Animal Magnetism*, 1779), animal magnetism is a force closely associated with biological life, which fills the entire universe and brings all things into a state of mutual influence. It forms a field around each living body, with poles like those of a magnet, and it ebbs and flows according to complex patterns. In the body, it affects the nervous system directly and all other parts of the body indirectly. It can be concentrated, dispersed, stored, and passed on from one strongly charged body to another. All of these proposals will seem completely familiar to those familiar with the teachings of occultism on vital energy or the etheric realm, and there is every reason to think that Mesmer himself—a member of at least one important magical order, the Orden des Gold- und Rosenkreuz (Order of the Gold and Rose Cross)— got his ideas from traditional sources. SEE ETHER; ORDEN DES GOLD- UND ROSENKREUZ.

Mesmer's ideas were first circulated in Vienna, where he worked as a physician, but won an international audience after he moved to Paris in 1778. Within a year of his arrival the Austrian doctor and his discoveries were being talked about all over France, and were subjected to vitriolic attacks in the medical and scientific press. By the time of Mesmer's death in 1815, there were mesmerist practitioners all over Europe and the United States. The condemnation of mesmerism by the orthodox science of the time drove mesmerists into the welcoming arms of the occult scene.

During Mesmer's years in Paris, his teachings had become the core of a lodge organization, the Société de l'Harmonie Universelle (Society of Universal Harmony), with lodges all over France. Although the Société did not survive the French Revolution, most of its teachings and many of its members found their way into more overtly magical orders afterwards. In this context, Mesmer's ideas were enormously influential; many of the later staples of French occult theory, such as Eliphas Lévi's teachings concerning the Astral Light, are simply mesmerism in a new terminology. SEE LÉVI, ELIPHAS. SEE ALSO MESMER, FRANZ ANTON. FURTHER READING: DARNTON 1968, MESMER 1948.

Mesopotamian occultism. Mesopotamia, the "Land Between the Rivers" in the Tigris-Euphrates valley in what is now Iraq, Syria, and Turkey, was the setting of one of the earliest urban cultures known to history—and one of the most important sources of the Western occult traditions. Much of modern Western magic, nearly all of astrology, and many other branches of occult theory and practice have their roots in the cultures of ancient Mesopotamia.

Mesopotamian history covers more than four thousand years of intricate political and cultural developments, but only the broadest outline will be necessary here. The first known civilization in the Tigris-Euphrates valley, Sumer, emerged in the marshy lands around the northern end of the Persian Gulf before 3000 B.C.E. The Sumerians were conquered around 2300 B.C.E. by the people of Akkad, tribal nomads further north who used a Semitic language, but who proceeded to adopt much of Sumerian culture and kept Sumerian as a sacred language for religious purposes. Akkad went under in turn around 2180 B.C.E., and a long age of warfare ended with the rise of the city of Babylon on the lower Euphrates River around 1900 B.C.E. and the foundation of the Babylonian Empire around 1700 B.C.E. From that time until its fall to the Persian king Cyrus in 539 B.C.E., Babylon was the economic, cultural, and (with some interruptions) political capital of Mesopotamia. Further north, on the upper Tigris River, was Babylon's great rival, the harsh military empire of Assyria, which nonetheless shared many of the same cultural and religious traditions, and practiced much of the same magic.

Conquest by the Persians, then by the Greeks under Alexander the Great, and finally by the Roman Empire, ended the political independence of the region; centuries of warfare between Rome and a revived Persian empire ravaged the area, and the Muslim conquest in the middle of the seventh century C.E. finished the process of decline, although some elements of the old Mesopotamian lore survived and even flourished in Arab hands.

In what is now southeastern Turkey, the city of Harran, originally a Sumerian trading post, preserved substantial elements of Mesopotamian religious tradition into medieval times, but with the abandonment of Harran in the fourteenth century C.E. the last living connection with the Mesopotamian tradition was lost. SEE HARRAN.

Throughout this history, Mesopotamian magic and religion were rooted in the stars. From the earliest Sumerian records on, it's clear that the stars were gods and vice versa, and traditions of stellar omens and divination (precursors to the later science of astrology) were already being developed. The stellar focus of Mesopotamian magic dates back ultimately to a time even before Sumer, since names for planets used in Sumer—*Delebat* for Venus, *Sagmegar* for Jupiter, and others—are not actually Sumerian words, but came from some older language that has otherwise been entirely lost. Scholars have not yet been able to decipher them, or relate them convincingly to any known language family.

By Sumerian times, atronomer-priests had defined the three "Paths of Heaven" (the equatorial, northern, and southern skies) and identified them with the three great gods Anu, Enlil, and Ea, rulers respectively of the starry sky, the wind, and the waters. All these played an important part in traditions connected with the precession of the equinoxes—the slow turning of the Earth's axis that causes the sun's position at any given date to creep backwards through the zodiac. SEE PRECESSION OF THE EQUINOXES.

These ancient star-divinities came to share space with later planetary deities—Nabu (Mercury), Ishtar (Venus), Nergal (Mars), Marduk (Jupiter), and Enki (Saturn), as well as Sin and Shamash, the moon and sun respectively—and with various other gods and goddesses who emerged in different parts of Mesopotamia or were imported from elsewhere. The result was a busy and flexible polytheism that, at one time or another, included nearly every divinity known to the ancient Near East in its ambit. As with other ancient religions, spirituality and magical practice were not distinguished from each other, and the surviving clay-tablet literature includes many spells and magically oriented prayers directed to celestial deities or, as often as not, to stars and planets directly.

The details of most Sumerian and Akkadian magical practice are lost to us. Babylon is another matter, since tens of thousands of clay tablets have survived in readable condition from Babylonian times, and the language was deciphered early in the nineteenth century. The Assyrians also left substantial clay tablet libraries, and one of them—the library of the Assyrian king Ashurbanipal (668–627 B.C.E.), who was deeply interested in magic—includes a wealth of magical lore, including detailed ritual texts. SEE ASHURBANIPAL.

Entire genres of magical ritual have survived in this way. One important type was *Namburbi* ("evil-dispelling") rituals, designed to ward off the effects of an evil omen. Another, *Maqlû* ("burning") rituals, involved figurines of demons, ghosts, or human enemies that were destroyed by fire; SEE MAQLÛ RITUALS; NAMBURBI RITUALS. Statue magic, which involved making and consecrating magical images for a wide range of purposes, was a highly developed art; SEE STATUES, MAGICAL. Less complex magical practices were also in common use; amulets shaped like a variety of animals helped to drive off evil spirits and bring good luck, and a wide range of charms, incantations, magical blessings, and counterspells were in everyday use.

While Mesopotamian magic as such was effectively extinct by the end of the Middle Ages, it left many legacies to later Western magical traditions. Astrology, while at least partly a Greek creation, was based on centuries of careful records of the sky compiled by Mesopotamian astronomers. To Mesopotamian magic, similarly, we owe the habit of assigning herbs, stones, and other substances to the seven planets, and in many cases the specific correspondences have come down more or less intact from Mesopotamian sources by way of later Greek manuscripts. The link between seven numerical magic squares and the seven planets is another inheritance from Mesopotamian magic, as is the traditional term *kamea* used for these squares. SEE MAGIC SQUARE. FURTHER READING: ABUSCH 1987, ABUSCH AND VAN DER TOORN 1999, REINER 1970, REINER 1995.

Metatron. The "Prince of the Countenance" and highest of the angels in Jewish occult doctrines, Metatron emerges out of the complex realm of Jewish angelology sometime in the first few centuries of the Common Era, replacing Michael as the chief angel of Heaven. His status was high enough that even in relatively orthodox writings, he is sometimes called "the lesser YHVH," and compared more to God than to the other angels.

There are two different traditions about Metatron's place in Heaven. One pictures him as an angel created at or before the creation of the world, and sees him as the most exalted spiritual power created by God. The other tradition insists that Metatron started out as the patriarch Enoch, who ascended alive into Heaven to become the angelic scribe of the good deeds of Israel. SEE ENOCH. Many later mystics and scholars accepted both of these traditions at the same time, and dealt with the resulting cognitive dissonance by insisting that there were actually two Metatrons. Two different spellings of the name were used to distinguish the two: MITTRVN for the primordial Metatron, MTTRVN for the former Enoch.

The origins of the name Metatron are uncertain at best. It may come from the Greek phrase *meta thronios*, "before the throne," or from the Persian god Mithras, who had essentially the same relation toward the Zoroastrian god Ahura Mazda.

In modern Cabalistic writings Metatron is the archangel of Kether, the first Sephirah of the Tree of Life. SEE KETHER. FURTHER READING: GREER 1997, SCHOLEM 1974.

mete-wand. A staff marked with measurements according to some traditional measuring system, important in systems of magic that rely on specific systems of measurement, proportion, or sacred geometry. Mete-wands are usually not consecrated, although some consecrated magical wands and staffs have measurements on them and double as mete-wands. SEE SACRED GEOMETRY; STAFF.

Middle Pillar exercise. One of the basic exercises of the Golden Dawn tradition and many related systems of magic, the Middle Pillar exercise involves visualizing five energy centers along the midline of the body, which correspond to five primary points on the Middle Pillar of the Cabalistic Tree of Life; SEE TREE OF LIFE. The five centers are:

Center	Color	Position in Body
Kether	White	Above crown of head
Daath	Gray	Throat
Tiphareth	Gold	Heart (or solar plexus)
Yesod	Violet	Genitals
Malkuth	Black (or green)	Soles of feet

Each center of the Middle Pillar is visualized as a sphere of colored light six to eight inches across. In the exercise, after the working space is cleared with the Lesser Banishing Ritual of the Pentagram, each center is visualized in turn, starting with the Kether center above the head, and the Name of God of the corresponding Sephirah is vibrated, usually four times. After all five centers have been established, currents of evergy are visualized circling through the aura along various pathways; the

exact details vary from one version of the exercise to another.

The Middle Pillar exercise can be found in outline in the Golden Dawn papers, but in its modern form it was devised by Golden Dawn magician Israel Regardie (1907–1985) and publicized in his books. It is widely considered to be the essential foundation for magical practice in the systems that use it, since the energy centers awakened by daily practice of the exercise allow energy to be brought through into ritual work and other forms of magical practice.

A number of variations on the standard Middle Pillar exercise have been introduced in recent decades, and other magical traditions have adopted similar exercises of their own. In the Aurum Solis tradition, for example, an exercise called the Rousing of the Citadels fills the place of the Middle Pillar exercise; SEE ROUSING OF THE CITADELS. Other magical traditions make use of the system of seven chakras imported from India. SEE ALSO CABALA; CHAKRA; GOLDEN DAWN, HERMETIC ORDER OF THE. FURTHER READING: GODDARD 1999, GREER 1997, REGARDIE 1970, REGARDIE 1979.

midheaven. In astrology, the degree of the zodiac at the highest point in the sky at the time for which a chart is cast. In natal astrology, the position of the midheaven is often used to interpret the highest goals or potentials a person may achieve in life. SEE ASTROLOGY; NATAL ASTROLOGY. FURTHER READING: CLEMENT 2001.

Minchiate deck. A deck of ninety-seven cards—forty-one trumps and fifty-six small cards—closely related to the tarot. The Minchiate deck was apparently devised in Florence sometime in the sixteenth century and was used in card games; the word *minchiate* probably derives from an old Italian term, *menchia*, meaning "game." There were several early forms of the Minchiate deck, some of which had as many as 120 cards.

The trumps of the Minchiate deck include most of the tarot trumps, but add several additional virtues, as well as the four elements and the twelve signs of the zodiac. The titles of the standard deck are as follows:

I. The Juggler
II. The Grand Duke

III. The Western Emperor

IV. The Eastern Emperor

V. The Lovers

VI. Temperance

VII. Fortitude

VIII. Justice

IX. The Wheel of Fortune

X. The Chariot

XI. The Hermit

XII. The Traitor

XIII. Death

XIV. The Devil

XV. The Tower

XVI. Hope

XVII. Prudence

XVIII. Faith

XIX. Charity

XX. Fire

XXI. Water

XXII. Earth

XXIII. Air

XXIV. Libra

XXV. Virgo

XXVI. Scorpio

XXVII. Aries

XXVIII. Capricorn

XXIX. Sagittarius

XXX. Cancer

XXXI. Pisces

XXXII. Aquarius

XXXIII. Leo

XXXIV. Taurus

XXXV. Gemini

XXXVI. The Star

XXXVII. The Moon

XXXVIII. The Sun

XXXIII. The World

XXXX. The Last Judgment

XXXXI. The Fool

The last six cards were traditionally printed without either name or number.

Very little attention has been paid to the Minchiate deck, except by students of the odder corners of tarot lore; however, a capable modern version of the deck was published in 1999 for divinatory use. SEE ALSO TAROCCHI DI MANTEGNA; TAROT. FURTHER READING: S. KAPLAN 1978, B. WILLIAMS 1999.

mirror, magic. A basic occult tool used for scrying and other forms of magical work, the magic mirror may be made and consecrated in a variety of ways, ranging from the simple to the complex. It was much used in nineteenth-century magical traditions, especially those that drew on the work of American magus P. B. Randolph (1825–1875); SEE RANDOLPH, PASCHAL BEVERLY.

In the present-day occult scene, magic mirrors are used by some Hermetic magicians, by initiates of a number of Wiccan and Neopagan traditions, and by Chaos magicians, especially those associated with the Illuminates of Thanateros—as well as by plenty of students of the occult who have simply come across the relevant lore and made it a part of their own workings. SEE ILLUMINATES OF THANATEROS (IOT). SEE ALSO CATOPTROMANCY; SCRYING. FURTHER READING: BESTERMAN 1965.

mistletoe. (*Viscum album*) A parasitic plant which grows on a range of hardwoods, mistletoe was the most sacred plant of the ancient Druids, who placed the highest value on it when it was found growing on an oak. In magical lore, it has the power to confer fertility and to banish hostile spirits.

Traditional humoral medicine considers it warm and dry in the third degree, and thus associated with fire. SEE ALSO DRUIDS; NATURAL MAGIC.

Mithraic Mysteries. One of the most influential and intriguing of the ancient Mysteries, the Mithraic Mysteries centered on a Persian god imported into the Roman Empire. Originally an ancient Indo-European deity associated with oaths and contracts, Mithras appears in very early sources from Iran (as Mithra) and India (as Mitra), and is even referred to in clay tablets from the ancient Hittite capital at Boghazkoy, in what is now Turkey. He was one of the few older gods to be incorporated as an angelic power in the monotheistic religion preached by Zoroaster in early Iran, and so became a significant figure in the religious life of the Middle East. Kings of several western Asian countries in classical times were named Mithradates, "gift of Mithra," and archeologists have found a respectable number of statues, temples, and coins bearing the image of the god.

His presence in the Western occult traditions, however, stems from his adoption by Romans sometime in the first century of the Common Era. Plutarch (46–after 120 C.E.), the great Greek Pagan scholar, believed that the Mithraic cult he knew had come into existence among the pirates of Cilicia, in what is now southeastern Turkey. This claim has generally been accepted by modern scholars, not least because Plutarch was reporting on events that happened not long before his time. Whatever the original source of the Mithraic cult, it became popular among intellectuals in Tarsus, the capital of Cilicia, and later among Roman soldiers and politicians throughout the empire.

The Mithraic Mysteries functioned in much the same way as the fraternal lodges of more recent centuries. Membership was limited to men, who passed through seven grades of initiation, each of which was associated with one of the seven planets:

Grade	Meaning	Planet
1. Corax	Raven	Mercury
2. Nymphus	Bridegroom	Venus
3. Miles	Soldier	Mars
4. Leo	Lion	Jupiter
5. Perses	Persian	Moon
6. Heliodromus	Sunrunner	Sun
7. Pater	Father	Saturn

Initiates met for initiation rituals and ceremonial meals of bread and wine in underground shrines decorated with the chief Mithraic emblem, the image of Mithras slaying a great bull. This image may point to the core of the Mithraic mysteries, for as David Ulansey has pointed out in a recent and influential book, the picture of Mithras and the bull—which also includes a set of minor figures, among them a snake, a dog, a scorpion, a raven, a lion, and a cup—is an accurate star map of a particular section of the heavens, centering on the constellations Taurus and Perseus.

It has been suggested that the inner secret of Mithraism was related to the precession of the equinoxes, the slow wobble of Earth's axis that moves the sun's position at the equinoxes and solstices back through the zodiac at a rate of one sign every 2,150 years. Precession had been discovered (or rediscovered) by the Greek astronomer Hipparchus (c. 190–126 B.C.E.), and an age that saw the stars as gods might well have been awed by the discovery that the entire structure of the cosmos seemed to be wheeling around them. SEE CYCLES, COSMIC; PRECESSION OF THE EQUINOXES.

The Mysteries of Mithras flourished throughout the Roman Empire in the second and third centuries of the Common Era, but were suppressed along with other Pagan religious traditions on the rise of Christianity to political power in the fourth and fifth centuries. There was at least one nineteenth-century attempt to revive a version of the Mithraic Mysteries, which seems to have gone nowhere; the tradition's masculine bias seems to have prevented any attempts at reviving it within the modern Neopagan movement. FURTHER READING: CLAUSS 2000, ULANSEY 1989.

Mohsian Tradition. American Wiccan tradition, founded in California in the early 1960s by Bill and Helen Mohs, using materials drawn from the 1734 Tradition, the Plant Bran, and Gardnerian Wicca. Around 1969, the eclectic system practiced by the Mohs and their coven began to be called the "American Tradition" or "Eclectic American Tradition"; the term "Mohsian" emerged in the early 1970s. SEE GARDNERIAN WICCA; PLANT BRAN; 1734 TRADITION (UNDER S).

Mohsian covens celebrate the eight sabbats and hold Esbats on the night of the full moon; they work the standard three-degree system, with an outer court rite of dedication preceding the first degree, and the Gardnerian rituals are used for initiation. FURTHER READING: DAVIES 2001.

mojo. In hoodoo, a mojo or mojo bag (also known as a "toby" or "hand") is the most common form of amulet, consisting of a cloth bag—typically made of red flannel—

into which various magically effective substances are placed. *SEE* HOODOO.

monad. (Greek, "unit") In a variety of philosophies, some of them occult, a term for the central spiritual spark at the core of each living being. The term entered philosophical use by way of the work of the German polymath Gottfried Wilhelm Leibnitz (1646–1716), who held that monads—unconscious in the "inanimate" world, half-conscious in plants and animals, and fully conscious in humanity—were the fundamental building blocks of the entire cosmos. It was adopted by a number of mystical movements, mostly German, in the eighteenth and nineteenth centuries as a convenient term that lacked a specific anchor in existing theologies. From there it seems to have passed to Theosophy, which made much use of it.

Equivalent concepts in other Western esoteric systems include the *yechidah* or "Only One" of Cabalistic theory, and the *synteresis* or divine spark discussed by Plotinus and other Platonist thinkers. *SEE* CABALA; PLATONISM. *SEE ALSO* SPIRIT.

Monas Hieroglyphica. (Latin, "hieroglyphic monad") Esoteric symbol devised by John Dee and publicized in a book of the same title published in 1564. The Monas consisted of the planetary symbol of Mercury combined with the zodiacal symbol of Aries, but all seven planetary symbols could be derived from it. The highly obscure text of Dee's book suggests that new systems of alchemy, astrology, proportion, optics, and other sciences (occult and mundane) can be derived from the study of the symbol.

Little seems to have been done with the monad since Dee's time, but it was occasionally used as an emblem by the early Rosicrucians, and has cropped up in a range of other occult traditions. *SEE ALSO* DEE, JOHN. FURTHER READING: DEE 1986, JOSTEN 1964.

Monas Hieroglyphica

moon. One of the seven traditional astrological planets, the moon in the birth chart represents the emotional and instinctive side of the self. In astrological terms the moon rules the sign Cancer, is exalted in Taurus, is in her detriment in Capricorn, and in her fall in Scorpio. *SEE* ASTROLOGY.

In alchemy, the moon is a common symbol for silver, and also represents the albedo or white phase of the Great Work. *SEE* ALCHEMY.

Astrological symbol of the moon

Moon, the. The eighteenth Major Arcanum of the tarot, commonly illustrated with an image of a dog and a wolf baying at the rising moon. In the Golden Dawn tradition, this Arcanum corresponds to the Hebrew letter Qoph, while the French tradition associates it with Tzaddi. Its common divinatory meanings include deceit, delusion, intuition, and the unknown.

Its magical title is "Ruler of Flux and Reflux, Child of the Sons of the Mighty." *SEE ALSO* TAROT.

Tarot trump the Moon (Universal Tarot)

moon crown. In Wicca, a headband bearing a crescent moon, usually of metal and almost always with two points upwards, worn by a High Priestess. The equivalent headdress of a High Priest is the horn crown. *SEE* HIGH PRIESTESS; HORN CROWN; WICCA.

Mopses, Order of. Quasi-Masonic order founded in Cologne, Germany, in 1738 in response to the Catholic Church's first major condemnation of Freemasonry (the bull *Eminente Apostolatus Specula*, issued by Pope Clement XII on April 28, 1738). The order was set up to allow Catholics who were interested in Masonic lodge membership to belong to a similar organization that was not under the ban of the church. It spread through much of Catholic Europe, with lodges active in France, the Netherlands, Germany, and Austria in the 1840s.

Unlike most Masonic organizations, the Order of Mopses admitted women as well as men to membership. Its name referred to a popular breed of lapdog, which was also its emblem—a sign that members may not have taken Mopsism quite as seriously as Masons have often taken their lodge activities. It seems to have faded out of existence by the end of the eighteenth century. *SEE ALSO* FREEMASONRY; LODGE, FRATERNAL.

Mór. (Old Irish, "sea") An alternate name for the Ogham letter Phagos. *SEE* PHAGOS, OGHAM.

Morya, Master. *SEE* EL MORYA, MASTER.

motto, magical. In many contemporary magical systems, a name taken by a magician, either at the time of his or her first initiation or at some later point. Originally the magical motto was simply an alias, used to conceal one's identity at a time when being publicly engaged in magical practice was problematic. By the late nineteenth century, however, when the magical motto in its present form emerged, the motto had developed the secondary purpose of expressing the magician's central purpose or spiritual orientation.

Magical mottoes are typically in Latin, Greek, Hebrew, or Enochian, and may consist of anything from one word to an entire sentence. Very often, a magician will be referred to by the initials of his or her magical motto—thus, *Soror* (Sister) *D. N. F.* rather than *Deo Non Fortuna* (Latin for "By God, not by chance," the motto of English occultist Violet Firth and the source of her pen name, Dion Fortune).

The magical mottoes of other famous magicians may give some idea of the options. Aleister Crowley's motto was *Perdurabo* (Latin, "I will endure to the end"); Allan Bennet's was *Iehi Aour* (Hebrew, "Let there be light"); William Butler Yeats' was *Deus Est Demon Inversus* (Latin, "God is the Devil Inverted," and its initials spell out the Latin word *Dedi*, "I have given").

The custom of taking magical mottoes may have influenced the modern Neopagan custom of taking Craft names. *SEE* CRAFT NAME. *SEE ALSO* LODGE, MAGICAL.

Mount Shasta. *SEE* SHASTA, MOUNT.

Mu. A lost continent allegedly located in the central Pacific up to 13,000 years ago, Mu has an unusually complicated history—even for lost continents, which is saying something. Its origins can be traced back to Diego de Landa, a sixteenth-century Spanish monk who arrived in the Yucatan Peninsula with the conquistadors and played an important role in wiping out most of what remained of classical Mayan culture. At the same time, he attempted to write down the Mayan alphabet for European scholars to examine.

Unfortunately for his efforts, the Mayan language didn't have an alphabet. It had, instead, an elegant system of hieroglyphics with signs standing for sounds, words, and abstract concepts. Bishop de Landa apparently didn't ask enough questions to find this out, and simply copied out a set of signs whose names in Mayan sounded roughly equivalent to the letters of the Latin alphabet.

In 1864, de Landa's copy of the Mayan "alphabet" came into the hands of Charles-Étienne Brasseur de Bourbourg (1814–1874), an eccentric French scholar. Brasseur proceeded to work out and publish a "translation" of one of the three surviving Mayan codices, which seemed to be talking about some sort of violent volcanic disaster in a place called "Mu, Land of Mud." (The codex in question is actually a set of astrological tables once used by Mayan priests to track the influences of the planet Venus.) Brasseur's work was borrowed by Atlantis theorists Ignatius Donnelly (1831–1901) and Augustus Le Plongeon (1826–1908), both of whom claimed that Mu was actually Atlantis.

The birth of Mu as a lost continent of its own was the work of James Churchward, whose previous contribution to the literary world had been a hunting and fishing guide to northeast Maine. His 1925 opus *The Lost Continent of Mu* was supposedly based on two different sets of tablets, one from central America and the other from India, which had originated in the lost continent. Mu, according to Churchward, had been the original home of humankind, a large land mass in the middle of the Pacific, stretching roughly from Easter Island to the Marianas. At its height it had a population of some 64 million people, ruled by a priest-king called the Ra, and sent out colonies to various parts of the Old and New Worlds. The catastrophe that overwhelmed Mu was the result of underground "gas-belts" that suddenly deflated, plunging the Land of Mud to the bottom of the sea.

Even scholars supportive of the lost continent hypothesis have found Mu an embarrasment, as Churchward's books are full of obvious misstatements and errors, and his extravagant claims have precisely no evidence to back them. Certain branches of the occult community have adopted Mu into their versions of occult history, however, and Mu has also been routinely confused in occult and New Age circles with another lost continent, Lemuria—no mean feat, given that they supposedly existed in entirely different oceans. SEE ALSO LOST CIVILIZATIONS; OCCULT HISTORY. FURTHER READING: CHURCHWARD 1931, DE CAMP 1970.

Muinn. (Old Irish, "back") The eleventh letter of the Ogham alphabet, with the sound-value *m*. It corresponds to the grapevine among trees, the titmouse among birds, the color "variegated" (Irish *mbracht*), and the number six. In Robert Graves' version of the Ogham tree-calendar, its month runs from September 3 to September 30. SEE OGHAM.

Ogham letter Muinn

multiplication. In alchemy, a process by which a small amount of an alchemically active substance is increased in amount and power. The Philosopher's Stone, according to alchemical texts, could be put through the process of multiplication several times, with each one creating more of the stone with a greater power of changing base metals to gold. Alchemical symbolism assigns this process to

the zodiacal sign Aquarius. SEE ALCHEMY; PHILOSOPHER'S STONE.

mundane astrology. The astrology of nations and communities, and arguably the oldest of all the branches of astrology, documented back to the second millennium B.C.E. in Babylonian records. Mundane astrology was in constant use from ancient times up to the coming of the Scientific Revolution, and many of the great astrologers of ancient, medieval, Renaissance, and early modern history were deeply involved in attempts to read the future history of the world as written in the stars.

The personal, psychological focus of much of modern astrology has downplayed its importance in more recent times, but it is still practiced; for example, the Y2K computer crisis of January 2000 was accompanied by learned analyses in the astrological press, using the classical methods of mundane astrology to predict whether the world's computer systems would or would not come unhinged at midnight on December 31, 1999.

Three primary approaches make up the armory of traditional mundane astrology. The first of these, and the one most practiced at present, is based on the birth charts of political leaders, and charts for the foundation of cities, nations, and the like. This approach is closely based on natal astrology, the most popular branch of astrology in modern times, and uses essentially the same methods. SEE NATAL ASTROLOGY; PROGRESSIONS; TRANSITS.

The second basic approach is far and away the most ancient aspect of astrology still in use, drawing on the same celestial apparitions—eclipses and comets—that ancient star-priests once used to predict calamity in the city-states of Mesopotamia. By the Middle Ages, the standard approaches to comet and eclipse interpretation included drawing up a horoscope for the beginning of the eclipse, and assessing the symbolic meanings of visual phenomena associated with it (for example, colors and light effects in the case of eclipses, and shape and visual appearance in the case of comets).

The effects of eclipses and comets extend for a substantial period after the actual event. In one common scheme, lunar eclipses have effects lasting as many months as there are minutes in the eclipse's duration, while solar eclipses hold sway for as many years as minutes in the eclipse. Comets are particularly long-acting, and their effects can be traced out over several decades.

The third traditional method, which apparently entered the Western astrological tradition by way of ancient Persian starlore, pays attention to the conjunctions of the two outermost of the traditional planets, Jupiter and Saturn. These come into conjunction approximately every twenty years, and their conjunctions are about 120 degrees apart on the zodiac, forming a great triangle—or, to use the traditional term, a trigon. Because of the way the four traditional elements relate to the zodiacal signs, all three points of the trigon fall into signs that share the same element. Over time, though, the points of the trigon slowly shift around the zodiac, and about every 240 years the trigon's points move from sign to sign and, in the same moment, from one element to another.

This shift of the trigon from element to element, according to the theory of conjunctions, marks the passage from one age of the world to another. The shift of the trigon from water signs to fire signs in 1603, for example, is held to have ushered in the end of Renaissance culture, the dawn of modern science, and the rise of Britain to world dominance, while the shift from fire to earth 240 years later marked the beginning of the age of materialism and the rise of America to the position of global power. The next shift, into the signs governed by air, will happen in the 2080s; according to the theory of conjunctions, another nation will begin the giddy rise to global power shortly after this time.

In some schemes, systems of mundane astrology are fitted into the much vaster perspectives of cosmic cycles of history. For example, the precession of the equinoxes—the slow wobble in Earth's axis that moves the sun slowly backwards through the zodiac relative to the seasons—is commonly integrated into mundane astrology as a vast but diffuse background factor. Discussions of the Age of Aquarius in recent years show that this aspect of mundane astrology is far from forgotten even today. *SEE* CYCLES, COSMIC; PRECESSION OF THE EQUINOXES. *SEE ALSO* ASTROLOGY. FURTHER READING: GENEVA 1995.

Murray hypothesis. The claim that medieval witchcraft was the survival of a Pagan religion from pre-Christian times had been proposed by several other writers before the time of British scholar Margaret Murray (1862–1963), but her widely read books played a central role in propagating it—and, not incidentally, in preparing the ground for the rise of modern Wicca.

Murray was an Egyptologist, a student of the famous Sir Flinders Petrie, who was stranded in London by the outbreak of the First World War and took up the study of medieval witchcraft more or less as a way to pass the time. Following the lead of Sir James Frazer's *The Golden Bough* (1890), which interpreted a wide range of myths and rituals as survivals of an archaic "fertility religion," she became convinced that the witchcraft trials of the late Middle Ages and early modern period represented the deliberate destruction of a fertility religion exactly like the ones Frazer had described. She published several papers on these themes in scholarly journals between 1917 and 1920, and 1921 saw the release of her first and most famous book on the subject, *The Witch-Cult in Western Europe.*

The book stated, and claimed to prove, that witchcraft across most of Western Europe had been a Pagan religion worshipping a horned god of fertility, meeting in thirteen-person covens on the four quarter days of Candlemas, May Day, Lammas, and All Hallows. This religion, Murray claimed, had remained the faith of the majority of the rural lower classes until the seventeenth century, when it had finally been suppressed by violent persecution.

She went on to develop the picture of the medieval witch cult in two other books, *The God of the Witches* (1931) and *The Divine King in England* (1954). The latter argued that every one of the medieval kings of England had actually been a supporter of the witch religion, and interpreted several centuries' worth of political assassinations and deaths in war as the ceremonial killing of the Divine King or his substitute at regular intervals—another idea borrowed from Frazer.

Although it took some years for her ideas about witchcraft to catch on, by the late 1940s the Murray hypothesis was widely accepted by scholars, and all through the 1950s and 1960s hers was the most commonly held theory about the nature of medieval witchcraft. It was only after her death in 1963 that scholarly opinion began to shift, prompted by renewed studies of the original source material—mostly records of witchcraft trials—that Murray had used to back up her thesis.

These studies demonstrated that Murray had shamelessly manipulated the data, leaving out passages that contradicted her theories, and presenting details that only appeared in one or a few cases as though they were universal (see Cohn 1975, and Oates and Wood 1998, for details). While the demolition of the Murray hypothesis has been accepted almost universally in the scholarly realm, however, many people in the current Pagan scene still treat Murray's books (and her theory) as beyond questioning. *SEE ALSO* WITCH; WITCHCRAFT. FURTHER READING: COHN 1975, HUTTON 1999, MURRAY 1921, MURRAY 1933, MURRAY 1954, OATES AND WOOD 1998.

Murrell, James. English magician, 1780–1860. Born in Rochford, Essex, in the middle of one of England's most witch-haunted districts, Murrell was the seventh son of a seventh son. The only member of his family to receive an education, he was apprenticed to a surveyor, and later worked as a pharmacist's assistant before returning to Rochdale around 1812. He set himself up as a shoemaker in the village, but later abandoned that profession for that of cunning man; *SEE* CUNNING MAN/WOMAN. He was famous all through the region for casting horoscopes, curing diseases with herbal medicine, summoning angels, exorcising evil spirits, and breaking curses.

His library of magical books, which was kept in a locked chest, provides a fascinating glimpse of the fusion of high and folk magic during the dark ages of rationalism. It included books on astrology and astronomy, a handbook of geomancy, a copy of Culpeper's herbal annotated in Murrell's own hand, and a manual for evoking spirits. Some of these books apparently came to Murrell from an older source; one notebook, the only part of his library that still exists today, consists of horoscopes and magical lore collected by a seventeenth-century magician named Neoboad. FURTHER READING: MAPLE 1970.

myrrh. (*Balsamodendron* spp.) The fragrant gum of several species of trees native to Arabia and east Africa, used for incense since ancient times. Its bitter scent makes it a traditional symbol of mourning, and it has often been assigned to Binah, the third Sephirah of the Tree of Life;

SEE BINAH. In traditional humoral medicine, it is considered to be warm and dry in the third degree, and thus associated with the element of fire. *SEE ALSO* NATURAL MAGIC.

Mysteries, the. Among the most famous aspects of ancient Greek and Roman religion, the Mysteries were traditional initiation rituals, many of them handed down from much earlier times. There were a variety of Mysteries available in the Greek world, and some students of mystical lore in ancient times made a habit of being initiated into as many of them as possible.

The most famous of all the Mysteries were the Eleusinian Mysteries, which were enacted once each year in the small town of Eleusis, not far from Athens; *SEE* ELEUSINIAN MYSTERIES. They were associated with the myth of Demeter's search for her daughter Persephone. More widespread were the Bacchic Mysteries, which centered on the myths of Dionysus; at their height, during the heyday of the Roman Empire, there were Bacchic congregations throughout the Empire, even in relative backwaters such as Britain. Other mysteries that had a wide popularity in classical times include those of Cybele, the Magna Mater or Great Mother, which spread from what is now Turkey; those of Isis, born of the fusion of Greek and Egyptian religion in the years after Alexander the Great's conquest of Egypt; and those of Mithras, which were unusual in only being open to men. *SEE* MITHRAIC MYSTERIES.

The initiation rites of the Mysteries were secret, and only scattered references and visual images survive to allow modern scholars to guess at what was involved. In the early stages of the ceremony, there were various ceremonies, some for purification and some for symbolic purposes; for example, initiates of the Eleusinian Mysteries bathed in the sea and sacrificed pigs to purify themselves, and they traveled on foot from Athens to Eleusis along a route, the Sacred Way, with several stops to commemorate various events in the myth of Demeter and Persephone. There seem to have been tests and terrifying sights, and then the revelation of the core secret of the Mystery—something that was seen, according to the accounts. In the Bacchic Mysteries, for example, what was seen was a huge phallus in a winnowing basket. What that meant, and what significance it had to those who had passed through the initiation ceremony, we can only guess.

Most of the Mysteries involved only a single stage of initiation. The Eleusinian Mysteries were different in having two phases, the *Myesis* or Lesser Mysteries and the *Teletai* or Greater Mysteries. The Mithraic Mysteries were a good deal more complex; they had seven degrees of initiation, each associated with one of the seven planets known to the ancient world.

The Mysteries were an important feature of Pagan religion in the ancient world and, like most of the other aspects of classical Paganism, they apparently went out of existence as Christianity took control of the Roman world and Pagan spiritual practices were outlawed. Certain elements of the Mysteries were preserved in magical circles, as attested by the Graeco-Egyptian magical papyri; *SEE* GRAECO-EGYPTIAN MAGICAL PAPYRI. Important elements of the Greek terminology used in the papyri is borrowed directly from the Mysteries, and there are entire rituals—for example, the so-called "Mithras Liturgy"—that seem to have been borrowed directly from Mystery rites. Since many of the more philosophical Greek and Roman magicians also sought initiation into the Mysteries, such borrowings were certainly possible, and they may have allowed some fragments of Mystery practice to pass into later magical traditions. Attempts to show specific borrowings from the Mysteries in later occultism, though, have been problematic at best so far.

Very little attention appears to have been paid to the Mysteries during the Middle Ages and the Renaissance, but the public emergence of Freemasonry in the early eighteenth century made rituals of initiation a subject of greater interest. This interest showed itself in several ways. First, attempts were made to claim (on essentially no evidence) that Freemasonry or some other fraternal order was the lineal descendant of a particular Mystery tradition or, as often as not, of the Mysteries as a whole. Second, new lodge rituals were constructed based on the scraps of surviving information about the Mysteries, a project that may have reached its zenith with the invention of the Seventh Degree of the Patrons of Husbandry, a full-scale Victorian attempt at reenacting the Eleusinian Mysteries. Third, the Mysteries were interpreted by reading back the habits and traditions of eighteenth- and nineteenth-century fraternal lodges into ancient Greece and Rome. *SEE* LODGE, FRATERNAL; GRANGE, THE (PATRONS OF HUSBANDRY). All three of these had important effects on the development of the mythic history of occultism as it developed in the modern period; *SEE* OCCULT HISTORY. *SEE ALSO* PAGANISM. FURTHER READING: BURKERT 1987, GRAF 1997.

N

Nachash. (Hebrew NChSh, "serpent") The serpent of the Tree of Knowledge, the chief villain of the Book of Genesis, has had a curious role in Cabalistic symbolism. By gematria—the Cabalistic process of adding together the number values of the letters of a word, and comparing the result with those of other words—Nachash, which adds to 358, is equal to MShICh, Meshiach or Messiah. Some Gnostics equated the serpent of Eden with the Redeemer, but whether they made use of this equation is not known; *SEE* GNOSTICISM.

In Cabalistic symbolism, Nachash—the serpent who tempted Adam and Eve—is contrasted with Nehushtan, the brazen serpent raised on a pole by Moses in the desert, which is also seen as the serpent of the Tree of Life; *SEE* NEHUSHTAN. Eliphas Lévi and other magical theorists have also identified Nachash as the dangerous and deceptive lower astral, with Nehushtan as the redemptive upper astral; *SEE* ASTRAL PLANE.

nadir. The point on an astrological chart corresponding to the heavens directly beneath the Earth at the moment for which the chart is cast. Planets, signs, and other important points at or near the nadir correspond to deep-seated, often unconscious forces at work in the personality or the situation. *SEE* ASTROLOGY.

Nakhiel. In the lore of ceremonial magic, the planetary intelligence of the sun. His corresponding planetary spirit is Sorath. *SEE* INTELLIGENCE, PLANETARY.

Namburbi rituals. (Akkadian, "banishing evil") A type of magical ceremony practiced in Babylonia, Assyria, and several other Mesopotamian cultures, which were used to dispell the predicted results of an evil omen. *SEE* MESOPOTAMIAN OCCULTISM.

Napoleon's Book of Fate. This simplified variant of geomancy was a popular method of divination in the nineteenth century, due principally to its supposed connection with Napoleon Bonaparte. To use the *Book of Fate,* the diviner chooses one of thirty-two stock questions, then makes five random rows of dots or dashes with a pen. The first twelve dots or dashes are marked off and the remainder counted; an odd number is marked with a single dot, an even number with two dots. The resulting pattern of dots is then looked up in a table, which directs the diviner to a page containing a sentence answering the original question.

According to Herman Kirchenhoffer, its nineteenth-century translator (or inventor), the *Book of Fate* was found in an ancient Egyptian tomb by one of the scholars who accompanied Napoleon Bonaparte in his 1801 invasion of Egypt, translated by a learned Copt, and used by Napoleon himself as an infallible guide to the future until he lost it at the Battle of Leipzig in 1813. Since no one, Copt or otherwise, could read ancient Egyptian documents at that time—Jean François Champollion's initial translation of the Rosetta Stone text did not appear until 1821—there is good reason to doubt the accuracy of the story. The popularity of geomancy and related systems of divination in all the Arab countries, however, makes it at least possible that the *Book of Fate* may have some Egyptian connection. *SEE ALSO* GEOMANCY. FURTHER READING: COLMER 1994.

Naronia. In the occult philosophy of the Hermetic Brotherhood of Luxor (H. B. of L.), an important cycle in the human soul governed by astrological forces. Each year, when the sun transits the point it occupied at the time of an individual's birth, the life energies and potentials of that individual's soul are held to be reenergized. Each month, when the moon transits the same point in the heavens, those energies and potentials are magnetized and filled with magical energies. Magical workings done by a magician at the time of this solar-lunar interaction are particularly effective for inner development.

It has been suggested that the Naronia cycle of the female partner was used as the key to sexual magic by the H. B. of L., and possibly also by P. B. Randolph, the source of much of the brotherhood's sexual occultism. *SEE* RANDOLPH, PASCHAL BEVERLY. *SEE ALSO* HERMETIC BROTHERHOOD OF LUXOR (H. B. OF L.). FURTHER READING: GODWIN ET AL. 1995.

natal astrology. Also called genethliac astrology, this is the most widely known branch of astrological practice and, in most modern societies, the only one known to the general public. Natal astrology seeks to understand the character and destiny of an individual by examining a chart of the heavens erected for the moment of his or her birth.

The basic principles of natal astrology have been established for centuries, and are widely known even to people who have little astrological background. The sign of the zodiac in which the sun was placed at the time of birth is the sun sign, and has the strongest influence on the natal chart. The sign in which the moon was placed determines the moon sign, and the point of the horizon rising on the eastern horizon at the moment of birth determines the ascendant or rising sign. While specific interpretations vary, many astrologers hold that the sun sign determines the public face, the moon sign shows instinctive and unconscious factors in the personality, while the rising sign reveals the real self.

Each of the other planets rules over an aspect of the personality—for example, Mercury governs communication, and Venus the emotions—and the signs in which these planets appear show how each of these aspects expresses itself. The relation of the signs to the four traditional elements also allows a chart to have elemental meanings; the planets may be distributed more or less evenly among the elements, or they may be clustered in one or two. The position of the ascendant also determines the location of the twelve houses—abstract divisions of the sky through which the signs and planets circle—which mark out different spheres of life in which the signs and planets act. *SEE* HOUSE, ASTROLOGICAL. Finally, if the planetary positions form aspects—specific geometrical relationships—with one another, this can either bring the effects of the planets into harmony or place them at loggerheads. *SEE* ASPECT, ASTROLOGICAL.

Natal astrology is thus a good deal more complex than the sort of simplistic sun sign astrology that appears in newspaper horoscope columns. In earlier times, astrologers claimed to be able to read the health, career, fortunes, and death of a person from his or her natal chart. Most current astrologers avoid claims of this sort, and concentrate on interpreting the chart in terms of personality and potentials.

A natal chart is the basis for most forms of progression, which allows important periods in a person's life to be predicted in advance. *SEE* PROGRESSIONS. *SEE ALSO* ASTROLOGY.

nation sack. In traditional hoodoo, a cloth bag worn by women under their clothes, and used to hold magical items. The nation sack originated in Memphis, Tennessee; "traditional Memphis-style nation sacks" can be purchased from some hoodoo suppliers nowadays, though just how traditional they and their contents are is anyone's guess. The origin of the name is unknown. *SEE* HOODOO.

National Socialism. Well before its fiery demise in 1945, the National Socialist ("Nazi") movement in Germany was already being linked with occult traditions, and in recent decades a sizeable literature has come into print in most Western languages claiming various connections between Nazism and the occult. Most of this literature is worthless from a factual point of view—full of obvious errors, major distortions of fact, and large helpings of fantasy and fabrication. In the resulting furor, the handful of works of serious historical scholarship on the subject have received little attention, and the actual evidence for Nazi occultism has been largely neglected.

A central task in discussing the occult dimensions of Nazism, then, is that of clearing away the jungle of misinformation that has grown up around the Third Reich's ruins. There is, for example, not a scrap of evidence that Hitler or any other important Nazi officials were particularly interested in the so-called "Spear of Destiny" that allegedly pierced the side of Jesus of Nazareth, and the best-selling book that introduced this claim includes a blizzard of similar provable inaccuracies. Similarly, the suggestion that the Nazis were puppets of sinister Tibetan adepts and the claim that they were in contact with superbeings from inside the hollow Earth are relevant to the study of twentieth-century occult folklore, but have nothing to do with what was going on in Germany between 1919 and 1945.

Behind all the smoke, however, is a certain amount of fire. While the more extreme claims about occult influence on Nazism (and vice versa) can be discarded, a certain core of hard fact remains. The following points have been solidly documented:

(a) The ideology of Nazi Germany was largely borrowed from German and Austrian occult societies involved in Ariosophy, a racist offshoot of Theosophy that emerged around the beginning of the twentieth century;

(b) The Nazi Party itself was originally organized as a political arm of the Thule-Gesellschaft, a secret society closely connected to the most important German Ariosophical magical order;

(c) Important members of the Nazi Party, including Hitler himself, were directly and personally involved in occult studies of one sort or another.

These three points all by themselves make it clear that the occult dimension of Nazism cannot simply be dismissed. While many other factors came together in Germany in the 1920s and 1930s to unleash Nazism on the world, the contribution of Ariosophy and certain other elements of the Western occult traditions was not a minor one.

The origins of Nazism, then, can be traced to Ariosophy, an occult movement that emerged in Austria and Germany around the beginning of the twentieth century; SEE ARIOSOPHY. The central figure in the emergence of Ariosophy was Guido von List, an Austrian writer and occultist who reintroduced the study of the runes to modern occultism, and whose writings glorified the ancient Germanic tribes and their magical wisdom. According to List, this wisdom had been the possession of the Armanen, a priestly caste among the ancient Germans. List also dabbled in prophecy, and in the latter part of his life wrote at length about *die Stärke von Oben*, "the strong one from above," who would soon appear and liberate the Aryan race from its alleged Jewish oppressors. The Guido von List Society, founded by List's admirers, combined an interest in German Pagan religion and magic with strong racist and right-wing political views. Its inner circle, the HAO or Höhere Armanenorden (Higher Armanen Order), practiced magical rituals based on List's theories. SEE ARMANEN; LIST, GUIDO VON.

Associated with List was another Austrian occultist, Jörg Lanz von Liebenfels, a defrocked monk who argued that modern humanity was the product of interbreeding between ancient Aryan supermen and sexually perverted subhuman dwarfs. A founding member of the Guido von List Society and the publisher of one of Austria's major racist magazines, *Ostara*, Lanz von Liebenfels went on to start a magical order of his own, the Ordo Novi Templi (Order of New Templars) or ONT, which required that applicants pass racial purity tests before joining, and which developed a complex liturgy of rituals devoted to restoring the lost Aryan electrical-psychic powers in its members. SEE LANZ VON LIEBENFELS, JÖRG; ORDO NOVI TEMPLI (ONT).

In Germany, these same currents of thought found a ready market in anti-Semitic and nationalist circles before the First World War. Around 1910, the German Ariosophist Hermann Pohl began to assemble the materials for an occult order, the Germanenorden, which was formally founded in 1912. Partly a secret political movement and partly a magical society, the Germanenorden borrowed heavily from Guido von List's ideas. Differences between occult and political wings of the order led to a schism in 1916. SEE GERMANENORDEN.

In 1917, the Munich branch of the Germanenorden Walvater—the more occult wing—came under the leadership of the adventurer Rudolf von Sebottendorf, who increased its membership more than sevenfold and gave it the public alias of Thule-Gesellschaft, the Thule Society. During the attempted Communist revolution in Bavaria that followed Germany's defeat in the First World War, the Thule Society played a central role in organizing right-wing resistance to the Communists. SEE THULE-GESELLSCHAFT.

The Thule Society also organized a political party, the Deutsche Arbeiterpartei (DAP) or German Workers Party, to organize the more conservative sections of the working class. On the evening of September 12, 1919, an Austrian veteran named Adolf Hitler came to a DAP meeting and got into a heated political discussion there. A few days later, the party invited him to join. Guido von List's "strong one from above" had made his appearance.

Hitler himself had a substantial acquantance with the occult. According to a friend of his Vienna days, occultism, oriental religions, and astrology made up a significant part of the future Führer's reading. During his years in Vienna, he was also a regular subscriber to Lanz von Liebenfels' magazine Ostara, and once visited the Ariosophist to fill out his collection of back issues. Hitler's writings and recorded comments show that he had nothing but contempt for the völkisch wing of Ariosophy, the branch that sought to revive ancient Germanic paganism and folk tradition, but a great deal of Lanz von Liebenfels' racial ideology and political program found its way into Hitler's own plans. SEE HITLER, ADOLF.

Throughout the early stages of his rise to power, Hitler was helped by members of the Thule Society, whose connections to wealthy and influential right-wing Bavarians proved crucial as the small-time, poorly organized DAP transformed itself into the Nationalsozialistische Deutsche Arbeiterpartei (NSDAP) or National Socialist German Workers Party. A special role was played by Dietrich Eckart, an Ariosophical occultist and writer, who was not actually a member of the Thule Society but was closely associated with many Thule leaders. Eckart lent Hitler books, helped him polish his rhetoric and his manners, and guided the early stages of Hitler's career. A number of books have alleged that Eckart was also Hitler's occult mentor and initiator and, while this has not been proven, Eckart was certainly qualified for the role.

Another significant figure was Rudolf Hess (1894–1987), a Thule Society member who also belonged to the French right-wing occult group Les Veilleurs and may have passed information between these two groups;

SEE VEILLEURS, LES. Not long after Hitler's appearance, Hess became an important member of the Nazi Party, rising to the position of Deputy Führer, which he held until 1941. Hess was a serious occultist by any standard, a student of astrology and of the Anthroposophical teachings of Rudolf Steiner.

On the night of May 10, 1941, as part of a series of events that still has never been adequately explained by historians, Hess boarded a Luftwaffe ME–110 night fighter and flew to Scotland. The date was an astrologically important one—Mercury, Venus, Jupiter, Saturn, and Uranus were all conjunct the sun, with Mars squaring them all and a full moon approaching opposition—and according to several accounts, Hess was wearing a collection of talismans and magical gear when he made the trip. The purpose for his journey remains unknown, though there has been a good deal of speculation. Imprisoned by the British authorities during the war, he was sentenced to life imprisonment at Nuremberg and held in Berlin's Spandau prison until his death in 1987.

Yet another important figure in the interface between Nazism and the occult was Heinrich Himmler (1900–1945), who joined the NSDAP in 1919 and became head of the SS, then a volunteer corps of Nazis who served as Hitler's private security force, in 1929. Deeply involved in occult studies, Himmler believed himself to be the reincarnation of the medieval German king Heinrich I, and was interested in the völkisch and Pagan side of the Ariosophical movement. Under his leadership, the SS took on many of the characteristics of an Ariosophical magical order.

In 1933, Himmler took over Wewelsburg, a dilapidated medieval castle, and turned it into a Nazi ritual center where senior SS officers gathered three or four times a year for ritual work and occult meditations. In 1935 he organized a special SS research bureau, the Ahnenerbe. While it branched out to include a vast array of research projects, the Ahnenerbe's primary mission was research into Germanic prehistory, and it amassed huge archives on witchcraft, Freemasonry, and many other topics of occult interest. SEE SS.

The exact role of these occult involvements of Nazi leaders in the actual workings of the Nazi state, the conduct of its war machine, and the planning and execution of the Holocaust is a matter of heated debate. Attempts to define the Nazi program as purely occult are as misleading as those which ignore every aspect of occultism in the Third Reich. The contemporary English occultist Dion Fortune, who probably had as much experience with the contemporary magical scene as anyone alive at the time, commented perceptively:

> There are two schools of thought in the entourage of the Fuehrer—those who believe in the invincibility of physical force and rely on mundane plane organization to achieve their ends; and the relatively small and apparently obscure group of those who realize that there are subtle forces that can be enlisted to serve their ends. Hitler himself uses both as his instruments. (Fortune 1993, p. 60.)

In the end, neither the physical nor the occult side of Nazism proved able to defend the Third Reich from the whirlwind of violence it unleashed on itself, and evidence that might have settled the question of the occult dimensions of Nazism disappeared as Allied bomber fleets flattened Germany's cities and Allied armies occupied the rubble. The last opportunity for knowledge may have been the Nuremberg War Crimes trials, and other factors closed off this possibility, probably for good. According to Airey Neave, one of the British prosecutors in the trials, a very large quantity of evidence bearing on the occult side of Nazism was deliberately suppressed by the International Military Tribunal as too bizarre to be admitted. It was felt that such evidence might allow Nazi war criminals to plead insanity and escape punishment for their crimes. FURTHER READING: FORTUNE 1993, GOODRICK-CLARKE 1992, HAKL 2000, HITLER 1974, LUMSDEN 1997.

natural magic. One of the two great divisions of Western magical practice, the other being ritual or ceremonial magic; *SEE* CEREMONIAL MAGIC. Natural magic deals with the magical powers of physical substances—herbs, stones, resins, metals, perfumes, and the like. It has generally been much less controversial than ritual magic, and has been practiced openly even at times when even a rumor of involvement in ritual magic was enough to cause imprisonment and death.

The principle governing natural magic in the Western occult tradition is the great Hermetic axiom "As above, so below." Every object in the material world, according to this dictum, is a reflection of astrological and spiritual powers. By making use of these material reflections, the natural magician concentrates or disperses particular powers of the higher levels of being; thus a stone or an herb associated with the sun is infused with the magical energies of the sun, and wearing that stone or hanging that herb on the wall brings those energies into play in a particular situation.

The philosophy and practice of natural magic are both closely associated with astrology and humoral medicine. *SEE* ASTROLOGY; HUMORS. *SEE ALSO* MAGIC. FURTHER READING: AGRIPPA 1993, GREER 2000.

Naudhr. *SEE* NAUTHIZ.

Nauthiz. (Old Germanic, "need, constraint") The tenth rune of the elder futhark, corresponding to the concepts of restriction, necessity, and fate. Some modern runemasters associate it with Skuld, the third of the Norns or goddesses of fate, who represents the future. Its sound-value is *n*. *SEE* ELDER FUTHARK.

In the Anglo-Saxon futhorc, the same rune takes on the name Nyd (Old English, "need") and has essentially the same meanings and value. The Old English rune-poem comments that need oppresses the heart, but can be a source of help and salvation to those who pay attention to it in time. *SEE* ANGLO-SAXON FUTHORC.

In the younger futhorc, this rune is named Naudhr (Old Norse, "need") and has the same meanings and sound. The Old Norse rune-poem gives it the memorable image of a naked man chilled by frost. *SEE* YOUNGER FUTHARK.

In the Armanen runic system, finally, this rune is named Not (modern German, "need, suffering") and corresponds to the concept of need, the god Heimdall, the mother, and the zodiacal sign Scorpio. Its magical power, from the rune-charm of the Old Norse *Havamal*, is the ability to calm hatred in the heart of a warrior. *SEE* ARMANEN RUNES.

Rune Nauthiz (Nyd, Naudhr, Not)

Nazi occultism. *SEE* NATIONAL SOCIALISM.

necromancy. (Greek *nekromanteia*, from *nekros*, "dead," and *manteia*, "divination") The art of divination through contact with the spirits of the dead; more generally, any magical operation that makes use of the souls of dead human beings. The term "necromancy" has also sometimes been used loosely to mean any form of magic of which the speaker disapproves.

Necromancy has ancient roots in the Western occult traditions, and played a fairly large part in certain branches of magical practice in classical times. Literary sources, including the Bible, the *Odyssey*, and the Babylonian *Epic of Gilgamesh*, include passages where rituals for summoning and communicating with the dead were practiced. Binding tablets, magical lead tablets written with curses and deposited in graves or dropped in wells in order to get them to the underworld, were an important part of the arsenal of the ancient Greek sorcerer, and often had connections to necromantic magic; *SEE* BINDING TABLET.

In the Middle Ages, by contrast, most people who wanted to get into contact with unauthorized spiritual powers summoned devils rather than the dead; it was at this time that goetia, originally a term for necromancy, came to mean the art of conjuring demons. *SEE* GOETIA. There were some exceptions, however, and the practice of necromancy was a living tradition in England until the Scientific Revolution. The Elizabethan wizard and astrologer Simon Forman is known to have practiced it, and the same is rumored of Edward Kelly, John Dee's scryer and magical partner. *SEE* FORMAN, SIMON; KELLY, EDWARD.

The general loss of interest in necromancy lasted until 1848, when communication with the dead became fashionable once again with the rise of the Spiritualist movement; *SEE* SPIRITUALISM. The complex relationship between Spiritualism and the broader occult community played itself out in this issue, as in others. Occult writings from the late nineteenth and early twentieth century range in attitude from glowing support of Spiritualism, through cautious interest or the suggestion that Spiritualists were handling real powers in a clumsy way, to rabid denunciations of the entire movement.

At present, a few magical traditions make use of necromantic practices of one sort or another, while most others either ignore the subject or discourage its practice. At least one popular handbook of witchcraft published in the twentieth century gives detailed instructions for rituals of necromancy, and some modern Pagan traditions include evocations of the spirits of the dead as part of the ceremony of Samhain—one of the eight sabbats of modern Pagan practice—though these are generally treated in a symbolic sense rather than a magical one. *SEE* SAMHAIN. Spiritualism still continues as an independent religious movement, and some aspects of the New Age movement have taken up its habit of consulting the dead; *SEE* NEW AGE MOVEMENT. *SEE ALSO* DIVINATION. FURTHER READING: E. BUTLER 1949, HUSON 1970.

Necronomicon. A fictional book of evil magic invented by the American fantasy-horror writer H. P. Lovecraft (1891–1937). According to Lovecraft, the *Necronomicon* was written by the mad Arab Abdul Alhazred in Damascus in A.D. 730, translated into Latin by Olaus Wormius and into English by John Dee in the sixteenth century, and lurks in the closed stacks of select libraries. It is said to contain the secret lore of the Old Ones—monstrous, tentacled extraterrestrial entities who once ruled the Earth and who now wait until "the stars are right" to wrap their slimy tentacles about the planet once again. Copies of the *Necronomicon* play an important part in several of Lovecraft's stories and novels, and in the writings of his numerous imitators.

The title is usually translated as "Book of Dead Names," but this is inaccurate—*necro-* and the ending *-icon* are Greek, and so *nom-* is from Greek *nomos*, "law," not Latin *nomen*, "name." More correct translations might be "Book of the Laws of the Dead," "Book of the Laws of Death," or possibly "Book of Dead Laws."

It should be stressed that the *Necronomicon* was entirely the invention of a pulp fantasy author of the twentieth century, and had no existence anywhere before Lovecraft's time. In the last decades of the twentieth century, however, at least three different versions of the *Necronomicon* were manufactured and published in the occult market. The most popular of them, by the pseudonymous "Simon," had a mass market paperback run of respectable size.

Entities from Lovecraft's stories—Cthulhu, Azathoth, and the like—have also put in an appearance in supposedly serious works of magical theory and practice. The British occultist Kenneth Grant, whose writings are perhaps the closest approach to Lovecraft's esthetic within the present-day magical community, has argued that while the *Necronomicon* has no physical reality, it has a reality on the inner levels and can be accessed in the dream state. In addition, the modern tradition of Chaos magic—which explicitly denies the reality of supernatural beings, and considers them to be simply symbols useful in magical workings—has drawn on the *Necronomicon* and other Lovecraftian materials as a source of imagery. *SEE* CHAOS MAGIC. *SEE ALSO* FANTASY OCCULTISM. FURTHER READING: GRANT 1980, SIMON 1980.

Nehushtan. (Hebrew NChShThN, "brass object") In the Bible (Numbers 21:8–9), the serpent of brass made by Moses and set up on a pole to cure the Israelites of the venomous bites of fiery serpents in the wilderness. The word *Nehushtan*, "thing of brass," contains a Hebrew pun, for the first three letters (NChSh) mean "serpent" and the last two (ThN) mean "dragon."

Christian commentators have generally interpeted the brazen serpent as a prefigure of Christ, who was lifted up on a pole (more or less) to cure human beings of the "snakebite" of original sin. This interpretation is less hamhanded than it sounds, since the Hebrew words for "Messiah" (MShICh) and "serpent" (NChSh) have the same numerical value. *SEE* GEMATRIA.

In some magical writings, the brazen serpent Nehushtan is identified with the positive and redemptive powers of the upper astral, while the serpent of the Tree of Knowledge, Nachash, is identified with the negative powers of the lower astral. *SEE* NACHASH.

nemyss. (ancient Egyptian *nemes*) The standard Egyptian headdress during pharaonic times, the nemyss (also spelled "nemiss" and "nemes" in English) in its simplest form is a square or rectangle of cloth, often striped, with one edge reinforced by a band that ends in ties. The band is placed across the forehead with the cloth going up over the head; the two ties are pulled around and tied together behind the head, and the cloth is then allowed to fall down onto the shoulders. Nemysses are worn in the Hermetic Order of the Golden Dawn, in some Druid groups, and in certain modern Pagan groups working with Egyptian traditions.

Neopaganism. A general term for the Pagan and quasi-Pagan movements that became public in much of the Western world in the second half of the twentieth century. Many of these movements claim connections, historical or spiritual, with earlier Pagan traditions in Europe, although the existence of these connections has been forcefully challenged by scholars. For information on traditional Western polytheistic religion, *SEE* PAGANISM.

It has sometimes been claimed that the term "Neopagan" was invented by a particular Pagan religious group in California in the 1970s, but it actually dates back nearly a century before that time. The term was already in use by the 1890s, when literary critics such as F. W. Barry used it as a label for writers who rejected Puritan morality and Christian religion in favor of imagery and ideas drawn from ancient Greek and Celtic sources. By 1908 a group of artists and poets at Cambridge was using the term for itself, and the Cambridge Neo-Pagans continued as a minor force in British cultural circles into the 1920s.

Barry's devoutly Christian condemnation of the "Neo-pagan" writers and poets of his time may have been more on target than he realized, for some figures on that end of the cultural spectrum had long since moved from Pagan art to Pagan spirituality. Earlier in the nineteenth century, the poet Thomas Jefferson Hogg was widely known among his friends for performing rituals to worship the Greek gods, while the painter Edward Calvert, whose scenes from ancient Greek legend and history were popular all through the late nineteenth century, erected an altar to Pan in his back yard and offered libations of wine to the goat-footed god. *SEE* PAN. They were by no means the first European intellectuals to pass from an admiration of classical culture to the worship of classical gods.

The first known examples actually date back to the Renaissance, and the emergence of a revived Druidry in England and Wales in the eighteenth century was a significant sign; *SEE* DRUIDS. Freemasonry, with its claims of a connection to the ancient Mysteries, also helped lay the groundwork for the later revival; SEE FREEMASONRY. It was the great English Platonist Thomas Taylor (1758–1835), however, whose open rejection of Christianity in favor of a revival of Pagan spirituality and Platonist theurgy seems to have launched the nineteenth-century Neopagan movement in Britain; SEE TAYLOR, THOMAS. By the middle of the nineteenth century, following in his footsteps and that of several others, a small but noticeable Neopagan subculture existed in most of the countries of Western Europe.

This subculture was intellectual, largely urban, college-educated, and familiar with recent trends in scholarship on mythology and religion. Many of its members were involved in other aspects of alternative thought and lifestyle, with interests ranging from vegetarianism through occultism to various schemes of Utopian social reform. In short, it was very much like the present-day Neopagan scene, and utterly unlike the peasant cunning folk who came to play such a large part in the mythologies of the later Neopagan revival; SEE CUNNING MAN/WOMAN.

The Victorian revival of Paganism drew heavily on the vast nineteenth-century surge of interest in folklore and mythology, which brought about the rediscovery of Germanic and Celtic myth and legend, as well as the first great collections of folklore relating to magic and popular religious practices. It also drew on the growing interest in Asian religions, an interest that became a major cultural phenomenon with the foundation of the Theosophical Society in 1875 and the arrival of the first Buddhist missionaries in England and America a few decades later. SEE THEOSOPHICAL SOCIETY.

A final factor, and a crucial one, was the spread of occult philosophy and practice in the last quarter of the nineteenth century. Here again, the Theosophical Society played an important role, and two other organizations—the Hermetic Brotherhood of Luxor and the Hermetic Order of the Golden Dawn—also had much to do with the development of the nineteenth-century occult revival, which had been launched in France by the magician and scholar Eliphas Lévi in 1845. SEE GOLDEN DAWN, HERMETIC ORDER OF THE; HERMETIC BROTHERHOOD OF LUXOR (H. B. OF L.); LÉVI, ELIPHAS. While the occultism of that period was rarely Pagan in any explicit sense, it challenged Christian doctrine at almost every point. Under Blavatsky's leadership, the Theosophical Society was intensely hostile to Christian teachings and did nothing to disguise the fact. The Golden Dawn went further, invoking Pagan deities from Egyptian sources in its rituals and equating Osiris and Jesus in its instructional papers.

Thus, at the end of the nineteenth century, Christianity was no longer the only game in town, and a variety of people and small groups—most of them closely connected with occult traditions of one sort or another—began to take up more vocal and more explicitly Pagan stances in the early years of the twentieth century. Edward Carpenter (1844–1929), who abandoned a career as an Anglican minister to preach socialism and Pagan religion, was one of many examples; his brash masterpiece *Civilization: Its Cause and Cure* (1906) called for the renewal of Pagan worship in sacred groves and on mountaintops. Similarly, British author Kenneth Grahame, whose children's book *The Wind in the Willows* contains one of the best-loved evocations of the presence of Pan in all of literature, described himself in his 1904 *Pagan Papers* as a faithful Pagan following "the old religion."

The Pagan revival had its largest impact in the English-speaking and German-speaking countries. As a result, Britain and Germany both had openly Pagan groups worshipping in public between the two world wars. The British groups still mostly drew on ancient Greek traditions, while the German groups were devoted to a revived Teutonic Paganism that too often shaded over into Ariosophy and racism; SEE ARIOSOPHY.

Youth groups associated with Woodcraft, a quasi-Pagan movement founded in America in 1902, also played an important part in the rising interest in Paganism. In its original form, Woodcraft drew on Native American symbolism and traditions, but the European branches of the movement replaced much of this with local Pagan traditions; SEE WOODCRAFT.

A major shift in the Neopagan scene came with the repeal of Britain's antiquated Witchcraft Act in 1951. Shortly afterwards, British newspaper readers were startled and titillated to read of covens of witches worshipping in the nude ("skyclad") in their own country. A retired colonial official, Gerald Gardner, presented himself as the inheritor of an ancient tradition called Wicca; his two books on the subject and his frequent appearances in the media gave his claims enormous publicity. *SEE* GARDNER, GERALD BROUSSEAU; WICCA. Within a short time several other witches were claiming, in the newspapers and elsewhere, to have inherited their own independent traditions of witchcraft. *SEE* COCHRANE, ROBERT; SANDERS, ALEC. The origins of these traditions have been hotly disputed, but there is little reason to doubt that they grew out of the earlier Neopagan underground, inspired by Margaret Murray's hypothesis that medieval witchcraft had been a survival of an ancient Pagan fertility religion; *SEE* MURRAY HYPOTHESIS.

The great cultural convulsions of the Sixties took Wicca from a relatively small presence on the cultural fringe to a religious movement on an international scale, and opened the door to a proliferation of other Pagan revivals. While Pagan spirituality was never one of the central themes of the Sixties counterculture, there were enough points of contact between the two that Wicca surged in popularity. The emergence of feminism as a major cultural force in the 1970s also helped foster the spread of a religious movement that gave reverence to female images of the divine and offered positions of honor to women.

The last three decades of the twentieth century saw the unfolding of four major trends in the Neopagan movement. First of all was the sheer growth in the number of people identifying themselves as Pagan in western Europe, North America, and Australasia. While estimates vary wildly, a rough guess based on the average of various surveys suggests that by 2000, there were between half a million and one million people in the Western world who considered themselves to be Pagans. This by itself raised Neopaganism to the level of a significant social force.

The second trend was the emergence of a plethora of new Pagan traditions and approaches. Starting in the 1970s, Wicca and its close equivalents were joined in the Neopagan community by groups and individuals worshipping Celtic, Norse, Greek, Egyptian, Hawaiian, and Slavic gods and goddesses—to name only a few of the more popular sides of the Pagan revival. *SEE* ASATRU;

CELTIC RECONSTRUCTIONISM; DRUIDRY. A less impressive side to this trend was the emergence of quasi-Pagan systems that drew their inspiration from fantasy fiction and the media; *SEE* FANTASY OCCULTISM.

The third trend, an even more powerful force for diversity, was a shift from a group-centered, initiatory model of Pagan practice to a more individual approach based on self-initiation and solitary practice. The publication of Scott Cunningham's *Wicca: A Guide for the Solitary Practitioner* (1988) marked an important phase in this shift. Although the book was attacked by many important figures in the Wiccan community when it first appeared, this first major guide to solitary Wiccan practice ran through more than twenty-five printings in the twelve years following, and was widely imitated by other writers in the field. *SEE* CUNNINGHAM, SCOTT. The impact of this and other books of the same kind has been measured in the growth of "solitaries" as a widely recognized class of Pagan worshippers.

The fourth trend was the emergence of the Pagan festival as a major nexus for the growing Neopagan subculture. Modeled partly on science-fiction conventions and partly on medieval reenactment events—both products of subcultures that overlapped significantly with the Pagan scene—Pagan festivals sprang up in the 1980s and 1990s, partly as an opportunity for Pagans to socialize, worship, and learn together, and partly as a substitute for more permanent forms of organization within the Pagan community—a project which had been attempted various times with very limited success.

With the coming of the twenty-first century, the Neopagan movement stands at a crossroads. The spread of Neopagan religion, and the emergence of a certain number of mature and capable spokespersons within the movement, have brought it a level of social acceptance it has never before had. J. K. Rowling's astonishingly popular Harry Potter novels represent only the most visible part of a flood of positive images of witches, magicians, and Pagans in popular media.

At the same time, other religious alternatives such as Spiritualism and Theosophy have made similar gains in the past, and then faded out again with shifts in cultural fashions. It remains to be seen if the modern Pagan revival can consolidate its gains and establish itself as a viable spiritual movement over the long term. FURTHER READING: ADLER 1986, HUTTON 2000, CUNNINGHAM 1988, HUTTON 1999, JONES AND PENNICK 1995, SEZNEC 1953.

Neoplatonism. SEE PLATONISM.

nephesh. (Hebrew NPhSh, "soul") In Cabalistic lore, the lowest part of the soul, corresponding to the animal levels of consciousness. In the Golden Dawn system, the nephesh was termed the Automatic Consciousness, and relates to the etheric or vital body. SEE ETHERIC BODY; SUBTLE BODIES.

Neptune. Discovered in 1846, Neptune is the second of the outer planets to be revealed since the invention of the telescope. Like Uranus, which rocked the astrological world sixty-five years earlier, Neptune presented a difficult puzzle to astrologers, who had to figure out its influences and effects without the benefit of previous astrological research. The current astrological picture of Neptune assigns it to artistic creativity, visionary experiences, idealism, the imagination, and psychoactive drugs. Neptune rules the sign Pisces (formerly assigned to Jupiter), and is in its detriment in Virgo. SEE ASTROLOGY.

Astrological symbol of Neptune

neshamah. (Hebrew NShMH, "soul") In Cabalistic theory, one of the higher aspects of the human soul, corresponding to the third Sephirah, Binah. The neshamah, or supernal understanding, is one of the three parts of the soul—along with the chiah and yechidah—that remain above the Abyss and comprise the Higher Genius. In some sources, all three of these higher aspects of the self are referred to collectively as the neshamah. SEE CABALA; CHIAH; YECHIDAH.

Neshiah. (Hebrew NShIH, "pasture, meadow") In Cabalistic lore, the fourth of the seven earths, corresponding to the Sephirah Tiphareth. SEE EARTHS, SEVEN.

Netzach. (Hebrew NtzCh, "victory") The seventh Sephirah of the Cabalistic Tree of Life, located on the bottom of the Pillar of Mercy. Its standard symbolism is as follows:

Name of God: YHVH TzBAVTh, Tetragrammaton Tzabaoth (Lord of Armies).

Archangel: HANIAL, Haniel (Grace of God).

Angelic Host: ThRShIShIM, Tarshishim (Brilliant Ones).

Astrological Correspondence: NVGH, Nogah (Venus).

Tarot Correspondence: The four Sevens of the pack.

Elemental Correspondence: Fire.

Magical Image: A beautiful naked woman.

Additional Symbol: The rose.

Additional Title: The Gate of the Mysteries.

Colors: in Atziluth—amber.

in Briah—emerald.

in Yetzirah—bright yellow-green.

in Assiah—olive flecked with gold.

Correspondence in the Microcosm: The emotions, as part of Ruach (the conscious self).

Correspondence in the Body: The left hip.

Grade of Initiation: 4=7, Philosophus.

Qlippoth: AaRB TzRQ, A'arab Tzereq (the Ravens of Dispersion.)

Its text from the *Thirty-two Paths of Wisdom* runs, "The Seventh Path is called the Occult Intelligence because it is the refulgent splendor of all the intellectual virtues, which are perceived by the eyes of the intellect and the contemplations of faith." SEE ALSO CABALA; TREE OF LIFE.

Neuburg, Victor. English poet and magician, 1883–1940. Born in London to a wealthy Jewish family, he left school in 1899, spent the next seven years working for his family's import business while he wrote and published his first significant poems, and entered Trinity College at Cambridge in 1906, determined to pursue a literary career. While an undergraduate, he met Aleister Crowley and quickly became one of the Beast's disciples and lovers. He was initiated into the A∴A∴, Crowley's magical order, in early 1909, with the magical motto *Omnia Vincam* ("I will conquer all"), and in the summer of that year underwent a magical retirement under Crowley's tutelage at Boleskine House.

From 1909 to 1914 Neuburg was heavily involved in all of Crowley's activities, helping to edit the *Equinox* (to which he also contributed essays and poetry), and carrying out a series of magical workings with Crowley. Two of these are of particular importance: he was with the Beast in the Algerian desert through the working that produced Crowley's book *The Vision and the Voice*, and he also cooperated with Crowley in the famous Paris Working of 1914, in which he and Crowley used sex magic to invoke Mercury and Jupiter.

After the conclusion of the Paris Working, Neuburg broke with Crowley. Whether he had finally lost patience with the Beast's monumental ego or whether there was some more specific cause is impossible to tell, as neither man discussed the matter afterwards. Crowley is said to have responded to Neuburg's departure by ritually cursing him. After a nervous breakdown, a stint in the army during World War I, and an unsuccessful marriage, Neuburg went on to a successful career as a poet and editor. He seems to have had no further involvement in magic after his separation from Crowley. SEE ALSO ARGENTEUM ASTRUM (A∴A∴); CROWLEY, ALEISTER. FURTHER READING: FULLER 1990, NEUBURG 1990.

New Age movement. Among the most recent offshoots of the Western occult traditions, the New Age movement emerged in Britain in the 1970s among a loose network of people interested in alternative lifestyles and spiritualities. Many members of this network had been involved in "contactee" organizations—groups of people associated with the UFO phenomenon, who claimed to be in contact with extraterrestrial higher intelligences—during the 1950s and 1960s. The contactee movement during those years had been awash with apocalyptic prophecies of a New Age about to dawn, heralded by vast planetary catastrophes.

During the 1970s, a new interpretation of this idea evolved within the British network just mentioned. This idea was the suggestion that instead of waiting hopefully for the New Age to dawn, it would be more useful to live as though it had already arrived. People in the network set out to enact the New Age in daily life, and thereby help create it by inspiring others and showing that alternatives to the status quo were available. From the original circles where it was first proposed, the idea and a growing body of associated practices spread to wider alternative circles, first in Britain, then in America; by the middle of the 1980s it was functioning on a global scale.

As a movement based on opposition to existing social, cultural, and spiritual ideas, rather than on any specific doctrine of its own, the New Age has defined itself by what it is not, rather than by what it is. The resulting movement is less a single phenomenon than a grab-bag of miscellaneous beliefs united mostly by the fact that they have been more or less rejected by the scientific and cultural mainstream. Thus UFOs, channeling, alternative health care methods, shamanism, reincarnation, Goddess worship, lost civilizations, kundalini yoga, earth mysteries, transpersonal psychology, perpetual motion schemes, the Gaia hypothesis, conspiracy theories, pyramidology, and many other equally diverse topics are all grist for the New Age mill.

This diversity makes it difficult to point to any particular set of beliefs or activities as central to the New Age movement. Still, the movement's status as a reaction against the cultural status quo provides it with a certain unity. It also serves as a connection with its historical roots.

One of the most interesting things about the New Age, in fact, is just how little of it is new. Most of the elements of the modern New Age movement were just as central to the alternative scene in Britain and America a century ago, when channelers were still called mediums, believers in ancient Goddess-worshipping matriarchies were reading Jane Harrison rather than Marija Gimbutas, physical culture and Swedish massage filled the roles of Feldenkrais training and shiatsu, and conspiracy theorists discussed czarist Russia's sinister plans rather than those of the equally sinister New World Order. It may be symptomatic that one of the most popular alternative periodicals in Britain in 1900 was titled *The New Age*.

One particular source for current New Age ideas deserves particular mention. The complicated cosmology developed by the Theosophical Society in the late nineteenth and early twentieth centuries, largely based on H. P. Blavatsky's monumental *The Secret Doctrine* (1888), includes the great majority of the ideas now central to the New Age movement, and also embodies the same across-the-board rejection of conventional ideas of science and spirituality. The entire New Age movement has been characterized as "Theosophy plus therapy," and while this is an oversimplification—there are a number of important New Age elements, such as channeling, which fall into neither of these categories—the label has a substantial element of truth to it. *SEE* THEOSOPHICAL SOCIETY; THEOSOPHY.

The relation between the Western occult traditions and the New Age movement is a contentious issue, in large part because many present-day occultists and Pagans respond with horror to the suggestion that their traditions have anything to do with the New Age scene. Once again, though, the same relationship between a core of serious teachings on the one hand, and a much broader but much shallower penumbra of popularizations on the other, has been a factor in the history of occultism for a very long time. Alchemists in the Middle Ages wrote about the hordes of "puffers," inept would-be alchemists interested only in making gold, who were bringing the alchemical art into disrepute. Centuries later, occultists of the Victorian period shook their heads at the excesses and follies of the mesmerist and Spiritualist movements, both of which drew heavily from occult traditions. *SEE* MESMERISM; SPIRITUALISM.

The New Age movement is simply the most recent example of the same process. For all its awkward features, it has played an important role in recent decades in providing audiences and support to worthwhile systems of alternative medicine and spiritual practice, and in spreading occult perspectives out into Western culture as a whole. *SEE ALSO* AGHARTA; ATLANTIS; CYCLES, COSMIC; GAIA HYPOTHESIS; GLASTONBURY; LEMURIA; LOST CIVILIZATIONS; MATRIARCHIES, ANCIENT; MU; NEW THOUGHT; OCCULT HISTORY; SHASTA, MOUNT. FURTHER READING: FERGUSON 1980, HANEGRAAF 1996.

New England Covens of Traditionalist Witches (NECTW). American witchcraft tradition, founded or made public by Gwen Thompson of New Haven, Connecticut, in the late 1960s. Thompson claimed a family tradition of witchcraft reaching back many generations, and the system of witchcraft derived from her teachings is strongly influenced by popular occultism of a variety of types. Mostly active on the eastern coast of North America, the NECTW tradition has received little attention but seems to have had a great deal of influence on some aspects of the American Pagan scene.

NECTW covens observe the eight sabbats and celebrate esbats at full moons. Circles are held outdoors whenever possible. The tradition emphasizes ecology, herbalism, divination, and magical practice. FURTHER READING: DAVIES 2001.

New Reformed Orthodox Order of the Golden Dawn (NROOGD). *SEE* GOLDEN DAWN, NEW REFORMED ORTHODOX ORDER OF THE (NROOGD).

New Thought. A spiritual movement, founded in America in the middle of the nineteenth century but presently active in many countries, which places the highest priority on the power of human thought. According to New Thought, illness and suffering are the product of negative thought patterns, and can be banished by replacing these thought patterns with other, positive ones.

The New Thought movement evolved from nineteenth-century American offshoots of Mesmerism, especially as formulated by P. P. Quimby and Mary Baker Eddy. *SEE* CHRISTIAN SCIENCE; MESMERISM; QUIMBY, PHINEAS PARKHURST. Its roots also include the Transcendentalist movement in early nineteenth-century New England; *SEE* TRANSCENDENTALISM. A movement rather than an organization, New Thought spread primarily through books and lecturers and encompassed a diversity of approaches, some borrowed from occult traditions and others derived from psychology, Christianity, and other ideologies of personal growth. At certain times—for example, in the middle decades of the twentieth century—there has been a fair overlap between New Thought circles and practitioners of occult traditions, while at other times the two have appealed to different audiences and have found few points of contact.

Many New Thought ideas have been taken up in the more recent New Age movement; *SEE* NEW AGE MOVEMENT.

Newton, Isaac. English scientist and alchemist, 1642–1727. Born to a poor family in a small Lancashire village, Newton was fascinated with mathematics and alchemy from an early age. He attended the village school, won entry into the Grantham grammar school, and in 1660 began studies at Cambridge University, where he studied mathematics and alchemy. His mathematical studies led, before his graduation in 1666, to his discovery of the binomial theorem, the invention of calculus, and other major achievements. His success in alchemy was equally marked, reaching the stage of the "peacock's tail" in the Great Work.

In 1667 he became a fellow of Trinity College, Cambridge, and pursued studies in gravitation, optics, alchemy, and biblical chronology. Like most alchemists, he was secretive about his discoveries, and most of his major publications came in the last decades of his life. His work on gravitation and cosmology, the *Principia Mathematica*, was published in 1687; his work on optics did not see print until 1704, and his work on biblical chronology and prophecy was published in two volumes after his death in 1728 and 1733. His work on alchemy remained unpublished until the late twentieth century.

Newton's alchemical activities became an embarrassment in the eighteenth century and afterwards, since alchemy—like the rest of the Western occult traditions—was dismissed as nonsense after the triumph of scientific rationalism in the early eighteenth century, and Newton himself was held up as a secular patron saint of the new scientific ideology. Thus very little attention has been paid to his long and systematic alchemical researches until quite recently, and many biographers of Newton still downplay a main interest of his life. *SEE ALSO* ALCHEMY. FURTHER READING: DOBBS 1975, DOBBS 1991.

Ngetal. (Old Irish, meaning uncertain) The thirteenth letter of the Ogham alphabet, with the sound-value *ng*. It corresponds to reed or broom among trees, the goose among birds, and the color green; it has no numerical value. In Robert Graves' version of the Ogham tree-calendar, its month extends from October 29 to November 25. *SEE* OGHAM.

Ogham letter Ngetal

Nichols, Philip Peter Ross. British educator, author, and occultist, 1902–1975. Born in Norfolk, Nichols attended Cambridge from 1921 to 1924, graduating with a degree in history, and spent most of his professional life as principal of Carlisle and Gregson's, a private school. He was an accomplished watercolorist and poet, and published several books of verse. His literary output also includes articles on occult topics in the *Occult Observer*, one of the central British magazines in the field in the postwar era, and a role in preparing the seminal English translation and revision of Paul Christian's *The History of Magic*, published in 1952.

A devout if eccentric Christian active in the Anglican Church, Nichols appears to have come to occultism late in life, largely by way of his friendship with Gerald Gardner, the founder of Wicca. The two men were members of the same nudist colony before and during the Second World War; *SEE* GARDNER, GERALD BROUSSEAU. After the war, he became involved in Martinism; *SEE* MARTINISM. He was also involved in the alternative Christian movement, and in 1962 was made Archdeacon of the Isles in the Ancient Catholic Church by Archbishop Tugdual. *SEE* INDEPENDENT BISHOPS.

His occult interests took a new turn in 1954, when he joined the Ancient Druid Order and was elevated to the office of Scribe, or secretary of the order. In 1964, on the death of Chosen Chief Robert MacGregor-Reid and the election of Thomas Maughan to the chiefship, Nichols and a group of dissident members left the ADO and formed a new organization, the Order of Bards Ovates and Druids (OBOD). Nichols was elected Chosen Chief of the new order, a post he retained until his death, and spent much of his free time teaching and writing for the order. His unexpected death in 1975 threw OBOD into confusion and led to a nine-year hiatus in its activities.

SEE ALSO ORDER OF BARDS OVATES AND DRUIDS (OBOD). FURTHER READING: CARR-GOMM 2002, NICHOLS 1990.

Nichsa. In the lore of ceremonial magic, the king of the undines or water elementals. SEE ELEMENTAL.

nine. Nine in the Cabala is Yesod, the ninth Sephirah, and also the number of the letter Teth. Names of God with nine letters include YHVH TzBAVTh, Tetragrammaton Tzabaoth; YHVH TzDQNV, Tetragrammaton Tzidqenu; and ALHIM GBVR, Elohim Gibor. SEE CABALA.

Nine in Renaissance magical symbolism is sacred to the Muses, and is the number of the celestial spheres and the orders of angels. SEE ALSO ARITHMOLOGY. FURTHER READING: MCLEAN 1994, WATERFIELD 1988, WESTCOTT 1984.

Nine Unknown Men. In nineteenth- and twentieth-century occult writings and conspiracy theories, the secret masters of the world. Their relation to the Great White Lodge, another organization contending for the same role in the cosmos, is unclear. SEE GREAT WHITE LODGE; MASTERS.

Nion. (Old Irish, meaning uncertain) The fifth (in Boibeloth) or third (in Beth-Luis-Nion) letter of the Ogham alphabet, also spelled Nuinn, with the sound-value *n*. It corresponds to the ash among trees, the snipe among birds, the color clear (Gaelic *necht*) and the number thirteen. In Robert Graves' version of the Ogham tree-alphabet, its month runs from February 18 to March 17. SEE OGHAM.

Ogham letter Nion

nirvanic plane. SEE ATMIC PLANE.

niter. In the alchemical theory of the late Renaissance and early modern period, an essential vital substance that coalesces in the air out of the primal creative fire of nature. Niter descends in rain and other forms of precipitation, and dew collected when the sun is in the zodiacal signs Aries and Taurus contains high amounts in very pure form.

In one sense, niter is a term for saltpeter (potassium nitrate, KNO_3), a mineral much used in Renaissance and early modern alchemy. As usual with alchemy, however, it is almost impossible to be sure when the term refers to the mineral, when it refers to a subtle energy of life, or when it refers to some lost concept large enough to include both.

Niter's place in alchemical theory was largely the result of the Polish alchemist Michael Sendivogius (1566–1636), who made niter the center of his own approach to alchemy. He referred to niter as the beginning and key of all chemical knowledge, and used it to obtain the Mercury of the Philosophers, the essential principle of fluidity that is the key to alchemical transmutation. SEE MERCURY; SENDIVOGIUS, MICHAEL.

In seventeenth- and eighteenth-century alchemy, niter was paired with salt in a cyclical vision of the world closely akin to the ideas of modern ecology. According to this view, niter descended from the heavens to the earth, was absorbed by the earth, and there was transmuted into salt. The salt rose up again from earth to heaven, and was changed back into niter by the energies of the sun.

When saltpeter is heated, it gives off oxygen in large quantities. There is evidence that alchemists knew that the vapor given off by saltpeter could sustain life, and the alchemist Cornelis Drebbel apparently made use of this to accomplish his famous feat of sailing underwater in a wooden submarine propelled by twelve oarsmen from Westminster to Greenwich. SEE DREBBEL, CORNELIS.

Other terms for niter include aerial niter, chalybs, and central salt. The terms *magnesia*, *our salt*, and *water which does not wet the hands* were sometimes used for niter and sometimes for other substances. SEE ALSO ALCHEMY. FURTHER READING: SZYDLO 1994.

nodes, lunar. The points at which the orbit of the moon intersects the ecliptic, the apparent path of the sun through the heavens, as seen from Earth. Due to the complex movements of the moon, these points revolve along the zodiac from east to west, taking about 18.5 years to complete one circuit.

The position of the two lunar nodes was of high importance in medieval and Renaissance astrology, and is still much used in Arabic and Hindu astrological practice. The northern node—the point at which the moon crosses the ecliptic from south to north—is called caput draconis, the head of the dragon, and has a favorable quality related to those of Jupiter and Venus. The southern node, where the moon moves southward across the ecliptic, is cauda draconis, the tail of the dragon; its quality is unfavorable, related to those of Saturn and Mars.

Both affect houses and enter into aspects in the same way as planets. They are held by some modern astrologers to reveal how the subject of a birth chart relates to other people; others use the north node as a guide to where the subject's potential can be put to use, while the south node suggests areas of unavoidable limitation.

The traditional names for the two lunar nodes, Cauda Draconis and Caput Draconis, are also names for two of the sixteen geomantic figures. SEE GEOMANCY. SEE ALSO ASTROLOGY.

Nogah. In Cabalistic symbolism, the celestial sphere of Venus; the manifestation of Netzach, the seventh Sephirah of the Tree of Life, in the world of Assiah. SEE ASSIAH; NETZACH.

Norton, Rosaleen. Australian artist and occultist, 1917–1979. Born in Dunedin, New Zealand, to a sea captain and his devout Episcopalian wife, she moved to Sydney, Australia, with her family at the age of seven and spent most of her life in that city. At age three, she began to draw and to have psychic experiences, setting in motion both of her life's driving passions. A lifelong habit of eccentricity also got started early, and she was expelled from grammar school when the school authorities decided she was a bad influence on other pupils.

She studied art at East Sydney Technical College, and left home in her teen years, settling in Sydney's bohemian King's Cross neighborhood, where she made a modest living posing for artists. In 1935 she married Beresford Conroy, another young bohemian, with whom she traveled around Australia's east coast. The marriage did not survive the Second World War, and the two divorced shortly after Conroy returned from military service.

From her teen years, Norton was a keen reader of occult literature, and practiced self-hypnosis and automatic drawing. These had a powerful influence on her art, which combined occult and sexual imagery. Both these factors, in turn, routinely got her in trouble with the authorities. At her first major exhibition, in Melbourne in 1949, four paintings were seized by the police for obscenity. Norton won the ensuing court case, but the publication of a book of her paintings and drawings, *The Art of Rosaleen Norton* (1952), landed her back in court again, and this time the judge ruled that a page in the book had to be cut out of all unsold copies and destroyed.

A fixture of the King's Cross district all through the 1950s and 1960s, condemned by many and admired by others, she became increasingly reclusive toward the end of her life. She finally died in 1979 of cancer.

Her work and artistic career have been compared to those of Austin Osman Spare, whose interests and outlook were much the same; SEE SPARE, AUSTIN OSMAN. FURTHER READING: DRURY 1993.

Norton, Thomas. English alchemist, fl. fifteenth century C.E. Almost nothing is known about this most widely read of English alchemists, the author of the *Ordinall of Alchemy*, written in 1477. According to information in the *Ordinall*, he was a native of Bristol, and was initiated into the mysteries of alchemy by an older master of the art at the age of twenty-eight. A tradition among alchemists claims that Norton's master was George Ripley, Canon of Bridlington, another important English alchemist.

Norton's *Ordinall*, a long poem on alchemy, is among the most complete discussions of alchemical work in existence, and covers everything from the basic theory of the art to details of labor relations and good recipes for fireproof pottery. It was salvaged and put into general circulation by Elias Ashmole (1617–1692), who gave it pride of place in his collection of English alchemical verse, *Theatrum Chemicum Brittanicum* (1652); SEE ASHMOLE, ELIAS. SEE ALSO ALCHEMY.

Nostradamus. (Michel de Nostredame) French physician, astrologer, and diviner, 1503–1566. Perhaps the most famous of all prophets, Nostradamus was born in St.

Remy, France, to a family of Jewish converts to Christianity. He received an excellent education, mastering Latin, Greek, Hebrew, mathematics, astrology, and medicine, and taking a medical degree at Montpellier. Thereafter he worked as a physician in southern France. He settled at Agen and married a local girl, but plague struck the town and his wife died. Thereafter, he resumed a wandering life, and apparently began the divinatory work that would give him lasting fame.

In 1547 he finally settled down at Salon la Craux in Provence, marrying a wealthy widow, Anne Ponsart Gemelle. This marriage proved less ill-omened than his first, and produced six children. Starting in 1551, he began to produce yearly almanacs that included predictions for the coming year. In 1555 appeared the first edition of his great work, *Les Prophéties de M. Michel Nostradamus*, containing 350 quatrains (four-line verses). The final edition of his work, with a full 1000 quatrains, appeared two years after his death.

His prophecies, according to the account in the first two quatrains, were obtained by scrying, using a bowl of water on a tripod as a reflecting surface; SEE SCRYING. They are written in an exceptionally obscure style, full of words borrowed from other languages, and have been interpreted and reinterpreted in different ways for centuries. Some appear to be remarkably accurate predictions of events centuries after Nostradamus' time, others are so cryptic that it's anyone's guess what they mean, and still others have failed to turn out as predicted; the "Great King of Terror" expected in 1999, for example, does not seem to have put in an appearance.

Faked versions of the prophecies of Nostradamus, many of them devised to support specific political or military ends, have been in circulation for quite some time. In the Second World War, both German and Allied intelligence services produced and circulated bogus Nostradamus prophecies as weapons in the propaganda war. SEE ALSO DIVINATION.

Not. SEE NAUTHIZ.

notariqon. (Hebrew, from Latin *notarius*, "shorthand writer") In Cabala, a method of analyzing and constructing Hebrew words by means of acronyms. By means of notariqon, a Cabalist can analyze a word by treating it as an acronym for a phrase or sentence. For example, the word *chen*, "grace," which is spelled in Hebrew חן, ChN, is treated in Cabalistic writings as a notariqon for the phrase *chokmah nistorah*, "secret wisdom." Thus whenever the Jewish scriptures refer to grace, Cabalists claim that the presence of the secret wisdom of the Cabala is actually what's being discussed.

The same process can be made use of in the opposite direction, in order to create words of power that sum up the energies of a phrase or sentence. The sentence *Ateh gibor le-olam, Adonai*, "Mighty art Thou forever, Lord," is condensed in this way into the word AGLA, which is commonly used in Cabalistic ceremonial magic. SEE AGLA.

Notariqon is one of the three standard methods used in traditional Cabalistic analysis of scripture; SEE ALSO GEMATRIA; TEMURAH; CABALA.

Notory Art. A nearly forgotten branch of medieval and Renaissance magic, the Notory Art or *ars notoria* was used to learn different branches of knowledge without the time and difficulty of studying them in the usual way. There were several different manuals of the Notory Art in circulation. In most of them, the practitioner would stare fixedly at a complicated diagram while reciting a magical conjuration. While it seems unlikely that this procedure would have suddenly filled the practitioner's head with information about a previously unknown subject, the Notory Art may well have been able to produce an artificial version of inborn talent, or the sort of intuitive understanding that makes it possible for large amounts of data to be learned and mastered in a short time.

Many of the textbooks of the Notory Art were ascribed to King Solomon, the supreme magician of medieval legend, who supposedly received the entire art directly from God. SEE SOLOMON. Despite this, or possibly because of it, church authorities considered the Notory Art to be among the most reprehensible forms of magic, and condemned it repeatedly. Very few books on the subject have survived. FURTHER READING: THORNDYKE 1923, R. TURNER 1998.

Nuinn. An alternative name for the Ogham letter Nion. SEE NION.

Nun. (Hebrew NIN, "fish") The fourteenth letter of the Hebrew alphabet, a single letter with the sound-value *n*. Its numerical values are 50 in its ordinary form and 700 in its final form. Its standard magical correspondences are as follows:

> *Path on the Tree of Life:* Path 24, Tiphareth to Netzach.
>
> *Astrological Correspondence:* Scorpio, the Scorpion.
>
> *Tarot Correspondence:* Trump XIII, Death.
>
> *Part of the Cube of Space:* The southwestern edge.
>
> *Colors:* in Atziluth—greenish blue.
>
> > in Briah—dull brown.
> >
> > in Yetzirah—very dark brown.
> >
> > in Assiah—livid indigo-brown, like a beetle's shell.

The text of the *Thirty-two Paths of Wisdom* assigned to Nun runs as follows: "The Twenty-fourth Path is the Imaginative Intelligence, and it is so called because it gives a likeness to all the similitudes which are created in like manner similar to its own harmonious elegancies." *SEE ALSO* CABALA; HEBREW ALPHABET.

Hebrew letter Nun, left, and its final form, right

nwyvre. (Welsh *nwyfre*, "brightness, energy, sky") In many of the branches of modern Druidry, the term ny-wfre or nwyvre is used as a term for magical or spiritual energy. It is especially common as a term for the subtle energy that flows through the Earth. *SEE* DRUIDS; LEYS.

Nyd. *SEE* NAUTHIZ.

oak. (*Quercus* spp.) The most important sacred tree in most Indo-European cultures, the oak is among the largest of Europe's forest trees and has played an equally massive role in tree lore and magic throughout the history of the Western occult traditions. It is more often hit by lightning than any other European tree—"Beware the oak, it draws the stroke" is an English proverb—and so has long been sacred to gods of thunder and lightning such as Thor, Taranis, and Zeus.

The oak was held especially sacred by the Druids, and is the tree corresponding to Duir, the seventh letter of the Ogham alphabet. *SEE* DRUIDS; OGHAM.

In modern magical practice, oak is attributed to the planet Jupiter, and is used primarily when working with Pagan thunder gods; a chaplet of oak leaves may be worn to invoke divinities of this sort. An oaken wand or staff makes a good tool for any form of weather magic, or for workings with earth energies. *SEE ALSO* NATURAL MAGIC.

Oak King. In some modern Wiccan and Pagan traditions, the representative of the bright half of the year, who contends eternally with the Holly King, the representative of the dark half of the year, for the favors of the Goddess. The Oak King, along with the other elements of this mythology, was introduced to modern Paganism by the English poet Robert Graves, whose *The White Goddess* (1948) was a basic sourcebook for the entire Neopagan movement. *SEE* NEOPAGANISM; WICCA.

ob. (Hebrew, "sorcerer") In magical philosophy, one of the three forms of fire, associated with magnetism and electricity on the physical level and with the negative, magnetic form of subtle fire on the etheric level. In some sources this form of fire is associated with black magic, necromancy, and death. The other two forms of fire are od and aur. *SEE* AUR; ETHER; OD.

In the Hermetic Brotherhood of Luxor and occult traditions descending from it, Ob was the name given for the "ruling spiritual hierophant" of the sinister Dark Satellite. The word was also associated, via dubious etymology, with Oberon, obsession, Obeah, and various other terms associated with spirits and negative magic. *SEE* DARK SATELLITE; HERMETIC BROTHERHOOD OF LUXOR (H. B. OF L.).

obsession. A form of attack by a hostile spirit, obsession is a process by which an entity of some nature dominates the consciousness of a human being or animal. It is distinct from possession, in which the personality of the victim is replaced or suppressed and the entity takes complete control of the victim's body. In obsession, by contrast, the victim remains conscious and retains bodily control, but his or her thoughts and feelings are pushed in a particular direction by the entity.

The classic symptoms of obsession include a period of chills and drowsiness, followed by the presence of some intrusive pattern of thoughts, feelings, or both, which grow stronger and more insistent over time. Exorcism is usually needed to drive out an obsessing entity, and most magical traditions have rituals that can be used for this purpose. *SEE* EXORCISM. *SEE ALSO* POSSESSION. FURTHER READING: FORTUNE 1930, REGARDIE 1971.

occult history. Alternative versions of history presented by occultists as the "real" history of the occult tradition or the world as a whole. While extremely common for the last century and a half, these versions are a relatively recent addition to Western occultism. Through ancient times, the Middle Ages, and the Renaissance, there seems to be no evidence that students of the occult in the Western world had opinions about history noticeably different from those of the ordinary people or the scholarly historians of their societies.

Occult history seems to have started to emerge after 1614, when Isaac Casaubon published evidence that dated the *Corpus Hermeticum* to sometime after the birth of Christ. Up to that time, students of the Hermetic writings (along with everybody else) had believed them to be authentic Egyptian teachings dating back to the time of Moses, if not before. *SEE* CORPUS HERMETICUM; HERMETICISM.

Casaubon's publication was part of the widespread attack on Renaissance magical philosophy that ended the Renaissance and helped usher in the Scientific Revolution. Many occultists of the time, recognizing the political dimension of the attack, rejected Casaubon's conclusions and insisted that the *Corpus Hermeticum* was ancient Egyptian wisdom, no matter what orthodox historians said.

The rest of the seventeenth century saw little more in the way of occult history. The eighteenth century, on the other hand, marked the public emergence of Freemasonry, which sparked a historical industry that hasn't quit yet. Though all the evidence suggests that Freemasonry started out as exactly what it originally claimed to be—a trade union of stonemasons with a set of medieval guild rituals—members from the gentry and aristocracy found so working-class an origin embarrassing, and went to work trying to find something more romantic. Some of the results—the supposed connection between the Freemasons and the Knights Templar, for example, or the idea that Masonry can be traced back to ancient Egypt—are still in circulation to this day, despite an impressive lack of evidence to support them. *SEE* FREEMASONRY; KNIGHTS TEMPLAR.

Along these same lines, the founders and promoters of other lodge organizations—many inspired by Freemasonry, some with independent origins—went to work all through the eighteenth and nineteenth centuries, producing impressive pedigrees for their own traditions. By the mid-nineteenth century, it was a poor excuse for a lodge, whether occult or fraternal, that couldn't claim to trace its origins back to ancient Egypt, Moses, the original Druids, or some equally romantic source. All these claims were elaborated and combined in various ways, giving rise to a view of history in which occult lodges were seen as the one enduring factor in the swirling tides of historical change.

The French Revolution at the end of the eighteenth century sent these speculations spinning off in new directions. Several conservative writers, unable to believe that the French people could have actually wanted to overthrow one of the most corrupt and ineffective monarchies in Europe, insisted that the revolution must have been the product of a vast and sinister conspiracy against monarchy and Christianity. The Bavarian Illuminati, a short-lived and unsuccessful secret society in Germany, was for some reason chosen by the Abbé Barruel—the first major figure in modern conspiracy theory—to play the villain of the piece. *SEE* BAVARIAN ILLUMINATI. While most of the resulting furore took place outside the occult traditions of the West, elements of conspiracy theory have spilled back into occultism at intervals and provided raw materials for fabricators of occult history.

The nineteenth century saw occult history swell in other ways, as a variety of figures on the fringes of Victorian culture challenged accepted ideas. Some of them, such as Charles Darwin, were accepted by the educated establishment and brought about sweeping revisions in the way Western cultures looked at the world. Others remained on the fringes, and contributed to a growing collection of alternative viewpoints that were rejected by professional scholars and scientists but developed a following outside the official institutions of learning.

One figure that made a massive contribution to occult history in this way was Ignatius Donnelly (1831–1901), a Minnesota congressman turned alternative historian who brought Plato's account of Atlantis out of relative obscurity and argued that the lost continent had actually existed. His 1882 book *Atlantis, or the Antediluvian World* relied on Victorian scientific hypotheses that were discarded during his lifetime, but its basic ideas have been copied endlessly since it first came out. *SEE* ATLANTIS; LOST CIVILIZATIONS. His second great book, *Ragnarok, or the Age of Fire and Gravel* (1882), proposed that the Earth had collided with a comet in prehistoric times—another idea that has found an enthusiastic following in more recent versions of occult history.

The dominant figure in nineteenth-century occult history, though, was Helena Petrovna Blavatsky (1831–1891), the founder of the Theosophical Society. Blavatsky's influential writings and lectures had as a central theme the complete inadequacy of the Victorian world picture; she rejected materialist science and orthodox religion with equal force. As an alternative, she built up a vision of the world that combined very nearly everything that had been rejected by the official science and scholarship of her time. Lost continents, secret societies, the claim that the works of William Shakespeare were actually written by Francis Bacon, theories of evolution in which animals were descended from man rather than vice versa, and much more along the same lines filled Blavatsky's massive works, along with a great deal of lore from the Western magical traditions and Eastern mysticism. *SEE* BLAVATSKY, HELENA PETROVNA; THEOSOPHY.

Blavatsky's version of occult history swept all before it, and for a century—from 1875 to 1975—there were few occult movements in the Western world that didn't include references to Atlantis, Lemuria, and the masters of the Great White Lodge somewhere in their instructional papers. The idea that these things were a central part of the occult tradition was rarely questioned.

In the last quarter of the twentieth century, however, a large number of occult movements began breaking away from the Theosophical version of occult history. In the Hermetic tradition and such related movements as Thelema, a rising interest in authentic knowledge about older systems of magic made occult history, with its shaky foundations in the realm of fact, less interesting. An increased focus on magical practice, as distinct from occult theory, in this wing of the community also fed into this change, as students of the occult found themselves wondering what the lore of Atlantis had to do with the practical work of magical training. In the Neopagan movement, by contrast, many people rejected the occult history of the Theosophists in order to build up a new and different version, in which ancient matriarchies and the survival of Pagan traditions over millennia played the central role. *SEE* MATRIARCHIES, ANCIENT; PAGANISM; WICCA.

Ironically, as large elements of the occult community were moving away from the Theosophical version of occult history, that version found a new audience in the burgeoning New Age movement. *SEE* NEW AGE MOVEMENT. Nearly all of the "secrets of the past" that were the stock in trade of occultists in the early twentieth century have been revamped and put back to work as elements of modern New Age ideology. There is thus every reason to think that occult history will be around for a long time to come. FURTHER READING: BLAVATSKY 1888, DE CAMP 1970, J. GODWIN 1993, J. GODWIN 1994, KAFTON-MINKEL 1989.

Och. One of the seven Olympian spirits, Och is associated with the sun, and rules over 28 of the 196 provinces of Heaven. The period of history ruled by Och ran from 920 to 1410 C.E. *SEE* OLYMPIAN SPIRITS.

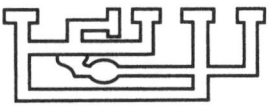

Olympian spirit Och

octatopos. (Greek, "eight place") In ancient astrology, a system in which there were eight rather than twelve houses in the zodiac. The meanings were identical to the first eight houses of the modern house system. *SEE* HOUSE, ASTROLOGICAL.

od. (Hebrew AVD, "fire") In magical philosophy, one of the three forms of fire, associated with ordinary flame on the physical level and with the positive, electric form of subtle fire on the etheric level. In some sources this form of fire is associated with white magic, healing, and life. The other two forms of fire are ob and aur. *SEE* AUR; ETHER; OB.

The physicist and psychic researcher Karl von Reichenbach borrowed the word *od* from older sources as a term for the subtle energy he discovered in his experiments with magnets and clairvoyant vision. In this usage, it is a general term for etheric energy. The expanded form *odyle* is sometimes used with the same meaning. *SEE* REICHENBACH, KARL VON.

Odd Fellowship. A fraternal and charitable society with rituals and symbolism comparable to those of Freemasonry, Odd Fellowship emerged in working-class circles in England sometime before 1650, and gradually spread to become one of the world's largest fraternal orders. Three major Odd Fellows orders exist at present: the Grand United Order of Odd Fellows (GUOOF) and the Manchester Unity Order of Odd Fellows (MUOOF), both primarily English, and the Independent Order of Odd Fellows (IOOF), based in North America but with lodges in Europe, Australasia, and Latin America as well.

Very little information survives about the origins of Odd Fellowship, or about the origin and meaning of its quirky name, though many theories have been proposed. By the late seventeenth century, when documentary evidence first appears, there were Odd Fellow lodges in many English cities. Odd Fellowship spread to North America, Europe, and Australasia in the nineteenth century, and reached its greatest size and influence around 1900.

Odd Fellowship still survives on a small scale in most Western countries today. Membership is open to men and women of good character who believe in a Supreme Being and are loyal to their country. The Grand United Order still has separate units for men and women, while the Manchester Unity and (as of January 1, 2001) the Independent Order admit both men and women to regular Odd Fellows lodges.

Symbolism, rituals, and teachings vary substantially from order to order. In the IOOF, the following degrees are worked:

> *Odd Fellows Lodge*
>> Initiatory Degree
>> First Degree, or Degree of Friendship
>> Second Degree, or Degree of Love
>> Third Degree, or Degree of Truth

> *Encampment (Third Degree required*
>> *for admission)*
>> Patriarchal Degree
>> Golden Rule Degree
>> Royal Purple Degree

> *Canton (Royal Purple Degree required*
>> *for admission)*
>> Patriarchs Militant Degree

> *Grand Body Degrees (Completion of term as*
>> *presiding officer of lodge or encampment*
>> *required for admission)*
>> Grand Lodge Degree
>> Grand Encampment Degree

Odd Fellowship is in no sense an occult organization; its rituals and teachings are largely drawn from the Bible, and are intended to teach basic ethical concepts such as fidelity, brotherly love, tolerance, and justice. Its main functions throughout its history have been charitable work in the community and mutual aid among its members.

Still, like most fraternal orders, it has served as a template for occult lodges; this was especially the case in America in the late nineteenth and early twentieth centuries, when the IOOF was the largest fraternal organization in the country. The process seems to have worked the other way as well, and some degree of occult symbolism can be traced in Odd Fellow books of the time. It is unlikely to be an accident, for example, that the Independent Order has ten degrees and twenty-two emblems in its degree structure, paralleling the Cabalistic Tree of Life with its ten Sephiroth and twenty-two Paths. *SEE* CABALA. *SEE ALSO* FREEMASONRY; LODGE, FRATERNAL. FURTHER READING: GROSH 1871, STILLSON 1897.

odic shield. In magical theory and practice, a field of etheric energy established around the outer edge of the human aura to protect the user from hostile magic or the assaults of spirits. Several different methods have been used to establish and maintain an odic shield. The shroud of concealment, which is used in rituals of invisibility, is a closely related phenomenon. *SEE* AURA; SHROUD OF CONCEALMENT. FURTHER READING: SADHU 1959.

Oera Linda Book. First published in 1871, but allegedly containing documents thousands of years old, the *Oera Linda Book* claims to present the actual history of Atlantis (or "Atland," the term used in the book), which it locates in the North Sea. It dates Atland's destruction to 2193 B.C.E., and explains how survivors founded a powerful maritime empire near the mouth of the Rhine, ruled by an Earth Mother and colleges of virgin priestesses. Eventually the rule of the Earth Mothers gave way to that of kings, and the empire crumbled before waves of invaders from the east.

The book, supposedly written in an archaic Frisian dialect, was allegedly passed down in the Over den Linden family for some six thousand years before finally coming to Cornelius Over den Linden, who was given it by his aunt in 1848; the first translations into modern Frisian and Dutch were made in 1871, and an English translation was published in 1876. All the evidence suggests, however, that it was simply faked, either by Over den Linden or by J. O. Ottema, who paid for the "translation." Its account of an ancient Frisian empire contradicts all available archeological and linguistic evidence and is full of the standard details of nineteenth-century historical fakery. For example, Pagan gods are presented as historical figures in standard euhemerist style; *SEE* EUHEMERISM. (For another good example of the genre, *SEE* AGHARTA.)

Although the *Oera Linda Book* has nothing explicitly to do with occultism, it has intersected the Western occult traditions at least twice, in very different ways. German occultists connected to the Ariosophical movement of the early twentieth century made much use of it as a basis for their claims of Germanic spiritual supremacy, and Atland thus became accepted as historical fact during the Nazi era. *SEE* ARIOSOPHY; NATIONAL SOCIALISM. More recently, the Oera Linda Book has become the central inspiration for at least one English magical organization, the Ordo Anno Mundi (OAM), which traces its initiatory lineage to Frisian-descended canal folk in the English midlands. *SEE ALSO* ATLANTIS; LOST CIVILIZATIONS; OCCULT HISTORY.

Ogdoadic Tradition. *SEE* AURUM SOLIS.

Ogham. An archaic alphabet used in Ireland, Scotland, and Britain for inscriptions on standing stones and other surfaces. It consists of twenty regular letters formed of notches cut across one or both sides of the edge of a standing stone (or any other line), plus five additional letters with more complicated shapes. It was traditionally written in vertical lines, starting from the bottom.

According to the fourteenth-century *Book of Ballymote*, Ogham was invented by Ogma Sun-face during the reign of Bres, son of Elatha, king of Ireland. The first thing ever written in it was the letter Beith (B) repeated seven times on a piece of birch, as a warning to Lug son of Ethliu that his wife would be carried away into faeryland. An alternate account in the same source claims that it was invented by Fenius Farsaidh, along with the Irish language, shortly after the events at the Tower of Babel described in the Book of Genesis.

There are two different versions of the Ogham, called Boibeloth and Beth-Luis-Nion, which differ in the names given to the letters and the order of several letters in the first series. (Both of these names are also used for late and rather clumsy "secret alphabets" clearly derived from the English alphabet.) While the Beth-Luis-Nion letter names are all but universal in modern Pagan practice, the Boibeloth letter order is the most common, and there is a good deal of confusion between the two.

Name (Sound Value): Tree

Beith (B): Birch

Luis (L): Rowan

Fearn (V): Alder

Saille (S): Willow

Nion (N): Ash

Huath (H): Hawthorn

Duir (D): Oak

Tinne (T): Holly

Coll (C): Hazel

Quert (Q): Apple

Muin (M): Vine

Gort (G): Ivy

Ngetal (Ng): Reed

Straif (Z): Blackthorn

Ruis (R): Elder

Ailm (A): Fir

Onn (O): Gorse

Ur (U): Heather

Eadha (E): Aspen

Ioho (I): Yew

Koad: Grove

Oir: Spindle

Uilleand: Honeysuckle

Iphin: Gooseberry

Phagos: Beech

The old Irish sources give a wide array of symbols, phrases, correspondences, and metaphors for the different Ogham letters. Examples include word-Oghams, in which poetic phrases represent letters; sow-Ogham, in which different colors and locations of pigs represent letters; fortress-Ogham, bird-Ogham, color-Ogham, and church-Ogham, all of which use names or words beginning with the letter in question; dog-Ogham, in which from one to five dogs of different types stand for the letters in their series; and so on. Different ways of writing Ogham, many of them deliberately confusing, are also to be found. All of these seem to be methods of secret communication, which allowed trained bards to weave hidden messages into their poems for other bards to read.

The first surviving traces of Ogham date from Ireland in the fifth century C.E., where it was used on gravestones. While conventional historians are agreed that it must have been invented shortly before this time, there is little evidence for this claim, and the alphabet may have been used on more perishable writing materials for centuries prior to that time. References to Ogham in Irish epic poetry dating from Pagan times suggest that it was commonly used for magic and divination, as well as for more mundane purposes.

The spread of church Latin drove Ogham out of common use by the early Middle Ages, but it survived as an element of traditional bardic lore until the hedge-schools of Ireland were forced out of existence by English repression in the eighteenth century. Thereafter, it was an obscure curiosity known to a handful of scholars until 1948, when Robert Graves' epochal *The White Goddess* introduced it to a wider public.

Graves drew connections between the Ogham and traditions of goddess worship, and also linked many of the Ogham letters to a thirteen-month calendar; *SEE* **OGHAM TREE-CALENDAR.** More recently, the Ogham has been converted into a system of card divination, and at least two Ogham-based decks are available as of this writing. The Ogham has become a standard element of the lore of most modern Druid traditions and is fairly widely used in other Neopagan traditions inspired by the Celts. *SEE ALSO* DRUIDS; FIONN'S WINDOW. FURTHER READING: CALDER 1917, GRAVES 1966, MCMANUS 1991.

Ogham tree-calendar. According to English poet Robert Graves, an archaic lunar calendar of thirteen months once used all over the ancient world in matriarchal times. Introduced in 1948 in his book *The White Goddess*, the tree-calendar has become a fixture of modern Paganism, and appears frequently in books on Celtic traditions and Druidry.

Graves' version of the Ogham tree-calendar runs as follows:

1. Beith (Birch): December 24–January 20
2. Luis (Rowan): January 21–February 17
3. Nion (Ash): February 18–March 17
4. Fearn (Alder): March 18–April 14
5. Saille (Willow): April 15–May 12
6. Huath (Hawthorn): May 13–June 9
7. Duir (Oak): June 10–July 7
8. Tinne (Holly): July 8–August 4
9. Coll (Hazel): August 5–September 1
10. Muin (Grapevine): September 2–September 29
11. Gort (Ivy): September 30–October 27
12. Ngetal (Reed): October 28–November 24
13. Ruis (Elder): November 25–December 22
    Mistletoe: December 23, Midwinter Day

More recently, alternative attributions of the Ogham letters to the cycle of the year have been suggested by Colin and Liz Murray and by John King, but neither of these has caught on as well as Graves'.

While the Ogham tree-calendar is a perfectly valid ritual calendar, and has been used effectively by a wide range of modern Pagans, it should be said that there is no evidence whatsoever that it existed before Graves "discovered" it. An ancient Druidic calendar discovered in France, the Coligny calendar, follows a very different scheme; *SEE* COLIGNY CALENDAR.

It's also inaccurate to describe the Ogham tree-calendar as a "lunar calendar," though the term is often used. The lunar cycle is approximately 29.5 days long, not the 28 days allowed by Graves' calendar, and so the moon and the calendar are out of step throughout the year. Like most modern calendars, the Ogham tree-calendar is actually a solar calendar; that is, it tracks the solar year of 365 days exactly, where real lunar calendars match the cycles of the moon exactly, and fit the solar year only by adding an extra month or two every few years. *SEE ALSO* OGHAM. FURTHER READING: GRAVES 1966, J. KING 1994, MURRAY & MURRAY 1989.

Oir. (Old Irish, "spindle") The second of five additional letters in the Ogham alphabet, used to represent the vowel combination *oi* or the consonant *th*. It corresponds to the spindle among trees, but lacks the extended symbolism of the twenty regular Ogham letters. *SEE* OGHAM.

Ogham letter Oir

Olam Yesodoth. (Hebrew AaLM YSVDVTh, "world of elements") In Cabalistic lore, the planet Earth as the celestial sphere assigned to the tenth Sephirah of the Tree of Life, Malkuth the Kingdom. An alternative name is Cholem Yesodoth, "breaker of foundations." Israel Regardie has suggested, quite sensibly, that this latter name is the result of poor knowledge of Hebrew on the part of Cabalistic magicians; the initial *Ayin* of "Olam" could have been written as "Gh," an alternative sound of *Ayin*, and then misread as "Ch" by some later reader or transcriber. *SEE* MALKUTH.

Old Europe. *SEE* MATRIARCHIES, ANCIENT.

Old One. *SEE* GOD, THE.

Old Religion. In modern Wiccan sources, a common term for Wicca, reflecting its claim to be older than Christianity (the "new religion"). The term appears in Charles Godfrey Leland's *Aradia, or the Gospel of the Witches* (1899) as a term for the witch-cult he described, and was also used by Gerald Gardner for Wicca.

While traditional Pagan religions did exist long before Christianity, of course, there is little evidence supporting the claim that Wicca existed before the mid-twentieth century. Some modern Wiccans, accepting the idea of a recent origin for their religion, have taken to calling it "the New Religion" instead. *SEE* NEOPAGANISM; PAGANISM; WICCA.

Old Ways. A general term for Pagan spirituality and lifestyles, mostly used by those who accept claims that modern Neopagan traditions date from before Christianity. *SEE* OLD RELIGION.

Olympian spirits. Also known as Olympic spirits, these seven entities rule over the 196 provinces of Heaven, and also govern the world in turn for periods of 490 years each. Their names are Aratron, Bethor, Phaleg, Och, Hagith, Ophiel, and Phul. They first appear in the sixteenth-century *Arbatel of Magic*, and have been a staple fixture of occult writings ever since. *SEE ALSO* ARBATEL OF MAGIC, THE; *AND THE NAMES OF THE INDIVIDUAL SPIRITS*.

om. *SEE* AUM.

omens. Events in the outer world with divinatory meaning, the basis of the oldest and most widespread of all systems of divination. Nearly every ancient culture paid detailed attention to omens and their interpretation. A great deal of Mesopotamian omen lore has survived in the clay-tablet libraries recovered by archeologists, although little of this has been translated.

Greek and Roman omen lore is more available to speakers of modern languages, and several intact treatises—notably Marcus Tullius Cicero's detailed *De Divinatione* (*On Divination*)—can be found in good translations. The omen lore of these two cultures differed somewhat, but there were sizeable overlaps. Both paid much attention to augury, or divination by the flight of birds, and hieromancy, or divination by the entrails (especially the liver) of animals sacrificed to the gods. Another common form of divination was cledonomancy, which used words overheard as a source of omens. *SEE* CLEDONOMANCY; SACRIFICE.

The Pagan peoples outside Rome's imperial boundaries were at least as devoted to omen lore as their Latin-speaking neighbors. The Roman historian Tacitus, writing in the first century of the Common Era, comments that Germanic tribes of his time watched the behavior of sacred horses for omens, and he and the much later Norse sagas agree in suggesting that Germanic peoples also paid much attention to augury by the flight of birds. The custom of trial by combat, which remained common in the Christian Middle Ages, started out as a Pagan Germanic custom related to omen lore; it was held that the gods would show their decision by the victory of one of two warriors.

In the Middle Ages, despite Christian disapproval of most methods of divination, omen lore was still carefully studied. Surviving manuscripts from several European countries include charts for predicting the future from the calls of birds, from the date and direction of thunder, and from many other signs. Like most traditional methods of divination, however, the art of reading omens dropped from general use at the time of the Scientific Revolution, and it has seen very little attention since that time. *SEE ALSO* DIVINATION. FURTHER READING: H. DAVIDSON 1981, FLACELIERE 1965, KIECKHEFER 1989, MORRISON 1981.

Önd. In some modern magical traditions drawing on northern Paganism, a term for vital force or etheric energy; *SEE* ETHER.

one. In Pythagorean number lore, one—the monad—is not a number but the *source* of number. Its titles include "artificer," "modeler," "matrix," "matter," and "Prometheus," as the source of all numerical forms; "androgyne," since it is neither even nor odd (to the Pythagoreans, three was the first odd number); "chaos," "obscurity," and "darkness," since no distinct number can be found within it; "ship" and "chariot," since it contains all other things inside it; and "Proteus," since it becomes all things. As the lord and ruler of numbers, it was assigned to Zeus.

One in Cabalistic symbolism is Kether, Crown, the first Sephirah, and is also the number of the letter Aleph. Both Aleph and the letter Yod, the source of all Hebrew letters, are considered Names of God in Cabalistic thinking, and as such are the Names of one letter each. *SEE* CABALA.

One in Renaissance magical symbolism is the number of God, the sun, the heart, the Philosopher's Stone, and the phoenix; it represents unity, piety, concord, and friendship. It is also the number of the *anima mundi* or Soul of the World. SEE ALSO ARITHMOLOGY. FURTHER READING: MCLEAN 1994, WATERFIELD 1988, WESTCOTT 1984.

Onn. (Old Irish, "ash tree") The seventeenth letter of the Ogham alphabet, with the sound-value *o*. It corresponds to gorse among trees, the cormorant among birds, the color dun, and the number four. In Robert Graves' version of the Ogham tree-calendar, it is associated with the spring equinox. SEE OGHAM.

Ogham letter Onn

Ophiel. One of the seven Olympic spirits, Ophiel is associated with the planet Mercury, and rules over 14 of the 196 provinces of Heaven. Ophiel is the ruler of the world during the present period of history, which began in 1900 and will end in 2390 C.E. SEE OLYMPIAN SPIRITS.

Olympian spirit Ophiel

opposition. In astrology, an angle of 180 degrees between planets or other significant points in the heavens. Astrological forces in opposition are in direct conflict with one another, pulling in opposite directions on the personality or the energies of the period of time in which the opposition has its effect. SEE ASPECT, ASTROLOGICAL; ASTROLOGY.

oracles. The word "oracle" is used nowadays for nearly any form of divination. In ancient times, however, it referred to Pagan religious centers used for the purpose of divination. The most widely known oracles of the ancient world were in Greece, but there were others throughout the eastern Mediterranean area.

The most famous of all oracles was at Delphi, where a priestess seated on a three-legged stool entered into trance and gave answers that were held to be inspired by a deity—in historical times, Apollo, but Greek records suggest that the oracle had been sacred to a succession of goddesses in earlier times. Ancient accounts claim that the Pythia, as the oracular priestess was called, went into trance as a result of fumes rising from a chasm in the earth. Archeologists, however, have found no trace of such a cleft in their excavations at Delphi, and the source of the Pythia's inspiration remains a mystery.

Access to the Pythia was relatively expensive—two-thirds of a day's wages for a private enquiry in the fifth century B.C.E.—and also infrequent; oracles were only available on nine days of the year. For a lesser fee, the Pythia would perform sortilege, or divination by lots; this could either give a yes-no answer or provide a selection between alternatives set out by the querent and marked on the lots. Black and white beans were generally used.

Other widely known Greek oracles were at Dodona, where priestesses interpreted the rustling of leaves in a sacred oak grove as signs of the will of Zeus, and at Epidaurus, where a dream-oracle of Asclepius provided the sick with visionary instructions on how to cure their illnesses. Pausanias, a Greek travel writer of the second century C.E., discussed dozens of other oracles in his entertaining *Description of Greece*; most of these were small local shrines where a wide range of divination methods were practiced. In many cases these oracles involved something much closer to omen reading than the formal pronouncements of the Pythia; SEE OMENS.

There were also books of oracles, attributed to ancient prophets such as Bakis and Musaeus, which served much the same function in ancient times that the prophecies of Nostradamus do at present; SEE NOSTRADAMUS. Specialists in these collections, called *chresmologoi*, were routinely called on to offer advice in public decisions.

Most of the oracles fell out of use after the beginning of the Common Era, due to the spread of astrology and other means of divination; SEE ASTROLOGY. The rise of Christianity to political power in the fourth century C.E. finished the process. The old oracles were all consecrated to Pagan gods, and were suppressed by force. SEE PAGANISM. SEE ALSO DIVINATION. FURTHER READING: FLACELIERE 1965, MORRISON 1981.

Orange Ray. In occult philosophy, the fifth of the Seven Rays, the primary creative energies of the cosmos. The Orange Ray is the ray of science and knowledge. In Theosophical lore, the Orange Ray is directed by the Master Hilarion, a chohan of the Great White Lodge. Its symbolic gem is topaz. *SEE* HILARION, MASTER. *SEE ALSO* RAYS, SEVEN.

Orbis Solis. (Latin, "orb of the sun") In the Aurum Solis system of magic, the third lowest of the six energy centers of the human body, related to the Sephirah Tiphareth and located at the heart. In the Rousing of the Citadels, an Aurum Solis exercise equivalent to the Middle Pillar exercise, it is visualized as a yellow sphere, half of which projects forward from the front of the chest. Its Name of Power is YHVH ALVH VDAaTh, Tetragrammaton Eloah va-Daath.

It corresponds to the heart chakra and to the Tiphareth center of the Middle Pillar exercise. *SEE* AURUM SOLIS; MIDDLE PILLAR EXERCISE; ROUSING OF THE CITADELS.

Ordains. (From the phrase "Be it ordained") In Wicca, rules of practice and conduct within a given tradition, normally written out in the tradition's version of the Book of Shadows. *SEE* BOOK OF SHADOWS.

Orden des Gold- und Rosenkreuz. (Order of the Gold and Rose Cross) German Masonic Rosicrucian order, an important link in the development of occult lodge systems. The details of its origin are obscure, but it was apparently founded by the German alchemist Hermann Fichtuld in the late 1750s.

Candidates for membership were required to be Master Masons. There were nine degrees of initiation (see below). Members studied alchemical and mystical literature, and at least attempted to practice metallic alchemy.

> *Degree:* 1, 9. *Title:* Magus. *Sign:* Urim, Thummim, and Shemhamphorash. *Symbol:* Equilateral triangle. *Name in Brotherhood:* Luxianus Renaldus de Perfectis.
>
> *Degree:* 2, 8. *Title:* Magister. *Sign:* Cross of gold enameled blue, with diamonds. *Symbol:* Compass. *Name in Brotherhood:* Pedemontanus de Rebis.

> *Degree:* 3, 7. *Title:* Adeptus Exemptus. *Sign:* Cross of gold, enameled with the four chief colors. *Symbol:* Hitakel. *Name in Brotherhood:* Ianus de Aure Campis.
>
> *Degree:* 4, 6. *Title:* Adeptus Major. *Sign:* Cross of gold, enameled red with gold edge. *Symbol:* Phrath. *Name in Brotherhood:* Sphaere Fontus a Sales.
>
> *Degree:* 5, 5. *Title:* Adeptus Minor. *Sign:* Cross of silver, enameled yellow with silver edge. *Symbol:* Pison. *Name in Brotherhood:* Hodos Camlionis.
>
> *Degree:* 6, 4. *Title:* Philosophus. *Sign:* Cross of silver, enameled with a black edge. *Symbol:* Gihon. *Name in Brotherhood:* Pharus Illuminans.
>
> *Degree:* 7, 3. *Title:* Practicus. *Sign:* Cross of silver, enameled black with silver edge. *Symbol:* Wetharetz. *Name in Brotherhood:* Monoceros de Astris.
>
> *Degree:* 8, 2. *Title:* Theoreticus. *Sign:* Orb of crystal, white and gold. *Symbol:* Mayim. *Name in Brotherhood:* Porajus de Rejectis.
>
> *Degree:* 9, 1. *Title:* Junior. *Sign:* A gold ring with symbols. *Symbol:* Aesh. *Name in Brotherhood:* Pereclinus de Faustis.

The Gold- und Rosenkreuz achieved a level of influence few other occult orders have ever managed when some of its aristocratic members succeeded in recruiting Frederick William, the Prussian crown prince, in 1781. On the death of Frederick the Great in 1786, several members of the order were elevated to high positions in the government. They were largely responsible for Frederick William's conservative religious and cultural policies, which were sharply at odds with those of Frederick the Great.

On Frederick William's death in 1797, the Rosicrucian faction at court was dismissed. The Gold- und Rosenkreuz continued in existence for some time thereafter—a manuscript dating from 1802, *Aleph* by the pseudonymous Archarion, includes many of the order's themes. Its end was as obscure as its origin, but it has been suggested that it went under in the convulsions of the Napoleonic Wars. *SEE ALSO* FREEMASONRY; ROSICRUCIANS. FURTHER READING: MCINTOSH 1987.

Order of Bards Ovates and Druids (OBOD). Druidic order based in England, currently the largest Druid organization in the world. The Order of Bards Ovates and Druids was founded in 1964 by dissident members of the Ancient Druid Order, one of the major British Druid groups of the time. OBOD's first Chosen Chief, Philip Ross Nichols, reorganized the ritual structure of the new order, adding the four Celtic fire festivals and a winter solstice rite to the Ancient Druid Order's equinox and summer solstice rituals, and conferring the three grades of Bard, Ovate, and Druid.

Both Nichols and the Pendragon of the new order, Vera Chapman, had connections to the Kindred of the Kibbo Kift, the most colorful of the English Woodcraft groups in the period between the two world wars. As a result, Woodcraft ideas about the importance of ecology and the natural world, and a number of ritual elements, entered OBOD practice and have become common in a number of more recent Druid organizations in Britain and elsewhere. *SEE* KIBBO KIFT, KINDRED OF THE; WOODCRAFT.

On Nichol's death in 1975, the order quickly passed into abeyance. It was refounded in 1988 by a group of former members led by Philip Carr-Gomm, and began offering its teachings and ceremonies by correspondence. This approach proved very popular, and in the years immediately following the order's renewal it gained members not only in Britain but also in continental Europe, North America, and Australasia. It currently has some sixty local groups worldwide. *SEE ALSO* DRUIDS; NICHOLS, PHILIP PETER ROSS; SABBAT. FURTHER READING: CARR-GOMM 1993, NICHOLS 1990.

Order of the Star in the East. *SEE* STAR IN THE EAST, ORDER OF THE.

Order of Woodcraft Chivalry (OWC). English quasi-Pagan organization, founded in 1916 by Ernest Westlake and his adult children Aubrey and Margaret as an alternative to the Boy Scouts. The OWC was based largely on Ernest Thompson Seton's Woodcraft movement in the United States, but used Anglo-Saxon and Celtic lore in place of the Native American traditions central to Seton's work. Like other Woodcraft organizations, the OWC taught physical, mental, and spiritual renewal through contact with nature; *SEE* WOODCRAFT.

The Westlakes were heavily influenced by the writings of classicist Jane Harrison, who introduced the idea of ancient matriarchies to the English-speaking world; *SEE* MATRIARCHIES, ANCIENT. Pan, Artemis, and Dionysus were considered to be the patron deities of the order, and a good deal of Pagan material found a place in the order's rituals and symbolism. There was an inner circle for adults, based on Seton's Red Lodge, which apparently offered three degrees of initiation.

The OWC was primarily active in the New Forest area of England, and had a Forest School at Godshill in the New Forest itself. It has been suggested by several authors that the original New Forest coven of witches that initiated Gerald Gardner may actually have been an OWC offshoot. *SEE* GARDNER, GERALD BROUSSEAU.

The OWC remains active at present in a quiet way. Its present leadership firmly denies that the order has anything to do with the occult. *SEE ALSO* KIBBO KIFT, KINDRED OF THE. FURTHER READING: EDGELL 1992, WEBB 1976.

Ordo Novi Templi (ONT). (Latin, "Order of New Templars") An Aryan racist and anti-Semitic magical order founded by the Austrian occultist Jörg Lanz von Liebenfels in 1907, and active in Germany, Austria, and Hungary until the beginning of World War II. Based on Lanz's theory of "theozoology," which held that modern human races derive from different degrees of interbreeding between godlike "theozoa" and sexually degenerate subhuman dwarfs, the ONT developed a complex liturgy and organizational structure, most of it the product of Lanz's pen. *SEE* LANZ VON LIEBENFELS, JÖRG.

ONT ritual centered on the three monastic offices of Matins, Prime, and Compline, which were celebrated daily with Aryan hymns, readings, psalms, and devotional images. The total liturgy comprised seven hefty volumes by the time it reached its complete form in the mid-1920s.

Requirements for membership were equally complex. Candidates for ONT membership had to pass through a test of "racial purity." Those with purity scores of less than 50 percent were limited to the lowest order, that of

Servers; those who scored above 50 percent could advance through the order of Novices to Masters (50 to 75 percent purity) or Canons (75–100 percent); Masters or Canons who founded a new chapter of the order were advanced to the rank of Presbyter, and if the chapter grew to include more than five Masters or Canons the founder advanced to the highest order, that of Priors.

Despite all these intricacies, the ONT was tolerably successful as magical orders go, with a maximum membership around 300 and as many as five chapters operating at any given time, and reached its zenith between 1925 and 1935. Despite its racist and anti–Semitic stance, it was banned along with nearly all other occult organizations by the Nazi government in the late 1930s. It was quietly revived after the war and remains active today. *SEE ALSO* ARIOSOPHY. FURTHER READING: GOODRICK-CLARKE 1992.

Ordo Templi Orientis (OTO). (Latin, "Order of Oriental Templars") One of the largest magical orders in the world today, the Ordo Templi Orientis emerged from the complicated world of central European fringe Masonry in the early twentieth century. Its beginnings date back to 1895, when Freemasons Carl Kellner (1851–1905), a wealthy Austrian industrialist, and Theodor Reuss (1855–1923), a journalist and former opera singer, began discussing the possibility of forming a "Masonic Academy" of esoteric studies.

Kellner was a serious student of yoga and Tantrism, and claimed to have studied sexual esotericism in the 1880s from three teachers—the Sufi Soliman ben Aifa and the Hindu tantrikas Bhima Sena Pratapa and Mahatma Agamya Paramahamsa. On the other hand, both men were involved in the Hermetic Brotherhood of Luxor, an English magical order of the time which taught a system of sex magic based on the work of American occultist P. B. Randolph. *SEE* HERMETIC BROTHERHOOD OF LUXOR (H. B. OF L.); RANDOLPH, PASCHAL BEVERLY. The methods of sex magic later taught by the OTO bear a close enough relationship to Randolph's methods that the existence of Kellner's Asian teachers has been called into doubt on more than one occasion.

In 1902 Kellner and Reuss contacted John Yarker, a prolific English marketer of Masonic degrees, and bought a charter to set up a lodge of the Rite of Memphis and Misraim, a variant of Masonry that offered no less than 99 degrees to its initiates. The following year, a prospectus for a new order, the Ordo Templi Orientis, was published. The project made little progress, however, until a year after Kellner's death in 1905. The year 1906 saw the official founding of the order, and Reuss worked on its rituals and structure for the next six years, meanwhile gathering a small number of members.

In 1912 the new order went public, offering ten degrees:

I°: Prüfling (Probationer)

II°: Minerval

III°: Johannis-(Craft-) Freimauer (Craft Freemason, or Freemason of St. John)

IV°: Schottischer-(Andreas-) Mauer (Scottish Mason, or Mason of St. Andrew)

V°: Rose Croix-Mauer (Rose Croix Mason)

VI°: Templer-Rosenkreuzer (Templar-Rosicrucian)

VII°: Mystischer Templer (Mystic Templar)

VIII°: Orientalisher Templer (Oriental Templar)

IX°: Vollkommener Illuminat (Perfect Illuminatus)

X°: Rex Supremus (Supreme King)

The sexual mysticism of the H. B. of L., the core of Reuss' system, was taught in the VIII° and IX°; specifically, methods of magical masturbation made up the core of the VIII° curriculum, while ritual intercourse belonged to the IX°. The grade of X° was purely administrative, and was given to the head of the OTO in a country.

The year 1912 saw another major event in OTO history, for it was in this year that Reuss encountered Aleister Crowley and elevated him to the position of Rex Supremus for Britain and Ireland. *SEE* CROWLEY, ALEISTER. Crowley immediately went to work building up a British branch of the order under the name Mysteria Mystica Maxima (MMM). His reputation was already bad enough in the British occult community that he found only a limited number of takers for the new order—a detail that did not prevent him from making sweeping claims about its size and influence. Crowley's protegé Charles Stansfield Jones founded the first lodge in North America, Agape Lodge in Vancouver, Canada, in 1914; in 1916 he was appointed North American head of the order. *SEE* ACHAD, FRATER.

Within a few years of his advancement to X°, Crowley began revising Reuss' rituals to make them conform more closely to his philosophy of Thelema. He also re-named most of the degrees and added several intermediate steps, using titles imported from or modeled on various Scottish Rite degrees:

0°: Minerval

I°: M. (Entered Apprentice Mason)

II°: M.. (Fellow Craft Mason)

III°: M.·. (Master Mason)

PM (Past Master)

IV°: Companion of the Holy Royal Arch of Enoch

Prince of Jerusalem

Knight of the East and of the West

V°: Sovereign Prince of Rose Croix, Knight of the Pelican and Eagle

Member of the Senate of Knight Hermetic Philosophers, Knights of the Red Eagle

VI°: Illustrious Knight (Templar) of the Order of Kadosch, and Companion of the Holy Graal

Grand Inquisitor Commander, Member of the Grand Tribunal

Prince of the Royal Secret

VII°: Very Illustrious Sovereign Grand Inspector General

Member of the Supreme Grand Council

VIII°: Perfect Pontiff of the Illuminati

IX°: Initiate of the Sanctuary of the Gnosis

X°: Rex Summus Sanctissimus (Supreme and Most Holy King)

Reuss soon came to regret placing Crowley in so powerful a position in the order. By 1915 he was in correspondence with H. Spencer Lewis, an American occultist who would later found the esoteric order AMORC. *SEE* ANCIENT MYSTICAL ORDER ROSAE CRUCIS (AMORC);

LEWIS, HARVEY SPENCER. Reuss provided Lewis with an OTO charter, and made a variety of moves to try to use Lewis to counter Crowley's influence. In 1921, to side-step the claims of Crowley and Jones to exclusive OTO jurisdiction in Britain and North America, Reuss took the further step of making Lewis a member of the European branch of the order, and of raising him to the honorary degrees of 33°, 90°, 95° and VII° in the Scottish Rite, Rite of Memphis, Rite of Misraim, and OTO respectively. Around this time Reuss and Crowley had a final falling-out, and Crowley proclaimed himself Outer Head of the order. Lewis, for his part, had little interest in getting involved in the increasingly complex internal politics of the OTO, and distanced himself from Reuss as he began developing his own organization.

Reuss' death in 1921 left no clear successor, and few of the order's branches managed to survive for long. (Crowley's English branch certainly did not; it had gone out of existence after a police raid in 1917, although Crowley initiated a handful of new members before his death in 1947.) The events of the next several decades are a thicket of claims, counterclaims, and accusations involving a dozen different claimants to OTO headship, which there is neither room nor need to summarize here. In the English-speaking world, Crowley's standing as OTO head was widely accepted, although by his death in 1947 the OTO under his jurisdiction consisted of one small lodge in Pasadena, California, which dissolved a few years later. The fight over Crowley's legacy was just as contentious as Reuss' had been, and for some twenty years thereafter the OTO consisted of a handful of people scattered over two continents, few of whom were on speaking terms with any of the others, and even fewer of whom were apparently working the OTO rituals at all.

This state of affairs began to change in 1969, when an American, Grady McMurtry (1918–1985), under the title Hymenaeus Alpha, announced that he had been given charters by Crowley to act as his Caliph or deputy while visiting the Beast in England in 1943. The existence and validity of these charters is a topic of endless and bitter dispute throughout the current OTO scene, though it is clear that McMurtry was in contact with Crowley during the Beast's last years, and had some form of authority over the one American OTO lodge.

Notwithstanding these disputes, McMurtry proceeded to resurrect the OTO and turn it into one of the larger magical lodge organizations of the twentieth century. In the process, he managed to provide Crowley's ideas with a far larger audience than the Beast himself had ever been able to find. The great majority of the revival of Thelema in North America and Europe in the last quarter of the twentieth century can be credited to the revived OTO.

The last years of McMurtry's Caliphate saw his OTO embroiled in a variety of legal challenges. Shortly before McMurtry's death in 1985, the order under his headship was awarded sole rights to the original order's trademarks and copyrights, a ruling that still stands as of this writing.

On McMurtry's death, he was succeeded by a senior OTO member who has chosen not to make his name public, and who functions as Caliph under the title of Hymenaeus Beta. There have been, predictably, further disputes, schisms, and squabbles since that time, but the OTO under his leadership has nonetheless continued to be one of the largest and most active occult orders in the world. There are also a number of other orders, most of them small, claiming the OTO inheritance in various parts of the world. *SEE ALSO* CROWLEY, ALEISTER; THELEMA. FURTHER READING: CARTER 1999; F. KING 1972.

orgone. In the thought of Wilhelm Reich, a subtle energy present in all living tissue, which can be concentrated or dispersed by various means; one of the many names for ether. *SEE* ETHER.

Os. (Old English, "mouth") The fourth rune of the Anglo-Saxon futhorc, Os is a variant of Ansuz, the third run of the elder futhark, and shares its meanings. Its sound-value, however, is *o*. *SEE* ANGLO-SAXON FUTHORC; ANSUZ.

Anglo-Saxon rune Os

Os. The fourth rune of the Armanen runic system, representing the mouth. Its correspondences include the god

Odin, the child, and the zodiacal sign Cancer; its magical power, taken from the rune-charm in the Old Norse *Havamal*, is the power to break fetters and shackles. Its sound-value is *o*. *SEE* ARMANEN RUNES.

Armanen rune Os

Osiris. (ancient Egyptian *Usir*) One of the most important Egyptian gods, the lord of eternity, the god of death and resurrection, the first king of Egypt, and the most popular of gods all through Egypt's history. He was the sixth member of the Ennead or company of the gods of Heliopolis. While other gods held higher positions in the Egyptian pantheon or in the rituals surrounding the pharaohs and the great temples, Osiris was the most important of the gods to the ordinary people.

The mythology of Osiris recounted how he had been slain by his brother Set, brought back to life by his wife Isis, slain a second time, and had then passed to the land of the dead to become lord of the Otherworld. To share in the resurrection of Osiris was the hope of every devout Egyptian. The dead were called "Osiris" in ritual, and all the spells and prayers that had been used to restore Osiris to life were put to use in Egyptian funeral rites preparing the dead for their journey through the underworld to Amentet, the realm of the virtuous dead. Since Osiris was also an agricultural god—his first death is, among other things, the planting of the seed, his second the harvesting and grinding of the ripe grain—his rites and festivals had much to do with the seasonal rhythms of farming and played a central role in everyday life.

In the Hermetic Order of the Golden Dawn, which drew heavily on Egyptian symbolism, the myth of Osiris was a pervasive underlying pattern in the rituals of the Outer Order, and in the Portal Grade—the transition between Outer and Inner Orders—the gathering of the symbols of the elements on the altar is linked to the gathering of the parts of Osiris' body by Isis. The Hierophant, the presiding officer in the Outer Order rituals, takes on the visualized godform of Osiris during ritual work. *SEE* GOLDEN DAWN, HERMETIC ORDER OF THE. *SEE ALSO*

Ostara. Pagan Germanic goddess of spring, whose name is the origin of the English word "Easter" and its German equivalent "Oster." Effectively nothing of Ostara's myths, traditions, or symbolism have survived.

Many modern Pagans use the name Ostara for the spring equinox, one of the eight sabbats of modern Paganism. *SEE* EQUINOX; SABBAT. It was also the name of a Austrian occult magazine, issued by Jörg Lanz von Liebenfels during the first decades of the twentieth century, which had a major influence on Adolf Hitler. *SEE* HITLER, ADOLF; LANZ VON LIEBENFELS, JÖRG.

Othila. (Old Germanic, "estate, land") The twenty-third or twenty-fourth rune of the elder futhark, representing one's homeland or ancestral territory. In the writings of some modern runemasters, it is associated with the god Odin. Its sound-value is *o*. Its position in the elder futhark is uncertain, as it exchanges places with the rune Daeg in different accounts. *SEE* ELDER FUTHARK.

The same rune, renamed Ethel (Old English, "estate"), is the twenty-third rune of the Anglo-Saxon futhorc, with essentially the same meanings. Its sound-value is *oe*. *SEE* ANGLO-SAXON FUTHORC.

Rune Othila

OTO. *SEE* ORDO TEMPLI ORIENTIS (OTO).

Ouija. (from French *oui* and German *ja*, both meaning "yes") Among the most popular divination methods in the modern Western world, the Ouija was patented in 1891 by Elijah H. Bond. A year later the patent was purchased by William Fuld, who modified the board, took out a second patent, and made a fortune manufacturing and selling the device. His Baltimore Talking Board Company sold all rights to the Ouija to Parker Brothers, a game company, in 1966.

The Ouija consists of a rectangular board twelve by eighteen inches in size, marked with letters, numbers, and other signs, and a pointer on small wheels that allow it to roll freely across the board. The participants each place the fingertips of one hand on the pointer, and wait for a message. The Ouija answers by movements of the pointer, which points to a series of letters and numbers.

These movements result from small, unconscious motions of the hands of the participants. What guides those motions is a matter of much debate; materialists argue that they are the result of psychological automatisms, while others suggest that spiritual entities prompt and direct the movements of the pointer. Whatever the actual source, Ouija communications are routinely extended and meaningful, and in some cases rise to the status of literature. James Merrill's award-winning poetic trilogy *The Changing Light at Sandover*, well over 500 pages in length, is largely composed of communications received by way of a homemade Ouija apparatus. An even larger body of work was communicated through the Ouija by an entity calling herself Patience Worth, and included five commercially successful full-length novels, a play, two short stories, and 2,500 poems.

Very little of what comes by way of Ouija sessions is of this level of quality, though; most is relatively dull, and can be inaccurate and misleading. The Ouija has also been accused of serving as a conduit for demonic possession and negative spiritual influences. Many of these latter claims come from fundamentalist Christian sources, and are based on the common fundamentalist habit of vilifying any spiritual phenomenon outside their control.

There are enough accounts of psychic and spiritual trouble that began with Ouija experimentation, though, that definite caution may well be appropriate. As with any means of interacting with the subtle planes of being, Ouija should not be treated as a game or toy; and prayers, invocations, or methods of magical self-defense should be used to prevent negative outcomes. *SEE ALSO* DIVINATION; SPIRITUALISM. FURTHER READING: HUNT 1985, MERRILL 1992.

ouroboros. (Greek, "tail biter") The serpent who swallows his own tail, a common image in magic and alchemy from ancient times to the present. It appears to be Egyptian in origin—for example, it appears in the tomb furnishings of Tutankhamen—but spread over much of the Western world by late classical times.

It has had a variety of meanings. In alchemy, it has usually represented the process of circulation, in which a substance is distilled, the distillate poured back onto the residue, and the process repeated. *SEE* ALCHEMY; CIRCULATION.

Outer Court. In modern occult and Pagan terminology, a semipublic group operated by a magical order, coven, or other magical body. Individuals interested in membership are invited to join the Outer Court organization, where they learn the rudiments of theory and practice in the system taught by the sponsoring group. After a time, those Outer Court members who show themselves to be suitable candidates for membership in the sponsoring group are invited to join. The Outer Court thus serves as a filter for potential members as well as a forum for basic training.

In the 1980s and 1990s, a set of rituals assembled by the Pagan Way organization, an American Neopagan body, became common as Outer Court training material in many American Wiccan and Pagan traditions. *SEE* PAGAN WAY. *SEE ALSO* COVEN; LODGE, MAGICAL; NEOPAGANISM; WICCA.

ovate. (Latin *ovatus*, from Old Gaulish; cognate to Gaelic *fáith*, "seer") According to Greek and Roman sources, a subordinate class of Druids concerned with divination and natural philosophy. Essentially nothing is known about the original ovates beyond the fact of their existence.

During the Druidic revival of the eighteenth and nineteenth centuries, the word "ovate" was thought to be related to Latin *ovum*, "egg," and Druid orders founded in this period often used it as the name for the first step of their degree systems, with the grades of Bard and Druid following in that order. More recent scholarship, based more on Irish than on Latin sources, has revised this arrangement, and most Druid orders founded in the twentieth century make an ovate grade the second step in their degree systems when they use the traditional terms at all. *SEE ALSO* DRUIDS.

Pachad. (Hebrew PChD, "fear") An alternative name for Geburah, the fifth Sephirah of the Cabalistic Tree of Life. *SEE* GEBURAH.

pact. The idea of making a pact with the Devil, or selling one's soul in exchange for magical powers or earthly wealth, is an invention of Christian legend, and first appears in Christian tradition in late Roman times. Among the earliest accounts is the story of Theophilus, the church treasurer in Adana, who was said to have sold his soul to the Devil in the early sixth century in exchange for being made bishop of Adana. The tale of his dealings with Satan, his repentance, and his eventual salvation was repeated and elaborated for centuries. *SEE* THEOPHILUS OF ADANA.

The idea of the diabolic pact had major impacts on the history of magic. According to orthodox Christian doctrine, magic was only possible through pacts made with the Devil. The church fathers Origen (185–254 C.E.) and Augustine of Hippo (354–430 C.E.) both argued in favor of this theory, which received the stamp of approval of Thomas Aquinas (1227–1274), the most important Catholic theologian of the Middle Ages.

During the later Middle Ages, this idea became central to the Christian theory of witchcraft, and served as a major justification for the horrors inflicted on accused witches during the Burning Times. It was agreed by theologians and witch-hunters alike that since magic required a pact with the Devil, anyone who practiced magic must have made an implicit pact, even if they had no knowledge of having done so; this sort of thinking

was used to justify defining magic as a form of heresy, and provided a weapon for persecutors that was almost impossible to evade. Detailed discussions of the pact and its nature appeared in witch-hunting handbooks such as the *Malleus Maleficarum* (1486), and written pacts were sometimes exhibited in witchcraft trials—although how these were extracted from Satan's filing cabinets is not clear. *SEE* BURNING TIMES.

The popularity of the pact concept, especially after it found its classic form in the Faust legends, eventually guaranteed that it would work its way into magical practice, especially in the murky realm of goetia. *SEE* FAUST LEGEND; GOETIA; GRIMOIRE. Early grimoires—"grammars" of magic—such as the *Key of Solomon* present the goetic magician as the absolute master of spirits, commanding and banishing them rather than bartering with them. Some late grimoires such as the *Grand Grimoire*, on the other hand, include instructions on making the best deal possible with the powers of Hell, or suggest ways by which a pact, once made, can be evaded by the clever magician. For obvious reasons, these traditions—never widespread in magical circles even at their height—dropped entirely out of use by the time of the nineteenth-century magical revival and have been ignored ever since.

Ideas about pacts with the Devil remain current among modern fundamentalist Christians, who seem to have learned very little since the fifteenth century, and may be encountered in those areas of modern folklore strongly influenced by fundamentalist beliefs. The "Satanic ritual abuse" furor of the late twentieth century is a good example of this latter, and references to "pacts with Satan" indistinguishable from that of Theophilus can be found in some Christian sources on this subject. *SEE* SATANIC RITUAL ABUSE. *SEE ALSO* SATANISM. FURTHER READING: E. BUTLER 1949, P. PALMER 1936.

Pagan Way. One of the major sources of modern American Paganism, the Pagan Way movement was launched in 1970 by Joseph Wilson, an American witch stationed with the US Air Force in England. In response to the growing popularity of Wicca and other Pagan traditions, Wilson and a group of other active Pagans and Wiccans decided to create a form of Pagan worship that would be open to all who were interested. Most of the rituals were composed by American Gardnerian Ed Fitch.

The Pagan Way rituals were intentionally put in the public domain, and have been copied, adapted, and reshaped by dozens if not hundreds of American and Canadian Pagan groups. No particular organizational structure was included in the original system; a pair of Gardnerian witches in Chicago, Donna Cole and Herman Enderle, filled the gap by organizing the first formal Pagan Way grove. Throughout most of the 1970s, Pagan Way groves could be found in most American cities and many less urban areas as well.

The more political Pagan scene of the 1980s had less room for the loosely formed Pagan Way movement, and the number and size of Pagan Way groves decreased sharply. The rituals have remained in circulation, however, and a number of Wiccan covens have set up Pagan Way groves as Outer Court training circles, to train prospective members and assess their potential as coven members. *SEE* OUTER COURT. *SEE ALSO* NEOPAGANISM.

Paganism. (From Latin *paganus*, "rural") A general term for the traditional polytheistic religious traditions of Europe and the Mediterranean basin. The word was later applied to all religions other than Christianity, Judaism, and Islam, and has also been borrowed by many groups and people in the modern Neopagan revival, some of which claim connections to ancient Paganism. For the origins and history of these latter movements, *SEE* NEOPAGANISM.

The controversies and difficulties around the concept of Paganism begin with the word itself. The term *paganus* was originally applied by Christians to followers of the traditional religions of the Roman Empire; it was apparently never used by followers of these religions as a label for themselves. Nor is it clear at all why this particular label was chosen. It has been suggested that it referred to Pagans as rural rustics, "hicks," who held to the older religions after the urban population had converted to Christianity; that it was a piece of Roman soldiers' slang, meaning roughly "civilian," and thus came to be used for someone not enrolled in the army of Christ; or that it meant followers of the religion of the *pagus*, the local unit of government in the Roman Empire. No firm decision among these possibilities has yet emerged from scholarly disputes.

Another major source of difficulty in understanding Paganism is that outside of the literate cultures of the Mediterranean basin, which left a number of theological and liturgical writings that still survive, nearly everything we know about Paganism was written down by Christian authors more interested in denouncing Pagan ideas and practices than understanding them. Some modern Pagan writers have compared the situation to trying to understand Jewish theology and practice if the only sources one had to go on were published by the Third Reich. Still, the clues that remain have been fitted together with the evidence of archeology and cross-cultural comparisons to make some conclusions fairly certain.

Perhaps the most important key to understanding ancient, classical, and medieval Paganism was that there was never one "Paganism." Rather, there were "Paganisms," hundreds or even thousands of them, forming a wildly diverse patchwork of belief and practice that extended across the pre-Christian world. No single generalization is true of them all. Some worshipped goddesses, while others did not; some were polytheistic, while others worshipped a single deity; and still others had objects of worship that are difficult to fit into the modern category of "deity" at all.

Practice was as diverse as theology. While there were common patterns of ritual and devotion, every deity had his or her quirks and habits, and in many cases different temples had their own unique traditions of ceremony. In the Greco-Roman world, the focus of most surviving documentation, animal sacrifice was the most common form of Pagan ritual, and the scraps of information that survive about Celtic and Germanic Pagan ritual suggest that sacrificial offerings of various sorts were also central in these very different cultural settings; SEE SACRIFICE. Still, there were many other traditional rites and practices in these Pagan areas, and even within the broad label of "animal sacrifice" there was constant variation. Elsewhere—for example, in Mesopotamia and Egypt, both of which contributed much to classical Pagan thought and practice—entirely different theological and ritual traditions flourished, and no doubt there were many other wildly different threads in the tapestry of ancient Paganism that have fallen through the gaps in historical records and are lost completely.

In such an environment, religious diversity ran riot. What can most confidently be said of classical Pagan religions, as they appear in the historical sources, is that they were deeply rooted in the life and traditions of local communities. Each city or rural area had its own particular gods and spirits, who were honored with their own traditional rites. Certain deities had a wider appeal and were popular across large regions, and a few such as the divine twins Castor and Pollux were all but universally revered across the classical world.

There was little if any sense of exclusiveness. Travelers routinely offered sacrifice to the gods of the towns they visited, and a priest or priestess of one divinity would as a matter of course take part in offerings to others. The political and economic structures of the classical world, in turn, were deeply intertwined with Pagan religious life; in Rome, for example, most political figures had religious duties, and the Senate usually met inside temples.

The dominant role of community in classical Paganism turned out to be one of its most serious weaknesses, once the stability of the Roman world began to break down. During the latter half of the third century, a period of severe economic and political crisis throughout the empire, records show that many Pagan religious organizations were severely affected. The Arval Brothers of Rome are one example of many. They were a college of twelve Pagan priests who worshipped the ancient goddess Dea Dia, using a litany dating from around the fifth century B.C.E.; according to legend they had been founded by Romulus himself. They lost three-fourths of their rev-

enues in 241 C.E., struggled on until 304 when the last inscriptions of their activities are dated, and then apparently went out of existence.

Economic troubles of this sort had a major impact on the survival of Paganism, because they left Pagan religions vulnerable to the rise of a rival force. Christianity emerged in the course of the first century of the Common Era as a radical break with traditional Pagan ways. It rejected all gods besides its own, classifying them either as lifeless nonentities or as demonic forces—or sometimes, inconsistently, as both. It required its members to renounce many of the public ceremonies and activities that kept the classical world functioning. It also urged members to recruit converts by any available means.

Christianity's isolation from the wider community was a source of weakness in its earliest days, and fostered widespread suspicions that played a large part in spurring on the Pagan persecutions of Christianity. As the political and economic structures of the Roman world broke apart, however, this source of vulnerability turned into a source of strength. The collapse of other religious traditions left it an increasingly open field. By 312 C.E., the Christian church included a large enough fraction of the population of the empire that the Emperor Constantine legalized it in order to enlist its political support.

Constantine's Edict of Milan was the first stage in a series of swings that convulsed the religious side of the Roman world. Under Constantine, the Christian church quickly gained wealth and political power, and began to use it to attempt to suppress other religious traditions. An edict of Constantine's successor Constantius in 341 banned sacrifices to Pagan gods; in 351 all Pagan temples were ordered closed, and entry to them was forbidden on pain of death. A decade later Constantius was succeeded by the Pagan emperor Julian, whose short reign saw a massive Pagan backlash against Christianity. This backlash was spearheaded by the rise of Platonist theurgy, a new religious and philosophical movement that sought to create a mystical Platonic theology in which all traditional Pagan observances could find a place. Led by major Platonist philosophers such as Iamblichus of Chalcis and Proclus, the theurgical movement provided the last systematic opposition to Christianity in the Roman world, and was strongly supported by Julian, himself a theurgist.

SEE IAMBLICHUS OF CHALCIS; PLATONISM; PROCLUS; THEURGY.

Julian's death in 363 ushered in a short period of uneasy truce, but by 380 the Christians were secure enough in power to begin legal measures against Paganism once again, and the year 391 saw the ban on sacrifices renewed. By 435 offering sacrifices to the gods was a capital offense. In 571, Justinian completed the process by legislation that stripped civil rights from all non-Christians, barred Pagans from all teaching positions, and nullified any will that left anything to a Pagan person or organization.

There was also a great deal of direct violence against Pagans from the late fourth century onwards. Some of this was carried out by government troops acting under the new laws, but much more was unofficial, carried out by the Christian church itself. As Christianity grew in power and gained control over local law enforcement, mobs of monks became the shock troops of the new religious order, burning Pagan temples and attacking people who were known or suspected to be Pagans. One famous victim was the philosopher Hypatia of Alexandria, who was dragged from her chariot and hacked to pieces by a crowd of monks urged on by the Christian bishop of Alexandria. Her case was one of scores that can be traced in the records of the time.

Despite these pressures, Christianity was still a minority religion in the empire until after 450, and Paganism continued to hold fast in certain areas and in certain social milieus much longer. The upper classes remained largely Pagan well into the fifth century, defending their traditional faiths in the face of steadily increasing political and religious pressure. As late as 536, Pagans secretly opened the gates of the ancient Temple of Janus to call down help from the gods when Rome was besieged. A handful of important Pagan centers, including the Academy at Athens and the great temple of Isis at Philae in Egypt, remained publicly active into the sixth century, when they were finally closed by the Emperor Justinian.

Pagan practice endured longest in the countryside, where old habits died hard. In many regions of Italy, peasants kept offering sacrifices to their local gods despite all the church could do; Christian writings from the fifth and sixth centuries express constant frustration at the persistence of Pagan cults in Tuscany and in the northern regions near the Alps. Gaul was similar, and Eligius of Noviomagus still found it necessary to denounce the worship of Roman gods, the veneration of springs and trees, and the celebration of the Pagan festival of the Kalends of January in Provence in the seventh century. Rural Greece was even more resolutely Pagan, and it was not until the ninth century that the last Pagan regions of Greece saw forced baptisms and the imposition of church hierarchy.

Outside of the area dominated by Roman culture, Christianity spread slowly at first. A few Germanic tribes, such as the Goths, were converted in the fourth century C.E., but the rest of northern and western Europe fell under Christian control more slowly. Much of France was still Pagan into the eighth century, western Germany and England until the ninth, Scandinavia until the eleventh, and Baltic countries such as Latvia and Lithuania until the eighteenth.

In the face of the strong Pagan presence in Europe, Christian missionaries developed an effective set of methods for seizing religious control over an area. The first priority was getting a local foothold via the construction of a monastery. Monastic schools, which offered the lure of literacy and classical education to the children of the local nobility, assisted with the next step, which was the conversion of the political leadership. The next stage involved legal measures to establish Christianity and prohibit other religions. Finally, as churches and monasteries were established throughout the new territory, Pagan religious practices could be suppressed more and more completely by persuasion or force. At any given time, different parts of Europe were at different stages in this process—with living Pagan traditions continuing until the last stage was finally complete.

This slow process left substantial areas of Europe largely Pagan until the high Middle Ages, as mentioned above, and might have been vulnerable to Pagan countermeasures if these had been carried out effectively. The Pagan religions, however, were never able to stage an effective counterattack. Their traditional tolerance of other gods and teachings left them constantly vulnerable to Christian incursions, and they lacked—even in the Roman world, where Pagan religions were most organized—the sort of self-supporting structure that allowed

Christianity to keep up a steady pressure toward universal control. Competing religions that did have solid organization and a willingness to reject Christianity outright—Islam, Judaism, and Manichaeism—proved the point by surviving, in the first two cases, or going under only in the face of overwhelming violence, in the last. *SEE* CATHARS; MANICHAEISM.

The Pagan subcultures of Christian Europe can thus be traced with increasing difficulty up to the time of the Reformation, when the last traces died out amid the savage religious warfare and social upheavals of a chaotic age. The sources in any case are sparse, since literacy was almost entirely a Christian monopoly.

Most of the few solid sources of information on the survival of Pagan practices in medieval Europe are found in penitentials—handbooks meant for Christian priests, which gave detailed descriptions of common sins and the penances to be assigned to those who confessed to them. One particularly rich source is the *Corrector* of Burchard, bishop of Worms, which was written around A.D. 1000.

In Burchard's time, centuries after the official Christianization of western Germany, peasants might still be caught making offerings to sacred springs and trees, worshipping the sun and the moon, or performing Pagan rituals at the wake for a dead person. The penances Burchard prescribed for these actions were relatively mild—a peasant who made an offering at a Pagan holy spring, for instance, would be absolved after thirty days' penance of bread and water. (For the sake of comparison, adultery rated a full year on bread and water.)

The forms of Pagan practice listed in the penitentials, and other medieval sources, fall into a few clear categories. Magical rituals with Pagan or quasi-Pagan overtones, nearly all of them aimed at purely practical goals, formed one large category. Throughout the Middle Ages, huge amounts of once-Pagan folk magic remained in practice, much of it lightly Christianized by inserting the Trinity and the saints in place of Pagan gods and spirits, and the more Christian forms of this magic were accepted by most church officials as perfectly harmless. Overtly Pagan magic, on the other hand, was forbidden, and penalties for its practice gradually harshened until they were caught up in the frenzied witch hunts of the Burning Times.

Survivals of Pagan religious ritual, such as leaving offerings at holy places or celebrating festivals that were not part of the church calendar, formed a much smaller category of Pagan activities, and one that faded out relatively early. By the thirteenth century, such practices had been entirely absorbed into various forms of folk Christian practice, such as the veneration of local saints and holy relics.

A third category, found across Europe in one form or another, comprises a specific set of traditions that have only recently been explored in any detail. These first emerge in the penitential literature in scattered references from the tenth century, and play an important part in the genesis of the witch-hunting hysteria of the Burning Times. In these traditions, groups of people—most often, but not exclusively, women—took part in visionary journeys at night in the company of a mysterious goddess. *SEE* CANON EPISCOPI. It is difficult to connect this third category with older traditions of European Paganism, and they may have had another origin.

While some writers (see particularly Ginzburg 1991) argue that these accounts are records of archaic shamanistic traditions that had survived from the distant past, it is also possible that they were a new arrival on the European scene. Quite a few tribal peoples spilled out of the Asian steppes into Europe during the early Middle Ages, and might have brought shamanistic traditions of this sort with them. In any case, these traditions seem to have had a good deal to do with the origins of the legendary Witches' Sabbath, but much less in common with any historically recorded Western Pagan tradition. *SEE* SABBATH, WITCHES'; WITCH.

All these phenomena were mostly active in the early Middle Ages, and faded out of existence by the time of the Reformation. Traditions of folk magic and dissenting religion in western Europe from the early modern period onward have been documented in vast detail, but these show no trace of any coherent Pagan tradition of the sort claimed by some current Pagan revivalists. Rather, the gods and goddesses had become figures of literature, remembered mostly because educated people learned Latin (and sometimes Greek) and read ancient poetry that referred to them. Ironically, this turned out to be the foundation for the modern revival of Pagan worship, since the old gods and goddesses remained widely enough known to attract new worshippers among urban intellectual circles as Christianity began to lose its grip on the Western world. *SEE* NEOPAGANISM; GOD, THE; GODDESS, THE.

While it is just possible that some modern Neopagan movements have a direct historical connection to ancient Pagan religions, no serious evidence has yet been produced to document this. The evidence suggests, rather, that modern Neopaganism is a revival, not a continuation, and draws on older Pagan traditions primarily by way of literary sources.

It must be remembered, though, that the validity of the Neopagan movement does not depend on a continuous history. A revived religion can easily be as relevant, as meaningful, and as powerful as one with an uninterrupted history. The fact that the Pagan gods and goddesses were not worshipped for a time, as some modern Pagan theologians have pointed out, does not make them nonexistent or powerless, nor make reverence to them a waste of effort. *SEE ALSO* MAGIC, PERSECUTION OF; MYSTERIES, THE. FURTHER READING: ARMSTRONG 1986, CHUVIN 1989, GEFFCKEN 1978, GINZBURG 1991, HUTTON 1999, JOLLY 1996, JONES AND PENNICK 1995, LELAND 2002, MACMULLEN 1984, MERRIFIELD 1987, MILIS 1998, SEZNEC 1953.

palindromes. Palindromes are words that read the same forwards and backwards. Little more than a source of parlor games in modern times, palindromes were once important in magic, and some of the more important barbarous names in ancient magical texts were palindromes. The word of power *ablanathanalba* is the most common of these, but monstrously long magical palindromes such as "aberamenthôouthlerthexanaxethrelthuoôthenemareba" and "iaeôbaphrenemounothilarikriphiaeyeaiphirkiralithonuomenerphabôeai" were also used. (In working these out, remember that *th* and *ph* are both single letters in Greek.)

The use of magical palindromes seems to have died out around the time of the fall of the Roman Empire. *SEE ALSO* BARBAROUS NAMES. FURTHER READING: BETZ 1986.

Palladian Order. The subject of a massive hoax launched in 1884 by French writer Gabriel Jorgand-Pagés, a prolific author of pornography, muckraking journalism, and anti-Catholic polemic under the pen name Léo Taxil. On the publication that year of an encyclical by Pope Leo XIII attacking Freemasonry, Taxil (as he is usually called in historical works) suddenly announced that he had reconciled himself to the church. He sought absolution, undertook a lengthy penance, and began to write a series of books exposing a diabolical secret order hidden away in the depths of Freemasonry.

According to Taxil, the inner core of Freemasonry was the sinister Palladian Order, a supersecret organization of Satanist sex fiends. In their meetings, Palladists summoned the Devil, committed an assortment of blasphemies and sacrileges, and practiced every kind of sexual excess. They also allegedly supported the British Empire—a charge that, all by itself, was enough to define them as willing servants of Satan in the eyes of conservative French Catholics.

Taxil's breathless prose told of orgiastic rites in lodges in India, hidden factories inside the Rock of Gibraltar churning out Satanic paraphernalia, and séances at which Asmodeus rubbed ectoplasmic elbows with the ghost of Voltaire. At the head of it all was Albert Pike, the "Sovereign Pontiff of Universal Freemasonry," who sat at the center of a vast spiderweb of Masonic-Satanic conspiracy in Charleston, South Carolina.

Improbable as all this was, it instantly won plenty of believers in the overheated world of late nineteenth-century French Catholicism. Palladism became an instant topic of conversation all over France. As Taxil continued to write in this vein, he was publicly supported by important Catholic clergymen, and finally received a private audience with the pope in 1887.

As the Palladian furor heated up, several other authors chimed in, bringing out their own shocking revelations of the activities of the Palladists. Much was made of a schism between Luciferians—allegedly Gnostic dualists who identified Lucifer as the god of light and spirit, while Adonai, the Christian god, was the god of matter and darkness—and Satanists, who simply took orthodox Christian theology and stood it on its head. A new name entered the lists of the secret heads of Palladism: Diana Vaughan, the Grand Priestess, who was supposedly descended from a mating between the seventeenth-century alchemist Thomas Vaughan and a female demon. Word circulated that Vaughan was in France, and a periodical—published, curiously, by Taxil—duly emerged under her name to preach Palladism to the enraged and tittilated French public.

In 1895, Catholic newspaper headlines blared the unbelievable: Diana Vaughan had renounced her Palladian connections and converted to Catholicism. A new periodical from Taxil's presses, *Mémoires d'une ex-Palladiste* (*Memoirs of an ex-Palladist*), recounted her change of heart and recorded the sinister ceremonies over which she had formerly presided. Readers were treated to accounts of serpents slithering sensuously over the bare breasts of female Masons, and glimpses of the inner power struggles of the Palladian Order—struggles which involved important European political figures.

In 1897, after much pleading from journalists and the Catholic hierarchy, Taxil announced that Diana Vaughan was prepared to emerge from hiding and make a public appearance. A hall in Paris was rented, and every seat quickly sold out. When the hour of Vaughan's planned appearance arrived, though, it was Taxil who mounted the stage.

He proceeded to inform the entire audience that he had made complete fools of them for more than a decade. The Palladian Order and all its outrageous activities were creations of his imagination. Diana Vaughan was a typist who had worked for Taxil, and who had agreed to lend her name and photograph to further his hoax. Most of the other authors who had chimed in with Palladian revelations were simply pen names belonging to Taxil and one of his friends. The whole thing was a fraud from beginning to end, launched for the purpose of showing the world just how gullible the Catholic Church really was.

As can be imagined, a riot followed these remarks, and the hall had to be cleared by the police. Some devout Catholics convinced themselves that Taxil had been lying, and a certain amount of Palladist-hunting continued for a few years. On the other side of the equation were Freemasons in Italy who wanted to join the Palladian Order and spent years thereafter trying to get in contact with it.

The legacy of the Palladist hoax was surprisingly important. They include the word "Satanist," which entered the English language for the first time during the Palladist furor. Taxil's claims are still quoted now and then as fact by anti-Masonic conspiracy theorists and fundamentalist Christians, including such luminaries as American televangelist Pat Robertson. More generally, Taxil's image of a vast conspiracy focused on sex and devil worship played a major role in redefining Satanism in the twentieth century, where it influenced cultural phenomena as different as Anton Szandor LaVey's Church of Satan and the Satanic ritual abuse furor of the 1980s and 1990s.

A new wrinkle in the Palladist story is the appearance of a so-called New Order of the Palladium, whose manifesto appeared in 2001. The New Order claims descent from the Palladist Order of the 1880s, as well as the Bavarian Illuminati and the obscure Renaissance occultist Johannes Pantheus; SEE BAVARIAN ILLUMINATI; VOARCHADUMIA. What, if anything, lies behind these undocumented claims is anyone's guess. SEE CHURCH OF SATAN; SATANIC RITUAL ABUSE. SEE ALSO FREEMASONRY; PIKE, ALBERT; SATANISM. FURTHER READING: ANONYMOUS 2001, MEDWAY 2001, RIGGS 1997.

Pallas. An asteroid sometimes used in astrology, assigned by some astrologers to the sign Virgo and by others to Libra. SEE ASTEROIDS.

palmistry. The art of divination by means of the lines and form of the human hand, also known as chiromancy. Palmistry is one of the oldest surviving forms of divination. It was apparently invented in India, where it is attested in Vedic writings that date from before 1800 C.E. From there it traveled east to China and Japan, where it is still much practiced, and west via Persian and Middle Eastern peoples to Europe, which it reached in Hellenistic times. Aristotle and Pliny mentioned it, and a treatise (unfortunately now lost) was written on the subject in Greek around 250 B.C.E.

The palmist's art seems to have been lost to the West during the fall of the Roman Empire, but returned in the late Middle Ages by way of the Arabs, who mastered it along with many other divination systems. Heavily practiced in the Renaissance, it was the subject of writings by Robert Fludd and Paracelsus, among others; SEE FLUDD, ROBERT; PARACELSUS. Like most Western divination systems, though, it lost a great deal of ground with the Scientific Revolution and was mostly forgotten by 1750.

The revival of palmistry was set in motion by two French diviners, Casimir d'Arpentigny and Adrien Desbarolles, who published books on palmistry in 1839 and 1859 respectively. Their works won palmistry a new following and laid the foundation of most modern systems of palm reading. Another major influence on modern palmistry was Louis Hamon, alias Cheiro, whose *The Language of the Hand* (1897) remains a classic; *SEE* CHEIRO. Despite the competition from Tarot cards, astrology, and more recently minted divination systems, palmistry remains popular today.

The various features of the hand provide the competent palmist with a wide assortment of symbols and sources of information. The general shape of the hand and the relative proportions of fingers and palm provide a general overview of character, with the shapes and sizes of the individual fingers providing more specific information; the divisions (called "phalanxes") of the fingers, the "mounts" or fleshy areas at the bases of the fingers, and the lines crossing the palm all have their stories to tell. Many of these features are closely associated with astrological symbolism—for example, the thumb and the "mount" at the base of the thumb correspond to Venus and reveal information about the querent's vital energy and emotional life, while the little finger and its "mount" correspond to Mercury and show the querent's mental development and characteristics.

Unlike astrology and Tarot divination, palmistry has rarely been incorporated into the broader Western occult tradition as a subject for study. The one major exception is in classical Jewish Cabala, which abounds in detailed texts of palmistry. Some of these date to the first few centuries of the Common Era, and were part of the Ma'aseh Merkabah, a system of Jewish mysticism older than the Cabala itself; *SEE* MA'ASEH MERKABAH. Several chapters of the Zohar deal with palmistry, and the great Cabalist Isaac Luria had a reputation as an expert palmist. *SEE* LURIA, ISAAC.

Like many other aspects of the Jewish Cabala, Cabalistic palmistry never found a way into the Hermetic Cabala. Like tassomancy (tea-leaf reading) and divination with playing cards, palmistry has survived and flourished primarily in the less exalted social setting of professional divination, and remains a major force in that field today. FURTHER READING: CAMPBELL 1996, CHEIRO 1987, GETTINGS 1965, SCHOLEM 1974.

Pan. (Greek, "all") The horned and horny goat-god of ancient Greek mythology, the primary model for the Christian Devil and a major presence in the modern Pagan revival. Despite the meaning of his name, Pan was a relatively minor god in ancient Greece, a herdsmen's divinity mostly worshipped in the rural region of Arcadia. Christian chroniclers reported in scandalized tones that his worshippers offered sacrifices with their genitals uncovered.

Pan's rise to prominence actually began in Victorian Britain, when poets and intellectuals connected to the Romantic movement turned him into the central symbol of everything contemporary British culture was not. The extrordinary craze for Pan, fauns, and satyrs in British literature in the late nineteenth and early twentieth centuries has been the subject of more than one critical study.

To a large degree, Pan has served as the major inspiration for the God of modern Wicca, whose horns, virility, and animal qualities are all closely aligned with the dancing goat-god. *SEE* GOD, THE. FURTHER READING: MERIVALE 1969.

pantacle. An alternative spelling of "pentacle," replacing the Greek root *penta-*, the number five, with *panta-*, "all." *SEE* PENTACLE.

Papus. (Gérard Encausse) French physician and occultist, 1865–1916. Born in Spain to a French chemist and his Spanish wife, he came to Paris with his family at the age of four and was educated there, finally taking a medical degree and working as a physician. He was attracted to the occult from an early age, and spent much of his free time at the Bibliothèquê National, reading old books on magic and alchemy.

In the early 1880s he was active in Parisian Theosophical circles, but found the increasingly Asiatic turn of Theosophy little to his taste and left the society before the middle of the decade. By this time he had already been initiated into Martinism, and in 1884 he and fellow

Martinist Pierre Augustin Chaboseau formed the Martinist Order. In 1891, the two became founding members of the Supreme Council of the Martinist Order, an umbrella group that became the largest single Martinist group in the world until after Papus' death in 1916. *SEE* MARTINISM.

In 1888 Papus published his first book, *Traitè élémentaire de science occulte* (*Elementary Treatise on Occult Science*) and launched a journal, *L'Initiation*. By this time he was a leading figure in Paris occult circles, and joined in the same year with Stanislaus de Guaita, the "Sâr" Peladan, and other occult figures to found the most influential of France's nineteenth-century magical orders, le Rose+Croix Kabbalistique (The Kabbalistic Rose Cross). *SEE* GUAITA, STANISLAUS DE; PELADAN, JOSEPHIN. Later in his life, Papus founded another occult organization, the Independent Group for Esoteric Studies, which carried out researches into ghosts, occult folklore, and Spiritualism as well as ceremonial magic.

His major works include *Traité méthodique de la science occulte* (*Systematic Treatise on Occult Science*, 1891), *Le Tarot de Bohémiens* (*The Tarot of the Gypsies*, 1889), and the posthumous *Traité méthodique de la magie pratique* (*Systematic Treatise of Practical Magic*, 1924). FURTHER READING: DECKER ET AL. 1996, PAPUS 2000, PAPUS N.D.

Paracelsus. (Philippus Aureolus Theophrastus Bombastus Paracelsus von Hohenheim) Swiss alchemist, physician, and occultist, 1493–1541. A physician's son from a remote mountain village in Switzerland, he grew up among miners and country folk, and developed early on a respect for traditional folklore and a contempt for established intellectual authorities. His mother died when he was nine, and his father relocated to Villach, in what is now part of Slovenia, where he found work teaching in the mining school. Young Theo von Hohenheim eagerly studied alchemy and mineralogy, and also attended monastic schools, where he gained a solid grounding in Latin.

At the age of fourteen, he left home to study, and in the usual fashion of the time attended several universities before receiving his bachelor's degree from the University of Vienna in 1511. He went on to medical school at the University of Ferrara, where he is thought to have received a medical degree around 1516. Thereafter he set out on a series of travels. Working as an army surgeon, he traveled through most of Europe, going east as far as central Asia, west to Spain and Britain, and south to Egypt. He finally returned to Villach in 1524, but set out almost immediately thereafter on another series of wanderings through central Europe.

A difficult, arrogant man with a severe alcohol problem, Paracelsus had a talent for alienating friends and making enemies, and as a result he was never able to settle anywhere for long. In 1526, as a result of his early publications and several notable cures, Paracelsus was appointed professor of medicine at the University of Basel, where he enlivened his lectures by publicly burning the works of Galen and Avicenna, the standard medical texts of the time. By 1528 he had quarreled so violently with the Basel city government that he had to escape from the town by night, and resumed his wandering life.

Much of his effort in the years that followed the Basel debacle was devoted to writing books expounding his theories of medicine, magic, and alchemy. Oporinus, his secretary at the time, commented: "He could not be found sober an hour or two together, in particular after his departure from Basel. Nevertheless, when he was most drunk and came home to dictate to me, he was so consistent and logical that a sober man could not have improved upon his manuscripts" (quoted in Pachter 1951, p. 155). His books went on to win a popularity he himself never managed. In 1540, his health failing, he settled in Salzburg, Austria, where he died of a stroke a year later while drinking at an inn.

Paracelsus was responsible for a massive reorientation of alchemy, one that has continued to the present. To him, the central purpose of alchemy was the creation of herbal and chemical medicines to cure disease. He became the founder of modern spagyrics, and his approaches to spagyric theory and practice are still standard today; *SEE* SPAGYRICS. In alchemical theory, he introduced the concept of the Three Principles: salt, sulphur, and mercury; *SEE* MERCURY; SALT; SULPHUR. His medical system, which was largely based on alchemy, saw the human body as an alchemical laboratory in which the *archeus*, the essential vital spirit centered in the stomach, transmuted food and drink into the substance of a human body.

In magic, Paracelsus was the first writer to classify elemental spirits into the four types of salamanders (fire), undines (water), sylphs (air), and gnomes (earth)—in fact, he invented the word "gnome." *SEE* ELEMENTAL. *SEE ALSO* ALCHEMY. FURTHER READING: GRELL 1998, PACHTER 1951, PAGEL 1958, PARACELSUS 1976, PARACELSUS 1990, WOOD 2000.

Paralda. In ceremonial magic, the king of the sylphs, the air elementals. *SEE* ELEMENTAL.

Paroketh. (Hebrew PRKTh, "veil") In Cabala, the "Veil of the Sanctuary," a barrier in consciousness separating the four lowest Sephirah of the Tree of Life from Tiphareth and the Sephirah above it. The opening of the Veil symbolizes the transition from ordinary human awareness to the higher awareness of adeptship. *SEE* ADEPT; CABALA; TIPHARETH.

In the Golden Dawn tradition, the word "Paroketh" was the password of the Portal Grade, which corresponds to the opening of the Veil. *SEE* GOLDEN DAWN, HERMETIC ORDER OF THE; PHRATH.

Parsons, Jack. (Marvel Whiteside Parsons) American rocket scientist and occultist, 1914–1952. Born in Los Angeles to a couple who separated almost immediately after his birth, Parsons was raised by his mother and maternal grandparents and received a private school education, but dropped out after two years at the University of Southern California and never received a degree. A boyhood interest in pyrotechnics led him into a career in rocketry when his skill with gunpowder rockets won him a job at the Guggenheim Aeronautical Laboratory, later Jet Propulsion Laboratories (JPL). There he played a major role in creating America's first effective rocketry program and helped develop jet-assisted takeoff units for the Army Air Corps and navy.

His interest in the occult also dated back to his teen years, but was reawakened when he encountered a book by Aleister Crowley in 1939. He began attending meetings of the local Ordo Templi Orientis lodge shortly thereafter, and was initiated in the Minerval Degree in 1941. *SEE* ORDO TEMPLI ORIENTIS (OTO).

In 1942, Parsons leased a large house in a wealthy Pasadena neighborhood, and "The Parsonage" soon became a center for the local avant-garde, as well as the headquarters of the OTO lodge. Despite a succession of minor local scandals and investigations by Pasadena police looking for a "black magic cult," this arrangement continued for most of a decade.

Parsons corresponded with OTO head Aleister Crowley (1875–1947) at great length. He also struck up a friendship with the writer L. Ron Hubbard, later the founder of Scientology, and according to surviving documents the two engaged in extensive magical rituals together before quarreling and going their separate ways in 1946. Shortly after the quarrel he also resigned from the OTO due to disagreements with Crowley's autocratic style.

In his later years Parsons was in financial trouble fairly often, and lost his government security clearance twice. In 1949, after an extensive magical working, he became convinced that he was the Antichrist. He began work on two post-OTO projects, the Gnosis and the Witchcraft; both of them were magical religions based on a simplified version of Crowley's teachings.

These projects were still in the early stages of development when Parsons died in a massive explosion at his home in 1952. The official verdict was death by accident; evidence suggests that he was handling mercury fulminate, a highly unstable explosive, in his home laboratory and accidently dropped a container. Suggestions that it might have been either suicide or murder have remained unproven.

After his death, and particularly in the years since the emergence of the Sixties counterculture, Parsons became something of a folk hero in the more radical side of the occult community, and he remains a name to conjure with in the American magical scene. FURTHER READING: CARTER 1999, PARSONS 1989.

Part of Fortune. In astrology, the most important of the Arabian Parts, abstract points on an astrological chart which govern specific aspects of human life. The Part of Fortune is found by measuring the distance between the sun and the moon, and going the same distance away from the ascendant. It governs good luck and, in particular, wealth. *SEE* ARABIAN PARTS; ASTROLOGY.

In geomancy, which borrows much astrological symbolism, the Part of Fortune is found by adding up the total number of points in the twelve houses of a geomantic chart, and subtracting twelve repeatedly until a number between one and twelve is left. This number is the number of the house of the chart where the Part of Fortune is found. It is a symbol of money. SEE GEOMANCY. FURTHER READING: ZOLLER 1989.

partzufim. (Hebrew, "personifications") In Cabala, five powers or divine personalities, each of which corresponds to one or more of the Sephiroth of the Tree of Life. The partzufim play an important role in the more esoteric branches of Cabalistic theory and speculation, especially in the work of Isaac Luria and his followers. SEE LURIA, ISAAC. SEE ALSO CABALA.

Name	Translation	Sephiroth
Arikh Anpin	Greater Face	Kether
Abba	Father	Chokmah
Aima	Mother	Binah
Zauir Anpin	Lesser Face	Chesed–Yesod
Kallah	Bride	Malkuth

Pasqually, Martines de. French mystic and occultist, 1727–1774. Born in Grenoble to a Spanish father and a French mother, he was apparently of Jewish ancestry. Little is known about his childhood and upbringing, or about his occult training; even the date and place of his initiation into Freemasonry remain unknown. He first appears in historical records in 1754, when he founded a Masonic lodge in Montpellier, and traveled through much of France over the next decade, initiating students in Paris, Lyon, Bordeaux, Marseilles, Toulouse, and Avignon, and founding several more lodges.

In 1766, Pasqually went to Paris to try to obtain some formal sanction for his new version of Masonry. At that time, however, the Grand Loge de France was racked by internal crises, and finally dissolved completely in December of that year after a fight broke out at a Grand Loge session and the police prohibited further meetings. Amid the confusion, Pasqually met Jean-Baptiste Willermoz, a wealthy merchant and active Mason from Lyon, who became Pasqually's most important student.

With Willermoz' help, Pasqually organized his own order, called La Franc-Maçonnerie des Chevaliers Maçons Élus Coens de l'Univers (Freemasonry of Knight Masons, Elect Priests of the Universe), with himself as Sovereign Master. A young French nobleman, Louis-Claude de Saint-Martin, became Pasqually's secretary and soon took on a leading role in the order as well. SEE SAINT-MARTIN, LOUIS-CLAUDE DE.

In the years that followed, Pasqually communicated to his disciples a complex system of initiations and instructional materials, together with a system of ceremonial magic used by members of the higher grades. With Saint-Martin's help, the barely literate Pasqually also wrote an essay, *"Traité de la réintégration des êtres"* (*"Treatise on the reintegration of beings"*), which expounded the theory and meaning of the Élus Coens system.

Pasqually had no means of support other than his Masonic connections, and his financial difficulties and large debts became a source of embarrassment to many of his disciples. In 1772, he left France for Haiti, where his two brothers-in-law were wealthy colonists, and where he hoped to make enough money to cover his debts and enable himself to devote the rest of his life to the work of the order. He died suddenly in Port-au-Prince in 1774. According to contemporary reports, at the moment of his death, his image appeared to his wife in Bordeaux. SEE ALSO ÉLUS COENS; MARTINISM. FURTHER READING: HUBBS 1971.

pastos. (Greek, "chest, coffin") The chest in which, according to ancient Egyptian myth, the god Osiris was imprisoned and slain by his evil brother Set; SEE OSIRIS. In the Golden Dawn, the same term was used for the symbolic coffin of Christian Rosenkreutz, which was identified with that of Osiris. SEE VAULT OF CHRISTIAN ROSENKREUTZ.

pathotisme. In the teachings of Max and Alma Theon's Groupe Cosmique, a technique of inner plane working combining polarity work with astral projection. Two people are involved, one a clairvoyant or sensitive, the other a magician; the operation is said to work best in most cases when the sensitive is female and the magician male. The sensitive enters trance and makes contact with inner plane sources of wisdom, while the magician provides guidance and occult protection against hostile powers, and writes down the communications as they are received. Using this technique, the Theons received more than 10,000 pages of material, which formed the core of the Groupe Cosmique's system.

The technique of pathotisme has much in common with the sort of polarity working done by Dion Fortune and other magicians of her circle a little later; SEE FORTUNE, DION; POLARITY. The origins of the method, however, are probably to be traced to the writings of Mary Ann Atwood, who describes a similar system in her *Suggestive Inquiry into the Hermetic Mystery* (1850). While most copies of this book were burned by the author within weeks of its publication, and it was not reprinted until 1918, a few copies escaped destruction and could be found in English occult circles in the late nineteenth century. SEE ATWOOD, MARY ANN. SEE ALSO THEON, MAX. FURTHER READING: RHONE 2000.

Patrons of Husbandry (Grange, the). SEE GRANGE, THE (PATRONS OF HUSBANDRY).

Patrizi, Francesco. Croatian philosopher and occultist, 1529–1597. Born to an aristocratic family in the town of Cherso in Dalmatia, in what is now part of Croatia and was then in the Venetian Republic, Patrizi was educated at the universities of Ingolstadt and Padua, where he encountered and rebelled against the philosophy of Aristotle. A chance encounter with a Franciscan friar brought him into contact with the writings of the great Italian Platonist Marsilio Ficino; SEE FICINO, MARSILIO. This sparked in Patrizi a lifelong passion for Platonic and Hermetic philosophy. SEE HERMETICISM; PLATONISM.

After leaving Padua in 1562, Patrizi worked for a time as the manager of an estate on Cyprus, involved himself in a series of unsuccessful business ventures, and traveled to Spain in 1575, where he sold a collection of rare Greek manuscripts to the Spanish king Philip II. In 1577 he finally found a haven at the court of Ferrara, one of the leading Italian city-states of the time, where he taught Platonic philosophy, translated several important Greek Platonist works into Latin, and composed a massive work of his own, modestly titled *Nova de Universis Philosophia* (*New Philosophy of Everything*), in which he proposed that Aristotle's philosophy and the writings of Thomas Aquinas should be set aside by the Catholic Church, to be replaced by the writings of Plato and the *Corpus Hermeticum.*

In 1592 Patrizi's project seemed to loom tantalizingly within reach, as he was appointed by Pope Clement VIII to the newly created chair of Platonist philosophy at the papal university in Rome. Once there, however, he found himself embroiled in the complicated politics of the papal Curia, and his "new philosophy of everything" ended up being formally condemned as heretical. Patrizi's friends in the Curia saw to it that he was permitted to keep teaching, but his career as a philosopher was effectively over, and he died a few years later in Rome. With his death, and the rise of the hardline Counter-Reformation movement within Catholicism, the Christian Hermeticism of the Renaissance was effectively at an end. FURTHER READING: BRICKMAN 1941, LEIJENHORST 1998.

Peh. (Hebrew PH, "mouth") The twenty-seventh letter of the Hebrew alphabet, one of the seven double letters, Peh represents the sounds *p* and *ph*. Its numerical value is 80, and it has a final value of 800. Its standard correspondences are as follows:

> *Path of the Tree of Life:* Path 27, Netzach to Hod.
> *Astrological Correspondence:* Mars.
> *Tarot Correspondence:* Trump XVI, the Tower.
> *Part of the Cube of Space:* The north face.
> *Colors:* in Atziluth—scarlet.
> 　　in Briah—red.
> 　　in Yetzirah—Venetian red.
> 　　in Assiah—bright red, rayed with azure
> 　　　and emerald.

Its corresponding text from the *Thirty-two Paths of Wisdom* runs as follows: "The Twenty-seventh Path is the Exciting Intelligence, and it is so called because through it every existent being receives its spirit and motion." SEE ALSO HEBREW ALPHABET.

Hebrew letter Peh, left,
and its final form, right

Peladan, Joséphin. French novelist, art critic, and occult theorist, 1859–1918. Born in Lyon, the perennial hotbed of French occult movements, Peladan came from a family background that combined intense Catholicism and wide-ranging if eccentric scholarship. To this he added a fascination with the quasi-Catholic occult teachings of Eliphas Lévi. After studying at Jesuit colleges in Avignon and Nîmes, failing his baccalaureate exams, and moving to Paris, he began a literary career.

Before his twenty-fifth birthday Peladan had already made his reputation by way of scathing critiques of the officially approved Academic painters and their rivals, the Impressionists. His reviews argued for a return to the ideals and standards of the Italian Renaissance, defended the Symbolist painters of the time and demanded a renewal of mystical, idealist, and spiritually motivated art. He soon became a significant figure in avant-garde circles, giving himself the title Sâr (Chaldean for "prince") and affecting ornate robes.

The Sâr's first novel, *Le Vice Suprême* (*The Supreme Vice*), was published in 1884 and became an instant bestseller, running through more than twenty printings before the end of the century. Its main characters, the sexually rapacious Princess Léonora d'Este and the androgynous, celibate Magus Mérodack, and its use of Cabalistic and magical symbolism caught the interest of audiences already fascinated by writers of the Decadent school. It also set in motion one of the most significant magical careers of the period—that of Stanislaus de Guaita, who wrote to Peladan in 1884: "It is your *Vice Suprême* that revealed to me . . . that the Kabbala and high magic could be something other than a trick." *SEE* GUAITA, STANISLAUS DE.

By 1886, Peladan and Guaita had both become part of the circle of young men interested in magic who gathered at Edmond Bailly's bookshop La Librairie de l'Art Indépendant. In May 1888, they became founding members of a magical order, Le Rose+Croix Kabbalistique (The Cabalistic Rose Cross), with seats on the governing Council of Twelve. In July of the same year, on a visit to Bayreuth to watch Wagner's *Parsifal*, Peladan was struck by sudden inspiration, and saw a way to combine his interest in the occult with his commitment to art. The result of this inspiration was the Salons de la Rose+Croix, exhibitions of symbolist art held annually from 1892 to 1897.

The first salon was a major success, but the revolution Peladan hoped to carry out did not happen. The Sâr was a difficult, dogmatic personality with a talent for making enemies, and he managed to alienate most of his supporters within a short time. He split with the Rose+Croix Kabbalistique over issues of theology in 1890, and founded his own order, the Rose+Croix Catholique—later titled l'Ordre de la Rose+Croix, du Temple et du Graal (the Order of the Rose+Cross, the Temple and the Grail)—which attracted few members. He quarreled with the patron who provided most of the funding for the first salon, the Comte de la Rochefoucauld, while the salon was in progress; later salons could not muster the resources that made the first a dazzling cultural event. More devastating to the Sâr's hopes, the favorable public reaction to the salons failed to make an enduring impact on the artistic currents of the time. The academic and Impressionist schools continued to flourish, and Peladan's school simply became one more relatively minor movement in the busy artistic scene.

After the sixth salon in 1897, Peladan called a halt to his crusade. His magical order, never much more than a forum for his own ideas, quietly faded away. He continued to write novels, plays, and critical articles, but was all but forgotten at the time of his death. *SEE ALSO* SALONS DE LA ROSE+CROIX. FURTHER READING: PINCUS-WITTEN 1976.

pelican. In medieval legend, the pelican nourished its young by wounding itself in the chest and allowing them to drink its blood. Originally a feature of Christian bestiaries, this detail of legend was adopted by a variety of mystics and alchemists during the Middle Ages and Renaissance as a symbol of self-sacrifice and self-transformation. The Rosicrucian movement of the seventeenth century and after made particularly heavy use of the pelican as an emblem, often pairing it with the eagle or the phoenix; *SEE* ROSICRUCIANS. The eagle and pelican are still paired in the traditional jewel of the eighteenth degree of Scottish Rite Masonry, the Rose-Croix of Heredom; *SEE* FREEMASONRY.

The term *pelican* was also used for a piece of alchemical glassware, which had a tube leaving its top and re-entering further down its side. This was used for the process of continuous distillation, a staple technique of medieval and Renaissance alchemy. The resemblance of the tube to the pelican gashing its own chest with its beak seems to have been the origin of the name. *SEE* ALCHEMY.

Pelley, William Dudley. American journalist, fascist, and occultist, 1890–1965. Born in Lynn, Massachusetts, the only son of a Methodist minister, Pelley was unable to finish school due to his family's poverty and worked at factory jobs in his teen years. Reading formed his only recreation, and this gave him a sufficient command of English to earn him a job as junior reporter with a local newspaper at the age of eighteen. His articles were well received, and in less than a decade he was writing for large national weekly magazines such as *Colliers'* and *Red Book*. He married in 1911, and seemed to be on his way to a conventional journalistic career.

In 1918 he was sent to Russia by the *Saturday Evening Post* to cover the Russian Revolution. His experiences there left him with a hatred of communism and a conviction that a sinister conspiracy of Jews was somehow behind it all. By the time he returned to America in 1920, he had become deeply committed to fascist political ideas. His wife divorced him in 1921, and he moved to California, where he found a successful niche as a novelist and Hollywood screenwriter.

In 1925, while staying in a cabin in the mountains, he had a mystical experience in which he felt himself called to lead a vast spiritual-political movement. His account of his experience, published in 1928 in *American Magazine* as "My Seven Minutes in Eternity," was enormously popular and brought him thousands of letters. In the aftermath of his experience, he found himself receiving spiritual teachings communicated by a disembodied voice; these ultimately totaled over one and a half million words of occult philosophy.

The teachings he received by these means, and communicated through a series of books and periodicals, were an idiosyncratic mix of Christianity, New Thought, and fascist ideology. *SEE* CHRISTIAN OCCULTISM; NEW THOUGHT. He drew extensively on prophecies of world history deduced from the Great Pyramid; convinced that the Second Coming of Christ would occur in 2001, he believed that his followers needed to stockpile arms and food in order to

take part in the final battle against the powers of evil—whom he identified, predictably, with the Jews.

In 1930 he moved to Asheville, North Carolina, where he established a publishing firm and began organizing weekly study groups for his teachings. In 1931 he brought these together into an organization called the League of the Liberators. In 1933, one day after Adolf Hitler became chancellor of Germany, Pelley founded a paramilitary organization, the Silver Shirts or SS, with which he hoped to follow the Nazi example. *SEE* HITLER, ADOLF; NATIONAL SOCIALISM.

The Silver Shirts organization attracted, at its peak, some 100,000 members, but Pelley's efforts to use it as a springboard to a fascist America were undercut by the approach of the Second World War and rising anti-Nazi sentiment in America. In the 1940 election he ran for president, but received a negligible share of the vote. In 1942, after printing pro-German statements in his paper *Roll Call*, Pelley was arrested by federal agents, tried for sedition, and jailed. In his absence the Silver Shirts collapsed. He was paroled in 1952 on condition that he stay out of politics, and shortly thereafter founded a new organization called Soulcraft. He continued to write and teach until a short time before his death in 1965.

Although Pelley was a forgotten figure by the final decades of the twentieth century, his legacy looms surprisingly large. Several of the most important current figures in the extremist right, including Aryan Nations founder Richard Girnt Butler, began their political careers in the Silver Shirts and retained a large amount of Pelley's teachings in their own ideologies. Much of the modern Christian Identity movement, in fact, can trace its origins to Pelley's ideas. *SEE* CHRISTIAN IDENTITY. FURTHER READING: BARKUN 1994, LOBB 1999.

Pennsylvania Dutch magic. Traditions of occultism preserved by German-American communities in rural Pennsylvania; the phrase "Pennsylvania Dutch" is a garbling of "Pennsylvania Deutsch"—that is, Pennsylvania German. Unlike many immigrant communities in North America, the Pennsylvania Dutch have preserved a surprising amount of their traditional magical lore. Like folk magic traditions from around the world, this lore includes both natural and ceremonial magic, and concentrates primarily on healing and other practical tasks.

The Pennsylvania Dutch communities, with their close ties to Germany, served as a major channel by which European magical texts made their way from central Europe across the Atlantic. Probably the most famous grimoire to end up in Pennsylvania Dutch hands this way is the *Sixth and Seventh Books of Moses*, a manual of Christian Cabalistic magic, which was originally written in Germany sometime in the eighteenth century, and entered into circulation among the Pennsylvania Dutch by the time of the American Revolution. In English translation, it went on to become the most famous of magical textbooks in Pennsylvania Dutch magic as well as in hoodoo. *SEE* SIXTH AND SEVENTH BOOKS OF MOSES.

Hex signs, a set of traditional emblems put up on barns and houses to drive away hostile magic and bring good luck, are among the most widely known elements of Pennsylvania Dutch magic.

The terms *braucherei* (literally, "using") and *hexerei* ("hexing") are commonly used in Pennsylvania Dutch communities for their traditional magical practices.

Some attempts have been made to incorporate Pennsylvania Dutch magic into one branch or another of the current Neopagan revival, but such projects have met with little interest in the Pagan community. *SEE* NEOPAGANISM. *SEE ALSO* CUNNING MAN/WOMAN. FURTHER READING: RAVENWOLF 1996, THORSSON 1998.

pentacle. One of the four standard working tools or magical weapons of the ceremonial magician, representing the element of earth. The term "pantacle" is also used for the same item. Its usual form is a disk of wax, wood, or metal bearing a pentagram or some other symbolic pattern. It is used to command, concentrate, and represent the forces of earth in ceremonial workings. *SEE* EARTH, ELEMENT OF.

The pentacle as a symbol of elemental earth

pentagram. The most important symbol in modern magical practice, the pentagram has an ancient and complex history. It has been used in many cultures as a protective symbol, credited with the power to banish evil spirits and bring good luck. It is found in Babylonian clay tablets dating from the first millennium B.C.E.

Pythagoras (c. 570–c. 495 B.C.E.), one of the first major figures in the Western occult traditions, made it an important emblem of physical and mental harmony. The Pythagorean Brotherhood is known to have used it as an identifying mark, often with one letter of the Greek word ΥΓΕΙΑ, "health," written in each of the five points. A signet ring bearing the pentagram was apparently worn by members of the brotherhood. *SEE* PYTHAGORAS.

By the early Middle Ages the pentagram had been incorporated into the standard range of Christian symbolism, associated with the five books of Moses, the five stones used by David against Goliath, and so on. It was often used as a protection against elves, hostile spirits, and the evil eye. The anonymous author of *Sir Gawain and the Green Knight* made a gold pentagram on red the coat of arms of Sir Gawain. The poem relates the five points to the five wounds of Christ, the five joys of the Virgin Mary, the keenness of Gawain's five senses, the strength of his five fingers, and the five knightly virtues of liberality, loving-kindness, continence, courtesy, and piety. *SEE* CHRISTIAN OCCULTISM.

In the Renaissance and early modern periods, the Pythagorean symbolism of the pentagram was rediscovered, and the pentagram itself became a common symbol for the medical profession. Magical writings of the same period gave it new importance as the Shield of Solomon, and Renaissance magi such as Paracelsus identified it as the "Seal of the Microcosm," paired with the hexagram or Seal of Solomon as the "Seal of the Macrocosm." In the early eighteenth century, it was adopted by Freemasonry and, as the "blazing star," appears on the eastern wall of Masonic lodges around the world. *SEE* FREEMASONRY.

The pentagram rose to a higher status among magical symbols in the nineteenth century, when Eliphas Lévi and other leading lights of the magical renaissance adopted it. Lévi redefined it as the emblem of the supremacy of spirit over the four elements, and made much of its power to command spirits. *SEE* LÉVI, ELIPHAS. It was nonetheless after his time, in the shadowy realm of magical lodges and traditions that led up to the Golden Dawn, that the pentagram was developed into a major ritual tool; SEE PENTAGRAM, RITUALS OF THE. The publicity given to it by the Golden Dawn and its successor orders, along with Lévi's writings, made the pentagram the most famous magical symbol of the twentieth century, and Wicca and other twentieth-century Neopagan movements readily adopted it. There seems to be no evidence, though, that it was a Pagan symbol before the creation of Wicca in the late 1940s.

In modern magical tradition, the meaning and use of the pentagram varies depending on whether it has one point or two points upwards. The most common interpretation is that the pentagram with one point upwards represents the power of spirit over the realm of the material elements, and is used to invoke angels and good spirits. The inverted pentagram with two points upwards, by contrast, is held to represent the domination of spirit by matter, and is used to call forth the powers of evil. Many magical traditions insist that the inverted pentagram should never be used at all. There are alternative ways of interpreting upright and inverted pentagrams, however.

The different points of the pentagram are associated with the five elements. The most common scheme is that introduced by the Golden Dawn, as shown below.

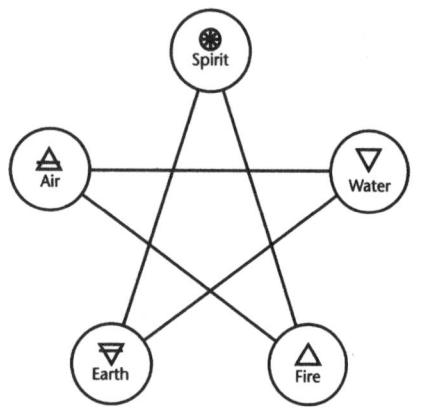

The assignment of elements to the points of the pentagram

The magical powers of the pentagram have been linked to its remarkable geometrical properties, which are derived from those of the Golden Proportion. All the proportions and relationships between lines and line segments in a properly drawn pentagram are either equal to the Golden Proportion or closely derived from it. SEE GOLDEN PROPORTION.

The pentagram is also a common emblem in many contexts that have nothing at all to do with magic. Most of the "stars" in the world's flags, including that of the United States, are pentagrams. The pentagram also appears in the corporate logo of Texaco Oil. An inverted pentagram marked with mysterious symbols and the sinister-looking word FATAL is the emblem of the Order of the Eastern Star, an American Masonic auxiliary; despite this emblem's suggestive appearance, its meaning is depressingly innocuous. SEE EASTERN STAR, ORDER OF THE. SEE ALSO HEXAGRAM. FURTHER READING: SCHOUTEN 1968.

The pentagram

Pentagram, Rituals of the. In the Hermetic Order of the Golden Dawn, and most subsequent magical traditions in the English-speaking world, a set of rituals using the symbolism of the pentagram to invoke or banish elemental energies. The basic format of all the pentagram rituals begins with the Cabalistic Cross, a short ritual based on the conventional Christian sign of the cross; SEE CABALISTIC CROSS.

The magician then goes to the eastern quarter of the ritual space and traces a pentagram in the air with a magical weapon or with his or her hand, then traces a quarter circle in the air, at shoulder or chest height, around to the southern quarter. Another pentagram is traced in the south, and another quarter of the circle traced from south to west. The process continues until the magician has traced a complete circle around himself or herself, marked with pentagrams at the four quarters.

The magician then goes to the center, faces east, and says the following words:

Before me, Raphael;

Behind me, Gabriel;

To my right hand, Michael;

To my left hand, Auriel;

For about me flame the pentagrams,

And upon me shines the six-rayed star.

(There are at least two variants of the last line—*And above me shines the six-rayed star* and *And in the column stands the six-rayed star.* Which of these is the original version is impossible to say from the existing evidence.)

The magician then repeats the Cabalistic Cross, completing the ritual.

The effect of the ritual is completely dependent on the exact pentagrams that are used in the four quarters. Depending on the point at which one starts tracing and the direction traced, the pentagram can invoke or banish the energies of earth, water, air, fire, active spirit, and passive spirit. In the most advanced forms of pentagram ritual, one of the spirit pentagrams and one of the elemental pentagrams are traced in each quarter, and accompanied by gestures symbolizing the Adeptus Minor grade and the corresponding elemental grades respectively. SEE ALSO HEXAGRAM, RITUALS OF THE; PENTAGRAM. FURTHER READING: GREER 1997, REGARDIE 1971.

Pentagrammaton. In Christian Cabala and a variety of related traditions, the name of Jesus spelled with five Hebrew letters, either יהשוה, YHShVH (pronounced Yeheshua) or יהושה, YHVShH (pronounced Yehovashah). This is understood as the descent of the letter ש, Shin, representing Spirit, into the Tetragrammaton יהוה, YHVH, representing the realm of the four elements; it also represents the transformation of the angry and jealous God of the Old Testament into the God of love preached by Jesus of Nazareth, a transformation seen by Christian Cabalists as a result of the incarnation of God in Christ. SEE CHRISTIAN OCCULTISM.

The Pentagrammaton and its symbolism were worked out by early Christian Cabalists, and played an important part in the magical Christianity proposed by the Italian Cabalist and Hermeticist Giovanni Pico della Mirandola (1463–1494); SEE PICO DELLA MIRANDOLA, GIOVANNI. It was also an important feature of Rosicrucian mysticism and was inherited by the Hermetic Order of the Golden Dawn, which used it in a number of its rituals. It has since been used by a wide range of magical traditions, often without any recognition of its Christian origins. SEE GOLDEN DAWN, HERMETIC ORDER OF THE; ROSICRUCIANS. SEE ALSO TETRAGRAMMATON.

Peorth. SEE PERTH.

Perth. (Old Germanic, meaning uncertain) The fourteenth rune of the elder futhark, this rune has been at the center of a great deal of confusion and controversy, both in scholarly circles and in the runic revival. Unlike the other rune names, which can readily be translated, the word *perth* does not seem to have survived into later Germanic languages and has no certain Indo-European cognates; thus, nobody knows for sure exactly what it means. The rune did not make it into the younger futhark, which has the largest surviving body of runic lore connected with it, and the Old English rune-poem (which includes it under the name Peorth) mentions only that whatever it is, it brings joy and laughter to warriors sitting in the beerhall.

Suggestions have ranged all over the map. One of the most plausible is that it was a piece from a board game; we know that a variety of board games were played all over barbarian Europe until chess, which arrived from the Middle East, pushed nearly all of them to oblivion. "Beer" is an obvious suggestion, but is linguistically impossible. Another ingenious suggestion comes from modern runemaster Freya Aswynn, who suggests "Birth" as a translation, and claims that the Anglo-Saxon rune-poem was revised by Christian scribes, and originally referred not to warriors in the beerhall but to mothers in the birthing room. Unfortunately, the evidence of linguistics is against this clever suggestion as well.

Perhaps the most practical approach is the one taken by many modern rune diviners, who simply use Perth as a symbol of the unknown and mysterious. While this is certainly not what it meant in Pagan times, it seems to work well in practice. SEE ALSO ANGLO-SAXON FUTHORC; ELDER FUTHARK. FURTHER READING: ASWYNN 1998.

Rune Perth

Pertho. *SEE* PERTH.

Phagos. (Old Irish, "beech tree") The last of the five *forfedha* or additional letters in the Ogham alphabet, used to represent the vowel combination *ae* or the consonants *k* and *x*; also known as Mór, "Sea." It corresponds to the beech among trees, but lacks the extended symbolism of the twenty regular Ogham letters. *SEE* OGHAM.

The name Phagos is also sometimes used for the fourth of the forfedha, Iphin. *SEE* IPHIN.

Ogham letter Phagos

Phaleg. One of the seven Olympian spirits, Phaleg is associated with the planet Mars and rules 35 of the 196 provinces of Heaven. The period of history ruled by Phaleg extended from 430 to 920 C.E. *SEE* OLYMPIAN SPIRITS.

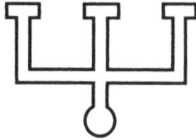

Olympian spirit Phaleg

phallic religion. A fixation (and in large part an invention) of eighteenth- and nineteenth-century European scholars, phallic religion was the worship of the powers of fertility in the form of the penis. Hinduism, with its use of the *lingam* or phallic stone as an emblem of the god Shiva, provided a basis for an extensive and often pornographic literature, published in small private editions, in which scholars traced penis-worship across the globe and throughout time. Writings concerning phallic religion played an important role in the evolution of the Romantic image of the witch, and thus in the prehistory of modern Wicca and Neopaganism. *SEE* NEOPAGANISM. FURTHER READING: J. GODWIN 1994.

Pheryllt. According to some modern Druid groups, a secret order of ancient Druid alchemists once located on and around Mt. Snowdon in northern Wales. Evidence

for their historical existence seems to be entirely absent, and the best evidence suggests that these "Druid alchemists" are the product of simple mistranslation.

The word *Pheryllt* (modern Welsh *fferyllydd*) started out as a medieval Welsh garbling of the name *Vergil* (which is unpronounceable in Welsh), and has its roots in the medieval idea that the Roman poet Vergil, author of the *Aeneid* and other works, had been a master magician; *SEE* VERGIL. The name gradually became a common term for one who made potions, and in modern times is the standard Welsh term for a chemist or pharmacist. It seems likely that recent occultists with a poor grasp of medieval Welsh, finding references to the "books of Vergil" in old Welsh sources, read "Pheryllt" in its modern sense and set the myth of the ancient Druid-alchemists in motion.

During the eighteenth, nineteenth, and early twentieth centuries, however, Druidic organizations mixed thoroughly with other branches of the occult community in Britain and France, and the idea of the Pheryllt led some Druid orders to adopt a great deal of alchemical lore into their teachings and symbolism. As a result, whether or not there were Druid alchemists in ancient times, they unquestionably exist at present. *SEE ALSO* ALCHEMY; DRUIDS.

Philosopher's Stone. The great goal of alchemical practice, the Philosopher's Stone or *medicina metallorum* ("medicine of metals") is a substance with the power to transmute base metals into pure gold. According to alchemical writings, it also has the power to cure all human diseases, to turn ordinary stones into gemstones, and to make glass flexible. It is described in Renaissance and early modern accounts as a fine but very heavy powder the color of rubies. The exact composition of the Philosopher's Stone is the supreme secret of practical alchemy.

Properly speaking, the Philosopher's Stone or Red Stone is only one, if the most important, of several different stones that are discussed in alchemical writings. The White Stone is an earlier result of the same process that produces the Red Stone, and has the power to turn base metals to pure silver. In spagyric or herbal alchemy, the vegetable stone is much discussed; it is a fixed substance that contains the highest possible level of healing virtue from the original plant. According to some writers, it also separates an herbal tincture into its three principles (the sulphur, salt, and mercury of the plant) without the difficult operations usually needed for the purpose. *SEE* SPAGYRICS. *SEE ALSO* ALCHEMY; FLAMEL, NICHOLAS; VEGETABLE STONE.

philtre. An obsolete word for "potion," used in some modern occult groups. *SEE* NATURAL MAGIC.

Phorlakh. In ceremonial magic, the angel of the element of earth; also spelled Furlac. *SEE* ANGEL.

Phrath. (Hebrew PRTh) According to Genesis 2:14, the last of the four rivers that flow out of Paradise, identified with the actual river Euphrates. In the Golden Dawn tradition, Phrath is associated with the element of earth, and the section of the Middle Pillar from Yesod to Tiphareth. The word Phrath is also given as a password to the Philosophus, and serves as the foundation of the word Paroketh, the password of the Portal Grade. *SEE* CABALA; GOLDEN DAWN, HERMETIC ORDER OF THE; PAROKETH.

Phul. One of the seven Olympian spirits, Phul is associated with the moon and rules over seven of the 196 provinces of Heaven. The period of history governed by Phul was from 1040 to 550 B.C.E., and she will rule again from 2390 to 2880 C.E. *SEE* OLYMPIAN SPIRITS.

Olympian spirit Phul

phylactery. An amulet or talisman worn on the body, usually for magical protection. The term is often used to translate Hebrew *tefillin*, the little cases containing scriptural verses worn by orthodox Jews, but phylacteries can take a wide range of forms, from strips of writing material bound about a head or limb to jewels, stones, or other objects worn on a cord or band. *SEE ALSO* AMULET; TALISMAN.

physical culture. A nineteenth- and twentieth-century movement in Europe and North America devoted to physical health through exercise, diet, and a more natural lifestyle. Although the physical culture movement was not, strictly speaking, part of the Western occult traditions, many occultists of the same period were also involved with physical culture, and occult teachings and physical culture systems borrowed heavily from one another in many cases.

The physical culture movement rose as a response to the dismal state of health common in the early nineteenth century. The sweeping social and cultural changes of the two previous centuries had shifted much of the population from the countryside to sprawling, polluted cities, depriving them of fresh air and natural foods while consigning them to repetitive industrial labor, to equally repetitive housework, or to sedentary lifestyles. The standard diet in most of the Western world consisted almost entirely of meat, fat, and starch. Clothing styles, especially for women, were so constricting that they actually deformed the body. Some measure of the problem can be taken from the fact that constipation was considered America's most severe health crisis in the nineteenth and early twentieth centuries.

Dominant trends in theology and culture devalued the body and physical activity in favor of the "purer" life of the mind. The Romantic movement of the late eighteenth century, however, rejected this and brought a new attention to the life of the body. By the 1820s, new systems of exercise—the Jahn exercises from Germany, and Per Henrik Ling's gymnastics from Sweden—were attracting students from all over the Western world. A Swiss army officer, Phokion Heinrich Clias, became one of the first professional exercise teachers in 1822, establishing a thriving school in London, which taught both men and women. By the 1830s books and articles on different systems of exercise were becoming common.

By the second half of the nineteenth century, as a result, teachers of physical culture could be found in most cities in the Western world, and books and correspondence courses on the subject were readily available. They made up part of a broad range of self-improvement literature and educational resources, which also drew on many elements of the occult traditions of the time. Many writers and teachers in the physical culture movement included instructions on breathing, visualization, the training of the will, and similar subjects that were identical to those being offered by occult orders at the same time.

One major figure linking physical culture and occultism was Genevieve Stebbins, the most famous American teacher of the Delsarte system of exercise and physical training. Alongside her successful career as an exercise teacher, theatrical performer, and writer, she was a member of the Hermetic Brotherhood of Luxor (H. B. of L.), one of the most important magical orders of the nineteenth century. Her books include a great deal of magical training, including breathing exercises and ways of working with subtle energy. SEE HERMETIC BROTHERHOOD OF LUXOR (H. B. OF L.); STEBBINS, GENEVIEVE.

Another figure on the same lines was William Walker Atkinson (1862–1932), one of the coauthors of *The Kybalion* and a member of the Golden Dawn, who also published works on physical culture under the pen name Yogi Ramacharaka; SEE ATKINSON, WILLIAM WALKER. The redoubtable Joseph Greenstein, who performed as a vaudeville strongman under the name "the Mighty Atom" and developed a system of physical exercise based on his study of the Cabala, is another; SEE GREENSTEIN, JOSEPH L.

The physical culture movement thrived in the first half of the twentieth century but fell on hard times in the 1950s. Postwar culture, especially in America, had little interest in the complete development of the self offered by classic physical culture systems, and the links between physical culture and occultism made many people shy away from the older movement. In its place emerged a new approach to exercise, championed by figures such as Joe Weider. This new bodybuilding aimed at a visually impressive body rather than a strong and healthy one. Natural foods and heavy weights gave way to steroids, supplements, and exercises designed to inflate the muscles with fluid for maximum bulk.

This cosmetic approach to exercise remains standard at most North American gyms. The older traditions survived, however, and went through a modest renaissance in the 1990s and 2000s, gaining new adherents and giving rise to a "backyard gym" movement devoted to the methods of the old-time strongmen. Whether any of physical culture will find its way back into use in the occult community, though, remains to be seen. FURTHER READING: RUYTER 1999, SPIELMAN 1998, STEBBINS 1893, TODD 1998.

physical plane. In magical philosophy, the universe known to modern science, consisting of physical matter and energy. This is understood as the lowest level of reality and the end product of the cosmic process of Creation. It receives form and life from the next higher plane, the etheric plane. SEE ETHERIC PLANE.

physiognomy. The art of reading and interpreting facial features, physiognomy was among the most common arts of analyzing character and foretelling destiny in the Middle Ages and Renaissance, but is almost completely forgotten today. Like palmistry, with which it has much in common, the art of physiognomy assigns each part of the face to a different aspect of personality. Thus, for example, large ears were considered to betoken a good memory, while baldness was associated with intelligence. Some systems of physiognomy considered not only the face but the rest of the body as well.

Like so much of the Western occult tradition, physiognomy reached Europe by way of the Arabs in the Middle Ages, although its original sources are less clear. It dropped out of use around the time of the Scientific Revolution, and has received very little attention in occult circles since that time. There is essentially nothing on the subject in modern English. SEE ALSO PALMISTRY.

Picatrix. An Arabic handbook of Hermetic magic, originally titled *Ghayat el-Hakim* or "The Goal of the Wise" and (falsely) attributed to the Arab philosopher al-Majriti. Translated into Spanish in 1256, it found its way into Latin shortly thereafter, and under the title *Picatrix* went on to become one of the most influential magical handbooks in the medieval and Renaissance periods.

Much of the text deals with the proper construction of talismans to draw down the power of the stars and planets for various practical purposes. It also contains passages defending magic against the criticisms leveled against it and presenting it as a valid, important, and even holy art. These passages, some of them derived from

Hermetic literature, played an important role in inspiring the magical revival of the Renaissance. *SEE ALSO* GRI-MOIRE. FURTHER READING: YATES 1964.

Pickingill, George. English folk magician, 1816– 1909. A farm worker who spent most of his life in the village of Canewdon in Essex, Pickingill had a substantial reputation as a "cunning man" and was the subject of many stories, both in his lifetime and afterwards. Canewdon itself was a traditional haunt of witches, a reputation Pickingill appears to have exploited to the full. He was apparently feared by nearly everyone in the region. During the harvest, according to old accounts, he would go out into the fields and threaten to bewitch the threshing machinery; farmers bribed him with beer to go away, and he is said to have ended every day dead drunk.

It has been claimed in Wiccan publications that Pickingill was a hereditary Wiccan High Priest with a lineage going back to 1071. He is said to have founded nine covens, of which one was the New Forest coven that allegedly initiated Gerald Gardner in 1939. The same sources name him as the teacher of the phallic-religion theorist Hargrave Jennings and the coauthor, with Jennings, of the famous Cipher manuscript used to found the Hermetic Order of the Golden Dawn. Pickingill is also supposed to have initiated Allan Bennett and Aleister Crowley into the Craft. None of these claims have any basis in historical evidence, the claim that Hargrave Jennings wrote the Cipher manuscript is provably incorrect, and the entire account looks suspiciously like the sort of retroactive recruitment that has been a staple of occult history for centuries. *SEE* CIPHER MANUSCRIPT; CROW-LEY, ALEISTER; CUNNING MAN/WOMAN; OCCULT HISTORY. *SEE ALSO* WICCA. FURTHER READING: MAPLE 1970, VA-LIENTE 1987.

Pico della Mirandola, Giovanni. Italian philosopher and magician, 1463–1494. Born into a noble family, Pico began the study of canon law at Bologna in his early teens but found philosophy more to his taste, and traveled widely through Italy and France, attending lectures at numerous universities. In 1484, he moved to Florence, where he met Marsilio Ficino and became part of the Platonic Academy founded by Ficino under the patronage of the Medicis. Despite his youth, Pico quickly be-

came one of the Academy's leading lights, and absorbed the heady mix of Hermetic occultism and Platonic mystical philosophy for which Ficino was already becoming famous. *SEE* FICINO, MARSILIO; HERMETICISM.

Pico's occult studies were not limited to these, however. Fluent in Hebrew, he was a close friend of several noted Jewish scholars, including Elia del Medigo and Flavius Mithridates. His writings show that he was thoroughly familiar with the elements of Cabalistic thought and practice, and had some knowledge of the Zohar and the mystical letter combinations of Abraham Abulafia. Pico seems to have been the first to make the Cabala part of the developing Renaissance magical synthesis, and thus stands at the fountainhead of much of the later Western magical tradition. *SEE* CABALA.

In the year 1486, full of enthusiasm, Pico went to Rome equipped with nine hundred theses or "conclusions" that he offered to defend in public debate. Taken together, his theses formed a manifesto of Christian occultism. He defended natural and angelic magic, arguing that "no science more effectively proves the divinity of Christ than magic and Cabala" (quoted in Yates 1964, p. 105). As might be expected, this and similar statements brought down a firestorm of theological criticism on his head.

The great public debate never happened, and Pico was forced to publish a defense of his orthodoxy the next year. This did not quiet the controversy, and Pope Innocent VIII appointed a commission of theologians to look into the matter. In 1487, several of Pico's theses were proclaimed heretical; Pico himself was forced to make a formal submission and retraction, and a papal bull was issued condemning all nine hundred theses and forbidding their publication. Pico was imprisoned for a time, though Lorenzo de Medici managed to win his release. He remained in Florence, where he wrote the *Heptaplus*, a Cabalistic meditation on the seven days of Creation.

In 1493, Pico's position was sharply improved when a new pope, Alexander VI, reversed the findings of the commission and absolved both him and his works from any suspicion of heresy. He wrote a final book, *Disputations against Divinatory Astrology*, in which he condemned the use of astrology to foretell the future but defended Ficino's astrological natural magic. He died after a sudden illness in 1494. FURTHER READING: FARMER 1998, YATES 1964, YATES 1979.

Pietro di Abano. Italian physician, scholar, astrologer, and magician, 1250–1316. Born in the small town of Abano near Padua, he was the son of Constantio di Abano, a notary. The details of his upbringing and schooling are not clear, but he spent some years studying at the University of Paris, where he won a stellar reputation as a scholar, but also ran into trouble with the Inquisition over his interest in astrology.

He is known to have traveled to Constantinople, where he found manuscripts of Aristotle and Dioscorides unknown in the West, and is said to have traveled to Spain, England, and Scotland as well. By 1307 he was teaching at the University of Padua, where he spent the rest of his life.

His many books included important translations and original works on astrology, astrological medicine, and physiognomy—the art of divining character by facial features. *SEE* ASTROLOGY; PHYSIOGNOMY. Like most physicians of his time, he held that astrology was an essential part of medicine, and he also wrote at length on natural magic, discussing the ways that natural substances could draw down occult influences from the stars and planets. *SEE* NATURAL MAGIC. He has also been credited with a book on geomancy and several important textbooks of magic, although many scholars consider these to be forgeries.

Pietro di Abano lived during one of the most fateful transitions in the history of magic in the West. He grew up in an age when astrology, natural magic, and many other branches of occultism could be practiced freely. By the time of his death, all these subjects were increasingly controversial; not long afterwards, in 1327, the burning of Cecco di Ascoli marked the beginning of the Inquisition's war on magic. Later in the fourteenth century Pietro's body was removed from its coffin and publicly burned. *SEE* MAGIC, PERSECUTION OF. FURTHER READING: GREER 1999, THORNDYKE 1923.

Pike, Albert. American soldier, author, Freemason, and occultist, 1809–1891. Born in Massachusetts, the son of an alcoholic cobbler, he showed promise as a scholar

from his childhood, learning Hebrew, Latin, and Greek in his teen years. He easily passed his entrance exams at Harvard but was unable to afford tuition, and in 1831 left Massachusetts for the frontier. Winding up in Fort Smith, Arkansas, he taught school for a time, edited a newspaper, and became a lawyer. In 1834 he married Ann Hamilton, and her money enabled him to go into politics. In 1846, during the Texas war of independence, he led a band of volunteers against the Mexican army at the battle of Buena Vista. He also found friends among the local Native American tribes and represented them in court against the federal government.

Pike became a Freemason during his time in Arkansas, and joined the Scottish Rite—at that time one of the smallest Masonic bodies, with fewer than a thousand members in the United States—in 1853. His scholarship and classical background led the Supreme Council of the Rite's Southern Jurisdiction to appoint him to a five-man committee charged with revising the rituals. The committee never met, but Pike took on the task himself, studying most of what was then known about the Western world's occult heritage in the process. His massive revision was complete in draft by 1859. That same year, with the resignation of Supreme Commander Albert Mackey, Pike became the head of the Southern Jurisdiction of the Scottish Rite.

When the Civil War began in 1861, he sided with the Confederacy and was appointed commissioner of Indian affairs by Jefferson Davis. Placed in command of Native units, with the rank of brigadier general, he found himself caught between loyalties when his Confederate superiors gave him orders he felt violated the treaty rights of his Native soldiers. In July of 1862 he resigned his command and published an open letter to the tribes accusing the Confederate government of ignoring its treaty obligations. In response, he was arrested and jailed, then released as the Confederacy's western defenses collapsed in the late fall of 1862.

Out of money, in constant danger from the soldiers of both sides, and with his marriage in ruins, Pike fled to a cabin in the Ozark hills with his books and remained there until 1868, intensively studying the Cabala, the Hindu and Zoroastrian scriptures, and what was known about the Gnostics. In the process, he revised the Scottish

Rite rituals further, expanding them to include large portions of occult tradition.

In 1868 Pike left Arkansas for Washington, D.C., where he spent the rest of his life, living in a simple room paid for by the Supreme Council and devoting nearly all his time to the Scottish Rite, to other fraternal involvements, and to esoteric scholarship. He died in 1891. *SEE ALSO* FREEMASONRY. FURTHER READING: CARNES 1989, DUNCAN 1961, PIKE 1871.

pilebogar. In some English folk traditions of magic, a staff with a forked upper end into which a crystal or a hen's egg painted red is inserted. Pilebogars are used to dispell disruptive magical energies. *SEE ALSO* CUNNING MAN/WOMAN. FURTHER READING: PENNICK 1989.

Pisces. (Latin, "fishes") The twelfth and last sign of the zodiac, a mutable water element of feminine polarity. In Pisces, Jupiter has the rulership (or in some modern versions, Neptune); Venus is exalted, and Mercury is in both detriment and fall. Pisces rules the feet. *SEE* ZODIAC.

The sun is in Pisces approximately from February 19 to March 20. People with this sun placement are traditionally intuitive, imaginative, idealistic, and kind; they can also be weak and vague, on the one hand, or completely dishonest and deceptive on the other.

In the Golden Dawn tarot system, this sign corresponds to Trump XVIII, the Moon. *SEE* MOON, THE; TAROT.

Astrological symbol of Pisces

Pison. (Hebrew PIShVN) According to Genesis 2:11–12, the first of four rivers that flow out of Paradise. In the Golden Dawn tradition, Pison is associated with the element of fire and the Pillar of Severity. *SEE* CABALA.

planes. In occult jargon, different levels or dimensions of existence, of which the physical plane perceived by the five ordinary senses is one. The others can be contacted and experienced by various magical or mystical methods.

There are many different accounts of the planes of existence in Western esoteric writings and traditions. The number of planes is subject to much disagreement—different systems list anywhere from three to forty-nine planes—as are the relations between the different planes, and between the planes and different realms of human experience. Among the planes most often discussed in Western occult writings are the physical, etheric, astral, mental, and spiritual planes.

According to some magical philosophies, the universe in its totality forms a spectrum between absolute spirit and its complte manifestation in matter, and "planes" are more or less arbitrary divisions of the spectrum, just as the colors of the rainbow are more or less arbitrary divisions of the spectrum of light. This theory would account for the diversity of different systems of planes, as well as the common features that unite them. *SEE ALSO* ASTRAL PLANE; ETHERIC PLANE; MENTAL PLANE; PHYSICAL PLANE; SPIRITUAL PLANE.

planets. In astrology and magic, a term for all celestial bodies visible from Earth that move in regular orbits across the background of stars. The sun and moon are thus considered planets by astrologers and occultists, though not by modern astronomers.

Before the invention of the telescope, seven planets were known. In their traditional order, these were the moon, Mercury, Venus, the sun, Mars, Jupiter, and Saturn. When it was believed that the Earth was the center of the known universe, this was also thought to be their order of increasing distance from the Earth, with the moon closest and Saturn farthest away.

The discovery of the additional planets Uranus, Neptune, and Pluto posed a challenge to astrology, and it took decades of careful work in each case to determine the astrological influence of these previously unknown bodies. Several asteroids, such as Ceres and Pallas, and Chiron, a massive comet-like body between the orbits of Saturn and Uranus, have also been included in some recent versions of astrology, though their role remains more hotly debated. Finally, a number of probably fictional "unknown planets" including Vulcan or Hephaestus, a planet supposedly closer to the sun than Mercury, and Lilith, a never-observed "dark moon" of the Earth, have been used by a few astrologers. *SEE* ASTROLOGY *AND THE NAMES OF INDIVIDUAL PLANETS.*

Plant Bran. (Welsh, "family of Bran") British witchcraft tradition, tracing its descent and deriving most of its approach from Robert Cochrane's Clan of Tubal-Cain. Plant Bran has made an effort to avoid publicity, and as a result little accurate information seems to be available about it. It remains active as of this writing, with most covens to be found in Britain. *SEE* COCHRANE, ROBERT; CLAN OF TUBAL-CAIN.

Plato. (Aristocles of Athens) Greek philosopher, 427–347 B.C.E. The most influential philosopher in the history of the Western world, Plato was born in Athens to an aristocratic family that traced its descent to the last king of Athens; his actual name was Aristocles, but he was given the nickname Plato (Greek *platon*, "broad") because of the width of his shoulders. In his youth he was a noted athlete, competing in wrestling in the Isthmian Games at Corinth, and was educated as a poet and dramatist. At the age of twenty he encountered the philosopher Socrates, and became his chief disciple from that time until 399, when Socrates was executed by the Athenian government.

After Socrates' death, Plato went to Megara, where he studied philosophy together with his friend Euclid, who was later famous for his writings on geometry. From there he traveled around the Mediterranean world, visiting Egypt, Cyrene (in what is now Tunisia), Italy, and Sicily in search of philosophical wisdom. While in Sicily he offended the dictator of Syracuse, Dionysius, and was sold into slavery, but a friend found him in Aegina and bought his freedom. He then returned to Athens, where he founded his school, the Academy. Except for two later visits to Sicily, he remained in Athens, teaching and writing, for the rest of his life.

Plato was strongly influenced by his teacher Socrates, but also by the teachings of the Pythagorean school, and the philosophy he taught to his students at the Academy and wove into his writings was a fusion of the two. Certainly geometry and the other disciplines of the quadrivium were taught at the Academy, which had a sign over the door saying "Let no one ignorant of geometry enter here." *SEE* PYTHAGORAS; QUADRIVIUM.

References in ancient times to a set of "unwritten doctrines" passed on by lectures at the Academy suggest that the Pythagorean system came to be the theoretical core of his system, while Socrates' method of teaching by question and answer became the core method. Plato's dialogues, which have often been treated as detailed discussions of his own opinions, are literary works intended for a popular audience, and there is a great deal of scholarly debate about how much of Plato's developed philosophy they contain. *SEE* PLATONISM.

Plato's reputation has risen and fallen many times over the centuries between his time and the present, with some ages considering him the ideal philosopher and master of wisdom while others have dismissed him as a crackpot. His traditional birthday on November 8 is still celebrated by many Platonists with a feast. FURTHER READING: FINDLAY 1974, FINDLAY 1978, PLATO 1961.

Platonism. The philosophical movement founded by Plato, which lived on after him to become the single most influential philosophy in the history of the Western world. Platonism has powerfully influenced a wide range of Pagan, Jewish, Christian, Muslim, and nonreligious thinkers over more than two millennia. It also became far and away the most important philosophical basis for the Western occult traditions, and for two thousand years after Plato's time the vast majority of scholarly magic was grounded directly or indirectly on Platonist ideas about the universe.

Plato (427–347 B.C.E.), the founder of Platonist philosophy, was heavily influenced by the earlier Pythagorean school and by a range of earlier Greek philosophers. *SEE* EMPEDOCLES OF ACRAGAS; PYTHAGORAS. He saw the central problem of philosophy as the relation between the ever-changing world perceived by the senses—the realm of Becoming, in his terms—and the timeless realities of the spirit, the realm of Being. The core of his philosophy was the concept that everything perceived by the senses is a reflection or projection of some essential pattern in the realm of Being. He called these essential patterns Forms or Ideas, and taught that given the right forms of training, they could be experienced directly by the human mind.

During his lifetime, Plato founded a school, the Academy, that carried on his teachings and developed his philosophy for centuries after his death. At first centered on the Academy in Athens, Platonism gradually spread more widely, and by the beginning of the Common Era had adherents throughout the Mediterranean world. One of these, Philo of Alexandria (c. 20 B.C.E.–after 39 C.E.), launched the tradition on a trajectory that would have important consequences for the future. Philo was a Jew, a member of one of Alexandria's most prominent Jewish families, and he set himself the goal of making sense of Jewish scriptures and traditions in the light of Platonic philosophy. The result was successful enough to give rise to many later projects along the same lines, fusing Platonism not only with Judaism but also with Christianity and Islam.

The same broad diffusion of Platonist ideas that led to Philo's project also found its way into occult circles. Pythagoras and some of his successors had probably been magicians in every sense of the word, and although Plato was deeply suspicious of magical practices, his philosophy was quickly put to use by magicians as a way of making sense of their own traditions. The *Chaldean Oracles* of Julianus the Theurgist, a major magical text of the early Common Era, is deeply imbued with Platonist ideas. *SEE* CHALDEAN ORACLES; JULIANUS THE THEURGIST. Similarly, Platonism found its way into a range of spiritual traditions closely related to the occultism of the time. Both Gnosticism and Hermeticism were deeply influenced by Platonism; in fact, a section of Plato's dialogue *The Republic*, translated into Coptic, was included by one sect of ancient Gnostics in the holy books of the Nag Hammadi library. *SEE* GNOSTICISM; HERMETICISM.

In the early third century C.E. Platonism underwent a major shift with the appearance of Plotinus (c. 205–270 C.E.), who became effectively the second founder of the tradition. In his essays, collected after his death by his disciple Porphyry of Tyre as *The Enneads*, he reworked Plato's vision of the worlds of Being and Becoming into a system of four worlds. In his thought, the realm of Becoming was divided into the *hylic world* or world of matter, and the *psychic world* or world of ordinary consciousness, while the realm of Being was separated into the *noetic world*, the level of the Forms, and the *henadic world*, the level of the ultimate unity behind all things. A mystic

and a visionary, Plotinus began what modern scholars call the Neoplatonist movement, which turned Platonism more directly toward the realms of spirituality and the occult. *SEE* PLOTINUS.

By the time of Plotinus, a new force—Christianity—was beginning to make itself felt in the Roman world, and Platonism became one of the major centers of opposition to the new creed. Plotinus' student Porphyry wrote a book titled *Against the Christians*, every copy of which was destroyed after Christianity seized power in the fourth century. On a wider scale was the project of Iamblichus of Chalcis (died 330), the great fourth-century Platonist, who set out to redefine Platonism as the foundation of a unified Paganism that could resist Christian inroads. *SEE* IAMBLICHUS OF CHALCIS. Proclus (412–485), the last great Pagan Platonist of the ancient world, drew on Iamblichus' work in devising a Pagan Platonist theology that made room for every aspect of traditional Pagan practice. *SEE* PROCLUS.

Iamblichus and Proclus, like most Platonists in the last two centuries of the ancient world, were followers of a new tradition in Platonism, the theurgical tradition. Theurgists combined philosophical study with magical and religious ritual; they taught that just as the rational side of the self needed to be trained through logic and philosophy, the nonrational side needed to be purified and healed through ritual means. Nearly all the major defenders of Paganism in the classical world's final centuries were deeply involved in theurgy. *SEE* THEURGY.

Ironically, though, the same Platonist ideas that were being used by Iamblichus and Proclus to illuminate traditional Pagan rites were also being used, at the same time, by a handful of Christian philosophers and theologians to make sense of their very different tradition. Origen (185–254 C.E.), an important Christian thinker of the third century, was a fellow-student of Plotinus in the Platonic schools of Alexandria; he was only one of a series of Christian Platonists who shaped what would be a major influence on Christian theology and philosophy. Among the most important of these was an anonymous writer who called himself Dionysius the Areopagite (c. sixth century C.E.). Pseudo-Dionysius, as he is usually called, replaced Pagan gods with Christian angels to rework Proclus' theurgical Platonism into a system that was central to most Christian mysticism until the time of the Reformation a thousand years later.

Largely because of its adoption by Christianity, Platonism was essentially the only classical philosophy to survive the fall of Rome in a living form. In the Byzantine Empire, centered on Constantinople (modern Istanbul), the works of Plato and his followers remained in circulation, and the Eastern Orthodox Church drew heavily on Platonism as it developed its theology and philosophy. To this day a very strong Platonist streak can be traced in all the Orthodox churches.

Western Europe was another matter. Greek was for all practical purposes a lost language in the West, and the Latin Platonist writings that survived the fall of Rome were fairly meager: a partial Latin translation of Plato's dialogue *Timaeus* survived, along with a few other texts by later writers. On the other hand, many of the early Christian Platonists were central to the learning of the early medieval Catholic Church.

Crucial figures included Augustine, bishop of Hippo in North Africa (354–430 C.E.), far and away the most influential theologian of the age; Martianus Capella (fifth century C.E.), whose encyclopedic *Marriage of Philology and Mercury* was the most popular textbook of the liberal arts well into the high Middle Ages; and pseudo-Dionysius the Aropagite, mentioned earlier in this article. These were all Platonists of one sort or another, and their writings provided the core resources drawn on by early medieval philosophers.

For the first four centuries or so after the fall of Rome, philosophers of any sort were few and far between in the West; in an age of drastic instability and violence, most scholars were concerned with preserving and passing on the basic elements of education, and with Christian theology. With the rise of a more stable society after Charlemagne (742–814), the founder of the Holy Roman Empire, opportunities for scholarship broadened.

John Scotus Eriugena (ninth century C.E.), the first great medieval Platonist, taught at the court of Charles the Bald, king of France, and produced a series of important works and translations from Greek into Latin; he was familiar with most of the important Platonist works and

attempted, with mixed results, to introduce Platonist ideas into the Christianity of his time. After him came a long and distinguished line of Christian Platonists, who developed most of what is now classified as early medieval philosophy along Platonist lines.

The tradition of Christian Platonism was eclipsed in the twelfth and thirteenth centuries, though, by the rediscovery of Aristotle's writings, which were translated out of Arabic into Latin starting in the middle of the twelfth century. Aristotle's rationalist thought won wide acceptance in educated circles and even, once it was Christianized by Thomas Aquinas, in the church itself. Platonism, and mysticism generally, remained influential in the Franciscan Order and in a few other contexts, but it remained for the Renaissance to tip the balance back.

At the same time as Platonist thought was losing influence in the Christian world, however, it played an important role in launching a major new movement in Judaism. Jewish mystical circles in the south of France in the eleventh century were strongly influenced by Platonist writings, as well as by older Jewish mystical systems—the Ma'aseh Berashith or "Work of Creation," and the Ma'aseh Merkabah or "Work of the Chariot." The fusion of these teachings, primarily in the circle of Isaac the Blind (died c. 1235), gave rise to the Cabala; *SEE* CABALA; MA'ASEH BERASHITH; MA'ASEH MERKABAH.

It was not until the fifteenth century, however, that Platonism rose back into widespread prominence in the West. The coming of the Renaissance awakened a renewed interest in ancient philosophy, and the recovery of the complete works of Plato—first translated from Greek to Latin by the Florentine scholar and occultist Marsilio Ficino (1433–1499)—spurred a widespread fad for Platonism. *SEE* FICINO, MARSILIO.

Over the next century and a half, most of the other classics of Platonist thought came back into circulation. At the same time, both Hermeticism and the Cabala entered scholarly circles across Europe; the *Corpus Hermeticum* had been translated by Ficino just before Plato, and Ficino's younger contemporary Giovanni Pico della Mirandola (1463–1494) was responsible for publicizing the Cabala. *SEE* CORPUS HERMETICUM; HERMETICISM; PICO DELLA MIRANDOLA, GIOVANNI. Scholars across Europe quickly recognized the connections among these traditions—and the links that tied all of them to occult theory and practice.

The result was Renaissance Hermeticism, a widely popular and intensely magical way of thought that drew its theology from the Cabala and the Christian Platonists of earlier centuries, its mythology from Hermeticism, and its philosophy straight from Platonism by way of Plotinus and the late classical theurgists. It played a dominant role in most of the major occult works of the time. Widely influential, it was also bitterly attacked by its opponents, and it became one of the major forces in an age of free-wheeling intellectual warfare.

By the end of the sixteenth century, the intellectual battle lines hardened into a three-way struggle among Renaissance Hermeticism, the scholastic Aristotelianism of the universities, and the first formulations of what was then called "the mechanical philosophy" and is now called modern scientific materialism. Over the century that followed, the last of these gradually won out in the West. Platonism underwent one last major revival in the seventeenth century, when the Cambridge Platonists in England turned to Christian Platonism as a weapon against materialist philosophies. Henry More (1614–1687), the leading light of the movement, and a number of others struggled to defend the reality of the spiritual, and managed at least to ensure that Christian Platonism would remain a viable option within the Anglican Church.

The Cambridge Platonist revival faded out in the early eighteenth century, and thereafter the "mechanical philosophy" of Descartes, Bacon, and Newton held the field. For most of the following three centuries Platonism was largely ignored in the Western world, except by scholars and educated occultists. One major exception was Thomas Taylor (1758–1835), the great English Platonist and Pagan, who translated nearly all the surviving Platonist writings from ancient Greek into English. *SEE* TAYLOR, THOMAS. His efforts played a central role in launching the Neopagan revival in nineteenth-century Britain, which was directly ancestral to the modern Pagan movement, and he was also a major source drawn on by the Transcendentalists in America. *SEE* NEOPAGAN-ISM; TRANSCENDENTALISM.

Taylor's translations and his bold promotion of a Platonized Paganism as "the true religion of mankind" found few takers in the occult community of his time, however, and the reading lists offered by magical orders of the next century or so include essentially none of the standard Platonist canon. The same general neglect of Platonism in occult circles has continued to the present. It remains to be seen whether Western occultism has finally broken with what was once its core philosophy, or whether occultists of some future time will once again draw on Platonism as a resource for their work. FURTHER READING: CARABINE 2000, CASSIRER 1953, DILLON 1977, FINDLAY 1974, FINDLAY 1978, GERSH 1986, MEBANE 1989, PATRIDES 1970, SHAW 1995, D. WALKER 1972, WALLIS 1972, WETHERBEE 1973.

Plotinus. Greek-Egyptian philosopher, c. 205–270 C.E. Plotinus was the most important and influential philosopher of the Neoplatonic school. Little is known about his early life, as he preferred not to talk about himself. According to the biography written by his student Porphyry of Tyre, he was a native of Egypt; he decided to devote himself to philosophy at the age of twenty-eight, and after a time he spent visiting different teachers spent eleven years studying with the Neoplatonist Ammonius in Alexandria. In 243, hoping to travel into the East, he accompanied the army of the Emperor Gordian on a military expedition against the Persians. Gordian was assassinated by his own soldiers, and Plotinus escaped with some difficulty and made his way to Rome, where he began teaching publicly in 244. He remained in Rome until shortly before his death. His pupil Porphyry later collected and edited his writings into a single volume, *The Enneads*, which became the single most important source for later Platonist thought.

Plotinus himself was a mystic rather than a magician, and saw no need for ritual or symbolic methods in the quest for inner transformation; in his view, ethical virtue and disciplined reasoning were all that was needed. On the other hand, his writings assume the effectiveness of magic and present an explanation for its powers that later, more magically oriented Platonists found useful. His philosophical system became central to nearly all later approaches to Platonism, and also played an important role in the development of esoteric Christian traditions. *SEE ALSO* PLATONISM. FURTHER READING: DECK 1967, HADOT 1993, PLOTINUS 1992, RIST 1967, WALLIS 1972.

Pluto. The outermost named planet (so far) in our solar system, Pluto was discovered in 1930, although it was predicted in the late nineteenth century on the basis of wobbles in the orbit of Neptune. Like the other outer planets, Uranus and Neptune, Pluto has presented a challenge to astrologers, since it has no place in the traditions of classical astrology. Current astrological theory assigns it to the unconscious, to death and renewal, to profound transformation and destruction. Pluto rules the sign Scorpio, which was formerly allotted to Mars, and is in its detriment in placid Taurus. *SEE* ASTROLOGY.

Astrological symbol of Pluto

polarity. In occult writings, especially those influenced by English magician Dion Fortune (1890–1946) and her students, the framework of energies surrounding human sexuality. All things, according to polarity theory, have a male (projective) and a female (receptive) aspect, and all energies follow a circular pattern in which they descend from the creative source through one entity, project through that entity's male aspect, are received by the female aspect of another entity, and return through the second entity to the source.

Physical sexuality is one expression of this pattern, but far from the only one. The traditional occult lore of subtle bodies and the planes of being add further complexity, for each being is primarily male on certain planes and primarily female on others.

Among human beings, for example, men are (obviously) male on the physical plane and the closely related etheric plane, but most tend to be receptive or female on the astral plane (the level of the emotions), male again on the mental plane, and female on the spiritual plane. Women, in turn, are female on the physical and etheric planes, but tend to be male or active on the astral, receptive on the mental, and active on the spiritual. *SEE* SUBTLE BODIES.

In magical workings, polarity can be used as a source of power, usually by pairing men and women and making use of the subtle energy currents between them. In most systems of polarity magic, however, direct sexual contact between partners engaging in polarity work is held to drain the energies down to the physical level, where they cannot be used effectively for magical purposes. *SEE ALSO* FORTUNE, DION; SEX AND OCCULTISM. FURTHER READING: FORTUNE 1930.

polar shifts. *SEE* CYCLES, COSMIC.

poppet. A doll made to represent a person who is the target of a magical working. Poppets, also known as "voodoo dolls," are one of the most enduring features of practical magic; examples survive from ancient Egyptian times, and poppet magic is still much used today. In practice, various magical means are used to identify the poppet with the target of the working.

Poppet magic is most famous as a way of working harmful magic—for example, by inserting pins into the poppet to cause pain or illness in the corresponding part of the victim—but can also be used for many other magical workings. A pair of poppets may be bound together for love workings, while a single poppet may be bound with string or thread to keep an individual from harming others. Healing can also be done with poppet magic. *SEE ALSO* CUNNING MAN/WOMAN; HOODOO.

Populus. (Latin, "people") A geomantic figure governed by the moon. Populus is a neutral figure in divination, traditionally described as "good with good and evil with evil." *SEE* GEOMANCY.

Geomantic figure Populus

Posism. In the teachings of American occultist P. B. Randolph, the third and final phase of the process of magic, consisting of a receptive state in which the awareness is held perfectly empty and open. The preceding phases are called Volantia and Decretism. *SEE* DECRETISM; RANDOLPH, PASCHAL BEVERLY; VOLANTIA.

In the teachings of the Hermetic Brotherhood of Luxor, which drew heavily on Randolph's work, Posism was renamed Reception. The two prior phases were termed Formation and Execution. SEE HERMETIC BROTHERHOOD OF LUXOR (H. B. OF L.).

possession, demonic. A state in which the body of a human being (or occasionally another living organism) is taken over by a demonic entity. Possession by demons is found in folklore and magical traditions from around the world and throughout recorded history, although the details of the experience have a large cultural component, varying particularly by religion. The classic Western form, made famous by the movie version of *The Exorcist*, is rarely found outside of a close association with Christianity.

The more traditional Christian denominations have long practiced the art of exorcism as a treatment for possession, and the office of exorcist is one of the traditional minor orders. SEE HOLY ORDERS. In the Middle Ages and Renaissance, such practices tended to stray across the border into overt magic, and exorcists who became interested in doing more with demons than driving them out made up a significant part of the goetic underworld of the Middle Ages. SEE CHRISTIAN OCCULTISM; GOETIA. SEE ALSO DEMON; EXORCISM; OBSESSION. FURTHER READING: GOODMAN 1988, GREER 2001.

pralaya. In Theosophy, an interval of dissolution and latency. Each pralaya alternates with a manvantara, or period of manifestation. Manvantaras and pralayas form the building blocks of the Theosophical doctrine of cosmic cycles. SEE CYCLES, COSMIC; MANVANTARA; THEOSOPHY.

prana. (Sanskrit, "breath") A term for breath and/or vital energy borrowed from classical Hindu sources by Theosophy, and from Theosophy by a sizeable number of occult groups in the nineteenth and twentieth centuries. It seems to be essentially identical with the Western magical concept of ether. SEE ETHER; ETHERIC BODY.

pranayama. (Sanskrit, "control of breath") The traditional term for breathing exercises in Hindu yoga, borrowed (along with some of the exercises themselves) by a variety of occult groups and teachers in the nineteenth

and twentieth centuries. There are a wide range of pranayama exercises in Hindu sources, but only a few of these have been taken up in Western magical traditions.

One very common pranayama in Western sources is simple rhythmic breathing. The most popular form of this is the fourfold breath, in which the breath is drawn in to the count of four, held for the same count, breathed out to the same count, and held out for the same count.

Alternate-nostril breathing is also taught in a number of modern Western magical traditions. In this, the breath is drawn in one side of the nose and expelled through the other, then back in through the second side and out through the first, the fingers opening and closing the nostrils on each side by pressing against the sides of the nose.

In traditional yoga and modern magical practice alike, pranayama is used to balance, stabilize, and calm the subtle bodies of the practitioner, improving physical and emotional health and laying the foundations for meditation. SEE MEDITATION. SEE ALSO BREATH; YOGA. FURTHER READING: CROWLEY 1991, SADHU 1959.

precession of the equinoxes. A slow shift in the positions of the Earth's axis relative to the sun and the fixed stars, precession is the source of a great deal of myth, speculation, and esoteric theory. The Earth's axis is tilted at an angle of just over twenty-three degrees relative to its orbit around the sun, and at this period of history its northern end points toward the star Polaris. Over long periods of time, though, the direction of the axis turns in a slow counterclockwise circle. As a result, the pole star gradually changes over time. So do the apparent positions of the sun among the stars at the solstices and equinoxes, since these are determined by the relation between the Earth's angle of tilt, on the one hand, and the plane of its orbit around the sun on the other.

Estimates vary concerning the actual length of the cycle, but the traditional figure—25,950 years to complete one full circle—is close to modern guesses. At this rate, the points of the equinoxes and solstices slip backwards one degree along the zodiac every seventy-two years.

These changes have an enormous impact on the patterns of the night sky. Four thousand years ago, when ancient Egypt and Sumeria were flourishing, the pole star was not Polaris but Alpha Draconis (a star not far from the handle of the Big Dipper), and on the day of the spring equinox, the sun was in the constellation Taurus. At present, the Earth's north pole points to Polaris, and the sun rises in the early degrees of Pisces at the spring equinox; in another four thousand years or so, the pole star will be Alpha Cepheus, part of the house-shaped constellation on the other side of the sky from the Big Dipper, and the springtide sun will rise near the border between Capricorn and Sagittarius.

The current consensus in the world of official scholarship is that precession was first discovered around 128 B.C.E. by the Greek astronomer Hipparchus. A persistent minority of scholars, though, has pointed out that this claim is not only unproven but unlikely. In ages when the movements of the stars were used to track the seasons and predict times for successful hunting and gathering, or for planting and harvesting crops, changes caused by precession would have become apparent within a relatively small number of generations.

These scholars have argued that astronomical lore played a central part in mythology, since in cultures without writing, mythic narratives offered the one sure way of passing on information from generation to generation. A strong case can be made that certain features found in myths all over the world are the remnants of an ancient language of astronomical symbolism with deep ties to religion and spirituality.

Even those who accept the Hipparchan discovery of precession have come to admit that a certain amount of precessional lore may have had an important role in ancient religion. In particular, the otherwise obscure symbolism of the Mithraic Mysteries has been shown to make perfect sense when read as a response to precession. SEE MITHRAIC MYSTERIES.

Outside the realm of official scholarship, precession has played a much more significant role in theory and symbolism. Comparisons between the sun's motion around the zodiac and the much slower movements of precession led in ancient times to the concept of the precessional cycle as a Great Year. The twelve months of that year were marked by the passage of the point of the spring equinox through each of the twelve zodiacal signs in turn.

This concept has been the most persistent and widespread form of precessional symbolism in the Western occult traditions. Christian symbolism has routinely been interpreted in precessional terms; Pisces, which took over the spring equinoctial point around the time of the birth of Jesus, and Virgo, which took over the autumn point at the same time, are reflected in the fish-symbol of the earliest Christians and the virgin Mary. SEE CHRISTIAN OCCULTISM. The Age of Aquarius so heavily popularized in the Sixties is simply the month of the Great Year into which we are now gradually moving, as the equinoctial point shifts out of Pisces and into Aquarius. SEE AQUARIUS, AGE OF.

Discussions of precession in occult sources often combine or confuse precession with various other real or hypothetical cosmic cycles, and with changes in the angle of tilt of Earth's axis—another major concern of occult theorists in the nineteenth century. A simple lack of astronomical knowledge seems to be behind many of these confusions. SEE ALSO APOCATASTASIS; CYCLES, COSMIC. FURTHER READING: DE SANTILLANA 1977, EVANS 1998, FIDELER 1993, ULANSEY 1989.

Prieure de Sion. (Priory of Sion) French esoteric semi-secret society, allegedly founded in 1178 by the creators of the Knights Templar as guardians of a secret bloodline descended from Jesus of Nazareth via Mary Magdalene. It is claimed that this bloodline became the royal house of France during the Merovingian period (476–750 C.E.), remained in existence after losing the throne, and survives to the present day in the person of one Pierre Plantard, current head of the priory. Despite a severe shortage of evidence, numerous widely publicized books based on these claims have seen print over the last few decades.

The Priory of Sion was actually founded by Plantard in 1956, borrowing its name from a Catholic religious order that was absorbed by the Jesuits in 1617, and fabricating an impressive history for itself in the time-honored manner; SEE OCCULT HISTORY. Plantard and several other founding members of the Priory had been longtime members of Alpha Galates, an esoteric society with connections to French right-wing political movements and a record of collaboration with the Nazis during the Second World War. Articles in the Priory's magazine *Circuit*, aside from those concerning Plantard's genealogy and exalted personal qualities, have to do with many of the standard themes of French conservative esotericism—myth, astrology, assorted political schemes, and the need for French national renewal through a revival of the spirit of chivalry.

The priory is apparently more or less dormant at present, although persons claiming to be its representatives still attempt to promote its viewpoint in various forums. SEE ALSO ALPHA GALATES; GRAIL, HOLY; JESUS OF NAZARETH. FURTHER READING: BAIGENT ET AL. 1982, RICHARDSON 1999, WILSON 1988.

Priory of Sion. *SEE* PRIEURE DE SION.

Principles, Three. *SEE* THREE PRINCIPLES.

Proclus. Greek philosopher, 412–485. The last great theoretician of Pagan Platonism, Proclus was born to an aristocratic family in Constantinople, by that time the capitol of the eastern half of the Roman Empire. His parents, Patricius and Marcella, were from Lycia in Asia Minor, and returned there shortly after Proclus was born. He attended grammar school in the Lycian town of Xanthus, then went to Alexandria to pursue an education in rhetoric and law. On a visit to Constantinople, he had a vision of the goddess Athena, who urged him to take up philosophy. After his return to Alexandria, he followed the advice of the goddess, studying Neoplatonic philosophy with Olympiodorus the Younger and mathematics with Heron.

His travels took him next to Athens, where he became a student at the Academy, studying with Plutarch and Syrianus. Except for a year of exile in Lydia, which was forced on him by the opposition of the Christians, he spent the rest of his life in Athens, and became head of the Academy in his turn.

His literary output was substantial; he wrote some forty significant books, as well as a variety of hymns, poems, and other minor works. According to his student and biographer Marinus of Smyrna, he wrote some 700 lines a day, meanwhile teaching four lessons daily to his students and keeping all the holy days in both the Greek and the Egyptian religious calendars. He was normally a vegetarian, but ate small amounts of meat at sacrifices when the honor of the gods demanded it.

His philosophical teaching was the last and most complex statement of Pagan Neoplatonism. Taking the system of Iamblichus as a starting point, he worked out its internal logic and applied this to every detail, seeking a way of understanding the universe that was both logically consistent and mystically valid. His major work *The Elements of Theology* took this quest to its furthest extreme, demonstrating each aspect of Neoplatonist theory by a series of logical proofs.

His work was influential in its time among Pagan intellectual circles, and also had a powerful influence on the early Christian Neoplatonists. Its abstruseness and complexity has left it outside the mainstream of occult thought in more recent centuries, however. SEE ALSO PAGANISM; PLATONISM; THEURGY. FURTHER READING: GEFFCKEN 1978, MARINUS 1986, PROCLUS 1963, SIORVANES 1966.

progressions. In astrology, a set of methods used to project important events and trends in a person's life by manipulating the birth chart. The most common method of progression in present-day use is the secondary progression, which starts from birth and takes each day that follows as a representation of one year in the life of the birth chart's subject. To figure out the astrological trends during the thirty-fifth year of a person's life, in other words, an astrologer can erect a chart for the time of birth on the thirty-fifth day of that person's life, and compare the positions of the planets with those on the birth chart. This "year-for-a-day" approach is relatively arbitrary but has been used with success for many years.

Two other forms of progression can be encountered sometimes: tertiary progression, which makes each day equal to one lunar period (27.32 days), and minor progression, which makes each lunar period equal to one year in the subject's life.

Progressions by any of these methods are often combined with transits—the positions of the planets in the actual year of the subject's life being considered, seen in relation to the natal chart—for purposes of interpretation. *SEE* TRANSITS. *SEE ALSO* ASTROLOGY; DIRECTION.

projection. In alchemy, the final step in the Great Work, the process by which the Philosopher's Stone is heated together with a base metal and converts it to silver or gold. Alchemical symbolism assigns this process to the zodiacal sign Pisces. *SEE* ALCHEMY; PHILOSOPHER'S STONE.

Puella. (Latin, "girl") A geomantic figure governed by Venus. Puella is favorable in most divinatory questions, but unfavorable for divinations involving money. *SEE* GEOMANCY.

Geomantic figure Puella

Puer. (Latin, "boy") A geomantic figure governed by Mars. Puer is favorable in divinatory questions involving love and conflict, but unfavorable for most others. *SEE* GEOMANCY.

Geomantic figure Puer

Pymander, Divine. *SEE* CORPUS HERMETICUM.

Pythagoras. Greek philosopher and mathematician, c. 570–c. 495 B.C.E. According to the four ancient accounts of his life, Pythagoras was a native of Samos, but left his homeland as a young man in search of knowledge. After studying philosophy with Thales of Miletus and Pherecydes of Syros, he is said to have traveled to Egypt, Babylonia, and several other countries, where he studied traditional religious and mystical lore with priests in a variety of temples. He then emigrated to Crotona, a Greek colonial city in southern Italy, where he spent most of the rest of his life. In Crotona he founded a secret society, later known as the Pythagorean Brotherhood, which passed on his teachings and also played an important role in the political life of the community. Around 500 B.C.E., popular unrest over the brotherhood's political influence led to widespread rioting, and many of the brotherhood were killed. Pythagoras himself fled to Metapontum, where he died a few years later.

The teachings Pythagoras brought with him to Crotona were communicated under vows of secrecy, and there has been much dispute ever since about just what they included. Accounts in classical literature credit Pythagoras with discoveries in mathematics, geometry, and music theory, but also with miracles of the type claimed for other ancient magicians, such as Apollonius of Tyana; *SEE* APOLLONIUS OF TYANA. Belief in reincarnation, insistence on a vegetarian diet, a detailed system of number mysticism, and a variety of moral and philosophical maxims were also ascribed to him by ancient sources.

In many ways Pythagoras can be seen as the founder, or at least the first historical figure, of Western occult tradition. Certainly many of the factors central to his biography—the search for wisdom in exotic countries, the idea that a secret initiatory society is the proper context for esoteric teachings, the fatal lure of political involvement—as well as many of the specific teachings attributed to him have remained standard features of occultism in the West ever since his time. *SEE ALSO* ARITHMANCY; QUADRIVIUM; SACRED GEOMETRY. FURTHER READING: BURKERT 1972, GORMAN 1979, GUTHRIE 1987, PHILIP 1966.

Qabala. *SEE* CABALA.

Qebehsenuf. (ancient Egyptian *qbhsnuf*) One of the four Canopic gods, the sons of Horus, who had guardianship of the vital organs of the deceased. He has the head of a hawk, governs the western quarter of the world, and guards the liver and gall bladder. He is associated with the goddess Sekhet, and was also called "the Bloodletter." *SEE* CANOPIC GODS.

In the Golden Dawn tradition, Qebehsenuf (under the older spelling Kabexnuf) is one of the invisible guardians of the temple, and is stationed in the southwest. *SEE* GOLDEN DAWN, HERMETIC ORDER OF THE; INVISIBLE STATIONS. FURTHER READING: BUDGE 1967, REGARDIE 1971.

Qesheth. (Hebrew QShTh, "bow") In most versions of the Cabalistic Tree of Life, three Paths rise from the lowest Sephirah, Malkuth, to Spheres further up the Tree. The Golden Dawn allocation of Hebrew letters to Paths assigns these Paths to the letters Qoph, Shin, and Tau, which spell out the word *qesheth*—the Hebrew word for "rainbow," and also for the sort of bow used with arrows. Both these meanings are used frequently in the symbolism of the Golden Dawn Cabala, the first to represent the shimmering colors of the astral plane, the second with reference to the Twenty-fifth Path, the "Path of the Arrow," which rises from Yesod to Tiphareth. *SEE* ASTRAL PLANE; CABALA.

Qlippoth. (Hebrew, "shells," "husks") In Cabalistic lore, the "Lords of Unbalanced Force," demonic entities from a former universe who have survived into the present one. The Qlippoth are the subject of a vast and sometimes contradictory body of demonological lore, originating in Jewish sources but borrowed and in some areas expanded by later occult theorists. Like most Hebrew words, Qlippoth has a variety of English spellings; Kelippoth is another that is commonly used.

According to Cabalistic texts, the Qlippoth originated as the ruling powers of a universe that came before this one, a realm of unbalanced force that was destroyed in the early stages of the creation of the cosmos. In Cabalistic writings from before the time of Isaac Luria (1534–1572), the Qlippoth are sometimes pictured in Neoplatonic terms as the last link in the chain of emanation, the furthest thing from God that still has enough of the divine creative power in it to exist at all. Other passages, more metaphorical, relate the Qlippoth to the Tree of Life as the bark relates to the living wood of an actual tree—the natural and necessary result of the organic process of creation, like excrement, the dregs of wine, or the dross that remains after gold has been refined.

It is often suggested in Cabalistic writings that evil is simply the manifestation of the Sephirah Geburah (Severity) taken too far and separated from its proper balancing power of Chesed (Mercy); *SEE* GEBURAH; SEPHIROTH. The sense of the Qlippoth as a natural part of existence reaches its zenith in the Zoharic comment that everything is a "shell" or "husk" when seen from a higher level of existence, and the kernel in the shell when seen from a lower one.

The teachings of Isaac Luria and his school introduced a radically different understanding of the Qlippoth. In Luria's Cabala, the orderly process of Creation was interrupted by disaster; the vessels meant to contain the seven Sephiroth from Chesed to Malkuth were inadequate, and shattered in the face of the descending current of creative light. From the shards of these vessels, brought to life by the sparks of divine light still caught in them, the Qlippoth came into being. The rescue of the sparks of light from their imprisonment in the Kingdom of Shells is the great theme of Luria's Cabala, and has much in common with much older Gnostic mythologies. *SEE* GNOSTICISM; LURIA, ISAAC.

The Qlippoth in their totality make up the Sitra Achra or "Other Side," the realm of the demons. This realm and its inhabitants are lavishly described in Cabalistic literature. The school of Burgos in the early Spanish Cabala, and the successors of Isaac Luria, were particularly active in this Cabalistic demonology.

Ten orders of Qlippoth, corresponding to the ten Sephiroth of the Tree of Life, are the best known. Thaumiel, the Two Contending Forces, oppose the unity of Kether; Augiel, who "attach themselves to living and material appearances," correspond to Chokmah; Satariel, the Concealers, correspond to Chokmah. To Chesed correspond Ga'ashekelah, the Disturbers or Breakers in Pieces; to Geburah, Golohab, the Burners with Fire; to Tiphareth, Tagiriron, the Disputers, while to Netzach and Hod correspond respectively Aareb Tzereq, the Ravens of Dispersion, and Samael, the Liars. Yesod has Gamaliel, the Obscene Ones, while Malkuth has Lilith, the Woman of Night. Each of these has its own traditional form and attributions, which may be found under its own entry elsewhere in this encyclopedia.

The lore of the Qlippoth received a great deal of attention in Jewish Cabalistic circles and Hermetic occult lodges alike—for example, a detailed paper on the subject was once part of the curriculum of the Hermetic Order of the Golden Dawn. In recent years, in keeping with the general modern habit of romanticizing evil, a certain number of ceremonial magicians have taken this attention in practical directions. English magician Kenneth Grant, for example, has published several books on magical workings involving the Qlippoth, whom he identifies

with the entities in H. P. Lovecraft's fictional grimoire, the *Necronomicon; SEE* NECRONOMICON. *SEE ALSO* CABALA. FURTHER READING: GRANT 1980, MATHERS 1983, SCHOLEM 1974.

Qoph. (Hebrew QVP, "back of the head) The nineteenth letter of the Hebrew alphabet, Qoph is one of the single letters, with a sound-value that has no English equivalent—like a *k* made in the back of the throat—and the numerical value of 100. Its standard magical symbolism is as follows:

> *Path of the Tree of Life:* Path 29, Netzach to Malkuth.
>
> *Astrological Correspondence:* Pisces, the Fishes.
>
> *Tarot Correspondence:* Trump XVIII, the Moon.
>
> *Part of the Cube of Space:* The lower south edge.
>
> *Colors:* in Atziluth—magenta.
>
> in Briah—buff, flecked with silver-white.
>
> in Yetzirah—pale translucent pinkish-brown.
>
> in Assiah—brownish-gray stone.

The corresponding section from the *Thirty-two Paths of Wisdom* is as follows: "The Twenty-ninth Path is the Corporeal Intelligence, so called because it forms every body which is formed beneath all the worlds, and the increment of them." *SEE ALSO* CABALA; HEBREW ALPHABET.

Hebrew letter Qoph

quadrivium. (Latin, "four roads") The four ancient sciences of number, usually listed as arithmetic, geometry, music, and astronomy. These categories should not be understood in a purely scientific mode, however. "Arithmetic" in earlier times included a great deal of number symbolism, and what would now be called arithmology and arithmancy; "geometry" included the sort of mystical perspectives now classified as sacred geometry; "music" included all the arts, and focused primarily on harmonious number relationships; and "astronomy" included not merely astrology but also the various ways of tracking the cycles of time.

The sciences that later became the quadrivium were first formulated in the Western world by the Pythagorean Brotherhood, which drew on older Egyptian and Mesopotamian lore, and were organized into a set of four in the late classical period. By the dawn of the Middle Ages, the quadrivium was enshrined as the second stage of a liberal education, following the trivium, which consisted of Latin grammar, logic, and rhetoric. The trivium and quadrivium formed the seven liberal arts, and remained central to education throughout the Western world until the dawn of the modern age. They played a particularly important role in Renaissance occultism, and it may have been because of this connection that the quadrivium fell into neglect after the triumph of materialist philosophies in the seventeenth century. *SEE ALSO* ARITHMOLOGY; ASTROLOGY; PYTHAGORAS; SACRED GEOMETRY. FURTHER READING: HENINGER 1974.

Quert. (Old Irish, "rags") The tenth letter in the Ogham alphabet, with the sound-value *q*. It corresponds to the apple among trees, the hen among birds, the color mouse-brown (Gaelic *quiar*) and no number. In Robert Graves' version of the Ogham tree-calendar, it shares the month from August 6 to September 2 with the letter Coll. *SEE* OGHAM.

Ogham letter Quert

Questing Beast. *SEE* GLATISANT.

Quimby, Phineas Parkhurst. American physician and occultist, 1802–1866. Born in New Hampshire, he spent most of his life in the small town of Belfast, Maine. In 1838, during the height of the American craze for mesmerism, he became interested in Mesmer's discoveries and began a successful career as a mesmeric physician. In the last years of his life, however, he became convinced that all physical illness was actually the result of wrong attitudes and ideas on the part of the patient, and could be cured by replacing these ideas with correct ones.

Among his patients during this final phase of his career was Mary Baker Eddy, who later went on to found Christian Science on exactly the same principle. Though Eddy denied being influenced by Quimby or anybody else, a collection of the older healer's papers (the so-called "Quimby manuscripts") has been an underground classic in circles on the fringe of Christian Science for more than a century. *SEE* CHRISTIAN SCIENCE. *SEE ALSO* NEW AGE MOVEMENT.

quinance. In astrology, a section of the zodiac five degrees wide; half a decan, or one-sixth of a zodiacal sign. In some older astrological sources, each quinance has a ruling planet, and certain other symbolism. Little use is made of them in modern astrology, however. *SEE* ASTROLOGY; DECANS.

quincunx. In astrology, an aspect formed by two planets at an angle of 150 degrees, or five whole signs apart. It was introduced by French astrologer Jean-Baptiste Morin (1583–1656). A minor and offbeat aspect, it is ignored by many astrologers, although others pay close attention to it. Its most common interpretation is as a signal of interactions that don't quite work, or that proceed in unexpected and unsettling directions. *SEE* ASPECT, ASTROLOGICAL.

quintile. In astrology, an aspect formed by two planets at an angle of 72 degrees, or one-fifth of the zodiac. It was introduced to astrology by German astrologer Johannes Kepler (1571–1630). A minor aspect, it relates to talent and also to power, and is considered generally favorable. *SEE* ASPECT, ASTROLOGICAL.

R

Ra Hoor Khuit. (Ancient Egyptian *Re Heru-khuti*, "Ra as Horus of both horizons") In Aleister Crowley's magico-religious system of Thelema, the divinity ruling over the New Aeon announced to the world by the revealing of the Book of the Law in 1904. "Ra Hoor Khuit" is a now-obsolete transliteration of Re Herukhuti or Ra Horakhte, an aspect of the solar god Re much worshipped in the New Kingdom period of ancient Egyptian history.

According to Crowley's writings, Ra Hoor Khuit is the active manifestation of the New Aeon's ruling divinity, paired with the passive manifestation Hoor-parkraat; the two together make up the synthetic deity Heru-ra-ha. *SEE ALSO* CROWLEY, ALEISTER; THELEMA.

Rad. *SEE* RAIDO.

Raido. (Old Germanic, "journey") The fifth rune of the Elder Futhark, associated with journeys, especially on horseback; with advice and counsel; and with the god Hermod. Its sound-value is *r*. *SEE* ELDER FUTHARK.

The same rune, under the name Rad (Old English, "ride"), is the fifth rune of the Anglo-Saxon futhorc, and has the same meanings and sound value. *SEE* ANGLO-SAXON FUTHORC.

Under the name Reidh (Old Norse, "riding"), with the same meanings and sound-value, the same rune also has the fifth place in the younger futhark. The rune poems point out sensibly enough that what is joy to the rider is hard work for the horse!

Under the name Rit, finally, the same rune is the fifth of the Armanen runes, and represents a wheel. It is associated with Ragnarok, the twilight of the gods, with the zodiacal sign Leo, and with the power to stop the flight of arrows, spears, and stones, as described in Odin's rune-charm in the Old Norse Havamal. *SEE* ARMANEN RUNES.

Rune Raido (Rad, Reidh, Rit)

Rakoczy, the Master. *SEE* SAINT-GERMAIN, COMTE DE.

Ramacharaka, Yogi. *SEE* ATKINSON, WILLIAM WALKER.

Randolph, Paschal Beverly. American occultist, 1825–1875. Born and raised in the Five Points, the most notorious slum area of nineteenth-century New York, Randolph was the illegitimate child of Flora Clark, a poor black woman, and William Beverly Randolph, a white man who may have been connected to the wealthy Randolph family of Virginia. His father abandoned the relationship in Randolph's earliest years, if not before, and his mother died when Randolph was six or seven years old. Thereafter he led a precarious existence, spending a time in the almshouse of New York's Bellevue Hospital, working as a bootblack, and begging from door to door.

As a teenager he worked as a cabin boy on an Atlantic merchant brig. Around 1845, he settled for a time in upstate New York, working as a barber. There he encountered Spiritualism and became first a convert, then a medium, holding séances regularly by 1853. *SEE* SPIRI-TUALISM. He also carried on a sideline as a "clairvoyant physician" specializing in sexual problems. By 1854 he had also launched a literary career with a novel, *Waa-gu-Mah*, which has since been lost. The year 1855 saw him travel to England, France, and Germany, where he contacted Spiritualists and occultists of various sorts, and learned about magic mirrors and hashish—two things that would occupy much of his career. By the end of the year he was back in America, but in 1857 he crossed the Atlantic again, and in 1861 and 1862 he returned to the Old World and traveled east as far as Egypt and Palestine.

All through this period he was developing a complicated and unique occult philosophy based on sex, clairvoyant experience, and the development of occult powers. In 1858 he turned on Spiritualism, denouncing it as passive "vampirism" of the medium by evil spirits, and for a while traveled on the anti-Spiritualist lecture circuit, attacking Spiritualism as earnestly as he had praised it a few years earlier. For a short time he was involved with a Christian church, but moved on to Rosicrucian and occult practices by the early 1860s. After a period involved in politics during and after the Civil War, he turned his attention entirely toward occultism, writing numerous books and pamphlets on the subject and attempting several times to found a magical order to carry on his teachings.

Each of his many books on the subject presented his philosophy from different viewpoints, and different books routinely contradict one another. Still, the basic outlines remained the same. All souls, or "atomonads," are spun off by the central spiritual sun and evolve gradually through countless worlds before achieving human incarnation; after a human life, the evolution of the soul continued on other worlds. Basic training for the aspiring mage included "volantia" (calm focused concentration), "decretism" (unity of will), and "posism" (a state of receptivity), and the development of clairvoyance through exercises using the magic mirror. More advanced was "blending," a form of conscious trance in which the mage and a spiritual entity shared possession of the mage's body and awareness; to Randolph, this was the key to communicating with higher spiritual realms. *SEE* BLENDING; DECRETISM; POSISM; VOLANTIA.

The supreme mystery of magic in Randolph's system, though, was sexual. At the moment of mutual orgasm, an act of will carried out by both partners had almost unlimited powers. Randolph insisted that women were capable of experiencing sexual pleasure and orgasm—a point loudly denied by many physicians and moralists during his lifetime—and criticized men who did nothing to provide their lovers with pleasure.

The origins of his teachings are a subject of much dispute. He clearly drew much from Spiritualist theoreticians of the time, and particularly from Andrew Jackson Davis; *SEE* DAVIS, ANDREW JACKSON. Later in life, he claimed to have been initiated by Rosicrucians, and also by the "Ansairee" (al-Nusa'iri), a heretical offshoot of Islam active then as now in Syria. In his own writings, however, he also admitted to having made up these connections out of whole cloth to give his own ideas the borrowed dignity of an ancient tradition. In this he was following the time-honored occult tradition of historical dishonesty; *SEE* OCCULT HISTORY.

Unfortunately Randolph's considerable creativity and intelligence were more than overbalanced by his arrogance, egotism, and uncontrolled temper. Subject to violent mood swings, he had a genius for offending friends and making enemies, and very few of his students remained in contact with him for long. He founded several magical orders to pass on his teachings, but most blew up within months of their foundation due to disputes set in motion by Randolph himself. His personal life was equally unstable, filled with a string of failed marriages and relationships. In his last years his mood swings grew increasingly erratic, and in 1875 he committed suicide while in a period of extreme depression.

After his death, various elements of Randolph's teachings were taken up by the Hermetic Brotherhood of Luxor, the Fraternitas Rosae Crucis, and the Societas Rosicruciana in America, among other groups. *SEE* FRA-TERNITAS ROSAE CRUCIS (FRC); HERMETIC BROTHER-HOOD OF LUXOR (H. B. OF L.); SOCIETAS ROSICRUCIANA IN AMERICA (SRIA). Strong echoes of some of his teachings also appear in the early writings of H. P. Blavatsky, while his sexual teachings (which Blavatsky rejected) went on to become the central magical teaching of the Ordo Templi Orientis. *SEE* BLAVATSKY, HELENA PETRO-

VNA; ORDO TEMPLI ORIENTIS (OTO). FURTHER READING: DEVENEY 1997, RANDOLPH 1874.

Raphael. (Hebrew RPAL, "God has healed") One of the most important archangels of traditional Jewish, Christian, and magical lore, Raphael first appears in the apochryphal Book of Tobit, in which he accompanies Tobias from Nineveh to Media and helps him defeat the machinations of the demon Asmodeus. He is variously assigned to the Sephirah Tiphareth or Hod, and thus serves as angelic ruler of either the sun or Mercury. According to Cabalistic sources, his original name was Labbiel, and was given the name Raphael when he assisted God in the creation of Adam. *SEE* ARCHANGEL.

Raqia. (Hebrew RQIAa, "firmament") In Cabalistic lore, the second of the seven heavens, corresponding to the Sephirah Hod. *SEE* HEAVENS, SEVEN.

Rashith ha-Gilgalim. (Hebrew, "beginnings of wheelings") The highest of the celestial spheres in Cabalistic cosmology, corresponding to the Sephirah Kether in the world of Assiah. Its astrological equivalent in pre-Copernican times was the *primum mobile*, the sphere beyond the stars that was held to be the source of all celestial motion. More recent opinion is divided, with some schools assigning it to the Milky Way galaxy while others equate it with the planet Neptune. *SEE* KETHER; TREE OF LIFE.

Rays, Seven. In occult philosophy of the nineteenth and twentieth centuries, the seven primary creative energies in the cosmos, corresponding to the seven colors of the spectrum. Teachings concerning the Seven Rays were first developed in Theosophy, but spread quickly outside the Theosophical fold to become one of the most common ways of classifying the subtle levels and forces of the universe in occult circles throughout the Western world.

1. Red. *Characteristic:* Power. *Master:* El Morya. *Magical Path:* Shamanism, "primitive" magic.
2. Blue. *Characteristic:* Wisdom. *Master:* Kuthumi. *Magical Path:* Meditation.
3. Yellow. *Characteristic:* Intelligence. *Master:* Venetian Chohan. *Magical Path:* Astrology and other forms of divination.
4. Green. *Characteristic:* Beauty. *Master:* Serapis. *Magical Path:* Nature mysticism, physical and etheric exercises.
5. Orange. *Characteristic:* Knowledge. *Master:* Hilarion. *Magical Path:* Alchemy.
6. Violet. *Characteristic:* Love. *Master:* Jesus. *Magical Path:* Devotional mysticism.
7. Indigo. *Characteristic:* Transcendance. *Master:* Comte de Saint-Germain. *Magical Path:* Ceremonial magic.

The Rays are still much used in Theosophically inspired branches of occultism, and may also be found in the New Age movement. The widespread rejection of Theosophy by many modern occultists, however, has caused the lore of the Rays to be neglected by many other elements of the occult community. *SEE* THEOSOPHY. *SEE ALSO ENTRIES ON EACH RAY (BY COLOR).* FURTHER READING: LEADBEATER 1925.

Raziel. (Hebrew RZIAL, "secret of God") In Cabalistic lore, the archangel of the Secret Wisdom, supposed author of the Sepher Raziel, and revealer of the Mysteries to Adam, Enoch, Noah, and Solomon. According to Rabbinic sources, he stands on Mount Horeb each day and proclaims the secrets of men to all mankind. He corresponds to the Sephirah Chokmah in the world of Briah. *SEE* ARCHANGEL; BRIAH; CHOKMAH.

Reclaiming Tradition. An influential movement in recent American Paganism, the Reclaiming Tradition took shape in San Francisco in the early 1980s around a series of classes offered by feminist witches Starhawk and Diane Baker. A number of these classes developed into covens, and these and other like-minded individuals evolved into the Reclaiming Collective over the course of the decade. The Collective incorporated as a nonprofit religious corporation in 1990. In the late 1990s, the collective aspect of the organization was dissolved and replaced by the Wheel, a council made of spokespersons from Reclaiming Tradition cells (roughly comparable to covens in other Pagan traditions).

Unlike most other branches of the occult community, the Reclaiming Collective is intensely political, combining Pagan religious and magical practice with left-wing political activism, particularly in the areas of environmentalism and feminism. Many of the more traditional aspects of modern Paganism, in turn, are downplayed; initiation is an optional event and follows no fixed pattern, ritual forms are improvised on the spot, and there is no particular pantheon of deities common to Reclaiming practitioners. The basic Reclaiming approach has been summarized as EIEIO: Ecstatic, Improvisational, Ensemble, Inspired, and Organic.

By way of summer intensive "Witch Camps," which are held in many parts of the world, and its periodical *Reclaiming Quarterly*, the Reclaiming Tradition has had a significant influence on Pagan culture in North America and some parts of Europe. In terms of organized groups, however, it remains largely a San Francisco Bay area movement. *SEE ALSO* DIANIC WICCA; NEOPAGANISM; WOMEN'S INTERNATIONAL TERRORIST CONSPIRACY FROM HELL (WITCH). FURTHER READING: STARHAWK 1989.

Red Lion. An important image in alchemical symbolism, the red lion generally refers to sulphur, one of the three alchemical principles; it may also refer to gold, or to sulphuric acid. As with alchemical terminology in general, though, no one definition will fit every use of the term, and it is usually an open question exactly what is meant by any given appearance of it.

A document titled "Trismosin's Alchemical Process, called the Red Lion" was published several times in the Renaissance and at least once in modern times. The process outlined in this document is said to produce the Philosopher's Stone; what it actually produces is several ounces of gold fulminate, a highly unstable and dangerous explosive. The would-be alchemist is then told to grind the fulminate to powder in a mortar, and throw it onto molten metal! It's hard to tell whether these suicidal instructions are meant to decrease the number of ignorant alchemists in the world, or are simply an unusually vicious practical joke. *SEE ALSO* ALCHEMY. FURTHER READING: TRISMOSIN N.D.

Red Ray. In occult philosophy, the first of the Seven Rays, the primary creative energies of the cosmos. The Red Ray is the ray of power. In Theosophical lore, the Red Ray is under the direction of the Master El Morya, a chohan of the Great White Lodge. Its symbolic gem is the diamond. *SEE* EL MORYA, MASTER. *SEE ALSO* RAYS, SEVEN.

Red Stone. *SEE* PHILOSOPHER'S STONE.

Rede, Wiccan. *SEE* WICCAN REDE.

Reformed Druids of North America (RDNA). One of the first major Pagan organizations of the modern period, the RDNA may also be the most influential religious movement ever set in motion by college students. It originated in 1963 at Carleton College, a private college in Minnesota, which required all students to attend religious services of some sort each Sunday. A group of students decided to protest this requirement by forming a religion of their own, the Reformed Druids of North America ("Reformed" in that it no longer practiced blood sacrifice). A basic liturgy and theology were put together, and the group held services outdoors each Sunday during the 1963–4 school year.

The next year, the religious services requirement was officially dropped by the college authorities, but members of the RDNA continued to meet and expand what had become a living tradition of nature worship. As members left Carleton and headed elsewhere, new groves of the RDNA sprang up in various places. Never a large organization—at its height, the RDNA had twelve active groves—it was nonetheless a major influence on Druid and other Pagan groups in North America, and many of the most active current Druid organizations today trace their origins to an RDNA source. *SEE* AR NDRAIOCHT FEIN (ADF).

The RDNA pantheon includes Dalon ap Landu, god of groves; Grannos, god of healing; Braciaca, god of malt; Belenos, god of the sun; Sirona, goddess of rivers; Taranis, god of thunder and lightning; Llyr, god of the sea; and Danu, goddess of fertility. All these are secondary to the two great powers, Be'al, who represents abstract Spirit, and the Earth Mother. This somewhat eclectic pantheon is more than matched by the RDNA liturgy or Order of Worship, which has much in common with liberal Protestant Christian religious services, includes readings from a global assortment of spiritual texts, and culminates in a rite of communion in which either the Waters of Life (Irish whiskey) or the Waters of Sleep (ordinary water) are partaken by all present. The two basic tenets of Reformed Druidism are as follows:

1. The object of the search for religious truth, which is a universal and never-ending search, may be found through the Earth-Mother; which is Nature; but this is one way among many.

2. And great is the importance, which is a spiritual importance, of Nature, which is the Earth-Mother; for it is one of the objects of Creation, and with it do people live, yea, even as they do struggle through life are they come face to face with it.

These are often presented in a more simplified form as:

1. Nature is good!

2. Likewise, Nature is good!

Exactly how seriously any of this was meant or taken is an open question. The RDNA's sense of humor has always been among its strongest assets; its original history, the *Druid Chronicles*, is written entirely in a mock-biblical style, and the rite of ordination for one of its levels of priesthood includes picking up the candidate and tossing him or her into the nearest body of water.

The RDNA remains active at present, not least at Carleton College, where the fortieth anniversary of the Reform was celebrated in 2003. There are a variety of closely related groups listed on RDNA websites, including the Hasidic Druids of North America, the Reformed Druids of North Asia, and the Recombinant Druids of North America, which range from the moderately active to the probably imaginary. Given that at least one fully recognized RDNA grove consists entirely of trees, it's hard to say. *SEE ALSO* DRUIDRY. FURTHER READING: ADLER 1986, HANSEN 1995, REFORMED DRUIDS OF NORTH AMERICA 2003.

Regardie, Israel. (Regudy, Francis Israel) American occultist, 1907–1985. Born in London's East End slums, Regardie emigrated to the United States with his parents in 1921 and grew up in Washington, D. C. In his teen years, he developed an interest in the occult, which he pursued through reading in the Library of Congress and through membership in the Societas Rosicruciana in America, where he was initiated as a Zelator. *SEE* SOCIETAS ROSICRUCIANA IN AMERICA (SRIA). At the age of

twenty he encountered the writings of Aleister Crowley; deeply impressed, he wrote to Crowley, met him a short time later in Paris, and found himself with a job as Crowley's secretary.

His employment with Crowley lasted until 1931, when Crowley ran out of money; the two remained on cordial terms until 1937, when an explosive quarrel blew their friendship apart permanently. By this time he had already written two books, the short but useful Cabalistic study *A Garden of Pomegranates* (1932) and the much more substantial *The Tree of Life* (1932), which remains one of the major works on the theory of the Golden Dawn system of magic. These won him entry into English magical circles, and in 1934 he was initiated into the Hermes Temple of the Stella Matutina, one of the Golden Dawn's successor orders.

His stay in Hermes Temple was brief. He rose rapidly through the grades to the rank of Theoricus Adeptus Minor, but was appalled by what he saw as the ignorance and incompetence of the Temple Chiefs and adepts. He noted with dismay that many elements of the original Golden Dawn system had been withdrawn from circulation, and that important papers had been hidden or even destroyed. He also objected harshly to the English magical scene's emphasis on inner plane contacts, which he saw as a misdirection of effort as well as a source of delusion.

In 1935 he quit the Stella Matutina and returned to America with his collection of Golden Dawn papers. He had decided that the only way to save the order's magical system from what he saw as its unworthy keepers was to make all of it public. The resulting work, titled *The Golden Dawn*, was issued in four volumes by Aries Press in Chicago between 1937 and 1940.

After his return to America, he took up the study of psychology, went through a course of Freudian psychoanalysis, and soon gravitated to the system created by Wilhelm Reich, which he felt had deep connections to magic. *SEE* REICH, WILHELM. He also studied chiropractic and massage, and established a practice as a therapist. A resident of Los Angeles for many years, he retired to Sedona, Arizona, where he spent his last years working with a variety of younger Golden Dawn magicians. *SEE ALSO* CROWLEY, ALEISTER; GOLDEN DAWN, HERMETIC ORDER

OF THE; STELLA MATUTINA, ORDER OF THE. FURTHER READING: KNIGHT 2000, REGARDIE 1972, SUSTER 1990.

Reghini, Arturo. Italian author, mathematician, and occultist, 1878–1946. Born in Florence in an aristocratic family, Reghini studied mathematics at the University of Pisa, and while there made contact with the thriving Italian occult scene. In 1898, he and H. P. Blavatsky's friend Elizabeth Cooper-Oakley founded the Italian branch of the Theosophical Society; SEE THEOSOPHICAL SOCIETY. While still deeply involved in Theosophy, Reghini also entered the world of high-degree Masonry, receiving initiation in the Rite of Memphis and Misraim in 1902. He soon took on a leadership role in the complex politics of Italian Masonry, and helped organize the Italian Philosophical Rite of Masonry, a branch of the Craft that tried to find middle ground between the radical left and radical right. SEE FREEMASONRY.

During the years from the new century's beginning to the start of the First World War, Reghini was a notable presence in the Italian occult community. He served as the editor of two important journals, *Ignis* and *Atanor*, publishing articles by luminaries such as René Guénon and Julius Evola. His own writings on Masonry, Pythagorean sacred mathematics, and Pagan spirituality were widely influential.

The outbreak of the First World War disrupted Reghini's esoteric career, and in 1919 the Philosophical Rite merged into one of the existing Masonic jurisdictions. Reghini himself served in the army. In the aftermath of war, the rising power of Benito Mussolini's Fascist Party became the major issue of the day in Italian Freemasonry. Many Italian Masons, Reghini among them, gave cautious support to the fascists, but following Mussolini's seizure of power in 1922 they soon found that the new regime was anything but appreciative of their help. In 1924 the Fascist Party declared that Masonic affiliation was incompatible with party membership, and the next year organized violence against Masons and lodges broke out. Reghini's protests against this, and against the alliance between the Fascist Party and the Catholic Church, had little effect on government policy.

From 1928 on, when he was forced out of his job as a mathematics teacher, until his death in 1946, Reghini lived in semi-retirement, writing and teaching about Pythagorean mathematics and spirituality. His works remain important in continental European occult traditions but have been essentially ignored in the English-speaking world. SEE ALSO PYTHAGORAS; QUADRIVIUM. FURTHER READING: THOMAS 1997.

Regulus. The brightest star in the constellation Leo, also known as Cor Leonis (the Heart of the Lion). In the Golden Dawn version of astrology, the zodiac was calculated beginning with Regulus as 0 degrees Leo. SEE GOLDEN DAWN, HERMETIC ORDER OF THE.

Some accounts of the astrological ages of the world date the coming of the Age of Aquarius to the entrance of Regulus into the zodiacal sign Virgo, which is predicted to happen in 2012. SEE AQUARIUS, AGE OF; PRECESSION OF THE EQUINOXES.

Reich, Wilhelm. Austrian psychologist, 1897–1957. Born into a middle-class Jewish family in Vienna, Reich graduated with high grades from a technical high school in 1915. After a stint in the Austrian army, serving on the Italian front, he attended medical school at the University of Vienna, qualifying as a physician in 1922. While still a student, he developed an interest in sexology and psychoanalysis, and became a member of the Vienna Psychological Society.

As a result of work at the University Neurological Clinic, where he pursued postgraduate studies, he became convinced that the body as well as the mind needed to be included in psychological therapy. This led him to the creation of a form of therapy he called "vegetotherapy" (from its focus on the autonomic or vegetative nervous system), which combined Freudian analysis with deep tissue massage.

In the late 1920s he flirted with Marxism, joining the Communist Party and arguing that the sexual liberation of the masses was the first step toward their economic liberation. With the dawn of the 1930s, these issues became less central to his work as he pursued researches into the basis of sexual energy. By the end of the decade, he had become convinced that he had discovered a new form of energy—orgone, the basic life-force of the universe—and devoted the rest of his life to a series of increasingly strange researches and writings about it. *SEE* ORGONE.

Reich moved to the United States before the Second World War. By this time he had developed orgone accumulators—large upright boxes made of alternating layers of metal and wood—and lost no time in advertising and selling them through the mail. This brought the unfriendly attentions of the Food and Drug Administration, which prohibited him from selling his equipment. This he ignored, and the legal troubles that followed ended with his death in prison in 1957.

The last part of his life was given over to theories and experiments that even his more enthusiastic followers tend to avoid discussing. He became convinced that an orgone-powered device of his invention could disintegrate clouds in midair, and then turned it on UFOs, having discovered that Earth was a battlefield in a cosmic war between flying saucers—one set of saucers, he proclaimed, was trying to steal the Earth's orgone, while another set was trying to replace it.

Whatever the value of these later theories, his system of vegetotherapy proved effective, and both this and his writings became popular among occultists in the latter part of the twentieth century. His orgone has been identified with Mesmer's animal magnetism, Reichenbach's Odic force, and Eliphas Lévi's Astral Light, all of which it closely resembles, as another rediscovery of the etheric energy known to magicians for centuries. *SEE* ETHER; MESMER, FRANZ ANTON; LÉVI, ELIPHAS; REICHENBACH, KARL VON. FURTHER READING: REICH 1942.

Reichenbach, Karl von. Austrian scientist, 1788–1869. One of the scientifically minded noblemen who thronged continental Europe in the eighteenth and early nineteenth centuries, Baron Reichenbach was the scion of a distinguished and wealthy family of Austrian aristocracy, and spent most of his life either in Vienna or his family seat, Castle Riesenberg, a short distance away. He had a distinguished career as a chemist, being responsible among other things for the discovery of paraffin.

Later in life, the Baron turned his attention to the still-mysterious phenomena of magnetism, and discovered that certain sensitive individuals were able to see a faint light emanating from the poles of a magnet. Further experiments led him to the conviction that the light and other effects, far from being a mere side effect of magnetism, was the sign of another form of energy, which he called od or odic force. Reichenbach carried out extensive experiments on the odic force, using a variety of sensitives, and published extensively on the subject. Despite harsh and often wildly inaccurate criticism from the scientific mainstream of the time, he continued his researches into od up to the time of his death. *SEE* OD. FURTHER READING: REICHENBACH 1965.

Reidh. *SEE* RAIDO.

reincarnation. The belief that souls of the dead are reborn in other bodies, human or animal; also called transmigration. Far and away the most common teaching on the afterlife in Western occult traditions, reincarnation has a very long pedigree in the West. Pythagoras (c. 570–c. 495 B.C.E.), arguably the first major historical figure in the Western occult traditions, not only believed in reincarnation but claimed to remember a series of his own previous lives, including one during the Trojan War. *SEE* PYTHAGORAS. His prestige, and the adoption of the same belief by Plato in his dialogue *The Republic*, made reincarnation a standard belief in the more mystically oriented Platonist circles throughout antiquity. *SEE* PLATONISM. The ancient Druids are also believed to have taught reincarnation as an element in their traditional lore; *SEE* DRUIDS.

The rise of Christianity, with its insistence on eternal salvation or damnation after a single lifetime, forced the idea of reincarnation into an underground existence. Several Gnostic sects appear to have taught the doctrine, but after the suppression of Gnosticism in the last centuries of the Roman Empire, the orthodox ideas of Heaven and Hell defined the nature of the afterlife for nearly everyone in the Western world for centuries. *SEE* GNOSTICISM.

The one living tradition that retained a belief in reincarnation during the Middle Ages was the Cabala; *SEE* CABALA. The idea of reincarnation seems to have entered Jewish thought sometime in the first few centuries of the Common Era, but it was a minority view at best until the rise of the Cabala; most of the important medieval Jewish philosophers rejected it. In early Cabalistic texts such as the *Bahir*, on the other hand, reincarnation is presented as a reality, although these early writings seem to be unsure what to make of it. Several of these sources suggest that reincarnation is a punishment for specific sins, rather than the usual form of the afterlife for all.

By the late fifteenth century, though, the idea of reincarnation had been widely accepted in Jewish Cabalist circles, and some Cabalistic writers included the possibility of animal incarnations in their treatment of the subject. The great Cabalist Joseph ben Shalom Ashkenazi (fl. early fourteenth century) and his followers taught that reincarnation was a reality throughout the universe, and that everything from Sephiroth and angels down to inorganic matter passed through an endless cycle of transformations, descending from on high to the depths and then returning to the heights.

The Cabalistic version of reincarnation gained another wrinkle in the teachings of Isaac Luria and his school. In this doctrine, all souls were held to be part of Adam Qadmon, the Primordial Human, but different souls or "sparks" came from different "limbs" and "roots" within that body. People whose souls belonged to the same root had a natural affinity for one another, and shared a common spiritual task, which was the redemption of their root. *SEE* LURIA, ISAAC.

The revival of reincarnation outside Cabalistic circles was largely a result of the same revival of Greek and Roman spiritual literature that played such a large part in launching the Renaissance itself. Ancient accounts of Pythagorean and Platonist philosophy reintroduced the concept to the Western world. The development of contacts with India, especially after the beginning of English colonialism there in the eighteenth century, strengthened the influence of the doctrine and led a few esoteric traditions to adopt it. By the beginning of the nineteenth century, at least two English traditions—the Greek Pagan revival launched by Thomas Taylor (1758–1835), and those Druid groups influenced by the Welsh polymath Iolo Morganwg (Edward Williams, 1747–1826)—had adopted reincarnation as an article of faith. *SEE* DRUIDS; NEOPAGANISM; TAYLOR, THOMAS.

By the late nineteenth century, the occult community was sharply divided between believers in a standard Christian afterlife, on the one hand, and proponents of reincarnation on the other. Opponents of reincarnation denounced it in heated terms—one nineteenth-century Spiritualist described it as a "repulsive and unnatural doctrine" disseminated by "missionaries of Satan." The Spiritualist movement itself split over the issue, with followers of French Spiritualist Allan Kardec (H. L. D. Rivail, 1804–1869), who accepted reincarnation, forming a separate movement under the name of "Spiritism." *SEE* KARDEC, ALLAN; SPIRITISM; SPIRITUALISM.

Other nineteenth-century occult organizations such as the Hermetic Brotherhood of Luxor also rejected reincarnation, holding that human souls proceed on to other realms of being after a single life. This same viewpoint was upheld by none other than H. P. Blavatsky, founder of the Theosophical Society, in her first major book, *Isis Unveiled* (1877)—though she changed her views later. Nonetheless, as the Theosophical Society and Asian mystical traditions rose to dominance in the alternative spirituality scene, reincarnation became an increasingly common view of the afterlife, and Christian and quasi-Christian ideas of Heaven were increasingly pushed aside; *SEE* THEOSOPHY.

Most current occult traditions treat reincarnation as a simple matter of fact. Reincarnation has also become the standard interpretation of the afterlife among modern Pagans of nearly all stripes. Wiccans can trace the idea back to Charles Godfrey Leland, whose 1899 book *Aradia, or the Gospel of the Witches* is among the primary sources for Wiccan traditions. An earlier book by Leland (*Etruscan Roman Remains*, 1892) discusses an Italian tradition found among witch families, according to which sorcerers and witches are reborn among their own biological descendants. *SEE* LELAND, CHARLES GODFREY; NEOPAGANISM.

The theory of reincarnation has also been accepted generally among followers of the New Age movement. *SEE* NEW AGE MOVEMENT. FURTHER READING: LELAND 2002, SCHOLEM 1974.

repercussion. In magical tradition, the most important danger in etheric projection, shapeshifting, and other forms of out-of-body experience that make use of etheric substance. If a body of transformation formed in this way is struck by a etherically conductive metal such as silver or iron, the damage done to the body will be mirrored in the physical body of the projector. If the conductive material is driven through the center of the transformation body, the projector risks instant death.

Repercussion is a constant feature of the folklore of shapeshifting, and magicians in the nineteenth and early twentieth centuries insisted that these accounts were based on reality. Little has been said about repercussion since the rise of more psychological approaches to magic, however. *SEE ALSO* ETHERIC BODY; ETHERIC PROJECTION; LYCANTHROPY.

Resh. (Hebrew, "head") The twentieth letter of the Hebrew alphabet, a double letter with the sound-value *r* and the number-value 200. Its standard occult correspondences are as follows:

> *Path of the Tree of Life:* Path 30, Hod to Yesod.
> *Astrological Correspondence:* The Sun.
> *Tarot Correspondence:* Trump XIX, the Sun.
> *Part of the Cube of Space:* The southern face of the cube.
> *Colors:* in Atziluth—orange.
> in Briah—golden yellow.
> in Yetzirah—rich amber.
> in Assiah—amber, rayed with red.

Its text from the *Thirty-two Paths of Wisdom* runs as follows: "The Thirtieth Path is the Collecting Intelligence, and is so called because astrologers deduce from it the judgement of the stars and the celestial signs, and the perfections of their science, according to the rules of their resolutions." *SEE ALSO* CABALA; HEBREW ALPHABET.

Hebrew letter Resh

retrograde. In astrology, the apparent movement of a planet backwards through the zodiac. This happens at least once a year to all the planets, and as many as four times a year to fast-moving Mercury. The effect is an optical illusion caused by the Earth's own movement around the sun. When the Earth speeds past the slower planets further out, they appear to fall back against the background of the stars; the inner planets Mercury and Venus appear to move backwards when they are on the same side of the sun as the Earth and go rushing past our world.

Retrogrades play an important part in several branches of astrology. When a planet is retrograde, its influence is muted and subject to complications. Many people find that when Mercury is retrograde, for example, communications and travel—both of which are ruled by Mercury—often suffer from unexpected delays and difficulties. *SEE ALSO* ASTROLOGY.

Reuchlin, Johannes. German scholar and Cabalist, 1455–1522. In childhood his fine singing voice earned him a place in the chapel choir of the Margrave of Baden. Attending the palace school, he showed such promise in scholarship that the Margrave appointed him traveling companion to his son Friedrich, and this enabled Reuchlin to attend the University of Paris, where Friedrich was sent in 1473. He mastered Latin, Greek, and Hebrew at Paris, and wrote a Latin dictionary that was published in 1478. That same year he went to Orleans to study law, supporting himself by teaching ancient languages. In 1481 he returned to Germany and accepted a position at the University of Tübingen.

He soon gained a reputation as the best legal mind in Germany, and in 1490 took part in a diplomatic mission to Italy, where he met Pico della Mirandola and other Florentine Hermeticists; *SEE* PICO DELLA MIRANDOLA, GIOVANNI. His Hebrew studies were equally famous, and included intensive study of Cabalistic writings. His first book on the Cabala, *De Verbo Mirifico* (*On the Wonder-Working Word*), included a detailed account of Cabalistic angel magic and analyzed the name of Jesus by way of the Tetragrammaton. *SEE* PENTAGRAMMATON; TETRAGRAMMATON.

In 1509 he became the center of a continent-wide controversy when Johann Pfefferkorn, a converted Jew, and several officers of the Inquisition proposed to the Emperor Maximilian that all Jewish books except the Old Testament should be seized and burnt. Maximilian consulted Reuchlin, the foremost Hebrew scholar in Germany, and on his advice rejected the plan. Pfefferkorn and his associates then turned their attention to Reuchlin, charging him with heresy in Inquisition courts and in a series of scurrilous pamphlets. Reuchlin's friends, who included many influential scholars and members of the nobility, rallied around him, and the battle was on.

The legal side of the dispute was not settled until 1516, when the pope himself ordered all proceedings against Reuchlin dismissed. That same year saw the publication of *Epistolae Obscurorum Virorum* (*Letters of Obscure Men*), a brilliant and merciless parody of the case against Reuchlin, which was concocted and anonymously published by several of Reuchlin's friends. The *Letters* made Reuchlin's opponents the laughingstock of Europe and helped keep attacks on Christian Cabalists at bay for the rest of the sixteenth century.

In the last phases of the controversy, Reuchlin published his second and most important Cabalistic book, *De Arte Cabalistica* (*On the Cabalistic Art*, 1517). This was the first comprehensive treatise of Christian Cabala, and covers most of the Cabalistic tradition as it then existed. In 1518 he took a position at the University of Ingolstadt, and taught there until shortly before his death. FURTHER READING: REUCHLIN 1993, YATES 1979.

rising on the planes. In Golden Dawn magic and some other modern magical traditions, a standard magical practice for spiritual development. In the standard Golden Dawn form, the magician sits in a balanced and stable position, holding the lotus wand in both hands, with the lotus flower at its top pointed at his or her forehead. In imagination, the magician then rises up out of his or her physical body and begins to ascend the Middle Pillar of the Cabalistic Tree of Life, seeking to move up the levels of being and come into contact with higher spiritual realities.

Rising on the planes has been taken sometimes to involve full-scale astral projection, sometimes to refer to a variety of scrying in the spirit vision; both approaches work well in practice. Different traditions derived from the Golden Dawn have taken the method in a variety of directions, but the sense of rising up through the levels of being remains a constant feature. *SEE ALSO* ASTRAL PROJECTION; GOLDEN DAWN, HERMETIC ORDER OF THE; SCRYING. FURTHER READING: CROWLEY 1976, REGARDIE 1971.

risting. (Old Norse *rist*, "cut, carve") In modern rune magic, the term used for the act of engraving or carving one or more runes into a hard surface. Rune-risting is an important part of most current runic traditions; pieces of wood, horn, or other hard substances play much the same part in these that talismans of substances such as paper and parchment play in Hermetic magic. *SEE ALSO* RUNES; TALISMAN. FURTHER READING: PENNICK 1989, THORSSON 1998.

Rit. *SEE* RAIDO.

ritual magic. *SEE* CEREMONIAL MAGIC.

root race. In Theosophy and occult systems influenced by it, one of seven successive human or quasi-human races whose evolutions and tribulations make up the history of the Earth. The first root race, the Polarian, lived on the "Imperishable Sacred Continent" at the north pole and was barely in physical incarnation at all, having bodies made of "fire-mist." The second, the Hyperborean, lived on a continent that now makes up part of northern Asia, and was physical enough to invent sexual reproduction. Third came the Lemurians, who were ape-like, telepathic giants, some of them egg-laying and others four-armed. Fourth were the Atlanteans, more or less human in the current sense of the word, who were the ancestors of most of the present non-white population of the world. The "Aryan race" (that is to say, the peoples of Europe, the Middle East, and India) is the fifth, and two more root races are to come before the present humanity finishes its time on this planet and moves to Mercury to progress further along the evolutionary ladder.

Each root race, according to the Theosophical teaching, has a manu, who is its ruler and physical progenitor; a bodhisattva, who is responsible for its religious life; and a variety of other officials who are all members of the Great White Lodge, the secret brotherhood that superintends the spiritual evolution of the Earth. The manu and bodhisattva of the fifth root race are Vaivasvata and Maitreya, respectively. In the twenty-sixth century, when the sixth root race is scheduled to appear in California, the Masters El Morya and Kuthumi will be promoted to manu and bodhisattva of the new turn of the evolutionary spiral.

The doctrine of root races has much in common with the racial ideologies popular in late nineteenth- and early twentieth-century science, and was eagerly adopted by occult racists such as the Ariosophists to justify their ideologies. SEE ARIOSOPHY. SEE ALSO THEOSOPHY. FURTHER READING: J. GODWIN 1993, LEADBEATER 1925.

rootwork. An alternate name for hoodoo, especially common in the Atlantic coastal states. SEE HOODOO.

rose. (*Rosa* spp.) The most important symbolic flower in the Western tradition, the rose appears constantly in occult imagery, not least because of its association with the Rosicrucian movement; SEE ROSICRUCIANS. While its meanings vary widely, the rose generally represents love in all its forms, from the most spiritual levels of compassion to the most earthy of passions. It is balanced by the lily, the symbol of purity. SEE LILY. FURTHER READING: WILKINS 1969.

Rosencreutz, Christian. Legendary founder of the Rosicrucian order (1378–1484). The *Fama Fraternitatis*, the first of the original Rosicrucian documents, is the only source concerning his biography, and refers to him throughout simply as C. R. or C. R. C. His full name was first published in the *Chemical Wedding of Christian Rosenkreutz*, the third of the documents. His name has been variously spelled; the spelling used in this entry is the most common.

According to the Fama's account, Rosencreutz was born in Germany to a noble but penniless family. At the age of five he entered a monastery, where he learned Greek and Latin. While still in his teens, he eagerly set out on a pilgrimage to the Holy Land with an elder brother of the same monastery, whose initials were P. A. L.

The journey was interrupted by the death of P. A. L. in Cyprus, but Rosencreutz was unwilling to turn back and continued to Damascus, hoping to go on from there to Jerusalem. He was prevented from doing so "by reason of the feebleness of his body"—although the same source later comments on his strong constitution—and won favor with the Turks in Damascus because of his skill in medicine.

While in Damascus, he learned of Damear (modern Dhamar), a city of wise men in Arabia, where wonders were wrought and the secrets of nature disclosed. Changing his travel plans, he paid a group of Arabs to take him to Damear. There, according to the *Fama*, the inhabitants greeted him as though they had long expected him, called him by his name, and showed him secrets from the monastery where he had grown up. He stayed in Damear for three years, studying medicine and mathematics, and improving his command of Arabic. Then he traveled by way of Egypt to the city of Fez, where he spent two years studying magic and Cabala. SEE DAMEAR; FEZ.

Completing his studies, he went to Spain, hoping to share what he had learned with the scholars of Europe. This hope was disappointed, and his discoveries were rejected and laughed at, not only in Spain but elsewhere in Europe. So, finally, Rosencreutz returned to Germany where, after five years of further studies, he sought out three brothers from his old monastery and with them formed the Fraternity of the Rosy Cross. Four more, one of them Rosencreutz' nephew, were brought into the fraternity at a later time. While the majority of the brethren traveled throughout the world, Rosencreutz remained at the headquarters of the fraternity, the Collegium Spiritus Sancti, until the time of his death, and was buried there in a concealed underground vault. The rediscovery of this vault and of Rosencreutz' uncorrupted body in 1604 was the occasion for the publication of the Rosicrucian manifestoes, and became the central narrative of the movement.

The second of the original documents, the *Confessio Fraternitatis*, adds nothing of substance to the biography just given. The third, the *Chemical Wedding*, is a complex alchemical fable narrated by Rosencreutz in the first person, but its relationship to the figure described in the *Fama* is uncertain.

There have been various efforts to argue that Rosencreutz was an actual historical figure. Some Theosophists claimed him as an earlier incarnation of the Comte de Saint-Germain, and a painting by Rembrandt—"The Polish Rider," painted c. 1655—has been identified as a portrait either of the Comte or of Rosencreutz himself. Other writers have proposed that Paracelsus or the Polish alchemist Michael Sendivogius were the original on which the portrait of Rosencreutz was based. Such claims are hard to disprove but have little evidence to support them. *SEE ALSO*: SAINT-GERMAIN, COMTE DE; MASTERS; ROSICRUCIANS; VAULT OF CHRISTIAN ROSEN-CREUTZ. FURTHER READING: ALLEN 1968, J. GODWIN 1991, MCINTOSH 1987.

Rosicrucian Fellowship. American Rosicrucian organization, founded in 1907 by Max Heindel (Carl Louis Grashof), a Danish-American Theosophist who had studied with Rudolf Steiner before the latter broke with Theosophy; *SEE* STEINER, RUDOLF. Originally founded in Columbus, Ohio, the fellowship attracted interest primarily in the west coast states. In 1910, following the promptings of a vision, Heindel moved the fellowship's headquarters to Oceanside, California, where it remains to this day.

The fellowship offers correspondence courses in various branches of Western occult tradition, and also keeps several books in print, including Heindel's *The Rosicrucian Cosmo-Conception*, the core text of the fellowship's teaching. It also publishes a popular ephemeris for astrologers. *SEE ALSO* ROSICRUCIANS. FURTHER READING: HEINDEL 1909, MCINTOSH 1987.

Rosicrucian Order of the Crotona Fellowship (ROCF). British magical order, originally founded in 1911 as the Order of the Twelve by English actor and occultist George Alexander Sullivan. It was disbanded early in the First World War due to wartime restrictions on travel and publishing, but restarted as the ROCF in 1920, with Sullivan again at the helm.

The ROCF drew its membership almost entirely from the Co-Masonic movement, a branch of Fremasonry that admits womem as well as men to membership, and included a number of minor Theosophical celebrities, including Mabel Besant-Scott, the daughter of Annie Besant. *SEE* FREEMASONRY; THEOSOPHICAL SOCIETY. More ambitious than most of the other British orders between the wars, it established a system of nine degrees in three chapters, along with a range of subsidiary bodies such as the Ecclesia, the Templum, and the Academia Rosae Crucis, which offered a range of study courses in occult subjects. The most ambitious of its projects was the Theatricum, also known as "The First Rosicrucian Theatre in England," which produced and performed plays written by Sullivan.

Sullivan himself was unquestionably the driving force behind the organization. He took the magical name Aureolis and gave himself the somewhat garbled Latin title of Magi Supremus; claiming to be the Comte de Saint-Germain, he insisted that he (as Francis Bacon) had written the plays attributed to Shakespeare, and proclaimed himself immortal. Unfortunately he spoiled the effect somewhat by dying in 1942, after which the ROCF quietly dissolved.

The ROCF, despite its ambitions, would be little more than a footnote in occult history except for the later career of one of its members, a wealthy Englishman who had retired in the New Forest area after making his fortune in the East Indies. This member later claimed that an inner circle among the ROCF's membership were initiated into a surviving tradition of Pagan religion that had been passed down since ancient times—a tradition called Wicca. His name, of course, was Gerald Gardner. *SEE* GARDNER, GERALD BROUSSEAU; WICCA.

Rosicrucians. In Western occult tradition, a secret order of adepts using the symbol of the Rose Cross. Many different groups and teachers have claimed the Rosicrucian legacy over the years, creating a thick cloud of confusion around the subject.

The first mention of the Rosicrucian Order dates from the year 1614, when a booklet was published by Wilhelm Wessel in the German city of Cassel. The full title of the booklet is worth quoting: *Universal and General Reformation of the Whole Wide World; together with the Fama Fraternitatis of the Praiseworthy Fraternity of the Rosy Cross, written to all the Learned and Rulers of Europe; also a short reply sent by Herr Haselmayer, for which he was seized by the Jesuits and condemned to a galley; now put into print and communicated to all true hearts*. The first part of this booklet, the "Universal and General Reformation," is a German translation of one chapter of Traiano Boccalini's *Ragguagli di Parnasso* (1612); this is a scathing satire in which Apollo sets out to reform the world, listens to the harebrained schemes of a variety of wise men, and finally limits his reform to new laws governing the price of vegetables. There follows the *Fama Fraternitatis* or "Announcement of the Fraternity," which proclaims the existence of a secret Fraternity of the Rose Cross, describes the life of its founder Christian Rosencreutz and the discovery of the vault in which he and many of the secrets of the fraternity were buried, and invites all like-minded people to contact the Fraternity and share in its wisdom and alchemical wealth. The final item, Herr Haselmayer's letter, is an attempt to make contact with the order.

The *Fama's* publication ignited an extraordinary furor all over Europe. Conservatives denounced the mysterious order, skeptics questioned its existence, Hermeticists defended it, and plenty of people tried to take it up on its offer of membership. Books, pamphlets, broadsheets, letters, and other publications on the subject came from presses all over Europe.

A second pamphlet emerged in 1615 from the same press. This was titled *A Short Consideration of the More Secret Philosophy, written by Philip à Gabella, student of Philosophy, now published for the first time along with the Confession of the R. C. Fraternity.* The "Short Consideration" was an essay on magical philosophy based on John Dee's *Monas Hieroglyphica* (1564); the *Confessio,* which followed it, expanded on the material in the Fama from a somewhat more doctrinaire Lutheran standpoint. *SEE DEE, JOHN; MONAS HIEROGLYPHICA.*

A year later, with the controversy still at full boil, the third "manifesto"—titled *Chymische Hochzeit Christiani Rosenkreutz Anno 1549 (The Chemical Wedding of Christian Rosencreutz, Year 1549)*—was published by Lazarus Zetzner, a Strasburg printer. Not actually a manifesto at all, the *Chemical Wedding* is an alchemical and allegorical fable, narrated in the first person by Christian Rosencreutz himself, which describes his journey to visit the wedding of a mysterious king and queen and the pomp and complex ceremonies that surround this event, culminating in the death and resurrection of the bride and bridegroom.

All three of these original publications were issued anonymously. The third, the *Chemical Wedding,* was apparently the first one to be written, and its author was Johann Valentin Andreae. In later life a sober Lutheran minister, Andreae was a college student at the time he wrote the *Chemical Wedding,* involved in Hermeticist circles at the University of Tübingen; his father and brother were both alchemists. In his autobiography, which he wrote late in life and which remained unpublished until 1799, he admitted to having written the *Chemical Wedding*

a few years after beginning his studies at Tübingen in 1601; an entry in another of his writings fixes the date of authorship as 1605. Its publication in 1616 occurred at the hands of a "false brother," according to Andreae's account, and occasioned Andreae a good deal of embarrassment; he had been appointed to his first church post only two years before, and was busy trying to put the more scandalous parts of his college career behind him. Additional evidence supports this account, and Andreae's authorship of the *Chemical Wedding* is accepted by virtually all scholars. *SEE ANDREAE, JOHANN VALENTIN.*

The *Fama* and *Confessio* are a more complex affair. While Andreae may have had a hand in them and certainly knew the people involved, he was not acting alone. At the time when they were written (c. 1608–1610), Andreae was a member of a circle of Christian Hermeticists around the Paracelsian physician Tobias Hess (1568–1614), and—again, by way of comments in one of Andreae's writings—we know that Hess wrote at least part of the *Confessio.* The two manifestos may be by a number of authors working together, a common practice at the time.

The purpose of the two manifestos has given rise to endless speculation, but an important clue in the matter has received too little attention. The *Fama,* the first of the manifestos, did not appear alone; it was published with a translation of an Italian satire. (The translation itself was made by Christoph Besold, another important Hermeticist in Tübingen and a close friend of Andreae's.) The *General Reformation* is a mordant mythological satire on schemes of social reform; it is followed by a manifesto proclaiming, among other things, a mythological scheme for social reform. It's hard to miss the implication that the entire project was intended as a joke.

Certainly this was Andreae's opinion. He referred to the Rosicrucian writings consistently in later years as a *ludibrium,* a word that can mean "joke," "comedy," "play," or "mockery." In one of his writings (*Mythologiae Christiana,* 1618) he makes a curious comment about the "comedy" having involved "an entire change of actors." This is apparently what happened. What had started out within Andreae's circle of friends had spun out of their control within a short time of the first publication. What began as an ornate joke, of the sort much practiced at the time, became something (or, rather, several somethings) much more serious. Writers unconnected with the original circle began to borrow the Rosicrucian symbolism and story as a framework for Lutheranism, alchemical and magical teachings, or millennarian prophecies of the approaching end of the world.

There also seems to have been a political dimension, one that would have disastrous consequences. While the original manifestos were being written, a complex political intrigue centering on Friedrich V, Prince Palatine of the Rhine, was coming to fruition. Friedrich was one of the leading lights among the Protestant monarchs of the period. Rudolf II, king of Bohemia and Holy Roman Emperor, had abdicated in 1611, and his successor Matthias died only five years later. Since the Bohemian crown was elective, not hereditary, Friedrich's advisers and supporters were busily positioning him as future king of Bohemia, with the imperial crown a tantalizing possibility. The scheme failed catastrophically; Friedrich was crowned king of Bohemia in 1619, but he and his allies were overwhelmed by Catholic armies in the Battle of the White Mountain in 1620. The Palatinate was overrun later the same year, and Friedrich was driven into lifelong exile in Holland.

Under Friedrich, the Palatinate of the Rhine had become a major center not only of Lutheranism but of Hermetic and alchemical influences. Not only the Rosicrucian manifestos but other Hermetic publications of the same period may have played a part in a deliberate propaganda scheme to foster a Lutheran–Hermetic movement backing Friedrich and opposing the House of Habsburg, the champions of the Catholic reaction.

The Thirty Years War, which broke out in the aftermath of Friedrich's failed gamble, effectively ended the German occult revival of the period, and whatever might have been behind the Rosicrucian manifestoes seems to have gone into hiding or out of existence at that time. Only in England and the Scandinavian countries, where the Catholic Church had definitively lost power decades earlier, did writers who aligned themselves with the Rosicrucian movement remain active. Even there, the movement (if it was a movement) seems to have petered out by the end of the seventeenth century.

The resurgence of Rosicrucian orders in the next century was set in motion by the spread of Freemasonry, which emerged from obscurity in England in the second decade of the eighteenth century and spread to most European countries within a few decades afterward. As Masonic initiates began adding to the three original degrees of Entered Apprentice, Fellow Craft, and Master Mason, nearly all the traditional secret societies and Mystery cults of the past were ransacked for inspiration, and Rosicrucianism was not exempt. The result was a flurry of Masonic Rosicrucian orders from the eighteenth century to the present. *SEE* FREEMASONRY; ORDEN DES GOLD- UND ROSENKREUTZ; SOCIETAS ROSICRUCIANA IN ANGLIA (SRIA).

Similar motives in the massive occult renaissance of the late nineteenth and early twentieth centuries gave rise to a new outpouring of Rosicrucian organizations. The Hermetic Order of the Golden Dawn in England and the Rose+Croix Kabbalistique in France, which between them played a dominant role in the turn-of-the-century European occult scene, claimed Rosicrucian lineage and made much use of Rosicrucian symbolism. *SEE* GOLDEN DAWN, HERMETIC ORDER OF THE. "Sâr" Josephin Peladan, whose occult-inspired art shows were the toast of late nineteenth-century Paris, drew on the same source. *SEE* PELADAN, JOSÉPHIN; SALONS DE LA ROSE+ CROIX.

In the first decades of the twentieth century, America saw the rise of a series of large-scale Rosicrucian magical orders that operated on the correspondence-course principle, and taught the basics of occult philosophy and practice to two generations of American magicians. *SEE* ANCIENT MYSTIC ORDER ROSAE CRUCIS (AMORC); FRATERNITAS ROSAE CRUCIS (FRC); ROSICRUCIAN FELLOWSHIP; SOCIETAS ROSICRUCIANA IN AMERICA (SRIA). Another twentieth-century addition to the Rosicrucian ranks was Austrian occultist Rudolf Steiner (1861–1925), who made use of Rosicrucian traditions in his voluminous writings on occult theory and practice. The Rosicrucian tradition even has a place in the prehistory of modern Wicca; *SEE* ROSICRUCIAN ORDER OF THE CROTONA FELLOWSHIP (ROCF). Further Roscrucian developments can probably be expected in the twenty-first century as well.

In the last two centuries, in keeping with the grand occult tradition of falsifying history, various accounts of the origins of Rosicrucianism have been circulated tracing it back to ancient Egypt, Atlantis, or some similarly remote period; at least one currently active Rosicrucian order claims that the tradition dates back to the heretic pharaoh Akhenaten in the fourteenth century B.C.E. *SEE* AKHENATEN. Sadly, these claims have no trace of historical evidence to back them, and represent yet another off-shoot of the rich legacy of occult pseudo-history. *SEE* OCCULT HISTORY. *SEE ALSO* FLUDD, ROBERT; MAIER, MICHAEL; ROSENCREUTZ, CHRISTIAN. FURTHER READING: ÅKERMAN 1998, DICKSON 1998, MCINTOSH 1987, YATES 1972.

Rousing of the Citadels. The variant of the Middle Pillar exercise used in the Aurum Solis magical system. It differs from the standard Middle Pillar primarily in using an additional center at the middle of the brow, and in placing the centers on the front of the body, projecting out from the skin or (in the case of the Flos Abysmi center) entirely outside the body.

The six centers used in the Rousing of the Citadels are as follows:

Center	Meaning	Location
Corona Flammae	Crown of Flame	Above head
Uncia Coeli	Ounce of Heaven	Brow
Flos Abysmi	Flower of the Abyss	Throat
Orbis Solis	Orb of the Sun	Heart
Cornua Lunae	Horns of the Moon	Genitals
Instita Splendens	Splendid Border	Between feet

SEE ALSO AURUM SOLIS; MIDDLE PILLAR EXERCISE; *AND THE NAMES OF THE INDIVIDUAL CENTERS.* FURTHER READING: DENNING AND PHILLIPS 1978.

rowan. (*Sorbus aucuparia*) An important tree in magical tradition, the rowan is also known as the mountain ash; a small, shrubby tree with leaves divided into many leaflets and bright red berries, it is found through most of the Northern Hemisphere. Rowan has been much used as a protection against hostile magic and uncanny beings.

In the Ogham tree-alphabet of the ancient Celts, rowan is associated with the letter Luis. *SEE* LUIS; OGHAM.

Royal Stars. In astrology and occult symbolism generally, the four stars Aldebaran, Regulus, Antares, and Fomalhaut. In Sumerian times, these four bright and highly visible stars marked the sun's positions at the equinoxes and solstices, although due to precession of the equinoxes this is no longer true; *SEE* PRECESSION OF THE EQUINOXES.

In the Adeptus Exemptus ritual of the Hermetic Order of the Golden Dawn, emblems of these four stars are tied onto the body of the candidate at different points in the ceremony. *SEE* ADEPTUS EXEMPTUS.

An alternative name of the Royal Stars is the Watchers of the Heavens; *SEE* WATCHERS, THE.

ruach. (Hebrew RVCh, "breath, spirit") In Cabala and many magical traditions, a term commonly used for spirit, with the same origin and many of the same ambiguities as the English word. *SEE* SPIRIT.

In the Golden Dawn tradition and in many Cabalistic sources, *ruach* was used as a term for the ordinary conscious self, composed of intellect, emotion, imagination, will, and memory. It is guided from above by the spiritual self or neshamah, and links downward to the physical body by way of the vital body or automatic consciousness, the *nephesh*. *SEE* NEPHESH; NESHAMAH. *SEE ALSO* CABALA.

Ruach Elohim. (Hebrew, RVCh ALHIM, "spirit of God") In Cabala, the divine spirit. The letters of these two words add up to the number 300, the number of the Hebrew letter Shin; this detail of gematria plays a large role in that letter's symbolism and meaning. *SEE* GEMATRIA; SHIN.

Rubeus. (Latin, "red") A geomantic figure governed by Mars. Rubeus is usually considered an unlucky figure, except for questions related to passion and debauchery. *SEE* GEOMANCY.

Geomantic figure Rubeus

Rudhyar, Dane. (Daniel Chennevière) French–American astrologer, composer, artist, and occultist, 1895–1985. Born in Paris to a wealthy family, Rudhyar was a child prodigy who graduated with a degree in philosophy at age sixteen and published a well-regarded book on the French composer Claude Debussy two years later. Exempt from military service due to poor health, he left France in 1916 for America, changing his name to Dane Rudhyar and settling in New York, where he quickly became a rising star in the American musical scene. An important figure in American Modernism, a movement in classical music active in the 1920s, he also wrote scores for several Hollywood movie productions.

In 1931, he suddenly left New York, dropped all contacts with the musical world, and settled in Santa Fe, New Mexico. There he pursued the study of astrology, a long-time interest, and took up the study of Alice Bailey's occult philosophy, joining her Arcane School. *SEE* ARCANE SCHOOL, THE; ASTROLOGY; BAILEY, ALICE. By 1933 he was writing monthly articles for respected astrological publications, and in 1936 he published what is generally considered his masterwork, *The Astrology of Personality*, which was dedicated to Bailey and originally published by her publishing house. In this work, he predicted the discovery of a planetary body between Saturn and Uranus; just over forty years later, this prediction proved correct when Charles Kowal discovered the giant comet Chiron in the location Rudhyar had predicted. *SEE* CHIRON.

Rudhyar also became a noted painter in the late 1930s, and wrote two novels and several volumes of verse. Married four times, he spent much of the rest of his life in New Mexico and California, writing some thirty books on astrology, philosophy, music, and art. He was the founder of humanistic astrology, a movement within modern astrology that rejects a scientific approach to astrological forces in favor of one based on depth psychology and holistic philosophy. His death in San Francisco at the age of ninety brought eulogies from around the astrological world. FURTHER READING: RUDHYAR 1970.

rue. (*Ruta graveolens*) An herb native to the Mediterranean area, much used in traditional natural magic. It is a common protective herb against hostile magic and will banish evil spirits. Hunter's lore holds that if you rub an arrow with rue, it will always find its mark. *SEE ALSO* NATURAL MAGIC.

Ruis. (Old Irish, "redden") The fifteenth letter of the Ogham alphabet, with the sound-value *r*. It corresponds to the elder among trees, the rook among birds, the color red, and the number fifteen. In Robert Graves' version of the Ogham tree-calendar, its month runs from November 26 to December 22. *SEE* OGHAM.

Ogham letter Ruis

Ruler, elemental. In Cabalistic magic, a class of spirits who govern the four elements, placed above the elemental kings but below the angels of the elements. Their role in the elemental realm is equivalent to that of the planetary intelligences, similarly placed between the planetary angels and the planetary spirits. The four rulers are Seraph (fire), Tharsis (water), Aral (air), and Kerub (earth); these four names derive from those of the Angelic Hosts of four of the Sephiroth of the Tree of Life. *SEE ALSO* ARAL; KERUB; SERAPH; THARSIS.

runes. (Old Norse *run*, "secret") A group of ancient alphabets used by Germanic and Scandinavian peoples as a system of writing for practical purposes and as a magical and divinatory tool. The oldest known system of runes, the elder futhark of twenty-four letters, apparently originated sometime before 50 C.E., the date of the oldest known runic artifact. (The term *futhark*, used for a runic alphabet, is made up of the sound-values of the first six letters.) An expanded version, the Anglo-Saxon futhorc of either twenty-nine or thirty-three letters, was in use by 400 C.E. Among the peoples of Scandinavia, by contrast, the runic alphabet evolved in the other direction, simplifying into the younger futhark of sixteen runes.

Scholars have argued for more than a century about the origin of the runes, with Greek, Latin, and Etruscan alphabets being suggested as the original source of the runic letters. It's clear, however, that runes were deeply connected with Germanic magical traditions from the beginning, as the meaning of "rune" suggests.

The Roman historian Tacitus, in his account of the German tribes (the *Germania*, written in 98 C.E.), mentioned in passing a system of divination using *notae* ("signs"). Pieces of wood from a nut-bearing tree were marked with the notae, and three of these were drawn and interpreted. The first known runic artifact, a brooch found at Meldorf in Germany, dates from around 50 C.E., so Tacitus' comment may be a reference to runic (or proto-runic) divination.

Later runic inscriptions, including the impressive runestones found across southern Scandinavia, also include magical words of power and long, incomprehensible passages similar to the *nomina barbara* of contemporary magic further south. *SEE* ALU; BARBAROUS NAMES; LAUKAR; LINA. Norse sagas and other written material from the last years of the runic tradition present the runes as magical through and through, and the god Odin is credited with their discovery. Runemasters, called *erilar* in the time of the elder futhark, apparently played a major role in the magical and spiritual life of the Germanic tribespeople of the Age of Migrations (c. 300–c. 800 C.E.), as their later Norse equivalents did until the Christianization of Scandinavia in the eleventh century.

With the coming of Christianity and the Latin alphabet, the runes gradually dropped out of use. Runic inscriptions from the Middle Ages often include elements from classical, Arabic, and medieval magical traditions, showing that the native magic of the north was fading out of memory. By the beginning of the Renaissance, rune lore survived only in fragmentary form in a handful of manuscript sources.

The rediscovery of the runes began with the work of the great Renaissance scholar and magician Johannes Bureus (1568–1652) in Sweden, who put the tools of contemporary classical scholarship to work on the surviving relics of Pagan Scandinavian culture. *SEE* BUREUS, JOHANNES. Remnants of Anglo-Saxon runic lore also caught the attention of English antiquaries from the Renaissance onwards.

The revival of the runes as a major presence in the Western occult tradition, however, began with the work of Guido von List (1848–1919), the seminal figure in the modern Teutonic revival. *SEE* LIST, GUIDO VON. In 1902, while recovering from an eye operation, List underwent a mystical experience in which the runes played an important part. Out of this experience, he devised a somewhat idiosyncratic system of eighteen runes based on a passage from the *Elder Edda* in which the god Odin recounts the runes' secret powers. This system remains popular in the German-speaking countries, but has had little following in the rest of the world. Another dominant figure in German runic studies was Friedrich Marby (1882–1966), who developed a method of runic yoga as part of a complex and impressive system of rune mysticism and magic. *SEE* MARBY, FREIDRICH BERNHARD.

Rune studies in the English-speaking world, on the other hand, progressed little until the rise of the first major Teutonic Pagan movements in the early 1970s, and remained a concern of very few for some years thereafter. The publication of Ralph Blum's *The Book of Runes* in 1978 changed this situation. While Blum's work has been harshly criticized as shallow and inaccurate, it served to introduce the runes to a widespread audience and created a market for more substantial studies of rune lore. The decades since that time have seen a flowering of rune studies, in conjunction with the development and spread of the Teutonic Pagan revival. *SEE* ASATRU. *SEE ALSO* ANGLO-SAXON FUTHORC; ARMANEN RUNES; ELDER FUTHARK; YOUNGER FUTHARK. FURTHER READING: ASWYNN 1998, DAVIDSON 1981, FLOWERS 1986, LIST 1988, THORSON 1989B, THORSSON 1998.

Ruta. According to Theosophical lore, one of the two islands that were left after the first, partial flooding of Atlantis, the other being Daitya. The Theosophical version of Atlantis was taken over by many other occult systems of the late nineteenth and early twentieth centuries, and references to the Island of Ruta can be found there, as well as in fantasy fiction. *SEE ALSO* ATLANTIS.

Sabaoth. (Hebrew TzBAVTh, "army") An element in several biblical and Cabalistic Names of God (for example, ALHIM TzBAVTh, Elohim Tzabaoth, "Elohim of Hosts") that was mistaken for an independent Name by Hellenistic magicians and used freely in ancient, medieval and modern magic. The spelling "Sabao" is also found in some ancient sources, particularly in Gnostic and Graeco-Egyptian magical writings. *SEE* GNOSTICISM; GRAECO-EGYPTIAN MAGICAL PAPYRI. *SEE ALSO* CABALA.

sabbat. A traditional term for a meeting of witches, borrowed by the modern Pagan revival; for information on older traditions, *SEE* SABBATH, WITCHES'. In modern Pagan practice, the sabbats are the eight major festivals of the wheel of the year, the Pagan sacred calendar, and consist of the solstices, the equinoxes, and four "cross-quarter" days located approximately halfway between these. The sabbats have a variety of names in different Pagan traditions, but Samhain, Yule, Imbolc, Ostara, Beltane, Litha, Lammas, and Mabon are the most common set. A division into greater sabbats—the cross-quarter days—and lesser sabbats—the solstices and equinoxes—is common in many traditions.

> *Sabbat:* Samhain. *Alternative Names:* Hallowmass, Winternight. *Date:* October 31.
>
> *Sabbat:* Yule. *Alternative Names:* Winter Solstice, Alban Arthuan. *Date:* December 21.
>
> *Sabbat:* Imbolc. *Alternative Names:* Oimelc, Brigid, Candlemas, Disting. *Date:* February 2.
>
> *Sabbat:* Ostara. *Alternative Names:* Spring Equinox, Alban Eiler. *Date:* March 21.
>
> *Sabbat:* Beltane. *Alternative Names:* Roodmas, Walburga. *Date:* May 1.
>
> *Sabbat:* Litha. *Alternative Names:* Summer Solstice, Midsummer, Alban Heruin. *Date:* June 21.
>
> *Sabbat:* Lammas. *Alternative Names:* Lughnasadh, Thingtide. *Date:* August 1.
>
> *Sabbat:* Mabon. *Alternative Names:* Autumn Equinox, Winter Finding, Alban Elued. *Date:* September 21.

While some of the eight individual sabbats have ancient roots, the modern Pagan calendar as a whole is a twentieth-century creation. The diverse origins of the standard current names of the sabbats are a good sign that the list is a modern creation put together from written sources: *Samhain*, *Beltane*, and *Imbolc* are terms taken from Irish Gaelic; *Yule* and *Lammas* are Old English; *Ostara* is Old German; *Mabon* is medieval Welsh; and *Litha* was taken from the fantasy fiction of J. R. R. Tolkien and appears nowhere else. *SEE* BELTANE; IMBOLC; LAMMAS; LITHA; MABON; OSTARA; SAMHAIN; YULE.

Historical records of the festivals are an equally diverse lot. The celebrations of Beltane and Samhain are well attested in a range of Celtic sources, and a list of the four cross-quarter days, treated as a set, are found in a few old Irish sources. Festivals on or around the solstices are common to most cultures around the world. There is no evidence, however, that the equinoxes were celebrated in Pagan Europe, and plenty of evidence that a wide assortment of other festivals that are not part of the modern Pagan year-wheel played a much more important role.

To judge from the fertility rites and folk festivals that appear in old records or survive today, the ancient Pagan calendar of festivals was as complex, localized, and diverse as every other aspect of ancient Paganism. None of this, equally, makes the current sabbats inappropriate as a ritual calendar for modern Pagans, and a set of ceremonies equally spaced around the year has much to recommend it in practical terms. SEE ALSO NEOPAGANISM; PAGANISM; WICCA. FURTHER READING: FARRAR AND FARRAR 1981, HUTTON 1994.

Sabbath, Witches'. In the folklore of medieval witchcraft, the supposed meetings to which witches flew to worship the Devil and perform magical activities. Sabbats occurred on various dates—there was no fixed calendar in the witch-hunting manuals or other contemporary sources—and involved varying activities, among which feasting, dancing, killing and eating infants, and lovemaking with other witches and/or demons were fairly standard. The word *sabbath* has been variously explained by scholars of witchcraft, but most modern researchers agree that it was borrowed from the Hebrew word *shabbat*, "sabbath," as part of the common Christian habit of lumping all non-Christians together as worshippers of the Christian Devil.

In witch trials, admission that one had attended a sabbath was important in proving guilt, and detailed, leading questions on the subject were on most of the standard lists used during interrogation of suspected witches. Since torture was nearly always used in these last, colorful descriptions of the sabbath and its activities were readily forthcoming. The comparison to current ideas of "Satanic ritual abuse," evidence for which is routinely extracted by way of lists of detailed, leading questions fed to "survivors" under hypnosis or intense psychological pressure, has not escaped a number of modern scholars of the subject. SEE SATANIC RITUAL ABUSE.

It is evident that the sabbath of the witch-hunting manuals had no historical reality whatsoever, and was cobbled together out of European folklore and traditional Christian claims about other religions—claims which, ironically, had been directed at Christianity itself in Roman times. It has been argued, however, that large parts of the sabbath myth borrowed from a set of poorly understood medieval traditions of spiritual flight in the company of a nocturnal goddess. SEE CANON EPISCOPI. SEE ALSO BURNING TIMES; MAGIC, PERSECUTION OF; PAGANISM. FURTHER READING: COHN 1975, GINZBURG 1991.

Sabian symbols. A set of emblems, one for each of the 360 degrees of the zodiac, used by some modern astrologers as an aid to chart interpretation. A recent addition to astrology, the Sabian symbols were devised in 1925 by the American astrologer Marc Edmund Jones and the clairvoyant Elsie Wheeler. They were first circulated by Jones in lessons given out to members of the Sabian Assembly, the school of astrology and esoteric thought he operated, and then published in his book *The Sabian Symbols in Astrology* (1953). In 1973, astrologer Dane Rudhyar published an expanded and reinterpreted version of the symbols in his *An Astrological Mandala*; this has become the most commonly used version in modern astrological practice.

The flavor of the Sabian symbols can be gauged by a few examples. One degree Aries is "A woman just risen from the sea. A seal is embracing her." In Rudhyar's interpretation, it represents "Emergence of new forms and of the potentiality for consciousness" (Rudhyar 1974 p. 49). sixteen degrees Virgo is "In the zoo, children are brought face to face with an orangutan"; the meaning is "A direct confrontation with the 'wild' power of primordial nature within oneself" (Ibid., p. 160). Twenty-eight degrees Pisces is "A fertile garden under the full moon reveals a variety of full-grown vegetables"; the interpretation is "The full satisfaction of the individual's basic needs" (Ibid., p. 286).

The Sabian symbols have also been used on their own as a divinatory tool, using various random methods to select a single symbol, which is then interpreted. SEE ALSO ASTROLOGY. FURTHER READING: JONES 1953, RUDHYAR 1974.

Sachiel. In ceremonial magic, the angel of the planet Jupiter. SEE ANGEL.

sacred geometry. In modern occult circles, the most common term for the branch of occult theory and practice focusing on geometrical form as a way of symbolizing, experiencing, and contacting spiritual levels of existence. A complex and erudite branch of occultism, sacred geometry is among the least well-known of occult traditions nowadays, although there has been a steady subcurrent of interest in it for many centuries.

In essence, sacred geometry is simply geometry as it was practiced throughout the Western world from ancient times until the coming of the Scientific Revolution. In ancient, medieval, and Renaissance times, geometrical forms and relationships were seen as an expression of the deep, archetypal structure of reality, and students of geometry were taught to experience geometric processes as the unfolding, in space and time, of spiritual realities.

These same patterns could equally be put to work in architecture and art. According to the theory of sacred geometry, when this is done, the spiritual force represented by the geometries of a building or an artwork affects people who encounter it, whether or not they know how to interpret the geometrical language. Greek temples and Gothic cathedrals, both of which were designed and built using the canons of sacred geometry, provide evidence of how well this works in practice.

The history of sacred geometry in the Western occult tradition begins with Pythagoras of Samos (c. 570–c. 495 B.C.E.), who traveled to Egypt and Babylon to study mathematics and philosophy, and founded a semisecret society that taught geometry as a spiritual discipline. SEE PYTHAGORAS. His followers, who scattered across the Mediterranean world in the aftermath of the anti-Pythagorean riots of the early fifth century B.C.E., took his geometrical lore with them.

Vitruvius, the one important Roman writer on architecture whose book survived the Middle Ages, quotes Pythagorean geometrical lore extensively; SEE VITRUVIUS. The masons' guilds of the Middle Ages, from which Freemasonry is descended, also preserved a great deal of what is now sacred geometry; SEE FREEMASONRY.

The Christian church found that older traditions of sacred geometry could easily be converted to Christian use, and there is some reason to think that geometrical and mathematical symbolism are woven into many passages in the New Testament itself. Until the Reformation—and well after it, in some areas—churches were universally designed and built with an eye to geometrical symbolism. SEE CHRISTIAN OCCULTISM.

A combination of traditional masons' lore and rediscovered classical documents came together in the Renaissance to launch a massive revival of sacred geometry. Internationally famous scholars such as the Venetian friar Francesco Giorgi (1466–1540) published important works on the subject, most of which have never been translated out of Latin; SEE GIORGI, FRANCESCO. The practical applications of geometry were not neglected; Giorgi was a consultant on architectural symbolism, and a century later the renowned Dutch swordsman Gerard Thibault (1574–1629) published a book expounding an effective system of swordsmanship based on sacred geometry; SEE THIBAULT, GERARD.

Like most branches of the Western occult traditions, sacred geometry fell on hard times with the coming of the Scientific Revolution. It was preserved mostly in the more occult end of Freemasonry, which kept enough contact with its roots to retain a fascination with geometrical symbolism. Several important books on sacred geometry and related principles were published in the eighteenth and nineteenth centuries, of which William Stirling's *The Canon* (1897) was the most influential; SEE STIRLING 1999.

The modern revival of sacred geometry began with the work of one man, René "Aour" Schwaller de Lubicz (1887–1961), whose studies of Gothic cathedrals and ancient Egyptian monuments led him to an intensive study of traditional geometry and the publication of a series of massive and difficult books on the subject; SEE SCHWALLER DE LUBICZ, RENÉ A. Later, in the late 1960s and early 1970s, a number of English writers studying leys and earth mysteries came across Stirling's *The Canon* and similar works, and began work along similar lines; SEE LEYS. The current revival is fairly modest but has produced a number of excellent books and several beautifully designed buildings.

In earlier times, sacred geometry was considered to be part of the quadrivium, the four branches of occult mathematics. SEE ARITHMOLOGY; GOLDEN PROPORTION; QUADRIVIUM. FURTHER READING: FIDELER 1993, HANCOX 1992, LAWLOR 1982, PENNICK 1979, STIRLING 1999.

sacrifice. The primary religious ritual of ancient Pagan religions, in which offerings—most often, though not always, livestock—were made at the altar of one or more gods. In the case of the livestock, the god or gods received a part of the offering, while the rest was generally cooked and shared amongst the worshippers. Other forms of sacrifice included throwing valuables into bodies of water or casting them down wells or ritual pits.

Detailed information on sacrificial rituals in ancient Greece and Rome has survived in classical literature. These, together with scattered information and archeological finds from the rest of Europe, and cross-cultural parallels from other Indo-European cultures such as ancient Persia and Vedic India, have allowed the Pagan sacrificial rituals of other Western cultures to be reconstructed in some detail.

The basic theory of ancient sacrifice was summed up concisely by the Romans in the phrase *do ut des*—"I give that you might give." Sacrifice was part of an exchange of gifts between the gods and humanity; the gods gave fertility to crops and livestock, and people gave back a portion of these things in exchange. Besides grain and livestock, other items of value might be offered; most of the Pagan religions of the Mediterranean basin made use of incense as an offering, for example, while the ancient Celts were famous for throwing gold and silver into rivers and lakes as offerings to their deities.

Sacrifice was also closely connected to divination. The entrails of livestock who were offered to the gods were inspected by diviner priests, who read them—especially the liver, which was associated with sky gods such as Jupiter—as an omen of the gods' response to the offering. This practice was known variously as haruspicy, hieromancy, or hepatoscopy. The behavior of the flames during the burning of any burnt offering was also watched as an omen. The movements of incense smoke and the crackling of grain offerings in the fire were also used to judge whether or not the gods had accepted the offering. *SEE* DIVINATION; OMENS.

In Judaism, sacrificial rituals very similar to those of their Pagan neighbors were practiced up until the final destruction of the Temple of Jerusalem in 70 C.E., and details of the rituals can still be found in the Old Testament and its Jewish commentaries. Much of the symbolism of Christianity is actually based on these ancient ritual forms, with Jesus of Nazareth playing the role of sacrificial lamb.

The rise of the Christian church to dominance in the last years of the classical period saw older traditions of sacrifice suppressed in most of the Western world. At first, this was justified by the idea that the sacrifice of Jesus had made all further sacrifice unnecessary. Later, in the Middle Ages, Christian theologians redefined "sacrifice" as the act of giving up some form of pleasure in order to prove how much one loves God. This would have been incomprehensible to a Pagan Roman, who might have wondered what benefit a god could get from watching a worshipper make himself or herself miserable; nonetheless, it remains a very common understanding (or misunderstanding).

Very few branches of the modern Neopagan revival have made much use of traditional ideas of sacrifice. Among the exceptions are some Norse and Celtic Reconstructionist groups, and a handful of Druid groups such as Ar nDraiocht Fein (ADF). *SEE* AR NDRAIOCHT FEIN (ADF); ASATRU; CELTIC RECONSTRUCTIONISM. The offerings used in these groups consist of grain, alcoholic beverages, cooked food, and jewelry, along with songs and poetry. A few groups have gone to the extent of baking imitation animals of bread and offering these up in an imitation of the time-honored fashion. *SEE ALSO* PAGANISM. FURTHER READING: FLACELIERE 1965, MERRIFIELD 1987.

Sadhu, Mouni. (Sudowski, Dymitr) Polish occultist, c. 1898–1966. Born in St. Petersburg to a Polish Catholic father and a German Theosophist mother, he had an ordinary childhood, but his formal schooling ended with the Russian Revolution that followed. As a cadet in the White (anti-Communist) army after the war, he saw combat, and escaped to Poland after the White forces collapsed in 1919. Joining the Polish army as a lieutenant, he probably fought in the Polish-Soviet war of 1920–1921.

War's end found Sudowski in Warsaw, where he worked at the post office and took up occult studies with the Polish branch of the Theosophical Society; *SEE* THEOSOPHICAL SOCIETY. By the late 1920s he had founded a study circle of his own, which focused its efforts on the tarot system devised by Grigorii Mebes (1869–1930). He also made contact with Martinist circles in Warsaw and Paris, and apparently joined several other occult societies as well; *SEE* MARTINISM.

After the sudden conquest of Poland by Germany in 1939, Sudowski became a collaborator with the Nazi occupation government. At war's end, he fled to Germany to escape the Soviets, and from there traveled by way of a Catholic monastery in Paris to Brazil—in all likelihood using the same network of secret routes that allowed so many other Nazis and Nazi sympathizers to escape Europe after the Third Reich's collapse.

While in Brazil he studied yoga at a commune at Curitiba organized by followers of Indian guru Ramana Maharshi. In 1949 he went to Tiruvannamalai, India, where Maharshi's ashram was located, and studied meditation with Maharshi for six months before moving on to Melbourne, Australia, where he spent the rest of his life.

His time in India inspired Sudowski to take the pen name Mouni Sadhu, under which he wrote a book about his time with Maharshi, *In Days of Great Peace* (1957). Other books followed, returning more and more to the occult studies of his youth. The most important of these was *The Tarot* (originally published 1962), which expounds a detailed system of occult theory and practice, using the twenty-two trumps of the tarot deck as a framework. Much of the material in the book comes from Mebes' writings on the subject.

Sudowski also organized several study groups in Melbourne and Sydney, and his house in the Melbourne suburb of Box Hill was a meeting place for many local students of the occult. He died after a short illness in 1966. FURTHER READING: DECKER AND DUMMETT 2002, SADHU 1962.

Sagittarius. (Latin, "archer") The ninth sign of the zodiac, a mutable fire sign of masculine polarity. In Sagittarius, Jupiter has the rulership and Mercury is in his detriment. This sign rules the hips, thighs, and liver.

The sun is in Sagittarius approximately from November 23 to December 21. People with this sun placement are traditionally optimistic, jovial, and honest, with a strong philosophical bent; they may also be irresponsible, tactless, and impractical.

In the Golden Dawn tarot system, Sagittarius corresponds to Trump XIV, Temperance. *SEE* TAROT; TEMPERANCE. *SEE ALSO* ASTROLOGY.

Astrological symbol of Sagittarius

Saille. (Old Irish, "willow") The fourth (in Boibeloth) or fifth (in Beth-Luis-Nion) letter of the Ogham alphabet, with the sound-value *s*. Saille corresponds to the willow among trees, the hawk among birds, the color "fine-colored" (Gaelic *sodath*), and the number sixteen. In Robert Graves' version of the Ogham tree-alphabet, its month runs from April 15 to May 12. *SEE* OGHAM.

Ogham letter Saille

Saint-Germain, Comte de. European adventurer, 1691?–1784. Very little is known for certain about this extraordinary person. The late eighteenth century was an age when the courts of Europe were full of exotic personalities who lived by their wits. It was the time of Casanova, Cagliostro, and the gender-bending Chevalier d'Eon, to name only a few of the most dazzling lights in the firmament of adventurers, but the individual who called himself the Comte de Saint-Germain (as well as Count Bellamare, Count Surmont, the Marquis of Montferrat, Chevalier Schöning, General Soltikov, Count Tsarogy, Lord Weldon, and many other aliases) stood head and shoulders above them all.

He was fluent in at least six languages, a brilliant raconteur and conversationalist as well as a skilled musician, painter, chemist, and physician, and had the useful trick of being able to write equally well with both hands. He was also compulsively boastful and vain, surprisingly inept as a diplomat, and not above some exceptionally shady financial dealings. One way or another, he left his mark on Europe for nearly five decades.

The circumstances of his birth and upbringing are completely unknown. Late in his life he claimed to be the son and heir of Francis Rakoczy, the last independent prince of Transylvania, born in 1691 and raised in the house of the last of the Medici. A comparison between Saint-Germain's portraits and those of Francis Rakoczy show what could be a family resemblance. Other stories current in his lifetime claim that he was the illegitimate son of a king of Portugal, the son of a Savoyard tax-collector named Rotondo, the son of Jewish physician from Alsatia named Wolff, or the son of an Arabian princess and a *jinn*. The facts of the matter will probably never be known.

The first certain date in his biography is 1735, when he was in Holland and wrote a letter that has been preserved in the British Museum. He was also seen in Holland in 1739. The year 1743 saw him arrive in England, where he made a stir at court. In 1745, during the Jacobite rebellion of that year, a rival for some lady's affection slipped a letter in his pocket implicating him in a pro-Stuart conspiracy, and then had him arrested; the plot was amateurish enough that he was released almost at once.

His whereabouts from 1745 to 1757 are far from certain; some reports place him in Vienna, while he himself claimed to have visited India twice during that time. In 1757 he was in Paris, and quickly became a fixture at court, where his manners and wit made him a favorite of King Louis XV. In 1760, that monarch entrusted him with a secret mission to Holland, where he was to make contact with representatives of the British government and explore the possibility of peace between Britain and France, then in the midst of the Seven Years War. Saint-Germain apparently could not resist boasting publicly about his mission, and bungled the negotiations as well; when news of this reached Paris, orders were issued for Saint-Germain's arrest, and he barely escaped a trip to the Bastille.

He fled to England, then to Germany. By 1762 he was back in Holland, where he extracted nearly 100,000 gulden from a local industrialist for the rights to secret methods of manufacturing dyes and tanning leather, then disappeared without passing on the supposed secrets. During the Russo-Turkish war of 1768–1774, he was in Italy, and provided the Russian navy with a recipe for his famous healing tea—a mild laxative made from senna pods—which earned him a honorary rank as a Russian

general. The year 1774 saw him back in Germany, in sharply reduced circumstances, living off a succession of German noblemen who were enraptured by Saint-Germain's still powerful charm. He died in 1784 in the home of Prince Charles of Hesse-Cassel.

The mystery Saint-Germain cultivated lived on after him, and his reputation grew uncontrollably after his death. While eminent Masons and Rosicrucians who knew him were convinced that he was not a member of either society, later Masonic and occult theorists claimed him as an adept of the Mysteries, and the rise of Theosophy saw him turned into a Mahatma and the Head Of All True Freemasonry or H. O. A. T. F. (He himself once claimed that he had been initiated into Masonry at one point, but had forgotten the signs and passwords—which is perhaps not the best recommendation for high Masonic standing.) His last host, Charles of Hesse-Casel, reported that when the two of them talked about philosophy or religion, Saint-Germain held purely materialist views and rejected both religion and occultism.

An important addition to the Saint-Germain legend was made by the publication in 1836 of the supposed memoirs of the Countess d'Adhémar, a member of Marie-Antoinette's court on the eve of the French Revolution. These recount Saint-Germain's appearances after his supposed death, and his attempts to warn the French court about the coming of the Revolution. Although they have been endlessly requoted by occult writers, the memoirs themselves are fraudulent; they were invented by the remarkable Étienne Léon de Lamothe-Langon, a nineteenth-century French hack writer who made a living by forging memoirs of famous people. (This was not Lamothe-Langon's only contribution to occult history. He also invented a series of fourteenth-century witch trials in southern France, which were considered genuine until the 1970s.)

Saint-Germain has thus become an important figure in the list of Hidden Masters, and his career has been worked over and improved by the usual methods of occult history; *SEE* OCCULT HISTORY.

Theosophical lore identifies him as the Master Rakoczy, the chohan or chief adept of the Seventh or Indigo Ray, the mysterious ray of ceremonial magic and elemental power. According to these sources, his identities in previous incarnations include the Greek Neoplatonist Proclus; Christian Rosencreutz, the founder of the Rosicrucians; and both Roger and Francis Bacon, among others. *SEE* INDIGO RAY; THEOSOPHY.

In Theosophy, and in several other esoteric movements such as Guy Ballard's I AM Activity, his name remains one to conjure with. The absorption of occult ideas into the New Age movement has given him some presence in New Age circles as well. *SEE* BALLARD, GUY; MASTERS. *SEE ALSO* CAGLIOSTRO, COUNT ALESSANDRO. FURTHER READING: BUTLER 1948, FULLER 1988, LEADBEATER 1925, PATAI 1994.

St. John's-wort. Among the most important herbs in traditional European folk magic, St. John's-wort (*Hypericum perforatum*) was used to banish evil spirits and ward off ill luck. Large amounts of the flowering herb were gathered on St. John's Eve (June 23) each year and piled over bonfires; cattle were then driven through the resulting clouds of smoke to keep them safe from elves and other dangerous entities. A branch that had been "smoked" in this manner made a common talisman against spirits and hostile magic, and was believed to confer protection to a house and all who dwelt there until the following St. John's Eve.

Some herbalists in recent years have claimed that this herb was originally St. Joan's-wort, and that the name was changed to that of a male saint out of of sexism. Unfortunately for this theory, medieval herbals started referring to *herba Sancti Johannes* several centuries before the birth of the first St. Joan. *SEE ALSO* NATURAL MAGIC. FURTHER READING: GREER 2000, MACER 1949.

Saint-Martin, Louis-Claude de. French philosopher and mystic, 1743–1803. Born at Amboise into an impoverished family of the French nobility, Saint-Martin suffered from poor health through much of his childhood. His father, a cold and ambitious man, attempted to force him into a public career in the hope of recouping the family's fortunes. He attended the Jesuit school at Pontlevoi, then was sent by his father to law school at Orléans. After six months working as a lawyer, he rebelled, and prevailed on his father to allow him to take up a military career. He received an officer's commission with the régiment de Foix, which was stationed first at Tours and then at Bordeaux.

Most of the officers of the regiment were Freemasons, and many of them belonged to the Élus Coens order of Martines de Pasqually. *SEE* ÉLUS COENS; PASQUALLY, MARTINES DE. One of this latter group, a captain of grenadiers named Grainville, brought Saint-Martin into contact with Pasqually, and the young nobleman was initiated into the Élus Coens in 1765, an event that Saint-Martin later considered the turning point of his life.

Saint-Martin was troubled by the ceremonial magic practiced by Pasqually and his followers, but found in Pasqually's philosophical and spiritual teachings a rich source of illumination. In 1768 he became the presiding officer of the Bordeaux lodge of the Élus Coens, and in 1771 he ended his military career and became Pasqually's private secretary. When Pasqually left France for Haiti in 1772, Saint-Martin and Jean-Baptiste Willermoz effectively took over management of the order, and Pasqually's death in 1774 left them in charge. Saint-Martin moved to Lyons in 1773 and lodged with Willermoz, assisting the latter in the affairs of the order while he worked on his first book, *Des Erreurs et de la Vérité* (*On Errors and On the Truth*). This work presented Pasqually's philosophy in a highly obscure, symbolic language.

Des Erreurs was an immediate success in Masonic and magical circles, at least in part because nobody was able to figure out just what it meant, and it won Saint-Martin entry into high society. His learning, intelligence, and ready wit made him a success in the salons of Paris, and won him the support of influential figures. At the insistence of his growing circle of friends and followers, he wrote a second book, *Tableau Naturel des Rapports qui Existent Entre Dieu, L'homme et l'Univers* (*Natural Table of the Relationships that Exist Among God, Man, and the Universe*), which explained the material in *Des Erreurs* more clearly, and was published in 1782. Though his relationship with Willermoz was becoming strained by this time, the latter took copies of *Tableau Naturel* with him to the great Masonic convention in Wilhelmsbad in 1784 and handed them out to all and sundry.

In 1784, like so many others, Saint-Martin became fascinated by the work of Franz Anton Mesmer, then newly arrived in Paris. *SEE* MESMER, FRANZ ANTON. He joined Mesmer's lodge, and carried out experiments in mesmerism with the Marquis de Puységur, but soon lost interest in the phenomenon, deciding that it had little to do with the spiritual quest at the center of his own work.

In 1787, in the course of travels that took him to England, Germany, Switzerland, and Italy, he encountered the ideas of Jakob Böhme, which he found very much to his taste. *SEE* BÖHME, JAKOB. After mastering the difficult German of Böhme's treatises, he plunged deep into the study of the theosopher's writings and proceeded to translate many of Böhme's works into French. His encounter with Böhme also convinced him to make a final break with the magical and Masonic world of Willermoz and the Élus Coens, and he formally resigned from all his Masonic involvements in 1790.

When his father died in 1792, he returned to Amboise and lived there for most of his remaining years, busy with his writings and translations. Despite his aristocratic background, he welcomed the French Revolution as a necessary purification, and as a result escaped the mass executions that befell so many of the nobility. He died peacefully in 1803. *SEE ALSO* MARTINISM; THEOSOPHY. FURTHER READING: HUBBS 1971.

Saint-Yves d'Alveydre, Joseph-Alexandre. French occultist, 1842–1909. Perhaps the most eccentric of the many astonishing figures of the nineteenth-century French occult renaissance, Saint-Yves was the teacher of Papus, the doyen of Parisian occult circles for half a century, and the creator of the famous Archéomètre—"the key to all the religions and sciences of antiquity" and the "synthetic reformation of all contemporary arts," according to its inventor. An egomaniac's egomaniac, fond of seeing himself as a pivotal figure in the evolution of the entire cosmos, Saint-Yves' talents as a musician and an occultist came surprisingly close to living up to his pretensions.

He was born in Paris, the son of a doctor. His talent for music showed itself early, and he attracted attention in his schoolboy days for his skill as an organist. His relationship with his parents was a difficult one, made more so in his teens by sharp disagreements over his future. He was interested in a literary career, but his father intended

him for the military. The outcome was a brief and unsuccessful stint as a military physician, followed by several years of voluntary exile on the island of Jersey in the English Channel. In 1871, in the chaotic aftermath of the Franco-Prussian War, he returned to France and was able to find a job in the government.

In 1877 he married Marie-Victoire de Riznich, a wealthy and aristocratic widow who was a friend of the Empress Eugenie, wife of the former French head of state Napoleon III. It was an advantageous match, as her money freed him from the necessity to work for a living and enabled him to devote his time to music, occult studies, and utopian politics. In the latter field he devised a system he called "Synarchy," which has remained popular in French occult sources ever since.

In 1885 he set out to learn Sanskrit, and found as teacher one Haji Sharif, a parrot-shop proprietor in Le Havre who had left India at the time of the rebellion of 1857. A competent Sanskritist, Sharif also had teachings of another sort to offer, and introduced Saint-Yves to ideas about the hidden city of Agharta and its mysterious language and alphabet, Vattanian. This latter was apparently Sharif's own invention, although Agharta's roots are in the speculative fantasies of Louis Jacolliot and, through him, to a largely forgotten eighteenth- and nineteenth-century literature in which European mythologies were reworked into supposed histories of the distant past. *SEE* AGHARTA; EUHEMERISM.

Within a short time Saint-Yves and his teacher quarreled, but the former had another route to information about Agharta—astral projection, which he used to spy out the hidden city's secrets. These were duly described in his book *Mission de l'Inde en Europe* (*The Mission of India in Europe*), which he published at his own expense in 1886. Within weeks of the publication, worried that he had given away too much, he recalled the entire edition and had all but two copies destroyed. It was finally republished a year after his death. This was one of a number of books in which he discussed the "missions" of a variety of different groups: the sovereigns of Europe, the workers, the Jews, and so forth. All of these, like *Mission de l'Inde*, took a mix of Synarchy and nineteenth-century Christian Hermeticism as their foundation.

The lessons in Vattanian proved to be the key to much more. The twenty-two letters of the Vattanian alphabet, interpreted by way of the Cabala and information received from the spirit of his wife after her death in 1895, became the foundation of the great Archéomètre, a mandala of correspondences in which the numbers three, seven, and twelve structure an array of colors, musical notes, numbers, astrological forces, and Hebrew and Vattanian letters. All this was released to the public in 1900, on the occasion of the International Spiritist and Spiritualist Congress in Paris on September 26 of that year, and in exhaustive detail in a book, *L'Archéomètre*, edited by Papus and finally published in 1912.

After his wife's death, Saint-Yves lived in seclusion in Versailles, devoting his time to esoteric studies and to the training of a small number of students, of whom Papus was the most prominent. He died in 1909, still hard at work on the Archéomètre and its related philosophical system. *SEE ALSO* PAPUS. FURTHER READING: J. GODWIN 1994, J. GODWIN 1995.

Saklas. (Aramaic, "fool") In Gnostic theology, a name of the chief of the archons and creator of the fallen, material world. *SEE* GNOSTICISM; IALDABAOTH.

salamanders. In the lore of ceremonial magic, the elemental spirits of fire. Their king is Djin. (The word "salamander" is also used for a class of small, lizardlike animals related to frogs, since these latter live in decaying wood and sometimes crawl out from the midst of burning logs.) *SEE* ELEMENTAL.

Salons de la Rose+Croix. Occultism-inspired art shows held annually in Paris over a six-year period from 1892 to 1897, under the direction of the Rosicrucian author and critic Joséphin Peladan, which showcased artworks with mystical, occult, and mythological themes. At that time the French art world revolved around the annual salon sponsored by La Société des artistes français, a conservative organization of academic painters who systematically excluded Impressionists, Symbolists, and other rebels against official standards. The "Sâr" Peladan (as he styled himself) had made his career with devastating reviews of the salon's artists, who in his words, "push[ed] mediocrity beyond the limits of all decency" (Pincus-Witten 1976, p. 40). The creation of the Salons de la Rose+Croix marked a further extension of his crusade, and formed the high-water mark of the Symbolist movement in art.

The first Salon de la Rose+Croix opened on March 9, 1892, in the Galeries Durand-Ruel, 11 rue Le Peletier, Paris, to the sound of the Prelude to Wagner's *Parsifal* and the scent of incense and roses. Sixty-three artists had works on display. Enormous crowds turned out, so large that the traffic jam of carriages forced the police to close the street. Five evenings during the salon's run were devoted to musical soirees, in which Wagner's work shared space with that of Erik Satie, the official composer of Peladan's Rosicrucian order, who wrote three "Sonneries de la Rose+Croix" for the occasion. By all accounts, the exhibition was a magnificent spectacle from beginning to end.

By the time the salon closed on April 11, however, Peladan had managed to quarrel with the Comte de Rochefoucauld, his chief financial backer, and the Sâr and Satie parted company several months later. The later Salons de la Rose+Croix were never able to reach the standard set by the first. The hold of the official salon had been successfully broken, but the chief beneficiaries of the Sâr's victory were the Impressionists and other avant-garde artists, who rejected Peladan's approach completely. Other salons of Idealist and Symbolist art were being organized. In 1897, after the sixth Salon de la Rose+Croix met with favorable but tepid reviews, Peladan announced that there would be no more. *SEE ALSO* PELADAN, JOSÉPHIN; SATIE, ERIK. FURTHER READING: PINCUS-WITTEN 1976.

salt. A word with several different meanings in Western occult tradition, "salt" may refer either to common table salt (sodium chloride, NaCl) or to any of a wide range of other inorganic salts used in alchemy and alternative medicine. Common salt is nearly always the meaning of the term in magic, and in ancient and modern Pagan practice. In alchemy and related fields such as spagyrics, on the other hand, the word "salt" has a much wider range of meanings.

Common salt is used in magic primarily as a means of purification. In modern Pagan usage, salt is used as a means of purification, and may either be mixed with water that is used to purify a ritual circle, or sprinkled on the ground directly. In some traditions, a bowl of salt is placed on the altar as an emblem of the element of earth. *SEE* NEOPAGANISM. Ceremonial magicians also use salt as a purifying substance.

The twelve mineral salts that form most of the inorganic substance in the human body, under the title "cell salts," have been put to use as medicines in a system of healing with important connections to occultism and alchemy. *SEE* CELL SALTS.

In alchemy, salt is one of the Three Principles of Paracelsian alchemical theory; it represents the principle of solidity and stability. Every substance contains its own salt, which consists of those portions which remain behind when the substance is heated to a high temperature. In spagyrics, for example, the salt of an herb is extracted by macerating (soaking) the herb in alcohol for an extended period, pouring off the alcohol, burning the remaining herb, and then calcining it at a high temperature until it is reduced to white ash; *SEE* CALCINATION. The ash is macerated in more alcohol, and then filtered out; the alcohol is allowed to evaporate, and the salt of the herb crystallizes out in the evaporation dish. *SEE* ALCHEMY; SPAGYRICS.

Samael. (Hebrew, "blindness of God") From the early centuries of the Common Era, the most common Jewish term for the Devil. He is identified with the snake that tempted Eve, and is the guardian spirit of both the Roman Empire and Christianity. Together with Lilith, his spouse, he rules over the *sitra achra*, the "Other Side" or realm of the powers of evil.

As with so much of the traditional lore, though, these neat summaries cover a chaos of alternative claims. Samael is also the angel of death and, as such, a faithful servant of God; he is the angel whom God sent to fetch the soul of Moses—in some sources, at least. In other writings, Samael is the angel of the planet Mars, or the archangel of Geburah, the fifth Sephirah of the Cabalistic Tree of Life, though this role is more often filled by Kamael instead. Nor is Lilith Samael's only mate; the demons Naamah, Agrat bat Mahlah, and Eisheth Zenunim are all described in various places as Samael's mate and as the queen of the demons.

To add to the confusion, in Cabalistic lore, the Samael or Liars (plural) are the Qlippoth or demonic powers associated with Hod, the eighth Sephirah of the Tree of Life. Their traditional appearance is that of dull-colored dogs with the heads of demons. Their cortex or realm in the Kingdom of Shells is called Theuniel, and their archdemon is Adramelek. *SEE* QLIPPOTH.

As an individual angel (or demon), Samael was borrowed by the Gnostics in the first three or four centuries of the Common Era as another name for Ialdabaoth, the ruler of the archons and creator of the fallen material world. *SEE* IALDABAOTH.

According to Cabalistic lore, whatever Samael's current relation to the divine, he is likely to end up on the right side eventually. At the end of the present cycle of time, Samael will repent and become an angel of holiness, and lose the letter Mem (מ) from his name; he will then be named Sael, which is one of the seventy-two holy names of God from the Shemhamphorash. Mem stands here for *maveth*, "death," and after this transformation death and suffering will be no more. *SEE* APOCATA-STASIS; SHEMHAMPHORASH.

Samech. (Hebrew SMK, "prop") The fifteenth letter of the Hebrew alphabet, a single letter with the sound-value *s* and the numerical value sixty. Its standard magical symbolism is as follows:

Path of the Tree of Life: Twenty-fifth, from Tiphareth to Yesod.

Astrological Correspondence: Sagittarius, the Archer.

Tarot Correspondence: Trump XIV, Temperance.

Part of the Cube of Space: Upper west edge.

Colors: in Atziluth—blue.

in Briah—yellow.

in Yetzirah—green.

in Assiah—deep vivid blue.

The corresponding text from the *Thirty-two Paths of Wisdom* runs as follows: "The Twenty-fifth Path is the Intelligence of Probation or Temptation, and it is so called because it is the primary temptation by which the Creator trieth all righteous persons." *SEE ALSO* CABALA; HEBREW ALPHABET.

Hebrew letter Samech

Samhain. The beginning and end of the year in the old Celtic calendar, falling around the beginning of November in modern terms. Samhain is the oldest documented festival of Celtic Paganism; the Coligny calendar, a Druid calendar from ancient Gaul, includes the "three nights of Samonios." *SEE* COLIGNY CALENDAR.

Samhain was traditionally associated with the spirits of the dead, who were believed to walk the world at that time. After the arrival of Christianity, the feast of Samhain became All Hallow's Day. The evening before it, the modern Halloween, retained much of the same symbolism.

In modern Pagan usage, Samhain is one of the eight sabbats of the year-wheel, and is held on or around November 1. It is especially consecrated to the spirits of the dead, and to the deities most closely associated with death (who vary widely from one Neopagan pantheon to another). In some traditions, the celebration of Samhain includes the summoning of the dead; *SEE* NECROMANCY. Other traditions deal with their presence in a more symbolic manner. *SEE ALSO* SABBAT.

Sanat Kumara. In the lore of Theosophy and related systems of occult philosophy, the Lord of the World, the spiritual ruler of the Earth and the head of the Great White Lodge. The word "Kumara" is said to mean "Lord," while Sanat is the personal name of this being. A Lord of the Flame from the planet Venus, Sanat Kumara came to the Earth in a chariot of fire about six and a half million years ago, during Lemurian times, to take up his position. There were two other Lords of the World before him. Three other Lords of the Flame assist him in his work.

The not dissimilar title "Lord of this World" has, of course, been used for the Christian Devil, who also has strong associations with flame and the planet Venus, and who is said to have descended in fire to this world from elsewhere at an early point in earthly history. It may not be accidental that "Sanat" and "Satan" are fairly transpar-ent anagrams of each other. *SEE* SATAN. FURTHER READING: LEADBEATER 1925. *SEE ALSO* GREAT WHITE LODGE; THEOSOPHY.

Sandalphon. (Hebrew SNDLPhVN, meaning uncertain) One of the primary archangels in Jewish and Cabalistic angelology. Sandalphon is said in Jewish writings to have originally been the prophet Elijah, who ascended into heaven in a fiery chariot, but is also described as the twin brother of Metatron and the left-hand, feminine cherub of the Ark of the Covenant. He (or she) is the archangel of Malkuth, the tenth sphere of the Tree of Life. *SEE* ARCHANGEL; MALKUTH; METATRON.

Sanders, Alec. English witch, 1926–1988. A controversial and theatrical figure, Sanders claimed that he was raised in a Pagan family and was initiated into the tradition at the age of seven, when he unexpectedly walked in on his Welsh grandmother as she was performing a ritual. He also claimed to have been elected "King of the Witches" by an assembly of 1,623 English witches in 1965.

Documentary evidence, on the other hand, indicates that in 1961 he wrote to a Gardnerian coven in England, commenting, "To be a witch is something that I have always wanted—and yet I have never been able to contact anybody who could help me" (Valiente 1989, pp. 165–6). He was apparently initiated by a Gardnerian coven about a year later. As for the title "King of the Witches," it and the assembly of witches seem to have come entirely out of Sanders' active imagination.

Details on his early life are sparse, and there are many conflicting stories in circulation, most of them apparently started by Sanders himself. Other than the letter mentioned above, he first surfaced in the British tabloid press in 1961, when he initiated a candidate into his coven in full view of three press photographers, using a ritual he had made up for the occasion from bits of a medieval grimoire. The resulting publicity got him fired from his job as a maintenance man for a Manchester library.

He was rarely out of sight of the press for long after that, and after he moved to London in 1967 he attracted a large number of students and initiates. His High Priestess and wife was the former Maxine Morris, who was eighteen when they were handfasted in 1965. Most of the current lineages of Alexandrian Wicca trace their roots to people initiated by Sanders in this period. In 1973, however, he and Maxine divorced, and he moved to the seaside town of Bexhill in Sussex, where he continued to chase publicity with limited success until his death from lung cancer in 1988.

While Sanders' showmanship, overt dishonesty, and fondness for the limelight gave him a poor reputation among British witches during his lifetime, many people who went on to become major figures in British Wicca from the 1970s on were initiated and taught by him, and the Alexandrian tradition remains one of the larger and more active branches of Wicca today. SEE ALSO ALEXANDRIAN WICCA. FURTHER READING: VALIENTE 1989.

Sangreal. SEE GRAIL, HOLY.

Sangreal Sodality. A magical tradition founded by British occultist William Gray, beginning in 1982 with the publication of the first of four books outlining the teachings and practices of the tradition. Gray devised these books as "a unique experiment in spiritual sociology" (Gray 1983, p. ix)—the creation of a Western esoteric movement from the ground up. Readers of the books were encouraged to practice the meditations and rituals of the system, organize groups to work with the Sangreal teachings, and contact Gray himself as a first step toward networking with other Sangreal students.

The Sangreal system is defined as a specifically Western esoteric system; west is its holy direction, and materials from outside of Europe are rigorously excluded. The term "Sangreal" is read both as "sang real" (royal blood) and "san greal" (Holy Grail); both of these refer to the sacred kings of the past, who sacrificed themselves for the benefit of their communities, and provide a model for the Sodality's rituals, teachings, and orientation. Gray's own version of the Cabala, which assigns English letters to the Paths of the Tree of Life, is the basis of much of its advanced theory and practice. A core ritual, the Sangreal Sacrament, and a wide range of additional ceremonies are part of the system; full details on all of these can be found in Gray's books.

Gray's experiment had a modest success, with a series of Sangreal Sodality groups established in Britain and the United States. While it has not become a large move-

ment by any means, there are still a variety of groups and people working with the system as of this writing. SEE ALSO GRAIL, HOLY; GRAY, WILLIAM G. FURTHER READING: GRAY 1982, GRAY 1983, GRAY 1984, GRAY 1985.

Satan. (Hebrew, "accuser") In Christian myth and theology, an angel who rebelled against God and became the Prince of Darkness, Lord of this World, and leader of the forces of evil. In most Western occult traditions, Satan is a relatively minor figure, and many branches of Western occultism specifically deny that a single, conscious power of evil exists. Christian occultism, and the Christian heresy of Satanism, are important exceptions; some systems of goetic magic also find room for Satan in their demonologies. SEE CHRISTIAN OCCULTISM; GOETIA; SATANISM.

Satan has a possible echo in Theosophical lore, where the Lord of the World—the spiritual ruler of the Earth and head of the Great White Lodge—is Sanat Kumara (literally "Lord Sanat"), a Lord of the Flame who descended to Earth from Venus in a fiery chariot some six million years ago. SEE GREAT WHITE LODGE; SANAT KUMARA. SEE ALSO AHRIMAN; LUCIFER.

Satanic ritual abuse. The subject of a flurry of accusations, rumors, panics, and criminal charges that appeared, starting in the 1980s, in most of the countries of the Western world. According to proponents of these claims, a vast underground network of Satanists permeates the modern world, sacrificing, torturing, and sexually abusing children by the thousands or millions, raising funds through sales of pornography and drugs, infiltrating and corrupting the police and the courts, and disseminating Satanic ideas into society by way of rock music and Dungeons & Dragons roleplaying games. The entire frenzy bears an uncomfortable similarity to the witchcraft panics that marked the Burning Times, and it is probably not an accident that Satanic ritual abuse claims have been used as the basis for persecution of occultists and Pagans. SEE BURNING TIMES; MAGIC, PERSECUTION OF.

All through the twentieth century, various figures—most of them closely connected with conservative Christianity—claimed that an invisible underground of Devil worshippers was at work in the modern world. These claims seem to have originated with Léo Taxil's Palladian hoax in late nineteenth-century France; *SEE* PALLADIAN ORDER. In twentieth-century America, however, very few people outside of the fundamentalist churches seem to have paid attention to such allegations until 1980, when a new factor entered the picture.

That factor was the publication of a book, *Michelle Remembers* by Michelle Smith and Lawrence Padzer, which claimed that Smith had been sexually abused and tortured by a cult of Satanists in Victoria, British Columbia. Smith claimed to have witnessed human sacrifice and cannibalism, and alleged that horns and a tail had been surgically implanted on her body (she claimed she had later ripped them out). All this had surfaced while Smith was in therapy with Padzer, a conservative Catholic and former missionary who had treated her for multiple personality disorder, converted her to Catholicism, and later married her.

Michelle Remembers quickly became a bestseller, and several other "Satanic cult survivors" surfaced around the same time with their own stories of sex, torture, and human sacrifice. Laurel Wilson, a teacher from Bakersfield, California, alleged that she had been a baby-producing "breeder" for a Satanist cult, and wrote a successful book, *Satan's Underground*, under the pseudonym Lauren Stratford. Another successful "survivor" was Christian minister Mike Warnke, who by 1991 had parlayed his book *The Satan Seller* and his claim to have been a Satanic high priest into a six-figure income from lectures and book royalties. The year 1984 saw the publication of what would become the standard handbook for "survivors" in therapy, *The Courage to Heal*, and the modern ritual-abuse industry was born.

Criminal charges against supposed Satanic abusers were not long behind. The first case erupted in suburban Los Angeles in 1983, where the mother of a two-year-old accused staff members at the McMartin day care center of sexual assault. The mother was diagnised as schizophrenic two years later, but in the meantime the authorities had moved in. An unlicensed therapist who claimed to be an expert in ritual abuse was called in to interview some four hundred preschool-age children. Her methods included asking leading questions, repeating the same questions over and over again when the answers didn't support the accusations of abuse, threatening children and calling them "bad" when they did not report abuse, and giving them presents when they did. The result was 135 counts of molestation against seven staff members, the longest and most expensive criminal trial in American history, and no convictions.

Defendants in other Satanic abuse trials were considerably less fortunate. In a Texas trial in 1986, for example, child care worker Michelle Noble was convicted and sentenced to life plus 311 years for sexually abusing children; the only evidence was the testimony of several children, extracted by methods similar to those used in the McMartin case. (In 1988, she managed to win a new trial, and was acquitted on all counts.) Similarly extreme sentences on similarly scant evidence were handed down in a number of other cases; many of these, similarly, were overturned on appeal.

More complex were cases of alleged Satanic ritual abuse which were supposedly repressed from memory by victims in childhood, and then recovered by therapeutic techniques years or decades later. The entire subject of "repressed memories" is a subject of massive scientific controversy at present. What is clear, though, is that methods used by many therapists in the pursuit of "repressed memories" could be used as textbook examples of ways to distort and redefine memory. Patients are told that their recovery depends on being able to remember being abused, handed books such as *Michelle Remembers* as guides to what they ought to be remembering, subjected to hypnosis and powerful drugs such as sodium amytal, and put in therapy groups where intense emotional pressure is put on them to support other patients' claims to victimhood by coming up with "repressed memories" of their own. The results have included thousands of accusations by adults against their elderly parents. More recently, a number of therapists have been successfully sued for malpractice for these approaches to "therapy."

The furor gave rise to a curious alliance between social workers and therapists, on the one hand, and fundamentalist Christian organizations on the other. Some of the therapists involved in the field come to it from liberal or even radical feminist political stances. Still, it is interesting (and may be significant) that the targets of the Satanic ritual abuse frenzy make up a laundry list of things fundamentalist Christian leaders had been attacking for a decade or more prior to the first accusations—Wicca and other Pagan religions; occultism in general; rock music; "occult" fantasy fiction and related games such as Dungeons & Dragons; and day care centers, which permit women to work outside the home.

Certainly attempts were made by fundamentalist groups to use Satanic ritual abuse accusations to target Wiccan and other Pagan groups, as well as the few actual Satanist organizations in the United States. The only professed Satanists caught up in the frenzy, however, were Michael and Lilith Aquino of the Temple of Set; SEE TEMPLE OF SET. Accused of participating in the ritual abuse of children in San Francisco, the Aquinos defended themselves with gusto and proved that they had been in Washington, D.C., at the time the alleged abuse had taken place. No charges ever actually filed against them, and two authors who published books alleging the Aquinos' guilt found themselves facing libel suits and settled out of court.

By the late 1980s Satanic ritual abuse accusations had become the center of a growing industry. Cadres of "experts," most of them without any relevant professional training, were holding seminars for law enforcement officers, social workers, and therapists across North America; TV and print media were drawing large audiences with shocking claims about Satanic activities; foundations, associations, and Christian ministries, dedicated to fighting the vast Satanic conspiracy, were raising millions of dollars; therapists and social workers had discovered that helping people "recover repressed memories" of Satanic ritual abuse could be turned into a lucrative line of work. All that was missing was evidence that Satanic ritual abuse was actually happening.

This sheer lack of evidence was among the most striking features of the entire phenomenon. Consistently, police investigations of alleged Satanic ritual abuse found no bodies of sacrifice victims, no traces of blood where sacrifices had allegedly taken place, no evidence that children who had been allegedly tortured and raped had suffered physical injuries or sexual contact, and no Satanic paraphernalia or ritual equipment. Supporters of Satanic ritual abuse allegations, for their part, claim that the absence of evidence simply shows how clever the Satanists are.

Support for the Satanic ritual abuse industry began to wane in the United States in the early 1990s. The failure of most ritual abuse prosecutions to stand up in court was one cause of this, but much of it was the work of investigative journalists and detectives who took a harder look at the allegations. Reporters for *Cornerstone* magazine, an evangelical Christian monthly, investigated the claims of "Lauren Stratford" and published a scathing article in 1989 documenting a mass of contradictions between her claims and provable facts. Another article in the same magazine in 1993 did a similar background check on Mike Warnke and produced much the same results. Several widely circulated books tackled the entire Satanic ritual abuse furor and detailed the inaccuracies and lack of evidence involved. More damning still was FBI specialist Ken Lanning's 1992 official report on 300 cases of alleged Satanic ritual abuse, which dissected the entire frenzy and found no evidence behind any of it.

By this time, however, Satanic ritual abuse claims had spread to England and several other European countries. The English outbreak was largely the result of the Reachout Trust, an evangelical Christian organization whose officially stated purpose is "to promote a Bible based Christianity by any means expedient" (quoted in Medway 2001, p. 231). Social workers in Britain and other European countries were also involved in passing on American ideas about Satanic ritual abuse. The result was much the same as in the United States: a flurry of loudly publicized cases, followed by sweeping legal charges that ultimately collapsed due to lack of evidence.

By the late 1990s, as a result, police and courts throughout most of the Western world had become wary of Satanic ritual abuse claims, and few cases were brought to trial after that time. Supporters of the Satanist hunt responded by claiming that the criminal justice system was under Satanist control. Attempts were made to broaden the hunt by accusing the Freemasons, the CIA, and alien beings from other worlds of colluding with the Satanists, or engaging in ritual abuse or mind-control conspiracies on their own.

As of this writing, charges of Satanic ritual abuse are still being made, primarily by fundamentalist Christian groups and in private networks of "survivors" and their therapists. Outside these limited circles, very few people seem to be listening, but the risk that this modern-day witch hunt might resume some day cannot be dismissed by occultists. SEE ALSO SATANISM. FURTHER READING: CARLSON ET AL. 1989, MEDWAY 2001, NATHAN AND SNEDEKER 1995, PENDERGRAST 1995, SMITH AND PADZER 1980, VICTOR 1993.

Satanism. A Christian heresy that worships Satan, the power of evil in Christian mythology, rather than the Trinity, and embraces those actions and attitudes classified by more orthodox Christian sects as "sinful." Satanism has been a subject for Christian fantasies and paranoias for nearly two thousand years, and its influence as a catchall for Christian ideas about evil, sexuality, and other people's religions has been vast. Satanism in practice, on the other hand, has been relatively rare, and seems to have been generated almost entirely by Christian propaganda against it.

The idea that there are people who worship Satan seems to have emerged very early in Christianity, largely as a way of attacking Pagan religions in the Roman Empire. Much early Christian propaganda insisted that Pagan gods and goddesses were simply nonexistent. Since Pagan temples and priests reported miracles about as often as Christians did, however, there was a steady undercurrent of claims that the Pagan deities were actually demons in the service of Satan. These conflicting claims were applied in turn to every other religion Christianity encountered during its ancient, medieval, and modern expansions; Judaism, Islam, and the various European Pagan religions were all at different times classified as worship of nonexistent beings, as Devil worship, or (inconsistently) as both at the same time.

In ancient and medieval Christian literature, Pagans and Jews alike were routinely accused of deliberately summoning demons for nefarious purposes. Two of the most important early Christian legends about magic— the stories of Saint Cyprian of Antioch and Theophilus of Adana—had, respectively, a Pagan and a Jewish sorcerer as important characters, and both summoned the Christian Devil by magical arts. These legends, and the pattern of thought behind them, played an important role in laying the groundwork for later beliefs in Satanism. SEE CYPRIAN OF ANTIOCH, SAINT; THEOPHILUS OF ADANA.

The idea that a secret underground of Satanists actually existed within Christian society, however, was a creation of the fourteenth century, and developed out of a series of conspiracy panics that swept medieval Europe during that time. In the wake of the Black Death of 1347–1351 C.E., in particular, claims went around that various people—Jews, lepers, Muslims—had conspired to unleash the plague on Christendom. Toward the end of the century, a new set of rumors emerged in what is now western Switzerland, claiming that a secret sect of Satan worshippers met at night to invoke the Devil, murder babies, engage in orgiastic sex, and direct harmful magic at their neighbors. The resulting panics launched the age of trials and executions that modern Pagans call the Burning Times. SEE BURNING TIMES.

Ironically, the vast publicity given to these supposed Satanic conspiracies came to function as a sort of unintentional propaganda for Satanism, and as the hold of Christianity on the Western world slackened, a certain number of people appear to have been attracted to Satanism because of its apparent promises of worldly power and pleasure. One example of this sort of Satanism surfaced in the "Affair of the Poisons" in late seventeenth-century France. Those implicated in this massive scandal included important members of the nobility, as well as King Louis XIV's mistress Madame de Montespan; the participants were present at Black Masses in which a naked woman (on several occasions, Mme. de Montespan herself) was used for the altar and various demons were invoked. The ringleaders of the group were also involved in prostitution, poisoning, and providing abortions. It's uncertain how seriously they took the Satanic ceremonies they provided, and it may have simply been a form of exotic entertainment for bored aristocrats.

In the same way, other examples of Satanism in practice are subject to doubts as to just how seriously the practitioners meant what they were doing. The Hell Fire Club, a collection of upper-class Englishmen in the eighteenth century whose tastes extended to Gothic ceremonies as well as alcohol and orgies, is a good case in point; SEE HELL FIRE CLUB. Activities along the same lines occurred in France and Belgium in the late nineteenth century, as part of the fashionable decadence of the fin-de-siècle period. J.-K. Huysmans, author of the horror classic *Là-Bas*, reported being present at several Black Masses, and there is no reason to doubt his testimony on the subject.

Another confusing factor is the habit of accusing any occultist who practiced sex magic of Satanism. The Abbé Boullan, a scandalous figure defrocked by the church for promoting a variety of Catholic sex magic, was accused on that basis alone of being a Satanist pure and simple. *SEE* BOULLAN, JOSEPH-ANTOINE.

Aleister Crowley, who has commonly been termed a Satanist but actually worshipped the quasi-Egyptian pantheon of his own religion of Thelema, is a similar case—although Crowley's claim to be the Great Beast 666 at least gave Christians some reason to confuse his religion with Satanism. *SEE* CROWLEY, ALEISTER; THELEMA. Neither of these men can be called a Satanist in any strict sense of the word, but both are still cited as Satanists in popular books on the subject.

The emergence of modern Satanism was largely the result of a massive hoax carried out by the French journalist Léo Taxil in the late nineteenth century. Taxil, a left-wing journalist and writer of pornography, suddenly announced in 1884 that he had been reconciled to the Roman Catholic Church, and proceeded to publish a flurry of writings detailing a vast Satanic organization, the Palladian Order, which was associated with Freemasonry.

After several years and a great deal of hullaballoo, in which many prominent Catholic leaders lent the anti-Palladian crusade their full support, Taxil let the other shoe drop by announcing in a large public meeting that the whole thing was a fraud, cooked up to demonstrate just how gullible and superstitious the Catholic Church was. The legacies of the hoax included the word "Satanism," which first entered the English language in media accounts of the Palladian affair, and a major boost to the idea of Satanic conspiracies in the minds of conservative Christians who refused to believe that they had been deceived. *SEE* PALLADIAN ORDER.

The first public Satanic religious organization did not surface until 1966, when Anton Szandor LaVey (1930–1997) founded the Church of Satan in San Francisco. As much a work of showmanship as a serious religion, the Church of Satan derived much of its philosophy from the writings of Ayn Rand and used the trappings of Satanism mostly as a source of publicity. LaVey's media presence, however, spawned plenty of copycat groups who took their Devil worship more literally, and also gave rise to a schismatic group, the Temple of Set, dedicated to the serious practice of the Left-Hand Path. *SEE* CHURCH OF SATAN; LAVEY, ANTON SZANDOR; TEMPLE OF SET.

The 1960s and 1970s also saw the large-scale renewal of claims by conservative Christians that secret conspiracies of Satanists were at work in American society, committing horrible crimes and encouraging sex, violence, and liberalism. These claims burst out of the fundamentalist subculture in the early 1980s with the beginning of the Satanic ritual abuse furor. The closest approach to the Burning Times in the Western world in recent centuries, the frenzy of accusations and prosecutions that resulted from claims of Satanic ritual abuse put dozens of people in jail on the basis of testimony extracted from children and adults by very questionable methods, and without a trace of corroborating evidence. *SEE* SATANIC RITUAL ABUSE.

The 1980s also saw the emergence of Satanism as a small but highly visible subculture among American teenagers. Drawing their inspiration mostly from Anton LaVey's *Satanic Bible*, from the most popular of the *Necronomicon* forgeries in circulation, and from other more or less Satan-related ideas and images in current music and popular culture, adolescent Satanists became a focus for a good deal of debate and consternation in the media, the educational industry, and conservative Christian circles. The fact that a few disturbed teens committed violent crimes under the cloak of Satanism did nothing to decrease the furor. Like the folklore about Satanic ritual abuse, though, Satanism as an adolescent subculture had far more to do with pop culture than with the historical current of Satanist tradition and practice. *SEE* FANTASY OCCULTISM; NECRONOMICON. FURTHER READING: KING 1971B, MEDWAY 2001, MORIARTY 1992.

Satariel. (Hebrew SAThARIAL, "Concealers of God") In the lore of the Cabala, the Satariel or Concealers are the Qlippoth or demonic powers associated with Binah, the third Sephirah of the Tree of Life. Their traditional form is that of a gigantic, veiled head with horns and eyes seen dimly through the veil, followed about by evil centaurs. Their archdemon is Lucifuge. *SEE* QLIPPOTH.

Sat B'hai, Order of the. English order, titled in full "The Royal Oriental Order of Sikha (Apex) and the Sat B'hai." The Sat B'hai was founded around 1871 by Captain J. H. Lawrence-Archer, an English Freemason who had served in India. It seems to have had little more than a paper existence until 1875, when Kenneth Mackenzie joined and brought with him several other stalwarts of the British fringe Masonry scene, including Francis Irwin and the indefatigable John Yarker.

As originally created by Lawrence-Archer, the order consisted of little more than a hierarchy of exalted titles. Mackenzie worked up a series of initiation rituals for the order, but his attempts to recruit members and establish the order in Britain had little effect. By 1879 Mackenzie had washed his hands of it, although Irwin and a circle of his Masonic associates kept it in existence on a small scale for some years thereafter.

The Sat B'hai claimed an Indian ancestry and used vaguely Hindu terminology in a framework mostly derived from Freemasonry. Lodges were called "Ashayams," and the seven degrees were those of Arch Mute, Arch Auditor, Arch Scribe, Arch Herald, Arch Minister, Arch Courier, and Arch Censor. All these had their symbols, emblems, mystic names, and titles. Admission to the lowest three grades, from Arch Mute through Arch Scribe, was open to men and women of good character, but the higher four grades were accessible only to Masons, and Arch Couriers and Arch Censors had to be Master Masons. *SEE ALSO* MACKENZIE, KENNETH ROBERT HENDERSON. FURTHER READING: HOWE 1997.

Satie, Erik. French musician and composer (1866–1925). Described by Igor Stravinsky as "the oddest person I have ever known," Erik Satie was for a time the official composer of the Rose+Croix Catholique, the Rosicrucian order founded by philosopher and art critic Joséphin Peladan, and had numerous contacts in the Paris occult scene of the late nineteenth century.

Born in Honfleur in Normandy, where his uncle Adrien had a reputation as a local character, Satie studied at the Paris Conservatoire and thereafter lived a bohemian life in Paris, supporting himself as a cafe pianist and composer-for-hire. Sometime in the late 1880s, he became an associate of Peladan, and the composer's three "Sonneries de la Rose+Croix" were performed at the opening of the first Salon de la Rose+Croix in 1892. He broke with the Sâr later that same year, and for a time worked with Jules Bois—another figure in the Paris occult scene—whose play *La Porte Heroique du Ciel* (*The Heroic Gate of the Sky*) was accompanied by music written by Satie.

Satie's occult involvements seem to have faded out by the late 1890s, replaced by a quirky Catholic mysticism and a range of other eccentricities. The works named above, and a few others composed around the same time, represent his major contribution to the occult tradition. *SEE ALSO* PELADAN, JOSÉPHIN; SALONS DE LA ROSE+CROIX.

sator arepo tenet opera rotas. The most famous of all magical squares, the so-called "Rotas-Sator square" dates back to Roman times, when it was much used in protective magic. Its origins are completely unknown, although various proposals have been made. It commonly takes this form:

It thus reads the same way vertically as horizontally, upwards and downwards, left and right. Written out as a sentence, in addition, it is a palindrome—that is, it reads the same forwards as backwards—and this works just as well when the individual words are placed in reverse order (*rotas opera tenet arepo sator*).

The words can be interpreted in Latin as "Arepo the sower holds the works of the wheels." What this means is anybody's guess.

It has been pointed out that the same letters can be reorganized into the following:

```
        A
        P
        A
        T
        E
        R
A P A T E R N O S T E R O
        O
        S
        T
        E
        R
        O
```

In other words, the Latin for "our father," plus *A* and *O* for alpha and omega, repeated twice. Whether this has any relevance for the magic square's origins, or whether it is simply a coincidence, has been the subject of much argument among scholars. *SEE ALSO* BARBAROUS NAMES; PALINDROMES. FURTHER READING: MERRIFIELD 1987.

Saturn. One of the seven traditional planets of astrology, Saturn in a birth chart represents limitations and challenges as well as areas of stability. In astrological symbolism, Saturn rules the signs Capricorn and Aquarius (although modern astrologers often assign Aquarius to Uranus); he is exalted in Libra, in his detriment in Cancer and Leo, and in his fall in Aries. *SEE* ASTROLOGY.

In alchemy, Saturn is a common symbol for lead, and is also used to represent the nigredo or black phase of the Great Work. *SEE* ALCHEMY.

Astrological symbol of Saturn

School of Night. A circle of Elizabethan noblemen and their friends, devoted to occult philosophy, Pythagorean mathematics, heretical religion, and experimental science. The membership of the school was drawn from the friends and allies of Sir Walter Raleigh, and included Raleigh himself, Thomas Hariot, the poet George Chapman, and Henry Percy, Earl of Northumberland, who was called "the Wizard Earl" by contemporaries. The

playwright Christopher Marlowe has also been associated with the school.

William Shakespeare, who was supported by Raleigh's opponent Robert, Earl of Essex, gave the school the name by which it is known to scholars in a passage of *Love's Labours Lost*—a play which, among many other things, was a lampoon directed at Raleigh ("Armado" in the play) and his circle. What name the school had among its members, if any, is unknown. FURTHER READING: BRADBROOKE 1965, YATES 1979.

Schwaller de Lubicz, René A. French occultist and sacred geometer, 1887–1961. Born René Schwaller in Alsace, de Lubicz arrived in Paris in 1905 and became part of the occult scene there, joining the Theosophical Society and devoting his time to the study of alchemy and the symbolism of the Gothic cathedrals. He was befriended and adopted by the Lithuanian-French poet O. V. de Lubicz-Milosz, and had connections with the circle of alchemists around the mysterious Fulcanelli. According to de Lubicz, Fulcanelli's most famous book, *Le Mystère des Cathédrales*, was based on material Fulcanelli plagiarized from him. *SEE* FULCANELLI.

In 1919, in the aftermath of the First World War, de Lubicz became the leader of a group called Les Veilleurs ("the Watchmen"), which combined occult interests with a right-wing political agenda and anti-Semitic ideas. Its membership included Rudolf Hess, then living in Paris, who went on to pursue the same type of magical politics on the other side of the Rhine in later decades. *SEE* NATIONAL SOCIALISM.

In the early 1920s, de Lubicz handed over leadership of *Les Veilleurs* and moved to St. Moritz, Switzerland, where he founded Suhalia, a community with craft workshops and alchemical laboratories. He worked there until 1927, when he relocated to Majorca; the Suhalia community dissolved at his departure.

At the beginning of the Spanish Civil War in 1936, de Lubicz relocated to Egypt, where an encounter with ancient Egyptian sculpture convinced him that the same teachings he had encountered in old alchemical texts could be traced in far more detail in the sacred geometries of pharaonic Egypt. The rest of his life was spent in writing a series of works expounding the esoteric philosophies and geometries of Egyptian art and architecture. He spent the last years of his life in Grasse, in the south of France, where he died in 1961. *SEE ALSO* SACRED GEOMETRY. FURTHER READING: VANDENBROECK **1987.**

Scorpio. (Latin, "scorpion") The eighth sign of the zodiac, a fixed water sign of feminine polarity. In Scorpio, the ruler is Mars (or, in some modern versions, Pluto); no planet is exalted, Venus is in her detriment, and the moon is in her fall. Scorpio governs the reproductive system.

The sun is in Scorpio approximately from October 24 to November 22. People with this sun placement are traditionally intense, passionate, and energetic, with strong emotions and intuitions; they can also be jealous, obsessive, and vindictive.

In the Golden Dawn tarot system, Scorpio corresponds to Trump XIII, Death. *SEE* DEATH; TAROT.

Astrological symbol of Scorpio

Scot, Michael. Scottish scholar and astrologer, c. 1175–1235. Michael Scot was the most important intellectual figure in Western Europe in the early thirteenth century. His place and date of birth are uncertain, although a tradition holds that he was born at Balwearie Castle in Fife. He is thought to have studied at Oxford and Paris, but the first certain date in his life is August 18, 1217, when he completed a Latin translation of an important astronomical treatise by the Arab writer al-Bitrûgi.

He was living in Toledo at the time, in the heart of Muslim Spain, among the community of European scholars who were spearheading the transmission of Arabic learning to the West. Scot also translated important works by Aristotle and Averroes during his stay at Toledo. By 1220 he was in Italy, where he won the favor of Pope Honorius III, who provided him with church income. The early 1220s saw him teaching astronomy and astrology at the University of Paris. Sometime in the late 1220s or early 1230s, he entered the service of the Holy Roman Emperor Friedrich II, for whom he wrote three books: *Liber Introductorius*, a beginning textbook of

astrology; *Liber particularis*, a book of questions and answers about astrology; and *Liber Physiognomiae*, dealing with the art of physiognomy—a common medieval method of divination by the shape of the body and face. *SEE* PHYSIOGNOMY. He was still in the service of the emperor at the time of his death.

Scot's writings condemn magic harshly as "the mistress of all iniquity and evil," but he clearly knew a great deal about the theory and practice of the subject. His *Liber Introductorius* includes such things as a list of words of power for commanding spirits, a method of calculating the proper hours for summoning them, and the names of the angels of the seven planets, the spirits of the seven celestial spheres, and the guardians of the seven metals. Whether or not he was a practicing magician is open to question, but for centuries after his death he was credited with vast magical and divinatory powers. FURTHER READING: THORNDYKE **1965.**

Scottish Rite. *SEE* FREEMASONRY.

scourge. In the more traditional branches of Wicca, the initiate is scourged forty times as part of the initiation rituals of the first degree. This is repeated in the second degree, but the initiate then scourges the initiator one hundred twenty times, in illustration of the "law of threefold return." Most covens at present use a scourge with soft leather thongs, which makes the act symbolic at best. *SEE* WICCA.

scrying. The art of receiving clairvoyant perceptions, either through a reflective surface such as a crystal ball or magic mirror, or through the unaided imagination. An important element in magical and divinatory practice since ancient times, scrying is well attested in classical and ancient sources and is still much practiced today. The best scholarly survey of the subject (Bestermann 1965) documents it from ancient times to the present and includes references to scrying practices from every inhabited continent.

Magic mirrors and crystals were used for scrying in ancient Greece, as well as more unusual devices such as a bronze shield with oil poured on it. It was not common in Rome, but is referred to in a few Roman records. Arabic methods, imported into the Western world during the Middle Ages, included using a soot-blackened thumbnail or a pool of ink in the palm of the hand. These and other methods were widely used in Europe from the Dark Ages onward. The Christian church generally denounced the practice, although Saint Remigius (437–533 C.E.), the first archbishop of Rheims, is said to have divined in a glass of wine. In terms of Western occult history, scrying was practiced by a good many of the major figures in medieval and Renaissance magic, and luminaries such as Trithemius and Paracelsus wrote on the subject. SEE PARACELSUS; TRITHEMIUS, JOHANNES. The tradition of scrying with the largest impact on later occultism, though, emerged in Britain, with the Elizabethan wizard John Dee (1527–1608) as one of its first major figures. Dee was not a scryer himself, but carried out magical operations to summon spirits into a crystal or mirror, where a succession of scryers—among them the famous Edward Kelly (1555–1597)—reported on their words and actions. SEE DEE, JOHN; KELLY, EDWARD. This approach was very common in British occult practice for several centuries after Dee's time. At the same time, a parallel folk tradition of crystal scrying remained very much in evidence, and most scryers in this tradition made do on their own. SEE CUNNING MAN/WOMAN.

In the nineteenth century, important occultists such as Frederick Hockley and P. B. Randolph carried out much of their work using crystals and mirrors, and toward the end of the century the Hermetic Brotherhood of Luxor popularized Randolph's methods widely. SEE HERMETIC BROTHERHOOD OF LUXOR (H. B. OF L.); HOCKLEY, FREDERICK; RANDOLPH, PASCHAL BEVERLY. In the same century, Joseph Smith, founder of the Mormon religion, worked as a scryer before taking up his prophetic work, and according to his own account, translated the Book of Mormon from "reformed Egyptian" to English with the aid of a pair of scrying crystals. SEE SMITH, JOSEPH. Spiritualists and Mesmerists also worked extensively with crystals and magic mirrors. SEE MESMERISM; SPIRITUALISM.

In the Hermetic Order of the Golden Dawn, and in most later groups following the Golden Dawn tradition, methods of scrying using reflective surfaces were little used. Instead, "scrying in the spirit vision" was practiced. This involved learning to visualize an image and use it as a doorway to pass through in the imagination. The result, with practice, is a vivid daydream-like experience in which images are seen and information received, much as in other kinds of scrying. The tattvas—a set of elemental emblems borrowed from Hindu sources—the tarot trumps, and the Enochian tablets were the major targets of scrying in the spirit vision in Golden Dawn practice. SEE ENOCHIAN MAGIC; GOLDEN DAWN, HERMETIC ORDER OF THE; TAROT; TATTVAS.

The prestige of the Golden Dawn made its approach to scrying widely popular in the twentieth century. Also pushing in the same direction was the prominence of Jungian psychology among occultists; "active imagination," a practice very similar to Golden Dawn "scrying in the spirit vision," is a major element in Jungian practice. SEE JUNGIAN PSYCHOLOGY.

Nonetheless, both approaches to scrying are still common in the occult community today. Scrying crystals and magic mirrors are widely available from occult supply stores, and a wide range of occult traditions—from old-fashioned hoodoo to Chaos magic—offer instruction in their use. The Golden Dawn approach of "scrying in the spirit vision" is also much practiced, in Golden Dawn–derived groups and also in a range of other occult traditions. SEE ALSO DIVINATION; MIRROR, MAGIC. FURTHER READING: BESTERMAN 1965, DEVENEY 1997, FLACELIERE 1965, REGARDIE 1971.

seasonal tides. In some magical teachings, the four seasons are referred to as tides, and given special names representing the energies active during the corresponding times of the year. The system goes as follows:

> Spring (March 21–June 20): Tide of Sowing
>
> Summer (June 21–September 22): Tide of Reaping
>
> Autumn (September 23–December 22): Tide of Planning
>
> Winter (December 23–March 20): Tide of Destruction

In the Aurum Solis system of magic, this same system appears in identical form. The names of the Aurum Solis seasonal tides—Tempus Sementis (spring), Tempus Messis (summer), Tempus Consilii (autumn), and Tempus

Eversionis (winter)—are simply the terms above translated into Latin. *SEE* AURUM SOLIS.

This system is sometimes confused with the tattvic tides, which are elemental patterns of energy that cycle through the Earth's etheric body every two hours. *SEE* TATTVIC TIDES. FURTHER READING: W. BUTLER 1959, DENNING AND PHILLIPS 1978.

seax. In modern northern Neopaganism, a ritual knife, usually single-edged and often a good deal larger than the athame common in Wicca and other Pagan traditions. It serves as one of the chief working tools of the northern Pagan magician. *SEE* ASATRU.

Seax-Wica. A branch of Wicca created by Gardnerian initiate Raymond Buckland in 1973. Originally for his own use, it was adopted by a large number of students over the years, especially after the publication of Buckland's book on the subject, *The Tree: The Complete Book of Saxon Witchcraft* (1974). Buckland also operated a correspondence course on Seax-Wica for many years; the course is still available under other management as of this writing.

Unlike many modern Wiccan traditions, Seax-Wica claims no direct connection with ancient Pagan traditions, but Anglo-Saxon symbolism was borrowed as the basis for the system. The Goddess and God are called Freya and Woden. There are no degrees of initiation or oaths of secrecy, and the rituals have been published in full. Coven members are elected to serve in a priestly role for a term of a year and a day, as a way of preventing abuses of power.

Students of Seax-Wica begin as *Theows* or non-initiates, who may attend coven meetings by invitation. Those accepted for training become *Ceorls*, and those who are initiated have the title of *Gesith*. Any Gesith may found a coven, and any person may take the title of Gesith and start a coven from the ground up by learning the Seax-Wica teachings from Buckland's book or correspondence course, performing a rite of self-dedication, and beginning to train and initiate others.

There are currently Seax-Wica covens throughout Europe, North America, and Australasia, as well as in other countries. *SEE ALSO* WICCA. FURTHER READING: BUCKLAND 1974.

Second Death. In magical theory, the second and most important phase of the dying process, following the First Death (the death of the physical body) by hours, days, or weeks. The occult understanding of death is complex, and derives from the equally complex occult lore of the subtle body. *SEE* SUBTLE BODY.

According to most occult traditions, the lower bodies—physical, etheric, and astral—separate from the immortal part of the self in that order. The separation of the etheric body or body of vital energy is the crucial phase, since this body makes it possible for the self to remain in contact with the world of ordinary matter. Before the Second Death, the dead person may function as a ghost or a vampire, or even reanimate the physical body under certain rare conditions; after it, the immortal parts of the self go on to the afterlife, while the rest decays. *SEE ALSO* ETHERIC REVENANT; VAMPIRE.

Secret Chiefs. *SEE* MASTERS.

Seg. In the Cabala, the secret name of the world of Briah. The numerical values of its letters add up to sixty-three, which is also the sum of YVD HI VAV HI, the spelling of the Tetragrammaton in Briah. *SEE* BRIAH, TETRAGRAMMATON.

seidhkona. (Old Norse, "*seidhr* woman") In ancient Norse tradition and, in some modern Asatru circles, a woman who practices seidhr. *SEE* SEIDHR.

seidhr. (also "seith") In ancient and modern Norse Paganism, a tradition of trance work used to contact other realms and bring through messages from the gods and spirits. According to Norse legend, seidhr was originally the special gift of the goddess Freyja, who taught it to Odin. References in the sagas and histories suggest that it was traditionally practiced by women and had a somewhat dubious reputation.

The practitioner, called *volva* (seeress), *seidhkona* (seidhr-woman), or *spakona* (prophetess), sat on a seat raised above the ground on a platform. Around the platform was a group of singers, who sang magical songs. The costume of a volva is described in the Saga of Erik the Red; it included a blue cloak decorated with jewels and straps or hangings, a hood, catskin gloves trimmed with white fur, calfskin boots with the hair side outwards, glass beads, a leather pouch full of magical charms, and a staff with brass bindings and a knob at one end.

In modern Asatru, the practice of seidhr has been revived, drawing heavily on modern ideas about shamanism. A drum is used to help induce an altered state in the practitioner, who visualizes a journey to one of the mythic realms of Norse Pagan tradition, and comes into contact with one or more spiritual beings. The most widely practiced approach to seidhr in present-day Asatru was pioneered by American Pagan writer and practitioner Diana Paxson, and involves a group pathworking through the worlds of Norse cosmology, followed by the entry of one member of the group through the gate of Hella, the underworld goddess. The chosen member then sits on a platform, enters into trance, and answers questions.

There is a good deal of similarity between seidhr and Spiritualist mediumship; *SEE* SPIRITUALISM. *SEE ALSO* ASATRU; DIVINATION; GALDOR. FURTHER READING: ASWYNN 1998, BLAIN 1999, DAVIDSON 1981, ENRIGHT 1996, THORSSON 1998.

seith. *SEE* SEIDHR.

self-initiation. A process by which a person who does not have access to formal ritual initiation, or who chooses not to seek initiation for some reason, carries out an approximation of the same process on his or her own. In self-initiation, solo ritual work and a variety of training exercises replace the more traditional initiation rituals conferred by a group.

The validity of self-initiation has been hotly disputed in some circles, but the practice has become a standard part of the current occult scene. A wide range of books outlining methods of self-initiation in different traditions are in print as of this writing. The emergence of the solitary practitioner as an important element of the modern magical and Pagan scene has helped to drive the popularity of self-initiation practices. *SEE ALSO* INITIATION.

semiquintile. In astrology, a minor aspect formed by two planets at an angle of thirty-six degrees. It is associated with talent, and has a mild favorable influence. *SEE* ASPECT, ASTROLOGICAL.

semisextile. In astrology, a minor aspect formed by two planets at an angle of thirty degrees. It is a neutral aspect, associated with opportunities that may or may not be taken up. *SEE* ASPECT, ASTROLOGICAL.

semisquare. In astrology, a minor aspect formed by two planets at an angle of forty-five degrees. It is among the strongest of the minor aspects, and has a somewhat unfavorable effect, representing sources of difficulty or tension. *SEE* ASPECT, ASTROLOGICAL.

Sendivogius, Michael. (Michal Sedziwoj) Polish aristocrat and alchemist, 1566–1636. The child of rural Polish nobility, Sendivogius was educated in Krakow, at that time the capital of Poland and a center of alchemical and occult studies. In the 1580 and early 1590s he traveled abroad to complete his studies, attending classes at the universities of Leipzig, Vienna, and Altdorf. In 1593 he moved to Prague and took a position at the court of the Holy Roman Emperor Rudolf II, who was passionately interested in alchemy and the occult. In Prague, Sendivogius made contact with Michael Maier, another of the great alchemists of the age. *SEE* MAIER, MICHAEL. Aside from alchemy, Sendivogius also took a part in diplomatic relations between the emperor and Poland's King Zygmunt III.

The year 1604 marked a high point in Sendivogius' alchemical career. In that year, according to contemporary sources, he successfully transmuted base metal into gold in the presence of Rudolf II and a crowd of other witnesses. The same year also saw the publication of his most important alchemical text, *Novum Lumen Chymicum* (*A New Light of Alchemy*), which earned him a Europe-wide reputation as an alchemical philosopher.

This fame was not without its disadvantages. The next year Sendivogius was invited to visit Friedrich, duke of Württemburg, only to find himself imprisoned by the duke and his court alchemist in an effort to force him to yield alchemical secrets. Intervention by the emperor and the king of Poland finally won Sendivogius his freedom after several harrowing months.

He returned to his homeland, where he spent the years from 1607 to 1616, and then traveled to Germany and Austria, settling in Vienna in 1619 at the court of Rudolf's successor, Ferdinand II, where he stayed until

1624. His last years were spent back in Poland, where he died in 1636.

Sendivogius was one of the last major original thinkers in Renaissance alchemy, and his books were widely read and quoted by alchemists until the coming of the Scientific Revolution. His most important concept was the aerial niter, an essential vital spirit present in the atmosphere. This concept led to the development of niter-salt theory, the last great theoretical system in traditional alchemy, and also may have enabled Sendivogius' contemporary Cornelis Drebbel to design and test an effective submarine, with alchemical air-purifying equipment, in 1621. *SEE* DREBBEL, CORNELIS; NITER. *SEE ALSO* ALCHEMY. FURTHER READING: PRINKE 1990, SZYDLO 1994.

separation. In alchemy, the process of dividing a substance into the three alchemical principles of mercury, sulphur, and salt (which are not the same as the common substances with these names; *SEE* MERCURY; SALT; SULPHUR). There are a wide range of methods for accomplishing separation in alchemy. Alchemical symbolism assigns this process to the zodiacal sign Scorpio. *SEE* ALCHEMY.

Sepher Yetzirah. (Hebrew, "Book of Formation") The oldest document currently part of the Cabalistic canon, the Sepher Yetzirah traditionally dates back to the time of Abraham, the forefather of the Jewish people. Its actual origins are much disputed, but a date sometime between 100 B.C.E. and 900 C.E. is considered probable by most modern scholars. It was probably the product of a writer or school practicing the Ma'aseh Berashith, a system of Jewish mysticism dating from the early Common Era, which was ancestral to the Cabala; *SEE* MA'ASEH BERASHITH.

The Sepher Yetzirah is a symbolic and mystical commentary on the twenty-two letters of the Hebrew alphabet, providing a range of correspondences for each letter, and outlining a series of meditative practices that combine the letters in different ways. Much later Cabalistic letter-mysticism has been developed from the Sepher Yetzirah, and the complex letter-combinations of the Cabalist Abraham Abulafia (1240–after 1292) are particularly dependent on this ancient source. *SEE* ABULAFIA, ABRAHAM. The Cube of Space, a three-dimensional diagram relating the Hebrew letters to the dimensions of space, is also derived from the Sepher Yetzirah; *SEE* CUBE OF SPACE.

The Sepher Yetzirah was considered to be the key document in the creation of the golem; *SEE* GOLEM. *SEE ALSO* CABALA; HEBREW ALPHABET. FURTHER READING: A. KAPLAN 1990.

Sephiroth. (Hebrew, "numerations") In Cabala, the ten emanations of God forming the Cabalistic Tree of Life; the singular form of the word is Sephirah. The doctrine of the Sephiroth is at the core of the Cabala, and forms the chief element that distinguishes the Cabala from earlier forms of Jewish mysticism such as the Ma'aseh Berashith and Ma'aseh Merkabah. *SEE* MA'ASEH BERASHITH; MA'ASEH MERKABAH.

The original idea of ten special powers or manifestations of the divine is older than the Cabala, and both this idea and the term Sephiroth itself appear in the *Sepher Yetzirah*, a very ancient text that probably derives from the Ma'aseh Berashith; *SEE* SEPHER YETZIRAH. The early stages of the Cabala's evolution saw various names and atributes being applied to the Sephiroth. By the mid-thirteenth century the standard set of names had been settled, but a great deal of variation still exists among different Cabalistic traditions when it comes to the Names of God and other attributions that correspond to the Sephiroth.

The following names and attributions are standard in many branches of Western occultism:

> *Number:* 1. *Name:* Kether. *Meaning:* Crown.
> *Astrological Attribution:* Primum Mobile.
>
> *Number:* 2. *Name:* Chokmah. *Meaning:* Wisdom.
> *Astrological Attribution:* Sphere of Stars.
>
> *Number:* 3. *Name:* Binah. *Meaning:* Understanding.
> *Astrological Attribution:* Saturn.
>
> *Number:* 4. *Name:* Chesed. *Meaning:* Mercy.
> *Astrological Attribution:* Jupiter.
>
> *Number:* 5. *Name:* Geburah. *Meaning:* Severity.
> *Astrological Attribution:* Mars.
>
> *Number:* 6. *Name:* Tiphareth. *Meaning:* Beauty.
> *Astrological Attribution:* Sun.
>
> *Number:* 7. *Name:* Netzach. *Meaning:* Victory.
> *Astrological Attribution:* Venus.

Number: 8. *Name:* Hod. *Meaning:* Glory. *Astrological Attribution:* Mercury.

Number: 9. *Name:* Yesod. *Meaning:* Foundation. *Astrological Attribution:* Moon.

Number: 10. *Name:* Malkuth. *Meaning:* Kingdom. *Astrological Attribution:* Earth.

In older Cabalistic writings, the Sephiroth are also called "sayings," "names," "lights," "powers," "crowns," "stages," "garments," "mirrors," and many other terms as well. They are also seen as the limbs or bodily parts of Adam Qadmon, the Primordial Human; *SEE* ADAM.

As this flurry of names suggests, the Sephiroth have many different aspects. Each Sephirah contains an entire Tree of Life within itself. As the old Cabalistic texts put it, each Sephirah "descends into itself," creating an infinity of realms and worlds inside itself. There are thus hidden worlds of mercy, justice, beauty, and so on, unfolding endlessly within each of the Sephiroth.

In the modern Hermetic and Pagan versions of the Cabala, the Sephiroth are often equated with the gods and goddesses of various Pagan religions. *SEE ALSO ENTRIES FOR THE INDIVIDUAL SEPHIROTH;* CABALA; TREE OF LIFE. FURTHER READING: FORTUNE 1984, GREER 1996, SCHOLEM 1974.

Seraph. In Cabalistic magic, ruler of the element of fire. His name is derived from that of the Seraphim, the angelic host assigned to the Sephirah Geburah. *SEE* RULER, ELEMENTAL; SERAPHIM.

Seraphim. (Hebrew, "fiery serpents") An order of angels variously assigned by different systems of angelology. In the Cabala, the Seraphim correspond to Geburah, the fifth sphere of the Tree of Life, and are seen as angels of judgment. In Christian angelology, by contrast, the Seraphim are the highest of the nine orders of angels, and are preeminently angels of love. *SEE* ANGEL; GEBURAH.

Serapis, Master. In the lore of Theosophy and related systems of occult teaching, one of the Masters of the Great White Lodge, the secret brotherhood that supervises the spiritual evolution of the Earth. The Master Serapis is the chohan or chief adept of the Fourth or Green Ray, the ray of harmony, beauty, nature, and the arts. *SEE ALSO* GREEN RAY; MASTERS; THEOSOPHY.

Servants of the Light (SOL). International magical order founded in 1965 by English occultists W. E. Butler and Gareth Knight, both former students of Dion Fortune and members of her magical order, the Society of the Inner Light. *SEE* BUTLER, W. E.; FORTUNE, DION; INNER LIGHT, SOCIETY OF THE. Originally known as the Helios Course on the Practical Qabalah, it became a full-fledged magical order in 1975, when Knight bowed out of the organization to pursue other occult interests, and changed its name to the Servants of the Light School of Occult Science. On Butler's death in 1978, the position of Director passed to Dolores Ashcroft-Nowicki, who heads the order as of this writing.

The SOL's teachings are very much in the Dion Fortune tradition, and those familiar with Fortune's writings will recognize the flavor at once. The SOL operates a correspondence course on Cabalistic magic, presents workshops on magical ritual and related subjects, and confers initiations by way of local lodge organizations. There are presently fifteen lodges of the SOL, located in Britain, continental Europe, and North America, as well as four independent lodges associated with the order. *SEE ALSO* LODGE, MAGICAL.

sesquiquintile. In astrology, a minor aspect formed by two planets at an angle of 108 degrees. It is considered a mildly favorable aspect, related to talent. *SEE* ASPECT, ASTROLOGICAL.

sesquisquare. In astrology, a minor aspect formed by two planets at an angle of 135 degrees. It is considered mildly unfavorable. *SEE* ASPECT, ASTROLOGICAL.

Setne Khamwas. Egyptian magician-priest, c. 1300–c. 1245 B.C.E. The son of the pharaoh Ramses II and his principal queen, Isis-neferet, Setne Khamwas (also spelled Setne Khamu'ast) served as a soldier in his youth and went on to a career in the priesthood, rising to the position of High Priest of Ptah at Memphis. A likely heir to the throne, he died ten years before his extremely long-lived father. He became one of the great magicians of Egyptian legend, and stories were still being told about him more than a thousand years after his death.

During Dion Fortune's tenure as head of the Fraternity of the Inner Light, Setne Khamwas was apparently one of the inner plane contacts who played a role in the fraternity's work. *SEE* INNER LIGHT, SOCIETY OF THE. FURTHER READING: FOWDEN 1986, RICHARDSON 1985.

seven. Seven in the Cabala is Netzach, the seventh Sephirah, and the number of the letter Zayin. Of the number seven, the Sepher Yetzirah comments that "God has loved and blessed the number seven more than anything beneath heaven." There are seven double letters in the Hebrew alphabet, seven angels who stand in the presence of God, seven heavens, seven earths, and seven hells. Names of God with seven letters include ARARITA, Ararita, and AShR AHIH, Asher Eheieh. *SEE* CABALA.

Seven in Christian symbolism is the number of the sacraments and the canonical hours. The Book of Revelation is awash with sevens: seven candlesticks, seven stars, seven crowns, seven churches in Asia, seven seals, seven horns, seven eyes, seven spirits of God, seven angels with seven trumpets, seven heads of the dragon, seven mountains with seven kings sitting on them, and seven thunders that announce the end. There are seven petitions in the Lord's Prayer, and seven words that Jesus uttered on the cross.

Seven in Renaissance magical symbolism is sacred to the Holy Spirit. It is called the vehicle of human life, and is the number of the planets, the virtues, the days of the week, and the gifts of the Holy Spirit. *SEE ALSO* ARITHMOLOGY. FURTHER READING: MCLEAN 1994, WATERFIELD 1988, WESTCOTT 1984.

1734 Tradition. A North American witchcraft tradition with British roots, the 1734 Tradition emerged out of the work of Robert Cochrane (1931–1966), a British witch who claimed initiation in a family tradition of witchcraft. Cochrane was a major figure in the British witchcraft scene of the early 1960s, a maverick of sorts whose system of witchcraft—the Clan of Tubal-Cain—was sharply different from the then-dominant Gardnerian approach. *SEE* CLAN OF TUBAL-CAIN; COCHRANE, ROBERT.

In the mid-1960s, Cochrane entered into a correspondence with an American student, Joseph Wilson. Cochrane's letters were full of riddles, poetry, hints, and half-answered questions, and Wilson and a number of his friends and associates developed their own system based on these evasive directions. Copies of the letters were

widely circulated, giving rise to many different branches of the tradition.

Current members of the 1734 Tradition refer to it as a British-Celtic or Celtic-Eclectic system. The number 1734 is not, as has sometimes been asserted, a date, or the address of Cochrane's original High Priestess. It is a cryptogram that conceals the name of the High Goddess of the system, as 1737 conceals the name of the High God.

Present-day practitioners of the 1734 Tradition use meditation and visionary experience as central tools in their work. Like Cochrane's original coven, they work outdoors whenever possible. Unlike Cochrane himself, whose experiments with native psychedelic plants led to his death, current 1734 initiates apparently do not use narcotics or hallucinogens in their rites. *SEE ALSO* WITCHCRAFT.

sex and occultism. Like practically every other human activity, occultism has its points of contact with human sexuality. Most versions of occult philosophy hold that the sexual energies in the human organism are an expression of the primal creative powers of the universe. From this common starting point, though, the occult traditions of the West have tended to take two very different paths. Some occult systems propose that the energies of sex should be prevented from finding their ordinary outlet, and redirected into other uses. Others suggest that the energies should be allowed to express themselves in lovemaking, but that lovemaking itself can be used as a vehicle for magical operations.

Both these approaches can be traced back to ancient times. Surviving records concerning the Gnostics suggest that some of them practiced ascetic disciplines that involved redirecting sexual energies up the spine to the brain; this was referred to, in a metaphor drawn from Jewish sources, as "the waters of the Jordan flowing uphill." Such methods apparently required perfect celibacy. Other Gnostics, by contrast, seem to have practiced ritual lovemaking, and tasted the mingled sexual fluids as a form of communion. *SEE* GNOSTICISM.

Whether anything of the sort was practiced in the occultism of medieval or Renaissance Europe is anyone's guess. The grimoires—handbooks of medieval and early modern magic, mostly concerned with the art of summoning demons—often require periods of celibacy, of a few days or more, before ritual workings, but make no other references to sex. The same is true of the much more complex literature of Renaissance high magic. *SEE* GRIMOIRE; HERMETICISM.

The literature of medieval alchemy is full of sexual symbolism, and has often been identified as a coded language discussing sexual practices. Like most attempts to redefine alchemy as something other than a laboratory art, though, this interpretation falters through simple lack of evidence. Legal and theological condemnations of alchemy, which were not infrequent during the Middle Ages, accuse alchemists of fraud and other crimes, but sexual immorality never seems to enter into the picture. If there was a sexual component to alchemy, it seems to have centered on suppressing and redirecting the sexual energies, not expressing them; a number of sources, including Ben Jonson's satirical but well-informed play *The Alchemist* (1612), refer to the idea that the alchemical work fails in the presence of any expression of sexual desire. *SEE* ALCHEMY.

Certainly, though, esoteric approaches to sex were common in certain mystical movements on the edge of occultism. The Cabala, originally a system of mystical Jewish interpretation of Scripture and ritual, had developed a distinctive sexual practice by the close of the Middle Ages; *SEE* CABALA. As described in Cabalistic texts such as the *Iggeret ha-Qodesh* (*Holy Letter*), a short instructional work probably dating from the late medieval period, this involved lovemaking on the eve of the Sabbath as a way of participating in the union of God and the Shekinah, the personified divine presence in the world. This latter union was understood by many highly orthodox Jewish writers of the time in frankly sexual terms, and sex itself never took on the same negative cast in Judaism that it did in Christianity. *SEE* SHEKINAH.

As Cabala was the dominant current in Jewish thought from the middle of the sixteenth century to the middle of the nineteenth, these sexual teachings became extremely widespread among observant Jews. The development of the Christian Cabala, starting in the fifteenth century, and the purely magical Hermetic Cabala beginning in the sixteenth, spread these ideas in gentile communities as well, but evidence for actual practice of Ca-

balistic sexual techniques among Christian and Hermetic Cabalists is hard to find until some centuries later.

By the eighteenth century, methods of sexual practice were in use in some occult circles, and the nineteenth saw a major flowering of sexual occultism. Some eighteenth- and nineteenth-century thinkers reinterpreted ancient Paganism as a worship of sexual energies, with the penis and vagina as the primary sacred symbols; books about "phallic religion," as the theory was called, existed in an underground where scholarship and pornography overlapped. Another figure in the same underworld was Edward Sellon (1818–1866), fencing master, travel agent, pornographer, and author of one of the more indecent autobiographies in existence, *The Ups and Downs of Life* (1867). Sellon was also responsible for *Annotations on the Sacred Writings of the Hindoos* (1865), the first detailed presentation of Hindu tantric sexual theory and practice in English. *SEE* PHALLIC RELIGION.

About this same time, the most common modern approach to occult sexual practice had its origins in the mind of an American occultist of African descent, Paschal Beverly Randolph (1825–1875). A Spiritualist and a student of the "animal magnetism" of Austrian occultist and physician Franz Anton Mesmer (1734– 1815), Randolph devised a method of magical practice involving heterosexual intercourse, in which both partners concentrated intensely on the goal of the working at the moment of mutual orgasm. *SEE* RANDOLPH, PASCHAL BEVERLY.

Randolph hinted at his methods in his books, but passed on the actual methods to a number of students. After his death, Randolph's system was taken up by the Hermetic Brotherhood of Luxor (H. B. of L.), one of the most important magical orders of the late nineteenth century; *SEE* HERMETIC BROTHERHOOD OF LUXOR (H. B. OF L.). The H. B. of L.'s members included two German occultists, Carl Kellner (1851–1905) and Theodor Reuss (1855–1923), who adapted Randolph's teachings further and made them the central secret of a new occult order, the Ordo Templi Orientis (OTO); *SEE* ORDO TEMPLI ORIENTIS (OTO).

In 1912 the OTO recruited its most famous member, English occultist and self-proclaimed Beast of Revelation

Aleister Crowley (1875–1947). Crowley, for whom the word "oversexed" might well have been invented, took to sexual magic at once, and proclaimed it as the essential secret of all magic and religion. Crowley's bisexuality led him to rework Randolph's system to include homosexual as well as heterosexual lovemaking. Crowley also invented a practice he called "eroto-comatose lucidity," which consisted of repeated orgasm until sheer exhaustion propelled him into trance. SEE CROWLEY, ALEISTER; TRANCE.

From Crowley, in turn, Randolph's system passed to Gerald Gardner (1884–1964), who studied with Crowley during the last year of the Beast's life. Gardner reworked and simplified Randolph's sexual mysticism while devising his new religion, Wicca. As a result, what started out as the occult teaching of a nineteenth-century African-American magician is now presented by many modern Pagan groups as an ancient Pagan tradition handed down in England since prehistoric times. SEE GARDNER, GERALD BROUSSEAU; GREAT RITE; WICCA.

The other side of sexual occultism also underwent a great deal of development in the nineteenth and twentieth centuries. Both the Theosophical Society and the Hermetic Order of the Golden Dawn, the H. B. of L.'s main rivals in the occult scene of the late nineteenth century, discouraged sex magic, and so did most of the other occult organizations of the time. In America, in particular, the idea that absolute celibacy was a crucial element of occult practice found deep roots, and organizations such as Hiram Butler's Esoteric Fraternity taught that celibacy all by itself would lead to spiritual development. SEE ESOTERIC FRATERNITY.

Along the same lines, if noticeably weirder, was the teaching of Thomas Lake Harris (1823–1906), an erstwhile Swedenborgian minister whose Brotherhood of the New Life taught a system of spiritual development in which diet, breathing exercises, and absolute celibacy allowed thousands of happy, health-giving faeries to dwell inside the body of the practitioner, who had the added privilege of intensely erotic "counterpartal unions" with spiritual beings. Harris, always one to practice what he preached, wrote love poetry by the ream to his angelic "counterpart," by whom he claimed to have had three spirit-children. SEE HARRIS, THOMAS LAKE.

Harris' system derived in part from an extensive lore concerning human matings with spirits. This lore had its origins in a satirical novel, Le Comte de Gabalis, by the Abbé de Montfaucon de Villars (1635–1673), which made fun of seventeenth-century occultism by claiming that it was all about sex with elemental spirits. Despite the novel's tone of high mockery, a surprising number of later occultists missed the joke and treated it as a serious presentation of occult truths. As a result, attempts at "counterpartal" relationships were common enough in the occult scene that a number of nineteenth- and twentieth-century occultists issued warnings against the practice. SEE COMTE DE GABALIS, LE; FANTASY OCCULTISM.

One of these latter was Dion Fortune (1890–1946), whose work on sex is probably the most thoroughly developed system of sexual magic to come out of the occult tradition in the twentieth century. Fortune, like almost all occult theorists on the subject, argued that sexual energies are an expression of the primary creative energies of the cosmos; they can be expressed through physical lovemaking or through interactions on any of the other levels of being. Fortune's sexual methods focus on redirecting creative force away from physical sex, but without the contempt for sexuality often seen on the celibate side of the debate; especially in her later work, Fortune treats erotic energies as a neutral force that can be directed toward or away from lovemaking, depending on circumstances and needs. SEE FORTUNE, DION; POLARITY.

At the present time just about every possible occult approach to sex can be found in the spiritual marketplaces of the Western world. Systems preaching the benefits of total celibacy appear cheek by jowl with systems that propose Bacchanalian orgies as the proper expression of human sexual energies, and with every nuance in between. The one thing that can be said with certainty is that the aspiring occultist can choose nearly any level or type of sexual activity, and consider himself or herself in line with at least one tradition.

The entire subject of sex and occultism has been made even more complex by a set of popular myths about the interface between magic and sex; like most fantasies about the occult, these have been reflected from time to time in the behavior of some occultists. These myths are almost entirely the creation of Christianity, and have their roots in that religion's extremely conflicted attitude toward human sexuality.

From the time of Jesus of Nazareth on, many versions of Christianity have responded to sex with fear, disgust, contempt, and obsessive fascination. The origins of this odd mix of attitudes is complex and heavily disputed by scholars. One result, however, is that for the last two thousand years, Christians have frequently assumed that anything non-Christian is primarily about sex.

Examples can be quoted endlessly. Medieval accounts of heretics and witches centered on the wild sexual escapades that supposedly took place at heretics' conventicles and the Witches' Sabbath, just as Victorian missionaries titillated audiences with tales of "Pagan orgies" in the far corners of the world. In the same way, many conservative Christians nowadays are convinced that the world is full of Devil-worshippers who spend most of their time engaging in perverted sexual activities—an attitude that has much to do with the imaginary epidemic of "Satanic ritual abuse" in recent years. *SEE* SATANIC RITUAL ABUSE.

It is worth noting that this sort of ideology has proven to be a fertile source of Satanism for at least four hundred years. Faced with claims that Satanists spend their time engaging in wild sexual orgies, and presented with Christian ideologies that reject nearly all human pleasures as sinful, a noticeable number of Christians over the years have decided that the grass is greener on the other side of the theological fence. It is not accidental that Aleister Crowley was born and raised in the Plymouth Brethren, one of the narrowest of nineteenth-century Evangelical sects. Many of the modern teenage Satanists whose antics occupy the tabloid press come from similar backgrounds. *SEE* SATANISM. FURTHER READING: COHEN 1976, CROWLEY 1976, FORTUNE 1930, J. GODWIN 1994, GODWIN ET AL. 1995, KING 1972B.

sextile. In astrology, an arc of sixty degrees between two planets or points. A sextile aspect gives rise to a mildly harmonious relationship between the affected energies. *SEE* ASPECT, ASTROLOGICAL; ASTROLOGY.

Seymour, Charles Richard Foster. Irish occultist, 1880–1943. Born in Galway to a family in the landed gentry, he graduated from Trinity College in Dublin in 1899 and started a military career with a commission in the British Army's Hampshire Regiment. After serving with distinction in the Boer War, he transferred to the Indian Army. The First World War saw him in what was then British East Africa, where he was wounded in action against German colonial forces. During his military career he also served as an interpreter for the British diplomatic mission in Moscow and as a teacher in the Indian Army staff college at Quetta. He retired from the army in 1927 and returned to college, receiving his M.A. degree in 1929.

Throughout his military career he was an active Freemason, belonging to regimental lodges, and was a member of the Grand Lodge of Scotland. It seems to have been by way of Masonic contacts that he came into contact with Dion Fortune's Fraternity of the Inner Light. He was initiated in 1933, rose through the grades quickly, and by 1934 held the newly created office of Executive Officer with full responsibility for running the fraternity's training and testing program. He also took on a large share of the fraternity's public lectures and wrote articles for its magazine. *SEE* FORTUNE, DION; INNER LIGHT, SOCIETY OF THE.

In 1937 he began intensive magical work with Christine Campbell Thompson, another member of the Fraternity, picking up a range of inner plane contacts and bringing through material from Atlantean and Celtic sources. As this work expanded, Seymour's interest in the Fraternity of the Inner Light diminished, though he remained an active member of the Fraternity until the outbreak of war in 1939. During the Second World War, Seymour and Thompson both worked with a small Golden Dawn–derived temple in London, and continued their own private work. These activities came to an end with Seymour's sudden death from cerebral hemmhorage in 1943. FURTHER READING: ASHCROFT-NOWICKI 1986, KNIGHT 2000, RICHARDSON 1985.

Shaare Moth. (Hebrew, "gates of death") In Cabalistic lore, the third of the seven hells, corresponding to the Sephirah Netzach. *SEE* HELLS, SEVEN.

Shabbathai. (Hebrew, "Saturn") In Cabala, the planet Saturn, the celestial sphere corresponding to Binah in the world of Assiah. SEE ASSIAH; BINAH.

Shad Barshemoth ha-Shartathan. In ceremonial magic, the Spirit of Spirits of the moon. Its governing Intelligence of Intelligences is Malkah be-Tarshishim ve-ad Ruachoth Shechalim. SEE SPIRIT.

Shambhala. In Tibetan legend and tradition, a city located somewhere north of Tibet, in the largely uninhabited lands of central Asia, ruled by a line of enlightened kings. Its name is also spelled Shamballah, Shambhalla, and Schamballah in Western sources. By whatever spelling, Shambhala in Tibetan traditions is the source of the Kalachakra teachings, an important system of Tibetan Buddhist theory and practice. According to some accounts, a messianic king named Rigden-jyepo will one day ride forth from Shambhala to vanquish the forces of evil and conquer the world.

Theosophy adopted Shambhala early on, and there are references to the hidden city in both *Isis Unveiled* and *The Secret Doctrine*. According to accounts in later Theosophical literature, Shambhala was a city founded by the manu of the fifth root race about 70,000 B.C.E., on the shores of the Gobi Sea opposite the fabled White Island. Inspired by these passages, the Theosophist and central Asian traveler Nicholas Roerich made several expeditions in search of Shambhala, and never surrendered the belief that Rigden-jyepo would soon appear.

Attempts to relate Shambhala to Agharta, the other central Asian occult center of nineteenth- and twentieth-century occult speculation, were not uncommon and tended to stray in one of two directions. Some writers have equated the two with each other, while others have seen them as distinct, or even competing, centers of occult influence. SEE AGHARTA. Perhaps the furthest journey in this direction may be found in the works of Trevor Ravenscroft, who interpreted them both as centers of cosmic evil but, drawing on Rudolf Steiner's distinctive cosmology, identified them with Steiner's two warring evil forces. Agharta, in this view, is a center of the Luciferic influence, the arrogant rejection of matter in favor of the intellect; Shambhala, in turn, is the center

of the Ahrimanic influence of absolute materialism. SEE AHRIMAN; ANTHROPOSOPHY; LUCIFER.

The popularity of Shambhala in Theosophical circles and related twentieth-century movements has ensured it a welcome in current New Age circles, and a great deal of talk about Shambhala may still be heard in the New Age community today. It thus represents yet another example of the New Age's legacy to Theosophy. SEE NEW AGE MOVEMENT. SEE ALSO OCCULT HISTORY. FURTHER READING: BERNBAUM 1980, GODWIN 1993.

Shasta, Mount. Volcanic peak in northern California, 14,162 feet high, a central feature in several modern American occult traditions. Important in the legends of local native tribes as a haunt of faery-like creatures and hairy giants of the sasquatch type, it seems to have first entered into Western occult lore with the appearance of Frederick Oliver's novel *A Dweller on Two Planets* (first published in 1894), which described a hidden citadel of Atlantean Masters within the peak. Oliver claimed that the story was absolute truth, received telepathically by him from a Master named Phylos the Thibetan. Oliver's account became highly popular with the occult and Theosophical communities in America, and the idea of a hidden city of Masters inside Shasta quickly passed into general circulation.

By the 1930s the role of the mountain in occult circles was secure, and most occult teachers of the time included it in their systems. H. Spencer Lewis, founder of the Rosicrucian order AMORC, published a book in 1931—*Lemuria: The Lost Continent of the Pacific*—which claimed the mountain as the highest peak of ancient Lemuria, joined to the North American continent by continental drift, and riddled with caverns in which Lemurian masters preserved their ancient wisdom. Long-time residents of the Mount Shasta area have reported that several search parties were sent from AMORC headquarters in San Jose during the 1930s in the hope of finding the hidden entrances to the Lemurian colony. SEE ANCIENT MYSTICAL ORDER ROSAE CRUCIS (AMORC).

It was also during the 1930s that Guy Ballard, founder of the I AM movement, reported meeting the Comte de Saint-Germain on the peak; SEE BALLARD, GUY. The I AM organization still has a large piece of property not far from Mt. Shasta City, and performs a pageant about the life of the Master Jesus there in August each year.

As a result of Shasta's reputation, several small towns around the foot of the mountain have been centers of occultism for many decades, and in recent years have received a new influx of people connected with the New Age movement. Stories of the hidden cities Ilethelme and Yaktayvia, said to be located on or in the peak, are still much discussed, and it's claimed that UFOs are routinely spotted going in and out of the mountain. What, if anything, is behind all this exuberant mythology is anyone's guess. *SEE ALSO* LEMURIA; NEW AGE MOVEMENT; OCCULT HISTORY. FURTHER READING: KAFTON-MINKEL **1989**, PHYLOS THE TIBETAN **1929**.

Shaver mystery. In September 1943, a letter from one "S. Shaver" arrived at the office of the pulp science-fiction magazine *Amazing Stories*, announcing the discovery of an "ancient language" called Mantong that, suggested the author, "seems to me to be definite proof of the Atlantis legend." It went into the trash but was fished out by *Amazing*'s editor—the legendary Ray Palmer—and published in the December 1943 issue of the magazine. The reader response was favorable enough that Palmer wrote to the author asking for more information.

What he got was a clumsily typed 10,000-word letter titled "A Warning to Future Man." The author gave his full name, Richard S. Shaver, and recounted a jumbled tale of an underground world of tunnels and caves full of psychotic subterranean dwarfs called "deros"—Mantong for detrimental robots—who used ancient Lemurian "telaug" (telepathic augmentation) and "sex-stim" rays, among other devices, to torment dwellers on the surface. Palmer recognized a gold mine when he saw it, rewrote the letter into a 31,000-word story titled "I Remember Lemuria!" and published it in the March 1945 issue. The issue promptly sold out, and *Amazing* was deluged with 2,500 letters a month from readers who wanted to know more about the sinister deros, or recounted tales of their own dero encounters.

From 1945 until 1948, when Palmer's bosses told him to drop the "Shaver mystery" and return the magazine to its original science-fiction focus, accounts of the deros' wicked doings and the secret history of the Earth filled *Amazing*'s pages. One issue, June 1947, was devoted entirely to the subject. More orthodox science-fiction fans were outraged, but the Shaver stories developed a cult following of their own. When Palmer left *Amazing* in 1948 to found *Fate Magazine*, Shaver fans and the newly hatched UFO scene provided him with a ready market for "true stories of the strange, the unusual, the unknown."

The Shaver mystery drew heavily on a variety of traditional and Theosophical occult themes, and many of its elements were adopted into belief systems on the fringes of the occult community. In the more paranoid wing of the New Age movement, in particular, the deros and their secret world of tunnels remain a living presence. *SEE* NEW AGE MOVEMENT. *SEE ALSO* DEROS; GNOMES; MANTONG; THEOSOPHY. FURTHER READING: CHILDRESS **1999**, KAFTON-MINKEL **1989**, SHAVER **1948**.

Shechaqim. (Hebrew, "clouds") In Cabalistic lore, the third of the seven heavens, corresponding to the Sephirah Netzach. *SEE* HEAVENS, SEVEN.

Shekinah. (Hebrew, "presence") Originally a term for the presence of God, especially as manifested in the Temple of Jerusalem, this word gradually became the name of a feminine aspect of God corresponding to Malkuth, the tenth Sephirah of the Cabalistic Tree of Life. *SEE* CABALA; MALKUTH. The Shekinah is seen as the creative presence of God within the manifested universe. Originally belonging to the world of Briah, she is in exile in Assiah as a result of the Fall. *SEE* FALL, THE.

In some of the more mythological Cabalistic schools, the relationship of the Shekinah to God takes on the shape of a romantic melodrama spun out against the background of the creation and destruction of the universe, with God and the Shekinah as lovers fated to a long series of separations and reconciliations on their way to the final eschatological state of connubial bliss. It has been suggested that this pattern of thought represents a legacy from the goddess myths of archaic Hebrew polytheism.

Whether this is true or not, for centuries now, devout Cabalistic Jews have made love on the night of the sabbath with the intention of both participating in, and furthering, the reconciliation and love of God and his Shekinah. The well-known Cabalistic document *Iggeret Haqodesh*, or *Holy Letter*, gives detailed instructions on the contemplations and practices that are to accompany this bit of Tantric Judaism. *SEE* SEX AND OCCULTISM. *SEE ALSO* CABALA. FURTHER READING: COHEN 1976, PATAI 1967.

Shemhamphorash. (Hebrew *Shem ha-mephoresh*, "divided name") One of the more intricate products of Cabalistic analysis of the Jewish scriptures, the Shem-hamphorash consists of seventy-two three-letter sequences constructed from three verses of the Book of Exodus. In the original Hebrew, Exodus 14:19, 14:20, and 14:21 each contain exactly seventy-two letters; to turn this into the Shemhamphorash, the first verse is written from right to left (as ordinary Hebrew), the second beneath it from left to right, and the third beneath the second from right to left. The seventy-two sections of the name are then read off in vertical columns.

In practice, the three-letter segments of the name are used as divine names in their own right, or filled out with the traditional angelic suffixes -el or -iah to become the names of seventy-two angels, who are assigned to the quinances of the zodiac; *SEE* QUINANCE. Each of these angels is associated with a verse from the Psalms, and may be invoked for specific purposes. For example, the eighth angel of the Shemhamphorash, Kehethel, who governs the second quinance of Virgo, also rules over agriculture, hunting, rural environments, and mystical practice, and can be invoked by the recitation of Psalm 94:6.

This limited use of the name is probably best, as Cabalistic tradition insists that, correctly pronounced, the complete Shemhamphorash will cause the entire universe to shatter. *SEE ALSO* CABALA. FURTHER READING: D. GODWIN 1989, PAPUS 1977.

Shemittoth. *SEE* CYCLES, COSMIC.

Sheol. (Hebrew, "depth, abyss") In Cabalistic lore, the seventh and lowest of the seven hells, corresponding to the three Supernal Sephiroth. *SEE* HELLS, SEVEN.

shewstone. A crystal or gem used for scrying. *SEE* SCRYING.

Shin. (Hebrew, "tooth") The twenty-first letter of the Hebrew alphabet, one of the three mother letters, with a sound-value of *sh* and a numerical value of 300. Its standard magical symbolism is as follows:

> *Path of the Tree of Life:* Thirty-first Path, Hod to Malkuth.
>
> *Astrological Correspondence:* Fire.
>
> *Tarot Correspondence:* Trump XX, Judgement.
>
> *Part of the Cube of Space:* North-south axis.
>
> *Colors:* in Atziluth—glowing scarlet orange.
>
> in Briah—vermilion.
>
> in Yetzirah—scarlet, flecked with gold.
>
> in Assiah—vermilion, flecked with crimson and emerald.

The corresponding text of the *Thirty-two Paths of Wisdom* runs as follows: "The Thirty-first Path is the Perpetual Intelligence, and why is it so called? Because it regulates the motions of the Sun and Moon in their proper order, each in an orbit convenient for it."

Shin is also a common Cabalistic symbol for the spirit of God, since the phrase *ruach ha-qodesh*, "holy spirit," adds to 300—the numerical value of the letter Shin—by gematria. *SEE* GEMATRIA. This has been borrowed into Christian Cabala as well, and the letter Shin is added to the Tetragrammaton to create the Pentagrammaton or Cabalistic name of Jesus. *SEE* PENTAGRAMMATON. *SEE ALSO* CABALA; HEBREW ALPHABET.

Hebrew letter Shin

Shroud of Concealment. In Golden Dawn magic, a shell of etheric substance built up around the magician by intensive ritual work that prevents other people from perceiving the magician. The creation of the Shroud of Concealment is fundamental to the Golden Dawn method of magical invisibility. The technique is closely related to the odic shield of other magical systems. *SEE* ETHER; GOLDEN DAWN, HERMETIC ORDER OF THE; ODIC SHIELD. FURTHER READING: GREER 1997, REGARDIE 1971.

Sialam, Sleep of. In nineteenth- and early twentieth-century occult writings, the highest form of magical trance, in which a specially chosen and prepared person enters into an expanded state of awareness and is able to prophesy the future. The term first surfaced in Western occultism in *Ravalette*, an 1863 novel by American occultist P. B. Randolph, as "the Sleep of Sialam Boaghiee," but seems to have been of Indian origin.

It was later borrowed by most of the important occult writers of the late nineteenth century, including H. P. Blavatsky (who refers coyly to the "Sleep of ★ ★ ★" in *Isis Unveiled* [Blavatsky 1877, v. 1, pp. 357–358]) and the Hermetic Brotherhood of Luxor. *SEE* HERMETIC BROTHERHOOD OF LUXOR (H. B. OF L.).

In his book on the tarot (Crowley 1969, p. 98), Aleister Crowley connected Trump XII, the Hanged Man, to the "Sleep of Shiloam," which is probably the same thing. *SEE* CROWLEY, ALEISTER; HANGED MAN, THE. FURTHER READING: DEVENY 1997, RANDOLPH 1874.

siddhi. (Sanskrit, "attainment") In Theosophy and other traditions drawing on Hindu sources, a supernormal power resulting from the systematic practice of spiritual disciplines. Like most other systems of mysticism, Theosophy has tended to strongly discourage the pursuit of siddhis for their own sake, pointing out that the development of such powers is a distraction from the real work of inner transformation, and can also lead to the inflation of the ego. *SEE* MAGIC; THAUMATURGY; THEOSOPHY; THEURGY.

Sig. *SEE* SOL.

sigil. (Latin *sigillum*, "seal") An abstract symbol, created by any of several different methods, which is used in magic either as the signature of a spirit or magical force, or as the symbolic representation of the outcome desired by the magician.

In ancient, medieval, and Renaissance magic, the standard way of making and using sigils started with the *kameas* or magic squares of the seven planets. Hebrew or Greek names of spirits were converted into numbers—both these languages use alphabets that have numerical value—and the numbers located on the relevant magic square, dividing by 10 or 100 where necessary to bring

the numbers down to those present in the magic square. Linked by a line in connect-the-dots fashion, the numbers on the square give rise to an abstract lineal figure, which is the sigil of the spirit. This can be (and was) traced in the air, marked on the ground with chalk or a sword's point, written on talismans, or otherwise manipulated as a representation of the spirit or force for which it stood. *SEE* MAGIC SQUARE.

These methods, and others related to them, remained in use in the great magical revival of the nineteenth and early twentieth centuries. In the Hermetic Order of the Golden Dawn, for example, the great Rose Cross Lamen—an essential item of magical equipment, made and worn by each Adeptus Minor of the Order—had a rose containing the twenty-two Hebrew letters in a set order; *SEE* LAMEN. Among its other uses, this was the basis for "Sigils from the Rose," which were made by drawing a line from letter to letter and using the resulting zigzag shape.

In the last few decades, however, a sharply different form of sigil magic has become more common, especially in avant-garde occult circles in Britain, Germany, and America. This new approach has its roots in the work of English artist and occultist Austin Osman Spare (1886–1956). Spare's personal (and very idiosyncratic) system of magic, the Zos Kia Cultus, involved sigils made by combining English letters or geometrical shapes to symbolize whatever the magical working was meant to accomplish. Intense concentration on a sigil of this sort, particularly at the moment of orgasm, was used to focus the magical will on the goals of the working. *SEE* SPARE, AUSTIN OSMAN; ZOS KIA CULTUS.

Spare's methods have become popular in modern Chaos magic circles, in large part because they do not require belief in any form of deity or spiritual being. As a result, most of the references to sigil magic in the current occult community deal with this approach, rather than the older meaning of the word. FURTHER READING: REGARDIE 1971, U. D. 1991.

Sigil. (Anglo-Saxon rune) *SEE* SOL.

signatures, doctrine of. In traditional Western occultism and herb lore, the belief that the medical and magical virtues of an herb may be found symbolized in some way in the herb's color, shape, or other qualities. For example, the bright yellow flowers of dandelions, because they are the color of jaundice, are held to label the plant as good for liver complaints—which, in fact, it is.

There are at least three forms of the doctrine of signatures, which may be found in occult writings of the ancient, medieval, and early modern periods. First is the medical version of the doctrine, as shown in the example above, in which the signature present in the plant indicates its particular healing virtues.

The second version is astrological, and holds that the ruling planet of any herb can be identified by its physical qualities. Thus, for example, herbs with ferny, much-divided leaves are assigned to Venus, and those with golden flowers are usually solar. (Dandelion, again, is an example; many of the old herbals assign it to the sun.) This has important medical implications, since the planetary ruler of an herb is a significant factor in the old, astrological approach to herbal medicine; it also serves to point out magical applications for herbs and other plants.

The third version of the doctrine of signatures is mystical, and is particularly associated with the tradition launched by the German mystic Jakob Böhme (1575–1624). In one of Böhme's mystical experiences, he found himself able to read the medical and mystical powers of every plant in a field at a glance, though this ability departed when he emerged from the mystical state. In works written by his followers, this vision became the basis of a version of the doctrine of signatures that was purely mystical in application, pointing toward the possibilities of transcendent knowledge to be gained by spiritual practice. SEE BÖHME, JAKOB; THEOSOPHY. SEE ALSO NATURAL MAGIC. FURTHER READING: TOBYN 1997, WOOD 2000.

Sirius. The brightest star in Earth's sky, with a magnitude of 1.6, Sirius is located in the mouth of the constellation Canis Major. It has had various roles in occult traditions, ancient as well as modern. Its place in ancient and medieval starlore generally derived closely from its relationship to the calendar. In ancient Egypt, for example, it was associated with the goddess Isis, and its first rising just before dawn at that time marked the coming of the Nile flood. (This has since changed due to the precession of the equinoxes; SEE PRECESSION OF THE EQUINOXES.)

In modern occult tradition, Sirius has had a rather stranger part to play. The writings of Dion Fortune and other members of her school identify Sirius as the "Sun behind the Sun," and represents the higher self of the Solar Logos or indwelling spiritual power of our sun; SEE SOLAR LOGOS. It is also considered the Sphere of the Greater Masters; SEE MASTERS. SEE ALSO FORTUNE, DION; INNER LIGHT, SOCIETY OF THE. Certain magical workings in this tradition are timed by the rising of Sirius or its arrival at the midheaven.

In occult writings, Sirius is often called Sothis, which is a Greek rendering of its ancient Egyptian name. SEE ALSO ASTROLOGY.

sistrum. A musical instrument used in ancient Egyptian ritual, the sistrum is a variety of rattle, consisting of a frame which supports several parallel rods. The rods pass through the centers of metal disks, which slide back and forth freely. The frame has a handle fastened to it. The sistrum is shaken rhythmically to produce a delicate chiming. In ancient Egypt, it was sacred to the goddesses Isis and Hathor. SEE ALSO ISIS.

six. In Platonic and Pythagorean symbolism, six is associated with Amphitrite, the wife of the sea god Poseidon; with Hekate, the three-faced guardian of crossroads; and with Thalia, one of the Muses. Its titles include "marriage," "peace," "reconciliation," and "cosmos," because it is the result of the joining of opposites, being the product of two (the first even number) multiplied by three (the first odd number), as well as "perfect" and "equal-limbed," since it is the sum of all its factors—$1 + 2 + 3 = 6$. It is associated with healing, fertility, and beauty.

In the Cabala, six is Tiphareth, Beauty, the sixth Sephirah of the Tree, and also the number of the letter Vau. The Name of God with six letters is AL GBVR, El Gibor. SEE CABALA.

In Renaissance magical symbolism, six is the number of perfection, of redemption, and of humanity. FURTHER READING: MCLEAN 1994, WATERFIELD 1988, WESTCOTT 1984.

Sixth and Seventh Books of Moses. A magical handbook of German origin, first published in Stuttgart in 1849, which went on to become one of the most famous magical books in American folk magic and hoodoo. The text of the supposed *Sixth and Seventh Books* takes up only twenty-two pages in the most common edition, the remaining 168 pages being filled up with essays on magical history and theory, collections of Cabalistic talismans, explanations of the magical use of the Psalms, and similar material.

Copies of the *Sixth and Seventh Books* in manuscript were in circulation in Pennsylvania and other German-settled areas of North America in colonial times. The Stuttgart edition was being reprinted by American publishers by the 1850s, and an English translation was available by 1880. Within a decade it was in use among hoodoo practitioners in the United States and the West Indies, and its reputation in the hoodoo community has grown to legendary proportions. SEE ALSO GRIMOIRE; HOODOO; PENNSYLVANIA DUTCH MAGIC. FURTHER READING: ANONYMOUS 1910, K. HAYES 1997.

skyclad. In Wicca and other modern Neopagan traditions, a ritual term meaning "naked." The word is an exact translation of the Sanskrit *digambara*, used by several sects of Jain and Hindu ascetics who renounce clothing along with all other worldly goods. Although it has been claimed by some in the Wiccan and Neopagan scene as a traditional term in use for centuries in the West, no trace of it appears in Western occult sources before the emergence of modern Wicca. it seems to have been introduced by Gerald Gardner, the founder of Wicca, who got it from English-language sources on tantra. SEE GARDNER, GERALD BROUSSEAU; WICCA.

Smith, Harry. American eccentric and occultist, 1923–1991. Born in Portland, Oregon, in a family of Theosophists, he grew up near the small town of Bellingham, Washington; his father worked in a cannery and his mother taught school at the nearby Lummi reservation. Contact with the Lummi nation sparked an interest in anthropology, which he studied at the University of Washington in 1943–1944, but left without taking a degree. In 1946 he moved to San Francisco and became part of the Beat scene of the late 1940s, establishing a reputation as one of the most innovative experimental filmmakers of the time. He also began the study of

magic, contacting Charles Stansfield Jones among others. SEE ACHAD, FRATER.

In 1950 he moved to New York City, where he pursued a variety of interests with his usual combination of enthusiasm and wild disorder. The year 1952 saw the publication of his most important work, the epochal *Anthology of American Folk Music* issued by Folkways, which brought together scores of forgotten recordings from the 1920s and 1930s and is widely credited with launching the folk music movement of the 1950s and 1960s. His talents as a painter landed him one of the first shows by an American artist at the Louvre, a two-person show shared with French Surrealist Marcel Duchamp. He also assembled the world's largest collection of paper airplanes, which he donated to the Smithsonian Institution, and became one of the world's major experts on string figures.

Smith rarely had much money, and spent more than he had on alcohol, drugs, and a variety of eccentricities. His involvement in the occult was intense but just as odd as the rest of his life—for example, he devoted months of study to comparing the internal structure of the Enochian tablets to the traditional "setts" or weaving patterns of Highland Scots tartans, and devised a set of elemental tablets that combined both systems. SEE ENOCHIAN MAGIC.

In his last years he became a welcome presence at meetings of the Ordo Templi Orientis (OTO), and was consecrated as a bishop in the OTO's Gnostic church, the Ecclesia Gnostica Catholica, in 1986. SEE ORDO TEMPLI ORIENTIS (OTO). His financial situation became easier as a result of liberal donations from old friends such as the poet Allen Ginsburg and a generous annual grant from the Grateful Dead. He also held the position of Shaman in Residence at the Naropa Institute in Boulder, Colorado, in his final years. He died in New York City in 1991. FURTHER READING; IGLIORI 1996, SINGH AND CROSON 1998.

Smith, Joseph. American magician, prophet, and founder of the Church of Jesus Christ of Latter-day Saints, 1805–1844. Born into a rural farm family in Vermont, and raised in the "Burned-Over District" of upstate New York—an area famous for its religious revivals, and later the seedbed of Spiritualism—Smith was introduced to the practice of magic from an early age. His father, Joseph Smith Sr., was a dowser and treasure hunter, possessed a magical dagger engraved with the sigil of Mars, and according to one account belonged to an apocalyptic sect of dowsers who predicted the end of the world in 1802. *SEE* DOWSING.

By the age of thirteen, Joseph Jr. was experimenting with a dowsing rod, and a few years later he began scrying with a shewstone; *SEE* SCRYING; SHEWSTONE. He was actively involved throughout his teen years in attempts to find buried treasure by magical means, and was brought to court in 1826 and 1830 under laws that classed magicians and seers as "disorderly persons." He apparently studied magic with Luman Walters, a physician and treasure hunter who had been to Europe and studied animal magnetism.

None of this was out of the ordinary for the area in which he grew up. Upstate New York was a hotbed of folk magic, dowsing, and treasure hunting all through the eighteenth and early nineteenth centuries, and scholars have documented dozens of magical practitioners active in the area during Smith's youth.

In 1820, at the age of fourteen, Smith had his first vision, in which a pillar of light descended on him and a divine voice told him his sins were forgiven and warned him not to join any existing sect. In 1823, in a second visionary experience, the angel Moroni appeared to him and told him of golden plates hidden in a nearby hill. Moroni named several conditions that had to be met before the plates could be obtained. It took Smith four years to meet the conditions, but according to his testimony and that of other family members, in the early hours of September 22, 1827, he and his wife Emma obtained the plates.

Smith translated the plates, which were said to be written in "reformed Egyptian," by means of a pair of crystals that Mormon teachings identify with the biblical Urim and Thummim. The result of the translation was the Book of Mormon, which was published in 1830. The Church of Jesus Christ of Latter-Day Saints, more generally known as the Mormon Church, was founded the same year.

Over the next fourteen years, the church expanded substantially. Smith led his followers from upstate New York to Kirtland, Ohio, and then to Nauvoo, Missouri, in search of a place where they could be safe from religious persecution. In 1844 he was murdered by a mob in Carthage, Missouri.

During the years between 1830 and his death, Smith received over a hundred further revelations, and established most of Mormon theology and practice. This body of teaching included the temple endowment rituals—a set of initiation ceremonies which Mormons believe to be the original form of the ancient mysteries, and which many non-Mormon scholars believe were copied from Freemasonry. *SEE* FREEMASONRY.

Smith also studied Cabala from Alexander Neibahr, a Jew from Alsace who moved to England, converted first to Christianity and then to the Mormon Church, and moved to Nauvoo, Illinois, where he became a close associate of the Mormon prophet. Neibahr published a series of articles in the Mormon periodical *Times and Seasons*, explaining elements of Cabalistic doctrine, and quoting at length from important Cabalistic texts such as the Zohar. Many of the concepts of Mormon theology appear to have come from this source. *SEE* CABALA.

There seems to have been little in the way of practical occultism in Joseph Smith's career after the founding of his church. Still, one piece of evidence suggests that his early involvement in magic had not entirely worn off. At the time of his death, a medallion was found on his body. Photographs of the medallion, which still exists, prove it to be a standard talisman of Jupiter as described in the writings of Cornelius Agrippa. *SEE* TALISMAN. FURTHER READING: BRODIE 1971, BROOKE 1994, QUINN 1987.

Smith, Pamela Colman. English artist and occultist, 1878–1951. The creator of the most influential occult tarot deck of modern times, Smith was born in Middlesex, England, to prosperous American parents, and spent her childhood in various parts of England, the West Indies, and America, as a result of her father's career. An actor in her teen years, she toured with Ellen Terry's famous Lyceum Theatre, then enrolled in the Pratt Institute in 1893 and graduated in 1897 with a degree in art. Her career began well, with a string of contracts for book illustrations and Christmas cards, but she was never able to make a steady income from her art. Her work was in the Symbolist style, which was popular at the turn of the century but lost favor rapidly thereafter. SEE SALONS DE LA ROSE+CROIX.

She moved to England in 1899 and soon made the acquaintance of Irish poet and Golden Dawn member William Butler Yeats; SEE YEATS, WILLIAM BUTLER. It was Yeats who brought her into contact with the Hermetic Order of the Golden Dawn, which she joined in 1901, taking the magical motto *Quod Tibi Id Aliis* ("To Others As To Yourself "). In the factional divisions that split the order thereafter, however, she sided with Arthur Edward Waite, joining his Independent and Rectified Rite in 1903.

It was Waite who commissioned, in 1909, a tarot deck based on his researches into the cards. He had encountered, in the fifteenth-century Italian Sola-Busca tarot deck, the idea of assigning visual images to the small cards as well as the Major Arcana, and had devoted years of personal study and research to the tarot and Hermetic philosophy. The two collaborated closely on the deck, Waite supplying the symbolism but Smith handling all other aspects of the designs. The deck was first published by Rider in 1910, and under the name of the Rider-Waite deck, it became the most successful and influential tarot deck of the twentieth century.

Smith's involvement in occultism faded out not long after the publication of the deck, and she became a Roman Catholic in 1911. She continued to eke out a living by book illustrations, sales of prints and paintings, and professional storytelling, the latter drawing on the Jamaican folk tales she had learned in childhood. The vast cultural changes set in motion by the First World War, however, and her own lack of business sense left her all but destitute; the frenetic society of the Jazz Age had little time for the quiet, mystical character of her art.

A small trust fund enabled her and a close friend, Nora Lake, to survive in a small flat in an isolated town in Cornwall, but by the time she died her debts were so extensive that the sale of all her possessions covered approximately a quarter of the total. Although she became a Fellow of the Royal Society of Arts in 1948, she and her work were almost totally forgotten by the time of her death in 1951. SEE ALSO TAROT. FURTHER READING: S. KAPLAN 1990.

Societas Rosicruciana in America (SRIA). (Latin, "Rosicrucian Society in America") American Rosicrucian order, founded in 1907 as a schism from the Societas Rosicruciana in Civitatibus Foederatis (SRICF), the American branch of the Societas Rosicruciana in Anglia (SRIA); SEE SOCIETAS ROSICRUCIANA IN ANGLIA (SRIA). The SRICF, like its parent body, limited membership to Master Masons, but several of its American members wished to open the doors to non-Masons. Sylvester C. Gould, a member of the Boston college of the SRCF, broke with the older organization and organized the Societas Rosicruciana in America in 1907. On his death two years later, another ex-member of the Boston college, Dr. George Winslow Plummer (1877–1944), took charge of the new organization.

Plummer, under the title Khei X°, reshaped the SRIA into a pattern that would become all but universal among American occult orders in the first three-quarters of the twentieth century. A correspondence course formed the backbone of the new structure, with a selection of books serving both as expansions of the course and recruitment tools. A magazine available to members only assisted with communication. Members who completed the basic course were encouraged to join local groups—Colleges, in the SRIA—which offered a series of initiations. This program was a definite success, and by 1930 eighteen Colleges in all had received charters, though not all of them were still in operation at that time.

On Plummer's death in 1944, the leadership of the SRIA passed to his widow, Gladys Plummer, generally known by her religious title Mother Serena. Serena died in 1989, and was succeeded by Sister Lucia Grosch, the current head. The SRIA remains very quietly in existence, with a base in New York State and a scattering of members across North America. SEE ALSO ROSICRUCIANS. FURTHER READING: KHEI 1920, MCINTOSH 1987.

Societas Rosicruciana in Anglia (SRIA). (Latin, "Rosicrucian Society in England") British Masonic Rosicrucian order, founded in 1866 by English Freemason Robert Wentworth Little. The order drew extensively on the traditions of the Rosicrucian orders of eighteenth-century Germany, borrowing the degree structure of the Orden des Gold- und Rosenkreuz (Order of the Golden and Rosy Cross); *SEE* ORDEN DES GOLD- UND ROSENKREUZ. According to its official history, it was founded on the basis of documents found by Little in Freemasons' Hall in London, but later searches for the documents in question by SRIA member William Wynn Westcott turned up nothing.

A Scottish branch, the Societas Rosicruciana in Scotia, was organized shortly after the founding of the Metropolitan College in London, and the next few decades saw the opening of additional colleges (the SRIA term for local lodges) in Bristol, Manchester, Sheffield, and Newcastle. An Australian college opened in 1878, and 1880 saw the founding of an American branch, the Societas Rosicruciana in Civitatibus Foederatis (Rosicrucian Society of the United States, SRICF). This last body suffered a schism in 1907 on the part of members who wished to dispense with the requirement of Masonic membership, and gave rise to the Societas Rosicruciana in America (which also uses the initials SRIA); *SEE* SOCIETAS ROSICRUCIANA IN AMERICA (SRIA).

The original SRIA acquired perhaps its most significant member in 1880, when William Wynn Westcott joined the order. He soon became head of the Metropolitan College and in 1891 took charge as Supreme Magus. Well before that time, his interest in magical lodge work and practical occultism had found another expression when he and fellow SRIA member Samuel "MacGregor" Mathers founded the Hermetic Order of the Golden Dawn. *SEE* GOLDEN DAWN, HERMETIC ORDER OF THE; MATHERS, SAMUEL LIDDELL. When Westcott withdrew from involvement in his creation, however, he remained active in the SRIA for the remainder of his life.

Members of the SRIA and its international branches were (and still are) required to be Master Masons in good standing. The order's interests, as revealed in nearly a century and a half of publications, are philosophical and esoteric, but seem to stop well short of practical occultism. The SRIA remains quietly active at present. *SEE ALSO* ROSICRUCIANS. FURTHER READING: J. GODWIN 1994, HOWE 1997.

Society of the Inner Light. *SEE* INNER LIGHT, SOCIETY OF THE.

Sol. (Old Norse, "sun") The eleventh rune of the younger futhark, representing the sun as the source of light and life. Its sound-value is *s*. *SEE* YOUNGER FUTHARK.

The same rune, renamed Sigil, is the sixteenth rune in the Anglo-Saxon futhorc, and has the same meaning; the Old English rune-poem describes it as the sun, which guides fishermen home from their journeys.

Under the name Sig, finally, the same rune represents victory as the eleventh rune of the Armanen rune system. Its power, drawn from the rune-charm of the Old Norse *Havamal*, is the ability to lead in battle and return home unhurt. It corresponds to the god Njord and the zodiacal sign Aquarius, and has the sound-value *s*. This was the rune used by the SS as one of their primary symbols. *SEE* ARMANEN RUNES; SS. *SEE ALSO* SOWELU.

Rune Sol (Sigil, Sig)

Solar Logos. In the writings of Dion Fortune and some of her students, the Solar Logos is the god of the solar system, identified with the sun. The Solar Logos is understood to be a being of the same kind, although of a far higher evolutionary level, as the entities (including human beings) that inhabit the solar system it creates and rules. Inhabitants of a solar system who evolve to a sufficient degree become Solar Logoi themselves and create new solar systems of their own. *SEE ALSO* FORTUNE, DION; INNER LIGHT, SOCIETY OF THE. FURTHER READING: FORTUNE 2000.

Solar Pitris. In Theosophy, a group of Dhyan Chohans (enlightened beings) who transcended the human level of being in previous Manvantaras, or cycles of evolution, and who assisted the evolution of present-day humanity by stimulating the development of conscious thinking during the time of the third root race. They are also known as Lords of the Flame. *SEE* ROOT RACE; THEOSOPHY.

solar return. In astrology, the moment that the sun returns to the same position it held when a given person was born. Because the modern calendar does not track the sun's movement precisely, the exact date and time of the solar return will usually not be the same as the date and time of birth, but will fall within a day or so to either side. A horoscope drawn up for the moment of the solar return can be used, especially in comparison with the birth chart of the same person, to predict trends and events in the coming year.

Some astrologers also use the lunar return, which occurs each lunar month when the moon reaches the same position it held in the birth chart, as a month-by-month guide to trends and events. SEE ALSO ASTROLOGY.

solitary practitioner. In modern Pagan and magical parlance, a person who practices magic or a Pagan religion on his or her own, rather than belonging to a coven, lodge, or other working group. Historically, most magical practitioners have carried on their careers alone or, at most, in the company of a few students or assistants. The material in the Graeco-Egyptian magical papyri, the best surviving source for magical practice in the ancient world, is written for solo practice, as are most of the rites outlined in Arabic magical texts such as the *Picatrix* and their medieval European descendants. SEE GRAECO-EGYPTIAN MAGICAL PAPYRI; GRIMOIRE; PICATRIX. The few records of magical training that exist suggest that it was passed from master to apprentice, without the presence of any larger group.

The emergence of the magical lodge, coven, or working group as the standard setting for magical training and practice was a product of the fusion between occultism and fringe Freemasonry in the eighteenth and nineteenth centuries. By the late nineteenth century, magical lodges such as the Hermetic Brotherhood of Luxor and the Hermetic Order of the Golden Dawn presented themselves as custodians of secret traditions of initiation only available to their members. SEE GOLDEN DAWN, HERMETIC ORDER OF THE; HERMETIC BROTHERHOOD OF LUXOR (H. B. OF L.). Wicca, and most of its relatives in the modern Pagan revival, made essentially the same claim at the time of their appearance in the middle and late twentieth century. SEE NEOPAGANISM; WICCA.

The result of these developments was an attitude, very common among occultists and Pagans in the middle years of the twentieth century, that belonging to an organization was essential if one wanted to become a "real" magician, witch, or the like. This led to a great deal of deception and bad faith, as people who sought to create their own magical and Pagan paths found it necessary to lie about the sources of their systems in order to get their work taken seriously. SEE FAMILY TRADITION; GRANDMOTHER STORY.

Solitary work within the Hermetic magical community never quite fell completely out of fashion, since there were always a certain number of books outlining methods of magical practice for the individual working alone; SEE BARDON 1962. In the Pagan community, however, the rise of the solitary practitioner can be dated to a specific event—the 1988 publication of Scott Cunningham's book *Wicca: A Guide for the Solitary Practitioner.* SEE CUNNINGHAM, SCOTT. Harshly denounced by many prominent Wiccans, it nonetheless went on to become a 500,000-copy bestseller, and launched an entire subculture within the modern Pagan movement. While traditionalists within the Wiccan community still reject the idea of self-initiation and solitary practice, "solitaries" appear to be here to stay as a large segment of modern Paganism. SEE ALSO NEOPAGANISM; SELF-INITIATION. FURTHER READING: BARDON 1962, CUNNINGHAM 1988.

Solomon. King of Israel, c. 986–c. 933 B.C.E. A son of David, the second king of Israel, by his favorite wife Bathsheba, Solomon ascended the throne on his father's death and reigned for forty years. His reign marked the high point of the Israelite kingdom, largely due to his father's successes, his own careful management of commerce and revenue, and the temporary weakness of Egypt and Babylonia, the great powers of the eastern Mediterranean area. With the assistance of his ally Hiram, king of Tyre, he built the first and most famous Temple of Jerusalem; SEE TEMPLE OF SOLOMON. In the last years of his reign, the expenses of his court, his building projects, and the maintenance of a large army created a rising current of unrest, and after his death a rebellion split the kingdom into the two states of Judah and Israel.

Biblical accounts of Solomon stress his wisdom and universal knowledge, and that reputation gradually spread to encompass the occult branches of knowledge. By Roman times, Solomon had acquired a reputation as the supreme master of magic; a bronze talismanic disk excavated from the Roman-era port at Ostia bears an image of him stirring an enchanter's cauldron with a long ladle. In the first century of the Common Era, the Jewish writer Josephus was already referring to books on the invocation of demons under Solomon's name.

In the Middle Ages and later, a large number of books of magic were attributed to him. The most famous of all the grimoires, the *Key of Solomon*, was credited to him, along with the *Lesser Key of Solomon* or *Lemegeton*, the *Shemhamphorash of Solomon the King*, the *Testament of Solomon*, the *Book of the Throne of Solomon*, the *Book of Solomon on Gems and Spirits*, and many other occult titles, most of which did not escape the Christian church's strenuous attempts to find and burn them. *SEE* GRIMOIRE; KEY OF SOLOMON; LEMEGETON; SHEM HA-MEPHORESH. Solomon was also considered in medieval times to be the founder of the Notory Art; *SEE* NOTORY ART.

It probably deserves to be mentioned that there is actually no evidence that Solomon himself had any involvement with magical practices at all, and his magical reputation is another example of the retrospective recruitment so common in occult history. *SEE* OCCULT HISTORY. FURTHER READING: E. BUTLER 1949, THORNDYKE 1923.

Sons of Belial. *SEE* BELIAL, SONS OF.

Sophia. (Greek, "wisdom") The spirit, goddess, or personification of wisdom, a figure who has played many different roles in Western occult tradition. In Greek and Hebrew, the words for wisdom (respectively, *sophia* and *chokmah*) are both grammatically feminine, and this quirk of language encouraged the concept of "wisdom" to take on the role of a goddess in cultures and religions where goddesses as such were prohibited.

Sophia was one of the central figures in Gnostic myth. According to the *Apocalypse of John* and other classic Gnostic scriptures, she was the last of the aeons or divine powers of the spiritual realm. Desiring to create by herself, without the cooperation of her consort or the permission of higher entities, she gave birth to the evil demiurge Ialdabaoth. This action brought about her fall into matter, and this fall and her eventual restoration to the spiritual realm make up the core movement of the Gnostic myth of creation and redemption.

In some branches of modern goddess spirituality and the New Age movement, Sophia has been redefined and brought back into prominence as a feminine counterpart to the masculine images of the divine more common in Judaism and Christianity. *SEE ALSO* GNOSTICISM; IALDABAOTH. FURTHER READING: FIDELER 1985, LAYTON 1987, C. MATTHEWS 1991.

Sorath. In the lore of ceremonial magic and geomancy, the planetary spirit of the sun. Its governing intelligence is Nakhiel. *SEE* SPIRIT.

Sowelu. (Old Germanic, "sun") The sixteenth rune of the elder futhark, representing light, energy, and the sun. It represents the sun as the source of life, as well as the soul as the principle of individual life. Modern rune scholars relate it to the Germanic sun goddess Sunna and to the gods Thor and Baldur. Its sound-value is *s*. *SEE* ELDER FUTHARK. *SEE ALSO* SOL.

Rune Sowelu

spagyrics. The most commonly practiced branch of alchemy in the modern world, spagyrics is the art of herbal alchemy—the creation of medicines from herbs by alchemical processes. The term *spagyrics* comes from the Greek verbs *spao*, to draw out or divide, and *ageiro*, to join or gather together. This refers to the central process of spagyric art, and indeed of all alchemy: *solve et coagula*, which in modern language might be translated "separate and reunite."

Spagyric methods of preparing medicines have been a part of alchemy since ancient times, and are much used in the traditional healing systems of India, China, and the Arabic world. In Europe, they seem to have been quietly practiced through the late Middle Ages and the

Renaissance, but leapt into prominence in the wake of Paracelsus (1493–1541); SEE PARACELSUS. A physician as well as an alchemist, Paracelsus wrote voluminously on spagyric techniques, publishing detailed instructions for the would-be practitioner. His writings, as well as those of later Paracelsian alchemists such as Johann Rudolf Glauber (1604–1668), remain fundamental to modern spagyric theory and practice.

Like most branches of alchemy, spagyrics received little attention during and after the Scientific Revolution. The usefulness of spagyric medication, though, kept a current of interest alive. In the 1850s and 1860s, the German homeopathic physician Carl Friedrich Zimpel (1800–1878) became the first important modern spagyrist, using the writings of Paracelsus and Glauber to produce spagyric medicines. More recently, a variety of spagyrists in Europe, America, Australia, and elsewhere have introduced spagyric medicine to the alternative health care field, and there are a number of good practical books on the market at present.

Spagyric practice is based on Paracelsus' theory of the Three Principles—mercury, sulphur, and salt—which are present in all things. SEE MERCURY; SALT; SULPHUR. The Principles are not the same as the minerals commonly called by their names. In a plant, for example, the "sulphur" consists primarily of the essential oil and other volatile substances; the "mercury" consists of ethyl alcohol, which is a matured form of the sugary sap of plants; and the "salt" consists of minerals and other substances that remain behind when the plant is burnt.

In spagyric processes, these three constituents are taken apart, purified, and recombined. The methods for doing this range from the very simple to the extremely complex. The simplest method presently used involves simply macerating (soaking) an herb in alcohol to extract the sulphur and mercury from the salt, pouring off the alcohol tincture, burning the leftover vegetable matter, heating it intensely until it is reduced to a white ash (which contains the salt), grinding the ash and combining it with the alcohol tincture. The next step up the ladder of complexity is to use distillation to purify the sulphur-mercury blend and filtration and evaporation to purify the salt. From there, the options widen out into an extensive array of processes for managing a more complete separation or purifying the separated constituents more thoroughly before recombining them. One common process is circulation, in which the same tincture is distilled over and over again, and each time returned to the undistilled vegetable matter to macerate before being distilled once more.

There are a variety of different products that can be produced by spagyric methods. An elixir is a spagyric product made from several different plants. A clyssus is a product made from a single plant, and properly speaking includes all parts of the plant—root, stem, leaf, flower, and seed. A vegetable stone, the highest and most difficult achievement in spagyrics, is a clyssus that has been brought to the highest level of potency, and fixed into a hard, stonelike mass by the application of heat.

Like homeopathic medicines, which they resemble in effects although not in the mode of preparation, spagyric medicines have wide-reaching effects on the physical, subtle, and mental aspects of the human body, and are generally taken in small doses. SEE HOMEOPATHY. SEE ALSO ALCHEMY; CLYSSUS; ELIXIR; VEGETABLE STONE. FURTHER READING: ALBERTUS 1974, JUNIUS 1985.

Spare, Austin Osman. English artist and occultist, 1886–1956. Born into a working-class London family, Spare displayed a remarkable talent for painting and drawing from an early age, and won a scholarship to the Royal College of Art in Kensington. One of his drawings was exhibited at the Royal Academy while he was in his teens.

To his artistic talents, though, Spare added a lifelong fascination with the occult, sparked in boyhood by his friendship with a local witch and diviner named Margaret Paterson. While he produced art of high quality on ordinary themes, much of his time and energy was devoted to weird paintings and drawings that expressed the world of spirits and powers he dealt with daily in his magical work. The reaction of the public and the press to these artworks cut short his career as a conventional artist, although he was always able to find work.

Spare's magic was intensely personal and idiosyncratic, based on the idea that the most ancient levels of the subconscious mind contain archaic superhuman powers that can be accessed by magical means. Through what he called the "Formula of Atavistic Resurgence," these powers could be brought into manifestation. The techniques of his magic included the construction of sigils from words and names, and a form of masturbatory sex-magic in which concentrated awareness was focused on a sigil at the moment of orgasm. Spare systematized this combination of approaches into a system of magic called the Zos Kia Cultus; *SEE* ZOS KIA CULTUS.

An intensely solitary man, Spare enjoyed the company of cats more than that of people, and spent the last three decades of his life leading a reclusive existence in the slums of South London. After his death, his magical discoveries were taken up by avant-garde occultists in England and elsewhere, and more recently have played a major role in the theory and practice of Chaos magic. *SEE* CHAOS MAGIC. FURTHER READING: GRANT 1974.

sphere of sensation. In the Golden Dawn system of magic, the aura; primarily the human aura, but the phrase is also used for the auras of minerals, plants, animals, and entire planets. According to Golden Dawn teaching documents, the sphere of sensation is a representation in miniature of the entire cosmos surrounding the Earth, and also contains the Tree of Life expanded into a three-dimensional-form. *SEE ALSO* ASCENDANT; AURA. FURTHER READING: REGARDIE 1971.

spiral dance. In modern Pagan practice, a dance in which the participants spiral into the center of the circle and out again. While there are variations, the participants typically spiral counterclockwise into the center of the circle, then clockwise out to the periphery.

Some current Pagan sources claim that the spiral dance was practiced in ancient times and has been passed down through the centuries but, as usual, such claims seem to have no basis in fact. The spiral dance as currently practiced was apparently pioneered in the 1970s by the New Reformed Orthodox Order of the Golden Dawn (NROOGD), a California Pagan organization that emerged out of a college class on Paganism. It has since spread through much of the Neopagan movement. *SEE ALSO* NEOPAGANISM.

spirit. Among the most diffuse and difficult terms in Western thought, the word "spirit" and its related adjective, "spiritual," have been used in occult tradition as a label for many different phenomena and beings. The word has at least three primary meanings in a Western magical context, two of them in some level of contradiction to each other, and many more nuances and shades of meaning than can be dealt with here.

The English word "spirit" is a borrowing from the Latin *spiritus*, which means "wind" or "breath" and also appears in English as the root of words such as "respiration." Like many terms having the same general meaning—Hebrew *ruach*, Greek *pneuma*, Sanskrit *prana*, and Chinese *ch'i*, among others—it came to be used as a word for a subtle power acting in the world. Some of these words (such as prana and ch'i) took on the general meaning of life energy, while others (such as ruach) took on a meaning having more to do with the supernatural realm.

The word *spiritus*, by contrast, went both ways at once. Ancient Romans used spiritus to mean life energy, vitality, and verve, as we might speak of a spirited horse or describe somebody as being in high spirits; they also used spiritus for individual supernatural beings, as we might describe a ghost as a spirit; equally, under the influence of Stoic philosophy or Christian theology, they used spiritus to stand for the highest and deepest aspect of the cosmos, as we do when we use the word "spiritual." All three of these meanings have played important roles in occult thought.

Spirit has, among its other meanings, been incorporated into the system of the four elements as a fifth, higher element. *SEE* ELEMENTS, MAGICAL; SPIRIT, ELEMENT OF. FURTHER READING: S. SMITH 1988.

spirit, element of. In magical symbolism, the fifth of the five elements, corresponding to the underlying fabric of space-time and to the point of balance among the qualities and humors. As with all the elements, there are varying attributions to the element of spirit, but the following are standard in most current Western occult systems:

> *Symbol:* ✴
>
> *Names of God:* אהיה, AHIH, Eheieh (active), אגלא, AGLA, Agla (passive).
>
> *Archangels:* מתתרון, MTTRVN, Metatron (active), סנדלפון, SNDLPVN, Sandalphon (passive).

Direction: Center.

Qualities: Union of all qualities.

Nature: Balance.

SEE ALSO DIRECTIONS IN OCCULTISM; ELEMENTS, MAGICAL; HUMORS.

spirit, planetary. In the lore of ceremonial magic, one of seven spiritual beings associated with the seven planets of ancient astrology, and subordinate to the seven planetary intelligences. In some traditional sources, the intelligence of each planet is described as good, while the spirit is considered evil; in others, the spirit is simply a blind force, which requires the guidance of the intelligence if it is to accomplish good.

The seven planetary spirits are traditionally invoked in geomantic divination. SEE GEOMANCY. SEE ALSO INTELLIGENCE, PLANETARY.

Planet	Spirit
Saturn	Zazel
Jupiter	Hismael
Mars	Bartzabel
Sun	Sorath
Venus	Kedemel
Mercury	Taphthartharath
Moon	*Spirit:* Chashmodai
	Spirit of Spirits: Shad Barshemoth ha-Shartathan

Note: the moon is governed by multiple spirits, of which Chashmodai is the most important in magical terms. Shad Barshemoth ha-Shartathan is the Spirit of Spirits, or collective personality, of the spirits of the moon.

Spiritism. An offshoot of Spiritualism founded by French medium and occult researcher Allan Kardec (1804–1869), which differs from its parent by the acceptance of reincarnation and several other theories rejected by mainstream Spiritualism. SEE REINCARNATION. Spiritism remains a living tradition in France, Britain, America, Australasia, and the Philippines, but its greatest success has been in Brazil, where Kardec's teachings have been combined with African-derived Umbanda mystical traditions to give rise to a lively and complex movement that

nowadays is one of the largest religious forces in the country. SEE ALSO KARDEC, ALLAN; SPIRITUALISM.

spiritual body. In magical philosophy, the highest aspect of the human individual, the synteresis or divine spark that forms the core of each person and exists eternally. Conscious awareness of the spiritual body—or to put things in another way, the reflection of the spiritual body's awareness down through the levels of the self into ordinary awareness—is considered the highest level of magical attainment, and brings with it total mastery of the powers and potentials of the self. SEE ALSO SPIRITUAL PLANE.

spiritual plane. In occult philosophy, the highest of the levels of being, the primary level of creative power from which all other planes unfold. As with all the planes of occult theory, the spiritual plane is "above" other planes only in a metaphorical sense; in reality, all the planes interpenetrate the realm of physical matter experienced by the senses. The spiritual plane is considered to be beyond space, time, and human understanding, and so most occult writers have the common sense not to try to say much about it. SEE ALSO SPIRITUAL BODY.

Spiritualism. The most important occult-derived movement of the nineteenth century, Spiritualism is traditionally considered to have begun in 1848, when the Fox sisters in Hydesville, New York, began to receive messages from the dead by way of loud rapping noises. Their accounts, and the experiences of others who heard the same raps and were able to carry on conversations with the unseen noisemakers, launched first a local, then a national, and finally an international furor. Other people found themselves able to communicate with the spirits of the dead, first by means of similar noises and then, more and more often, by trance techniques borrowed from the earlier mesmerist movement. By the early 1850s tens of thousands of Americans were attending séances, listening to the words of spirits as communicated by entranced mediums, and discarding earlier religious beliefs in favor of a new, if often vague, Spiritualist gospel.

The actual origins of Spiritualism go back long before the time of the Fox sisters, however, into the complex realm of early nineteenth-century American folk religion and occultism. The same region of upstate New York that saw the birth of Spiritualism had earned the name of "the Burnt-over District" as a result of its frequent and enthusiastic religious revivals, and twenty years before had been the launching point for another religion, Mormonism; SEE SMITH, JOSEPH. Local folklore included the idea that ghosts and spirits could communicate by knocking or rapping. Even the idea of communicating with the dead by means of an entranced medium was fairly well known; mesmerism had been imported to the United States from France by the dawn of the nineteenth century, and mesmerized "sensitives" were holding communications with the spirits of dead sages long before the Fox house in Hydesville started resounding with raps. The teachings of Swedish mystic Emmanuel Swedenborg were also influential in setting the stage for Spiritualism. SEE MESMERISM; SWEDENBORG, EMMANUEL.

In effect, the media furor over the Fox sisters and their spirit conversations served as a catalyst to bring attention to something that had been taking shape for many years already. Once brought into the public spotlight, however, the Spiritualist movement burgeoned, winning tens of thousands of converts and for a time threatening to unseat Christianity from its dominance over American culture. In the early 1850s the movement jumped the Atlantic to Britain and France, and quickly established itself in those European countries that allowed religious freedom.

The teachings of the movement varied wildly depending on the utterances of particular mediums. The general principles, though, were much the same across the spectrum. Orthodox notions of heaven and hell were rejected in favor of a vision of an afterlife of perpetual improvement. All spiritual entities, in most versions of Spiritualism, either started out as human beings or passed through the human stage of being on their way to the higher vistas of evolution. Spirits were not cut off from the material world after death, it was held, but had access to a wide range of information hidden from the living. They could also sometimes cause physical or quasi-physical phenomena to occur during séances.

One major theoretical split in the Spiritualist movement opened up between Christian Spiritualists, who accepted the divinity of Jesus and some elements of Chris-

tian doctrine, and those who rejected Christianity completely in favor of a purely Spiritualist theology, largely drawn from Swedenborg, the eccentric French thinker Charles Fourier, and the American visionary Andrew Jackson Davis. SEE DAVIS, ANDREW JACKSON; FOURIER, CHARLES. Later on, toward the end of the nineteenth century, a new schism came into being over the question of reincarnation, with a minority following the lead of French philosopher Allan Kardec and supporting the idea of rebirth while most Spiritualists rejected it heatedly. SEE KARDEC, ALLAN; REINCARNATION; SPIRITISM.

Far and away the most bitter controversies, however, opened up over the reality and validity of spiritualistic experiences themselves. From the earliest days of the movement, mediums were accused of producing the "spirit noises" by fraudulent means. The emergence of mediumship as the central way of communicating with spirits led to charges that the "spirits" were simply the products of delusion or overheated imaginations. While a few mediums were apparently able to produce effects that still have not been explained by science, the movement as a whole was never able to produce the conclusive proof of communication from the other world that it sought.

As a result, Spiritualism never quite managed to unseat Christianity as the majority faith of the Western world, and by the end of the nineteenth century had settled into its present role as another minority religious group, with varying relations to Christian orthodoxy on the one hand and occultism on the other. A loose network of independent mediums, each with his or (more commonly) her coterie of followers, forms the largest part of the Spiritualist scene, but there are also organized churches, in which séances are combined with broadly Protestant worship services, and camps, where visitors and residents can partake of a smorgasbord of séances, lectures, and training programs. There have been widespread allegations of massive fraud in connection with the modern Spiritualist movement, but it seems clear that many mediums are sincere in their beliefs. FURTHER READING: BARROW 1986, KEENE 1997, MOORE 1977.

spiritus loci. (Latin, "spirit of the place") In ancient Pagan traditions, the spiritual being inhabiting a particular geographical region. Some modern magical writers have misinterpreted the phrase to mean "place where a spirit manifests," which would properly be *locus spiritus*.

spiritus mundi. (Latin, "spirit of the world") In medieval and Renaissance philosophy and alchemy, and later occult teachings, the second of three essential parts of the universe, uniting the *anima mundi* or Soul of the World with the *corpus mundi* or Body of the World. In modern terms, *spiritus mundi* might better be translated "subtle energy body of the world," since the Latin term *spiritus*, depending on context, can mean either a level of being above the soul or, as here, one that connects the soul to matter.

In alchemical and magical thought, the *spiritus mundi* is understood to be an intangible, constantly moving substance or energy flowing through all things, shaping the material substances of the world in accordance with the patterns of the anima mundi. It can be collected by alchemists in dew primarily, and in all forms of precipitation generally, especially when the sun is in the zodiacal signs Aries and Taurus (March 21–May 20). *SEE* ALCHEMY; NITER. *SEE ALSO* ANIMA MUNDI; CORPUS MUNDI. FURTHER READING: KIRCHWEGER 2001.

Sprengel, Anna. The fictitious German adept who, according to claims circulated by the founders of the Hermetic Order of the Golden Dawn, authorized the order's founding. The letters supposedly written by her to William Wynn Westcott have been shown to be forged by someone with a poor command of German. *SEE* GOLDEN DAWN, HERMETIC ORDER OF THE.

square. In astrology, an arc of ninety degrees separating two planets or points in the heavens. The square aspect gives rise to a "hard," conflict-laden relationship between the affected energies. *SEE* ASPECT, ASTROLOGICAL.

SS. (Schutzstaffel) (German, "protection squad") The infamous "Black Order" of Nazi Germany, the SS started out in 1925 as a small group of diehard Nazis who served as a volunteer bodyguard to Adolf Hitler. For the first few years of its existence, it was a small organization mostly under the control of the SA (Sturmabteilung) or Brownshirts, the private army of toughs recruited by the Nazi party for use in street brawls against Communist and Socialist Red Guards.

In 1929, a series of political struggles and resignations advanced Heinrich Himmler to the post of SS commander. Himmler, a colorless young man with the manners of a college professor, was a student of the occult with a lifelong interest in the racist occultism called Ariosophy. *SEE* ARIOSOPHY. He convinced Hitler that the fledgling SS could become an elite force within the Nazi party, and began reshaping the Führer's bodyguard into something that was more than half a magical order.

Strong similarities connect the SS as it developed under Himmler with such earlier Ariosophical orders as the Ordo Novi Templi and the Thule-Gesellschaft. *SEE* ORDO NOVI TEMPLI (ONT); THULE-GESELLSCHAFT. The swastika and dagger, the symbols of the Thule Society, reappeared as the swastika armband and ceremonial dagger worn by every SS man, and the racial guidelines governing admission into the ONT were copied by the SS. The most famous symbol of the SS, the double S-rune, was drawn from Ariosophical lore; it was the eleventh rune of the Armanen runic system, Sol, and stood for victory. *SEE* ARMANEN RUNES; SOL.

The same combination of political activism and occult studies, focusing on Germanic Pagan traditions interpreted through an Ariosophical filter, formed the basic outlook of the SS. Strict membership standards and discipline, closely paralleling those of the Ariosophical movements, set the SS apart from the roughneck SA storm troopers, and a complex system of symbolism and ritual was gradually evolved. Most SS members remained unpaid volunteers, but a small full-time staff was organized, and this expanded as the Nazi party grew from a fringe movement to the most powerful force in German politics.

In 1933, shortly after Hitler's accession to power, the SS and SA were given police powers, and some 27,000 people were rounded up and interned in the first concentration camps. The unreliability of the SA made a loyal and dependable military force essential to the Nazi leadership, and the camps also needed to be guarded by reliable guards. In response, the SS created a new branch, the Waffen-SS or Armed SS, which included Hitler's bodyguard, sizeable military detachments, and guards for the new camps. Both Waffen-SS and regular SS detachments took part in the infamous "Night of the Long

Knives" in 1934, when the SA's leadership was rounded up and murdered at Hitler's command.

Himmler's plans for the SS aimed at the creation of a *Deutsche Männerordern* or Order of German Manhood, selected for discipline, character, racial purity, and political reliability. Most members worked at other jobs and attended SS meetings once or twice a week, on evenings or weekends, where they listened to lectures on Nazi theory and practiced military drill. Even orthodox historians have referred to the SS as "Nazi Freemasonry," and in fact many aspects of Masonry and other fraternal orders were copied by Himmler and incorporated into the SS system.

The SS also had its more esoteric side. Three separate departments of the SS headquarters staff were devoted wholly or partly to research into occult, Pagan, or Ariosophical themes. The most important of these was the *Ahnenerbe Forschungs- und Lehrgemeinschaft*, the Society for Ancestral Heritage Research and Education, usually referred to simply as the Ahnenerbe. This branch of the SS employed scores of historians, archeologists, and occultists, including such important occult figures as Julius Evola, and carried out detailed research programs into the history of German witchcraft, runic magic, and Freemasonry. *SEE* EVOLA, JULIUS.

The innermost esoteric aspects of the SS took shape in the seclusion of Wewelsburg, a castle in the German province of Westphalia that Himmler rebuilt as the ceremonial center of the SS. He and twelve handpicked senior SS members gathered there several times a year. What exactly went on at the castle is anybody's guess; Wewelsburg and all its contents were destroyed on Himmler's orders in April of 1945, when the Third Reich was on the verge of collapse. It seems probable, given Himmler's occult interests, that the Wewelsburg meetings had at least some magical elements, and possible that the castle was the center of the organized magical core of the Third Reich whose existence was suspected by so many occultists at the time.

With the collapse of Nazi power and the suicide or execution of most of the Nazi hierarchy, the SS disintegrated, and those of its members who survived the aftermath of the war and the Nuremberg trials scattered far and wide. How much of the "Black Order" may have survived in Latin American exile is anybody's guess, but so far, at least, the inner occult secrets of the SS seem to have remained safely lost. *SEE ALSO* HITLER, ADOLF; NATIONAL SOCIALISM. FURTHER READING: LUMSDEN 1997.

staff. Among the most common tools of traditional Western magic, the staff is little used in modern occult traditions but seems to be staging a modest comeback in recent years with the revival of interest in folk traditions of magic. In one sense, the staff is simply a much larger equivalent of the wand, but its size and solidity makes it much better suited to outdoor workings.

Traditionally, a staff should be cut from living wood, carefully dried, and fashioned by hand by the person who intends to use it. Whole saplings were often used for this purpose. In any case, prayers, invocations, and offerings to the tree-spirit are standard. Different woods are used for different magical purposes, but the lore of woods differs significantly from tradition to tradition.

Many different types of staff have been used in the various branches of Western magical practice. The croomstick, a staff with a bent upper end like a shepherd's crook or an ordinary cane, is an important instrument in some English folk magic traditions, while the stang, a staff with a forked top, has been adopted by some traditions of modern witchcraft. Other traditional wands, including mete-wands and pilebogars, have received less attention in recent years. *SEE* CROOMSTICK; METE-WAND; PILEBOGAR; STANG. *SEE ALSO* WAND. FURTHER READING: PENNICK 1989.

Stan. (Old English, "stone") The thirty-second rune of the Anglo-Saxon futhorc, representing an altar of stone. It is not mentioned in the Old English rune-poem, which ends with the twenty-ninth rune. Its sound-value is *st*. *SEE* ANGLO-SAXON FUTHORC.

Rune Stan

stang. A wooden staff ending in a fork, used in a number of modern Pagan traditions as a working tool. The stang seems to have been introduced to the Neopagan movement by Robert Cochrane (1931–1966), who claimed to have inherited a family tradition from the distant past; *SEE* CLAN OF TUBAL-CAIN; COCHRANE, ROBERT; FAMILY TRADITION. In Cochrane's Clan of Tubal-Cain, the stang was one of the principal working tools, and served as a symbol of the Horned God. Some other Wiccan traditions that use it attribute it to the Goddess instead, with the fork serving as a vaginal symbol.

The stang is often placed in the quarter of the circle corresponding to the season of the year—that is, east in spring, south in summer, west in autumn, and north in winter—during ritual. It can function as a temporary altar, with various symbolic items hung on it for the duration of a ritual. *SEE ALSO* ALTAR; STAFF. FURTHER READING: VALIENTE 1989.

Star, the. The seventeenth Major Arcanum of the tarot, this card showed a variety of different pictures in the early days of the tarot but in most modern decks has a distinctive image: a nude woman kneeling at the edge of a pool of water, pouring water from two vessels, one onto the ground and one into the water. One or more stars shines in the night sky overhead. In the Golden Dawn system, this trump is assigned to the Hebrew letter Tzaddi, while the French system assigns it to Peh. In divination, its meanings commonly include hope, unexpected help, and spiritual guidance.

Its magical title is "Daughter of the Firmament, Dweller Between the Waters." *SEE ALSO* TAROT; TZADDI.

Tarot trump the Star (Universal Tarot)

Star in the East, Order of the. An offshoot of Theosophy, the Order of the Star in the East was founded in 1911 as a vehicle for the claim that Jiddu Krishnamurti, the son of a servant at the Theosophical Society headquarters in Adyar, India, was the coming World Teacher of the New Age. Heavily backed by Annie Besant and C. W. Leadbeater, at that time heads of the Theosophical Society, the order grew and flourished, reaching a total membership of well over 100,000. It was not entirely welcome to many old-line Theosophists, though, and several groups—including most of the German section of the society, led by its president, Rudolf Steiner—split with the Theosophical Society over its championing of Krishnamurti and the order. *SEE* ANTHROPOSOPHY; STEINER, RUDOLF.

The order came to an abrupt halt in 1929 at the hands of Krishnamurti himself. Addressing a rally of order members, he proclaimed that "truth is a pathless land," denied that he was the World Teacher, and dissolved the order. This act of uncommon courage sent the Theosophical Society into a tailspin from which it has never really recovered. After the dissolution of the order, Krishnamurti went on to spend the rest of his life teaching and writing about his personal philosophy, which has little in common either with Theosophy or with the Western occult tradition. *SEE ALSO* THEOSOPHICAL SOCIETY; THEOSOPHY.

statues, magical. The construction and consecration of statues charged with magical force, and often inhabited by an indwelling life and consciousness, was an important part of the magical traditions of the ancient and classical world. The most famous description of the process is in the Hermetic dialogue *Asclepius*, but the practice was far from a monopoly of Hermeticism. Egyptian, Mesopotamian, Greek, and many other magical traditions practiced it systematically. In most of these cultures, every statue of a god or goddess used in religious rites was ceremonially brought to life by magic.

The methods used to prepare and consecrate magical statues varied to some degree in different cultures and times, but there were substantial common patterns. Some statues were considered to be consecrated by being made in the traditional image of a god or spirit. Others were consecrated by various simple rituals; in ancient Greece, for example, it was held that a stone could be made into the dwelling of a god by anointing it with oil and draping it with wreaths and garlands. More complex and more ambitious methods inserted magically potent substances in the statue itself, and then consecrated the statue with sacrificial rituals.

In ancient and classical sources, full-sized magical statues included animal guardians, set up to protect gates and doors; images of beneficent divinities, used to provide helpful spiritual powers with a physical dwelling; images of dangerous divinities, used for the same purpose or to drive away plagues or invasions; and images of dangerous gods or of earthly enemies, who were bound and buried to weaken their power to cause harm. Smaller images, similar to the poppets or voodoo dolls of later magical traditions, were also much used in Greek and Roman times, especially along with binding tablets; *SEE* BINDING TABLET. *SEE ALSO* EGYPTIAN OCCULTISM; MESOPOTAMIAN OCCULTISM. FURTHER READING: FARAONE 1992, WALKER AND DICK 2001.

Stebbins, Genevieve. American actress, teacher, and occultist, 1857–c. 1935. Born in San Francisco to a middle-class family, she took up acting in childhood, and at eighteen went to New York to pursue a theatrical career. By 1877, she had become involved with the Delsarte system of voice and movement training, which was entering a period of high popularity in America at that time. In 1885 she left the stage for a career as a Delsarte teacher, performer, and writer, founding a school in New York and presenting the Delsarte exercises throughout the northeastern states.

She was briefly married to Joseph Thompson, an attorney, but the marriage was dissolved in 1892. By that time Stebbins was apparently already a member of one of the surviving offshoots of the Hermetic Brotherhood of Luxor, although the date she joined is unclear. *SEE* HERMETIC BROTHERHOOD OF LUXOR (H. B. OF L.). In 1893 she married an English journalist and surveyor named Norman Astley, who shared her interest in the occult, and in the same year her most important work, *Dynamic Breathing and Harmonic Gymnastics*, was published. It combines the Delsarte system with the Swedish health exercises of Per Henrik Ling (1776–1839), and fused these with what she called "the breathing and the mental imagery which have been the common property of every

mystic and occult fraternity under the sun" (quoted in Ruyter 1999, p. 95). Most of this latter material seems to have reached her by way of H. B. of L. sources, and shows important parallels with the order's teachings. Astley himself had previously worked with Thomas Burgoyne, a founder of the Hermetic Brotherhood of Luxor, and assisted him in the production of his one book, *The Light of Egypt* (1889); *SEE* BURGOYNE, THOMAS HENRY.

Stebbins retired from active teaching and performing in 1907, and she and her husband moved to northern California, where they became active in occult circles. They assisted Elbert Benjamine (C. C. Zain) in organizing the Church of Light to pass on the H. B. of L. teachings. *SEE* CHURCH OF LIGHT; ZAIN, C. C. Her last books, a work of occult philosophy titled *The Quest of the Spirit* and a comprehensive exercise manual, *The Genevieve Stebbins System of Physical Training*, were both published in 1913. The precise dates of her death and Astley's have so far eluded researchers. *SEE ALSO* PHYSICAL CULTURE. FURTHER READING: RUYTER 1999, STEBBINS 1893, STEBBINS 1913.

Steganographia. A book written by the German scholar and mage Johannes Trithemius (1462–1516), and famous during the following two centuries. Apparently a grimoire for summoning spirits and demons, it is actually a textbook of cryptography, the science of codes and ciphers. Many different methods of secret writing, along with instructions for using them and examples of their use, are concealed in long strings of gibberish included in what appear to be magical invocations.

For example, one invocation—*Pamersiel Anoyr Madrisel Ebrasothean Abrulges Itrasbiel Nadres Ormenu Itules Rabion Hamorphiel*—though it looks like a fine example of a magical invocation, is actually an instruction for a simple cipher. The first and last words are what cryptographers call "nulls"—that is, meaningless. If one takes every other letter of the rest of the invocation, however, the result is "nym die ersten Bugstaben de omni uerbo," which is a mix of Latin and medieval German for "take the first letter of every word." The hidden message communicated using this cipher would be spelled out by the first letter of each word in an innocuous-looking message: "Wisdom extols all that Thou art, Celestial King, and teaches new observances of nature," which sounds like part of a devotional meditation, would mean "we attack at noon."

The *Steganographia* was circulated in manuscript form for nearly a century after its author's death; a letter from the Elizabethan magus John Dee (1527–1608) mentions that huge sums of money had been offered for it in Europe. It was finally printed in 1606, and several handbooks of secret writing based on it were published later in the seventeenth century. Many people, however, never got past the fake "magic" that was used to conceal the codes; the book was condemned by the Spanish Inquisition, and helped give its author a long-lived reputation as a sorcerer. *SEE ALSO* TRITHEMIUS, JOHANNES. FURTHER READING: SHUMAKER 1982.

Steiner, Rudolf. Austrian philosopher and occultist, 1861–1925. Steiner was born in what is now Slovenia, and spent his childhood in a succession of towns scattered across much of the Austro-Hungarian Empire, where his father, a railway employee, was posted. He attended high school and college in Vienna, where he encountered Theosophy and progressive thought. During these years he also met and studied with Felix Kogutski, a local herbalist.

He made a name for himself as a student of the works of Goethe, and in 1883 was invited to edit all Goethe's scientific writings for the standard edition. *SEE* GOETHE, JOHANN WOLFGANG VON. In 1890, after the successful completion of this massive task, he moved to Weimar in Germany to work at the Goethe Archive there, and in the next few years he published several works of philosophy, including his doctoral dissertation, *The Philosophy of Freedom.*

In 1897 he moved to Berlin to become the editor of the *Magazin für Literatur*, and soon became a significant figure in the German capitol's intellectual circles. He married Anna Eunicke, a widow with whom he had lodged at Weimar, in 1899; this marriage was not a success, and she left him in 1906. During this same period, he returned to his old interest in Theosophy, and soon was giving lectures on esoteric philosophy at Theosophical venues in Berlin and elsewhere. Another Theosophist, the actress Marie von Sivers, became a close friend and confidante—a detail that cannot have helped his relationship with his wife. He and Sivers married in 1914, a few years after his first wife's death.

In 1906, as Steiner's own ideas of "spiritual science" were solidifying, he contacted Theodor Reuss—who founded the Ordo Templi Orientis that same year—and received a charter for a lodge of the Order of Memphis and Misraim. Steiner's plan seems to have been to establish an organization to teach the system he was developing. This project was overshadowed in 1911 when he was elected president of the German section of the Theosophical Society. The society's backing of Jiddu Krishnamurti as the new World Teacher was more than Steiner could tolerate, though, and in 1913 he led most of Germany's Theosophists out of the society and into a new organization of his own founding, the Anthroposophical Society. *SEE* STAR IN THE EAST, ORDER OF THE.

The new society grew steadily in the confusions of World War I and its aftermath, and established its headquarters in Dornach, Switzerland, in 1921. From this center, Steiner lectured and wrote voluminously for the last few years of his life. His output covered not only occult philosophy and training but also farming, education, medicine, and the arts. He died in 1925. *SEE ALSO* ANTHROPOSOPHY; THEOSOPHY. FURTHER READING: STEINER 1933, STEINER 1995.

Stella Matutina, Order of the. (Latin, "morning star") Magical order founded by Robert Felkin and other Golden Dawn adepts after the disintegration of the original Hermetic Order of the Golden Dawn in 1903. Under Felkin's direction, it established temples in London, Bristol, and several other British cities, and with the help of poet and magus William Butler Yeats revised the original GD ceremonies into the forms most commonly used today. *SEE* YEATS, WILLIAM BUTLER. The Stella Matutina quickly became the largest of the direct Golden Dawn successor groups, and also turned out to be the longest-lived.

The Stella Matutina had 123 members by 1915, and added several additional grade ceremonies not used in the original Golden Dawn. The Adeptus Major (6°=5$^\square$), Adeptus Exemptus (7°=4$^\square$), and Magister Templi (8°=3$^\square$) grades were created in 1913 and brought into use in the years immediately following. The order also made contact with the Anthroposophical Society, headed by Rudolf Steiner, and drew on Steiner's work for some of its teachings. *SEE* ANTHROPOSOPHY; STEINER, RUDOLF.

In 1916, after receiving an invitation from a group of New Zealand occultists, Felkin relocated to New Zealand to found a new branch of the Stella Matutina under the name Smaragdum Thalasses ("emerald of the sea"). He left the Stella Matutina in England under the direction of Christine Stoddart, William Reason, and F. N. Heazell as chiefs. The New Zealand temple flourished, and remained active into the 1970s.

The order in England, by contrast, ran into severe problems. In 1918 and 1919, Stoddart became convinced that Satanic forces were at work behind the Stella Matutina, and her increasingly erratic denunciations launched a series of bitter disputes that wrecked the Amoun Temple in London, the head temple of the order. The Stella Matutina never really recovered from this last flurry of disputes, although several temples survived for decades after the dust had settled. Stoddart later abandoned the order completely, became a conservative Christian, and published two books claiming that the Stella Matutina was part of a vast international Satanist-Communist-Zionist conspiracy using sexual energies to control the world.

Another Stella Matutina member who went in unexpected directions was Israel Regardie, who was invited to join the surviving Bristol temple after the publication of his book *The Tree of Life* in 1932. After rising through the grades of the order, Regardie became disgusted with what he saw as the incompetence and lack of understanding of the temple chiefs; he noted that large parts of the original Golden Dawn curriculum had already been withdrawn from circulation, and feared that the rest might follow. Regardie therefore published all the Golden Dawn material he could find in four volumes as *The Golden Dawn*. The publication of the once-secret teachings made it possible for people interested in the Golden Dawn system to make use of it without involving themselves in the increasingly stifling internal politics of surviving branches of the order, and this seems to have hastened the demise of several remaining temples.

At least one temple of the Stella Matutina, the Bristol temple, seems nevertheless to have survived into the 1970s, and the order's New Zealand offshoot was still active into the same decade. There have been various claims that other Stella Matutina lodges may have kept working longer still. Given the habitual secrecy of the Golden Dawn tradition, the facts of the matter may never be known for certain. SEE ALSO GOLDEN DAWN, HERMETIC ORDER OF THE. FURTHER READING: HARPER 1974, REGARDIE 1971, ZALEWSKI 1988.

Stoeckhlin, Chonrad. German horse wrangler and shaman, 1549–1587. An inhabitant of the small village of Oberstdorf in the Bavarian Alps, Stoeckhlin became the village horse wrangler in 1567, inheriting the job from his father. Shortly after the death of a friend in 1578, Stoeckhlin began having visionary experiences, first of the friend's ghost, then of an angel dressed in white with a red cross on its forehead. After the angel's first appearance, Stoeckhlin began going into trance four times a year, at the time of the ember days; SEE EMBER DAYS. During these trances he would travel through the air for many hours with a group of other men and women called the *Nachtschar* ("night troop").

Stoeckhlin also claimed the abilities to heal illnesses and detect witches as a result of these journeys. In 1586, a year of bad weather and epidemic disease, he was asked by the villagers to identify the person responsible, and named an elderly local woman, Anna Enzenbergerin. The accusation was forwarded to the court of the archbishop of Augsburg, which ordered both Enzenbergerin and Stoeckhlin to be imprisoned on suspicion of witchcraft. Enzenbergerin died as a result of torture, while Stoeckhlin confessed to the charges after several sessions of severe torture and was burned at the stake on January 23, 1587. Sixteen other villagers followed him to the stake, and seven others died from the effects of torture before they could be executed.

The case of Chonrad Stoeckhlin bears numerous similarities to that of the Friulian benandanti, the "followers of Diana" described in the ninth-century Canon *Episcopi*, and other Pagan traditions in various corners of medieval Europe. SEE BENANDANTI; CANON EPISCOPI; HERODIAS. FURTHER READING: BEHRINGER 1998.

Stoicism. One of the most important philosophical movements of the ancient world, Stoicism took its name from the *Stoa Poikile* or "Painted Colonnade" on the northwest corner of the central square of Athens. There, beginning sometime in the early third century B.C.,

Zeno of Citium—founder of the Stoic philosophy—gave his lectures. The core of his teaching was that inner attitudes and choices, not external things, were the cause of happiness or unhappiness. By mastering the wayward habits of the mind, rigorously examining assumptions and judgments, and governing action by reason, Zeno argued, it was possible to live a life in harmony with nature.

Later Stoic teachers such as Cleanthes of Assos, Chrysippus of Soli, Musonius Rufus, and Epictetus expanded this teaching into a fully developed system of theory and practice, divided into three branches—logic, physics (meaning the study of nature in all its manifestations, not merely physics in the modern sense), and ethics. Stoic teaching held that all existing things are animated by *pneuma* or vital breath in various states of tension. The individual human soul in Stoic thought is simply part of the universal *pneuma*; the souls of those who attain self-mastery possess an internal tension that enabled them to survive death, while the "slack" soul of the average man simply diffuses into nothingness after the death of the body. Stoic theory also traced out vast cycles of time in which the universe, created and destroyed each time out of primal fire, endlessly repeated the same history down to the smallest detail. *SEE* APOCATASTASIS.

In terms of practice, the Stoic path in its developed form prescribed three intensive disciplines of awareness. The discipline of perception involved carefully examining the activities of the mind to shake off the habit of projecting inner emotional states onto outer experiences; the discipline of will involved assessing all acts of intention to be sure they were in keeping with reason and appropriate to the situation; the discipline of desire involved acceptance of the universe as it unfolds at each moment, and detachment from the results of action. Stoic belief in the primacy of fate also led many Stoics to the study of astrology, as well as other traditional systems of prophecy and divination.

For a period of four centuries, roughly from 200 B.C.E. to 200 C.E., Stoicism was among the most influential ways of thought and life in the ancient world, attracting followers throughout the Mediterranean area. Its international appeal can be judged from the fact that one important Stoic writer of the first century C.E., Chaeremon, was an Egyptian priest as well as a Stoic philosopher. *SEE* CHAEREMON. It played a major part in providing a philosophical basis for magic throughout the ancient world, and Stoic concepts pervade such esoteric writings as the *Corpus Hermeticum*; *SEE* CORPUS HERMETICUM.

Stoicism lost ground in the later years of the Roman Empire, as Christianity and mystical philosophies such as Neoplatonism rose to dominance. Substantial elements of Stoic theory, however, were absorbed into the Neoplatonist synthesis, into some branches of astrology, and into certain other occult traditions, where they have remained a significant factor ever since. FURTHER READING: ARNOLD 1911, AURELIUS 1909, EPICTETUS 1909, HADOT 1998, MATES 1953, RIST 1969, SAMBURSKY 1959.

Straif. (Old Irish, "sulphur") The fourteenth letter of the Ogham alphabet, with a sound-value of *z* or *str*. It corresponds to blackthorn among trees, the thrush among birds, and the color "bright" (Gaelic *sorcha*); it has no numerical value. In Robert Graves' version of the Ogham tree-calendar, it shares the month from April 16 to May 13 with the letter Saille. *SEE* OGHAM.

Ogham letter Straif

Strength. The eleventh (traditionally) or eighth (in most modern decks) Major Arcanum of the tarot. In most decks, this card bears the image of a woman either opening or closing the mouth of a lion. In the Golden Dawn tradition, this Arcanum is assigned to the Hebrew letter Teth, while the French system assigns it to Cheth. Its common meanings in divination include power and the ability to overcome obstacles.

Its magical title is "Daughter of the Flaming Sword, Leader of the Lion." *SEE ALSO* TAROT.

Tarot trump Strength (Universal Tarot)

Stuart, House of. A former royal house of Scotland and England, deeply enmeshed in the early history of Freemasonry and in several currents of European occultism. Originally a Breton family named Fitzlaad, which crossed the channel in 1066 with William the Conqueror, the Stuarts (also spelled Stewarts) took their more famous name after becoming hereditary stewards of Scotland in the twelfth century, and gained the Scots throne in 1371. In 1603, on the death of Elizabeth I of England, the Stuart James VI of Scotland united the Scots and English thrones as James I of Great Britain, bringing the dynasty to its apogee.

None of the later Stuarts were particularly gifted as kings, and persistent habits of arrogance and overconfidence made their rule over the united kingdoms a troubled one. In the 1630s, James' son Charles I attempted to suspend England's Parliamentary system and impose an autocratic government, but was defeated in the English Civil War of 1640–1645 and executed by the victorious Parliament in 1649. Charles' son was restored to the throne as Charles II in 1666; his brother and successor, James II, attempted to carry out some of his father's autocratic ideas and was driven from the throne by the revolution of 1688. Charles II's two sisters, Mary and Anne, took the throne in turn thereafter but died without heirs. On Anne's death in 1714 the throne of Great Britain was given to George of Hanover, a minor German prince descended from the Stuarts by way of a daughter of James I.

The heirs of James II—his son James, the "Old Pretender," and his grandson Charles, the "Bonnie Prince Charlie" of Highland song and legend—made numerous attempts to oust the Hanoverian dynasty, culminating in armed risings in 1715 and 1745. These efforts were backed by France, which was at war with England during much of this time, and supported by Scottish Highland clans struggling for cultural survival. English troops crushed both risings, and repressive laws enacted in the wake of "the Forty-Five" broke the back of the clan system and eliminated the Highlanders as a military threat.

After France and Britain signed the Peace of Aix-la-Chapelle in 1748, the French withdrew their support from the Stuarts and the hope of a Stuart restoration was essentially over. Charles Stuart himself lingered on until 1788, when he died from the effects of chronic alcoholism and syphilis, leaving no legitimate heirs. As his brother Henry had entered the priesthood, Charles' death marked the effective end of the Stuart line.

The connections between the House of Stuart and occult traditions are highly complex. Both James I and Charles I were responsible for harsh legislation against magical practice—James himself was the author of a book, *Daemonologie*, which insisted on the reality and diabolical nature of witchcraft and urged the execution of witches—but both were heavily involved in the more political forms of Renaissance Hermeticism, using magical approaches to art, architecture, drama, and ceremony in an attempt to strengthen their regimes. Under Charles I, these activities reached their culmination in a grandiose plan to rebuild London as a Hermetic City of the Sun, centered on a rebuilt St. Paul's Cathedral made over in the image of the Temple of Solomon. The project collapsed with the outbreak of civil war in 1640, and very few traces of the Stuart building program were left standing after the victory of the Parliamentary rebels.

Neither Charles II nor James II seem to have had much interest in the occult tradition, nor did James' son, the "Old Pretender"; all three were devout Catholics, and seem to have accepted the church's increasingly stringent bans on esoteric study and practice. The Old Pretender's son is another matter. Whether or not Charles Stuart was personally involved in occultism remains an open question, but the intrigues of the Jacobites (as the supporters of the exiled Stuarts were called) had a significant impact on the occult movement of the time.

The burgeoning Masonic movement of the early eighteenth century, with its oaths of secrecy and its international spread, offered substantial possibilities for political intrigue, and there is evidence that the Scottish Rite of Freemasonry—which first emerged in France in the years leading up to the rising of 1745—may have started out as a vehicle for Jacobite activities. The connection between the Stuart dynasty and high-level Masonry was sufficiently strong, at least in French Masonic circles, that the redoubtable Martines de Pasqually—one of the seminal figures in the origins of Martinism—founded his magical order on the basis of a charter supposedly signed by Bonnie Prince Charlie. SEE MARTINISM; PASQUALLY, MARTINES DE.

The romantic aura of the Jacobite cause ensured that interest in the Stuarts, as well as attempts to make use of their reputation and legacy, would survive the extinction of the Stuart line itself. During the late nineteenth century, a number of prominent occultists avowed the Jacobite cause, and tracts were circulated supporting the claims of minor European nobles with traces of Stuart ancestry. Samuel Mathers of Golden Dawn fame included Jacobitism among his interests; SEE MATHERS, SAMUEL LIDDELL.

There have also been a number of would-be Stuarts over the last two centuries. According to contemporary records, Charles Stuart died without any living heirs—his legitimate children suffered from congenital syphilis, and predeceased him—but most of these supposed Stuarts have claimed direct descent from him via various historically undocumented marriages, and expounded colorful accounts of the various conspiracies devoted to suppressing the truth about their royal heritage. SEE ALSO DREBBEL, CORNELIS; FREEMASONRY; KNIGHTS TEMPLAR; OCCULT HISTORY. FURTHER READING: HART 1994, SHUCHARD 1972.

sublimation. In alchemy, the process by which a solid substance is transformed into vapor by heating; the vapor may be condensed again into a sublimate. Alchemical symbolism assigns this process to the zodiacal sign Libra. SEE ALCHEMY.

subtle bodies. In occult philosophy, the several different nonphysical aspects of the self associated with the different planes of being; SEE PLANES. Different systems of occult teaching use a wide range of classifications and terminologies for the human subtle bodies. Common to all, though, is the idea that the core of the self is surrounded by a series of bodies of different levels of solidity, with the ordinary physical body being simply the coarsest and most visible of these bodies.

The theory of subtle bodies dates back at least as far as the ancient world, and was much discussed by late classical Platonists such as Iamblichus. SEE IAMBLICHUS OF CHALCIS; PLATONISM. The *Corpus Hermeticum*, the founding document of the Hermetic tradition, includes a mythic account in which the soul descending into incarnation gathers up subtle bodies from the planetary spheres through which it passes, and releases them again when it rises back upwards after death. SEE CORPUS HERMETICUM; HERMETICISM.

The Cabala includes a good deal of theory concerning the different levels of the human subtle body, which it divides into three broad sections: *neshamah*, the spiritual self; *ruach*, the conscious self; and *nephesh*, the body of life-energy. The first two of these are subdivided further. SEE CABALA; NEPHESH; NESHAMAH; RUACH.

In the magical traditions that have arisen since the beginning of the nineteenth century, theories and terminology have proliferated beyond counting. One common classification uses five levels: the physical body, made of ordinary matter; the etheric body, made of the subtle substance-energy of life, which forms the template on which the physical body is constructed; the astral body, made of a yet subtler substance, which is the medium of consciousness and the link by which stellar energies interact with the individual; the mental body, made of the substance of consciousness itself, which participates in the realm of the Platonic ideas; and the spiritual body, which is the essential and immortal core of the self. Other systems count more or fewer bodies than these five, however, and the same terms are sometimes used for entirely different levels of being. SEE ASTRAL BODY; ETHERIC BODY; MENTAL BODY; SPIRITUAL BODY. SEE ALSO SPHERE OF SENSATION.

succubus. (Latin, "one who lies under") In Western demonology, a spirit that seeks to have sexual relations with men. Monks, priests, and other men committed to the celibate life were believed to be particularly at risk from succubi. A detail reported in several sources is that succubi, although they take generally female shapes, are actually male and have penises. The counterpart of a succubus is an incubus; *SEE* INCUBUS. *SEE ALSO* DEMON.

sulphur. One of the *tria prima* or Three Principles of alchemy and spagyrics, sulphur is the principle of flammability and energy. Every substance contains its own sulphur, which consists of those portions that evaporate most readily when the substance is heated.

The use of sulphur as a category of substance in alchemy dates back to the early Arabic alchemist Geber (Jabir ibn Hayyan, 720–800 C.E.), who proposed that all metals were made of a sulphur and a mercury fused together. The Swiss alchemist and physician Paracelsus (1493–1541) expanded this theory by proposing salt as a third factor. *SEE* GEBER; MERCURY; PARACELSUS; SALT.

In spagyrics, the sulphur of an herb is extracted by macerating (soaking) the herb in alcohol for weeks or months, and then distilling off the alcohol. The part of the plant that vaporizes and recondenses with the alcohol is the sulphur of the plant. *SEE ALSO* ALCHEMY; SPAGYRICS.

Summerland. In nineteenth-century Spiritualism and twentieth-century Paganism, a term for the location where human souls go after death. In most forms of Spiritualism, the Summerland is little more than an alternative term for the Christian Heaven.

In modern Pagan practice, and in those Spiritualist traditions that accept reincarnation, the Summerland is a nonphysical realm in which the souls of the dead dwell before they are reborn into another physical body. Modern Pagan sources tend to picture the Summerland as a paradise inhabited by unicorns, faeries, and other legendary beings, full of natural beauty and abundance. *SEE ALSO* NEOPAGANISM; REINCARNATION; SPIRITUALISM.

Summoner. In some traditions of witchcraft, a male officer in a coven, usually the assistant to the High Priest and often the next in line for the High Priest's office. His implements of office are a black staff and a black robe. According to some sources, he was responsible for protect-

ing the High Priestess in case of trouble, and for guarding the coven's Book of Shadows. *SEE* BOOK OF SHADOWS.

Other names for the Summoner include the Guardian, the Black Man, the Man in Black, and Black Staff. *SEE ALSO* COVEN; HIGH PRIEST.

Sun. One of the seven planets of traditional astrology, the sun in a birth chart represents the self, and in particular the public self—the face one shows to the world. In astrological terms, the sun rules the sign Leo, is exalted in Aries, is in his detriment in Aquarius and in his fall in Libra. *SEE* ASTROLOGY.

In alchemy, the sun is a common symbol for gold, and also represents the rubedo or red phase of the Great Work. *SEE* ALCHEMY.

Astrological symbol of the sun

Sun, the. The nineteenth Major Arcanum of the tarot, generally showing an image of the sun, often with one or more children in a walled garden beneath it. In the Golden Dawn Tarot system, this Arcanum corresponds to the Hebrew letter Resh, while the French system assigns it to Qoph. Its interpretations are usually positive, including success, victory, healing, and happiness, but it can also traditionally represent sudden death.

Its magical title is "Lord of the Fire of the World." *SEE ALSO* RESH; TAROT.

Tarot trump the Sun (Universal Tarot)

Sun, Spiritual. A variety of occult traditions hold that the physical sun is an emblem or representation of a primal, spiritual sun, the source of all energy and life in the cosmos. The concept of the spiritual sun was a dominant theme in nineteenth-century occultism, where it often served as a more impersonal version of the Christian God.

The image of the "central sun," creating concentric shells of universes around itself, seems to have surfaced first in the writings of American mystic Andrew Jackson Davis (1926–1909), passed from his work into Spiritualism, and from there became part of the common language of nearly all nineteenth-century occult traditions. It was taken up by such figures as P. B. Randolph, Emma Hardinge Britten, and H. P. Blavatsky. However, the rise of Pagan spirituality in the twentieth century, with its radically different images of the divine, seems to have pushed the spiritual sun aside for the time being. SEE DAVIS, ANDREW JACKSON; SPIRITUALISM; THEOSOPHY. SEE ALSO SUN.

Surrealism. Twentieth-century artistic movement, centered in France, which drew significantly on occult traditions as a theoretical basis. Surrealism's roots were in the slightly earlier Dada movement, which set out to undermine all social and artistic standards as a protest against the inhumanity of the First World War. André Breton, who became the central figure in Surrealism, joined the Dadaists in Paris in the immediate postwar period, but broke with Dada in 1923, arguing that it had become too premeditated and predictable.

The first *Surrealist Manifesto*, penned by Breton, was published in 1924. It called for a rejection of rational, esthetic, and moral ideas in art, and the use of automatic writing, trance states, and other methods to get the conscious mind out of the way of the process of artistic creation. A second *Manifesto* emerged in 1929, and by that time the movement had attracted a number of significant poets and artists, including Antonin Artaud, Man Ray, and Max Ernst. The movement went through various ups and downs, became increasingly allied with Marxist ideology and hostile to occultism, and finally guttered out as a movement in the late 1940s. Several individuals in the movement, notably British artist Leonora Carring-

ton (1917–), have continued to work in a recognizeably Surrealist style with strong occult influences since that time.

Breton himself was heavily influenced by Eliphas Lévi and other magical writers, although he rejected the existence of spirits and objectively real magical forces, insisting instead that occult methods were simply ways to tap into the practitioner's own unconscious mind. Most Surrealists seem to have held similar opinions, although the deliberate murkiness of their theoretical statements make it hard to be sure. Certainly figures such as the American magician P. B. Randolph, forgotten nearly everywhere else in the twentieth century, remained known figures in the Surrealist movement; SEE RANDOLPH, PASCHAL BEVERLY.

A line from the nineteenth-century French poet Lautréamont, praised by Surrealists as the poetic image par excellence, gives some of the flavor of the movement: "As beautiful as the chance meeting, on a dissecting table, of a sewing machine and an umbrella" (Choucha 1991, p. 54). FURTHER READING: CHOUCHA 1991.

Swedenborg, Emmanuel. Swedish scientist and mystic, 1688–1772. The son of a bishop in the Swedish Lutheran Church, Swedenborg attended university at Uppsala, where he studed Hebrew from his brother-in-law, the Cabalist Erik Benzelius, and another Cabalist among the University staff, Johan Kemper. SEE CABALA. Swedenborg's chief interest at the time was in the new scientific thought, and he went on to become an engineer. After advanced studies in England, France, the Netherlands, and Germany, he launched Sweden's first scientific journal and took a position working for the government as an assessor of mines. Meanwhile, he wrote no fewer than 154 books on mathematics and the sciences. As a member of Sweden's educated upper class, close to the Swedish royal house and to important figures in the nobility, Swedenborg was involved in international diplomacy, and carried out secretive missions for the Swedish government in a number of European countries. Sweden and France both supported attempts to restore the House of Stuart to the British throne in 1715 and 1745; Swedenborg was apparently heavily involved in these efforts, and in the complex Masonic and magical intrigues that surrounded them. He is believed to have been a Freemason, though the records of his initiation have been lost. *SEE* FREEMASONRY; STUART, HOUSE OF.

In his late fifties, Swedenborg became fascinated with the study of what we now call psychology, recorded his dreams, and made use of breath control and mental concentration as a method of inner exploration. In 1744 he had an intense visionary experience which featured Jesus and Swedenborg's dead father. Another vision in 1745 left him convinced that he had a special spiritual mission to accomplish in the world.

The same systematic approach that he had learned as an engineer and scientist led him to make a comprehensive study of the Bible, correlating it with his own burgeoning spiritual experiences. These involved conversations with angels and other spiritual entities, who communicated a complex theological system and an account of the spiritual realms. All of this material Swedenborg wrote down and systematized.

The first fruit of these experiences was the twelve-volume opus *Arcana Coelestia* (*Celestial Secrets*), first published in 1749, in which Swedenborg described the nature of Heaven, Hell, and human destiny in immense detail. Over two hundred additional books on religious subjects followed. While *Arcana Coelestia* was published anonymously, the identity of its author slipped out after a few years, and the result was ceaseless controversy during the last third of his life. European intellectuals of the stature of Immanuel Kant and F. C. Oettinger were drawn into the debate over Swedenborg's visions, and in 1769 he and his work barely escaped condemnation by the Swedish Lutheran Church.

Swedenborg's visionary capacities extended to more practical details as well. According to contemporary accounts, he accurately described the details of a fire in Stockholm while attending a party more than a hundred miles away, and accurately foretold the deaths of several people, including himself. He died in London, while visiting friends there, on the date he had predicted. After his death, his works became the basis of a church, the Church of the New Jerusalem (more commonly known as the Swedenborgian Church), which has consistently struggled to distance itself from occultism and attain the highest possible degree of respectability. FURTHER READING: DOLE AND KIRVEN 1992, SCHUCHARD 1995, TROBRIDGE 1992.

sword, magical. One of the standard devices in the magical toolkit since early times, the magical sword is used to command, banish, and defeat spirits, especially in the practice of magical evocation. The *Key of Solomon*, the most famous of medieval grimoires, provides detailed instructions for preparing and consecrating no less than four magical swords, as well as a scimitar, a lance, a dagger, a poniard, and a collection of knives—the Solomonic magician entered the magical circle as heavily armed as a knight going to war. *SEE* KEY OF SOLOMON. Most other grimoires suggest a somewhat less topheavy collection of magical armament, but at least one sword was normally in evidence.

The replacement of the magic of the grimoires with the new, more spiritually oriented magic of the nineteenth-century occult renaissance saw the sword take on new forms, but it remained at least as important. The French magus Eliphas Lévi (1810–1875) included a discussion of the magical sword in his most important tome, *Dogme et Rituel de la Haute Magie* (*Doctrine and Ritual of High Magic*, 1845), the book that launched the modern magical revival, and the Hermetic Order of the Golden Dawn—whose work was the single most important influence on twentieth-century Western occultism—included a typically ornate set of instructions for making and consecrating a magical sword in its training papers. Golden Dawn alumnus Aleister Crowley (1875–1947) also wrote at length on the symbolism and uses of the magical sword. *SEE* CROWLEY, ALEISTER; GOLDEN DAWN, HERMETIC ORDER OF THE; LÉVI, ELIPHAS.

In most modern systems of ceremonial magic, the sword remains a standard and heavily used element of magical gear, and suggestions that it be replaced with something more meaningful in modern terms—a handgun has been proposed—have made little headway. Some of the more traditional Wiccan groups have retained the sword as a working tool; *SEE* WICCA.

Elsewhere in the Neopagan movement, however, the sword has largely fallen out of favor, in large part because of a different attitude toward spiritual beings than the one expressed in the grimoires and, to a lesser extent, in more recent traditions. Where most ceremonial magicians summon, command, and banish spirits, many modern Pagans feel it more appropriate to treat them as equals and allies, to be invited to the ritual circle and welcomed with offerings rather than ordered about.

The use of the magical sword is at least partly a function of natural magic. Many occult traditions claim that iron, especially when sharpened, is inimical to many types of spiritual entity. The most common understandings of the etheric realm suggest that iron, like other conductive metals, can short-circuit etheric bodies that lack the protection of a physical form. *SEE* ETHERIC BODY.

The magical trident, another common instrument of magicians, is closely related to the magical sword, and is sometimes referred to as a sword. *SEE* TRIDENT, MAGICAL. FURTHER READING: CROWLEY 1980, LEVI 1972, MATHERS 1888, REGARDIE 1971.

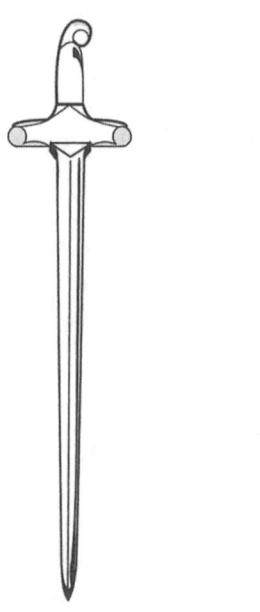

The sword of the magician serves as a defense against hostile spirits

Sworn Book of Honorius. A thirteenth-century grimoire, an important textbook of ritual magic throughout the later Middle Ages and Renaissance. According to its preface, it was compiled by one Honorius of Thebes at the behest of an assembly of eighty-nine master magicians from Naples, Athens, and Toledo as a summary of all known magical lore, and is to be passed on only to those who swear an oath of secrecy.

Like the *Picatrix*, which entered circulation in Europe around the same time, the *Sworn Book* presents a forceful and coherent defense of magic as a valid and moral art, which can only be mastered by those who are learned, disciplined, and pure of heart.

The actual author of the *Sworn Book*, and the date and place of its composition, are unknown. It was certainly in circulation in Paris by the early thirteenth century, when it was among the grimoires denounced by William of Auvergne, bishop of Paris. *SEE ALSO* GRIMOIRE. FURTHER READING: PETERS 1978, THORNDYKE 1923.

sylphs. In the lore of ceremonial magic, the elemental spirits of air. Their king is Paralda. *SEE* ELEMENTAL.

synastry. (Greek *syn-*, "together," + *astron*, "star") The branch of astrology concerned with exploring human relationships by comparing the birth charts and other astrological data of the people involved. While synastry is most often used to assess the potentials of a marriage or other close emotional relationship, it can also be used to sound out the possibilities of a business partnership or to explore family dynamics between parents and children, siblings, or other relatives.

As with every branch of astrology, the principles of synastry are complex, and cannot be quickly summarized. The sort of newspaper-astrology synastry that claims that certain sun signs are compatible, and others are not, is rejected by the vast majority of competent astrologers. In synastry, aspects between planets of one chart and those of the other are of critical importance, and the relation of planets on one chart to the ascendant, midheaven, and house cusps of the other may be equally so. Composite charts using the midpoints between each pair of planets—in other words, the degree of the zodiac halfway between a planet on one chart and the same planet on the other—are also used by some astrologers. *SEE ALSO* ASTROLOGY.

Tablet of Union. In the Enochian system of magic, a rectangular pattern of twenty letters, used to represent the element of spirit. Four divine names governing the four elements, and the names of three angels ruling over spirit, are extracted from it. *SEE* ENOCHIAN MAGIC.

```
E X A R P
H C O M A
N A N T A
B I T O M
```

Tablet of Union

Tagiriron. (Hebrew, ThGRIRVN, "Disputers") In Cabalistic lore, the Disputers or Wranglers, the Qlippoth or demonic power associated with Tiphareth, the sixth Sephirah of the Tree of Life. Their traditional form is described as vast giants wrestling with each other. *SEE* QLIPPOTH.

Talbot, Edward. *SEE* KELLY, EDWARD.

Taliahad. (Hebrew ThLIHD) In ceremonial magic, the angel of the element of water. Taliahad is invoked in the consecration of the cup in Golden Dawn magic. *SEE* ANGEL.

talisman. (Arabic *tilsam*, from Greek *tetelesmenon*, "that which has been consecrated") In magical lore, an object charged or consecrated with magical energies for the fulfillment of some specific purpose. Talismanic magic has had an important place in Western occultism since ancient times, and a dizzying variety of objects have been consecrated for various talismanic purposes.

Talismans can be traced in every magical tradition that has contributed to Western occultism. Ancient Egyptian priestly magicians had a wide range of talismanic methods at their disposal. For example, massive stone tablets were inscribed with healing spells and set in basins; those who were sick could pour water over the hieroglyphic carvings, drink the water, and benefit from the magic. More sinister rites were used to attack the foreign and domestic enemies of the Egyptian state; some of these made use of statues of enemy soldiers who were bound or maltreated and then buried in a secret place. *SEE* EGYPTIAN OCCULTISM.

Similar traditions could be found in the magical lore of the busy city-states of Mesopotamia, and the vast palace libraries of Ashurbanipal, the last great king of Assyria, include detailed instructions for a variety of talismanic magical workings. *SEE* ASHURBANIPAL; MESOPOTAMIAN OCCULTISM. The magicians of Sumer, Babylon, and other Mesopotamian cultures drew heavily on the astrological lore of the region, setting a precedent that has been followed by talismanic magicians ever since.

Ancient Greece and Rome had a remarkable range of talisman lore, including the making of magical statues; *SEE* STATUES, MAGICAL. A very common form of talismans was the binding tablet—a lead tablet that was dropped in wells, graves, caverns, and other points of ready access to the underworld to carry messages to the powers of the unseen and accomplish various forms of magic, usually hostile. *SEE* BINDING TABLET.

Talismans in the form now used in magic began to evolve toward the end of the classical period, with Egypt—where the art of writing had never quite lost its magical aura—as one focal point. The Graeco-Egyptian magical papyri, sorcerers' handbooks from the first few centuries of the common era, include instructions for making a variety of talismanic devices. It was after Egypt fell into Arab hands in the eighth century, though, that Muslim magicians began reshaping the lore they inherited from the ancient world, and evolved talismans of the sort that are still used today.

In this modern sense, a talisman is a piece of metal, paper, parchment, or some other material that can be engraved or written on. It is usually cut into a flat disk, although other shapes are known. Once made and marked with magically effective words and symbols, the talisman is consecrated in a formal ritual, and then concealed and left to do its work.

A talisman of Mercury, inscribed with Hebrew words of power, planetary symbols, and geometrical figures (top: front of talisman; bottom: back of talisman)

The methods used to consecrate a talisman vary widely in different traditions of magic. In medieval Arabic handbooks such as the *Picatrix*, and in many more recent works, the talisman is simply made of a metal with the right symbolism and held in the smoke of a specially compounded incense, then wrapped in silk and put away to work. *SEE* PICATRIX. The range of methods extends from this up to hugely complex techniques of the sort used by the Hermetic Order of the Golden Dawn, in which the magician can easily spend two hours reciting conjurations, vibrating divine names, evoking spirits, channeling energies, and putting the talisman through the equivalent of a lodge initiation ceremony. *SEE* GOLDEN DAWN, HERMETIC ORDER OF THE. Both these approaches, and many that fall between these extremes, work well in practice.

Talismans, according to standard occult theory, work because their material basis forms a "body" for the energies placed in them at the time of consecration. With this anchor on the physical plane, the talisman keeps on working steadily and mindlessly toward the fulfillment of whatever purpose it was created to accomplish. When a talisman has finished its work, therefore, or when the situation has changed and its energies are no longer needed, it must be ceremonially deconsecrated and the physical form destroyed.

While standard talismans of the type described above remain far and away the most common approach in use among ceremonial magicians, noticeably different approaches can be found among those who draw on folk magic traditions, especially those of American Hoodoo; *SEE* HOODOO. In this system, a mojo, toby, or hand—that is, a small cloth bag filled with magically active substances—may be used for most of the purposes classical talismans might fill. *SEE* MOJO. Other traditions draw on various forms of natural magic to accomplish the same things; *SEE* NATURAL MAGIC. *SEE ALSO* AMULET. FURTHER READING: FARAONE 1992, GREER 1997, REGARDIE 1971.

Taphthartharath. In ceremonial magic, the planetary spirit of Mercury. Its intelligence is Tiriel. *SEE* SPIRIT.

Tarocchi di Mantegna. A deck of cards related to the tarot, the Tarocchi di Mantegna deck is misnamed—it is neither a Tarocchi (tarot) deck, nor was it created by the Renaissance artist Andrea Mantegna. Rather, it is a fifty-card deck of unknown purpose, created at some point in the late fifteenth century, with some striking similarities to the tarot trumps. Two copies survive, and the famous German artist Albrecht Dürer (1471–1528) produced drawings based on twenty-two of the cards around the beginning of the sixteenth century.

The fifty cards of the Tarocchi di Mantegna are divided into five groups of ten, which correspond to human social classes, the Muses, the liberal arts, abstract principles and virtues, and astronomical spheres, respectively. They are titled, in the Renaissance-era Venetian dialect of Italian, as follows:

I. Misero (beggar)

II. Fameio (servant)

III. Artixan (artisan)

IV. Merchadante (merchant)

V. Zintilomo (gentleman)

VI. Chavalier (chevalier)

VII. Doxe (duke)

VIII. Re (king)

IX. Imperator (emperor)

X. Papa (pope)

XI. Caliope (Calliope, muse of epic poetry)

XII. Urania (muse of astronomy)

XIII. Terpsicore (Terpsichore, muse of dancing)

XIV. Erato (muse of erotic poetry)

XV. Polimnia (Polyhymnia, muse of hymns)

XVI. Talia (Thalia, muse of comedy)

XVII. Melpomene (muse of tragedy)

XVIII. Euterpe (muse of music)

XIX. Clio (muse of history)

XX. Apollo (divine patron of the arts)

XXI. Grammatica (grammar)

XXII. Loica (logic)

XXIII. Rhetorica (rhetoric)

XXIV. Geometria (geometry)

XXV. Aritmetricha (arithmetic)

XXVI. Musicha (music)

XXVII. Poesia (poetry)

XXVIII. Philosofia (philosophy)

XXIX. Astrologia (astrology)

XXX. Theologia (theology)

XXXI. Iliaco (spirit of the sun)

XXXII. Chronico (spirit of time)

XXXIII. Cosmico (spirit of the universe)

XXXIV. Temperancia (temperance)

XXXV. Prudencia (prudence)

XXXVI. Forteza (fortitude)

XXXVII. Iusticia (justice)

XXXVIII. Charita (charity)

XXXIX. Speranza (hope)

XXXX. Fede (faith)

XXXXI. Luna (moon)

XXXXII. Mercurio (Mercury)

XXXXIII. Venus

XXXXXIV. Sol (sun)

XXXXV. Marte (Mars)

XXXXVI. Iupiter (Jupiter)

XXXXVII. Saturno (Saturn)

XXXXVIII. Octava Spera (eighth sphere)

XXXXIX. Primo Mobile (first mover)

XXXXX. Prima Causa (first cause)

The Tarocchi di Mantegna seem to have been purely a phenomenon of the late fifteenth century and dropped out of use entirely thereafter. A few twentieth-century editions have been produced for collectors, but the deck as a whole has received little attention from modern occultists. SEE ALSO MINCHIATE; TAROT. FURTHER READING: S. KAPLAN 1978.

tarot. A deck of seventy-eight cards that comprise the most popular divinatory tool in modern occultism. The tarot is indispensible in many current systems of occult theory and practice. Aside from its use as a divinatory method, in which cards are dealt out from a shuffled deck and interpreted in various ways, the tarot is also used as a subject for meditation, a focus for scrying, and a convenient symbolic alphabet in many different branches of occult practice. SEE MEDITATION; SCRYING. Its role is a fairly recent one, however, and as little as two hundred years ago it was essentially unknown to most occultists.

The tarot deck consists of three groups of cards. First are twenty-two trumps or Major Arcana, each of which has a number, a title, and a traditional image. Second are the forty small cards or pip cards, ten cards each of four suits—wands or staves; cups; swords; and coins, disks, or pentacles—which correspond to the pip cards of an ordinary playing card deck. Last are the sixteen court cards—the king, queen, knight, and page or servant of each suit—which correspond to the face cards of the ordinary deck.

Well over a thousand different tarot decks have been designed and produced over the last few hundred years. Many variations of name, number, and imagery have arisen, especially among the trumps, the most enigmatic and symbolically rich part of the deck. The numbers and titles of the trumps in most modern occult tarot decks are as follows:

0. The Fool

I. The Magician

II. The High Priestess

III. The Empress

IV. The Emperor

V. The Hierophant

VI. The Lovers

VII. The Chariot

VIII. Strength

IX. The Hermit

X. The Wheel of Fortune

XI. Justice

XII. The Hanged Man

XIII. Death

XIV. Temperance

XV. The Devil

XVI. The Tower

XVII. The Star

XVIII. The Moon

XIX. The Sun

XX. Judgement

XXI. The Universe

The older decks tend to have little in the way of occult symbolism, while the more recent decks are often loaded with it to the bursting point. For instance, the Magician in older decks is generally called the Juggler or the Mountebank, and stands behind a random assortment of junk on a plank table, while most newer decks equip the Magician with an altar topped with the wand, cup, sword or dagger, and pentacle of the well-equipped ceremonial magician. Behind these changes lies the complex history of the tarot itself.

According to occult history, which has embroidered a rich fabric of fantasy around this subject, the tarot originated in ancient Egypt, and the word "tarot" itself is from the supposed ancient Egyptian words *tar*, "road," and *rosh* or *rog*, meaning "royal." This claim was introduced by a French scholar, Antoine Court de Gébelin (1728–1784), in a wildly popular book on ancient Egypt published in 1781, and it has been repeated in books on the tarot ever since.

Unfortunately Court de Gébelin wrote more than forty years before the Egyptian hieroglyphs were deciphered, and his "ancient Egyptian" terms came out of his own head. The ancient Egyptian words for "road" and "royal" are actually *w3t* and *nsw*, respectively. To judge by the standard modern dictionaries of Egyptian hieroglyphics, in fact, neither *tar* nor *rog* nor *rosh* are ancient Egyptian words at all. The word "tarot" is simply the French version of the older Italian name *tarocchi* or *tarocco*, a Renaissance slang term of unknown meaning; before 1500, the tarot deck was called *trionfi*, "triumphs" or "trumps."

Similar problems surround the other two common occult theories about the origins of the tarot—that it was invented and brought to Europe by the Gypsies, on the one hand, and that it was created by a convention of occultists meeting in the city of Fez, Morocco, in 1300. The first theory falls victim to the fact that the tarot was in circulation in Italy well before the first Gypsies arrived there. The second theory simply has no evidence whatsoever to support it; while it cannot be disproved—the convention might just possibly have taken place in such secrecy that no scrap of evidence remained for historians to find—the same sort of argument can be used to "prove" that the tarot was invented on Mars and reached Earth by way of flying saucers.

The actual history of the tarot begins in Renaissance Italy in the beginning of the fifteenth century. Around the middle of the previous century, playing cards had first been imported from the Arabic world, and had found an enthusiastic welcome among European gamblers. The deck introduced to Italy had the same number of suits, pip cards, and face cards as a modern deck, though it lacked a joker. Its suits were wands, cups, swords, and coins, still the standard suit marks in traditional Italian decks; the clubs, spades, hearts, and diamonds standard in English-speaking countries are a later French invention, and still another set of suits are standard in central Europe.

At some point in the first decades of the fifteenth century, someone at the ducal courts of Milan or Ferarra—possibly Marziano da Tortona, secretary to Filippo Maria Visconti, Duke of Milan—came up with the idea of adding further cards to the deck. In the card games of the time, trick-taking games ancestral to bridge and pinochle, these additional cards made play more lively by enabling players to trump any of the four ordinary suits.

A deck devised by Marziano da Tortona, probably before 1418, is described in a surviving letter. It had sixteen trump cards that featured a collection of classical Pagan gods. There were many other versions, though none has yet been proved to be earlier than Marziano's. By the 1440s, however, something closer to the later tarot deck was becoming standard, and by 1450—the probable date of the great Pierpont Morgan–Bergamo deck, the most complete of the early hand-painted decks—the number, names, and approximate order of the trumps had been more or less established.

It deserves to be pointed out that all the available evidence for these early tarot decks indicates that they were meant to be used in card games; the first references to tarot divination date from centuries later. As a game, tarot proved highly popular; it spread from Italy to France and Switzerland in the early sixteenth century, and from there to most of Europe by the beginning of the seventeenth. In the middle of the sixteenth century, according to one source, tarot was more popular than chess in France.

Cartomancy itself seems to have begun in the middle of the eighteenth century, and ordinary playing cards of various kinds were used. The first efforts at tarot divination apparently took place in Bologna, Italy, where a specialized tarot deck—the *Tarocco bolognese* of sixty-two cards—had become standard; a manuscript from before 1750 gives divinatory meanings for thirty-five of the cards. This had little influence on later occult interpretations of the tarot, however.

The occult tradition of the tarot had its origins in the writings of Antoine Court de Gébelin, the French scholar whose imaginary Egyptian terminology was mentioned above. A Freemason, a founding member of the deeply esoteric Philaléthes organization, and probably a member of Martinez de Pasqually's Élus Coens as well, he was deeply involved in the Paris esoteric scene. *SEE* **ÉLUS COENS; FREEMASONRY.** His magnum opus, *Le Monde Primitif* (*The Primitive World*), published in nine volumes between 1773 and 1782, argued that all modern languages, religions, and cultures were the descendants of the high culture of a primordial Golden Age, which he identified with ancient Egypt. In an essay in the eighth volume, he identified the tarot as an ancient Egyptian book, communicating secret teachings in the form of hieroglyphic emblems.

Court de Gébelin's assertions were quickly taken up by Etteila (Jean-Baptiste Aliette, 1738–1791), who had previously published a book on divination with the common thirty-two-card picquet deck. This book, published in 1770, referred in passing to divination with "les Taraux"; Etteila had perhaps heard of the Bolognese tradition. In 1782, the year that Court de Gébelin's essay on the tarot saw print, Etteila wrote a book on divination with tarot cards; barred from publication that year by the royal censors, it was resubmitted under a different title the next year and passed muster.

Thereafter Etteila produced a series of books on the subject, enlarging on the Egyptian mysteries of the tarot and the use of the cards in divination. In the process he pioneered the relation of tarot and astrology, and invented the phrase "the Book of Thoth" as a title for the deck. He established an organization, the Société des Interprètes du Livre de Thot (Society of Interpreters of the

Book of Thoth), to pass on his teachings, and his students and successors were important figures in the Paris occult underworld for half a century after his death. *SEE* ET-TEILA.

Despite all these previous contributions, it was Eliphas Lévi (Alphonse Louis Constant, 1810–1875), the architect of the nineteenth-century occult revival, who ensured that the tarot would become one of the core elements of modern occultism. He did this by noticing that the number of Major Arcana, twenty-two, was equal to the number of letters in the Hebrew alphabet, one of the essential elements of the Cabala—and by using this fact to fuse tarot and the Cabala so thoroughly that magicians ever since have seen the two as a unity. Lévi's great book, *Dogme et Rituel de la Haute Magie* (*Doctrine and Ritual of High Magic*, 1855) was structured along the lines of his Cabalist-tarot fusion—for example, the two parts (*Doctrine* and *Ritual*) each had twenty-two chapters, each of which dealt with matters suggested by the joint symbolism of the respective Hebrew letter and tarot trump. *SEE* CABALA; HEBREW ALPHABET; LÉVI, ELIPHAS.

The enormous popularity of Lévi's books inserted the study of the tarot firmly into the occult systems of the nineteenth century. The cards were taken up by the Hermetic Order of the Golden Dawn, the most influential of all magical orders of the period, and became central to the entire Golden Dawn system of magical theory and practice. *SEE* GOLDEN DAWN, HERMETIC ORDER OF THE. The Golden Dawn reworked Lévi's approach to the tarot, changing the attributions of the Hebrew letters to the trumps—Lévi had assigned Aleph, the first letter, to trump I, the Magician, and placed the Fool (trump 0) just before the Universe at the end of the sequence, while the Golden Dawn moved the Fool to the beginning and assigned Aleph to it. The Golden Dawn also massively expanded and systematized the symbolism of the deck, creating what has become the standard modern approach to the subject, and redesigned a number of the cards.

While the Golden Dawn's own secret tarot deck remained unpublished until the late twentieth century, two decks inspired by it played a major role in launching the twentieth-century craze for tarot cards. The first was designed by Golden Dawn alumnus Arthur Edward Waite (1857–1942) and painted by Pamela Colman Smith (1878–1951), a professional artist who belonged to Waite's branch of the Golden Dawn. Published by Rider & Co. in 1909, it became known as the Rider-Waite tarot, and went on to become the most popular tarot deck of the modern period. *SEE* SMITH, PAMELA COLMAN; WAITE, ARTHUR EDWARD.

Waite had encountered a late fifteenth-century tarot deck, the Sola-Busca deck, which had symbolic illustrations on all seventy-eight cards. Most other decks simply used different numbers of the suit signs to mark the small cards; the six of swords, for example, in most older decks has six swords on it and little or nothing else. Borrowing the Sola-Busca concept and, in many cases, the individual designs as well, Waite and Smith produced a deck that could be interpreted entirely on the basis of its visual images. This proved enormously popular, and most modern tarot decks have used the same approach.

The second influential deck inspired by the Golden Dawn version was the Thoth tarot, designed by British occultist Aleister Crowley (1875–1947) and executed by Lady Frieda Harris, an artist strongly influenced by Italian Futurism and other modernist currents in the art world of her time. Based on Crowley's Cabalistic erudition and his new, post-Christian religion of Thelema, the Thoth deck radically reshaped the imagery of the cards, and also broke with the habit of using medieval imagery for the cards. It was completed in 1944. *SEE* CROWLEY, ALEISTER; THELEMA.

The Thoth deck existed only as a set of paintings and illustrations in a book until the 1960s, when 250 copies of a two-color edition (the illustrations were printed entirely in blue, the back of the cards in red) was produced by the Sangreal Society, an esoteric organization based in Texas. The year 1969 saw the first color printing of the deck, of limited quality. It was not until 1977 that a new edition, made from the original paintings themselves, brought the Thoth tarot out in something close to its intended form.

During the 1970s, new tarot decks began to come onto the market in a steady trickle; in the 1980s, the trickle became a stream, and in the 1990s the stream turned into an overwhelming flood. As of this writing, scores of new decks find their way into print each year, to say nothing of the other, non-tarot divination decks—

most of them at least partly inspired by the tarot. There are Tarots based on every mythology from Chinese to ancient Mayan, every spiritual tradition from Wicca to Zen, and every artistic tradition from cave paintings to the work of Salvador Dali—to say nothing of unclassifiables such as the Herbal tarot, the Baseball tarot, the Alice in Wonderland tarot, the Lord of the Rings tarot, and so on. The literature on tarot has expanded accordingly, and followers of every Western spiritual tradition have access to texts expounding the philosophy and practice of the tarot in familiar terms.

In all this ebullient growth there have been a few dissenting voices. Some traditional Jewish Cabalists, and Jewish scholars of Cabalistic history such as Gershom Scholem, have steadfastly rejected the idea that the tarot has any connection to the Cabala at all. In the same way, some modern scholars of playing card history have dismissed the occult dimension of the tarot as nonsense.

Such views are correct, in that the tarot does seem to have started out as a clever addition to playing cards and nothing more. To define tarot forever in terms of its origins, though, is to approach it in a remarkably simple-minded way. Over more than two centuries, since it was first adopted by occultists in the late eighteenth century, the tarot has been steadily reworked and developed by those who saw its occult potential and were not afraid to bring that potential closer to reality. Whether or not the tarot was originally connected with the occult, in other words, it certainly is now—and the contributions of many occultists, diviners, and magicians have gone into making the modern tarot one of the most important elements of Western occult tradition. *SEE ALSO* DIVINATION; FEZ; *AND ENTRIES UNDER NAMES OF INDIVIDUAL CARDS OF THE MAJOR ARCANA.* FURTHER READING: DECKER ET AL. 1996, DUMMETT 1986, KAPLAN 1978, KAPLAN 1986, KAPLAN 1990, OLSEN 1994.

Tarrega, Ramon de. Spanish alchemist and magician, c. 1295–1371. He was born of Jewish parents in the Spanish town of Tarrega. According to his testimony before the Inquisition in 1370, he converted to Christianity at the age of twelve and entered the Dominican Order. At some point he studied medicine and became a capable physician, and around 1319 he wrote his first book, *De*

Secretis Naturae sive Quinta Essentia (*On the Secrets of Nature, or the Fifth Essence*), an important work of alchemical medicine. Numerous other books followed, most of them on alchemical subjects.

The details of his life and travels are poorly known, but comments in his books suggest that he was in Paris in 1319, in Montepllier in 1330, and in London in 1332, 1337, 1355, and 1357. According to an account commonly repeated in alchemical writings, he worked as an alchemist for England's King Edward III, and spent some time in the Tower of London before escaping to France.

At some point in the 1350s one of his books, a magical text titled *De Invocatione Daemonum* (*On the Invocation of Demons*), came to the attention of Dominican inquisitor Nicholas Eymeric (1320–1399) and was condemned as heretical. When Ramon returned to Spain, probably in 1367, he was brought before the Inquisition. In 1368 he was imprisoned in the Dominican monastery at Barcelona, where he remained for the rest of his life. He was formally condemned in 1371, and his books were ordered to be burnt. A short time after the arrival of the condemnation from Rome, Ramon was found dead in his cell.

His books managed to survive by the simple expedient of being attributed to someone else—in this case the Spanish mystic Ramon Lull (1232–1315), who thus ended up with an undeserved reputation as an alchemist. *SEE* LULL, RAMON. *SEE ALSO* ALCHEMY. FURTHER READING: PATAI 1994, PERIERA 1989.

Tarshishim. (Hebrew ThRShShIM, "chrysolites, glittering stones") In Cabalistic lore, an order of angels, sometimes assigned to the Sephirah Netzach. *SEE* ANGEL; NETZACH.

tassomancy. (Greek, *tassos*, "cup," and *manteia*, "divination") The art of divination by tea leaves. Rarely explored or practiced by those who define themselves as occultists, tassomancy remains an important divinatory system in folk tradition and among professional diviners.

In practicing tassomancy, the diviner takes a mostly empty cup of tea with tea leaves in the bottom, swirls the tea around so that the leaves are deposited on the sides of the cup, and interprets the images formed by the leaves.

Different positions around the cup stand for different time periods. There are also specialized teacups for tassomancy, in which the sides of the cup are marked off into segments, each with its own meaning. *SEE ALSO* DIVINATION. FURTHER READING: HEWITT 1999.

tattvas. A set of emblems of the elements borrowed into the Western magical tradition from Hindu sources, the tattvas (also known as tattwas) were introduced into Western occult practice by the Hermetic Order of the Golden Dawn, which borrowed them from Theosophical literature. There are five primary tattvas, as follows:

Name	Element	Color	Shape
Prithivi	Earth	Yellow	Square
Apas	Water	Silver	Crescent
Tejas	Fire	Red	Triangle
Vayu	Air	Blue	Circle
Akasha	Spirit	Black	Oval

Earth tattva

Water tattva

Fire tattva

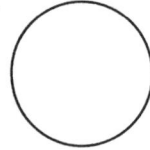

Air tattva

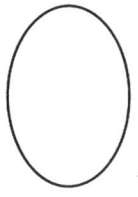

Spirit tattva

These are used to construct twenty-five combined tattvas, which are made simply by laying a small image of one tattva on a larger image of the other. For example, Fire of Water (Tejas of Apas) is a small red triangle superimposed on a silver crescent, while Water of Air (Apas of Vayu) is a small silver crescent superimposed over a blue circle.

The tattvas were heavily used in the Golden Dawn as a tool for training clairvoyance; students would sit and concentrate on a tattva—primary or combined—and then shift the gaze to a blank white wall, where the phantom image of the tattva in complementary colors would appear. With practice, this can be turned into an imaginary doorway through which the clairvoyant can pass into the elemental realm symbolized by the tattva. The practice spread out of Golden Dawn circles relatively early and now plays a part in many magical training programs.

The system of Hindu esotericism that included the tattvas also provided the Golden Dawn with the lore of the tattvic tides; *SEE* TATTVIC TIDES. *SEE ALSO* CLAIRVOYANCE; ELEMENTS, MAGICAL. FURTHER READING: REGARDIE 1971.

tattvic tides. A system of energy tides that moves through the Earth's etheric body, cycling from east to west. There are five phases in the tattvic tides, which take their names from the five tattvas; *SEE* TATTVAS.

The system of tattvic tides was originally borrowed into Western occultism from Hindu Tantrism by way of an early Theosophical book, *Nature's Finer Forces* by Rama Prasad; a summary of this book was circulated as a teaching document in the Hermetic Order of the Golden Dawn in that order's early years. Later on, the tattvic tides were also adopted by the Aurum Solis and renamed "velocia" (Latin, "swift ones"). *SEE* AURUM SOLIS; GOLDEN DAWN, HERMETIC ORDER OF THE.

The cycle of tattvic tides begins at dawn with the Akasha tattva, which represents Spirit. This is said to be "in course" for twenty minutes, and is followed by the Vayu or Air tattva. After another twenty minutes comes the Tejas or Fire tattva, then the Apas or Water tattva, and finally the Prithivi or Earth tattva, each at twenty-minute intervals. The whole cycle takes a total of two hours, and repeats itself twelve times in the course of a day and night.

In magical practice, the tattvic tides are used in elemental workings in much the same way as the planetary hours are used in planetary magic. Workings of a particular element, or for purposes that harmonize with some elemental influence, are done while the corresponding tattva is in course.

Some confusion exists between the tattvic tides and a set of seasonal tides discussed in some magical writings. SEE SEASONAL TIDES. FURTHER READING: DENNING AND PHILLIPS 1988, REGARDIE 1971.

tattwas. SEE TATTVAS.

Tau. (Hebrew TV, "cross") The twenty-second and last letter of the Hebrew alphabet, a double letter with the sound-values *t* and *th*. Its numerical value is 400, and its standard magical symbolism is as follows:

> *Path of the Tree of Life:* Path 32, from Yesod to Malkuth.
>
> *Astrological Correspondence:* The planet Saturn.
>
> *tarot Correspondence:* Trump XXI, The World.
>
> *Part of the Cube of Space:* The center.
>
> *Colors:* in Atziluth—indigo.
>
>> in Briah—black.
>>
>> in Yetzirah—bluish black.
>>
>> in Assiah—black rayed with blue.

The corresponding text from *The Thirty-two Paths of Wisdom* runs: "The Thirty-second Path is the Administrative Intelligence, and is so called because it directs and associates the seven planets in all their operations, each of them in its own due course." SEE ALSO CABALA; HEBREW ALPHABET.

Hebrew letter Tau

Taurus. (Latin, "bull") The second sign of the zodiac, a fixed earth sign of feminine polarity. In Taurus, Venus is the ruler, the moon is exalted, and Mars in is his detriment. This sign governs the throat and neck. SEE ZODIAC.

The sun is in Taurus approximately from April 21 to May 21. People with this sun placement are traditionally reliable, steady, calm, persistent, and capable of hard work; they can also be greedy, possessive, and intolerant of change.

In the Golden Dawn tarot system, Taurus corresponds to Trump V, the Hierophant. SEE HIEROPHANT, THE; TAROT.

Astrological symbol of Taurus

Taylor, Thomas. English philosopher and Pagan, 1758–1835. Born in London to working-class parents, he was a sickly child and was taken to Staffordshire at the age of six as a result of ill health. Returning to London three years later, he was enrolled at St. Paul's School, and quickly showed a talent for classical languages and a fascination with philosophy. His father wished him to become a Protestant minister, a profession that held less than no interest for Taylor. He spent three years in his teens working at a dockyard and two more as the assistant to a minister, during which time he worked further on his mastery of languages.

At the age of twelve, he met Mary Morton, the daughter of a local coal merchant, and the two fell in love. Remarkably, the relationship proved lifelong. When Taylor was twenty, Mary's father decided to marry her to a wealthy man, and she and Taylor responded by arranging to get married at once. They had no money at all, and Taylor was forced to work for a time as an usher at a private school, then found a position at a bank. He spent nights in study, first learning mathematics and chemistry, then the works of Aristotle, and finally the writings of Plato and Plotinus. These last converted him not only to Platonic philosophy but also to an unabashed Greek Paganism, which he practiced and upheld publicly for the rest of his life.

During this time, he published his first book, a mathematical treatise, and designed an ever-burning lamp, which he demonstrated at Freemasons' Tavern in London. The demonstration ended with a fire that nearly burnt down the building, but brought him to the attention of wealthy patrons who enabled him to quit his job and begin working full time as a writer and translator. The result was a steady stream of capable, erudite English translations that eventually included every significant work of Platonist philosophy and Greek mythology, as well as many other important philosophical works.

These translations and his lectures on Platonism brought Taylor into contact with artistic and scholarly circles in England and elsewhere. He became assistant secretary of the Society of Arts, a position that paid his bills while requiring little of his time, and counted as friends major artists of the time such as William Blake and John Flaxman. His open Paganism, which extended to the point of pouring libations of wine to Jupiter and sacrificing lambs to a variety of Greek gods, brought down on him the denunciations of Christian critics. He responded in kind, publicly dismissing Christianity as a "bastardized and barbarous" religion which would someday give way to a renewal of the Platonized Paganism he loved.

His works were enormously influential in Britain, where they became standard reading for two generations of Romantic poets, and in America, where they were prized by the Transcendentalists; SEE TRANSCENDENTALISM. His overt Paganism also had a major impact in Britain, where revived Greek Paganism became a living tradition among poets and intellectuals during and after Taylor's lifetime, and played an important part in setting the stage for the modern Neopagan revival; SEE NEOPAGANISM. SEE ALSO PAGANISM; PLATONISM. FURTHER READING: TAYLOR 1969, TAYLOR 1972.

Tebel. (Hebrew ThBL, "world") In Cabalistic lore, one of the seven earths, corresponding (with Cheled) to Yesod and Malkuth. SEE CHELED; EARTHS, SEVEN.

Tebel Vilon Shamayim. SEE VILON.

Teiwaz. SEE TIWAZ.

telesmatic imagery. In ceremonial magic, a visualized image used to represent a magical force. The use of telesmatic imagery can be traced back to ancient times, when specialized images of gods and spirits were imagined in ritual work, with attributes and symbols that helped represent the energies channeled through them in magical work. Ancient magical handbooks such as the Graeco-Egyptian magical papyri frequently instruct the magician to imagine a god or a spirit according to an exact description, of which every detail has some symbolic meaning. SEE GRAECO-EGYPTIAN MAGICAL PAPYRI.

This tradition was carried onwards by the Arabic magicians of the Middle Ages, and passed into Europe with the transmission of Arabic magical handbooks such as the *Picatrix*; SEE PICATRIX. It was probably the source of the bizarre descriptions of demons in the grimoires of late medieval and early modern Europe, although the key to interpretation had been lost in this latter case and very few attempts to decode this particular symbolic language seem to have been made in modern times. SEE GOETIA; GRIMOIRE.

The transformations of magical theory in the nineteenth-century magical renaissance favored a more analytical, interpretive approach to imagery, and the vast confusion of traditional magical imagery gave way, in at least some cases, to something more coherent. In the Hermetic Order of the Golden Dawn, which played an important role in this trend, traditional telesmatic images were supplemented or replaced by a system which built up images based on letters of the Hebrew alphabet. This approach permitted magicians trained in the system to manufacture telesmatic images at will for any desired magical energy. SEE GOLDEN DAWN, HERMETIC ORDER OF THE.

The Golden Dawn system was borrowed by some of its successor orders and imitators but, like many of the more complex dimensions of the order's system, it has seen little use in recent years. Meanwhile, many practicing magicians have made use of the bizarre imagery of the old grimoires, but few seem to have realized that these images were probably intended to communicate specific information about the forces they symbolize. FURTHER READING: GREER 1997, REGARDIE 1971.

Temperance. The fourteenth Major Arcanum of the tarot, commonly showing a woman or angel pouring liquid from one vessel to another; this is a conventional Renaissance emblem of temperance, and represents the old custom of watering down strong wine to make it less intoxicating. In the Golden Dawn system, this Arcanum is assigned to the Hebrew letter Samech, while the French system assigns it to Nun. Its common divinatory meanings are combination of forces, reconciliation, moderation, and arbitration.

The magical title for this Arcanum is "Daughter of the Reconcilers, the Bringer Forth of Life." SEE ALSO TAROT.

Tarot trump Temperance (Universal tarot)

Templars. SEE KNIGHTS TEMPLAR.

temple, magical. In modern occult practice, the space in which magical operations are carried out. Despite the impressive title, most "magical temples" in present-day occultism are spare bedrooms converted to magical use, with magical circles or other diagrams traced on the floor and appropriate symbolic decorations on the walls, when they are not simply magicians' living rooms or bedrooms put to use for magical practice. Several useful books are available giving detailed instructions for assembling the equipment necessary for a magical temple.

The term *magical temple* is also used in the Golden Dawn tradition, as well as some others, for a magical lodge. SEE LODGE, MAGICAL. FURTHER READING: CICERO AND CICERO 1992, WANG 1980.

Temple of Set. International magical order dedicated to the Left-Hand Path, founded in 1975 by Michael Aquino and a group of former members of the Church of Satan; SEE CHURCH OF SATAN. Less colorful but far more serious than its parent organization, the Temple of Set is one of the few currently active organizations presenting a detailed philosophical and practical system of what, by almost every other branch of the Western occult traditions, would be considered evil magic.

Based in San Francisco, the Temple of Set offers six degrees of initiation: Setian I°, Adept II°, Priest/Priestess of Set III°, Magister/Magistra Templi IV°, Magus/Maga V°, and Ipsissimus/Ipsissima VI°. The first of these is a probationary degree, the second the principal degree in which work is done. The remaining degrees are specialized religious offices that are conferred by the Temple hierarchy. Members who join and are admitted to the first degree are required to qualify for the second within two years or face loss of membership.

Local groups within the temple are Pylons; some of these are geographically localized, while others are "correspondence Pylons" that draw their membership from around the world. The temple also has a series of orders, which are special-interest groups focusing on specific magical arts, or the magical traditions of particular cultures. The most widely known of the orders is the Order of the Trapezoid, which makes use of occult material previously used by German National Socialist occultists; SEE NATIONAL SOCIALISM. As of this writing there are apparently nine orders in existence.

Temple of Set writings draw a distinction between consciousness-worshipping religions—the class to which the temple belongs—and nature-worshipping religions, a class which includes nearly all others. These latter are considered to be emotional crutches for those unable or unwilling to stand up for themselves, and renunciation of all other religious commitments is one of the conditions for advancement to the second degree in the temple. Antinomianism—that is, rejection and denial of conventional morality—is seen as an essential part of the process of breaking free of the "herd mentality," and self-discipline, intellectual clarity, and individual autonomy are other important elements of the Setian path.

Magical workings are done to accomplish the personal will of the magician. The idea that magic (or other actions) should be carried out in harmony with the universe, or the will of God or the gods, is rejected completely.

The goal of the Setian path is the attainment of individual godhood, which is understood as eternal, isolated self-consciousness, separate from nature and the natural universe. It is interesting to note that this goal is fairly close to the concept of eternal damnation accepted by mystics and philosophers in many of the world's major religions.

Setians hold that the present aeon, the Aeon of Set, began with the founding of the Temple of Set in 1975, and that the Word of the aeon is *Xeper* (pronounced "kheffer"), an ancient Egyptian word meaning "to come into being." *SEE* AEON. *SEE ALSO* SATANISM.

Temple of Solomon. The most important building in Western occult symbolism, the Temple of Solomon was built in Jerusalem in the middle of the tenth century B.C.E. It was a rectangular building of stone, cedar, and gold, 60 cubits (about 103 feet) long, 20 cubits (around 34 feet) wide, and 30 cubits (around 52 feet) high. The entrance faced east, and was flanked by two brass pillars named Jachin ("stability") and Boaz ("strength"). Within was the sanctuary, 40 cubits long, and beyond that the Holy of Holies, the inner chamber in which the Ark of the Covenant and a few other sacred items were kept. The Holy of Holies was off limits to all but the High Priest himself, who entered it once a year.

The temple was destroyed in 586 B.C.E. by the Assyrian Empire after an unsuccessful rebellion on the part of the Jews, and it remained in ruins for some seventy years, during which the Assyrian Empire gave way to a short-lived Babylonian Empire and much of the population of Israel was deported to Babylon. When the Babylonian

Empire fell to the Persians, the new conquerors allowed the Jews to return home, and a new temple was built along the lines of the old. This was massively remodeled by Herod the Great, king of Judea, starting about 20 B.C.E., and destroyed down to the foundations in 70 C.E. by the Romans.

The detailed descriptions of the temple and its furnishings in the Old Testament (1 Kings 5:15–7:51 and 2 Chronicles 1:18–5:1) have prompted speculation, calculation, and fantasy for well over two thousand years. The medieval Knights Templar had their original headquarters on the site of the temple and took their name from it; *SEE* KNIGHTS TEMPLAR. The core mythology of Freemasonry centers on the building of the temple, and Masons whose enthusiasm exceeds their historical knowledge still sometimes claim that Masonry can trace its foundations to the time of Solomon; *SEE* FREEMASONRY. The measurements and proportions of the temple, as described in the scriptural passages listed above, have also been heavily drawn on by students of the Cabala and sacred geometry from the Middle Ages onward. *SEE* CABALA; SACRED GEOMETRY. *SEE ALSO* SOLOMON. FURTHER READING: STIRLING 1999, YATES 1979.

Temple ov Psychick Youth, Thee (TOPY). British avant-garde magical order, founded in 1981 by industrial music performer Genesis P-Orridge. As much a work of performance art as a traditional occult society, TOPY derived its magical system partly from P-Orridge's interest in body modification and extreme experiences, partly from the work of English magician Austin Osman Spare (1886–1956); *SEE* SPARE, AUSTIN OSMAN. Its manifesto, the *Grey Book*, proclaims majick (the preferred TOPY spelling) as a liberating activity that uses "implicit powers of thee human brain (neuromancy) linked with guiltless sexuality focused through thee will structure (sigils)," and explicitly rejects "mystification, gods or demons" (TOPY n.d.). TOPY documents consistently use "thee" for "the," "ov" for "of," "coum" for "come," and several other nonstandard spelling habits, in an effort, as TOPY members might put it, to majickally overcoum thee grip ov thee habitual and conventional. In organizational terms, TOPY is a non-hierarchical tribal network with very little in the way of visible structure. During its period of greatest popularity, from 1980 to 1992, nearly the only semblance of organization it had was P-Orridge himself, who served as de facto head of the temple between stints on the road with his music group, Psychic TV. After P-Orridge relinquished leadership of the temple in 1992 and attempted (without noticeable effect) to dissolve it, the temple evolved a nonstructured structure consisting of three Stations (in Britain, Europe, and the United States) and a scattering of local groups called Access Points. It became registered as a nonprofit religious organization in 1993.

The rituals and teachings of TOPY, like those of most Chaos magic systems, are founded on an attempt to strip magical practice of all theistic and dogmatic elements, in favor of a purely technical approach. Orgasm, body fluids, and chanting play a central role. Members of TOPY, in order to become initiates of the temple, are required to create a sigil by writing down a favorite sexual fantasy and anointing it with three different body fluids and hair from two body areas at the twenty-third hour of the twenty-third day of the month. The sigil is then sent into headquarters, where according to TOPY it serves to build up a reservoir of psychic energy for members to draw on. When this has been done twenty-three times, the person who does so is an Initiate. Initiates take majickal names that consist of the names "Coyote," "Kali," or "Eden" followed by a number.

TOPY reached its highest degree of publicity in 1992, when British police raided P-Orridge's home in Brighton, hoping to find evidence of Satanic ritual abuse; SEE SATANIC RITUAL ABUSE. The material found there, although it did not include anything relating to Satanic ritual abuse, did keep the British tabloids busy for months, and probably attracted more people to TOPY than any of the temple's own publicity projects.

The temple remains active at present, with Access Points in a variety of American, British, and European cities. It boasts a substantial online presence as well. SEE ALSO CHAOS MAGIC. FURTHER READING: KINNEY 1994, TOPY N.D.

Temple Solaire. (Solar Temple) Occult organization founded in 1984 by Belgian occultist and homeopath Luc Jouret (1947–1994), drawing on materials from the French Templar revival of the nineteenth and twentieth centuries. A successful figure in the alternative healing scene in France, Switzerland, and Canada, Jouret made contact with the diverse occult communities in Geneva, Switzerland, and Montreal, Quebec. He was briefly a member of the Renewed Order of the Temple, a Neo-Templar order headed by right-wing politician Julien Origas. Jouret left the Renewed Order of the Temple in 1984 and founded his own organization immediately thereafter. SEE KNIGHTS TEMPLAR.

To the occult teachings standard in French Neo-Templar orders, Jouret added his own interest in alternative health, and a growing concern that environmental pollution would lead to a catastrophe that would destroy the Earth. By the late 1980s he and other members of his group were in contact with survivalists and Christian "end time" groups in Canada and the United States. The Temple Solaire concealed itself behind two spiritual groups, Club Amenta and Club Archédia, which made no reference to Jouret's growing apocalyptic fantasies.

Despite this concealment, the actual intentions of the Temple Solaire leaked out, largely through the revelations of disgruntled ex-members. Both Club Amenta and Club Archédia were dissolved, and several Temple members—including Jouret—were brought up on charges of possessing illegal weapons. Jouret and his remaining followers retreated to isolated bases in Switzerland and Canada. There, on October 5, 1994, fifty-three members of the Temple Solaire, adults and children, died of gunshot wounds, many of them self-inflicted. Jouret's body was among those found in the Swiss base. He left behind a series of papers claiming that he and the other members of the temple were leaving behind their physical bodies in order to escape the Earth on the eve of its destruction. SEE ALSO CHRISTIAN IDENTITY.

Tempus Consilii. (Latin, "time of planning") The Aurum Solis name for the season of autumn. SEE AURUM SOLIS; SEASONAL TIDES.

Tempus Eversionis. (Latin, "time of destruction") The Aurum Solis name for the season of winter. SEE AURUM SOLIS; SEASONAL TIDES.

Tempus Messis. (Latin, "time of harvest") The Aurum Solis name for the season of summer. *SEE* AURUM SOLIS; SEASONAL TIDES.

Tempus Sementis. (Latin, "time of sowing") The Aurum Solis name for the season of spring. *SEE* AURUM SOLIS; SEASONAL TIDES.

temurah. (Hebrew, "permutation") One of the three classical methods of Cabalistic analysis, temurah is a method by which one Hebrew letter may be replaced by another. In one sense, this forms a simple substitution cipher—or, rather, a whole series of them, since there are many different systems of temurah. In Cabalistic analysis, the letters of a word can be transformed through temurah to create another word, which can be seen as the "hidden meaning" of the first word.

For example, the method of temurah known as Atbash (in Hebrew, AThBSh, from its first two pairs) turns each letter of the Hebrew alphabet into its equivalent on the alphabet's other end—thus Aleph, the first letter, becomes Tau, the last letter, and vice versa; Beth, the second letter, becomes Shin, the next to last letter, and so on. If we take Baphomet, the name of the idol supposedly worshipped by the Knights Templar, and transliterate it into Hebrew, the result is בפומת, BPhVMTh. If this is put through temurah using Atbash, the result is שופיא. SVPhIA, Sophia or Divine Wisdom. Whether or not this is what the name Baphomet was actually intended to conceal is anybody's guess—which points up the major problem of temurah as an interpretive tool. *SEE* BAPHOMET; KNIGHTS TEMPLAR.

Among the most widely used forms of temurah is Aiq Beker, also called the Cabala of Nine Chambers; *SEE* AIQ BEKER. *SEE ALSO* CABALA; GEMATRIA; NOTARIQON.

ten. In Pythagorean number symbolism, ten is the completion of number, and all the important number ratios in Pythagorean practice are derived from it. Its titles include "All," "Fate," "Eternity," "Trust," and "God." There are ten points in the tetractys, the core Pythagorean number diagram; *SEE* TETRACTYS.

In the Cabala, ten is Malkuth, the tenth Sephirah, and also the number of the letter Yod. It is also the number of Sephiroth in the Tree of Life as a whole. The Name of God with ten letters is ALHIM TzBAVTh, Elohim Tzabaoth. *SEE* CABALA.

In Renaissance magical symbolism, ten is called the end and completion of numbers. It is the number of perfection, and represents the power of multiplicity. *SEE ALSO* ARITHMOLOGY. FURTHER READING: MCLEAN 1994, WATERFIELD 1988, WESTCOTT 1984.

terms, astrological. A set of correspondences between five of the seven traditional planets and various segments of the zodiac; the sun and moon have no terms. Terms are of different lengths, and follow no easily understood scheme. For example, the first six degrees of Aries are the term of Jupiter; the next eight (from 7 to 14 degrees) are the term of Venus; next comes the term of Mercury, from 15 to 21 degrees; after that are the terms of Mars, from 22 to 26 degrees, and Saturn from 27 to 30 degrees.

The terms were introduced to astrology in ancient Greek times, and form (along with decans and dodecatemoria) one of the mostly forgotten complexities of ancient astrology. *SEE* DECANS; DODECATEMORY. The terms are primarily used nowadays in horary astrology. *SEE ALSO* ASTROLOGY; HORARY ASTROLOGY. FURTHER READING: APPLEBY 1985.

Terrebia. *SEE* GAIA HYPOTHESIS.

Teth. (Hebrew TTh, "serpent") The ninth letter of the Hebrew alphabet, a single letter with the sound-value *t*. Its numerical value is nine, and its standard magical symbolism is as follows:

> *Path of the Tree of Life:* Path 19, from Chesed to Geburah.
>
> *Astrological Correspondence:* Leo.
>
> *tarot Correspondence:* Trump VIII, Strength.
>
> *Part of the Cube of Space:* The southeast edge.
>
> *Colors:* in Atziluth—lemon yellow.
>
> in Briah—deep purple.
>
> in Yetzirah—gray.
>
> in Assiah—reddish amber.

The corresponding text of the *Thirty-two Paths of Wisdom* runs: "The Nineteenth Path is the Intelligence of the secret of all the activities of the spiritual beings, and is so called because of the influence that is diffused by it from the most high, exalted, and sublime glory." *SEE ALSO* CABALA; HEBREW ALPHABET.

Hebrew letter Teth

tetractys. In Pythagorean number mysticism, a triangular arrangement of ten points or numbers, arranged in rows of one, two, three, and four, as follows:

Pythagoreans called this "the fount and root of visible nature," and swore their most solemn oaths by it. It played roughly the same role in Pythagorean symbolism in ancient times and the Renaissance as the Tree of Life plays in modern Cabalism. In particular, it was used as a key to the quadrivium, the four Pythagorean disciplines of mystical mathematics—arithmetic, geometry, music, and astronomy; *SEE* QUADRIVIUM. For example, the four rows of points represented the numbers one, two, three, and four, the foundations of Pythagorean number theory. Similarly, they could be used to construct the three basic intervals in music theory—the octave, which is formed by a 1:2 ratio in string length; the fifth, formed by a 2:3 ratio; and the fourth, formed by a 3:4 ratio.

The tetraktys appears in various forms in the symbolism and imagery of Western occultism. Like most aspects of the Pythagorean tradition, however, it has received little attention in the occult community in recent years. *SEE ALSO* PYTHAGORAS. FURTHER READING: GUTHRIE 1987, HENINGER 1974.

Tetragrammaton. (Greek, "word of four letters") The most holy of the names of God in Cabala, as well as in the Jewish religion, the Tetragrammaton consists of the four letters יהוה (Yod, Heh, Vau, Heh). Most modern scholars give its pronunciation as Yahweh, while an older tradition with roots in the early Christian church transliterates it as Jehovah (which in classical Latin, the language in which this version was first written, is pronounced Yehowah). Many modern magicians "pronounce" it, even in ritual practice, simply by spelling it out letter by letter. Observant Jews do not pronounce it at all, and where it occurs in the scriptures, the name Adonai ("Lord") is read instead.

The word itself is probably an archaic form of the Hebrew verb "to be," and may mean something like "He Who Is." Especially in the old pronunciation "Yehowah," though, it bears a close resemblance to a whole family of names of gods and holy words in various ancient traditions—for example, the Roman title of Jupiter, Jove (in classical Latin, pronounced "Yoweh") or the Gnostic divine name IAO. The whole tradition may have its roots in the ancient use of vowel sequences as words of power; *SEE* VOWELS.

In the Cabala, which has taken the Tetragrammaton as one of its major themes, an immense and complex symbolism has been developed out of it. The four Cabalistic worlds of Atziluth, Briah, Yetzirah, and Assiah each correspond to one of the letters of the Name, which has a special pronunciation in each world; this, in turn, gives rise to the secret name of the world. *SEE* ASSIAH; ATZILUTH; BRIAH; YETZIRAH. The letters of the Tetragrammaton are also rearranged by Cabalists into a total of twelve names of power, called the Twelve Banners of the Name, each of which corresponds to one of the twelve tribes of Israel, the twelve signs of the zodiac, and so forth. All these permutations have their magical uses.

The English poet Robert Graves, whose work with the ancient Celtic Ogham alphabet brought it to the attention of the modern Pagan movement, claimed that the correct pronunciation of the Tetragrammaton could be found in Ogham sources. His version was YIEUOAO; this does not seem to have caught on in occult circles, however. *SEE* OGHAM. *SEE ALSO* BARBAROUS NAMES; CABALA; HEBREW ALPHABET. FURTHER READING: TYSON 1998.

TGAOTU. Masonic abbreviation for the phrase "the Great Architect of the Universe," sometimes used in ritual texts outside of Masonry and occasionally mistaken for a *nomen barbarum*. One of Dion Fortune's essays recounts her discovery of a ritual that seemed to address the divine by the "holy name" Tegatoo; this proved, on further research, to be TGAOTU. SEE FREEMASONRY; BARBAROUS NAMES.

Tharsis. In Cabalistic magic, ruler of the element of water. Her name is derived from that of the Tharsishim or Tarshishim, the angelic host corresponding (in some accounts) to the Sephirah Netzach. SEE RULER, ELEMENTAL; TARSHISHIM; TREE OF LIFE.

thaumaturgy. (Greek *thaumaturgeia*, from *thaumata*, "wonders," and *ergon*, "work") The branch of magical practice directed toward causing change in the universe of experience. It is contrasted with theurgy, the branch of magical practice directed toward the transformation of the magician. SEE MAGIC.

In some modern Pagan traditions, "thaumaturgy" is used to mean magic that is done without invoking divine energies, while "theurgy" is magic in which the gods are invoked. SEE ALSO THEURGY.

Thaumiel. (Hebrew ThAVMIAL, "Twins of God") In Cabalistic lore, the Qlippoth or demonic powers associated with Kether, the first Sphere of the Tree of Life. The traditional form of the Thaumiel is giant dual heads with batlike wings, but no bodies. SEE QLIPPOTH.

Thelema. (Greek, "will") A religion founded by English magus Aleister Crowley (1875–1947) and propagated by his followers since his death. The central text of Thelema is the *Book of the Law*, which was revealed to Crowley in 1904 by a disembodied intelligence named Aiwass; SEE BOOK OF THE LAW.

The central teaching of Thelema is that every soul is eternal, and possesses a "True Will" or essential purpose that is the law under which it lives. During each incarnation, the soul seeks to find and accomplish its true will. Any action in harmony with one's true will is good, whether or not it corresponds to ordinary ideas of morality, while every action not in harmony with one's true will is wrong. In the standard Thelemite phrasing, "Thou hast no right but to do thy will."

Another aspect of Thelemite belief has to do with cosmic cycles in which a succession of gods or ruling spiritual powers replaces one another at the helm of the cosmos. The writing of the *Book of the Law*, according to Thelema, marked the end of the Aeon of Osiris—an age in which virtue consisted of sacrifice and self-abasement—and the beginning of the Aeon of Horus, the age of the Crowned and Conquering Child, in which will and the unabashed fulfilment of desires are the dominant themes. The aeons seem to be roughly equivalent to the twelve great months of the cycle of precession. SEE CYCLES, COSMIC; PRECESSION OF THE EQUINOXES.

Most organized Thelemic activity at present is associated with the Ordo Templi Orientis (OTO), a magical lodge organization taken over by Crowley in the 1920s and reshaped into a vehicle for the Thelemite revelation. SEE ORDO TEMPLI ORIENTIS (OTO). The Gnostic Mass, a ritual written by Crowley, is celebrated by most OTO groups as the principal public rite of Thelema. SEE ALSO CROWLEY, ALEISTER. FURTHER READING: CROWLEY 1975, DUQUETTE 1993.

Theon, Max. European? occultist, c. 1848–1927. One of the most enigmatic figures in modern occult history, Theon successfully concealed most of the details about his origin from contemporary and modern researchers. His name may originally have been Louis Maximilian Bimstein, and he was probably of Jewish ancestry, though whether he came from eastern Europe or the Middle East is disputed. Certainly he seems to have been in Poland at the time of the unsuccessful anti-Russian risings of 1863. Beyond that, his early biography is a blank.

He was apparently in Paris in 1870, and in England by 1873. There he established a business as a spiritual healer, and in 1885 married Mary Ware, a spiritualist medium and lecturer who had founded an organization called the Universal Philosophical Society during the previous year. SEE SPIRITUALISM.

In 1884, Theon had already set in motion a much more important organization, with an advertisement in a new reprint of the *Corpus Hermeticum*; SEE CORPUS HERMETICUM. This invited "Students of the Occult Science, Searchers after Truth, and Theosophists" to apply for membership in an occult brotherhood. That brotherhood was the Hermetic Brotherhood of Luxor (H. B. of L.), which grew to become one of the major occult organizations of the nineteenth-century magical revival and played a central role in the prehistory of such later occult societies as the Ordo Templi Orientis and the Church of Light. *SEE* HERMETIC BROTHERHOOD OF LUXOR (H. B. OF L.).

After launching the brotherhood, Theon seems to have left its management almost entirely to his disciple Peter Davidson (1837–1915) and Davidson's associate T. H. Burgoyne (c. 1855–c. 1895). *SEE* BURGOYNE, THOMAS HENRY. In 1886, just in time to avoid the scandal that largely wrecked the H. B. of L., Theon moved to what was then the French colony of Algeria, where he and his wife settled at Tlemcen. Their home became the headquarters of a new organization, the Groupe Cosmique. The Groupe published a journal, the *Revue Cosmique*, and developed an extensive occult philosophy that was very influential in France.

The *Philosophie Cosmique*, embodied in more than 10,000 pages of text, has substantial similarities to the teachings Theon introduced by way of the H. B. of L. Sexual magic was dropped, however, to be replaced with material drawn from Hindu sources, and with an increased focus on the goal of physical immortality. Increasingly central to Theon's work in this last phase of his career was "pathotisme," which he claimed was the ancient form of magnetism (in Mesmer's sense of the word), and combined polarity work with inner plane experience through trance, as a way of obtaining occult knowledge. *SEE* MESMERISM; PATHOTISME; POLARITY.

Theon, true to form, published most of the *Philosophie Cosmique* under the pseudonym Aia Aziz, and continued to avoid the limelight even while managing a sizeable esoteric organization. His death in 1927 remains one of the few details about him that is known with some degree of certainty. FURTHER READING: GODWIN ET AL. 1995, RHONE 2000.

Theophilus of Adana. In Christian legend, the original example of a person who made a pact with the Devil. While the story is set in the early sixth century C.E., it was apparently written between 650 and 850 and all evidence suggests that it is a work of pious fiction with no basis in history.

According to the story, Theophilus was the steward of the church of Adana. When the bishop of Adana died, he was asked to take the position, but he insisted that he did not feel worthy of the office and wished to remain steward. Another man was elected, and the new bishop proceeded to replace Theophilus and appoint a new steward. Resentment and pride worked on Theophilus for months, and finally he went to a Jewish sorcerer who lived in the town. The sorcerer summoned the Devil, and Theophilus signed and sealed a paper denying Christ and the Virgin Mary in exchange for being restored to his position.

The next day, Theophilus found himself summoned to the bishop's house and restored to his position. After a time, though, guilt began to gnaw at him; he repented, and proceeded to invoke the Virgin Mary with prayer and fasting. The Virgin miraculously gave Theophilus back the paper he had signed, and Theophilus, confessing his sins and distributing all his wealth to the poor, died and was carried off to Heaven.

The written pact in the tale was simply a statement that Theophilus rejected Christ and the Virgin—that is, the two primary figures in Christian mythology. It took a history of elaborations and developments to shape this into the diabolic pact of later Christian legend. *SEE* PACT. *SEE ALSO* SATANISM. FURTHER READING: P. PALMER 1936.

Theosebia. *SEE* ZOSIMUS OF PANOPOLIS.

theosophical reduction. *SEE* AIQ BEKER.

Theosophical Society. The single most important force in the nineteenth-century renaissance of occultism, the Theosophical Society was founded in 1875 in New York City by Helena Petrovna Blavatsky, Colonel H. S. Olcott, and several other people interested in occult matters. For the first few years of its existence, it was indistinguishable from the hundreds of other small occult groups throughout the Western world at that time, and for a time even had the standard lodge hardware of passwords, grades, and recognition signs. In Blavatsky, though, it had a resource no other group could match, and with the publication of her first book *Isis Unveiled* (1877) the fledgling society was on its way to international prominence.

Isis Unveiled was largely based on existing Western occult teachings; unlike later Theosophical writings, for instance, it rejected the idea of reincarnation except in special cases, and spoke approvingly of practical occultism. *SEE* REINCARNATION. Its very similarity to other occult systems in the contemporary West, though, limited its spread, and for the first decade or so the society was relatively small.

In late 1878 Blavatsky, Olcott, and a few other Theosophists left New York and, after a brief stay in England, arrived in India in 1879 and established a base at Adyar, near Madras. During the next few years the society was closely linked to the Arya Samaj, a movement for Hindu national and religious renewal. Blavatsky's writings and publicity activities brought a steady stream of European visitors, and an assortment of minor miracles tittilated the press.

In 1884 Blavatsky and Olcott returned to England, where they lectured to huge crowds and launched the Theosophical Society in Europe on a massive scale. While they were away, Blavatsky's housekeeper in Adyar contacted local journalists with details of how she and her husband had faked "miracles" at Blavatsky's behest. The prestigious Society for Psychical Research sent an investigator at once. Before Blavatsky could return home, the investigator had turned up damning evidence of deliberate fakery. The resulting scandal was carried by newspapers on five continents but did little to slow the society's meteoric growth.

Blavatsky returned to London as the furor over the faked "phenomena" died down, and spent the last years of her life there, managing the society and organizing an inner circle, the Esoteric Section, which offered instruction in certain kinds of practical occultism and may have been intended to compete with magical orders such as the Hermetic Brotherhood of Luxor and the Hermetic Order of the Golden Dawn. *SEE* GOLDEN DAWN, HERMETIC ORDER OF THE; HERMETIC BROTHERHOOD OF LUXOR (H. B. OF L.).

She also devoted much time to writing a second vast book, *The Secret Doctrine*. Heavily influenced by her study of Hindu and Buddhist writings, *The Secret Doctrine* takes the form of a huge commentary on the *Stanzas of Dzyan*, which Blavatsky claimed was the oldest book in the world. In the course of elucidating the *Stanzas*, *The Secret Doctrine* unfolds a sprawling cosmology of rays, rounds, planes, root races, lost continents, and immortal sages. In an about-face from *Isis Unveiled*, *The Secret Doctrine* (like all Blavatsky's work after her time in India) embraced reincarnation and rejected practical occultism in favor of philosophical study, meditation, and devotion to the Mahatmas. In the process it set the tone for most of what became standard Theosophical teaching.

On Blavatsky's death in 1891, the society descended into a series of disputes over leadership and direction. The new head of the order, Annie Besant, had vast energy and enthusiasm but little tact and less ability to compromise, and under her leadership the society suffered a series of devastating schisms. In 1895 most of America's Theosophists formed a new organization under the leadership of William Quan Judge. The year 1909 saw the departure of G. R. S. Mead, a close friend of Blavatsky and a highly respected occult scholar, who founded the Quest Society in London, and the same year the United Lodge of Theosophists was founded in Los Angeles by Robert Crosbie and another body of dissidents. In 1913, the president of the German section of the Theosophical Society, Rudolf Steiner, took more than 90 percent of Germany's Theosophists with him into his new Anthroposophical Society.

Several of these schisms had their roots in some of the new directions Besant and her close associate, C. W. Leadbeater, took the society. Besant had been initiated into Co-Masonry, a small Masonic order that admitted women as well as men, and promoted it through Theosophical channels; Leadbeater had become a bishop in the Liberal Catholic Church, a mystical Christian group with roots in the clerical underworld of independent bishops. *SEE* FREEMASONRY; INDEPENDENT BISHOPS; LIBERAL CATHOLIC CHURCH (LCC). For a variety of reasons, both these involvements gave offense to many longtime Theosophists.

More serious over the long term was the Order of the Star in the East, founded by Besant to promote Jiddu Krishnamurti—the son of a servant at the Theosophical Society headquarters in Adyar—as the Messiah of the New Age. Founded in 1911, the order was extremely successful for a time, but it collapsed suddenly in 1929 when Krishnamurti himself disavowed the claims being made in his name. *SEE* STAR IN THE EAST, ORDER OF THE.

This last blow came close to wrecking the society, and its membership plunged to 33,000 by 1935. It survived, however, and has continued its work on a small scale, elaborating the teachings bequeathed to it by Blavatsky and carrying out several successful publishing ventures. SEE ALSO BLAVATSKY, HELENA PETROVNA; THEOSOPHY. FURTHER READING: BLAVATSKY 1877, BLAVATSKY 1888, GODWIN ET AL. 1995.

theosophy (Christian mystical). (Greek *theosopheia*, "divine wisdom") A tradition of Christian occultism dating from the sixteenth century, and unrelated to the teachings of the Theosophical Society (founded in 1875); for the latter, SEE THEOSOPHY.

The word "theosophy" first appears in the writings of Greek Neoplatonists such as Porphyry and Iamblichus, where it means "wisdom concerning the gods." In Christian writers of the Middle Ages, it was a synonym for "theology." Late in the Renaissance, however, it came to be used for a new movement of thought that combined classic Christian mysticism with alchemical ideas, and often with various other branches of occult theory and practice.

To this new theosophy, God, nature, and humanity all shared similar deep structures, which could be traced by way of the doctrine of correspondences. The processes that transformed lead into gold in the alchemical retort were mirrored by those that transformed the unredeemed human soul through illumination in the retort of the human body. In the writings of the more daring theosophers, these same processes were also traced within the evolving being of God himself. The teachings of theosophy thus formed a bridge between Christian mysticism and occult practice of various kinds, especially alchemy.

This theosophical tradition emerged in Germany in the late sixteenth century with the writings of Valentin Weigel (1533–1588), who combined the Christian mysticism of the great Rhineland mystics such as Meister Eckhart with the new alchemical synthesis of Paracelsus; SEE PARACELSUS. The mystical alchemist Heinrich Khunrath (1560–1605), whose *Amphitheatrum Sapientiae Aeternae* (*Amphitheater of Eternal Wisdom*) was a major influence on the early Rosicrucians, and Gerhard Dorn (c.

1530–c. 1584), the first important editor and commentator on the works of Paracelsus, were also important early figures in the movement.

The writings of Jakob Böhme (1575–1624), the mystical shoemaker of Görlitz, gave definite form to theosophy and became the classic theosophic texts. Böhme's teachings, a fusion of alchemical ideas and Christian mysticism sparked by his own ecstatic visionary experiences, became enormously popular in seventeenth-century occult circles. SEE BÖHME, JAKOB.

The seventeenth century was in many ways the golden age of theosophy. In Germany, important theosophers of this period included Johann Georg Gichtel (1638–1710) and Gottfried Arnold (1666–1714). The most important English theosophers were Jane Leade (1623–1704) and John Pordage (1608–1681), who were central to an active circle of theosophers and Böhme students in London. Holland contributed Johann Baptist van Helmont (1618–1699), who was also a celebrated alchemist. In France, the movement gave rise to the quietist mysticism of Pierre Poiret (1646–1719) and Antoinette Bourignon (1616–1680). Most of these writers were heavily influenced by Böhme. All through this period, the works of Böhme and of contemporary theosophers were an important influence on alchemical and occult circles throughout Europe.

The dawn of the eighteenth century saw some decline in the popularity of theosophy, although important writers such as Friedrich Christoph Oettinger (1702–1782) kept the current alive. Toward the end of the eighteenth century, spurred by the Romantic movement, new interest in the tradition burst out over much of Europe. The writings of Louis-Claude de Saint-Martin (1743–1803), the "Unknown Philosopher," played an important part in this trend. Saint-Martin was a pupil of the magician Martines de Pasqually and an initiate of Pasqually's magical Ordre du Élus Coens; his translations of Böhme as well as his original writings introduced theosophic ideas to a wide audience in Masonic and occult circles. SEE ÉLUS COENS; PASQUALLY, MARTINES DE; SAINT-MARTIN, LOUIS-CLAUDE DE.

In the early nineteenth century, theosophy was an important element in the Naturphilosophie movement in Germany, which sought to create a form of science that would not be hostile to the spirit, and produced the greatest of the later theosophers, Franz von Baader (1765–1841). It also played an important part in sparking the occult revival of the late nineteenth century. The scale and popular impact of that revival, however, quickly overshadowed the theosophic tradition, and with the creation of the Theosophical Society in 1875—an organization which borrowed the word "theosophy" while making very little use of classical theosophic teachings—theosophy became a relatively minor factor in modern occultism.

Important elements of theosophical teaching still play a significant role in Martinism, in Rudolf Steiner's Anthroposophy, and in a handful of other traditions. The late twentieth century also saw the anonymous publication of the deeply theosophical text *Meditations on the Tarot* by Valentin Tomberg (1900–1973), which has had a substantial influence in occult circles and may yet bring classical theosophy to a wider audience. *SEE* TOMBERG, VALENTIN. *SEE ALSO* CHRISTIAN OCCULTISM. FURTHER READING: FAIVRE 2000, GIBBONS 1996, VERSLUIS 1998, VERSLUIS 2000.

Theosophy. The teachings of the Theosophical Society, founded in 1875 by Helena Petrovna Blavatsky, and unrelated to the older tradition of Christian theosophy; for the latter, *SEE* THEOSOPHY (CHRISTIAN MYSTICAL).

It is difficult to summarize the immense body of Theosophical teachings in a short space. Theosophical writings frame a vision of reality in which the entire cosmos and everything in it comes into existence out of the primal void at intervals, and eventually returns to the void. A period of manifestation is called a *manvantara*, and a period of latency in the void is a *pralaya*. The prodigious lengths of manvantaras and pralayas have been worked out to exact figures in Theosophical literature. *SEE* CYCLES, COSMIC.

In this cycling cosmos, monads—basic units of consciousness—descend from the primal unity to enter into evolution. They begin at the lowest possible level, the third elemental kingdom, which (like the other two elemental kingdoms) is invisible to us because it functions on planes below the ones we can perceive. After evolving through the three elemental kingdoms, each monad en-

ters the mineral kingdom, progressing from there to the vegetable, animal, and human kingdoms, learning the lessons of each level in turn. When the human level has been outgrown, monads become Dhyan Chohans (sometimes spelled Dhyani-Chohans), spiritual beings living on planes above our limits of perception, who fill a dizzyingly complex hierarchy of spiritual powers entrusted with myriad functions within the universe.

In the course of this upward journey, monads reincarnate through a chain of seven globes or worlds, which are arranged on the fourth, fifth, sixth, and seventh planes of the cosmos. Our world is the fourth and most material globe of its chain, and is the reincarnation of a former chain—now dead—whose fourth globe is our moon. Monads start their incarnations on the first globe of a chain, and incarnate there until their work is finished, then move on to the next. A complete circuit of the globes of a chain is a round, and seven rounds must be completed before a monad is able to pass from one level (such as the human kingdom) to the next; present-day humanity is in the fourth globe of its fourth round.

In the process of learning the lessons of this stage of the journey, furthermore, the group of monads comprising humanity must pass through seven root races, each of which has seven subraces. Aryan humanity is of the fifth root race, while other races belong to the fourth or Atlantean root race. The sixth root race is due to appear in California sometime in the twenty-sixth century. *SEE* ROOT RACE.

The fifth root race has been around for about one million years, while the earlier root races are assigned to much more ancient periods of time and had a variety of radically different forms—the Lemurians, for example, were four-armed, three-eyed, and egg-laying. As a consequence of this, Theosophical teaching stands the conventional idea of evolution on its head; instead of humanity evolving from animals, all mammals are held to have devolved from the various human root races.

The monads that have already completed the transition to the status of Dhyan Chohan, as mentioned above, fill various roles in the enormously complex hierarchy of Dhyan Chohans. The Lunar Pitris, for example, are those who completed their seven rounds on the chain of globes associated with the moon, and were then assigned to create the bodies for the new humanity of the Earth chain. The Solar Pitris or Lords of the Flame, in turn, finished their rounds on earlier chains, and were responsible for awakening the minds of humanity during the time of the third root race. The manus, one of whom is assigned to guide each root race, fall somewhere between the Solar and Lunar Pitris in the scheme of things. Higher still on the ladder of being are the seven Watchers or Planetary Logoi who keep watch over the seven globes of a chain, and above them is the Solar Logos who presides over an entire planetary system—who is in turn the subordinate of other, higher powers.

More closely connected to the ordinary life of humanity is the Great White Lodge, consisting of human adepts who have progressed far beyond the ordinary human level. The Great White Lodge is currently headed by Sanat Kumara, who is a Lord of the Flame from Venus and took up his position about six and a half million years ago; SEE SANAT KUMARA. Beneath him are Gautama, the buddha of the fifth root race, and three assistant pratyeka buddhas; the manu of the current root race, Vaivasvata, and his second-in-command or bodhisattva, Maitreya; and various other figures. Other important figures of the lodge are the seven chohans of the Rays: El Morya, Kuthumi, the Venetian Chohan, Hilarion, Serapis, Jesus, and the Comte de Saint-Germain. SEE GREAT WHITE LODGE.

It may come as no surprise, in turning from the theory of Theosophy to its practice, that one of the major activities of Theosophical organizations is education in this immense cosmology. Blavatsky's books are studied intensively by Theosophists, and there are also useful summaries, of which the most popular is Geoffrey Barborka's *The Divine Plan* (1964). Meditation is also taught and practiced in Theosophical classes. Most forms of practical occultism are strongly discouraged, however, and students are encouraged instead to focus their efforts on meditation, study, and devotion to the work of the Masters. Although not precisely a requirement, vegetarianism is common and highly encouraged in Theosophical circles.

Nearly all the teachings of Theosophy are derived from Blavatsky's second major book, *The Secret Doctrine*, written after her trip to India and her adoption of many concepts from Buddhist and Hindu sources. Her earlier opus, *Isis Unveiled* (1877), actually presents a rather different cosmology and spirituality in which reincarnation is a rare event and practical magic is encouraged. Much of the material in this earlier book has strong similarities to the concepts circulated by earlier nineteenth-century occultists such as P. B. Randolph and Emma Hardinge Britten. SEE BRITTEN, EMMA HARDINGE; RANDOLPH, PASCHAL BEVERLY.

During what might well be called the "Theosophical Century," from 1875 to 1975, the teachings of Theosophy had a massive impact across the spectrum of Western occultism, and very few of the occult traditions and orders founded during those years found themselves able to do without some version of Theosophy's evolutionary cycles, lost continents, and hidden Masters. In the last quarter of the twentieth century, as part of a general refocusing of the occult tradition away from grand systems of occult philosophy and toward renewed attention to practical work, these Theosophical echoes have become a good deal less common. The rise of the Neopagan revival, with its radically different occult history of Pagan survivals and ancient matriarchies, also diverted attention away from the root races and planetary rounds of Theosophical lore. SEE MATRIARCHIES, ANCIENT; NEOPAGANISM.

Ironically, though, the abandonment of Theosophical ideas by large parts of the occult community occurred at the same time that these ideas were adopted by a new cultural phenomenon. The New Age movement, which crystallized in the 1970s and burst into popular consciousness in the 1980s, has borrowed a large part of its interests and characteristic approaches from Theosophy. The entire New Age movement has been characterized as "Theosophy plus therapy," and although this is an oversimplification it contains a good deal of truth. SEE NEW AGE MOVEMENT. SEE ALSO BLAVATSKY, HELENA PETROVNA; THEOSOPHICAL SOCIETY. FURTHER READING: BARBORKA 1964, BLAVATSKY 1888, LEADBEATER 1925.

theurgy. (Greek *theurgeia*, from *theos*, "god," and *ergeia*, "work") In ancient times, the magical wing of Platonism, which adopted ceremonial magic and traditional religious ritual as a process of purification needed to cleanse the lower aspects of the self and lay the foundation for the higher work of philosophical contemplation. Theurgy evolved as a distinct school in the first centuries of the Common Era, as part of the same fusion of Platonic philosophy and popular occultism that also brought about the creation of Hermeticism and many Gnostic traditions. *SEE* GNOSTICISM; HERMETICISM. The major figure in the formulation of theurgy was Iamblichus of Chalcis (?–c. 330); *SEE* IAMBLICHUS OF CHALCIS.

The theurgists led what was very nearly the last organized resistance against Christianity in the classical world. Julian, the last Pagan emperor of Rome, was a committed theurgist and a close student of Iamblichus' writings, and the great resurgence of Pagan thought and practice in the fourth century relied heavily on theurgy as both a philosophical stance and a basis for mutual toleration and support. Even after the political defeat of Paganism, theurgists such as Proclus and Sosipatra continued to teach and practice. The tradition dwindled out slowly on the fringes of the Byzantine Empire, and there is reason to believe that it survived in outposts such as Harran until the Middle Ages; *SEE* HARRAN.

The language of theurgy and some of its practices were revived in the Renaissance in the wake of Marsilio Ficino's epochal translation of the Hermetic treatises. *SEE* CORPUS HERMETICUM; FICINO, MARSILIO. With the spread of knowledge about classical Platonism and Hermeticism in the Renaissance, theurgy became an important element in the occult traditions of the time, and is discussed at length in such classic Renaissance occult works as Heinrich Cornelius Agrippa's *Three Books of Occult Philosophy* (1531).

In recent usage, the term *theurgy* has come to refer to any form of magic that aims at the spiritual transformation of the magician—which, admittedly, was the primary goal of classical theurgy. *SEE* MAGIC. Several variant meanings also exist, however. In some French esoteric Christian systems, the word is used for a system of focused contemplative prayer that aims at practical as well as spiritual goals; *SEE* CHRISTIAN OCCULTISM. In some modern Pagan circles, it is used for any magical working that calls on the gods, as distinct from thaumaturgy, which uses the powers in natural substances or the magician himself or herself. *SEE* THAUMATURGY. *SEE ALSO*

PLATONISM. FURTHER READING: AGRIPPA 1993, GEFFCKEN 1978, JOHNSTON 1990, LEWY 1978, SADHU 1965.

Thibault, Gerard. Dutch painter, architect, physician, swordsman, and Hermeticist, 1574–1629. Born in Antwerp to a family of wool merchants, Thibault traveled as a young man to Sanlucar de Barrameda in the south of Spain, where he studied with masters of the Spanish style of swordsmanship—a system based on geometrical principles and linked to traditions of sacred geometry. In 1611, after returning home, he entered a competition against the acknowledged fencing masters of Holland and took first place, then faced and defeated all comers in a celebrated exhibition before Prince Maurice of Nassau.

His elaborate textbook of swordsmanship, *Academie de l'Espee* (1630), is based entirely on Renaissance sacred geometry. Its philosophical first chapter quotes at length from Cornelius Agrippa's *Three Books of Occult Philosophy* and several other occult texts of the time, and its complex diagrams include a range of Hermetic and Pythagorean symbolism.

After Thibault's death, his system of esoteric swordsmanship was largely forgotten, although the complex geometrical diagrams used to illustrate his book were studied and expanded by later Masonic students of sacred geometry. *SEE ALSO* SACRED GEOMETRY. FURTHER READING: BYROM 1992, DE LA FONTAINE VERWEY 1978, THIBAULT 1998.

Thirty-two Paths of Wisdom. A traditional Jewish mystical text related to the Sepher Yetzirah, of uncertain authorship, probably written sometime between the seventh and tenth centuries of the Common Era. The *Thirty-two Paths of Wisdom* consists of thirty-two short passages describing each Path as a particular "intelligence" or state of consciousness. In the modern magical Cabala, these passages are sometimes called (inaccurately) "Yetziratic texts," since the *Thirty-two Paths of Wisdom* has commonly been included in editions of the Sepher Yetzirah since the late Middle Ages. *SEE* SEPHER YETZIRAH.

Thorn. *SEE* THURISAZ.

Thoth. (Ancient Egyptian *Djehuti*) The ancient Egyptian god of knowledge, magic, speech, and writing, god of the moon and prime minister of Heaven, Thoth was among the most complex and popular of the Egyptian gods, and was among those who claimed the title *weret-hekau*, "Great of Magic." In the years after the Greek conquest of Egypt in 323 B.C.E., Thoth was often equated with the Greek god Hermes, and from the fusion emerged Hermes Trismegistus, "Hermes the Thrice Great," the legendary founder of Hermeticism. SEE HERMES TRISMEGISTUS. SEE ALSO EGYPTIAN OCCULTISM. FURTHER READING: FOWDEN 1986.

thoughtform. In occult writings, an astral form created, deliberately or accidentally, by the power of human thought. According to a common magical teaching, any conception held in the mind for a long time or with sufficient energy takes shape on the astral plane as a thoughtform, and if reinforced with emotional or etheric energies, will gradually descend the planes to take shape on the physical plane. This is a primary formula of practical magic when used consciously and with intent. Worked unintentionally, as when a person broods on a fear and thus brings it into manifestation in his or her life, it is a potent source of human misery. SEE ASTRAL PLANE.

three. In Pythagorean number lore, three is the first actual number, since it has a beginning, a middle, and an end; one and two are considered to be basic principles of number rather than numbers in their own right. It represents two-dimensional space, since three points determine a plane. Its titles include "wisdom," "piety," and "friendship."

In the Cabala, three is Binah, Understanding, the third Sephirah of the Tree of Life. It is also the number of the letter Gimel. There are three mother letters in the Hebrew alphabet. Names of God containing three letters include ShDI, Shaddai, and HUA, Hu. SEE CABALA.

In Renaissance magical symbolism, three is the holiest and most powerful of numbers. It is the number of perfection and of ideal forms, and is associated with the Holy Trinity. FURTHER READING: MCLEAN 1994, WATERFIELD 1988, WESTCOTT 1984.

Three Principles. In Renaissance and modern alchemy, the three basic constituents of matter, called sulphur, mercury, and salt, though not to be identified with the physical substances of the same name. Sulphur is the volatile and energizing principle, mercury the fluid and mediating principle, salt the solid and stabilizing principle; all three are considered by alchemists to be present in every material substance. SEE ALCHEMY; MERCURY; SALT; SULPHUR.

The teaching of the Three Principles evolved from an older teaching in Arabic and medieval European alchemy in which metals were considered to be composed of a combination of sulphur and mercury. The differences among metals were a function of different levels of purity of these two substances; only when the purest form of both united underground was gold formed. This teaching was first widely promulgated by the Arabian alchemist Jabir ibn Hayyan; SEE GEBER.

In spagyric alchemy, the form of medicinal alchemy that works with herbs, the sulphur of a plant consists of its essential oils and other volatile compounds; the mercury is its sap or, in fermented form, pure alcohol; the salt is the solid material that remains when the plant is burned. SEE SPAGYRICS.

Three Worlds. A variety of systems of three worlds or realms of being can be found in Western occult traditions. Many of them seem to have no connection other than the number itself, which is an important symbolic number in all Indo-European cultures.

In Druidry, a system of three worlds has been adopted from the writings of Iolo Morganwg (1747–1826). In this system, which is basic to Morganwg's teachings on spiritual evolution, each soul comes into being out of the cauldron of Annwn or mineral existence into the first world, called Abred, which is the world of plant and animal life. Souls that progress through the circles of Abred reach the human level at last, and through the attainment of wisdom make the transition to the second world, Gwynfydd, the world of angelic or enlightened life. Above Gwynfydd is Ceugant, the third world, the unfathomable realm of the divine. SEE DRUIDRY.

In French Martinist teachings, another set of three worlds is used as a framework for magical theory and practice. These are the mental world or world of the

Archetype, the astral world or world of Humanity, and the physical world or world of Nature. SEE MARTINISM. FURTHER READING: NICHOLS 1990, SADHU 1962.

threefold return. A teaching common to most modern Pagan traditions, the law of threefold return states that any magical action, positive or negative, rebounds with threefold intensity on the magician. Concern with the moral dimension of magic is a relatively modern phenomenon in Western magical traditions, and many systems of magical practice from the Middle Ages and before pay little attention to ethical issues; the magic of the grimoires, like that of the Graeco-Egyptian magical papyri, aims at goals ranging across the spectrum from healing and blessing to death curses and erotic magic intended to extract sexual favors from the unwilling. Despite this, a good deal of evidence supports the idea that the regular use of magic for selfish and/or destructive ends backfires on the magician, and the law of threefold return is probably a wise rule of thumb for the practicing occultist. SEE GRAECO-EGYPTIAN MAGICAL PAPYRI; GRIMOIRE; MAGIC.

Thule. In ancient Greek and Roman geographical writings, a distant island somewhere to the north of Britain, also known as Ultima Thule ("Furthest Thule"). In some nineteenth-century German ideologies, the name was borrowed for an alleged lost Arctic homeland of the Aryan peoples, also known as Arktogäa; in this form it became a fixture of Ariosophical and other proto-Nazi German occult movements. SEE ARIOSOPHY; ARKTOGĀA; THULE-GESELLSCHAFT.

Thule-Gesellschaft. (Thule Society) The final link in the chain of occult orders and secret societies that led to Nazism, the Thule-Gesellschaft originated as the Bavarian branch of the Germanenorden, an important Ariosophist magical order of the early twentieth century; SEE ARIOSOPHY; GERMANENORDEN. Before 1917, the Germanenorden in Bavaria had accomplished very little, but in that year the charismatic adventurer Rudolf von Sebottendorf joined the order and turned his considerable energies toward recruiting new members, boosting Bavarian membership from 200 to over 1500 by the fall of 1918.

Due to the chaotic political climate, the order rented rooms and carried on its activities in Bavaria under the alias of the Thule Society. Under that name, it carried on the Germanenorden's distinctive mix of Ariosophical racist occultism and right-wing political activism.

In November of 1918, bled white by four years of war, faced with mutinies in the army and widespread civil unrest, Germany's government collapsed. In Bavaria, a socialist coalition took power, then lost it to a hardline communist faction headed by Russian emigrés. Munich was the scene of assassinations, firing squad executions, and pitched battles between left-wing and right-wing forces. All through this period, the Thule Society played a central role in organizing and supporting the conservative side. Thule members stockpiled weapons, forged railway passes, and organized a sizeable militia unit—the Kampfbund Thule—which took an active part in the fighting that ended the Bavarian Soviet Republic in May of 1919.

Another step taken by the Thule Society at this time had wider consequences. At Sebottendorf's urging, Thule members Karl Harrer and Anton Drexler formed a discussion group among Munich workers in the fall of 1918. In January 1919, in response to the communist seizure of power, the discussion group transformed itself into a political party, the Deutsche Arbeiterpartei ("German Workers Party") or DAP. In February of 1920, it changed its name to Nationalsozialistische Deutsche Arbeiterpartei, best known then and thereafter as the Nazi Party. By then it was already well on its way to becoming a mass movement, and it had gained its most important member, an intense, awkward young Austrian veteran named Adolf Hitler.

All through the 1920s, the Thule Society continued to play an important role in the growth and direction of the Nazi movement, and Thule members helped Hitler make connections with wealthy conservatives in Bavaria and elsewhere. An associate of the Thule Society, the anti-Semitic playwright and journalist Dietrich Eckart, took on a mentor role for Hitler that ended only with Eckart's death in 1923. The web of connections leading out from the Thule Society reached as far as India, where A. K. Mukherji—the friend and, later, husband of neo-Nazi theologian Savitri Devi—was aware of the society's work and introduced Devi to Dietrich Eckart's writings. *SEE* DEVI, SAVITRI.

The Thule Society seems to have gone out of existence around 1925, although details are hard to come by (a constant hazard in the history of secret orders). Nearly all its membership, functions, and projects were transferred more or less directly to its erstwhile offspring, the Nazi party. The inner symbolic and magical dimensions of the Thule Society, which it had inherited from the Germanenorden, were taken on in large part by the SS after Heinrich Himmler took the latter over in 1929; *SEE* SS. *SEE ALSO* HITLER, ADOLF; NATIONAL SOCIALISM. FURTHER READING: GOODRICK-CLARKE 1998.

thurible. An older term for an incense burner, still used in some magical writings. The standard thurible is a shallow bowl or cup of metal half full of sand; charcoal is put on the sand and lit, and incense burned on the charcoal.

Thurisaz. (Old Germanic, "giant") The third rune of the elder futhark, corresponding to disruptive power, opposition, and primal energy. It represents the giants, mighty but usually dimwitted figures of Germanic mythology who represent the hostile forces of nature. Thurisaz is also the origin of the name of Thor, the strongest and most giantlike of the Aesir. Its sound-value is *th*. *SEE* ELDER FUTHARK.

The same rune, renamed Thurs (Old Norse, "giant"), is the third rune of the younger futhark, with the same meanings and sound-value as Thurisaz. *SEE* YOUNGER FUTHARK.

In the Anglo-Saxon futhorc, this rune takes the name Thorn (Old English, "thorn") but remains the third rune in the sequence. The Old English rune-poem speaks of the thorn as "exceedingly sharp" and "evil to the touch of a warrior." The rune's sound-value and general meanings are the same as in the elder and younger futharks. *SEE* ANGLO-SAXON FUTHORC.

In the Armanen runic system, finally, the same rune is named Thorn and stands for the thunderbolt. Its power in the rune-charm of the Old Norse *Havamal* is the ability to blunt the weapons of enemies at need. It corresponds to the god Thor, to the act of engendering, and to the zodiacal sign Gemini, and represents the sound *th*. *SEE* ARMANEN RUNES.

Rune Thurisaz (Thurs, Thorn)

Thurs. *SEE* THURISAZ.

thyrsus. A wand or ritual staff used in the ancient Greek mysteries, the thyrsus consists of a long, straight fennel stalk topped with a pine cone, and sometimes wound about with a grapevine. The thyrsus was primarily used in the Mysteries of Dionysus. *SEE* FENNEL; MYSTERIES, THE.

Tibetan, the. *SEE* DJWAL KUL, MASTER.

Tide of Destruction. A magical term for the season of winter. *SEE* SEASONAL TIDES.

Tide of Planning. A magical term for the season of autumn. *SEE* SEASONAL TIDES.

Tide of Reaping. A magical term for the season of summer. *SEE* SEASONAL TIDES.

Tide of Sowing. A magical term for the season of spring. *SEE* SEASONAL TIDES.

Tinne. (Old Irish, "iron bar") The eighth letter of the Ogham alphabet, with the sound-value *t*. It corresponds to the holly among trees, the starling among birds, the color dark gray and the number eleven. In Robert Graves' version of the Ogham tree-calendar, its month runs from July 9 to August 5. *SEE* OGHAM.

Ogham letter Tinne

Tiphareth. (Hebrew TPhARTh, "beauty") The sixth and central Sephirah of the Cabalistic Tree of Life, located in the center of the Pillar of Balance or Consciousness. Its standard correspondences are as follows:

Name of God: YHVH ALVH VDAaTh, Tetragrammaton Eloah va-Daath (Lord God of Knowledge).

Archangel: MKAL, Michael (He Who Is As God).

Angelic Host: MLKIM, Malakim (Kings).

Astrological Correspondence: ShMSh, Shemesh (the sun).

Tarot Correspondence: The four Sixes and four Knights or Princes of the pack.

Elemental Correspondence: Air.

Magical Images: A naked child; a crowned and throned king; a crucified man.

Additional Symbols: The cube, the cross of six squares, the truncated pyramid.

Additional Title: Microprosopus, the Lesser Countenance.

Colors: in Atziluth—clear rose pink.

in Briah—golden yellow.

in Yetzirah—rich salmon-pink.

in Assiah—golden amber.

Correspondence in the Microcosm: The imagination in Ruach.

Correspondence in the Body: The solar plexus.

Grade of Initiation: 5=6, Adeptus Minor.

Negative Power: ThGRIRVN, Tagiriron (the Disputers).

The corresponding passage in the *Thirty-two Paths of Wisdom* reads: "The Sixth Path is called the Mediating Intelligence, because in it are multiplied the influxes of the Emanations, for it causes that influence to flow into all the reservoirs of the blessings, with which these themselves are united." *SEE ALSO* CABALA; TREE OF LIFE.

Tir. *SEE* TIWAZ.

Tiriel. In ceremonial magic, the planetary intelligence of Mercury. Its subordinate planetary spirit is Taphthartharath. *SEE* INTELLIGENCE, PLANETARY.

Tit ha-Yon. (Hebrew TIT HYVN, "mire of mud") In Cabalistic lore, the fourth of the seven hells, corresponding to the Sephirah Tiphareth. *SEE* HELLS, SEVEN.

Tiwaz. (Old Germanic, "sky-god") The seventeenth rune of the elder futhark, corresponding to divine power, justice, confrontation, and courage. Also known as Teiwaz, Tiwaz is the Old Germanic equivalent of the Greek Zeus and the Latin *deus*, "god," and Tyr or Tiw—the equivalent figure in surviving Norse and Germanic mythologies—was the original supreme god of the Germanic tribes, a position later taken over by Odin. The sound-value of this rune is *t*. *SEE* ELDER FUTHARK.

The same rune, named Tyr, is the twelfth rune of the younger futhark, and under the name Tir, it is the seventeenth rune of the Anglo-Saxon futhorc. Its meanings and sound-value are identical to those of Tiwaz; the Old English rune-poem adds the useful detail that this rune corresponds to the planet Mars and/or the polestar. *SEE* ANGLO-SAXON FUTHORC; YOUNGER FUTHARK.

The same rune, finally, is the twelfth of the Armanen rune system under the name Tyr, and stands for the sword. Its power, from the rune-charm of the Old Norse *Havamal*, is to enable the dead to speak to the living. It corresponds to the god Vidar and to the zodiacal sign Pisces. *SEE* ARMANEN RUNES.

Rune Tiwaz (Tyr, Tir)

toby. *SEE* MOJO.

Tomberg, Valentin. Estonian occultist, 1900–1973. Tomberg was born in Saint Petersburg, where his father—an Estonian of German origins—was an official in the Tsarist government. French, German, and Russian were all spoken at home in his childhood. His mother died in the October Revolution of 1917. Shortly thereafter he moved to Estonia, and by 1925 was the president of the Estonian branch of the Anthroposophical Society. *SEE* ANTHROPOSOPHY.

He remained very active in Anthroposophy, lecturing widely, until Estonia was invaded by the Soviet Union in 1940. He managed to escape, and ended up in London, where he found a position with the BBC. During the war he converted to Catholicism, wrote two books on law, and began writing a series of works on esoteric thought. His most famous work, *Meditations on the Tarot*, was published anonymously in 1972.

Tomberg's works are important documents of Christian occultism, and *Meditations on the Tarot* in particular has become one of the classics of that tradition. His approach draws heavily on mainstream Christian mysticism, but also on theosophic writers such as Saint-Martin; SEE SAINT-MARTIN, LOUIS-CLAUDE DE; THEOSOPHY (CHRISTIAN MYSTICAL). Pierre Teilhard de Chardin's evolutionary mysticism also plays a significant role among his sources. SEE ALSO CHRISTIAN OCCULTISM. FURTHER READING: FAIVRE 2000, TOMBERG 1972.

Tower, the. The sixteenth Major Arcanum of the tarot, usually bearing the image of a tower struck by lightning, with two persons falling from it. Alternative names are "the House of God" and "the Lightning-Struck Tower." In the Golden Dawn system, it corresponds to the Hebrew letter Peh, while in the French system it corresponds to Ayin. Its common meanings include danger, crisis, destruction, and liberation.

Its magical title is "Lord of the Hosts of the Mighty." SEE ALSO TAROT.

Tarot trump the Tower (Universal tarot)

trance. A state of altered consciousness in which the person undergoing it loses awareness of ordinary reality. It may be produced by hypnosis, self-hypnosis, drugs, or other means. Most systems of Western occult practice include some degree of trance work, although the details vary widely. Quasi-occult traditions such as Spiritualism and the New Age movement also make much use of trance work of one sort or another. SEE NEW AGE MOVEMENT; SPIRITUALISM.

Practices such as scrying and astral projection, which make up an important branch of magical practice in some systems, depend on effective trance induction methods in order to work. SEE ASTRAL PROJECTION; SCRYING. SEE ALSO ATWOOD, MARY ANNE; PATHOTISME.

Transcendentalism. An eighteenth-century literary and spiritual movement in New England, Transcendentalism was among the first American mystical movements, and it also inaugurated the long and complex American love affair with Asian spiritual traditions. It first took shape around 1830 as a handful of writers and philosophers—among them Ralph Waldo Emerson (1803–1882), Henry Thoreau (1817–1862), and Bronson Alcott (1799–1888), the father of the famous children's author Louisa May Alcott—began to respond to German mystical philosophy, the translations of Platonist writings then issuing from the pen of Thomas Taylor in England, and the first reports of Hindu philosophy in English journals. SEE PLATONISM; TAYLOR, THOMAS.

Around 1836, when regular gatherings of a "Transcendental Club" started taking place at the house of George Ripley, a Unitarian minister in Boston, the movement took on coherent form. A journal, *The Dial*, was started in 1840; though it was never a financial success, and went under after four years, it was widely read and influential, and included the first Hindu writings ever published on American soil. The movement also spawned a commune, Brook Farm, which was founded in 1841 and remained in existence until 1857.

By the time Brook Farm failed, the movement had lost most of its momentum, although several of its members continued along the same path for the rest of their careers. During its lifetime, the impact of Transcendentalism was limited and most visible in the high volume of mockery and condemnation the movement received, from materialists and orthodox Christians alike. Still, the Transcendentalists blazed a trail that has been followed by movement after movement ever since; Spiritualism, New Thought, Theosophy, and the vast American "Journey to the East" of the 1960s and 1970s, in many ways, can best be seen as continuing responses to the Transcendentalist impulse. FURTHER READING: FROTHINGHAM 1876, GELDARD 1993, VERSLUIS 1993.

transits. In astrology, movements of the planets relative to the planetary positions in an existing chart. According to the fundamental theory of astrology, the state of the heavens at the moment of birth or origin leaves lasting traces on the person born or the thing created at that moment. Since the heavens continue to cycle after that moment, planets, zodiacal signs, and other factors pass through relationships with the astrological imprint left on the person or thing. These relationships and their effects are tracked by means of transits.

For example, every thirty years or so the planet Saturn returns to the same position in the zodiac. A person who is born when Saturn is at, say, fifteen degrees Taurus will have Saturn revisiting that position again around that person's thirtieth birthday. (The exact date can vary by as much as a few years, due to the effect of retrogrades and differing orbital speeds in different parts of Saturn's orbit around the sun.) This transit, called a Saturn return, typically brings important changes and challenges relating to whatever sign and house Saturn inhabits in the person's birth chart.

At any given point in time one or more planets will be transiting some aspect of a birth chart, and those astrologers who specialize in transit analysis can predict a great deal of the ups and downs of everyday life by tracking transits on a daily basis. More generally, however, the solar return—the return of the sun to its location in the natal chart—and the transits of Jupiter, Saturn, and the outer planets, are used to keep track of the general outlines of a person's life. SEE SOLAR RETURN. The transits of the outer planets are often combined with progressions; SEE PROGRESSIONS. SEE ALSO ASTROLOGY.

transmigration. SEE REINCARNATION.

transvection. In scholarly and theological writings, a term for the power of flight ascribed to witches and supernatural beings. The nature of transvection was heavily debated by Christian theologians all through the Burning Times, with one side insisting that it was an illusion caused by demons, while the other claimed with equal fervor that demons physically carried witches through the air.

In actual Pagan and magical practice during the Middle Ages, Renaissance, and early modern period, the power of flight seems to have been partly a matter of drugs and partly a matter of what would later be called astral projection. Flying ointments recorded in medieval and Renaissance writings include powerful hallucinogens, and experiments with these recipes in modern times have produced "trips" with many of the standard features of the Witches' Sabbat of folklore. In other cases, Pagan or quasi-Pagan groups such as the benandanti and the cults of Diana mentioned in the Canon *Episcopi* did their flying in a dream state, apparently without the help of drugs. SEE BENANDANTI; CANON EPISCOPI.

Tree of Knowledge. The Tree of Knowledge of Good and Evil, to give it its full name, plays a central role in the narrative of the Fall in the first chapters of the Book of Genesis. Adam and Eve are forbidden to eat of its fruit, and their decision to do so causes the Fall and deprives them of eternal life. SEE FALL, THE.

In Cabalistic theory, the Tree of Knowledge and the Tree of Life were held to be united until Adam separated them, an act which gave independent existence to evil. Early Cabalistic writings call this act "the cutting of the shoots," and identify it in one way or another with every significant sin mentioned in the Old Testament.

In writings of the nineteenth- and twentieth-century magical renaissance, the Tree of Knowledge is associated with the serpent Nachash and the lower astral, the realm of illusion. SEE ASTRAL PLANE; NACHASH; TREE OF LIFE.

Tree of Life. In the Cabala, the arrangement formed by the ten Sephiroth and twenty-two Paths. The Tree of Life is the primary symbolic pattern of modern Western occultism, heavily used even by groups and traditions that claim no connection whatsoever to the Cabala.

The Tree of Life evolved gradually in Cabalistic circles in Spain and southern France out of discussions about the relation of the ten Sephiroth to one another. The essential arrangement of the Sephiroth was settled by the fourteenth century, but the relationship between the Sephiroth and the Paths remained open to debate for centuries thereafter, and there are still several different

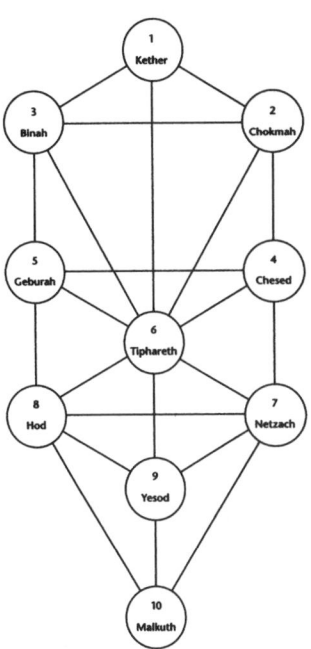

Tree of Life; the lines are the Paths and the circles are the Sephiroth

versions of the Tree in use at present, differing in the position and attributions of the Paths.

Various classifications of levels or stages within the Tree have been in circulation over the course of the Cabala's development. One very early division, discussed by the Spanish Cabalist Azriel of Gerona (fl. early thirteenth century), defines the topmost triangle of the Sephiroth as "intellectual," the next triangle as "mental," and the lowest triangle as "natural." (These terms are drawn from medieval metaphysics, and have caused a good deal of confusion in more recent times, since "intellect" in medieval thought meant roughly what "spiritual intuition" means nowadays.)

Another division, important in early writings but not much in evidence in the modern tradition, divided the Tree in half, with the upper five Sephiroth (Kether through Geburah) representing hidden powers and the lower five (Tiphareth through Malkuth) representing revealed powers. A somewhat similar division, more popular in recent writings, divides the three uppermost Sephiroth (the "Three Supernals") from the seven lower ones (the "Sephiroth of the Building"), which correspond to

the seven days of the creation of the world in the Book of Genesis; between these is fixed a barrier, the Abyss.

Yet another division, much used in modern Cabala, divides the Tree according to the four worlds of the Cabala. In this system, the first Sephirah, Kether, belongs to the world of Atziluth; the second and third, Chokmah and Binah, belong to the world of Briah; the fourth through ninth belong to the world of Yetzirah; and the last, Malkuth, belongs to the world of Assiah. Alternatively, each of these worlds is often assigned a Tree of its own. *SEE* FOUR WORLDS.

Also very important, throughout the history of Cabalistic thought, is the division of the Tree into three pillars. The right-hand pillar, comprising Chokmah, Chesed, and Netzach, is called the Pillar of Mercy or of Force. The left-hand pillar, comprising Binah, Geburah, and Hod, is called the Pillar of Severity or of Form. The central pillar, comprising Kether, Tiphareth, Yesod, and Malkuth, is called the Pillar of Mildness, Equilibrium, or Consciousness, or simply the Middle Pillar. The first two pillars are commonly associated with the two pillars of King Solomon's Temple, Jachin and Boaz. *SEE* BOAZ; JACHIN; TEMPLE OF SOLOMON.

In writings of the nineteenth- and twentieth-century magical renaissance, the Tree of Life is identified with the serpent Nehushtan and the upper astral, the realm of purification. *SEE* ASTRAL PLANE; NEHUSHTAN; TREE OF KNOWLEDGE. *SEE ALSO* CABALA; SEPHIROTH. FURTHER READING: FORTUNE 1984, GREER 1996, SCHOLEM 1974.

triads. In traditional Welsh bardic lore, short texts used to classify a wide range of legendary, legal, technical, and practical information. Up to the sixteenth century, when the old traditions of oral instruction collapsed as a result of the introduction of printing, apprentice bards in Wales memorized hundreds of triads as a mental index for the lore they were required to learn. Of particular importance were the *Trioedd Ynys Prydein* (*Triads of the Island of Britain*), which included important details from myth and legend, and the *Trioedd Cerdd* (*Bardic Triads*), which covered rules of the bardic art. An example from the *Trioedd Ynys Prydein* is this:

The three noble shoemakers of the island of Britain:

Caswallawn son of Beli, when he went to Rome
to seek Fflur;

Manawyddan son of Llyr, when the enchantment was
on Dyved;

Llew Llaw Gyffes, when he and Gwydion sought arms
and a name from his mother Arianrhod.

An example from the *Trioedd Cerdd* is this:

Three things that give breadth to a poet:

Knowledge of histories;

The bardic art;

A store of ancient verse.

The *Trioedd Ynys Prydein* refer to a wide range of myths and legends, many of which have been lost or survive only in fragmentary form. It has been argued on fairly solid grounds that at least some of this material dates back to Druidic lore.

The triads have received surprisingly little attention from the modern Pagan revival, although they have been drawn on by several modern Druid orders and a few of the more learned Celtic Neopagan groups. The overwhelming popularity of Irish and Scottish traditions among modern Celtophiles, and the corresponding neglect of other Celtic cultures, probably has a good deal to do with the general neglect of the triads. *SEE ALSO* BARD. FURTHER READING: BROMWICH 1961.

triangle of manifestation. In goetic magic, a triangle drawn on the floor or ground outside the magical circle, generally to the north, as the location in which a summoned spirit is expected to manifest. Triangles of manifestation in traditional grimoires are marked with divine names, and often surround a censer that burns incense corresponding to the type of spirit being summoned. *SEE* GOETIA; GRIMOIRE.

Several modern magicians have suggested that the triangle of manifestation in the old grimoires was actually the frame of a magic mirror, in which the summoned spirit appeared. *SEE* MIRROR, MAGIC.

tribes of Israel. According to the Bible (Genesis 49:2–28), the twelve tribes of Israel were descended from ten sons of Jacob—Reuben, Simeon, Judah, Zebulun, Is-

sachar, Dan, Gad, Asher, Naphtali, and Benjamin—and two of Jacob's grandsons, Ephraim and Manasseh. Since ancient times, attempts have been made to assign the twelve tribes to the twelve signs of the zodiac, on the basis of the blessings given to each tribe's ancestor by Jacob, and to each tribe by Moses (Deuteronomy 33:6–25). These correspondences play a part in some systems of Cabalistic symbolism, especially eighteenth- and nineteenth-century Masonic Cabalism.

Name of Tribe	Mathers/Pike	Halevi
Judah	Leo	Aries
Issachar	Cancer	Taurus
Zebulun	Capricorn	Gemini
Reuben	Aquarius	Cancer
Simeon	Pisces	Leo
Gad	Aries	Virgo
Ephraim	Taurus	Libra
Manasseh	Gemini	Scorpio
Benjamin	Sagittarius	Sagittarius
Dan	Scorpio	Capricorn
Asher	Libra	Aquarius
Naphtali	Virgo	Pisces

The first set of attributions given in the table is the most common, and may be found in Golden Dawn sources as well as Albert Pike's immense masonic compendium *Morals and Dogma*. The second is used by the modern Jewish Cabalist Z'ev ben Shimon Halevi, and may be found in a few other sources.

The breastplate of the High Priest, which has twelve jewels on it, is also associated with the twelve tribes, and there have been a number of different methods of relating the two. *SEE* BREASTPLATE OF THE HIGH PRIEST. *SEE ALSO* CABALA; ZODIAC. FURTHER READING: D. GODWIN 1991, HALEVI 1980, MATHERS 1983, PIKE 1871.

trident, magical. An instrument much used in several European traditions of Hermetic magic, the magical trident is a weapon used to command, banish, or destroy hostile entities. It is usually made of iron or steel, with three sharp points and a handle of wood or some other nonconductive material. According to the lore of natural magic, sharp points of iron can discharge the etheric substance that makes up the bodies of certain types of hostile spirits. FURTHER READING: BARDON 1967, SADHU 1962.

The magical trident

trigon. In astrology, the triangular figure traced out in the zodiac by conjunctions of Jupiter and Saturn, which occurs approximately every twenty years. Due to the relationship of the four traditional elements to the signs of the zodiac, all three points of the trigon are in signs of the same element; old books on astrology thus speak of the "watery trigon" or the "fiery trigon," indicating periods when the conjunctions of Jupiter and Saturn all occurred in, respectively, watery or fiery signs.

Every 240 years, the conjunctions of these two planets shift from one set of signs to another, and thus change their elemental symbolism. In traditional mundane astrology, this shift represents the end of one age of the world and the beginning of another. SEE CYCLES, COSMIC; MUNDANE ASTROLOGY. SEE ALSO ASTROLOGY.

trine. In astrology, an aspect of 120 degrees between two planets or significant points. A trine is normally a favorable or "easy" aspect, fostering a harmonious relationship between the two factors involved. SEE ASPECT; ASTROLOGICAL.

Trismegistus, Hermes. SEE HERMES TRISMEGISTUS.

Tristitia. (Latin, "sorrow") A geomantic figure governed by Saturn. In divination, favorable for foundations and building projects, but unfavorable for most other questions. SEE GEOMANCY.

Geomantic figure Tristitia

Trithemius, Johannes. German humanist and occultist, 1462–1516. Born Johann Heidenberg in the town of Trittenheim, from which his Latin pen name derived, Trithemius decided at age fifteen to devote his life to scholarship despite the opposition of his stepfather. Leaving home, he wandered through northwestern Germany and the Netherlands before entering the University of Heidelberg, where he studied with some of the foremost scholars of the day. After graduating in 1482, Trithemius set out to revisit his family but was forced by a snowstorm to take shelter in the Benedictine monastery of Saint Martin at Sponheim. Powerfully attracted by the monastic life there, he took novice's vows as soon as the snowstorm ended, and by the age of twenty-one was elected abbot of the monastery, a position he held for the next twenty-three years. A brilliant scholar and a collector of books, he became renowned throughout Europe, and the leading literary scholars of the time frequented Sponheim during his tenure there.

His substantial literary output included works on mystical theology, church history, monastic reform, and humanist studies. These were overshadowed, however, when word leaked out that he had composed a book on steganography—the art of secret communication—that apparently relied on magical invocations. While he was never officially censured by the Catholic Church, the furor that arose forced him to conceal the manuscript of the *Steganographia*, and the third part of it was never completed. SEE STEGANOGRAPHIA.

In 1505 he left the monastery at Sponheim, where he and the monks had become increasingly at odds, and became the abbot of the monastery of Saint Jacob at Würzburg. There he wrote several other books, including *Polygraphia*, a more conventional handbook of ciphers and secret writing; *De Septem Secundeis* (*On the Seven Secondary Powers*), a deeply magical tract about the influence of the seven planetary angels over the cycles of human history, and several books supporting the persecution of witches. This latter may seem surprising to modern eyes, but he consistently argued that ceremonial magic was entirely compatible with Catholic orthodoxy, while witchcraft—which, like most of his contemporaries, he interpreted as Devil worship—was not. He died in 1516. FURTHER READING: BRANN 1999, SHUMAKER 1982.

trivium. *SEE* QUADRIVIUM.

Tuatha de Danaan. (Irish, "Children of the Goddess Dana") The most important of the many and varied races of Irish supernatural beings. According to the *Book of Invasions*, the primary source for Irish mythological history, the Tuatha de Danaan were a race of wizards who migrated to Ireland from four cities—Gorias, Falias, Finias, and Murias—in the north of the world. They conquered Ireland from the Fir Bolg, an earlier race of invaders, and spent much of the time of their dominance contending with the monstrous Fomorians. They were finally dispossessed by the Milesians, the ancestors of the current Irish, and retreated underground, becoming the Sidhe or faery folk of Irish legend. *SEE* FAERY.

According to most students of Irish folklore and myth, the Tuatha de Danaan were simply the gods of Pagan Ireland, who were turned into historical figures after the coming of Christianity by the process of euhemerism; *SEE* EUHEMERISM. Many Irish customs relating to the Tuatha de Danaan appear to be the remains of ancient traditions of worship. In many modern Celtic Pagan traditions, various important members of the Tuatha de Danaan are worshipped as divinities. FURTHER READING: EVANS-WENTZ 1966.

Tubal-Cain, Clan of. *SEE* CLAN OF TUBAL-CAIN.

twelve. In the Cabala, twelve is the number of the banners or permutations of the Tetragrammaton. There are twelve single letters in the Hebrew alphabet.

In Christian symbolism, twelve is the number of the Apostles, of the prophets, and of the gates of the New Jerusalem.

In Renaissance magical symbolism, twelve is the number of grace and perfection, and of the signs of the zodiac. *SEE ALSO* ARITHMOLOGY. FURTHER READING: MCLEAN 1994, WATERFIELD 1988, WESTCOTT 1984.

two. To the Pythagoreans, two was the first movement away from unity, and thus bears the titles "daring," "impulse," and "recklessness." It was seen not as a number at all in the strict sense of the word, but as one of the two principles from which number unfolds. As the principle of separation, they called it "anguish," "endurance," and "hardship." As the source of even numbers, it was called "justice." Because they saw it as a movement toward being and a development from the seed of unity, it was called "Nature." Since even numbers were feminine in Pythagorean thought, two was assigned to Isis, Rhea, and Demeter.

In Cabalistic thought, two is Chokmah, "Wisdom," the second Sephirah of the Tree of Life. It is also the number of the Hebrew letter Beth. Names of God with two letters include AL, El, and YH, Yah. *SEE* CABALA.

In Renaissance magical symbolism, two is the number of marriage and of the human microcosm, and represents the creation of matter. It is associated with the two cherubim on the ark of the covenant and the two tablets of the Mosaic law. *SEE ALSO* ARITHMOLOGY. FURTHER READING: MCLEAN 1994, WATERFIELD 1988, WESTCOTT 1984.

two-headed doctor. In African-American tradition, a term sometimes used for a hoodoo doctor. *SEE* HOODOO.

Typhon. In ancient Greek mythology, the last and most terrible enemy of Zeus, also called Typhoeus. Typhon was the son of Gaia and Tartarus, born after Zeus defeated the Titans and became lord of the universe. A storm god, Typhon had a hundred fire-breathing serpent heads on his shoulders. Shortly after his birth, he attacked Olympus, and after a long battle was defeated, maimed, and cast down to Hades by Zeus.

After the Greek conquest of Egypt under Alexander the Great, Typhon came to be identified with Apep or Apophis, the monstrous sun-devouring snake of Egyptian myth. This connection became part of the standard approach to Egyptian myth in later Western cultures, and plays a role in the symbolism of the Golden Dawn tradition, among other branches of occultism. FURTHER READING: HESIOD 1973, REGARDIE 1971.

Tyr. *SEE* TIWAZ.

Tzaddi. (Hebrew TzDI, "fishhook") The eighteenth let-ter of the Hebrew alphabet, one of the single letters, with the sound-value *ts* and the numerical value of 90 (in its final form, 900). Its standard magical symbolism is as fol-lows:

Path of the Tree of Life: Path 28, Netzach to Yesod.

Astrological Correspondence: Aquarius, the Water Carrier.

Tarot Correspondence: Trump XVII, the Star.

Part of the Cube of Space: The upper south edge.

Colors: in Atziluth—violet.

in Briah—sky blue.

in Yetzirah—bluish mauve.

in Assiah—white tinged with purple.

Its corresponding section in the *Thirty-two Paths of Wisdom* reads as follows: "The Twenty-eighth Path is called the Natural Intelligence, and by it the nature of all that exists beneath the Sun is completed and perfected." *SEE ALSO* CABALA; HEBREW ALPHABET.

Hebrew letter Tzaddi, left, and its final form, right

Tzadkiel. (Hebrew TzDQIAL, "justice of God") In the Cabala, the archangel associated with Chesed, the fourth Sephirah of the Tree of Life, in the world of Briah. *SEE* ARCHANGEL; BRIAH; CHESED.

Tzaphkiel. (Hebrew TzPhQIAL, "contemplation of God") In the Cabala, the archangel associated with Binah, the third Sephirah of the Tree of Life, in the world of Briah. *SEE* ARCHANGEL; BINAH; BRIAH.

Tzedek. (Hebrew TzDQ, "justice") The Hebrew word for the planet Jupiter, used in ceremonial magic as the magical name of the sphere of Jupiter. *SEE* JUPITER.

Tzelmoth. (Hebrew TzLMVTh, "shadow of death") In Cabalistic lore, the second of the seven hells, associated with the Sephirah Hod. *SEE* HELLS, SEVEN.

U

Uilleand. (Old Irish, "honeysuckle") The third of five additional letters in the Ogham alphabet, used to represent the vowel combination *ui* or the consonant *p*. It corresponds to the honeysuckle among trees, but lacks the complex symbolism of the twenty regular Ogham letters. *SEE* OGHAM.

Ogham letter Uilleand

Uncia Coeli. (Latin, "ounce of heaven") In the Aurum Solis system of magic, the second highest of the six energy centers of the human body, located in the middle of the brow. In the Rousing of the Citadels, an Aurum Solis exercise roughly equivalent to the Middle Pillar exercise, it is visualized as a dove-gray sphere, half of which projects forward from the brow. Its Name of Power is YHVH ALHIM, Tetragrammaton Elohim.

It corresponds to the third eye chakra, but has no relation to either the Sephiroth of the Tree of Life or the centers of the Middle Pillar exercise. *SEE* AURUM SOLIS; MIDDLE PILLAR EXERCISE; ROUSING OF THE CITADELS.

uncrossing. In hoodoo, the process of removing a curse from someone; the opposite of crossing. The term has been adopted into several other magical traditions in recent times. *SEE* CROSSING; HOODOO.

undines. In the lore of ceremonial magic, the elementals of water. Their king is Nichsa. *SEE* ELEMENTAL.

Ur. (Old Irish, "earth") The eighteenth letter of the Ogham alphabet, with the sound-value *u*. It corresponds to heather among trees, the lark among birds, the color of resin (Gaelic *usgdha*), and the number five. In Robert Graves' version of the Ogham tree-calendar, it is related to the summer solstice. *SEE* OGHAM.

Ogham letter Ur

Ur. (rune) *SEE* URUZ.

Uranus. Discovered by Sir William Herschel in 1781, Uranus was the first of the outer planets to be revealed by the telescope. Its discovery led to many years of discussion and research on the part of astrologers, who had no place for it in the neat symbolic structure of classical astrology. In modern astrological thought, however, Uranus represents the power of radical change and disruption, and is associated with rebellions, inventions, new technologies, alternative sexualities, and countercultures. He rules the sign Aquarius, and is in his detriment in Leo. *SEE ALSO* ASTROLOGY.

Astrological symbol of Uranus

Ursa Major. (Latin, "great bear") Also known as the Big Dipper, the brightest and most visible of the polar constellations in the Northern Hemisphere, Ursa Major has had a substantial role in mythology and magic for thousands of years. That role has much to do with the symbolism of the north pole, for in the past Ursa Minor was even closer to the pole than it is now.

Precession, the slow wobble of the Earth's axis that produces the astrological ages, also shifts the location of the celestial pole (the point in the heavens directly above Earth's North Pole) through a vast circle of sky over a period of some 25,920 years. Polaris is the current pole star, but until the Middle Ages the four stars in the "bowl" of the Big Dipper were actually closer to the celestial pole. These may have been the symbolic four cities of the Tuatha de Danaan in Irish legend, located at the north of the world; they may also have formed Caer Pedryvan, the mythic castle "four times revolving" which is the hiding place of the Cauldron of Rebirth in the mystical Welsh poem *Preiddeu Annwn*. *SEE* PRECESSION OF THE EQUINOXES.

In the Graeco-Egyptian magical papyri, the constellation of the Great Bear is related to the goddess Artemis, who evolved in late classical times into an underworld goddess closely related to Hekate, Persephone, and the Babylonian death goddess Ereshkigal. An invocation of Ursa Major for general magical purposes can be found in the Graeco-Egyptian magical papyri (PGM VII 686–702); *SEE* GRAECO-EGYPTIAN MAGICAL PAPYRI. Artemis herself was in one sense a bear goddess, as the rituals at her temple at Brauron in Greece make clear.

Little of this ancient polar lore has survived into modern occult tradition, but a number of magical systems have assigned Ursa Major a significant role for other reasons. Several magical traditions heavily influenced by Theosophy have borrowed, as Theosophy did, the traditional Hindu link between the seven principal stars of Ursa Major and the Seven Rishis or primordial sages. These stars and sages are said to hold the evolutionary patterns for seven planets, of which Earth is one. *SEE* THEOSOPHY.

The same seven stars are also said to be the source of the essential pattern of the Round Table, which was brought to Earth by Merlin for King Arthur. *SEE* ARTHURIAN LEGENDS. FURTHER READING: J. GODWIN 1993, KNIGHT 1983.

Uruz. (Old Germanic, "wild ox") The second rune of the elder futhark and, under the name Ur, of the younger futhark, Anglo-Saxon futhorc, and Armanen runic alphabet as well. In the elder futhark and Anglo-Saxon futhorc it corresponds to the huge and ferocious aurochs, an extinct species of wild ox, and with concepts of primal strength and vitality; the Old English rune-poem speaks of the aurochs roaming the moorlands and fighting with its horns. The rune represents the sound *u*, and is associated by some modern runemasters with the god Thor. *SEE* ANGLO-SAXON FUTHORC; ELDER FUTHARK.

In the younger futhark, this rune is named Ur, which means "slag" or "drizzle." It is associated with tenacity and purification. *SEE* YOUNGER FUTHARK.

In the Armanen runic system this rune, named Ur, represents primordial force. Its power, out of the rune-charm from the Old Norse *Havamal*, is to bring healing. It corresponds to the god Uller, to the mother, and to the zodiacal sign Taurus, and stands for the sound *u*. *SEE* ARMANEN RUNES.

Rune Uruz (Ur)

V

Vaivasvata Manu. In Theosophical lore, the manu or ruler of the present, fifth root race, the Aryan race. *SEE* MANU; THEOSOPHY.

Valentinus, Basilius. German alchemist, dates unknown. The author of several of the most influential works in the later alchemical tradition, Basilius Valentinus is described in alchemical writings as a Benedictine monk in the monastery of Saint Peter in Erfurt, but no record of his existence has yet to come to light in the detailed records of the Benedictine Order. It is also claimed that he lived in the latter part of the fifteenth century, though internal evidence dates his books to the beginning of the sixteenth.

Valentinus' legacy consists entirely of his writings, which were first published around 1600. His most important works were the *Triumphal Chariot of Antimony* (1604), which is considered by historians of science to be the first monograph ever written on a particular chemical element, and the *Twelve Keys*, first published in 1599, which present a complex symbolic allegory of the alchemical process. *SEE ALSO* ALCHEMY.

Valiente, Doreen. English witch and author, 1922–1999. Among the most influential figures in modern Wiccan history, Valiente was born in south London but raised in the West Country, where witchcraft folklore was a significant part of everyday life well into the twentieth century. Her parents were devout Christians who attempted to raise her in that faith, sending her to a convent school; she walked out at age fifteen and refused to return.

Her interest in the occult dated to her childhood, and she was already casting simple spells in her teen years. Shortly after the repeal of the Witchcraft Act in 1951, she contacted Cecil Williamson, then owner of a museum of witchcraft on the Isle of Man, hoping to make contact with a witch. Williamson put her in touch with Gerald Gardner (1884–1964), the founder of Wicca, who initiated her in 1953; *SEE* GARDNER, GERALD BROUSSEAU. Valiente became Gardner's High Priestess shortly thereafter, and played a major role in revising the original Wiccan rituals, excising substantial passages borrowed from the works of Aleister Crowley (1875–1947). *SEE* BOOK OF SHADOWS; CROWLEY, ALEISTER. Her works include the standard version of the Charge of the Goddess, which is used by most modern Wiccan traditions.

She left Gardner's coven in 1957 to start the first of her own. In 1964 she was initiated by Robert Cochrane into the Clan of Tubal-Cain, a tradition of witchcraft that Cochrane claimed to have inherited through his family since ancient times. *SEE* CLAN OF TUBAL-CAIN; COCHRANE, ROBERT. She broke with Cochrane a few years later over his increasingly erratic behavior.

For the remainder of her life, Valiente was active in English Wiccan circles; she wrote a number of books on the subject of Wicca, and by her last years was widely seen as the grande dame of English Wicca. In 1972, she successfully lobbied Parliament to prevent the reenactment of the Witchcraft Act. She spent her last years in Sussex, where she died of cancer in 1999. *SEE ALSO* WICCA. FURTHER READING: HUTTON 1999, VALIENTE 1987, VALIENTE 1989.

vampire. In occult lore, a type of etheric revenant that survives by preying on the life energy of living human beings. The vampire of occult lore has little in common with the animated, blood-sucking corpse of modern horror media, although accounts by occultists vary significantly and there has been some penetration of media stereotypes into occult writing in recent decades.

Most occult discussions of vampirism, though, stress that the vampire leaves its grave in an etheric rather than a physical form, and drinks life energy rather than physical blood. The term *vampire*—often qualified as *psychic* vampire—is also sometimes used for living human beings who have learned the trick of parasitizing other people's etheric bodies and draining their life force.

A good deal of attention has been paid to vampirism by some occult writers, partly because of the possibilities of gothic horror inherent in the subject and partly because it can be used to illuminate certain details of the composition of the human subtle bodies and the nature of the after-death experience. FURTHER READING: FORTUNE 1930, GREER 2001, LÉVI 1972.

Van Van oil. A common ingredient in hoodoo magic, Van Van oil is used to wash floors for magical protection, to anoint mojo bags, to dress candles, and to carry out a wide range of other magical workings. There are several different formulas; one common recipe calls for an infusion of lemon grass in olive oil. Much of the commercial Van Van oil on the market, on the other hand, consists of a mixture of lemon juice and wood alcohol. SEE HOODOO. FURTHER READING: MALBROUGH 1986.

Vau. (Hebrew VV, "nail") The sixth letter in the Hebrew alphabet, a single letter with the sound-values *v, u,* and *w* (depending on the Hebrew dialect) and the numerical value of six. Also spelled Vav, its standard magical symbolism is as follows:

> *Path of the Tree of Life:* Path 16, Chokmah to Chesed.
>
> *Astrological Correspondence:* Taurus, the Bull.
>
> *Tarot Correspondence:* Trump V, the Hierophant.
>
> *Part of the Cube of Space:* The southeast edge.

> *Colors:* in Atziluth—red-orange.
>
> in Briah—deep indigo.
>
> in Yetzirah—deep warm olive.
>
> in Assiah—rich brown.

The corresponding section of the *Thirty-two Paths of Wisdom* runs as follows: "The Sixteenth Path is the Triumphal or Eternal Intelligence, so called because it is the pleasure of the Glory, beyond which is no other Glory like to it, and it is called also the paradise prepared for the righteous." SEE ALSO CABALA; HEBREW ALPHABET.

Hebrew letter Vau (Vav)

Vault of Christian Rosencreutz. According to the *Fama Fraternitatis,* the first of the seventeenth-century Rosicrucian manifestoes, a chamber of seven sides, each five feet wide and eight feet high, in which Christian Rosencreutz—the legendary founder of the Rosicrucian Order—was buried. On its walls, floor, and ceiling were written the secrets of the universe, and it contained a variety of books and occult devices. The story of its rediscovery is central to the narrative of the *Fama.*

The idea of a secret tomb in which an important occult figure lies dead but uncorrupted, surrounded by tomes of magical lore, is an old one in Western occult tradition and long predates the Rosicrucian manifestoes. The Greek magician Apollonius of Tyana, according to Arabic sources, was said to have learned his wisdom by discovering the hidden tomb of Hermes Trismegistus. The tombs of Adam, his son Seth, and a variety of other figures have collected similar legends, and Merlin's enclosure in an *esplumoir* at the end of his earthly life is a related image. SEE APOLLONIUS OF TYANA; MERLIN.

For its Adeptus Minor initiation ritual, the Hermetic Order of the Golden Dawn uses a replica of the Vault of Christian Rosencreutz and reenacts the vault's rediscovery and opening in the course of the ritual. SEE ADEPTUS MINOR. SEE ALSO ROSENKREUTZ, CHRISTIAN; ROSICRUCIANS. FURTHER READING: ALLEN 1968, MCLEAN 1985.

vegetable stone. The highest goal of spagyric alchemy, corresponding in some ways to the Philosopher's Stone in the alchemy of metals. A vegetable stone is made from a particular type of plant that is subjected to a complex process of separation, purification, and recombination, and is then fixed into a hard, stonelike form by means of heat.

A properly prepared vegetable stone has the highest degree of healing power of which the original plant is capable. According to some writers, it also separates an herbal tincture into its three principles (the sulphur, salt, and mercury of the plant) without the difficult operations usually needed for the purpose. SEE SPAGYRICS. FURTHER READING: ALBERTUS 1974, JUNIUS 1985.

vegetarianism. The belief that meat should be excluded from human diet. Since ancient times, certain branches of the Western occult tradition have insisted that eating animal flesh is incompatible with spiritual development. The first Western tradition known to have required vegetarianism is the Pythagorean brotherhood, founded by Pythagoras of Samos before 500 B.C.E.; SEE PYTHAGORAS. There is some question as to whether vegetarianism was one of Pythagoras' own teachings, as ancient accounts vary on the subject. Certainly, though, the Pythagorean teacher and philosopher Empedocles of Acragas (active in the fifth century B.C.E.) condemned the eating of meat in his surviving writings, and later Pythagoreans treated vegetarianism as an essential part of their discipline. SEE EMPEDOCLES OF ACRAGAS.

Outside of Pythagorean circles, very few Western occultists practiced vegetarianism until the nineteenth century, when the Theosophical Society imported Hindu ideas on the subject to a Western audience; SEE THEOSOPHICAL SOCIETY. Since that time, Western occult movements can be divided roughly into those that insist on vegetarianism and those that do not, with the more Theosophical and meditative falling generally into the first category, and those more focused on ritual magic into the second.

Some of the latter, though, specifically condemn the practice. The writings of English occultist Dion Fortune (1898–1946), for example, insist that a vegetarian diet tends to make most people from Western backgrounds too sensitive for ordinary life, much less the psychic strains involved in ceremonial magic. As with most of the details of magical practice, the question of a vegetarian diet is probably best left to the personal choice of the magician. SEE ALSO BEANS.

Veil of the Sanctuary. In King Solomon's temple in ancient Israel, a veil separating the Holy of Holies, where the Ark of the Covenant was kept, from the rest of the temple's interior. The veil was originally part of the furnishings of the tabernacle built by the Israelites during their wanderings, and was blue, purple, and scarlet, ornamented with cherubim; the specifications are given in Exodus 26:31–33. According to Matthew 27:51, Mark 15:38, and Luke 23:45, the Veil of the Sanctuary tore from top to bottom at the time of the crucifixion of Jesus of Nazareth.

In mystical and occult writings, the Veil of the Sanctuary has been used as a metaphoric label for the limitations of awareness that prevent human beings from directly perceiving divine realities. In the Cabala, the Veil of the Sanctuary was positioned on the Tree of Life just below Tiphareth, the sixth Sephirah. SEE CABALA; TREE OF LIFE. In the Golden Dawn tradition, the Portal grade represented passage through the Veil of the Sanctuary on the way to Tiphareth, and "Paroketh," the Hebrew name of the veil, was used as a password of the grade. SEE GOLDEN DAWN, HERMETIC ORDER OF THE; PAROKETH. SEE ALSO TEMPLE OF SOLOMON.

Veilleurs, Les. (French, "the Watchmen") French occult-political group active between the two world wars. Les Veilleurs emerged from the Paris occult scene in 1919, preaching a mix of esoteric spirituality, right-wing politics, and anti-Semitism. Its membership included R. A. Schwaller de Lubicz, the group's founder and first leader, who went on to become a central figure in the modern revival of sacred geometry; Rudolf Hess, later an important official in the Nazi Party; and O. V. de Lubicz-Milosz, the French-Lithuanian poet. SEE NATIONAL SOCIALISM; SCHWALLER DE LUBICZ, RENÉ A.

velocia. (Latin, "swift ones") The term used for the tattvic tides in the magical system of the Aurum Solis. SEE AURUM SOLIS; TATTVAS.

Venetian Chohan. In the lore of Theosophy and related systems of occult teaching, one of the Masters of the Great White Lodge, the secret brotherhood that superintends the spiritual evolution of the Earth. The Venetian Chohan, whose name does not seem to appear in published sources, is the chohan or chief adept of the Third or Yellow Ray, the ray of intelligence and of astrological forces. *SEE ALSO* MASTERS; THEOSOPHY; YELLOW RAY.

Venus. One of the seven traditional planets of astrology, Venus in a birth chart is associated with love, relationships, and the feminine side of the personality. She rules the signs Taurus and Libra, is exalted in Pisces, is in her detriment in Scorpio and Aries, and in her fall in Virgo. *SEE* ASTROLOGY.

In alchemy, Venus is a common symbol for copper. *SEE* ALCHEMY.

Astrological symbol of Venus

Vergil. (Publius Vergilius Maro). Roman poet, 70 B.C.E.–19 C.E. Born in rural northern Italy to a family of humble origins but respectable wealth, he attended school in Cremona, Naples, and Rome, and embarked on a literary career. In 42 B.C.E. he became part of the literary circle around Maecenas, the freedman and unofficial prime minister of Octavian (later Augustus Caesar, first emperor of Rome, 63 B.C.E.–14 C.E.). The patronage of Octavian, already one of the two most powerful men in Rome, enabled Vergil to devote his time completely to writing, and allowed him to produce his major poetic works—the *Eclogues*, a collection of ten pastoral poems; the *Georgics*, a celebration of the cycles of nature and the agricultural year; and the *Aeneid*, his last and most famous work, an epic drama about the origins of the Roman people. On a research trip to Greece to collect local color for a revision of parts of the *Aeneid*, he caught a fever. Returning to Italy by ship, he died shortly after landing at Brundisium (modern Brindisi).

As far as any ancient source reports, Vergil had nothing whatsoever to do with any sort of magic or oc-

cultism. It is thus among the ironies of history that legends of the Middle Ages turned him into the supreme sorcerer of ancient times. This seems to have come about by way of a confusion with a shadowy figure of the early Middle Ages, Vergil of Seville. Whatever the details, the figure of Vergil the Enchanter was a common one in medieval writings. By another ironic twist of fate, these legends—by way of a Welsh mistranslation—ended up creating a nonexistent book and an equally nonexistent order of Druid alchemists in the imagination of some modern Druid writers. *SEE* PHERYLLT.

Vesta. An asteroid sometimes used in astrology. It has been assigned to the zodiacal sign Virgo. *SEE* ASTEROIDS.

Via. (Latin, "way") A geomantic figure governed by the moon. In divination, Via is a figure of mixed character, fortunate for journeys but unfortunate in many other questions. *SEE* GEOMANCY.

```
•
•
•
•
```

Geomantic figure Via

vibration. In ceremonial magic, a mode of pronouncing divine names and other words of power for maximum effect. It consists of chanting or intoning the words in such a way as to set up a trembling or buzzing sensation in the body. According to instructional papers, it is best learned by practicing with simple vowel sounds, altering the tone and the shape of the mouth until the required effect begins to show itself. With practice, the sensation can be focused on any location inside or outside of the physical body, and magical energies maximize at the location where it is focused. *SEE ALSO* VIBRATORY FORMULA OF THE MIDDLE PILLAR. FURTHER READING: GREER 1997, REGARDIE 1971.

vibratory formula of the Middle Pillar. In the Golden Dawn magical system, a ritual technique for invoking divine energies. It is performed by standing with the arms extended to the side in the form of a cross, drawing in a deep breath, and mentally pronouncing the divine name to be invoked in the heart. The name is visualized as descending along the centerline of the body to the energy center between the feet, then rising up again suddenly and passing out through the mouth; at the same time, the magician makes the Sign of the Enterer and vibrates the name forcefully, expelling all the breath from his or her lungs. The magician then makes the Sign of Silence and contemplates the invoked force.

A similar practice called the Calyx is one of the standard techniques of Aurum Solis ritual, and relates to the Aurum Solis version of the Middle Pillar exercise, the Rousing of the Citadels. *SEE* AURUM SOLIS; ROUSING OF THE CITADELS.

The Golden Dawn papers warn that this technique should only be attempted with divine names, as performing it with the names of elementals or demons will bring about obsession. *SEE* OBSESSION. *SEE ALSO* GOLDEN DAWN, HERMETIC ORDER OF THE; VIBRATION. FURTHER READING: DENNING AND PHILLIPS 1981, GREER 1997, REGARDIE 1971.

Vilon. (Hebrew VILVN, "veil") In Cabalistic lore, the first and lowest of the seven heavens, corresponding to the Sephiroth Yesod and Malkuth. *SEE* HEAVENS, SEVEN.

Violet Flame. According to the Ascended Masters teachings, a system of twentieth-century popular American occultism, a magical energy derived from the Violet Ray; *SEE* RAYS, SEVEN. The Violet Flame has the capacity to transform and transmute energy, and students of the Ascended Master teachings visualize themselves surrounded and filled with the Violet Flame while repeating decrees for protection and spiritual development. *SEE* ASCENDED MASTERS' TEACHINGS; DECREE.

Violet Ray. In occult philosophy, the sixth of the Seven Rays, the primary creative energies of the cosmos. The Violet Ray is the ray of love and devotional mysticism. In Theosophical lore, the Violet Ray is directed by the Master Jesus, one of the chohans of the Great White Lodge. Its symbolic gem is the ruby. *SEE* JESUS OF NAZARETH. *SEE ALSO* RAYS, SEVEN.

virginity. Narrowly defined, the state of a living being who has not experienced sexual intercourse; more broadly, the state of any object or substance that has not yet been used for any particular purpose. In the broad sense, virginity is often a requirement of materials used in traditional magical operations. Virgin wax, parchment, clothing, and the like are routinely called for by the grimoires, on the grounds that these materials need to be free of the influence of any other form of activity, so that the energies of the ritual may be uncontaminated.

Virginity in the narrow sense also has a place in the older magical traditions. According to some sources, the clairvoyant or scryer used in a magical operation must be a virgin, in order for the visions that are evoked to be pure and accurate. The fact that many of the old sources simply require a child below the age of puberty is a reminder that premarital sex was as common in earlier eras as it is today. *SEE ALSO* POLARITY; SEX AND OCCULTISM.

Virgo. (Latin, "virgin") The sixth sign of the zodiac, a mutable earth sign of feminine polarity. In Virgo, Mercury has the rulership and is also in his exaltation; Jupiter is in his detriment, and Venus is in her fall. Virgo rules the nervous system and intestines.

The asteroids Ceres and Vesta, and by some authorities Juno and Pallas, are assigned to this sign as well. *SEE* ASTEROIDS.

The sun is in Virgo approximately from August 24 to September 22. People with this sun placement are traditionally diligent and perceptive, with a keen eye for detail and a habit of modesty; they can also be fussy, perfectionistic, and tense.

In the Golden Dawn tarot system, Virgo corresponds to Trump IX, the Hermit. *SEE* HERMIT, THE; TAROT. *SEE ALSO* ZODIAC.

Astrological symbol of Virgo

Vision, A. Book by occultist and poet William Butler Yeats (1865–1939), presenting an innovative system of occult philosophy based on twenty-eight phases of the moon. The system was derived from automatic writing and mediumistic communications by Yeats' wife Georgie, starting in 1917 and continuing for more than a decade thereafter. The entities who passed on the system, named by Yeats only as "the communicators," presented it specifically as a set of "metaphors for poetry."

The core conception of *A Vision* is the duality in the human soul between the Primary, which is objective and relates to the world of facts, and the Antithetical, which is subjective and relates to the world of the imagination. The Primary expresses itself in the individual as the Creative Mind, which seeks to understand the Body of Fate, the sum total of facts that affect the individual. The Antithetical expresses itself as the Will, which seeks to bring into being the Mask, the object or ideal of all that the individual desires.

Different points on the cycle of twenty-eight phases combine different proportions of Primary and Antithetical, and produce different personality types, each with its distinctive type of Will, Mask, Creative Mind, and Body of Fate. Each soul works its way around the cycle from the pure Primary of Phase 1 (the New Moon) to the pure Antithetical of Phase 15 (the Full Moon) and back again. This same cycle also governs the movement of the soul between incarnations, and the movement of historical cycles of 1,000- and 2,000-year lengths.

A Vision was originally issued in a limited, private edition in 1925, and circulated among Yeats' occultist friends and contacts. A heavily revised and expanded version was brought out for the general public in 1937. It has been studied primarily by scholars of Yeats' poetry since that time, although some use has been made of it by astrologers as a way of interpreting lunar positions in the horoscope. SEE ASTROLOGY; MOON. SEE ALSO YEATS, WILLIAM BUTLER. FURTHER READING: YEATS 1956.

vital body. SEE ETHERIC BODY.

vital energy. SEE ETHER.

vitriol. A fundamental term in alchemy with a wide range of meanings. In the most basic physical sense, vitriol is a term for several different hydrated metallic sulfate salts—copper sulfate ($CuSO_4$), or blue vitriol; iron sulfate ($FeSO_4$), or green vitriol; and zinc sulfate ($ZnSO_4$), or white vitriol—which are produced chemically by treating metals with sulfuric acid. As usual with alchemy, however, the term has also been given other meanings.

The word "vitriol" has also been used since medieval times as shorthand for the Latin phrase *Visita interiora terrae rectificando invenies occultum lapidem,* "Visit the interior of the earth, by rectifying you will find the hidden stone." SEE ALSO ALCHEMY.

Vitruvius. (Marcus Vitruvius Pollio) Roman architect and engineer, active in the first century C.E. His dates of birth and death are not known, and the only details of his career that survive are those he gives himself in his surviving work, the *Ten Books on Architecture.* He apparently worked for Augustus Caesar as a military engineer before settling down to a civilian career as an architect, and writing down his ideas on architecture.

Vitruvius was very much a practical builder rather than a theorist, but—like all architects of his time—he made use of basic Pythagorean rules of geometry and proportion in his design work, and covered many of these in his book. Its rediscovery in the mid-fifteenth century played a major role in the revival of sacred geometry and Pythagorean thought during the Renaissance. SEE PYTHAGORAS; SACRED GEOMETRY. FURTHER READING: VITRUVIUS 1960.

Voarchadumia. According to the book of the same name—*Voarchadumia Contra Alchimiam: Ars Distincta ab Archimia, et Sophia, Cum Additionibus, Proportionibus, Numeris, et Figuris Opportunis Joannis Augustini Panthei Veneti Sacerdotis* (*Voarchadumia Against Alchemy: An Art Distinct from Archemy and Wisdom, with Additions, Proportions, Numbers, and Opportune Figures, by Johannes Augustinus Pantheus, Priest in Venice*), to give it the glory of its full title—the supreme art of transmutation, differing from ordinary alchemy. It is difficult to determine from Pantheus' book exactly how Voarchadumia differs from alchemy, and very few other writers seem to have made any use of the distinction.

Voarchadumia was a central concern of John Dee (1527–1608), the most important English magician of the Elizabethan period, who heavily annotated his copy of Pantheus' book and used major elements of Pantheus' approach in his early books *Propaedumata Aphoristica* (1558) and *Monas Hieroglyphica* (1564). SEE DEE, JOHN.

While Voarchadumia has been one of the most thoroughly forgotten of occult concepts, the recently published manifesto of one occult order claims mastery of "the Voarchadumic art" as well as a lineal descent from Pantheus himself—evidence, perhaps, that modern occultists are paying more attention to historical sources than those of the recent past. What lies behind this improbable claim is anyone's guess. SEE PALLADIAN ORDER. SEE ALSO ALCHEMY. FURTHER READING: ANONYMOUS 2001, YATES 1964.

void of course. In astrology, the condition of a planet that has passed through its last aspect in a given sign of the zodiac. When a planet is void of course, its influence is limited until it enters the next sign, and matters relating to that planet may not go well if started during the void of course period.

In modern astrology, periods when the moon is void of course are considered particularly important. Since the moon goes around the zodiac in about 29.5 days, it is void of course up to fourteen times in a month, with void of course periods lasting anything from a fraction of a minute to several days. During these times, according to astrologers, it is a bad idea to make plans or to try to start any new project, as nothing will come of it. SEE ALSO ASTROLOGY.

Volantia. In the teachings of American occultist P. B. Randolph (1825–1875), the first of three stages of magical practice, consisting of intense mental focus on visualized imagery; the following stages were Decretism and Posism; SEE DECRETISM; POSISM. The magical student was taught Volantia by staring at a white card with a black circle on it, then looking at a blank wall and concentrating on the afterimage. The goal to be sought is the ability to see an imagined object, with the eyes open, with as much clarity and exactness as though the object were physically present. SEE RANDOLPH, PASCHAL BEVERLY.

In the Hermetic Brotherhood of Luxor, which borrowed liberally from Randolph's work, this stage was renamed Formation. The other stages were Execution and Reception. SEE HERMETIC BROTHERHOOD OF LUXOR (H. B. OF L.).

Voodoo. Also spelled Vodu, Vodun and Vodoun, a Caribbean religion with roots in West African traditions brought to the New World by enslaved African people. Like so many African traditions, Voodoo was treated with undeserved contempt by most European and American scholars until the late twentieth century, and the word came to be used as a synonym for "magic" or "superstition" in many areas. Confusion with hoodoo, a distinct tradition of African-American folk magic that developed in the American South, has added to this. While a few attempts have been made to draw Voodoo into certain Western magical syntheses, it remains a distinct religious system that should be studied on its own, or with other African and African-diaspora traditions. SEE ALSO HOODOO.

vowels. In ancient times, sequences of vowels were used by the priests and magicians of a variety of nations as chants or words of power. Most of the documentation that survives on the topic is Greek, but Greek writers themselves claimed that the use of vowels was an ancient Egyptian practice. Vowel sequences are much used in the Graeco-Egyptian magical papyri, and also appear in ancient Gnostic writings. SEE GNOSTICISM; GRAECO-EGYPTIAN MAGICAL PAPYRI.

Ancient Greek has seven vowels, which were identified with the seven planets, the seven diatonic notes of the musical octave, and various other sequences of seven; unfortunately the exact correspondences have not survived in any ancient source, and a variety of schemes have been proposed.

Many of the divine names and holy words of ancient religions and magical traditions are also made of vowels. The Gnostic Name of God, IAO, and the Roman title of Jupiter, Jove (pronounced "Yoweh" in classical Latin) are two examples, and the Tetragrammaton, the most sacred Jewish name of God, is probably another. SEE TETRAGRAMMATON. FURTHER READING: D. GODWIN 1991.

Voynich manuscript. Perhaps the most mysterious book in the world, this manuscript surfaced in 1912 in Frascati, Italy, in the bottom of an old chest at a Jesuit school. The American book dealer Wilfred Voynich bought it that same year, and brought it back to the United States. After passing through the hands of several owners, it was donated to Yale University in 1969.

The manuscript is a volume of 204 pages, six by nine inches in size, written in what is either a fiendishly difficult cipher or an unknown language. There were once another twenty-eight pages, but these are now lost. The writing looks like ordinary medieval script at first glance, but is actually in an alphabet of its own, one with twenty-nine letters, which has never been found in any other source. Along with the closely written text are little ink drawings in multiple colors, showing plants, astronomical constellations, and nude women in bathtubs.

With the manuscript was a letter dated August 19, 1666, from one Johannes Marcus Marci, rector of Prague University, to the famous Jesuit scholar and linguist Athanasius Kircher in Rome, explaining that the manuscript had been bought many years previously by Emperor Rudolf II for no less a sum than 600 ducats, and asking Kircher—an expert on codes—to try to make sense of it.

How it got to Prague remains a mystery, although there are clues that link the manuscript to a major figure in the Western esoteric tradition. Originally there were no page numbers in the manuscript, but someone made up that omission in the sixteenth century. The handwriting has been identified as that of John Dee, the great Elizabethan scholar and magician, who spent several years in Prague during the reign of Rudolf II. Clearly Dee had it in his possession at one point, and Dee's son Arthur Dee is on record as mentioning a book written entirely in "hieroglyphics" that his father had during his time in Prague. SEE DEE, ARTHUR; DEE, JOHN. Whether Dee brought it with him from his home, where he had England's largest library, or whether it came to him in the course of his travels, is impossible to say.

There have been many different attempts at decoding the manuscript, and successful decipherments have been reported several times. Unfortunately none of these have succeeded in presenting a convincing case for their accuracy. Even an attempt by the National Security Agency to break the code with the aid of a Cray-6 supercomputer produced no useful result. It remains one of the major unsolved enigmas of our time. FURTHER READING: BRUMBAUGH 1978.

vril. In Edward Bulwer-Lytton's novel *The Coming Race* (1873), a mysterious energy extracted from the atmosphere by the Vril-ya, inhabitants of an underground civilization. Wielded through a vril-staff, a metal wand, vril could accomplish almost anything. The term was borrowed almost immediately by occultists as another name for etheric energy. SEE ETHER. FURTHER READING: ANONYMOUS 1911, BULWER-LYTTON 1873, KAFTON-MINKEL 1989.

Vril Society. In the modern mythology of Nazi occultism, an organization—also referred to as the "Luminous Lodge"—based in Berlin and supposedly deeply involved in the origins and direction of the Nazi Party. Like much of the mythology in question, this claim mixes a small amount of fact with a much larger helping of speculation and straightforward fiction.

According to an article published in 1947 by Willy Ley—a German rocket engineer who fled the Nazis in 1933 and became a successful science writer in the United States—a small organization called the Wahrheitsgesellschaft ("Truth Society") existed in Berlin between the wars. It devoted its time to the study of vril, and taught that the secret of vril could be divined by contemplating the structure of an apple sliced in half. Since an apple cut horizontally shows a pentagram at the center, formed by the seeds and core structure, the teachings of the Wahrheitsgesellschaft were presumably in line with occult tradition generally. Their size and level of organization may be judged by the fact that their magazine, according to Ley, managed to put out only one issue. SEE ALSO NATIONAL SOCIALISM; VRIL. FURTHER READING: J. GODWIN 1993, LEY 1947, PAUWELS AND BERGIER 1968.

Vulcan. A hypothetical planet inside the orbit of Mercury, predicted in the nineteenth century on the basis of wobbles in Mercury's movements; it is sometimes also called Hephaestus, the Greek name of the same blacksmith god. The planet was never actually seen, and the variations in the observed orbit of Mercury found another explanation when Einstein's theory of relativity showed that gravitational bending of light accounts for it. Nonetheless, a handful of modern astrologers continue to use old tables for the predicted positions of Vulcan, and use it in their chart interpretations. SEE ASTROLOGY; LILITH.

Waite, Arthur Edward. English author and occultist, 1857–1942. Born in Brooklyn, New York, the illegitimate son of an Englishwoman and an American ship captain, Waite moved to England with his mother in 1859 and was raised in the Roman Catholic Church. He received a limited education, and began working as a clerk at the age of fifteen. He was a voracious reader, however, with a taste for philosophy and theology, and by his late teens was writing poetry, essays, and stories for publication.

In 1878 he encountered Spiritualism, and spent several years deeply immersed in the Spiritualist movement; *SEE* SPIRITUALISM. By the early 1880s he had returned to Catholicism, and to a strong interest in Christian mysticism, but remained fascinated with the byways of the occult for the rest of his life. His first occult book, an anthology of writings by the French magus Eliphas Lévi (1810–1875), was published in 1886. *SEE* LÉVI, ELIPHAS. A string of further titles followed, exploring the Rosicrucian tradition, the legends of the Holy Grail, alchemy, Freemasonry, and an assortment of other topics.

His interest in the occult was not limited to writing books about it. In 1891, after a previous application was rejected, he became a member of the Hermetic Order of the Golden Dawn, taking the motto *Sacramentum Regis* ("Sacrament of the King"). He rose to the Philosophus grade, the highest grade of the Outer Order, but left the order in 1893. Readmitted in 1896, he entered the Second Order in 1899. In the troubles that overtook the order after the revolt of 1900, Waite played a dubious role, supporting the rebels and then leading a faction that attempted to seize control of the entire order.

Failing to achieve this, Waite's faction founded a separate organization, the Independent and Rectified Rite of the Golden Dawn, which discarded much of the magical teachings of the original order in favor of a form of Christian mysticism flavored with Cabalistic and occult elements. Internal dissensions broke up the Independent and Rectified Rite in 1914, and the next year Waite and a group of former members of the rite founded the Fellowship of the Rose Cross, with a heavily reworked version of the original rituals. This body continued to operate throughout Waite's life, and has been reactivated in recent years.

Waite's most important contribution to the occult, though, was his role in the creation of the Rider-Waite tarot deck, the twentieth century's most popular and influential deck. In his researches into the tarot, Waite had encountered an obscure fifteenth-century deck, the Sola-Busca deck, which gave complex images to the small cards as well as the Major Arcana. Pamela Colman Smith (1878–1951), a skilled Symbolist artist and member of the Independent and Rectified Rite, illustrated the cards according to Waite's designs. The deck was published in 1909 and has rarely been out of print since that time. *SEE* SMITH, PAMELA COLMAN; TAROT.

Less widely known is the fact that Waite designed a second tarot deck, which was executed in 1920 and 1921 as a series of watercolor paintings by his associate John Brahms Trinick (1890–1974), an artist and Christian mystic of Australian origin. This deck was used in the Fraternitas Rosae Crucis as a set of images for meditation and contemplation, but never published as a deck; some of the images have recently been reprinted in Decker and Dummett 2002.

A number of other tarot decks, including the Universal Waite deck used to illustrate this encyclopedia, have used Waite's work with Pamela Colman Smith as their basis.

Waite combined his career in occultism with an extremely active professional life as a writer, journalist, and editor, and was also an enthusiastic Freemason, having entered Masonry in 1901. He continued to write and publish, and to preside over meetings of the Fellowship, up to the final months of his life. *SEE ALSO* GOLDEN DAWN, HERMETIC ORDER OF THE. FURTHER READING: DECKER AND DUMMETT 2002, GILBERT 1987.

wand. Far and away the most common magical instrument in legend, as well as in actual magical practice, the magical wand was originally one of many devices in the toolkit of the ancient and medieval ceremonial magician. In the *Key of Solomon*, the most famous of the medieval grimoires, it is one of more than a dozen tools carried by the magus and his five disciples, although its importance is marked by the fact that the magus himself, and not one of the disciples, must carry it. *SEE* KEY OF SOLOMON. Many other grimoires give it a lesser place, or omit it altogether.

The writings of French magician Eliphas Lévi (1810–1875), who kickstarted the nineteenth-century magical revival, paid much attention to the wand as a symbol of the will, and it was Lévi who assigned the wand to the element of fire, still its most common attribution. Following his lead, the Hermetic Order of the Golden Dawn and its successor groups paid much attention to the wand, and Golden Dawn alumnus Aleister Crowley (1875–1947) wrote at length on the wand's symbolism and uses. *SEE* CROWLEY, ALEISTER; GOLDEN DAWN, HERMETIC ORDER OF THE; LÉVI, ELIPHAS. Other twentieth-century mages such as Franz Bardon also worked extensively with the wand as a magical tool; *SEE* BARDON, FRANZ.

At present, the wand is used primarily in those magical traditions that trace their ancestry or inspiration to the major nineteenth- and twentieth-century orders of ceremonial magic. In the Neopagan movement, its place is generally taken by the athame, although some of the more traditional Wiccan systems find a place for the wand. *SEE* ATHAME; NEOPAGANISM. *SEE ALSO* LOTUS WAND. FURTHER READING: CROWLEY 1980, MATHERS 1888, REGARDIE 1971.

Example of a wooden wand; the wand is a symbol of elemental fire

wandering bishops. *SEE* INDEPENDENT BISHOPS.

waning. Decreasing or dwindling. In magical writings, the word is often used of the moon during the second half of the lunar month, from full moon to new moon. *SEE* MOON.

warding. Protecting or guarding, often in a magical sense. A warding spell is a magical working designed to protect or prevent access to a person, place, or thing. *SEE ALSO* BANISHING.

Wards, Setting. In the magical system of the Aurum Solis, the basic pattern of protective ritual, used in the same way as (and largely derived from) the Golden Dawn Lesser Banishing Ritual of the Pentagram; *SEE* PENTAGRAM, RITUALS OF THE. There are two versions: the Setting of the Wards of Power, which may be done in Hebrew or Greek, and the slightly different Setting of the Wards of Adamant, which is done in Latin. SEE AURUM SOLIS.

A fictional magical operation of the same name, but with a completely different form, was invented by the fantasy author Katherine Kurtz in her popular Deryni novels. Like several other elements of current fantasy fiction, it has been borrowed and put to use by some people in the modern magical community. SEE FANTASY OCCULTISM.

warlock. (Old English *waerloga*, "oathbreaker") An Anglo-Saxon insult, which came to be used against people who practiced magic. Later, the word became a common term for a magician, usually restricted to men. The idea that "warlock" was the male equivalent of "witch" seems to be an eighteenth-century notion. SEE WITCH.

Warner, William John. SEE CHEIRO.

Watcher on the Threshold. Among the more colorfully named concepts in magical philosophy, the Watcher on the Threshold is an entity or experience—definitions vary—which stands in the way of the early stages of progress in magical training. The term seems to have emerged in early nineteenth-century occult circles, and was publicized by occult novelist Edward Bulwer-Lytton (1803–1873) in his famous work *Zanoni*, originally published in 1842.

The exact nature of the Watcher is a matter of much dispute. Bulwer-Lytton described it as the sum total of the magician's bad habits and past actions. Many magical theorists have identified the Watcher as the ego's fear of growth and change, which must be met and overcome before significant progress on the magical path can be gained. In the writings of the Aurum Solis system of magic, the Watcher is seen as a misunderstood reflection of the higher self itself, turned into a figure of fear by the lower self's misunderstandings. SEE AURUM SOLIS.

In the occult philosophy of Alice Bailey, the Watcher on the Threshold is the sum total of illusion, glamour, and maya—that is, the distortions of thought, feeling, and action, respectively—which each individual has built up over past lives and must confront in the process of initiation. SEE GLAMOUR.

Whatever its actual nature, though, the experience of the Watcher is something nearly every aspirant to magical training encounters at some point in the early stages of his or her quest. Boredom, irritation, distractions, and a hundred other emotional obstacles to continued magical study and practice loom before the would-be mage. If these are resisted or explored by way of introspection, they give way to stark, paralyzing fear, often of overwhelming intensity.

The only way to overcome the Watcher is to keep on studying and practicing magic despite it all. After a relatively short period, the fear and the obstacles give way, and the first real potential for magical power begins to surface. FURTHER READING: BAILEY 1950, W. BUTLER 1962.

Watchers, the. Spiritual entities in various magical traditions, ancient and modern. In ancient Jewish and Christian esoteric traditions, the Watchers were a class of fallen angel, identified with the "sons of God" who mated with the daughters of men in Chapter 6 of the Book of Genesis. They are also called the Grigori, which is simply the Greek equivalent of "watchers." Various Gnostic traditions made use of this imagery; SEE GNOSTICISM.

In some modern magical traditions, "the Watcher" is a term for an artificial elemental built up by a working magical lodge, which guards and protects the lodge against intrusions from outside. SEE LODGE, MAGICAL.

In modern Pagan practice, the Watchers are conceptualized as entities guarding and witnessing at the four quarters of the magical circle, protecting the circle and keeping watch over the portals to other realms of being. While they are not usually named, there is a detailed symbolism involving them. The Watcher of the East corresponds to the spring equinox and the star Aldebaran; the Watcher of the South to the summer solstice and the star Regulus; the Watcher of the West to the autumn equinox and the star Antares; and the Watcher of the North to the winter solstice and the star Fomalhaut. SEE ROYAL STARS. The Watchers are associated with the four watchtowers, which play a role in the opening and closing ceremonies of many Wiccan and Pagan rituals. SEE WATCHTOWERS.

watchtowers. In modern Pagan practice, manifestations of the four directional powers, usually corresponding to the four elements and other aspects of the fourfold symbolism that plays so important a role in current Pagan magical practice. The four watchtowers are imagined far beyond the magical circle in the four directions. Each functions as a protective power for the circle, as well as a portal to other realms of being.

The watchtowers are presided over by the Watchers; *SEE* WATCHERS, THE. In most rituals for casting a magical circle in modern Paganism, calls to the watchtowers play an important part.

The four watchtowers cannot be traced in Pagan practice before the twentieth century, and are probably a borrowing from Golden Dawn magic, where the four Enochian watchtowers play a similar part in some ritual workings. *SEE* WATCHTOWERS, ENOCHIAN.

watchtowers, Enochian. Four tables of letter-combinations used in the Enochian system of magic, corresponding to the four elements. In many modern versions of Enochian magic, the four watchtowers are set up in the four quarters of the magical temple and used as gateways for the manifestation of elemental force.

The description of the tables as "watchtowers" is based on a vision received by Edward Kelly during the original Enochian workings, in which he perceived four great towers at the quarters of the earth, from which the angels of the watchtowers came forth. *SEE ALSO* ENOCHIAN MAGIC. FURTHER READING: REGARDIE 1971, R. TURNER 1989.

water, element of. In magical symbolism, one of the four (or five) elements, corresponding to matter in the liquid state, to the cold and moist qualities, and to the phlegmatic humor. As with all the elements, there are varying attributions to the element of water, but the following are standard in most current Western occult systems:

Symbol: ▽

Letter of Tetragrammaton: ה, Heh

Name of God: אל, AL, El (God)

Archangel: גבריאל, GBRIAL, Gabriel (Strength of God)

Angel: תליהד, TLIHD, Taliahad

Ruler: תרשים, ThRShIS, Tharsis

Elemental King: Nichsa

Elementals: Undines

Hebrew Name of Element: מים, MIM, Mayim

Direction: מערב, MAaRB, Mearab, the West

Season: Autumn

Time of Day: Sunset

Qualities: Cold and wet

Nature: Union

SEE ALSO DIRECTIONS IN OCCULTISM; ELEMENTS, MAGICAL; HUMORS.

waxing. Increasing or growing. In magical writings, this word is often applied to the moon during the first half of the lunar month, from the new moon to the full moon. *SEE* MOON.

Welsh Traditional witchcraft. An American Pagan tradition founded in New York City in the early 1970s, based on Celtic lore, primarily the Welsh legends included in the *Mabinogion*. Closely akin to most American Wicca of the time, it celebrates the eight sabbats, holds esbats on the full moon, and worships the Great Mother and the Horned God—the former under the names Arianrhod, Blodeuwedd, and Ceridwen, the latter as Mabon and Cernunnos. Welsh Traditional groups are called groves rather than covens, wear robes, and use green ritual cords. The sword is an important ritual tool in the system.

Welsh Traditional witchcraft had its largest influence in the 1970s and early 1980s, but there are still groves and individuals working in the tradition today over much of the United States. *SEE ALSO* MABINOGION; WICCA.

Wesak festival. In the lore of Theosophy and related systems of occult teaching, a celebration held by the Great White Lodge on the full moon of the Hindu month of Vaisakh (approximately May in the Western calendar), in a hidden valley on the northern slope of the Himalayas. The spectacle is described in some detail in C. W. Leadbeater's *The Masters and the Path*, which also includes a large color illustration of the Wesak festival, based on Leadbeater's astral visits there. What reality the festival has outside of Theosophical teaching is a matter of personal opinion and experience. SEE ALSO GREAT WHITE LODGE; MASTERS. FURTHER READING: LEADBEATER 1925.

Westcott, William Wynn. English occultist, 1848– 1925. Born at Leamington, Warwickshire, the son and nephew of physicians, Westcott studied medicine in his turn. In 1871, on graduating, he joined his uncle's medical practice, and the same year began what would be a lifelong involvement with Masonry.

By 1879 he had become fascinated with occultism, and left medical practice to spend two years of intensive study of Cabalistic, Hermetic, alchemical, and Rosicrucian writings. While he later described this period as a "life of retirement," he stayed sufficiently connected with the world to marry and to join the Societas Rosicruciana in Anglia (SRIA)—two milestones that both occurred in early 1880.

In 1881 he moved to London and entered the civil service as a deputy coroner. The following decade was a busy period in his life, and saw Westcott's occult involvements expand steadily. In 1883 he became a member of the Society of Eight, a secretive group dedicated to alchemy and other occult studies, which had been founded by the erratic occultist Kenneth Mackenzie. He also lectured on Cabala and Hermeticism to Anna Kingsford's Hermetic Society. In 1886, on the death of Kenneth Mackenzie, he took over and revived the Swedenborgian Rite of Masonry, and in the process obtained several parcels of records, rituals, and assorted papers from Mackenzie's widow.

It may have been in this way that Westcott obtained the so-called Cipher Manuscript, which became the foundation of his most enduring legacy, the Hermetic Order of the Golden Dawn. In the summer of 1887, according to his diary, Westcott worked out the cipher and decoded the manuscript, passing the results on to Samuel Mathers for review in September of that year. By early October, Westcott and Mathers were already planning a magical order based on the manuscript material. At some point during this period, Westcott also apparently forged the "Anna Sprengel" letters, which were presented to other members of the Golden Dawn as proof of the new order's pedigree. In March 1888 the Hermetic Order of the Golden Dawn was formally instituted, celebrated its first equinox ceremony, and initiated its first Neophytes.

Westcott, under the mottoes *Non Omnis Moriar* ("I shall not wholly die") and *Sapere Aude* ("Dare to be wise"), was one of the three Ruling Chiefs of the Hermetic Order of the Golden Dawn, wrote many of its instructional papers, and remained a leading figure in the order until 1897. In March of that year he was forced to resign from Golden Dawn office; his superiors in the Home Office had been informed of his membership in a magical order, and had demanded that he choose between his order and his job. His departure left Mathers in control of the order, and thus contributed largely to the crises that beset the order a few years later.

The Golden Dawn was by no means his only esoteric involvement in this period. In 1892 he became Supreme Magus of the SRIA, a position he held until his death; for a time, he was also actively involved in the Esoteric Section of the Theosophical Society, and gave lectures on the Cabala to Theosophical audiences. He seems to have withdrawn from active involvement in Theosophy around the time of his departure from the Golden Dawn.

In 1918 Westcott retired and moved to Durban, South Africa, to live with his daughter and son-in-law. He remained active in Masonic circles, and continued his studies, correspondence, and writing until his death in 1925. SEE ALSO CIPHER MANUSCRIPT; FREEMASONRY; GOLDEN DAWN, HERMETIC ORDER OF THE; MACKENZIE, KENNETH ROBERT HENDERSON; SOCIETAS ROSICRUCIANA IN ANGLIA (SRIA). FURTHER READING: GILBERT 1983C.

Wheel of Fortune. The tenth Major Arcanum of the tarot, the Wheel of Fortune was a traditional allegorical image in the Middle Ages, representing the rising and falling tides of fortune in life. Most versions of the tarot arcanum show a wheel with a variety of figures rising and falling on it. In the Golden Dawn Tarot system, this Arcanum is assigned to the Hebrew letter Kaph, while the French system assigns it to Yod. Its common meanings in divination include change of fortune, a moderate degree of happiness, transition, and evolution.

Its magical title is "Lord of the Forces of Life." *SEE ALSO* TAROT.

Tarot trump Wheel of Fortune (Universal Tarot)

wheel of the year. *SEE* SABBAT.

White Eagle Lodge. An international esoteric organization founded in 1936 by medium Grace Cooke and her husband Ivan as a vehicle for the teachings transmitted through Mrs. Cooke by her spirit guide, White Eagle. Operating at first out of rented quarters in London, the lodge purchased land in rural Hampshire after the Second World War and established a domed temple there in 1974. Its history has been one of modest but steady growth. Two additional temples have been founded, one in Texas and the other in Queensland, Australia, and more than a dozen lodges and study groups working with the White Eagle teachings can be found in various parts of the world.

The White Eagle Lodge defines itself as an nondenominational Christian church founded to give practical expression to the White Eagle teaching. Members practice meditation and spiritual healing, and there are inner Brotherhood groups at temples and lodges that carry on ritual work. Published works on the White Eagle teaching have something of a Theosophical flavor, with the Seven Rays, the chakras, vegetarianism, and talk about the Master Jesus much in evidence. *SEE* THEOSOPHY.

The emblem of the White Eagle Lodge is a six-pointed star at the center of an equal-armed cross, surrounded by a circle. FURTHER READING: HODGSON 1983, LIND 1984.

White Pillar. *SEE* JACHIN.

Wica. Gerald Gardner's original spelling of Wicca, used by him in the late 1940s and early 1950s and abandoned in favor of "Wicca" after that. *SEE* WICCA.

Wicca. The most successful and influential of the twentieth-century Neopagan movements, with a bewildering variety of traditions and branches. Wicca and its many offshoots have become the dominant force in the occult community throughout the English-speaking world in recent years. Its origins and history before 1951, however, are the subject of continuing controversy.

Its original creator or discoverer, Gerald Gardner, claimed that it was the original pre-Christian religion of the British Isles, handed down in secret for centuries. These claims were largely based on the theories of witchcraft researcher Margaret Murray, a friend of Gardner's, and they have been repeated and expanded by numerous Wiccans since his time. *SEE* GARDNER, GERALD BROUSSEAU; MURRAY HYPOTHESIS.

According to this account, Wicca was descended from the most ancient religion of the British Isles, the worship of a primeval goddess of fertility; later, a Horned God, lord of animals and the male aspect of fertility, was worshipped alongside the Goddess. On the arrival of Christianity, the upper classes converted to the new faith but the rural folk remained loyal to their Old Religion, gathering in covens on their traditional holy days to celebrate the powers of life and practice their magic. The witchcraft persecutions, according to this view, were Christian attempts to stamp out the Old Religion, but Wiccan covens survived in isolated areas. It was one of these surviving covens, Gardner claimed, that he encountered in the New Forest in the late 1930s. *SEE* CLUTTERBUCK, DOROTHY; ROSICRUCIAN ORDER OF THE CROTONA FELLOWSHIP (ROCF).

Gardner was not the first person to make such a claim, nor was he the last. Several older Pagan revivals, including the Druid orders founded in eighteenth-century Britain and the proto-Nazi Armanen system of Guido von List, traced their roots back to Pagan times along similar lines. *SEE* DRUIDRY; LIST, GUIDO VON. In the years since Wicca's public emergence, a substantial number of people have come forward claiming to possess the same sort of secret Pagan traditions handed down from the distant past, preserved within particular families (so-called "family traditions" or "fam-trads") or organized on a larger scale. *SEE* FAMILY TRADITION; GRANDMOTHER STORY. As of this writing, there are well over a hundred different Wiccan, quasi-Wiccan, or Pagan traditions that claim to be able to trace their origins to ancient times in this way.

However, many present-day Wiccans, and essentially all outside researchers, find the claim of an ancient origin for Wicca impossible to accept. The evidence for this more skeptical position is fairly strong. It has been shown, for example, that all the elements of Wicca were available to Gardner from sources in the British occult scene of his time, including the Woodcraft movement, Druidry, and the teachings of Aleister Crowley. *SEE* CROWLEY, ALEISTER; WOODCRAFT. Scholars have also shown that the actual pre-Christian religions of the British Isles and elsewhere have essentially nothing in common with modern Wicca; *SEE* PAGANISM.

Whatever the actual origins of Wicca—and the truth of the matter may never be known for certain—it has established a large and growing presence in the English-speaking world. The first known Wiccan covens were founded by Gardner and his direct students in England in the late 1940s and early 1950s. Within a short time of the publication of Gardner's books on Wicca, several other people came forward, claiming to have inherited family traditions of witchcraft. *SEE* COCHRANE, ROBERT; SANDERS, ALEC. While all these traditions were the subject of hostile media campaigns, they grew steadily in the 1950s and 1960s, and explosively in the years that followed.

The first Wiccan groups in the United States were founded in the early 1960s, but it was not until the great cultural explosion of the late Sixties that Wicca began to make significant headway in North America. The 1970s was in many ways the heyday of traditional Wicca in the United States, and saw a proliferation of Gardnerian and Alexandrian covens, as well as other homegrown traditions inspired by Gardner's writings and similar sources.

The 1980s brought a new current, with the rise of an intensely political, feminist Wicca, of which Dianic Wicca and San Francisco's Reclaiming Collective are typical forms. *SEE* DIANIC WICCA; RECLAIMING TRADITION. At the same time, along with the rest of the Neopagan scene, Wicca has expanded hugely, and covens of one sort or another can be encountered almost everywhere in North America; the Bible Belt itself increasingly sports a pentagram on the buckle.

Internationally, Wicca has established a sizeable presence in Australia, Canada, New Zealand, and several western European countries. There are also some Wiccan covens and solitary practitioners in Japan, Latin America, and in American military bases around the world.

In recent years, the Wiccan movement has become ever more diverse, as Wiccan traditions and other forms of modern Paganism have blended together freely; many groups calling themselves Wiccan have essentially nothing in common with the movement launched by Gerald Gardner in the early 1950s.

In an environment this diverse, few generalizations can be made about modern Wicca. The following points refer primarily to what is sometimes called "traditionalist Wicca"—that is, Wicca that remains fairly close to Gardner's original teachings.

Wicca is a duotheistic religion—that is, it worships two deities, a God and a Goddess, whose names vary widely in different branches of the movement and are usually among the secrets passed on during initiation. The God is horned, and associated with the Greek deity Pan and the Celtic Cernunnos. The Goddess has the three forms of Maiden, Mother, and Crone, and is associated primarily with the moon; her ancient equivalents include Diana, Hecate, and Isis. Both are powers of fertility and nature, and their mating is the creative polarity from which all things are born. *SEE* GOD, THE; GODDESS, THE.

Teachings and traditions about the God and Goddess make up a part of the lore of Wicca, which is passed on to members through a grade system of three degrees. Male students are traditionally initiated by a woman, female students by a man. Each degree is preceded by a course of study that covers a range of magical exercises and teachings drawn from various sources, most of them modern.

In those Wiccan traditions that still follow Gardner's approach fairly closely, initiates of the first degree are titled "Priest and Witch of the Great Goddess"; those of the second are titled "Witch Queen" if female and "Magus" if male, while third-degree initiates have the title "High Priestess" or "High Priest." The first-degree initiation includes forty strokes with a scourge, an oath of secrecy, and the presentation of the "working tools of the Art." In the second degree, the candidate is again scourged forty times, and then scourges the initiator one hundred twenty times, symbolizing the "law of threefold return"; thereafter, the Legend of the Goddess is either read or acted out, and the candidate is introduced to the powers of the four elements. The third degree, for its part, centers on ritual lovemaking between the candidate and the initiator within the consecrated circle; in some traditions this is done in symbolic form only, by dipping the athame into a chalice of wine.

An important part of Wiccan magic is the Great Rite, or ritual sex. In the original Gardnerian tradition, at least, the methods involved were very closely akin to those taught by P. B. Randolph, and later adapted by the Ordo Templi Orientis for its IX°—that is, heterosexual intercourse with both participants concentrating and visualizing on the purpose of the rite (Valiente 1978, pp. 147–148). *SEE* GREAT RITE; SEX AND OCCULTISM.

Alongside the degree ceremonies and training process, the activities of a coven include a calendar of eight sabbats or seasonal rituals—the four greater sabbats of Candlemas or Imbolc (February 2), May Eve or Beltane (April 30), Lammas or Lughnasadh (August 1) and Halloween or Samhain (October 31), and the four lesser sabbats, which are the solstices and equinoxes—as well as regular monthly meetings or esbats, which are held on the night of the full moon. *SEE* ESBAT; SABBAT. When climate and circumstances permit, these ceremonies are done in the nude, or "skyclad" in Wiccan jargon; *SEE* SKYCLAD. Robes are often worn in less favorable weather when working outdoors.

Standard equipment for Wiccans includes the athame, or black-hilted knife, which is the major working tool; the wand or staff; the cauldron; the pentacle; and the witch's garter, a length of scarlet cord that is normally worn tied above the left knee when not in use. These correspond to the elements of air, fire, water, earth, and spirit, respectively.

Although Wiccan initiations include oaths of secrecy, most of the material covered by these oaths has been published numerous times. According to Doreen Valiente, one of Gardner's High Priestesses, the rituals in use in Gardner's coven in 1953 were "practically identical" to those included in Gardner's novel *High Magic's Aid*, published in 1949 (Valiente 1978, p. 14). Later books by Gardner, Valiente, and other figures in the Wiccan community have given out a great deal of information about Wicca's tenets and practices, and may be consulted for details. *SEE ALSO* HIGH PRIEST; HIGH PRIESTESS. FURTHER READING: BRACELIN 1960, GARDNER 1949, HESELTON 2000, HUTTON 2000, VALIENTE 1987, VALIENTE 1989.

Wiccan Rede. A poem of fifty-two lines, originally written by Gwen Thompson in the 1960s and circulated among members of the New England Covens of Traditionalist Witches (NECTW). Like many early Wiccan poems and invocations, it was borrowed widely and without attribution, and may be found in many sources as an "ancient Wiccan teaching." It includes ethical principles, magical rules, lore of the moon and the winds, and practical advice.

The term "Wiccan rede" is also used for the central ethical rule of Wicca, which is taken from the last two lines of the poem, and has been borrowed by most modern Pagan groups in one form or another. It runs:

> *Eight words the Wiccan Rede fulfill:*
> *An ye harm none, do what ye will.*

As with most of Wiccan tradition, there seems to be no evidence that this rule as such is older than the mid-twentieth century, although it closely echoes Crowley's "Do what thou wilt shall be the whole of the law; love is the law, love under will." *SEE* CROWLEY, ALEISTER. *SEE ALSO* NEW ENGLAND COVENS OF TRADITIONALIST WITCHES (NECTW); WICCA.

Wiccaning. The Wiccan equivalent of christening, a ceremony to bless a newborn child and place it under the protection of the God and Goddess. In most versions of the Wiccaning ceremony, the child is presented to the four watchtowers, anointed with blessed oil or holy water and passed through the smoke of burning incense; *SEE* WATCHTOWERS. He or she is also given a secret Craft name, which is used until the child is old enough to choose his or her own Craft name; SEE CRAFT NAME.

A similar rite practiced by non-Wiccan Pagan groups is called Paganing. SEE NEOPAGANISM. SEE ALSO WICCA.

widdershins. A Scottish dialect term for counterclockwise movement. In traditional lore from most of Europe, moving around something in a widdershins direction was unlucky, and could be used deliberately to curse someone.

In modern magical practice, widdershins movement is used to disperse and dissolve energies. Many traditions use it in the process of closing down a magical working, to disperse any energy left over from the rite.

The opposite of widdershins in current Pagan usage is deosil; SEE DEOSIL.

will. Perhaps the most important concept in modern magic, will is understood by most practicing occultists as the fundamental energy behind magical action. The theory of the magical will was introduced by French magus Eliphas Lévi (1810–1875) in his influential *Dogme et Rituel de la Haute Magie* (*Doctrine and Ritual of High Magic*, 1845), the book that launched the modern magical revival, and has been borrowed effectively unchanged by most magical writers and theorists since that time. SEE LÉVI, ELIPHAS.

The will may be defined as the part of the self that chooses, decides, or intends. The central key to all magic, as understood by Lévi and subsequent writers, is learning to will a single thing strongly, with complete mental focus, for an extended period. Symbolism, either imagined or expressed in physical form, is used to channel the energies of the will toward the chosen target, and ritual methods and energy work are used to take care of secondary factors (such as banishing unwanted influences from the magical circle) or to embody the will on one or another plane of existence—but the will remains central.

Lévi's concept of the magical will was profoundly influenced by the writings of the German philosopher Arthur Schopenhauer (1788–1860), whose major book *The World as Will and Representation* (1818) argued that the human will is a facet or expression of a universal will, and that all things that are perceived by the senses or the mind—all "representations," in Schopenhauer's terms—are simply expressions of different aspects or "grades" of the will. Schopenhauer was among the few nineteenth-century thinkers outside the magical community to accept the reality and power of magic, and his essay "On the Will in Nature" includes a survey of Hermetic and Paracelsian magical writings.

A wide range of exercises for training and developing the will are taught in ceremonial magic traditions in the modern world. These represent a small fraction of the total body of methods in circulation in the late nineteenth and early twentieth centuries, when the idea of training the will was practiced in circles that had little or nothing to do with the occult. The physical culture movement, which was as focused on developing conscious control over the body as it was on increasing sheer physical strength and stamina, played a large part in this development; SEE PHYSICAL CULTURE. FURTHER READING: CROWLEY 1976, CROWLEY 1980, HADDOCK 1918, LÉVI 1972.

Williams, Charles. English poet, writer, and occultist, 1886–1945. Born to a middle-class family in London, he moved with his family to St. Albans in childhood. He was a devout Anglican from his earliest years on, and as a child loved to spend time in church. After an ordinary education, he attended University College, London, for two years. Thereafter he worked in the book trade, first at a small bookshop and then at the Oxford University Press in London, rising to the position of editor.

His first volume of poetry was published in 1912, and was followed by several others. In the meantime he had begun work on poems based on the Arthurian legends. This led him to A. E. Waite's writings on the Holy Grail, and from there to Waite's other works, with their quirky blend of Christian theology and Hermetic high magic. Williams contacted Waite directly in 1915, and in 1917 applied for membership in Waite's Fellowship of the Rosy Cross, an offshoot of the Hermetic Order of the Golden Dawn. SEE GOLDEN DAWN, HERMETIC ORDER OF THE; WAITE, ARTHUR EDWARD.

He was initiated on September 21, 1917, taking the motto *Qui Sitit Veniat* ("Who is thirsty, let him come"), and rose quickly through the grades of the fellowship. At the fall equinox of 1923 he was installed as Master of the

Temple—a rank equivalent to Hierophant in the original Golden Dawn—for a term of six months, and took the same position again in the fall of 1924. He remained an active member until 1927.

In 1922 he began to offer evening lectures through a London continuing-education program, and soon became an enormously popular speaker on Christian literature and theology. He gathered a following, mostly of younger women, who were attracted both by his charisma and his mystical approach to Anglican Christianity. In 1939, he formulated this group into an order, the Companions of the Coinherence, drawing the name from one of the central concepts of his theology—the idea that all beings share a common life and gain salvation through one another. SEE COMPANIONS OF THE COINHERENCE.

Williams' career as a writer and poet was deeply influenced both by his occult studies and by his Christian beliefs. He wrote seven novels with themes drawn from Christian occultism, and his two collections of Arthurian poems, *Taliessin Through Logres* and *The Region of the Summer Stars*, both contain poems that include detailed descriptions of Golden Dawn magical operations such as Rising on the Planes. He also wrote a history of witchcraft, called simply *Witchcraft* (1941), with a chapter on high magic deeply permeated with ideas drawn from Waite and from Dion Fortune's work on sexual polarity as well.

In 1939, on the outbreak of the Second World War, Williams was evacuated to Oxford along with the entire London branch of the Oxford University Press. There he made connections, through his friend C. S. Lewis, with the Inklings, an informal literary society that included Lewis and J. R. R. Tolkien among its members. Williams was probably the source for much of the occult material in Lewis' space trilogy (*Out of the Silent Planet*, *Perelandra*, and *That Hideous Strength*), which was written during the war years. Williams' health failed unexpectedly toward war's end, and he died after a routine surgical operation a few days after the German surrender in 1945. SEE ALSO CHRISTIAN OCCULTISM. FURTHER READING: HADFIELD 1959, WILLARD 1995, WILLIAMS 1941, WILLIAMS 1954.

Wirth, Oswald. (Joseph Paul Oswald) Swiss occultist, 1860–1943. Born in Brienz, Switzerland, to Alsatian parents who fled their homeland after the revolutions of 1848, Wirth was raised Catholic but became interested in mesmerism in his teen years. After leaving home and working for a time as a bookkeeper in London, he moved to France, where he became a Freemason and took up a career as a mesmeric healer.

In 1887 he met Stanislaus de Guaita, the leading figure in the French occult revival of the time, and became his personal secretary and close friend. SEE GUAITA, STANISLAUS DE. Involvement with Guaita brought him into the thick of the Parisian occult scene, and he was a founding member of the Ordre de la Rose+Croix Kabbalistique, the premier Parisian magical lodge, which was organized in 1888. In 1889, prompted by Guaita, Wirth issued a tarot deck based on contemporary French occult symbolism, and contributed an essay on the astronomical symbolism of the tarot to Papus' book *The Tarot of the Bohemians*.

Guaita died of a drug overdose in 1897, and friends of Wirth found him a position at the library of the French government's Colonial Office. For the next forty years, he continued to write extensively on occult and Masonic subjects, and in 1927 came up with a second tarot deck, based on essentially the same principles as his earlier deck but with a more complex symbolic structure.

When the Germans invaded France in 1940, Wirth was on vacation in the Ardennes—the focal point of the invasion—with his sister and niece. They managed to escape to southern France, where he settled at Vienne, south of Lyons. There Wirth died in 1943. FURTHER READING: DECKER AND DUMMETT 2002, WIRTH 1985.

witch. The most emotionally loaded of the terms used for a practitioner of magic in English, the word "witch" has been the subject of heated controversies in the modern Pagan scene. In Old English, all agree, it was originally spelled *wicce* (the feminine form) or *wicca* (the masculine), and meant a person who divines or casts spells. Beyond that point, the arguments begin.

According to the folk etymology introduced by Wicca's founder or discoverer Gerald Gardner, and accepted by many modern Pagans, *wicce* derives from an old

Indo-European root meaning "wise," and witchcraft is therefore "the craft of the wise." Scholars of historical linguistics have rejected this claim, pointing out that it violates several known phonological laws, and it has been pointed out that "wise one" is actually the literal meaning of a completely different word for a magical practitioner—*wizard*.

An alternative interpretation, more generally accepted by scholars but heatedly rejected by many Wiccans, holds that *wicce* descends from a different root, one meaning "to bend or twist." Since Old English, like all Indo-European languages, puts a strong moral overlay on the opposition between "straight" and "twisted," this is a good deal less complimentary than it looks.

The disputes about the word are not limited to its etymology. In modern usage, it has at least four mutually contradictory meanings:

(1) In many parts of the Pagan community, "witch" means exactly the same thing as "Wiccan"—that is, a follower of some form of the Pagan religion of Wicca. It is often capitalized when this meaning is intended, just as "Christian," "Jew," and other terms for followers of a particular religion are capitalized. *SEE* WICCA.

(2) In other parts of the Pagan community, "witch" means a folk magician—what in Britain not long ago would have been called a "cunning man" or "cunning woman," a person who had an extensive knowledge of practical magic, together with other skills such as herbalism. In circles that use this meaning, a sharp distinction is drawn between "witchcraft," which is a tradition of practical magic, and "Wicca," which is a religion. *SEE* CUNNING MAN/WOMAN; NATURAL MAGIC.

(3) Among anthropologists and other academics, by contrast, "witch" means a person who is a source of noxious supernatural power. Most traditional cultures around the world believe that some people have an inborn power to curse others; this often has nothing to do with the practice of magic. Since early in the twentieth century, anthropologists have used the word "witch" as a label for people identified as one of these innate cursers, while "sorcerer" is the label for a person who practices magical rituals. While these uses are arbitrary, they have become very common among scholars of every kind. *SEE* EVIL EYE.

(4) Among conservative Christians, finally, the word "witch" means roughly what it did to church officials during the Burning Times: a member of an evil cult that worships the Devil. Even in recent years, Christian Fundamentalists have made repeated attempts to use the word "witch" to redefine Wiccans and other Pagans as Satanists, and to blame them for alleged cases of Satanic ritual abuse. *SEE* MAGIC, PERSECUTION OF; SATANIC RITUAL ABUSE.

Given the extremely mixed messages communicated by the word "witch," some Pagans in recent decades have argued that it should be abandoned in favor of "Wiccan," "Pagan," or some other less controversial label. *SEE ALSO* NEOPAGANISM.

Witch. When capitalized, this much-debated word usually means a follower of some form of the Pagan religion of Wicca; the capitalization is meant to put it on the same level as other labels for religious believers, such as "Christian" and "Jew." *SEE* WICCA; WITCH.

witch ball. A glass ball several inches across, usually blue, green, or violet, used to banish the evil eye and other forms of hostile magic. Some contain pins and needles to disperse negative energies, while others are empty. As late as the end of the nineteenth century, witch balls were hung in windows, though this was often for decorative purposes; as with so many magical customs, the original purpose was gradually forgotten, leaving nothing but a puzzling custom. FURTHER READING: MERRIFIELD 1987.

witch bottle. A common method of magical protection in English and colonial American folk magic, a witch bottle is a glass bottle filled with nails, broken glass, and other sharp objects. The maker of the witch bottle then fills the remaining air space in the bottle with his or her own urine, and buries the bottle in his or her yard.

In modern accounts of this magical method, the witch bottle is preventive; hostile magical energies sent against the maker are safely absorbed by the bottle instead. The older tradition used it as a defense against hostile spells that had actually been cast, and claimed that the caster would be unable to urinate as long as the bottle was left sealed.

Another form of witch bottle, used as a more drastic means of defense against hostile magic, involves bottling up the urine of a victim of enchantment, sealing it tightly, and placing the bottle in a roaring fire. When the bottle exploded, according to tradition, the hostile magician would die suddenly.

Witch bottles have been common enough in Britain that archeologists routinely find them buried near the foundations of churches. This form of magical protection was especially popular in the seventeenth and eighteenth centuries. SEE ALSO CUNNING MAN/WOMAN. FURTHER READING: MERRIFIELD 1987.

Witch persecutions. SEE BURNING TIMES; MAGIC, PERSECUTION OF.

witchcraft. Literally, the craft practiced by witches; SEE WITCH. The term is used in several different senses in the modern occult and Pagan communities. Neopagan groups who identify with medieval witches but claim to be unrelated to modern Wicca often use it as an identifying label for themselves, while it is also used by some for European folk magic, as distinct from the Pagan religion of Wicca. In other contexts, it is used as a more general word for magic. SEE CUNNING MAN/WOMAN; WICCA.

Witches' ladder. A cord tied with thirteen knots used to keep track of repetitions during chanting or meditation, along the lines of a Catholic or Buddhist rosary. The knots are slipped through the fingers one at a time. SEE CORD; WICCA.

Witches' Sabbath. SEE SABBATH, WITCHES'.

Witta. A modern Pagan tradition created in America in the late twentieth century, and popularized by Pagan author Edain McCoy in two books. Although Witta claims ancient Irish roots, the word *Witta* itself is impossible to pronounce in Irish, which does not double the letter *t* and has no letter *w*. The tradition also includes English practices, such as dancing around the maypole, which were never practiced by the native Irish. SEE MAYPOLE.

Like most modern Pagan traditions, it celebrates the eight sabbats and holds monthly meetings at the full moon. It uses the names Brighid and Lugh for the God-dess and God, but encourages practitioners to offer worship to any traditional Irish god or goddess. There are no degrees of initiation. A relatively small tradition, Witta has an organized presence in several US states and a scattering of solitary practitioners elsewhere. SEE ALSO NEO-PAGANISM; WICCA. FURTHER READING: MCCOY 1993.

Women's International Terrorist Conspiracy From Hell (WITCH). A short-lived movement in the counter-culture of the late 1960s, WITCH was founded on All Hallow's Eve of 1968 and consisted almost entirely of young women attending college. WITCH manifestos presented it as a revolutionary guerrilla organization, proclaiming that witches and Gypsies were the original guerrilla fighters against oppression. Like so many of the radical youth movements of the Sixties, though, the activities of WITCH were far less militant than the rhetoric, and WITCH members contented themselves with dressing up in black robes and pointed hats for demonstrations.

According to the WITCH literature, any woman could become a witch by repeating the words "I am a Witch" three times, and thinking about what that meant. This claim has not generally been recognized by other traditions of witchcraft.

WITCH seems to have faded quietly out of existence in the early 1970s, along with the rest of the Sixties' counterculture. Attempts have been made to revive the movement at intervals since that time, apparently with little success. SEE ALSO DIANIC WICCA; RECLAIMING TRADITION.

Woodcraft. Quasi-Pagan youth movement organized in 1902 by Canadian-American nature writer Ernest Thompson Seton (1860–1946). One of the first back-to-nature movements in the Western world, Woodcraft borrowed heavily from Native American ritual and tradition in an effort to bridge the widening gap between human beings and the natural world, and to teach values of self-discipline and cooperation to young people.

Highly successful in its first years, Woodcraft grew from a single "tribe" of forty-two in 1902 to some 200,000 members in 1910, the year that the Boy Scouts of America (BSA) was founded. Under pressure from the

BSA's wealthy and influential founders, Seton brought his group into the Boy Scout fold, but this alliance broke up in 1915 over differences in goals. Seton refounded his Woodcraft League in 1916 and opened Woodcraft tribes to girls as well as boys, also founding Woodcraft Clubs for adults and a semisecret inner order, the Red Lodge or Sun Lodge, which was devoted to the more mystical side of Woodcraft and had three degrees of initiation.

Seton soon had an international following, with groups founded on Woodcraft lines active in Britain and central Europe. The British Woodcraft groups, the Order of Woodcraft Chivalry and the Kindred of the Kibbo Kift, both played an important role in the prehistory of modern Wicca. SEE KIBBO KIFT, KINDRED OF THE; ORDER OF WOODCRAFT CHIVALRY (OWC); WICCA.

Woodcraft had a strongly Pagan character, including certain features that would be instantly recognized by most present-day Pagans. Woodcraft members met in a ritually cast circle, with four lamps in the four directions to mark the quarters, which had their sacred symbols and colors as well. Near the center was an image of the Red God, the horned spirit of the "Buffalo Wind" that called overcivilized humanity back to its wild origins. Wakanda, the Great Spirit, and Maka Ina, Mother Earth, were also reverenced in Woodcraft ceremonials.

Although it was a major rival to the Boy Scouts at its peak in the 1920s, Woodcraft went into a decline during the Great Depression and the Second World War, and Seton's death in 1946 left it rudderless. There are still a small number of Woodcraft groups in North America and Britain, and a sizeable movement in the Czech Republic. Most of Seton's legacy, however, remains forgotten and unexplored by modern Pagans. FURTHER READING: GREER AND COOPER 1998, SETON 1920, SETON 1926.

World, the. The twenty-first (or twenty-second) Major Arcanum of the tarot, also called "the Universe" in some decks. Its imagery varies in early decks, although most recent decks have a nude or partly nude woman dancing in an oval space at the center, surrounded by various symbolic designs. In the Golden Dawn and French systems of tarot symbolism alike, this Arcanum is assigned to the Hebrew letter Tau.

The magical title of this Arcanum is "Great One of the Night of Time." SEE ALSO TAROT; TAU.

Tarot trump the World (Universal Tarot)

Wronski, Joseph-Marie-Hoené. Polish polymath and occultist, 1776–1853. The son of the royal architect to the last King of Poland, Wronski began a military career and distinguished himself in the defense of Warsaw in 1794 against Prussian and Russian armies. In 1797 he left the army and went to Germany, where he studied philosophy, mathematics, and law. The year 1800 found him in France, beginning a long and eccentric publishing career with several studies of Kant's philosophy. In 1803, by his own account, he discovered the Absolute, and the rest of his life was spent writing and publishing increasingly elaborate and obscure books about his insights, carrying on bitter disputes with the ever-increasing list of people he thought had slighted him or ignored his achievements, and teaching a handful of students, of whom Eliphas Lévi is the most famous. He died in abject poverty.

Wronski's system of thought is unusually difficult even by the standards of nineteenth-century philosophy. According to Wronski, the Law of Creation—a numerical structure based principally on the numbers three and seven, which governs the unfolding of all things out of the polarity between Spirit and Nothingness—comes into manifestation in the world of experience by way of the Law of Progress. The interplay between these two laws gives rise to a dizzying array of trinities and septenaries that spread out to embrace every imaginable phenomenon. There are reasons for believing that this structure has roots in the Cabala, which was much studied in Poland by Jews and non-Jews alike during Wronski's youth.

Among his most intriguing creations was a "Prognomètre," a complex machine for predicting the future through the application of the Law of Creation. It and its method of operation were among Wronski's most jealously guarded secrets. After Wronski's death, the "Prognomètre" came into the hands of Eliphas Lévi, who discovered his teacher's device in a secondhand shop; what happened to it after Lévi's death seems to be unknown. *SEE ALSO* LÉVI, ELIPHAS. FURTHER READING: J. GODWIN 1995.

Wunjo. (Old Germanic, "joy") The eighth rune of the elder futhark, corresponding to the concepts of joy, success, and perfection. It represents the sound *w*. Some modern runemasters associate this rune with the god Odin, others with Ullr. *SEE* ELDER FUTHARK.

The same rune, named Wynn (Old English, "joy") is the eighth rune of the Anglo-Saxon futhorc. The Old English rune-poem relates it to joy without suffering, sorrow, or anxiety. *SEE* ANGLO-SAXON FUTHORC.

Rune Wunjo (Wynn)

Wynn. *SEE* WUNJO.

Xaos magic. *SEE* CHAOS MAGIC.

yarthkin. In English folk belief, a hostile or malevolent earth spirit, which can be kept at bay by appropriate magical workings. *SEE ALSO* GNOME; HYTERSPRITE.

year and a day. In modern Wicca and many modern Pagan traditions, the period of time that must be spent studying a given degree or grade before the next one can be received. Measuring time by a period of one year and one day is a very old habit in England. In medieval English law, for example, if a wounded person died within a year and a day of the injury, the one responsible for the wound could be charged with murder.

In his book *The White Goddess*, an important sourcebook for the twentieth-century Pagan revival, Robert Graves argues that "a year and a day" originally referred to a traditional calendar in which the day of the winter solstice was not part of any month. *SEE ALSO* OGHAM TREE-CALENDAR. FURTHER READING: GRAVES 1966.

Yeats, William Butler. Irish poet and occultist, 1865–1939. Born in Dublin, the son of an artist, Yeats spent most of his first eight years in rural Sligo, Ireland, then attended school in London and Dublin. Poor grades put a university education out of reach, and he attended art school for a little over a year. By the time he left school he had decided on a career as a poet.

His interest in occultism dated nearly as far back as his commitment to poetry. In 1885, the year he first published verse, he helped found a Dublin Hermetic Society for the study of occultism, oriental religions, and philosophy. In 1887, on moving to London, he joined the Theosophical Society and advanced to its inner Esoteric Section in 1888, though he left in 1890. *SEE* THEOSOPHICAL SOCIETY; THEOSOPHY.

His Theosophical connections, however, led him to the Hermetic Order of the Golden Dawn, which played a much more substantial role in his life. He was initiated as a Neophyte in 1890, shortly before his departure from the Theosophical Society, and rapidly ascended through the grades of the order, attaining the grade of Adeptus Minor at the beginning of 1893. *SEE* GOLDEN DAWN, HERMETIC ORDER OF THE. He and Samuel Mathers, one of the order's founders, became close personal friends, and the two of them—together with Mathers' wife Moina and Maud Gonne, an Irish political activist and Yeats' sometime lover—worked together on plans for an Irish occult order, the Castle of Heroes; *SEE* CASTLE OF HEROES.

In the crisis of leadership that nearly destroyed the order in 1900, Yeats took an active role in organizing the revolt against Mathers, and emerged from the struggle as one of the leaders of the order. In the difficulties that followed the revolt, he tried to keep the order to a moderate course, and when the order finally broke apart in 1903 he became a member of the largest of the successor groups, the Stella Matutina. He remained active in it until 1922, when the London lodge foundered. *SEE* STELLA MATUTINA, ORDER OF THE.

Before that time, he had begun a more personal exploration of the unseen world. In 1917, Yeats married Georgie Hyde-Lees, and within a few days of their marriage his wife surprised him by deciding to experiment with automatic writing. The messages that came through outlined an entire system of occult philosophy based on twenty-eight symbolic phases of the moon. A book presenting the system, *A Vision*, was privately published in 1925, and then thoroughly revised and published again in 1937. Much of his poetry, from the beginning of the communications on, borrowed from the imagery of the system. *SEE* VISION, A.

Yeats' occult activities took place in the midst of one of the most successful poetic careers in modern history, a career that won Yeats the 1923 Nobel Prize in literature and gave the twentieth century some of its most widely read and respected poems. Yeats himself passed judgment on his magical studies in a 1892 letter to John O'Leary:

> If I had not made magic my constant study I could not have written a single word of my Blake book, nor would *The Countess Kathleen* have ever come to exist. The mystical life is the centre of all that I do and all that I think and all that I write (Yeats 1955b, p. 211).

After Ireland won independence in 1921, Yeats served in the Irish Senate before failing health forced him to step down. He died in southern France in 1939. FURTHER READING: HARPER 1974, YEATS 1955A, YEATS 1956.

yechidah. (Hebrew YChDH, "only one") In Cabalistic theory, the highest aspect of the human soul, corresponding to the Sephirah Kether, and included in the neshamah. The yechidah corresponds to the Neoplatonist concept of the *scintilla* or *synteresis*, the spark of divine light at the center of the self. *SEE* CABALA; NESHAMAH; NEOPLATONISM.

Yellow Ray. In occult philosophy, the third of the Seven Rays, the basic creative energies of the universe. The Yellow Ray is the ray of intelligence, and its chief characteristic is adaptability; it corresponds to the Buddhist concept of "skillful means," the adaptation of all available resources in the quest for enlightenment. The Yellow Ray is also closely connected with astrology and other systems for determining the influences of time. *SEE* ASTROLOGY.

In Theosophical lore, the Yellow Ray is under the direction of the Venetian Chohan, a Master of the Great White Lodge. Its symbolic gem is the emerald. *SEE* VENETIAN CHOHAN. *SEE ALSO* RAYS, SEVEN.

Yesod. (Hebrew YSVD, "foundation") The ninth Sephirah of the Cabalistic Tree of Life, located on the Middle Pillar between Tiphareth and Malkuth. Its standard magical symbolism is as follows:

Name of God: ShDI AL ChI, Shaddai El Chai (Almighty Living God).

Archangel: GBRIAL, Gabriel (Strength of God).

Angelic Host: KRVBIM, Kerubim, Powers of the Elements.

Astrological Correspondence: LBNH, Levanah (the Moon).

Tarot Correspondence: The four Nines of the pack.

Elemental Correspondence: Air.

Magical Image: A beautiful and very strong naked man.

Additional Title: The Treasure House of Images.

Colors: in Atziluth—indigo.

in Briah—violet.

in Yetzirah—very dark purple.

in Assiah—citrine flecked with azure.

Correspondence in the Microcosm: The nephesh.

Correspondence in the Body: The genitals.

Grade of Initiation: 2=9, Theoricus

Negative Power: GMLIAL, Gamaliel, the Obscene Ones.

The corresponding passage from the *Thirty-two Paths of Wisdom* reads as follows: "The Ninth Path is the Pure Intelligence, so called because it purifies the Numerations; it proves and corrects the designing of their representation, and disposes the unity with which they are combined without diminution or division." *SEE ALSO* CABALA; TREE OF LIFE.

Yetzirah. (Hebrew ITzIRH, "formation") In the Cabala, the third of the four worlds, associated with the angelic level of being and the Vau of Tetragrammaton. It is represented on the Tree of Life as a whole by ten orders of angels, but corresponds most closely with the six Sephiroth from Chesed through Yesod. In Yetzirah, the Tetragrammaton is spelled YVD HA VAV HA, and the secret name of the world of Yetzirah is Mah. *SEE* CABALA; MAH; TETRAGRAMMATON.

Yod. (Hebrew YVD, "hand, fist") The tenth letter of the Hebrew alphabet, a single letter with the sound-values *i* and *y* and the numerical value of ten. Its standard magical symbolism is as follows:

> *Path of the Tree of Life:* Path 20, Chesed to
>   Tiphareth.
> *Astrological Correspondence:* Virgo, the Virgin.
> *Tarot Correspondence:* Trump IX, the Hermit.
> *Part of the Cube of Space:* The lower north edge.
> *Colors:* in Atziluth—yellowish green.
>   in Briah—slate grey.
>   in Yetzirah—greenish grey.
>   in Assiah—plum.

The corresponding passage from the *Thirty-two Paths of Wisdom* reads as follows: "The Twentieth Path is the Intelligence of Will, and is so called because it is the means of preparation of all and each created being, and by this intelligence the existence of the Primordial Wisdom becomes known." *SEE ALSO* CABALA; HEBREW ALPHABET.

Hebrew letter Yod

yoga. (Sanskrit, "yoke, joining") In Hindu tradition, any of a wide array of systems of spiritual training and practice designed to bring about the state of enlightenment. The best-known form of yoga is hatha yoga, a system of physical and spiritual exercise in which the body is placed in special postures to facilitate relaxation, balance, health, and meditation. Hatha yoga itself is simply one element of *raja* ("royal") yoga, also called *ashtanga* ("eight-limbed") yoga, a system of spiritual development in which postures, breathing exercises, moral development,

and meditation practice are combined to lead to the experience of *samadhi* or union with the divine.

Yoga has been a subject of great fascination to Western occultists for several centuries, since Western travelers in India first began to bring back reports of the mystical practices of Hindu yogins. References to yogic practices can be found in ancient Greek and Roman sources, and such figures as Pythagoras and Apollonius of Tyana were said to have traveled to India in order to study the wisdom of the East. *SEE* APOLLONIUS OF TYANA; PYTHAGORAS.

The British conquest of India in the late eighteenth century launched a new wave of interest in yoga, as English officials reported back on the fascinating physical and spiritual abilities possessed by some Hindu yogins. Until the end of the nineteenth century, however, very little accurate was known about yogic practices, and a great deal of misinformation was circulated. The American occultist and physical culturist William Walker Atkinson (1862–1932), for example, wrote a series of books on yoga in the first decades of the twentieth century under the name Yogi Ramacharaka; the material in these books had essentially nothing to do with yoga, but was drawn from contemporary occultism, New Thought, and physical culture practices. *SEE* ATKINSON, WILLIAM WALKER; PHYSICAL CULTURE.

The rise of Theosophy in the last decades of the nineteenth century opened the door to a more accurate perception of yoga. The Theosophical Society led the way by sponsoring and publishing English translations of basic yoga texts, and presenting basic instructions on yogic meditation in a series of popular books. *SEE* THEOSOPHICAL SOCIETY. Starting in the early twentieth century, as a result of this interest, a series of Hindu yogic practitioners traveled to America and Europe and launched the modern Western yoga movement. At the same time, a number of Westerners wrote important books on the subject, which were widely circulated. Two authors who were particularly influential in the Western occult scene were Sir John Woodroffe, whose original works and translations of classic yoga texts introduced the concept of the chakras to Western occultism, and Aleister Crowley, whose influential books

Book Four (1911) and *Eight Lectures on Yoga* (1939) presented a system of yoga based on classical Hindu texts but fitted to Western students. *SEE* CHAKRA; CROWLEY, ALEISTER.

By the last decades of the twentieth century, competent instruction in classical yoga could be found in most large cities in the Western world, and books, videos, and other resources on the subject were even more widely available. Many Western occult traditions have made active use of these resources, and various forms of yoga now play a significant role in several Western occult systems. FURTHER READING: CROWLEY 1980, CROWLEY 1991.

Yogi Ramacharaka. *SEE* ATKINSON, WILLIAM WALKER.

younger futhark. The system of runes used in the Scandinavian countries during the Viking Age, the younger futhark was a condensation and simplification of the elder futhark, reducing twenty-four runes into sixteen and simplifying many of the individual runes. Much more is known about this system of runes than about the other traditional runic alphabets (the elder futhark and the Anglo-Saxon futhorc), since it stayed in use much later and was standard in Iceland, where most of the surviving Pagan Teutonic lore is found.

Original sources of material on the younger futhark include two rune-poems, one Norwegian and the other Icelandic, as well as a range of more fragmentary sources in surviving poetry, sagas, and runic inscriptions. *SEE ALSO* ANGLO-SAXON FUTHORC; ELDER FUTHARK; FUTHARK; RUNES. FURTHER READING: THORSSON 1998.

Rune	Sound Value	Name	Meaning
ᚠ	F	Fe	Wealth
ᚢ	U	Ur	Rain
ᚦ	Th	Thurs	Giant
ᚨ	A	As	God Odin
ᚱ	R	Reidh	Journey
ᚲ	K	Kaun	Sore
ᚼ	H	Hagall	Hail
ᚾ	N	Naudhr	Need
ᛁ	I	Is	Ice
ᛆ	Á	Ar	Plenty
ᛋ	S	Sol	Sun
ᛏ	T	Tyr	God Tyr
ᛒ	B	Bjarkan	Birch Tree
ᛘ	M	Madhr	Man
ᛚ	L	Logr	Water
ᛦ	Y	Yr	Yew Tree

Yr. (Anglo-Saxon rune) (Old English, "axe") The twenty-seventh rune of the Anglo-Saxon futhorc, described in the Old English rune-poem as a reliable weapon on horseback. It represents the sound *y*. *SEE* ANGLO-SAXON FUTHORC.

Rune Yr

Yr. (Younger Futhark rune) (Old Norse, "yew tree") Yr is the sixteenth and last rune of the younger futhark, standing for endings, for eternal life and sudden death. It represents the sound *r*. *SEE* YOUNGER FUTHARK.

The same rune is also the sixteenth rune of the Armanen runic system, and represents the rainbow. Its magical power, from the rune-charm of the Old Norse *Havamal*, is to charm and bind the hearts of the young. It corresponds to the god Ymir and to the child, and represents the sound *y*. *SEE* ARMANEN RUNES.

Rune Yr

Yule. In modern Paganism, the most common name for the midwinter solstice, one of the eight sabbats of the Pagan ceremonial year. *SEE* SABBAT.

Z

Zain, C. C. (Elbert Benjamine) American astrologer and occultist, 1882–1951. The child of a respected Iowa physician, his name was originally Benjamin Williams. He attended public schools and received a bachelor's degree in biology from Iowa State University.

His interest in occultism dated from 1898, after seeing a performance by a traveling hypnotist and mentalist. Two years later he cast his first horoscope, beginning what would be a lifelong involvement in astrology, and made contact with the Brotherhood of Light, one of the surviving fragments of the Hermetic Brotherhood of Luxor. *SEE* HERMETIC BROTHERHOOD OF LUXOR (H. B. OF L.). In 1909, he was asked to become a member of the governing council of the brotherhood, and for all practical purposes was placed in charge of what was at that time a small and struggling organization.

In 1914 he began work on a correspondence course that would teach the brotherhood's system of occult philosophy and practice. He moved to Los Angeles in 1915, and devoted his time to establishing the Brotherhood of Light. Helping him in this work was former Brotherhood of Light member Genevieve Stebbins, who had been a major figure in the occult wing of the physical culture movement. *SEE* PHYSICAL CULTURE; STEBBINS, GENEVIEVE.

He married Elizabeth Dorris in 1916, and began teaching classes to the public in 1918. Since occult teaching and writing did not earn a living for Benjamine and his family, he worked at a wide range of jobs—commercial fisherman, cowboy, lumberman, and ranch foreman, among others. He also found time for hiking and camping, and was involved in establishing the first bird sanctuary in the Los Angeles area.

The correspondence course was finally completed in 1934. By that time Benjamine had founded a new organization, the Church of Light, which was incorporated in 1932. Benjamine spent the remainder of his life in Los Angeles, teaching classes and managing the Church of Light. He died in 1951. *SEE ALSO* CHURCH OF LIGHT. FURTHER READING: GIBSON 1996.

Zanoni. The central character of Edward Bulwer-Lytton's novel of the same name, first published in 1842. Closely modeled on the Comte de Saint-Germain, Zanoni is a mysterious and immortal adept, one of the last two members of an ancient Chaldean magical order. His adventures, which end with his willing death in the midst of the French Revolution, involve most of the clichés and many of the details of nineteenth-century occultism.

The character of Zanoni, and Bulwer-Lytton's novel generally, had a powerful influence on occultists for most of a century after the novel's publication. Samuel Mathers, one of the founding members of the Hermetic Order of the Golden Dawn, modeled himself on Zanoni to a sometimes embarrassing degree, and used "Zan" and "Zanoni" as nicknames. *SEE* MATHERS, SAMUEL LIDDELL. *SEE ALSO* SAINT-GERMAIN, COMTE DE. FURTHER READING: BULWER-LYTTON N.D., J. GODWIN 1994.

Zarathustra. *SEE* ZOROASTER.

Zata, Elman. In Rosicrucian lore, one of the three highest Chiefs of the Rosicrucian Order. In the Adeptus Minor ritual of the Hermetic Order of the Golden Dawn, he is described as an Arab, and said to have died at the age of 463. *SEE* ALVERDA, HUGO; BRY, FRANCISCUS DE. *SEE ALSO* GOLDEN DAWN, HERMETIC ORDER OF.

Zauir Anpin. (Hebrew ZAVIR ANPIN, "small face") In Cabalistic thought, one of the Partzufim or Personifications of the Tree of Life, also known as Microprosopus or the Lesser Countenance. Zauir Anpin represents God as an entity present and active in the universe, represented by the Tetragrammaton, YHVH. Since the Hebrew phrase "small face" also implies "short-tempered," Zauir Anpin is identified in many Cabalistic writings with the angry and jealous god of the Old Testament.

On the Tree of Life, Zauir Anpin is represented by the six Sephiroth from Chesed to Yesod. *SEE* TREE OF LIFE. *SEE ALSO* CABALA.

Zayin. (Hebrew ZIN, "sword") The seventh letter of the Hebrew alphabet, a single letter with a sound-value of *z* and a numerical value of seven. Its standard magical symbolism is as follows:

> *Path of the Tree of Life:* Path 17, Binah to Tiphareth.
> *Astrological Correspondence:* Gemini, the Twins.
> *Tarot Correspondence:* Trump VI, the Lovers.
> *Part of the Cube of Space:* The upper east edge.
> *Colors:* in Atziluth—orange.
>> in Briah—pale mauve.
>> in Yetzirah—color of new yellow leather.
>> in Assiah—reddish grey tinged with mauve.

The corresponding text from the *Thirty-two Paths of Wisdom* reads as follows: "The Seventeenth Path is the Disposing Intelligence, which provides faith to the righteous, and they are clothed with the holy spirit by it, and it is called the foundation of excellence in the state of higher things." *SEE ALSO* CABALA, HEBREW ALPHABET.

Hebrew letter Zayin

Zazel. In ceremonial magic, the planetary spirit of Saturn. Its governing intelligence is Agiel. *SEE* SPIRIT.

Zebul. (Hebrew ZBVL, "dwelling") In Cabalistic lore, the fourth of the seven heavens, associated with the Sephirah Tiphareth. *SEE* HEAVENS, SEVEN.

zenith. (Arabic *al-zenit*, "height") In a horoscope, the highest point of the zodiac as seen from a given place and time; also called midheaven. In the Northern Hemisphere, the zenith is that point of the zodiac due south of the viewer at the moment for which the horoscope is erected. Many house systems locate the cusp of the tenth house at the zenith. *SEE* ASTROLOGY.

zodiac. (Greek *kyklos zodiakos*, "circle of animals") In astrology, the circle traced by the sun in its apparent movement through the heavens as seen from Earth, divided into twelve sectors named after constellations through which the circle passes. These twelve sectors are the well-known signs of the zodiac:

Name	Glyph	Symbol
Aries	♈	ram
Taurus	♉	bull
Gemini	♊	twins
Cancer	♋	crab
Leo	♌	lion
Virgo	♍	virgin
Libra	♎	scales
Scorpio	♏	scorpion
Sagittarius	♐	archer
Capricorn	♑	goat
Aquarius	♒	water bearer
Pisces	♓	fishes

There is an important difference between the zodiac and the twelve constellations that have given its signs their names. The constellations are of varying widths, as opposed to the signs, which are all thirty-degree segments of space. Furthermore, due to the precession of the equinoxes, the constellations gradually move through the zodiac over time, so that the stars of the constellation Pisces are now visible in the section of the heavens labeled Aries. *SEE* PRECESSION OF THE EQUINOXES.

Each of the twelve signs has its own relation to the other factors of astrology. The planets, in particular, have their own complex friendships and enmities among the signs. Each sign has a planetary ruler, and a planet in a sign it rules is at maximum strength. When a planet is in a sign opposite a sign it rules, the planet is in its detriment, and at minimum strength. Each planet also has a sign in which it is exalted, and a planet in its exaltation has its most positive expression; a planet in the sign opposite the sign of its exaltation is in its fall, and has its most negative expression.

The zodiac, despite its Greek name, is like most of astrology a Mesopotamian invention. It is one of several different ways of dividing up the path of the sun through the heavens in ancient astrology; the decans, an Egyptian system of thirty-six divisions, was much used in ancient times as well. SEE DECANS. SEE ALSO ASTROLOGY AND ENTRIES FOR THE ZODIACAL SIGNS.

zodiac, terrestrial. In modern occult lore, a zodiacal pattern laid out on the landscape on a vast scale in prehistoric times, and discoverable by careful study of maps and aerial photos. The first such zodiac was either discovered or invented, depending on one's viewpoint, by Katherine Maltwood in the 1920s and announced in her book *A Guide to Glastonbury's Temple of the Stars* in 1929. According to Maltwood, the outlines of a colossal image of the zodiac, similar to the modern version although not quite identical with it, could be traced out in landforms, old paths, rivers, and earthworks over several square miles of territory near Glastonbury.

The fit between the landscape and the zodiac traced out by Maltwood is impressive, although skeptics have pointed out that many of the features that outline the zodiacal figures are provably modern, and many other features that do not contribute to her patterns are quietly ignored. Official archeology has consistently rejected the Glastonbury zodiac on these grounds as the geographical equivalent of a Rohrshach inkblot, while many people in the alternative-archeology community continue to embrace it as a genuine prehistoric artifact.

Since the publication of Maltwood's book, additional zodiacs have been found in other places in England and elsewhere. One has even been found in west London; although the features tracing it out date only from the late nineteenth century, its discoverer has suggested that the pattern was there all along on the inner planes, and simply descended into full manifestation by way of the architects of Victorian London. SEE ALSO LEYS. FURTHER READING: MALTWOOD 1929, MICHELL 1969.

Zohar. (Hebrew, "Splendor") The most important of all Cabalistic books, the Zohar is more a collection than a single treatise, comprising a series of separate tractates that fills five volumes in the standard printed editions. It presents itself as the recorded discussions of Simeon bar Yochai, an important Jewish mystical teacher of the second century C.E., with his companions and friends. This attribution was accepted by most Cabalists up to recent times, and by the sixteenth century the legend had grown up that the Zohar as it now exists was a fragment of the original work, which had once been forty camel loads in size.

Linguistic and literary evidence, however, shows the Zohar to be a much more recent work, and all modern scholars agree that it was actually written by Moses de Leon (died 1305), a Jewish Cabalist who lived for most of his life in the small town of Guadalajara in Spain. It was composed in stages between 1270 and 1300, and most of it was in circulation by the time of its author's death.

Vast, rambling, and diffuse, the Zohar is impossible to summarize and nearly as difficult to interpret. It assumes a very substantial background in Old Testament lore as well as Jewish legal, theological, philosophical, and mystical thought. Much of it consists of commentaries on scriptural verses, but these are interwoven with expositions on various parts of Cabalistic doctrine, narratives about the activities of Simeon bar Yochai and his companions, legendary stories, and a range of other material. Most of the themes and ideas of the traditional Jewish Cabala are covered in the course of the text.

The Zohar consists of a main portion, which is a Cabalistic commentary on the sections of the Torah read each week in Jewish worship, interspersed with several dozen shorter pieces on a dizzying array of subjects, from the creation of the universe to the practice of palmistry. Several of these latter may not have been written by Moses de Leon at all, but were composed by later writers and mistaken for portions of the Zohar.

This sort of mistake was almost unavoidable because of the way the Zohar was "published." It was released by its author piecemeal, with the earliest parts going into circulation before 1281 (the date of the first quotation in another Cabalistic text) while other parts did not appear until at least a decade later. For several centuries manuscript collections of different parts of the Zohar were in circulation, and each Cabalist made do with whatever parts he was able to obtain. By the fifteenth century, complete manuscripts existed, and it was these that were used for the first printed versions, issued by competing Italian publishers in Mantua and Cremona in 1558–1560.

The Zohar was originally written in Aramaic, the common language of Palestine during the second century C.E., as part of Moses de Leon's attempt to present his views as those of Simeon bar Yochai. Important parts of the Zohar were translated into Latin by the French mystic Guillaume Postel and by the German occultist Christian Knorr von Rosenroth; the latter's work served as the basis for Samuel Mathers' English translation of three portions, first published in 1898 as *The Kabbalah Unveiled*, which has been a principal source of Zoharic lore for the English-speaking occult community ever since. SEE ALSO CABALA. FURTHER READING: MATHERS 1968, SCHOLEM 1941, SCHOLEM 1974, SPERLING AND SIMON 1931–4.

Zoroaster. Prophet and founder of the Zoroastrian religion, dates unknown; his name is given as Zarathushtra in the Avestan tongue, the language of the oldest Zoroastrian writings, and Zardusht in the later Pahlavi scriptures. Almost nothing is known for certain about his life. Even the period in which he lived is a matter of conjecture; modern estimates range from the seventh to the seventeenth centuries B.C.E., while the ancient Greeks held that he had lived 5,000 years before the fall of Troy. The Gathas—the oldest part of the Zoroastrian scriptures—are written in an Iranian dialect so archaic that it is close kin to Vedic Sanskrit, and even the more recent Younger Avesta contains references to stone (rather than metal) knives and arrowheads, so the possibility of a very ancient date for Zoroaster cannot be ruled out.

The legends surrounding him claim that he was born of a virgin, and laughed aloud at the moment of his birth. After a childhood and youth menaced by supernatural evil and filled with miracles and austerities, he received his first revelation from Ahura Mazda, the spirit of Truth, at the age of thirty. Seven further revelations were granted him over the course of the following years. He spent ten solitary years wandering and preaching the gospel of Ahura Mazda, opposed constantly by the Kigs and Karaps, the priests of the older Iranian religion. He finally converted a local king named Vishtaspa, and with this support succeeded in establishing his new religion. His followers launched a series of holy wars against the Kigs and Karaps, and in the course of these, at the age of seventy-seven, Zoroaster was killed.

The Greeks and Romans knew of Zoroaster dimly as a master wizard, the first of the Magi and the founder of astrology and magic. An ancient Greek scholion to one of Plato's dialogues comments about him that "some say he was a Greek, or a man of that nation that came from the continent on the other side of the great sea"—a comment that seems to refer either to Atlantis or to the continent that, in Greek thought, lay beyond Atlantis on the far side of the Atlantic Ocean. SEE ATLANTIS. Much of late classical mysticism and magic was backdated to him, a process that reached its culmination when the Chaldean Oracles of Julianus the Theurgist—an important magical text of the second century C.E.—was attributed to him; SEE CHALDEAN ORACLES. Many of the references to Zoroaster in later magical writings drew on this image, with its heavy burden of occult history; SEE OCCULT HISTORY. FURTHER READING: BUTLER 1948, MEHR 1991, SETTEGAST 1990, ZAEHNER 1961.

zorvoyance. In the writings of American magician P. B. Randolph (1825–1875), the form of clairvoyance that perceives the entities of the "middle Spaces"—in standard occult terminology, the astral plane. SEE ASTRAL PLANE; CLAIRVOYANCE; RANDOLPH, PASCHAL BEVERLY. SEE ALSO AETHAEVOYANCE.

Zos. In the magical philosophy of Austin Osman Spare (1886–1956), one of the two primary principles. Zos represents the physical body in all its aspects, and is symbolized by the hand. Zos was also Spare's magical name. SEE KIA; SPARE, AUSTIN OSMAN; ZOS KIA CULTUS.

Zos Kia Cultus. The magical philosophy devised by British artist and occultist Austin Osman Spare (1886–1956). Its two central principles were Zos, which represented the physical body in all its aspects, and Kia, the "atmospheric I," which represented the soul and spirit. Zos was symbolized by the hand, and Kia by the eye or the phallus. The masturbatory implications of the symbolic union of Zos and Kia were not accidental, as ritual masturbation was an important part of Spare's magical toolkit.

The Cultus seems to have been practiced, in its original form, only by Spare himself, but it has played a very important role in the origins of Chaos magic. *SEE* CHAOS MAGIC; ILLUMINATES OF THANATEROS (IOT). *SEE ALSO* SPARE, AUSTIN OSMAN.

Zosimus of Panopolis. Egyptian alchemist, fl. c. 300 C.E. Little is known about the circumstances of his life. He was born at Panopolis in Upper Egypt and later lived in Alexandria, and from one of his writings we know that he once visited Memphis to inspect an ancient alchemical furnace in a temple there. He quotes several earlier alchemical writers at length, and had a particularly high respect for Maria the Jewess; *SEE* MARIA.

Zosimus' writings are clear sources of evidence that alchemy, whether or not it had a mystical dimension from the beginning, certainly had one by the beginning of the fourth century. Deeply influenced by Hermetic writings, which he quotes in several places, he saw alchemy as a way of spiritual purification and transformation, and recorded intense dream-experiences full of alchemical imagery.

Several of his works are addressed to a woman named Theosebia, apparently an influential teacher of alchemy in her own right. He seems to have disagreed with her sharply about the issue of alchemical secrecy. In the manner of later alchemical teachers, Theosebia taught students in small groups sworn to secrecy. Zosimus, by contrast, insisted that the alchemical mysteries were so important and so necessary to human spiritual growth that they should never be veiled in secrecy. We know nothing else whatsoever about Theosebia, but it seems clear that her point of view in this controversy won out. *SEE ALSO* ALCHEMY; HERMETICISM. FURTHER READING: FOWDEN 1986, PATAI 1994.

FINIS CORONAT OPUS

BIBLIOGRAPHY

Abraham, Lyndy, "Arthur Dee, 1579–1651: A Life," *Cauda Pavonis* 13/2 (1994), 1–14.

Abusch, I. Tzvi, *Babylonian Witchcraft Literature* (Atlanta: Scholars Press, 1987).

Abusch, Tzvi, and Karel van der Toorn, eds., *Mesopotamian Magic* (Groningen: Styx, 1999).

Adams, Alison, and Stanton J. Linden, eds., *Emblems and Alchemy* (Glasgow: Glasgow Emblem Studies, 1998).

Adler, Margot, *Drawing Down the Moon* (Boston: Beacon, 1986).

Agrippa, Henry Cornelius, *Three Books of Occult Philosophy*, ed. Donald Tyson (St. Paul: Llewellyn, 1993).

Aho, Wayne, *The Politics of Righteousness* (Seattle: U. of Washington Press, 1990).

Åkerman, Susanna, *Rose Cross Over the Baltic* (Leiden: Brill, 1998).

Albertus, Frater, *Alchemist's Handbook* (N.Y.: Weiser, 1974).

Alciatus, Andreus, *Works*, ed. Peter M. Daly and Virginia W. Callahan, 2 vols. (Toronto: Univ. of Toronto Press, 1985).

Aldred, Cyril, *Akhenaten, King of Egypt* (London: Thames and Hudson, 1988).

Allen, Michael B., *The Platonism of Marsilio Ficino* (Berkeley: U. of California Press, 1984).

Allen, Paul A., ed., *A Christian Rosenkreutz Anthology* (Blauvelt, N.Y.: Rudolf Steiner Publications, 1968).

AMORC (Ancient Mystic Order Rosae Crucis), *Rosicrucian Manual* (San Jose, Calif.: AMORC, 1948).

Anderson, William, *Green Man* (San Francisco: HarperCollins, 1990).

Anonymous, *Manifesto of the New Order of the Palladium* (Rochester, N.Y.: New Order of the Palladium, 2001).

Anonymous, *The Sixth and Seventh Books of Moses* (Chicago: de Laurence, 1910).

Anonymous, *Tabula Smaragdina* (Laytonville, Calif.: Smithtown Press, 1988).

Anonymous, *Vril or Vital Magnetism* (Chicago: McClurg, 1911).

Anson, Peter F., *Bishops at Large* (London: Faber & Faber, 1964).

Anton, Ted, *Eros, Magic, and the Murder of Professor Culianu* (Evanston, Ill.: Northwestern UP, 1996).

Appleby, Derek, *Horary Astrology* (Wellingborough, Northamptonshire: Aquarian, 1985).

Armstrong, A. H., ed. *Classical Mediterranean Spirituality* (N.Y.: Crossroad, 1986).

Arnold, E. Vernon, *Roman Stoicism* (London: Routledge & Kegan Paul, 1911).

Ashcroft-Nowicki, Dolores, *The Forgotten Mage* (Wellingborough: Aquarian, 1986).

Ashmole, Elias, *Theatrum Chemicum Brittanicum* (London: J. Grismond for Nathaniel Brooke, 1652).

Assmann, Jan, *Egyptian Solar Religion in the New Kingdom*, tr. Anthony Alcock (London: Kegan Paul, 1995).

Aswynn, Freya, *Northern Mysteries and Magick* (St. Paul: Llewellyn, 1998).

Atwood, Mary Ann, *A Suggestive Inquiry into the Hermetic Mystery* (Belfast: William Tait, 1918).

Aurelius, Marcus, *The Meditations of Marcus Aurelius*, tr. George Long (N.Y.: Collier, 1909).

Avalon, Arthur (John Woodroffe), *The Serpent Power* (N.Y.: Dover, 1974).

Axelrod, Alan, *The International Encyclopedia of Secret Societies and Fraternal Orders* (N.Y.: Facts on File, 1997).

Baigent, Michael, Richard Leigh, and Henry Lincoln, *Holy Blood, Holy Grail* (N.Y.: Delacorte, 1982).

Bailey, Alice, *A Treatise on White Magic* (N.Y.: Lucis Trust, 1951).

———, *Glamour: A World Problem* (N.Y.: Lucis Trust, 1950).

Barber, Malcolm, *The Cathars* (Harlow, Essex: Longman, 2000).

———, *The New Knighthood: A History of the Order of the Temple* (Cambridge: Cambridge UP, 1994).

Barborka, Geoffrey, *The Divine Plan* (Adyar: Theosophical Publishing House, 1964).

Bardon, Franz, *Initiation Into Hermetics* (Kettig uber Koblenz: Osiris-Verlag, 1962).

———, *The Key to the True Quabbalah* (Wuppertal: Dieter Ruggeberg, 1971).

———, *The Practice of Magical Evocation* (Graz: Rudolf Pravica, 1967).

Beresford Ellis, Peter, *The Druids* (London: Constable, 1994).

Barkun, Michael, *Religion and the Racist Right: The Origins of the Christian Identity Movement* (Chapel Hill, N.C.: Univ. of North Carolina Press, 1994).

Baron, Frank, *Doctor Faustus: From History to Legend* (Munich: Wilhelm Fink, 1978).

Barrett, William, and Theodore Besterman, *The Divining Rod* (N.Y.: University Books, 1968).

Barry, Jonathan, Marianne Hester, and Gareth Roberts, ed., *Witchcraft in Early Modern Europe* (Cambridge: Cambridge UP, 1996).

Barrow, Logie, *Independent Spirits: Spiritualism and English Plebeians 1850–1910* (London: Routledge & Kegan Paul, 1986).

Barton, Tamsyn, *Ancient Astrology* (London: Routledge, 1994); cited as Barton 1994a.

———, *Power and Knowledge: Astrology, Physiognomics, and Medicine in the Roman Empire* (Ann Arbor: Univ. of Michigan Press, 1994); cited as Barton 1994b.

Bath, Michael, *Speaking Pictures: English Emblem Books and Renaissance Culture* (London: Longman 1994).

Behringer, Wolfgang, *Shaman of Oberstdorf: Chonrad Stoeckhlin and the Phantoms of the Night*, tr. H. C. Erik Midelfort (Charlottesville: UP of Virginia, 1998).

Bendit, Lawrence J., and Phoebe D. Bendit, *The Etheric Body of Man* (Wheaton, Ill.: Quest, 1977).

Benes, Peter, ed., *Wonders of the Invisible World: 1600–1900* (Boston: Boston University, 1995); cited as Benes 1995a.

———, "Fortunetellers, Wise Men, and Magical Healers in New England, 1644–1850," in Benes 1995a, 127–148; cited as Benes 1995b.

Bennett, J. G., *Enneagram Studies* (York Beach, Maine: Weiser, 1983).

Benz, Ernst, *The Mystical Sources of German Romantic Philosophy*, tr. Blair R. Reynolds and Eunice M. Paul (Allison Park, Pa.: Pickwick, 1983).

Bernbaum, Edwin, *The Way to Shambhala* (N.Y.: Anchor, 1980).

Best, Michael R., and Frank H. Brightman, eds., *The Book of Secrets of Albertus Magnus of the Virtues of Herbs, Stones and Certain Beasts, Also a Book of the Marvels of the World* (Oxford: Clarendon Press, 1973).

Besterman, Theodore, *Crystal-Gazing* (New Hyde Park, N.Y.: University Books, 1965).

Betz, Hans Dieter, *The Greek Magical Papyri in Translation* (Chicago: U. of Chicago, 1986).

Blain, Jenny, and Robert Wallis, "Men and 'Women's Magic': Gender, Seidhr and 'Ergi'," *Pomegranate* 9 (August 1999), 4–16.

Blau, Joseph Leon, *The Christian Interpretation of the Cabala in the Renaissance* (N.Y.: Columbia UP, 1944).

Blavatsky, Helena Petrovna, *Isis Unveiled* (N.Y.: Bouton, 1877).

———, *The Secret Doctrine* (Adyar: TPH, 1888).

Boehme, Jakob, *Essential Readings*, ed. Robin Waterfield (Wellingborough: Aquarian, 1989).

———, *The Way to Christ* (N.Y.: Paulist, 1978).

Bonner, Andrew, *Selected Works of Ramon Lull*, 2 vols. (Princeton: Princeton UP, 1985).

Boyd, Hamish, M.D., *Introduction to Homeopathic Medicine* (New Canaan, Conn.: Keats, 1981).

Bradbrooke, Muriel C., *The School of Night* (N.Y.: Russell & Russell, 1965).

Bracelin, Jack, *Gerald Gardner: Witch* (London: Octagon, 1960).

Brann, Noel L., *Trithemius and Magical Theology* (Albany: SUNY, 1999).

Brickman, George, *An Introduction to F. Patrizi's Nova de Universis Philosophia* (Ph.D. diss., Columbia University, 1941).

Briggs, Robin, *Witches and Neighbors* (London: HarperCollins, 1996).

Britten, Emma Hardinge, *Autobiography of Emma Hardinge Britten* (Manchester: John Heywood, 1900).

Brodie, Fawn M., *No Man Knows My History* (N.Y.: Alfred A. Knopf, 1971).

Bromwich, Rachel, *Trioedd Ynys Prydein: The Welsh Triads* (Cardiff: University of Wales Press, 1961).

Brooke, John L., *The Refiner's Fire: The Making of Mormon Cosmology, 1644–1844* (Cambridge: Cambridge UP, 1994).

———, "'The True Spiritual Seed': Sectarian Religion and the Persistence of the Occult in Eighteenth-Century New England," in Benes 1995a, 107–126.

Brumbaugh, Robert, ed., *The Most Mysterious Manuscript* (Carbondale, Ill.: Univ. of Southern Illinois Press, 1978).

Brzustowicz, Richard, *The Mandrake Tradition* (MA Thesis, University of Washington, 1974).

Buber, Martin, *The Legend of the Baal-Shem* (Princeton: Princeton UP, 1955).

Buckland, Raymond, *Practical Candleburning Rituals* (St. Paul: Llewellyn, 1970).

———, *The Tree: The Complete Book of Saxon Witchcraft* (St. Paul: Llewellyn, 1974).

———, *Witchcraft from the Inside* (St. Paul: Llewellyn, 1975).

Budge, E. A. Wallis, *The Egyptian Book of the Dead* (N.Y.: Dover, 1967).

Bulwer-Lytton, Edward, *The Coming Race* (London: n.p., 1873.)

———, *Zanoni* (Philadelphia: Wanamaker, n.d.).

Buranelli, Vincent, *The Wizard from Vienna* (N.Y.: Coward, McCann and Geoghan, 1975).

Burkert, Walter, *Ancient Mystery Cults* (Cambridge, Mass.: Harvard UP, 1987).

———, *Lore and Science in Ancient Pythagoreanism*, tr. Edwin L. Minar Jr. (Cambridge, Mass.: Harvard UP, 1972).

Burr, Timothy, *BISBA* (Trenton: Hercules, 1965).

Butler, E. M., *The Fortunes of Faust* (Cambridge: Cambridge UP, 1952).

———, *The Myth of the Magus* (Cambridge: Cambridge UP, 1948).

———, *Ritual Magic* (Cambridge: Cambridge UP, 1949).

Butler, Jon, "The Dark Ages of American Occultism, 1760–1848," in Kerr and Crow (1983), 58–78.

Butler, W. E., *Apprenticed to Magic* (Wellingborough: Aquarian, 1962).

———, *How to Read the Aura, Practice Psychometry, Telepathy and Clairvoyance* (Rochester, Vt.: Destiny, 1987).

———, *Lords of Light* (Rochester, Vt.: Destiny, 1990).

———, *The Magician: His Training and Work* (No. Hollywood, Calif.: Wilshire, 1959).

Calder, George, tr., *Auraicept na n-Éces: The Scholar's Primer* (Edinburgh: John Grant, 1917).

Cammell, C. R., *Aleister Crowley: The Man, The Mage, The Myth* (London: Richards, 1951).

Campanella, Tommaso, *The City of the Sun*, tr. Daniel J. Donno (Berkeley: U. of California Press, 1981).

Campbell, Edward D., *The Encyclopedia of Palmistry* (N.Y.: Perigee, 1996).

Campion, Nicholas, *The Great Year: Astrology, Millenarianism and History in the Western Tradition* (N.Y.: Arkana, 1994).

Carabine, Deirdre, *John Scottus Eriugena* (Oxford: Oxford UP, 2000).

Cardan, Jerome, *The Book of My Life*, tr. J. Stoner (London: n.p., 1931).

Carey, George W., *The Biochemic System of Medicine* (New Delhi, India: B. Jain, 1996).

———, and Inez E. Perry, *The Zodiac and the Salts of Salvation* (N.Y.: Weiser, 1932).

Carlson, Shawn, Gerald LaRue, etc., *Satanism in America: How the Devil Got Much More Than His Due* (El Cerrito, Calif.: Gaia, 1989).

Carnes, Mark C., *Secret Ritual and Manhood in Victorian America* (New Haven, Conn.: Yale UP, 1989).

Carr-Gomm, Philip, *The Druid Way* (Shaftesbury, Dorset: Element, 1993).

———, ed., *The Druid Renaissance* (London: Thorsons, 1996).

———, *In the Grove of the Druids: The Druid Teachings of Ross Nichols* (London: Watkins, 2002).

Carroll, Peter, *Liber Null and Psychonaut* (York Beach, Maine: Weiser, 1978).

Carter, John (pseud.), *Sex and Rockets: The Occult World of Jack Parsons* (Venice, Calif.: Feral, 1999).

Case, Paul Foster, *The Tarot: A Key to the Wisdom of the Ages* (Richmond, Va.: Macoy, 1947).

———, *The True and Invisible Rosicrucian Order* (York Beach, Maine: Weiser, 1985).

Cassirer, Ernst, *The Platonic Renaissance in England*, tr. James P. Pettigrove (Austin, Tex.: U. of Texas Press, 1953).

Chadwick, Henry, *Priscillian of Avila: The Occult and the Charismatic in the Early Church* (Oxford: Clarendon Press, 1976)

————, *The Early Church* (London: Penguin, 1993).

Chadwick, Nora K. *The Druids* (Cardiff: U. of Wales Press, 1966).

Chapman, Janine, *Quest for Dion Fortune* (York Beach, Maine: Weiser, 1993).

Charmasson, Therese, *Recherches sur une Technique Divinatoire: La Geomancie dans l'Occident Medieval* (Geneva: Librairie Droz, 1980).

Charpentier, Louis, *The Mysteries of Chartres Cathedral* (N.Y.: Avon, 1972).

Cheiro, *The Language of the Hand* (N.Y.: Prentice-Hall, 1987).

Childress, David Hatcher, and Richard Shaver, *Lost Continents and the Hollow Earth* (Kempton, Ill.: Adventures Unlimited, 1999).

Choucha, Nadia, *Surrealism and the Occult* (Oxford: Mandrake, 1991).

Christian, Paul, *The History and Practice of Magic*, tr. James Kirkup and Julian Shaw (London: Forge Press, 1952).

Churchward, James, *The Lost Continent of Mu* (N.Y.: Ives Washburn, 1931).

Chuvin, Pierre, *A Chronicle of the Last Pagans*, tr. B. A. Archer (Cambridge, Mass.: Harvard UP, 1989).

Cicero, Chic, and Sandra Tabatha Cicero, *Secrets of a Golden Dawn Temple* (St. Paul: Llewellyn, 1992).

Clauss, Manfred, *The Roman Cult of Mithras*, tr. Richard Gordon (N.Y.: Routledge, 2000).

Clow, Barbara Hand, *Chiron* (St. Paul: Llewellyn, 1988).

Clulee, Nicholas H., *John Dee's Natural Philosophy* (N.Y.: Routledge, 1988).

Cohen, Seymour J., *Iggeret HaKodesh, the Holy Letter* (N.Y.: Ktav, 1976).

Cohn, Norman, *Europe's Inner Demons* (New York: Basic Books, 1975).

Colmer, Michael, *Napoleon's Book of Fate* (London: Blandford, 1994).

Colquhon, Ithell, *Sword of Wisdom* (London: Spearman, 1975).

Crowley, Aleister, *Atlantis Liber LI: The Lost Continent* (n.p.: Dove Press, 1970).

————, *Book Four* (York Beach, Maine: Weiser, 1980).

————, *The Book of Thoth* (York Beach, Maine: Weiser, 1969).

————, *The Confessions of Aleister Crowley: An Autohagiography* (repr. London: Arkana, 1989).

————, *Eight Lectures on Yoga* (Scottsdale, Ariz.: New Falcon, 1991).

————, *The Law Is for All* (St. Paul: Llewellyn, 1975).

————, *Magick in Theory and Practice* (N.Y.: Dover, 1976).

————, *777 and Other Qabalistic Writings of Aleister Crowley* (York Beach, Maine: Weiser, 1973).

Culianu, Ioan P., *Eros and Magic in the Renaissance* (Chicago: U of Chicago Press, 1997).

Cunningham, Scott, *Magical Herbalism* (St. Paul: Llewellyn, 1982).

————, *Wicca: A Guide for the Solitary Practitioner* (St. Paul: Llewellyn, 1988).

Curl, James Stevens, *The Art and Architecture of Freemasonry* (Woodstock, N.Y.: Overlook, 1993).

Darnton, Robert, *Mesmerism and the End of the Enlightenment in France* (Cambridge, Mass.: Harvard UP, 1968).

Darrah, John, *Paganism in Arthurian Romance* (Woodbridge, Suffolk: Boydell, 1994).

Davidson, Gustav, *A Dictionary of Angels* (N.Y.: Macmillan, 1967).

Davidson, Hilda Ellis, "The Germanic World," in Loewe and Blacker 1981.

Davies, Morganna, and Aradia Lynch, *Keepers of the Flame: Interviews with Elders of Traditional Witchcraft in America* (Providence, R.I.: Olympian, 2001).

Dawson, Warren R., *A Leechbook or Collection of Medical Recipes of the Fifteenth Century* (London: Macmillan, 1934).

de Camp, L. Sprague, *Lost Continents* (N.Y.: Dover, 1970).

Deck, John N., *Nature, Contemplation and the One* (Toronto: Univ. Toronto Press, 1967).

Decker, Ronald, Thierry DePaulis, and Michael Dummett, *A Wicked Pack of Cards: Origins of the Occult Tarot* (N.Y.: St. Martin's, 1996).

Decker, Ronald, and Michael Dummet, *A History of the Occult Tarot 1870–1970* (New York: St. Martin's, 2002).

Dee, John, *The Hieroglyphic Monad* (Edmonds, Wash.: Sure Fire, 1986).

De la Fontaine Verwey, Herman, "Gerard Thibault and his *Academie de l'Espee*," *Quarendo* 8 (Leiden: E. J. Brill, 1978).

Della Porta, Giambattista, *Natural Magick* (New York, Basic Books, 1957).

DeLuce, Robert, *Horary Astrology* (n.p.: DeLuce, 1932).

de Montfaucon de Villars, N., *Comte de Gabalis* (repr. Mokelumne Hill, Calif.: Health Research, 1963).

Denning, Melita, and Osborne Phillips, *The Apparel of High Magick* (St. Paul: Llewellyn, 1975); cited as Denning and Phillips 1975a.

————, *Mysteria Magica* (St. Paul: Llewellyn, 1981).

————, *Robe and Ring* (St. Paul: Llewellyn, 1974).

————, *The Sword and the Serpent* (St. Paul: Llewellyn, 1975); cited as Denning and Phillips 1975b.

————, *The Triumph of Light* (St. Paul: Llewellyn, 1978).

de Santillana, Giorgio, and Hertha von Dechend, *Hamlet's Mill* (Boston: David R. Godine, 1977).

Deveny, John, *Paschal Beverly Randolph* (Albany, N.Y.: SUNY, 1997).

Devi, Savitri, *The Lightning and the Sun* (Calcutta: the author, 1958).

Dickson, Donald R., *The Tessera of Antilia: Utopian Brotherhoods and Secret Societies in the Early Seventeenth Century* (Leiden: Brill, 1998).

Dillon, John. *The Middle Platonists* (Ithaca: Cornell UP, 1977).

Dobbs, Betty Jo Teeter, *Foundations of Newton's Alchemy, or, "The Hunting of the Greene Lyon"* (Cambridge: Cambridge UP, 1975).

————, *The Janus Faces of Genius: The Role of Alchemy in Newton's Thought* (Cambridge: Cambridge UP, 1991).

Dole, George F., and Robert H. Kirven, *A Scientist Explores Spirit* (N.Y.: Swedenborg Foundation, 1992).

Donnelly, Ignatius, *Atlantis: The Antediluvian World* (Blauvelt, N.Y.: Steinerbooks, 1973).

Drakeford, Mark, *Social Movements and their Supporters* (N.Y.: Saint Martin's, 1997).

Drury, Neville, *Pan's Daughter* (Oxford: Mandrake, 1993).

Dummett, Michael, *The Visconti-Sforza Tarot Cards* (N.Y.: George Braziller, 1986).

Duncan, Robert L., *Reluctant General: The Life and Times of Albert Pike* (N.Y.: Dutton, 1961).

Duquette, Lon Milo, *Aleister Crowley's Illustrated Goetia* (Phoenix: New Falcon, 1992).

———, *The Magic of Thelema* (York Beach, Maine: Weiser, 1993).

Dzielska, Maria, *Apollonius of Tyana in Legend and History* (Rome: "L'Erma" de Breitschneider, 1986).

Eberly, John, "We Can Build You: The Homunculus in Alchemical Tradition," *Caduceus—The Hermetic Quarterly* (Spring 1997) Vol. 3, No. 1, 23–33.

Edgell, Derek, *The Order of Woodcraft Chivalry 1916–1949* (Lewiston, N.Y.: Mellen, 1992).

Eisler, Riane, *The Chalice and the Blade* (San Francisco: Harper & Row, 1987).

Eller, Cynthia, *Living in the Lap of the Goddess* (N.Y.: Crossroads, 1993).

———, *The Myth of Matriarchal Prehistory* (Boston: Beacon, 2000).

Elworthy, Frederick, *The Evil Eye* (N.Y.: Collier, 1971).

Enright, Michael J., *Lady with a Mead Cup* (Dublin: Four Courts, 1996).

Epictetus, *The Golden Sayings of Epictetus*, tr. Hastings Crossley (N.Y.: Collier, 1909).

Evans, James, *The History and Practice of Ancient Astronomy* (N.Y.: OUP, 1998).

Evola, Julius, *Revolt Against the Modern World*, tr. Guido Stucco (Rochester, Vt.: Inner Traditions International, 1995).

———, *The Yoga of Power*, tr. Guido Stucco (Rochester, Vt.: Inner Traditions International, 1992).

Faivre, Antoine, *The Eternal Hermes: From Greek God to Alchemical Magus* (Grand Rapids, Mich.: Phanes, 1995).

———, *Theosopy, Imagination, Tradition: Studies in Western Esotericism*, translated by Christine Rhone (Albany, N.Y.: State University of New York Press, 2000).

Fandrich, Ina Johanna, "The Mysterious Voodoo Queen Marie Laveau: A Study of Spiritual Power and Female Leadership in Nineteenth Century New Orleans" (Ph.D dissertation, Temple University, 1994).

Fanger, Claire, ed., *Texts and Traditions of Medieval Ritual Magic* (University Park: Pennsylvania State UP, 1998).

Faraone, Christopher A., *Talismans and Trojan Horses: Guardian Statues in Ancient Greek Myth and Ritual* (N.Y.: OUP, 1992).

Farmer, S. A., *Syncretism in the West: Pico's 900 Theses* (Tempe, Ariz.: MRTS, 1998).

Farrar, Stewart, and Janet Farrar, *Eight Sabbats for Witches* (London: Robert Hale, 1981).

———, *The Witches' God* (Custer, Wash.: Phoenix, 1989).

———, *The Witches' Goddess* (Custer, Wash.: Phoenix, 1986).

———, *The Witches' Way: Principles, Rituals, and Beliefs of Modern Witchcraft* (London: Robert Hale, 1984).

Fideler, David R., *Jesus Christ, Sun of God* (Wheaton, Ill.: Quest, 1993).

———, "The Passion of Sophia: An Early Gnostic Creation Myth," *Gnosis* 1 (Fall 1985), 16–22.

Findhorn Community, the, *The Findhorn Garden* (N.Y.: Harper & Row, 1975).

Findlay, J. N., *Plato and Platonism: An Introduction* (N.Y.: Quadrangle, 1978).

———, *Plato: The Written and Unwritten Doctrines* (London: Routledge and Kegan Paul, 1974).

Flaceliere, Robert, *Greek Oracles*, tr. Douglas Garman (N.Y.: W. W. Norton, 1965).

Flamel, Nicolas, *Nicholas Flamel: His Exposition of the Hieroglyphicall Figures* (N.Y.: Garland, 1994).

Flint, Valerie, *The Rise of Magic in Early Medieval Europe* (Princeton: Princeton UP, 1996).

Flowers, Stephen, *Runes and Magic* (Berne: Peter Lang, 1986).

Fludd, Robert, *Robert Fludd: Essential Readings*, ed. William H. Huffman (London: Aquarian, 1992).

Forrest, Isadora, *Isis Magic* (St. Paul: Llewellyn, 2000).

Fortune, Dion, *Applied Magic and Aspects of Occultism* (Wellingborough: Aquarian, 1987); cited as Fortune 1987a.

———, *The Cosmic Doctrine* (York Beach, Maine: Weiser, 2000).

———, *Esoteric Orders and Their Work and the Training and Work of the Initiate* (Wellingborough: Aquarian, 1987); cited as Fortune 1987b.

———, *Glastonbury* (Wellingborough: Aquarian, 1989).

———, *The Magical Battle of Britain* (Bath: Golden Gates, 1993).

———, *The Mystical Qabalah* (York Beach, Maine: Weiser, 1984).

———, *Psychic Self-Defence* (London: Rider, 1930).

Foster, George M., *Hippocrates' Latin American Legacy: Humoral Medicine in the New World* (Amsterdam: Gordon and Breach, 1994).

Fowden, Garth, *The Egyptian Hermes* (Cambridge: Cambridge UP, 1986).

Frazer, James, *The Golden Bough* (N.Y.: Macmillan, 1922).

Frejer, B. Ernest, ed., *The Edgar Cayce Companion* (Virginia Beach: ARE, 1995).

Frew, Donald H., "Harran: Last Refuge of Classical Paganism," *Pomegranate* 9 (August 1999), 17–29.

Frothingham, Octavius Brooks, *Transcendentalism in New England* (N.Y.: Putnam, 1876).

Fulcanelli, *Fulcanelli: Master Alchemist: Le Mystère des Cathédrales* (Albuquerque, N.M.: Brotherhood of Light, 1986).

Fuller, Jean Overton, *The Comte de St. Germain* (London: East-West, 1988).

———, *The Magical Dilemma of Victor Neuburg* (Oxford: Mandrake, 1990).

Gager, John G., ed., *Curse Tablets and Binding Spells from the Ancient World* (Oxford: OUP, 1992).

Galbreath, Robert, "Explaining Modern Occultism," in Kerr and Crow 1983, 11–37.

Gallagher, E. V., *Divine Man or Magician? Celsus and Origen on Jesus* (Chico, Calif.: Scholars Press, 1982).

Gantz, Jeffrey, tr., *The Mabinogion* (London: Penguin, 1976).

Gardner, Adelaide, *Meditation: A Practical Study* (Wheaton, Ill.: TPH, 1968).

Gardner, Gerald, *Witchcraft Today* (London: Rider, 1954).

———, *The Meaning of Witchcraft* (London: Rider, 1959).

Geffcken, Johannes, *The Last Days of Greco-Roman Paganism*, tr. Sabine MacCormack (New York: North-Holland, 1978).

Geldard, Richard, *The Esoteric Emerson* (Hudson, N.Y.: Lindisfarne, 1993).

Geneva, Ann, *Astrology and the Seventeenth-Century Mind* (Manchester: Manchester UP, 1995).

Geoffrey of Monmouth, *The History of the Kings of Britain*, tr. Lewis Thorpe (London: Penguin, 1966).

Gerald of Wales, *The Journey Through Wales / The Description of Wales* (London: Penguin, 1978).

Gersh, Stephen, *Middle Platonism and Neoplatonism: The Latin Tradition*, 2 vols. (Notre Dame, Ind.: Univ. Notre Dame Press, 1986).

Gettings, Fred, *The Book of the Hand* (London: Hamlyn, 1965).

Ghyka, Matila, *The Geometry of Art and Life* (N.Y.: Dover, 1977).

Gibbons, B. J., *Gender in Mystical and Occult Thought* (Cambridge: Cambridge UP, 1996).

Gibson, Christopher, "The Religion of the Stars: The Hermetic Philosophy of C. C. Zain," *Gnosis* 38 (Winter 1996), 58–63.

Gilbert, R. A., *A. E. Waite, Magician of Many Parts* (Wellingborough: Crucible, 1987).

———, *The Golden Dawn Companion* (Wellingborough: Aquarian, 1986).

———, *The Golden Dawn: Twilight of the Magicians* (Wellingborough: Aquarian, 1983); cited as Gilbert 1983a.

———, *The Magical Mason: Forgotten Hermetic Writings of William Wynn Westcott, Physician and Magus* (Wellingborough: Aquarian, 1983); cited as Gilbert 1983c.

———, ed., *The Sorcerer and His Apprentice: Unknown Hermetic Writings of S. L. MacGregor Mathers and J. W. Brodie-Innes* (Wellingborough: Aquarian, 1983); cited as Gilbert 1983b.

Gimbutas, Marija, *The Civilization of the Goddess* (San Francisco: HarperSanFrancisco, 1991).

———, *The Language of the Goddess* (San Francisco: Harper & Row, 1989).

Ginzburg, Carlo, *Ecstasies: Deciphering the Witch's Sabbath* (N.Y.: Pantheon, 1991).

———, *The Night Battles: Witchcraft and Agrarian Cults in the Sixteenth and Seventeenth Centuries* (N.Y.: Penguin, 1985).

Goddard, David, *The Tower of Alchemy* (York Beach, Maine: Weiser, 1999).

Godwin, David, "Astrological Attributions of the Twelve Tribes," *The Qabalistic Messenger* 1:1 (December 1991), 1–5.

———, "The Breastplate of the High Priest," *The Qabalistic Messenger* 1:3 (June 1992), 1–3.

———, *Godwin's Cabalistic Encyclopedia* (St. Paul: Llewellyn, 1989).

Godwin, Joscelyn, *Arktos: The Polar Myth in Science, Symbolism, and Nazi Survival* (Grand Rapids, Mich.: Phanes, 1993).

———, tr., *The Chemical Wedding of Christian Rosenkreutz* (Grand Rapids, Mich.: Phanes, 1991).

———, *Music and the Occult: French Musical Philosophies, 1750–1950* (Rochester, N.Y.: U. of Rochester Press, 1995).

———, *The Mystery of the Seven Vowels* (Grand Rapids, Mich.: Phanes, 1991).

———, *Robert Fludd* (Boulder, Colo.: Shambhala, 1979).

———, *The Theosophical Enlightenment* (Albany: SUNY, 1994).

Godwin, Joscelyn, Christian Chanel, and John P. Deveny, *The Hermetic Brotherhood of Luxor* (York Beach, Maine: Weiser, 1995).

Goodison, Lucy, and Christine Morris, eds., *Ancient Goddesses: The Myth and the Evidence* (London: British Museum, 1998).

Goodman, Felicitas D., *How About Demons? Possession and Exorcism in the Modern World* (Bloomington, Ind.: Indiana UP, 1988).

Goodrick-Clarke, Nicholas, *Hitler's Priestess* (N.Y.: New York UP, 1998).

———, *The Occult Roots of Nazism: Secret Aryan Cults and their Influence on Nazi Ideology* (N.Y.: New York UP, 1992).

Gorman, Peter, *Pythagoras: A Life* (London: Routledge and Kegan Paul, 1979).

Graf, Fritz, *Magic in the Ancient World*, tr. Franklin Philip (Cambridge, Mass.: Harvard UP, 1997).

Grafton, Anthony, *Cardano's Cosmos* (Cambridge, Mass.; Harvard UP, 1999).

Grant, Kenneth, *Images and Oracles of Austin Osman Spare* (London: Muller, 1974).

———, *Outside the Circles of Time* (London: Frederick Muller, 1980).

Graves, Robert, *The White Goddess* (N.Y.: Farrar, Strauss & Giroux, 1966).

Gray, William G., *Concepts of Qabalah* (York Beach, Maine: Weiser, 1984).

———, *Sangreal Ceremonies and Rituals* (York Beach, Maine: Weiser, 1985).

———, *The Sangreal Sacrament* (York Beach, Maine: Weiser, 1983).

———, *Western Inner Workings* (York Beach, Maine: Weiser, 1982).

Green, Tamara M., *The City of the Moon God: Religious Traditions of Harran* (Leiden: Brill, 1992).

Greer, John Michael, *Circles of Power: Ritual Magic in the Western Tradition* (St. Paul: Llewellyn, 1997).

———, *Earth Divination, Earth Magic* (St. Paul: Llewellyn, 1999).

———, *Monsters* (St. Paul: Llewellyn, 2001).

———, *Natural Magic* (St. Paul: Llewellyn, 2000).

———, "Osiris and Christ," in Chic Cicero and Sandra Tabatha Cicero, eds., *The Magical Pantheons* (St. Paul: Llewellyn, 1998).

———, *Paths of Wisdom: The Magical Cabala in the Western Tradition* (St. Paul: Llewellyn, 1996).

———, and Gordon Cooper, "The Red God: Woodcraft and the Origins of Wicca," *Gnosis* 48 (Summer 1998), 50–58.

Greer, Mary K., *Women of the Golden Dawn* (Rochester, Vt.: Park Street, 1995).

Grell, Ole Peter, ed., *Paracelsus: The Man and His Reputation* (Leiden: Brill, 1998).

Grieve, Maud, *A Modern Herbal* (London: Jonathan Cape, 1931).

Griffiths, Bill, *Aspects of Anglo-Saxon Magic* (Hockwold-cum-Wilton, Norfolk: Anglo-Saxon Books, 1996).

Grosh, A. B., *The Odd Fellows Manual* (Philadelphia: Theodore Bliss & Co., 1871).

Gruffydd, W. J., *Rhiannon* (Cardiff: University of Wales Press, 1953).

Guénon, René, *The Lord of the World* (Ellingstring: Coombe Springs, 1983).

Guirdham, Arthur, *The Great Heresy* (Jersey: Neville Spearman, 1977).

Gullan-Whur, Margaret, *The Four Elements* (London: Century, 1987).

Guthrie, Kenneth Sylvan, ed. and trans., *The Pythagorean Sourcebook and Library* (Grand Rapids, Mich.: Phanes, 1987).

Haddock, Frank Channing, *Power of Will* (Meriden, Conn.: Pelton, 1918).

Hadfield, Alice Mary, *An Introduction to Charles Williams* (London: R. Hale, 1959).

Hadot, Pierre, *Plotinus, or the Simplicity of Vision*, tr. Michael Chase (Chicago: U. Chicago Press, 1993).

———, *The Inner Citadel*, tr. Michael Chase (Cambridge, Mass.: Harvard UP, 1998).

Hakl, Hans Thomas, *Unknown Sources: National Socialism and the Occult*, tr. Nicholas Goodrick-Clarke (Edmonds, Wash.: Holmes, 2000).

Halevi, Z'ev ben Shimon, *Kabbalah and Exodus* (Boulder: Shambhala, 1980).

Hall, Manly Palmer, *The Lost Keys of Freemasonry* (Los Angeles: PRS, 1937).

———, *The Secret Teachings of All Ages* (Los Angeles: PRS, 1988).

Hamill, John, *The Rosicrucian Seer* (Wellingborough: Aquarian, 1986).

Hancox, Joy, *The Byrom Collection: Renaissance Thought, the Royal Society, and the Building of the Globe Theatre* (London: Jonathan Cape, 1992).

Hanegraaff, Wouter J., *New Age Religion and Western Culture* (Leiden: E. J. Brill, 1996).

Hansen, Daniel, *American Druidism: A Guide to American Druid Groups* (Seattle: Peanut Butter, 1995).

Hapgood, Charles, *Maps of the Ancient Sea Kings* (N.Y.: Dutton, 1979).

Haq, Syed Nomanul, *Names, Natures and Things: The Alchemist Jabir ibn Hayyan and his "Kitab al Ahjar" (Book of Stones)* (Boston: Kluwer, 1994).

Hargrave, John, *The Confession of the Kibbo Kift* (London: Duckworth, 1927).

Harkness, Deborah E., *John Dee's Conversations with Angels* (Cambridge: Cambridge UP, 1999).

Harper, George Mills, *Yeats's Golden Dawn* (London: Macmillan, 1974).

Harrington, David, and deTraci Regula, *Whispers of the Moon: The Life and Work of Scott Cunningham* (St. Paul: Llewellyn, 1996).

Harris, Eleanor L., *Ancient Egyptian Divination and Magic* (York Beach, Maine: Weiser, 1998).

Harrison, Jane, *Prolegomena to the Study of Greek Religion* (Cambridge: Cambridge UP, 1903).

Hart, Vaughan, *Art and Magic at the Court of the Stuarts* (London: Routledge, 1994).

Haskins, Jim, *Voodoo and Hoodoo* (New York, Stein and Day, 1978).

Hayes, Kevin J., *Folklore and Book Culture* (Knoxville: Univ. of Tennessee Press, 1997).

Hayes, T. Wilson, *Winstanley the Digger* (Cambridge, Mass.: Harvard UP, 1979).

Heindel, Max, *The Rosicrucian Cosmo-Conception* (Oceanside, Calif.: Rosicrucian Fellowship, 1909).

Heninger, S. K., *Touches of Sweet Harmony: Pythagorean Cosmology and Renaissance Poetics* (San Marino, Calif.: Huntington Library, 1974).

Heselton, Philip, *Wiccan Roots: Gerald Gardner and the Modern Wiccan Revival* (Chievely, Berks.: Capall Bann, 2000).

Hesiod, Theogony, trans. Dorothea Wender, *In Hesiod and Theognis* (N.Y.: Penguin, 1973).

Hewitt, William W., *Tea Leaf Reading* (St. Paul: Llewellyn, 1999).

Hill, Christopher, *The Religion of Gerrard Winstanley: Past and Present Supplement 5* (Oxford: Past and Present Society, 1978).

Hillgarth, J. N., *Ramon Lull and Lullism in 14th Century France* (Oxford: Oxford UP, 1971).

Hitler, Adolf, *Mein Kampf*, tr. Ralph Manheim (London: Hutchinson, 1974).

Hodgson, Joan, *A White Eagle Lodge Book of Health and Healing* (Liss, Hampshire, England: White Eagle Pub. Trust, 1983).

Hodson, Geoffrey, *Fairies at Work and at Play* (London: TPH, 1976); cited as Hodson 1976a.

————, *The Kingdom of the Gods* (Wheaton, Ill.: Quest, 1976); cited as Hodson 1976b.

Hoeller, Stephan A., *The Gnostic Jung and the Seven Sermons to the Dead* (Wheaton, Ill.: TPH, 1982).

————, "A Sage for All Seasons," *Gnosis* 18 (Winter 1991), 10–11.

Hohmann, John George, *Pow-Wows or the Long Lost Friend* (Forestville, CA: Lucky Mojo Curio Co., 1992).

Holmyard, Eric John, *Alchemy* (Harmondsworth: Penguin, 1957).

Hornung, Erik, *Conceptions of God in Ancient Egypt*, tr. John Baines (London: Routledge & Kegan Paul, 1982).

Howe, Ellic, *Fringe Masonry in England, 1870–1885* (Edmonds, Wash.: Holmes, 1997).

———, *The Magicians of the Golden Dawn* (London: Routledge & Kegan Paul, 1972).

Hubbs, Joanna, *An Analysis of Martinism in the Last Quarter of the Eighteenth Century* (Ph.D. dissertation, University of Washington, 1971).

Hull, J. M., *Hellenistic Magic and the Synoptic Tradition* (London: SCM, 1974).

Hulse, David Allen, *New Dimensions for the Cube of Space* (York Beach, Maine: Weiser, 2000).

Hunt, Stoker, *Ouija: The Most Dangerous Game* (N.Y.: Barnes and Noble, 1985).

Huson, Paul, *Mastering Herbalism* (N.Y.: Stein and Day, 1974).

———, *Mastering Witchcraft* (N.Y.: Putnam, 1970).

Hutton, Ronald, "The Discovery of the Modern Goddess," in Pearson 1998, 89–100.

———, *Stations of the Sun: A History of the Ritual Year in England* (Oxford: Oxford UP, 1994).

———, *The Triumph of the Moon: A History of Modern Pagan Witchcraft* (Oxford: Oxford UP, 1999).

Idel, Moshe, *Golem: Jewish Magical and Mystical Traditions on the Artificial Anthropoid* (Albany: SUNY Press, 1990).

———, *The Mystical Experience in Abraham Abulafia* (Albany: SUNY Press, 1988).

Igliori, Paola, ed., *American Magus Harry Smith: A Modern Alchemist* (N.Y.: Inanout, 1996).

Jenkins, Geraint H., *Facts, Fantasy and Fiction: The Historical Vision of Iolo Morganwg* (Aberystwyth: Canolfan Uwchefrydiau Cymreig a Cheltaidd Prifysgol Cymry, 1997).

Johnson, K. Paul, *The Masters Revealed: Madame Blavatsky and the Myth of the Great White Lodge* (Albany, N.Y.: SUNY, 1994).

Johnston, Sarah Iles, *Hekate Soteira* (Atlanta: Scholars Press, 1990).

Jolly, Karen Louise, *Popular Religion in Late Saxon England; Elf Charms in Context* (Chapel Hill: U. of North Carolina Press, 1996).

Jones, Evan, and Doreen Valiente, *Witchcraft: A Tradition Renewed* (Custer, Wash.: Phoenix, 1990).

Jones, Prudence, and Nigel Pennick, *A History of Pagan Europe* (London: Routledge, 1995).

Jones, W. R., "'Hill-Diggers' and 'Hell-Raisers': Treasure Hunting and the Supernatural in Old and New England," in Benes 1995a, 97–106.

Josten, C. H., "A Translation of John Dee's 'Monas Hieroglyphica' (Antwerp, 1564), with an Introduction and Annotations," *Ambix* 12 (1964), 84–221.

Judith, Anodea, *Wheels of Life* (St. Paul: Llewellyn, 1987).

Judith, Anodea, and Selene Vega, *The Sevenfold Journey: Reclaiming Mind, Body and Spirit Through the Chakras* (Freedom, Calif.: Crossing, 1993).

Jung, Carl Gustav, *Memories, Dreams, Reflections*, ed. Aniela Jaff (N.Y.: Pantheon, 1962).

Junius, Manfred M., *Practical Handbook of Plant Alchemy* (N.Y.: Inner Traditions International, 1985).

Kafton-Minkel, Walter, *Subterranean Worlds* (Port Townsend, Wash.: Loompanics, 1989).

Kalogera, Lucy Shepard, *Yeats's Celtic Mysteries* (Ph.D. dissertation, Florida State University, 1977).

Kaplan, Aryeh, tr., *The Bahir* (York Beach, Maine: Weiser, 1979).

———, *Meditation and Kabbalah* (York Beach, Maine: Weiser, 1982).

———, *Sefer Yetzirah: The Book of Creation in Theory and Practice* (York Beach, Maine: Weiser, 1990).

Kaplan, Stuart, *The Encyclopedia of Tarot, Volume I* (Stamford, Conn.: US Games, 1978).

———, *The Encyclopedia of Tarot, Volume II* (Stamford, Conn.: US Games, 1986).

———, *The Encyclopedia of Tarot, Volume III* (Stamford, Conn.: US Games, 1990).

Kardec, Allen, *The Spirit's Book* (Albuquerque, N.M.: Brotherhood of Life, 1989).

Keeley, Lawrence H., *War Before Civilization: The Myth of the Peaceful Savage* (Oxford: Blackwell, 1996).

Keene, M. Lamar, *The Psychic Mafia* (Amherst, N.Y.: Prometheus, 1997).

Keizer, Lewis S., *The Wandering Bishops* (Santa Cruz, Calif.: Academy of Arts and Humanities, 1976).

Kent, James Tyler, *Lectures on Homeopathic Philosophy* (1900; repr. Berkeley, Calif.: North Atlantic, 1979).

Kerenyi, C., *Eleusis* (N.Y.: Bollingen Foundation, 1967).

Kerr, Howard, and Charles L. Crow, *The Occult In America: New Historical Perspectives* (Urbana, Ill.: U. of Illinois Press, 1983).

Khei X° (George Winslow Plummer), *Rosicrucian Fundamentals* (N.Y.: Flame, 1920).

Kieckhefer, Richard, *European Witch Trials* (Berkeley, Calif.: Univ. California Press, 1976).

———, *Forbidden Rites: A Necromancer's Manual of the Fifteenth Century* (University Park: Pennsylvania State Univ. Press, 1998).

———, *Magic in the Middle Ages* (Cambridge: Cambridge UP, 1989).

King, Francis, ed., *Astral Projection, Ritual Magic, and Alchemy* (London: Spearman, 1971); cited as King 1971a.

———, *The Magical World of Aleister Crowley* (London: Arrow, 1977).

———, *Modern Ritual Magic: The Rise of Western Occultism* (Dorset: Prism, 1989).

———, *The Secret Rituals of the O.T.O.* (London: Spearman, 1972).

———, *Sexuality, Magic, and Perversion* (London: Spearman, 1971); cited as King 1971b.

———, *The Magical World of Aleister Crowley* (Oxford: Mandrake, 1991).

King, Godfré Ray (pseud. of Ray Ballard), *Unveiled Mysteries* (Saint Germain Press, 1934).

King, John, *The Celtic Druids' Year* (London: Blandford, 1994).

Kingsford, Anna, and Edward Maitland, *The Perfect Way: or, the Finding of Christ* (London: Watkins, 1882).

Kirchweger, Anton Joseph, *Aurea Catena Homeri* (Edmonds, Wash.: Holmes, 2002).

Klimkeit, Hans-Joachim, *Gnosis on the Silk Road: Gnostic Texts from Central Asia* (San Francisco: HarperSanFrancisco, 1993).

Knight, Gareth, *Dion Fortune and the Inner Light* (Loughborough: Thoth, 2000).

———, *The Secret Tradition in Arthurian Legend* (Wellingborough: Aquarian, 1983).

Konstantinos, *Summoning Spirits* (St. Paul: Llewellyn, 1997).

Kors, Alan Charles, and Edward Peters, *Witchcraft in Europe 400–1700: A Documentary History* (Philadelphia: Univ. Pennsylvania Press, 2001).

Kramer, Heinrich, and Jacob Sprenger, *Malleus Maleficarum*, tr. Montague Summers (N.Y.: Dover, 1971).

Küntz, Darcy, ed., *The Complete Golden Dawn Cipher Manuscript* (Edmonds, Wash.: Holmes, 1996).

———, *The Golden Dawn Source Book* (Edmonds, Wash.: Holmes, 1996).

Lady Sheba, *The Book of Shadows* (St. Paul: Llewellyn, 2000).

Lawlor, Robert, *Sacred Geometry: Philosophy and Practice* (N.Y.: Thames & Hudson, 1982).

Layton, Bentley, *The Gnostic Scriptures* (Garden City, N.Y.: Doubleday, 1987).

Leadbeater, C. W., *The Chakras* (Wheaton, Ill.: Quest, 1974).

———, *Man, Visible and Invisible* (Wheaton, Ill.: Quest, 1971).

———, *The Masters and the Path* (Adyar: TPH, 1925).

———, *The Science of the Sacraments* (Adyar: TPH, 1920).

Leek, Sybil, *Diary of a Witch* (New York: Prentice-Hall, 1968).

Leijenhorst, Cees, "Francesco Patrizi's Hermetic Philosophy," in van den Broeck and Hanegraaf 1998, 125–146.

Leland, Charles Godfrey, *Aradia, or the Gospel of the Witches* (N.Y.: Samuel Weiser, 1974).

———, *Etruscan Roman Remains in Popular Tradition* (repr. London: Kegan Paul, 2002).

Leo, Alan, *Astrology for All* (Rochester, Vt.: Inner Traditions, 1989); cited as Leo 1989a.

———, *Esoteric Astrology* (Rochester, Vt.: Inner Traditions, 1989); cited as Leo 1989b.

Lethbridge, T. C., *Witches* (N.Y.: Citadel, 1962).

Levack, Brian P., *The Witch-Hunt in Early Modern Europe* (London: Longman, 1995).

Lévi, Eliphas, *Transcendental Magic*, tr. Arthur Edward Waite (York Beach, Maine: Weiser, 1972).

Lewy, Hans, *Chaldaean Oracles and Theurgy* (Paris: Études Augustiniennes, 1978).

Ley, Willy, "Pseudoscience in Naziland," *Amazing Science Fiction* 39 (May 1947), 90–98.

Lind, Ingrid, *The White Eagle Inheritance* (Wellingborough: Turnstone, 1984).

Lindsay, Jack, *Origins of Astrology* (N.Y.: Barnes & Noble, 1972).

———, *The Origins of Alchemy in Greco-Roman Egypt* (London: Frederick Muller, 1970).

List, Guido von, *The Secret of the Runes,* tr. Stephen Flowers (Rochester, Vt.: Destiny, 1988).

Lobb, David, "Fascist Apocalypse: William Pelley and Millennial Extremism" (paper presented to the fourth annual conference of the Center for Millennial Studies, 1999).

Loewe, Michael, and Carmen Blacker, eds., *Oracles and Divination* (Boulder, Colo.: Shambhala, 1981).

Lomer, Georg, *Seven Hermetic Letters*, tr. Gerhard Hanswille and Franca Gallo (Salt Lake City: Merkur, 1997).

Long, Carolyn Morrow, *Spiritual Merchants: Religion, Magic, and Commerce* (Memphis, Tenn.: Univ. of Tennessee Press, 2001).

Lovelock, James E., *Gaia: A New Look at Life on Earth* (N.Y.: Oxford UP, 1979).

Lumsden, Robin, *Himmler's Black Order: A History of the SS, 1923–1945* (Stroud, Gloucestershire: Sutton, 1997).

Macdonald, Michael-Albion, *De Nigromancia attributed to Roger Bacon* (Gillette, N.J.: Heptangle, 1988).

Macer, *A Middle English Translation of Macer Floridus De Viribus Herbarum*, tr. Gosta Frisk (Uppsala: Almqvist and Wiksells, 1949).

MacFarlane, Alan, *Witchcraft in Tudor and Stuart England* (Prospect Heights: Waveland, 1991).

MacMullen, Ramsay, *Christianizing the Roman Empire* (New Haven, Conn.: Yale UP, 1984).

MacNulty, W. Kirk, *Freemasonry* (London: Thames & Hudson, 1991).

Maier, Michael, *Atalanta Fugiens*, tr. and ed. Joscelyn Godwin (Grand Rapids, Mich.: Phanes, 1989).

Malaclypse the Younger (Greg Hill), *Principia Discordia* (San Francisco: Rip Off Press, 1970).

Malbrough, Ray T., *Charms, Spells, and Formulas* (St. Paul: Llewellyn, 1986).

———, *The Magical Power of the Saints* (St. Paul: Llewellyn, 1998).

Maltwood, Katherine, *A Guide to Glastonbury's Temple of the Stars* (London: James Clark, 1929).

Maple, Eric, *The Dark World of Witches* (N.Y.: Pegasus, 1970).

Marenbon, John, *Early Medieval Philosophy 480–1150: An Introduction* (Routledge & Kegan Paul, 1983).

Marinus of Samaria, *The Life of Proclus* (Grand Rapids, Mich.: Phanes, 1986).

Mates, B., *Stoic Logic* (Berkeley: U. of California, 1953).

Mathers, Samuel Liddell, trans., *The Kabbalah Unveiled* (repr. York Beach, Maine: Weiser, 1968).

———, *The Key of Solomon the King* (London: George Redway, 1888).

———, "The Qlippoth of the Qabalah," in Gilbert 1983, 23–29; cited as Mathers 1983.

———, *The Sacred Magic of Abra-Melin the Mage* (repr. N.Y.: Causeway, 1974).

Matthaei, R., ed., *Goethe's Color Theory* (N.Y.: Van Nostrand, 1971).

Matthews, Caitlin, *Sophia, Goddess of Wisdom* (N.Y.: Mandala, 1991).

Matthews, John, *The Bardic Source Book* (London: Blandford, 1998).

———, *The Celtic Seers Source Book* (London: Blandford, 1999).

———, *The Druid Source Book* (London: Blandford, 1996).

Matthews, John, and Marion Green, *The Grail Seekers Companion* (Wellingborough: Aquarian, 1986).

McCoy, Edain, *Witta: An Irish Pagan Tradition* (St. Paul: Llewellyn, 1993).

McIntosh, Christopher, *The Rosicrucians: The History and Mythology of an Occult Order* (Wellingborough: Aquarian, 1987).

McLean, Adam, ed., *A Compendium on the Rosicrucian Vault* (Tysoe, Warwickshire: Hermetic Research Trust, 1985).

———, *The Magical Calendar* (Grand Rapids: Phanes, 1994).

———, *A Treatise on Angel Magic* (Grand Rapids: Phanes, 1990).

McManus, Damian, *A Guide to Ogham* (Maynooth: An Sagart, 1991).

Mead, G. R. S., *Apollonius of Tyana* (New Hyde Park, N.Y.: University Books, 1966).

———, *Thrice Greatest Hermes* (repr. York Beach, Maine: Weiser, 1992).

Means, Laurel, ed., *Medieval Lunar Astrology* (Lewiston, N.Y.: Edwin Mellen Press, 1993).

Mebane, John S., *Renaissance Magic and the Return of the Golden Age* (Lincoln: U. of Nebraska Press, 1989).

Medway, Gareth, *Lure of the Sinister: The Unnatural History of Satanism* (New York: New York UP, 2001).

Meeks, Dimitri, and Christine Favard-Meeks, *Daily Life of the Egyptian Gods*, tr. G. M. Goshgarian (Ithaca, N.Y.: Cornell UP, 1996).

Mehr, Farhang, *The Zoroastrian Tradition* (Rockport, Mass.: Element, 1991).

Merivale, Patricia, *Pan the Goat-God: His Myth in Modern Times* (Cambridge, Mass.: Harvard UP, 1969).

Merrifield, Ralph, *The Archeology of Ritual and Magic* (London: Batsford, 1987).

Merrill, James, *The Changing Light at Sandover: A Poem* (N.Y.: Knopf, 1992).

Mesmer, Franz Anton, *Mesmerism* (London: Macdonald, 1948).

Michell, John, *City of Revelation* (N.Y.: David McKay, 1972).

———, *The View Over Atlantis* (N.Y.: Ballantine, 1969).

Milis, Ludo J. R., ed., *The Pagan Middle Ages* (Woodbridge: Boydell, 1998).

Miles, Dillwyn, *The Secret of the Bards of the Isle of Britain* (Llandybie, Wales: Gwasg Dinefwr, 1992).

Montgomery, John Warwick, *Cross and Crucible: Johann Valentin Andreae (1586–1654), Phoenix of the Theologians* (The Hague: Martinus Nijhoff, 1973).

Moore, R. Laurence, *In Search of White Crows: Spiritualism, Parapsychology, and American Culture* (N.Y.: Oxford UP, 1977).

Morgan, Owen, *The Light of Britannia* (Cardiff: Daniel Owen, n.d.).

Moriarty, Anthony, *The Psychology of Adolescent Satanism* (Westport, Conn.: Praeger, 1992).

Morrison, J. S., "The Classical World," in Loewe and Blacker (1981).

Moura, Ann, *Green Witchcraft* (St. Paul: Llewellyn, 1996).

———, *Green Witchcraft III: The Manual* (St. Paul: Llewellyn, 2000).

Murray, Colin, and Liz Murray, *The Celtic Tree Oracle* (London: Rider, 1989).

Murray, Margaret, *The Witch Cult in Western Europe* (Oxford: Oxford UP, 1921).

———, *The God of the Witches* (Oxford: Oxford UP, 1933).

———, *The Divine King in England* (London: Faber & Faber, 1954).

Mylonas, George E., *Eleusis and the Eleusinian Mysteries* (Princeton: Princeton UP, 1961).

Nathan, Debbie, and Michael Snedeker, *Satan's Silence: Ritual Abuse and the Making of a Modern American Witch Hunt* (N.Y.: Basic, 1995).

Nauert, Charles G., *Agrippa and the Crisis of Renaissance Thought* (Urbana, Ill.: U. of Illinois Press, 1965).

Nethercot, A. H., *The First Five Lives of Annie Besant* (London: Hart-Davis, 1961).

———, *The Last Four Lives of Annie Besant* (London: Hart-Davis, 1963).

Neuburg, Victor, *The Triumph of Pan* (1910; repr. London: Skoob, 1990).

Newman, Barbara, "God and the Goddesses: Vision, Poetry and Belief in the Middle Ages," in *Poetry and Philosophy in the Middle Ages* (Leiden: Brill, 2001), 173–196.

Nichols, Ross, *The Book of Druidry* (London: Aquarian, 1990).

Noll, Richard, *The Aryan Christ: The Secret Life of Carl Jung* (N.Y.: Random House, 1997).

———, *The Jung Cult: Origins of a Charismatic Movement* (Princeton: Princeton UP, 1994).

Oates, Caroline, and Juliette Wood, *A Coven of Scholars: Margaret Murray and Her Working Methods* (London: Folklore Society, 1998).

Olsen, Christina, Carte da Trionfi: *The Development of Tarot in Fifteenth-Century Italy* (Ph.D. dissertation, Univ. of Pennsylvania, 1994).

Ossendowski, Ferdinand, *Men, Beasts, and Gods* (N.Y.: Dutton, 1922).

Owen, A. L., *The Famous Druids: A survey of three centuries of English literature on the Druids* (Oxford: Clarendon, 1962).

Pachter, Henry M., *Magic into Science: The Story of Paracelsus* (N.Y.: Henry Schuman, 1951).

Padfield, Peter, *Himmler: Reichsführer-SS* (London: Macmillan, 1990).

Pagel, Walter, *Paracelsus: An Introduction to Philosophical Medicine in the Era of the Renaissance* (Basel: Karger, 1958).

Pagels, Elaine, *The Gnostic Gospels* (N.Y.: Random House, 1979).

Pallis, Marco, "Ossendowski's Sources," *Studies in Comparative Religion* 15 (1983), 30–41.

Palmer, Helen, *The Enneagram* (San Francisco: Harper & Row, 1988).

Palmer, Philip Mason, *The Sources of the Faust Tradition* (N.Y.: Oxford UP, 1936).

Papus (Gerard Encausse), *The Qabalah* (Wellingborough: Thorsons, 1977).

———, *The Tarot of the Bohemians*, tr. A. J. Morton (No. Hollywood, Calif.: Wilshire, n.d.).

Paracelsus, *Essential Readings*, ed. Nicholas Goodrick-Clarke (Wellingborough: Crucible, 1990).

———, *The Hermetic and Alchemical Writings of Aureolus Philippus Theophrastus Bombast of Hohenheim, called Paracelsus the Great*, ed. and tr. Arthur Edward Waite, 2 vols. (repr. Berkeley, Calif.: Shambhala, 1976).

Parker, Derek, *Familiar to All: William Lilly and Astrology in the Seventeenth Century* (London: Jonathan Cape, 1975).

Parsons, Jack, *Freedom Is a Two-Edged Sword* (Phoenix: New Falcon, 1989).

Partner, Peter, *The Murdered Magicians: The Templars and Their Myth* (Oxford: OUP, 1982).

Patai, Raphael, *The Jewish Alchemists* (Princeton: Princeton UP, 1994).

———, *The Hebrew Goddess* (N.Y.: Bantam, 1967).

Patrides, C. A., ed., *The Cambridge Platonists* (Cambridge, Mass.: Harvard UP, 1970).

Pauwels, Louis, and Jacques Bergier, *The Morning of the Magicians* (N.Y.: Avon, 1968).

Pearson, Joanne, Richard H. Roberts, and Geoffrey Samuel, eds., *Nature Religion Today: Paganism in the Modern World* (Edinburgh: Edinburgh UP, 1998).

Pendergrast, Mark, *Victims of Memory* (Hinesburg, Vt.: Upper Access, 1995).

Pennell, Elizabeth Robins, *Charles Godfrey Leland: A Biography* (London: Hamlyn, 1906).

Pennick, Nigel, *The Ancient Science of Geomancy* (London: Thames & Hudson, 1979).

———, *Games of the Gods* (York Beach, Maine: Weiser, 1989).

———, *Practical Magic in the Northern Tradition* (Wellingborough: Aquarian, 1989).

———, and Paul Devereaux, *Lines on the Landscape* (London: Robert Hale, 1989).

Periera, Michela, *The Alchemical Corpus Attributed to Raymond Lull* (London: Warburg Institute, 1989).

Peters, Edward, *The Magician, the Witch and the Law* (np: University of Pennsylvania Press, 1978).

Pettis, Chuck, *Secrets of Sacred Space* (St. Paul: Llewellyn, 1999).

Philip, J. A., *Pythagoras and Early Pythagoreanism* (Toronto: Univ. Toronto Press, 1966).

Phillips, Osborne, *Aurum Solis Initiation Ceremonies and Inner Magical Techniques* (Loughborough, Leics.: Thoth, 2001).

Phylos the Tibetan (Frederick S. Oliver), *A Dweller on Two Planets* (Los Angeles: Poseid, 1929).

Piersen, William D., "Black Arts and Black Magic: Yankee Accommodations to African Religion," in Benes 1995a, 34–43.

Piggott, Stuart, *The Druids* (London: Thames & Hudson, 1968).

Pike, Albert, *Morals and Dogma of the Ancient and Accepted Scottish Rite of Freemasonry* (Charleston, S.C.: Supreme Council 33°, 1871).

Pincus-Witten, Robert, *Occult Symbolism in France: Joséphin Peladan and the Salons de la Rose-Croix* (N.Y.: Garland, 1976).

Plato, *Collected Dialogues*, ed. Edith Hamilton and Huntington Cairns (Princefon: Princeton UP, 1961).

Plotinus, *The Enneads*, tr. Stephen MacKenna (Burdett, N.Y.: Larson, 1992).

Prinke, Rafal, "Michael Sendivogius and Christian Rosenkreutz: The Unexpected Possibilities," *The Hermetic Journal* 1990, 72–98.

Proclus, *The Elements of Theology*, tr. E. R. Dodds (Oxford: Oxford UP, 1963).

Quinn, D. Michael, *Early Mormonism and the Magic World View* (Salt Lake City: Signature, 1987).

Ramacharaka, Yogi (William Walker Atkinson), *Science of Breath* (Chicago: Yogi Pub. Society, 1905).

Randolph, Paschal Beverly, *Eulis!* (Toledo: Randolph, 1874).

Raoult, Michel, "The Druid Revival in Brittany, France, and Europe," in Carr-Gomm (1996).

Rauschning, Hermann, *Hitler Speaks* (London: Butterworth, 1939).

Ravenwolf, Silver, *American Folk Magic* (St. Paul: Llewellyn, 1996).

Read, John, *Prelude to Chemistry* (N.Y.: Macmillan, 1937).

Redford, Donald B., *Akhenaten, the Heretic King* (Princeton: Princeton UP, 1984).

Reformed Druids of North America, *A Reformed Druid Anthology II* (Washington, D.C.: Drynemeton Press, 2003).

Regardie, Israel, *Ceremonial Magic* (Wellingborough: Aquarian, 1980).

———, *Foundations of Practical Magic* (Wellingborough: Aquarian, 1979).

———, *The Golden Dawn* (St. Paul: Llewellyn 1971).

———, *The Middle Pillar* (St. Paul: Llewellyn, 1970).

———, *What You Should Know About the Golden Dawn* (St. Paul: Llewellyn, 1972).

Regula, deTraci, *The Mysteries of Isis* (St. Paul: Llewellyn, 1994).

Reich, Wilhelm, *The Function of the Orgasm* (N.Y.: World Publications, 1942).

Reichenbach, Karl von, *Psycho-Physiological Researches* (repr. Mokelumne Hill, Calif.: Health Sciences, 1965).

Reiner, Erica, *Astral Magic in Babylonia* (Philadelphia: American Philosophical Society, 1995).

———, *Surpu: A Collection of Sumerian and Akkadian Incantations* (Osnabruck: Biblio-Verlag, 1970).

Reuchlin, Johann, *On the Art of the Cabala*, tr. Martin and Sarah Goodman (Lincoln, NB: Bison, 1993).

Rhone, Christine, "Mira Alfassa: A Western Occultist in India," *Pomegranate* 13 (2000), 38–42.

Richardson, Alan, *Dancers to the Gods* (Wellingborough: Aquarian, 1985).

Richardson, Robert, *The Unknown Treasure: The Priory of Sion Fraud and the Spiritual Treasure of Rennes-le-Chateau* (Houston: Northstar, 1999).

Riggs, Brian, "The Pope and the Pornographer," *Gnosis* 44 (Summer 1997), 46–50.

Rist, J. M., *Plotinus: The Road to Reality* (Cambridge: Cambridge UP, 1967).

———, *Stoic Philosophy* (Cambridge: Cambridge UP, 1969).

Ritner, Robert Kriech, *The Mechanics of Ancient Egyptian Magical Practice, Studies in Ancient Oriental Civilization #54* (Chicago: U. of Chicago, 1993).

Roberts, J. M., *The Mythology of the Secret Societies* (London: Secker and Warburg, 1972).

Roberts, Marie Mulvey, and Hogh Ormsby-Lennon, *Secret Texts: The Literature of Secret Societies* (N.Y.: AMS, 1995).

Robinson, James M., ed., *The Nag Hammadi Library* (N.Y.: HarperCollins, 1988).

Roche de Coppens, Peter, *The Nature and Use of Ritual* (St. Paul: Llewellyn, 1987).

Rossner, John, *In Search of the Primordial Tradition and the Cosmic Christ* (St. Paul: Llewellyn, 1989).

Rowse, A. L., *Sex and Society in Shakespeare's Age: Simon Forman the Astrologer* (N.Y.: Scribners, 1974).

Rudhyar, Dane, *An Astrological Mandala* (N.Y.: Vintage, 1974).

———, *The Astrology of Personality* (Garden City, N.Y.: Doubleday, 1970).

Russell, Jeffrey Burton, *Witchcraft in the Middle Ages* (Ithaca, N.Y.: Cornell UP, 1972).

Ruyter, Nancy Lee Chalfa, *The Cultivation of Body and Mind in Nineteenth-Century American Delsartism* (Westport, Conn.: Greenwood, 1999).

Sadhu, Mouni, *Concentration* (No. Hollywood: Wilshire, 1959).

———, *The Tarot* (No. Hollywood: Wilshire, 1962).

———, *Theurgy, the Art of Effective Worship* (London: George Allen & Unwin, 1965).

Sambursky, S., *Physics of the Stoics* (London: Routledge & Kegan Paul, 1959).

Schaya, Leo, *The Universal Meaning of the Kabbalah*, tr. Nancy Pearson (N.Y.: Viking, 1958).

Schneider, Heinrich, *Quest for Mysteries: The Masonic Background for Literature in Eighteenth-Century Germany* (Ithaca: Cornell, 1947).

Schneider, Herbert W., and George Lawton, *A Prophet and a Pilgrim* (New York: Columbia UP, 1942)

Schoch, Robert M., *Voices of the Rocks: A Scientist Looks at Catastrophes and Ancient Civilizations* (New York: Harmony, 1999).

Scholem, Gershom, *The Kabbalah* (New York: Quadrangle, 1974).

———, *Major Trends in Jewish Mysticism* (New York: Schocken, 1941).

Schouten. J., *The Pentagram as a Medical Symbol* (Nieuwkoop: De Graaf, 1968).

Schuchard, Marsha Keith, "Yeats and the Unknown Superiors: Swedenborg, Falk, and Cagliostro," in Roberts and Ormsby-Lennon (1995), 114–168.

———, "Freemasonry, Secret Societies, and the Continuity of the Occult Traditions in English Literature" (Doctoral dissertation, University of Texas at Austin, 1975).

Scott-Elliott, Walter, *The Story of Atlantis & the Lost Lemuria* (London, England: Theosophical Publishing House, 1925).

Seton, Ernest Thompson, *The Book of Woodcraft and Indian Lore* (Garden City, N.Y.: Doubleday, 1926).

———, *Two Little Savages* (Garden City, N.Y.: Doubleday, 1920).

Settegast, Mary, *Plato Prehistorian* (Hudson, N.Y.: Lindisfarne, 1990).

Seward, Desmond, *The Monks of War* (N.Y.: Penguin, 1995).

Seznec, Jean, *The Survival of the Pagan Gods* (N.Y.: Pantheon, 1953).

Shaver, Richard S., *I Remember Lemuria* (Evanston, Ill.: Venture, 1948).

Shaw, Gregory, *Theurgy and the Soul: The Neoplatonism of Iamblichus* (University Park, Pa.: PSU Press, 1995).

Shea, Robert, and Robert Anton Wilson, *The Eye in the Pyramid* (N.Y.: Dell, 1975).

———, *The Golden Apple* (N.Y.: Dell, 1975).

———, *Leviathan* (N.Y.: Dell, 1975).

——, *The Illuminatus Trilogy* (3 vols.) (New York: Dell, 1975).

Shumaker, Wayne, *Renaissance Curiosa* (Binghamton, N.Y.: MRTS, 1982).

Simon (pseudonym), *The Necronomicon* (New York: Avon, 1980).

Simoons, Frederick J., *Plants of Life, Plants of Death* (Madison: University of Wisconsin Press, 1998).

Singer, June, "A Necessary Heresy: Jung's Gnosticism and Contemporary Gnosis," *Gnosis* 4 (Spring 1987), 11–19.

Singh, Rani, and Steve Croson, eds., *Think of the Self Speaking: Harry Smith, Selected Interviews* (N.Y.: Cityful, 1998).

Siorvanes, Lucas, *Proclus: Neo-Platonic Philosophy and Science* (Edinburgh: Edinburgh UP, 1966).

Skinner, Stephen, *Terrestrial Astrology* (London: Routledge & Kegan Paul, 1980).

Smith, Michelle, and Laurence Padzer, *Michelle Remembers* (N.Y.: Pocket, 1980).

Smith, Morton, *Jesus the Magician* (San Francisco: Harper & Row, 1978).

Smith, Pamela H., *The Business of Alchemy: Science and Culture in the Holy Roman Empire* (Princeton: Princeton UP, 1994).

Smith, Steven G., *The Concept of the Spiritual* (Philadelphia: Temple UP, 1988).

Smoley, Richard, "The Emerald Tablet," *Gnosis* 40 (Summer 1996), 17–19.

Spence, Lewis, *The Problem of Atlantis* (N.Y.: Brentano, 1921).

Sperling, Harry, and Maurice Simon, trans., *The Zohar* (5 vols.) (London: Soncino, 1949).

Spielman, Ed, *The Spiritual Journey of Joseph L. Greenstein, the Mighty Atom: World's Strongest Man* (Cobb, Calif.: First Glance, 1998).

Stebbins, Genevieve, *Dynamic Breathing and Harmonic Gymnastics* (N.Y.: Edgar S. Werner, 1893).

——, *The Quest of the Spirit* (N.Y.: Edgar S. Werner, 1913).

Steiner, Rudolf, *A Way of Self-Knowledge* (Hudson, N.Y.: Anthroposophic Press, 1999).

——, *Goethe the Scientist* (N.Y.: Anthroposophic Press, 1950).

——, *How to Know Higher Worlds* (Hudson, N.Y.: Anthroposophic Press, 1994).

——, *Intuitive Thinking as a Spiritual Path* (Hudson, N.Y.: Anthroposophic Press, 1995).

——, *The Anthroposophical Movement* (London: Anthroposophic Press, 1933).

Stevenson, David, *The Origins of Freemasonry: Scotland's Century 1590–1710* (Cambridge: Cambridge UP, 1988).

Stewart, Randall, ed., *Sortes Astrampsychus* (Munich: K. G. Saur, 2001).

Stewart, R. J., *Advanced Magical Arts* (Shaftesbury: Element, 1988).

——, *Living Magical Arts* (Poole: Blandford, 1987).

——, *The Mystic Life of Merlin* (London: Arkana, 1986; cited as Stewart 1986a).

——, *The Prophetic Vision of Merlin* (London: Arkana, 1986; cited as Stewart 1986b).

——, *Robert Kirk, Walker Between Worlds* (Shaftesbury: Element, 1990).

——, *The Way of Merlin* (London: Aquarian, 1991).

Stillson, Henry L., ed., *The History of Odd Fellowship* (Boston: Fraternity Publishing Co., 1897).

Stirling, William, *The Canon: An Exposition of the Pagan Mystery Perpetuated in the Cabala as the Rule of All the Arts* (repr. York Beach, Maine: Weiser, 1999).

Sugrue, Thomas, *There Is a River* (N.Y.: Dell, 1973).

Suster, Gerald, *Crowley's Apprentice: The Life and Ideas of Israel Regardie* (York Beach, Maine: Weiser, 1990).

Szydlo, Zbigniew, *Water Which Does Not Wet Hands* (Warsaw: Polish Academy of Sciences, 1994).

Taavitsainen, Irma, *Middle English Lunaries: A Study of the Genre* (Helsinki: Mémoires de la Société Neophilologique de Helsinki XLVII, 1988).

Taylor, Thomas, *The Theoretic Arithmetic of the Pythagoreans* (N.Y.: Weiser, 1972).

———, *Thomas Taylor the Platonist*, ed. Kathleen Raine and George Mills Harper (Princeton: Princeton UP, 1969).

Tester, S. J., *A History of Western Astrology* (Woodbridge, Sussex: Boydell, 1987).

Theon of Smyrna, *Mathematics Useful for Understanding Plato*, tr. Robert and Deborah Lawlor (San Diego, Calif.: Wizards Bookshelf, 1979).

Thibault, Gerard, *Academy of the Sword*, Vol. 1 trans. John Michael Greer (Seattle: Fir Mountain, 1998).

Thomas, Dana Lloyd, "A Modern Pythagorean," *Gnosis* 44 (Summer 1997), 52–59.

Thompson, R. Campbell, *The Devils and Evil Spirits of Babylonia* (London: Luzac, 1903).

Thorndyke, Lynn, *A History of Magic and Experimental Science* (N.Y.: Columbia UP, 1923).

———, *Michael Scot* (London: Nelson, 1965).

Thorsson, Edred, *A Book of Troth* (St. Paul: Llewellyn, 1989); cited as Thorsson 1989a.

———, *Fire and Ice* (St. Paul: Llewellyn, 1990).

———, *Northern Magic* (St. Paul: Llewellyn, 1998).

———, *Rune Might: Secret Practices of the German Rune Magicians* (St. Paul: Llewellyn, 1989); cited as Thorsson 1989b.

"Three Initiates," *The Kybalion* (Chicago: Yogi Pub. Society, 1912).

Tobyn, Graeme, *Culpeper's Medicine* (Shaftesbury, Dorset: Element, 1997).

Todd, Jan, *Physical Culture and the Body Beautiful* (Macon, Ga.: Mercer UP, 1998).

Tolkien, J. R. R., "Tree and Leaf," in *The Tolkien Reader* (New York: Ballantine, 1966).

Tolstoy, Nikolai, *The Quest for Merlin* (Boston: Little, Brown, 1985).

Tomberg, Valentin, *Meditations on the Tarot: A Journey into Christian Hermeticism* (published anonymously, New York: Amity House, 1972).

TOPY (Thee Temple ov Psychick Youth), *The Grey Book* (undated photocopy; available on various Internet sites).

Torrens, R. G., *The Secret Rituals of the Golden Dawn* (Wellingborough: Aquarian, 1973).

Towers, Eric, *Dashwood—The Man and the Myth* (Wellingborough: Crucible, 1987).

Townley, Kevin, *The Cube of Space: Container of Creation* (Boulder: Archive Press, 1993).

Trismosin, Solomon, *Splendor Solis: Alchemical Treatises of Solomon Trismosin* (London: Kegan Paul, Trench, Trubner & Co., n.d.).

Trobridge, George, *Swedenborg: Life and Teaching* (N.Y.: Swedenborg Foundation, 1992).

Trowbridge, W. R. H., *Cagliostro* (N.Y.: Brentano's, 1910).

Turner, Henry Ashby, Jr., *Hitler: Memoirs of a Confidant* (New Haven, Conn.: Yale UP, 1985).

Turner, Robert, *Ars Notoria*, ed. Darcy Küntz (Edmonds, Wash.: Holmes, 1998).

———, *Elizabethan Magic* (Shaftesbury, Dorset: Element, 1989).

Tyson, Donald, *Tetragrammaton* (St. Paul: Llewellyn, 1998).

U. D., Frater, *Practical Sigil Magic* (St. Paul: Llewellyn, 1991).

Ulansey, David, *The Origin of the Mithraic Mysteries* (Oxford: Oxford UP, 1989).

Valiente, Doreen, *Witchcraft for Tomorrow* (Custer, Wash.: Phoenix, 1987).

———, *The Rebirth of Witchcraft* (Custer, Wash.: Phoenix, 1989).

VandenBroeck, André, *Al-Kemi: Hermetic, Occult, Political, and Private Aspects of R. A. Schwaller de Lubicz* (Hudson, N.Y.: Lindisfarne, 1987).

van den Broeck, Roelof, "The Cathars: Medieval Gnostics?", in van den Broeck and Hanegraaf 1998, 87–108.

———, and Wouter J. Hanegraaf, eds., *Gnosis and Hermeticism from Antiquity to Modern Times* (Albany, N.Y.: SUNY Press, 1998).

van der Horst, Pieter Willem, *Chaeremon: Egyptian Priest and Stoic Philosopher* (Leiden: Brill, 1984).

———, et al., *The Use of Sacred Books in the Ancient World* (Leuven: Peeters, 1998).

van Oort, Johannes, "Manichaeism: Its Sources and Influences on Western Christianity," in van den Broeck and Hanegraaf 1998, 37–52.

Versluis, Arthur, *American Transcendentalism and Asian Religions* (Oxford: Oxford UP, 1993).

———, "Christian Theosophic Literature of the Seventeenth and Eighteenth Centuries," in van den Broeck and Hanegraaf 1998, 217–236.

———, *Wisdom's Children: A Christian Esoteric Tradition* (Albany: SUNY Press, 2000).

Victor, Jeffrey S., *Satanic Panic* (Chicago: Open Court, 1993).

Vitruvius (M. Vitruvius Pollio), *The Ten Books On Architecture*, tr. Morris Hicky Morgan (N.Y.: Dover, 1960).

Wakefield, W. L., and A. P. Evans, *Heresies of the High Middle Ages: Selected Sources Translated and Annotated* (London: Columbia UP, 1969).

Walker, Christopher, and Michael Dick, *The Induction of the Cult Image in Ancient Mesopotamia* (Helsinki: SAALT, 2001).

Walker, Daniel P., *The Ancient Theology: Studies in Christian Platonism from the Fifteenth to the Eighteenth Centuries* (Ithaca: Cornell UP, 1972).

———, *Spiritual and Demonic Magic from Ficino to Campanella* (London: Warburg Institute, 1958).

Wallis, R. T., *Neoplatonism* (N.Y.: Scribners, 1972).

Wang, Robert, *The Secret Temple* (N.Y.: Weiser, 1980).

Waterfield, Robin, trans., *The Theology of Arithmetic* (Grand Rapids: Phanes, 1988).

Watkins, Alfred, *The Old Straight Track* (London: Methuen, 1925).

Webb, James, *The Occult Establishment* (La Salle, Ind.: Open Court, 1976).

Wehr, Gerhard, *An Illustrated Biography of C. G. Jung*, tr. Michael Kohn (Boston: Shambhala, 1989).

Westcott, William Wynn, "Chess Shatranji and Chaturanga," in R. A. Gilbert, *The Magical Mason* (Wellingborough: Aquarian, 1983).

———, *The Occult Power of Numbers* (Van Nuys, Calif.: Newcastle, 1984).

Wetherbee, Winthrop, tr., *The Cosmographia of Bernardus Sylvestris* (N.Y.: Columbia UP, 1973).

Whitehead, Nicholas, *Patterns in Magical Christianity* (Albuquerque, N.M.: Sun Chalice, 1995).

Wilding, Michael, "Edward Kelly: A Life," *Cauda Pavonis* 18 (1999), 1–26.

Wilkins, Eithne, *The Rose-Garden Game* (London: Gollancz 1969).

Willard, Thomas, "Acts of the Companions: A.E. Waite's Fellowship and the Novels of Charles Williams," in Roberts, Marie Mulvey, and Hugh Ormsby-Lennon, eds., *Secret Texts: The Literature of Secret Societies* (New York: AMS Press, 1995).

Williams ab Ithel, John, *Barddas* (York Beach, Maine: Weiser, 2004).

Williams, Brian, *The Minchiate Tarot* (Rochester, Vt.: Destiny, 1999).

Williams, Charles, *Taliessin Through Logres and the Region of the Summer Stars* (London: Oxford UP, 1954).

———, *Witchcraft* (London: Faber and Faber, 1941).

Williams, Thomas A., *Eliphas Lévi: Master of Occultism* (University, Ala.: University of Alabama Press, 1975).

Wilmshurst, W. L., *The Meaning of Masonry* (N.Y.: Bell, 1980).

Wilson, Robert Anton, "The Priory of Sion: Jesus, Freemasons, Extraterrestrials, The Gnomes of Zurich, Black Israelites and Noon Blue Apples," *Gnosis* 6 (Winter 1988), 30–39.

Wirth, Oswald, *The Tarot of the Magicians* (York Beach, Maine: Weiser, 1985).

Witemeyer, Barbara, *Ernest Thompson Seton Woodcraft Groups in England* (Santa Fe: the author, 1994).

Wood, Matthew, *Vitalism: The History of Herbalism, Homeopathy, and Flower Essences* (Berkeley, Calif.: North Atlantic, 2000).

Wright, Machaelle Small, *Perelandra Garden Workbook* (Jeffersonton, Va.: Perelandra, 1987).

Yates, Frances, *The Art of Memory* (Chicago: U. of Chicago Press, 1966).

———, *Giordano Bruno and the Hermetic Tradition* (Chicago: U. of Chicago Press, 1964).

———, *The Occult Philosophy in the Elizabethan Age* (London: Routledge & Kegan Paul, 1979).

———, *The Rosicrucian Enlightenment* (London: Routledge & Kegan Paul, 1972).

———, *Theatre of the World* (Chicago: U. of Chicago Press, 1969).

Yeats, William Butler, *Autobiographies* (N.Y.: Macmillan, 1955; cited as Yeats 1955a).

———, *A Vision* (N.Y.: Macmillan, 1956).

———, *The Letters of W. B. Yeats,* ed. Allan Wade (N.Y.: Macmillan, 1955); cited as Yeats 1955b.

Young-Eisendrath, Polly, and Terence Dawson, eds., *The Cambridge Companion to Jung* (Cambridge: Cambridge UP, 1997).

Yronwode, Catherine, *Hoodoo Herb and Root Magic* (Forestville, Calif.: Lucky Mojo Curio Co., 2002).

Zain, C. C., *Church of Light Correspondence Course* (Los Angeles: Church of Light, 1914–1934).

Zalewski, Patrick J., *Secret Inner Order Rituals of the Golden Dawn* (Phoenix: Falcon, 1988).

———, and Chris Zalewski, *The Equinox and Solstice Ceremonies of the Golden Dawn* (St. Paul: Llewellyn, 1992).

Zaehner, R. C., *The Dawn and Twilight of Zoroastrianism* (N.Y.: Putnam, 1961).

Zohar. See Sperling 1931.

Zoller, Robert, *The Arabic Parts in Astrology* (Rochester, Vt.: Inner Traditions International, 1988).

GET MORE AT LLEWELLYN.COM

Visit us online to browse hundreds of our books and decks, plus sign up to receive our e-newsletters and exclusive online offers.

- • Free tarot readings • Spell-a-Day • Moon phases
- • Recipes, spells, and tips • Blogs • Encyclopedia
- • Author interviews, articles, and upcoming events

GET SOCIAL WITH LLEWELLYN

Find us on Facebook

www.Facebook.com/LlewellynBooks

Follow us on twitter™

www.Twitter.com/Llewellynbooks

GET BOOKS AT LLEWELLYN

LLEWELLYN ORDERING INFORMATION

Order online: Visit our website at www.llewellyn.com to select your books and place an order on our secure server.

Order by phone:
- • Call toll free within the U.S. at 1-877-NEW-WRLD (1-877-639-9753)
- • Call toll free within Canada at 1-866-NEW-WRLD (1-866-639-9753)
- • We accept VISA, MasterCard, and American Express

Order by mail:
Send the full price of your order (MN residents add 6.875% sales tax) in U.S. funds, plus postage and handling to: Llewellyn Worldwide, 2143 Wooddale Drive Woodbury, MN 55125-2989

POSTAGE AND HANDLING:

STANDARD (U.S. & Canada):
(Please allow 12 business days)
$25.00 and under, add $4.00.
$25.01 and over, FREE SHIPPING.

INTERNATIONAL ORDERS (airmail only):
$16.00 for one book, plus $3.00 for each additional book.

Visit us online for more shipping options. Prices subject to change.

FREE CATALOG!

To order, call
1-877-NEW-WRLD
ext. 8236
or visit our website

Secrets of the Lost Symbol:
The Unauthorized Guide to Secret Societies,
Hidden Symbols & Mysticism

JOHN MICHAEL GREER

Secrets of the Lost Symbol is an essential resource for Dan Brown fans who want to know the facts behind the fiction.

From *Abramelin the Mage* to the *Zohar*, this encyclopedic unofficial companion guide to *The Lost Symbol* uncovers the forgotten histories of arcane traditions that have shaped—and still inhabit—our modern world.

Discover the truth about Freemasonry—a major theme in Brown's best-selling novel—including its rituals, temples, and infamous members such as the legendary Albert Pike. Get the real story behind the Rosicrucians, the Temple of Solomon, and ancient occult rites.

978-0-7387-2169-9, 240 pp., 5 x 7 $9.95

Monsters:
An Investigator's Guide to Magical Beings

JOHN MICHAEL GREER

Most of us don't believe that entities such as vampires, shapeshifters, and faeries really exist. Even those who study UFOs or psychic powers dismiss them as unreal.

The problem is, people still keep running into them.

What do you do when the world you think you inhabit tears open, and something terrifying comes through the gap? Join ceremonial magician John Michael Greer as he takes you on a harrowing journey into the reality of the impossible. In *Monsters* he examines the most common types of beings still encountered in the modern world, surveying what is known about them and how you can deal with their antics.

- Breaks new ground in the study of the paranormal using folklore, magical philosophy, and actual experience as guides
- The only book that explores monsters and magical beings from the viewpoint of a practicing magician
- Provides techniques of magical self-defense for those times when monsters pose a threat to human health, safety, or sanity
- Explores the fine art of investigating a reported monster sighting
- Identifies the nine types of monsters: vampires, ghosts, werewolves (and other shapeshifters), faeries, mermaids, dragons, spirits, angels, and demons

0-7387-0050-9, 320 pp., 7½ x 9⅛ $19.95

Atlantis:
Ancient Legacy, Hidden Prophecy

JOHN MICHAEL GREER

Is there anything our modern industrial society can learn from the story of Atlantis, a legend that has endured for two thousand years?

From the dialogues of Plato to the modern age of Atlantology, esteemed occultist John Michael Greer traces the evolution of this controversial story about a great civilization drowned by the sea. See how this fascinating legend was reshaped by modern occultists and pioneers of the "rejected knowledge" movement. Greer also proposes his own revolutionary theory—based on Plato's accounts, human history, and geological science—of a civilization doomed by natural disasters at the end of the last Ice Age.

As the threat of global warming makes headlines today, Greer poses the ultimate question: is the legend of Atlantis a legacy of the distant past, or a prophecy of our own future?

978-0-7387-0978-9, 264 pp., 6 x 9, illus.

$21.95

The UFO Phenomenon:
Fact, Fantasy and Disinformation

JOHN MICHAEL GREER

Do UFOs exist? Are the lights and strange craft in our skies aliens from other galaxies—or the product of fraud, delusion, or mistaken identity?

John Michael Greer, a respected authority on occult traditions, reveals the secret hidden at the center of the UFO labyrinth. This meticulously researched guide plunges into the thick of the controversy with an unexpected and compelling approach to the UFO mystery. Moving beyond the familiar debate between those who believe that UFOs are extraterrestrial in origin and those who believe UFOs do not exist at all, this unique work goes further to examine stranger and more rewarding topics—the nature of apparitions, the history of secret American aerospace technologies, the mythology of progress, and the role of popular culture in defining experienced reality.

978-0-7387-1319-9, 6 x 9, 264 pp. $16.95

Encyclopedia of Natural Magic

JOHN MICHAEL GREER

Natural magic is the ancient and powerful art of using material substances—herbs, stones, incenses, oils, and much more—to tap into the hidden magical powers of nature, transforming your surroundings and yourself.

Not just a cookbook of spells, the *Encyclopedia of Natural Magic* provides an introduction to the philosophy underlying this system. It also gives detailed information on 176 different herbs, trees, stones, metals, oils, incenses, and other substances, and offers countless ways to put them to magical use. With this book and a visit to your local herb store, rock shop, or backyard garden, you're ready to enter the world of natural magic!

0-7387-0674-4, 312 pp., 7 ½ x 9 ⅛, illus. $18.95

Three Books of Occult Philosophy

Completely Annotated, with Modern Commentary—

The Foundation Book of Western Occultism

HENRY CORNELIUS AGRIPPA
EDITED AND ANNOTATED BY
DONALD TYSON

Agrippa's *Three Books of Occult Philosophy* is the single most important text in the history of Western occultism. Occultists have drawn upon it for five centuries, although they rarely give it credit. First published in Latin in 1531 and translated into English in 1651, it has never been reprinted in its entirety since. Photocopies are hard to find and very expensive. Now, for the first time in 500 years, *Three Books of Occult Philosophy* will be presented as Agrippa intended. There were many errors in the original translation, but occult author Donald Tyson has made the corrections and has clarified the more obscure material with copious notes.

This is a necessary reference tool not only for all magicians, but also for scholars of the Renaissance, Neoplatonism, the Western Kabbalah, the history of ideas and sciences and the occult tradition. It is as practical today as it was 500 years ago.

0-87542-832-0, 1,024 pp., 7 x 10 $49.95